CHILD DEVELOPMENT

CHILD DEVELOPMENT

TWELFTH EDITION

John W. Santrock

Uiversity of Texas at Dallas

McGraw Hill

Boston   Burr Ridge, IL   Dubuque, IA   Madison, WI   New York   San Francisco   St. Louis
Bangkok   Bogotá   Caracas   Kuala Lumpur   Lisbon   London   Madrid   Mexico City
Milan   Montreal   New Delhi   Santiago   Seoul   Singapore   Sydney   Taipei   Toronto

McGraw-Hill
Higher Education

CHILD DEVELOPMENT

Published by McGraw-Hill, an imprint of The McGraw-Hill Companies, Inc., 1221 Avenue of the Americas, New York, NY 10020. Copyright © 2009, 2007, 2004, 2001, 1996, 1992, 1989, 1987, 1982. All rights reserved. No part of this publication may be reproduced or distributed in any form or by any means, or stored in a database or retrieval system, without the prior written consent of The McGraw-Hill Companies, Inc., including, but not limited to, in any network or other electronic storage or transmission, or broadcast for distance learning.

This book is printed on acid-free paper.

1 2 3 4 5 6 7 8 9 0 VNH/VNH 0 9 8

ISBN: 978-0-07-337063-7
MHID: 0-07-337063-0

Vice President and Editor in Chief: *Michael Ryan*
Publisher: *Michael J. Sugarman*
Director of Development: *Dawn Groundwater*
Developmental Editor: *Maureen Spada*
Editorial Coordinator: *Jillian Allison*
Executive Marketing Manager: *James R. Headley*
Supplements Editor: *Emily Pecora*
Production Editors: *Melissa Williams/Marilyn Rothenberger*
Manuscript Editor: *Beatrice Sussman*
Interior Designer: *Pam Verros*
Cover Designer: *Laurie Entringer*
Photo Researcher: *LouAnn Wilson*
Media Project Manager: *Jennifer Blankenship*
Senior Production Supervisor: *Tandra Jorgensen*
Composition: *10/12 Times New Roman by Aptara, Inc.*
Printing: *Printed on 45# Pub Matte Plus by R.R. Donnelley & Sons*

Cover photos, L to R: Royalty-free/Corbis, Royalty-free/Corbis, © Veer; Royalty-free/Corbis.

Credits: The credits section for this book begins on page C-1 and is considered an extension of the copyright page.

Library of Congress Cataloging-in-Publication Data
Santrock, John W.
    Child Development / John W. Santrock. — 12th ed.
        p. cm.
    Includes biographical references and indexes
    ISBN: 978-0-07-337063-7; ISBN: 0-07-337063-0
        1. Child developmental   2. Child psychology   I. Title.
BF713.526 2008
155—dc22   2008566343

www.mhhe.com

With special appreciation to my wife, Mary Jo;
my children, Tracy and Jennifer;
and my grandchildren, Jordan and Alex

About the Author

John W. Santrock

John Santrock received his Ph.D. from the University of Minnesota in 1973. He taught at the University of Charleston and the University of Georgia before joining the Program in Psychology and Human Development at the University of Texas at Dallas, where he currently teaches a number of undergraduate courses.

John has been a member of the editorial boards of *Child Development* and *Developmental Psychology*. His research on father custody is widely cited and used in expert witness testimony to promote flexibility and alternative considerations in custody disputes. John also has authored these exceptional McGraw-Hill texts: *Psychology* (7th edition), *Children* (10th edition), *Adolescence* (12th edition), *Life-Span Development* (12th edition), and *Educational Psychology* (4th edition).

For many years, John was involved in tennis as a player, teaching professional, and coach of professional tennis players. He has been married for more than 35 years to his wife, Mary Jo, who is a realtor. He has two daughters—Tracy, who is studying to become a financial planner at Duke University, and Jennifer, who is a medical sales specialist at Medtronic. He has one granddaughter, Jordan, age 17, and two grandsons, Alex, age 4, and Luke, age 3. Tracy recently completed the New York Marathon, and Jennifer was in the top 100 ranked players on the Women's Professional Tennis Tour. In the last decade, John also has spent time painting expressionist art.

John Santrock (center) teaching an undergraduate psychology course.

Brief Contents

Contents

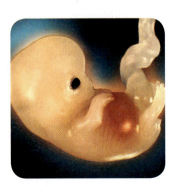

SECTION 5

SOCIAL CONTEXTS OF DEVELOPMENT 413

Expert Consultants

Child development has become an enormous, complex field and no single author, or even several authors, can possibly keep up with the rapidly changing content in the many different areas of child development. To solve this problem, author John Santrock sought the input of leading experts about content in numerous aspects of child development. The experts provided detailed evaluations and recommendations for a chapter (or chapters) in their areas of expertise. The biographies and photographs of the experts, who literally represent a who's who in the field of child development, follow.

Robert Sternberg

Dr. Sternberg, widely recognized as one of the world's leading experts on the cognitive aspects of children's development, is currently is Dean of the School of Arts and Sciences and Professor of Psychology at Tufts University. He is also Honorary Professor of Psychology in the Department of Psychology at the University of Heidelberg, Heidelberg, Germany. Prior to Tufts, Dr. Sternberg was IBM Professor of Psychology and Education in the Department of Psychology, Professor of Management in the School of Management, and Director of the Center for the Psychology of Abilities, Competencies, and Expertise at Yale. This Center, now relocated to Tufts, seeks to have an impact on science, education, and society. He is a former president of the American Psychological Association and is president-elect of the International Association for Cognitive Education and Psychology. Dr. Sternberg received his Ph.D. from Stanford University in 1975 and his B.A. summa cum laude, *Phi Beta Kappa,* with honors with exceptional distinction in psychology, from Yale University in 1972. He also holds honorary doctorates from numerous universities including the University of Heidelberg (Germany), Complutense University of Madrid (Spain); University of Leuven (Belgium); University of Cyprus; University of Paris V (France); and St. Petersburg State University (Russia). Dr. Sternberg is the author of more than 1,200 journal articles, book chapters, and books, and has received over $20 million in government and other grants and contracts for his research. The central focus of his research is on intelligence, creativity, and wisdom, and he also has studied love and close relationships as well as hate. This research has been conducted in five different continents. Among his many awards are the Sir Francis Galton Award from the International Association of Empirical Aesthetics; the Arthur W. Staats Award from the American Psychological Foundation and the Society for General Psychology; and the E. L. Thorndike Award for Career Achievement in Educational Psychology from the Society for Educational Psychology of the American Psychological Association (APA). He has been listed in the *APA Monitor on Psychology* as one of the top 100 psychologists of the twentieth century, and is listed by the ISI as one of its most highly cited authors (top 1/2%) in psychology and psychiatry.

Diane Hughes

Dr. Hughes is a leading expert on diversity and children's development. Following her doctoral work at the University of Michigan, she became a Professor in the Department of Psychology at New York University and currently is a faculty member in the Steinhardt Department of Applied Psychology at New York University. Dr. Hughes is a community and developmental psychologist who examines ethnicity and race as contexts for parenting and adolescent development. Dr. Hughes seeks to discover how parents from a range of ethnic backgrounds communicate information about ethnicity and race in the course of their everyday routines and practices. She and her colleagues have been awarded multi-million-dollar grants from the National Science Foundation to establish and maintain the Center for Research on Culture, Development, and Education at New York University.

The narrative for this chapter (Chapter 17, "Culture and Diversity") is interesting and engaging. The coverage is broad, but all of it seems highly relevant to understanding cultural influences on development . . . it is great to see issues of culture, ethnicity, immigrant status, and SES get such extensive coverage in a course textbook.

—DIANE HUGHES

Michael Lewis

Dr. Lewis is widely recognized as one of the word's leading experts on emotional and self development. His current position is University Distinguished Professor of Pediatrics and Psychiatry, and Director of the Institute for the Study of Child Development at Robert Wood Johnson Medical School—University of Medicine and Dentistry of New Jersey. He is also Professor of Psychology, Education, and Biomedical Engineering at Rutgers University. His research has focused on normal and deviant emotional and intellectual development. His highly influential books include *Social Cognition and the Acquisition of the Self; Children's Emotions and Moods; Shame: The Exposed Self;* and *Altering Fate: Why the Past Does Not Predict the Future.* In addition, Dr. Lewis has authored four research monographs and edited 31 books, including the recent *Introduction*

to Infant Development (coauthored with Alan Slater) (2nd ed.). He also has published more than 350 articles and chapters in research journals and scholarly texts. Dr. Lewis has served as consulting editor for a number of leading research journals, including *SRCD Monographs, Child Development, Developmental Psychology,* and *Infant Behavior and Development.* He is a Fellow in a number of organizations, including the American Psychological Association and the Japan Society for the Promotion of Society. Dr. Lewis currently is working on two books: *The Role of Consciousness in Children's Development* and *Little White Lies and Then Some.*

> *The narrative (Chapter 10, "Emotional Development") is up-to-date, impressively so . . . good coverage for an undergraduate text.*
>
> —MICHAEL LEWIS

Joan Grusec

Dr. Grusec is one of the world's leading experts on family processes and children's socialization. She obtained her Ph.D. from Stanford University and has been a Professor of Psychology at the University of Toronto for a number of years. Her long-standing research interests and contributions have focused on the influence of parenting on children's socialization as well as determinants of parenting practices. She is the author or editor of several books, including *Parenting and Children's Internalization of Values* (coedited with Leon Kuczynski) and *Handbook of Socialization* (coedited with Paul

Hastings). Dr. Grusec also coauthored (with Daphne Bugental) the chapter, "Socialization Processes," in the *Handbook of Child Psychology.* She also has been associate editor of *Developmental Psychology.*

> *I think the chapter (Chapter 14, "Families") does a truly excellent job of reviewing research in the area of families and the role of parents and siblings in children's development. The revision is impressively up-to-date, well organized, and clearly presented. It's obvious why this book has lasted through so many revisions.*
>
> —JOAN GRUSEC

Beverly Goldfield

Dr. Goldfield is a leading expert on language development. She received her Ed.D. in human development from Harvard University Graduate School of Education and was a postdoctoral Fellow in the Psychology Department at Harvard. Dr. Goldfield is currently a Professor in the Psychology Department at Rhode Island College. She has published extensively in the field of language development with research inter-

ests in the intersection of infant social and cognitive skills, social support, and early lexical development.

> *. . . the narrative is clearly written and is a good mix of summary findings of some research areas and more detailed presentations of some key studies, in which the author also explains some of the methodology involved in the studies.*
>
> —BEVERLY GOLDFIELD

Kirby Deater-Deckard

Dr. Deater-Deckard is a leading expert on gene-environment processes. His current title is Professor and Director of Graduate Programs in Psychology at Virginia Polytechnic Institute and State University (Virginia Tech). Dr. Deater-Deckard obtained his Ph.D. at the University of Virginia under the direction of Sandra Scarr, completed a postdoctorate at Vanderbilt University, held a research position at the Institute

of Psychiatry in London, and was a Professor at the University of Oregon. His research focuses on the development of individual differences in childhood and adolescence, with emphasis on gene-environment processes and parenting. He has published numerous research articles in leading journals and book chapters in the areas of developmental psychology and child development. Dr. Deater-Deckard coedited *Gene-Environment Processes in Social Behaviors and Relationships* and *Immigrant Families,* and he authored *Parenting Stress.* Dr. Deater-Deckard is joint editor of the *Journal of Child Psychology and Psychiatry* and on the editorial boards of *Journal of Family Psychology; Parenting: Science and Practice;* and *Infant and Child Development.* He also is currently a coinvestigator on an NICHD grant that involves a twin study of environmental influences on early reading.

> The chapter (Chapter 2, "Biological Beginnings") *reflects the latest and most important research in the field and does this very well.*
>
> **—KIRBY DEATER-DECKARD**

Phyllis Bronstein

Dr. Bronstein is a leading expert on gender development. Her current title is Professor Emerita of Psychology at the University of Vermont. Dr. Bronstein has had a long-term interest in gender development across the childhood, adolescent, and adult years. Her publications include a book on fatherhood and two books on integrating gender and multiculturalism into the psychology curriculum, as well as numerous articles and chapters on gender role socialization in the family and women's career development within academia. Dr. Bronstein has recently been given the opportunity to observe early gender development firsthand, with the birth of her grandson.

> . . . The chapter (Chapter 12, "Gender") *offers balanced, thorough, and up-to-date information about the topic of gender in the context of development.*
>
> **—PHYLLIS BRONSTEIN**

Gustavo Carlo

Dr. Carlo is a leading expert on moral development. He currently holds the position of Professor of Developmental Psychology at the University of Nebraska–Lincoln. Dr. Carlo obtained his Ph.D. from Arizona State University. His main research interest focuses on prosocial and moral behavior in children and adolescents, especially on the personality, parenting, and sociocultural correlates of prosocial behaviors. Dr. Carlo's research has been published in numerous journals such as *Child Development, Developmental Psychology, Journal of Personality and Social Psychology,* and *Journal of Research on Adolescence.* He has also published several book chapters, including a chapter on altruism in the recently published *Handbook of Moral Development.* He coedited (with Carolyn Pope Edwards) the 51st Nebraska Symposium on Motivation volume on *Moral Development Through the Life Span* and has edited several special journal issues on moral development. He is past associate editor for the *Journal of Research on Adolescence.*

> The coverage of major issues in moral development is comprehensive and up-to-date . . . . The chapter (Chapter 13, "Moral Development") provides excellent breadth and depth—the discussion is well thought out and understandable.
>
> **—GUSTAVO CARLO**

Linda Smolak

Dr. Smolak is a leading expert on children's health and nutrition. She currently is the Samuel B. Cummings Jr. Professor of Psychology at Kenyon College. Her research focuses on the development of body image and eating problems in girls and boys. She has special interests in the roles of gender and sociocultural issues in the development of these problems. Her recent publications included being coeditor of *The Prevention of Eating Problems and Eating Disorders* and coeditor of the forthcoming book, *Body Image, Eating Disorders, and Obesity in Youth* (2nd ed.).

> . . . I think the chapter (Chapter 4, "Physical Development and Health") *is very up-to-date and cites good, recent research.*
>
> **—LINDA SMOLAK**

Candice Mills

Dr. Mills is a leading expert on social cognition in children's development. She obtained her Ph.D. in developmental psychology from Yale University and currently is an Assistant Professor in the School of Behavioral and Brain Sciences at the University of Texas at Dallas. Dr. Mills' research explores how children evaluate the knowledge and beliefs of others as well as themselves, and what changes over the course of development. Her recent publications (with coauthor Frank Keil) include articles in these research journals: *Cognition, Psychological Science,* and *Journal of Experimental Child Psychology.* For the current edition of *Life-Span Development,* Dr. Mills updated and expanded the section on children's theory of mind.

> The additions to this textbook show the remarkable advances made in the field the last several years. Students will also benefit from the learning system, which encourages them to preview each chapter's main themes and then review and reflect on the learning goals for each chapter.
>
> **—CANDICE MILLS**

Preface

Preparing a new edition of *Child Development* is both a joy and a challenge. I enjoy revising this text because I continue to learn more about children and because the feedback from students and instructors has been consistently enthusiastic. The challenge of revising a successful text is always to continue meeting readers' needs and expectations, while keeping the material fresh and up-to-date. For the twelfth edition of *Child Development*, at the request of adopters and reviewers, I have significantly shortened the book, reduced the number of chapters from 18 to 17, expanded coverage in a number of key areas, including diversity and development of the brain, incorporated the latest research and applications, and fine-tuned aspects of the book that make learning easier and more engaging.

A MORE STREAMLINED BOOK

In recent years, child development texts have gotten increasingly longer. Many instructors have told me that they have found it impossible to cover everything in a comprehensive child development text in a single semester. Through elimination or reduction of dated or less central topics and extensive rewriting, I have significantly reduced the length of the text.

REDUCTION IN NUMBER OF CHAPTERS FROM 18 TO 17

As part of reducing the book's length, at the request of adopters and reviewers, I decreased the number of chapters in *Child Development*, twelfth edition, from 18 to 17 by highlighting the main topics in Chapters 1 ("Introduction") and 2 ("The Science of Child Development") in the eleventh edition and combined them into a single opening chapter. This reduction in chapters provides a more manageable set of chapters for a semester-length course without losing core content.

RESEARCH

Above all, a text on child development must include a solid research foundation. Accomplishing this goal involved extensive research updating, obtaining detailed feedback from some of the world's leading experts on various content areas of child development, and *Research in Child Development* interludes.

Recent Research

This edition of *Child Development* presents the latest, most contemporary research on the biological, cognitive, and socioemotional aspects of children's lives and includes more than 1,200 citations from 2006, 2007, 2008, and 2009. Later in the Preface, I highlight the main content changes on a chapter-by-chapter basis.

Expert Research Consultants

Child development has become an enormous, complex field and no single author, or even several authors, can possibly be an expert in many different areas of child development. To solve this problem, I sought the input of leading experts in many different research areas of child development. The experts provided me with detailed evaluations and recommendations for a chapter, or chapters, in their area(s) of expertise. The expert research consultants for *Child Development*, twelfth edition, are:

Expert	*Chapters and Topics*
Kirby Deater-Deckerd *Virginia Tech*	Chapter 2: Biological Beginnings
Linda Smolak *Kenyon College*	Chapter 4: Physical Development and Health
Candice Mills *University of Texas at Dallas*	Chapter 7: Information Processing
Robert J. Sternberg *Tufts University*	Chapter 8: Intelligence
Beverly Goldfield *Rhode Island College*	Chapter 9: Language Development
Michael Lewis *Rutgers University*	Chapter 10: Emotional Development
Phyllis Bronstein *University of Vermont*	Chapter 12: Gender
Gustavo Carlo *University of Nebraska*	Chapter 13: Moral Development
Joan Grusec *University of Toronto*	Chapter 14: Families
Diane Hughes *New York University*	Chapter 17: Culture and Diversity

Research Interludes

The *Research in Child Development* interludes appear once in each chapter and provide a more in-depth look at research related to a topic in the chapter. I call them interludes rather than boxes because they follow directly in the text after they have been introduced. In most instances, they consist of a description of a research study, including the identity of the participants, the methods used to obtain data, and the main results. In most cases, they are research studies that have been conducted in the twenty-first century. Because students often have more difficulty reading about research studies than other text material, I wrote these with an eye toward student understanding.

Among the new *Research* interludes in the new edition are:

Chapter 4: Physical Activity in Young Children Attending Preschools

Chapter 11: Adolescents' Self-Images

Chapter 13: Fast Track

APPLICATIONS

It is important to not only present the scientific foundations of child development to students, but also to provide applied examples of concepts, and to give students a sense that the field of child development has personal meaning for them.

Caring for Children Interludes

In addition to giving special attention throughout the text to health and well-being, parenting, and education applications, the twelfth edition of *Child Development* includes *Caring for Children* interludes. They describe important strategies for nurturing and improving the lives of children. Among the new and updated *Caring for Children* interludes in the new edition are:

Chapter 1: Updated Improving Family Policy

Chapter 3: New: From Waterbirth to Music Therapy

Chapter 6: New: Tools of the Mind

Chapter 16: Updated "I Have a Dream"

Careers in Child Development

Instructors and students have provided extremely positive feedback about the emphasis on careers in child development in the text. The twelfth edition continues this emphasis. *Careers in Child Development* profiles describe an individual whose career relates to the chapter's content. Most of these profiles have a photograph of the person at work.

In the eleventh edition, a *Careers in Child Development* section was incorporated into Chapter 1. Combining the first two chapters from the eleventh edition in the twelfth edition resulted in the *Careers in Child Development* section now following Chapter 1 as a Careers Appendix. The Careers Appendix describes a number of careers in education/research, clinical/counseling, medical/nursing/physical development, and family/relationships categories.

Culture and Diversity

In addition, this text has always emphasized culture and diversity, and this tradition continues in this edition. Coverage of culture and diversity appears in every chapter, and the twelfth edition also includes a separate chapter, "Culture and Diversity" (Chapter 17), that focuses on cross-cultural comparisons, socioeconomic status, and ethnicity. Also, *Diversity in Child Development* interludes are new in this edition. They appear once in each chapter and focus on a topic related to the chapter's content. Among the topics of the Diversity interludes are:

Chapter 3: Cultural Beliefs About Pregnancy, including recent views on beliefs in Latino and Asian cultures

Chapter 9: Bilingual Education, with substantial updating of this topic (Snow & Yang, 2006)

Chapter 12: Gender Roles Across Cultures

Chapter 14: Acculturation and Ethnic Minority Parenting

Chapter 16: Early Childhood Education in Japan and Developing Countries

Chapter 17: Computers, the Internet, and Sociocultural Diversity

I expanded the coverage of diversity in a number of places in the twelfth edition. New or expanded coverage of diversity is described later in the preface in the chapter-by-chapter changes.

ACCESSIBILITY AND INTEREST

Many students today juggle numerous responsibilities in addition to their coursework. To help them make the most of their study time, I have made this book as accessible as possible without watering down the content. The writing, organization, and learning system of *Child Development* will engage students and provide a clear foundation in child development.

Writing and Organization

For *Child Development*, twelfth edition, every sentence, every paragraph, and every section of every chapter was carefully considered and, if appropriate, moved, streamlined, expanded, or eliminated in order to integrate new research and to make the book more accessible.

The Learning System

I strongly believe that students not only should be challenged to study hard and think more deeply and productively about child development, but also should be provided with an effective way to learn the content. Instructors and students continue to provide extremely positive feedback about the book's learning system and student-friendly presentation.

Students often struggle to find the main ideas in their courses, especially in child development, which includes so much material. This book's learning system centers on learning goals that, together with the main text headings, keep the key ideas in front of the reader from the beginning to the end of the chapter. Each chapter has no more than five main headings and corresponding learning goals, which are presented side-by-side in the chapter-opening spread. At the end of each main section of a chapter, the learning goal is repeated in a feature called Review and Reflect, which prompts students to review the key topics in the section and poses a question to encourage them to think critically about what they have read. At the end of the chapter, under the heading Reach Your Learning Goals, the learning goals guide students through the chapter review that is organized by the chapter's main headings.

In addition to the verbal tools just described, visual organizers, or maps, that link up with the learning goals are presented at the beginning of each major section in the chapter. The complete learning system, including many additional features not mentioned here, is illustrated in a section titled *To the Student*, which follows this Preface on page 000.

CHAPTER-BY-CHAPTER CHANGES

I made a number of changes in all 17 chapters of *Child Development*, twelfth edition. The highlights of these changes follow.

CHAPTER 1
INTRODUCTION

- Combined two chapters from the eleventh edition into a shorter, single opening chapter at the request of instructors
- Inclusion of new main section: Caring for Children
- Significant updating of research and citations
- Revised definition of gender based on expert consultant Diane Halpern's input
- Expanded discussion of poverty and children
- Updated coverage of improving family policy (Coltrane & others, 2008; Conger & Conger, 2008)
- New *Diversity in Child Development* interlude: Gender, Families, and Children's Development
- New Figure 1.3: Percentage of Children Around the World Who Have Never Been to School of Any Kind
- Updated poverty statistics for U.S. children (Federal Interagency Forum on Child and Family Statistics, 2007)
- New comparison of child poverty rates in the United States, Canada, and Sweden
- Description of recent research revealing the cumulative effects of poverty on physiological indices of stress in children (Evans & Kim, 2007)
- New discussion of research on poverty and children's development, including new research Figure 1.5
- Moved coverage of *Careers in Child Development* to an Appendix that follows Chapter 1
- Expanded discussion of research on children from ethnic minority backgrounds (Coltrane & others, 2008)
- New *Research in Child Development* interlude: Research Journals

CHAPTER 2
BIOLOGICAL BEGINNINGS

- Extensive line-by-line rewriting of chapter and inclusion of a number of new introductions to topics and transitions between topics for improved clarity and understanding
- Extensive research and citation updating
- Description of recent search documenting how stress hormones can damage DNA (Flint & others, 2007)
- Updated material on continued lowering of number of genes that humans possess (about 20,500) (Ensembl Human, 2008)
- Description of recent research on characteristics of boys with Klinefelter syndrome (Ross & others, 2008)
- Updated and expanded coverage of fragile X syndrome, including a new photograph of a boy with fragile X syndrome (Ono, Farzin, & Hagerman, 2008)
- Inclusion of recent research on cognitive deficits in boys with fragile X syndrome (Hooper & others, 2008)
- New coverage of underutilization of the only drug (hydroxyurea) approved to treat sickle-cell anemia in adolescents and adults, plus current research that is under way to determine if the drug is effective in treating babies
- Description of recent large-scale study that found no difference in pregnancy loss between chronic villus sampling and amniocentesis (Caughey, Hopkins, & Norton, 2006).
- Expanded coverage of phenylketonuria and how its link with nutrition reflects the principle of heredity-environment interaction
- Description of recent research review on how genetic counseling clients interpret risk (Sivell & others, 2008)
- New section on extensive recent research on the potential for using noninvasive prenatal diagnosis (NIPD) as an alternative to chorionic villus sampling and amniocentesis (Avent & others, 2008; Finning & Chitty, 2008)
- New Figure 2.7, showing a fetal MRI
- New coverage of recent national study on the influence of the woman's age on the success rate of in vitro fertilization, including new Figure 2.8
- New *Diversity in Child Development* interlude: The Increased Diversity of Adopted Children and Adoptive Parents
- New description of two recent meta-analyses—one that focused on behavioral problems and mental health referrals in adopted and nonadopted children (Juffer & van IJzendoorn, 2005) and one that examined the cognitive development of adopted and nonadopted children (van IJendoorn, Juffer, & Poelhuis, 2005)
- Coverage of recent study of the antisocial behavior of adopted and nonadopted young adults (Grotevant & others, 2006)
- New coverage of recent large-scale study on adoption and learning disabilities (Altarac & Saroha, 2007)

- Description of recent research review on the self-esteem of adopted and nonadopted children, and transracial and same-race adoptees (Juffer & van IJzendoorn, 2007)
- Updated and expanded discussion of the epigenetic view (Gottlieb, 2007), including criticisms of the heredity-environment correlation view

 ## CHAPTER 3
PRENATAL DEVELOPMENT AND BIRTH

- Extensive rewriting of chapter on a line-by-line basis and rearrangement of some sections (placing Assessing the Newborn before Low Birth Weight and Preterm Infants, for example) to improve clarity and understanding
- Extensive editing and updating of chapter based on recommendations by expert consultant Maria Hernandez-Reif
- Considerable research and citation updating
- Important new section on development of the brain in the prenatal period, including a photo (Figure 3.4) of the tubular appearance of the human nervous system six weeks after conception (Moulson & Nelson, 2008)
- New discussion of neural tube defects and what characterizes anencephaly and spina bifida
- Description of two recent research studies, indicating that exercise in pregnancy is linked to reduced risk of preterm birth (Hegaard & others, 2008; Juhl & others, 2008)
- Coverage of a highly successful home nurse visitation program, the Nurse Family Partnership, created by David Olds and his colleagues (2007), that has produced positive outcomes for mothers and their children
- Inclusion of information from recent research review of aspirin and reproductive outcomes (James, Brancazio, & Price, 2008)
- Coverage of recent study on caffeine intake during pregnancy and risk for miscarriage (Weng, Odouli, & Li, 2008)
- Change of label from FAS to FASD (fetal alcohol spectrum disorders) in keeping with recently developed terminology and expanded coverage of FASD (Olson, King, & Jirikowic, 2008)
- Description of recent research on impaired memory development in children with FASD (Pei & others, 2008)
- Description of recent research on continuing negative outcomes of FASD in early adulthood (Spohr, Willms, & Steinhausen, 2007)
- Inclusion of recent research on extent of reduction in alcohol intake in non-Latino White and African American women when they become pregnant (Morris & others, 2008)
- Description of recent research on maternal smoking and inattention/hyperactivity in children (Obel & others, 2008)

- Coverage of recent research on harmful effects of cocaine use during pregnancy on growth, language development, and attention (Accornero & others, 2007; Lewis & others, 2007; Richardson, Goldschmidt, & Willford, 2008)
- Inclusion of information about recent study that revealed negative neonatal outcomes following exposure to methamphetamine in the prenatal period (Smith & others, 2008)
- Description of recent study on prenatal marijuana exposure and lower intelligence in childhood (Goldschmidt & others, 2008)
- Updated and revised conclusions about effects of marijuana use by pregnant women on offspring (de Moares & others, 2006; Williams & Ross, 2007)
- Inclusion of recent research on continuous versus late methadone treatment during pregnancy and neonatal outcomes (Burns & others, 2007)
- Discussion of recent research on maternal lead exposure during pregnancy and infant mental development (Hu & others, 2007)
- Coverage of recent analysis proposing that fetal programming from an overweight pregnant woman is likely linked to offspring being overweight in childhood and adolescence (McMillen & others, 2008)
- Expanded coverage of diabetes during pregnancy and outcomes for offspring, including recent research review on maternal diabetes and increased risk of metabolic disease in offspring (Doblado & Moley, 2007; Langer, 2008a)
- Updated research on fetal mercury exposure and developmental outcomes (Axelrad & others, 2007; Xue & others, 2007)
- Description of recent research review on maternal stress during pregnancy and negative developmental outcomes in offspring (Talge & others, 2007)
- Coverage of recent research on links between negative mood changes in pregnant women and physiological changes in the fetus (Glynn & others, 2008)
- Updated coverage of trends in cesarean delivery (National Center for Health Statistics, 2007)
- Description of recent national study comparing neonatal death rates of cesarean delivery with no labor complications to neonatal deaths rates involving planned vaginal delivery (MacDorman & others, 2008)
- New *Caring for Children* interlude: From Waterbirth to Music Therapy (Field, 2007)
- Coverage of factors involved in why poverty continues to contribute to preterm birth in the United States (Goldenberg & Nagahawatte, 2008)
- Considerably expanded and updated material on consequences of preterm birth (Foster-Cohen & others, 2007; Johnson, 2007)
- Description of recent study linking preterm birth with dropping out of school (Swamy, Osbye, & Skjaerven, 2008)

- Description of recent MRI study of brain deficiencies in children born very preterm (Narberhus & others, 2008)

- Updated research about use of progestin in reducing risk of preterm birth (Fonseca & others, 2007; Rouse & others, 2007; Thornton, 2007)

- Coverage of recent study that revealed a substantial reduction in preterm birth when women took folic acid for one year prior to delivering (Bukowski & others, 2008)

- Description of two recent experimental studies revealing benefits of kangaroo care (Gathwala, Singh, & Balhara, 2008; Suman, Udani, & Nanavati, 2008)

- New coverage of recent survey on techniques used in the NICU (Field & others, 2006)

- Updated coverage of the *Research in Child Development* interlude on Tiffany Field's massage therapy research, including recent research on effects of massage therapy on preterm infants' stress behaviors, with new Figure 3.10 illustrating the results (Hernandez-Reif, Diego, & Field, 2007)

- New coverage of sleep deprivation experienced by postpartum women, including new Figure 3.11 (Gunderson & others, 2008; National Sleep Foundation, 2007)

- Expanded and updated description of postpartum depressed mothers' patterns of interaction with their infants (Teti & Towe-Goodman, 2008)

- Coverage of recent study of mothers' postpartum depression, preterm/full-term infants, and maternal synchrony (Feldman & Eidelman, 2007)

- Discussion of recent national research study on links between postpartum depression and the way mothers interact with their infants (Paulson, Dauber, & Leiferman, 2006)

- Description of unsettled issue of optimal course of therapy for the depressed, breast feeding mother, and breast fed infant (Field, 2008)

 CHAPTER 4
PHYSICAL DEVELOPMENT AND HEALTH

- New chapter-opening *Images of Child Development,* The Story of Angie and Her Weight, highlighting the increasing problem of being overweight in childhood

- Significantly updated and expanded coverage of increased interest in body image in adolescence, including recent research (Gillen, Lefkowitz, & Shearer, 2006; Neumark-Sztainer & others, 2006)

- Inclusion of information about recent study on early-maturing girls and trying cigarettes and alcohol without their parents' knowledge (Westling & others, 2008)

- Updated coverage of development of the brain (Fischer & Immordino-Yang, 2008; Moulson & Nelson, 2008)

- Expanded description of function of myelination and new Figure 4.11, showing myelination of axons (Dubois & others, 2008; Fair & Schlagger, 2008)

- Expanded and updated discussion of links between spurts in brain activity and cognitive functioning (Immordino-Yang & Fischer, 2007)

- Inclusion of new material on increasing focal activation of the brain in middle and late childhood (Durston & others, 2006)

- Significant updating of brain changes to include thickening of the corpus callosum in adolescence (Toga, Thompson, & Sowell, 2006)

- Description of recent research that revealed link between volume of the amygdala in young adolescents and their aggressive behavior when interacting with parents (Whittle & others, 2008)

- Coverage of recent research on changes in the brain in adolescence and resistance to peer pressure (Paus & others, 2008)

- New description of issues involved in whether information about brain changes in adolescence can be applied to whether adolescents should be given a death sentence or not (Ash, 2006)

- Updated and expanded material on sleep patterns in infancy (Sadeh, 2008)

- Description of recent research on factors related to infant night waking (DeLeon & Karraker, 2007)

- Expanded discussion of REM sleep in infancy, and question raised about whether we can know for sure whether infants dream

- Updated and expanded discussion of shared sleeping and SIDS controversy (Bajanowski & others, 2008; Mitchell, 2007)

- Expanded and updated research on SIDS, including recent information about the role of the neurotransmitter serotonin and abnormal brain stem functioning (Shani, Fifer, & Myers, 2007)

- New coverage of recent research showing that babies who use a pacifier when they go to sleep are less likely to experience SIDS (Li & others, 2006; Mitchell, Blair, & L'Hoir, 2006)

- Expanded and updated description of young children's recommended sleep patterns (National Sleep Foundation, 2008)

- Inclusion of recent research on link between inadequate sleep and injuries that require attention in preschool children (Koulouglioti, Cole, & Kitzman, 2008)

- Description of recent longitudinal study on characteristics linked to young children having bad dreams (Simard & others, 2008)

- Inclusion of recent research on bedtime sleep resistance and problem behaviors in children (Carvalho Bos & others, 2008)

- Description of recent research on short sleep duration and being overweight in childhood (Nixon & others, 2008; Patel & Hu, 2008)

- Discussion of recent national survey on factors linked to whether children get adequate sleep or not (Smaldone, Honig, & Byrne, 2007)

- Coverage of recent studying linking inadequate sleep in adolescence to negative health-related behaviors (Chen, Wang, & Jeng, 2006)

- New discussion of recent research on percentage of over-weight babies in the United States, including new Figure 4.18 (Kim & others, 2006)

- Inclusion of material from recent research review by the American Academy of Pediatrics indicating no link between breast feeding and children's allergies (Greer & others, 2008)

- Extensive updating, revision, and expansion of material on breast feeding based on recent large-scale research review (Agency for Healthcare Quality and Research, 2007)

- Description of recent research linking longer breast feeding with lower incidence of metabolic syndrome in midlife women (Ram & others, 2008)

- Discussion of an important issue related to the correlational nature of breast versus bottle feeding studies (Agency for Healthcare Quality and Research, 2007)

- Coverage of recent information about breast feeding and type 2 diabetes (Ip & others, 2007)

- Inclusion of information from recent national survey of young children's consumption of fat in their diet (Kranz, Lin, & Wagstaff, 2007)

- New discussion of the role of caregiver feeding behavior and styles in young children's eating behavior (Black & Hurley, 2007; Black & Lozoff, 2008)

- Updated material on increase in overweight children in many countries around the world (Chan, 2008; Li & others, 2008)

- Description of recent study linking high levels of watching TV with being overweight in childhood (Wells & others, 2008)

- Expanded and updated coverage of developmental outcomes of children who are overweight

- Description of recent study on how peers perceived obese children (Zeller, Reiter-Purtill, & Ramey, 2008)

- Description of recent study indicating percent of over-weight male and female adolescents who become obese adults (Wang & others, 2008)

- Recent research on iron deficiency anemia in children and their affective behavior (Lozoff & others, 2007)

- Expanded and updated coverage of young children's nutrition in low-income families (Bryce & others, 2008; Sausenthaler & others, 2007)

- Coverage of recent large-scale U.S. study on percentage of children 2 to 19 years of age who have weight problems and recent leveling off in overweight categories (Odgen, Carroll, & Flegal, 2008)

- Discussion of recent study on parents' misperceptions of their children's overweight (Eckstein & others, 2006)

- Coverage of increased concern about sedentary lifestyles of children in a number of countries around the world (Fogelholm, 2008; Liu & others, 2008)

- Inclusion of information about three recent studies focused on increasing young children's physical activity (Beets & Foley, 2008; Bower & others, 2008; Trost, Fees, & Dzewaltowski, 2008)

- Coverage of recent research on benefits of an intensive resistance training program on reducing children's body fat and increasing their muscle strength (Benson, Torode, & Fiatarone Singh, 2008)

- Inclusion of recent research indicating amount of daily physical activity that is associated with lower odds of child-hood obesity (Wittmeier, Mollard, & Kriellaars, 2008)

- Description of recent study linking aerobic exercise to an increase in planning skills in overweight children (Davis & others, 2007)

- Coverage of recent study indicating a gender difference in adolescents in meeting U.S. guidelines for physical activity (Butcher & others, 2008)

- New *Research in Child Development* interlude: Physical Activity in Young Children Attending Preschools

- New description of recent trend in reducing physical activity opportunities in preschool and kindergarten programs (American Academy of Pediatrics, 2006)

- Discussion of recent data from the National Youth Risk Survey on adolescents' exercise patterns with a special focus on gender and ethnic variations, including new Figure 4.21 (MMWR, 2006)

- At the request of reviewers and adopters, the chapter has more material focused on children's development and less emphasis is given to adolescents

CHAPTER 5
MOTOR, SENSORY, AND PERCEPTUAL DEVELOPMENT

- New *Diversity in Child Development* interlude: Cultural Variations in Guiding Infants' Motor Development

- Description of recent research on infants' walking patterns and their occasional large steps (Badaly & Adolph, 2008)

- Updated coverage of cultural variation in infant motor development (Adolph, 2008)

- Description of recent study linking children's physical fitness and the mastery of motor skills (Haga, 2008)

- New material on link between Mexican youths' participation in sports and their lower incidence of being overweight or obese (Salazar-Martinez & others, 2006)

- New information about importance of exercising fine motor skills (Needham, 2008)

- Updated information about development of visual acuity in young infants (Aslin & Lathrop, 2008)

- New discussion of recent research on face perception in young infants (Kelly & others, 2007a, b; Slater, Field, & Hernandez-Reif, 2007)

- Revised and updated discussion of color vision in infancy (Aslin & Lathrop, 2008)

- New section: Nature, Nurture, and the Development of Infants' Visual Perception (Kellman & Arterberry, 2006)

- New description of research on visual expectations in early childhood, including new Figure 5.10

- New coverage of developmental changes in stereoacuity during infancy (Birch & others, 2005; Takai & others, 2005)

- Updated discussion of early screening for hearing problems (Korres & others, 2008)

- New material on otitis media (Park & others, 2008)

CHAPTER 6
COGNITIVE DEVELOPMENTAL APPROACHES

- Rewriting of Piaget material for improved student understanding

- Revised, improved Figure 6.5 on Piaget's three mountains task that provides students with a better understanding of the concept of egocentrism

- Recent revised interpretation of A-not-B error (Clearfield & others, 2006)

- Updated and expanded evaluation of Piaget's view of infant cognitive development (Slater, Field, & Hernandez-Reif, 2007)

- Expanded analysis of object permanence, including Meltzoff and Moore's (2008; Moore & Meltzoff, 2008) criticisms of the violation of expectations method as an accurate measure of object permanence

- Description of recent research on the personal fable and adolescent adjustment (Aalsma, Lapsley, & Flannery, 2006)

- Rewriting of Vygotsky material for improved student understanding

- New *Caring for Children* interlude, Tools of the Mind (Bodrova & Leong, 2007; Hyson, Copple, & Jones, 2006)

- New Figure 6.11 on Tools of the Mind approach

- New *Diversity in Child Development* interlude: Guided Participation and Cultural Contexts

- Expanded description of criticisms of Vygotsky (Gauvain, 2008)

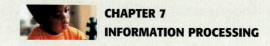

CHAPTER 7
INFORMATION PROCESSING

- New coverage of joint attention and its role in infants' language development

- Coverage of recent research on emergence of gaze following in infants, including a new Figure 7.2, showing the research setting and sequence involved in the study (Brooks & Meltzoff, 2005)

- New description of recent research indicating that an increase in processing speed precedes an increase in working memory capacity (Kail, 2007)

- Expanded and updated coverage of attention, including developmental changes in orienting/investigative process and sustained attention (Courage & Richards, 2008)

- Expanded and updated discussion of habituation and its importance in infant development (Slater, Field, & Hernandez-Reif, 2007)

- New coverage of advances in executive attention and sustained attention in early childhood (Rothbart & Gartstein, 2008)

- New description of exercises used in some European kindergartens to improve young children's attention (Mills & Mills, 2000; Posner & Rothbart, 2007)

- Connection of improved attention of elementary school children to increased focal activation in the prefrontal cortex (Durston & others, 2006)

- Updated discussion of the important role of attention in school readiness (NICHD Early Child Care Research Network, 2005; Posner & Rothbart, 2007)

- Coverage of recent study documenting a link between attentional problems in childhood and aspects of information processing in late adolescence (Friedman & others, 2007)

- Updated discussion of working memory and its link to a number of aspects of children's learning and development (Andersson & Lyxell, 2007; Baddeley, 2007a, b; Cowan, 2007)

- New *Diversity in Child Development* interlude: Culture and Children's Memory (Bauer, 2006; Cole, 2006)

- New discussion of connections between development of the brain and development of memory in infancy, including new Figure 7.7 (de Haan & Martinos, 2008; Nelson, 2008)

- Recent recommendations for three changes to improve interviewing techniques with children to reduce their suggestibility (Bruck, Ceci, & Principe, 2006)

- Updated discussion of Michael Pressley's (Pressley & Harris, 2006; Pressley & Hilden, 2006; Pressley & others, 2007) views on strategy instruction in education

- Expanded and updated coverage of concept formation and categorization in infancy (Quinn, Bhatt, & Hayden, 2008)

- New Figure 7.11 showing stimuli in research on categorization in infancy

- Description of recent research on early development of intense interests in particular categories, including strong gender differences, including new Figure 7.12 (DeLoache, Simcock, & Macari, 2007)

- Expanded and updated coverage of children's scientific thinking (Lehrer & Schauble, 2006)

- Description of recent research on more than 107,000 students in 41 countries linking family, economic, and cultural influences to science achievement (Chiu, 2007)

- Much expanded and updated description of the young child's theory of mind with considerable input from leading expert Candice Mills

- Description of recent study linking infant attention to 4-year-olds' theory of mind (Wellman & others, 2008)

- Coverage of recent study linking young children's theory of mind competence with later metamemory skills (Lockl & Schneider, 2007)

- New discussion of reasons to question false-belief understanding as a pivotal point in development of a theory of mind

- New Figures 7.15 and 7.16, showing stimuli used in theory of mind research

- New section: Theory of Mind and Autism (Fernyhough, 2008; Harris, 2006)

- Updated evaluation and commentary about Fostering a Community of Learners (Lehrer & Schauble, 2006)

- Reduced coverage of cognitive changes in information processing in adolescence to allow expanded coverage of children's information processing

CHAPTER 8
INTELLIGENCE

- New chapter-opening *Images of Child Development:* The Story of Shiffy Landa

- New *Diversity in Child Development* interlude: Larry P.: Intelligent, but Not on Intelligence Tests

- Revised description of what intelligence is, including variations on what Vygotsky and Gardner might include in their definitions

- Updated discussion of the Wechsler scales to include recently introduced composite indexes such as the Verbal Comprehension Index, Working Memory Index, and Processing Speed Index

- New coverage of Sternberg's view on wisdom, how it is linked to his triarchic theory, and his emphasis that wisdom should be taught in schools (Sternberg, 2008c, 2009b)

- Inclusion of new material on Sternberg's (2006) Rainbow assessment, reflecting his triarchic theory of intelligence, to improve the prediction of college students' grade-point average beyond the SAT

- Considerable editing and updating of discussion of intelligence based on feedback from expert consultant Robert J. Sternberg

- Inclusion of recent research on assessment of emotional intelligence and its prediction of high school students' grades (Gil-Olarte Marquez, Palomera Martin, & Brackett, 2007)

- New material on increased interest in emotional intelligence, as well as criticism of the concept (Cox & Nelson, 2008)

- Expanded and updated coverage of evaluating tests of general intelligence and concept of *g* in comparison to concept of multiple intelligences, including Sternberg's (2007a) most recent position on these topics

- New description of Sternberg and his colleagues (Sternberg & Grigorenko, 2008b; Zhang & Sternberg, 2008) that there are no culture-fair tests, only culture-reduced tests

- Deleted coverage of group intelligence tests

- Deleted discussion of older studies of genetic influence on intelligence in favor of more recent studies

- New description of the Bayley-III, including its two new scales—socioemotional and adaptive—that are assessed by questionnaires given to the infant's primary caregiver (Lennon & others, 2008)

- New discussion of gifted education, including recent concerns that the No Child Left Behind policy may be harming students who are gifted (Clark, 2008; Cloud, 2007)

- Inclusion of new strategies parents and teachers can use to encourage students' creativity: (1) build students' self-confidence, (2) encourage students to take risks, and (3) guide students to be persistent and delay gratification

CHAPTER 9
LANGUAGE DEVELOPMENT

- Extensive editing and updating of chapter based on input from leading experts Jean Berko Gleason, Beverly Goldfield, and John Bonvillian

- Movement of babbling before recognizing language sounds in the section on how language develops in infancy

- New section on gestures to indicate their importance in early language development and expansion of this topic

- Expanded discussion of infants' understanding of words before speaking first word

- New material on cross-linguistic differences in early acquisition of verbs in English, Mandarin Chinese, Korean, and Japanese

- Expanded discussion of early word learning to include individual variations in use of whole phrases and referential/expressive distinction

- New material on explanations for young children's rapid word learning, including fast mapping and other processes (Gershkoff-Stowe & Hahn, 2007)

- Expanded and updated coverage of 3-year-olds' phonological advances (Aktar & Herold, 2008; Menn & Stoel-Gammon, 2009)

- New coverage of Michael Tomasello's (2006) interactionist view of language that stresses the role of intentions

- Substantially updated and revised *Research in Child Development* interlude: Family Environment and Young Children's Language Development—including recent research indicating that type of maternal speech, vocabulary, and gestures are more important that the sheer amount of verbal input in predicting children's vocabulary development in low-income families (Pan & others, 2005)

- New *Careers in Child Development* profile: Sharla Peltier, Speech Pathologist

- Coverage of recent study on importance of social interaction in advancing the language of infants, including new research Figure 9.10 (Goldstein, King, & West, 2003)

- Expanded and updated discussion of language development in early childhood, including increased emphasis on the regularities in which young children acquire their particular language (Berko Gleason, 2009)

- Added emphasis on critical role that phonological skills play in becoming a competent reader

- New coverage of importance of having a good vocabulary to competence at reading comprehension (Berninger & Abbott, 2005)

- New section: Early Literacy (Giorgis & Glazer, 2009; Morrow, 2009)

- Expanded material on importance of fluency in reading and which factors improve fluency (Mayer, 2008)

- Coverage of recent study focused on factors involved in a school in which students showed high achievement in reading and writing (Pressley & others, 2007b)

- Heightened emphasis on importance of teachers in development of students' writing skills based on observations made by Michael Pressley and his colleagues (2007b)

- Updated and expanded coverage of writing skills (Graham, 2009; Harris & others, 2008)

- Discussion of recent meta-analysis of the most effective intervention factors in improving writing quality of fourth-through twelfth-grade students (Graham & Perin, 2007)

- Coverage of recent research review in which cognitive processes used in one language transfer more easily to learning a second language (Bialystok, 2007)

- Expanded and updated discussion of research indicating more complex conclusions about whether there are sensitive periods in learning a second language (Thomas & Johnson, 2008)

- New *Diversity in Child Development* interlude: Bilingual Education; substantial updating and revision of this topic (Snow & Yang, 2006)

- Significantly updated coverage of children with Williams syndrome, including recent research (Mervis & Becerra, 2007; Zitzer-Comfort & others, 2007)

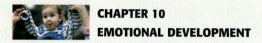 **CHAPTER 10**
EMOTIONAL DEVELOPMENT

- Extensive rewriting of chapter for improved student understanding, including addition of numerous concrete examples of concepts and more descriptions of infants' behaviors and emotions

- New material on cultural variations in emotion in East Asian and non-Latino White children and variations in how parents in these cultures differ in their socialization of children in regard to emotion (Cole & Tan, 2007)

- Revised discussion of appearance of early emotions based on experts Joseph Campos and Michael Lewis, including coverage of controversy about timing and sequence of early emotions (Campos, 2005; Lewis, 2007)

- New description of research on emergence of jealousy in infancy, including new research Figure 10.3 (Hart & Carrington, 2002)

- Updated and expanded description of separation protest in infants (Kagan, 2008)

- Expanded and updated coverage of infant smiling, including new Figure 10.4 on showing the characteristics of an intense smile by a 6-month-old (Messinger, 2008)

- Description of recent research review on swaddling (van Sleuwen & others, 2007)

- New discussion of developmental changes in temperament characteristics (Rothbart & Gartstein, 2008)

- Description of recent research on factors that benefited children with a difficult temperament (Bradley & Corwyn, 2008)

- Inclusion of new material on links between infant fear and guilt, empathy, and low aggression in childhood (Rothbart, 2007)

- New section on children's ability to cope with stress, especially in the face of such circumstances as terrorist attacks (Klingman, 2006; Saarni & others, 2006)

- Description of recent research revealing links between high reactive/low reactive infants, inhibited temperament in infancy, and developmental outcomes in adolescence (Kagan & others, 2007)

- Coverage of recent research on emotion-dismissing parents and children's poor emotion regulation (Lunkenheimer, Shields, & Cortina, 2007)

- Deleted section on coping and stress; moved discussion of coping with stress to Development of Emotion section

- Reduced coverage of adolescence in Development of Emotion section to allow for expanded and more focused information about children at the request of adopters and reviewers

- Important new major section: Social Orientation/ Understanding, including coverage of infants' developing social interest, locomotion, joint attention, and social referencing (Laible & Thompson, 2007; Thompson, 2008)

- New discussion of recent research on becoming a social partner with a peer in 1- and 2-year-olds, including a photograph (Figure 10.7) of the research setting and task (Brownell, Ramani, & Zerwas, 2006)

- Description of recent study on links between joint attention in infancy and social competence at 30 months of age (Vaughn Van Hecke & others, 2007)

- New section: Infants' Social Sophistication and Insight (Thompson, 2008)

- New description of Bowlby's internal working model of attachment

- New commentary about how recent findings regarding infants' earlier social understanding may be linked to understanding goals and intentions in Bowlby's phase 3 of attachment rather than phase 4 (Thompson, 2008)

- Coverage of recent longitudinal study on infant attachment and cognitive development in the elementary school years (O'Connor & McCartney, 2007)

- New Figure 10.10 on dramatic increase in percentage of U.S. fathers staying at home full-time with their children and results of recent study of stay-at-home fathers (Wong & Rochlen, 2008)

- New Figure 10.11 on primary care arrangements for children under 5 years of age with employed mothers (Clarke-Stewart & Miner, 2008)

- Inclusion of recent research on positive outcomes that develop when low-income parents select higher-quality child care (McCartney & others, 2007)

- Description of recent research on quality of child care and children's vocabulary development (Belsky & others, 2007)

- Expanded discussion of cultural variations in attachment (Saarni & others, 2006)

- New *Diversity in Child Development* interlude: Child-Care Policies Around the World, including very recent information related to childbirth (Tolani & Brooks-Gunn, 2008)

CHAPTER 11
THE SELF AND IDENTITY

- New discussion of why studying the self in infancy is difficult based on the view of leading expert Ross Thompson (2007)

- New description of young children's use of psychological traits in their self-descriptions at about 4 to 5 years of age (Thompson, 2006)

- Expansion of section on Self-Understanding, to Self-Understanding and Understanding Others, including new

introduction on how young children are more psychologically sophisticated than used to be thought (Laible & Thompson, 2007; Thompson, 2006)

- New *Diversity in Child Development* interlude: Multiple Selves and Sociocultural Contexts

- Added definition of social cognition

- Extensively revised, updated, and reorganized discussion of self-understanding in early childhood and middle and late childhood

- Coverage of research on how even 4-year-olds understand that people will sometimes make statements that aren't true to get what they want or to avoid trouble (Gee & Heyman, 2007; Lee & others, 2002)

- Expanded explanation of why young children have unrealistically positive self-descriptions (Thompson, 2008)

- Description of recent research on the age at which young children take into account the relative frequency of errors informants make in deciding whether to trust the person (Pasquini & others, 2007)

- New *Research in Child Development* interlude: Adolescents' Self-Images

- Inclusion of information about recent study linking low self-esteem in childhood with depression in adolescence and early adulthood (Orth & others, 2008)

- Coverage of recent study on link between relationship authenticity and increase in self-esteem during adolescence (Impett & others, 2008)

- Coverage of recent research studies on self-esteem in adolescence and emerging adulthood (Galambos, Barker, & Krahn, 2006; Trzesniewski & others, 2006)

- New discussion of James Cote's (2006) view on identity development in emerging adulthood

- New description of ethnic identity in emerging adulthood based on Jean Phinney's (2006) recent ideas

- Inclusion of recent research on ethnic identity in Navajo adolescents (Jones & Galliher, 2007)

- Coverage of recent study on bicultural identity of Mexican American adolescents (Devos, 2006)

CHAPTER 12
GENDER

- New *Diversity in Child Development* interlude: Gender Roles Across Cultures

- Revised and updated definition of gender so as to not exclude biological factors, based on input from leading gender expert, Diane Halpern

- Considerable editing of chapter based on feedback from leading gender expert, Phyllis Bronstein

- New coverage of differential socialization of adolescent boys and girls by mothers and fathers (Bronstein, 2006)

- Description of recent research on gender stereotyping of emotions (Durik & others, 2006)

- Coverage of recent research on gender differences in the HPA axis following stress (Uhart & others, 2006)

- Description of recent research view on visuospatial differences in boys and girls (Halpern & others, 2007)

- Coverage of recent national assessments indicating that U.S. girls have much stronger literacy skills (reading, writing) than U.S. boys, who are only slightly better than U.S. girls in math and science (National Assessment of Educational Progress, 2007)

- Updating of discussion of relational aggression, including research that indicates relational aggression comprises a greater percentage of girls' total aggression than is the case for boys (Putallaz & others, 2007; Young, Boye, & Nelson, 2006)

- Updated coverage of Hyde's (2005, 2007a, b) genders similarities view

- Updated description of gender differences in school achievement (Halpern, 2006)

 CHAPTER 13
MORAL DEVELOPMENT

- New chapter-opening story on Jewel Cash, a 16-year-old teenage dynamo and community involvement exemplar

- Coverage of recent research review of cross-cultural studies of Kohlberg's moral judgment stages, including the role of perspective taking (Gibbs & others, 2007)

- Updated summary of experts' conclusions about gender and Gilligan's approach to moral thinking (Hyde, 2005, 2007; Walker, 2006)

- New *Diversity in Child Development* interlude: Moral Reasoning in the United States and India

- New section on young children's development of a conscience (Kochanska & Aksan, 2007)

- Coverage of recent study linking early mutually responsive orientation between parents and their infant, decrease in power assertive discipline in early childhood, and a increase in the young child's internalization and self-regulation (Kochanska & others, 2008)

- New section on importance of relational quality in role of parenting in children's moral development (Laible & Thompson, 2007)

- New sections on use of proactive strategies and conversational dialogue by parents in encouraging their children's moral development (Thompson, McGinley, & Meyer, 2006)

- New *Caring for Children* interlude: Parenting Recommendations for Raising a Moral Child

- Inclusion of recent information about 40 of 50 states now having mandates regarding character education (Nucci & Narvaez, 2008)

- Coverage of recent acceptance of using a care perspective as part of character education (Noddings, 2008; Sherblom, 2008)

- New material on two conditions that improve the likelihood that service learning will generate positive outcomes for youth (Nucci, 2006)

- Description of recent study on service learning and academic adjustment (Schmidt, Shumow, & Kackar, 2007)

- Inclusion of recent study of gender differences in service learning (Webster & Worrell, 2008)

- New section on cheating, including recent research and information about why students cheat and strategies for preventing cheating (Anderman & Murdock, 2007; Stephens, 2008)

- New section on integrative moral education (Narváez, 2008)

- New discussion of early-onset and late-onset antisocial behavior and their links with outcomes in emerging adulthood (Schulenberg & Zarrett, 2006)

- Description of recent research on maternal monitoring and lower incidence of delinquency in Latino girls (Loukas, Suizzo, & Prelow, 2007)

- Coverage of recent study linking early child abuse with delinquency (Lansford & others, 2007)

- Inclusion of recent research studies on the role of peer rejection and deviant peers in predicting delinquency (Bowman, Prelow, & Weaver, 2007; Vitaro, Pedersen, & Brendgen, 2007)

- New material on importance of self-control and intelligence in whether adolescents will become delinquents or not (Koolhof & others, 2007)

- New *Research in Child Development* interlude: Fast Track, providing very recent information about an extensive intervention with high-risk kindergarten children and outcomes of the intervention in adolescence (Conduct Problems Prevention Research Group, 2007; Dodge & the Conduct Problems Prevention Research Group, 2007)

- New major section: Religious and Spiritual Development

- New coverage of first-year college students' religiousness (Pryor & others, 2007)

- New section on religion and identity development in adolescence and emerging adulthood (Kroger, 2007; Templeton & Eccles, 2006)

- Expanded and updated coverage of the positive role of religion in adolescent development (Cotton & others, 2006)

- Description of recent large-scale random sample connecting religiosity in adolescents to lower levels of problem behaviors (Sinha, Cnaan, & Gelles, 2006)

- Coverage of recent World Values Survey (Lippman & Keith, 2006)

- Description of recent research on percentage of U.S. parents with children at home who pray with their children and send their children to religious education programs (Pew Research Center, 2008)

- Discussion of recent study of changes in religiousness and attending religious services from 14 to 25 years of age, including new Figure 13.5 (Koenig, McGue, & Iacono, 2008)

- Coverage of recent study of Indonesian Muslim 13-year-olds' religious involvement and social competence (French & others, 2008)

CHAPTER 14
FAMILIES

- Connection of turn-taking and games like peek-a-boo to joint attention by the caregiver and infant, and connection to discussion of joint attention in Chapter 7, "Information Processing" (Tomasello & Carpenter, 2007)

- Expansion of material on emotion in family processes, including recent research on effectiveness of distinctive parenting responses depending on the domain involved (Davidoff & Grusec, 2006)

- Coverage of recent research on the Bringing Baby Home workshop in the transition to parenting section (Shapiro & Gottman, 2005)

- Expanded description of parenting adaptations in middle and late childhood, especially in supporting and stimulating children's academic achievement (Huston & Ripke, 2006)

- Much expanded coverage of parents as managers of children's lives, including recent research review of family management and African American children's academic achievement (Mandara, 2006)

- Discussion of recent research on links between parenting styles and psychosocial maturity and academic achievement (Steinberg, Blatt-Eisengart, & Cauffman, 2006)

- Discussion of increasing number of recent research studies that have found negative developmental outcomes for children who have been physically punished by their parents (Bender & others, 2007; Mulvaney & Mebert, 2007)

- Description of recent study on coparenting and young children's effortful control (Karreman & others, 2008)

- New coverage of data indicating that child neglect occurs up to three times as often as child abuse (Benoit, Coolbear, & Crawford, 2008)

- New information about abnormal stress hormone levels in children who have been maltreated (Gunnar & Fisher, 2006), including new Figure 14.4

- Description of recent research linking attachment in adolescence with patterns of intimacy in emerging adulthood (Mayseless & Scharf, 2007)

- New material included from Laurie Kramer's (2006) research on how frequently siblings have conflicts, how parents react when siblings have conflicts, and teaching siblings skills to improve their sibling interaction

- Inclusion of recent research on mediating training for parents and positive sibling outcomes (Smith & Ross, 2007)

- New description of three main characteristics of sibling relationships in adolescence (Dunn, 2007)

- Coverage of recent research on siblings (Kim & others, 2007)

- Updated coverage of birth order, based on recent review (Paulhus, 2008)

- Coverage of Ann Crouter's (2006) recent research on link between parents' poor conditions at work and negative parenting

- New description of link between working mothers and reduction in children's (especially girls') gender stereotyping (Goldberg & Lucas-Thompson, 2008)

- Description of recent research review on participation in organized activities and positive outcomes for children and youth (Mahoney, Harris, & Eccles, 2006)

- Description of Paul Amato's (2006) longitudinal research on adult outcomes of individuals who experienced their parents' divorce in childhood and adolescence

- Inclusion of information about recent study on increased depression in adolescent daughters in divorced families (Ormel & others, 2008)

- Added commentary that problems children from divorced families experience often stem from active marital conflict in the predivorce period (Thompson, 2008)

- Discussion of E. Mavis Hetherington's (2006) recent conclusions about which type of stepfamily arrangement is linked to better adjustment in children and adolescents

- New *Diversity in Child Development* interlude: Acculturation and Ethnic Minority Parenting

- New description of low-income families having less resources than higher-income families (Conger & Dogan, 2007; Patterson & Hastings, 2007)

CHAPTER 15
PEERS

- New *Diversity in Child Development* interlude: Cross-Cultural Comparisons of Peer Relations

- Discussion of two recent longitudinal studies on links between peer competence and popularity in middle and late childhood and work success and romantic relationships in adulthood (Collins & van Dulmen, 2006; Huesmann & others, 2006)

- Discussion of three recent studies that illustrate the link between affiliating with deviant, antisocial peers and drug use, delinquency, and depression (Connell & Dishion, 2006; Laird & others 2005; Nation & Heflinger, 2006)

- Expanded and updated description of links between parent and peer relations (Allen & Antonishak, 2008)

- New description of poor parenting skills as precursors of children becoming rejected by peers (Shaw & others, 2006)

- Coverage of recent longitudinal research on marital quality, attachment security, and children's peer relations (Lucas-Thompson & Clarke-Stewart, 2007)

- Discussion of recent research studies on bullying (Brunstein & others, 2007; Nylund & others, 2007)

- New description of three widely used bullying intervention programs

- Description of how increased use of electronic media has resulted in less time for play in childhood (Linn, 2008)

- Updated coverage of social play (Sumaroka & Bernstein, 2008)

- Expanded coverage of pretend play, including Catherine Garvey's (2000) and Angeline Lillard's (2007) views

- Expanded and updated material on which adolescents are most likely to conform to their peers (Prinstein, 2007; Prinstein & Dodge, 2008)

- Discussion of recent research on age differences in resistance to peer influence (Steinberg & Monahan, 2007)

- Commentary about developmental changes in reputation-based crowds in adolescence (Collins & Steinberg, 2006)

- Updated and expanded coverage of variation in quality of friendships and developmental outcomes (Crosnoe & others, 2008; Rubin, Fredstrom, & Bowker, 2008)

- New description of research on characteristics of friends and initiation of sexual intercourse (Sieving & others, 2006)

- Description of recent research on girls and friendships with older boys (Poulin & Pedersen, 2007)

- New section: Gender and Friendship, including recent research findings

- Inclusion of material on the positive aspect of girls' friendships with achievement-oriented best friends and how this is linked to taking math courses in high school (Crosnoe & others, 2008)

- Coverage of recent research indicating importance of friends' grade-point average in adolescent development (Cook, Deng, & Morgano, 2007)

- Discussion of recent research on friendship, co-rumination, and depression in adolescence (Rose, Carlson, & Waller, 2007)

- At the request of adopters and reviewers, deleted final section on dating and romantic relationships

 CHAPTER 16
SCHOOLS AND ACHIEVEMENT

- New coverage of recent conclusions by experts in educational psychology that the most effective teachers often use both constructivist and direct instruction approaches (Bransford & others, 2006)

- New *Diversity in Child Development* interlude: Early Childhood Education in Japan and Developing Countries (Roopnarine & Metingdogan, 2006)

- Updated and expanded coverage of Montessori programs (Hyson, Copple, & Jones, 2006; Whitescarver, 2006)

- Update on number of states providing education for 3- and 4-year-old children and percentage of 3- and 4-year-old children who attend center-based programs (NAEYC, 2005)

- Description of how not all developmentally appropriate programs show significant benefits for children and recent changes in the concept of developmentally appropriate education (Hyson, 2007)

- Updated material on Project Head Start, including information about it being the largest federally funded program for U.S. children (Hagen & Lamb-Parker, 2008)

- Description of recent data on positive outcomes of the Perry Preschool program for individuals at age 40 (Schweinhart & others, 2005)

- New coverage of issue involving whether the United States should have universal preschool education (Zigler, Gilliam, & Jones, 2006)

- Description of recent study comparing discipline problems in sixth-graders in middle school with sixth-graders in elementary schools (Cook & others, 2008)

- Updated statistics on school dropouts, including substantial decrease in Latino dropouts since 2000 (National Center for Education Statistics, 2008a)

- New *Caring for Children* interlude: "I Have a Dream" ("I Have a Dream" Foundation, 2008), including recent evaluation of the Houston "I Have a Dream" program

- Description of recent initiative by the Bill and Melinda Gates Foundation (2006, 2008) to reduce the dropout rate in schools with high dropout rates by keeping high-risk students with the same teachers across the high school years

- Considerable editing of material on children with disabilities, based on expert consultant Karen Harris' recommendations

- Updated description of percentage of students with disabilities receiving special services (National Center for Education Statistics, 2008b)

- Revised definition of learning disabilities to more closely approximate U.S. government's definition

- Coverage of trends in percentage of students with learning disabilities who receive special services (National Center for Education Statistics, 2007)

- New description of variation that occurs across states and school systems in how learning disabilities are defined and diagnosed (Bender, 2008)

- New discussion of causes of learning disabilities and increasing research emphasis on the brain's role in learning disabilities, including new Figure 16.4 (Shaywitz, Gruen, & Shaywitz, 2007)

- Description of recent intensive 16-week instruction program that increased reading skills of first-grade students with severe reading problems who had not responded to adequately to reading instruction (Simos & others, 2007)

- Added description of how an ADHD diagnosis requires that the characteristics appear early in childhood and be debilitating for the child

- New material on how school teams are not supposed to diagnose ADHD and why (Bender, 2008)

- New material documenting a three-year delay in thickening of the cerebral cortex in children with ADHD, including new Figure 16.5

- Updated coverage of new stimulant and nonstimulant drugs that are being evaluated in treatment of ADHD (Bhatara & Aparasu, 2007; Faraone, 2007)

- New material on the important role the teacher plays in monitoring the effectiveness of an ADHD student's medication (Thompson, Moore, & Symons, 2007)

- New coverage of very recent interest in the role that exercise might play in ADHD (Ratey, 2006; Tantillo & others, 2006)

- New section, Autism Spectrum Disorders, including research linking autism spectrum disorders to genetic mutations on chromosome 16 in approximately 1 out of 100 cases of these disorders (Weiss & others, 2008).

- New Figure 16.6, showing percentage of U.S. students with disabilities who spend time in the regular classroom in a recent school year (National Center for Education Statistics, 2007)

- New description of 2004 reauthorization of IDEA and its link with No Child Left Behind legislation (Hallahan & Kauffman, 2006)

- New section on the role of interest in achievement (Wigfield & others, 2006)

- New section on the role of cognitive engagement and responsibility in achievement (Blumenfeld, Kempler, & Krajcik, 2006)

- New section, Some Final Thoughts About Intrinsic and Extrinsic Motivation (Cameron & Pierce, 2008; Schunk, 2008)

- New section, Mindset, describing Carol Dweck's (2006, 2007) recent emphasis on the importance of children developing a growth rather than a fixed mindset

- Coverage of recent study on gender differences in mastery and performance orientations (Kenney-Benson & others, 2006)

- Inclusion of information about recent study illustrating importance of mastery goals in students' effort in mathematics (Chouinrad, Karsenti, & Roy, 2007)

- New description of how the U.S. government's No Child Left Behind legislation promotes performance rather than mastery orientation

- New coverage that emphasizes how mastery and performance goals aren't always mutually exclusive and that for many children combining mastery and performance goals orientations benefits them (Anderman, 2007; Schunk, Meece, & Pintrich, 2008)

- Coverage of recent study on academic profiles of adolescents with low and high self-efficacy (Bassi & others, 2007)

- New section on expectations in achievement, including discussion of teachers and parents' expectations, as well as children's expectations (Benner & Mistry, 2007)

- Description of recent observational study of teachers in twelve classrooms to determine learning factors involved in classrooms in which teachers have high, average, or low expectations for students (Rubie-Davis, 2007)

- Coverage of recent study indicating that teachers' positive expectations help to protect students from negative influence of low parental expectations (Wood, Kaplan, & McLoyd, 2007)

- Description of recent study that revealed link between instructional and socioemotional support and first-grade students' achievement (Perry, Donohue, & Weinstein, 2007)

- New description of lack of resources to support learning in homes of students from low-income families (Schunk, Meece, & Pintrich, 2008)

- Discussion of recent improvements U.S. adolescents have made in math and science comparisons with their counterparts in other countries (Gonzales & others, 2004)

CHAPTER 17
CULTURE AND DIVERSITY

- Description of recent study on cultural variation in children's social organization and work on a task in a group (Mejia-Arauz & others, 2007)

- New coverage of recent analysis by Carolyn Tamis-LeMonda and her colleagues (2008) that describes the importance of cultural values in parenting practices and how in many families children are reared in a context of individualistic and collectivistic values

- Inclusion of information about recent study linking neighborhood disadvantage, parenting behavior, and child outcomes (Kohen & others, 2008)

- Updated U.S. poverty statistics for U.S. children (Federal Interagency Forum on Child and Family Statistics, 2008)

- Inclusion of very recent data on much higher percentage of children living in poverty in female-headed households compared with married families (Federal Interagency Forum on Child and Family Statistics, 2008)

- Description of recent study on persistent poverty and physiological indications of stress in children (Evans & Kim, 2007)

- Updated statistics on percent of children in African American, Latino, and non-White Latino families living in poverty (Federal Interagency Forum on Child and Family Statistics, 2008)

- New coverage of recent research by Aletha Huston and her colleagues (Huston & others, 2006) on intervening in impoverished families

- Description of recent changes in the Quantum Opportunities program and its expansion by the Eisenhower Foundation (2008)

- Updating of material on acculturation and adolescent problems (Gonzales & others, 2006, 2007)

- New Figure 17.5, showing percentage of adolescents in various ethnic groups in 2000 and projected figures for 2100

- Expanded and updated coverage of material on family duty, obligation, and stress in children and adolescents from different immigrant groups (Hayashino & Chopra, 2009; Kagitcibasi, 2006)

- Inclusion of recent studies linking discrimination of African American and Latino adolescents to more problems and lower-level academic achievement, including new Figure 17.6, showing types of racial hassles African American adolescents experience (DeGarmo & Martinez, 2006; Sellers & others, 2006)

- Description of recent research on discrimination of Chinese American children by their peers (Rivas, Hughes, & Way, 2008)

- New coverage of Mark Bauerlein's (2008) recent book, *The Dumbest Generation,* and discussion of how the digital age might be affecting the current generation of adolescents

- New material on dramatic increase in media multitasking by children and youth and how if this is factored into media-use figures, children and adolescents now use electronic media an average of eight hours per day (Roberts & Foehr, 2008)

- Extensively updated coverage of use of various media by adolescents based on recent national survey, including new Figure 17.7 on use of various media by children and adolescents (Rideout, Roberts, & Foehr, 2005)

- Coverage of recent study of TV watching from $2\frac{1}{2}$ to $5\frac{1}{2}$ years of age and its link to whether children show social and behavioral problems (Mistry & others, 2007)

- Description of recent research on link between watching violent TV shows in early childhood and antisocial behavior in elementary school (Christakis & Zimmerman, 2007)

- New material included from recent research review of electronic media use and learning in infancy and childhood (Kirkorian, Anderson, & Wartella, 2008)

- New information about one positive aspect of video game use—improvement in visuospatial skills (Schmidt & Vandewater, 2008)

- Updated coverage of electronic media programs and children's prosocial behavior (Wilson, 2008)

- Coverage of recent national survey of U.S. 10- to 17-year-olds' unwanted exposure to online pornography (Wolak, Mitchell, & Finkelhor, 2007)

- New section: The Online Social Environment of Children and Adolescents

- Discussion of recent study on conversation themes in online adolescent chat rooms (Subrahmanyam, Smaahel, & Greenfield, 2006)

- New coverage of MySpace and Facebook, exploring the powerful role these two Internet sites are playing in the social networking of adolescents and college students

- New information about youths' communication with strangers on the Internet and cyberbullying (Subrahmanyam & Greenfield, 2008)

- New *Diversity in Child Development* interlude: Computers, the Internet, and Sociocultural Diversity

- Description of recent innovations in use of videoconferencing and e-mail to connect U.S. students with students in other countries, including new photograph

- Description of recent study linking home Internet use by adolescents in low-income families to positive academic outcomes (Jackson & others, 2006)

ACKNOWLEDGMENTS

I very much appreciate the support and guidance provided to me by many people at McGraw-Hill. Beth Mejia, Publisher, has done a marvelous job of directing and monitoring the development and publication of this text. Mike Sugarman, Executive Editor, has brought a wealth of publishing knowledge and vision to bear on improving my texts. Maureen Spada has done an excellent job as the Developmental Editor in handling the page-by-page changes and other editorial matters in this new edition. Dawn Groundwater, Director of Development, has done a superb job of organizing and monitoring the many tasks necessary to move this book through the editorial process. Jillian Allison, Editorial Coordinator, has once done a competent job of obtaining reviewers and handling many editorial chores. James Headley, Marketing Manager, has contributed in numerous positive ways to this book. Beatrice Sussman once again did a terrific job as the book's copy editor. Marilyn Rothenberger did a superb job in coordinating the book's production.

I also want to thank my wife, Mary Jo, our children, Tracy and Jennifer, and my grandchildren, Jordan, Alex, and Luke, for their wonderful contributions to my life and for helping me to better understand the marvels and mysteries of children's development.

Special thanks go to the many reviewers of twelfth edition of this text. Their extensive contributions have made this is far better book.

REVIEWERS

I owe a special gratitude to the reviewers who provided detailed feedback about the book.

Expert Consultants

Kirby Deater-Deckerd, *Virginia Tech;* Linda Smolak, *Kenyon College;* Candice Mills, *University of Texas at Dallas;* Robert J. Sternberg, *Tufts University;* Beverly Goldfield, *Rhode Island College;* Michael Lewis, *Rutgers University;* Phyllis Bronstein, *University of Vermont;* Gustavo Carlo, *University of Nebraska;* Joan Grusec, *Univeristy of Toronto;* Diane Hughes, *New York University*

Twelfth Edition Reviewers

Kristine Anthis—*Southern Connecticut State University*
Brein K. Ashdown—*St. Louis University*
Jann Belcher—*Utah Valley State College*
Bryan Bolea—*Grand Valley State University*
Teresa Bossert-Braasch—*McHenry County College*
Albert Bramante—*Union County College*
Jo Ann Burnside—*Richard J Daley College*
Catherine Caldwell-Harris—*Boston University*
Victoria Candelora—*Brevard Community College*
Lisa R. Caya—*University of Wisconsin—La Crosse*
Darlene DeMarie—*University of South Florida*
Ruth Doyle—*Casper College*
Sean Duffy—*Rutgers University*
Karen Falcone—*San Joaquin Delta College*
Gary Feng—*Duke University*
Janet Frick—*University of Georgia*
Kate Fogarty—*University of Florida—Gainsville*
Dale Fryxell—*Chamainde University*
Eugene Geist—*Ohio University*
Renee Ha—*University of Washington*
Joyce Hemphill—*University of Wisconsin*
Alice Honig—*Syracuse University*
Stephen Hupp—*Southern Illinois University—Edwardsville*
Hsin-Hui Lin—*University of Houston—Victoria*
Gretchen S. Lovas—*Susquehanna University*
Barbara Aldis Patton—*University of Houston—Victoria*
Winnie Mucherah—*Ball State University*
Cynthia Rickert—*Dominican College*
Jaynati Roy—*Southern Conneticut State University*
Donna Ruiz—*University of Cincinnati*
Margot Underwood—*College of DuPage*
Kourtney Valliancourt—*New Mexico State University*

Reviewers of Previous Editions

Ruth L. Ault, *Davidson College;* Mary Ballard, *Appalachian State University;* William H. Barber, *Midwestern State University;* Marjorie M. Battaglia, *George Mason University;* Wayne Benenson, *Illinois State University;* Michael Bergmire, *Jefferson College;* David Bernhardt, *Carleton University;*

Kathryn Norcross Black, *Purdue University;* Elain Blakemore, *Indiana University;* Susan Bland, *Niagara County Community College;* Amy Booth, *Northwestern University;* Marc Bornstein, *National Institute of Child Health and Human Development;* Megan E. Bradley, *Frostburg State University;* Maureen Callahan, *Webster University;* D. Bruce Carter, *Syracuse University;* Elaine Cassel, *Marymount University, Lord Fairfax Community College;* Lisa Caya, *University of Wisconsin—LaCrosse;* Steven Ceci, *Cornell University;* Theodore Chandler, *Kent State University;* Dante Cicchetti, *University of Rochester;* Audry E. Clark, *California State University, Northridge;* Debra E. Clark, *SUNY–Cortland;* Robert Cohen, *The University of Memphis;* John D. Coie, *Duke University;* Cynthia Garcia Coll, *Wellesley College;* W. Andrew Collins, *University of Minnesota;* Robert C. Coon, *Louisiana State University;* Roger W. Coulson, *Iowa State University;* William Curry, *Wesleyan College;* Fred Danner, *University of Kentucky;* Marlene DeVoe, *Saint Cloud State University;* Denise M. DeZolt, *Kent State University;* K. Laurie Dickson, *Northern Arizona University;* Daniel D. DiSalvi, *Kean College;* Diane C. Draper, *Iowa State University;* Jerry Dusek, *Syracuse University;* Beverly Brown Dupré, *Southern University at New Orleans;* Glen Elder, Jr., *University of North Carolina;* Claire Etaugh, *Bradley University;* Dennis T. Farrell, *Luzerne County Community College;* Saul Feinman, *University of Wyoming;* Tiffany Field, *University of Miami;* Oney Fitzpatrick, Jr., *Lamar University;* Jane Goins Flanagan, *Lamar University;* L. Sidney Fox, *California State University—Long Beach;* Douglas Frye, *University of Virginia;* Janet A. Fuller, *Mansfield University;* Irma Galejs, *Iowa State University;* Mary Gauvain, *University of California, Riverside;* John Gibbs, *Ohio State University;* Colleen Gift, *Highland Community College;* Margaret S. Gill, *Kutztown University;* Hill Goldsmith, *University of Wisconsin—Madison;* Cynthia Graber, *Columbia University;* Nira Grannott, *University of Texas at Dallas;* Stephen B. Graves, *University of South Florida;* Donald E. Guenther, *Kent State University;* Julia Guttmann, *Iowa Wesleyan College;* Robert A. Haaf, *University of Toledo;* Robin Harwood, *Texas Tech University;* Susan Harter, *University of Denver;* Craig Hart, *Brigham Young University;* Elizabeth Hasson, *Westchester University;* Rebecca Heikkinen, *Kent State University;* Joyce Hemphill, *University of Wisconsin;* Shirley-Anne Hensch, *University of Wisconsin;* Stanley Henson, *Arkansas Technical University;* Alice Honig, *Syracuse University;* Cynthia Hudley, *University of California—Santa Barbara;* Vera John-Steiner, *University of New Mexico;* Helen L. Johnson, *Queens College;* Kathy E. Johnson, *Indiana University—Purdue University Indianapolis;* Seth Kalichman, *Loyola University;* Kenneth Kallio, *SUNY—Geneseo;* Maria Kalpidou, *Assumption College;* Daniel W. Kee, *California State University—Fullerton;* Christy Kimpo, *University of Washington;* Melvyn B. King, *SUNY—Cortland;* Claire Kopp, *UCLA;* Deanna Kuhn, *Columbia University;* John Kulig, *Northern Illinois University;* Janice Kupersmidt, *University of North Carolina;* Michael Lamb, *National Institute of Child Health and Human Development;* Daniel K. Lapsley, *University of Notre Dame;* David B. Liberman, *University of Houston;* Robert Lickliter, *Florida*

International University; **Marianna Footo Linz,** *Marshall University;* **Pamela Ludemann,** *Framingham State College;* **Kevin MacDonald,** *California State University—Long Beach;* **Virginia A. Marchman,** *University of Texas at Dallas;* **Saramma T. Mathew,** *Troy State University;* **Barbara McCombs,** *University of Denver;* **Dottie McCrossen,** *University of Ottawa;* **Sheryll Mennicke,** *Concordia College, St. Paul;* **Carolyn Meyer,** *Lake Sumter Community College;* **Dalton Miller-Jones,** *NE Foundation for Children;* **Marilyn Moore,** *Illinois State University;* **Carrie Mori,** *Boise State University;* **Brad Morris,** *Grand Valley State University;* **Winnie Mucherah,** *Ball State University;* **John P. Murray,** *Kansas State University;* **Dara Musher-Eizenman,** *Bowling Green State University;* **José E. Nanes,** *University of Minnesota;* **Sherry J. Neal,** *Oklahoma City Community Center;* **Larry Nucci,** *University of Illinois at Chicago;* **Daniel J. O'Neill,** *Briston Community College;* **Randall E. Osborne,** *Southwest Texas State University;* **Margaret Owen,** *University of Texas at Dallas;* **Robert Pasnak,** *George Mason University;* **Barba Patton,** *University of Texas—Victoria;* **Judy Payne,** *Murray State University;* **Elizabeth Pemberton,** *University of Delaware;* **Herb Pick,** *University of Minnesota;* **Kathy Lee Pillow,** *Arkansas State University, Beebe;* **Nan Ratner,** *University of Maryland;* **Brenda Reimer,** *Southern Missouri State University;* **John Reiser,** *Vanderbilt University;* **Cosby Steele Rogers,** *Virginia Polytechnic Institute and State University;* **Kimberly A. Gordon Rouse,** *Ohio State University;* **Kenneth Rubin,** *University of Maryland;* **Alan Russell,** *Flinders University;* **Carolyn Saarni,** *Sonoma State University;* **Douglas B. Sawin,** *University of Texas, Austin;* **Krista Schoenfeld,** *Colby Community College;* **Ed Scholwinski,** *Southwest Texas State University;* **Dale Schunk,** *Purdue University;* **Bill M. Seay,** *Louisiana State University;* **Matthew J. Sharps,** *California State University, Fresno;* **Marilyn Shea,** *University of Maine, Farmington;* **Susan Shonk,** *SUNY—College of Brockport;* **Susan Siaw,** *California Polytechnic Institute—Pomona;* **Robert Siegler,** *Carnegie Mellon University;* **Evelyn D. Silva,** *Cosumnes River College;* **Mildred D. Similton,** *Pfeiffer University;* **Dorothy Justus Sluss,** *Virginia Polytechnic Institute and State University;* **Janet Spence,** *University of Texas—Austin;* **Melanie Spence,** *University of Texas—Dallas;* **Richard Sprott,** *California State University, East Bay;* **Mark S. Strauss,** *University of Pittsburgh;* **Margaret Szewczyk,** *University of Chicago;* **Ross Thompson,** *University of California—Davis;* **Donna J. Tyler Thompson,** *Midland College;* **Marion K. Underwood,** *University of Texas—Dallas;* **Cherie Valeithian,** *Kent State University;* **Jaan Valsiner,** *Clark University;* **Robin Yaure,** *Pennsylvania State—Mont Alto;* **Elizabeth Vera,** *Loyola University—Chicago;* **Lawrence Walker,** *University of British Columbia;* **Kimberlee L. Whaley,** *Ohio State University;* **Belinda M. Wholeben,** *Northern Illinois University;* **Frederic Wynn,** *County College of Morris*

SUPPLEMENTS

The supplements listed here may accompany *Child Development,* twelfth edition. Please contact your McGraw-Hill representative for details concerning policies, prices, and availability.

For the Instructor

The instructor side of the Online Learning Center at http://www.mhhe.com/santrockcd12e contains the Instructor's Manual, Test Bank files, PowerPoint slides, Image Gallery, and other valuable material to help you design and enhance your course. Ask your local McGraw-Hill representative for your password.

Instructor's Manual *by Ralph Carlini, University of Massachusetts—Darmouth* Each chapter of the Instructor's Manual is introduced by a Total Teaching Package Outline. This fully integrated tool helps instructors more easily locate and choose among the many resources available for the course by linking each element of the Instructor's Manual to a particular teaching topic within the chapter. These resources include chapter outlines, suggested lecture topics, classroom activities and demonstrations, critical thinking exercises, critical thinking questions, implications for guidance, and service learning resources.

Test Bank and Computerized Test Bank *by Diane Powers, Iowa Central Community College* This comprehensive Test Bank includes more than 2,000 multiple-choice questions and 5-10 essay questions per chapter. Organized by chapter, the questions are designed to test factual, applied, and conceptual understanding and are keyed to Bloom's taxonomy. All test questions are compatible with EZ Test, McGraw-Hill's Computerized Test Bank program.

PowerPoint Slides *by Len Mendola, Adelphia University* These presentations cover the key points of each chapter and include charts and graphs from the text. They can be used as is, or you may modify them to meet your specific needs.

CPS Questions These questions, formatted for use with the interactive Classroom Performance System, are organized by chapter and designed to test factual, applied, and conceptual understanding. These test questions are also compatible with EZTest, McGraw-Hill's Computerized Test Bank program.

McGraw-Hill's Visual Asset Database for Lifespan Development ("VAD") McGraw-Hill's Visual Assets Database for Lifespan Development (VAD 2.0) (www.mhhe.com/vad) is an on-line database of videos for use in the developmental psychology classroom, created specifically for instructors. You can customize classroom presentations by downloading the videos to your computer and showing the videos on their own or insert them into your course cartridge or PowerPoint presentations. All of the videos are available with or without captions. Ask your McGraw-Hill representative for access information.

Multimedia Courseware for Child Development *Charlotte J. Patterson, University of Virginia* This video-based set of two CD-ROMS covers classic and contemporary experiments in child development. Respected researcher Charlotte J. Patterson selected the content and wrote accompanying modules that can be assigned to students. These modules include suggestions for additional projects as well as a testing component. Multimedia Courseware can be packaged with the text at a discount.

Annual Editions: Child Growth and Development 08/09

This reader is a collection of articles on topics related to the latest research and thinking in human development. Annual Editions are updated regularly and include useful features such as a topic guide, an annotated table of contents, unit overviews, and a topical index.

Taking Sides: Clashing Views in Childhood and Society

Current controversial issues are presented in a debate-style format designed to stimulate student interest and develop critical thinking skills. Each issue is thoughtfully framed with an issue summary, an issue introduction, and a postscript.

Cases in Child and Adolescent Development for Teachers

Containing more than 40 cases, *Case Studies in Child and Adolescent Development for Teachers* brings developmental issues to life. The reality-based cases address a variety of developmental issues, giving students an opportunity to think critically about the way development influences children everyday.

For the Student

Online Learning Center (OLC)   This companion website, at http://www.mhhe.com/santrockcd12e offers a wide variety of student resources. **Multiple Choice, True/False, and Internet Exercises** reinforce key principles and cover all the major concepts discussed throughout the text. Entirely different from the test items in the Test Bank, these quiz questions, written by

Meghan Bradley at Frostburg State University, have been written to assess students but also to help them learn. Key terms from the text are reproduced in a **Glossary of Key Terms** where they can be accessed in alphabetical order for easy reference and review. **Decision Making Scenarios** present students with the opportunity to apply the information in the chapter to realistic situations, and see what effects their decisions have. Streamable online **Videos** reinforce chapter content.

CourseSmart is a new way for faculty to find and review eTextbooks. It's also a great option for students who are interested in accessing their course materials digitally and saving money. CourseSmart offers thousands of the most commonly adopted textbooks across hundreds of courses from a wide variety of higher education publishers. It is the only place for faculty to review and compare the full text of a textbook online, providing immediate access without the environmental impact of requesting a print exam copy. At CourseSmart, students can save up to 50% off the cost of a print book, reduce their impact on the environment, and gain access to powerful web tools for learning, including full text search, notes and highlighting, and email tools for sharing notes between classmates.

To the Student

This book provides you with important study tools to help you more effectively learn about children's development. Especially important is the learning goals system that is integrated throughout each chapter. In the visual walk-through of features, pay special attention to how the learning goals system works.

THE LEARNING GOALS SYSTEM

Using the learning goals system will help you to learn the material more easily. Key aspects of the learning goals system are the learning goals, chapter maps, Review and Reflect, and Reach Your Learning Goals sections, which are all linked together. At the beginning of each chapter, you will see a page that includes both a chapter outline and three to six learning goals that preview the chapter's main themes and underscore the most important ideas in the chapter. Then, at the beginning of each major section of a chapter, you will see a mini–chapter map that provides you with a visual organization of the key topics you are about to read in the section. At the end of each section is Review and Reflect, in which the learning goal for the section is restated, a series of review questions related to the mini–chapter map are asked, and a question that encourages you to think critically about a topic related to the section appears. At the end of the chapter, you will come to a section titled Reach Your Learning Goals. This includes all of the main headings, a restatement of the chapter's learning goals, and a summary of the chapter's content that is directly linked to the chapter outline at the beginning of the chapter and the questions asked in the Review part of Review and Reflect within the chapter. The Reach Your Learning Goals section essentially provides brief answers to the questions asked in the within-chapter Review sections.

CHAPTER-OPENING OUTLINE AND LEARNING GOALS

MINI–CHAPTER MAP

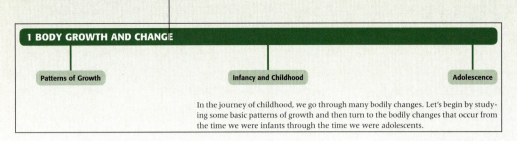

1 BODY GROWTH AND CHANGE

Patterns of Growth   Infancy and Childhood   Adolescence

In the journey of childhood, we go through many bodily changes. Let's begin by studying some basic patterns of growth and then turn to the bodily changes that occur from the time we were infants through the time we were adolescents.

REVIEW AND REFLECT

Review and Reflect: Learning Goal 1

1 Discuss Historical Views and the Modern Era of Child Development

REVIEW

- What is development? How has childhood been perceived through history?
- What are the key characteristics of the modern study of child development?

REFLECT

- Now that you have studied historical views of childhood and the beginning of the modern era in child development, what do you think are some of the major changes in the topics child development researchers study today compared with what psychologists such as G. Stanley Hall, Alfred Binet, and Arnold Gesell studied in the early twentieth century?

REACH YOUR LEARNING GOALS

Reach Your Learning Goals

Physical Development and Health

1   BODY GROWTH AND CHANGE: DISCUSS DEVELOPMENTAL CHANGES IN THE BODY

Patterns of Growth

- Human growth follows cephalocaudal and proximodistal patterns. In a cephalocaudal pattern, the fastest growth occurs at the top—the head. Physical growth in size, weight, and feature differentiation occurs gradually, moves from the top to the bottom. In a proximodistal pattern, growth begins at the center of the body and then moves toward the extremities.

Infancy and Childhood

- Height and weight increase rapidly in infancy and then take a slower course during childhood. The average North American newborn is 20 inches long and weighs $7\frac{1}{2}$ pounds. Infants grow about 1 inch per month during their first year. In early childhood, girls are only slightly smaller and lighter than boys. Growth is slow and consistent in middle and late childhood, and head circumference, waist circumference, and leg length decrease in relation to body height.

Adolescence

- Puberty is a rapid maturation involving hormonal and body changes that occur primarily in early adolescence puberty began coming on earlier in the twentieth century. There are wide individual variations in the age at which puberty begins. Heredity plays an important role in determining puberty. Key hormones involved in puberty are testosterone and estradiol. Rising testosterone levels in boys cause voice changes, enlargement of external genitals, and increased height. In girls, increased levels of estradiol influence breast and uterine development and skeletal change. Key physical changes of puberty include a growth spurt as well as sexual maturation. The growth spurt occurs on the average about two years sooner for girls than for boys. Adolescents are preoccupied with their bodies and develop images of their bodies. Adolescent girls have more negative body images than adolescent boys. Early maturation favors boys during adolescence, but in adulthood late-maturing boys have a more successful identity. Early-maturing girls are vulnerable to a number of problems including eating disorders, smoking, and depression.

OTHER LEARNING SYSTEM FEATURES

IMAGES OF CHILD DEVELOPMENT
The Story of . . .

Each chapter opens with a high-interest story that is linked to the chapter's content.

Ted Kaczynski, the convicted Unabomber, traced his difficulties to growing up as a genius in a kid's body and not fitting in when he was a child.

Images of Child Development
The Stories of Ted Kaczynski and Alice Walker

Ted Kaczynski sprinted through high school, not bothering with his junior year and making only passing efforts at social contact. Off to Harvard at age 16, Kaczynski was a loner during his college years. One of his roommates at Harvard said that he avoided people by quickly shuffling by them and slamming the door behind him. After obtaining his Ph.D. in mathematics at the University of Michigan, Kaczynski became a professor at the University of California at Berkeley. His colleagues there remember him as hiding from social circumstances—no friends, no allies, no networking.

After several years at Berkeley, Kaczynski resigned and moved to a rural area of Montana, where he lived as a hermit in a crude shack for 25 years. Town residents described him as a bearded eccentric. Kaczynski traced his own difficulties to growing up as a genius in a kid's body and sticking out like a sore thumb in his surroundings as a child. In 1996, he was arrested and charged as the notorious Unabomber, America's most wanted killer. Over the course of 17 years, Kaczynski had sent 16 mail bombs that left 23 people wounded or maimed, and 3 people dead. In 1998, he pleaded guilty to the offenses and was sentenced to life in prison.

Research in Child Development

IN VITRO FERTILIZATION AND DEVELOPMENTAL OUTCOMES IN ADOLESCENCE

A longitudinal study examined 34 in vitro fertilization families, 49 adoptive families, and 38 families with a naturally conceived child (Golombok, MacCallum, & Goodman, 2001). Each type of family included a similar portion of boys and girls. Also, the age of the young adolescents did not differ according to family type (mean age of 11 years, 11 months).

Children's socioemotional development was assessed by (1) interviewing the mother and obtaining detailed descriptions of any problems the child might have; (2) administering a Strengths and Difficulties questionnaire to the child's mother and teacher; and (3) administering the Social Adjustment Inventory for Children and Adolescents, which examines functioning in school, peer relationships, and self-esteem.

No sigificant differences between the children from the in vitro fertilization, adoptive, and naturally conceiving families were found. The results from the Social Adjustment Inventory for Children and Adolescents are shown in Figure 2.9. Another study also revealed no psychological differences between IVF babies and those not conceived by IVF, but more research is needed to reach firm conclusions in this area (Hahn & DiPietro, 2001).

RESEARCH IN CHILD DEVELOPMENT INTERLUDE

One *Research in Child Development* interlude appears in every chapter. The Research interludes describe a study or program and are designed to acquaint you with how research on child development is conducted.

CARING FOR CHILDREN INTERLUDE

Every chapter has one *Caring for Children* interlude, which provides applied information about parenting, education, or health and well-being related to a topic in the chapter.

Caring for Children

FROM WATERBIRTH TO MUSIC THERAPY

The effort to reduce stress and control pain during labor has recently led to an increase in the use of some older and some newer nonmedicated techniques (Field, 2007; Simkin & Bolding, 2004; Smith & others, 2006). These include waterbirth, massage, acupuncture, hypnosis, and music therapy.

Waterbirth

Waterbirth involves giving birth in a tub of warm water. Some women go through labor in the water and get out for delivery, others remain in the water for delivery. The rationale for waterbirth is that the baby has been in an amniotic sac for many months and that delivery in a similar environment is likely to be less stressful for the baby and the mother. Mothers get into the warm water when contractions become closer together and more intense. Getting into the water too soon can cause labor to slow or stop. Reviews of research have indicated mixed results for waterbirths (Field, 2007; Pinette, Wax, & Wilson, 2004). In one comparison of almost 6,000 landbirths and more than 3,500 waterbirths, waterbirths resulted in a lower incidence of

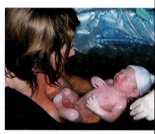

What characterizes the use of waterbirth in delivering a baby?

DIVERSITY IN CHILD DEVELOPMENT INTERLUDE

Once each chapter, a *Diversity in Child Development* interlude appears to provide information about diversity related to a chapter topic.

Diversity in Child Development

CULTURAL BELIEFS ABOUT PREGNANCY

All cultures have beliefs and practices that surround life's major events, and one such event is pregnancy. When a woman who immigrated to the United States becomes pregnant, the beliefs and practices of her native culture may be as important as, or more so than, those of the mainstream U.S. culture that now surrounds her. The conflict between cultural tradition and Western medicine may pose a risk for the pregnancy and a challenge for the health-care professional who wishes to give proper care while respecting the woman's values.

The American Public Health Association (2006) has identified a variety of cultural beliefs and practices that are observed among various immigrant groups, such as:

- **Food cravings.** Latin American, Asian, and some African cultures believe that it is important for a pregnant woman's food cravings to be satisfied because they are

KEY TERMS AND GLOSSARY

Key terms appear in boldface. Their definitions appear in the margin near where they are introduced.

Patterns of Growth

During prenatal development and early infancy, the head constitutes an extraordinarily large portion of the total body (see Figure 4.1). Gradually, the body's proportions change. Why? Growth is not random. Instead, it generally follows two patterns: the cephalocaudal pattern and the proximodistal pattern.

The **cephalocaudal pattern** is the sequence in which the fastest growth always occurs at the top—the head. Physical growth in size, weight, and feature differentiation

cephalocaudal pattern The sequence in which the fastest growth occurs at the top—the head—with physical growth in size, weight, and feature differentiation gradually working from top to bottom.

KEY TERMS

evolutionary psychology 55	genotype 60	behavior genetics 71	active (niche-picking) genotype-environment correlations 72
chromosomes 57	phenotype 60	twin study 71	
DNA 57	Down syndrome 61	adoption study 71	shared environmental experiences 73
genes 58	Klinefelter syndrome 62	passive genotype-environment correlations 71	
mitosis 59	fragile X syndrome 62		nonshared environmental experiences 73
meiosis 59	Turner syndrome 62	evocative genotype-environment correlations 72	
fertilization 59	XYY syndrome 62		epigenetic view 73
zygote 59	phenylketonuria (PKU) 62		
	sickle-cell anemia 62		

Key terms also are listed and page-referenced at the end of each chapter.

Key terms are alphabetically listed, defined, and page-referenced in a Glossary at the end of the book.

A

accommodation Piagetian concept of adjusting schemes to fit new information and experiences.

acculturation Cultural changes that occur when one culture comes in contact with another culture.

active (niche-picking) genotype-environment correlations Correlations that exist when children seek out environments they find compatible and stimulating.

androgyny The presence of masculine and feminine characteristics in the same person.

anger cry A cry similar to the basic cry but with more excess air forced through the vocal cords.

animism A facet of preoperational thought; the belief that inanimate objects have lifelike qualities and are capable of action.

A-not-B error Also called AB̄ error, this occurs when infants make the mistake of selecting the familiar hiding place (A) rather than the new hiding place (B) as they progress into

and little verbal exchange is allowed. This style is associated with children's social incompetence, including a lack of initiative and weak communication skills.

authoritative parenting This style encourages children to be independent but still places limits and controls on their actions. Extensive verbal give-and-take is allowed, and parents are warm and nurturant toward the child. This style is associated with children's social competence, including being achievement oriented and self-reliant.

Sleep that knits up the ravelled sleave of care . . . Balm of hurt minds, nature's second course. Chief nourisher in life's feast.

—WILLIAM SHAKESPEARE
English Playwright, 17th Century

The Sleep/Wake Cycle   When we were infants, sleep consumed more of our time than it does now (Sadeh, 2008; Taveras & others, 2008). Newborns sleep 16 to 17 hours a day, although some sleep more and others less—the range is from a low of about 10 hours to a high of about 21 hours, although the longest period of sleep is not always between 11 P.M. and 7 A.M. Although total sleep remains somewhat consistent for young infants, their sleep during the day does not always follow a rhythmic pattern. An infant might change from sleeping several long bouts of 7 or 8 hours to three or four shorter sessions only several hours in duration. By about 1 month of age, most infants have begun to sleep longer at night. By 6 months of age, they usually have moved closer to adultlike sleep patterns, spending their longest span of sleep at night and their longest span of waking during the day (Sadeh, 2008).

The most common infant sleep-related problem reported by parents is night waking. Surveys indicate that 20 to 30 percent of infants have difficulty going to sleep at night and night waking (Sadeh, 2008). What factors are involved in infant night waking? Infant night-waking problems have consistently been linked to excessive parental

QUOTATIONS

These appear occasionally in the margins to stimulate further thought about a topic.

CRITICAL-THINKING AND CONTENT QUESTIONS IN PHOTOGRAPH CAPTIONS

Most photographs have a caption that ends with a critical-thinking or knowledge question in italics to stimulate further thought about a topic.

Singer Celine Dion became pregnant through in vitro fertilization and gave birth to her son Rene-Charles in 2001.

tion and Down syndrome (Avent & others, 2008; Hahn, Zhong, & Holzgreve, 2008). Being able to detect an offspring's sex and various diseases and defects so early raises ethical concerns about couples' motivation to terminate a pregnancy (Newsom, 2008; van den Heuvel & Marteau, 2008).

Technical challenges still characterize the use of NIPD, but its benefit in reducing risk make it an attractive diagnostic candidate (van der Schoot, Hahn, & Chitty, 2008). The main technical challenge is to efficiently separate out the fetal cells, which comprise only about one of every million cells in a mother's blood.

Infertility and Reproductive Technology

Recent advances in biological knowledge have also opened up many choices for infertile people. Approximately 10 to 15 percent of couples in the United States experience infertility, which is defined as the inability to conceive a child after 12 months of regular intercourse without contraception. The cause of infertility can rest with the woman or the man (Kumar & others, 2006). The woman may not be ovulating (releasing eggs to be fertilized), she may be producing abnormal ova, her fallopian tubes, by which ova normally reach the womb, may be blocked, or she may have a disease that prevents implantation of the embryo into the uterus. The man may produce too few sperm, the sperm may lack motility (the ability to move adequately), or he may have a blocked passageway (Hesmet & Lo, 2006).

In the United States, more than 2 million couples seek help for infertility every year. In some cases of infertility, surgery may correct the cause; in others, hormone-based

Appendix

Careers in Child Development

Each of us wants to find a rewarding career and enjoy the work we do. The field of child development offers an amazing breadth of career options that can provide extremely satisfying work.

If you decide to pursue a career in child development, what career options are available to you? There are many. College and university professors teach courses in areas of child development, education, family development, nursing, and medicine. Teachers impart knowledge, understanding, and skills to children and adolescents. Counselors, clinical psychologists, nurses, and physicians help parents and children of different

In the upcoming sections, we will profile careers in four areas: education and research; clinical and counseling; medical, nursing, and physical development; and families and relationships. These are not the only career options in child development, but they should provide you with an idea of the range of opportunities available and information about some of the main career avenues you might pursue. In profiling these careers, we will address the amount of education required, the nature of the training, and a description of the work.

CAREERS IN CHILD DEVELOPMENT APPENDIX

A *Careers in child Development* appendix that describes a number of careers appears following Chapter 1.

CAREERS IN CHILD DEVELOPMENT PROFILES

Throughout the book, *Careers in Child Development* profiles feature a person working in a child development field related to the chapter's content.

Careers in Child Development

Holly Ishmael, Genetic Counselor

Holly Ishmael is a genetic counselor at Children's Mercy Hospital in Kansas City. She obtained an undergraduate degree in psychology and then a master's degree in genetic counseling from Sarah Lawrence College.

Genetic counselors, like Ishmael, work as members of a health-care team, providing information and support to families with birth defects or genetic disorders. They identify families at risk by analyzing inheritance patterns and explore options with the family. Some genetic counselors, like Ishmael, become specialists in prenatal and pediatric genetics; others might specialize in cancer genetics or psychiatric genetic disorders.

Ishmael says, "Genetic counseling is a perfect combination for people who want to do something science-oriented, but need human contact and don't want to spend all of their time in a lab or have their nose in a book" (Rizzo, 1999, p. 3).

Genetic counselors have specialized graduate degrees in the areas of medical genetics and counseling. They enter graduate school with undergraduate backgrounds from a variety of disciplines, including biology, genetics, psychology, public health, and social work. There are

approximately thirty graduate genetic counseling programs in the United States. If you are interested in this profession, you can obtain further information from the National Society of Genetic Counselors at www.nsgc.org.

Holly Ishmael (*left*) in a genetic counseling session.

KEY PEOPLE

The most important theorists and researchers in each chapter are listed and page-referenced at the end of each chapter.

KEY PEOPLE

Thomas Bouchard 54	Albert Bandura 56	Sandra Scarr 72	Gilbert Gottlieb 73
Charles Darwin 55	Steven Jay Gould 57	Robert Plomin 73	
David Buss 56	David Moore 58	Judith Harris 73	

E-LEARNING TOOLS

This feature appears at the end of each chapter and consists of three parts: *Taking It To the Net* Internet problem-solving exercises, *Health and Well-Being, Parenting, and Education Exercises,* which provide an opportunity to practice decision-making skills related to real-world applications, and *Video Clips* relevant to a chapter's content. By going to the Online Learning Center for this book, you can complete these valuable and enjoyable exercises and find many learning activities to improve your knowledge and understanding of the chapter.

E-LEARNING TOOLS

To help you master the material in this chapter, you'll find a number of valuable study tools at the Online Learning Center for *Child Development,* twelfth edition (**www.mhhe.com/santrockcd12**).

Taking It to the Net

Research the answers to these questions:

1. Ahmahl, a biochemistry major, is writing a psychology paper on the potential dilemmas that society and scientists may face as a result of decoding the human genome. What are some of the main issues or concerns that Ahmahl should address in his class paper?

2. Brandon and Katie are thrilled to learn that they are expecting their first child. They are curious about the genetic makeup of their unborn child and want to know (a) what disorders might be identified through prenatal genetic testing; and (b) which tests, if any, Katie should undergo to help determine this information.

3. Greg and Courtenay have three boys. They would love to have a girl. Courtenay read that there is a clinic in Virginia where you can pick the sex of your child. How successful are such efforts? Would you want to have this choice available to you?

Health and Well-Being, Parenting, and Education Exercises

Build your decision-making skills by trying your hand at the health and well-being, parenting, and education exercises.

Video Clips

The Online Learning Center includes the following video for this chapter:

- *Interview with Adoptive Parents*
  An interview with a couple that adopted a second child.

CHILD DEVELOPMENT

ONE

THE NATURE OF CHILD DEVELOPMENT

In every child who is born, under no matter what circumstances, and of no matter what parents, the potentiality of the human race is born again.

—JAMES AGEE
American Writer, 20th Century

Examining the shape of childhood allows us to understand it better. Every childhood is distinct, the first chapter of a new biography in the world. This book is about children's development, its universal features, its individual variations, its nature at the beginning of the twenty-first century. *Child Development* is about the rhythm and meaning of children's lives, about turning mystery into understanding, and about weaving together a portrait of who each of us was, is, and will be. In Section 1, you will read one chapter: "Introduction" (Chapter 1).

1

*We reach backward
to our parents and
forward to our
children and through
their children to a
future we will never
see, but about which
we need to care.*

—CARL JUNG
Swiss Psychoanalyst, 20th Century

LEARNING GOALS

◆ Discuss historical views and the
modern era of child development.

◆ Identify five areas in which
children's lives need to be
improved, and explain the roles
of resilience and social policy in
children's development.

◆ Discuss the most important
processes, periods, and issues in
development.

◆ Summarize why research is
important in child development, the
main theories of child development,
and research methods, designs,
and challenges.

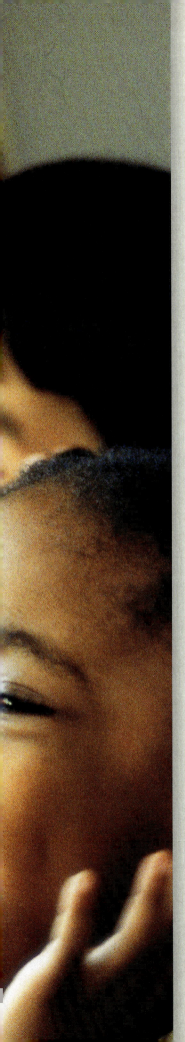

INTRODUCTION

CHAPTER OUTLINE

Images of Child Development
The Stories of Ted Kaczynski and Alice Walker

Ted Kaczynski, the convicted Unabomber, traced his difficulties to growing up as a genius in a kid's body and not fitting in when he was a child.

Ted Kaczynski sprinted through high school, not bothering with his junior year and making only passing efforts at social contact. Off to Harvard at age 16, Kaczynski was a loner during his college years. One of his roommates at Harvard said that he avoided people by quickly shuffling by them and slamming the door behind him. After obtaining his Ph.D. in mathematics at the University of Michigan, Kaczynski became a professor at the University of California at Berkeley. His colleagues there remember him as hiding from social circumstances—no friends, no allies, no networking.

After several years at Berkeley, Kaczynski resigned and moved to a rural area of Montana, where he lived as a hermit in a crude shack for 25 years. Town residents described him as a bearded eccentric. Kaczynski traced his own difficulties to growing up as a genius in a kid's body and sticking out like a sore thumb in his surroundings as a child. In 1996, he was arrested and charged as the notorious Unabomber, America's most wanted killer. Over the course of 17 years, Kaczynski had sent 16 mail bombs that left 23 people wounded or maimed, and 3 people dead. In 1998, he pleaded guilty to the offenses and was sentenced to life in prison.

A decade before Kaczynski mailed his first bomb, Alice Walker spent her days battling racism in Mississippi. She had recently won her first writing fellowship, but rather than use the money to follow her dream of moving to Senegal, Africa, she put herself into the heart and heat of the civil rights movement. Walker had grown up knowing the brutal effects of poverty and racism. Born in 1944, she was the eighth child of Georgia sharecroppers who earned $300 a year. When Walker was 8, her brother accidentally shot her in the left eye with a BB gun. Since her parents had no car, it took them a week to get her to a hospital. By the time she received medical care, she was blind in that eye, and it had developed a disfiguring layer of scar tissue. Despite the counts against her, Walker overcame pain and anger and went on to win a Pulitzer Prize for her book *The Color Purple*. She became not only a novelist but also an essayist, a poet, a short-story writer, and a social activist.

What leads one individual, so full of promise, to commit brutal acts of violence and another to turn poverty and trauma into a rich literary harvest? If you have ever wondered why people turn out the way they do, you have asked yourself the central question we will explore in this book.

Alice Walker won the Pulitzer Prize for her book *The Color Purple*. Like the characters in her book, Walker overcame pain and anger to triumph and celebrate the human spirit.

PREVIEW

Why study children? Perhaps you are or will be a parent or teacher, and responsibility for children is or will be a part of your everyday life. The more you learn about children and the way researchers study them, the better you can guide them. Perhaps you hope to gain an understanding of your own history—as an infant, as a child, and as an adolescent. Perhaps you accidentally came across the course description and found it intriguing. Whatever your reasons, you will discover that the study of child development is provocative, intriguing, and informative. In this first chapter, we will explore historical views and the modern study of child development, why caring for children is so important, examine the nature of development, and outline how science helps us to understand it.

1 CHILD DEVELOPMENT—YESTERDAY AND TODAY

Historical Views of Childhood   **The Modern Study of Child Development**

What do we mean when we speak of an individual's development? **Development** is the pattern of change that begins at conception and continues through the life span. Most development involves growth, although it also includes decay. Anywhere you turn today, the development of children captures public attention. Historically, though, interest in the development of children has been uneven.

Historical Views of Childhood

Childhood has become such a distinct period that it is hard to imagine that it was not always thought of as markedly different from adulthood. However, in medieval Europe laws generally did not distinguish between child and adult offenses. After analyzing samples of art along with available publications, historian Philippe Ariès (1962) concluded that European societies prior to 1600 did not give any special status to children (see Figure 1.1).

Were children actually treated as miniature adults with no special status in medieval Europe? Ariès primarily sampled aristocratic, idealized subjects, which might have been misleading. Childhood probably was recognized as a distinct phase of life more than Ariès believed, but his analysis helped to highlight cultural differences in how children are viewed and treated.

Throughout history, philosophers have speculated at length about the nature of children and how they should be reared. The ancient Egyptians, Greeks, and Romans held rich conceptions of children's development. More recently in European history, three influential philosophical views portrayed children in terms of original sin, tabula rasa, and innate goodness:

- In the **original sin view**, especially advocated during the Middle Ages, children were perceived as being born into the world as evil beings. The goal of child rearing was to provide salvation, to remove sin from the child's life.

- Toward the end of the seventeenth century, the **tabula rasa view** was proposed by English philosopher John Locke. He argued that children are not innately bad but, instead, are like a "blank tablet." Locke believed that childhood experiences are important in determining adult characteristics. He advised parents to spend time with their children and to help them become contributing members of society.

- In the eighteenth century, the **innate goodness view** was presented by Swiss-born French philosopher Jean-Jacques Rousseau. He stressed that children are inherently good. Because children are basically good, said Rousseau, they should be permitted to grow naturally, with little parental monitoring or constraint.

Today, the Western view of children holds that childhood is a highly eventful and unique period of life that lays an important foundation for the adult years and is markedly different from them. Most current approaches to childhood identify distinct periods in which children master specific skills and tasks that prepare them for adulthood. Childhood is no longer seen as an inconvenient waiting period during which adults must suffer the incompetencies of the young. Instead, we protect children from the stresses and responsibilities of adult work through strict child labor laws. We handle their crimes in a special system of juvenile justice. We also have provisions for helping children when families fail. In short, we now value childhood as a special time of growth and change, and we invest great resources in caring for and educating children.

FIGURE 1.1 Historical Perception of Children. European paintings centuries ago often depicted children as miniature adults. *Do these artistic creations indicate that earlier Europeans did not view childhood as a distinct period?*

development The pattern of movement or change that begins at conception and continues through the life span.

original sin view Advocated during the Middle Ages, the belief that children were born into the world as evil beings and were basically bad.

tabula rasa view The idea, proposed by John Locke, that children are like a "blank tablet."

innate goodness view The idea, presented by Swiss-born French philosopher Jean-Jacques Rousseau, that children are inherently good.

Children are the legacy we leave for the time we will not live to see.

—Aristotle
Greek Philosopher, 4th Century B.C.

The Modern Study of Child Development

The modern era of studying children began with some important developments in the late 1800s (Cairns & Cairns, 2006). Since then, the study of child development has evolved into a sophisticated science with major theories, as well as elegant techniques and methods of study that help organize our thinking about children's development. This new era began during the last quarter of the nineteenth century when a major shift took place—from a strictly philosophical approach to human psychology to an approach that includes systematic observation and experimentation.

Most of the influential early psychologists were trained either in the natural sciences such as biology or medicine or in philosophy. The natural scientists valued experiments and reliable observations; after all, experiments and systematic observation had advanced knowledge in physics, chemistry, and biology. But these scientists were not at all sure that people, much less children or infants, could be studied in this way. Their hesitation was due, in part, to a lack of examples to follow in studying children. In addition, philosophers of the time debated, on both intellectual and ethical grounds, whether the methods of science were appropriate for studying people.

The deadlock was broken when some daring thinkers began to try new methods of studying infants, children, and adolescents. For example, near the turn of the century, French psychologist Alfred Binet invented many tasks to study attention and memory. He used them to study his own daughters, other normal children, children with mental retardation, children who are gifted, and adults. Eventually, he collaborated in the development of the first modern test of intelligence (the Binet test). At about the same time, G. Stanley Hall pioneered the use of questionnaires with large groups of children. In one investigation, Hall tested 400 children in the Boston schools to find out how much they "knew" about themselves and the world, asking them such questions as "Where are your ribs?"

Later, during the 1920s, many child development research centers were created and their professional staffs began to observe and chart a myriad of behaviors in infants and children. Research centers at the Universities of Minnesota, Iowa, California at Berkeley, Columbia, and Toronto became famous for their investigations of children's play, friendship patterns, fears, aggression and conflict, and sociability. This work became closely associated with the so-called child study movement, and a new organization, the Society for Research in Child Development, was formed at about the same time.

Another ardent observer of children was Arnold Gesell. With his photographic dome (shown in Figure 1.2), Gesell (1928) could systematically observe children's behavior without interrupting them. He strove for precision in charting what a child is like at specific ages.

Gesell not only developed sophisticated strategies for studying children, but also had provocative views on children's development. His views were strongly influenced by Charles Darwin's evolutionary theory (Darwin had made the scientific study of children respectable when he developed a baby journal for recording systematic observations of children). Gesell argued that certain characteristics of children simply "bloom" with age because of a biological, maturational blueprint.

Evolutionary theory also influenced G. Stanley Hall. Hall (1904) argued that child development follows a natural evolutionary course that can be revealed by child study. He theorized that child development unfolds in stages, with distinct motives and capabilities at each stage. Later in the chapter, you will see that today there is considerable debate about how strongly children's development is determined by biology and by environment, and the extent to which development occurs in stages or not.

The direct study of children, in which investigators directly observe children's behavior, conduct experiments, and obtain information about children by questioning their parents and teachers, had an auspicious start in the work of these child study experts. The flow of information about children, based on direct study, has only increased since that time. Methodological advances in observation, as well as the introduction of experimentation and the development of major theories, characterize the achievements

FIGURE 1.2 Gesell's Photographic Dome. Cameras rode on metal tracks at the top of the dome and were moved as needed to record the child's activities. Others could observe from outside the dome without being seen by the child.

of the modern era. Later in the chapter, we will spend considerable time describing the major theories and research methods of the field of child development today.

Review and Reflect: Learning Goal 1

 Discuss Historical Views and the Modern Era of Child Development

REVIEW

- What is development? How has childhood been perceived through history?
- What are the key characteristics of the modern study of child development?

REFLECT

- Now that you have studied historical views of childhood and the beginning of the modern era in child development, what do you think are some of the major changes in the topics child development researchers study today compared with what psychologists such as G. Stanley Hall, Alfred Binet, and Arnold Gesell studied in the early twentieth century?

*Ah! What would the world be to us
If the children were no more?
We should dread the desert behind us
Worse than the dark before.*

—HENRY WADSWORTH LONGFELLOW
American Poet, 19th Century

---

2 CARING FOR CHILDREN

Improving the Lives of Children   **Resilience, Social Policy, and Children's Development**

Caring for children is an important theme of this text. To think about why caring for children is so important, we will explore why it is beneficial to study children's development and some areas in which children's lives need to be improved, and explore the roles of resilience and social policy in children's development.

Improving the Lives of Children

If you were to pick up a newspaper or magazine in any U.S. town or city, you might see headlines like these: "Political Leanings May Be Written in the Genes," "Mother Accused of Tossing Children into Bay," "Gender Gap Widens," and "FDA Warns About ADHD Drug." Researchers are examining these and many other topics of contemporary concern. The roles that health and well-being, parenting, education, and sociocultural contexts play in child development, as well as how social policy is related to these issues, are a particular focus of this textbook.

Health and Well-Being   Does a pregnant woman endanger her fetus if she has a few beers a week? How does a poor diet affect a child's ability to learn? Are children exercising less today than in the past? What roles do parents and peers play in whether adolescents abuse drugs? Throughout this text, we will discuss many questions like these regarding health and well-being. Investigating these questions and their answers are important goals for just about everyone.

Health professionals today recognize the power of lifestyles and psychological states in health and well-being (Fahey, Insel, & Roth, 2009; Hahn, Payne, & Lucas, 2009). In every chapter of this book, issues of health and well-being are integrated into our discussion.

Careers in Child Development

Luis Vargas, Clinical Child Psychologist

Luis Vargas is Director of the Clinical Child Psychology Internship Program and a professor in child and adolescent psychiatry at the University of New Mexico School of Medicine. Luis obtained an undergraduate degree in psychology from Trinity University in Texas and a Ph.D. in clinical psychology at the University of Nebraska–Lincoln.

Vargas' work includes assessing and treating children, adolescents, and their families, especially when a child or adolescent has a serious mental disorder. Vargas also trains mental health professionals to provide culturally responsive and developmentally appropriate mental health services. In addition, he is interested in cultural and assessment issues with children, adolescents, and their families.

Vargas' clinical work is heavily influenced by contextual and ecological theories of development (which we will discuss later in this chapter). His first undergraduate course in human development, and subsequent courses in development, contributed to his decision to pursue a career in clinical child psychology.

Following this chapter you can read about many careers in child development, including more about the field of child clinical psychology.

Also, at appropriate places throughout the book we will provide profiles of individuals in various child development careers.

Luis Vargas (*left*) conducting a child therapy session.

Clinical psychologists are among the health professionals who help people improve their well-being. In the *Careers in Child Development* profile, you can read about clinical psychologist Luis Vargas, who helps adolescents with problems. A *Careers* Appendix that follows Chapter 1 describes the education and training required to become a clinical psychologist and other careers in child development.

Parenting   Can two gay men raise a healthy family? Are children harmed if both parents work outside the home? Do adopted children fare as well as children raised by their biological parents? How damaging is divorce to children's development? We hear many controversial questions like these related to pressures on the contemporary family (Parke & others, 2008; Wallerstein, 2008). We'll examine these questions and others that provide a context for understanding factors that influence parents' lives and how effectively they rear their children. How parents, as well as other adults, can make a positive difference in children's lives is another major theme of this book.

You might be a parent someday or might already be one. You should take seriously the importance of rearing your children, because they are the future of our society. Good parenting takes considerable time. If you plan to become a parent, commit yourself day after day, week after week, month after month, and year after year to providing your children with a warm, supportive, safe, and stimulating environment that will make them feel secure and allow them to reach their full potential as human beings. The poster at the left that states "Children learn to love when they are loved" and reflects this theme.

Children learn to love when they are loved

Understanding the nature of children's development can help you become a better parent (Fiese & Winter, 2008; Grusec, Almas, & Willoughby, 2008). Many parents learn parenting practices from their parents. Unfortunately, when parenting practices and child-care strategies are passed from one generation to the next, both desirable and undesirable ones are usually perpetuated. This book and your instructor's lectures in this course can help you become more knowledgeable about children's development and sort through which practices in your own upbringing you should continue with your own children and which you should abandon.

Education There is widespread agreement that something needs to be done to improve the education of our nation's children (Ballentine & Hammock, 2009; Nieto & Bode, 2008). Among the questions involved in improving schools are: Are U.S. schools teaching children to be immoral? Are they failing to teach them how to read and write and calculate adequately? Should there be more accountability in schools, with accountability of student learning and teaching assessed by formal tests? Have schools become too soft and watered down? Should they make more demands on and have higher expectations of children? Should schooling involve less memorization and more attention to the development of children's ability to process information more efficiently? Should schools focus only on developing the child's knowledge and cognitive skills, or should they pay more attention to the whole child and consider the child's socioemotional and physical development as well? For example, should schools be dramatically changed so that they serve as a locus for a wide range of services? These services might include primary health care, child care, preschool education, parent education, recreation, and family counseling, as well as traditional educational activities, such as learning in the classroom. In this text, we will examine such questions about the state of education in the United States and consider recent research on solutions to educational problems.

Sociocultural Contexts and Diversity Health and well-being, parenting, and education—like development itself—are all shaped by their sociocultural context (Taylor & Whittaker, 2009; Tolani & Brooks-Gunn, 2008). The term **context** refers to the settings in which development occurs. These settings are influenced by historical, economic, social, and cultural factors. Four contexts that we will pay special attention in this text are culture, ethnicity, socioeconomic status, and gender.

Culture encompasses the behavior patterns, beliefs, and all other products of a particular group of people that are passed on from generation to generation. Culture results from the interaction of people over many years. A cultural group can be as large as the United States or as small as an isolated Appalachian town. Whatever its size, the group's culture influences the behavior of its members (Matsumoto & Juang, 2008; Shiraev & Levy, 2007). **Cross-cultural studies** compare aspects of two or more cultures. The comparison provides information about the degree to which development is similar, or universal, across cultures, or is instead culture-specific (Kagitcibasi, 2007; Rothbaum & Trommsdorff, 2007).

Ethnicity (the word *ethnic* comes from the Greek word for "nation") is rooted in cultural heritage, nationality, race, religion, and language. African Americans, Latinos, Asian Americans, Native Americans, Polish Americans, and Italian Americans are a few examples of ethnic groups. Diversity exists within each ethnic group (Gollnick & Chinn, 2009; Kottak & Kozaitis, 2008). Contrary to stereotypes, not all African Americans live in low-income circumstances; not all Latinos are Catholics; not all Asian Americans are high school math whizzes (Banks, 2008; Spring, 2008).

Socioeconomic status (SES) refers to a person's position within society based on occupational, educational, and economic characteristics. Socioeconomic status implies certain inequalities. Generally, members of a society have (1) occupations that vary in prestige, and some individuals have more access than others to higher-status occupations; (2) different levels of educational attainment, and some individuals have more access than others to better education; (3) different economic resources; and (4) different levels of power to influence a community's institutions. These differences in the ability to control resources and to participate in society's rewards produce unequal opportunities (Philipsen, Johnson & Brooks-Gunn, 2009).

Gender Gender is another key dimension of children's development (Blakemore, Berenbaum, & Liben, 2009; Matlin, 2008). **Gender** refers to the characteristics of people as males

Shown here are two Korean-born children on the day they became U.S. citizens. Asian American children are the fastest-growing group of ethnic minority children.

context The settings, influenced by historical, economic, social, and cultural factors, in which development occurs.

culture The behavior patterns, beliefs, and all other products of a group that are passed on from generation to generation.

cross-cultural studies Comparisons of one culture with one or more other cultures. These provide information about the degree to which children's development is similar, or universal, across cultures, and to the degree to which it is culture-specific.

ethnicity A characteristic based on cultural heritage, nationality, race, religion, and language.

socioeconomic status (SES) The grouping of people with similar occupational, educational, and economic characteristics.

gender The characteristics of people as males and females.

and females. How you view yourself, your relationships with other people, your life and your goals is shaped to a great extent by whether you are male or female and how your culture defines what is appropriate behavior for males and females.

Each of these dimensions of the sociocultural context—culture, ethnicity, SES, and gender—influence how children develop, as discussions in later chapters will demonstrate. We will explore, for example, questions such as

- Do infants around the world form attachments with their parents in the same way, or do these attachments differ from one culture to another?
- Does poverty influence the likelihood that young children will be aggressive?
- Is there a parenting style that is universally effective, or does the effectiveness of different types of parenting vary across ethnic groups?
- How does gender influence children's peer relationships?

In the United States, the sociocultural context has become increasingly diverse in recent years. Its population includes a grater variety of cultures and ethnic groups than ever before. This changing demographic tapestry promises not only the richness that diversity produces but also difficult challenges in extending the American dream to all individuals (Banks, 2008; Nieto & Bode, 2008). We will discuss sociocultural contexts and diversity in each chapter. In addition, a *Diversity in Child Development* interlude appears in every chapter. The first *Diversity* interlude, which focuses on gender, families, and children's development around the world, follows.

Diversity In Child Development

GENDER, FAMILIES, AND CHILDREN'S DEVELOPMENT

Around the world, the experiences of male and female children and adolescents continue to be quite different (Kagitcibasi, 2007; UNICEF, 2008). One analysis found that a higher percentage of girls than boys around the world have never had any education (UNICEF, 2004) (see Figure 1.3). The countries with the fewest females being educated are in Africa, where in some areas, girls and women are receiving no education at all. Canada, the United States, and Russia have the highest percentages of educated women. In developing countries, 67 percent of women over the age of 25 (compared with 50 percent of men) have never been to school. At the beginning of the twenty-first century, 80 million more boys than girls were in primary and secondary educational settings around the world (United Nations, 2002).

In many countries, adolescent females have less freedom to pursue a variety of careers and engage in various leisure acts than males. Gender differences in sexual expression are widespread, especially in India, Southeast Asia, Latin America, and Arab countries, where there are far more restrictions on the

FIGURE 1.3 Percentage of Children 7 to 18 Years of Age Around the World Who Have Never Been to School of Any Kind. When UNICEF(2004) surveyed the education that children around the world are receiving, it found that far more girls than boys receive no formal schooling at all.

Muslim school in Middle East with boys only.

sexual activity of adolescent females than males. In certain areas around the world, these gender differences do appear to be narrowing over time. In some countries, educational and career opportunities for women are expanding, and in some parts of the world control over adolescent girls' romantic and sexual relationships is weakening. However, in many countries females still experience considerable discrimination, and much work is needed to bridge the gap between the rights of males and females.

In certain parts of the world, children grow up in closely knit families with extensive extended-kin networks "that provide considerable support and emphasize a traditional way of life" (Brown & Larson, 2002). For example, in Arab countries, children and adolescents are required to adopt strict codes of conduct and loyalty. However, in Western countries such as the United States, children and adolescents are growing up in much larger numbers in nontraditional families. Parenting in Western countries is less authoritarian than in the past.

"Some of the trends that are occurring in many countries around the world involve increased family mobility, migration to urban areas, smaller families, fewer extended-family households, and increases in mothers' employment" (Brown & Larson, 2002). Unfortunately, many of these changes may reduce the ability of families to provide time and resources for children and adolescents.

Resilience, Social Policy, and Children's Development

Some children develop confidence in their abilities despite negative stereotypes about their gender or their ethnic group. And some children triumph over poverty or other adversities. They show *resilience* (Gutman, 2008). Think back to the chapter-opening story about Alice Walker. In spite of racism, poverty, her low socioeconomic status, and a disfiguring eye injury, she went on to become a successful author and champion for equality.

Are there certain characteristics that make children like Alice Walker resilient? Are there other characteristics that make children like Ted Kaczynski, who despite his intelligence and education, become a killer? After analyzing research on this topic, Ann Masten and her colleagues (2004, 2006, 2007; Masten, Burt, & Coatsworth, 2006) concluded that a number of individual factors, such as good intellectual functioning, influence resiliency. In addition, as Figure 1.4 shows, their families and resources outside the children's families tend to show certain features. For example, resilient children are likely to have a close relationship to a caring parent figure and bonds to caring adults outside the family.

Should governments also take action to improve the contexts of children's development and aid their resilience? **Social policy** is a government's course of action designed to promote the welfare of its citizens. The shape and scope of social policy related to children are tied to the political system. The values held by citizens and elected officials, the nation's economic strengths and weaknesses, and partisan politics all influence the policy agenda.

Out of concern that policymakers are doing too little to protect the well-being of children, researchers increasingly are undertaking studies that they hope will lead to wise and effective decision making about social policy (Conger & Conger, 2008; Crane & Heaton, 2008). Children who grow up in poverty represent a special concern (Johnson, Tarrant, & Brooks-Gunn, 2008). In 2006, approximately 17.4 percent of U.S. children were living in families below the poverty line (Federal Interagency Forum on Child and Family Statistics, 2007). This is an increase from 2001 (16.2 percent) but down from a peak of 22.7 percent in 1993. The U.S. figure of 17.4 percent of children living in poverty is much higher than those from other industrialized nations. For example, Canada has a child poverty rate of 9 percent and Sweden has a rate of 2 percent. As indicated in Figure 1.5, one study found that a higher percentage of children in poor families than in middle-income families in the United States were exposed to family turmoil, separation

Source	Characteristic
Individual Child	Good intellectual functioning; Appealing, sociable, easygoing disposition; Self-confidence, high self-esteem; Talents; Faith
Child's Family	Close relationship to caring parent figure; Authoritative parenting: warmth, structure, high expectations; Socioeconomic advantages; Connections to extended supportive family networks
Resources Outside the Child's Family	Bonds to caring adults outside the family; Connections to positive organizations; Attending effective schools

FIGURE 1.4 Characteristics of Resilient Children and Their Contexts

social policy A government's course of action designed to promote the welfare of its citizens.

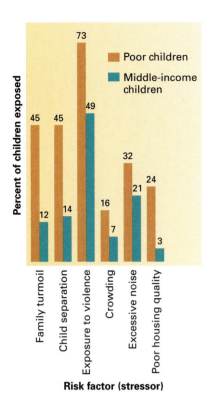

FIGURE 1.5 Exposure to Six Stressors Among Poor and Middle-Income Children. One study analyzed the exposure to six stressors among poor children and middle-income children (Evans & English, 2002). Poor children were much more likely to face each of these stressors.

from a parent, violence, crowding, excessive noise, and poor housing (Evans & English, 2002). A recent study also revealed that the more years children spent living in poverty, the more their physiological indices of stress were elevated (Evans & Kim, 2007). What can we do to lesson the effect of these stressors on the lives of children and those who care for them? To read more about improving the lives of children through social policies, see the *Caring for Children* interlude that follows.

Caring for Children

IMPROVING FAMILY POLICY

In the United States, the national government, state governments, and city governments all play a role in influencing the well-being of children (Children's Defense Fund, 2007; Corbett, 2007; Murnane, 2007). When families fail or seriously endanger a child's well-being, governments often step in to help (Ross & Kirby, 2006). At the national and state levels, policymakers for decades have debated whether helping poor parents ends up helping their children as well. Researchers are providing some answers by examining the effects of specific policies (Coltrane & others, 2008; Gupta, Thorton, & Huston, 2008).

For example, the Minnesota Family Investment Program (MFIP) was designed in the 1990s primarily to affect the behavior of adults—specifically, to move adults off the welfare rolls and into paid employment. A key element of the program was that it guaranteed that adults who participated in the program would receive more money if they worked than if they did not. When the adults' income rose, how did that affect their children? A study of the effects of MFIP found that increases in the incomes of working poor parents were linked with benefits for their children (Gennetian & Miller, 2002). The children's achievement in school improved, and their behavior problems decreased.

Developmental psychologists and other researchers have examined the effects of many other government policies. They are seeking ways to help families living in poverty improve their well-being, and they have offered many suggestions for improving government policies (Conger & Conger, 2008; Johnson, Tarrant, & Brooks-Gunn, 2008).

These children live in a slum area of a small Vermont town where the unemployment rate is very high because of a decline in industrial jobs. *What should be the government's role in improving the lives of these children?*

Review and Reflect: Learning Goal 2

2 Identify Five Areas in Which Children's Lives Need to be Improved, and Explain the Roles of Resilience and Social Policy in Children's Development

REVIEW

- What are several aspects of children's development that need to be improved?
- What characterizes resilience in children's development? What is social policy, and how can it impact children's lives?

REFLECT

- Imagine what your development as a child would have been like in a culture that offered fewer or distinctively different choices than your own? How might your development have been different if your family was significantly richer or poorer than it was?

3 DEVELOPMENTAL PROCESSES, PERIODS, AND ISSUES

| Biological, Cognitive, and Socioemotional Processes | Periods of Development | Issues in Development |

Each of us develops in certain ways like *all* other individuals, like *some* other individuals, and like *no* other individuals. Most of the time, our attention is directed to a person's uniqueness, but psychologists who study development are drawn to both our shared characteristics and what makes us unique. As humans, we all have traveled some common paths. Each of us—Leonardo da Vinci, Joan of Arc, George Washington, Martin Luther King, Jr., and you—walked at about the age of 1, engaged in fantasy play as a young child, and became more independent as a youth. What shapes this common path of human development, and what are its milestones?

Biological, Cognitive, and Socioemotional Processes

The pattern of human development is created by the interplay of several processes—biological, cognitive, and socioemotional. **Biological processes** produce changes in an individual's body. Genes inherited from parents, the development of the brain, height and weight gains, motor skills, and the hormonal changes of puberty all reflect the role of biological processes in development.

Cognitive processes refer to changes in an individual's thought, intelligence, and language. The tasks of watching a mobile swinging above a crib, putting together a two-word sentence, memorizing a poem, solving a math problem, and imagining what it would be like to be a movie star all involve cognitive processes.

Socioemotional processes involve changes in an individual's relationships with other people, changes in emotions, and changes in personality. An infant's smile in response to her mother's touch, a child's attack on a playmate, another's development of assertiveness, and an adolescent's joy at the senior prom all reflect socioemotional development.

Biological, cognitive, and socioemotional processes are intricately intertwined (Diamond, 2007). Consider a baby smiling in response to its mother's touch. Even this simple response depends on biological processes (the physical nature of the touch and responsiveness to it), cognitive processes (the ability to understand intentional acts), and socioemotional processes (smiling often reflects positive emotion and smiling helps to connect infants with other human beings).

We typically will study each type of process—biological, cognitive, and socioemotional—in separate chapters of the book. For each period of development, we will explore how the process influences children's development. However, keep in mind that you are studying the development of an integrated human child who has only one interdependent mind and body (see Figure 1.6).

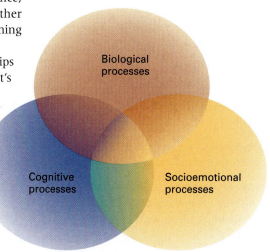

FIGURE 1.6 Changes in Development Are the Result of Biological, Cognitive, and Socioemotional Processes. The processes interact as individuals develop.

biological processes Changes in an individual's body.

cognitive processes Changes in an individual's thought, intelligence, and language.

socioemotional processes Changes in an individual's relationships with other people, emotions, and personality.

Periods of Development

For the purposes of organization and understanding, a child's development is commonly described in terms of periods, which are given approximate age ranges. The most widely used classification of developmental periods describes a child's development in terms of the following sequence: the prenatal period, infancy, early childhood, middle and late childhood, and adolescence.

The **prenatal period** is the time from conception to birth, roughly a nine-month period. During this amazing time, a single cell grows into an organism, complete with a brain and behavioral capabilities.

Infancy is the developmental period that extends from birth to about 18 to 24 months of age. Infancy is a time of extreme dependence on adults. Many psychological activities are just beginning—the ability to speak, to coordinate sensations and physical actions, to think with symbols, and to imitate and learn from others.

Early childhood is the developmental period that extends from the end of infancy to about 5 to 6 years of age; sometimes this period is called the preschool years. During this time, young children learn to become more self-sufficient and to care for themselves, they develop school readiness skills (following instructions, identifying letters), and they spend many hours in play and with peers. First grade typically marks the end of this period.

Middle and late childhood is the developmental period that extends from about 6 to 11 years of age; sometimes this period is referred to as the elementary school years. Children master the fundamental skills of reading, writing, and arithmetic, and they are formally exposed to the larger world and its culture. Achievement becomes a more central theme of the child's world, and self-control increases.

Adolescence is the developmental period of transition from childhood to early adulthood, entered at approximately 10 to 12 years of age and ending at about 18 to 19 years of age. Adolescence begins with rapid physical changes—dramatic gains in height and weight; changes in body contour; and the development of sexual characteristics such as enlargement of the breasts, development of pubic and facial hair, and deepening of the voice. The pursuit of independence and an identity are prominent features of this period of development. More and more time is spent outside of the family. Thought becomes more abstract, idealistic, and logical.

Today, developmentalists do not believe that change ends with adolescence (Baltes, Lindenberger, & Staudinger, 2006; Birren, 2007; Schaie, 2007). They describe development as a lifelong process. However, the purpose of this text is to describe the changes in development that take place from conception through adolescence. All of these periods of development are produced by the interplay of biological, cognitive, and socioemotional processes (see Figure 1.7).

Issues in Development

Many questions about children's development remain unanswered. For example, what exactly drives the biological, cognitive, and socioemotional processes of development, and how does what happens in infancy influence middle childhood or adolescence? Despite all of the knowledge that researchers have acquired, debate continues about the relative importance of factors that influence the developmental processes and about how the periods of development are related. The most important issues in the study of children's development include nature and nurture, continuity and discontinuity, and early and later experience.

Nature and Nurture   The **nature-nurture issue** involves the debate about whether development is primarily influenced by nature or by nurture (D'Onofrio, 2008; Rutter, 2007). *Nature* refers to an organism's biological inheritance, *nurture* to its environmental experiences. Almost no one today argues that development can be explained by nature alone or by nurture alone. But some ("nature" proponents) claim that the most important

---

prenatal period The time from conception to birth.

infancy The developmental period that extends from birth to about 18 to 24 months.

early childhood The developmental period that extends from the end of infancy to about 5 to 6 years of age, sometimes called the preschool years.

middle and late childhood The developmental period that extends from about 6 to 11 years of age, sometimes called the elementary school years.

adolescence The developmental period of transition from childhood to early adulthood, entered at approximately 10 to 12 years of age and ending at 18 to 19 years of age.

nature-nurture issue Involves the debate about whether development is primarily influenced by nature or nurture. The "nature" proponents claim biological inheritance is the most important influence on development; the "nurture" proponents claim that environmental experiences are the most important.

Periods of Development

Prenatal period	Infancy	Early childhood	Middle and late childhood	Adolescence

Biological processes

Cognitive processes

Socioemotional processes

Processes of Development

FIGURE 1.7 Processes and Periods of Development. Development moves through the prenatal, infancy, early childhood, middle and late childhood, and adolescence periods. These periods of development are the result of biological, cognitive, and socioemotional processes.

influence on development is biological inheritance, and others ("nurture" proponents) claim that environmental experiences are the most important influence.

According to the nature proponents, just as a sunflower grows in an orderly way—unless it is defeated by an unfriendly environment—so does a person. The range of environments can be vast, but evolutionary and genetic foundations produce commonalities in growth and development (Buss, 2008; Hartwell, 2008). We walk before we talk, speak one word before two words, grow rapidly in infancy and less so in early childhood, and experience a rush of sexual hormones in puberty. Extreme environments—those that are psychologically barren or hostile—can stunt development, but nature proponents emphasize the influence of tendencies that are genetically wired into humans (Balasubramanian, Koontz, & Reynolds, 2008).

By contrast, other psychologists emphasize the importance of nurture, or environmental experiences, to development (Grusec & Hastings, 2007; Maccoby, 2007). Experiences run the gamut from the individual's biological environment (nutrition, medical care, drugs, and physical accidents) to the social environment (family, peers, schools, community, media, and culture). For example, a child's diet can affect how tall the child grows and even how effectively the child can think and solve problems. Despite their genetic wiring, a child born and raised in a poor village in Bangladesh and a child in the suburbs of Denver are likely to have different skills, different ways of thinking about the world, and different ways of relating to people.

Continuity and Discontinuity Think about your own development for a moment. Did you become the person you are gradually, like the seedling that slowly, cumulatively grows into a giant oak? Or did you experience sudden, distinct changes, like the caterpillar that changes into a butterfly (see Figure 1.8)?

The **continuity-discontinuity issue** focuses on the extent to which development involves gradual, cumulative change (continuity) or distinct stages (discontinuity).

Continuity

Discontinuity

FIGURE 1.8 Continuity and Discontinuity in Development. Is human development more like that of a seedling gradually growing into a giant oak or more like that of a caterpillar suddenly becoming a butterfly?

continuity-discontinuity issue The issue regarding whether development involves gradual, cumulative change (continuity) or distinct stages (discontinuity).

For the most part, developmentalists who emphasize nurture usually describe development as a gradual, continuous process, like the seedling's growth into an oak. Those who emphasize nature often describe development as a series of distinct stages, like the change from caterpillar to butterfly.

Consider continuity first. As the oak grows from seedling to giant oak, it becomes more oak—its development is continuous. Similarly, a child's first word, though seemingly an abrupt, discontinuous event, is actually the result of weeks and months of growth and practice. Puberty, another seemingly abrupt, discontinuous occurrence, is actually a gradual process occurring over several years.

Viewed in terms of discontinuity, each person is described as passing through a sequence of stages in which change is qualitatively rather than quantitatively different. As the caterpillar changes to a butterfly, it is not more caterpillar, it is a different kind of organism—its development is discontinuous. Similarly, at some point a child moves from not being able to think abstractly about the world to being able to. This change is a qualitative, discontinuous change in development, not a quantitative, continuous change.

Early and Later Experience   The **early-later experience issue** focuses on the degree to which early experiences (especially in infancy) or later experiences are the key determinants of the child's development. That is, if infants experience harmful circumstances, can those experiences be overcome by later, positive ones? Or are the early experiences so critical—possibly because they are the infant's first, prototypical experiences—that they cannot be overridden by a later, better environment? To those who emphasize early experiences, life is an unbroken trail on which a psychological quality can be traced back to its origin (Kagan, 1992, 2000). In contrast, to those who emphasize later experiences, development is like a river, continually ebbing and flowing.

The early-later experience issue has a long history and continues to be hotly debated among developmentalists (Posada, 2008). Plato was sure that infants who were rocked frequently become better athletes. Nineteenth-century New England ministers told parents in Sunday afternoon sermons that the way they handled their infants would determine their children's later character. Some developmentalists argue that, unless infants experience warm, nurturing care during the first year or so of life, their development will never quite be optimal (Sroufe, 2007).

In contrast, later-experience advocates argue that children are malleable throughout development and that later sensitive caregiving is just as important as earlier sensitive caregiving. A number of developmentalists stress that too little attention has been given to later experiences in development (Baltes, 2009; Schaie, 2007). They accept that early experiences are important contributors to development, but no more important than later experiences. Jerome Kagan (2000) points out that even children who show the qualities of an inhibited temperament, which is linked to heredity, have the capacity to change their behavior. In his research, almost one-third of a group of children who had an inhibited temperament at 2 years of age were not unusually shy or fearful when they were 4 years of age (Kagan & Snidman, 1991).

People in Western cultures, especially those influenced by Freudian theory, have tended to support the idea that early experiences are more important than later experiences (Chan, 1963; Lamb & Sternberg, 1992). The majority of people in the world do not share this belief. For example, people in many Asian countries believe that experiences occurring after about 6 to 7 years of age are more important to development than are earlier experiences. This stance stems from the long-standing belief in Eastern cultures that children's reasoning skills begin to develop in important ways during middle childhood.

Evaluating the Developmental Issues   Most developmentalists recognize that it is unwise to take an extreme position on the issues of nature and nurture, continuity and discontinuity, and early and later experiences. Development is not all nature or all nurture, not all continuity or all discontinuity, and not all early or later experiences (D'Onofrio, 2008). Nature and nurture, continuity and discontinuity, and early and

What is the nature of the early and later experience issue?

early-later experience issue The issue of the degree to which early experiences (especially infancy) or later experiences are the key determinants of the child's development.

later experiences all play a part in development through the human life span. Along with this consensus, there is still spirited debate about how strongly development is influenced by each of these factors (Laible & Thompson, 2007; Plomin, DeFries, & Fulker, 2007). Are girls less likely to do well in math mostly because of inherited characteristics or because of society's expectations and because of how girls are raised? Can enriched experiences during adolescence remove deficits resulting from poverty, neglect, and poor schooling during childhood? The answers also have a bearing on social policy decisions about children and adolescents, and consequently on each of our lives.

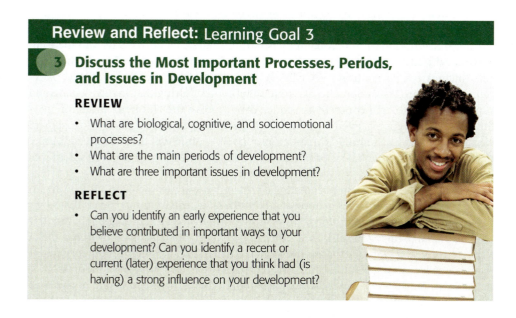

Review and Reflect: Learning Goal 3

3 **Discuss the Most Important Processes, Periods, and Issues in Development**

REVIEW

- What are biological, cognitive, and socioemotional processes?
- What are the main periods of development?
- What are three important issues in development?

REFLECT

- Can you identify an early experience that you believe contributed in important ways to your development? Can you identify a recent or current (later) experience that you think had (is having) a strong influence on your development?

4 THE SCIENCE OF CHILD DEVELOPMENT

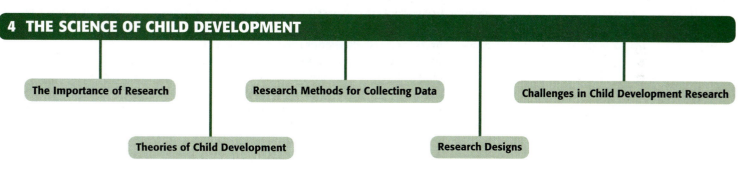

The Importance of Research

Theories of Child Development

Research Methods for Collecting Data

Research Designs

Challenges in Child Development Research

In this section, we introduce the theories and methods that are the foundation of the science of child development. We describe why research is important in understanding children's development and examine the main theories of children's development. We also consider the methods and research designs used when studies of children are conducted. At the end of the section, we explore some of the ethical challenges and biases that researchers must guard against to protect the integrity of their results and respect the rights of the participants in their studies.

The Importance of Research

Some people have difficulty thinking of child development as a science like physics, chemistry, and biology. Can a discipline that studies how parents nurture children, how peers interact, the developmental changes in children's thinking, and whether watching TV hour after hour is linked with being overweight, be equated with disciplines that study the molecular structure of a compound and how gravity works? Is child development really a science? The answer is yes. Science is defined not by *what*

*S*cience *refines everyday thinking.*

—**ALBERT EINSTEIN**
German-born American Physicist, 20th Century

it investigates, but by *how* it investigates. Whether you're studying photosynthesis, butterflies, Saturn's moons, or children's development, it is the way you study that makes the approach scientific or not.

Scientific research is objective, systematic, and testable. It reduces the likelihood that information will be based on personal beliefs, opinions, and feelings (Jackson, 2008; Rosnow & Rosenthal, 2008). Scientific research is based on the **scientific method**, an approach that can be used to discover accurate information. It includes these steps: conceptualize the problem, collect data, draw conclusions, and revise research conclusions and theory.

The first step, *conceptualizing a problem*, involves identifying the problem. At a general level, this may not seem like a difficult task. However, researchers must go beyond a general description of the problem by isolating, analyzing, narrowing, and focusing more specifically on what they want to study. For example, a team of researchers decide to study ways to improve the achievement of children from impoverished backgrounds. Perhaps they choose to examine whether mentoring that involves sustained support, guidance, and concrete assistance can improve the children's academic performance. At this point, even more narrowing and focusing takes place. For instance, what specific strategies should the mentors use? How often will they see the children? How long will the mentoring program last? What aspects of the children's achievement will be assessed?

As part of the first step in formulating a problem to study, researchers often draw on *theories* and *develop hypothesis*. A **theory** is an interrelated, coherent set of ideas that helps to explain and to make predictions. For example, a theory on mentoring might attempt to explain and predict why sustained support, guidance, and concrete experience make a difference in the lives of children from impoverished backgrounds. The theory might focus on children's opportunities to model the behavior and strategies of mentors, or it might focus on the effects of individual attention, which might be missing in the children's lives. A **hypothesis** is a specific testable assumption or prediction. A hypothesis is often written as an *if-then* statement. In our example, a sample hypothesis might be: If children from impoverished backgrounds are given individual attention by mentors, the children will spend more time studying and make higher grades. Testing a hypothesis can inform researchers whether or not a theory may be accurate.

The second step in the scientific method is to *collect information (data)*. In the study of mentoring, the researchers might decide to conduct the mentoring program for six months. Their data might consist of classroom observations, teachers' ratings, and achievement tests given to the mentored children before the mentoring began and at the end of six months of mentoring.

Once data have been collected, child development researchers use *statistical procedures* to understand the meaning of the data (Sprinthall, 2007). Then they try to *draw conclusions*. In this third step, statistics help to determine whether or not the researchers' observations are due to chance.

After data have been collected and analyzed, researchers compare their findings with those of other researchers on the same topic. The final step in the scientific method is revising *research conclusions and theory*.

Theories of Child Development

A wide range of theories makes understanding children's development a challenging undertaking (Newman & Newman, 2007). Just when you think one theory has the most helpful explanation of children's development, another theory crops up and makes you rethink your earlier conclusion. To keep from getting frustrated, remember that child development is a complex, multifaceted topic. No single theory has been able to account for all aspects of child development. Each theory contributes an important piece to the child development puzzle. Although the theories sometimes disagree, much of their information is complementary rather than contradictory. Together they let us see the total landscape of development in all its richness.

---

scientific method An approach that can be used to obtain accurate information. It includes these steps: (1) conceptualize the problem, (2) collect data, (3) draw conclusions, and (4) revise research conclusions and theory.

theory An interrelated, coherent set of ideas that helps to explain and make predictions.

hypotheses Specific assumptions and predictions that can be tested to determine their accuracy.

We will briefly explore five major theoretical perspectives on development: psychoanalytic, cognitive, behavioral and social cognitive, ethological, and ecological. As you will see, these theoretical approaches examine in varying degrees the three major processes involved in children's development: biological, cognitive, and socioemotional.

Psychoanalytic Theories   **Psychoanalytic theories** describe development as primarily unconscious (beyond awareness) and heavily colored by emotion. Psychoanalytic theorists emphasize that behavior is merely a surface characteristic and that a true understanding of development requires analyzing the symbolic meanings of behavior and the deep inner workings of the mind. Psychoanalytic theorists also stress that early experiences with parents extensively shape development. These characteristics are highlighted in the psychoanalytic theory of Sigmund Freud.

Freud's Theory   Freud (1917) proposed that personality has three structures: the id, the ego, and the superego. The *id* is the Freudian structure of personality that consists of instincts, which are an individual's reservoir of psychic energy. In Freud's view, the id is totally unconscious; it has no contact with reality. As children experience the demands and constraints of reality, a new structure of personality emerges—the *ego*. It deals with the demands of reality and is called the "executive branch" of personality because it uses reasoning to make decisions. The id and the ego have no morality—they do not take into account whether something is right or wrong. The *superego* is the Freudian structure of personality that is the moral branch of personality, the part that considers whether something is right or wrong. Think of the superego as what we often refer to as our "conscience."

As Freud listened to, probed, and analyzed his patients, he became convinced that their problems were the result of experiences early in life. He thought that as children grow up, their focus of pleasure and sexual impulses shifts from the mouth to the anus and eventually to the genitals. As a result, we go through five stages of psychosexual development: oral, anal, phallic, latency, and genital (see Figure 1.9). Our adult personality, Freud claimed, is determined by the way we resolve conflicts between sources of pleasure at each stage and the demands of reality.

Freud's theory has been significantly revised by a number of psychoanalytic theorists. Many contemporary psychoanalytic theorists point out that Freud overemphasized sexual instincts; they place more emphasis on cultural experiences as determinants of an individual's development. Unconscious thought remains a central theme, but most contemporary psychoanalysts maintain that conscious thought plays a greater role than Freud envisioned. Next, we will outline the ideas of an important revisionist of Freud's ideas—Erik Erikson.

Erikson's Psychosocial Theory   Erik Erikson (1902–1994) recognized Freud's contributions but stressed that Freud misjudged some important dimensions of human development. For one thing, Erikson (1950, 1968) said we develop in *psychosocial*

Sigmund Freud, the pioneering architect of psychoanalytic theory. *What are some characteristics of Freud's theory?*

psychoanalytic theories Describe development as primarily unconscious and heavily colored by emotion. Behavior is merely a surface characteristic, and the symbolic workings of the mind have to be analyzed to understand behavior. Early experiences with parents are emphasized.

Oral Stage	Anal Stage	Phallic Stage	Latency Stage	Genital Stage
Infant's pleasure centers on the mouth.	Child's pleasure focuses on the anus.	Child's pleasure focuses on the genitals.	Child represses sexual interest and develops social and intellectual skills.	A time of sexual reawakening; source of sexual pleasure becomes someone outside the family.
Birth to 1½ Years	*1½ to 3 Years*	*3 to 6 Years*	*6 Years to Puberty*	*Puberty Onward*

FIGURE 1.9 Freudian Stages

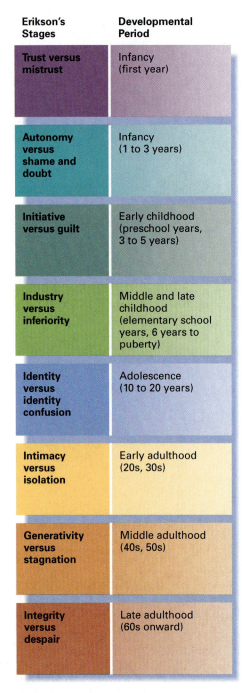

Erikson's Stages	Developmental Period
Trust versus mistrust	Infancy (first year)
Autonomy versus shame and doubt	Infancy (1 to 3 years)
Initiative versus guilt	Early childhood (preschool years, 3 to 5 years)
Industry versus inferiority	Middle and late childhood (elementary school years, 6 years to puberty)
Identity versus identity confusion	Adolescence (10 to 20 years)
Intimacy versus isolation	Early adulthood (20s, 30s)
Generativity versus stagnation	Middle adulthood (40s, 50s)
Integrity versus despair	Late adulthood (60s onward)

FIGURE 1.10 Erikson's Eight Life-Span Stages

Erikson's theory Includes eight stages of human development. Each stage consists of a unique developmental task that confronts individuals with a crisis that must be resolved.

stages, rather than in *psychosexual* stages, as Freud maintained. According to Freud, the primary motivation for human behavior is sexual in nature; according to Erikson, it is social and reflects a desire to affiliate with other people. According to Freud, our basic personality is shaped in the first five years of life; according to Erikson, developmental change occurs throughout the life span. Thus, in terms of the early versus later experience issue described earlier in this chapter, Freud argued that early experience is far more important than later experiences, whereas Erikson emphasized the importance of both early and later experiences.

In **Erikson's theory**, eight stages of development unfold as we go through life (see Figure 1.10). At each stage, a unique developmental task confronts individuals with a crisis that must be resolved. According to Erikson, this crisis is not a catastrophe but a turning point marked by both increased vulnerability and enhanced potential. The more successfully an individual resolves the crises, the healthier development will be.

Trust versus mistrust is Erikson's first psychosocial stage, which is experienced in the first year of life. Trust in infancy sets the stage for a lifelong expectation that the world will be a good and pleasant place to live.

After gaining trust in their caregivers, infants begin to discover that their behavior is their own. They start to assert their sense of independence, or autonomy. If infants are restrained too much or punished too harshly, they are likely to develop a sense of shame and doubt. This is Erikson's second stage of development, *autonomy versus shame and doubt*, which occurs in late infancy and toddlerhood (1 to 3 years).

Initiative versus guilt, Erikson's third stage of development, occurs during the preschool years. As preschool children encounter a widening social world, they face new challenges that require active, purposeful behavior. Children are asked to assume responsibility for their bodies, their behavior, their toys, and their pets, and they take initiative. Feelings of guilt may arise, though, if the child is irresponsible and is made to feel too anxious.

Industry versus inferiority is Erikson's fourth developmental stage, occurring approximately in the elementary school years. Children's initiative brings them in contact with a wealth of new experiences. As they move into middle and late childhood, they direct their energy toward mastering knowledge and intellectual skills. At no other time is the child more enthusiastic about learning than at the end of early childhood's period of expansive imagination. The danger is that the child can develop a sense of inferiority—feeling incompetent and unproductive.

During the adolescent years, individuals are faced with finding out who they are, what they are all about, and where they are going in life. This is Erikson's fifth developmental stage, *identity versus identity confusion*. Adolescents are confronted with many new roles and adult statuses—vocational and romantic, for example. If they explore roles in a healthy manner and arrive at a positive path to follow in life, then they achieve a positive identity. If parents push an identity on adolescents, and if adolescents do not adequately explore many roles and define a positive future path, then identity confusion reigns.

Intimacy versus isolation is Erikson's sixth developmental stage, which individuals experience during the early adulthood years. At this time, individuals face the developmental task of forming intimate relationships. Erikson describes *intimacy* as finding oneself yet losing oneself in another. If the young adult forms healthy friendships and an intimate relationship with another, intimacy will be achieved; if not, isolation will result.

Erik Erikson with his wife, Joan, an artist. Erikson generated one of the most important developmental theories of the twentieth century. *Which stage of Erikson's theory are you in? Does Erikson's description of this stage characterize you?*

Generativity versus stagnation, Erikson's seventh developmental stage, occurs during middle adulthood. By *generativity* Erikson means primarily a concern for helping the younger generation to develop and lead useful lives. The feeling of having done nothing to help the next generation is stagnation.

Integrity versus despair is Erikson's eighth and final stage of development, which individuals experience in late adulthood. During this stage, a person reflects on the past. Through many different routes, the person may have developed a positive outlook in most or all of the previous stages of development. If so, the person's review of his or her life will reveal a life well spent, and the person will feel a sense of satisfaction—integrity will be achieved. If the person had resolved many of the earlier stages negatively, the retrospective glances likely will yield doubt or gloom—the despair Erikson described.

Each of Erikson's stages has a "positive" pole, such as trust, and a "negative" pole, such as mistrust. In the healthy solution to the crisis of each stage, the positive pole dominates, but Erikson stressed that some exposure or commitment to the negative side is sometimes inevitable. For example, learning to trust is an important outcome of Erikson's first stage, but you cannot trust all people under all circumstances and survive. We will discuss Erikson's theory again in the chapters on socioemotional development.

Evaluating the Psychoanalytic Theories   The contributions of psychoanalytic theories include these ideas:

- Early experiences play an important part in development.
- Family relationships are a central aspect of development.
- Personality can be better understood if it is examined developmentally.
- The mind is not all conscious; unconscious aspects of the mind need to be considered.
- In Erikson's theory, changes take place in adulthood as well as in childhood.

These are some criticisms of psychoanalytic theories:

- The main concepts of psychoanalytic theories have been difficult to test scientifically.
- Much of the data used to support psychoanalytic theories come from individuals' reconstruction of the past, often the distant past, and are of unknown accuracy.
- The sexual underpinnings of development are given too much importance (especially in Freud's theory).
- The unconscious mind is given too much credit for influencing development.
- Psychoanalytic theories present an image of humans that is too negative (especially in Freud's theory).
- Psychoanalytic theories are culture- and gender-biased, treating Western culture and males as the measure for evaluating everyone (especially in Freud's theory).

Cognitive Theories   Whereas psychoanalytic theories stress the importance of the unconscious, cognitive theories emphasize conscious thoughts. Three important cognitive theories are Piaget's cognitive developmental theory, Vygotsky's sociocultural cognitive theory, and information-processing theory.

Piaget's Cognitive Developmental Theory   **Piaget's theory** states that children actively construct their understanding of the world and go through four stages of cognitive development. Two processes underlie the four stages of development in Piaget's theory: organization and adaptation. To make sense of our world, we organize our experiences. For example, we separate important ideas from less important ideas, and we connect one idea to another. In addition to organizing our observations and experiences, we *adapt*, adjusting to new environmental demands (Byrnes, 2008; Carpendale, Muller, & Bibok, 2008).

Jean Piaget, the famous Swiss developmental psychologist, changed the way we think about the development of children's minds. *What are some key ideas in Piaget's theory?*

Piaget's theory States that children actively construct their understanding of the world and go through four stages of cognitive development.

Sensorimotor Stage	Preoperational Stage	Concrete Operational Stage	Formal Operational Stage
The infant constructs an understanding of the world by coordinating sensory experiences with physical actions. An infant progresses from reflexive, instinctual action at birth to the beginning of symbolic thought toward the end of the stage.	The child begins to represent the world with words and images. These words and images reflect increased symbolic thinking and go beyond the connection of sensory information and physical action.	The child can now reason logically about concrete events and classify objects into different sets.	The adolescent reasons in more abstract, idealistic, and logical ways.
Birth to 2 Years of Age	*2 to 7 Years of Age*	*7 to 11 Years of Age*	*11 Years of Age Through Adulthood*

FIGURE 1.11 Piaget's Four Stages of Cognitive Development

Piaget (1954) also held that we go through four stages in understanding the world (see Figure 1.11). Each stage is age-related and consists of a distinct way of thinking, a *different* way of understanding the world. Thus, according to Piaget, the child's cognition is *qualitatively* different in one stage compared with another. What are Piaget's four stages of cognitive development like?

The *sensorimotor stage*, which lasts from birth to about 2 years of age, is the first Piagetian stage. In this stage, infants construct an understanding of the world by coordinating sensory experiences (such as seeing and hearing) with physical, motoric actions—hence the term *sensorimotor*.

The *preoperational stage*, which lasts from approximately 2 to 7 years of age, is Piaget's second stage. In this stage, children begin to go beyond simply connecting sensory information with physical action and represent the world with words, images, and drawings. However, according to Piaget, preschool children still lack the ability to perform what he calls *operations*, which are internalized mental actions that allow children to do mentally what they previously could only do physically. For example, if you imagine putting two sticks together to see whether they would be as long as another stick, without actually moving the sticks, you are performing a concrete operation.

The *concrete operational stage*, which lasts from approximately 7 to 11 years of age, is the third Piagetian stage. In this stage, children can perform operations that involve objects, and they can reason logically as long as reasoning can be applied to specific or concrete examples. For instance, concrete operational thinkers cannot imagine the steps necessary to complete an algebraic equation, which is too abstract for thinking at this stage of development.

The *formal operational stage*, which appears between the ages of 11 and 15 and continues through adulthood, is Piaget's fourth and final stage. In this stage, individuals move beyond concrete experiences and think in abstract and more logical terms. As part of thinking more abstractly, adolescents develop images of ideal circumstances. They might think about what an ideal parent is like and compare their parents to this ideal standard. They begin to entertain possibilities for the future and are fascinated with what they can be. In solving problems, they become more systematic, developing hypotheses about why something is happening the way it is and then testing these hypotheses. This is a brief introduction to Piaget's theory. It is provided here, along with other theories, to give you a broad understanding. In Chapter 6, "Cognitive Developmental Approaches," we will return to Piaget and examine his theory in more depth.

Vygotsky's Sociocultural Cognitive Theory   Like Piaget, the Russian developmentalist Lev Vygotsky (1896–1934) argued that children actively construct their knowledge. However, Vygotsky (1962) gave social interaction and culture far more important roles in cognitive development than Piaget did. **Vygotsky's theory** is a sociocultural cognitive theory that emphasizes how culture and social interaction guide cognitive development.

Vygotsky portrayed the child's development as inseparable from social and cultural activities (Gredler, 2008; Holzman, 2009). He argued that development of memory, attention, and reasoning involves learning to use the inventions of society, such as language, mathematical systems, and memory strategies. Thus in one culture, children might learn to count with the help of a computer; in another, they might learn by using beads. According to Vygotsky, children's social interaction with more-skilled adults and peers is indispensable to their cognitive development (Alvarez & del Rio, 2007). Through this interaction, they learn to use the tools that will help them adapt and be successful in their culture. For example, if you regularly help a child learn how to read, you not only advance a child's reading skills but also communicate to the child that reading is an important activity in their culture.

Vygotsky's theory has stimulated considerable interest in the view that knowledge is *situated* and *collaborative* (Bodrova & Leong, 2007; Gauvain, 2008). In this view, knowledge is not generated from within the individual but rather is constructed through interaction with other people and objects in the culture, such as books. This suggests that knowledge can best be advanced through interaction with others in cooperative activities.

Vygotsky's theory, like Piaget's, remained virtually unknown to American psychologists until the 1960s, but eventually both became influential among educators as well as psychologists. We will further examine Vygotsky's theory in Chapter 6.

There is considerable interest today in Lev Vygotsky's sociocultural cognitive theory of child development. *What were Vygotsky's basic ideas about children's development?*

The Information-Processing Theory   Early computers may be the best candidates for the title of "founding fathers" of information-processing theory. Although many factors stimulated the growth of this theory, none was more important than the computer. Psychologists began to wonder if the logical operations carried out by computers might tell us something about how the human mind works. They drew analogies between a computer's hardware and the brain and between computer software and cognition.

This line of thinking helped to generate **information-processing theory**, which emphasizes that individuals manipulate information, monitor it, and strategize about it. Unlike Piaget's theory but like Vygotsky's theory, information-processing theory does not describe development as stage-like. Instead, according to this theory, individuals develop a gradually increasing capacity for processing information, which allows them to acquire increasingly complex knowledge and skills (Halford, 2008; Vallotton & Fischer, 2008).

Robert Siegler (2006), a leading expert on children's information processing, states that thinking is information processing. In other words, when individuals perceive, encode, represent, store, and retrieve information, they are thinking. Siegler emphasizes that an important aspect of development is learning good strategies for processing information. For example, becoming a better reader might involve learning to monitor the key themes of the material being read.

Evaluating the Cognitive Theories   The primary contributions of cognitive theories are:

1. They present a positive view of development, emphasizing conscious thinking.
2. They (especially Piaget's and Vygotsky's) emphasize the individual's active construction of understanding.
3. Piaget's and Vygotsky's theories underscore the importance of examining developmental changes in children's thinking.
4. The information-processing theory offers detailed descriptions of cognitive processes.

These are some criticisms of cognitive theories:

1. Piaget's stages are not as uniform as he theorized. Piaget also underestimated the cognitive skills of infants and overestimated the cognitive skills of adolescents.

Vygotsky's theory A sociocultural cognitive theory that emphasizes how culture and social interaction guide cognitive development.

information-processing theory Emphasizes that individuals manipulate information, monitor it, and strategize about it. Central to this theory are the processes of memory and thinking.

2. The cognitive theories do not give adequate attention to individual variations in cognitive development.

3. Information-processing theory does not provide an adequate description of developmental changes in cognition.

4. Psychoanalytic theorists argue that the cognitive theories do not give enough credit to unconscious thought.

Behavioral and Social Cognitive Theories

At about the same time as Freud was interpreting patients' unconscious minds through their early childhood experiences, Ivan Pavlov and John B. Watson were conducting detailed observations of behavior in controlled laboratory settings. Their work provided the foundations of *behaviorism*, which essentially holds that we can study scientifically only what can be directly observed and measured. Out of the behavioral tradition grew the belief that development is observable behavior that can be learned through experience with the environment (Bugental & Grusec, 2006; Watson & Tharp, 2007). In terms of the continuity-discontinuity issue discussed earlier in this chapter, the behavioral and social cognitive theories emphasize continuity in development and argue that development does not occur in stage-like fashion. The three versions of the behavioral approach that we will explore are Pavlov's classical conditioning, Skinner's operant conditioning, and Bandura's social cognitive theory.

Pavlov's Classical Conditioning   In the early 1900s, the Russian physiologist Ivan Pavlov (1927) knew that dogs innately salivate when they taste food. He became curious when he observed that dogs salivate to various sights and sounds before eating their food. For example, when an individual paired the ringing of a bell with the food, the bell ringing subsequently elicited salivation from the dogs when it was presented by itself. With this experiment, Pavlov discovered the principle of *classical conditioning*, in which a neutral stimulus (in our example, ringing a bell) acquires the ability to produce a response originally produced by another stimulus (in our example, food).

In the early twentieth century, John Watson demonstrated that classical conditioning occurs in human beings. He showed an infant named Albert a white rat to see if he was afraid of it. He was not. As Albert played with the rat, a loud noise was sounded behind his head. As you might imagine, the noise caused little Albert to cry. After several pairings of the loud noise and the white rat, Albert began to cry at the sight of the rat even when the noise was not sounded (Watson & Rayner, 1920). Albert had been classically conditioned to fear the rat. Similarly, many of our fears may result from classical conditioning: fear of the dentist may be learned from a painful experience, fear of driving from being in an automobile accident, fear of heights from falling off a high chair when we were infants, and fear of dogs from being bitten.

Skinner's Operant Conditioning   Classical conditioning may explain how we develop many involuntary responses such as fears, but B. F. Skinner argued that a second type of conditioning accounts for the development of other types of behavior. According to Skinner (1938), through *operant conditioning* the consequences of a behavior produce changes in the probability of the behavior's occurrence. A behavior followed by a rewarding stimulus is more likely to recur, whereas a behavior followed by a punishing stimulus is less likely to recur. For example, when a person smiles at a child after the child has done something, the child is more likely to engage in the activity than if the person gives the child a nasty look.

According to Skinner, such rewards and punishments shape development. For example, Skinner's approach argues that shy people learned to be shy as a result of experiences they had while growing up. It follows that modifications in an environment can help a shy person become more socially oriented. Also, for Skinner the key

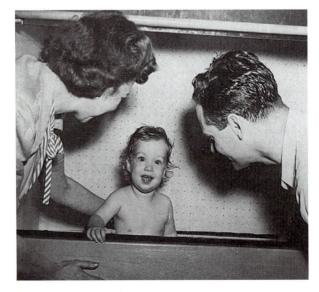

B. F. Skinner was a tinkerer who liked to make new gadgets. The younger of his two daughters, Deborah, was raised in Skinner's enclosed Air-Crib, which he invented because he wanted to control her environment completely. The Air-Crib was sound-proofed and temperature-controlled. Debbie, shown here as a child with her parents, is currently a successful artist, is married, and lives in London. *What do you think about Skinner's Air-Crib?*

aspect of development is behavior, not thoughts and feelings. He emphasized that development consists of the pattern of behavioral changes that are brought about by rewards and punishments.

Bandura's Social Cognitive Theory   Some psychologists agree with the behaviorists' notion that development is learned and is influenced strongly by environmental interactions. However, unlike Skinner, they argue that cognition is also important in understanding development. **Social cognitive theory** holds that behavior, environment, and cognition are the key factors in development.

American psychologist Albert Bandura (1925–) is the leading architect of social cognitive theory. Bandura (2001, 2007, 2008, 2009) emphasizes that cognitive processes have important links with the environment and behavior. His early research program focused heavily on *observational learning* (also called *imitation* or *modeling*), which is learning that occurs through observing what others do. For example, a young boy might observe his father yelling in anger and treating other people with hostility; with his peers, the young boy later acts very aggressively, showing the same characteristics as his father's behavior. A girl might adopt the dominant and sarcastic style of her teacher, saying to her younger brother, "You are so slow. How can you do this work so slowly?" Social cognitive theorists stress that people acquire a wide range of behaviors, thoughts, and feelings through observing others' behavior and that these observations form an important part of children's development.

What is *cognitive* about observational learning in Bandura's view? He proposes that people cognitively represent the behavior of others and then sometimes adopt this behavior themselves.

Bandura's (2001, 2007, 2008, 2009) most recent model of learning and development includes three elements: behavior, the person/cognition, and the environment. An individual's confidence that he or she can control his or her success is an example of a person factor; strategies are an example of a cognitive factor. As shown in Figure 1.12, behavior, person/cognition, and environmental factors operate interactively. Behavior can influence person factors and vice versa. Cognitive activities can influence the environment, the environment can change the person's cognition, and so on.

Evaluating the Behavioral and Social Cognitive Theories   Contributions of the behavioral and social cognitive theories include:

- Their emphasis on the importance of scientific research
- Their focus on environmental determinants of behavior
- The identification and explanation of observational learning (by Bandura)
- The inclusion of person/cognitive factors (in social cognitive theory)

Criticisms of the behavioral and social cognitive theories include the objections that they give:

- Too little emphasis on cognition (in Pavlov's and Skinner's theories)
- Too much emphasis on environmental determinants
- Inadequate attention to developmental changes
- Inadequate consideration of human spontaneity and creativity

Behavioral and social cognitive theories emphasize the importance of environmental experiences in human development. Next we turn our attention to a theory that underscores the importance of the biological foundations of development—ethological theory.

Ethological Theory   American developmental psychologists began to pay attention to the biological bases of development thanks to the work of European zoologists who pioneered the field of ethology. **Ethology** stresses that behavior is strongly influenced

Albert Bandura has been one of the leading architects of social cognitive theory. *What is the nature of his theory?*

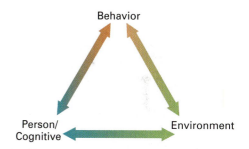
FIGURE 1.12 Bandura's Social Cognitive Model. The arrows illustrate how relations between behavior, person/cognition, and environment are reciprocal rather than unidirectional.

social cognitive theory The view of psychologists who emphasize behavior, environment, and cognition as the key factors in development.

ethology Stresses that behavior is strongly influenced by biology, is tied to evolution, and is characterized by critical or sensitive periods.

Konrad Lorenz, a pioneering student of animal behavior, is followed through the water by three imprinted greylag geese. Describe Lorenz's experiment with the geese. *Do you think his experiment would have the same results with human babies? Explain.*

by biology, is tied to evolution, and is characterized by critical or sensitive periods. These are specific time frames during which, according to ethologists, the presence or absence of certain experiences has a long-lasting influence on individuals.

European zoologist Konrad Lorenz (1903–1989) helped bring ethology to prominence. In his best-known experiment, Lorenz (1965) studied the behavior of greylag geese, which will follow their mothers as soon as they hatch.

In a remarkable set of experiments, Lorenz separated the eggs laid by one goose into two groups. One group he returned to the goose to be hatched by her. The other group was hatched in an incubator. The goslings in the first group performed as predicted. They followed their mother as soon as they hatched. However, those in the second group, which saw Lorenz when they first hatched, followed him everywhere, as though he were their mother. Lorenz marked the goslings and then placed both groups under a box. Mother goose and "mother" Lorenz stood aside as the box lifted. Each group of goslings went directly to its "mother." Lorenz called this process *imprinting*, the rapid, innate learning within a limited critical period of time that involves attachment to the first moving object seen.

At first, ethological research and theory had little or nothing to say about the nature of social relationships across the *human* life span, and the theory stimulated few studies with people. Ethologists' viewpoint that normal development requires that certain behaviors emerge during a *critical period*, a fixed time period very early in development, seemed to be overstated.

However, John Bowlby's work (1969, 1989) illustrated an important application of ethological theory to human development. Bowlby argued that attachment to a caregiver over the first year of life has important consequences throughout the life span. In his view, if this attachment is positive and secure, the infant will likely develop positively in childhood and adulthood. If the attachment is negative and insecure, children's development will likely not be optimal. Thus, in this view the first year of life is a *sensitive period* for the development of social relationships. In Chapter 10, "Emotional Development," we will explore the concept of infant attachment in greater detail.

Contributions of ethological theory include:

- Increased focus on the biological and evolutionary basis of development
- Use of careful observations in naturalistic settings
- Emphasis on sensitive periods of development

These are some criticisms of ethological theory:

- Concepts of critical and sensitive periods perhaps too rigid
- Too strong an emphasis on biological foundations

- Inadequate attention to cognition
- Better at generating research with animals than with humans

Another theory that emphasizes the biological aspects of human development—evolutionary psychology—will be presented in Chapter 2, "Biological Beginnings," along with views on the role of heredity in development.

Ecological Theory   Whereas ethological theory stresses biological factors, ecological theory emphasizes environmental factors. One ecological theory that has important implications for understanding children's development was created by Urie Bronfenbrenner (1917–2005).

Bronfenbrenner's ecological theory (1986, 2000, 2004; Bronfenbrenner & Morris, 1998, 2006) holds that development reflects the influence of several environmental systems. The theory identifies five environmental systems (see Figure 1.13):

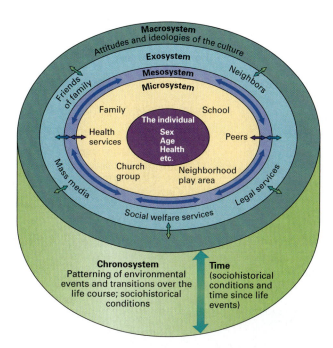

FIGURE 1.13 Bronfenbrenner's Ecological Theory of Development. Bronfenbrenner's ecological theory consists of five environmental systems: microsystem, mesosystem, exosystem, macrosystem, and chronosystem.

- *Microsystem:* The setting in which the individual lives. These contexts include the person's family, peers, school, neighborhood, and work. It is in the microsystem that the most direct interactions with social agents take place—with parents, peers, and teachers, for example.

- *Mesosystem:* Relations between microsystems or connections between contexts. Examples are the relation of family experiences to school experiences, school experiences to church experiences, and family experiences to peer experiences. For example, children whose parents have rejected them may have difficulty developing positive relations with teachers.

- *Exosystem:* Links between a social setting in which the individual does not have an active role and the individual's immediate context. For example, a husband's or child's experience at home may be influenced by a mother's experiences at work. The mother might receive a promotion that requires more travel, which might increase conflict with the husband and change patterns of interaction with the child.

- *Macrosystem:* The culture in which individuals live. Remember from earlier in this chapter that culture refers to the behavior patterns, beliefs, and all other products of a group of people that are passed on from generation to generation. Remember also that cross-cultural studies—the comparison of one culture with one or more other cultures—provide information about the generality of development (Shiraev & Levy, 2007).

- *Chronosystem:* The patterning of environmental events and transitions over the life course, as well as sociohistorical circumstances (Schaie, 2007). For example, divorce is one transition. Researchers have found that the negative effects of divorce on children often peak in the first year after the divorce (Hetherington, 1993, 2006). By two years after the divorce, family interaction is less chaotic and more stable. As an example of sociohistorical circumstances, consider how the opportunities for women to pursue a career have increased during the last thirty years.

Bronfenbrenner (2000, 2004; Bronfenbrenner & Morris, 1998, 2006) has added biological influences to his theory and now describes it as a *bioecological* theory. Nonetheless, ecological, environmental contexts still predominate in Bronfenbrenner's theory.

The contributions of ecological theory include (1) a systematic examination of macro and micro dimensions of environmental systems, (2) attention to connections between environmental settings (mesosystem), and (3) consideration of sociohistorical influences on development (chronosystem).

Urie Bronfenbrenner developed ecological theory, a perspective that is receiving increased attention. *What is the nature of ecological theory?*

Bronfenbrenner's ecological theory An environmental systems theory that focuses on five environmental systems: microsystem, mesosystem, exosystem, macrosystem, and chronosystem.

THEORY	ISSUES		
	Nature and nurture	**Early and later experience**	**Continuity and discontinuity**
Psychoanalytic	Freud's biological determinism interacting with early family experiences; Erikson's more balanced biological/cultural interaction perspective	Early experiences in the family very important influences	Emphasis on discontinuity between stages
Cognitive	Piaget's emphasis on interaction and adaptation; environment provides the setting for cognitive structures to develop. Vygotsky's theory involves interaction of nature and nurture with strong emphasis on culture. The information-processing approach has not addressed this issue extensively; mainly emphasizes biological/environment interaction.	Childhood experiences important influences	Discontinuity between stages in Piaget's theory; no stages in Vygotsky's theory or the information-processing approach
Behavioral and Social Cognitive	Environment viewed as the main influence on development	Experiences important at all points in development	Continuity with no stages
Ethological	Strong biological view	Early experience very important, which can contribute to change early in development; after early critical or sensitive period has passed, stability likely to occur	Discontinuity because of early critical or sensitive period; no stages
Ecological	Strong environmental view	Experiences involving the five environmental systems important at all points in development	No stages but little attention to the issue

FIGURE 1.14 A Comparison of Theories and Issues in Child Development

These are some criticisms of ecological theory: (1) too little attention to biological foundations of development, even with the added discussion of biological influences; and (2) inadequate attention to cognitive processes.

An Eclectic Theoretical Orientation   No single theory described in this chapter can explain entirely the rich complexity of children's development, but each has contributed to our understanding of development. Psychoanalytic theory best explains the unconscious mind. Erikson's theory best describes the changes that occur in adult development. Piaget's, Vygotsky's, and the information-processing views provide the most complete description of cognitive development. The behavioral and social cognitive and ecological theories have been the most adept at examining the environmental determinants of development. The ethological theories have highlighted biology's role and the importance of sensitive periods in development.

In short, although theories are helpful guides, relying on a single theory to explain development is probably a mistake. This book instead takes an **eclectic theoretical orientation**, which does not follow any one theoretical approach but rather selects from each theory whatever is considered its best features. In this way, you can view the study of development as it actually exists—with different theorists making different assumptions, stressing different empirical problems, and using different strategies to discover information. Figure 1.14 compares the main theoretical perspectives in terms of how they view important developmental issues in children's development.

Research Methods for Collecting Data

If they follow an eclectic orientation, how do scholars and researchers determine that one feature of a theory is somehow better than another? The scientific method

eclectic theoretical orientation An orientation that does not follow any one theoretical approach, but rather selects from each theory whatever is considered the best in it.

discussed earlier in this chapter provides the guide. Recall that the steps in the scientific method involve conceptualizing the problem, collecting data, drawing conclusions, and revising research conclusions and theories. Through scientific research, the features of theories can be tested and refined.

Whether we are interested in studying attachment in infants, the cognitive skills of children, or the peer relations of adolescents, we can choose from several ways of collecting data. Here we outline the measures most often used, including their advantages and disadvantages, beginning with observation.

A researcher observes teacher-child interaction through a one-way mirror in a child-care program.

Observation   Scientific observation requires an important set of skills (Gay, Mills, & Airasian, 2009; Jackson, 2008). Unless we are trained observers and practice our skills regularly, we might not know what to look for, we might not remember what we saw, we might not realize that what we are looking for is changing from one moment to the next, and we might not communicate our observations effectively.

For observations to be effective, they have to be systematic. We have to have some idea of what we are looking for. We have to know whom we are observing, when and where we will observe, how the observations will be made, and how they will be recorded.

Where should we make our observations? We have two choices: the laboratory and the everyday world.

When we observe scientifically, we often need to control certain factors that determine behavior but are not the focus of our inquiry (Rosnow & Rosenthal, 2008). For this reason, some research in life-span development is conducted in a **laboratory**, a controlled setting with many of the complex factors of the "real world" removed. For example, suppose you want to observe how children react when they see other people act aggressively. If you observe children in their homes or schools, you have no control over how much aggression the children observe, what kind of aggression they see, which people they see acting aggressively, or how other people treat the children. In contrast, if you observe the children in a laboratory, you can control these and other factors and therefore have more confidence about how to interpret your observations.

Laboratory research does have some drawbacks, however, including the following:

- It is almost impossible to conduct research without the participants' knowing they are being studied.
- The laboratory setting is unnatural and therefore can cause the participants to behave unnaturally.
- People who are willing to come to a university laboratory may not fairly represent groups from diverse cultural backgrounds.
- People who are unfamiliar with university settings, and with the idea of "helping science" may be intimidated by the laboratory setting.
- Some aspects of children's development are difficult if not impossible to examine in the laboratory.
- Laboratory studies of certain types of stress may even be unethical.

Naturalistic observation provides insights that we sometimes cannot achieve in the laboratory. **Naturalistic observation** means observing behavior in real-world settings, making no effort to manipulate or control the situation. Child development researchers conduct naturalistic observations in homes, child-care centers, schools, neighborhoods, malls, and other contexts.

Naturalistic observation was used in one study that focused on conversations in a children's science museum (Crowley & others, 2001). Parents were more than three times as likely to engage boys than girls in explanatory talk while visiting exhibits at the science museum, suggesting a gender bias that encourages boys more than girls to

laboratory A controlled setting in which many of the complex factors of the "real world" are removed.

naturalistic observation Observing behavior in real-world settings.

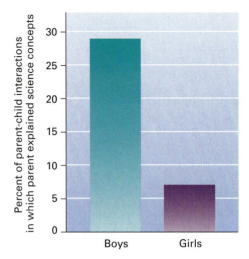

FIGURE 1.15 Parents' Explanations of Science to Sons and Daughters at a Science Museum. In a naturalistic observation study at a children's science museum, parents were more than three times more likely to explain science to boys than to girls (Crowley & others, 2001). The gender difference occurred regardless of whether the father, the mother, or both parents were with the child, although the gender difference was greatest for fathers' science explanations to sons and daughters.

Mahatma Gandhi was the spiritual leader of India in the middle of the twentieth century. Erik Erikson conducted an extensive case study of his life to determine what contributed to his identity development. *What are some limitations of the case study approach?*

standardized test A test with uniform procedures for administration and scoring. Many standardized tests allow a person's performance to be compared with the performance of other individuals.

be interested in science (see Figure 1.15). In another study, Mexican American parents who had completed high school used more explanations with their children when visiting a science museum than Mexican American parents who had not completed high school (Tenenbaum & others, 2002).

Survey and Interview Sometimes the best and quickest way to get information about people is to ask them for it. One technique is to *interview* them directly. A related method is the *survey* (sometimes referred to as a questionnaire), which is especially useful when information from many people is needed (Nardi, 2006). A standard set of questions is used to obtain people's self-reported attitudes or beliefs about a particular topic. In a good survey, the questions are clear and unbiased, allowing respondents to answer unambiguously.

Surveys and interviews can be used to study a wide range of topics from religious beliefs to sexual habits to attitudes about gun control to beliefs about how to improve schools. Surveys and interviews today are conducted in person, over the telephone, and over the Internet.

One problem with surveys and interviews is the tendency of participants to answer questions in a way that they think is socially acceptable or desirable rather than telling what they truly think or feel (Creswell, 2008). For example, on a survey or in an interview some individuals might say that they do not take drugs even though they do.

Standardized Test A **standardized test** has uniform procedures for administration and scoring. Many standardized tests allow a person's performance to be compared with the performance of other individuals—thus they provide information about individual differences among people (Gregory, 2007). One example is the Stanford-Binet intelligence test, which is described in Chapter 8, "Intelligence." Your score on the Stanford-Binet test tells you how your performance compares with that of thousands of other people who have taken the test.

Standardized tests also have three key weaknesses. First, they do not always predict behavior in nontest situations. Second, standardized tests are based on the belief that a person's behavior is consistent and stable, yet personality and intelligence—two primary targets of standardized testing—can vary with the situation. For example, individuals may perform poorly on a standardized intelligence test in an office setting but score much higher at home, where they are less anxious. This criticism is especially relevant for members of minority groups, some of whom have been inaccurately classified as mentally retarded on the basis of their scores on intelligence tests. A third weakness of standardized tests is that many psychological tests developed in Western cultures might not be appropriate in other cultures (Matsumoto & Juang, 2008). The experiences of people in differing cultures may lead them to interpret and respond to questions differently.

Case Study A **case study** is an in-depth look at a single individual. Case studies are performed mainly by mental health professionals when, for either practical or ethical reasons, the unique aspects of an individual's life cannot be duplicated and tested in other ways. A case study provides information about one person's fears, hopes, fantasies, traumatic experiences, upbringing, family relationships, health, or anything that helps the psychologist understand the person's mind and behavior. In later chapters, we discuss vivid case studies, such as that of Michael Rehbein, who had much of the left side of his brain removed at 7 years of age to end severe epileptic seizures.

Case histories provide dramatic, in-depth portrayals of people's lives, but remember that we must be cautious when generalizing from this information. The subject of a case study is unique, with a genetic makeup and personal history that no one else shares. In addition, case studies involve judgments of unknown reliability. Psychologists who conduct case studies rarely check to see if other psychologists agree with their observations.

Physiological Measures   Researchers are increasingly using *physiological measures* when they study children's development (Hofheimer & Lester, 2008; Moulson & Nelson, 2008). For example, as puberty unfolds, the blood levels of certain hormones increase. To determine the nature of these hormonal changes, researchers take blood samples from willing adolescents (Dorn & others, 2006).

Another physiological measure that is increasingly being used is neuroimaging, especially *functional magnetic resonance imaging (fMRI)*, in which electromagnetic waves are used to construct images of a person's brain tissue and biochemical activity (Nelson, Thomas, & de Haan, 2006) (see Figure 1.16). We will have much more to say about neuroimaging and other physiological measures at various points in this book.

Research Designs

Suppose you want to find out whether the children of permissive parents are more likely than other children to be rude and unruly. The data-collection method that researchers choose often depends on the goal of their research. The goal may be simply to describe a phenomenon, or it may be to describe relationships between phenomena, or to determine the causes or effects of a phenomenon.

Perhaps you decide that you need to observe both permissive and strict parents with their children and compare them. How would you do that? In addition to a method for collecting data, you would need a research design. There are three main types of research design: descriptive, correlational, and experimental.

Descriptive Research   All of the data-collection methods that we have discussed can be used in **descriptive research**, which aims to observe and record behavior. For example, a researcher might observe the extent to which people are altruistic or aggressive toward each other. By itself, descriptive research cannot prove what causes some phenomenon, but it can reveal important information about people's behavior (Given, 2008).

Correlational Research   In contrast to descriptive research, correlational research goes beyond describing phenomena to provide information that will help us to predict how people will behave. In **correlational research**, the goal is to describe the strength of the relationship between two or more events or characteristics. The more strongly the two events are correlated (or related or associated), the more effectively we can predict one event from the other (Kraska, 2008).

For example, to study if children of permissive parents have less self-control than other children, you would need to carefully record observations of parents' permissiveness and their children's self-control. The data could then be analyzed statistically to yield a numerical measure, called a **correlation coefficient**, a number based on a statistical analysis that is used to describe the degree of association between two variables. The correlation coefficient ranges from +1.00 to −1.00. A negative number means an inverse relation. For example, researchers often find a negative correlation between permissive parenting and children's self-control. By contrast, they often find a positive correlation between parental monitoring of children and children's self-control.

The higher the correlation coefficient (whether positive or negative), the stronger the association between the two variables. A correlation of 0 means that there is no association between the variables. A correlation of −.40 is stronger than a correlation of +.20 because we disregard whether the correlation is positive or negative in determining the strength of the correlation.

A caution is in order, however. Correlation does not equal causation (Aron, Aron, & Coups, 2008; Christensen, 2007). The correlational finding just mentioned does not mean that permissive parenting necessarily causes low self-control in children. It might mean that a child's lack of self-control caused the parents to simply throw up their arms in despair and give up trying to control the child. It might also mean that

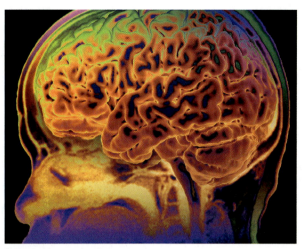

FIGURE 1.16 Magnetic Resonance Imaging

case study An in-depth look at a single individual.

descriptive research Has the purpose of observing and recording behavior.

correlational research The goal is to describe the strength of the relationship between two or more events or characteristics.

correlation coefficient A number based on statistical analysis that is used to describe the degree of association between two variables.

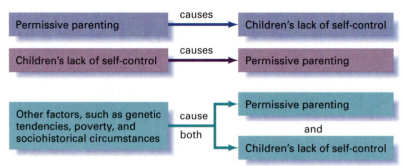

Observed correlation

As permissive parenting increases, children's self-control decreases.

Possible explanations for this correlation

Permissive parenting — causes → Children's lack of self-control

Children's lack of self-control — causes → Permissive parenting

Other factors, such as genetic tendencies, poverty, and sociohistorical circumstances — cause both → Permissive parenting

and

Children's lack of self-control

FIGURE 1.17 Possible Explanations for Correlational Data. An observed correlation between two events cannot be used to conclude that one event caused the other. Some possibilities are that the second event caused the first event or that a third, unknown event caused the correlation between the first two events.

other factors, such as heredity or poverty, caused the correlation between permissive parenting and low self-control in children. Figure 1.17 illustrates these possible interpretations of correlational data.

Throughout this book you will read about numerous correlational research studies. Keep in mind how easy it is to assume causality when two events or characteristics merely are correlated.

Experimental Research   To study causality, researchers turn to *experimental research*. An **experiment** is a carefully regulated procedure in which one or more factors believed to influence the behavior being studied are manipulated while all other factors are held constant. If the behavior under study changes when a factor is manipulated, we say that the manipulated factor has caused the behavior to change. In other words, the experiment has demonstrated cause and effect. The cause is the factor that was manipulated. The effect is the behavior that changed because of the manipulation. Nonexperimental research methods (descriptive and correlational research) cannot establish cause and effect because they do not involve manipulating factors in a controlled way (Martin, 2008).

Independent and Dependent Variables   Experiments include two types of changeable factors, or variables: independent and dependent. An independent variable is a manipulated, influential, experimental factor. It is a potential cause. The label independent is used because this variable can be manipulated independently of other factors to determine its effect. One experiment may include several independent variables.

A dependent variable is a factor that can change in an experiment, in response to changes in the independent variable. As researchers manipulate the independent variable, they measure the dependent variable for any resulting effect.

For example, suppose that you conducted a study to determine whether aerobic exercise by pregnant women changes the breathing and sleeping patterns of newborn babies. You might require one group of pregnant women to engage in a certain amount of exercise each week; the amount of exercise is thus the independent variable. When the infants are born, you would observe and measure their breathing and sleeping patterns. These patterns are the dependent variable, the factor that changes as the result of your manipulation.

Experimental and Control Groups   Experiments can involve one or more experimental groups and one or more control groups. An experimental group is a group whose experience is manipulated. A control group is a comparison group that is as much like the experimental group as possible and that is treated in every way like the

experiment A carefully regulated procedure in which one or more of the factors believed to influence the behavior being studied are manipulated while all other factors are held constant.

experimental group except for the manipulated factor (independent variable). The control group serves as a baseline against which the effects of the manipulated condition can be compared.

Random assignment is an important principle for deciding whether each participant will be placed in the experimental group or in the control group. Random assignment means that researchers assign participants to experimental and control groups by chance. It reduces the likelihood that the experiment's results will be due to any preexisting differences between groups (Martin, 2008). In the example of the effects of aerobic exercise by pregnant women on the breathing and sleeping patterns of their newborns, you would randomly assign half of the pregnant women to engage in aerobic exercise over a period of weeks (the experimental group) and the other half to not exercise over the same number of weeks (the control group). Figure 1.18 illustrates the nature of experimental research.

Time Span of Research

Researchers in child development have a special concern with studies that focus on the relation of age to some other variable. To do this, they study different individuals of different ages and compare them or they study the same individuals as they age over time.

Cross-Sectional Approach   The **cross-sectional approach** is a research strategy in which individuals of different ages are compared at one time. A typical cross-sectional study might include a group of 5-year-olds, 8-year-olds, and 11-year-olds. The groups can be compared with respect to a variety of dependent variables: IQ, memory, peer relations, attachment to parents, hormonal changes, and so on. All of this can be accomplished in a short time. In some studies, data are collected in a single day. Even in large-scale cross-sectional studies with hundreds of participants, data collection does not usually take longer than several months to complete.

The main advantage of the cross-sectional study is that researchers don't have to wait for children to grow older. Despite its efficiency, the cross-sectional approach has its drawbacks. It gives no information about how individual children change or about the stability of their characteristics. It can obscure the increases and decreases of development—the hills and valleys of growth and development.

Longitudinal Approach   The **longitudinal approach** is a research strategy in which the same individuals are studied over a period of time, usually several years or more. For example, if a study of self-esteem were conducted longitudinally, the same children might be assessed three times—at 5, 8, and 11 years of age, for example. Some longitudinal studies take place over shorter time frames, even just a year or so.

Longitudinal studies provide a wealth of information about such important issues as stability and change in development and the importance of early experience for later development, but they are not without their problems (Hofer & Sliwinski, 2006). They are expensive and time-consuming. Also, the longer the study lasts, the more participants drop out. For example, children's families may move, get sick, lose interest, and so forth. Those who remain in the study may be dissimilar to those who drop out, biasing the results. Those individuals who remain in a longitudinal study over a number of years may be more compulsive and conformity-oriented, for example, or they might have more stable lives.

Theories are often linked with a particular research method, or methods. Therefore, methods that researchers use are associated with their particular theoretical approach. Figure 1.19 illustrates connections between research methods and theories.

So far we have discussed many aspects of scientific research in child development. In the *Research in Child Development* interlude that follows, you can read about the journals where this research is published.

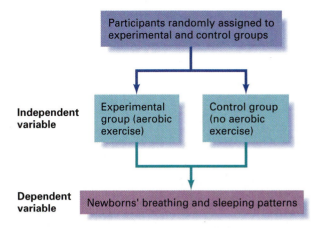

FIGURE 1.18 Principles of Experimental Research. Imagine that you decide to conduct an experimental study of the effects of aerobic exercise by pregnant women on their newborns' breathing and sleeping patterns. You would randomly assign pregnant women to experimental and control groups. The experimental group women would engage in aerobic exercise over a specified number of sessions and weeks. The control group would not. Then, when the infants are born, you would assess their breathing and sleeping patterns. If the breathing and sleeping patterns of newborns whose mothers were in the experimental group are more positive than those of the control group, you would conclude that aerobic exercise caused the positive effects.

cross-sectional approach A research strategy in which individuals of different ages are compared at one time.

longitudinal approach A research strategy in which the same individuals are studied over a period of time, usually several years or more.

FIGURE 1.19 Connections of Research Methods to Theories

Research Method	Theory
Observation	• All theories emphasize some form of observation. • Behavioral and social cognitive theories place the strongest emphasis on laboratory observation. • Ethological theory places the strongest emphasis on naturalistic observation.
Interview/survey	• Psychoanalytic and cognitive studies (Piaget, Vygotsky) often use interviews. • Behavioral, social cognitive, and ethological theories are the least likely to use surveys or interviews.
Standardized test	• None of the theories discussed emphasize the use of this method.
Physiological measures	• None of the theories discussed address psychophysiological measures to any significant degree.
Case study	• Psychoanalytic theories (Freud, Erikson) are the most likely to use this method.
Correlational research	• All of the theories use this research method, although psychoanalytic theories are the least likely to use it.
Experimental research	• The behavioral and social cognitive theories and the information-processing theories are the most likely to use the experimental method. • Psychoanalytic theories are the least likely to use it.
Cross-sectional/ longitudinal methods	• No theory described uses these methods more than any other.

Research in Child Development

RESEARCH JOURNALS

Regardless of whether you pursue a career in child development, psychology, or some related scientific field, you can benefit by learning about the journal process. As a student you might be required to look up original research in journals. As a parent, teacher, or nurse you might want to consult journals to obtain information that will help you understand and work more effectively with people. And as an inquiring person, you might look up information in journals after you have heard or read something that piqued your curiosity.

A journal publishes scholarly and academic information, usually in a specific domain—like physics, math, sociology, or, our current interest, child development. Scholars in these fields publish most of their research in journals, which are the source of core information in virtually every academic discipline.

An increasing number of journals publish information about child development. Among the leading journals in child development are *Developmental Psychology, Child Development, Developmental Psychopathology, Pediatrics, Pediatric Nursing, Infant Behavior and Development, Journal of Research on Adolescence, Human Development*, and many others. Also, a number of journals that do not focus solely on development include articles on various aspects of human development. These journals include *Journal of*

Educational Psychology, Sex Roles, Journal of Cross-Cultural Research, Journal of Marriage and the Family, Exceptional Children, and *Journal of Consulting and Clinical Psychology.*

Every journal has a board of experts who evaluate articles submitted for publication. Each submitted paper is accepted or rejected on the basis of such factors as its contribution to the field, methodological excellence, and clarity of writing. Some of the most prestigious journals reject as many as 80 to 90 percent of the articles submitted.

Journal articles are usually written for other professionals in the specialized field of the journal's focus; therefore, they often contain technical language and terms specific to the discipline that are difficult for nonprofessionals to understand. Their organization often takes this course: abstract, introduction, method, results, discussion, and references.

The *abstract* is a brief summary that appears at the beginning of the article. The abstract lets readers quickly determine whether the article is relevant to their interests. The *introduction* introduces the problem or issue that is being studied. It includes a concise review of research relevant to the topic, theoretical ties, and one or more hypotheses to be tested. The *method* section consists of a clear description of the subjects evaluated in the study, the measures used, and the procedures that were followed. The method section should be sufficiently clear and detailed so that by reading it another researcher could repeat or replicate the study. The *results* section reports the analysis of the data collected. In most cases, the results section includes statistical analyses that are difficult for nonprofessionals to understand. The *discussion* section describes the author's conclusions, inferences, and interpretation of what was found. Statements are usually made about whether the hypotheses presented in the introduction were supported, limitations of the study, and suggestions for future research. The last part of the journal article, called *references*, includes bibliographic information for each source cited in the article. The references section is often a good source for finding other articles relevant to the topic that interests you.

Where do you find journals such as those we have described? Your college or university library likely has some of them, and some public libraries also carry journals. Online resources such as PsycINFO, which can facilitate the search for journal articles, are available to students on many campuses.

Research journals are the core of information in virtually every academic discipline. Those shown here are among the increasing number of research journals that publish information about child development. *What are the main parts of a research article that presents findings from original research?*

Challenges in Child Development Research

The scientific foundation of research in child development helps to minimize the effect of research bias and maximize the objectivity of the results. Still, subtle challenges remain for each researcher to resolve. One is to ensure that research is conducted in an ethical way; another is to recognize, and try to overcome, deeply buried personal biases.

Conducting Ethical Research   The explosion in technology has forced society to grapple with looming ethical questions that were unimaginable only a few decades ago. The same line of research that enables previously sterile couples to have children might someday let prospective parents "call up and order" the characteristics they prefer in their children or tip the balance of males and females in the world. For example, should embryos left over from procedures for increasing fertility be saved or discarded? Should people with inheritable fatal diseases (such as Huntington disease) be discouraged from having their own biological children?

Researchers also face ethical questions both new and old. They have a responsibility to anticipate the personal problems their research might cause and to at least inform the participants of the possible fallout. Safeguarding the rights of research participants is a challenge because the potential harm is not always obvious (Myers & Hansen, 2006).

Ethics in research may affect you personally if you ever serve as a participant in a study. In that event, you need to know your rights as a participant and the responsibilities of researchers to assure that these rights are safeguarded.

If you ever become a researcher in child development yourself, you will need an even deeper understanding of ethics. Even if you only carry out experimental projects in psychology courses, you must consider the rights of the participants in those projects.

Today, proposed research at colleges and universities must pass the scrutiny of a research ethics committee before the research can be initiated. In addition, the American Psychological Association (APA) has developed ethics guidelines for its members. The code of ethics instructs psychologists to protect their participants from mental and physical harm. The participants' best interests need to be kept foremost in the researcher's mind (Fisher, 2009; Jackson, 2008). APA's guidelines address four important issues: informed consent, confidentiality, debriefing, and deception.

- *Informed consent.* All participants must know what their participation will involve and what risks might develop. For example, participants in a study on dating should be told beforehand that a questionnaire might stimulate thoughts about issues in their relationship that they have not considered. Participants also should be informed that in some instances a discussion of the issues might improve their relationship, but in others might worsen the relationship and even end it. Even after informed consent is given, participants must retain the right to withdraw from the study at any time and for any reason.

- *Confidentiality.* Researchers are responsible for keeping all of the data they gather on individuals completely confidential and, when possible, completely anonymous.

- *Debriefing.* After the study has been completed, participants should be informed of its purpose and the methods that were used. In most cases, the experimenter also can inform participants in a general manner beforehand about the purpose of the research without leading participants to behave in a way they think that the experimenter is expecting. When preliminary information about the study is likely to affect the results, participants can at least be debriefed after the study has been completed.

- *Deception.* This is an ethical issue that researchers debate extensively. In some circumstances, telling the participants beforehand what the research study is about substantially alters the participants' behavior and invalidates the researcher's data. In all cases of deception, however, the psychologist must ensure that the deception will not harm the participants and that the participants will be told the complete nature of the study (debriefed) as soon as possible after the study is completed.

Minimizing Bias Studies of children's development are most useful when they are conducted without bias or prejudice toward any particular group of people. Of special concern is bias based on gender and bias based on culture or ethnicity.

Gender Bias For most of its existence, our society has had a strong gender bias, a preconceived notion about the abilities of males and females that prevented individuals from pursuing their own interests and achieving their potential (Matlin, 2008; Smith, 2007). Gender bias also has had a less obvious effect within the field of child development. For example, it is not unusual for conclusions to be drawn about females' attitudes and behaviors from research conducted with males as the only participants.

Furthermore, when researchers find gender differences, their reports sometimes magnify those differences (Denmark & others, 1988). For example, a researcher might report that 74 percent of the boys in a study had high achievement expectations versus only 67 percent of the girls and go on to talk about the differences in some detail.

In reality, this might be a rather small difference. It also might disappear if the study were repeated, or the study might have methodological problems that don't allow such strong interpretations.

Pam Reid is a leading researcher who studies gender and ethnic bias in development. To read about Pam's interests, see the *Careers in Child Development* profile.

Careers in Child Development

Pam Reid, Educational and Developmental Psychologist

When she was a child, Pam Reid liked to play with chemistry sets. Reid majored in chemistry during college and wanted to become a doctor. However, when some of her friends signed up for a psychology class as an elective, she also decided to take the course. She was intrigued by learning about how people think, behave, and develop—so much so that she changed her major to psychology. Reid went on to obtain her Ph.D. in psychology (American Psychological Association, 2003, p. 16).

For a number of years' Reid, was a professor of education and psychology at the University of Michigan, where she also was a research scientist at the Institute for Research on Women and Gender. Her main focus has been on how children and adolescents develop social skills with a special interest in the development of African American girls (Reid & Zalk, 2001). In 2004, Reid became provost and executive vice-president at Roosevelt University in Chicago.

Pam Reid (center, back row) with some of the graduate students she mentored at the University of Michigan.

Cultural and Ethnic Bias   The realization that research on children's development needs to include more children from diverse ethnic groups has also been building (Graham, 1992, 2006). Historically, children from ethnic minority groups (African American, Latino, Asian American, and Native American) were excluded from most research in the United States and simply thought of as variations from the norm or average. If minority children were included in samples and their scores didn't fit the norm, they were viewed as confounds or "noise" in data and discounted. Given the fact that children from diverse ethnic groups were excluded from research on child development for so long, we might reasonably conclude that children's real lives are perhaps more varied than research data have indicated in the past.

Researchers also have tended to overgeneralize about ethnic groups (Banks, 2008; Nieto & Bode, 2008). **Ethnic gloss** is using an ethnic label such as African American or Latino in a superficial way that portrays an ethnic group as being more homogeneous than it really is (Trimble, 1988). For example, a researcher might describe a research sample like this: "The participants were 60 Latinos." A more complete description of the Latino group might be something like this: "The 60 Latino participants were Mexican Americans from low-income neighborhoods in the southwestern area of Los Angeles. Thirty-six were from homes in which Spanish is the dominant language spoken, 24 from homes in which English is the main language spoken. Thirty were born in the United States, 30 in Mexico. Twenty-eight described themselves as Mexican American, 14 as Mexican, 9 as American, 6 as Chicano, and 3 as Latino." Ethnic gloss can cause researchers to obtain samples of ethnic groups that are not representative of the group's diversity, which can lead to overgeneralization and stereotyping.

ethnic gloss Using an ethnic label such as African American or Latino in a superficial way that portrays an ethnic group as being more homogeneous than it really is.

Look at these two photographs, one of all White male children, the other of a diverse group of girls and boys from different ethnic groups, including some White children. Consider a topic in child development, such as parenting, cultural values, or independence seeking. *If you were conducting research on this topic, might the results of the study be different depending on whether the participants in your study were the children in the left or right photograph?*

Research on ethnic minority children and their families has not been given adequate attention, especially in light of their significant rate of growth (Coltrane & others, 2008). Until recently, ethnic minority families were combined in the category "minority," which masks important differences among ethnic groups as well as diversity within an ethnic group. At present and in the foreseeable future, the growth of minority families in the United States will be mainly due to the immigration of Latino and Asian families. Researchers need to take into account their acculturation level and generational status of parents and children, and how they influence family processes and child outcomes (Berry, 2007). More attention also needs to be given to biculturalism because the complexity of diversity means that some children of color identify with two or more ethnic groups (Phinney, 2006).

Review and Reflect: Learning Goal 4

4 Summarize Why Research Is Important in Child Development, the Main Theories of Child Development, and Research Methods, Designs, and Challenges

REVIEW

- What is scientific research, what is it based on, and why is scientific research on child development important?
- What are the main theories of child development?
- What are the main research methods for collecting data about children's development?
- What types of research designs do child development researchers use?
- What are some research challenges in studying children's development?

REFLECT

- Imagine that you are conducting a research study on the sexual attitudes and behaviors of adolescents. What ethical safeguards should you use in conducting the study?

Reach Your Learning Goals

Introduction

1 CHILD DEVELOPMENT—YESTERDAY AND TODAY: DISCUSS HISTORICAL VIEWS AND THE MODERN ERA OF CHILD DEVELOPMENT

Historical Views of Childhood

The Modern Study of Child Development

- Development is the pattern of change that begins at conception and continues through the life span; usually involves growth although it also involves decay. The history of interest in children is long and rich. Prior to the nineteenth century, philosophical views of childhood were prominent, including the notions of original sin, tabula rasa, and innate goodness.

- Today, we conceive of childhood as an important time of development. The modern era of studying children spans a little more than a century, an era in which the study of child development has become a sophisticated science. Methodological advances in observation as well as the introduction of experimentation and the development of major theories characterize the achievements of the modern era.

2 CARING FOR CHILDREN: IDENTIFY FIVE AREAS IN WHICH CHILDREN'S LIVES NEED TO BE IMPROVED, AND EXPLAIN THE ROLES OF RESILIENCE AND SOCIAL POLICY IN CHILDREN'S DEVELOPMENT

Improving the Lives of Children

Resilience, Social Policy, and Children's Development

- Health and well-being is an important area in which children's lives can be improved. Today, many children in the United States and around the world need improved health care. We now recognize the importance of lifestyles and psychological states in promoting health and well-being. Parenting is an important influence on children's development. One-parent families, working parents, and child care are among the family issues that influence children's well-being. Education can also contribute to children's health and well-being. There is widespread concern that the education of children needs to be more effective, and there are many views in contemporary education about ways to improve schools.

- Some children triumph over adversity—they are resilient. Researchers have found that resilient children are likely to have a close relationship with a parent figure and bonds to caring people outside the family. Social policy is a government's course of action designed to promote the welfare of its citizens. The poor conditions of life for a significant percentage of U.S. children, and the lack of attention to prevention of these poor conditions, point to the need for revised social policies.

3 DEVELOPMENTAL PROCESSES, PERIODS, AND ISSUES: DISCUSS THE MOST IMPORTANT PROCESSES, PERIODS, AND ISSUES IN DEVELOPMENT

Biological, Cognitive, and Socioemotional Processes

Periods of Development

- Three key processes of development are biological, cognitive, and socioemotional. Biological processes (such as genes inherited from parents) involve changes in an individual's body. Cognitive processes (such as thinking) consist of changes in an individual's thought, intelligence, and language. Socioemotional processes (such as smiling) include changes in an individual's relationships with others, in emotions, and in personality.

- Childhood's five main developmental periods are (1) prenatal—conception to birth, (2) infancy—birth to 18 to 24 months, (3) early childhood—end of infancy to about 5 to 6 years of age, (4) middle and late childhood—about 6 to 11 years of age, and (5) adolescence— begins at about 10 to 12 and ends at about 18 to 19 years of age.

Issues in Development	• The nature-nurture issue focuses on the extent to which development is mainly influenced by nature (biological inheritance) or nurture (environmental experience). Some developmentalists describe development as continuous (gradual, cumulative change), others describe it as discontinuous (a sequence of abrupt stages). The early-later experience issue focuses on whether early experiences (especially in infancy) are more important in development than later experiences. Most developmentalists recognize that extreme positions on the nature-nurture, continuity-discontinuity, and early-later experience issues are not supported by research. Despite this consensus, they continue to debate the degree to which each position influences children's development.

4 THE SCIENCE OF CHILD DEVELOPMENT: SUMMARIZE WHY RESEARCH IS IMPORTANT IN CHILD DEVELOPMENT, THE MAIN THEORIES OF CHILD DEVELOPMENT, AND RESEARCH METHODS, DESIGNS, AND CHALLENGES

The Importance of Research	• Scientific research is objective, systematic, and testable. Scientific research is based on the scientific method, which includes these steps: conceptualize the problem, collect data, draw conclusions, and revise theory. Scientific research on child development reduces the likelihood that the information gathered is based on personal beliefs, opinions, and feelings.
Theories of Child Development	• Psychoanalytic theories describe development as primarily unconscious and as heavily colored by emotion. The two main psychoanalytic theories in developmental psychology are Freud's and Erikson's. Freud also proposed that individuals go through five psychosexual stages—oral, anal, phallic, latency, and genital. Erikson's theory emphasizes eight psychosocial stages of development. The three main cognitive theories are Piaget's cognitive developmental theory, Vygotsky's sociocultural theory, and information-processing theory. Cognitive theories emphasize conscious thoughts. In Piaget's theory, children go through four cognitive stages: sensorimotor, preoperational, concrete operational, and formal operational. Vygotsky's sociocultural cognitive theory emphasizes how culture and social interaction guide cognitive development. The information-processing theory emphasizes that individuals manipulate information, monitor it, and strategize about it. Three versions of the behavioral and social cognitive theories are Pavlov's classical conditioning, Skinner's operant conditioning, and Bandura's social cognitive theory. Ethology stresses that behavior is strongly influenced by biology, is tied to evolution, and is characterized by critical or sensitive periods. Ecological theory is Bronfenbrenner's environmental systems view of development. It consists of five environmental systems: microsystem, mesosystem, exosystem, macrosystem, and chronosystem. An eclectic theoretical orientation does not follow any one theoretical approach, but rather selects from each theory whatever is considered the best in it.
Research Methods for Collecting Data	• Research methods for collecting data about child development include observation (in a laboratory or a naturalistic setting), survey (questionnaire) or interview, standardized test, case study, and physiological measures.
Research Designs	• Descriptive research aims to observe and record behavior. In correlational research, the goal is to describe the strength of the relationship between two or more events or characteristics. Experimental research involves conducting an experiment, which can determine cause and effect. An independent variable is the manipulated, influential, experimental factor. A dependent variable is a factor that can change in an experiment, in response to changes in the independent variable. Experiments can involve one or more experimental groups and control groups. In random assignment, researchers assign participants to experimental and control groups by chance. When researchers decide about the time span of their research, they can conduct cross-sectional or longitudinal studies.
Challenges in Child Development Research	• Researchers' ethical responsibilities include seeking participants' informed consent, ensuring their confidentiality, debriefing them about the purpose and potential personal consequences of participating, and avoiding unnecessary deception of participants. Researchers need to guard against gender, cultural, and ethnic bias in research. Every effort should be made to make research equitable for both females and males. Individuals from varied ethnic backgrounds need to be included as participants in child research, and overgeneralization about diverse members within a group must be avoided.

KEY TERMS

development 7
original sin view 7
tabula rasa view 7
innate goodness view 7
context 11
culture 11
cross-cultural studies 11
ethnicity 11
socioeconomic status
    (SES) 11
gender 11
social policy 13
biological processes 15
cognitive processes 15

socioemotional
    processes 15
prenatal period 16
infancy 16
early childhood 16
middle and late
    childhood 16
adolescence 16
nature-nurture issue 16
continuity-discontinuity
    issue 17
early-later experience
    issue 18
scientific method 20

theory 20
hypothesis 20
psychoanalytic theories 21
Erikson's theory 22
Piaget's theory 23
Vygotsky's theory 25
information-processing
    theory 25
social cognitive theory 27
ethology 27
Bronfenbrenner's ecological
    theory 29
eclectic theoretical
    orientation 30

laboratory 31
naturalistic observation 31
standardized test 32
case study 33
descriptive research 33
correlational research 33
correlation coefficient 33
experiment 34
cross-sectional approach 35
longitudinal approach 35
ethnic gloss 39

KEY PEOPLE

Philippe Ariès 7
John Locke 7
Jean-Jacques Rousseau 7
Alfred Binet 8
G. Stanley Hall 8

Arnold Gesell 8
Charles Darwin 8
Ann Masten 13
Jerome Kagan 18
Sigmund Freud 21

Erik Erikson 22
Jean Piaget 23
Lev Vygotsky 24
Robert Siegler 25
Ivan Pavlov 26

B. F. Skinner 26
Albert Bandura 27
Konrad Lorenz 28
Urie Bronfenbrenner 29

E-LEARNING TOOLS

To help you master the material in this chapter, you'll find a number of valuable study tools at the Online Learning Center for *Child Development,* twelfth edition (**www.mhhe.com/santrockcd12**).

Taking It to the Net

Research the answers to these questions:

1. George is teaching fourth grade. He wants his students to learn about the difficulties and challenges of being a child in colonial America. What was life like for children in the early history of our country?

2. Janice thinks that better and stricter gun control laws will help decrease violent crime among children. Her husband, Elliott, disagrees. Janice found a March 2000 Department of Justice study that provides support for her argument. What facts in the report can she point to in order to convince Elliott?

3. For his political science class, Darren has to track federal funding appropriations in the most recent Congress for any issue of his choice. He has chosen children's issues. How did children and families fare in terms of congressional appropriations in the first half of the 106th Congress?

Health and Well-Being, Parenting, and Education Exercises

Build your decision-making skills by trying your hand at the health and well-being, parenting, and education exercises.

Video Clips

The Online Learning Center includes the following videos for this chapter:

* *Career in Child Development*
  Dr. Lerner gives a humorous account of a decision to major in psychology in college.

* *Career in Developmental Psychology*
  Dr. Weinraub, one of the leading researchers on the NICHD Early Childcare Study, describes how she became interested in developmental psychology.

* *Ethical Issues in Studying Infants*
  Renowned infant researcher Albert Yonas, Department of Psychology, University of Minnesota, discusses the ethical issues he faces when studying infants.

Appendix

Careers in Child Development

Each of us wants to find a rewarding career and enjoy the work we do. The field of child development offers an amazing breadth of career options that can provide extremely satisfying work.

If you decide to pursue a career in child development, what career options are available to you? There are many. College and university professors teach courses in areas of child development, education, family development, nursing, and medicine. Teachers impart knowledge, understanding, and skills to children and adolescents. Counselors, clinical psychologists, nurses, and physicians help parents and children of different ages to cope more effectively with their lives and well-being. Various professionals work with families to improve the quality of family functioning.

Although an advanced degree is not absolutely necessary in some areas of child development, you usually can expand your opportunities (and income) considerably by obtaining a graduate degree. Many careers in child development pay reasonably well. For example, psychologists earn well above the median salary in the United States. Also, by working in the field of child development you can guide people in improving their lives, understand yourself and others better, possibly advance the state of knowledge in the field, and have an enjoyable time while you are doing these things.

If you are considering a career in child development, would you prefer to work with infants? Children? Adolescents? Parents? As you go through this term, try to spend some time with children of different ages. Observe their behavior. Talk with them about their lives. Think about whether you would like to work with children of this age in your life's work.

Another important aspect of exploring careers is to talk with people who work in various jobs. For example, if you have some interest in becoming a school counselor, call a school, ask to speak with a counselor, and set up an appointment to discuss the counselor's career and work.

Something else that should benefit you is to work in one or more jobs related to your career interests while you are in college. Many colleges and universities have internships or work experiences for students who major in such fields as child development. In some instances, these jobs earn course credit or pay; in others, they are strictly on a volunteer basis. Take advantage of these opportunities. They can provide you with valuable experiences to help you decide if this is the right career for you—and they can help you get into graduate school, if you decide you want to go.

In the upcoming sections, we will profile careers in four areas: education and research; clinical and counseling; medical, nursing, and physical development; and families and relationships. These are not the only career options in child development, but they should provide you with an idea of the range of opportunities available and information about some of the main career avenues you might pursue. In profiling these careers, we will address the amount of education required, the nature of the training, and a description of the work.

EDUCATION AND RESEARCH

Numerous career opportunities in child development involve education or research. These range from a college professor to early childhood educator to school psychologist.

College/University Professor

Courses in child development are taught in many programs and schools in college and universities, including psychology, education, nursing, child and family studies, social work, and medicine. The work that college professors do includes teaching courses either at the undergraduate or graduate level (or both), conducting research in a specific area, advising students and/or directing their research, and serving on college or university committees. Some college instructors do not conduct research as part of their job but instead focus mainly on teaching. Research is most likely to be part of the job description at universities with master's and Ph.D. programs. A Ph.D. or master's degree almost always is required to teach in some area of child development in a college or university. Obtaining a doctoral degree usually takes four to six years of graduate work. A master's degree requires approximately two years of graduate work. The training involves taking graduate courses, learning to conduct research, and attending and presenting papers at professional meetings. Many graduate students work as teaching or research assistants for professors in an apprenticeship relationship that helps them to become competent teachers and researchers.

If you are interested in becoming a college or university professor, you might want to make an appointment with your instructor in this class on child development to learn more about his or her profession and work. To read about the work of one college professor, see the *Careers in Child Development* profile.

Careers in Child Development

Valerie Pang, Professor of Teacher Education

Valerie Pang is a professor of teacher education of San Diego State University and formerly was an elementary school teacher. Like Dr. Pang, many professors of teacher education have a doctorate and have experience in teaching at the elementary or secondary school level.

Pang earned a doctorate at the University of Washington. She has received a Multicultural Educator Award from the National Association of Multicultural Education for her work on culture and equity. She also was given the Distinguished Scholar Award from the American Educational Research Association's Committee on the Role and Status of Minorities in Education.

Pang (2005) believes that competent teachers need to:

- Recognize the power and complexity of cultural influences on students.
- Be sensitive to whether their expectations for students are culturally biased.
- Evaluate whether they are doing a good job of seeing life from the perspective of students who come from different cultures.

Valerie Pang is a professor in the School of Education of San Diego State University and formerly an elementary school teacher. Valerie believes it is important for teachers to create a caring classroom that affirms all students.

Researcher

Some individuals in the field of child development work in research positions. In most instances, they have either a master's or Ph.D. in some area of child development. The researchers might work at a university, in some cases in a university professor's research program, in government at such agencies as the National Institute of Mental Health, or in private industry. Individuals who have full-time research positions in child development generate innovative research ideas, plan studies, carry out the research by collecting data, analyze the data, and then interpret it. Then, they will usually attempt to publish the research in a scientific journal. A researcher often works in a collaborative manner with other researchers on a project and may present the research at scientific meetings. One researcher might spend much of his or her time in a laboratory, whereas another researcher might work out in the field, such as in schools, hospitals, and so on.

Elementary School Teacher

The work of an elementary or secondary school teacher involves teaching in one or more subject areas, preparing the curriculum, giving tests, assigning grades, monitoring students' progress, conducting parent-teacher conferences, and attending in-service workshops. Becoming an elementary or secondary school teacher requires a minimum of an undergraduate degree. The training involves taking a wide range of courses with a major or concentration in education as well as completing a supervised practice-teaching internship.

Exceptional Children (Special Education) Teacher

A teacher of exceptional children spends concentrated time with individual children who have a disability or are gifted. Among the children a teacher of exceptional children might work with are children with learning disabilities, ADHD (attention deficit hyperactivity disorder), mental retardation, or a physical disability such as cerebral palsy. Some of this work will usually be done outside of the student's regular classroom, some of it will be carried out when the student is in the regular classroom. The exceptional children teacher works closely with the student's regular classroom teacher and parents to create the best educational program for the student. Becoming a teacher of exceptional children requires a minimum of an undergraduate degree. The training consists of taking a wide range of courses in education and a concentration of courses in educating children with disabilities or children who are gifted. Teachers of exceptional children often continue their education after obtaining their undergraduate degree and attain a master's degree.

Early Childhood Educator

Early childhood educators work on college faculties and have a minimum of a master's degree in their field. In graduate school, they take courses in early childhood education and receive supervisory training in child-care or early childhood programs. Early childhood educators usually teach in community colleges that award an associate degree in early childhood education.

Preschool/Kindergarten Teacher

Preschool teachers teach mainly 4-year-old children and kindergarten teachers primarily teach 5-year-old children. They usually have an undergraduate degree in education, specializing in early childhood education. State certification to become a preschool or kindergarten teacher usually is required.

Family and Consumer Science Educator

Family and consumer science educators may specialize in early childhood education or instruct middle and high school students about such matters as nutrition, interpersonal relationships, human sexuality, parenting, and human development. Hundreds of colleges and universities throughout the United States offer two- and four-year degree programs in family and consumer science. These programs usually include an internship requirement. Additional education courses may be needed to obtain a teaching certificate. Some family and consumer educators go on to graduate school for further training, which provides a background for possible jobs in college teaching or research.

Educational Psychologist

An educational psychologist most often teaches in a college or university and conducts research in such areas of educational psychology as learning, motivation, classroom management, and assessment. Most educational psychologists have a doctorate in education, which takes four to six years of graduate work. They help to train students who will take various positions in education, including educational psychology, school psychology, and teaching.

School Psychologist

School psychologists focus on improving the psychological and intellectual well-being of elementary and secondary school students. They may work in a centralized office in a school district or in one or more schools. They give psychological tests, interview students and their parents, consult with teachers, and may provide counseling to students and their families.

School psychologists usually have a master's or doctoral degree in school psychology. In graduate school, they take courses in counseling, assessment, learning, and other areas of education and psychology.

CLINICAL AND COUNSELING

There are a wide variety of clinical and counseling jobs that are linked with child development. These range from child clinical psychologist to adolescent drug counselor.

Clinical Psychologist

Clinical psychologists seek to help people with psychological problems. They work in a variety of settings, including colleges and universities, clinics, medical schools, and private practice. Some clinical psychologists only conduct psychotherapy, others do psychological assessment and psychotherapy, and some also do research. Clinical psychologists may specialize in a particular age group, such as children (child clinical psychologist).

Clinical psychologists have either a Ph.D. (which involves clinical and research training) or a Psy.D. degree (which involves only clinical training). This graduate training usually takes five to seven years and includes courses in clinical psychology and a one-year supervised internship in an accredited setting toward the end of the training. In most cases, they must pass a test to become licensed in a state and to call themselves a clinical psychologist

Psychiatrist

Like clinical psychologists, psychiatrists might specialize in working with children (child psychiatry) or adolescents (adolescent psychiatry). Psychiatrists might work in medical schools in teaching and research roles, in a medical clinic, or in private practice. In addition to administering drugs to help improve the lives of people with psychological problems, psychiatrists also may conduct psychotherapy. Psychiatrists obtain a medical degree and then do a residency in psychiatry. Medical school takes approximately four years and the psychiatry residency another three to four years. Unlike psychologists (who do not go to medical school) in most states, psychiatrists can administer drugs to clients.

Counseling Psychologist

Counseling psychologists work in the same settings as clinical psychologists, and may do psychotherapy, teach, or conduct research. In many instances, however, counseling psychologists do not work with individuals who have a severe mental disorder. A counseling psychologist might specialize in working with children, adolescents, and/or families.

Counseling psychologists go through much of the same training as clinical psychologists, although in a graduate program in counseling rather than clinical psychology. Counseling psychologists have either a master's degree or a doctoral degree. They also must go through a licensing procedure. One type of master's degree in counseling leads to the designation of licensed professional counselor.

School Counselor

School counselors help to identify students' abilities and interests, guide students in developing academic plans, and explore career options with students. They may help students cope with adjustment problems. They may work with students individually, in small groups, or even in a classroom. They often consult with parents, teachers, and school administrators when trying to help students with their problems.

High school counselors advise students on choosing a major, admissions requirements for college, taking entrance exams, applying for financial aid, and on appropriate vocational and technical training. Elementary school counselors are mainly involved in counseling students about social and personal problems. They may observe children in the classroom and at play as part of their work. School counselors usually have a master's degree in counseling.

Career Counselor

Career counselors help individuals to identify their best career options and guide them in applying for jobs. They may work in private industry or at a college/university. They usually interview individuals and give them vocational or psychological tests to help them provide students with information about careers that fit their interests and abilities. Sometimes they help individuals to create resumes or conduct mock interviews to help them feel comfortable in a job interview. They may create and promote job fairs or other recruiting events to help individuals obtain jobs.

Social Worker

Social workers often are involved in helping people with social or economic problems. They may investigate, evaluate, and attempt to rectify reported cases of abuse, neglect, endangerment, or domestic disputes. They can intervene in families if necessary and provide counseling and referral services to individuals and families.

Social workers have a minimum of an undergraduate degree from a school of social work that includes course work in various areas of sociology and psychology. Some social workers also have a master's or doctoral degree. They often work for publicly funded agencies at the city, state, or national level, although increasingly they work in the private sector in areas such as drug rehabilitation and family counseling.

In some cases, social workers specialize in a certain area, as is true of a medical social worker, who has a master's degree in social work (M.S.W.). This involves graduate course work and supervised clinical experiences in medical settings. A medical social worker might coordinate a variety of support services to people with a severe or long-term disability. Family-care social workers often work with families who need support services.

Drug Counselor

Drug counselors provide counseling to individuals with drug-abuse problems. They may work on an individual basis with a substance abuser or conduct group therapy sessions. They may work in private practice, with a state or federal government agency, with a company, or in a hospital setting. Some drug counselors specialize in working with adolescents or families. Most states provide a certification procedure for obtaining a license to practice drug counseling.

At a minimum, drug counselors go through an associates or certificate program. Many have an undergraduate degree in substance-abuse counseling, and some have master's and doctoral degrees.

MEDICAL, NURSING, AND PHYSICAL DEVELOPMENT

This third main area of careers in child development includes a wide range of careers in the medical and nursing areas, as well as jobs pertaining to improving some aspect of the child's physical development.

Obstetrician/Gynecologist

An obstetrician/gynecologist prescribes prenatal and postnatal care and performs deliveries in maternity cases. The individual also treats diseases and injuries of the female reproductive system. Obstetricians may work in private practice, in a medical clinic, a hospital, or in a medical school. Becoming an obstetrician/gynecologist requires a medical degree plus three to five years of residency in obstetrics/gynecology.

Pediatrician

A pediatrician monitors infants' and children's health, works to prevent disease or injury, helps children attain optimal health, and treats children with health problems. Pediatricians may work in private practice, in a medical clinic, in a hospital, or in a medical school. As a medical doctor, they can administer drugs to children and may counsel parents and children on ways to improve the children's health. Many pediatricians on the faculty of medical schools also teach and conduct research on children's health and diseases. Pediatricians have attained a medical degree and completed a three- to five-year residency in pediatrics.

Neonatal Nurse

A neonatal nurse is involved in the delivery of care to the newborn infant. The neonatal nurse may work to improve the health and well-being of infants born under normal circumstances or be involved in the delivery of care to premature and critically ill neonates.

A minimum of an undergraduate degree in nursing with a specialization in the newborn is required. This training involves course work in nursing and the biological sciences, as well as supervisory clinical experiences.

Nurse-Midwife

A nurse-midwife formulates and provides comprehensive care to selected maternity patients, cares for the expectant mother as she prepares to give birth and guides her through the birth process, and cares for the postpartum patient. The nurse-midwife also may provide care to the newborn, counsel parents on the infant's development and parenting, and provide guidance about health practices. Becoming a nurse-midwife generally requires an undergraduate degree from a school of nursing. A nurse-midwife most often works in a hospital setting.

Pediatric Nurse

Pediatric nurses have a degree in nursing that takes from two to five years to complete. Some also may obtain a master's or doctoral degree in pediatric nursing. Pediatric nurses take courses in biological sciences, nursing care, and pediatrics, usually in a school of nursing. They also undergo supervised clinical experiences in medical settings. They monitor infants' and children's health, work to prevent disease or injury, and help children attain optimal health. They may work in hospitals, schools of nursing, or with pediatricians in private practice or at a medical clinic. To read about the work of one pediatric nurse practitioner, see the *Careers in Child Development* profile.

Careers in Child Development

Katherine Duchen Smith, Nurse and Child-Care Health Consultant

Katherine Duchen Smith has a master's degree in nursing and works as a child-care health consultant. She lives in Ft. Collins, Colorado, and in 2004 was appointed as the public relations chair of the National Association of Pediatric Nurse Practitioners (NAPNAP), which has more than 6,000 members.

Smith provides health consultation and educational services to child-care centers, private schools, and hospitals. She also teaches in the Regis University Family Nurse Practitioner Program. Smith developed an interest in outreach and public-relations activities during her five-year term as a board member for the Fort Collins Poudre Valley Hospital System. Later, she became the organization's outreach consultant.

As child-care health consultants, nurses might provide telephone consultation and link children, families, or staff with primary care providers. In underserved areas, they might also be asked to administer immunizations, help chronically ill children access specialty care, or develop a comprehensive health promotion or injury prevention program for caregivers and families.

Katherine Duchen Smith (*left*), nurse and child-care health consultant, at a child-care center where she is a consultant.

Audiologist

An audiologist has a minimum of an undergraduate degree in hearing science. This includes courses and supervisory training. Audiologists assess and identify the presence and severity of hearing loss, as well as problems in balance. Some audiologists also go on to obtain a master's and/or doctoral degree. They may work in a medical clinic, with a physician in private practice, in a hospital, or in a medical school.

Speech Therapist

Speech therapists are health-care professionals who are trained to identify, assess, and treat speech and language problems. They may work with physicians, psychologists, social workers, and other health-care professionals as a team to help individuals with physical or psychological problems that include speech and language problems. Speech pathologists have a minimum of an undergraduate degree in the speech and hearing science or communications disorders area. They may work in private practice, in hospitals and medical schools, and in government agencies with individuals of any age. Some specialize in working with children or with a particular type of speech disorder.

Genetic Counselor

Genetic counselors work as members of a health-care team, providing information and support to families who have members with birth defects or genetic disorders and to families who may be at risk for a variety of inherited conditions. They identify families at risk and provide supportive counseling. They serve as educators and resource people for other health-care professionals and the public. Almost half work in university medical centers and another one-fourth work in private hospital settings.

Most genetic counselors enter the field after majoring in undergraduate school in such disciplines as biology, genetics, psychology, nursing, public health, and social work. They have specialized graduate degrees and experience in medical genetics and counseling.

FAMILIES AND RELATIONSHIPS

A number of careers are available for working with families and relationship problems. These range from being a child welfare worker to a marriage and family therapist.

Child Welfare Worker

A child welfare worker is employed by the child protective services unit of each state. The child welfare worker protects the child's rights, evaluates any maltreatment the child might experience, and may have the child removed from the home if necessary. A child social worker has a minimum of an undergraduate degree in social work.

Child Life Specialist

Child life specialists work with children and their families when the child needs to be hospitalized. They monitor the child patient's activities, seek to reduce the child's stress, help the child cope effectively, and assist the child in enjoying the hospital experience as much as possible. Child life specialists may provide parent education and develop individualized treatment plans based on an assessment of the child's development, temperament, medical plan, and available social supports.

Child life specialists have an undergraduate degree. As undergraduates, they take courses in child development and education and usually take additional courses in a child life program.

Marriage and Family Therapist

Marriage and family therapists work on the principle that many individuals who have psychological problems benefit when psychotherapy is provided in the context of a marital or family relationship. Marriage and family therapists may provide marital therapy, couple therapy to individuals in a relationship who are not married, and family therapy to two or more members of a family.

Marriage and family therapists have a master's or doctoral degree. They go through a training program in graduate school similar to that of a clinical psychologist but with the focus on marital and family relationships. To practice marital and family therapy in most states, it is necessary to go through a licensing procedure.

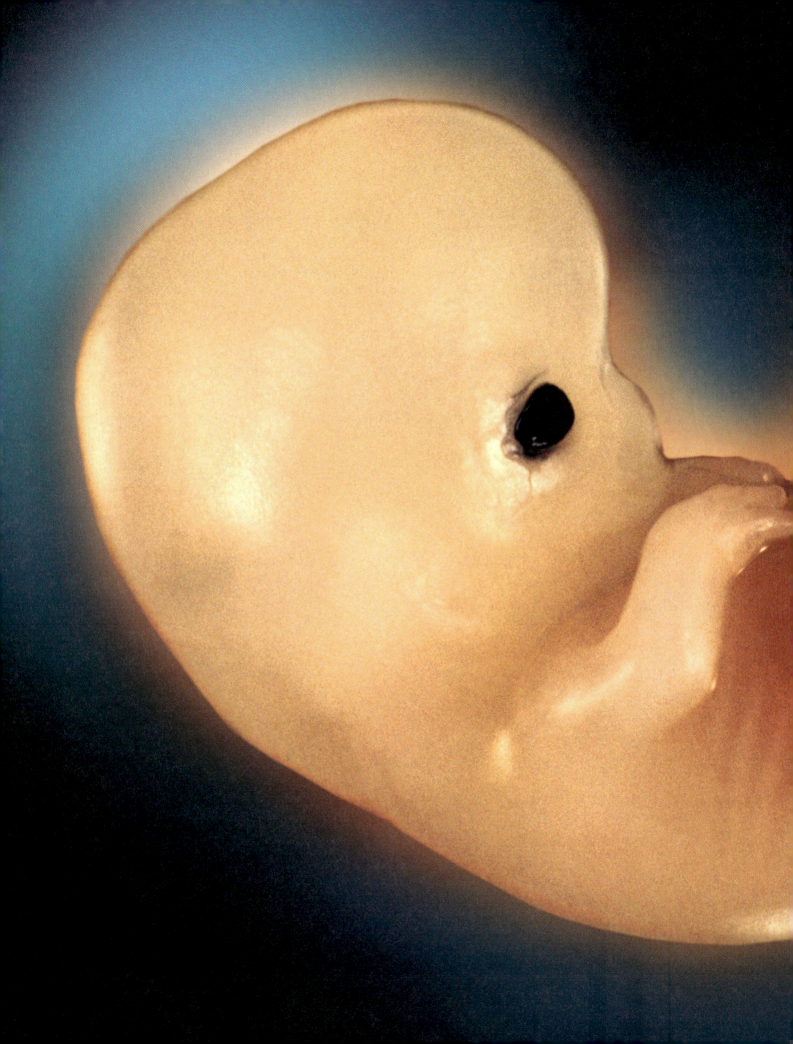

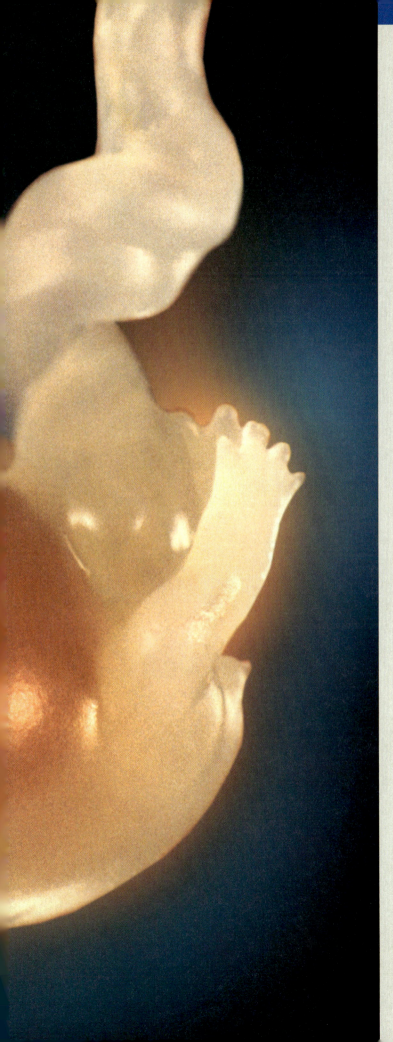

TWO

BIOLOGICAL PROCESSES, PHYSICAL DEVELOPMENT, AND PERCEPTUAL DEVELOPMENT

What endless questions vex the thought, of whence and whither, when and how.

—Sir Richard Burton
British Explorer, 19th Century

The rhythm and meaning of life involve beginnings, with questions raised about how, from so simple a beginning, complex forms develop, grow, and mature. What was this organism, what is this organism, and what will this organism be? In Section 2, you will read four chapters: "Biological Beginnings" (Chapter 2), "Prenatal Development and Birth" (Chapter 3), "Physical Development and Health" (Chapter 4), and "Motor, Sensory, and Perceptual Development" (Chapter 5).

2

There are one hundred and ninety-three living species of monkeys and apes. One hundred and ninety-two of them are covered with hair. The exception is the naked ape, self-named **Homo sapiens.**

—DESMOND MORRIS
British Zoologist, 20th Century

LEARNING GOALS

◆ Discuss the evolutionary perspective on development.

◆ Describe what genes are and how they influence human development.

◆ Identify some important reproductive challenges and choices.

◆ Explain some of the ways that heredity and environment interact to produce individual differences in development.

BIOLOGICAL BEGINNINGS

CHAPTER OUTLINE

Images of Child Development
The Stories of the Jim and Jim Twins

Jim Lewis (*left*) and Jim Springer (*right*).

Jim Springer and Jim Lewis are identical twins. They were separated at 4 weeks of age and did not see each other again until they were 39 years old. Both worked as part-time deputy sheriffs, vacationed in Florida, drive Chevrolets, had dogs named Toy, and married and divorced women named Betty. One twin named his son James Allan, and the other named his son James Alan. Both liked math but not spelling, enjoyed carpentry and mechanical drawing, chewed their fingernails down to the nubs, had almost identical drinking and smoking habits, had hemorrhoids, put on 10 pounds at about the same point in development, first suffered headaches at the age of 18, and had similar sleep patterns.

Jim and Jim do have some differences. One wears his hair over his forehead, the other slicks it back and has sideburns. One expresses himself best orally; the other is more proficient in writing. But, for the most part, their profiles are remarkably similar.

Another pair of identical twins, Daphne and Barbara, are called the "giggle sisters" because, after being reunited, they were always making each other laugh. A thorough search of their adoptive families' histories revealed no gigglers. The giggle sisters ignored stress, avoided conflict and controversy whenever possible, and showed no interest in politics.

Jim and Jim and the giggle sisters were part of the Minnesota Study of Twins Reared Apart, directed by Thomas Bouchard and his colleagues. The study brings identical twins (identical genetically because they come from the same fertilized egg) and fraternal twins (who come from different fertilized eggs) from all over the world to Minneapolis to investigate their lives. There the twins complete personality and intelligence tests, and they provide detailed medical histories, including information about diet and smoking, exercise habits, chest X-rays, heart stress tests, and EEGs. The twins are asked more than 15,000 questions about their family and childhood, personal interests, vocational orientation, values, and aesthetic judgments (Bouchard & others, 1990).

When genetically identical twins who were separated as infants show such striking similarities in their tastes and habits and choices, can we conclude that their genes must have caused the development of those tastes and habits and choices? Other possible causes need to be considered. The twins shared not only the same genes but also some experiences. Some of the separated twins lived together for several months prior to their adoption; some of the twins had been reunited prior to testing (in some cases, many years earlier); adoption agencies often place twins in similar homes; and even strangers who spend several hours together and start comparing their lives are likely to come up with some coincidental similarities (Joseph, 2006). The Minnesota study of identical twins points to both the importance of the genetic basis of human development and the need for further research on genetic and environmental factors (Lykken, 2001).

PREVIEW

The examples of Jim and Jim and the giggle sisters stimulate us to think about our genetic heritage and the biological foundations of our existence. However, organisms are not like billiard balls, moved by simple external forces to predictable positions on life's table. Environmental experiences and biological foundations work together to make us who we are. Our coverage of life's biological beginnings focuses on evolution, genetic foundations, challenges and choices regarding reproduction, and the interaction of heredity and environment.

1 THE EVOLUTIONARY PERSPECTIVE

Natural Selection and Adaptive Behavior   **Evolutionary Psychology**

In evolutionary time, humans are relative newcomers to Earth. As our earliest ancestors left the forest to feed on the savannahs, and then to form hunting societies on the open plains, their minds and behaviors changed, and they eventually established humans as the dominant species on Earth. How did this evolution come about?

Natural Selection and Adaptive Behavior

Natural selection is the evolutionary process by which those individuals of a species that are best adapted are the ones that survive and reproduce. To understand what this means, let's return to the middle of the nineteenth century, when the British naturalist Charles Darwin was traveling around the world, observing many different species of animals in their natural surroundings. Darwin, who published his observations and thoughts in *On the Origin of Species* (1859), noted that most organisms reproduce at rates that would cause enormous increases in the population of most species and yet populations remain nearly constant. He reasoned that an intense, constant struggle for food, water, and resources must occur among the many young born each generation, because many of the young do not survive. Those that do survive and reproduce, pass on their characteristics to the next generation. Darwin believed that these survivors are better *adapted* to their world than are the nonsurvivors (Johnson, 2008; Krogh, 2007). The best-adapted individuals survive to leave the most offspring. Over the course of many generations, organisms with the characteristics needed for survival make up an increased percentage of the population. Over many, many generations, this could produce a gradual modification of the whole population. If environmental conditions change, however, other characteristics might become favored by natural selection, moving the species in a different direction (Mader, 2009).

All organisms must adapt to particular places, climates, food sources, and ways of life. An eagle's claws are a physical adaptation that facilitates predation. *Adaptive behavior* is behavior that promotes an organism's survival in the natural habitat (Enger, 2007). For example, attachment between a caregiver and a baby ensures the infant's closeness to a caregiver for feeding and protection from danger, thus increasing the infant's chances of survival.

How does the attachment of this Vietnamese baby to its mother reflect the evolutionary process of adaptive behavior?

Evolutionary Psychology

Although Darwin introduced the theory of evolution by natural selection in 1859, his ideas only recently have become a popular framework for explaining behavior. Psychology's newest approach, **evolutionary psychology**, emphasizes the importance of adaptation, reproduction, and "survival of the fittest" in shaping behavior. "Fit" in this sense refers to the ability to bear offspring that survive long enough to bear offspring of their own (Rose & Rauser, 2007). In this view, natural selection favors behaviors that increase reproductive success, the ability to pass your genes to the next generation (Bjorklund, 2006, 2007).

evolutionary psychology Emphasizes the importance of adaptation, reproduction, and "survival of the fittest" in shaping behavior.

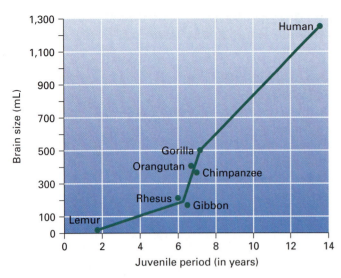

FIGURE 2.1 The Brain Sizes of Various Primates and Humans in Relation to the Length of the Juvenile Period. Compared with other primates, humans have both a larger brain and a longer childhood period. *What conclusions can you draw from the relationship indicated by this graph?*

David Buss (1995, 2000, 2004, 2008) has been especially influential in stimulating new interest in how evolution can explain human behavior. He points out that just as evolution shapes our physical features, such as body shape and height, it also pervasively influences how we make decisions, how aggressive we are, our fears, and our mating patterns. For example, assume that our ancestors were hunterers and gatherers on the plains and that men did most of the hunting and women stayed close to home gathering seeds and plants for food. If you have to travel some distance from your home in an effort to find and slay a fleeing animal, you need not only certain physical traits but also the ability for certain types of spatial thinking. Men born with these traits would be more likely than men without them to survive, to bring home lots of food, and to be considered attractive mates—and thus to reproduce and pass on these characteristics to their children. In other words, these traits would provide a reproductive advantage for males and, over many generations, men with good spatial thinking skills might become more numerous in the population. Critics point out that this scenario might or might not have actually happened.

Evolutionary Developmental Psychology Recently, interest has grown in using the concepts of evolutionary psychology to understand human development (Bjorklund, 2007; Brooker, 2009; Weaver, 2008). Next we discuss some ideas proposed by evolutionary developmental psychologists (Bjorklund & Pellegrini, 2002).

An extended childhood period evolved because humans require time to develop a large brain and learn the complexity of human societies (see Figure 2.1). Humans take longer to become reproductively mature than any other mammal. During this extended childhood period, they develop a large brain and the experiences needed to become competent adults in a complex society.

Many evolved psychological mechanisms are domain-specific. That is, the mechanisms apply only to a specific aspect of a person's makeup (Rubenstein, 2004). According to evolutionary psychology, information processing is one example. In this view, the mind is not a general-purpose device that can be applied equally to a vast array of problems. Instead, as our ancestors dealt with certain recurring problems such as hunting and finding shelter, specialized modules evolved that process information related to those problems. For example, a module for physical knowledge for tracking animals, a module for mathematical knowledge for trading, and a module for language.

Evolved mechanisms are not always adaptive in contemporary society. Some behaviors that were adaptive for our prehistoric ancestors may not serve us well today. For example, the food-scarce environment of our ancestors likely led to humans' propensity to gorge when food is available and to crave high-calorie foods, a trait that that might lead to an epidemic of obesity when food is plentiful.

Evaluating Evolutionary Psychology Although the popular press gives a lot of attention to the ideas of evolutionary psychology, it remains just one theoretical approach. Like the theories described in Chapter 1, it has limitations, weaknesses, and critics (Buller, 2005). Albert Bandura (1998), whose social cognitive theory was described in Chapter 1, acknowledges the important influence of evolution on human adaptation. However, he rejects what he calls "one-sided evolutionism," which sees social behavior as the product of evolved biology. An alternative is a *bidirectional view*, in which environmental and biological conditions influence each other. In this view, evolutionary pressures created changes in biological structures that allowed the use of tools, which enabled our ancestors to manipulate the environment, constructing new environmental conditions. In turn, environmental innovations produced new selection pressures that led to the evolution of specialized biological systems for consciousness, thought, and language.

In other words, evolution gave us bodily structures and biological potentialities; it does not dictate behavior. People have used their biological capacities to produce diverse cultures—aggressive and pacific, egalitarian and autocratic. As American scientist Steven Jay Gould (1981) concluded, in most domains of human functioning, biology allows a broad range of cultural possibilities.

Children in all cultures are interested in the tools that adults in their cultures use. For example, this 11-month-old boy from the Efe culture in the Democratic Republic of the Congo in Africa is trying to cut a papaya with an *apopau* (a smaller version of a machete). *Might the infant's behavior be evolutionary-based or be due to both biological and environmental conditions?*

Review and Reflect: Learning Goal 1

 Discuss the Evolutionary Perspective on Development

REVIEW

- How can natural selection and adaptive behavior be defined?
- What is evolutionary psychology? What are some basic ideas about human development proposed by evolutionary psychologists? How can evolutionary psychology be evaluated?

REFLECT

- Which is more persuasive to you: the views of evolutionary psychologists or their critics? Why?

2 GENETIC FOUNDATIONS OF DEVELOPMENT

- The Collaborative Gene
- Genes and Chromosomes
- Genetic Principles
- Chromosomal and Gene-Linked Abnormalities

How are characteristics that suit a species for survival transmitted from one generation to the next? Darwin did not know because genes and the principles of genetics had not yet been discovered. Each of us carries a "genetic code" that we inherited from our parents. Because a fertilized egg carries this human code, a fertilized human egg cannot grow into an egret, eagle, or elephant.

The Collaborative Gene

Each of us began life as a single cell weighing about one twenty-millionth of an ounce! This tiny piece of matter housed our entire genetic code—instructions that orchestrated growth from that single cell to a person made of trillions of cells, each containing a replica of the original code. That code is carried by our genes. What are genes and what do they do? For the answer, we need to look into our cells.

The nucleus of each human cell contains **chromosomes**, which are threadlike structures made up of deoxyribonucleic acid, or DNA. **DNA** is a complex molecule

chromosomes Threadlike structures that come in 23 pairs, one member of each pair coming from each parent. Chromosomes contain the genetic substance DNA.

DNA A complex molecule with a double helix shape that contains genetic information.

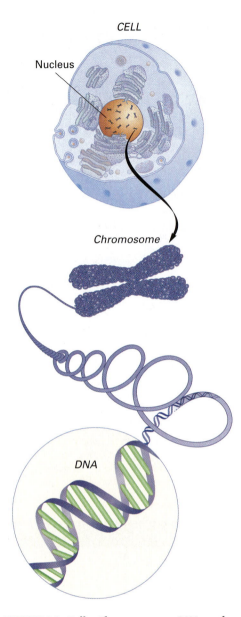

CELL

Nucleus

Chromosome

DNA

FIGURE 2.2 Cells, Chromosomes, DNA, and Genes. (*Top*) The body contains trillions of cells. Each cell contains a central structure, the nucleus. (*Middle*) Chromosomes are threadlike structures located in the nucleus of the cell. Chromosomes are composed of DNA. (*Bottom*) DNA has the structure of a spiraled double chain. A gene is a segment of DNA.

genes Units of hereditary information composed of short segments of DNA. Genes direct cells to reproduce themselves and manufacture the proteins that maintain life.

with a double helix shape, like a spiral staircase, and contains genetic information. **Genes**, the units of hereditary information, are short segments of DNA, as you can see in Figure 2.2. They direct cells to reproduce themselves and to assemble proteins. Proteins, in turn, are the building blocks of cells as well as the regulators that direct the body's processes (Hartwell, 2008; Hoefnagels, 2009).

Each gene has its own location, its own designated place on a particular chromosome. Today, there is a great deal of enthusiasm about efforts to discover the specific locations of genes that are linked to certain functions (Brooker, 2009; Weaver, 2008). An important step in this direction was accomplished when the Human Genome Project, and the Celera Corporation completed a preliminary map of the human *genome*—the complete set of developmental instructions for creating proteins that initiate the making of a human organism (U.S. Department of Energy, 2001).

One of the big surprises of the Human Genome Project was a report indicating that humans have only about 30,000 genes (U.S. Department of Energy, 2001). More recently, the number of human genes has been revised further downward to approximately 20,500 (Ensembl Human, 2008). Scientists had thought that humans had as many as 100,000 or more genes. They had also believed that each gene programmed just one protein. In fact, humans appear to have far more proteins than they have genes, so there cannot be a one-to-one correspondence between genes and proteins (Commoner, 2002; Moore, 2001). Each gene is not translated, in automaton-like fashion, into one and only one protein. A gene does not act independently, as developmental psychologist David Moore (2001) emphasized by titling his book *The Dependent Gene*.

Rather than being a group of independent genes, the human genome consists of many genes that collaborate both with each other and with nongenetic factors inside and outside the body. The collaboration operates at many points. For example, the cellular machinery mixes, matches, and links small pieces of DNA to reproduce the genes, and that machinery is influenced by what is going on around it.

A positive result from the Human Genome Project. Shortly after Andrew Gobea was born, his cells were genetically altered to prevent his immune system from failing.

Whether a gene is turned "on," working to assemble proteins, is also a matter of collaboration. The activity of genes (*genetic expression*) is affected by their environment (Gottlieb, 2007). For example, hormones that circulate in the blood make their way into the cell where they can turn genes "on" and "off." And the flow of hormones can be affected by environmental conditions, such as light, day length, nutrition, and behavior. Numerous studies have shown that external events outside of the original cell and the person, as well as events inside the cell, can excite or inhibit gene expression (Gottlieb, Wahlsten, & Lickliter, 2006). For example, one recent study revealed that an increase in the concentration of stress hormones such as cortisol produced a fivefold increase in DNA damage (Flint & others, 2007).

In short, a single gene is rarely the source of a protein's genetic information, much less of an inherited trait (Gottlieb, Wahlsten, & Lickliter, 2006; Moore, 2001).

Genes and Chromosomes

Genes are not only collaborative; they are enduring. How do the genes manage to get passed from generation to generation and end up in all of the trillion cells in the body? Three processes explain the heart of the story: mitosis, meiosis, and fertilization.

Calvin and Hobbes

by Bill Watterson

Mitosis, Meiosis, and Fertilization   All cells in your body, except the sperm and egg, have 46 chromosomes arranged in 23 pairs. These cells reproduce by a process called **mitosis**. During mitosis, the cell's nucleus—including the chromosomes—duplicates itself and the cell divides. Two new cells are formed, each containing the same DNA as the original cell, arranged in the same 23 pairs of chromosomes.

However, a different type of cell division—**meiosis**—forms eggs and sperm (or *gametes*). During meiosis, a cell of the testes (in men) or ovaries (in women) duplicates its chromosomes but then divides *twice*, thus forming four cells, each of which has only half of the genetic material of the parent cell. By the end of meiosis, each egg or sperm has 23 *unpaired* chromosomes.

During **fertilization**, an egg and a sperm fuse to create a single cell, called a **zygote** (see Figure 2.3). In the zygote, the 23 unpaired chromosomes from the egg and the 23 unpaired chromosomes from the sperm combine to form one set of 23 paired chromosomes—one chromosome of each pair from the mother's egg and the other from the father's sperm. In this manner, each parent contributes half of the offspring's genetic material.

Figure 2.4 shows 23 paired chromosomes of a male and a female. The members of each pair of chromosomes are both similar and different: Each chromosome in the pair contains varying forms of the same genes, at the same location on the chromosome. A gene for hair color, for example, is located on both members of one pair of chromosomes, in the same location on each. However, one of those chromosomes might carry the gene for blond hair; the other chromosome in the pair might carry the gene for brown hair.

Do you notice any obvious differences between the chromosomes of the male and the chromosomes of the female in Figure 2.4? The difference lies in the 23rd pair. Ordinarily, in females this pair consists of two chromosomes called *X chromosomes*; in males the 23rd pair consists of an X and a *Y chromosome*. The presence of a Y chromosome is what makes an individual male.

Sources of Variability   Combining the genes of two parents in offspring increases genetic variability in the population, which is valuable for a species because it provides more characteristics for natural selection to operate on (Hyde, 2009; Mader, 2009). In fact, the human genetic process creates several important sources of variability.

First, the chromosomes in the zygote are not exact copies of those in mother's ovaries and the father's testes. During the formation of the sperm and egg in meiosis, the members of each pair of chromosomes are separated, but which chromosome in the pair goes to the gamete is a matter of chance. In addition, before the pairs separate, pieces of the two chromosomes in each pair are exchanged, creating a new combination of genes on each chromosome. Thus, when chromosomes from the mother's egg and the father's sperm are brought together in the zygote, the result is a truly unique combination of genes (Raven & others, 2008).

If each zygote is unique, how do identical twins like those discussed in the opening of the chapter exist? *Identical twins* (also called monozygotic twins) develop from a single zygote that splits into two genetically identical replicas, each of which becomes

FIGURE 2.3 **A Single Sperm Penetrating an Egg at the Point of Fertilization**

mitosis Cellular reproduction in which the cell's nucleus duplicates itself with two new cells being formed, each containing the same DNA as the parent cell, arranged in the same 23 pairs of chromosomes.

meiosis A specialized form of cell division that occurs to form eggs and sperm (or gametes), each of which contains only half of the parent cell's genetic material.

fertilization A stage in reproduction whereby an egg and a sperm fuse to create a single cell, called a zygote.

zygote A single cell formed through fertilization.

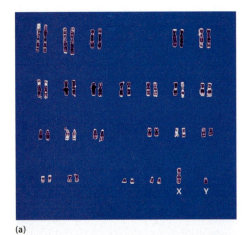

(a)

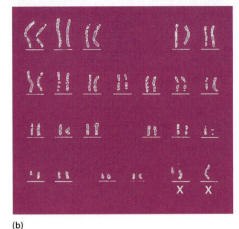

(b)

FIGURE 2.4 The Genetic Difference Between Males and Females. Set (*a*) shows the chromosome structure of a male, and set (*b*) shows the chromosome structure of a female. The last pair of 23 pairs of chromosomes is in the bottom right box of each set. Notice that the Y chromosome of the male is smaller than the X chromosome of the female. To obtain this kind of chromosomal picture, a cell is removed from a person's body, usually from the inside of the mouth. The chromosomes are stained by chemical treatment, magnified extensively, and then photographed.

genotype A person's genetic heritage; the actual genetic material.

phenotype The way an individual's genotype is expressed in observed and measurable characteristics.

a person. *Fraternal twins* (called dizygotic twins) develop from separate eggs and separate sperm, making them genetically no more similar than ordinary siblings.

Another source of variability comes from DNA. Chances, a mistake by cellular machinery, or damage from an environmental agent such as radiation may produce a *mutated gene,* which is a permanently altered segment of DNA (Enger, Ross, & Bailey, 2009).

Even when their genes are identical, however, people vary. The difference between genotypes and phenotypes helps us to understand this source of variability. All of a person's genetic material makes up his or her **genotype**. However, not all of the genetic material is apparent in our observed and measurable characteristics. A **phenotype** consists of observable characteristics. Phenotypes include physical characteristics (such as height, weight, and hair color) and psychological characteristics (such as personality and intelligence).

For each genotype, a range of phenotypes can be expressed, providing another source of variability (Gottlieb, 2007). An individual can inherit the genetic potential to grow very large, for example, but good nutrition, among other things, will be essential to achieving that potential.

Genetic Principles

What determines how a genotype is expressed to create a particular phenotype? Much is unknown about the answer to this question (Hartwell, 2008; Talaro, 2008). However, a number of genetic principles have been discovered, among them those of dominant-recessive genes, sex-linked genes, genetic imprinting, and polygenically determined characteristics.

Dominant-Recessive Genes Principle   In some cases, one gene of a pair always exerts its effects; it is *dominant*, overriding the potential influence of the other gene, called the *recessive* gene. This is the *dominant-recessive genes principle*. A recessive gene exerts its influence only if the two genes of a pair are both recessive. If you inherit a recessive gene for a trait from each of your parents, you will show the trait. If you inherit a recessive gene from only one parent, you may never know you carry the gene. Brown hair, farsightedness, and dimples rule over blond hair, nearsightedness, and freckles in the world of dominant-recessive genes.

Can two brown-haired parents have a blond-haired child? Yes, they can. Suppose that each parent has a dominant gene for brown hair and a recessive gene for blond hair. Since dominant genes override recessive genes, the parents have brown hair, but both are carriers of blondness and pass on their recessive genes for blond hair. With no dominant gene to override them, the recessive genes can make the child's hair blond.

Sex-Linked Genes   Most mutated genes are recessive. When a mutated gene is carried on the X chromosome, the result is called *X-linked inheritance*. It may have very different implications for males than females (Peterson, Wang, & Williams, 2008). Remember that males have only one X chromosome. Thus, if there is an altered, disease-creating gene on the X chromosome, males have no "backup" copy to counter the harmful gene and therefore may carry an X-linked disease. However, females have a second X chromosome, which is likely to be unchanged. As a result, they are not likely to have the X-linked disease. Thus, most individuals who have X-linked diseases are males. Females who have one changed copy of the X gene are known as "carriers," and they usually do not show any signs of the X-linked disease. Hemophilia and fragile X syndrome, which we will discuss later in the chapter, are examples of X-linked inheritance diseases (Pierce & others, 2007).

Genetic Imprinting   *Genetic imprinting* occurs when genes have differing effects depending on whether they are inherited from the mother or the father (Horsthemke & Buiting, 2008). A chemical process "silences" one member of the gene pair. For example, as a result of imprinting, only the maternally derived copy of a gene might be active,

Name	Description	Treatment	Incidence
Down syndrome	An extra chromosome causes mild to severe retardation and physical abnormalities.	Surgery, early intervention, infant stimulation, and special learning programs	1 in 1,900 births at age 20 1 in 300 births at age 35 1 in 30 births at age 45
Klinefelter syndrome (XXY)	An extra X chromosome causes physical abnormalities.	Hormone therapy can be effective	1 in 600 male births
Fragile X syndrome	An abnormality in the X chromosome can cause mental retardation, learning disabilities, or short attention span.	Special education, speech and language therapy	More common in males than in females
Turner syndrome (XO)	A missing X chromosome in females can cause mental retardation and sexual underdevelopment.	Hormone therapy in childhood and puberty	1 in 2,500 female births
XYY syndrome	An extra Y chromosome can cause above-average height.	No special treatment required	1 in 1,000 male births

FIGURE 2.5 Some Chromosomal Abnormalities. The treatments for these abnormalities do not necessarily erase the problem but may improve the individual's adaptive behavior and quality of life.

while the paternally derived copy of the same gene is silenced—or vice versa. Only a small percentage of human genes appear to undergo imprinting, but it is a normal and important aspect of development (Hampton, 2008). When imprinting goes awry, development is disturbed, as in the case of Beckwith-Wiedemann syndrome, a growth disorder, and Wilms tumor, a type of cancer (Gropman & Adams, 2007)

Polygenic Inheritance Genetic transmission is usually more complex than the simple example we have examined thus far (Hartwell, 2008; Lewis, 2007). Few characteristics reflect the influence of only a single gene or pair of genes. Most are determined by the interaction of many different genes; they are said to be *polygenically determined.* Even a simple characteristics such as height, for example, reflects the interaction of many genes, as well as the influence of the environment.

Chromosomal and Gene-Linked Abnormalities

Sometimes, abnormalities characterize the genetic process. Some of these abnormalities involve whole chromosomes that do not separate properly during meiosis. Other abnormalities are produced by harmful genes.

Chromosomal Abnormalities Sometimes, when a gamete is formed, the male sperm and the female ovum do not have their normal set of 23 chromosomes. The most notable examples involve Down syndrome and abnormalities of the sex chromosomes (see Figure 2.5).

Down Syndrome An individual with **Down syndrome** has a round face, a flattened skull, an extra fold of skin over the eyelids, a protruding tongue, short limbs, and retardation of motor and mental abilities (Fidler, 2008). The syndrome is caused by the presence of an extra copy of chromosome 21 (Visootsak & Sherman, 2007). It is not known why the extra chromosome is present, but the health of the male sperm or female ovum may be involved (Hodapp & Dykens, 2006).

Down syndrome appears approximately once in every 700 live births. Women between the ages of 16 and 34 are less likely to give birth to a child with Down syndrome than are younger or older women. African American children are rarely born with Down syndrome.

Sex-Linked Chromosomal Abnormalities Recall that a newborn normally has either an X and a Y chromosome, or two X chromosomes. Human embryos must possess at least one X chromosome to be viable. The most common sex-linked chromosomal abnormalities involve the presence of an extra chromosome (either an X or Y) or the absence of one X chromosome in females.

These athletes, many of whom have Down syndrome, are participating in a Special Olympics competition. Notice the distinctive facial features of the individuals with Down syndrome, such as a round face and a flattened skull. *What causes Down syndrome?*

Down syndrome A chromosomally transmitted form of mental retardation, caused by the presence of an extra copy of chromosome 21.

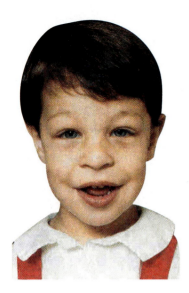

A boy with fragile X syndrome.

Klinefelter syndrome is a chromosomal disorder in which males have an extra X chromosome, making them XXY instead of XY (Itti & others, 2006). Males with this disorder have undeveloped testes, and they usually have enlarged breasts and become tall. A recent study revealed significant impairment in language, academic, attentional, and motor abilities in boys with Klinfelter syndrome (Ross & others, 2008). Klinefelter syndrome occurs approximately once in every 600 live male births.

Fragile X syndrome is a chromosomal disorder that results from an abnormality in the X chromosome, which becomes constricted and often breaks (Penagarikano, Mulle, & Warren, 2007). Mental deficiency often is an outcome, but it may take the form of mental retardation, a learning disability, or a short attention span. A recent study revealed that boys with fragile X syndrome were characterized by cognitive deficits in inhibition, memory, and planning (Hooper & others, 2008). This disorder occurs more frequently in males than in females, possibly because the second X chromosome in females negates the effects of the other abnormal X chromosome (Ono, Farzin, & Hagerman, 2008).

Turner syndrome is a chromosomal disorder in females in which either an X chromosome is missing, making the person XO instead of XX, or part of one X chromosome is deleted. Females with Turner syndrome are short in stature and have a webbed neck. They might be infertile and have difficulty in mathematics, but their verbal ability is often quite good (Murphy & Mazzocco, 2008). Turner syndrome occurs in approximately 1 of every 2,500 live females births.

The **XYY syndrome** is a chromosomal disorder in which the male has an extra Y chromosome (Isen & Baker, 2008). Early interest in this syndrome focused on the belief that the extra Y chromosome found in some males contributed to aggression and violence. However, researchers subsequently found that XYY males are no more likely to commit crimes than are XY males (Witkin & others, 1976).

Gene-Linked Abnormalities Abnormalities can be produced not only by an uneven number of chromosomes, but also by harmful genes (Presson & Jenner, 2008). More than 7,000 such genetic disorders have been identified, although most of them are rare.

Phenylketonuria (PKU) is a genetic disorder in which the individual cannot properly metabolize phenylalanine, an amino acid (Hvas, Nexos, & Nielsen, 2006). It results from a recessive gene and occurs about once in every 10,000 to 20,000 live births. Today, phenylketonuria is easily detected, and it is treated by a diet that prevents an excess accumulation of phenylalanine. If phenylketonuria is left untreated, however, excess phenylalanine builds up in the child, producing mental retardation and hyperactivity. Phenylketonuria accounts for approximately 1 percent of institutionalized individuals who are mentally retarded, and it occurs primarily in Whites.

The story of phenylketonuria has important implications for the nature-nurture issue. Although phenylketonuria is a genetic disorder (nature), how or whether a gene's influence in phenylketonuria is played out depends on environmental influences, as the disorder can be treated (nurture) (Ney & others, 2008; Schindler & others, 2001). That is, the presence of a genetic defect *does not* inevitably lead to the development of the disorder *if* the individual develops in the right environment (one free of phenylalanine) (Cipriano, Rupar, & Zaric, 2007). This is one example of the important principle of heredity-environment interaction. Under one environmental condition (phenylalanine in the diet), mental retardation results—but when other nutrients replace phenylalanine, intelligence develops in the normal range. The same genotype has different outcomes, depending on the environment (in this case, the nutritional environment).

Sickle-cell anemia, which occurs most often in African Americans, is a genetic disorder that impairs the body's red blood cells. Red blood cells carry oxygen to the body's cells and are usually shaped like a disk. In sickle-cell anemia, a recessive gene causes the red blood cell to beome a hook-shaped "sickle" that cannot carry oxygen properly and dies quickly. As a result, the body's cells do not receive adequate oxygen, causing anemia and early death (King, DeBrawa, & White, 2008). About 1 in 400 African American babies is affected by sickle-cell anemia. One in 10 African Americans is a carrier, as is 1 in 20 Latin Americans. A National Institutes of Health (2008) panel recently concluded that

Klinefelter syndrome A chromosomal disorder in which males have an extra X chromosome, making them XXY instead of XY.

fragile X syndrome A chromosomal disorder involving an abnormality in the X chromosome, which becomes constricted and often breaks.

Turner syndrome A chromosomal disorder in females in which either an X chromosome is missing, making the person XO instead of XX, or the second X chromosome is partially deleted.

XYY syndrome A chromosomal disorder in which males have an extra Y chromosome.

phenylketonuria (PKU) A genetic disorder in which the individual cannot properly metabolize phenylalanine, an amino acid. PKU is now easily detected—but, if left untreated, results in mental retardation and hyperactivity.

sickle-cell anemia A genetic disorder that affects the red blood cells and occurs most often in African Americans.

the only FDA-approved drug (hydroxyurea) to treat sickle-cell anemia in adolescents and adults is not widely used. Research is currently being conducted in a study named Baby HUG to determine if the drug works with babies.

Other diseases that result from genetic abnormalities include cystic fibrosis, diabetes, hemophilia, spina bifida, and Tay-Sachs disease (Dunn & others, 2008; Oakley, 2007). Figure 2.6 provides further information about these diseases. Someday, scientists may identify why these and other genetic abnormalities occur and discover how to cure them. The Human Genome Project has already linked specific DNA variations with increased risk of a number of diseases and conditions, including Huntington disease (in which the central nervous system deteriorates), some forms of cancer, asthma, diabetes, hypertension, and Alzheimer disease (Knowles, 2004).

Dealing with Genetic Abnormalities   Every individual carries DNA variations that might predispose the person to serious physical disease or mental disorder. But not all individuals who carry a genetic disorder display the disorder. Other genes or developmental events sometimes compensate for genetic abnormalities (Gottlieb, Wahlsten, & Lickliter, 2006). For example, recall the earlier example of phenylketonuria: Even though individuals might carry the genetic disorder of phenylketonuria, it is not expressed when phenylalanine is replaced by other nutrients in their diet.

Thus, genes are not destiny, but genes that are missing, nonfunctional, or mutated, can be associated with disorders (Gaff, Williams, & McInerney, 2008). Identifying such genetic flaws could enable doctors to predict an individual's risks, recommend healthy practices, and prescribe the safest and most effective drugs (Blaine & others, 2008). A decade or two from now, parents of a newborn baby may be able to leave the hospital with a full genome analysis of their offspring that reveals disease risks.

During a physical examination for a college football tryout, Jerry Hubbard, 32, learned that he carried the gene for sickle-cell anemia. Daughter Sara is healthy, but daughter Avery (in the print dress) has sickle-cell anemia. *If you were a genetic counselor, would you recommend that this family have more children? Explain.*

Name	Description	Treatment	Incidence
Cystic fibrosis	Glandular dysfunction that interferes with mucus production; breathing and digestion are hampered, resulting in a shortened life span.	Physical and oxygen therapy, synthetic enzymes, and antibiotics; most individuals live to middle age.	1 in 2,000 births
Diabetes	Body does not produce enough insulin, which causes abnormal metabolism of sugar.	Early onset can be fatal unless treated with insulin.	1 in 2,500 births
Hemophilia	Delayed blood clotting causes internal and external bleeding.	Blood transfusions/injections can reduce or prevent damage due to internal bleeding.	1 in 10,000 males
Huntington disease	Central nervous system deteriorates, producing problems in muscle coordination and mental deterioration.	Does not usually appear until age 35 or older; death likely 10 to 20 years after symptoms appear.	1 in 20,000 births
Phenylketonuria (PKU)	Metabolic disorder that, left untreated, causes mental retardation.	Special diet can result in average intelligence and normal life span.	1 in 10,000 to 1 in 20,000 births
Sickle-cell anemia	Blood disorder that limits the body's oxygen supply; it can cause joint swelling, as well as heart and kidney failure.	Penicillin, medication for pain, antibiotics, and blood transfusions.	1 in 400 African American children (lower among other groups)
Spina bifida	Neural tube disorder that causes brain and spine abnormalities.	Corrective surgery at birth, orthopedic devices, and physical/medical therapy.	2 in 1,000 births
Tay-Sachs disease	Deceleration of mental and physical development caused by an accumulation of lipids in the nervous system.	Medication and special diet are used, but death is likely by 5 years of age.	One in 30 American Jews is a carrier.

FIGURE 2.6 Some Gene-Linked Abnormalities

However, this knowledge might bring important costs as well as benefits. Who would have access to a person's genetic profile? An individual's ability to land and hold jobs or obtain insurance might be threatened if it is known that a person is considered at risk for some disease. For example, should an airline pilot or a neurosurgeon who is predisposed to develop a disorder that makes one's hands shake be required to leave that job early?

Genetic counselors, usually physicians or biologists who are well-versed in the field of medical genetics, understand the kinds of problems just described, the odds of encountering them, and helpful strategies for offseting some of their effects (Forrester & Merz, 2007; Latimer, 2007). A recent research review found that many individuals who receive genetic counseling find it difficult to quantify risk and tend to overestimate risk (Sivell & others, 2008). To read about the career and work of a genetic counselor, see the *Careers in Child Development* profile.

Careers in Child Development

Holly Ishmael, Genetic Counselor

Holly Ishmael is a genetic counselor at Children's Mercy Hospital in Kansas City. She obtained an undergraduate degree in psychology and then a master's degree in genetic counseling from Sarah Lawrence College.

Genetic counselors, like Ishmael, work as members of a health-care team, providing information and support to families with birth defects or genetic disorders. They identify families at risk by analyzing inheritance patterns and explore options with the family. Some genetic counselors, like Ishmael, become specialists in prenatal and pediatric genetics; others might specialize in cancer genetics or psychiatric genetic disorders.

Ishmael says, "Genetic counseling is a perfect combination for people who want to do something science-oriented, but need human contact and don't want to spend all of their time in a lab or have their nose in a book" (Rizzo, 1999, p. 3).

Genetic counselors have specialized graduate degrees in the areas of medical genetics and counseling. They enter graduate school with undergraduate backgrounds from a variety of disciplines, including biology, genetics, psychology, public health, and social work. There are approximately thirty graduate genetic counseling programs in the United States. If you are interested in this profession, you can obtain further information from the National Society of Genetic Counselors at www.nsgc.org.

Holly Ishmael (*left*) in a genetic counseling session.

Review and Reflect: Learning Goal 2

2 **Describe What Genes Are and How They Influence Human Development**

REVIEW

- What are genes?
- How are genes passed on?
- What basic principles describe how genes interact?
- What are some chromosomal and gene-linked abnormalities?

REFLECT

- What are some possible ethical issues regarding genetics and development that might arise in the future?

3 REPRODUCTIVE CHALLENGES AND CHOICES

Prenatal Diagnostic Tests   **Infertility and Reproductive Technology**   **Adoption**

The facts and principles we have discussed regarding meiosis, genetics, and genetic abnormalities are a small part of the recent explosion of knowledge about human biology. This knowledge not only helps us understand human development but also opens up many new choices to prospective parents, choices that can also raise ethical questions (Bromage, 2006).

Prenatal Diagnostic Tests

One choice open to prospective mothers is the extent to which they should undergo prenatal testing (Lenzi & Johnson, 2008). A number of tests can indicate whether a fetus is developing normally, including ultrasound sonography, fetal MRI, chorionic villus sampling, amnocentesis, maternal blood screening, and noninvasive prenatal diagnosis (NIPD). There has been a dramatic increase in research on the use of less invasive techniques, such as fetal MRI and NIPD, which pose lower risks to the fetus than more invasive techniques such as chorionic villus sampling and amniocentesis (Reddy, Filly, & Copel, 2008).

A 6-month-old infant poses with the ultrasound sonography record taken four months into the baby's prenatal development. *What is ultrasound sonography?*

Ultrasound Sonography An ultrasound test is often conducted seven weeks into a pregnancy and at various times later in pregnancy. *Ultrasound sonography* is a prenatal medical procedure in which high-frequency sound waves are directed into the pregnant woman's abdomen. The echo from the sounds is transformed into a visual representation of the fetus' inner structures. This technique can detect many structural abnormalities in the fetus, including microencephaly, a form of mental retardation involving an abnormally small brain; it can also determine the number of fetuses and give clues to the baby's sex (Gerards & others, 2008). There is virtually no risk to the woman or fetus in this test.

Fetal MRI The development of brain-imaging techniques has led to increasing use of *fetal MRI* to diagnose fetal malformations (Garel, 2008; Obenaver & Maestre, 2008) (see Figure 2.7). MRI stands for magnetic resonance imaging and uses a powerful magnet and radio images to generate detailed images of the body's organs and structures. Currently, ultrasound is still the first choice in fetal screening, but fetal MRI can provide more detailed images than ultrasound. In many instances, ultrasound will indicate a possible abnormality and then fetal MRI will be used to obtain a clearer, more detailed image (Muhler & others, 2007). Among the fetal malformations that fetal MRI may be able to detect better than ultrasound sonography are certain central nervous system, chest, gastrointestinal, genital/urinary, and placental abnormalities (Dietrich & Cohen, 2006; Fratelli & others, 2007; Laifer-Narin & others, 2007).

Chorionic Villus Sampling At some point between the tenth and twelfth weeks of pregnancy, chorionic villus sampling may be used to detect genetic defects and chromosomal abnormalities, such as the ones discussed in the previous section (Csaba, Bush, & Saphier, 2006). *Chorionic villus sampling (CVS)* is a prenatal medical procedure in which a small sample of the placenta (the vascular organ that links the fetus to the mother's uterus) is removed. Diagnosis takes about 10 days. There is a small risk of limb deformity when CVS is used.

Amniocentesis Between the fifteenth and eighteenth weeks of pregnancy, amniocentesis may be performed. *Amniocentesis* is a prenatal medical procedure in which a sample of amniotic fluid is withdrawn by syringe and tested for chromosomal or metabolic disorders (Nagel & others, 2007). The amnionic fluid is found

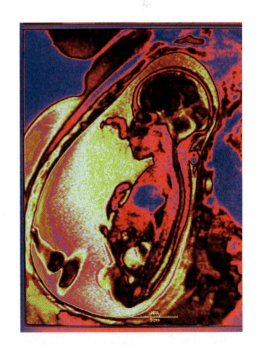

FIGURE 2.7 A Fetal MRI.

within the amnion, a thin sac in which the embryo is suspended. Ultrasound sonography is often used during amniocentesis so that the syringe can be placed precisely. The later amniocentesis is performed, the better its diagnostic potential. The earlier it is performed, the more useful it is in deciding how to handle a pregnancy (Pinette & others, 2004). It may take two weeks for enough cells to grow and amniocentesis test results to be obtained. Amniocentesis brings a small risk of miscarriage: about 1 woman in every 200 to 300 miscarries after amniocentesis.

Both amniocentesis and chorionic villus sampling provide valuable information about the presence of birth defects, but they also raise difficult issues for parents about whether an abortion should be obtained if birth defects are present (Quadrelli & others, 2007). Chorionic villus sampling allows a decision to made sooner, near the end of the first twelve weeks of pregnancy, when abortion is safer and less traumatic than later. Although earlier reports indicated that chorionic villus sampling brings a slightly higher risk of pregnancy loss than amniocentesis, a recent U.S. study of more than 40,000 pregnancies found that loss rates for CVS decreased from 1998–2003 and that there is no longer a difference in pregnancy loss risk between CVS and amniocentesis (Caughey, Hopkins, & Norton, 2006).

Maternal Blood Screening   During the sixteenth to eighteenth weeks of pregnancy, maternal blood screening may be performed. *Maternal blood screening* identifies pregnancies that have an elevated risk for birth defects such as spina bifida (a defect in the spinal cord) and Down syndrome (Palomaki & others, 2006). The current blood test is called the *triple screen* because it measures three substances in the mother's blood. After an abnormal triple screen result, the next step is usually an ultrasound examination. If an ultrasound does not explain the abnormal triple screen results, amniocentesis is typically used.

Noninvasive Prenatal Diagnosis (NIPD)   *Noninvasive prenatal diagnosis* (*NIPD*) is increasingly being explored as an alternative to such procedures as chorionic villus sampling and amniocentesis (Avent & others, 2008). At this point, NIPD has mainly focused on the isolation and examination of fetal cells circulating in the mother's blood and analysis of cell-free fetal DNA in maternal plasma (Finning & Chitty, 2008; Norbury & Norbury, 2008).

Researchers already have used NIPD to successfully test for genes inherited from a father that cause cystic fibrosis and Huntington disease. They also are exploring the potential for using NIPD to diagnose a baby's sex as early as five weeks after conception and Down syndrome (Avent & others, 2008; Hahn, Zhong, & Holzgreve, 2008). Being able to detect an offspring's sex and various diseases and defects so early raises ethical concerns about couples' motivation to terminate a pregnancy (Newsom, 2008; van den Heuvel & Marteau, 2008).

Technical challenges still characterize the use of NIPD, but its benefit in reducing risk make it an attractive diagnostic candidate (van der Schoot, Hahn, & Chitty, 2008). The main technical challenge is to efficiently separate out the fetal cells, which comprise only about one of every million cells in a mother's blood.

Infertility and Reproductive Technology

Recent advances in biological knowledge have also opened up many choices for infertile people. Approximately 10 to 15 percent of couples in the United States experience infertility, which is defined as the inability to conceive a child after 12 months of regular intercourse without contraception. The cause of infertility can rest with the woman or the man (Kumar & others, 2006). The woman may not be ovulating (releasing eggs to be fertilized), she may be producing abnormal ova, her fallopian tubes, by which ova normally reach the womb, may be blocked, or she may have a disease that prevents implantation of the embryo into the uterus. The man may produce too few sperm, the sperm may lack motility (the ability to move adequately), or he may have a blocked passageway (Hesmet & Lo, 2006).

In the United States, more than 2 million couples seek help for infertility every year. In some cases of infertility, surgery may correct the cause; in others, hormone-based

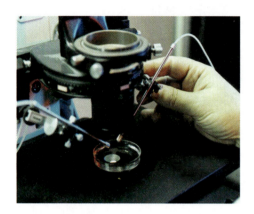

A technician using a micro-needle to inject human sperm into a human egg cell as part of an in vitro fertilization procedure. The injected sperm fertilizes the egg, and the resulting zygote is then grown in the laboratory until it reaches an early stage of embryonic development. Then it is implanted in the uterus.

Singer Celine Dion became pregnant through in vitro fertilization and gave birth to her son Rene-Charles in 2001.

drugs may improve the probability of having a child. Of the 2 million couples who seek help for infertility every year, about 40,000 try high-tech assisted reproduction. By far the most common technique used is *in vitro fertilization (IVF)*, in which eggs and a sperm are combined in a laboratory dish. If any eggs are successfully fertilized, one or more the resulting eggs is tranferred into the woman's uterus. A national U.S. study by the Centers for Disease Control and Prevention (2006) found the success rate of IVF depends on the mother's age (see Figure 2.8).

The creation of families by means of the new reproductive technologies raises important questions about the physical and psychological consequences for children (El-Toukhy, Khalaf, & Braude, 2006; Gurgan & Demirol, 2007). One result of fertility treatments is an increase in multiple births (Jones, 2007; Reddy & others, 2007). Twenty-five to 30 percent of pregnancies achieved by fertility treatments—including in vitro fertilization—now result in multiple births. Any multiple birth increases the likelihood that the babies will have life-threatening and costly problems, such as extremely low birth weight (Ito & others, 2006).

Not nearly as many studies have examined the psychological outcomes of IVF as the physical outcomes. To read about a study that addresses these consequences, see the *Research in Child Development* interlude that follows.

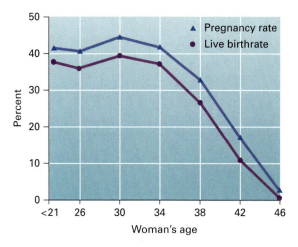

FIGURE 2.8 Success Rates of In Vitro Fertilization Vary According to the Woman's Age

Research in Child Development

IN VITRO FERTILIZATION AND DEVELOPMENTAL OUTCOMES IN ADOLESCENCE

A longitudinal study examined 34 in vitro fertilization families, 49 adoptive families, and 38 families with a naturally conceived child (Golombok, MacCallum, & Goodman, 2001). Each type of family included a similar portion of boys and girls. Also, the age of the young adolescents did not differ according to family type (mean age of 11 years, 11 months).

Children's socioemotional development was assessed by (1) interviewing the mother and obtaining detailed descriptions of any problems the child might have; (2) administering a Strengths and Difficulties questionnaire to the child's mother and teacher; and (3) administering the Social Adjustment Inventory for Children and Adolescents, which examines functioning in school, peer relationships, and self-esteem.

No sigificant differences between the children from the in vitro fertilization, adoptive, and naturally conceiving families were found. The results from the Social Adjustment Inventory for Children and Adolescents are shown in Figure 2.9. Another study also revealed no psychological differences between IVF babies and those not conceived by IVF, but more research is needed to reach firm conclusions in this area (Hahn & DiPietro, 2001).

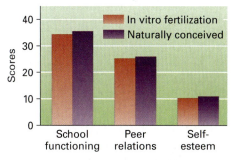

FIGURE 2.9 Socioemotional Functioning of Children Conceived Through In Vitro Fertilization or Naturally Conceived. This graph shows the results of a study that compared the socioemotional functioning of young adolescents who had either been conceived through in vitro fertilization (IVF) or naturally conceived (Golombok, MacCallum, & Goodman, 2001). For each type of family, the study included a similar portion of boys and girls and children of similar age (mean age of 11 years, 11 months). Although the means for the naturally conceived group were slightly higher, this is likely due to chance: There were no significant differences between the groups.

Adoption

Although surgery and fertility drugs can sometimes solve the infertility problem, another choice is to adopt a child (Bernard & Dozier 2008; Cohen & others, 2008). Adoption is the social and legal process by which a parent-child relationship is established between persons unrelated at birth. As we see next in the *Diversity in Child Development* interlude, an increase in diversity has characterized the adoption of children in the United States in recent years.

Diversity in Child Development

THE INCREASED DIVERSITY OF ADOPTED CHILDREN AND ADOPTIVE PARENTS

An increasing number of Hollywood celebrities are adopting children from developing countries. Actress Angelina Jolie recently adopted a baby girl, Zahara (*above*), in Ethiopia.

Several changes occurred during the last several decades of the twentieth century in the characteristics both of adopted children and of adoptive parents (Brodzinsky & Pinderhughes, 2002, pp. 280–282). Until the 1960s, most U.S. adopted children were healthy European American infants, who were adopted within a few days or weeks after birth. However, in recent decades, an increasing number of unmarried U.S. mothers decided to keep their babies, and the number of unwanted births decreased as contraception became readily available and abortion was legalized. As a result, the number of healthy European American infants available for adoption dropped dramatically. Increasingly, U.S. couples adopted children who were not European Americans, children from other countries, and children in foster care whose characteristics—such as age, minority status, exposure to neglect or abuse, or physical or mental health problems—"were once thought to be barriers to adoption" (p. 281).

Changes also have characterized adoptive parents. Until the last several decades of the twentieth century, most adoptive parents had a middle or upper socioeconomic status and were "married, infertile, European American couples, usually in their 30s and 40s, and free of any disability. Adoption agencies *screened out* couples who did not have these characteristics" (p. 281). Today, however, many adoption agencies *screen in* as many applicants as possible and have no income requirements for adoptive parents. Many agencies now permit single adults, older adults, and gay and lesbian adults to adopt children (Matthews & Cramer, 2006; Ryan, Pearlmutter, & Groza, 2004).

Do these changes matter? They open opportunities for many children and many couples, but possible effects of changes in the characteristics of parents on the outcomes for children are still unknown. For example, in one study, adopted adolescents were more likely to have problems if the adoptive parents had low levels of education (Miller & others, 2000). In another study, international adoptees showed fewer behavior problems and were less likely to be using mental health services than domestic adoptees (Juffer & van IJzendoorn, 2005). More research is needed before definitive conclusions can be reached about the changing demographic characteristics of adoption.

The changes in adoption practice over the last several decades make it difficult to generalize about the average adopted child or average adoptive parent. As we see next, though, some researchers have provided useful comparisons between adopted children and nonadopted children and their families.

How do adopted children fare after they are adopted? Children who are adopted very early in their lives are more likely to have positive outcomes than children adopted later in life. In one study, the later adoption occurred, the more problems the adoptees had. Infant adoptees had the fewest adjustment difficulties; those adopted after they were 10 years of age had the most problems (Sharma, McGue, & Benson, 1996).

In general, adopted children and adolescents are more likely to experience psychological and school-related problems than nonadopted children (Brodzinksy, Lang, & Smith, 1995; Brodzinsky & Pinderhuges, 2002). For example, a recent meta-analysis (a statistical procedure that combines the results of a number of studies) revealed that adoptees were far more likely to be using mental health services than their nonadopted counterparts. (Juffer & van IJzendoorn, 2005). Adopted children also showed more behavior problems than nonadoptees, but this difference was small. A recent large-scale study revealed that adopted children are more likely to have a learning disability than nonadopted children (Altarac & Saroha, 2007).

Do adopted children show differences in cognitive development as well? A meta-analysis of 62 studies involving almost 18,000 adopted children compared (1) the cognitive development of adopted children with that of children who remained in institutional care or in the birth family, and (2) the same group of adopted children to their current nonadopted siblings or peers in their current environment (van IJzendoorn, Juffer, & Poelhuis, 2005). In this meta-analysis, the adopted children scored higher on IQ tests and performed better in school than the children who stayed behind in institutions or with their birth famiilies. The IQ of adopted children did not differ from that of nonadopted peers or siblings in their current environment, but their school performance and language abilities were at lower levels, and they were more likely to have learning difficulties. Overall, the meta-analysis documented the positive influence of adoption on children's cognitive development and the normal intellectual ability of adopted children, but a lower level of performance in school.

Research that contrasts adopted and nonadopted adolescents has also found positive characteristics among the adopted adolescents. For example, in one study, although adopted adolescents were more likely than nonadopted adolescents to use illlicit drugs and to engage in delinquent behavior, the adopted adolescents were also less likely to be withdrawn and engaged in more prosocial behavior, such as being altruistic, caring, and supportive of others (Sharma, McGue, & Benson, 1996).

In short, the vast majority of adopted children (including those adopted at older ages, transracially, and across national borders) adjust effectively, and their parents report considerable satisfaction with their decision to adopt (Brodzinsky & Pinderhughes, 2002). In one recent national study, there were no differences in the antisocial behavior of adopted and nonadopted young adults (Grotevant & others, 2006). A recent research review of 88 studies also revealed no difference in the self-esteem of adopted and nonadopted children, as well as no differences between transracial and same-race adoptees (Juffer & IJzendoorn, 2007). Furthermore, adopted children fare much better than children in long-term foster care or in an institutional environment (Brodzinsky & Pinderhughes, 2002). To read more about adoption, see the *Caring for Children* interlude in which we discuss effective parenting strategies with adopted children.

Caring for Children

PARENTING ADOPTED CHILDREN

Many of the keys to effectively parenting adopted children are no different from those for effectively parenting biological children: Be supportive and caring, be involved and monitor the child's behavior and whereabouts, be a good communicator, and help the child to learn to develop self-control. However, parents of adopted children face some unique circumstances (Fontenot, 2007). These parents need to recognize the differences involved in adoptive family life, communicate about these differences, show respect for the birth family, and support the child's search for self and identity.

What are some strategies for parenting adopted children at different points in their development?

David Brodzinsky and Ellen Pinderhughes (2002, pp. 288–292) discussed how to handle some of the challenges that parents face when their adopted children are at different points in development:

- *Infancy.* Researchers have found few differences in the attachment that adopted and nonadopted infants form with their parents, but attachment can be compromised "when parents have difficulty in claiming the child as their own either because of unresolved fertility issues, lack of support from family and friends, and/or when their expectations about the child have not been met" (p. 288). Competent adoption agencies or counselors can help prospective adoptive parents develop realistic expectations.

- *Early childhood.* Because many children begin to ask where they came from when they are about 4 to 6 years old, this is a natural time to begin to talk in simple ways to children about their adoption status (Warshak, 2004). Some parents (although not as many as in the past) decide not to tell their children about the adoption. This secrecy may create psychological risks for the child if he or she later finds out about the adoption.

- *Middle and late childhood.* During the elementary school years, children begin to express "much more curiosity about their origins: *Where did I come from? What did my birthmother and birthfather look like? Why didn't they keep me? Where are they now? Can I meet them?*" (p. 290). As they grow older, children may become more ambivalent about being adopted and question their adoptive parents' explanations. It is important for adoptive parents to recognize that this ambivalence is normal. Also, problems may come from the desire of adoptive parents to make life too perfect for the adopted child and to present a perfect image of themselves to the child. The result too often is that adopted children feel that they cannot release any angry feelings and openly discuss problems (Warshak, 2004).

- *Adolescence.* Adolescents are likely to develop more abstract and logical thinking, to focus their attention on their bodies, and to search for an identity. These characteristics provide the foundation for adopted adolescents to reflect on their adoption status in more complex ways, to become "preoccupied with the lack of physical resemblance between themselves and others in the family" (p. 291), and to explore how the fact that they were adopted fits into their identity. Adoptive parents "need to be aware of these many complexities and provide teenagers with the support they need to cope with these adoption-related tasks" (p. 292).

Review and Reflect: Learning Goal 3

3 **Identify Some Important Reproductive Challenges and Choices**

REVIEW

- What are some common prenatal diagnostic tests?
- What are some techniques that help infertile people to have children?
- How does adoption affect children's development?

REFLECT

- We discussed a number of studies indicating that adoption is linked with negative outcomes for children. Does that mean that all adopted children have more negative outcomes than all nonadopted children? Explain.

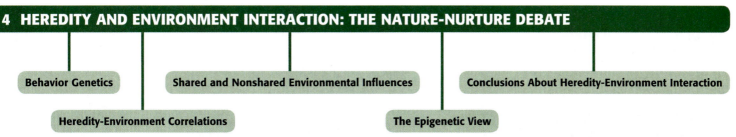

4   HEREDITY AND ENVIRONMENT INTERACTION: THE NATURE-NURTURE DEBATE

| Behavior Genetics | Shared and Nonshared Environmental Influences | Conclusions About Heredity-Environment Interaction |

| Heredity-Environment Correlations | The Epigenetic View |

Is it possible to untangle the influence of heredity from that of environment and discover the role of each in producing individual differences in development? When heredity and environment interact, how does heredity influence the environment, and vice versa?

Behavior Genetics

Behavior genetics is the field that seeks to discover the influence of heredity and environment on individual differences in human traits and development (Derks & others, 2008). Note that behavior genetics does not determine the extent to which genetics or the environment affects an individual's traits. Instead, what behavior geneticists try to do is to figure out what is responsible for the differences among people—that is, to what extent do people differ because of differences in genes, environment, or a combination of these? To study the influence of heredity on behavior, behavior geneticists often use either twins or adoption situations (Goldsmith, 2008).

In the most common **twin study**, the behavioral similarity of identical twins (who are genetically identical) is compared with the behavioral similarity of fraternal twins. Recall that although fraternal twins share the same womb, they are no more genetically alike than brothers or sisters. Thus by comparing groups of identical and fraternal twins, behavior geneticists capitalize on the basic knowledge that identical twins are more similar genetically than are fraternal twins (Wood & others, 2008). For example, one study found that conduct problems were more prevalent in identical twins than fraternal twins; the researchers concluded that the study demonstrated an important role for heredity in conduct problems (Scourfield & others, 2004).

However, several issues complicate interpretation of twin studies (Vogler, 2006). For example, perhaps the environments of identical twins are more similar than the environments of fraternal twins. Adults might stress the similarities of identical twins more than those of fraternal twins, and identical twins might perceive themselves as a "set" and play together more than fraternal twins do. If so, the influence of the environment on the observed similarities between identical and fraternal twins might be very significant.

In an **adoption study**, investigators seek to discover whether the behavior and psychological characteristics of adopted children are more like their those of their adoptive parents, who have provided a home environment, or more like those of their biological parents, who have contributed their heredity (Haugaard & Hazen, 2004; Loehlin, Horn, & Ernst, 2007). Another form of the adoption study compares adoptive and biological siblings.

Heredity-Environment Correlations

The difficulties that researchers encounter when they interpet the results of twin studies and adoption studies reflect the complexities of heredity-environment interaction. Some of these interactions are *heredity-environment correlations*, which means that individuals' genes may influence the types of environments to which they are exposed. In a sense, individuals "inherit" environments that may be related or linked to genetic "propensities" (Plomin, DeFries, & Fulker, 2007). Behavior geneticist Sandra Scarr (1993) described three ways that heredity and environment are correlated (see Figure 2.10):

- **Passive genotype-environment correlations** occur because biological parents, who are genetically related to the child, provide a rearing environment for the

Identical twins develop from a single fertilized egg that splits into two genetically identical organisms. Twin studies compare identical twins with fraternal twins. Fraternal twins develop from separate eggs, making them genetically no more similar than nontwin siblings. *What is the nature of the twin study method?*

behavior genetics The field that seeks to discover the influence of heredity and environment on individual differences in human traits and development.

twin study A study in which the behavioral similarity of identical twins is compared with the behavioral similarity of fraternal twins.

adoption study A study in which investigators seek to discover whether the behavior and psychological characteristics of adopted children are more like their adoptive parents, who provided a home environment, or more like their biological parents, who contributed their heredity. Another form of the adoption study is to compare adoptive and biological siblings.

passive genotype-environment correlations Correlations that exist when the biological parents, who are genetically related to the child, provide a rearing environment for the child.

Heredity-Environment Correlation	Description	Examples
Passive	Children inherit genetic tendencies from their parents, and parents also provide an environment that matches their own genetic tendencies.	Musically inclined parents usually have musically inclined children and they are likely to provide an environment rich in music for their children.
Evocative	The child's genetic tendencies elicit stimulation from the environment that supports a particular trait. Thus genes evoke environmental support.	A happy, outgoing child elicits smiles and friendly responses from others.
Active (niche-picking)	Children actively seek out "niches" in their environment that reflect their own interests and talents and are thus in accord with their genotype.	Libraries, sports fields, and a store with musical instruments are examples of environmental niches children might seek out if they have intellectual interests in books, talent in sports, or musical talents, respectively.

FIGURE 2.10 Exploring Heredity-Environment Correlations

child. For example, the parents might have a genetic predisposition to be intelligent and read skillfully. Because they read well and enjoy reading, they provide their children with books to read. The likely outcome is that their children, given their own inherited predispositions from their parents and their book-filled environment, will become skilled readers.

- **Evocative genotype-environment correlations** occur because a child's characteristics elicit certain types of environments. For example, active, smiling children receive more social stimulation than passive, quiet children do. Cooperative, attentive children evoke more pleasant and instructional responses from the adults around them than uncooperative, distractible children do.

- **Active (niche-picking) genotype-environment correlations** occur when children seek out environments that they find compatible and stimulating. *Niche-picking* refers to finding a setting that is suited to one's abilities. Children select from their surrounding environment some aspect that they respond to, learn about, or ignore. Their active selections of environments are related to their particular genotype. For example, outgoing children tend to seek out social contexts in which to interact with people, whereas shy children don't. Children who are musically inclined are likely to select musical environments in which they can successfully perform their skills. How these "tendencies" come about will be discussed shortly under the topic of the epigenetic view.

Scarr emphasizes that the relative importance of the three genotype-environment correlations changes as children develop from infancy through adolescence. In infancy, much of the environment that children experience is provided by adults. Thus, passive genotype-environment correlations are more common in the lives of infants and young children than they are for older children and adolescents who can extend their experiences beyond the family's influence and create their environments to a greater degree.

Notice that this analysis gives the preeminent role in development to heredity: The analysis describes how heredity may influence the types of environments that children experience. Critics argue that the concept of heredity-environment correlation gives heredity too much of a one-sided influence in determining development because it does not consider the role of prior environmental influences in shaping the correlation itself (Gottlieb, Wahlsten, & Lickliter, 2006). Before considering this criticism and a different view of the heredity-environment linkage, let's take a closer look at how behavior geneticists analyze the environments involved in heredity.

Shared and Nonshared Environmental Influences

Behavior geneticists have argued that to understand the environment's role in differences between people, we should distinguish between shared and nonshared

evocative genotype-environment correlations Correlations that exist when the child's genotype elicits certain types of physical and social environments.

active (niche-picking) genotype-environment correlations Correlations that exist when children seek out environments they find compatible and stimulating.

environments. That is, we should consider experiences that children share in common with other children living in the same home, and experiences that are not shared (Wardle & others, 2008).

Shared environmental experiences are siblings' common experiences, such as their parents' personalities or intellectual orientation, the family's socioeconomic status, and the neighborhood in which they live. By contrast, **nonshared environmental experiences** are a child's unique experiences, both within the family and outside the family, that are not shared with a sibling. Even experiences occurring within the family can be part of the "nonshared environment." For example, parents often interact differently with each sibling, and siblings interact differently with parents (Hetherington, Reiss, & Plomin, 1994). Siblings often have different peer groups, different friends, and different teachers at school.

Behavior geneticist Robert Plomin (2004) has found that shared environment accounts for little of the variation in children's personality or interests. In other words, even though two children live under the same roof with the same parents, their personalities are often very different. Further, Plomin argues that heredity influences the nonshared environments of siblings through the heredity-environment correlations we described earlier (Plomin & others, 2003). For example, a child who has inherited a genetic tendency to be athletic is likely to spend more time in environments related to sports, whereas a child who has inherited a tendency to be musically inclined is more likely to spend time in environments related to music.

What are the implications of Plomin's interpretation of the role of shared and nonshared environments in development? In the *Nurture Assumption*, Judith Harris (1998) argued that that what parents do does not make a difference in their children's and adolescents' behavior. Yell at them. Hug them. Read to them. Ignore them. Harris says it won't influence how they turn out. She argues that genes and peers are far more important than parents in children's and adolescents' development.

Genes and peers do matter, but Harris' descriptions of peer influences do not take into account the complexity of peer contexts and developmental trajectories (Hartup, 1999). In addition, Harris is wrong in saying that parents don't matter. For example, in the early child years parents play an important role in selecting children's peers and indirectly influencing children's development (Baumrind, 1999). A large volume of parenting literature with many research studies documents the importance of parents in children's development (Clarke-Stewart & Dunn, 2006; Grusec & Davidov, 2007; Maccoby, 2007; Parke & others, 2008). We will discuss parents' important roles throughout this book.

The Epigenetic View

Does the concept of heredity-environment correlation downplay the importance of environment in our development? The concept emphasizes how heredity directs the kind of environmental experiences individuals have. However, earlier in the chapter we discussed how genes are collaborative, not determining an individual's traits in an independent manner, but rather in an interactive manner with the environment. In line with the concept of a collaborative gene, Gilbert Gottlieb (2007; Gottlieb, Wahlsten, & Lickliter, 2006) emphasizes the **epigenetic view**, which states that development is the result of an ongoing, bidirectional interchange between heredity and the environment. Figure 2.11 compares the heredity-environment correlation and epigenetic views of development.

Let's look at an example that reflects the epigenetic view. A baby inherits genes from both parents at conception. During prenatal development, toxins, nutrition, and stress can influence some genes to stop functioning while others become stronger or weaker. During infancy, the same environmental experiences such as toxins, nutrition, stress, learning, and encouragement continue to modify genetic activity and the activity of the nervous system that directly underlies behavior (Gottlieb, 2005). Heredity and environment operate together—or collaborate—to produce a

Tennis stars Venus and Serena Williams. *What might be some shared and nonshared environmental experiences they had while they were growing up that contributed to their tennis stardom?*

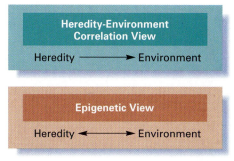

FIGURE 2.11 Comparison of the Heredity-Environment Correlation and Epigenetic Views

shared environmental experiences Siblings' common environmental experiences, such as their parents' personalities and intellectual orientation, the family's socioeconomic status, and the neighborhood in which they live.

nonshared environmental experiences The child's own unique experiences, both within the family and outside the family, that are not shared by another sibling. Thus, experiences occurring within the family can be part of the "nonshared environment."

epigenetic view Emphasizes that development is the result of an ongoing, bidirectional interchange between heredity and environment.

person's intelligence, temperament, height, weight, ability to pitch a baseball, ability to read, and so on (Gottlieb, Wahlsten, & Lickliter, 2006).

Conclusions About Heredity-Environment Interaction

If an attractive, popular, intelligent girl is elected president of her senior class in high school, is her success due to heredity or to environment? Of course, the answer is both.

The relative contributions of heredity and environment are not additive. That is, we can't say that such-and-such a percentage of nature and such-and-such a percentage of experience make us who we are. Nor is it accurate to say that full genetic expression happens once, around conception or birth, after which we carry our genetic legacy into the world to see how far it takes us. Genes produce proteins throughout the life span, in many different environments. Or they don't produce these proteins, depending in part on how harsh or nourishing those environments are.

The emerging view is that complex behaviors have some *genetic loading* that gives people a propensity for a particular developmental trajectory (Plomin, DeFries, & Fulker, 2007; Wardle & others, 2008). However, the actual development requires more: an environment. And that environment is complex, just like the mixture of genes we inherit (Grusec & Hastings, 2007; Parke & others, 2008). Environmental influences range from the things we lump together under "nurture" (such as parenting, family dynamics, schooling, and neighborhood quality) to biological encounters (such as viruses, birth complications, and even biological events in cells) (Greenough, 1997, 1999; Greenough & others, 2001).

Imagine for a moment that there is a cluster of genes somehow associated with youth violence (this example is hypothetical because we don't know of any such combination). The adolescent who carries this genetic mixture might experience a world of loving parents, regular nutritious meals, lots of books, and a series of masterful teachers. Or the adolescent's world might include parental neglect, a neighborhood in which gunshots and crime are everyday occurrences, and inadequate schooling. In which of these environments are the adolescent's genes likely to manufacture the biological underpinnings of criminality?

Review and Reflect: Learning Goal 4

4 **Explain Some of the Ways That Heredity and Environment Interact to Produce Individual Differences in Development**

REVIEW

- What is behavior genetics, and what two methods do behavior geneticists use to study heredity's influence on behavior?
- What are three types of heredity-environment correlations described by Scarr?
- What is meant by the concepts of shared and nonshared environmental experiences?
- What is the epigenetic view of development?
- What conclusions can be reached about heredity-environment interaction?

REFLECT

- Someone tells you that she has analyzed her genetic background and environmental experiences and reached the conclusion that environment definitely has had little influence on her intelligence. What would you say to this person about her ability to make this self-diagnosis?

Reach Your Learning Goals

Biological Beginnings

1 THE EVOLUTIONARY PERSPECTIVE: DISCUSS THE EVOLUTIONARY PERSPECTIVE ON DEVELOPMENT

Natural Selection and Adaptive Behavior

- Natural selection is the evolutionary process by which those individuals of a species that are best adapted survive and reproduce. Darwin proposed that natural selection fuels evolution. In evolutionary theory, adaptive behavior is behavior that promotes the organism's survival in a natural habitat.

Evolutionary Psychology

- Evolutionary psychology holds that adaptation, reproduction, and "survival of the fittest" are important in shaping behavior. Ideas proposed by evolutionary developmental psychology include the view that an extended childhood period is needed to develop a large brain and learn the complexity of human social communities. In addition, evolutionary psychology notes that evolved mechanisms are not always adaptive in contemporary society. Like other theoretical approaches to development, evolutionary psychology has limitations. Bandura rejects "one-sided evolutionism" and argues for a bidirectional link between biology and environment. Biology allows for a broad range of cultural possibilities.

2 GENETIC FOUNDATIONS OF DEVELOPMENT: DESCRIBE WHAT GENES ARE AND HOW THEY INFLUENCE HUMAN DEVELOPMENT

The Collaborative Gene

- Short segments of DNA constitute genes, the units of hereditary information that direct cells to reproduce and manufacture proteins. Genes act collaboratively, not independently.

Genes and Chromosomes

- Except in the sperm and egg, the nucleus of each human cell contains 46 chromosomes, which are composed of DNA. Genes are passed on to new cells when chromosomes are duplicated during the process of mitosis and meiosis, which are two ways in which new cells are formed. When an egg and a sperm unite in the fertilization process, the resulting zygote contains the genes from the chromosomes in the father's sperm and the mother's egg. Despite this transmission of genes from generation to generation, variability is created in several ways, including the exchange of chromosomal segments during meiosis, mutations, and the distinction between a genotype and a phenotype.

Genetic Principles

- Genetic principles include those involving dominant-recessive genes, sex-linked genes, genetic imprinting, and polygenic inheritance.

Chromosomal and Gene-Linked Abnormalities

- Chromosome abnormalities produce Down syndrome, which is caused by the presence of an extra copy of chromosome 21, as well as sex-linked chromosomal abnormalities such as Klinefelter syndrome, fragile X syndrome, Turner syndrome, and XYY syndrome. Gene-linked abnormalities involve harmful genes. Gene-linked disorders include phenylketonuria (PKU) and sickle-cell anemia. Genetic counseling offers couples information about their risk of having a child with inherited abnormalities.

3 REPRODUCTIVE CHALLENGES AND CHOICES: IDENTIFY SOME IMPORTANT REPRODUCTIVE CHALLENGES AND CHOICES

Prenatal Diagnostic Tests

- Some common prenatal diagnostic tests include ultrasound sonography, fetal MRI, chorionic villus sampling, amniocentesis, maternal blood screening, and noninvasive prenatal diagnosis, all of which can be used to determine whether a fetus is developing normally. There has been a dramatic increase in research on less invasive diagnosis, such as fetal MRI and NIPD.

Infertility and Reproductive Technology

- Approximately 10 to 15 percent of U.S. couples have infertility problems, some of which can be corrected through surgery or hormone-based fertility drugs. Additional options include in vitro fertilization and other more recently developed techniques.

Adoption

- Although adopted children and adolescents have more problems than their nonadopted counterparts, the vast majority of adopted children adapt effectively. When adoption occurs very early in development, the outcomes for the child are improved. Because of the dramatic changes that occurred in adoption in recent decades, it is difficult to generalize about the average adopted child or average adoptive family.

4   HEREDITY AND ENVIRONMENT INTERACTION: THE NATURE-NURTURE DEBATE: EXPLAIN SOME OF THE WAYS THAT HEREDITY AND ENVIRONMENT INTERACT TO PRODUCE INDIVIDUAL DIFFERENCES IN DEVELOPMENT

Behavior Genetics

- Behavior genetics is the field concerned with the influence of heredity and environment on individual differences in human traits and development. Methods used by behavior geneticists include twin studies and adoption studies.

Heredity-Environment Correlations

- In Scarr's heredity-environment correlations view, heredity directs the types of environments that children experience. She describes three genotype-environment correlations: passive, evocative, and active (niche-picking). Scarr argues that the relative importance of these three genotype-environment correlations changes as children develop.

Shared and Nonshared Environmental Influences

- Shared environmental experiences refer to siblings' common experiences, such as their parents' personalities and intellectual orientation, the family's socioeconomic status, and the neighborhood in which they live. Nonshared environmental experiences involve the child's unique experiences, both within a family and outside a family, that are not shared with a sibling. Many behavior geneticists argue that differences in the development of siblings are due to nonshared environmental experiences (and heredity) rather than shared environmental experiences.

The Epigenetic View

- The epigenetic view emphasizes that development is the result of an ongoing, bidirectional interchange between heredity and environment.

Conclusions About Heredity-Environment Interaction

- Complex behaviors have some genetic loading that gives people a propensity for a particular developmental trajectory. However, actual development also requires an environment, and that environment is complex. The interaction of heredity and environment is extensive. Much remains to be discovered about the specific ways that heredity and environment interact to influence development.

KEY TERMS

evolutionary psychology 55
chromosomes 57
DNA 57
genes 58
mitosis 59
meiosis 59
fertilization 59
zygote 59

genotype 60
phenotype 60
Down syndrome 61
Klinefelter syndrome 62
fragile X syndrome 62
Turner syndrome 62
XYY syndrome 62
phenylketonuria (PKU) 62
sickle-cell anemia 62

behavior genetics 71
twin study 71
adoption study 71
passive genotype-environment correlations 71
evocative genotype-environment correlations 72

active (niche-picking) genotype-environment correlations 72
shared environmental experiences 73
nonshared environmental experiences 73
epigenetic view 73

KEY PEOPLE

Thomas Bouchard 54
Charles Darwin 55
David Buss 56

Albert Bandura 56
Steven Jay Gould 57
David Moore 58

Sandra Scarr 72
Robert Plomin 73
Judith Harris 73

Gilbert Gottlieb 73

E-LEARNING TOOLS

To help you master the material in this chapter, you'll find a number of valuable study tools at the Online Learning Center for *Child Development*, twelfth edition (**www.mhhe.com/santrockcd12**).

Taking It to the Net

Research the answers to these questions:

1. Ahmahl, a biochemistry major, is writing a psychology paper on the potential dilemmas that society and scientists may face as a result of decoding the human genome. What are some of the main issues or concerns that Ahmahl should address in his class paper?

2. Brandon and Katie are thrilled to learn that they are expecting their first child. They are curious about the genetic makeup of their unborn child and want to know (a) what disorders might be identified through prenatal genetic testing; and (b) which tests, if any, Katie should undergo to help determine this information.

3. Greg and Courtenay have three boys. They would love to have a girl. Courtenay read that there is a clinic in Virginia where you can pick the sex of your child. How successful are such efforts? Would you want to have this choice available to you?

Health and Well-Being, Parenting, and Education Exercises

Build your decision-making skills by trying your hand at the health and well-being, parenting, and education exercises.

Video Clips

The Online Learning Center includes the following video for this chapter:

- *Interview with Adoptive Parents*
  An interview with a couple that adopted a second child.

3

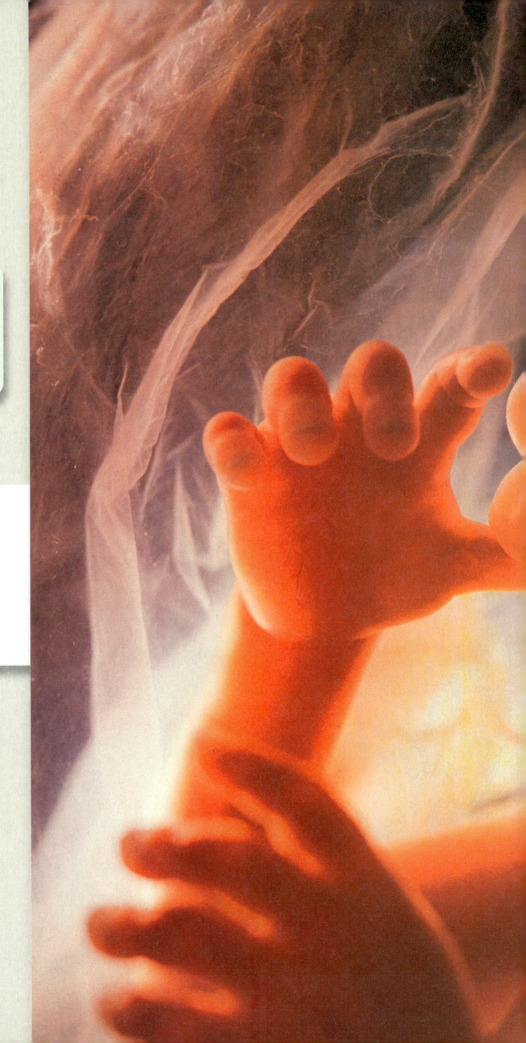

There was a star danced, and under that I was born.

—WILLIAM SHAKESPEARE
English Playwright, 17th Century

LEARNING GOALS

- Describe prenatal development.

- Discuss the birth process.

- Explain the changes that take place in the postpartum period.

PRENATAL DEVELOPMENT AND BIRTH

CHAPTER OUTLINE

Images of Child Development
The Story of Mr. Littles

Diana and Roger married when he was 38 and she was 34. Both worked full-time and were excited when Diana became pregnant. Two months later, Diana began to have some unusual pains and bleeding. Just two months into her pregnancy she had lost the baby. Diana thought deeply about why she was unable to carry the baby to full term. It was about the time she became pregnant that the federal government began to warn that eating certain types of fish with a high mercury content during pregnancy on a regular basis can cause a miscarriage. Now she eliminated these fish from her diet.

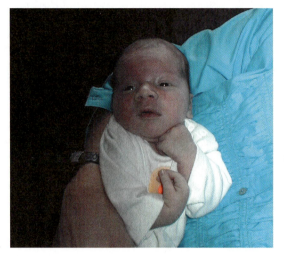

Alex, also known as "Mr. Littles."

Six months later, Diana became pregnant again. She and Roger read about pregnancy and signed up for birth preparation classes. Each Friday night for eight weeks they practiced simulated contractions. They talked about what kind of parents they wanted to be and discussed what changes in their lives the baby would make. When they found out that their offspring was going to be a boy, they gave him a name: Mr. Littles.

This time, Diana's pregnancy went well, and Alex, also known as Mr. Littles, was born. During the birth, however, Diana's heart rate dropped precipitously and she was given a stimulant to raise it. Apparently the stimulant also increased Alex's heart rate and breathing to a dangerous point, and he had to be placed in a neonatal intensive care unit (NICU).

Several times a day, Diana and Roger visited Alex in the NICU. A number of babies in the NICU who had a very low birth weight had been in intensive care for weeks, and some of these babies were not doing well. Fortunately, Alex was in better health. After several days in the NICU, his parents were permitted to take home a very healthy Alex.

PREVIEW

This chapter chronicles the truly remarkable developments from conception through birth. Imagine . . . at one time you were an organism floating in a sea of fluid in your mother's womb. Let's now explore what your development was like from the time you were conceived through the time you were born.

1 PRENATAL DEVELOPMENT

| The Course of Prenatal Development | Teratology and Hazards to Prenatal Development | Prenatal Care | Normal Prenatal Development |

Imagine how Alex ("Mr. Littles") came to be. Out of thousands of eggs and millions of sperm, one egg and one sperm united to produce him. Had the union of sperm and egg come a day or even an hour earlier or later, he might have been very different—maybe even of the opposite sex. *Conception* occurs when a single sperm cell from the male unites with an ovum (egg) in the female's fallopian tube in a process called fertilization. Over the next few months, the genetic code discussed in Chapter 2 directs a series of changes in the fertilized egg, but many events and hazards will influence how that egg develops and becomes tiny Alex.

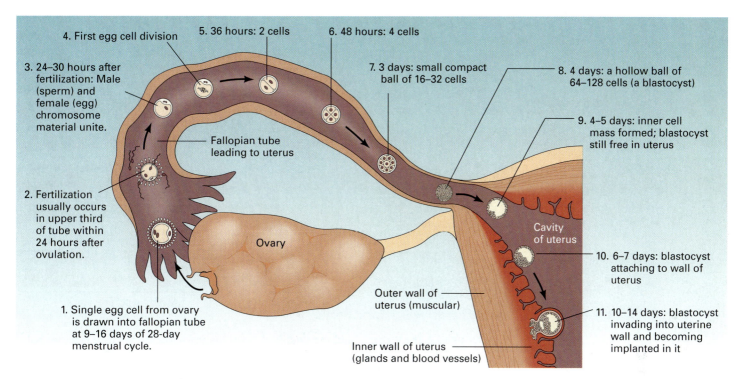

FIGURE 3.1 Significant Developments in the Germinal Period. Just one week after conception, cells of the blastocyst have already begun specializing. The germination period ends when the blastocyst attaches to the uterine wall. *Which of the steps shown in the drawing occur in the laboratory when in vitro fertilization (described in Chapter 3) is used?*

The Course of Prenatal Development

Prenatal development lasts approximately 266 days, beginning with fertilization and ending with birth. It can be divided into three periods: germinal, embryonic, and fetal.

The Germinal Period

The **germinal period** is the period of prenatal development that takes place in the first two weeks after conception. It includes the creation of the fertilized egg, called a zygote, cell division, and the attachment of the zygote to the uterine wall.

Rapid cell division by the zygote begins the germinal period (recall from Chapter 2 that this cell division occurs through a process called *mitosis*). By approximately one week after conception, the differentiation of these cells—their specialization for different tasks—has already begun. At this stage, the group of cells, now called the **blastocyst**, consists of an inner mass of cells that will eventually develop into the embryo and the **trophoblast**, an outer layer of cells that later provides nutrition and support for the embryo. *Implantation*, the attachment of the zygote to the uterine wall, takes place about 10 to 14 days after conception. Figure 3.1 illustrates some of the most significant developments during the germinal period.

The Embryonic Period

The **embryonic period** is the period of prenatal development from two to eight weeks after conception. During the embryonic period, the rate of cell differentiation intensifies, support systems for cells form, and organs appear.

This period begins as the blastocyst attaches to the uterine wall. The mass of cells is now called an *embryo*, and three layers of cells form. The embryo's *endoderm* is the inner layer of cells, which will develop into the digestive and respiratory systems. The *ectoderm* is the outermost layer, which will become the nervous system and brain, sensory receptors (ears, nose, and eyes, for example), and skin parts (hair and nails,

germinal period The period of prenatal development that takes place in the first two weeks after conception. It includes the creation of the zygote, continued cell division, and the attachment of the zygote to the uterine wall.

blastocyst The inner layer of cells that develops during the germinal period. These cells later develop into the embryo.

trophoblast The outer layer of cells that develops in the germinal period. These cells provide nutrition and support for the embryo.

embryonic period The period of prenatal development two to eight weeks after conception. During the embryonic period, the rate of cell differentiation intensifies, support systems for the cells form, and organs appear.

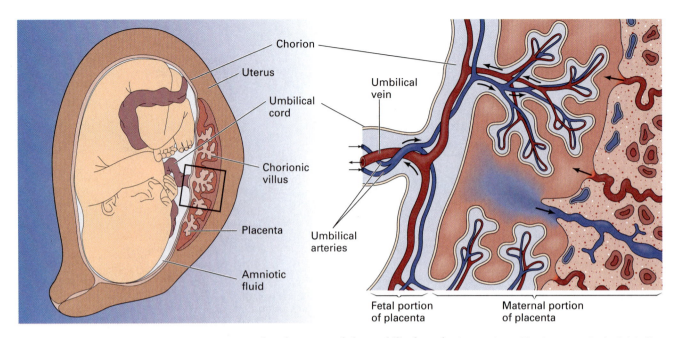

FIGURE 3.2 The Placenta and the Umbilical Cord. The area bound by the square in the left half of the illustration is enlarged in the right half. Arrows indicate the direction of blood flow. Maternal blood flows through the uterine arteries to the spaces housing the placenta, and it returns through the uterine veins to the maternal circulation. Fetal blood flows through the umbilical arteries into the capillaries of the placenta and returns through the umbilical vein to the fetal circulation. The exchange of materials takes place across the layer separating the maternal and fetal blood supplies, so the bloods never come into contact. *What is known about how the placental barrier works and its importance?*

for example). The *mesoderm* is the middle layer, which will become the circulatory system, bones, muscles, excretory system, and reproductive system. Every body part eventually develops from these three layers. The endoderm primarily produces internal body parts, the mesoderm primarily produces parts that surround the internal areas, and the ectoderm primarily produces surface parts.

As the embryo's three layers form, life-support systems for the embryo develop rapidly. These life-support systems include the amnion, the umbilical cord (both of which develop from the fertilized egg, not the mother's body), and the placenta. The **amnion** is like a bag or an envelope and contains a clear fluid in which the developing embryo floats. The amniotic fluid provides an environment that is temperature and humidity controlled, as well as shockproof. The **umbilical cord** contains two arteries and one vein, and connects the baby to the placenta. The **placenta** consists of a disk-shaped group of tissues in which small blood vessels from the mother and the offspring intertwine but do not join.

Figure 3.2 illustrates the placenta, the umbilical cord, and the blood flow in the expectant mother and developing organism. Very small molecules—oxygen, water, salt, food from the mother's blood, as well as carbon dioxide and digestive wastes from the offspring's blood—pass back and forth between the mother and embryo or fetus (Fowden & others, 2008). Large molecules cannot pass through the placental wall; these include red blood cells and harmful substances, such as most bacteria, maternal wastes, and hormones. The mechanisms that govern the transfer of substances across the placental barrier are complex and are still not entirely understood (Klieger, Pollex, & Koren, 2008; Nanovskaya & others, 2008).

By the time most women know they are pregnant, the major organs have begun to form. **Organogenesis** is the name given to the process of organ formation during the first two months of prenatal development. While they are being formed, the organs are especially vulnerable to environmental changes (Mullis & Tonella, 2008). In the third week after conception, the neural tube that eventually becomes the spinal

amnion The life-support system that is like a bag or envelope and contains a clear fluid in which the developing embryo floats.

umbilical cord The life-support system containing two arteries and one vein and connects the baby to the placenta.

placenta The life-support system that consists of a disk-shaped group of tissues in which small blood vessels from the mother and offspring intertwine but do not join.

organogenesis Organ formation that takes place during the first two months of prenatal development.

cord forms. At about 21 days, eyes begin to appear, and at 24 days the cells for the heart begin to differentiate. During the fourth week, the urogenital system becomes apparent, and arm and leg buds emerge. Four chambers of the heart take shape, and blood vessels appear. From the fifth to the eighth week, arms and legs differentiate further; at this time, the face starts to form but still is not very recognizable. The intestinal tract develops and the facial structures fuse. At eight weeks, the developing organism weighs about 1/30 ounce and is just over 1 inch long.

The Fetal Period   The **fetal period** is the prenatal period of development that begins two months after conception and lasts for seven months, on the average. Growth and development continue their dramatic course during this time (DiPietro, 2008).

Three months after conception, the fetus is about 3 inches long and weighs about 3 ounces. It has become active, moving its arms and legs, opening and closing its mouth, and moving its head. The face, forehead, eyelids, nose, and chin are distinguishable, as are the upper arms, lower arms, hands, and lower limbs. The genitals can be identified as male or female. By the end of the fourth month, the fetus has grown to 6 inches in length and weighs 4 to 7 ounces. At this time, a growth spurt occurs in the body's lower parts. For the first time the mother can feel arm and leg movements.

By the end of the fifth month, the fetus is about 12 inches long and weighs close to a pound. Structures of the skin have formed—toenails and fingernails, for example. The fetus is more active, and shows a preference for a particular position in the womb. By the end of the sixth month, the fetus is about 14 inches long and has gained another half pound to a pound. The eyes and eyelids are completely formed, and a fine layer of hair covers the head. A grasping reflex is present, and irregular breathing movements occur.

At about seven months, the fetus for the first time has a chance of surviving outside of the womb—that is, it is *viable*. But even when infants are born in the seventh month, they usually need help breathing. By the end of the seventh month, the fetus is about 16 inches long and now weighs about 3 pounds.

During the last two months of prenatal development, fatty tissues develop, and the functioning of various organ systems—heart and kidneys, for example—steps up. During the eighth and ninth months, the fetus grows longer and gains substantial weight—about another 4 pounds. At birth, the average American baby weighs $7\frac{1}{2}$ pounds and is about 20 inches long.

Figure 3.3 gives an overview of the main events during prenatal development. Notice that instead of describing development in terms of germinal, embryonic, and fetal periods, Figure 3.3 divides prenatal development into equal periods of three months, called *trimesters*. Remember that the three trimesters are not the same as the three prenatal periods we have discussed. The germinal and embryonic periods occur in the first trimester. The fetal period begins toward the end of the first trimester and continues through the second and third trimesters. Viability (the chances of surviving outside the womb) occurs at the beginning of the third trimester.

The Brain   One of the most remarkable aspects of the prenatal period is the development of the brain (Fair & Schlaggar, 2008; Moulson & Nelson, 2008). By the time babies are born, they have approximately 100 billion **neurons**, or nerve cells, which handle information processing at the cellular level in the brain. During prenatal development, neurons spend time moving to the right locations and are starting to become connected. The basic architecture of the human brain is assembled during the first two trimesters of prenatal development. The third trimester of prenatal development and the first two years of postnatal life are characterized by connectivity and functioning of neurons (Moulson & Nelson, 2008).

As the human embryo develops inside its mother's womb, the nervous system begins forming as a long, hollow tube located on the embryo's back. This pear-shaped *neural tube*, which forms at about 18 to 24 days after conception, develops out of the

T he history of man for nine months preceding his birth would, probably, be far more interesting, and contain events of greater moment than all three score and ten years that follow it.

—SAMUEL TAYLOR COLERIDGE
English Poet, Essayist, 19th Century

fetal period The prenatal period of development that begins two months after conception and lasts for seven months, on the average.

neurons Nerve cells, which handle information processing at the cellular level in the brain.

First trimester (first 3 months)			
Prenatal growth	**Conception to 4 weeks** • Is less than 1/10 inch long • Beginning development of spinal cord, nervous system, gastrointestinal system, heart, and lungs • Amniotic sac envelopes the preliminary tissues of entire body • Is called a "zygote"	**8 weeks** • Is just over 1 inch long • Face is forming with rudimentary eyes, ears, mouth, and tooth buds • Arms and legs are moving • Brain is forming • Fetal heartbeat is detectable with ultrasound • Is called an "embryo"	**12 weeks** • Is about 3 inches long and weighs about 1 ounce • Can move arms, legs, fingers, and toes • Fingerprints are present • Can smile, frown, suck, and swallow • Sex is distinguishable • Can urinate • Is called a "fetus"	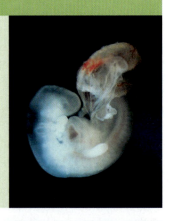

Second trimester (middle 3 months)			
Prenatal growth	**16 weeks** • Is about 6 inches long and weighs about 4 to 7 ounces • Heartbeat is strong • Skin is thin, transparent • Downy hair (lanugo) covers body • Fingernails and toenails are forming • Has coordinated movements; is able to roll over in amniotic fluid	**20 weeks** • Is about 12 inches long and weighs close to 1 pound • Heartbeat is audible with ordinary stethoscope • Sucks thumb • Hiccups • Hair, eyelashes, eyebrows are present	**24 weeks** • Is about 14 inches long and weighs 1 to 1½ pounds • Skin is wrinkled and covered with protective coating (vernix caseosa) • Eyes are open • Waste matter is collected in bowel • Has strong grip	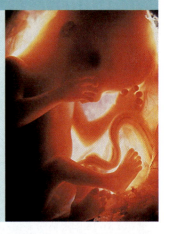

Third trimester (last 3 months)			
Prenatal growth	**28 weeks** • Is about 16 inches long and weighs about 3 pounds • Is adding body fat • Is very active • Rudimentary breathing movements are present	**32 weeks** • Is 16½ to 18 inches long and weighs 4 to 5 pounds • Has periods of sleep and wakefulness • Responds to sounds • May assume the birth position • Bones of head are soft and flexible • Iron is being stored in liver	**36 to 38 weeks** • Is 19 to 20 inches long and weighs 6 to 7½ pounds • Skin is less wrinkled • Vernix caseosa is thick • Lanugo is mostly gone • Is less active • Is gaining immunities from mother	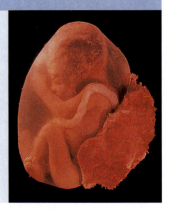

FIGURE 3.3 The Three Trimesters of Prenatal Development. Both the germinal and embryonic periods occur during the first trimester. The end of the first trimester as well as the second and third trimesters are part of the fetal period.

ectoderm. The tube closes at the top and bottom ends at about 24 days after conception. Figure 3.4 shows that the nervous system still has a tubular appearance six weeks after conception.

Two birth defects related to a failure of the neural tube to close are anencephaly and spina bifida. The highest regions of the brain fail to develop when fetuses have anencephaly and they die in the womb, during childbirth, or shortly after birth (Koukoura & others, 2006). Spina bifida results in varying degrees of paralysis of the lower limbs (Ghi & others, 2006). Individuals with spina bifida usually need assistive devices such as crutches, braces, or wheelchairs. A strategy that can help to prevent neural tube defects is for women to take adequate amounts of the B vitamin folic acid, a topic we will further discuss later in the chapter (Johnson, 2008; Ryan-Harshman & Aldoori, 2008).

In a normal pregnancy, once the neural tube has closed, a massive proliferation of new immature neurons begins to takes place about the fifth prenatal week and continues throughout the remainder of the prenatal period. The generation of new neurons is called *neurogenesis.* At the peak of neurogenesis, it is estimated that as many as 200,000 neurons are being generated every minute (Brown, Keynes, & Lumsden, 2001).

At approximately 6 to 24 weeks after conception, *neuronal migration* occurs (Couperus & Nelson, 2006). This involves cells moving outward from their point of origin to their appropriate locations and creating the different levels, structures, and regions of the brain (Hepper, 2007). Once a cell has migrated to its target destination, it must mature and develop a more complex structure.

At about 23 prenatal weeks, connections between neurons begin to occur, a process that continues postnatally (Moulson & Nelson, 2008). We will have much more to say about the structure of neurons, their connectivity, and the development of the brain in infancy in Chapter 4.

FIGURE 3.4 Early Formation of the Nervous System. The photograph shows the primitive, tubular appearance of the nervous system at six weeks in the human embryo.

Teratology and Hazards to Prenatal Development

For Alex, the baby discussed at the opening of this chapter, the course of prenatal development went smoothly. His mother's womb protected him as he developed. Despite this protection, the environment can affect the embryo or fetus in many well-documented ways.

General Principles A **teratogen** is any agent that can potentially cause a birth defect or negatively alter cognitive and behavioral outcomes. (The word comes from the Greek word *tera*, meaning "monster".) The field of study that investigates the causes of birth defects is called *teratology.* Teratogens include drugs, incompatible blood types, environmental pollutants, infectious diseases, nutritional deficiencies, maternal stress, advanced maternal and paternal age, and environmental pollutants. In fact, thousands of babies are born deformed or mentally retarded every year as a result of events that occurred in the mother's life as early as one or two months *before* conception. As we further discuss teratogens, you will see that factors related to the father also can influence prenatal development.

So many teratogens exist that practically every fetus is exposed to at least some teratogens. For this reason, it is difficult to determine which teratogen causes which problem. In addition, it may take a long time for the effects of a teratogen to show up. Only about half of all potential effects appear at birth.

The dose, genetic susceptibility, and the time of exposure to a particular teratogen influence both the severity of the damage to an embryo or fetus and the type of defect:

- *Dose.* The dose effect is rather obvious—the greater the dose of an agent, such as a drug, the greater the effect.
- *Genetic susceptibility.* The type or severity of abnormalities caused by a teratogen is linked to the genotype of the pregnant woman and the genotype of the embryo or fetus (Lidral & Murray, 2005). For example, how a mother metabolizes a particular drug can influence the degree to which the drug effects are transmitted to the embryo or fetus. Differences in placental membranes and placental transport also affect exposure. The extent to which an embryo or fetus is vulnerable to a teratogen may also depend on its genotype (Graham & Shaw, 2006).

These individuals are members of the Spina Bifida Association of Greater New Orleans. The association is made up of parents, family members, children, and adults with spina bifida, and health professionals who provide care for individuals born with spina bifida and their families.

teratogen From the Greek word *tera,* meaning "monster." A teratogen is any agent that potentially can cause a birth defect or negatively alter cognitive and behavioral outcomes. The field of study that investigates the causes of birth defects is called teratology.

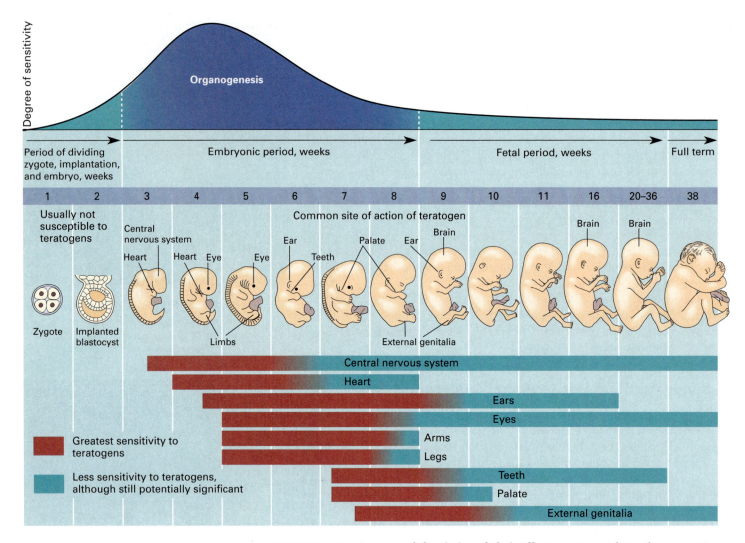

FIGURE 3.5 Teratogens and the Timing of Their Effects on Prenatal Development. The danger of structural defects caused by teratogens is greatest early in embryonic development. The period of organogenesis (red color) lasts for about six weeks. Later assaults by teratogens (blue-green color) mainly occur in the fetal period and instead of causing structural damage are more likely to stunt growth or cause problems of organ function.

- *Time of exposure.* Teratogens do more damage when they occur at some points in development than at others (Nava-Ocampo & Koren, 2007; Rifas-Shiman & others, 2006). Damage during the germinal period may even prevent implantation. In general, the embryonic period is more vulnerable than the fetal period.

Figure 3.5 summarizes additional information about the effects of time of exposure to a teratogen. The probability of a structural defect is greatest early in the embryonic period, when organs are being formed (Hill, 2007; Lu & Lu, 2008). Each body structure has its own critical period of formation. Recall from Chapter 1 that a *critical period* is a fixed time period very early in development during which certain experiences or events can have a long-lasting effect on development. The critical period for the nervous system (week 3) is earlier than for arms and legs (weeks 4 and 5).

After organogenesis is complete, teratogens are less likely to cause anatomical defects. Instead, exposure during the fetal period is more likely instead to stunt growth or to create problems in the way organs function. To examine some key teratogens and their effects, let's begin with drugs.

Prescription and Nonprescription Drugs   Many U.S. women are given prescriptions for drugs while they are pregnant—especially antibiotics, analgesics, and asthma medications (Riley & others, 2005). Prescription as well as nonprescription drugs, however, may have effects on the embryo or fetus that the women never imagined (Brent, 2008).

Prescription drugs that can function as teratogens include antibiotics, such as streptomycin and tetracycline; some antidepressants; certain hormones, such as progestin and synthetic estrogen; and Accutane (which often is prescribed for acne) (Garcia-Bournissen & others, 2008). Nonprescription drugs that can be harmful include diet pills and aspirin (Norgard & others, 2005). A recent research review indicated that low doses of aspirin pose no harm for the fetus but that high doses can contribute to maternal and fetal bleeding (James, Brancazio, & Price, 2008).

Psychoactive Drugs   *Psychoactive drugs* are drugs that act on the nervous system to alter states of consciousness, modify perceptions, and change moods. Examples include caffeine, alcohol, and nicotine, as well as illegal drugs such as cocaine, marijuana, and heroin (Alvik & others, 2006).

Caffeine   People often consume caffeine by drinking coffee, tea, or colas, or by eating chocolate (Bech & others, 2007). A review of studies on caffeine consumption during pregnancy concluded that a small increase in the risks for spontaneous abortion and low birth weight occurs for pregnant women consuming more than 150 milligrams of caffeine (approximately two cups of brewed coffee or two to three 12-ounce cans of cola) per day (Fernandez & others, 1998). (Low birth weight is linked to a variety of health and developmental problems, which we will discuss later in the chapter.) A recent study revealed that pregnant women who consumed 200 or more milligrams of caffeine a day had an increased risk of miscarriage (Weng, Odouli, & Li, 2008). Taking into account such results, the Food and Drug Administration recommends that pregnant women either not consume caffeine or consume it only sparingly.

Alcohol   Heavy drinking by pregnant women can be devastating to their offspring (Borowski & Niebyl, 2008). **Fetal alcohol spectrum disorders (FASD)** are a cluster of abnormalities and problems that appear in the offspring of mothers who drink alcohol heavily during pregnancy (Olson, King, & Jirkowic, 2008). The abnormalities include facial deformities and defective limbs, face, and heart. Some children with FASD have these body malformations but others don't. Most children with FASD are characterized by learning problems, and many are below average in intelligence with some being mentally retarded (Caley & others, 2008; Cuzon & others, 2008). A recent study revealed that children with FASD have impaired memory development (Pei & others, 2008). And another recent study revealed that as young adults individuals diagnosed with FASD in infancy were characterized by intellectual disability, limited occupational options, and dependent living (Spohr, Williams, & Steinhausen, 2007). Although women who drink heavily during pregnancy are at a higher risk of having a child with FASD, not all pregnant heavy drinkers have children with FASD.

Drinking alcohol during pregnancy, however, can have serious effects on offspring even when they are not afflicted with FASD (Pollard, 2007; Sayal & others, 2007). Serious malformations such as those produced by FASD are not found in infants born to mothers who are moderate drinkers, but even moderate drinking can have an effect on the offspring. In one study, children whose mothers drank moderately (one to two drinks a day) during pregnancy were less attentive and alert, even at 4 years of age (Streissguth & others, 1984). Also, one study found that pregnant women who had three or more drinks a day faced an increased risk of preterm birth (Parazzini & others, 2003). And in a longitudinal study, the more alcohol mothers drank in the first trimester of pregnancy, the more their children at 14 years of age fell behind on growth markers such as weight, height, and head size (Day & others, 2002).

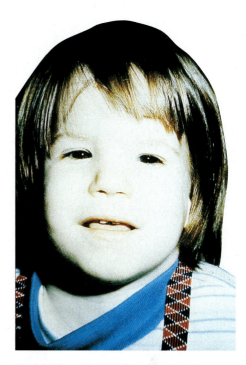

Fetal alcohol spectrum disorders (FASD) are characterized by a number of physical abnormalities and learning problems. Notice the wide-set eyes, flat cheekbones, and thin upper lip in this child with FASD.

fetal alcohol spectrum disorders (FASD) A cluster of abnormalities that appears in the offspring of mothers who drink alcohol heavily during pregnancy.

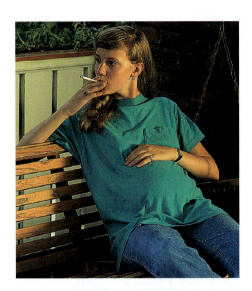

What are some links between expectant mothers' cigarette smoking and outcomes for their offspring?

What are some guidelines for alcohol use during pregnancy? Even drinking just one or two servings of beer or wine or one serving of hard liquor a few days a week can have negative effects on the fetus, although it is generally agreed that this level of alcohol use will not cause fetal alcohol syndrome. The U.S. Surgeon General recommends that *no* alcohol be consumed during pregnancy. And recent research suggests that it may not be wise to consume alcohol at the time of conception. One study revealed that intakes of alcohol by both men and women during the weeks of conception increased the risk of early pregnancy loss (Henriksen & others, 2004). And a recent study revealed that although both African American and non-Latino White women lowered their alcohol intake when they became pregnant, non-Latino White women lowered their alcohol intake more than African American women (Morris & others, 2008).

Nicotine   Cigarette smoking by pregnant women can also adversely influence prenatal development, birth, and postnatal development (Cooper & Moley, 2008; Shea & others, 2008). Preterm births and low birth weights, fetal and neonatal deaths, respiratory problems and sudden infant death syndrome (SIDS, also known as crib death) are all more common among the offspring of mothers who smoked during pregnancy (Roza & others, 2007). One study linked prenatal exposure to heavy smoking to nicotine withdrawal symptoms in newborns (Godding & others, 2004). A recent study also revealed that children whose mothers smoked during pregnancy were more likely to have a higher level of inattention and hyperactivity than children whose mothers did not smoke in pregnancy (Obel & others, 2008). Other research has found that prenatal exposure to cigarette smoking during pregnancy is related to increased incidence of attention deficit hyperactivity disorder at 5 to 16 years of age (Thapar & others, 2003). A recent research review also indicated that environmental tobacco smoke was linked to increased risk of low birth weight in offspring (Leonardi-Bee & others, 2008).

Intervention programs designed to help pregnant women stop smoking can reduce some of smoking's negative effects, especially by raising birth weights (Barron & others, 2007). A recent study revealed that women who quit smoking during pregnancy had offspring with higher birth weight than their counterparts who continued smoking (Jaddoe & others, 2008).

Cocaine   Does cocaine use during pregnancy harm the developing embryo and fetus? The most consistent finding is that cocaine exposure during prenatal development is associated with reduced birth weight, length, and head circumference (Smith & others, 2001). Also, in other studies, prenatal cocaine exposure has been linked to lower arousal, less effective self-regulation, higher excitability, and lower quality of reflexes at 1 month of age (Lester & others, 2002); to impaired motor development in the second year of life (Richardson, Goldschmidt, & Willford, 2008); to slower growth rate through 10 years of age (Richardson, Goldschmidt, & Larkby, 2008); to impaired language development and information processing (Beeghly & others, 2006; Lewis & others, 2007), including attention deficits in preschool children (Noland & others, 2005) and elementary school children (Accornero & others, 2007); and to learning disabilities at age 7 (Morrow & others, 2006).

Some researchers argue that these findings should be interpreted cautiously (Accornero & others, 2006). Why? Because other factors in the lives of pregnant women who use cocaine (such as poverty, malnutrition, and other substance abuse) often cannot be ruled out as possible contributors to the problems found in their children (Hurt & others, 2005). For example, cocaine users are more likely than nonusers to smoke cigarettes, use marijuana, drink alcohol, and take amphetamines.

Despite these cautions, the weight of research evidence indicates that children born to mothers who use cocaine are likely to have neurological and cognitive deficits (Field, 2007; Forrester & Mertz, 2007; Mayes, 2003; Shankaran & others, 2007). Cocaine use by pregnant women is not recommended.

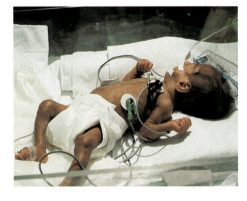

This baby was exposed to cocaine prenatally. What are some of the possible effects on development of being exposed to cocaine prenatally?

Methamphetamine Methamphetamine, like cocaine, is a stimulant, speeding up an individual's nervous system. Babies born to mothers who use methamphetamine, or "meth," during pregnancy are at risk for a number of problems, including high infant mortality, low birth weight, and developmental and behavioral problems (Forrester & Merz, 2007). A recent study revealed that meth exposure during prenatal development was linked to decreased arousal, increased stress, and poor movement quality in newborns (Smith & others, 2008). Meth use during pregnancy is increasing, and some experts conclude that it has become a greater problem in the United States than cocaine use (Elliott, 2004). A recent survey revealed that 5 percent of U.S. women used methamphetamine during their pregnancy (Arria & others, 2006).

Marijuana An increasing number of studies find that marijuana use by pregnant women has negative outcomes for offspring (de Moraes Barros & others, 2006; Huizink & Mulder, 2006; Williams & Ross, 2007). A research review concluded that marijuana use by pregnant women is related to deficits in memory and information processing in their offspring (Kalant, 2004). For example, in a longitudinal study, prenatal marijuana exposure was related to learning and memory difficulties at age 11 (Richardson & others, 2002). A recent study also revealed that prenatal marijuana exposure was linked to lower intelligence in children (Goldschmidt & others, 2008). Another study revealed that prenatal marijuana exposure was linked with depressive symptoms at 10 years of age (Gray & others, 2005). Further, a recent study indicated that prenatal exposure to marijuana was linked to marijuana use at 14 years of age (Day, Goldschmidt, & Thomas, 2006). In sum, marijuana use is not recommended for pregnant women.

Heroin It is well documented that infants whose mothers are addicted to heroin show several behavioral difficulties (Yang & others, 2006). The difficulties include withdrawal symptoms, such as tremors, irritability, abnormal crying, disturbed sleep, and impaired motor control. Many still show behavioral problems at their first birthday, and attention deficits may appear later in development. The most common treatment for heroin addiction methadone, is associated with very severe withdrawal symptoms in newborns (Binder & others, 2008). A recent study revealed that when compared with pregnant women who entered methadone treatment late (less than six months prior to birth), continuous methadone treatment during pregnancy was linked to improved neonatal outcomes (Burns & others, 2007).

Incompatible Blood Types Incompatibility between the mother's and father's blood type poses another risk to prenatal development. Blood types are created by differences in the surface structure of red blood cells. One type of difference in the surface of red blood cells creates the familiar blood groups—A, B, O, and AB. A second difference creates what is called Rh-positive and Rh-negative blood. If a surface marker, called the *Rh factor*, is present in an individual's red blood cells, the person is said to be Rh-positive; if the Rh marker is not present, the person is said to be Rh-negative. If a pregnant woman is Rh-negative and her partner is Rh-positive, the fetus may be Rh-positive. If the fetus' blood is Rh-positive and the mother's is Rh-negative, the mother's immune system may produce antibodies that will attack the fetus. This can result in any number of problems, including miscarriage or stillbirth, anemia, jaundice, heart defects, brain damage, or death soon after birth (Moise, 2005).

Generally, the first Rh-positive baby of an Rh-negative mother is not at risk, but with each subsequent pregnancy the risk increases. A vaccine (RhoGAM) may be given to the mother within three days of the first child's birth to prevent her body from making antibodies that will attack any future Rh-positive fetuses in subsequent pregnancies. Also, babies affected by Rh incompatibility can be given blood transfusions before or right after birth (Flegal, 2007).

An explosion at the Chernobyl nuclear power plant in the Ukraine produced radioactive contamination that spread to surrounding areas. Thousands of infants were born with health problems and deformities as a result of the nuclear contamination, including this boy whose arm did not form. *Other than radioactive contamination, what are some other types of environmental hazards to prenatal development?*

Environmental Hazards   Many aspects of our modern industrial world can endanger the embryo or fetus (Hertz-Picciotto & others, 2008; O'Connor & Roy, 2008). Some specific hazards to the embryo or fetus that are worth a closer look include radiation, toxic wastes, and other chemical pollutants (Orecchia, Lucignani, & Tosi, 2008; Raabe & Muller, 2008).

Radiation can cause a gene mutation (an abrupt, permanent change in DNA). Chromosomal abnormalities are elevated among the offspring of fathers exposed to high levels of radiation in their occupations (Schrag & Dixon, 1985). X-ray radiation also can affect the developing embryo or fetus, especially in the first several weeks after conception, when women do not yet know they are pregnant (Urbano & Tait, 2004). Possible effects include microencephaly (an abnormally small brain), mental retardation, and leukemia. Women and their physicians should weigh the risk of an X-ray when an actual or potential pregnancy is involved (Hurwitz & others, 2006; Menias & others, 2007). However, a routine diagnostic X-ray of a body area other than the abdomen, with the woman's abdomen protected by a lead apron, is generally considered safe (Loughlin, 2007).

Environmental pollutants and toxic wastes are also sources of danger to unborn children (Canfield & Jusko, 2008). Among the dangerous pollutants are carbon monoxide, mercury, and lead, as well as certain fertilizers and pesticides. Exposure to lead can come from lead-based paint that flakes off the walls of a home or from leaded gasoline emitted by cars on a nearby busy highway. Early exposure to lead can affect children's mental development (Yang & others, 2003). For example, in one study, 2-year-olds who prenatally had high levels of lead in their umbilical-cord blood performed poorly on a test of mental development (Bellinger & others, 1987). For example, a recent study revealed that a moderately high maternal lead level in the first trimester of pregnancy was linked to lower scores on an index of mental development in infancy (Hu & others, 2007).

Maternal Diseases   Maternal diseases and infections can produce defects in offspring by crossing the placental barrier, or they can cause damage during birth (Avgil & Ornoy, 2006). Rubella (German measles) is one disease that can cause prenatal defects. The greatest damage occurs if a mother contracts rubella in the third or fourth week of pregnancy, although infection during the second month is also damaging (Kobayashi & others, 2005). A rubella outbreak in 1964–1965 resulted in 30,000 prenatal and neonatal (newborn) deaths, and more than 20,000 affected infants were born with malformations, including mental retardation, blindness, deafness, and heart problems. Elaborate preventive efforts ensure that rubella will never again have such disastrous effects. A vaccine that prevents German measles is now routinely administered to children, and women who plan to have children should have a blood test before they become pregnant to determine if they are immune to the disease (Dontigny & others, 2008).

Syphilis (a sexually transmitted infection) is more damaging later in prenatal development—four months or more after conception. Rather than affecting organogenesis, as rubella does, syphilis damages organs after they have formed. Damage includes eye lesions, which can cause blindness, and skin lesions. When syphilis is present at birth, problems can develop in the central nervous system and gastrointestinal tract (Johnson, Erbelding, & Ghanem, 2007). Most states require that pregnant women be given a blood test to detect the presence of syphilis.

Another infection that has received widespread attention recently is genital herpes. Newborns contract this virus when they are delivered through the birth canal of a mother with genital herpes (Hollier & Wendel, 2008; Shapiro-Mendoza & others, 2008). About one-third of babies delivered through an infected birth canal die; another one-fourth become brain damaged. If an active case of genital herpes is detected in a pregnant woman close to her delivery date, a cesarean section can be performed (in which the infant is delivered through an incision in the mother's abdomen) to keep the virus from infecting the newborn (Baker, 2007).

AIDS is a sexually transmitted infection that is caused by the human immunodeficiency virus (HIV), which destroys the body's immune system. A mother can infect her offspring with AIDS in three ways: (1) during gestation across the placenta, (2) during delivery through contact with maternal blood or fluids, and (3) postpartum (after birth) through breast feeding. The transmission of AIDS through breast feeding is especially a problem in many developing countries (Lunney & others, 2008; UNICEF, 2008). Babies born to HIV-infected mothers can be (1) infected and symptomatic (show AIDS symptoms), (2) infected but asymptomatic (not show AIDS symptoms), or (3) not infected at all. An infant who is infected and asymptomatic may still develop HIV symptoms up until 15 months of age.

In the early 1990s, before preventive treatments were available, 1,000 to 2,000 infants were born with HIV infection each year in the United States. Since then, transmission of AIDS from mothers to the fetuses has been reduced dramatically (Boer & others, 2007; Boeving & Forsyth, 2008). Only about one-third as many cases of newborns with AIDS appear today as in the early 1990s. This decline is due to the increase in counseling and voluntary testing of pregnant women for HIV and to the use of zidovudine (AZT) by infected women during pregnancy, and for the infant after birth (Volmink & others, 2007). In many poor countries, however, treatment with AZT is limited, and HIV infection of infants remains a major problem (Chersich & others, 2008; Richardson & others, 2008).

The more widespread disease of diabetes, characterized by high levels of sugar in the blood, also affects offspring (Casson, 2006). A recent research review concluded that the offspring of diabetic mothers are at risk for metabolic disease (Doblado & Moley, 2007). And one study revealed that both chronic (long-standing) and gestational (onset or first recognition during pregnancy) diabetes were significant risks for cesarean delivery and preterm birth (Rosenberg & others, 2005). Women who have gestational diabetes also may deliver very large infants (weighing 10 pounds or more), and the infants may be at risk for diabetes themselves (Langer, 2008a).

Other Parental Factors   So far we have discussed a number of drugs, environmental hazards, maternal diseases, and incompatible blood types that can harm the embryo or fetus. Here we will explore other characteristics of the mother and father that can affect prenatal and child development: nutrition, age, and emotional states and stress.

Maternal Diet and Nutrition   A developing embryo or fetus depends completely on its mother for nutrition, which comes from the mother's blood (Derbyshire, 2007a, b). The nutritional status of the embryo or fetus is determined by the mother's total caloric intake, and her intake of proteins, vitamins, and minerals. Children born to malnourished mothers are more likely than other children to be malformed.

Being overweight before and during pregnancy can also put the embryo or fetus at risk, and an increasing number of pregnant women in the United States are overweight (Langer, 2008b; Reece, 2008). Researchers have found that obese women have a significant risk of fetal death (Nohr & others, 2005; Vyas & others, 2008). Recent studies indicate that pre-pregnancy maternal obesity doubles the risk of stillbirth and neonatal death, and is linked with defects in the central nervous system of offspring (Anderson & others, 2005; Frederick & others, 2007). Further, a recent analysis proposed that overnutrition in fetal life (due to overeating on the part of the pregnant woman) results in a series of neuroendocrine changes that in turn program the development of fat cells and the appetite regulation system (McMillen & others, 2008). In this analysis, it was

Because the fetus depends entirely on its mother for nutrition, it is important for the pregnant woman to have good nutritional habits. In Kenya, this government clinic provides pregnant women with information about how their diet can influence the health of their fetus and offspring. *What might the information about diet be like?*

predicted that such early fetal programming is likely linked to being overweight in childhood and adolescence.

One aspect of maternal nutrition that is important for normal prenatal development is folic acid, a B-complex vitamin (Goh & Koren, 2008). As we indicated earlier in the chapter, a lack of folic acid is linked with neural tube defects in offspring, such as spina bifida (Ryan-Harshman & Aldoori, 2008). A recent study of more than 34,000 pregnant women revealed that taking folic acid either alone or as part of a multivitamin for at least one year prior to conceiving was linked with a 70 percent lower risk of delivering from 20 to 28 weeks and a 50 percent lower risk of delivering between 28 to 32 weeks (Bukowski & others, 2008). Another study found that maternal use of folic acid and iron during the first month of pregnancy was associated with a lower risk of Down syndrome in offspring, although more studies are needed to confirm this connection (Czeizel & Puho, 2005). The U.S. Public Health Service recommends that pregnant women consume a minimum of 400 micrograms of folic acid per day (about twice the amount the average woman gets in one day). Orange juice and spinach are examples of foods rich in folic acid.

Eating fish is often recommended as part of a healthy diet, but pollution has made many fish a risky choice for pregnant women. Some fish contain high levels of mercury, which is released into the air both naturally and by industrial pollution (Fitzgerald & others, 2004). When mercury falls into the water, it can become toxic and accumulate in large fish, such as shark, swordfish, king mackerel, and some species of large tuna. Mercury is easily transferred across the placenta, and the embryo's developing brain and nervous system are highly sensitive to the metal (Gliori & others, 2006). Researchers have found that prenatal mercury exposure is linked to adverse outcomes, including miscarriage, preterm birth, and lower intelligence (Axelrad & others, 2007; Xue & others, 2007). The U.S. Food and Drug Administration (2004) gave the following recommendations for women of childbearing age and young children: Don't eat shark, swordfish, king mackerel or tilefish; eat up to 12 ounces (two average meals) a week of fish and shellfish that are lower in mercury, such as shrimp, canned light tuna, salmon, pollock, and catfish.

PCB-polluted fish also pose a risk to prenatal development (Korrick & Sagiv, 2008). PCBs (polychlorinated biphenyls) are chemicals that were used in manufacturing until they were banned in the 1970s in the United States, but they are still present in landfills, sediments, and wildlife. One study kept track of the extent to which pregnant women ate PCB-polluted fish from Lake Michigan and subsequently observed their children as newborns, young children, and at 11 years of age (Jacobson & others, 1984; Jacobson & Jacobson, 2002, 2003). The women who had eaten more PCB-polluted fish were more likely to have smaller, preterm infants who were more likely to react slowly to stimuli. As preschool children, their exposure to PCBs was linked with less effective short-term memory, and at age 11 with lower verbal intelligence and reading comprehension.

Maternal Age When possible harmful effects on the fetus and infant are considered, two maternal ages are of special interest: adolescence and 35 years and older (Chen & others, 2007a; Maconochie & others, 2007). One recent study revealed that the rate of stillbirth was elevated for adolescent girls and women 35 years and older (Bateman & Simpson, 2006).

The mortality rate of infants born to adolescent mothers is double that of infants born to mothers in their twenties. Although this high rate probably reflects the immaturity of the mother's reproductive system, poor nutrition, lack of prenatal care, and low socioeconomic status may also play a role (Lenders, McElrath, & Scholl, 2000). Prenatal care decreases the probability that a child born to an adolescent girl will have physical problems. However, adolescents are the least likely of women in all age groups to obtain prenatal assistance from clinics, pediatricians, and health services.

What are some of the risks for infants born to adolescent mothers?

Maternal age is also linked to the risk that a child will have Down syndrome (Soergel & others, 2006). As discussed in Chapter 2, an individual with *Down syndrome* has distinctive facial characteristics, short limbs, and retardation of motor and mental abilities. A baby with Down syndrome rarely is born to a mother 16 to 34 years of age. However, when the mother reaches 40 years of age, the probability is slightly over 1 in 100 that a baby born to her will have Down syndrome, and by age 50 it is almost 1 in 10.

When mothers are 35 years and older, risks also increase for low birth weight, for preterm delivery, and for fetal death (Delbaere & others, 2007; Fretts, Zera, & Heffner, 2008). One study found that low birth weight delivery increased 11 percent and preterm delivery increased 14 percent in women 35 years and older (Tough & others, 2002). In another study, fetal death was low for women 30 to 34 years of age but increased progressively for women 35 to 39 and 40 to 44 years of age (Canterino & others, 2004).

We still have much to learn about the role of the mother's age in pregnancy and childbirth (Montan, 2007). As women remain active, exercise regularly, and are careful about their nutrition, their reproductive systems may remain healthier at older ages than was thought possible in the past. For example, in a recent study, two-thirds of the pregnancies of women 45 years and older in Australia were free of complications (Callaway, Lust, & McIntrye, 2005).

Emotional States and Stress When a pregnant woman experiences intense fears, anxieties, and other emotions or negative mood states, physiological changes occur that may affect her fetus (Glynn & others, 2008; Talge & others, 2007). Maternal stress may increase the level of corticotropin-releasing hormone (CRH), a precursor of the stress hormone cortisol, early in pregnancy (Nakamura, Sheps, & Clara Arck, 2008). Elevated levels of CRH and cortisol in the fetus have been linked to premature delivery in infants (Field, 2007). A mother's stress may also influence the fetus indirectly by increasing the likelihood that the mother will engage in unhealthy behaviors, such as taking drugs and engaging in poor prenatal care.

The mother's emotional state during pregnancy can influence the birth process, too. An emotionally distraught mother might have irregular contractions and a more difficult labor, which can cause irregularities in the supply of oxygen to the fetus or other problems after birth. Babies born after extended labor also may adjust more slowly to their world and be more irritable.

High maternal anxiety and stress during pregnancy can have long-term consequences for the offspring. A recent research review indicated that pregnant women with high levels of stress are at increased risk for having a child with emotional or cognitive problems, attention deficit hyperactivity disorder (ADHD), and language delay (Talge & others, 2007). In this review, it was concluded that the type of stress that is most detrimental is still unknown, but research suggests stress in the woman's relationship with a partner is one candidate.

Positive emotional states also appear to make a difference to the fetus. Pregnant women who are optimistic thinkers have less adverse outcomes than pregnant women who are pessimistic thinkers (Loebel & Yali, 1999). Optimists are more likely to believe that they have control over the outcomes of their pregnancies.

Paternal Factors So far, we have discussed how characteristics of the mother—such as drug use, disease, diet and nutrition, age, and emotional states—can influence prenatal development and the development of the child. Might there also be some paternal risk factors? Indeed, there are several. Men's exposure to lead, radiation, certain pesticides, and petrochemicals may cause abnormalities in sperm that lead to miscarriage or diseases, such as childhood cancer (Fear & others, 2007). When fathers have a diet low in vitamin C, their offspring have a higher risk of birth defects and cancer (Fraga & others, 1991). Also, it has been speculated that, when fathers take cocaine, it may attach itself to sperm and cause birth defects, but the evidence

In one study, in China, the longer the fathers smoked, the greater the risk that their children would develop cancer (Ji & others, 1997). *What are some other paternal factors that can influence the development of the fetus and the child?*

for this effect is not yet strong. In one study, long-term use of cocaine by men was related to low sperm count, low motility, and a higher number of abnormally formed sperm (Bracken & others, 1990). Cocaine-related infertility appears to be reversible if users stop taking the drug for at least one year.

The father's smoking during the mother's pregnancy also can cause problems for the offspring. In one investigation, the newborns of fathers who smoked around their wives during the pregnancy were 4 ounces lighter at birth for each pack of cigarettes smoked per day than were the newborns whose fathers did not smoke during their wives' pregnancy (Rubin & others, 1986). In another study, in China, the longer the fathers smoked, the stronger the risk that their children would develop cancer (Ji & others, 1997). In yet another study, heavy paternal smoking was associated with the risk of early pregnancy loss (Venners & others, 2004).

The father's age also makes a difference (Maconochie & others, 2007; Yang & others, 2007). About 5 percent of children with Down syndrome have older fathers. The offspring of older fathers also face increased risk for other birth defects, including dwarfism and Marfan syndrome, which involves head and limb deformities.

There are also risks to offspring when both the mother and father are older (Dunson, Baird, & Colombo, 2004). In one study, the risk of an adverse pregnancy outcome, such as miscarriage, rose considerably when the woman was 35 years or older and the man was 40 years of age or older (de la Rochebrochard & Thonneau, 2002).

Prenatal Care

Although prenatal care varies enormously, it usually involves a defined schedule of visits for medical care, which typically include screening for manageable conditions and treatable diseases that can affect the baby or the mother (Mennuti, 2008). In addition to medical care, prenatal programs often include comprehensive educational, social, and nutritional services (Moos, 2006).

The education provided in prenatal care varies during the course of pregnancy. Those in the early stages of pregnancy, as well as couples who are anticipating a pregnancy, may participate in early prenatal classes (Davidson, London, & Ladewig, 2008). In addition to providing information on dangers to the fetus, early prenatal classes often discuss the development of the embryo and the fetus; sexuality during pregnancy; choices about the birth setting and care providers; nutrition, rest, and exercise; common discomforts of pregnancy and relief measures; psychological changes in the expectant mother and her partner; and factors that increase the risk of preterm labor and possible symptoms of preterm labor. Early classes also may include information about the advantages and disadvantages of breast feeding and bottle feeding (50 to 80 percent of expectant mothers decide how they will feed their infant prior to the sixth month of pregnancy). During the second or third trimester of pregnancy, prenatal classes focus on preparing for the birth, infant care and feeding, choices about birth, and postpartum self-care.

Good prenatal care involves exercising regularly. Exercise during pregnancy helps prevent constipation, conditions the body, and is associated with a more positive mental state (Rafla, Nair, & Kumar, 2008). However, it is important to remember not to overdo it. Pregnant women should always consult their physician before starting an exercise program.

Might the mother's exercise during pregnancy be related to the development of the fetus and the birth of the child? Few studies have been conducted on this topic, but several studies indicate that moderate exercise three to four times a week was linked to healthy weight gain in the fetus and a normal birth weight, whereas the risk of low birth weight increased for women who exercised intensely most days of the week and for women who exercised less than twice a week or not at all (Campbell & Mottola, 2001). Two recent studies confirmed that physical exercise during pregnancy

Many husbands, or coaches, take childbirth classes with their wives or friends.

is not linked to an increase in preterm birth rate (Hegaard & others, 2008; Juhl & others, 2008). In one of the studies, compared with sedentary pregnant women, women who engaged in light leisure time physical activity had a 24 percent reduced likelihood of preterm delivery, and those who participated in moderate to heavy leisure time physical activity had a 66 percent reduced risk of preterm delivery (Hegaard & others, 2008).

An innovative program that is rapidly expanding in the United States is CenteringPregnancy (Massey, Rising, & Ickovics, 2006; Moos, 2006). This program is relationship-centered and provides complete prenatal care in a group setting. CenteringPregnancy replaces traditional 15-minute physician visits with 90-minute peer group support settings and self-examination led by a physician or certified nurse-midwife. Groups of up to 10 women (and often their partners) meet regularly beginning at 12 to 16 weeks of pregnancy. The sessions emphasize empowering women to play an active role in experiencing a positive pregnancy.

A CenteringPregnancy program. This rapidly increasing program alters routine prenatal care by bringing women out of exam rooms and into relationship-oriented groups.

Some prenatal programs for parents focus on home visitation. Research evaluations indicate that the most successful home visitation program is the Nurse Family Partnership created by David Olds and his colleagues (2004, 2007). The Nurse Family Partnership involves home visits by trained nurses beginning in the second or third trimester of prenatal development. The extensive program consists of approximately 50 home visits from the prenatal period through 2 years of age. The home visits focus on the mother's health, access to health care, parenting, and improving the mother's life by providing her guidance in education, work and relationships. Research revealed that the Nurse Family Partnership has numerous positive outcomes, including fewer pregnancies, better work circumstances, and stability in relationship partners for the mother, and improved academic success and social development for the child (Olds & others, 2004, 2007).

Does prenatal care matter? Information about pregnancy, labor, delivery, and caring for the newborn can be especially valuable for first-time mothers (Flynn, Budd, & Modelski, 2008). Prenatal care is also very important for women in poverty because it links them with other social services (Hogan & others, 2007; Hueston, Geesey, & Diaz, 2008). The legacy of prenatal care continues after the birth because women who experience this type of care are more likely to get preventive care for their infants (Bates & others, 1994).

Research contrasting the experiences of mothers who had prenatal care and those who did not supports the significance of prenatal care (Chen & others, 2007b; Daniels, Noe, & Mayberry, 2006). One study found that U.S. women who had no prenatal care were far more likely than their counterparts who received prenatal care to have infants with low birth weight, increased mortality, and a number of other physical problems (Herbst & others, 2003). In other recent studies, low birth weight and preterm deliveries were common among U.S. mothers who received no prenatal care, and the absence of prenatal care increased the risk for preterm birth by almost threefold in both non-Latino White and African American women (Stringer & others, 2005).

Inadequate prenatal care may help explain a disturbing fact: Rates of infant mortality and low birth weight indicate that many other nations have healthier babies than the United States (Thornton & others, 2006). In many countries that have a lower percentage of low birth weight infants than the United States, mothers receive either free or very low cost prenatal and postnatal care, and can receive paid maternity leave from work that ranges from 9 to 40 weeks. In Norway and the Netherlands, prenatal care is coordinated with a general practitioner, an obstetrician, and a midwife.

Why do some U.S. women receive inadequate prenatal care? Sometimes the reasons are tied to the health-care system, to provider practices, and to their own individual and social characteristics (Magriples & others, 2008). Women who do not

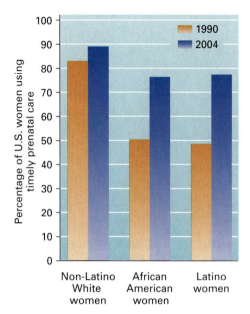

FIGURE 3.6 Percentage of U.S. Women Using Timely Prenatal Care: 1990 to 2004. From 1990 to 2004, the use of timely prenatal care increased by 7 percent (to 89.1) for non-Latino White women, by 25 percent (to 76.5) for African American women, and by 28 percent (to 77.4) for Latino women in the United States.

want to be pregnant, who have negative attitudes about being pregnant, or who unintentionally become pregnant are more likely to delay prenatal care or to miss appointments. As we noted earlier, adolescent girls are less likely than adult women to obtain prenatal care. Women living in poverty conditions are more likely to be obese, have diabetes and hypertension, smoke cigarettes and use illicit drugs, and be less likely to have regular prenatal care (Goldenberg & Nagahawatte, 2008). Within the United States, there are differences among ethnic groups both in the health of babies and in prenatal care (Madan & others, 2006; Wasserman, Bender, & Lee, 2007). In the 1980s, more than one-fifth of all non-Latino White mothers and one-third of all African American mothers did not receive prenatal care in the first trimester of their pregnancy, and 5 percent of White mothers and 10 percent of African American mothers received no prenatal care at all (Wegman, 1987).

The situation has been improving. From 1990 to 2004, the use of timely prenatal care increased for women from a variety of ethnic backgrounds in the United States, although non-Latino White women were still more likely to obtain prenatal care than African-American and Latino women (Martin & others, 2005) (see Figure 3.6). The United States needs more comprehensive medical and educational services to improve the quality of prenatal care and to reduce the number of low birth weight and preterm infants (Lu & Lu, 2008).

Cultures around the world have differing views of pregnancy than the United States. In the *Diversity in Child Development* interlude, we will explore these beliefs.

Diversity in Child Development

CULTURAL BELIEFS ABOUT PREGNANCY

All cultures have beliefs and practices that surround life's major events, and one such event is pregnancy. When a woman who immigrated to the United States becomes pregnant, the beliefs and practices of her native culture may be as important as, or more so than, those of the mainstream U.S. culture that now surrounds her. The conflict between cultural tradition and Western medicine may pose a risk for the pregnancy and a challenge for the health-care professional who wishes to give proper care while respecting the woman's values.

The American Public Health Association (2006) has identified a variety of cultural beliefs and practices that are observed among various immigrant groups, such as:

- *Food cravings.* Latin American, Asian, and some African cultures believe that it is important for a pregnant woman's food cravings to be satisfied because they are thought to be the cravings of the baby. If cravings are left unsatisfied, the baby might take on certain unpleasant personality and/or physical traits, perhaps characteristic of the food (Taylor, Ko, & Pan, 1999). As an example, in African cultures women often eat soil, chalk, or clay during pregnancy; this is believed to satisfy the baby's hunger as well as affirming soil as a symbol of female fertility (American Public Health Association, 2006).

- *"Hot-cold" theory of illness.* Many cultures in Latin America, Asia, and Africa characterize foods, medications, and illnesses as "hot" or "cold"; this has nothing to do with temperature or spiciness, but with traditional definitions and categories. Most of these cultures view pregnancy as a "hot" condition, although the Chinese view it as "cold" (Taylor Ko, & Pan, 1999). As a result, a woman may resist taking a prescribed medication because of concern that it could create too much "heat" and cause a miscarriage; in Indian culture iron-rich foods are also considered unacceptably "hot" for pregnant women (DeSantis, 1998).

- *Extended family.* In many immigrant cultures, the extended family is a vital support system, and health-care decisions are made based on the needs of the family over those of the individual. Western health-care providers need to be sensitive to this dynamic, which runs counter to today's practices of protecting patient confidentiality and autonomy.

- *Stoicism.* In many Asian cultures, stoicism is valued, as suffering is seen as part of life (Uba, 1992). Physicians are also viewed with great respect. As a result, a pregnant Asian woman may behave submissively and avoid voicing complaints to her health-care provider, but may privately fail to follow the provider's advice (Assanand & others, 1990).

Some cultures treat pregnancy simply as a natural occurrence; others see it as a medical condition (Walsh, 2006). How expectant mothers behave during pregnancy may depend in part on the prevalence of traditional home-care remedies and folk beliefs, the importance of indigenous healers, and the influence of health-care professionals in their culture. In various cultures women may consult herbalists and/or faith healers during pregnancy (Mbonye, Neema, & Magnussen, 2006).

Health-care workers should assess whether a woman's beliefs or practices pose a threat to her or the fetus. If they do, health-care professionals should consider a culturally sensitive way to handle the problem (Jansen, 2006).

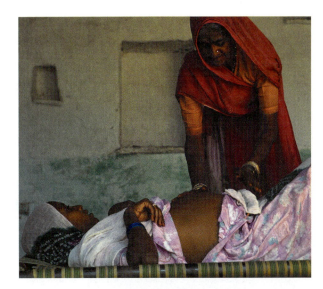

In India, a midwife checks on the size, position, and heartbeat of a fetus. Midwives deliver babies in many cultures around the world. *What are some cultural variations in prenatal care?*

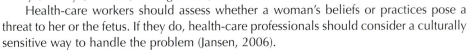

Normal Prenatal Development

Much of our discussion so far in this chapter has focused on what can go wrong with prenatal development. Prospective parents should take steps to avoid the vulnerabilities to fetal development that we have described. But it is important to keep in mind that most of the time, prenatal development does not go awry, and development occurs along the positive path that we described at the beginning of the chapter.

Review and Reflect: Learning Goal 1

1 **Describe Prenatal Development**

REVIEW

- What is the course of prenatal development?
- What are some of the main hazards to prenatal development?
- What are some good prenatal care strategies?
- Why is it important to take a positive approach to prenatal development?

REFLECT

- What can be done to convince women who are pregnant not to smoke or drink? Consider the role of health-care providers, the role of insurance companies, and specific programs targeted at women who are pregnant.

2 BIRTH

The Birth Process   Assessing the Newborn   Low Birth Weight and Preterm Infants

Nature writes the basic script for how birth occurs, but parents make important choices about conditions surrounding birth. We look first at the sequence of physical steps when a child is born.

The Birth Process

The birth process occurs in stages, occurs in different contexts, and in most cases involves one or more attendants.

Stages of Birth   The birth process occurs in three stages. The first stage is the longest of the three stages. Uterine contractions are 15 to 20 minutes apart at the beginning and last up to a minute. These contractions cause the woman's cervix to stretch and open. As the first stage progresses, the contractions come closer together, appearing every two to five minutes. Their intensity increases. By the end of the first birth stage, contractions dilate the cervix to an opening of about 4 inches, so that the baby can move from the uterus to the birth canal. For a woman having her first child, the first stage lasts an average of 12 to 14 hours; for subsequent children, this stage may be shorter.

The second birth stage begins when the baby's head starts to move through the cervix and the birth canal. It terminates when the baby completely emerges from the mother's body. With each contraction, the mother bears down hard to push the baby out of her body. By the time the baby's head is out of the mother's body, the contractions come almost every minute and last for about a minute. This stage typically lasts approximately 45 minutes to an hour.

Afterbirth is the third stage, at which time the placenta, umbilical cord, and other membranes are detached and expelled. This final stage is the shortest of the three birth stages, lasting only minutes.

Childbirth Setting and Attendants   In the United States, 99 percent of births take place in hospitals, a figure that has remained constant for several decades (Martin & others, 2005). Some women with good medical histories and low risk for problems may choose a delivery at home or in a freestanding birth center, which is usually staffed by nurse-midwives. Births at home are far more common in many other countries; for example, in Holland, 35 percent of the babies are born at home. Some critics worry that the U.S. tendency to view birth through a medical lens may lead to unnecessary medical procedures (Hausman, 2005).

Who helps a mother during birth varies across cultures. In U.S. hospitals, it has become the norm for fathers or birth coaches to be with the mother throughout labor and delivery. In the East African Nigoni culture, men are completely excluded from the childbirth process. When a woman is ready to give birth, female relatives move into the woman's hut and the husband leaves, taking his belongings (clothes, tools, weapons, and so on) with him. He is not permitted to return until after the baby is born. In some cultures, childbirth is an open, community affair. For example, in the Pukapukan culture in the Pacific Islands, women give birth in a shelter that is open for villagers to observe.

Midwives   Midwifery is the norm throughout most of the world (Tiran, 2008). In Holland, more than 40 percent of babies are delivered by midwives rather than doctors (Treffers & others, 1990). But in 2003, 91 percent of U.S. births were attended by physicians, and only 8 percent of women who delivered a baby were attended by a *midwife* (Martin & others, 2005). However, the 8 percent figure in 2003 represents a substantial

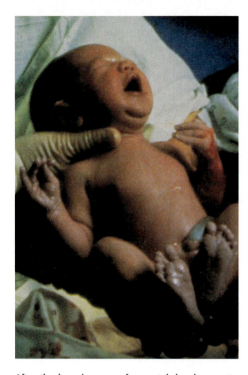

After the long journey of prenatal development, birth takes place. During birth the baby is on a threshold between two worlds. *What is the fetus/newborn transition like?*

A woman in the African !Kung culture giving birth in a sitting position. Notice the help and support being given by another woman. *What are some cultural variations in childbirth?*

increase from less than 1 percent of U.S. women attended by a midwife in 1975 (Martin & others, 2005). Ninety-five percent of the midwives who delivered babies in the United States in 2003 were certified nurse-midwives. Compared with physicians, certified nurse-midwives generally spend more time with patients during prenatal visits, place more emphasis on patient counseling and education, provide more emotional support, and are more likely to be with the patient one-on-one during the entire labor and delivery process, which may explain the more positive outcomes for babies delivered by certified nurse-midwives (Davis, 2005).

Doulas In many countries, a doula attends a childbearing woman. *Doula* is a Greek word that means "a woman who helps." A **doula** is a caregiver who provides continuous physical, emotional, and educational support for the mother before, during, and after childbirth. Doulas remain with the mother throughout labor, assessing and responding to her needs. Researchers have found positive effects when a doula is present at the birth of a child (Campbell & others, 2007; Stein, Kennell, & Fulcher, 2004). In a recent study, low-income pregnant women who were given doula support spent a shorter time in labor and their newborn had a higher health rating at one and five minutes after birth than their low-income counterparts who did not receive doula support (Campbell & others, 2006).

In the United States, most doulas work as independent providers hired by the expectant mother. Doulas typically function as part of a "birthing team," serving as an adjunct to the midwife or the hospital's obstetric staff (Dundek, 2006). Managed-care organizations are increasingly offering doula support as a part of regular obstetric care.

A doula assisting a birth. *What types of support do doulas provide?*

Methods of Childbirth U.S. hospitals often allow the mother and her obstetrician a range of options regarding their method of delivery. Key choices involve the use of medication, whether to use any of a number of nonmedicated techniques to reduce pain, and when to resort to a cesarean delivery (Downe, 2008).

Medication Three basic kinds of drugs that are used for labor are analgesia, anesthesia, and oxytocics.

Analgesia is used to relieve pain. Analgesics include tranquilizers, barbiturates, and narcotics (such as Demerol).

Anesthesia is used in late first-stage labor and during expulsion of the baby to block sensation in an area of the body or to block consciousness. There is a trend toward not using general anesthesia, which blocks consciousness, in normal births because a general anesthesia can be transmitted through the placenta to the fetus (Lieberman & others, 2005). An *epidural block* is regional anesthesia that numbs the woman's body from the waist down (Kukulu & Demirok, 2008). Even this drug, thought to be relatively safe, has come under recent criticism because it is associated with fever, extended labor, and increased risk for cesarean delivery (Birnbach & Ranasinghe, 2008).

Oxytocin is a synthetic hormone that is used to stimulate contractions; pitocin is the most widely used oxytocin (Ratcliffe, 2008). The benefits and risks of oxytocin as a part of childbirth continues to be debated (Vasdev, 2008). One recent large-scale Swedish study revealed that pregnant women who were given oxytocin during childbirth were more likely to have newborns with lower health ratings than pregnant women who were not given oxytocin during childbirth (Oscarsson & others, 2006).

Predicting how a drug will affect an individual woman and her fetus is difficult (Funai, Evans, & Lockwood, 2008). A particular drug might have only a minimal effect on one fetus yet have a much stronger effect on another. The drug's dosage also is a factor. Stronger doses of tranquilizers and narcotics given to decrease the mother's pain have a potentially more negative effect on the fetus than mild doses. It is important for the mother to assess her level of pain and have a voice in the decision of whether she should receive medication.

doula A caregiver who provides continuous physical, emotional, and educational support for the mother before, during, and after childbirth.

Natural and Prepared Childbirth For a brief time not long ago, the idea of avoiding all medication during childbirth gained favor in the United States. Instead, many women chose to reduce the pain of childbirth through techniques known as natural childbirth and prepared childbirth. Today, at least some medication is used in the typical childbirth, but elements of natural childbirth and prepared childbirth remain popular (Davidson, London, & Ladewig, 2008; Hogan & others, 2007).

Natural childbirth is the method that aims to reduce the mother's pain by decreasing her fear through education about childbirth and by teaching her to use breathing methods and relaxation techniques during delivery (Romano & Lothian, 2008). This approach was developed in 1914 by English obstetrician Grantley Dick-Read. Dick-Read believed that the doctor's relationship with the mother plays an important role in reducing her perception of pain and that the doctor should be present, providing reassurance, during her active labor prior to delivery.

French obstetrician Ferdinand Lamaze developed a method similar to natural childbirth that is known as **prepared childbirth**, or the Lamaze method. It includes a special breathing technique to control pushing in the final stages of labor, as well as more detailed education about anatomy and physiology than Dick-Read's approach provides. The Lamaze method has become very popular in the United States. The pregnant woman's partner usually serves as a coach, who attends childbirth classes with her and helps her with her breathing and relaxation during delivery.

Many other prepared childbirth techniques have been developed (Davidson, London, & Ladewig, 2008). They usually include elements of Dick-Read's natural childbirth or Lamaze's method, plus one or more other components. For instance, the Bradley method emphasizes the father's role as a labor coach (Signore, 2004). Virtually all of the prepared childbirth methods emphasize education, relaxation and breathing exercises, and support.

In sum, proponents of current prepared childbirth methods believe that when information and support are provided, women *know* how to give birth. To read about one nurse whose research focuses on fatigue during childbearing and breathing exercises during labor, see the *Careers in Child Development* profile. And to read about the increased variety of techniques now being used to reduce stress and control pain during labor, see the *Caring for Children* interlude.

natural childbirth Developed in 1914 by Dick-Read, this method attempts to reduce the mother's pain by decreasing her fear through education about childbirth and relaxation techniques during delivery.

prepared childbirth Developed by French obstetrician Ferdinand Lamaze, this childbirth strategy is similar to natural childbirth but includes a special breathing technique to control pushing in the final stages of labor and a more detailed anatomy and physiology course.

Careers in Child Development

Linda Pugh, Perinatal Nurse

Perinatal nurses work with childbearing women to support health and growth during the childbearing experience. Linda Pugh (Ph.D., R.N.C.) is a perinatal nurse on the faculty at the Johns Hopkins University School of Nursing. She is certified as an inpatient obstetric nurse and specializes in the care of women during labor and delivery. Pugh teaches nursing to both undergraduate and graduate students. In addition to educating professional nurses and conducting research, Pugh consults with hospitals and organizations about women's health issues.

Pugh's research interests include nursing interventions with low-income breast-feeding women, discovering ways to prevent and ameliorate fatigue during childbearing, and using effective breathing exercises during labor.

Linda Pugh (*right*) with a mother and her newborn.

Caring for Children

FROM WATERBIRTH TO MUSIC THERAPY

The effort to reduce stress and control pain during labor has recently led to an increase in the use of some older and some newer nonmedicated techniques (Field, 2007; Simpkin & Bolding, 2004; Smith & others, 2006). These include waterbirth, massage, acupuncture, hypnosis, and music therapy.

Waterbirth

Waterbirth involves giving birth in a tub of warm water. Some women go through labor in the water and get out for delivery, others remain in the water for delivery. The rationale for waterbirth is that the baby has been in an amniotic sac for many months and that delivery in a similar environment is likely to be less stressful for the baby and the mother. Mothers get into the warm water when contractions become closer together and more intense. Getting into the water too soon can cause labor to slow or stop. Reviews of research have indicated mixed results for waterbirths (Field, 2007; Pinette, Wax, & Wilson, 2004). In one comparison of almost 6,000 landbirths and more than 3,500 waterbirths, waterbirths resulted in a lower incidence of episiotomies (an incision made to widen the vagina for delivery), fewer perineal lacerations (the perineum is a muscle between the vagina and the rectum), fewer vaginal tears, and a lower rate of newborn complications (Geissbuehler, Stein, & Eberhard, 2004). Critics of waterbirth indicate that in some cases drowning and infectious disease may result (Pinnette & others, 2004). Waterbirth has been practiced more often in European countries such as Switzerland and Sweden in recent decades than in the United States but is increasingly being included in U.S. birth plans.

What characterizes the use of waterbirth in delivering a baby?

Massage

Massage is increasingly used as a procedure prior to and during delivery (Field, 2007; Kimber & others, 2008). Researchers have found that massage can reduce pain and anxiety during labor (Chang, Chen, & Huang, 2006; Eogan, Daly, & O'Herlihy, 2006; Wang & others, 2005). A recent research review concluded that massage reduces the incidence of perineal trauma (damage to genitalia) following birth (Beckmann & Garrett, 2006).

Acupuncture

Acupuncture, the insertion of very fine needles into specific locations in the body, is used as a standard procedure to reduce the pain of childbirth in China, although it only recently has begun to be used in the United States for this purpose (Pennick & Young, 2007). One research review indicated that only a limited number of studies had been conducted on the use of acupuncture in childbirth but that it appears to be safe and may have positive effects (Smith & Crowther, 2004). A recent study found that acupuncture lowered the need for medical inductions and cesarean deliveries (Duke & Don, 2005). Another recent study revealed that acupuncture resulted in less time spent in labor and a reduction in the need for oxytocin to augment labor (Gaudernack, Forbord, & Hole, 2006). Further research is needed to determine the effectiveness of acupuncture as a childbirth procedure (Lee & Chan, 2006).

Hypnosis

Hypnosis, the induction of a psychological state of altered attention and awareness in which the individual is unusually responsively to suggestions, is also increasingly being used during childbirth (Mottershead, 2006; Spencer, 2005). Some studies have indicated positive effects of hypnosis for reducing pain during childbirth (Barabasaz & Perez, 2007;

VandeVusse & others, 2007). However, some reviews indicate that further research is needed to determine the risks and benefits of this procedure (Cyna, McAuliffe, & Andrew, 2004; Simpkin & Bolding, 2004).

Music Therapy

Music therapy during childbirth, which involves the use of music to reduce stress and manage pain, is increasingly used (Cepeda & others, 2006; Chang & Chen, 2004). Few research studies have been conducted to determine its effectiveness (Simpkin & Bolding, 2004).

Cesarean Delivery   Normally, the baby's head comes through the vagina first. But if the baby is in a **breech position**, the baby's buttocks are the first part to emerge from the vagina. In 1 of every 25 deliveries, the baby's head is still in the uterus when the rest of the body is out. Breech births can cause respiratory problems. As a result, if the baby is in a breech position, what is called a cesarean section or a cesarean delivery is usually performed (Lee, El-Sayed, & Gould, 2008). In a **cesarean delivery**, the baby is removed from the mother's uterus through an incision made in her abdomen.

Cesarean deliveries are safer than breech deliveries. Cesarean deliveries also are performed if the baby is lying crosswise in the uterus, if the baby's head is too large to pass through the mother's pelvis, if the baby develops complications, or if the mother is bleeding vaginally. Cesarean deliveries can be life-saving, but they do bring risks. Compared with vaginal deliveries, they involve a higher infection rate, longer hospital stays, and the greater expense and stress that accompany any surgery. A recent national study of all U.S. live births and infant deaths from 1999 to 2002 revealed that cesarean deliveries with no labor complications resulted in a neonatal death rate that was 2.4 times that of planned vaginal deliveries (MacDorman & others, 2008).

The benefits and risks of cesarean sections continue to be debated (Declercq & others, 2008; Vendittelli & others, 2008). Some critics emphasize that too many babies are delivered by cesarean section in the United States (Chaillet & Dumont, 2007). More cesarean sections are performed in the United States than in any other country in the world. The cesarean delivery rate jumped 5 percent from 2002 to 2006 in the United States to 31 percent of all births, the highest level since these data began to be reported on birth certificates in 1989 (National Center for Health Statistics, 2007). Higher cesarean delivery rates may be due to a better ability to identify infants in distress during birth and the increase in overweight and obese pregnant women (Coleman & others, 2005). Also, some doctors may be overly cautious and recommend a cesarean delivery to defend against a potential lawsuit.

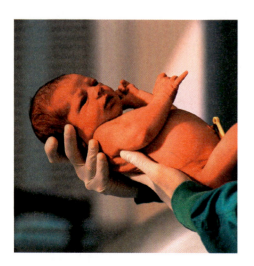

What is the transition from fetus to newborn like?

The Transition from Fetus to Newborn   Much of our discussion of birth so far has focused on the mother. Being born also involves considerable stress for the baby. During each contraction, when the placenta and umbilical cord are compressed as the uterine muscles draw together, the supply of oxygen to the fetus is decreased. If the delivery takes too long, the baby can develop *anoxia*, a condition in which the fetus or newborn has an insufficient supply of oxygen. Anoxia can cause brain damage (Smith, 2008).

The baby has considerable capacity to withstand the stress of birth. Large quantities of adrenaline and noradrenaline, hormones that protect the fetus in the event of oxygen deficiency, are secreted in stressful circumstances. These hormones increase the heart's pumping activity, speed up heart rate, channel blood flow to the brain, and raise the blood-sugar level. Never again in life will such large amounts of these hormones be secreted. This circumstance underscores how stressful it is to be born and also how well prepared and adapted the fetus is for birth (Van Beveren, 2007).

breech position   The baby's position in the uterus that causes the buttocks to be the first part to emerge from the vagina.

cesarean delivery   The baby is removed from the mother's uterus through an incision made in her abdomen.

Score	0	1	2
Heart rate	Absent	Slow—less than 100 beats per minute	Fast—100 to 140 beats per minute
Respiratory effort	No breathing for more than one minute	Irregular and slow	Good breathing with normal crying
Muscle tone	Limp and flaccid	Weak, inactive, but some flexion of extremities	Strong, active motion
Body color	Blue and pale	Body pink, but extremities blue	Entire body pink
Reflex irritability	No response	Grimace	Coughing, sneezing, and crying

FIGURE 3.7 The Apgar Scale. A newborn's score on the Apgar Scale indicates whether the baby has urgent medical problems. *What are some trends in the Apgar Scores of U.S. babies?*

At the time of birth, the baby is covered with what is called *vernix caseosa,* a protective skin grease. This vernix consists of fatty secretions and dead cells, thought to help protect the baby's skin against heat loss before and during birth.

Immediately after birth, the umbilical cord is cut and the baby is on its own. Before birth, oxygen came from the mother via the umbilical cord, but now the baby is self-sufficient and can breathe on its own. Now 25 million little air sacs in the lungs must be filled with air. These first breaths may be the hardest ones an individual takes.

Assessing the Newborn

Almost immediately after birth, after the baby and mother have become acquainted, a newborn is taken to be weighed, cleaned up, and tested for signs of developmental problems that might require urgent attention (Als & Butler, 2008). The **Apgar Scale** is widely used to assess the health of newborns at one and five minutes after birth. The Apgar Scale evaluates infants' heart rate, respiratory effort, muscle tone, body color, and reflex irritability. An obstetrician or a nurse does the evaluation and gives the newborn a score, or reading, of 0, 1, or 2 on each of these five health signs (see Figure 3.7). A total score of 7 to 10 indicates that the newborn's condition is good. A score of 5 indicates there may be developmental difficulties. A score of 3 or below signals an emergency and indicates that the baby might not survive. The percentage of U.S. newborns with five-minute Apgar scores of 9 or 10, indicating excellent health, increased slowly from 88.6 percent in 1978 to 91.1 percent in 2003 (Martin & others, 2005). In this survey, five-minute Apgar scores of 7 or less decreased from 2.1 percent in 1978 to 1.4 percent in 1993 but has been unchanged since.

The Apgar Scale is especially good at assessing the newborn's ability to respond to the stress of delivery and the new environment (Oberlander & others, 2008). It also identifies high-risk infants who need resuscitation. For a more thorough assessment of the newborn, the Brazelton Neonatal Behavioral Assessment Scale (NBAS) or the Neonatal Intensive Care Unit Network Neurobehavioral Scale (NNNS) may be used.

Named after pediatrician T. Berry Brazelton, the **Brazelton Neonatal Behavioral Assessment Scale (NBAS)** is performed within 24 to 36 hours after birth. It is also used as a sensitive index of neurological competence in the weeks or months after birth and as a measure in many studies of infant development (Mamtani, Patel, & Kulkarni, 2008). The NBAS assesses the newborn's neurological development, reflexes, and reactions to people. The newborn is an active participant, and the score is

Apgar Scale A widely used method to assess the health of newborns at one and five minutes after birth. The Apgar Scale evaluates infants' heart rate, respiratory effort, muscle tone, body color, and reflex irritability.

Brazelton Neonatal Behavioral Assessment Scale (NBAS) A test given within 24 to 36 hours after birth to assess newborns' neurological development, reflexes, and reactions to people.

based on the newborn's best performance. Sixteen reflexes, such as sneezing, blinking, and rooting, are assessed, along with reactions to circumstances, such as the infant's reaction to a rattle. (We will have more to say about reflexes in Chapter 4, when we discuss motor development in infancy.)

The examiner rates the newborn on each of 27 items. For example, item 15 is "cuddliness." The examiner uses nine categories to assessing cuddliness and scores the infant on a continuum that ranges from being very resistant to being held to being extremely cuddly and clinging. The 27 items of the NBAS are organized into four categories—physiological, motoric, state, and interaction. Based on these categories, the baby is also classified in global terms, such as "worrisome," "normal," or "superior" (Nugent & Brazelton, 2000).

A very low NBAS score can indicate brain damage, or stress to the brain that may heal in time. If an infant merely seems sluggish, parents are encouraged to give the infant attention and become more sensitive to the infant's needs. Parents are shown how the newborn can respond to people and how to stimulate such responses. These communications with parents can improve their interaction skills with both high-risk infants and healthy, responsive infants (Girling, 2006).

An "offspring" of the NBAS, the **Neonatal Intensive Care Unit Network Neurobehavioral Scale (NNNS)** provides a more comprehensive analysis of the newborn's behavior, neurological and stress responses, and regulatory capacities (Brazelton, 2004; Lester, Tronick, & Brazelton, 2004). Whereas the NBAS was developed to assess normal, healthy, term infants, Brazelton, along with Barry Lester and Edward Tronick, developed the NNNS to assess the at-risk infant. It is especially useful for evaluating preterm infants (although it may not be appropriate for those less than 30 weeks' gestational age) and substance-exposed infants (Boukydis & Lester, 2008; Smith & others, 2008).

Low Birth Weight and Preterm Infants

Different conditions that pose threats for newborns have been given different labels. We will examine these conditions and discuss interventions for improving outcomes of preterm infants.

Low Birth Weight, Preterm, and Small for Date Infants

Three related conditions pose threats to many newborns: low birth weight, being preterm, and being small-for-date. **Low birth weight infants** weigh less than $5\frac{1}{2}$ pounds at birth. *Very low birth weight* newborns weigh under 3 pounds and *extremely low birth weight* newborns under 2 pounds. **Preterm infants** are those born three weeks or more before the pregnancy has reached its full term—in other words, 35 or fewer weeks after conception. **Small for date infants** (also called *small for gestational age infants*) are those whose birth weight is below normal when the length of the pregnancy is considered. They weigh less than 90 percent of all babies of the same gestational age. Small for date infants may be preterm or full term. One study found that small for date infants had more than a fourfold risk of death (Regev & others, 2003).

The preterm birth rate in the United States increased 18 percent from 1990 to 2004 (Hoyert & others, 2006). One of every eight U.S. births is now preterm (Ashton, 2006). The increase in preterm birth is likely due to such factors as the increasing number of births to women 35 years and older, increasing rates of multiple births, increased management of maternal and fetal conditions (for example, inducing labor preterm if medical technology indicates it will increase the likelihood of survival), increased substance abuse (tobacco, alcohol), and increased stress (Goldenberg & Culcane, 2007). Ethnic variations characterize preterm birth. For example, in 2003, the likelihood of being born preterm was one in eight for all U.S. infants, but the rate was one in six for African American infants (Ashton, 2006).

A "kilogram kid," weighing less than 2.3 pounds at birth. *What are some long-term outcomes for weighing so little at birth?*

Neonatal Intensive Care Unit Neurobehavioral Scale (NNNS) An "offspring" of the NBAS, the NNNS provides a more comprehensive analysis of the newborn's behavior, neurological and stress responses, and regulatory capacities.

low birth weight infants An infant that weighs less than $5\frac{1}{2}$ pounds at birth.

preterm infants Those born three weeks or more before the pregnancy has reached its full term.

small for date infants Also called small for gestational age infants, these infants' birth weights are below normal when the length of pregnancy is considered. Small for date infants may be preterm or full term.

Recently, there has been considerable interest generated in the role that progestin might play in reducing preterm births (Basaran, 2008; Thornton, 2007). In one study, weekly injections of the hormone progesterone, which is naturally produced by the ovaries, lowered the rate of preterm births by one-third (Meis & Peaceman, 2003). Other recent studies provide further support for the use of progestin in the second trimester of pregnancy in reducing the risk of preterm delivery (Fonseca & others, 2007; Lamont & Jaggat, 2007). However, one recent study did not find a reduction in preterm labor when progestin was given to women who were pregnant with twins (Rouse & others, 2007). A recent survey indicated that the use of progestin to prevent preterm birth increased from 38 percent of maternal-fetal medicine specialists in 2003 to 67 percent in 2005 (Ness & others, 2006). Also, recall earlier in the chapter that a recent study revealed that taking folic acid either alone or as part of a multivitamin for one year prior to conceiving was linked to a substantial reduction in preterm birth (Bukowski & others, 2008).

The incidence of low birth weight varies considerably from country to country. In some countries, such as India and Sudan, where poverty is rampant and the health and nutrition of mothers are poor, the percentage of low birth weight babies reaches as high as 31 percent (see Figure 3.8). In the United States, there has been an increase in low birth weight infants in the last two decades. The U.S. low birth weight rate of 8.1 percent in 2004 is considerably higher than that of many other developed countries (Hoyert & others, 2006). For example, only 4 percent of the infants born in Sweden, Finland, Norway, and Korea are low birth weight, and only 5 percent of those born in New Zealand, Australia, and France are low birth weight.

The causes of low birth weight also vary. In the developing world, low birth weight stems mainly from the mother's poor health and nutrition (Lasker & others, 2005). Diseases such as diarrhea and malaria, which are common in developing countries, can impair fetal growth if the mother becomes infected while she is pregnant. In developed countries, cigarette smoking during pregnancy is the leading cause of low birth weight (Delpisheh & others, 2006; Hankins & Longo, 2006). In both developed and developing countries, adolescents who give birth when their bodies have not fully matured are at risk for having low birth weight babies (Malamitsi-Puchner & Boutsikou, 2006). In the United States, the increase in the number of low birth weight infants is thought to be due to such factors as the use of drugs, poor nutrition, multiple births, reproductive technologies, and improved technology and prenatal care that result in more high-risk babies surviving (Chen & others, 2007b; Hoyert & others, 2006).

Consequences of Preterm Birth and Low Birth Weight   Although most preterm and low birth weight infants are healthy, as a group they have more health and developmental problems than normal birth weight infants (Minde & Zelkowitz, 2008). Figure 3.9 shows the results of a recent Norwegian study indicating that the earlier preterm infants are born, the more likely they will drop out of school (Swamy, Osbye, & Skjaerven, 2008). Another recent study found that extremely preterm infants were more likely to show pervasive delays in early language development (such as vocabulary size and quality of word use) than very preterm infants, who in turn showed more early language delays than full-term infants (Foster-Cohen & others, 2007). A recent research review also revealed that very preterm infants had lower IQ scores, less effective information-processing skills, and were more at risk for behavioral problems than full-term infants (Johnson, 2007).

The number and severity of these problems increase when infants are born very early and as their birth weight decreases (Allen, 2008; Casey, 2008). Survival rates for infants who are born very early and very small have risen, but with this improved survival rate have come increases in rates of severe brain damage. The earlier the birth and the lower the birth weight, the greater the likelihood of brain injury.

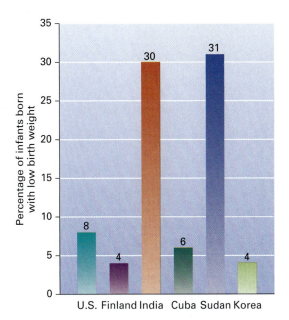

FIGURE 3.8 **Percentage of Infants Born with Low Birth Weight in Selected Countries**

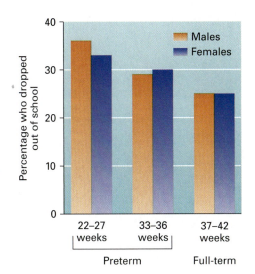

FIGURE 3.9 **Percentage of Preterm and Full-Term Birth Infants Who Dropped Out of School**

Approximately 7 percent of moderately low birth weight infants (3 pounds 5 ounces to 5 pounds 8 ounces) have brain injuries. This figure increases to 20 percent for the smallest newborns (1 pound 2 ounces to 3 pounds 5 ounces). A recent MRI study revealed that adolescents who had experienced very preterm birth were more likely to show reduced prefrontal lobe and corpus callosum functioning than full-term adolescents (Narberhaus & others, 2008). Low birth weight infants are also more likely than normal birth weight infants to have lung or liver diseases (Streubel, Donohue, & Aucott, 2008).

At school age, children who were born low in birth weight are more likely than their normal birth weight counterparts to have a learning disability, attention deficit hyperactivity disorder, or breathing problems such as asthma (Greenough, 2007; Joshi & Kotecha, 2007). One study revealed that 17-year-olds who were born with low birth weight were 50 percent more likely than normal birth weight individuals to have reading and mathematics deficits (Breaslau, Paneth, & Lucia, 2004). Approximately 50 percent of all low birth weight children are enrolled in special education programs.

Note that not all of these adverse consequences can be attributed solely to being born low in birth weight. Some of the less severe but more common developmental and physical delays occur because many low birth weight children come from disadvantaged environments (Malamitsi-Puchner & Boutsikou, 2006).

Nurturing Preterm Infants   Some effects of being born low in birth weight can be reversed. Intensive enrichment programs that provide medical and educational services for both the parents and children can improve short-term outcomes for low birth weight children (Minde & Zelkowitz, 2008). Federal laws mandate that services for school-age children be expanded to include family-based care for infants. At present, these services are aimed at children born with severe disabilities. The availability of services for moderately low birth weight children who do not have severe physical problems varies, but most states do not provide these services.

Currently, the two most popular neonatal intensive care unit (NICU) interventions that involve parents are breast feeding and **kangaroo care**, a way of holding a preterm infant so that there is skin-to-skin contact. Both of these interventions were uncommon until recently.

A recent survey revealed that breast feeding is now virtually universally encouraged for mothers with newborns in U.S. NICUs (Field & others, 2006). Recent surveys indicated that kangaroo care is used from 82 to 97 percent by nurses in NICUs (Engler & others, 2002; Field & others, 2006). Also in one of these surveys, massage therapy was used in 37 percent of the NICUs (Field & others, 2006).

Let's further examine kangaroo care and massage therapy. In kangaroo care, the baby, wearing only a diaper, is held upright against the parent's bare chest, much as a baby kangaroo is carried by its mother. Kangaroo care is typically practiced for two to three hours per day, skin-to-skin over an extended time in early infancy (Feldman & others, 2003; Johnson, 2007).

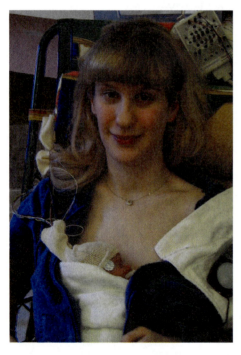

A new mother practicing kangaroo care. *What is kangaroo care?*

Why use kangaroo care with preterm infants? Preterm infants often have difficulty coordinating their breathing and heart rate, and the close physical contact with the parent provided by kangaroo care can help to stabilize the preterm infant's heartbeat, temperature, and breathing (Kennell, 2006; Ludington-Hoe & others, 2006). Further, preterm infants who experience kangaroo care have longer periods of sleep, gain more weight, decrease their crying, have longer periods of alertness, and earlier hospital discharge (Ludington-Hoe & others, 2006; Worku & Kassir, 2005). One study compared 26 low birth weight infants who received kangaroo care with 27 low birth weight infants who received standard medical/nursing care (Ohgi & others, 2002). At both 6 and 12 months of age, the kangaroo care infants were more alert and responsive, less irritable and fussy, and had a more positive mood. Another study found that preterm infants who received kangaroo care had better control of their arousal, more effectively attended to stimuli, and engaged in more sustained

kangaroo care   A way of holding a preterm infant so that there is skin-to-skin contact.

exploration during a toy session than a control group of preterm infants who did not receive kangaroo care (Feldman & others, 2002). And two recent experimental studies revealed that low birth weight infants randomly assigned to kangaroo mother care compared with traditional mother care gained more weight, were less likely to experience hypothermia and hypglycemia, were more strongly attached to their mother (Gathwala, Singh, & Balhara, 2008; Suman, Udani, & Nanavati, 2008). Increasingly kangaroo care is being recommended for full-term infants as well (Ferber & Makhoul, 2008).

Many preterm infants experience less touch than full-term infants because they are isolated in temperature-controlled incubators (Chia, Sellick, & Gans, 2006). The research of Tiffany Field has led to a surge of interest in the role that massage might play in improving the developmental outcomes for preterm infants. To read about her research, see the following *Research in Child Development* interlude.

Research in Child Development

TIFFANY FIELD'S RESEARCH ON MASSAGE THERAPY

Throughout history and in many cultures, caregivers have massaged infants. In Africa and Asia, infants are routinely massaged by parents or other family members for several months after birth. In the United States, interest in using touch and massage to improve the growth, health, and well-being of infants has been stimulated by the research of Tiffany Field (1998, 2001, 2003, 2007; Field, Diego, & Hernandez-Reif, 2007, 2008; Field & Diego, 2008; Field & others, 2006; Hernandez-Reif, Diego, & Field, 2007), director of the Touch Research Institute at the University of Miami School of Medicine.

In a recent study, preterm infants in a neonatal intensive care unit (NICU) were randomly assigned to a massage therapy group or a control group. For five consecutive days, the preterm infants in the massage group were given three 15-minute moderate pressure massages (Hernandez-Reif, Diego, & Field, 2007). Behavioral observations of the following stress behaviors were made on the first and last days of the study: crying, grimacing, yawning, sneezing, jerky arm and leg movements, startles, and finger flaring. The various stress behaviors were summarized in a composite stress behavior index. As indicated in Figure 3.10, massage had a stress-reducing effect on the preterm infants, which is especially important because they encounter numerous stressors while they are hospitalized.

In another study, Field and her colleagues (2004) taught mothers how to massage their full-term infants. Once a day before bedtime the mothers massaged the babies using either light or moderate pressure. Infants who were massaged with moderate pressure "gained more weight, were greater length, performed better on the orientation scale of the Brazelton, had lower Brazelton excitability and depression scores, and exhibited less agitation during sleep" (p. 435).

Field has demonstrated the benefits of massage therapy for infants who face a variety of problems. For example, preterm infants exposed to cocaine in utero who received massage therapy gained weight and improved their scores on developmental tests (Wheeden & others, 1993). In another investigation, newborns born to HIV-positive mothers were randomly assigned to a massage therapy group or to a control group that did not receive the therapy (Scafidi & Field, 1996). The massaged infants showed superior performance on a wide range of assessments, including daily weight

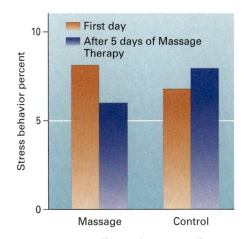

Shown here is Tiffany Field massaging a newborn infant. *What types of infants has massage therapy been shown to help?*

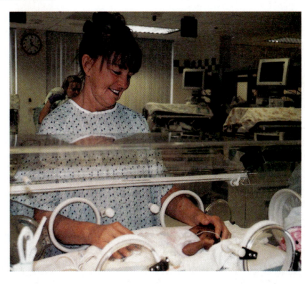

FIGURE 3.10 Effects of Massage Therapy on Stress Behavior in Newborns

gain. Another study investigated 1- to 3-month-old infants born to depressed adolescent mothers (Field & others, 1996). The infants of depressed mothers who received massage therapy had lower stress—as well as improved emotionality, sociability, and soothability—compared with the nonmassaged infants of depressed mothers.

In a recent review of the use of massage therapy with preterm infants, Field and her colleagues (2004) concluded that the most consistent findings involve two positive results: (1) increased weight gain, and (2) discharge from the hospital from three to six days earlier.

Infants are not the only ones who may benefit from massage therapy (Field, 2007). In other studies, Field and her colleagues have demonstrated the benefits of massage therapy with women in reducing labor pain (Field, Hernandez-Rief, Taylor, & others, 1997), with children who have arthritis (Field, Hernandez-Rief, Seligman, & others, 1997), with children who have asthma (Field, Henteleff, & others, 1998), with autistic children's attentiveness (Field, Lasko, & others, 1997), and with adolescents who have attention deficit hyperactivity disorder (Field, Quintino, & others, 1998).

Review and Reflect: Learning Goal 2

2 Discuss the Birth Process

REVIEW

- What are the three main stages of birth? What are some different birth strategies? What is the transition from fetus to newborn like for the infant?
- What are three measures of neonatal health and responsiveness?
- What are the outcomes for children if they are born preterm or with a low birth weight?

REFLECT

- If you are a female, which birth strategy do you prefer? Why? If you are a male, how involved would you want to be in helping your partner through pregnancy and the birth of your baby?

3 THE POSTPARTUM PERIOD

postpartum period The period after childbirth when the mother adjusts, both physically and psychologically, to the process of childbirth. This period lasts for about six weeks or until her body has completed its adjustment and returned to a near-prepregnant state.

Physical Adjustments

Emotional and Psychological Adjustments

Bonding

The weeks after childbirth present challenges for many new parents and their offspring. This is the **postpartum period**, the period after childbirth or delivery that lasts for about six weeks or until the mother's body has completed its adjustment and has returned to a nearly prepregnant state. It is a time when the woman adjusts, both physically and psychologically, to the process of childbearing.

The postpartum period involves a great deal of adjustment and adaptation. The baby has to be cared for. The mother has to recover from childbirth, to learn how to take care of the baby, and to learn to feel good about herself as a mother. The father needs to learn how to take care of his recovering wife, to learn how to take care of the baby, and to learn to feel good about himself as a father. Many health professionals believe that the best way to meet these challenges is with a family-centered approach that uses the family's resources to support an early and smooth adjustment to the newborn by all family members. The adjustments needed are physical, emotional, and psychological.

Physical Adjustments

A woman's body makes numerous physical adjustments in the first days and weeks after childbirth (London & others, 2007). She may have a great deal of energy or feel exhausted and let down. Most new mothers feel tired and need rest. Though these changes are normal, the fatigue can undermine the new mother's sense of well-being and confidence in her ability to cope with a new baby and a new family life (Runquist, 2007).

A concern is the loss of sleep that the primary caregiver experiences in the postpartum period (Gunderson & others, 2008; Signal & others, 2007). A recent analysis indicated that the primary caregiver loses as much as 700 hours of sleep in the first year following the baby's birth (Mass, 2008). In the 2007 Sleep in America Survey, a substantial percentage of women reported loss of sleep during pregnancy and in the postpartum period (National Sleep Foundation, 2007) (see Figure 3.11). The loss of sleep can contribute to stress, marital conflict, and impaired decision making (Meerlo, Sgoifo, & Suchecki, 2008). Even after their newborn begins to sleep better through the night by the middle of the baby's first year, many mothers report waking up several times a night even when their baby is asleep. Sleep experts say it takes several weeks to several months for parents' internal sleep clocks to adjust.

After delivery, a mother's body undergoes sudden and dramatic changes in hormone production. When the placenta is delivered, estrogen and progesterone levels drop steeply and remain low until the ovaries start producing hormones again. The woman will probably begin menstruating again in four to eight weeks if she is not breast feeding. If she is breast feeding, she might not menstruate for several months to a year or more, though ovulation can occur during this time. The first several menstrual periods following delivery might be heavier than usual, but periods soon return to normal.

Involution is the process by which the uterus returns to its prepregnant size five or six weeks after birth. Immediately following birth, the uterus weighs 2 to 3 pounds. By the end of five or six weeks, the uterus weighs 2 to $3\frac{1}{2}$ ounces. Nursing the baby helps contract the uterus at a rapid rate.

If the woman regularly engaged in conditioning exercises during pregnancy, exercise will help her recover her former body contour and strength. With a caregiver's approval, the new mother can begin some exercises as soon as one hour after delivery. A recent study found that women who maintained or increased their exercise from prepregnancy to postpartum had better maternal well-being than women who engaged in no exercise or decreased their exercise from prepregnancy to postpartum (Blum, Beaudoin, & Caton-Lemos, 2005).

Relaxation techniques are also helpful during the postpartum period. Five minutes of slow breathing on a stressful day in the postpartum period can relax and refresh the new mother, as well as the new baby.

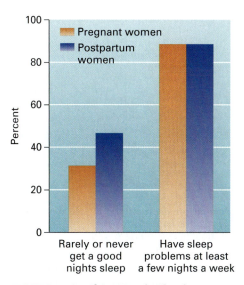

FIGURE 3.11 Sleep Deprivation in Pregnant and Postpartum Women

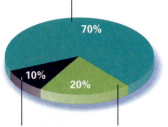

Postpartum blues
Symptoms appear 2 to 3 days after delivery and usually subside within 1 to 2 weeks.

Postpartum depression
Symptoms linger for weeks or months and interfere with daily functioning.

No symptoms

FIGURE 3.12 Postpartum Blues and Postpartum Depression Among U.S. Women. Some health professionals refer to the postpartum period as the "fourth trimester." Though the time span of the postpartum period does not necessarily cover three months, the term "fourth trimester" suggests continuity and the importance of the first several months after birth for the mother.

The postpartum period is a time of considerable adjustment and adaptation for both the mother and the father. Fathers can provide an important support system for mothers, especially in helping mothers care for young infants. *What kinds of tasks might the father of a newborn do to support the mother?*

postpartum depression Characteristic of women who have such strong feelings or sadness, anxiety, or despair that they have trouble coping with daily tasks in the postpartum period.

Emotional and Psychological Adjustments

Emotional fluctuations are common for mothers in the postpartum period. For some women, emotional fluctuations decrease within several weeks after the delivery, but other women experience more long-lasting emotional swings.

As shown in Figure 3.12, about 70 percent of new mothers in the United States have what are called "postpartum blues." About two to three days after birth, they begin to feel depressed, anxious, and upset. These feelings may come and go for several months after the birth, often peaking about three to five days after birth. Even without treatment, these feelings usually go away after one or two weeks.

For other women, emotional fluctuations persist and can produce feelings of anxiety, depression, and difficulty in coping with stress (Morrissey, 2007; Tam & Chung, 2007). Mothers who have such feelings, even when they are getting adequate rest, may benefit from professional help in dealing with their problems. Indications of a need for professional counseling about postpartum adaptation include excessive worrying, depression, extreme changes in appetite, crying spells, and inability to sleep.

Postpartum depression involves a major depressive episode that typically occurs about four weeks after delivery. In other words, women with postpartum depression have such strong feelings of sadness, anxiety, or despair that for at least a two-week period they have trouble coping with their daily tasks. Without treatment, postpartum depression may become worse and last for many months (Gjeringen, Katon, & Rich, 2008). About 10 percent of new mothers experience postpartum depression. Between 25 to 50 percent of these depressed new mothers have episodes that last six months or longer (Beck, 2002). If untreated, approximately 25 of these women are still depressed a year later.

Hormonal changes that occur after childbirth are believed to play a role in postpartum depression (Groer & Morgan, 2007; Jolley & others, 2007). Estrogen helps some women with postpartum depression, but estrogen also has some possible problematic side effects (Grigoriadis & Kennedy, 2002). Several antidepressant drugs are effective in treating postpartum depression and appear to be safe for breast feeding women (Horowitz & Cousins, 2006). Psychotherapy, especially cognitive therapy, also is an effective treatment of postpartum depression for many women (Beck, 2006; Lasiuk & Ferguson, 2005). Also, engaging in regular exercise may help in treating postpartum depression (Daley, Macarthur, & Winter, 2007).

One concern about postpartum depression is that breast feeding is less common among postpartum depressed women. They may not breast feed because of their concern about potentially negative effects of antidepressants that can be transmitted to their young infant through breast milk (Einarson & Ito, 2007). Currently, little research has been conducted on whether the positive effects of breast feeding might outweigh the positive effects of antidepressants for both the mother and the infant (Field, 2008).

Can a mother's postpartum depression affect the way mothers interact with their infants? Researchers have found that depressed mothers interact less with their infants and are less likely to respond to their infants' effort to get attention (Teti & Towe-Goodman, 2008). A recent national survey indicated that mothers who were depressed were 1.5 times more likely to provide less healthy feeding and sleeping practices for their newborns (Paulson, Dauber, & Leiferman, 2006). Another recent study revealed that postpartum depression was more common in mothers who had preterm than full-term infants (Feldman & Eidelman, 2007). In this study, with both preterm and full-term infants, mothers with postpartum depression showed a low level of maternal-infant synchrony.

Fathers also undergo considerable adjustment in the postpartum period, even when they work away from home all day (Cox, 2006; Pinheiro & others, 2006). Many fathers feel that the baby comes first and gets all of the mother's attention; some feel that they have been replaced by the baby.

A mother bonds with her infant moments after it is born. *How critical is bonding for the development of social competence later in childhood?*

To help the father adjust, parents should set aside some special time to be together with each other. The father's postpartum reaction also likely will be improved if he has taken childbirth classes with the mother and is an active participant in caring for the baby.

Bonding

A special component of the parent-infant relationship is **bonding**, the formation of a connection, especially a physical bond, between parents and the newborn in the period shortly after birth. Sometimes hospitals seem determined to deter bonding. Drugs given to the mother to make her delivery less painful can make the mother drowsy, interfering with her ability to respond to and stimulate the newborn. Mothers and newborns are often separated shortly after delivery, and preterm infants are isolated from their mothers even more than full-term mothers.

Do these practices do any harm? Some physicians believe that during the period shortly after birth, the parents and newborn need to form an emotional attachment as a foundation for optimal development in years to come (Kennell, 2006; Kennell & McGrath, 1999). Is there evidence that close contact between mothers and their newborn in the first several days after birth is critical for optimal development later in life? Although some research supports this bonding hypothesis (Klaus & Kennell, 1976), a body of research challenges the significance of the first few days of life as a critical period (Bakeman & Brown, 1980; Rode & others, 1981). Indeed, the extreme form of the bonding hypothesis—that the newborn must have close contact with the mother in the first few days of life to develop optimally—simply is not true.

Nonetheless, the weakness of the bonding hypothesis should not be used as an excuse to keep motivated mothers from interacting with their newborns. Such contact brings pleasure to many mothers. In some mother-infant pairs—including preterm infants, adolescent mothers, and mothers from disadvantaged circumstances—early close contact may establish a climate for improved interaction after the mother and infant leave the hospital.

Many hospitals now offer a *rooming-in* arrangement, in which the baby remains in the mother's room most of the time during its hospital stay. However, if parents choose not to use this rooming-in arrangement, the weight of the research suggests that this decision will not harm the infant emotionally (Lamb, 1994).

bonding The formation of a close connection, especially a physical bond, between parents and their newborn in the period shortly after birth.

Review and Reflect: Learning Goal 3

3 **Explain the Changes That Take Place in the Postpartum Period**

REVIEW

- What does the postpartum period involve? What physical adjustments does the woman's body make in this period?
- What emotional and psychological adjustments characterize the postpartum period?
- Is bonding critical for optimal development?

REFLECT

- If you are a female, what can you do to adjust effectively in the postpartum period? If you are a male, what can you do to help in the postpartum period?

Reach Your Learning Goals

Prenatal Development and Birth

1   PRENATAL DEVELOPMENT: DESCRIBE PRENATAL DEVELOPMENT

The Course of Prenatal Development

- Prenatal development is divided into three periods: germinal (conception until 10 to 14 days later), which ends when the zygote (a fertilized egg) attaches to the uterine wall; embryonic (two to eight weeks after conception), during which the embryo differentiates into three layers, life-support systems develop, and organ systems form (organogenesis); and fetal (two months after conception until about nine months, or when the infant is born), a time when organ systems have matured to the point at which life can be sustained outside of the womb. The growth of the brain during prenatal development is nothing short of remarkable. By the time babies are born, they have approximately 100 billion neurons, or nerve cells. Neurogenesis is the term that means the formation of new neurons. The nervous system begins with the formation of a neural tube at 18 to 24 days after conception. Proliferation and migration are two processes that characterize brain development in the prenatal period. The basic architecture of the brain is formed in the first two trimesters of prenatal development.

Teratology and Hazards to Prenatal Development

- Teratology is the field that investigates the causes of birth defects. Any agent that can potentially cause birth defects or negatively alters cognitive and behavioral outcomes is called a teratogen. The dose, genetic susceptibility, and time of exposure influence the severity of the damage to an unborn child and the type of defect that occurs. Prescription drugs that can be harmful include antibiotics. Nonprescription drugs that can be harmful include diet pills and aspirin. Legal psychoactive drugs that are potentially harmful to prenatal development include caffeine, alcohol, and nicotine. Fetal alcohol spectrum disorders are a cluster of abnormalities that appear in offspring of mothers who drink heavily during pregnancy. Even when pregnant women drink moderately (one to two drinks a day), negative effects on their offspring have been found. Cigarette smoking by pregnant women has serious adverse effects on prenatal and child development (such as low birth weight). Illegal psychoactive drugs that are potentially harmful to offspring include methamphetamine, marijuana, cocaine, and heroin. Incompatibility of the mother's and the father's blood types can also be harmful to the fetus. Environmental hazards include radiation, environmental pollutants, and toxic wastes. Syphilis, rubella (German measles), genital herpes, and AIDS are infectious diseases that can harm the fetus. Other parental factors include diet and nutrition, age, and emotional states and stress. A developing fetus depends entirely on its mother for nutrition. Maternal age can negatively affect the offspring's development if the mother is an adolescent or over 35. High stress in the mother is linked with less than optimal prenatal and birth outcomes. Paternal factors that can adversely affect prenatal development include exposure to lead, radiation, certain pesticides, petrochemicals, and a diet low in vitamin C.

Prenatal Care

- Prenatal care varies extensively but usually involves medical care services with a defined schedule of visits.

Normal Prenatal Development

- It is important to remember that, although things can and do go wrong during pregnancy, most of the time pregnancy and prenatal development go well.

2   BIRTH: DISCUSS THE BIRTH PROCESS

The Birth Process

- Childbirth occurs in three stages. The first stage, which lasts about 12 to 14 hours for a woman having her first child, is the longest stage. The cervix dilates to about 4 inches at the end of the first stage. The second stage begins when the baby's head moves through the cervix and ends with the baby's complete emergence. The third stage is afterbirth. Childbirth strategies involve the childbirth setting and attendants. In many countries, a doula attends a childbearing woman. Methods of delivery include medicated, natural and prepared, and cesarean. Being born involves considerable stress for the baby, but the baby is well prepared and adapted to handle the stress. Anoxia—insufficient oxygen supply to the fetus/newborn—is a potential hazard.Some children triumph over adversity—they are resilient. Researchers have found that resilient children are likely to have a close relationship with a parent figure and bonds to caring people outside the family. Social policy is a government's course of action designed to promote the welfare of its citizens. The poor conditions of life for a significant percentage of U.S. children, and the lack of attention to prevention of these poor conditions, point to the need for revised social policies.

Assessing the Newborn

- For many years, the Apgar Scale has been used to assess the newborn's health. The Brazelton Neonatal Behavioral Assessment Scale (NBAS) examines the newborn's neurological development, reflexes, and reactions to people. The Neonatal Intensive Care Unit Network Neurobehavioral Scale (NNNS) was created to assess the at-risk infant.

Low Birth Weight and Preterm Infants

- Low birth weight infants weigh less than $5\frac{1}{2}$ pounds and they may be preterm (born three weeks or more before the pregnancy has reached full term) or small for date (also called small for gestational age, which refers to infants whose birth weight is below norm when the length of pregnancy is considered). Small for date infants may be preterm or full term. Although most low birth weight infants are normal and healthy, as a group they have more health and developmental problems than normal birth weight infants. Kangaroo care and massage therapy have been shown to have benefits for preterm infants.

3   THE POSTPARTUM PERIOD: EXPLAIN THE CHANGES THAT TAKE PLACE IN THE POSTPARTUM PERIOD

Physical Adjustments

- The postpartum period is the name given to the period after childbirth or delivery. The period lasts for about six weeks or until the mother's body has completed its adjustment. Physical adjustments in the postpartum period include fatigue, involution (the process by which the uterus returns to its prepregnant size five or six weeks after birth), hormonal changes, and exercises to recover body contour and strength.

Emotional and Psychological Adjustments

- Emotional fluctuations on the part of the mother are common in this period, and they can vary a great deal from one mother to the next. Postpartum depression characterizes women who have such strong feelings of sadness, anxiety, or despair that they have trouble coping with daily tasks; without treatment, it may worsen and last for many months. Postpartum depression occurs in about 10 percent of new mothers. The father also goes through a postpartum adjustment.

Bonding

- Bonding is the formation of a close connection, especially a physical bond, between parents and the newborn shortly after birth. Early bonding has not been found to be critical in the development of a competent infant.

KEY TERMS

germinal period 81
blastocyst 81
trophoblast 81
embryonic period 81
amnion 82
placenta 82
umbilical cord 82
organogenesis 82
fetal period 83

neurons 83
teratogen 85
fetal alcohol spectrum
  disorders (FASD) 87
doula 99
natural childbirth 100
prepared childbirth 100
breech position 102
cesarean delivery 102

Apgar Scale 103
Brazelton Neonatal
  Behavioral Assessment
  Scale (NBAS) 103
Neonatal Intensive
  Care Unit Network
  Neurobehavioral Scale
  (NNNS) 104
low birth weight infants 104

preterm infants 104
small for date infants 104
kangaroo care 106
postpartum period 108
postpartum depression 110
bonding 111

KEY PEOPLE

David Olds 95   Ferdinand Lamaze 100   T. Berry Brazelton 103   Tiffany Field 107
Grantley Dick-Read 100

E-LEARNING TOOLS

To help you master the material in this chapter, you'll find a number of valuable study tools at the Online Learning Center for *Child Development*, twelfth edition (**www.mhhe.com/santrockcd12**).

Taking It to the Net

Research the answers to these questions:

1. Denise's sister, Doreen, is pregnant for the first time. Doreen is not particularly known for her healthy lifestyle. What particular things can Denise encourage Doreen to do in order to give birth to a healthy baby?

2. Sienne told her fiancé, Jackson, that he had better stop smoking before they begin trying to conceive a child. Why is Sienne concerned about Jackson's smoking and its effect on their children before they have even started planning their family?

3. Hannah, who gave birth to a healthy baby boy—her first child—two weeks ago, appears to her husband Sean to be sad, lethargic, and is having trouble sleeping. How can Sean determine if Hannah is just going through a natural period of postpartum "blues" or if she might be suffering from postpartum depression?

Health and Well-Being, Parenting, and Education Exercises

Build your decision-making skills by trying your hand at the health and well-being, parenting and education exercises.

Video Clips

The Online Learning Center includes the following videos for this chapter:

- *Midwifery*
  Here we learn about midwives and how they differ from obstetricians.

- *Childbirth Education Alternatives*
  A childbirth educator describes the types of childbirth classes that are available to expectant parents and the benefits of childbirth education.

- *Breast vs. Bottle Feeding*
  A discussion of the numerous benefits of breast feeding over bottle feeding.

4

That energy which makes a child hard to manage is the energy which afterward makes him a manager of life.

—HENRY WARD BEECHER
American Author, 19th Century

LEARNING GOALS

- ◆ Discuss developmental changes in the body.

- ◆ Describe how the brain changes.

- ◆ Summarize how sleep patterns change as children and adolescents develop.

- ◆ Characterize health in childhood.

PHYSICAL DEVELOPMENT AND HEALTH

CHAPTER OUTLINE

1 **BODY GROWTH AND CHANGE**
Patterns of Growth
Infancy and Childhood
Adolescence

2 **THE BRAIN**
Brain Physiology
Infancy
Childhood
Adolescence

3 **SLEEP**
Infancy
Childhood
Adolescence

4 **HEALTH**
Illness and Injuries Among Children
Nutrition and Eating Behavior
Exercise

Images of Child Development
The Story of Angie and Her Weight

The following comments are by Angie, an elementary-school-aged girl:

> When I was eight years old, I weighed 125 pounds. My clothes were the size that large teenage girls wear. I hated my body and my classmates teased me all the time. I was so overweight and out of shape that when I took at P.E. class my face would get red and I had trouble breathing. I was jealous of the kids who played sports and weren't overweight like I was.
>
> I'm nine years old now and I've lost 30 pounds. I'm much happier and proud of myself. How did I lose the weight? My mom said she had finally decided enough was enough. She took me to a pediatrician who specializes in helping children lose weight and keep it off. The pediatrician counseled my mom about my eating and exercise habits, then had us join a group that he had created for overweight children and their parents. My mom and I go to the group once a week and we've now been participating in the program for six months. I no longer eat fast food meals and my mom is cooking more healthy meals. Now that I've lost weight, exercise is not as hard for me and I don't get teased by the kids at school. My mom's pretty happy too because she's lost 15 pounds herself since we've been in the counseling program.

Not all overweight children are as successful as Angie at reducing their weight. Indeed, being overweight in childhood has become a major national concern in the United States (Sabin & Shield, 2008; Wardlaw & Smith, 2009). Later in the chapter, we will further explore being overweight in childhood, including its causes and outcomes.

PREVIEW

Think about how much you changed physically as you grew up. You came into this life as a small being but grew very rapidly in infancy, more slowly in childhood, and once again more rapidly during puberty. In this chapter, we will explore changes in body growth, the brain, and sleep. We also will examine children's health.

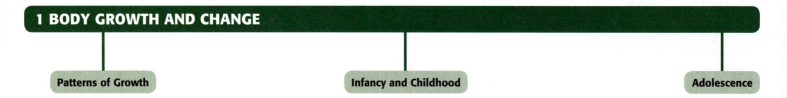

1 BODY GROWTH AND CHANGE

| Patterns of Growth | Infancy and Childhood | Adolescence |

In the journey of childhood, we go through many bodily changes. Let's begin by studying some basic patterns of growth and then turn to the bodily changes that occur from the time we were infants through the time we were adolescents.

Patterns of Growth

During prenatal development and early infancy, the head constitutes an extraordinarily large portion of the total body (see Figure 4.1). Gradually, the body's proportions change. Why? Growth is not random. Instead, it generally follows two patterns: the cephalocaudal pattern and the proximodistal pattern.

The **cephalocaudal pattern** is the sequence in which the fastest growth always occurs at the top—the head. Physical growth in size, weight, and feature differentiation

cephalocaudal pattern The sequence in which the fastest growth occurs at the top—the head—with physical growth in size, weight, and feature differentiation gradually working from top to bottom.

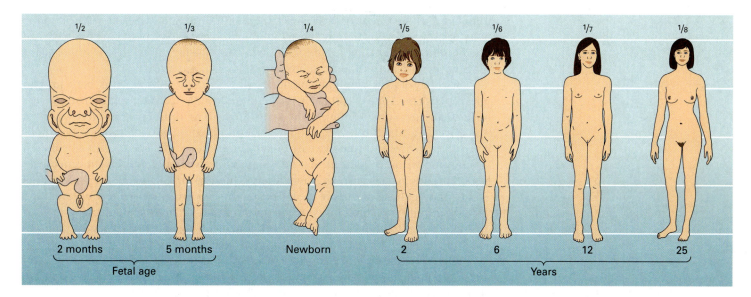

FIGURE 4.1 Changes in Proportions of the Human Body During Growth. As individuals develop from infancy through adulthood, one of the most noticeable physical changes is that the head becomes smaller in relation to the rest of the body. The fractions listed refer to head size as a proportion of total body length at different ages.

gradually works its way down from the top to the bottom—for example, from neck to shoulders, to middle trunk, and so on. This same pattern occurs in the head area; the top parts of the head—the eyes and brain—grow faster than the lower parts, such as the jaw.

Sensory and motor development also generally proceed according to the cephalo-caudal principle. For example, infants see objects before they can control their torso, and they can use their hands long before they can crawl or walk. However, one study found that infants reached for toys with their feet prior to using their hands (Galloway & Thelen, 2004). On average, infants first touched the toy with their feet when they were 12 weeks old and with their hands when they were 16 weeks old. We will have much more to say about sensory and motor development in Chapter 5.

The **proximodistal pattern** is the growth sequence that starts at the center of the body and moves toward the extremities. For example, muscle control of the truck and arms matures before control of the hands and fingers. Further, infants use their whole hand as a unit before they can control several fingers.

Infancy and Childhood

Height and weight increase rapidly in infancy (Lampl, 2008). Then, they take a slower course during the childhood years.

Infancy The average North American newborn is 20 inches long and weighs $7\frac{1}{2}$ pounds. Ninety-five percent of full-term newborns are 18 to 22 inches long and weigh between $5\frac{1}{2}$ and 10 pounds.

In the first several days of life, most newborns lose 5 to 7 percent of their body weight. Once infants adjust to sucking, swallowing, and digesting, they grow rapidly, gaining an average of 5 to 6 ounces per week during the first month. They have doubled their birth weight by the age of 4 months and have nearly tripled it by their first birthday. Infants grow about one inch per month during the first year, reaching approximately $1\frac{1}{2}$ times their birth length by their first birthday.

In the second year of life, infants' rate of growth slows considerably. By 2 years of age, infants weigh approximately 26 to 32 pounds, having gained a quarter to half a pound per month during the second year; now they have reached about one-fifth of their adult weight. The average 2-year-old is 32 to 35 inches tall, which is nearly one-half of adult height.

Early Childhood As the preschool child grows older, the percentage of increase in height and weight decreases with each additional year (Cooper & others, 2008). Girls are only slightly smaller and lighter than boys during these years. Both boys and girls

The bodies of 5-year-olds and 2-year-olds are different. Notice how the 5-year-old not only is taller and weighs more, but also has a longer trunk and legs than the 2-year-old. *What might be some other physical differences in 2- and 5-year-olds?*

proximodistal pattern The sequence in which growth starts at the center of the body and moves toward the extremities.

slim down as the trunks of their bodies lengthen. Although their heads are still somewhat large for their bodies, by the end of the preschool years most children have lost their top-heavy look. Body fat declines slowly but steadily during the preschool years. Girls have more fatty tissue than boys; boys have more muscle tissue.

Growth patterns vary individually (Burns & others, 2009). Think back to your preschool years. This was probably the first time you noticed that some children were taller than you, some shorter; some were fatter, some thinner; some were stronger, some weaker. Much of the variation is due to heredity, but environmental experiences are involved to some extent. A review of the height and weight of children around the world concluded that two important contributors to height differences are ethnic origin and nutrition (Meredith, 1978). Also, urban, middle-socioeconomic-status, and firstborn children were taller than rural, lower-socioeconomic-status, and later-born children. The children whose mothers smoked during pregnancy were half an inch shorter than the children whose mothers did not smoke during pregnancy. In the United States, African American children are taller than White children.

Why are some children unusually short? The culprits are congenital factors (genetic or prenatal problems), growth hormone deficiency, a physical problem that develops in childhood, or an emotional difficulty. When congenital growth problems are the cause of unusual shortness, often the child can be treated with hormones. Usually this treatment is directed at the pituitary, the body's master gland, located at the base of the brain. This gland secretes growth-related hormones. Physical problems during childhood that can stunt growth include malnutrition and chronic infections. However, if the problems are properly treated, normal growth usually is attained.

Middle and Late Childhood   The period of middle and late childhood—from about 6 to 11 years of age—involves slow, consistent growth. This is a period of calm before the rapid growth spurt of adolescence.

During the elementary school years, children grow an average of 2 to 3 inches a year. At the age of 8 the average girl and the average boy are 4 feet 2 inches tall. During the middle and late childhood years, children gain about 5 to 7 pounds a year. The average 8-year-old girl and the average 8-year-old boy weigh 56 pounds (National Center for Health Statistics, 2000). The weight increase is due mainly to increases in the size of the skeletal and muscular systems, as well as the size of some body organs. Muscle mass and strength gradually increase as "baby fat" decreases in middle and late childhood (Hockenberry & Wilson, 2009).

The loose movements and knock-knee of early childhood give way to improved muscle tone in middle and late childhood. Children also double their strength capacity during these years. The increase in muscular strength is due to heredity and to exercise. Because they have more muscle cells, boys tend to be stronger than girls.

Changes in proportions are among the most pronounced physical changes in middle and late childhood. Head circumference, waist circumference, and leg length decrease in relation to body height (Kliegman & others, 2007). A less noticeable physical change is that bones continue to harden during middle and late childhood; still, they yield to pressure and pull more than mature bones.

Adolescence

After slowing through childhood, growth surges during puberty. **Puberty** is a period of rapid physical maturation involving hormonal and bodily changes that occur primarily in early adolescence. The features and proportions of the body change as the individual becomes capable of reproducing. We will begin our exploration of puberty by describing its determinants and then examine important physical changes and psychological accompaniments of puberty.

Determinants of Puberty   Puberty is not the same as adolescence. For virtually everyone, puberty has ended long before adolescence is exited. Puberty is often thought of as the most important marker for the beginning of adolescence.

puberty A period of rapid physical maturation involving hormonal and bodily changes that take place primarily in early adolescence.

From *Penguin Dreams and Stranger Things,* by Berke Breathed. Copyright © 1985 by The Washington Post Company. By permission of Little, Brown & Company, Inc. and International Creative Management.

There are wide variations in the onset and progression of puberty. Puberty might begin as early as 10 years of age or as late as $13\frac{1}{2}$ for boys. It might end as early as 13 years or as late as 17 years.

In fact, over the years the timing of puberty has changed. Imagine a 3-year-old girl with fully developed breasts or a boy just slightly older with a deep male voice. That is what toddlers would be like by the year 2250 if the age at which puberty arrives were to continue decreasing as it did for much of the twentieth century. For example, in Norway, **menarche**—a girl's first menstruation—now occurs at just over 13 years of age, compared with 17 years of age in the 1840s (Petersen, 1979). In the United States—where children mature up to a year earlier than in European countries—the average age of menarche dropped an average of two to four months per decade for much of the twentieth century, to about $12\frac{1}{2}$ years today. Some researchers have found evidence that the age of puberty is still dropping for American girls; others suggest that the evidence is inconclusive or that the decline in age is slowing down (Archibald, Graber, & Brooks-Gunn, 2003; Hermann-Giddens, 2007). The earlier onset of puberty is likely the result of improved health and nutrition (Hermann-Giddens, 2007).

The normal range for the onset and progression of puberty is wide enough that, given two boys of the same chronological age, one might complete the pubertal sequence before the other one has begun it. For girls, the age range of menarche is even wider. It is considered within a normal range when it occurs between the ages of 9 and 15. Among the most important factors that influence the onset and sequence of puberty are heredity, hormones, and weight and body fat (Divall & Radovick, 2008).

Heredity Puberty is not an environmental accident. It does not take place at 2 or 3 years of age, and it does not occur in the twenties. Programmed into the genes of every human being is a timing for the emergence of puberty. Nonetheless, within the boundaries of about 9 to 16 years of age, environmental factors such as health, weight, and stress can influence the onset and duration of puberty.

Hormones Behind the first whisker in boys and the widening of hips in girls is a flood of hormones. **Hormones** are powerful chemical substances secreted by the endocrine glands and carried through the body by the bloodstream. In the case of puberty, the secretion of key hormones is controlled by the interaction of the hypothalamus, the pituitary gland, and the gonads (sex glands). The *hypothalamus* is a structure in the brain best known for monitoring eating, drinking, and sex. The *pituitary gland* is an important endocrine gland that controls growth and regulates other glands. The *gonads* are the sex glands—the testes in males, the ovaries in females.

The key hormonal changes involve two classes of hormones that have significantly different concentrations in males and females (Herbison & others, 2008; Richmond & Rogol, 2007). **Androgens** are the main class of male sex hormones. **Estrogens** are the main class of female hormones.

menarche A girl's first menstruation.

hormones Powerful chemical substances secreted by the endocrine glands and carried through the body by the bloodstream.

androgens The main class of male sex hormones.

estrogens The main class of female sex hormones.

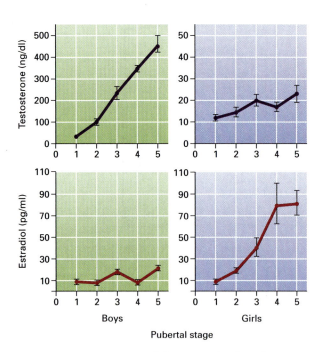

Testosterone is an androgen that is a key hormone in the development of puberty in boys. Throughout puberty, as their testosterone level rises, external genitals enlarge, height increases, and the voice changes (Wehkalampi & others, 2007). **Estradiol** is an estrogen that plays an important role in female pubertal development. As the estradiol level rises, breast development, uterine development, and skeletal changes occur. In one study, testosterone levels increased eighteenfold in boys but only twofold in girls across puberty; estradiol levels increased eightfold in girls but only twofold in boys across puberty (Nottleman & others, 1987) (see Figure 4.2).

Are there links between concentrations of hormones and adolescent behavior? Findings are inconsistent (Vermeersch & others, 2008). In any event, hormonal factors alone are not responsible for adolescent behavior (Graber, 2008). For example, one study found that social factors accounted for two to four times as much variance as hormonal factors in young adolescent girls' depression and anger (Brooks-Gunn & Warren, 1989). Hormones do not act independently; hormonal activity is influenced by many environmental factors, including parent-adolescent relationships. Stress, eating patterns, sexual activity, and depression can also activate or suppress various aspects of the hormone system (Dorn & others, 2006).

FIGURE 4.2 Hormone Levels by Sex and Pubertal Stage for Testosterone and Estradiol. The five stages range from the early beginning of puberty (stage 1) to the most advanced stage of puberty (stage 5). Notice the significant increase in testosterone in boys and the significant increase in estradiol in girls.

Growth Spurt Puberty ushers in the most rapid increases in growth since infancy. As indicated in Figure 4.3, the growth spurt associated with puberty occurs approximately two years earlier for girls than for boys. The mean beginning of the growth spurt in the United States today is 9 years of age for girls and 11 years of age for boys. Pubertal change peaks at an average of 11.5 years for girls and 13.5 years for boys. During their growth spurt, girls increase in height about 3.5 inches per year, boys about 4 inches.

Boys and girls who are shorter or taller than their peers before adolescence are likely to remain so during adolescence. At the beginning of adolescence, girls tend to be as tall as or taller than boys their age, but by the end of the middle school years most boys have caught up, or, in many cases, even surpassed girls in height. And even though height in elementary school is a good predictor of height later in adolescence, as much as 30 percent of the height of individuals in late adolescence is unexplained by height in the elementary school years.

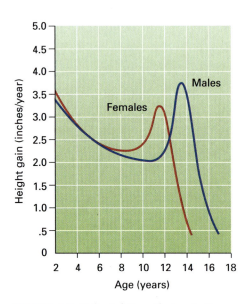

FIGURE 4.3 Pubertal Growth Spurt. On the average, the peak of the growth spurt that characterizes pubertal change occurs two years earlier for girls ($11\frac{1}{2}$) than for boys ($13\frac{1}{2}$).

Sexual Maturation Think back to the onset of your puberty. Of the striking changes that were taking place in your body, what was the first change that occurred? Researchers have found that male pubertal characteristics develop in this order: increase in penis and testicle size, appearance of straight pubic hair, minor voice change, first ejaculation (which usually occurs through masturbation or a wet dream), appearance of pubic hair, onset of maximum body growth, growth of hair in armpits, more detectable voice changes, and growth of facial hair. Three of the most noticeable areas of sexual maturation in boys are penis elongation, testes development, and growth of facial hair. The normal range and average age of development for these sexual characteristics, along with height spurt, is shown in Figure 4.4.

What is the order of appearance of physical changes in females? First, either the breasts enlarge or pubic hair appears. These are two of the most noticeable aspects of female pubertal development. Later, hair appears in the armpits. As these changes occur, the female grows in height, and her hips become wider than her shoulders. Her first menstruation (menarche) occurs rather late in the pubertal cycle; it is considered normal if it occurs between the ages of 9 and 15. Initially, her menstrual cycles may be highly irregular. For the first several years, she might not ovulate during every menstrual cycle. Some girls do not become fertile until two years after their periods begin. Pubertal females do not experience voice changes comparable to

testosterone An androgen that is a key hormone in boys' pubertal development.

estradiol An estrogen that is a key hormone in girls' pubertal development.

those in pubertal males. By the end of puberty, the female's breasts have become more fully rounded.

Body Image   One psychological aspect of physical change in puberty is certain: Adolescents are preoccupied with their bodies and develop images of what their bodies are like (Ayala & others, 2007). Preoccupation with body image is strong throughout adolescence, but it is especially acute during puberty, a time when adolescents are more dissatisfied with their bodies than in late adolescence (Graber & Brooks-Gunn, 2002).

Gender differences characterize adolescents' perceptions of their bodies (Jones, Bain, & King, 2008). In general, girls are less happy with their bodies and have more negative body images than boys throughout puberty (Bearman & others, 2006). As pubertal change proceeds, girls often become more dissatisfied with their bodies, probably because their body fat increases. In contrast, boys become more satisfied as they move through puberty, probably because their muscle mass increases (Bearman & others, 2006). Here is a sampling of recent research on body image in adolescence:

- *Appearance.* Adolescent males who evaluated their appearance more positively and who said appearance was very important to them were more likely to engage in risky sexy behavior, whereas adolescent females who evaluated their appearance more positively were less likely to engage in risky behavior (Gillen, Lefkowitz, & Shearer, 2006).

- *Physical and mental health problems.* A longitudinal study of more than 2,500 adolescents found that lower body satisfaction placed them at risk for poorer overall health (Neumark-Sztainer & others, 2006). Another study indicated that 12- to 17-year-old girls female patients in psychiatric hospitals who had a negative body image were more depressed, anxiety-prone, and suicidal than same-aged female patients who were less concerned about their body image (Dyl & others, 2006).

- *Best and worst aspects of being a boy or a girl.* The negative aspects of puberty for girls appeared in a recent study that explored 400 middle school boys' and girls' perceptions of the best and worst aspects of being a boy or a girl (Zittleman, 2006). In the views of the middle school students, at the top of the list of the worst things about being a girl was the biology of being female, which included such matters as childbirth, PMS, periods, and breast cancer. The middle school students said that aspects of discipline (such as getting into trouble and being blamed more than girls even when they were not at fault) are the worst things about being a boy. However, another aspect of physical development was at the top of the students' list of the best things about being a girl—appearance (which included choosing clothes, hairstyles, and beauty treatments). Students said the best thing about being a boy was playing sports.

Early and Late Maturation   Did you enter puberty early, late, or on time? When adolescents mature earlier or later than their peers, they often perceive themselves differently and their maturational timing is linked to their socioemotional development and whether they develop problems (Costello & others, 2007; Foster & Brooks-Gunn, 2008). In the Berkeley Longitudinal Study conducted some years ago, early-maturing boys perceived themselves more positively and had more successful peer relations than did late-maturing boys (Jones, 1965). The findings for early-maturing girls were similar but not as strong as for boys. When the late-maturing boys were in their thirties, however, they had developed a more positive identity than the early-maturing boys had (Peskin, 1967). Perhaps the late-maturing boys had more time to explore life's options, or perhaps the

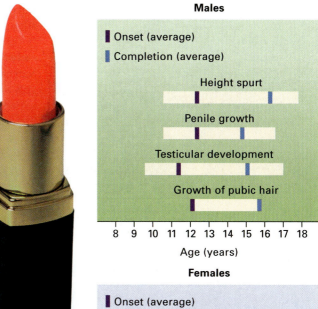

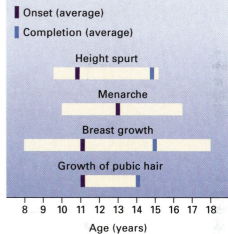

FIGURE 4.4 Normal Range and Average Development of Sexual Characteristics in Males and Females

What gender differences characterize adolescents' body image? What might explain the differences?

What are some outcomes of early and late maturation in adolescence?

early-maturing boys continued to focus on their physical status instead of paying attention to career development and achievement.

In recent years, an increasing number of researchers have found that early maturation increases girls' vulnerability to a number of problems (Biehl, Natsuaki, & Ge, 2007; Mendle, Turkheimer, & Emery, 2007). Early-maturing girls are more likely to smoke, drink, be depressed, have an eating disorder, request earlier independence from their parents, and have older friends; and their bodies are likely to elicit responses from males that lead to earlier dating and earlier sexual experiences. For example, a recent study revealed that early-maturing girls were more likely to try cigarettes and alcohol without their parents' knowledge (Westling & others, 2008). Apparently as a result of their social and cognitive immaturity, combined with early physical development, early-maturing girls are easily lured into problem behaviors, not recognizing the possible long-term effects of these on their development.

Review and Reflect: Learning Goal 1

1 Discuss Developmental Changes in the Body

REVIEW

- What are cephalocaudal and proximodistal patterns?
- How do height and weight change in infancy and childhood?
- What changes characterize puberty?

REFLECT

- Did you experience puberty early, late, or on time? How do you think this affected your social relationships and development?

2 THE BRAIN

| Brain Physiology | Infancy | Childhood | Adolescence |

In every physical change we have described so far, the brain is involved in some way. Structures of the brain help to regulate not only behavior but also metabolism, the release of hormones, and other aspects of the body's physiology.

Until recently, little was known for certain about how the brain changes as children develop. Not long ago, scientists thought that our genes determined how our brains were "wired" and that unlike most cells, the cells in the brain responsible for processing information stopped dividing early in childhood. Whatever brain your heredity dealt you, you were essentially stuck with it. This view, however, turned out to be wrong. Instead, the brain has plasticity, and its development depends on context (Fischer & Immordino-Yang, 2008; Moulson & Nelson, 2008). What we do can change the development of our brain.

The old view of the brain in part reflected the fact that scientists did not have the technology that could detect and map sensitive changes in the brain as it develops. The creation of sophisticated brain-scanning techniques has allowed better detection of these changes (Gilmore & others, 2007; Lee & others, 2007; Tumeh & others, 2007).

We described the amazing growth of the brain from conception to birth in Chapter 3. In this section, we initially will explore the basic structures and function of the brain, then examine developmental changes in the brain from infancy through adolescence.

Brain Physiology

The brain includes a number of major structures. The key components of these structures are *neurons*, the nerve cells that handle information processing, which we initially described in Chapter 3.

Structure and Function   Looked at from above, the brain has two halves, or hemispheres (see Figure 4.5). The top portion of the brain, farthest from the spinal cord, is known as the *forebrain*. Its outer layer of cells, the cerebral cortex, covers it like a cap. The *cerebral cortex* is responsible for about 80 percent of the brain's volume and is critical in perception, thinking, language, and other important functions.

Each hemisphere of the cortex has four major areas, called *lobes*. Although the lobes usually work together, each has a somewhat different primary function (see Figure 4.6):

- *Frontal lobes* are involved in voluntary movement, thinking, personality, and intentionality or purpose.
- *Occipital lobes* function in vision.
- *Temporal lobes* have an active role in hearing, language processing, and memory.
- *Parietal lobes* play important roles in registering spatial location, attention, and motor control.

Deeper in the brain, beneath the cortex, lie other key structures. These include the hypothalamus and the pituitary gland as well as the *amygdala*, which plays an important role in emotions, and the *hippocampus*, which is especially active in memory and emotion.

Neurons   How do these structures work? As we indicated, the neurons process information. Figure 4.7 shows some important parts of the neuron, including the *axon* and *dendrites*. Basically, an axon sends electrical signals away from the central part of the neuron. At tiny gaps called synapses the axon communicates with the dendrites of other neurons, which then pass the signals on. The communication in the synapse occurs through the release of chemical substances known as *neurotransmitters*.

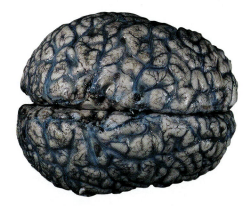

FIGURE 4.5 The Human Brain's Hemispheres. The two halves (hemispheres) of the human brain are clearly seen in this photograph.

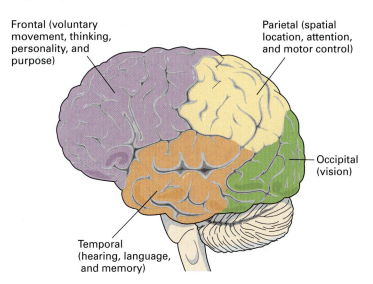

Frontal (voluntary movement, thinking, personality, and purpose)

Parietal (spatial location, attention, and motor control)

Occipital (vision)

Temporal (hearing, language, and memory)

FIGURE 4.6 The Brain's Four Lobes. Shown here are the locations of the brain's four lobes: frontal, occipital, temporal, and parietal.

FIGURE 4.7 The Neuron. (*a*) The dendrites receive information from other neurons, muscles, or glands. (*b*) Axons transmit information away from the cell body. (*c*) A myelin sheath covers most axons and speeds information transmission. (*d*) As the axon ends, it branches out into terminal buttons.

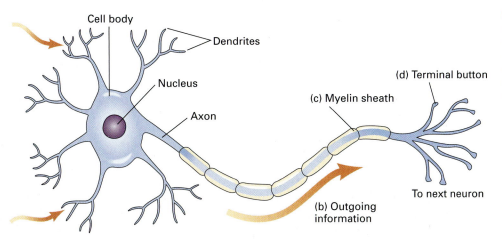

Cell body

Dendrites

Nucleus

Axon

(c) Myelin sheath

(d) Terminal button

(b) Outgoing information

To next neuron

(a) Incoming information

Most axons are covered by a myelin sheath, which is a layer of fat cells. The sheath helps impulses travel faster along the axon, increasing the speed with which information travels from neuron to neuron. The myelin sheath developed as the brain evolved. As brain size increased, it became necessary for information to travel faster over longer distances in the nervous system. We can compare the myelin sheath's development to the evolution of freeways as cities grew. A freeway is a shielded road and it keeps fast-moving, long-distance traffic from getting snarled by slow local traffic.

Which neurons get which information? Clusters of neurons known as *neural circuits* work together to handle particular types of information. The brain is organized in many neural circuits. For example, one neural circuit is important in attention and working memory (the type of memory that holds information for a brief time and is like a "mental workbench" as we perform a task) (Krimel & Goldman-Rakic, 2001). This neural circuit uses the neurotransmitter dopamine and lies in the prefrontal cortex area of the frontal lobes.

To some extent, the type of information handled by neurons depends on whether they are in the left or right hemisphere of the cortex (Bianco & others, 2008; Spironelli & Angrilli, 2008). Speech and grammar, for example, depend on activity in the left hemisphere in most people; humor and the use of metaphors depends on activity in the right hemisphere (Imada & others, 2007). This specialization of function in one hemisphere of the cerebral cortex or the other is called **lateralization**. However, most neuroscientists agree that complex functions such as reading or performing music involve both hemispheres. Labeling people as "left-brained" because they are logical thinkers and "right-brained" because they are creative thinkers does not correspond to the way the brain's hemispheres work. Complex thinking in normal people is the outcome of communication between both hemispheres of the brain (Liegois & others, 2008).

Infancy

As we saw in Chapter 3, brain development occurs extensively during the prenatal period. The brain's development is also substantial during infancy and later (Fischer, 2008; Nelson, 2007, 2008). Because the brain is still developing so rapidly in infancy, the infant's head should be protected from falls or other injuries, and the baby should never be shaken. *Shaken baby syndrome,* which includes brain swelling and hemorrhaging, affects hundreds of babies in the United States each year (Altimer, 2008; Squire, 2008).

Studying the brain's development in infancy is not easy. Even the latest brain-imaging technologies can't make out fine details—and these technologies can't be used on babies (Fair & Schlaggar, 2008). Position emission tomography (PET) scans (in which the amount of specially treated glucose in various areas of the brain is measured and then analyzed by computer) pose a radiation risk, and infants wriggle too much for magnetic resonance imaging (MRI) (in which a magnetic field is created around the body and radio waves are used to construct images of brain tissue and biochemical activity).

However, one researcher who is making strides in finding out more about the brain's development in infancy is Charles Nelson (2007, 2008; Nelson, Thomas, & de Haan, 2006; Nelson, Zeanah, & Fox, 2007). In his research, he attaches up to 128 electrodes to a baby's scalp (see Figure 4.8). He has found that even newborns produce distinctive brain waves that reveal they can distinguish their mother's voice from another woman's, even while they are asleep.

As an infant walks, talks, runs, shakes a rattle, smiles, and frowns, changes in its brain are occurring. Consider that the infant began life as a single cell and nine months later was born with a brain and nervous system that contained approximately 100 billion nerve cells, or neurons. What determines how those neurons are connected to communicate with each other?

Early Experience and the Brain

Children who grow up in a deprived environment may also have depressed brain activity (Nelson, Zeanah, & Fox, 2007; Reeb & others, 2008). As shown in Figure 4.9, a child who grew up in the unresponsive and unstimulating environment of a Romanian orphanage showed considerably depressed brain activity compared with a normal child.

lateralization Specialization of function in one hemisphere of the cerebral cortex or the other.

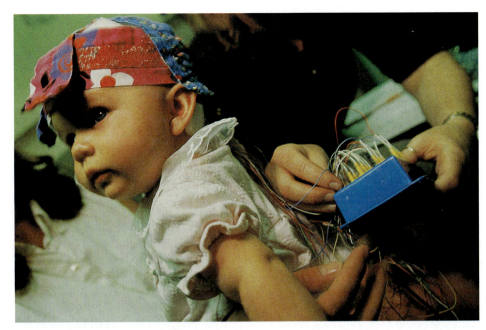

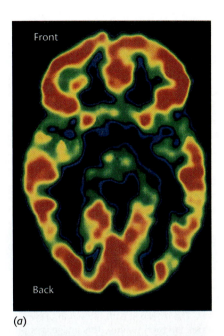

(a)

FIGURE 4.8 Measuring the Activity of an Infant's Brain. By attaching up to 128 electrodes to a baby's scalp to measure the brain's activity, Charles Nelson (2003, 2007; Nelson, Thomas, & de Haan, 2006) has found that even newborns produce distinctive brain waves that reveal they can distinguish their mother's voices from another woman's, even while they are asleep. *Why is it so difficult to measure infants' brain activity?*

Are the effects of deprived environments irreversible? There is reason to think the answer is no. The brain demonstrates both flexibility and resilience. Consider 14-year-old Michael Rehbein. At age 7, he began to experience uncontrollable seizures—as many as 400 a day. Doctors said the only solution was to remove the left hemisphere of his brain where the seizures were occurring. Recovery was slow, but his right hemisphere began to reorganize and take over functions that normally occur in the brain's left hemisphere, including speech (see Figure 4.10).

(a)

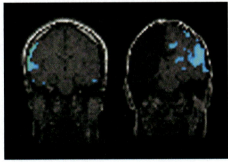

(b)

FIGURE 4.10 Plasticity in the Brain's Hemispheres. (a) Michael Rehbein at 14 years of age. (b) Michael's right hemisphere (*right*) has reorganized to take over the language functions normally carried out by corresponding areas in the left hemisphere of an intact brain (*left*). However, the right hemisphere is not as efficient as the left, and more areas of the brain are recruited to process speech.

(b)

FIGURE 4.9 Early Deprivation and Brain Activity. These two photographs are PET (positron emission tomography) scans (which use radioactive tracers to image and analyze blood flow and metabolic activity in the body's organs) of the brains of (a) a normal child and (b) an institutionalized Romanian orphan who experienced substantial deprivation since birth. In PET scans, the highest to lowest brain activity is reflected in the colors of red, yellow, green, blue, and black, respectively. As can be seen, red and yellow show up to a much greater degree in the PET scan of the normal child than the deprived Romanian orphan.

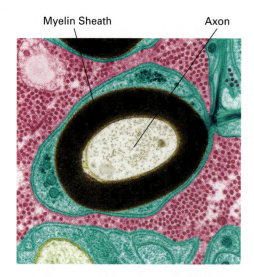

Myelin Sheath   Axon

FIGURE 4.11 A Myelinated Nerve Fiber. The myelin sheath, shown in brown, encases the axon (white). This image was produced by an electron microscope that magnified the nerve fiber 12,000 times. *What role does myelination play in the brain's development?*

Neuroscientists believe that what wires the brain—or rewires it, in the case of Michael Rehbein—is repeated experience. Each time a baby tries to touch an attractive object or gazes intently at a face, tiny bursts of electricity shoot through the brain, knitting together neurons into circuits. The results are some of the behavioral milestones we discuss in this chapter.

In sum, the infant's brain is waiting for experiences to determine how connections are made (Dalton & Bergenn, 2007). Before birth, it appears that genes mainly direct basic wiring patterns. Neurons grow and travel to distant places awaiting further instructions (Sheridan & Nelson, 2008). After birth, the inflowing stream of sights, sounds, smells, touches, language, and eye contact help shape the brain's neural connections (de Haan & Martinos, 2008; Nelson, 2007, 2008).

Changing Neurons   At birth, the newborn's brain is about 25 percent of its adult weight. By the second birthday, the brain is about 75 percent of its adult weight. Two key developments during these first two years involve the myelin sheath (the layer of fat cells that speeds up the electrical impulse along the axon) and connections between dendrites.

Myelination, the process of encasing axons with a myelin sheath, begins prenatally and continues after birth (Dubois & others, 2008; Fair & Schlagger, 2008) (see Figure 4.11). As we indicated earlier, this process increases the speed of processing information. Myelination for visual pathways occurs rapidly after birth, being completed in the first six months. Auditory myelination is not completed until 4 or 5 years of age. Some aspects of myelination continue even into adolescence. Indeed, the most extensive changes in myelination in the frontal lobes occur during adolescence (Giedd, 2008).

Dramatic increases in dendrites and synapses (the tiny gaps between neurons across which neurotransmitters carry information) also characterize the development of the brain in the first two years of life (see Figure 4.12). Nearly twice as many of these connections are made as will ever be used (Huttenlocher & others, 1991; Huttenlocher & Dabholkar, 1997). The connections that are used become strengthened and survive; the unused ones are replaced by other pathways or disappear (Nelson, Thomas, & de Haan, 2006). That is, connections are "pruned." Figure 4.13 vividly illustrates the growth and later pruning of synapses in the visual, auditory, and prefrontal cortex areas of the brain (Huttenlocher & Dabholkar, 1997).

As shown in Figure 4.13, "blooming and pruning" vary considerably by brain region in humans. For example, the peak synaptic overproduction in the area concerned with vision occurs about the fourth postnatal month, followed by a gradual pruning until the middle to end of the preschool years (Huttenlocher & Dabholkar, 1997). In areas of the brain involved in hearing and language, a similar, though somewhat later,

FIGURE 4.12 The Development of Dendritic Spreading. Note the increase in connectedness between neurons over the course of the first two years of life.
Reprinted by permission of the publisher from *The Postnatal Development of the Human Cerebral Cortex,* Vols. I-VII, by Jesse LeRoy Conel, Cambridge, Mass.: Harvard University Press, Copyright © 1939, 1975 by the President and Fellows of Harvard College.

myelination The process of encasing axons with a myelin sheath that increases the speed of processing information.

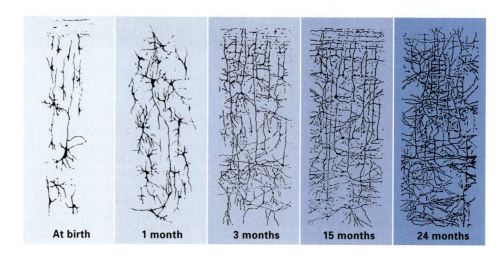

At birth   1 month   3 months   15 months   24 months

course is detected. However, in the *prefrontal cortex* (the area of the brain where higher-level thinking and self-regulation occur), the peak of overproduction occurs at just after 3 years of age. Both heredity and environment are thought to influence synaptic overproduction and subsequent pruning.

Changing Structures At birth, the hemispheres already have started to specialize: Newborns show greater electrical activity in the left hemisphere than in the right hemisphere when they are making or listening to speech sounds (Imada & others, 2007).

The areas of the brain do not mature uniformly (Nelson, 2007, 2008). Using the electroencephalogram (EEG), which measures the brain's electrical activity, researchers have found that a spurt in EEG activity occurs at about $1\frac{1}{2}$ to 2 years of age (Fischer & Bidell, 2006; Fischer & Rose, 1995). Other spurts seem to take place at about 9, 12, 15, and 20 years of age. Researchers stress that these spurts of brain activity may coincide with important changes in cognitive development. For example, the increase in EEG brain activity at $1\frac{1}{2}$ to 2 years of age is associated with an increase in the infant's capacity for conceptualization and language, and the spurts at 15 and 20 years of age are linked to increases in reflective thinking (Immordino-Yang & Fischer, 2007).

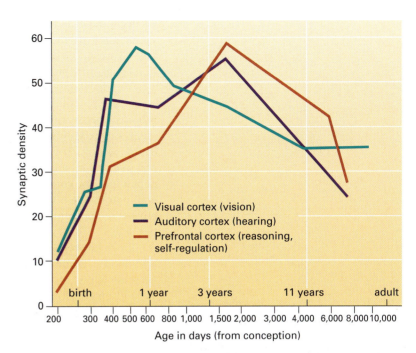

FIGURE 4.13 Synaptic Density in the Human Brain from Infancy to Adulthood. The graph shows the dramatic increase and then pruning in synaptic density for three regions of the brain: visual cortex, auditory cortex, and prefrontal cortex. Synaptic density is believed to be an important indication of the extent of connectivity between neurons.

Childhood

The brain and other parts of the nervous system continue developing through childhood and adolescence. These changes enable children to plan their actions, to attend to stimuli more effectively, and to make considerable strides in language development.

During early childhood, the brain and head grow more rapidly than any other part of the body. Figure 4.14 shows how the growth curve for the head and brain advances more rapidly than the growth curve for height and weight. Some of the brain's increase in size is due to myelination and some is due to an increase in the number and size of dendrites. Some developmentalists conclude that myelination is important in the maturation of a number of children's abilities (Fair & Schlaggar, 2008). For example, myelination in the areas of the brain related to hand-eye coordination is not complete until about 4 years of age. A functional magnetic resonance imaging (fMRI) study of children (mean age, 4 years) found that those who were characterized by developmental delay of motor and cognitive milestones had significantly reduced levels of myelination (Pujol & others, 2004). Myelination in the areas of the brain related to focusing attention is not complete until the end of the middle or late childhood.

Still, the brain in early childhood is not growing as rapidly as in infancy. However, the anatomical changes in the child's brain between the ages of 3 and 15 are dramatic. By repeatedly obtaining brain scans of the same children for up to four years, scientists have found that children's brains experience rapid, distinct bursts of growth (Thompson & others, 2000). The amount of brain material in some areas can nearly double in as little as one year, followed by a drastic loss of tissue as unneeded cells are purged and the brain continues to reorganize itself. The overall size of the brain does not increase dramatically from 3 to 15. What does dramatically change are local patterns within the brain (Thompson & others, 2000). From 3 to 6 years of age, the most rapid growth

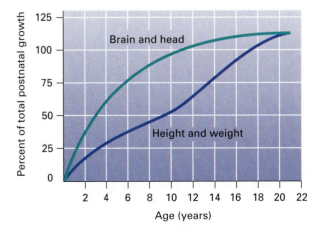

FIGURE 4.14 Growth Curves for the Head and Brain and for Height and Weight. The more rapid growth of the brain and head can easily be seen. Height and weight advance more gradually over the first two decades of life.

occurs in the frontal lobe areas involved in planning and organizing new actions and in maintaining attention to tasks. From age 6 through puberty, the most dramatic growth takes place in the temporal and parietal lobes, especially in areas that play major roles in language and spatial relations.

The development of the brain and opportunities to experience a widening world contribute to children's emerging cognitive abilities (Westermann & others, 2007). Scientists are beginning to chart connections between children's cognitive development, their changing brain structures, and the transmission of information at the level of the neuron. For example, we mentioned earlier that a neural circuit for attention and working memory is located in the prefrontal cortex and uses the neurotransmitter dopamine. The concentration of dopamine in a child's brain typically increases considerably from 3 to 6 years of age (Diamond, 2001). Perhaps this change, as well as rapid growth in the frontal lobe during this same period, is tied to the child's growing cognitive skills.

Links between the changing brain and children's cognitive development involve activation of some brain areas with some areas increasing in activation while others decrease (Dowker, 2006; Durston & Casey, 2006). One shift in activation that occurs as children develop in middle and late childhood is from diffuse, larger areas to more focal, smaller areas (Durston & others, 2006). This shift is characterized by synaptic pruning in which areas of the brain not being used lose synaptic connections and those being used show an increase in connections. In a recent study, researchers found less diffusion and more focal activation in the prefrontal cortex (the highest level of the frontal lobes) from 7 to 30 years of age (Durston & others, 2006). The activation change was accompanied by increased efficiency in cognitive performance, especially in *cognitive control*, which involves flexible and effective control in a number of areas. These areas include controlling attention, reducing interfering thoughts, inhibiting motor actions, and being flexible in switching between competing choices (Carver & others, 2001; Munkata, 2006).

Adolescence

Along with the rest of the body, the brain is changing during adolescence, but the study of adolescent brain development is in its infancy (Ernst & Mueller, 2008; McAnarney, 2008). As advances in technology take place, significant strides will also likely be made in charting developmental changes in the adolescent brain (Casey, Jones, & Hare, 2008; Whittle & others, 2008). What do we know now?

Using fMRI brain scans, scientists have recently discovered that adolescents' brains undergo significant structural changes (Eshel & others, 2007; Toga, Thompson, & Sowell, 2006). The **corpus callosum**, where fibers connect the brain's left and right hemispheres, thickens in adolescence and this improves adolescents' ability to process information (Giedd & others, 2006). We just described advances in the development of the **prefrontal cortex**—the highest level of the frontal lobes involved in reasoning, decision making, and self-control. The prefrontal cortex doesn't finish maturing until the emerging adult years, approximately 18 to 25 years of age, or later, but the **amygdala**—the seat of emotions such as anger—matures earlier than the prefrontal cortex. Figure 4.15 shows the locations of the corpus callosum, prefrontal cortex, and amygdala. A recent study of 137 early adolescents revealed a positive link between the volume of the amygdala and the duration of adolescents' aggressive behavior during interactions with parents (Whittle & others, 2008).

Leading researcher Charles Nelson (2003; Nelson, Thomas, & de Haan, 2006) points out that although adolescents are capable of very strong emotions their prefrontal cortex hasn't adequately developed to the point at which they can control

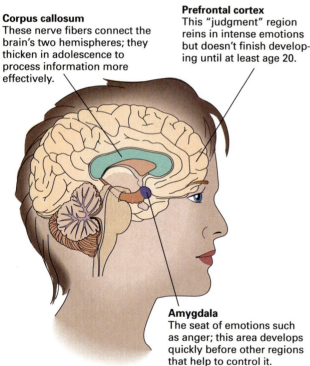

Corpus callosum
These nerve fibers connect the brain's two hemispheres; they thicken in adolescence to process information more effectively.

Prefrontal cortex
This "judgment" region reins in intense emotions but doesn't finish developing until at least age 20.

Amygdala
The seat of emotions such as anger; this area develops quickly before other regions that help to control it.

FIGURE 4.15 Changes in the Adolescent Brain

corpus callosum Where fibers connect the brain's left and right hemispheres.

prefrontal cortex The highest level of the frontal lobes that is involved in reasoning, decision making, and self-control.

amygdala The seat of emotions in the brain.

these passions. It is as if their brain doesn't have the brakes to slow down their emotions. Or consider this interpretation of the development of emotion and cognition in adolescents: "early activation of strong 'turbo-charged' feelings with a relatively un-skilled set of 'driving skills' or cognitive abilities to modulate strong emotions and motivations" (Dahl, 2004, p. 18).

Of course, a major issue is which comes first: biological changes in the brain or experiences that stimulate these changes (Lerner, Boyd, & Du, 2008). Consider a recent study in which the prefrontal cortex thickened, and more brain connections formed when adolescents resisted peer pressure (Paus & others, 2008). Scientists have yet to determine whether the brain changes come first or whether the brain changes are the result of experiences with peers, parents, and others. Once again, we encounter the nature/nurture issue that is so prominent in examining development.

Are there implications of what we now know about the adolescent's still developing brain for the legal system? For example, can the recent brain research we have just discussed be used to argue that because the adolescent's brain, especially the higher-level prefrontal cortex, is still developing, adolescents should not be given the death penalty? Some scientists argue that criminal behavior in adolescence should not be excused, but that adolescents should not be given the death penalty (Fassler, 2004). Other scientists, such as Jerome Kagan (2004), stress that whether adolescents should be given the death penalty is an ethical issue. Kagan also concludes that brain research does not show that adolescents have less responsibility for committing crimes. A similar stance is taken by some of the leading neuroscientists who study brain development in adolescence. Elizabeth Sowell (2004) says that scientists can't just do brain scans on adolescents and decide if they should be tried as adults. In 2005, the death penalty for adolescents (under the age of 18) was prohibited by the U.S. Supreme Court, but it still continues to be debated (Ash, 2006).

Lee Malvo was 17 years old when he and John Muhammad, an adult, went on a sniper spree in 2002, terrorizing the Washington, D.C., area and killing 10 people. A 2005 U.S. Supreme Court ruling stated that individuals who are 18 years of age and under, like Malvo, cannot be given the death penalty. *Are there implications for what scientists are learning about the adolescent's brain for legal decisions, such as the death penalty?*

Review and Reflect: Learning Goal 2

2 Describe How the Brain Changes

REVIEW

- What is the nature of brain physiology?
- How does the brain change in infancy?
- What characterizes the development of the brain in childhood?
- How does the brain change in adolescence, and how might this change be linked to adolescents' behavior?

REFLECT

- Numerous claims have been made that elementary and secondary education should be brain-based. Some journalists have even suggested that educators should look to neuroscientists for answers about how best to teach children and adolescents. Unfortunately, such bold statements are speculative at best and far removed from what neuroscientists actually know about the brain. Find an article on brain-based education in a magazine or on the Internet. Use your critical-thinking skills to evaluate the article's credibility. Does the author present research evidence to support the link between neuroscience and the brain-based method being recommended? Explain.

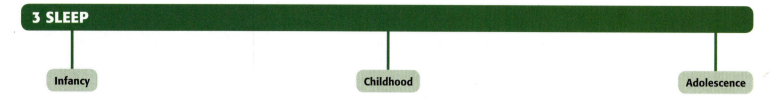

3 SLEEP

| Infancy | Childhood | Adolescence |

Sleep restores, replenishes, and rebuilds our brains and bodies. Some neuroscientists believe that sleep gives neurons used while we are awake a chance to shut down and repair themselves (National Institute of Neurological Disorders and Stroke, 2008). How do sleeping patterns change during the childhood years?

Infancy

How much do infants sleep? Are there any special problems that can develop regarding infants' sleep?

The Sleep/Wake Cycle   When we were infants, sleep consumed more of our time than it does now (Sadeh, 2008; Taveras & others, 2008). Newborns sleep 16 to 17 hours a day, although some sleep more and others less—the range is from a low of about 10 hours to a high of about 21 hours, although the longest period of sleep is not always between 11 P.M. and 7 A.M. Although total sleep remains somewhat consistent for young infants, their sleep during the day does not always follow a rhythmic pattern. An infant might change from sleeping several long bouts of 7 or 8 hours to three or four shorter sessions only several hours in duration. By about 1 month of age, most infants have begun to sleep longer at night. By 6 months of age, they usually have moved closer to adultlike sleep patterns, spending their longest span of sleep at night and their longest span of waking during the day (Sadeh, 2008).

The most common infant sleep-related problem reported by parents is night waking. Surveys indicate that 20 to 30 percent of infants have difficulty going to sleep at night and night waking (Sadeh, 2008). What factors are involved in infant night waking? Infant night-waking problems have consistently been linked to excessive parental involvement in sleep-related interactions with their infant (Sadeh, 2008). Also, a recent study of 9-month-old infants revealed that more time awake at night was linked to intrinsic factors such as daytime crying and fussing, and extrinsic factors such as being distressed when separated from the mother, breast feeding, and co-sleeping (DeLeon & Karraker, 2007).

Cultural variations influence infant sleeping patterns. For example, in the Kipsigis culture in Kenya, infants sleep with their mothers at night and are permitted to nurse on demand (Super & Harkness, 1997). During the day, they are strapped to their mothers' backs, accompanying them on daily rounds of chores and social activities. As a result, the Kipsigis infants do not sleep through the night until much later than American infants do. During the first eight months of postnatal life, Kipsigis infants rarely sleep longer than three hours at a stretch, even at night. This sleep pattern contrasts with that of American infants, many of whom begin to sleep up to eight hours a night by 8 months of age.

REM Sleep   In *REM sleep*, the eyes flutter beneath closed lids; in *non-REM sleep*, this type of eye movement does not occur and sleep is more quiet. Figure 4.16 shows developmental changes in the average number of total hours spent in REM and non-REM sleep. By the time they reach adulthood, individuals spend about one-fifth of their night in REM sleep, and REM sleep usually appears about one hour after non-REM sleep. However, about half of an infant's sleep is REM sleep, and

> *Sleep that knits up the ravelled sleave of care . . . Balm of hurt minds, nature's second course. Chief nourisher in life's feast.*
>
> —WILLIAM SHAKESPEARE
> **English Playwright, 17th Century**

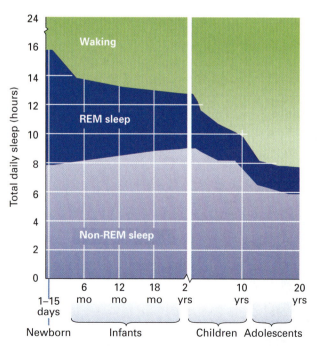

FIGURE 4.16 Developmental Changes in REM and Non-REM Sleep

infants often begin their sleep cycle with REM sleep rather than non-REM sleep (Sadeh, 2008). A much greater amount of time is taken up by REM sleep in infancy than at any other point in the life span. By the time infants reach 3 months of age, the percentage of time they spend in REM sleep falls to about 40 percent, and REM sleep no longer begins their sleep cycle.

Why do infants spend so much time in REM sleep? Researchers are not certain. The large amount of REM sleep may provide infants with added self-stimulation, since they spend less time awake than do older children. REM sleep also might promote the brain's development in infancy (Graven, 2006).

When adults are awakened during REM sleep, they frequently report that they have been dreaming—but when they are awakened during non-REM sleep, they are much less likely to report they have been dreaming (Cartwright & others, 2006; Dement, 2005). Since infants spend more time than adults in REM sleep, can we conclude that they dream a lot? We don't know whether infants dream or not, because they don't have any way of reporting dreams.

Shared Sleeping Sleeping arrangements for newborns vary from culture to culture (Alexander & Radisch, 2005). Sharing a bed with a mother is a common practice in many cultures, such as Guatamala and China, whereas in others, such as the United States and Great Britain, newborns sleep in a crib, either in the same room as the parents or in a separate room. In some cultures, infants sleep with the mother until they are weaned, after which they sleep with siblings until middle and late childhood (Walker, 2006). Whatever the sleeping arrangements, it is recommended that the infant's bedding provide firm support and that cribs should have side rails.

In the United States, sleeping in a crib in a separate room is the most frequent sleeping arrangement for an infant. In one cross-cultural study, American mothers said they have their infants sleep in a separate room to promote the infants' self-reliance and independence (Morelli & others, 1992). By contrast, Mayan mothers in rural Guatemala had infants sleep in their bed until the birth of a new sibling, at which time the infant would sleep with another family member or in a separate bed in the mother's room. The Mayan mothers believed that the co-sleeping arrangement with their infants enhanced the closeness of their relationship with the infants and were shocked when told that American mothers have their babies sleep alone.

Shared sleeping, or co-sleeping, is a controversial issue among experts (Sadeh, 2008). According to some child experts, shared sleeping brings several benefits: It promotes breast feeding and a quicker response to the baby's cries, and it allows the mother to detect potentially dangerous breathing pauses in the baby (McKenna & McDade, 2005; Pelayo & others, 2006). However, shared sleeping remains controversial, with some experts recommending it, others arguing against it (Mitchell, 2007; Newton & Vandeven, 2006; Pelayo & others, 2006). The American Academy of Pediatrics (AAP) Task Force on Infant Positioning and SIDS (2000) discourages shared sleeping. The Task Force concluded that bed sharing increases the risk that the sleeping mother will roll over onto her baby or increase the risk of sudden infant death syndrome (SIDS). Recent studies have found that bed sharing is linked with a greater incidence of SIDS, especially when parents smoke (Alm & others, 2006; Alexander & Radisch, 2005; Bajanowski & others, 2008). Also, shared sleeping is likely to place the infant at risk more if the caregivers are impaired by alcohol, smoking, or being overly tired (Baddock & others, 2007).

SIDS **Sudden infant death syndrome (SIDS)** is a condition that occurs when infants stop breathing, usually during the night, and die suddenly without an apparent cause. SIDS remains the highest cause of infant death in the United States, with nearly 3,000 infant deaths annually attributed to SIDS. Risk of SIDS is highest at 2 to 4 months of age (Centers for Disease Control and Prevention, 2008a).

sudden infant death syndrome (SIDS) A condition that occurs when an infant stops breathing, usually during the night, and suddenly dies without an apparent cause.

Is this a good sleep position for infants? Why or why not?

Since 1992, The American Academy of Pediatrics (AAP) has recommended that infants be placed to sleep on their backs to reduce the risk of SIDS, and the frequency of prone sleeping among U.S. infants has dropped dramatically (AAP Task Force on Infant Positioning and SIDS, 2000). Researchers have found that SIDS does indeed decrease when infants sleep on their backs rather than their stomachs or sides (Keens & Gemmill, 2008; Mitchell, Hutchinson, & Stewart, 2007; Sharma, 2007). Among the reasons given for prone sleeping being a high risk factor for SIDS are that it impairs the infant's arousal from sleep and restricts the infant's ability to swallow effectively (Ariagno, van Liempt, & Mirmiran, 2006).

In addition to sleeping in a prone position, researchers have found that the following are risk factors for SIDS:

- SIDS is less likely to occur in infants who use a pacifier when they go to sleep (Hauck, Omojokun, & Siadaty, 2006; Li & others, 2006; Mitchell, Blair, & L'Hoir, 2006)

- Low birth weight infants are 5 to 10 times more likely to die of SIDS than are their normal-weight counterparts (Horne & others, 2002).

- Infants whose siblings have died of SIDS are two to four times as likely to die of it (Lenoir, Mallet, & Calenda, 2000).

- Six percent of infants with *sleep apnea,* a temporary cessation of breathing in which the airway is completely blocked, usually for 10 seconds or longer, die of SIDS (McNamara & Sullivan, 2000).

- African American and Eskimo infants are four to six times as likely as all others to die of SIDS (Ige & Shelton, 2004).

- SIDS is more common in lower socioeconomic groups (Mitchell & others, 2000).

- SIDS is more common in infants who are passively exposed to cigarette smoke (Bajanowksi & others, 2008; Shea & Steiner, 2008).

- SIDS is more common if infants sleep in soft bedding (McGarvey & others, 2006).

- SIDS occurs more often in infants with abnormal brain stem functioning involving the neurotransmitter serotonin (Machaalani & Waters, 2008; Shani, Fifer, & Myers, 2007).

Childhood

Experts recommend that young children get 11 to 13 hours of a sleep each night (National Sleep Foundation, 2008). Most young children sleep through the night and have one daytime nap.

Following is a sampling of recent research on factors linked to children's sleep problems. A national survey indicated that children who do not get adequate sleep are more likely to show depressive symptoms, have problems at school, have a father in poor health, live in a family characterized by frequent disagreements and heated arguments, and live in an unsafe neighborhood than children who get adequate sleep (Smaldone, Honig, & Byrne, 2007). Another study revealed that marital conflict was linked to disruptions in children's sleep (El-Sheikh & others, 2006). Yet another study revealed that preschool children who did not get adequate sleep were more likely to experience injuries that required medical attention (Kouloughlioti, Cole, & Kitzman, 2008). And recent research indicates that short sleep duration in children is linked with being overweight (Nixon & others, 2008; Patel & others, 2008).

Not only is the amount of sleep children get important, but so is uninterrupted sleep. One study revealed that disruption in 4- to 5-year-old children's sleep (variability in amount of sleep, variability in bedtime, and lateness in going to bed) was linked to less optional adjustment in preschool (Bates & others, 2002). And a recent study found that bedtime resistance was associated with conduct problems or hyperactivity in children (Carvalho Bos & others, 2008).

Helping the child slow down before bedtime often contributes to less resistance in going to bed. Reading the child a story, playing quietly with the child in the bath, or letting the child sit on the caregiver's lap while listening to music are quieting activities.

Among the sleep problems that children can develop are nightmares and night terrors. Nightmares are frightening dreams that awaken the sleeper, more often toward the morning than just after the child has gone to bed at night. Almost every child has occasional nightmares, but persistent nightmares might indicate that the child is feeling too much stress during waking hours. A recent study revealed that preschool children who tended to have bad dreams were characterized by a difficult temperament at 5 months of age and anxiousness at 17 months of age (Simard & others, 2008).

Night terrors are characterized by sudden arousal from sleep and an intense fear, usually accompanied by a number of physiological reactions, such as rapid heart rate and breathing, loud screams, heavy perspiration, and physical movement (Bruni & others, 2008). In most instances, the child has little or no memory of what happened during the night terror. Night terrors are less common than nightmares and occur more often in deep sleep than do nightmares. Many children who experience night terrors return to sleep rather quickly. These sleep disruptions are not believed to reflect any emotional problems in children.

Adolescence

There has recently been a surge of interest in adolescent sleep patterns (Jenni & Lebourgeois, 2006; Owens & others, 2006). This interest focuses on the belief that many adolescents are not getting enough sleep, that there are physiological underpinnings to the desire of adolescents, especially older ones, to stay up later at night and sleep longer in the morning, and that these findings have implications for understanding when adolescents learn most effectively in school (Dahl & Lewin, 2002; Hansen & others, 2005; Yang & others, 2005). For example, a recent national survey found that 8 percent of middle school students and 14 percent of high school students are late for school or miss school because they oversleep (National Sleep Foundation, 2006). Also in this survey, 6 percent of middle school students and 28 percent of high school students fall asleep in U.S. schools on any given day.

Mary Carskadon and her colleagues (2002, 2004, 2005, 2006; Carskadon, Acebo, & Jenny, 2004) have conducted a number of research studies on adolescent sleep patterns. They found that adolescents sleep an average of 9 hours and 25 minutes when given the opportunity to sleep as long as they like. Most adolescents get considerably less sleep than this, especially during the week. This creates a sleep debt, which adolescents often try to make up on the weekend. The researchers also found that older adolescents are often more sleepy during the day than are younger adolescents. They concluded that this was not because of factors such as academic work and social pressures. Rather, their research suggests that adolescents' biological clocks undergo a hormonal phase shift as they get older. This pushes the time of wakefulness to an hour later than when they were young adolescents. The researchers found that this shift was caused by a delay in the nightly presence of the hormone *melatonin*, which is produced by the brain's pineal gland in preparation for the body to sleep. Melatonin is secreted at about 9:30 P.M. in younger adolescents but is produced approximately an hour later in older adolescents, which delays the onset of sleep.

Carskadon determined that early school starting times can result in grogginess and lack of attention in class and poor performance on tests. Based on this research, schools in Edina, Minnesota, made the decision to start classes at

In Mary Carskadon's sleep laboratory at Brown University, an adolescent girl's brain activity is being monitored. Carskadon (2005) says that in the morning, sleep-deprived adolescents' "brains are telling them its night time . . . and the rest of the world is saying it's time to go to school" (p. 19).

8:30 A.M. instead of 7:25 A.M. Discipline problems and the number of students who report an illness or depression have dropped. Test scores in Edina have improved for high school students, but not for middle school students, which supports Carskadon's idea that older adolescents are more affected by earlier school start times than younger adolescents are.

A longitudinal study further documented the negative outcomes of sleep loss during early adolescence (Fredriksen & others, 2004). The researchers examined the sleep patterns of 2,259 students from the sixth through the eighth grade. Over the course of the study, students who engaged in less sleep were more depressed and had lower self-esteem. Another recent study found that inadequate sleep during adolescence was linked to ineffective stress management, a low level of exercise, and having an unhealthy diet (Chen, Wang, & Jeng, 2006).

Review and Reflect: Learning Goal 3

3 **Summarize How Sleep Patterns Change as Children and Adolescents Develop**

REVIEW

- How can sleep be characterized in infancy?
- What changes occur in sleep during childhood?
- How does adolescence affect sleep?

REFLECT

- Did your sleep patterns start to change when you became an adolescent? Have they changed since you went through puberty? If so, how?

---

4 HEALTH

| Illness and Injuries Among Children | Nutrition and Eating Behavior | Exercise |

To some extent, the developmental path we have described so far in this chapter is the story of a mythical being, the average child. Whether a child experiences major bumps or detours on this path of physical growth and brain development depends to a great extent on the child's health. What are the major threats to the child's health today? We will look first at the major illnesses and injuries experienced by children and adolescents before turning to less obvious threats to healthy development: poor nutrition and eating habits, and lack of exercise. The formation of healthy habits in childhood, such as eating foods low in fat and cholesterol and engaging in regular exercise, not only has immediate benefits but also contributes to the delay or prevention of premature disability and mortality in adulthood—heart disease, stroke, diabetes, and cancer.

Illnesses and Injuries Among Children

To a pediatrician of the 1950s, the medical care available to children and adolescents today might seem like science fiction. New vaccinations and antibiotics as well as new tests and surgical techniques have helped to allow the emphasis in medical care to move toward prevention and outpatient care. Injuries and diseases can be treated far more effectively than in the past. The benefits of these advances, however, are distributed unevenly among the world's children. In this section, we first examine broad patterns in the causes of illness and death among children and adolescents and then turn to the difficulties faced by poor children in the United States and around the world.

Early Childhood   The story of children's health in the past 50 years is a shift away from fighting infectious diseases and to prevention and outpatient care (Alario & Birn Krant, 2008; Burns & others, 2009). In recent decades, vaccines have nearly eradicated disabling bacterial meningitis and have greatly reduced the incidence of measles, rubella, mumps, and chicken pox. In the effort to make a child's world safer, one of the main strategies is to prevent childhood injuries.

Young children's active and exploratory nature, coupled with being unaware of danger in many instances, often puts them in situations in which they are at risk for injuries. Most of young children's cuts, bumps, and bruises are minor, but some accidental injuries can produce serious impairment or even death (Andrews, Brouilette, & Brouilette, 2008). In the United States, motor vehicle accidents are the leading cause of death in young children, followed by cancer and cardiovascular disease (National Vital Statistics Report, 2004) (see Figure 4.17). In addition to motor vehicle accidents, other accidental deaths in children involve drowning, falls, burns, and poisoning (Lee & others, 2008).

Parental smoking is another major danger to children. Estimates indicate that approximately 22 percent of children and adolescents in the United States are exposed to tobacco smoke in the home. An increasing number of studies reach the conclusion that children are at risk for health problems when they live in homes in which a parent smokes (Hermann, King, & Weitzman, 2008). In one study, young children whose fathers smoked at home were more likely to have upper respiratory tract infections than those whose fathers did not smoke at home (Shiva & others, 2004). Children exposed to tobacco smoke in the home are more likely to develop wheezing symptoms and asthma than children in nonsmoking homes (Carlsen & Carlsen, 2008; Dong & others, 2008).

Middle and Late Childhood   For the most part, middle and late childhood is a time of excellent health (Van Dyck, 2007). Disease and death are less prevalent in this period than in early childhood and adolescence.

The most common cause of severe injury and death in middle and late childhood is motor vehicle accidents, either as a pedestrian or as a passenger (Lee & others, 2008). Using safety-belt restraints is important in reducing the severity of motor vehicle injuries. The school-age child's motivation to ride a bicycle increases the risk of accidents. Other serious injuries involve skateboards, roller skates, and other sports equipment.

Most accidents occur in or near the child's home or school (Robertson & South, 2007). The most effective prevention strategy is to educate the child about the hazards of risk taking and improper use of equipment (Snowdon & others, 2008). Appropriate safety helmets, protective eye and mouth shields, and protective padding are recommended for children who engage in active sports. Physically active school-age children are more susceptible to fractures, strains, and sprains than are their less active counterparts (Furnival, Street, & Schunk, 1999). Also, boys are more likely than girls to experience these injuries.

Caregivers play a key role in preventing childhood injuries (Schwebel, 2008). A recent study in four developing countries (Ethiopia, Peru, Vietnam, and India) revealed that depression in caregivers was consistently linked to children's risk of injury for all types of injury assessed (burns, serious falls, broken bones, and near-fatal injury) (Howe, Hutley, & Abramsky, 2006).

Children not only are vulnerable to injuries, they also may develop life-threatening diseases. Cancer is the second leading cause of death in children 5 to 14 years of age. Three percent of all children's deaths in this age period are due to cancer. Currently, 1 in every 330 children in the United States develops cancer before the age of 19. Morover, the incidence of cancer in children is increasing (Rubnitz & others, 2006).

Child cancers have a different profile from adult cancers. Adult cancers attack mainly the lungs, colon, breast, prostate, and pancreas. Child cancers mainly attack

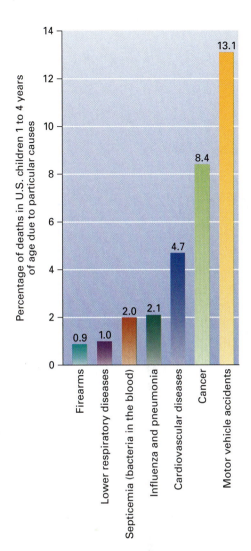

FIGURE 4.17 **Main Causes of Death in Children 1 through 4 Years of Age.** These figures show the percentage of deaths in U.S. children 1 to 4 years of age due to particular causes in 2002 (National Vital Statistics Reports, 2004).

the white blood cells (leukemia), brain, bone, lymph system, muscles, kidneys, and nervous system (Kennedy & D'Andrea, 2006).

The most common cancer in children is leukemia, a cancer of the tissues that make blood cells (Sanz, 2006). In leukemia, the bone marrow makes an abundance of white blood cells that don't function properly. They crowd out normal cells, making the child susceptible to bruising and infection.

Health, Illness, and Poverty Among the World's Children   The general statistics on children's health in the United States mask the special difficulties faced by the millions of U.S. children who live in poverty (Children's Defense Fund, 2007). In 2005, 17.8 percent of U.S. children were living in families below the poverty line (Federal Interagency Forum on Child and Family Statistics, 2007). An estimated 7 percent of U.S. children have no health care.

What is the best way to improve the health of children who live in poverty? Some experts argue that offering medical care is not enough. If you give an antibiotic to a child with a sore throat who then returns to a home where she will be cold and hungry, have you provided good health care? One approach to children's health aims to treat not only medical problems of the individual child but also the conditions of the entire family. In fact, some programs seek to identify children who are at risk for problems and then try to alter the risk factors in an effort to prevent illness and disease. The *Caring for Children* interlude describes one program that takes this ambitious approach.

Caring for Children

A HEALTHY START

The Hawaii Family Support/Healthy Start Program began in 1985 (Allen, Brown, & Finlay, 1992). It was designed by the Hawaii Family Stress Center in Honolulu, which already had been making home visits to improve family functioning and reduce child abuse for more than a decade. Participation is voluntary. Families of newborns are screened for family risk factors, including unstable housing, histories of substance abuse, depression, parents' abuse as a child, late or no prenatal care, fewer than 12 years of schooling, poverty, and unemployment. Healthy Start workers screen and interview new mothers in the hospital. They also screen families referred by physicians, nurses, and others. Because the demand for services outstrips available resources, only families with a substantial number of risk factors can participate.

Each new participating family receives a weekly visit from a family support worker. Each of the program's eight home visitors works with approximately 25 families at a time. The worker helps the family cope with any immediate crises, such as unemployment or substance abuse. The family also is linked directly with a pediatrician to ensure that the children receive regular health care. Infants are screened for developmental delays and are immunized on schedule. Pediatricians are notified when a child is enrolled in Healthy Start and when a family at risk stops participating.

The Family Support/Healthy Start Program recently hired a child development specialist to work with families of children with special needs. And, in some instances, the program's male family support worker visits a father to talk about his role in the family. The support workers encourage parents to participate in group activities held each week at the program center located in a neighborhood shopping center.

Over time, parents are encouraged to assume more responsibility for their family's health and well-being. Families can participate in Healthy Start until the child is 5 and enters public school.

The Hawaii Family Support/Healthy Start Program provides many home-visitor services for overburdened families of newborns and young children. *What are some examples of the home-visitor services in this program?*

What are some of the main causes of death in young children around the world?

Poverty in the United States is dwarfed by poverty in developing countries around the world. Each year UNICEF produces a report entitled *The State of the World's Children.* In a recent report, UNICEF (2006) concluded that the under-5 mortality rate is the result of a wide range of factors, including the nutritional health and health knowledge of mothers, the level of immunization, dehydration, availability of maternal and child health services, income and food availability in the family, availability of clean water and safe sanitation, and the overall safety of the child's environment.

The devastating effects on the health of young children occur in countries where poverty rates are high (UNICEF, 2007; Wagstaff & others, 2004). The poor are the majority in nearly one of every five nations in the world (UNICEF, 2006). They often experience lives of hunger, malnutrition, illness, inadequate access to health care, unsafe water, and a lack of protection from harm (Horton, 2006).

In the last decade, there has been a dramatic increase in the number of young children who have died because of HIV/AIDS transmitted to them by their parents (UNICEF, 2006). Deaths in young children due to HIV/AIDS especially occur in countries with high rates of poverty and low levels of education (Kalichman & others, 2005). For example, the uneducated are four times more likely to believe that there is no way to avoid AIDS and three times more likely to be unaware that the virus can be transmitted from mother to child (UNICEF, 2006).

Many of the deaths of young children around the world can be prevented by a reduction in poverty and improvements in nutrition, sanitation, education, and health services (UNICEF, 2008).

Nutrition and Eating Behavior

Poverty influences health in part through its effects on nutrition. However, it is not just children living in low-income families who have health-related nutrition problems; across the spectrum of income levels, a dramatic increase in the percent of U.S. children who are overweight has occurred.

Infancy   For the infant, the importance of receiving adequate energy and nutrients in a loving and supportive environment cannot be overstated (Black & Hurley, 2009; Schiff, 2009). Recall that from birth to 1 year of age, infants triple their weight and increase their length by 50 percent. Because infants vary in their nutrient reserves, body composition, growth

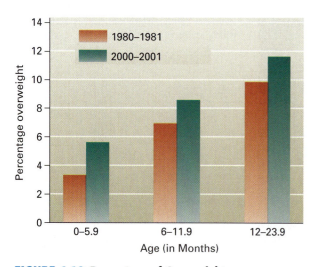

FIGURE 4.18 Percentage of Overweight U.S. Infants in 1980–1981 and 2000–2001. *Note:* Infants above the 95th percentile for their age and gender on a weight-for-height index were categorized as overweight.

rates, and activity patterns, their nutrient needs vary as well. However, because parents need guidelines, nutritionists recommend that infants consume approximately 50 calories per day for each pound they weigh—more than twice an adult's requirement per pound. For infants in the United States and other industrialized countries, the source of those calories rather than the amount is more likely to be an important concern.

A national study of more than 3,000 randomly selected 4- to 24-month-olds documented that many U.S. parents are aren't feeding their babies enough fruits and vegetables, but are feeding them too much junk food (Fox & others, 2004). Up to one-third of the babies ate no vegetables and fruit, frequently ate french fries, and almost half of the 7- to 8-month-old babies were fed desserts, sweets, or sweetened drinks. By 15 months, french fries were the most common vegetables the babies ate.

Are U.S. babies becoming increasingly overweight? A recent analysis revealed that in 1980, 3.4 percent of U.S. babies less than 6 months old were overweight, a percentage that increased to 5.9 percent in 2001 (Kim & others, 2006). As shown in Figure 4.18, as younger infants become older infants, an even greater percentage are overweight. Also in this study, in addition to the 5.9 percent of infant less than 6 months old who were overweight in 2001, another 11 percent were categorized as at risk for being overweight. In this study, infants were categorized as overweight if they were above the 95th percentile for their age and gender on a weight-for-height index; they were labeled at-risk for being overweight if they were between the 85th and 95th percentile.

In addition to eating too many french fries, sweetened drinks, and desserts, are there other factors that might explain this increase in overweight U.S. infants? A mother's weight gain during pregnancy and a mother's own high weight before pregnancy may be factors. One important factor likely is whether an infant is breast fed or bottle fed (Lawrence, 2008). Breast fed infants have lower rates of weight gain than bottle fed infants by school age, and it is estimated that breast feeding reduces the risk of obesity by approximately 20 percent (Li & others, 2007). Next, we explore other aspects of breast and bottle feeding.

Breast Versus Bottle Feeding   For the first 4 to 6 months of life, human milk or an alternative formula is the baby's source of nutrients and energy. For years, debate has focused on whether breast feeding is better for the infant than bottle feeding. The growing consensus is that breast feeding is better for the baby's health (Hosea Blewett & others, 2008; Lopez Alvarez, 2007). Since the 1970s, breast feeding by U.S. mothers has soared (see Figure 4.19). In 2004, more than two-thirds of U.S. mothers breast fed their newborns, and more than a third breast fed their 6-month-olds. The American Academy of Pediatrics (AAP) and the American Dietetic Association strongly endorse breast feeding throughout the infant's first year (AAP Work Group on Breastfeeding, 1997; James & Dobson, 2005).

What are some of the benefits of breast feeding? The following conclusions have been reached based on the current state of research:

Benefits for the Child

- *Gastrointestinal infections.* Breast fed infants have fewer gastrointestinal infections (Newburg & Walker, 2007).

- *Lower respiratory tract infections.* Breast fed infants have fewer lower respiratory tract infections (Ip & others, 2007).

- *Allergies.* A recent research review by the American Academy of Pediatrics indicated that there is no evidence that breast

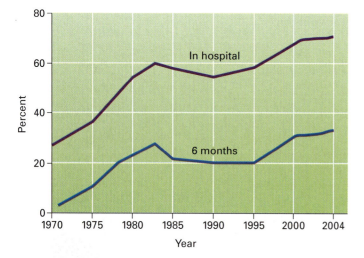

FIGURE 4.19 Trends in Breast Feeding in the United States: 1970–2004

feeding reduces the risk of allergies in children (Greer & others, 2008). The research review also concluded that modest evidence exists for feeding hyperallergenic formulas to susceptible babies if they are not soley breast fed.

- *Asthma*. The recent research review by the American Academy of Pediatrics concluded that exclusive breast feeding for three months protects against wheezing in babies, but whether it prevents asthma in older children is unclear (Greer & others, 2008).
- *Otitis media*. Breast fed infants are less likely to develop a middle ear infection (Rovers, de Kok, & Schilder, 2006).
- *Atopic dermatitis*. Breast fed babies are less likely to have this chronic inflammation of the skin (Snijders & others, 2007). The recent research review by the American Academy of Pediatrics also concluded that for infants with a family history of allergies, breast feeding exclusively for at least four months is linked to a lower risk of skin rashes (Greer & others, 2008).
- *Overweight and obesity*. Consistent evidence indicates that breast fed infants are less likely to become overweight or obese in childhood, adolescence, and adulthood (Moschonis, Grammatikaki, & Manios, 2007).
- *Diabetes*. Breast fed infants are less likely to develop type 1 diabetes in childhood (Ping & Hagopian, 2006) and type 2 diabetes in adulthood (Villegas & others, 2007).
- *SIDS*. Breast fed infants are less likely to experience SIDS (Ip & others, 2007).

In a large-scale research review, no conclusive evidence for the benefits of breast feeding was found for children's cognitive development and cardiovascular system (Agency for Healthcare Research and Quality, 2007).

Benefits for the Mother

- *Breast cancer*. Consistent evidence indicates a lower incidence of breast cancer in women who breast fed their infants (Shema & others, 2007).
- *Ovarian cancer*. Evidence also reveals a reduction in ovarian cancer in women who breast fed their infants (Jordan & others, 2008).
- *Type 2 diabetes*. Some evidence suggests a small reduction in type 2 diabetes in women who breast fed their infants (Ip & others, 2007).

In a large-scale research review, no conclusive evidence could be found for the maternal benefits of breast feeding on return to prepregnancy weight, osteoporosis, and postpartum depression (Agency for Healthcare Research and Quality, 2007). However, a recent study revealed that women who breast fed their infants had a lower incidence of metabolic syndrome (a disorder characterized by obesity, hypertension, and insulin resistance) in midlife (Ram & others, 2008).

Which women are least likely to breast feed? They include mothers who work full-time outside of the home, mothers under age 25, mothers without a high school education, African American mothers, and mothers in low-income circumstances (Heck & others, 2006; Merewood & others, 2007). In one study of low-income mothers in Georgia, interventions (such as counseling focused on the benefits of breast feeding and the free loan of a breast pump) increased the incidence of breast feeding (Ahluwalia & others, 2000). Increasingly, mothers who return to work in the infant's first year of life use a breast pump to extract breast milk that can be stored for later feeding of the infant when the mother is not present.

The AAP Work Group on Breastfeeding (1997) strongly endorses breast feeding throughout the first year of life. Are there circumstances when mothers should not breast feed? Yes, a mother should not breast feed (1) when the mother is infected with AIDS or some other infectious disease that can be transmitted through her milk, (2) if she has active tuberculosis, or (3) if she is taking any drug that may not be safe for the infant (Chatzimichael & others, 2007; Giglia & Binns, 2007; Vogler, 2006).

Human milk or an alternative formula is a baby's source of nutrients for the first four to six months. The growing consensus is that breast feeding is better for the baby's health, although controversy still swirls about the issue of breast feeding versus bottle feeding. *Why is breast feeding strongly recommended by pediatricians?*

Some women cannot breast feed their infants because of physical difficulties; others feel guilty if they terminate breast feeding early (Mozingo & others, 2000; Walshaw & Owens, 2006). Mothers may also worry that they are depriving their infants of important emotional and psychological benefits if they bottle feed rather than breast feed. Some researchers have found, however, that there are no psychological differences between breast fed and bottle fed infants (Ferguson, Harwood, & Shannon, 1987; Young, 1990). To read further about breast versus bottle feeding, see the *Diversity in Child Development* interlude.

Diversity in Child Development

LATONYA AND RAMONA: BREAST AND BOTTLE FEEDING IN AFRICA

Latonya is a newborn baby in Ghana. During her first days of life, she has been kept apart from her mother and bottle fed. Manufacturers of infant formula provide the hospital where she was born with free or subsidized milk powder. In the hospital, her mother has been persuaded to bottle feed rather than breast feed. When her mother leaves the hospital, she continues to bottle feed Latonya and overdilutes the milk formula with unclean water. Latonya's feeding bottles have not been sterilized. Latonya becomes very sick. She dies before her first birthday.

Ramona was born in Nigeria with a "baby-friendly" program. In this program, babies are not separated from their mothers when they are born, and the mothers are encouraged to breast feed them. The mothers are told of the perils that bottle feeding can bring because of unsafe water and unsterilized bottles. They also are informed about the advantages of breast milk, which include its nutritious and hygienic qualities, its ability to immunize babies against common illnesses, and its role in reducing the mother's risk of breast and ovarian cancer. Ramona's mother is breast feeding her. At 1 year of age, Ramona is very healthy.

For many years, maternity units in hospitals favored bottle feeding and did not give mothers adequate information about the benefits of breast feeding. In recent years, the World Health Organization and UNICEF have tried to reverse the trend toward bottle feeding of infants in many impoverished countries. They instituted the "baby-friendly" program in many countries. They also persuaded the International Association of Infant Formula Manufacturers to stop marketing their baby formulas to hospitals in countries where the governments support the baby-friendly initiatives (Grant, 1993). For the hospitals themselves, costs actually were reduced as infant formula, feeding bottles, and separate nurseries become unnecessary. For example, baby-friendly Jose Fabella Memorial Hospital in the Philippines reported saving 8 percent of its annual budget. Still, there are many places in the world where the baby-friendly initiatives have not been implemented (UNICEF, 2004).

The advantages of breast feeding in impoverished countries are substantial. However, these advantages must be balanced against the risk of passing HIV to the baby through breast milk if the mothers have the virus; the majority of mothers don't know that they are infected (De Baets & others, 2007; Dube & others, 2008). In some areas of Africa, more than 30 percent of mothers have HIV.

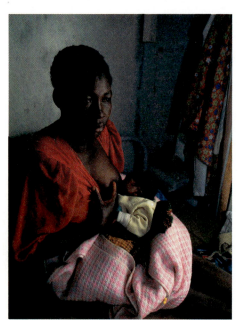

(Top) An HIV-infected mother breast feeding her baby in Nairobi, Africa. *(Bottom)* A Rhwandan mother bottle feeding her baby. *What are some concerns about breast versus bottle feeding in impoverished African countries?*

A further issue in interpreting the benefits of breast feeding was underscored in a recent large-scale research review (Agency for Healthcare Quality and Research, 2007). While highlighting a number of breast feeding benefits for children and mothers, the report issued a caution about breast feeding research: None of the findings imply causality. Breast versus bottle feeding studies are correlational, not experimental, and women who breast feed are wealthier, older, more educated, and likely more health-conscious than their bottle feeding counterparts, which could explain why breast fed children are healthier.

Malnutrition in Infancy   When they are severely malnourished, infants fail to grow adequately and they are listless. Very severe malnutrition usually takes the form of marasmus or kwashiorkor. **Marasmus** is severe malnutrition due to insufficient protein-calorie intake. Infants with marasmus have a shrunken, wasted, elderly appearance. **Kwashiorkor** is severe malnutrition caused by a deficiency in protein. The child's abdomen and feet swell with water. Otherwise, children with kwashiorkor may look well-fed. In fact, their vital organs are collecting whatever nutrients are present, depriving other parts of the body. The disease usually appears between 1 to 3 years of age. Marasmus and kwashiorkor are serious problems in developing countries, with as many as 50 percent of deaths under the age of 5 in these countries due to such severe protein-energy malnutrition (UNICEF, 2006).

Childhood   Poor nutrition in childhood can lead to a number of problems and occurs more in low-come than in higher-income families (Larson & others, 2008; Ruel & others, 2008). A special concern is the increasing epidemic of overweight children.

Malnutrition and Children in Low-Income Families   Malnutrition and even starvation are daily facts of life for children in many developing countries (UNICEF, 2008). Malnutrition also is a problem for U.S. children, with approximately 11 million preschool children experiencing malnutrition, placing their health at risk (Richter, 2004). One of the most common nutritional problems in early childhood is iron deficiency anemia, which results in chronic fatigue (Bartle, 2007; Ferrara & others, 2006). This problem results from the failure to eat adequate amounts of quality meats and dark green vegetables. Young children from low-income families are most likely to develop iron deficiency anemia (Shamah & Villalpando, 2006). A recent study revealed that Cunnigham preschool children with iron deficiency anemia were slower to display positive affect and touch novel toys for the first time than their nonanemic counterparts (Lozoff & others, 2007).

Poor nutrition is a special concern in the lives of young children from low-income families (Bryce & others, 2008; Cunnigham-Sabo & others, 2008). Many of these children do not get essential amounts of iron, vitamins, or protein (Walker & others, 2007). A recent study revealed that young children who had lower intakes of fresh fruit and vegetables cooked in olive oil, and higher intakes of canned fruit and vegetables and processed salad dressing, were more likely to come from lower-income, less educated families than higher-income, more educated families (Sausenthaler & others, 2007). In part, to address this problem in the United States, the Special Supplemental Nutrition Program for Women, Infants, and Children (WIC) serves approximately 7,500,000 participants in the United States. Positive influences on young children's nutrition and health have been found for participants in WIC (Herman & others, 2008). For example, one study found that participating in WIC was linked with a lower risk for being overweight in young Mexican American children (Melgar-Quinonez & Kaiser, 2004). In another study, participation in WIC was related to improved nutrition in preschool children, including higher intake of fruit and lower intake of added sugar from snacks (Siega-Riz & others, 2004). And a recent study revealed that WIC children who were anemic improved the most when they did not eat snacks and dried fruits (Swanson & others, 2007).

Eating Behavior and Parental Feeding Styles   For most children in the United States, insufficient food is not the key problem. Instead, poor nutrition as a result of unhealthy eating habits and being overweight threaten their present and future health (Bolling & Daniel, 2008; Reilly, 2009). A national assessment found that most children's diets need improvement (Federal Interagency Forum on Child and Family Statistics, 2002). In this assessment,

This Honduran child has kwashiorkor. Notice the telltale sign of kwashiorkor—a greatly expanded abdomen. *What are some other characteristics of kwashiorkor?*

marasmus Severe malnutrition caused by an insufficient protein-calorie intake, resulting in a shrunken, elderly appearance.

kwashiorkor Severe malnutrition caused by a protein-deficient diet, causing the feet and abdomen to swell with water.

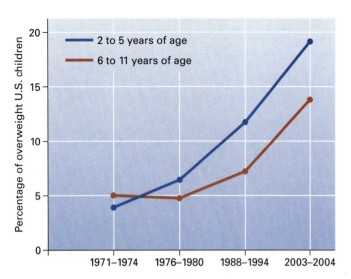

FIGURE 4.20 **The Increase in the Percentage of Overweight Children (Centers for Disease Control and Prevention, 2008b) in the United States**

only 27 percent of 2- to 5-year-old children were categorized as having good diets. Their diets worsened as they became older—only 13 percent of 6- to 9-year-old children had healthy diets. Although some health-conscious parents may be providing too little fat in their infants' and children's diets, other parents are raising their children on diets in which the percentage of fat is far too high (Schiff, 2009). And in a recent national survey, 4- to 18-year-olds often consumed the high-fat varieties of milk, yoghurt, cheese, ice cream, and dairy-based toppings (Kranz, Lin, Wagstaff, 2007).

Children's eating behavior is strongly influenced by their caregivers' behavior (Black & Hurley, 2007). Children's eating behavior improves when caregivers eat with children on a predictable schedule, model eating healthy food, make mealtimes pleasant occasions, and engage in certain feeding styles. Distractions from television, family arguments, and competing activities should be minimized so children can focus on eating. A sensitive/responsive caregiver feeding style is recommended, in which the caregiver is nurturant, provides clear information about what is expected, and appropriately responds to children's cues (Black & Hurley, 2007). Forceful and restrictive caregiver behaviors are not recommended. For example, a restrictive feeding style is linked to children being overweight (Black & Lozoff, 2008).

Overweight Children For most children in the United States and other developed nations, insufficient food is not the key problem. Instead, poor nutrition as a result of unhealthy eating habits and being overweight threaten their present and future health (Ventura & others, 2009; Wabitsch, 2009). As we saw earlier in our discussion of infants, the Centers for Disease Control and Prevention (2008b) has a category of obesity for adults but does not have an obesity category for infants, children, and adolescents because of the stigma the label may bring. Rather they have categories for being overweight or at risk for being overweight in childhood and adolescence.

The percentages of young children who are overweight or at risk for being overweight in the United States has increased dramatically in recent decades (see Figure 4.20), and the percentages are likely to grow unless changes occur in children's lifestyles (Ebbeling & Ludwig, 2008). A recent study revealed that in 2003 to 2006, 11 percent of U.S. 2- to 19-year-olds were obese, 16 percent were overweight, and 38 percent were at risk for being overweight (Ogden, Carroll, & Flegal, 2008). The good news from this large-scale study is that the percentages in these categories have started to level off rather than increase, as they had been doing in the last several decades.

It is not just in the United States that children are becoming more overweight. Recent surveys and policy prescriptions in Australia, mainland China, Hong Kong, and other countries indicate that children in many countries around the world are becoming more overweight (Chan, 2008; Li & others, 2008).

Being overweight in childhood is linked to being overweight in adulthood. In one study, a high percentage of children who were in the 95th percentile among their peers in terms of weight are still likely to be overweight when they are in their thirties (Guo & others, 2002). Another study revealed that girls who were overweight in childhood were 11 to 30 times more likely to be obese in adulthood than girls who were not overweight in childhood (Thompson & others, 2007).

Children who are overweight also are at risk for many medical and psychological problems (Freedman & others, 2007). Overweight children are at risk for developing pulmonary problems, such as sleep apnea (which involves upper airway obstruction), and hip problems (Tauman & Gozal, 2006). Diabetes, hypertension (high blood pressure), and elevated blood cholesterol levels also are common in children who are overweight (Plachta-Danielzik & others, 2008; Vohr & Boney, 2008). Once considered rare, hypertension in children has become increasingly common in overweight children (Thompson & others, 2007). Overweight children are three times more likely to develop hypertension than nonobese children (Sorof & Daniels, 2002). Overweight children with cardiovascular problems are more likely to come from low-socioeconomic-status families than higher-status ones (Longo-Mbenza & others, 2007). Social and psychological consequences of being overweight in childhood include low self-esteem, depression, and some exclusion of obese children from peer groups (Datar & Sturm, 2004; Gibson & others, 2008). A recent study revealed that obese children were perceived as less attractive, more tired, and more socially withdrawn than nonobese peers (Zeller, Reiter-Purtill, & Ramey, 2008).

What are some concerns about overweight children?

Both heredity and environment influence whether children will become overweight. Recent genetic analysis indicates that heredity is an important factor in children becoming overweight (Wardle & others, 2008). Overweight parents tend to have overweight children, even if they are not living in the same household (Wardlaw & Hempl, 2007). One study found that the greatest risk factor for being overweight at 9 years of age was a parent being overweight (Agras & others, 2004).

Environmental factors that influence whether children become overweight or not include the greater availability of food (especially food high in fat content), energy-saving devices, declining physical activity, parental monitoring of children's eating habits, the context in which a child eats, and heavy TV watching, (Byrd-Williams & others, 2008; Shoup & others, 2008). The American culture provides ample encouragement of overeating in children. Food is everywhere children go and easily accessed—in vending machines, fast-food restaurants, and so on (Rosenheck, 2008). Also, the portion size that children eat in meals in the United States has grown. Fast-food restaurants capitalize on this by providing families with the opportunity to "super size" their meals at a relatively lower cost for the extra food. And a recent study revealed a link between higher levels of watching TV with being overweight in childhood (Wells & others, 2008).

Many experts recommend a program that involves a combination of diet, exercise, and behavior modification to help children lose weight (Wittmeier, Mollar, & Kriellaars, 2008). As we learned in Angie's story at the beginning of the chapter, a combination of behavioral modification, a structured program, and positive parental involvement can effectively help overweight children.

Parents play an important role in children's eating habits and the likelihood they will become overweight or not (Black & Hurley, 2009; Ventura & others, 2009). One problem is that many parents do not recognize that their children are overweight. A recent study of parents with 2- to 17-year-old children found that few parents of overweight children perceived their children to be too heavy and were not worried about the children's weight (Eckstein & others, 2006). Another recent study revealed that Latino parents who monitored what their children ate had children who ate healthier foods and exercised more than their counterparts whose eating habits were not as closely monitored (Arrendondo & others, 2006). In another study, the context in which fourth- to sixth-grade children ate was linked with what they ate and their tendency to be overweight (Cullen, 2001). Children who ate with their families were more likely to eat lower-fat foods (such as low-fat milk and salad dressing and lean meats), more vegetables, and drank fewer sodas than children who ate alone. Overweight children ate 50 percent of their meals in front of a TV, compared with only 35 percent of normal-weight children.

In sum, healthy eating and an active rather than a sedentary lifestyle play important roles in children's development (Robbins, Power, & Burgess, 2008; Wabitsch, 2009). Pediatric nurses play an important role in the health of children, including providing advice to parents about ways to improve their children's eating habits and activity levels. To read about the work of one pediatric nurse, see the *Careers in Child Development* profile.

What can parents do to prevent their children from being overweight or obese?

Careers in Child Development

Barbara Deloin, Pediatric Nurse

Barbara Deloin is a pediatric nurse in Denver, Colorado. She practices nursing in the Pediatric Oral Feeding Clinic and is involved in research as part of an irritable infant study for the Children's Hospital in Denver. She also is on the faculty of nursing at the Colorado Health Sciences Center. Deloin previously worked in San Diego where she was coordinator of the Child Health Program for the County of San Diego.

Her research interests focus on children with special health-care needs, especially high-risk infants and children, and promoting positive parent-child experiences. Deloin was elected president of the National Association of Pediatric Nurse Associates and Practitioners for the 2000–2001 term.

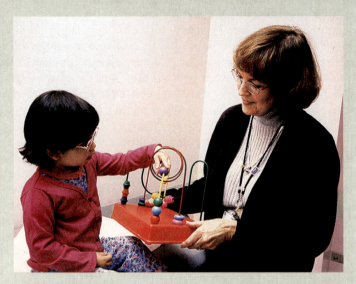

Barbara Deloin, working with a child with special health care needs.

Exercise

Because of their activity level and the development of large muscles, especially in the arms and legs, children need daily exercise (Timmons, Naylor, & Pfeiffer, 2008). However, children are not getting nearly enough exercise (Fahey, Insel, & Roth, 2009). A 1997 national poll found that only 22 percent of U.S. children in grades 4 through 12 were physically active for 30 minutes every day of the week (Harris, 1997). Their parents said their children were too busy watching TV, spending time on the computer, or playing video games to exercise much. Boys were more physically active at all ages than girls. In one historical comparison, the percentage of children involved in daily physical education (P.E.) programs in schools decreased from 80 percent in 1969 to 20 percent in 1999 (Health Management Resources, 2001). Educators and policy makers in many other countries around the world, including China, Finland, and Great Britain, have become extremely concerned about the sedentary lifestyles of many children in their countries (Fogelholm, 2008; Liu & others, 2008).

Television watching is linked with low activity and obesity in children (Gable, Chang, & Krull, 2007). A related concern is the dramatic increase in computer use by children. Reviews of research have concluded that the total time that children spend in front of a television or computer screen places them at risk for reduced activity and possible weight gain (Lajunen & others, 2007; Te Velde & others, 2007). One study revealed that children who watched two or more hours of TV a day were less likely to participate in organized physical activities and less likely to have two or more servings of fruit a day than their counterparts who watched less than two hours of TV a day (Salmon, Campbell, & Crawford, 2006). A longitudinal study found that a higher incidence of watching TV in childhood and adolescence was linked with being overweight, being less physically fit, and having higher cholesterol levels at 26 years of age (Hancox, Milne, & Poulton, 2004).

The following three recent studies address aspects of families and schools that influence young children's physical activity levels:

- Preschool children's physical activity was enhanced by family members engaging in sports together and by parents' perception that it was safe for their children to play outside (Beets & Foley, 2008).

- Preschool children's physical activity varied greatly across different child-care centers (Bower & others, 2008). Active opportunities, presence of fixed and portable play equipment, and physical activity training were linked to preschool children's higher physical activity in the centers.

- Incorporation of a "move and learn" physical activity curriculum increased the activity level of 3- to 5-year-old children in a half-day preschool program (Trost, Fees, & Dzewaltowski, 2008).

Researchers and educators are increasingly exploring strategies that will increase children's exercise participation (Floriani & Kennedy, 2008; Rink, 2009). Following are three recent studies that address ways to increase children's exercise:

- A high-intensity resistance training program decreased children's body fat and increased their muscle strength (Benson, Torode, & Fiatarone Singh, 2008).

- Forty-five minutes of moderate physical activity and 15 minutes of vigorous physical activity daily were related to decreased odds of children being overweight (Wittmeier, Mollard, & Kriellaars, 2008).

- Aerobic exercise was linked to increases in an important cognitive activity—planning—in overweight 9-year-old children (Davis & others, 2007).

Boys and girls become less active as they reach and progress through adolescence (Merrick & others, 2005). A study of more than 3,000 U.S. adolescents found that 34 percent were in the lowest fitness category (Carnethon, Gulati, & Greenland, 2005). Another study revealed that physical fitness in adolescence was linked to physical fitness in adulthood (Mikkelsson & others, 2006). In this study, distance running in adolescence was most predictive for adult fitness in males, whereas sit-ups were the most predictive for females.

Gender and ethnic differences in exercise participation rates are noteworthy, and they reflect the trend of decreasing exercise from early through late adolescence. A recent study revealed that 40 percent of female and 57 percent of male adolescents met U.S. guidelines for physical activity (Butcher & others, 2008). Another recent study found that Latino and African American 7- to 14-year-olds had lower aerobic fitness levels than their non-Latino White counterparts (Shaibi, Ball, & Goran, 2006). Also, as indicated in Figure 4.21, in the National Youth Risk Survey, non-Latino White boys exercised the most, African American girls the least (MMWR, 2006).

Here are some ways to get children and adolescents to exercise more:

- Improve physical fitness classes in schools.
- Offer more physical activity programs run by volunteers at school facilities.
- Have children plan community and school exercise activities that really interest them.
- Encourage families to focus on physical activity, and challenge parents to exercise more.

To read further about a research study focused on the importance of activities in young children's lives, see the *Research in Child Development* interlude.

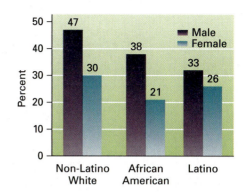

FIGURE 4.21 Exercise Rates of U.S. High School Students: Gender and Ethnicity. *Note*: Data are for high school students who were physically active doing any kind of physical activity that increased their heart rate and made them breathe hard some of the time for a total of at least 60 minutes a day on five or more of the seven days preceding the survey.

In 2007, Texas became the first state to test student's physical fitness. The student shown here is performing the trunk lift. Other assessments include aerobic exercise, muscle strength, and body fat. Assessments will be done annually.

Research in Child Development

PHYSICAL ACTIVITY IN YOUNG CHILDREN ATTENDING PRESCHOOLS

One study examined the activity level of 281 3- to 5-year-olds in nine preschools (Pate & others, 2004). The preschool children wore accelerometers, a small activity monitor, for four to five hours a day. Height and weight assessments of the children were made to calculate their body mass index (BMI).

Recently developed guidelines recommend the preschool children engage in two hours of physical activity per day, divided into one hour of structured activity and one hour of unstructured free-play (National Association for Sport and Physical Education, 2002). In this study, the young children participated in an average of 7.7 minutes per hour of moderate to vigorous activity, usually in a block of time when they were outside. Over the course of eight hours of a preschool day, these children would get approximately one hour of moderate and vigorous physical activity, only about 50 percent of the amount recommended. The researchers concluded that young children are unlikely to engage in another hour per day of moderate and vigorous physical activity outside their eight hours spent in preschool and thus are not getting adequate opportunities for physical activity.

Gender and age differences characterized the preschool children's physical activity. Boys were more likely to engage in moderate or vigorous physical activity than girls. Four- and five-year-old children were more likely to be sedentary than three-year-old children.

The young children's physical activity also varied according to the particular preschool they attended. The extent they participated in moderate and vigorous physical activity ranged from 4.4 to 10.2 minutes per hour across the nine preschools. Thus, the policies and practices of particular preschools influence the extent to which children engage in physical activity. The researchers concluded that young children need more vigorous play and organized activities. Unfortunately, there is a trend toward reducing time for physical activity, especially eliminating recess, in U.S. elementary schools that is trickling down to kindergarten and preschool programs. This decrease is part of a larger trend that involves narrowing early childhood programs to focus on academic learning and moving away from more comprehensive programs that focus on the whole child (Hyson, Copple, & Jones, 2006).

Review and Reflect: Learning Goal 4

 Characterize Health in Childhood

REVIEW

- What are the key health problems facing children?
- What are some important aspects of children's nutrition and eating behavior?
- What role does exercise play in children's development?

REFLECT

- What were your eating habits like as a child? In what ways are they similar or different to your current eating habits? Were your early eating habits a forerunner of whether or not you have weight problems today?

Reach Your Learning Goals

Physical Development and Health

1 BODY GROWTH AND CHANGE: DISCUSS DEVELOPMENTAL CHANGES IN THE BODY

Patterns of Growth

- Human growth follows cephalocaudal and proximodistal patterns. In a cephalocaudal pattern, the fastest growth occurs at the top—the head. Physical growth in size, weight, and feature differentiation occurs gradually, moves from the top to the bottom. In a proximodistal pattern, growth begins at the center of the body and then moves toward the extremities.

Infancy and Childhood

- Height and weight increase rapidly in infancy and then take a slower course during childhood. The average North American newborn is 20 inches long and weighs $7\frac{1}{2}$ pounds. Infants grow about 1 inch per month during their first year. In early childhood, girls are only slightly smaller and lighter than boys. Growth is slow and consistent in middle and late childhood, and head circumference, waist circumference, and leg length decrease in relation to body height.

Adolescence

- Puberty is a rapid maturation involving hormonal and body changes that occur primarily in early adolescence puberty began coming on earlier in the twentieth century. There are wide individual variations in the age at which puberty begins. Heredity plays an important role in determining puberty. Key hormones involved in puberty are testosterone and estradiol. Rising testosterone levels in boys cause voice changes, enlargement of external genitals, and increased height. In girls, increased levels of estradiol influence breast and uterine development and skeletal change. Key physical changes of puberty include a growth spurt as well as sexual maturation. The growth spurt occurs on the average about two years sooner for girls than for boys. Adolescents are preoccupied with their bodies and develop images of their bodies. Adolescent girls have more negative body images than adolescent boys. Early maturation favors boys during adolescence, but in adulthood late-maturing boys have a more successful identity. Early-maturing girls are vulnerable to a number of problems including eating disorders, smoking, and depression.

2 THE BRAIN: DESCRIBE HOW THE BRAIN CHANGES

Brain Physiology

- Each hemisphere of the brain's cerebral cortex has four lobes (frontal, occipital, temporal, and parietal) with somewhat different primary functions. Neurons are nerve cells in the brain that process information. Communication between neurons occurs through the release of neurotransmitters at gaps called synapses. Communication is speeded by the myelin sheath that covers most axons. Clusters of neurons, known as neural circuits, work together to handle particular types of information. Specialization of functioning does occur in the brain's hemispheres, as in speech and grammar, but for the most part both hemispheres are at work in most complex functions, such as reading or performing music.

Infancy

- Researchers have found that experience influences the brain's development. Early experience are very important in brain development, and growing up in deprived environments can harm the brain. Myelination continues through the childhood years, and even into adolescence for some brain areas such as the frontal lobes. Dramatic increases in denditric and synaptic connections occur in infancy. These connections are overproduced and later pruned.

Childhood

- During early childhood, the brain and head grow more rapidly than any other part of the body. Rapid, distinct bursts of growth occur in different areas of the brain from 3 to 15 years of age. One shift in brain activation in middle and late childhood is from diffuse, larger areas to more focal, smaller areas, especially in cognitive control.

Adolescence

- In adolescence, the corpus callosum thickens, and this improves information processing. Also, the amygdala, which is involved in emotions such as anger, develops earlier than the prefrontal cortex, which functions in reasoning and self-regulation. This gap in development may help to explain the increase in risk-taking behavior that characterizes adolescence.

3   SLEEP: SUMMARIZE HOW SLEEP PATTERNS CHANGE AS CHILDREN AND ADOLESCENTS DEVELOP

Infancy

- The typical newborn sleeps 16 to 17 hours a day. By 6 months of age, most infants have sleep patterns similar to those of adults. REM sleep occurs more in infancy than in childhood and adulthood. Sleeping arrangements vary across cultures, and there is controversy about shared sleeping. SIDS is a special concern in early infancy.

Childhood

- Most young children sleep through the night and have one daytime nap. It is recommended that preschool children sleep 11 to 13 hours each night and 5- to 12-year-old children 10 to 12 hours each night. Among sleep problems that may develop are nightmares and night terrors.

Adolescence

- Many adolescents stay up later than when they were children and are getting less sleep than they need. Research suggests that as adolescents get older, the hormone melatonin is released later at night, shifting the adolescent's biological clock. Inadequate sleep is linked to an unhealthy diet, low exercise level, depression, and ineffective stress management.

4   HEALTH: CHARACTERIZE HEALTH IN CHILDHOOD

Illness and Injuries Among Children

- In recent decades, vaccines have greatly reduced the incidence of many diseases that once were responsible for the deaths of many young children. The disorders most likely to be fatal during early childhood today are birth defects, cancer, and heart disease. Motor vehicle accidents are the number one cause of death in middle and late childhood followed by cancer. Parental smoking is a major danger for young children. For the most part, middle and late childhood is a time of excellent health. Caregivers play an important role in preventing childhood injuries. A special concern is the health of children living in poverty here and abroad. Improvements are needed in sanitation, nutrition, education, and health services in addition to a reduction in poverty. There also has been a dramatic increase in low-income countries in the number of children who have died because of HIV/AIDS being transmitted to them by their parents.

Nutrition and Eating Behavior

- The importance of adequate energy intake consumed in a loving and supportive environment in infancy cannot be overstated. Breast feeding is increasingly recommended over bottle feeding. Marasmus and kwashiorkor are diseases caused by severe malnutrition. Concerns about nutrition in childhood focus on fat content in diet and overweight children. The percentage of overweight children has increased dramatically in recent years. Being overweight increases a child's risk of developing many medical and psychological problems.

Exercise

- Most children and adolescents are not getting nearly enough exercise. Boys and girls become less active as they reach and progress through adolescence. TV watching and computer time place children and adolescents at risk for lower physical fitness and being overweight.

KEY TERMS

cephalocaudal pattern 118
proximodistal pattern 119
puberty 120
menarche 121
hormones 121

androgens 121
estrogens 121
testosterone 122
estradiol 122
lateralization 126

myelination 128
corpus callosum 130
prefrontal cortex 130
amygdala 130

sudden infant death
  syndrome (SIDS) 133
marasmus 143
kwashiorkor 143

KEY PEOPLE

Charles Nelson 126

E-LEARNING TOOLS

To help you master the material in this chapter, you'll find a number of valuable study tools at the Online Learning Center for *Child Development*, twelfth edition (**www.mhhe.com/ santrockcd12**).

Taking It to the Net

Research the answers to these questions:

1. June's only child, 12-year-old Suzanne, is starting to show all of the signs of puberty. What behavioral changes in Suzanne should June expect as a result of puberty?

2. Dana's part-time job involves helping in a community center's after-school program for inner-city elementary school children. Many of the children eat too much junk food, have low energy levels, and are overweight. She wants to implement an exercise program as part of each day's activities. What are some things that Dana should keep in mind?

3. Tom is the father of a 15-year-old high school student. He has petitioned his local school committee to change the school start time from 7:30 A.M. to 8:30 A.M. What could Tom use as a reason to delay the school start time?

Health and Well-Being, Parenting, and Education Exercises

Build your decision-making skills by trying your hand at the health and well-being, parenting and education exercises.

Video Clips

The Online Learning Center includes the following videos for this chapter:

- *Brain Development and Cognition*
Renowned infant brain researcher Charles Nelson describes findings from his research, showing that brain development influences cognitive development.

- *Influence of Brain Development in Puberty*
Dr. Ronald Dahl emphasizes the importance of considering the influence of brain development on puberty more so than hormones: "Puberty happens at the level of the brain."

- *Obesity*
Rebecca Roach, Registered Dietician, discusses reasons for the high rate of obesity in children today.

- *Talking About Drugs at Age 14*
Two adolescent girls express their views about drug use among teens.

5

A baby is the most complicated object made by unskilled labor.

—Anonymous

LEARNING GOALS

◆ Describe how motor skills develop.

◆ Outline the course of sensory and perceptual development.

◆ Discuss the connection of perception and action.

MOTOR, SENSORY, AND PERCEPTUAL DEVELOPMENT

CHAPTER OUTLINE

1

MOTOR DEVELOPMENT
The Dynamic Systems View

Reflexes

Gross Motor Skills

Fine Motor Skills

2

SENSORY AND PERCEPTUAL DEVELOPMENT
What Are Sensation and Perception?

The Ecological View

Vision

Hearing

Other Senses

Intermodal Perception

3

PERCEPTUAL-MOTOR COUPLING

Images of Child Development
The Stories of Stevie Wonder and Andrea Bocelli

Two "sensations": Stevie Wonder (*top*) and Andrea Bocelli (*bottom*). *How have they adopted to life without sight?*

In 1950, the newly born Steveland Morris was placed in an incubator in which he was given too much oxygen. The result was permanent blindness. In 1962, as 12-year-old singer and musician Stevie Wonder, he began a performing and recording career that has included such hits as "My Cherie Amour" and "Signed, Sealed, Delivered." At the beginning of the twenty-first century, his music is still perceived by some as "wondrous."

At age 12, Andrea Bocelli lost his sight in a soccer mishap. Today, now in his forties and after a brief career as a lawyer, Andrea has taken the music world by storm with his magnificent, classically trained voice.

Although Bocelli's and Stevie Wonder's accomplishments are great, imagine how very difficult it must have been for them as children to do many of the things we take for granted in sighted children. Yet children who lose one channel of sensation—such as vision—often compensate for the loss by enhancing their sensory skills in another area—such as hearing or touch. For example, researchers have found that blind individuals are more accurate at locating a sound source and have greater sensitivity to touch than sighted individuals (Bavelier & Neville, 2002; Forster, Eardley, & Eimer, 2007). In one study, blind children were more skillful than blindfolded sighted children at using hearing to detect walls (Ashmead & others, 1998). In this study, acoustic information was most useful when the blind children were within one meter of a wall—at which point, sound pressure increases.

PREVIEW

Think about what is required for children to find their way around their environment, to play sports, or to create art. These activities require both active perception and precisely timed motor actions. Neither innate, automatic movements nor simple sensations are enough to let children do the things they do every day. How do children develop perceptual and motor abilities? In this chapter, we will focus first on the development of motor skills, then on sensory and perceptual development, and on the coupling of perceptual-motor skills.

1 MOTOR DEVELOPMENT

The Dynamic Systems View   Reflexes   Gross Motor Skills   Fine Motor Skills

Most adults are capable of coordinated, purposive actions of considerable skill, including driving a car, playing golf, and typing effectively on a computer keyboard. Some adults have extraordinary motor skills, such as those involved in winning an Olympic pole vault competition, performing heart surgery, painting a masterpiece, or in the case of

Stevie Wonder, being extraordinarily talented at playing the piano. Look all you want at a newborn infant, and you will observe nothing even remotely approaching these skilled actions. How, then, do the motor behaviors of adults come about?

The Dynamic Systems View

Developmentalist Arnold Gesell (1934) thought his painstaking observations had revealed how people develop their motor skills. He had discovered that infants and children develop rolling, sitting, standing, and other motor skills in a fixed order and within specific time frames. These observations, said Gesell, show that motor development comes about through the unfolding of a genetic plan, or *maturation.*

Later studies, however, demonstrated that the sequence of developmental milestones is not as fixed as Gesell indicated and not due as much to heredity as Gesell argued (Adolph, 2008; Adolph & others, 2009; Adolph & Joh, 2007, 2008, 2009). In the 1990s, the study of motor development experienced a renaissance as psychologists developed new insights about *how* motor skills develop (Thelen & Smith, 1998, 2006). One increasingly influential theory is dynamic systems theory, proposed by Esther Thelen.

According to **dynamic systems theory**, infants assemble motor skills for perceiving and acting. Notice that perception and action are coupled according to this theory (Smith & Breazeal, 2007; Thelen, 1995, 2001; Thelen & Smith, 1998, 2006). To develop motor skills, infants must perceive something in the environment that motivates them to act and use their perceptions to fine-tune their movements. Motor skills represent solutions to the infant's goals (Bertenthal, 2008).

How is a motor skill developed according to this theory? When infants are motivated to do something, they might create a new motor behavior. The new behavior is the result of many converging factors: the development of the nervous system, the body's physical properties and its possibilities for movement, the goal the child is motivated to reach, and the environmental support for the skill (Bertenthal, 2008; von Hofsten, 2008). For example, babies learn to walk only when maturation of the nervous system allows them to control certain leg muscles, when their legs have grown enough to support their weight, and when they want to move.

Mastering a motor skill requires the infant's active efforts to coordinate several components of the skill. Infants explore and select possible solutions to the demands of a new task; they assemble adaptive patterns by modifying their current movement patterns. The first step occurs when the infant is motivated by a new challenge—such as the desire to cross a room—and gets into the "ballpark" of the task demands by taking a couple of stumbling steps. Then, the infant "tunes" these movements to make them smoother and more effective. The tuning is achieved through repeated cycles of action and perception of the consequences of that action. According to the dynamic systems view, even universal milestones, such as crawling, reaching, and walking, are learned through this process of adaptation: Infants modulate their movement patterns to fit a new task by exploring and selecting possible configurations (Adolph & Joh, 2007, 2008; Thelen & Smith, 2006).

To see how dynamic systems theory explains motor behavior, imagine that you offer a new toy to a baby named Gabriel (Thelen & others, 1993). There is no exact program that can tell Gabriel ahead of time how to move his arm and hand and fingers to grasp the toy. Gabriel must adapt to his goal—grasping the toy—and the context. From his sitting position, he must make split-second adjustments to extend his arm, holding his body steady so that his arm and torso don't plow into the toy. Muscles in his arm and shoulder contract and stretch in a host of combinations, exerting a variety of forces. He improvises a way to reach out with one arm and wrap his fingers around the toy.

Thus, according to dynamic systems theory, motor development is not a passive process in which genes dictate the unfolding of a sequence of skills over time. Rather, the infant actively puts together a skill to achieve a goal within the constraints set by the infant's body and environment. Nature and nurture, the infant and the environment, are all working together as part of an ever-changing system.

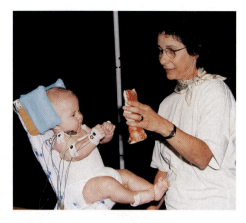

Esther Thelen is shown conducting an experiment to discover how infants learn to control their arms to reach and grasp for objects. A computer device is used to monitor the infant's arm movements and to track muscle patterns. Thelen's research is conducted from a dynamic systems perspective. *What is the nature of this perspective?*

How might dynamic systems theory explain the development of learning to walk?

dynamic systems theory A theory, proposed by Esther Thelen, that seeks to explain how motor behaviors are assembled for perceiving and acting.

*T*he experiences of the first three years of life are almost entirely lost to us, and when we attempt to enter into a small child's world, we come as foreigners who have forgotten the landscape and no longer speak the native tongue.

—SELMA FRAIBERG
Developmentalist and Child Advocate, 20th Century

Moro reflex

The Moro reflex usually disappears around three months.

rooting reflex A newborn's built-in reaction that occurs when the infant's cheek is stroked or the side of the mouth is touched. In response, the infant turns its head toward the side that was touched, in an apparent effort to find something to suck.

sucking reflex A newborn's built-in reaction of automatically sucking an object placed in its mouth. The sucking reflex enables the infant to get nourishment before it has associated a nipple with food.

Moro reflex A neonatal startle response that occurs in reaction to a sudden, intense noise or movement. When startled, the newborn arches its back, throws its head back, and flings out its arms and legs. Then the newborn rapidly closes its arms and legs to the center of the body.

grasping reflex A neonatal reflex that occurs when something touches the infant's palms. The infant responds by grasping tightly.

As we examine the course of motor development, we will describe how dynamic systems theory applies to some specific skills. First, though, let's examine how the story of motor development begins with reflexes.

Reflexes

The newborn is not completely helpless. Among other things, it has some basic reflexes (Pedroso, 2008). For example, the newborn automatically holds its breath and contracts its throat to keep water out. *Reflexes* are built-in reactions to stimuli; they govern the newborn's movements, which are automatic and beyond the newborn's control. Reflexes are genetically carried survival mechanisms. They allow infants to respond adaptively to their environment before they have had the opportunity to learn.

The rooting and sucking reflexes are important examples. Both have survival value for newborn mammals, who must find a mother's breast to obtain nourishment. The **rooting reflex** occurs when the infant's cheek is stroked or the side of the mouth is touched. In response, the infant turns its head toward the side that was touched in an apparent effort to find something to suck. The **sucking reflex** occurs when newborns automatically suck an object placed in their mouths. This reflex enables newborns to get nourishment before they have associated a nipple with food.

Another example is the **Moro reflex**, which occurs in response to a sudden, intense noise or movement. When startled, the newborn arches its back, throws back its head, and flings out its arms and legs. Then the newborn rapidly closes its arms and legs. The Moro reflex is believed to be a way of grabbing for support while falling; it would have had survival value for our primate ancestors.

Some reflexes—coughing, blinking, and yawning, for example—persist throughout life. They are as important for the adult as they are for the infant. Other reflexes, though, disappear several months following birth, as the infant's brain matures and voluntary control over many behaviors develops. The rooting, sucking, and Moro reflexes, for example, all tend to disappear when the infant is 3 to 4 months old.

The movements of some reflexes eventually become incorporated into more complex, voluntary actions. One important example is the **grasping reflex**, which occurs when something touches the infant's palms. The infant responds by grasping tightly. By the end of the third month, the grasping reflex diminishes, and the infant shows a more voluntary grasp. For example, when an infant sees a mobile turning slowly above a crib, it may reach out and try to grasp it. As its motor development becomes smoother, the infant will grasp objects, carefully manipulate them, and explore their qualities. An overview of the reflexes we have discussed, along with others, is given in Figure 5.1.

Although reflexes are automatic and inborn, differences in reflexive behavior are soon apparent. For example, the sucking capabilities of newborns vary considerably. Some newborns are efficient at forceful sucking and obtaining milk; others are not as adept and get tired before they are full. Most infants take several weeks to establish a sucking style that is coordinated with the way the mother is holding the infant, the way milk is coming out of the bottle or breast, and the infant's temperament (Blass, 2008).

Pediatrician T. Berry Brazelton (1956) observed how infants' sucking changed as they grew older. Over 85 percent of the infants engaged in considerable sucking behavior unrelated to feeding. They sucked their fingers, their fists, and their pacifiers. By the age of 1 year, most had stopped the sucking behavior, but as many as 40 percent of children continue to suck their thumbs after they have started school (Kessen, Haith, & Salapatek, 1970). Most developmentalists do not attach a great deal of significance to this behavior.

Reflex	Stimulation	Infant's Response	Developmental Pattern
Blinking	Flash of light, puff of air	Closes both eyes	Permanent
Babinski	Sole of foot stroked	Fans out toes, twists foot in	Disappears after 9 months to 1 year
Grasping	Palms touched	Grasps tightly	Weakens after 3 months, disappears after 1 year
Moro (startle)	Sudden stimulation, such as hearing loud noise or being dropped	Startles, arches back, throws head back, flings out arms and legs and then rapidly closes them to center of body	Disappears after 3 to 4 months
Rooting	Cheek stroked or side of mouth touched	Turns head, opens mouth, begins sucking	Disappears after 3 to 4 months
Stepping	Infant held above surface and feet lowered to touch surface	Moves feet as if to walk	Disappears after 3 to 4 months
Sucking	Object touching mouth	Sucks automatically	Disappears after 3 to 4 months
Swimming	Infant put face down in water	Makes coordinated swimming movements	Disappears after 6 to 7 months
Tonic neck	Infant placed on back	Forms fists with both hands and usually turns head to the right (sometimes called the "fencer's pose" because the infant looks like it is assuming a fencer's position)	Disappears after 2 months

FIGURE 5.1 Infant Reflexes. This chart describes some of the infant's reflexes.

Gross Motor Skills

Ask any parents about their baby, and sooner or later you are likely to hear about one or more motor milestones, such as "Cassandra just learned to crawl," "Jesse is finally sitting alone," or "Angela took her first step last week." Parents proudly announce such milestones as their children transform themselves from babies unable to lift their heads to toddlers who grab things off the grocery store shelf, chase a cat, and participate actively in the family's social life (Thelen, 1995, 2000). These milestones are examples of **gross motor skills**, which are skills that involve large-muscle activities, such as moving one's arms and walking.

The Development of Posture How do gross motor skills develop? As a foundation, these skills, like many other activities, require postural control (Adolph & others, 2008; Thelen & Smith, 2006). For example, to track moving objects, you must be able to control your head in order to stabilize your gaze; before you can walk, you must be able to balance on one leg.

Posture is more than just holding still and straight. In Thelen's (2000) view, posture is a dynamic process that is linked with sensory information from proprioceptive cues in the skin, joints, and muscles, which tell us where we are in space; from vestibular organs in the inner ear that regulate balance and equilibrium; and from vision and hearing.

Newborns cannot voluntarily control their posture. Within a few weeks, though, infants can hold their heads erect, and soon they can lift their heads while prone. By 2 months of age, babies can sit while supported on a lap or in an infant seat, but they cannot sit independently until they are 6 or 7 months of age. Standing also develops gradually during the first year of life. By about 8 months of age, infants usually learn to pull themselves up and hold on to a chair, and many can stand alone by about 10 to 12 months of age.

Learning to Walk Locomotion and postural control are closely linked, especially in walking upright (Adolph, 2008, 2009; Adolph & Joh, 2007, 2008). To walk upright, the

What are some developmental changes in posture during infancy?

gross motor skills Motor skills that involve large-muscle activities, such as moving one's arms and walking.

Newly crawling infant

Experienced walker

FIGURE 5.2 The Role of Experience in Crawling and Walking Infants' Judgments of Whether to Go Down a Slope. Karen Adolph (1997) found that locomotor experience rather than age was the primary predictor of adaptive responding on slopes of varying steepness. Newly crawling and walking infants could not judge the safety of the various slopes. With experience, they learned to avoid slopes where they would fall. When expert crawlers began to walk, they again made mistakes and fell, even though they had judged the same slope accurately when crawling. Adolph referred to this as the *specificity of learning* because it does not transfer across crawling and walking.

baby must be able both to balance on one leg as the other is swung forward and to shift the weight from one leg to the other.

Even young infants can make the alternating leg movements that are needed for walking. The neural pathways that control leg alternation are in place from a very early age, possibly even at birth or before. Infants engage in frequent alternating kicking movements throughout the first six months of life when they are lying on their backs. Also when 1-to 2-month-olds are given support with their feet in contact with a motorized treadmill, they show well-coordinated, alternating steps. Despite these early abilities, most infants do not learn to walk until about the time of their first birthday.

If infants can produce forward stepping movements so early, why does it take them so long to learn to walk? The key skills in learning to walk appear to be stabilizing balance on one leg long enough to swing the other forward and shifting the weight without falling. This is a difficult biomechanical problem to solve, and it takes infants about a year to do it.

When infants learn to walk, they typically take small steps because of their limited balance control and strength. However, a recent study revealed that infants occasionally take a few large steps that even exceed their leg length, and these large steps indicate increased balance and strength (Badaly & Adolph, 2008).

In learning to locomote, infants learn what kinds of places and surfaces are safe for locomotion (Adolph, 2008; Adolph & Joh, 2007, 2008, 2009; Adolph & others, 2009). Karen Adolph (1997) investigated how experienced and inexperienced crawling infants and walking infants go down steep slopes (see Figure 5.2). Newly crawling infants, who averaged about $8\frac{1}{2}$ months in age, rather indiscriminately went down the steep slopes, often falling in the process (with their mothers next to the slope to catch them). After weeks of practice, the crawling babies became more adept at judging which slopes were too steep to crawl down and which ones they could navigate safely. New walkers also could not judge the safety of the slopes, but experienced walkers accurately matched their skills with the steepness of the slopes. They rarely fell downhill, either refusing to go down the steep slopes or going down backward in a cautious manner. Experienced walkers perceptually assessed the situation—looking, swaying, touching, and thinking before they moved down the slope. With experience, both the crawlers and the walkers learned to avoid the risky slopes where they would fall, integrating perceptual information with the development of a new motor behavior. In this research, we again see the importance of perceptual-motor coupling in the development of motor skills.

Practice is especially important in learning to walk (Adolph, 2008, 2009). "Thousands of daily walking steps, each step slightly different from the last because of variations in the terrain and the continually varying biomechanical constraints on the body, may help infants to identify the relevant" combination of strength and balance required to improve their walking skills (Adolph, Vereijken, & Shrout, 2003, p. 495).

Figure 5.3 summarizes important accomplishments in gross motor skills during the first year, culminating in the ability to walk easily. The timing of these milestones, especially the later ones, may vary by as much as two to four months, and experiences can modify the onset of these accomplishments. For example, since 1992, when pediatricians began recommending that parents keep their infants supine at night, fewer babies crawl, and the age of onset of crawling is later (Davis & others, 1998). Also, some infants do not follow the standard sequence of motor accomplishments. For example, many American infants never crawl on their belly or on their hands and knees. They may discover an idiosyncratic form of locomotion before walking, such as rolling, or they might never locomote until they get upright (Adolph & Joh, 2008). In the African Mali tribe, most infants do not crawl (Bril, 1999).

According to Karen Adolph and Sarah Berger (2005), "The old-fashioned view that growth and motor development reflect merely the age-related output of maturation is,

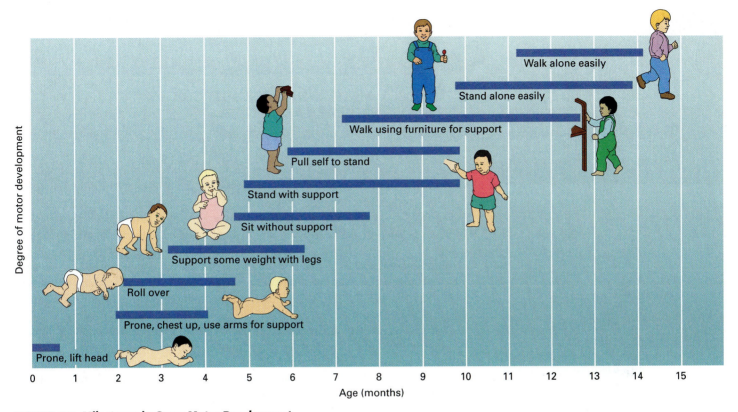

Walk alone easily

Stand alone easily

Walk using furniture for support

Pull self to stand

Stand with support

Sit without support

Support some weight with legs

Roll over

Prone, chest up, use arms for support

Prone, lift head

Degree of motor development

Age (months)

0 1 2 3 4 5 6 7 8 9 10 11 12 13 14 15

FIGURE 5.3 **Milestones in Gross Motor Development**

at best, incomplete. Rather, infants acquire new skills with the help of their caregivers in a real-world environment of objects, surfaces, and planes."

Development in the Second Year   The motor accomplishments of the first year bring increasing independence, allowing infants to explore their environment more extensively and to initiate interaction with others more readily. In the second year of life, toddlers become more motorically skilled and mobile. They are no longer content in a playpen and want to move all over the place. Child development experts believe that motor activity during the second year is vital to the child's competent development and that few restrictions, except for safety, should be placed on their adventures.

By 13 to 18 months, toddlers can pull a toy attached to a string and use their hands and legs to climb up a number of steps. By 18 to 24 months, toddlers can walk quickly or run stiffly for a short distance, balance on their feet in a squat position while playing with objects on the floor, walk backward without losing their balance, stand and kick a ball without falling, stand and throw a ball, and jump in place.

Can parents give their babies a head start on becoming physically fit and physically talented through structured exercise classes? Physical fitness classes for babies range from passive fare—with adults putting infants through the paces—to programs called "aerobic" because they demand crawling, tumbling, and ball skills. Pediatricians point out that when an adult is stretching and moving an infant's limbs, it is easy for them to go beyond the infant's physical limits without knowing it. Pediatricians also recommend that exercise for infants should not be the intense, aerobic variety. Babies cannot adequately stretch their bodies to achieve aerobic benefits.

In short, most infancy experts recommend against structured exercise classes for babies. But there are other ways of guiding infants' motor development. Caregivers in some cultures do handle babies vigorously, and this might advance motor development, as we discuss in the *Diversity in Child Development* interlude.

(*Top*) In the Algonquin culture in Quebec, Canada, babies are strapped to a cradle board for much of their infancy. (*Bottom*) In Jamaica, mothers massage and stretch their infants' arms and legs. *To what extent do cultural variations in the activity infants engage in influence the time at which they reach motor milestones?*

Diversity in Child Development

CULTURAL VARIATIONS IN GUIDING INFANTS' MOTOR DEVELOPMENT

Mothers in developing countries tend to stimulate their infants' motor skills more than mothers in more modern countries (Hopkins, 1991). Jamaican and Mali mothers regularly massage their infants and stretch their arms and legs (Adolph, 2008; Adolph, Karasik, & Tamis-LeMonda, 2009). Mothers in the Gusii culture of Kenya also encourage vigorous movement in their babies (Hopkins & Westra, 1988).

Do these cultural variations make a difference in the infant's motor development? When caregivers provide babies with physical guidance by physically handling them in special ways (such as stroking, massaging, or stretching) or by giving them opportunities for exercise, the infants often reach motor milestones earlier than infants whose caregivers have not provided these activities (Adolph, 2008). For example, Jamaican mothers expect their infants to sit and walk alone two to three months earlier than English mothers do (Hopkins & Westra, 1990).

Nonetheless, even when infants' motor activity is restricted, many infants still reach the milestones of motor development at a normal age. For example, Algonquin infants in Quebec, Canada, spend much of their first year strapped to a cradle board. Despite their inactivity, these infants still sit up, crawl, and walk within an age range similar to that of infants in cultures who have had much greater opportunity for activity.

Childhood The preschool child no longer has to make an effort to stay upright and to move around. As children move their legs with more confidence and carry themselves more purposefully, moving around in the environment becomes more automatic.

At 3 years of age, children enjoy simple movements, such as hopping, jumping, and running back and forth, just for the sheer delight of performing these activities. They take considerable pride in showing how they can run across a room and jump all of 6 inches. The run-and-jump will win no Olympic gold medals, but for the 3-year-old the activity is a source of pride.

At 4 years of age, children are still enjoying the same kind of activities, but they have become more adventurous. They scramble over low jungle gyms as they display their athletic prowess. Although they have been able to climb stairs with one foot on each step for some time, they are just beginning to be able to come down the same way.

At 5 years of age, children are even more adventuresome than they were at 4. It is not unusual for self-assured 5-year-olds to perform hair-raising stunts on practically any climbing object. They run hard and enjoy races with each other and their parents.

During middle and late childhood, children's motor development becomes much smoother and more coordinated than it was in early childhood. For example, only one child in a thousand can hit a tennis ball over the net at the age of 3, yet by the age of 10 or 11 most children can learn to play the sport. Running, climbing, skipping rope, swimming, bicycle riding, and skating are just a few of the many physical skills elementary school children can master. And, when mastered, these physical skills are a source of great pleasure and a sense of accomplishment. A recent study of 9-year-olds revealed that those who were more physically fit had a better mastery of motor skills (Haga, 2008). In gross motor skills involving large-muscle activity, boys usually outperform girls.

As children move through the elementary school years, they gain greater control over their bodies and can sit and pay attention for longer periods of time. However, elementary school children are far from being physically mature, and they need to

What are some developmental changes in children's motor development in early childhood and middle and late childhood?

be active. Elementary school children become more fatigued by long periods of sitting than by running, jumping, or bicycling (Rink, 2009). Physical action is essential for these children to refine their developing skills, such as batting a ball, skipping rope, or balancing on a beam. Children benefit from exercise breaks periodically during the school day on the order of 15 minutes every two hours (Keen, 2005). In sum, elementary school children should be engaged in active, rather than passive, activities.

Organized sports are one way of encouraging children to be active and to develop their motor skills. Schools and community agencies offer programs for children that involve baseball, soccer, football, basketball, swimming, gymnastics, and other sports. These programs may play a central role in children's lives. The *Caring for Children* interlude examines the role of parents in children's sports.

Caring for Children

PARENTS AND CHILDREN'S SPORTS

Participation in sports can have both positive and negative consequences for children (Cox, 2007; Singh & others, 2008). Participation can provide exercise, opportunities to learn how to compete, self-esteem, and a setting for developing peer relations and friendships. Further, participating in sports reduces the likelihood that children will become obese (Sturm, 2005). For example, in one recent study, Mexican youth who did not participate in sports were more likely to be overweight or obese than those who participated (Salazar-Martinez & others, 2006). Another study also revealed that participation in sports for three hours per week or more beyond regular physical education classes was related to increased physical fitness and lower fat mass in 9-year-old boys (Ara & others, 2004). However, sports also can bring pressure to achieve and win, physical injuries, a distraction from academic work, and unrealistic expectations for success as an athlete (Lawrence, Shaha, & Lillis, 2008; Siow, Cameron, & Garley, 2008).

High-pressure sports that involve championship play under the media spotlight cause special concern. Some clinicians and child developmentalists believe such activities put undue stress on children and teach them the wrong values—namely, a win-at-all-costs philosophy. Overly ambitious parents, coaches, and community boosters can unintentionally create a highly stressful atmosphere in children's sports (American Academy of Pediatrics Council on Sports Medicine and Fitness, McCambridge, & Stricker, 2008).

When the prestige of parents, an institution, or a community becomes the focus of the child's participation in sports, the danger of exploitation is clearly present. Programs oriented toward such purposes often require arduous training sessions over many months and years, frequently leading to sports specialization at too early an age. In such circumstances, adults often communicate the distorted view that the sport is the most important aspect of the child's life.

If parents do not become overinvolved, they can help their children build their physical skills and help them emotionally—for example, by discussing how to deal with a difficult coach, how to cope with a tough loss, and how to put in perspective a poorly played game. Parents should monitor their children as they participate in sports for signs of developing stress. If the problems appear to be beyond the intuitive skills of a volunteer coach or parent, consultation with a counselor or clinician may be needed. Also, the parent should be sensitive to whether a particular sport is the best one for the child and whether the child can handle its competitive pressures.

Here are some guidelines that can benefit both parents and coaches of children in sports (Women's Sports Foundation, 2001):

The Dos

- Make sports fun; the more children enjoy sports, the more they will want to play.
- Remember that it is okay for children to make mistakes; it means they are trying.

What are some of the possible positive and negative aspects of children's participation in sports?

- Allow children to ask questions about the sport, and discuss the sport in a calm, supportive manner.
- Show respect for the child's sports participation.
- Be positive and convince the child that he or she is making a good effort.
- Be a positive role model for the child in sports.

The Don'ts

- Yell or scream at the child.
- Condemn the child for poor play or continue to bring up failures long after they happen.
- Point out the child's errors in front of others.
- Expect the child to learn something immediately.
- Expect the child to become a pro.
- Ridicule or make fun of the child.
- Compare the child to siblings or to more talented children.
- Make sports all work and no fun.

Fine Motor Skills

Whereas gross motor skills involve large-muscle activity, **fine motor skills** involve finely tuned movements. Grasping a toy, using a spoon, buttoning a shirt, or doing anything that requires finger dexterity demonstrates fine motor skills.

Infancy Infants have hardly any control over fine motor skills at birth, but they have many components of what will become finely coordinated arm, hand, and finger movements (Rosenblith, 1992). The onset of reaching and grasping marks a significant achievement in infants' interactions (Van Hof, van der Kamp, & Savelsbergh, 2008). During the first two years of life, infants refine their reaching and grasping (Barrett & Needham, 2008; Barrett, Traupman, & Needham, 2008). Rachel Clifton and her colleagues (1993) demonstrated that infants do not have to see their own hands in order to reach for an object. They concluded that *proprioceptive* cues from muscles, tendons, and joints, not sight of the limb, guide reaching by 4-month-old infants. Initially, infants move their shoulders and elbows crudely, but later they move their wrists, rotate their hands, and coordinate their thumb and forefinger.

The infant's grasping system is very flexible. Infants vary their grip on an object, depending on its size and shape, as well as the size of their own hands relative to the object's size. Infants grip small objects with their thumb and forefinger (and sometimes their middle finger, too), whereas they grip large objects with all of the fingers of one hand or both hands.

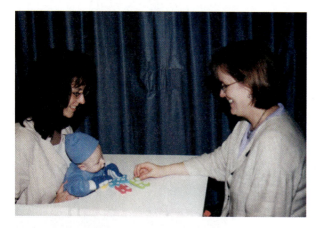

FIGURE 5.4 Infants' Use of "Sticky Mittens" to Explore Objects. Amy Needham and her colleagues (2002) found that "sticky mittens" enhanced young infants' object exploration skills.

Perceptual-motor coupling is necessary for the infant to coordinate grasping (Keen, 2005). Which perceptual system is most likely to be used in coordinating grasping varies with age. Four-month-old infants rely greatly on touch to determine how they will grip an object; 8-month-olds are more likely to use vision as a guide (Newell & others, 1989). This developmental change is efficient because vision lets infants preshape their hands as they reach for an object.

Experience plays a role in reaching and grasping (Needham, 2008). In one recent study, 3-month-old infants participated in play sessions wearing "sticky mittens" ("mittens with palms that stuck to the edges of toys and allowed the infants to pick up the toys") (Needham, Barrett, & Peterman, 2002, p. 279) (see Figure 5.4). Following the mitten sessions, these infants grasped and manipulated objects earlier in their development than a control group of infants who did not receive the "mitten" experience. The

fine motor skills Motor skills that involve more finely tuned movements, such as finger dexterity.

experienced infants looked at the objects longer, swatted at them more during visual contact, and were more likely to mouth the objects.

Just as infants need to exercise their gross motor skills, they also need to exercise their fine motor skills (Barrett, Davis, & Needham, 2007; Needham, 2008). Especially when they can manage a pincer grip, infants delight in picking up small objects. Many develop the pincer grip and begin to crawl at about the same time, and infants at this time pick up virtually everything in sight, especially on the floor, and put the objects in their mouth. Thus, parents need to be vigilant in regularly monitoring what objects are within the infant's reach (Keen, 2005).

Childhood As children get older, their fine motor skills improve (Sveistrup & others, 2008). At 3 years of age, children have had the ability to pick up the tiniest objects between their thumb and forefinger for some time, but they are still somewhat clumsy at it. Three-year-olds can build surprisingly high block towers, each block placed with intense concentration but often not in a completely straight line. When 3-year-olds play with a form board or a simple puzzle, they are rather rough in placing the pieces. When they try to position a piece in a hole, they often try to force the piece or pat it vigorously.

By 4 years of age, children's fine motor coordination is much more precise. Sometimes 4-year-old children have trouble building high towers with blocks because, in their desire to place each of the blocks perfectly, they upset those already stacked. By age 5, children's fine motor coordination has improved further. Hand, arm, and fingers all move together under better command of the eye. Mere towers no longer interest the 5-year-old, who now wants to build a house or a church, complete with steeple. (Adults may still need to be told what each finished project is meant to be.)

Increased myelination of the central nervous system is reflected in the improvement of fine motor skills during middle and late childhood. Recall from Chapter 4 that *myelination* involves the covering of the axon with a myelin sheath, a process that increases the speed with which information travels from neuron to neuron. By middle childhood, children can use their hands adroitly as tools. Six-year-olds can hammer, paste, tie shoes, and fasten clothes. By 7 years of age, children's hands have become steadier. At this age, children prefer a pencil to a crayon for printing, and reversal of letters is less common. Printing becomes smaller. At 8 to 10 years of age, children can use their hands independently with more ease and precision; children can now write rather than print words. Letter size becomes smaller and more even. At 10 to 12 years of age, children begin to show manipulative skills similar to the abilities of adults. The complex, intricate, and rapid movements needed to produce fine-quality crafts or to play a difficult piece on a musical instrument can be mastered. Girls usually outperform boys in fine motor skills.

A young girl using a pincer grip to pick up puzzle pieces.

Review and Reflect: Learning Goal 1

1 Describe How Motor Skills Develop

REVIEW
- What is the dynamic systems view of motor development?
- What are some reflexes of infants?
- How do gross motor skills develop?
- How do fine motor skills develop?

REFLECT
- How would you evaluate the benefits and drawbacks of allowing an 8-year-old to play for a town's soccer team?

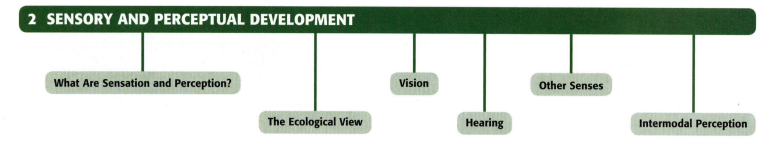

2 SENSORY AND PERCEPTUAL DEVELOPMENT

What Are Sensation and Perception?

Vision

Other Senses

The Ecological View

Hearing

Intermodal Perception

Right now, I am looking at my computer screen to make sure the words are being printed accurately as I am typing them. My perceptual and motor skills are working together. Recall that even control of posture uses information from the senses. And when people grasp an object, they use perceptual information about the object to adjust their motions.

How do these sensations and perceptions develop? Can a newborn see? If so, what can it perceive? What about the other senses—hearing, smell, taste, touch, and pain? What are they like in the newborn, and how do they develop? Can an infant put together information from two modalities, such as sight and sound? These are among the intriguing questions that we will explore in this section.

What Are Sensation and Perception?

How does a newborn know that her mother's skin is soft rather than rough? How does a 5-year-old know what color his hair is? Infants and children "know" these things as a result of information that comes through the senses. Without vision, hearing, touch, taste, smell, and other senses, we would be isolated from the world; we would live in dark silence, a tasteless, colorless, feelingless void.

Sensation occurs when information interacts with sensory *receptors*—the eyes, ears, tongue, nostrils, and skin. The sensation of hearing occurs when waves of pulsating air are collected by the outer ear and transmitted through the bones of the inner ear to the auditory nerve. The sensation of vision occurs as rays of light contact the eyes, become focused on the retina, and are transmitted by the optic nerve to the visual centers of the brain.

Perception is the interpretation of what is sensed. The air waves that contact the ears might be interpreted as noise or as musical sounds, for example. The physical energy transmitted to the retina of the eye might be interpreted as a particular color, pattern, or shape.

The Ecological View

For the past several decades, much of the research on perceptual development in infancy has been guided by the ecological view of Eleanor and James J. Gibson (E. Gibson, 1969, 1989, 2001; J. Gibson, 1966, 1979). They argue that we do not have to take bits and pieces of data from sensations and build up representations of the world in our minds. Instead, our perceptual system can select from the rich information that the environment itself provides.

According to the Gibsons' **ecological view**, we directly perceive information that exists in the world around us. Perception brings us into contact with the environment in order to interact with and adapt to it. Perception is designed for action. Perception gives people such information as when to duck, when to turn their bodies through a narrow passageway, and when to put their hands up to catch something.

In the Gibsons' view, all objects have **affordances**, which are opportunities for interaction offered by objects that are necessary to perform activities. A pot may afford you something to cook with, and it may afford a toddler something to bang. Adults immediately know when a chair is appropriate for sitting, when a surface is safe for walking, or when an object is within reach. We directly and accurately perceive

sensation Reaction that occurs when information contacts sensory receptors—the eyes, ears, tongue, nostrils, and skin.

perception The interpretation of sensation.

ecological view The view, proposed by the Gibsons, that people directly perceive information in the world around them. Perception brings people in contact with the environment in order to interact with it and adapt to it.

affordances Opportunities for interaction offered by objects that are necessary to perform activities.

these affordances by sensing information from the environment—the light or sound reflecting from the surfaces of the world—and from our own bodies through muscle receptors, joint receptors, and skin receptors, for example.

An important developmental question is, What affordances can infants or children detect and use? In one study, for example, when babies who could walk were faced with a squishy waterbed, they stopped and explored it, then chose to crawl rather than walk across it (Gibson & others, 1987). They combined perception and action to adapt to the demands of the task.

Similarly, as we described earlier in the section on motor development, infants who were just learning to crawl or just learning to walk were less cautious when confronted with a steep slope than experienced crawlers or walkers were (Adolph & Avolio, 2000). The more experienced crawlers and walkers perceived that a slope *affords* the possibility for not only faster locomotion but also for falling. Again, infants coupled perception and action to make a decision about what to do in their environment. Through perceptual development, children become more efficient at discovering and using affordances.

Studying the infant's perception has not been an easy task. The *Research in Child Development* interlude describes some of the ingenious ways researchers study the newborn's perception.

How would you use the Gibsons' ecological theory of perception and the concept of affordance to explain the role that perception is playing in this toddler's activity?

Research in Child Development

STUDYING THE NEWBORN'S PERCEPTION

The creature has poor motor coordination and can move itself only with great difficulty. Although it cries when uncomfortable, it uses few other vocalizations. In fact, it sleeps most of the time, about 16 to 17 hours a day. You are curious about this creature and want to know more about what it can do. You think to yourself, "I wonder if it can see. How could I find out?"

You obviously have a communication problem with the creature. You must devise a way that will allow the creature to "tell" you that it can see. While examining the creature one day, you make an interesting discovery. When you move an object horizontally in front of the creature, its eyes follow the object's movement.

The creature's head movement suggests that it has at least some vision. In case you haven't already guessed, the creature you have been reading about is the human infant, and the role you played is that of a researcher interested in devising techniques to learn about the infant's visual perception. After years of work, scientists have developed research methods and tools sophisticated enough to examine the subtle abilities of infants and to interpret their complex actions (Bendersky & Sullivan, 2007; Kellman & Arterberry, 2006).

Visual Preference Method

Robert Fantz (1963) was a pioneer in this effort. Fantz made an important discovery that advanced the ability of researchers to investigate infants' visual perception: Infants look at different things for different lengths of time. Fantz placed infants in a "looking chamber," which had two visual displays on the ceiling above the infant's head. An experimenter viewed the infant's eyes by looking through a peephole. If the infant was fixating on one of the displays, the experimenter could see the display's reflection in the infant's eyes. This allowed the experimenter to determine

FIGURE 5.5 Fantz' Experiment on Infants' Visual Perception. (*a*) Infants 2 to 3 weeks old preferred to look at some stimuli more than others. In Fantz' experiment, infants preferred to look at patterns rather than at color or brightness. For example, they looked longer at a face, a piece of printed matter, or a bull's-eye than at red, yellow, or white discs. (*b*) Fantz used a "looking chamber" to study infants' perception of stimuli.

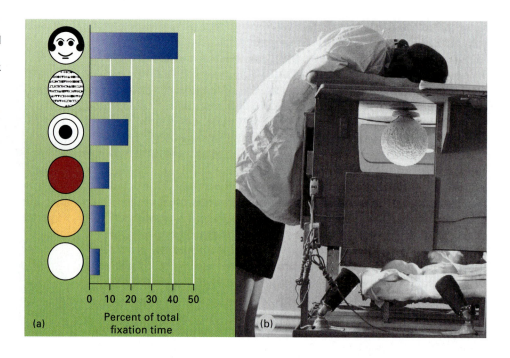

how long the infant looked at each display. Fantz (1963) found that infants only 2 days old look longer at patterned stimuli, such as faces and concentric circles, than at red, white, or yellow discs. Infants 2 to 3 weeks old preferred to look at patterns—a face, a piece of printed matter, or a bull's-eye—longer than at red, yellow, or white discs (see Figure 5.5). Fantz's research method—studying whether infants can distinguish one stimulus from another by measuring the length of time they attend to different stimuli—is referred to as the **visual preference method**.

Habituation and Dishabituation

Another way that researchers have studied infant perception is to present a stimulus (such as a sight or a sound) a number of times. If the infant decreases its response to the stimulus after several presentations, it indicates that the infant is no longer interested in the stimulus. If the researcher now presents a new stimulus, the infant's response will recover—indicating the infant could discriminate between the old and new stimulus (Snyder & Torrence, 2008).

Habituation is the name given to decreased responsiveness to a stimulus after repeated presentations of the stimulus. **Dishabituation** is the recovery of a habituated response after a change in stimulation. Newborn infants can habituate to repeated sights, sounds, smells, or touches (Rovee-Collier, 2004). Among the measures researchers use in habituation studies are sucking behavior (sucking stops when the young infant attends to a novel object), heart and respiration rates, and the length of time the infant looks at an object. Figure 5.6 shows the results of one study of habituation and dishabituation with newborns (Slater, Morison, & Somers, 1988).

High-Amplitude Sucking

To assess an infant's attention to sound, researchers often use a method called *high-amplitude sucking*. In this method, infants are given a nonnutritive nipple to suck, and the nipple is connected to "a sound generating system. Each suck causes a noise to be generated and the infant learns quickly that sucking brings about this noise. At first, babies suck frequently, so the noise occurs often. Then, gradually, they lose interest in hearing repetitions of the same noise and begin to suck less frequently. At this point, the experimenter changes the sound that is being generated. If the babies renew vigorous sucking, we infer that they have discriminated the sound change and are sucking more because they want to hear the interesting new sound" (Menn & Stoel-Gammon, 2005, p. 71).

visual preference method A method developed by Fantz to determine whether infants can distinguish one stimulus from another by measuring the length of time they attend to different stimuli.

habituation Decreased responsiveness to a stimulus after repeated presentations of the stimulus.

dishabituation The recovery of a habituated response after a change in stimulation.

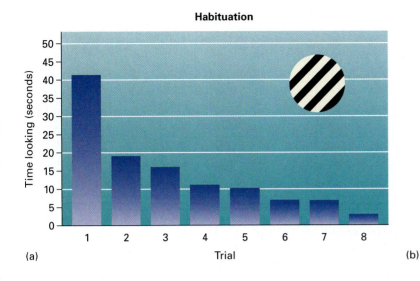

(a)

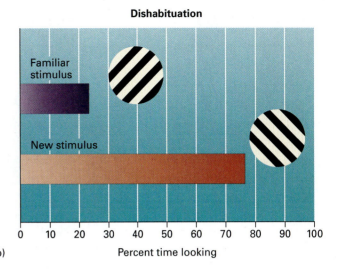

(b)

FIGURE 5.6 Habituation and Dishabituation. In the first part of one study, 7-hour-old newborns were shown the stimulus in (*a*). As indicated, the newborns looked at it an average of 41 seconds when it was first presented to them (Slater, Morison, & Somers, 1988). Over seven more presentations of the stimulus, they looked at it less and less. In the second part of the study, infants were presented with both the familiar stimulus to which they had just become habituated (*a*) and a new stimulus (shown in *b*, which was rotated 90 degrees). The newborns looked at the new stimulus three times as much as the familiar stimulus.

The Orienting Response and Tracking

A technique that can be used to determine if an infant can see or hear is the *orienting response*, which involves turning one's head toward a sight or sound (Keen, 2005). Another technique, *tracking*, consists of eye movements that follow (*track*) a moving object and can used to evaluate an infant's early visual ability, or a startle response can be used to determine an infant's reaction to a noise (Bendersky & Sullivan, 2007).

Equipment

Technology can facilitate the use of most methods for investigating the infant's perceptual abilities. Videotape equipment allows researchers to investigate elusive behaviors. High-speed computers make it possible to perform complex data analysis in minutes. Other equipment records respiration, heart rate, body movement, visual fixation, and sucking behavior, which provide clues to what the infant is perceiving. For example, some researchers use equipment that detects if a change in infants' respiration follows a change in the pitch of a sound. If so, it suggests that the infants heard the pitch change. Thus, scientists have become ingenious at assessing the development of infants, discovering ways to "interview" them even though they cannot yet talk.

Vision

Some important changes in visual perception with age can be traced to differences in how the eye itself functions over time. These changes in the eye's functioning influence, for example, how clearly we can see an object, whether we can differentiate its colors, at what distance, and in what light.

Infancy What do newborns see? How does visual perception develop in infancy?

Visual Acuity and Human Faces Psychologist William James (1890/1950) called the newborn's perceptual world a "blooming, buzzing confusion." A century later, we can safely say that he was wrong (Slater, Field, & Hernandez-Reif, 2007). Even the newborn perceives a world with some order. That world, however, is far different from the one perceived by the toddler or the adult.

Just how well can infants see? At birth, the nerves and muscles and lens of the eye are still developing. As a result, newborns cannot see small things that are far away. The newborn's vision is estimated to be 20/640 on the well-known Snellen chart used

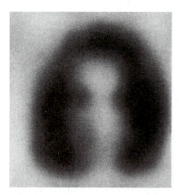  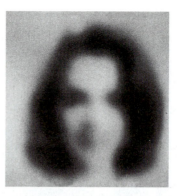 

FIGURE 5.7 Visual Acuity During the First Months of Life. The four photographs represent a computer estimation of what a picture of a face looks like to a 1-month-old, 2-month-old, 3-month-old, and 1-year-old (which approximates the visual acuity of an adult).

for eye examinations, which means that a newborn can see at 20 feet what a normal adult can see at 240 feet (Aslin & Lathrop, 2008). In other words, an object 20 feet away is only as clear to the newborn as it would be if it were 640 feet away from an adult with normal vision (20/20). By 6 months of age, though, on *average*, vision is 20/40 (Aslin & Lathrop, 2008).

Infants show an interest in human faces soon after birth (Aslin & Lathrop, 2008; Slater, Field, & Hernandez-Reif, 2007). Figure 5.7 shows a computer estimation of what a picture of a face looks like to an infant at different ages from a distance of about 6 inches. Infants spend more time looking at their mother's face than a stranger's face as early as 12 hours after being born (Bushnell, 2003). By 3 months of age, infants match voices to faces, distinguish between male and female faces, and discriminate between faces of their own ethnic group and those of other ethnic groups (Kelly & others, 2007a, b; Pascalis & Kelly, 2008).

Even very young infants soon change the way they gather information from the visual world, including human faces (Aslin & Lathrop, 2008). By using a special mirror arrangement, researchers projected an image of human faces in front of infants' eyes so that the infants' eye movements could be photographed (Maurer & Salapatek, 1976). As Figure 5.8 shows, the 2-month-old scans much more of the face than the 1-month-old, and the 2-month-old spends more time examining the internal details of the face. Thus, the 2-month-old gains more information about the world than the 1-month-old.

Color Vision The infant's color vision also improves (Aslin & Lathrop, 2008). By 8 weeks, and possibly by even 4 weeks, infants can discriminate some colors (Kelly, Borchert, & Teller, 1997). By 4 months of age, they have color preferences that mirror adults in some cases, preferring saturated colors such as royal blue over pale blue, for example (Bornstein, 1975). In part, these changes in vision reflect maturation. Experience, however, is also necessary for vision to develop normally. For example, one study found that experience is necessary for normal color vision to develop (Sugita, 2004). Early experience is also essential for the normal development of the ability to use the cues to depth and distance that come from binocular vision. *Binocular vision* combines into one image the two different views of the world received by our eyes because they are several inches apart; the difference between the images received by the two eyes provides powerful cues for distance and depth. Newborns do not have binocular vision; it develops at about 3 to 4 months of age (Slater, Field, & Hernandez-Reif, 2007). Researchers have found that deprivation of vision in one eye (called *monocular deprivation*) during infancy produces an irreversible loss of binocular depth perception (Billson, Fitzgerald, & Provis, 1985).

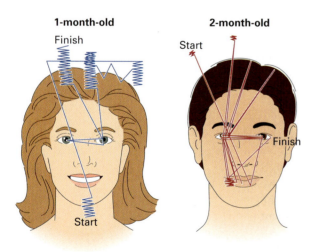

FIGURE 5.8 How 1- and 2-Month-Old Infants Scan the Human Face

Perceiving Patterns   What does the world look like to infants? Do they recognize patterns? As we saw in the *Research in Child Development* interlude, with the help of his "looking chamber," Robert Fantz (1963) revealed that infants look at different things for different lengths of time. Even 2- to 3-month-old infants prefer to look at patterned displays rather than non-patterned displays. For example, they prefer to look at a normal human face rather than one with scrambled features, and they prefer to look at a bull's-eye target or black-and-white stripes rather than a plain circle. Thus, research on visual preferences demonstrates that the newborn's visual world is not the "blooming, buzzing confusion" William James imagined.

Perceptual Constancy   Some perceptual accomplishments are especially intriguing because they indicate that the infant's perception goes beyond the information provided by the senses (Arterberry, 2008; Slater, Field, & Hernandez-Reif, 2007). This is the case in *perceptual constancy*, in which sensory stimulation is changing but perception of the physical world remains constant. If infants did not develop perceptual constancy, each time they saw an object at a different distance or in a different orientation, they would perceive it as a different object. Thus, the development of perceptual constancy allows the infant to perceive its world as stable. Two types of perceptual constancy are size constancy and shape constancy.

Size constancy is the recognition that an object remains the same even though the retinal image of the object changes. The farther away from us an object is, the smaller its image is on our eyes. Thus, the size of an object on the retina is not sufficient to tell us its actual size. For example, you perceive a bicycle standing right in front of you as smaller than the car parked across the street, even though the bicycle casts a larger image on your eyes than the car does. When you move away from the bicycle, you do not perceive it to be shrinking, even though its image on your retinas shrinks; you perceive its size as constant. But what about babies? Do they have size constancy? Researchers have found that babies as young as 3 months of age show size constancy (Bower, 1966; Day & McKenzie, 1973). However, at 3 months of age, this ability is not full-blown and continues to develop. As infants' binocular vision develops between 3 and 4 months of age, their ability to perceive size constancy improves (Aslin, 1987). Further progress in perceiving size constancy continues until 10 or 11 years of age (Kellman & Banks, 1998).

Shape constancy is the recognition that an object remains the same shape even though its orientation to us changes. Look around the room you are in right now. You likely see objects of varying shapes, such as tables and chairs. If you get up and walk around the room, you will see these objects from different sides and angles. Even though your retinal image of the objects changes as you walk and look, you will still perceive the objects as the same shape.

Do babies have shape constancy? As with size constancy, researchers have found that babies as young as 3 months of age have shape constancy (Bower, 1966; Day & McKenzie, 1973). Three-month-old infants, however, do not have shape constancy for irregularly shaped objects, such as tilted planes (Cook & Birch, 1984).

Depth Perception   Decades ago, the inspiration for what would become a classic experiment came to Eleanor Gibson as she was eating a picnic lunch on the edge of the Grand Canyon. She wondered whether an infant looking over the canyon's rim would perceive the dangerous drop-off and back up. She also was worried that her own two young children would play too close to the canyon's edge and fall off. Do even young children perceive depth?

To investigate this question, Eleanor Gibson and Richard Walk (1960) constructed a miniature cliff with a drop-off covered by glass in their laboratory. They placed infants on the edge of this visual cliff and had their mothers coax them to crawl onto the glass (see Figure 5.9). Most infants would not crawl out on the glass, choosing instead to remain on the shallow side, indicating that they could perceive depth.

FIGURE 5.9 Examining Infants' Depth Perception on the Visual Cliff. Eleanor Gibson and Richard Walk (1960) found that most infants would not crawl out on the glass, which indicated that they had depth perception.

size constancy Recognition that an object remains the same even though the retinal image of the object changes.

shape constancy Recognition that an object remains the same even though its orientation to us changes.

A 4-month-old in Elizabeth Spelke's infant perception laboratory is tested to determine if the baby knows that an object in motion will not stop in midair.

Exactly how early in life does depth perception develop? The 6- to 12-month-old infants in the visual cliff experiment had extensive visual experience. Do younger infants without this experience still perceive depth? Since younger infants do not crawl, this question is difficult to answer. As we noted earlier, infants develop the ability to use binocular cues to depth by about 3 to 4 months of age. Two- to 4-month-old infants show differences in heart rate when they are placed directly on the deep side of the visual cliff instead of on the shallow side (Campos, Langer, & Krowitz, 1970). However, these differences might mean that young infants respond to differences in some visual characteristics of the deep and shallow cliffs, with no actual knowledge of depth.

Researchers also are interested in fine-detail depth perception, which is called *stereoacuity* (Birch & others, 2005). A recent study using random-dot TV patterns showed that stereoacuity did not improve from 6 to 12 months of age but improved rapidly after one year of age (Takai & others, 2005).

Visual Expectations   By the time they are 3 months of age, infants not only see forms and figures but also develop expectations about future events. For example, Marshall Haith and his colleagues (Canfield & Haith, 1991; Haith, Hazen, & Goodman, 1988) presented pictures to infants in either a regular alternating (such as left, right, left, right) or an unpredictable sequence (such as right, right, left, right). When the sequence was predictable, the 3-month-old infants began to anticipate the location of the picture, looking at the side on which it was expected to appear. However, younger infants did not develop expectations about where a picture would be presented.

What kinds of expectations do infants form? Are we born expecting the world to obey basic physical laws, such as gravity, or when do we learn about how the world works? Experiments by Elizabeth Spelke (1991, 2000; Spelke & Hespos, 2001) have addressed these questions. She placed babies before a puppet stage and showed them a series of actions that are unexpected if you know how the physical world works—for example, one ball seemed to roll through a solid barrier, another seemed to leap between two platforms, and a third appeared to hang in midair (Spelke, 1979). Spelke measured and compared the babies' looking times for unexpected and expected actions. She concluded that, by 4 months of age, even though infants do not yet have the ability to talk about objects, move around objects, manipulate objects, or even see objects with high resolution, they can expect objects to be solid and continuous. However, at 4 months of age, infants do not expect an object to obey gravitational constraints (Spelke & others, 1992).

By 6 to 8 months, infants have learned to perceive gravity and support—that an object hanging on the end of a table should fall, that ball bearings will travel farther when rolled down a longer rather than a shorter ramp, and that cup handles will not fall when attached to a cup (Slater, Field, & Hernandez-Reif, 2007). As infants develop, their experiences and actions on objects help them to understand physical laws.

Nature, Nurture, and the Development of Infants' Visual Perception   There has been a longstanding interest in how strongly infants' visual perception is influenced by nature or nurture (Arterberry, 2008; Aslin & Lathrop, 2008). A recent analysis concluded that much of vision develops from innate (nature) foundations and that the basic foundation of many visual abilities can be detected at birth, whereas others unfold maturationally (Kellman & Arterberry, 2006). Environmental experiences (nurture) likely refine or calibrate many visual functions, and they may be the driving force behind some functions.

Childhood   Children become increasingly efficient at detecting the boundaries between colors (such as red and orange) at 3 to 4 years of age (Gibson, 1969). When they are about 4 or 5 years old, most children's eye muscles are developed enough for them to move their eyes efficiently across a series of letters. Many preschool children are farsighted, unable to see close up as well as they can see far away. By the time they enter the first grade, though, most children can focus their eyes and sustain their attention effectively on close-up objects.

After infancy, children's visual expectations about the physical world continue to develop. In one study, 2- to $4\frac{1}{2}$-year-old children were given a task in which the goal was to find a toy ball that had been dropped through an opaque tube (Hood, 1995). As shown in Figure 5.10, if the ball is dropped into the tube at the top right, it will land in the box at the bottom left. However, in this task, most of the 2-year-olds, and even some of the 4-year-olds, persisted in searching in the box immediately beneath the dropping point. For them, gravity ruled, and they had failed to perceive the end location of the curved tube.

How do children learn to deal with situations like that in Figure 5.10, and how do they come to understand other laws of the physical world? These questions are addressed by studies of cognitive development, which we will discuss in Chapters 6 and 7.

What are the signs of vision problems in children? They include rubbing the eyes, excessive blinking, squinting, appearing irritable when playing games that require good distance vision, shutting or covering one eye, and tilting the head or thrusting it forward when looking at something. A child who shows any of these behaviors should be examined by an ophthalmologist.

Approximately 1 in every 3,000 children is *educationally blind*, which means they cannot use their vision in learning and must use hearing and touch to learn. Almost one-half of these children were born blind, and another one-third lost their vision in the first year of life. Many children who are educationally blind, like Stevie Wonder and Andrea Bocelli, have normal intelligence and function very well academically with appropriate supports and learning aids. However, many educationally blind students have multiple disabilities and need a range of support services.

FIGURE 5.10 Visual Expectations About the Physical World. When young children see a ball dropped into the tube, many of them will search for it immediately below the dropping point.

Hearing

Can the fetus hear? What kind of changes in hearing take place in infancy?

The Fetus, Infant, and Child   During the last two months of pregnancy, the fetus can hear sounds as it nestles in its mother's womb: It hears the mother's voice, music, and so on (Kisilevsky & others, 2004; Morokuma & others, 2008). Two psychologists wanted to find out if a fetus that heard Dr. Seuss' classic story *The Cat in the Hat* while still in the mother's womb would prefer hearing the story after birth (DeCasper & Spence, 1986). During the last months of pregnancy, 16 women read *The Cat in the Hat* to their fetuses. Then shortly after they were born, the mothers read to them either *The Cat in the Hat* or a story with a different rhyme and pace, *The King, the Mice and the Cheese* (which was not read to them during prenatal development). Using the high-amplitude sucking method described earlier in the chapter, the researchers found that the infants sucked on a nipple in a different way when the mothers read the two stories, suggesting that the infants recognized the pattern and tone of *The Cat in the Hat* (see Figure 5.11). This study illustrates that an infant's brain has a remarkable ability to learn even before birth and reflects the ingenuity of researchers in assessing development.

Even newborns show a preference for certain sounds (Saffran, Werker, & Werner, 2006). Through experiments that measure sucking behavior, researchers have found that newborns prefer a recording of their mother's voice to the voice of an unfamiliar woman, their mother's native language to a foreign language, and the classical music of Beethoven to the rock music of Aerosmith (Flohr & others, 2001).

The newborn's hearing abilities are limited in several ways. Changes during infancy involve a sound's loudness, pitch, and localization.

Immediately after birth, infants cannot hear soft sounds quite as well as adults can; a stimulus must be louder to be heard by a newborn than by an adult (Trehub &

(a)

(b)

FIGURE 5.11 Hearing in the Womb.
(*a*) Pregnant mothers read *The Cat in the Hat* to their fetuses during the last few months of pregnancy. (*b*) When they were born, the babies preferred listening to a recording of their mothers reading *The Cat in the Hat*—as evidenced by their sucking on a nipple—rather than another story, *The King, the Mice and the Cheese.*

others, 1991). For example, an adult can hear a whisper from about 4 to 5 feet away, but a newborn requires that sounds be closer to a normal conversational level to be heard at that distance.

Infants are also less sensitive to the pitch of a sound than adults are. *Pitch* is the perception of the frequency of a sound. A soprano voice sounds high pitched, a bass voice low pitched. Infants are less sensitive to low-pitched sounds and are more likely to hear high-pitched sounds (Aslin, Jusczyk, & Pisoni, 1998). By 2 years of age, infants have considerably improved their ability to distinguish sounds with different pitches.

It is important to be able *localize* sounds, detecting their origins. Even newborns can determine the general location that a sound is coming from, but by 6 months of age, they are more proficient at localizing sounds. This ability continues to improve in the second year (Litovsky & Ashmead, 1997; Morrongiello, Fenwick, & Chance, 1990).

Our sensory-perceptual system seems built to give a special place to the sounds of language (Aslin, Clayards, & Bardhan, 2008). Newborns are especially sensitive to the sounds of human speech (Hollich, 2007). Babies are born into the world prepared to respond to the sounds of any human language. Even young infants can discriminate subtle phonetic differences, such as those between the speech sounds of *ba* and *ga*. Experience with the native language, however, has an effect on speech perception. In the second half of the first year of life, infants become "native listeners," especially attuned to the sounds of their native language (Jusczyk, 2002). In Chapter 9, "Language Development," we will further discuss development of infants' ability to distinguish the sounds they need for speech.

Most children's hearing is adequate, but early hearing screening in infancy needs to be conducted (Durieux-Smith, Fitzpatrick, & Whittingham, 2008; Korres & others, 2008). About 1 in 1,000 newborns are deaf (Mason & Hermann, 1998). Hearing aids or surgery can improve hearing for many of them (Davids & others, 2007).

Otitis media is a middle-ear infection that can impair hearing temporarily. If it continues too long, it can interfere with language development and socialization (Maruthy & Mannarukrishnaiah, 2008). As many as one-third of all U.S. children from birth to 3 years of age have three or more episodes. In some cases, the infection can develop into a more chronic condition in which the middle ear becomes filled with fluid, and this can seriously impair hearing. Treatments for otitis media include antibiotics and placement of a tube in the inner ear to drain fluid (Park & others, 2008; Zhou & others, 2008).

Other Senses

As we develop, we not only obtain information about the world from our eyes and our ears. We also gather information about the world through sensory receptors in our skin, nose, and tongue.

Touch and Pain   Do newborns respond to touch? Can they feel pain? Newborns do respond to touch. A touch to the cheek produces a turning of the head; a touch to the lips produces sucking movements.

Newborns can also feel pain (Field & Hernandez-Reif, 2008). If and when you have a son and need to consider whether he should be circumcised, questions about an infant's pain perception probably will become important to you. In some cultures, circumcision is performed on young boys about the third day after birth. Will a baby boy experience pain if he is circumcised in the days following his birth? An investigation by Megan Gunnar and her colleagues (1987) found that newborn infant males cried intensely during circumcision. The circumcised infant also displays amazing resiliency. Within several minutes after the surgery, they are able nurse and interact in a normal manner with their mothers. And, if allowed to, the newly circumcised newborn drifts into a deep sleep, which seems to serve as a coping mechanism.

For many years, doctors performed operations on newborns without anesthesia. This practice was accepted because of the dangers of anesthesia and because of the supposition that newborns do not feel pain. As researchers demonstrated that newborns can feel pain, the practice of operating on newborns without anesthesia is being challenged. Anesthesia now is used in some circumcisions (Taddio, 2008).

Smell and Taste   Newborns can differentiate odors (Doty & Shah, 2008). The expressions on their faces seem to indicate that they like the way vanilla and strawberry smell but do not like the smell of rotten eggs and fish (Steiner, 1979). In one investigation, 6-day-old infants who were breast fed showed a clear preference for smelling their mother's breast pad (MacFarlane, 1975) (see Figure 5.12). However, when they were 2 days old, infants did not show this preference, indicating that they require several days of experience to recognize this odor.

Sensitivity to taste might be present even before birth (Doty & Shah, 2008). When saccharin was added to the amniotic fluid of a near-term fetus, swallowing increased (Windle, 1940). In one study, even at only 2 hours of age, babies made different facial expressions when they tasted sweet, sour, and bitter solutions (Rosenstein & Oster, 1988) (see Figure 5.13). At about 4 months of age, infants begin to prefer salty tastes, which as newborns they had found to be aversive (Doty & Shah, 2008).

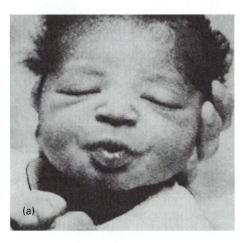

FIGURE 5.12 Newborns' Preference for the Smell of Their Mother's Breast Pad. In the experiment by MacFarlane (1975), 6-day-old infants preferred to smell their mother's breast pad rather than a clean one that had never been used, but 2-day-old infants did not show this preference, indicating that this odor preference requires several days of experience to develop.

Intermodal Perception

Imagine yourself playing basketball or tennis. You are experiencing many visual inputs: the ball coming and going, other players moving around, and so on. However, you are experiencing many auditory inputs as well: the sound of the ball bouncing or being hit, the grunts and groans, and so on. There is good correspondence between much of the visual and auditory information: When you see the ball bounce, you hear a bouncing sound; when a player stretches to hit a ball, you hear a groan.

We live in a world of objects and events that can be seen, heard, and felt. When mature observers simultaneously look at and listen to an event, they experience a unitary episode. All of this is so commonplace that it scarcely seems worth mentioning. But consider the task of very young infants with little practice at perceiving. Can they put vision and sound together as precisely as adults do?

Intermodal perception involves integrating information from two or more sensory modalities, such as vision and hearing. To test intermodal perception, Elizabeth Spelke (1979) showed 4-month-old infants two films simultaneously. In each film, a puppet jumped up and down, but in one of the films the sound track matched the puppet's dancing movements; in the other film, it did not. By measuring the infant's gaze, Spelke found that the infants looked more at the puppet whose actions were

intermodal perception The ability to relate and integrate information about two or more sensory modalities, such as vision and hearing.

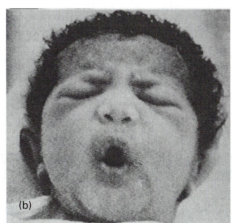
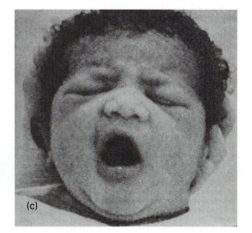

FIGURE 5.13 Newborns' Facial Responses to Basic Tastes. Facial expression elicited by (*a*) a sweet solution, (*b*) a sour solution, and (*c*) a bitter solution.

synchronized with the sound track, suggesting that they recognized the visual-sound correspondence. Young infants can also coordinate visual-auditory information involving people. In one study, $3\frac{1}{2}$-month-old infants looked more at their mother when they also heard her voice and longer at their father when they also heard his voice (Spelke & Owsley, 1979).

Might auditory-visual relations be coordinated even in newborns? Newborns do turn their eyes and their head toward the sound of a voice or rattle when the sound is maintained for several seconds (Clifton & others, 1981), but the newborn can localize a sound and look at an object only in a crude way (Bechtold, Bushnell, & Salapatek, 1979). Improved accuracy at auditory-visual coordination likely requires experience with visual and auditory stimuli.

The ability to connect information about vision with information about touch also develops in infancy. One-year-olds clearly can do this, and it appears that six-month-olds can, too (Acredolo & Hake, 1982). Whether still younger infants can coordinate vision and touch is yet to be determined.

Early exploratory forms of intermodal perception exist in newborns (Bahrick & Hollich, 2008; Sann & Streri, 2007). These exploratory forms of intermodal perception become sharpened with experience in the first year of life (Banks, 2005; Hollich, Newman, & Jusczyk, 2005). In the first six months, infants have difficulty connecting sensory input from different modes, but in the second half of the first year they show an increased ability to make this connection mentally. Thus, babies are born into the world with some innate abilities to perceive relations among sensory modalities, but their intermodal abilities improve considerably through experience (Bahrick & Hollich, 2008). As with all aspects of development, in perceptual development, nature and nurture interact and cooperate.

Review and Reflect: Learning Goal 2

 Outline the Course of Sensory and Perceptual Development

REVIEW

- What are sensation and perception?
- What is the ecological view of perception? What are some research methods used to study infant perception?
- How does vision develop?
- How does hearing develop?
- Through what senses can newborns gather information?
- What is intermodal perception, and how does it develop?

REFLECT

- What would you do to effectively stimulate the hearing of a 1-year-old infant?

3 PERCEPTUAL-MOTOR COUPLING

As we come to the end of this chapter, we return to the important theme of perceptual-motor coupling. The distinction between perceiving and doing has been a time-honored tradition in psychology. However, a number of experts on perceptual and motor development question whether this distinction makes sense

(Adolph & Joh, 2007, 2008; Thelen & Smith, 2006). The main thrust of research in Esther Thelen's dynamic systems approach is to explore how people assemble motor behaviors for perceiving and acting. The main theme of the ecological approach of Eleanor and James J. Gibson is to discover how perception guides action. Action can guide perception, and perception can guide action. Only by moving one's eyes, head, hands, and arms and by moving from one location to another can an individual fully experience his or her environment and learn how to adapt to it. Perception and action are coupled.

Babies, for example, continually coordinate their movements with perceptual information to learn how to maintain balance, reach for objects in space, and move across various surfaces and terrains (Adolph, 2008; Adolph & Joh, 2008; Thelen & Smith, 2006). They are motivated to move by what they perceive. Consider the sight of an attractive toy across the room. In this situation, infants must perceive the current state of their bodies and learn how to use their limbs to reach the toy. Although their movements at first are awkward and uncoordinated, babies soon learn to select patterns that are appropriate for reaching their goals.

Equally important is the other part of the perception-action coupling. That is, action educates perception (Adolph, 2008; Bertenthal, 2008). For example, watching an object while exploring it manually helps infants to discriminate its texture, size, and hardness. Locomoting in the environment teaches babies about how objects and people look from different perspectives, or whether surfaces will support their weight. Individuals perceive in order to move and move in order to perceive. Perceptual and motor development do not occur in isolation from each other but instead are coupled.

How are perception and action coupled in children's development?

Review and Reflect: Learning Goal 3

 3 **Discuss the Connection of Perception and Action**

REVIEW

- How are perception and motor actions coupled in development?

REFLECT

- Describe two examples, not given in the text, in which perception guides action. Then describe two examples, not given in the text, in which action guides perception.

Reach Your Learning Goals

Motor, Sensory, and Perceptual Development

1 MOTOR DEVELOPMENT: DESCRIBE HOW MOTOR SKILLS DEVELOP

The Dynamic Systems View

- Thelen's dynamic systems theory describes the development of motor skills as the assembling of behaviors for perceiving and acting. Perception and action are coupled. According to this theory, the development of motor skills depends on the development of the nervous system, the body's physical properties and its movement possibilities, the goal the child is motivated to reach, and environmental support for the skill. In the dynamic systems view, motor development is far more complex than the result of a genetic blueprint; the infant or child actively puts together a skill in order to achieve a goal within constraints set by the body and the environment.

Reflexes

- Reflexes—built-in reactions to stimuli—govern the newborn's movements. They include the sucking, rooting, and Moro reflexes—all of which typically disappear after three to four months. Some reflexes—such as blinking and yawning—persist throughout life; components of other reflexes are incorporated into voluntary actions.

Gross Motor Skills

- Gross motor skills involve large-muscle activities. Key skills developed during infancy include control of posture and walking. Gross motor skills improve dramatically in the childhood years. Boys usually outperform girls in gross motor skills involving large-muscle activity.

Fine Motor Skills

- Fine motor skills involve finely tuned movements. The onset of reaching and grasping marks a significant accomplishment. Fine motor skills continue to develop through the childhood years and by 4 years of age are much more precise. Children can use their hands as tools by middle childhood, and at 10 to 12 years of age start to show manipulative fine motor skills similar to those of adults.

2 SENSORY AND PERCEPTUAL DEVELOPMENT: OUTLINE THE COURSE OF SENSORY AND PERCEPTUAL DEVELOPMENT

What Are Sensation and Perception?

- Sensation occurs when information interacts with sensory receptors. Perception is the interpretation of sensation.

The Ecological View

- The Gibsons' ecological view states that people directly perceive information that exists in the world. Perception brings people in contact with the environment in order to interact and adapt to it. Affordances are opportunities for interaction offered by objects that are necessary to perform activities. Researchers have developed a number of methods to assess the infant's perception, including the visual preference method (which Fantz used to determine young infants' interest in looking at patterned over nonpatterned displays), habituation and dishabituation, high-amplitude sucking, and tracking.

Vision

- The infant's visual acuity increases dramatically in the first year of life. Infants show an interest in human faces soon after birth, and young infants systematically scan faces. Possibly by 4 weeks of age, infants can discriminate some colors. By 3 months of age, infants show size and shape constancy. In Gibson and Walk's classic study, infants as young as 6 months of age had depth perception. As visual perception develops, infants develop visual expectations. Much of vision develops from biological foundations, but environmental experiences can contribute to the development of visual perception. After infancy, children's visual expectations continue to develop, and further color differentiation occurs from 3 to 4 years of age. A number of children experience vision problems, and about 1 in every 3,000 children is educationally blind.

Hearing

- The fetus can hear several weeks prior to birth. Developmental changes in the perception of loudness, pitch, and localization of sound occur during infancy. Most children's hearing is adequate, but one special concern is otitis media.

Other Senses

Intermodal Perception

- Newborns can respond to touch and feel pain. Newborns can differentiate odors, and sensitivity to taste may be present before birth.

- Intermodal perception is the ability to relate and integrate information from two or more sensory modalities. Crude, exploratory forms of intermodal perception are present in newborns and become sharpened over the first year of life.

3 PERCEPTUAL-MOTOR COUPLING: DISCUSS THE CONNECTION OF PERCEPTION AND ACTION

- Perception and action are coupled—individuals perceive in order to move and move in order to perceive.

KEY TERMS

dynamic systems theory 155
rooting reflex 156
sucking reflex 156
Moro reflex 156
grasping reflex 156

gross motor skills 157
fine motor skills 162
sensation 164
perception 164
ecological view 164

affordances 164
visual preference
   method 166
habituation 166
dishabituation 166

size constancy 169
shape constancy 169
intermodal perception 173

KEY PEOPLE

Esther Thelen 155
T. Berry Brazelton 156
Karen Adolph 158

Rachel Clifton 162
Eleanor and James
   J. Gibson 164

Robert Fantz 165
William James 167
Richard Walk 169

Marshall Haith 170
Elizabeth Spelke 170
Megan Gunnar 172

E-LEARNING TOOLS

To help you master the material in this chapter, you'll find a number of valuable study tools at the Online Learning Center for *Child Development,* twelfth edition (**www.mhhe.com/santrockcd12**).

Taking It to the Net

Research the answers to these questions:

1. Ten-year-old Kristen is a new member of her soccer league's select team. Kristin's parents are reluctant to allow her to participate in a high-pressure, intensely competitive atmosphere. If they allow her to participate, what can they do to make it a healthy experience for themselves and Kristen?

2. Marianne has obtained a part-time job as a nanny for Jack, a 2-month-old boy. What can Marianne expect to see in terms of the child's sensory and motor development as she interacts with and observes Jack over the next several months?

3. Frank and Elise just received Elise's sonogram results—it's a boy. Frank wants them to circumcise their son. Elise does not want their baby to undergo this painful procedure. Frank was circumcised and assures Elise that he has no memory of the pain—if there was any. Is circumcision medically necessary? If Frank and Elise decide on circumcision, can their baby have some form of anesthesia?

Health and Well-Being, Parenting, and Education Exercises

Build your decision-making skills by trying your hand at the health and well-being, parenting, and education exercises.

Video Clips

The Online Learning Center includes the following videos for this chapter:

- *Grasping Reflex at 2 Weeks*
  The grasping reflex is demonstrated by a 2-week-old infant who holds tightly to an adult's pinky finger.

- *Auditory Tracking at 4 Months*
  A 4-month-old girl demonstrates auditory perception when she looks up at her mother, after hearing her mother call her name.

- *Gross Motor Ability in Second Year*
  At 18 months, Rose can step up on and off a large block without assistance.

- *Copying Shapes at Age 7*
  More advanced fine motor skills in middle childhood are demonstrated by this 7-year-old. With careful attention he copies a square, a triangle, and a circle.

COGNITION AND LANGUAGE

Learning is an ornament in prosperity, a refuge in adversity.

—ARISTOTLE
Greek Philosopher, 4th Century B.C.

Children thirst to know and understand. In their effort to know

and understand, they construct their own ideas about the

world around them. They are remarkable for their curiosity and

their intelligence. In Section 3, you will read four chapters:

"Cognitive Developmental Approaches" (Chapter 6),

"Information Processing" (Chapter 7), "Intelligence" (Chapter 8),

and "Language Development" (Chapter 9).

6

We are born capable of learning.

—Jean-Jacques Rousseau
*Swiss-Born French Philosopher,
18th Century*

LEARNING GOALS

◆ Discuss the key processes and four stages in Piaget's theory.

◆ Apply Piaget's theory to education and evaluate his theory.

◆ Identify the main concepts in Vygotsky's theory and compare it with Piaget's theory.

COGNITIVE DEVELOPMENTAL APPROACHES

CHAPTER OUTLINE

Images of Child Development
The Stories of Laurent, Lucienne, and Jacqueline

Jean Piaget, the famous Swiss psychologist, was a meticulous observer of his three children—Laurent, Lucienne, and Jacqueline. His books on cognitive development are filled with these observations. Here are a few of Piaget's observations of his children in infancy (Piaget, 1952):

- At 21 days of age, "Laurent found his thumb after three attempts: prolonged sucking begins each time. But, once he has been placed on his back, he does not know how to coordinate the movement of the arms with that of the mouth and his hands draw back even when his lips are seeking them" (p. 27).

- During the third month, thumb sucking becomes less important to Laurent because of new visual and auditory interests. But, when he cries, his thumb goes to the rescue.

- Toward the end of Lucienne's fourth month, while she is lying in her crib, Piaget hangs a doll above her feet. Lucienne thrusts her feet at the doll and makes it move. "Afterward, she looks at her motionless foot for a second, then recommences. There is no visual control of her foot, for the movements are the same when Lucienne only looks at the doll or when I place the doll over her head. On the other hand, the tactile control of the foot is apparent: after the first shakes, Lucienne makes slow foot movements as though to grasp and explore" (p. 159).

- At 11 months, "Jacqueline is seated and shakes a little bell. She then pauses abruptly in order to delicately place the bell in front of her right foot; then she kicks hard. Unable to recapture it, she grasps a ball which she then places at the same spot in order to give it another kick" (p. 225).

- At 1 year, 2 months, "Jacqueline holds in her hands an object which is new to her: a round, flat box which she turns all over, shakes, (and) rubs against the bassinet. . . . She lets it go and tries to pick it up. But she only succeeds in touching it with her index finger, without grasping it. She nevertheless makes an attempt and presses on the edge. The box then tilts up and falls again" (p. 273). Jacqueline shows an interest in this result and studies the fallen box.

- At 1 year, 8 months, "Jacqueline arrives at a closed door with a blade of grass in each hand. She stretches out her right hand toward the [door] knob but sees that she cannot turn it without letting go of the grass. She puts the grass on the floor, opens the door, picks up the grass again, and enters. But when she wants to leave the room, things become complicated. She puts the grass on the floor and grasps the doorknob. But then she perceives that in pulling the door toward her she will simultaneously chase away the grass which she placed between the door and the threshold. She therefore picks it up in order to put it outside the door's zone of movement" (p. 339).

For Piaget, these observations reflect important changes in the infant's cognitive development. Later in the chapter, you will learn that Piaget argued that infants go through six substages of development and that the behaviors you have just read about characterize those substages.

PREVIEW

Cognitive developmental approaches place a special emphasis on how children actively construct their thinking. They also focus heavily on how thinking changes from one point in development to another. In this chapter, we will highlight the cognitive developmental approaches of Jean Piaget and Lev Vygotsky.

1 PIAGET'S THEORY OF COGNITIVE DEVELOPMENT

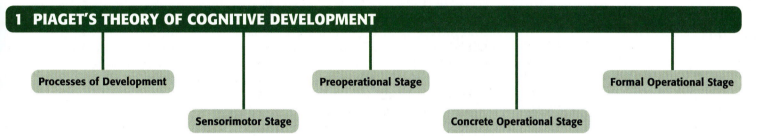

| Processes of Development | Preoperational Stage | Formal Operational Stage |
| Sensorimotor Stage | Concrete Operational Stage | |

Poet Nora Perry asks, "Who knows the thoughts of a child?" As much as anyone, Piaget knew. Through careful observations of his own three children—Laurent, Lucienne, and Jacqueline—and observations of and interviews with other children, Piaget changed perceptions of the way children think about the world.

Piaget's theory is a general, unifying story of how biology and experience sculpt cognitive development. Piaget thought that, just as our physical bodies have structures that enable us to adapt to the world, we build mental structures that help us to adapt to the world. *Adaptation* involves adjusting to new environmental demands. Piaget stressed that children actively construct their own cognitive worlds; information is not just poured into their minds from the environment. He sought to discover how children at different points in their development think about the world and how systematic changes in their thinking occur.

Processes of Development

What processes do children use as they construct their knowledge of the world? Piaget stressed that these processes are especially important in this regard: schemes, assimilation, accommodation, organization, equilibrium, and equilibration.

Schemes   Piaget (1954) said that as the child seeks to construct an understanding of the world, the developing brain creates **schemes**. These are actions or mental representations that organize knowledge. In Piaget's theory, behavioral schemes (physical activities) characterize infancy, and mental schemes (cognitive activities) develop in childhood (Lamb, Bornstein, & Teti, 2002). A baby's schemes are structured by simple actions that can be performed on objects such as sucking, looking, and grasping. Older children have schemes that include strategies and plans for solving problems. For example, a 5-year-old might have a scheme that involves the strategy of classifying objects by size, shape, or color. By the time we have reached adulthood, we have constructed an enormous number of diverse schemes, ranging from how to drive a car to balancing a budget to the concept of fairness.

In Piaget's view, what is a scheme? What schemes might this young infant be displaying?

schemes In Piaget's theory, actions or mental representations that organize knowledge.

I wish I could travel by the road that crosses the boby's mind, and out beyond all bounds; where messengers run errands for no cause between the kingdoms of kings of no history; where reason makes kites of her laws and flies them, and truth sets facts free from its fetters.

—RABINDRANATH TAGORE
Bengali Poet and Essayist, 20th Century

How might assimilation and accommodation be involved in infants' sucking?

assimilation Piagetian concept of the incorporation of new information into existing knowledge (schemes).

accommodation Piagetian concept of adjusting schemes to fit new information and experiences.

organization Piaget's concept of grouping isolated behaviors into a higher-order, more smoothly functioning cognitive system; the grouping or arranging of items into categories.

equilibration A mechanism that Piaget proposed to explain how children shift from one stage of thought to the next. The shift occurs as children experience cognitive conflict, or disequilibrium, in trying to understand the world. Eventually, they resolve the conflict and reach a balance, or equilibrium, of thought.

Assimilation and Accommodation   To explain how children use and adapt their schemes, Piaget proposed two concepts: assimilation and accommodation. Recall that **assimilation** occurs when children incorporate new information into their existing schemes. **Accommodation** occurs when children adjust their schemes to fit new information and experiences.

Think about a toddler who has learned the word *car* to identify the family's car. The toddler might call all moving vehicles on roads "cars," including motorcycles and trucks; the child has assimilated these objects into his or her existing scheme. But the child soon learns that motorcycles and trucks are not cars and fine-tunes the category to exclude motorcycles and trucks, accommodating the scheme.

Assimilation and accommodation operate even in very young infants. Newborns reflexively suck everything that touches their lips; they assimilate all sorts of objects into their sucking scheme. By sucking different objects, they learn about their taste, texture, shape, and soon. After several months of experience, though, they construct their understanding of the world differently. Some objects, such as fingers and the mother's breast, can be sucked, and others, such as fuzzy blankets, should not be sucked. In other words, they accommodate their sucking scheme.

Organization   To make sense out of their world, said Piaget, children cognitively organize their experiences. **Organization** in Piaget's theory is the grouping of isolated behaviors and thoughts into a higher-order system. Continual refinement of this organization is an inherent part of development. A boy who has only a vague idea about how to use a hammer may also have a vague idea about how to use other tools. After learning how to use each one, he relates these uses, grouping items into categories, and organizing his knowledge.

Equilibration and Stages of Development   **Equilibration** is a mechanism that Piaget proposed to explain how children shift from one stage of thought to the next. The shift occurs as children experience cognitive conflict, or disequilibrium, in trying to understand the world. Eventually, they resolve the conflict and reach a balance, or equilibrium, of thought. Piaget argued that there is considerable movement between states of cognitive equilibrium and disequilibrium as assimilation and accommodation work in concert to produce cognitive change. For example, if a child believes that the amount of a liquid changes simply because the liquid is poured into a container with a different shape—for instance, from a container that is short and wide into a container that is tall and narrow—she might be puzzled by such issues as where the "extra" liquid came from and whether there is actually more liquid to drink. The child will eventually resolve these puzzles as her thought becomes more advanced. In the everyday world, the child is constantly faced with such counterexamples and inconsistencies.

Assimilation and accommodation always take the child to a higher ground. For Piaget, the motivation for change is an internal search for equilibrium. As old schemes are adjusted and new schemes are developed, the child organizes and reorganizes the old and new schemes. Eventually, the organization is fundamentally different from the old organization; it is a new way of thinking, a new stage. The result of these processes, according to Piaget, is that individuals go through four stages of development. A different way of understanding the world makes one stage more advanced than another. Cognition is *qualitatively* different in one stage compared with another. In other words, the way children reason at one stage is different from the way they reason at another stage.

Each of Piaget's stages is age-related and consists of distinct ways of thinking. Piaget observed that there are four stages of cognitive development: sensorimotor, preoperational, concrete operational, and formal operational (see Figure 6.1).

Sensorimotor Stage

The **sensorimotor stage** lasts from birth to about 2 years of age. In this stage, infants construct an understanding of the world by coordinating sensory experiences (such as seeing and hearing) with physical, motoric actions—hence the term "sensorimotor." At the beginning of this stage, newborns have little more than reflexive patterns with which to work. At the end of the sensorimotor stage, 2-year-olds can produce complex sensorimotor patterns and use primitive symbols. We first will summarize Piaget's descriptions of how infants develop. Later we will consider criticisms of his view.

Substages   Piaget divided the sensorimotor stage into six substages: (1) simple reflexes; (2) first habits and primary circular reactions; (3) secondary circular reactions; (4) coordination of secondary circular reactions; (5) tertiary circular reactions, novelty, and curiosity; and (6) internalization of schemes (see Figure 6.2).

- *Simple reflexes*, the first sensorimotor substage, corresponds to the first month after birth. In this substage, sensation and action are coordinated primarily through reflexive behaviors, such as the rooting and sucking reflexes. Soon the infant produces behaviors that resemble reflexes in the absence of the usual stimulus for the reflex. For example, a newborn will suck a nipple or bottle only when it is placed directly in the baby's mouth or touched to the lips. But soon the infant might suck when a bottle or nipple is only nearby. The infant is initiating action and is actively structuring experiences in the first month of life.

- *First habits and primary circular reactions* is the second sensorimotor substage, which develops between 1 and 4 months of age. In this substage, the infant coordinates sensation and two types of schemes: habits and primary circular reactions.

    A *habit* is a scheme based on a reflex that has become completely separated from its eliciting stimulus. For example, infants in substage 1 suck when bottles are put to their lips or when they see a bottle. Infants in substage 2 might suck even when no bottle is present. A *circular reaction* is a repetitive action.

    A *primary circular reaction* is a scheme based on the attempt to reproduce an event that initially occurred by chance. For example, suppose an infant accidentally sucks his fingers when they are placed near his mouth. Later, he searches for his fingers to suck them again, but the fingers do not cooperate because the infant cannot coordinate visual and manual actions.

    Habits and circular reactions are stereotyped—that is, the infant repeats them the same way each time. During this substage, the infant's own body remains the infant's center of attention. There is no outward pull by environmental events.

- *Secondary circular reactions* is the third sensorimotor substage, which develops between 4 and 8 months of age. In this substage, the infant becomes more object-oriented, moving beyond preoccupation with the self. By chance, an infant might shake a rattle. The infant repeats this action for the sake of its fascination.

    The infant also imitates some simple actions, such as the baby talk or burbling of adults, and some physical gestures. However, the baby imitates only actions that he or she is already able to produce. Although directed toward objects in the world, the infant's schemes are not intentional or goal-directed.

- *Coordination of secondary circular reactions* is Piaget's fourth sensorimotor substage, which develops between 8 and 12 months of age. To progress into this substage, the infant must coordinate vision and touch, hand and eye. Actions become

Sensorimotor Stage   **0–2 Years**

Infants gain knowledge of the world from the physical actions they perform on it. Infants coordinate sensory experiences with these physical actions. An infant progresses from reflexive, instinctual action at birth to the beginning of symbolic thought toward the end of the stage.

Preoperational Stage   **2–7 Years**

The child begins to use mental representations to understand the world. Symbolic thinking, reflected in the use of words and images, is used in this mental representation, which goes beyond the connection of sensory information with physical action. However, there are some constraints on the child's thinking at this stage, such as egocentrism and centration.

Concrete Operational Stage   **7–11 Years**

The child can now reason logically about concrete events, understands the concept of conservation, organizes objects into hierarchical classes (classification), and places objects in ordered series (seriation).

Formal Operational Stage   **11–15 Years**

The adolescent reasons in more abstract, idealistic, and logical (hypothetical-deductive) ways.

FIGURE 6.1 Piaget's Four Stages of Cognitive Development

sensorimotor stage The first of Piaget's stages, which lasts from birth to about 2 years of age; infants construct an understanding of the world by coordinating sensory experiences (such as seeing and hearing) with motoric actions.

Substage	Age	Description	Example
1 Simple reflexes	Birth to 1 month	Coordination of sensation and action through reflexive behaviors.	Rooting, sucking, and grasping reflexes; newborns suck reflexively when their lips are touched.
2 First habits and primary circular reactions	1 to 4 months	Coordination of sensation and two types of schemes: habits (reflex) and primary circular reactions (reproduction of an event that initially occurred by chance). Main focus is still on the infant's body.	Repeating a body sensation first experienced by chance (sucking thumb, for example); then infants might accommodate actions by sucking their thumb differently than they suck on a nipple.
3 Secondary circular reactions	4 to 8 months	Infants become more object-oriented, moving beyond self-preoccupation; repeat actions that bring interesting or pleasurable results.	An infant coos to make a person stay near; as the person starts to leave, the infant coos again.
4 Coordination of secondary circular reactions	8 to 12 months	Coordination of vision and touch—hand-eye coordination; coordination of schemes and intentionality.	Infant manipulates a stick in order to bring an attractive toy within reach.
5 Tertiary circular reactions, novelty, and curiosity	12 to 18 months	Infants become intrigued by the many properties of objects and by the many things they can make happen to objects; they experiment with new behavior.	A block can be made to fall, spin, hit another object, and slide across the ground.
6 Internalization of schemes	18 to 24 months	Infants develop the ability to use primitive symbols and form enduring mental representations.	An infant who has never thrown a temper tantrum before sees a playmate throw a tantrum; the infant retains a memory of the event, then throws one himself the next day.

FIGURE 6.2 Piaget's Six Substages of Sensorimotor Development

This 17-month-old is in Piaget's stage of tertiary circular reactions. *What might the infant do to suggest that she is in this stage?*

more outwardly directed. Significant changes during this substage involve the coordination of schemes and intentionality. Infants readily combine and recombine previously learned schemes in a coordinated way. They might look at an object and grasp it simultaneously, or they might visually inspect a toy, such as a rattle, and finger it simultaneously, exploring it tactilely. Actions are even more outwardly directed than before. Related to this coordination is the second achievement—the presence of intentionality. For example, infants might manipulate a stick in order to bring a desired toy within reach, or they might knock over one block to reach and play with another one.

- *Tertiary circular reactions, novelty, and curiosity* is Piaget's fifth sensorimotor substage, which develops between 12 and 18 months of age. In this substage, infants become intrigued by the many properties of objects and by the many things that they can make happen to objects. A block can be made to fall, spin, hit another object, and slide across the ground. *Tertiary circular reactions* are schemes in which the infant purposely explores new possibilities with objects, continually doing new things to them and exploring the results. Piaget says that this stage marks the starting point for human curiosity and interest in novelty.

- *Internalization of schemes* is Piaget's sixth and final sensorimotor substage, which develops between 18 and 24 months of age. In this substage, the infant develops the ability to use primitive symbols. For Piaget, a *symbol* is an internalized sensory image or word that represents an event. Primitive symbols permit the infant to think about concrete events without directly acting them out or perceiving them. Moreover, symbols allow the infant to manipulate and transform the represented events in simple ways. In a favorite Piagetian example, Piaget's young daughter saw a matchbox being opened and closed. Later, she mimicked the event by opening and closing her mouth. This was an obvious expression of her image of the event.

Object Permanence   Imagine how chaotic and unpredictable your life would be if you could not distinguish between yourself and your world. This is what the life of a newborn must be like, according to Piaget. There is no differentiation between the self and world; objects have no separate, permanent existence.

By the end of the sensorimotor period, objects are both separate from the self and permanent. **Object permanence** is the understanding that objects and events continue to exist even when they cannot be seen, heard, or touched. Acquiring the sense of object permanence is one of the infant's most important accomplishments. According to Piaget, infants develop object permanence in a series of substages that correspond to the six substages of sensorimotor development.

How could anyone know whether an infant had a sense of object permanence or not? The principal way that object permanence is studied is by watching an infant's reaction when an interesting object disappears (see Figure 6.3). If infants search for the object, it is assumed that they believe it continues to exist.

Object permanence is just one of the basic concepts about the physical world developed by babies. To Piaget, children, even infants, are much like little scientists, examining the world to see how it works. The *Research in Child Development* interlude describes some of the ways in which adult scientists try to discover what these "baby scientists" are finding out about the world.

Research in Child Development

OBJECT PERMANENCE AND CAUSALITY

Two accomplishments of infants that Piaget examined were the development of object permanence and the child's understanding of causality. Let's examine two research studies that address these topics.

In both studies, Renée Baillargeon and her colleagues used a research method that involves *violation of expectations*. In this method, infants see an event happen as it normally would. Then, the event is changed in a way that violates what the infant expects to see. When infants look longer at the event that violates their expectations, it indicates they are surprised by it.

In one study focused on object permanence, researchers showed infants a toy car that moved down an inclined track, disappeared behind a screen, and then re-emerged at the other end, still on the track (Baillargeon & DeVoe, 1991) (see Figure 6.4a). After this sequence was repeated several times, something different occurred: A toy mouse was placed *behind* the tracks but was hidden by the screen while the car rolled by (b). This was the "possible" event. Then, the researchers created an "impossible event": The toy mouse was placed *on* the tracks but was secretly removed after the screen was lowered so that the car seemed to go through the mouse (c). In this study, infants as young as $3\frac{1}{2}$ months of age looked longer at the impossible event than at the possible event, indicating that they were surprised by it. Their surprise suggested that they remembered not only that the toy mouse still existed (object permanence) but its location.

Another study focused on infants' understanding of causality (Kotovsky & Baillargeon, 1994). In this research, a cylinder rolls down a ramp and hits a toy bug at the bottom of the ramp. By $5\frac{1}{2}$ and $6\frac{1}{2}$ months of age, after infants have seen how far the bug will be pushed by a medium-sized cylinder, their reactions indicate that they

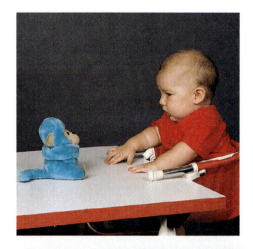

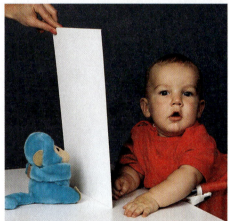

FIGURE 6.3 Object Permanence. Piaget argued that object permanence is one of infancy's landmark cognitive accomplishments. For this 5-month-old boy, "out of sight" is literally out of mind. The infant looks at the toy monkey (*top*), but when his view of the toy is blocked (*bottom*), he does not search for it. Several months later, he will search for the hidden toy monkey, reflecting the presence of object permanence.

object permanence The Piagetian term for one of an infant's most important accomplishments: understanding that objects and events continue to exist even when they cannot directly be seen, heard, or touched.

FIGURE 6.4 Using the Violation of Expectations Method to Study Object Permanence in Infants. If infants looked longer at (*c*) than at (*b*), researchers reasoned that the impossible event in (*c*) violated the infants' expectations and that they remembered that the toy mouse existed.

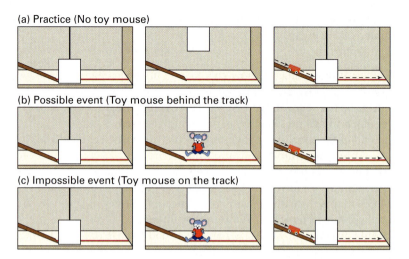

(a) Practice (No toy mouse)

(b) Possible event (Toy mouse behind the track)

(c) Impossible event (Toy mouse on the track)

understand that the bug will roll farther if it is hit by a large cylinder than if it is hit by a small cylinder. Thus, by the middle of the first year of life these infants understood that the size of a moving object determines how far it will move a stationary object that it collides with.

Evaluating Piaget's Sensorimotor Stage

Piaget opened up a new way of looking at infants with his view that their main task is to coordinate their sensory impressions with their motor activity. However, the infant's cognitive world is not as neatly packaged as Piaget portrayed it, and some of Piaget's explanations for the cause of change are debated. In the past several decades, sophisticated experimental techniques have been devised to study infants, and there have been a large number of research studies on infant development. Much of the new research suggests that Piaget's view of sensorimotor development needs to be modified (Carlson & Zelaso, 2008; Vallotton & Fischer, 2008).

The A-not-B Error

One modification concerns Piaget's claim that certain processes are crucial in transitions from one stage to the next. The data do not always support his explanations. For example, in Piaget's theory, an important feature in the progression into substage 4, *coordination of secondary circular reactions,* is an infant's inclination to search for a hidden object in a familiar location rather than to look for the object in a new location. For example, if a toy is hidden twice, initially at location A and subsequently at location B, 8- to 12-month-old infants search correctly at location A initially. But when the toy is subsequently hidden at location B, they make the mistake of continuing to search for it at location A. **A-not-B error** (also called A$\overline{\text{B}}$ error) is the term used to describe this common mistake. Older infants are less likely to make the A-not-B error because their concept of object permanence is more complete.

Researchers have found, however, that the A-not-B error does not show up consistently (Sophian, 1985). The evidence indicates that A-not-B errors are sensitive to the delay between hiding the object at B and the infant's attempt to find it (Diamond, 1985). Thus, the A-not-B error might be due to a failure in memory. Another explanation is that infants tend to repeat a previous motor behavior (Clearfield & others, 2006; Smith, 1999).

Perceptual Development and Expectations

A number of theorists, such as Eleanor Gibson (2001) and Elizabeth Spelke (1991; Spelke & Kinzler, 2007, 2008), maintain that infants' perceptual abilities are highly developed very early in development. For example, in Chapter 5 we discussed research that demonstrated the presence of intermodal perception—the ability to coordinate information from two more sensory modalities, such as vision and hearing—by $3\frac{1}{2}$ months of age, much earlier than Piaget would have predicted (Spelke & Owsley, 1979).

A-not-B error Also called A$\overline{\text{B}}$ error, this occurs when infants make the mistake of selecting the familiar hiding place (A) rather than the new hiding place (B) as they progress into substage 4 in Piaget's sensorimotor stage.

Research also suggests that infants develop the ability to understand how the world works at a very early age (Meltzoff, 2008; Oakes, 2008). For example, by the time they are 3 months of age, infants develop expectations about future events. Marshall Haith and his colleagues (Canfield & Haith, 1991; Haith, Hazen, & Goodman, 1988) presented pictures to infants in either a regular alternating sequence (such as left, right, left, right) or an unpredictable sequence (such as right, right, left, right). When the sequence was predictable, the 3-month-old infants began to anticipate the location of the picture, looking at the side on which it was expected to appear. However, younger infants did not develop expectations about where a picture would be presented.

What kinds of expectations do infants form? Are we born expecting the world to obey basic physical laws, such as gravity, or when do we learn about how the world works? Experiments by Elizabeth Spelke (1991, 2000; Spelke & Hespos, 2001) have addressed these questions. She placed babies before a puppet stage and showed them a series of actions that are unexpected if you know how the physical world works—for example, one ball seemed to roll through a solid barrier, another seemed to leap between two platforms, and a third appeared to hang in midair (Spelke, 1979). Spelke measured and compared the babies' looking times for unexpected and expected actions. She concluded that, by 4 months of age, even though infants do not yet have the ability to talk about objects, move around objects, manipulate objects, or even see objects with high resolution, they expect objects to be solid and continuous. However, at 4 months of age, infants do not expect an object to obey gravitational constraints (Spelke & others, 1992). Similarly, research by Renée Baillargeon and her colleagues (1995, 2004; Aguiar & Baillargeon, 2002) documents that infants as young as 3 to 4 months expect objects to be *substantial* (in the sense that other objects cannot move through them) and *permanent* (in the sense that objects continue to exist when they are hidden).

In sum, researchers conclude that infants see objects as bounded, unitary, solid, and separate from their background, possibly at birth or shortly thereafter, but definitely by 3 to 4 months of age, much earlier than Piaget envisioned. Young infants still have much to learn about objects, but the world appears both stable and orderly to them.

However, some critics, such as Andrew Meltzoff and Keith Moore (Meltzoff, 2008; Moore & Meltzoff, 2008), argue that Spelke's and Baillargeon's research relies on how long infants look at unexpected events and thus assess infants' *perceptual expectations* about where and when objects will reappear rather than tapping their *knowledge* about where the objects are when they are out of sight. Meltzoff (2008) points out that whether infants act on their perception is an important aspect of assessing object permanence and states that it does not appear that young infants can act on the information. Thus, Meltzoff (2008) concludes that whether longer looking time is a valid measure of object permanence and how early infants develop object permanence remains controversial.

By 6 to 8 months, infants have learned to perceive gravity and support—that an object hanging on the end of a table should fall, that ball-bearings will travel farther when rolled down a longer rather than a shorter ramp, and that cup handles will not fall when attached to a cup (Slater, Field, & Hernandez-Reif, 2007). As infants develop, their experiences and actions on objects help them to understand physical laws (Bremner, 2007).

Many researchers conclude that Piaget wasn't specific enough about how infants learn about their world and that infants are more competent than Piaget thought (Bremner, 2007; Spelke & Kinzler, 2008). As they have examined the specific ways that infants learn, the field of infant cognition has become very specialized. There are many researchers working on different questions, with no general theory emerging that can connect all of the different findings (Nelson, 1999). Their theories are local theories, focused on specific research questions, rather than grand theories like Piaget's (Kuhn, 1998). If there is a unifying theme, it is that investigators in infant development struggle with how developmental changes in cognition take place and the big issue of nature and nurture (Spelke & Kinzler, 2008).

How do today's researchers view infants' development differently than Piaget?

Preoperational Stage

The cognitive world of the preschool child is creative, free, and fanciful. The imagination of preschool children works overtime, and their mental grasp of the world improves. Piaget described the preschool child's cognition as *preoperational*. What did he mean?

Because Piaget called this stage preoperational, it might sound unimportant. Not so. Preoperational thought is anything but a convenient waiting period for the next stage, concrete operational thought. However, the label *preoperational* emphasizes that the child does not yet perform **operations**, which are internalized actions that allow children to do mentally what before they could do only physically. Operations are reversible mental actions. Mentally adding and subtracting numbers are examples of operations. *Preoperational thought* is the beginning of the ability to reconstruct in thought what has been established in behavior.

The **preoperational stage**, which lasts from approximately 2 to 7 years of age, is the second Piagetian stage. In this stage, children begin to represent the world with words, images, and drawings. Symbolic thought goes beyond simple connections of sensory information and physical action. Stable concepts are formed, mental reasoning emerges, egocentrism is present, and magical beliefs are constructed. Preoperational thought can be divided into substages: the symbolic function substage and the intuitive thought substage.

operations Internalized actions that allow children to do mentally what before they had done only physically. Operations also are reversible mental actions.

preoperational stage The second Piagetian developmental stage, which lasts from about 2 to 7 years of age, children begin to represent the world with words, images, and drawings.

symbolic function substage The first substage of preoperational thought, occurring roughly between the ages of 2 and 4. In this substage, the young child gains the ability to represent mentally an object that is not present.

egocentrism An important feature of preoperational thought, the inability to distinguish between one's own and someone else's perspective.

The Symbolic Function Substage The **symbolic function substage** is the first substage of preoperational thought, occurring roughly between the ages of 2 and 4. In this substage, the young child gains the ability to mentally represent an object that is not present. This ability vastly expands the child's mental world (Carlson & Zelazo, 2008). Young children use scribble designs to represent people, houses, cars, clouds, and so on; they begin to use language and engage in pretend play. However, although young children make distinct progress during this substage, their thought still has several important limitations, two of which are egocentrism and animism.

Egocentrism is the inability to distinguish between one's own perspective and someone else's perspective. The following telephone conversation between 4-year-old Mary, who is at home, and her father, who is at work, typifies Mary's egocentric thought:

Father: Mary, is Mommy there?

Mary: (Silently nods)

Father: Mary, may I speak to Mommy?

Mary: (Nods again silently)

Mary's response is egocentric in that she fails to consider her father's perspective before replying. A nonegocentric thinker would have responded verbally.

Piaget and Barbel Inhelder (1969) initially studied young children's egocentrism by devising the three mountains task (see Figure 6.5). The child walks

FIGURE 6.5 The Three-Mountains Task. The mountain model on the far left shows the child's perspective from view A, where he or she is sitting. The four squares represent photos showing the mountains from four different viewpoints of the model—A, B, C, and D. The experimenter asks the child to identify the photo in which the mountains look as they would from position B. To identify the photo correctly, the child has to take the perspective of a person sitting at spot B. Invariably, a child who thinks in a preoperational way cannot perform this task. When asked what a view of the mountains looks like from position B, the child selects Photo 1, taken from location A (the child's own view at the time) instead of Photo 2, the correct view.

Model of Mountains

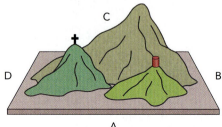

A
Child seated here

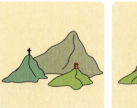

Photo 1
(View from A)

Photo 2
(View from B)

Photo 3
(View from C)

Photo 4
(View from D)

around the model of the mountains and becomes familiar with what the mountains look like from different perspectives, and she can see that there are different objects on the mountains. The child is then seated on one side of the table on which the mountains are placed. The experimenter moves a doll to different locations around the table, at each location asking the child to select from a series of photos the one photo that most accurately reflects the view the doll is seeing. Children in the preoperational stage often pick their own view rather than the doll's view. Preschool children frequently show perspective skills on some tasks but not others.

Animism, another limitation of preoperational thought, is the belief that inanimate objects have lifelike qualities and are capable of action (Gelman & Opfer, 2004). A young child might show animism by saying, "That tree pushed the leaf off, and it fell down" or "The sidewalk made me mad; it made me fall down." A young child who uses animism fails to distinguish the appropriate occasions for using human and nonhuman perspectives.

Possibly because young children are not very concerned about reality, their drawings are fanciful and inventive. Suns are blue, skies are yellow, and cars float on clouds in their symbolic, imaginative world. One 3½-year-old looked at a scribble he had just drawn and described it as a pelican kissing a seal (see Figure 6.6a). The symbolism is simple but strong, like abstractions found in some modern art. Twentieth-century Spanish artist Pablo Picasso commented, "I used to draw like Raphael but it has taken me a lifetime to draw like young children." In the elementary school years, a child's drawings become more realistic, neat, and precise (see Figure 6.6b). Suns are yellow, skies are blue, and cars travel on roads (Winner, 1986).

The Intuitive Thought Substage   The **intuitive thought substage** is the second substage of preoperational thought, occurring between approximately 4 and 7 years of age. In this substage, children begin to use primitive reasoning and want to know the answers to all sorts of questions. Consider 4-year-old Tommy, who is at the beginning of the intuitive thought substage. Although he is starting to develop his own ideas about the world he lives in, his ideas are still simple, and he is not very good at thinking things out. He has difficulty understanding events that he knows are taking place but which he cannot see. His fantasized thoughts bear little resemblance to reality. He cannot yet answer the question "What if?" in any reliable way. For example, he has only a vague idea of what would happen if a car were to hit him. He also has difficulty negotiating traffic because he cannot do the mental calculations necessary to estimate whether an approaching car will hit him when he crosses the road.

By the age of 5, children have just about exhausted the adults around them with "why" questions. The child's questions signal the emergence of interest in reasoning and in figuring out why things are the way they are. Following are some samples of the questions children ask during the questioning period of 4 to 6 years of age (Elkind, 1976):

"What makes you grow up?"

"What makes you stop growing?"

"Why does a lady have to be married to have a baby?"

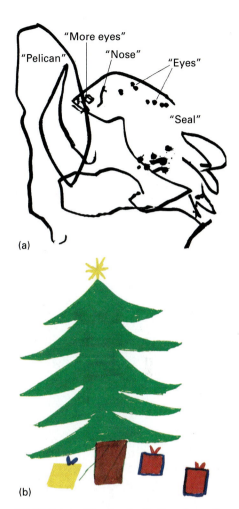

"I still don't have all the answers, but I'm beginning to ask the right questions."
© New Yorker Collection 1989 Lee Lorenz from cartoonbank.com. All rights reserved. Reprinted with permission.

FIGURE 6.6 The Symbolic Drawings of Young Children. (*a*) A 3½-year-old's symbolic drawing. Halfway into this drawing, the 3½-year-old artist said it was "a pelican kissing a seal." (*b*) This 11-year-old's drawing is neater and more realistic but also less inventive.

animism A facet of preoperational thought; the belief that inanimate objects have lifelike qualities and are capable of action.

intuitive thought substage The second substage of preoperational thought, occurring between approximately 4 and 7 years of age. Children begin to use primitive reasoning and want to know the answers to all sorts of questions.

"Who was the mother when everybody was a baby?"

"Why do leaves fall?"

"Why does the sun shine?"

Piaget called this substage *intuitive* because young children seem so sure about their knowledge and understanding yet are unaware of how they know what they know. That is, they know something but know it without the use of rational thinking.

Centration and the Limits of Preoperational Thought One limitation of preoperational thought is **centration**, a centering of attention on one characteristic to the exclusion of all others. Centration is most clearly evidenced in young children's lack of **conservation**, the awareness that altering an object's or a substance's appearance does not change its basic properties. For example, to adults, it is obvious that a certain amount of liquid stays the same, regardless of a container's shape. But this is not at all obvious to young children. Instead, they are struck by the height of the liquid in the container; they focus on that characteristic to the exclusion of others.

The situation that Piaget devised to study conservation is his most famous task. In the conservation task, a child is presented with two identical beakers, each filled to the same level with liquid (see Figure 6.7). The child is asked if these beakers have the same amount of liquid, and she usually says "yes." Then the liquid from one beaker is poured into a third beaker, which is taller and thinner than the first two. The child is then asked if the amount of liquid in the tall, thin beaker is equal to that which remains in one of the original beakers. Children who are less than 7 or 8 years old usually say "no" and justify their answers in terms of the differing height or width of the beakers. Older children usually answer "yes" and justify their answers appropriately ("If you poured the water back, the amount would still be the same").

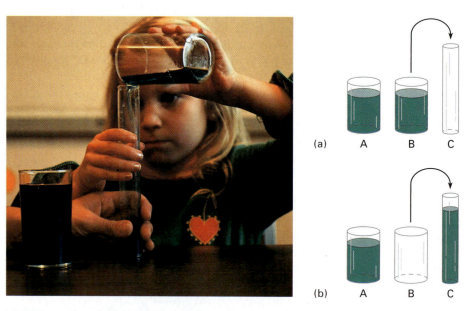

centration The focusing of attention on one characteristic to the exclusion of all others.

conservation The idea that altering an object's or substance's appearance does not change its basic properties.

FIGURE 6.7 Piaget's Conservation Task. The beaker test is a well-known Piagetian task to determine whether a child can think operationally—that is, can mentally reverse actions and show conservation of the substance. (*a*) Two identical beakers are presented to the child. Then, the experimenter pours the liquid from B into C, which is taller and thinner than A or B. (*b*) The child is asked if these beakers (A and C) have the same amount of liquid. The preoperational child says "no." When asked to point to the beaker that has more liquid, the preoperational child points to the tall, thin beaker.

Type of Conservation	Initial Presentation	Manipulation	Preoperational Child's Answer
Number	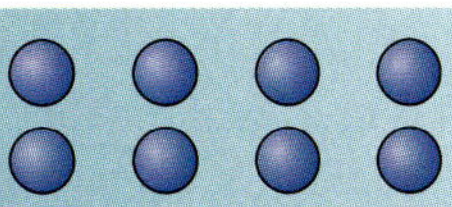 Two identical rows of objects are shown to the child, who agrees they have the same number.	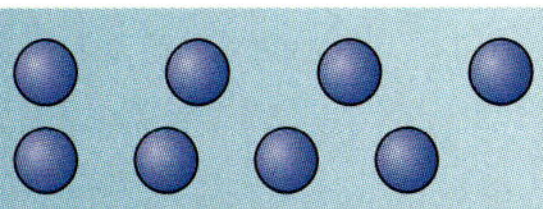 One row is lengthened and the child is asked whether one row now has more objects.	Yes, the longer row.
Matter	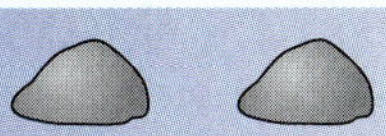 Two identical balls of clay are shown to the child. The child agrees that they are equal.	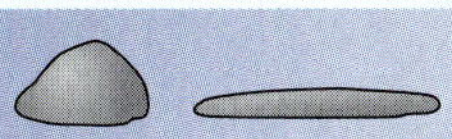 The experimenter changes the shape of one of the balls and asks the child whether they still contain equal amounts of clay.	No, the longer one has more.
Length	 Two sticks are aligned in front of the child. The child agrees that they are the same length.	 The experimenter moves one stick to the right, then asks the child if they are equal in length.	No, the one on the top is longer.

FIGURE 6.8 **Some Dimensions of Conservation: Number, Matter, and Length.** *What characteristics of preoperational thought do children demonstrate when they fail these conservation tasks?*

In Piaget's theory, failing the conservation-of-liquid task is a sign that children are at the preoperational stage of cognitive development. The preoperational child fails to show conservation not only of liquid but also of number, matter, length, volume, and area. Figure 6.8 portrays several of these.

Children often vary in their performance on different conservation tasks. Thus, a child might be able to conserve volume but not number.

Some developmentalists do not believe Piaget was entirely correct in his estimate of when children's conservation skills emerge. For example, Rochel Gelman (1969) showed that when the child's attention to relevant aspects of the conservation task is improved, the child is more likely to conserve. Gelman has also demonstrated that attentional training on one dimension, such as number, improves the preschool child's performance on another dimension, such as mass. Thus, Gelman suggests that conservation appears earlier than Piaget thought and that attention is especially important in explaining conservation.

Concrete Operational Stage

The **concrete operational stage**, which lasts approximately from 7 to 11 years of age, is the third Piagetian stage. In this stage, logical reasoning replaces intuitive reasoning as long as the reasoning can be applied to specific or concrete examples. For instance, concrete operational thinkers cannot imagine the steps necessary to complete an algebraic equation, which is too abstract for thinking at this stage of development. Children at this stage can perforsm *concrete operations*, which are reversible mental actions on real, concrete objects.

Conservation The conservation tasks demonstrate a child's ability to perform concrete operations. In the test of reversibility of thought involving conservation of matter (shown in Figure 6.8), a child is presented with two identical balls of clay. An experimenter rolls one ball into a long, thin shape; the other remains in its original ball shape. The child is then asked if there is more clay in the ball or in the long, thin piece of clay. By the time children reach the age 7 or 8, most answer that the amount of clay is the same. To answer this problem correctly, children have to imagine the clay ball rolling back into a ball after it has been changed into a long, thin shape; they have mentally reversed the action on the ball.

Concrete operations allow children to coordinate several characteristics rather than focus on a single property of an object. In the clay example, a preoperational

concrete operational stage Piaget's third stage, which lasts from approximately 7 to 11 years of age: children can perform concrete operations, and logical reasoning replaces intuitive reasoning as long as the reasoning can be applied to specific or concrete examples.

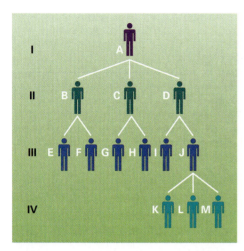

FIGURE 6.9 Classification: An Important Ability in Concrete Operational Thought. A family tree of four generations (*I to IV*): The preoperational child has trouble classifying the members of the four generations; the concrete operational child can classify the members vertically, horizontally, and obliquely (up and down and across). For example, the concrete operational child understands that a family member can be a son, a brother, and a father, all at the same time.

horizontal décalage Piaget's concept that similar abilities do not appear at the same time within a stage of development.

seriation The concrete operation that involves ordering stimuli along a quantitative dimension (such as length).

transitivity If a relation holds between a first object and a second object, and holds between the second object and a third object, then it holds between the first object and the third object. Piaget argued that an understanding of transitivity is characteristic of concrete operational thought.

formal operational stage Piaget's fourth and final stage, which occurs between the ages of 11 and 15; individuals move beyond concrete experiences and think in more abstract and logical ways.

child is likely to focus on height or width; a concrete operational child coordinates information about both dimensions. Conservation involves recognition that the length, number, mass, quantity, area, weight, and volume of objects and substances are not changed by transformations that merely alter their appearance.

Children do not conserve all quantities or conserve on all tasks simultaneously. The order of their mastery is number, length, liquid quantity, mass, weight, and volume. **Horizontal décalage** is Piaget's concept that similar abilities do not appear at the same time within a stage of development. During the concrete operational stage, conservation of number usually appears first and conservation of volume last. Also, an 8-year-old child may know that a long stick of clay can be rolled back into a ball but not understand that the ball and the stick weigh the same. At about 9 years of age, the child recognizes that they weigh the same, and eventually, at about 11 to 12 years of age, the child understands that the clay's volume is unchanged by rearranging it. Children initially master tasks in which the dimensions are more salient and visible, only later mastering those not as visually apparent, such as volume.

Classification   Many of the concrete operations identified by Piaget involve the ways children reason about the properties of objects. One important skill that characterizes concrete operational children is the ability to classify things and to consider their relationships. Specifically, concrete operational children can understand (1) the interrelationships among sets and subsets, (2) seriation, and (3) transitivity.

The ability of the concrete operational child to divide things into sets and subsets and understand their relationship is illustrated by a family tree of four generations (Furth & Wachs, 1975) (see Figure 6.9). This family tree suggests that the grandfather (A) has three children (B, C, and D), each of whom has two children (E through J), and that one of these children (J) has three children (K, L, and M). The concrete operational child understands that person J can, at the same time, be father, brother, and grandson. A child who comprehends this classification system can move up and down a level (vertically), across a level (horizontally), and up and down and across (obliquely) within the system.

Seriation is the ordering of stimuli along a quantitative dimension (such as length). To see if children can serialize, a teacher might haphazardly place eight sticks of different lengths on a table. The teacher then asks the children to order the sticks by length. Many young children put the sticks into two or three small groups of "big" sticks or "little" sticks, rather than a correct ordering of all eight sticks. Or they line up the tops of the sticks but ignore the bottoms. The concrete operational thinker simultaneously understands that each stick must be longer than the one that precedes it and shorter than the one that follows it.

Transitivity involves the ability to reason about and logically combine relationships. If a relation holds between a first object and a second object, and also holds between the second object and a third object, then it also holds between the first and third objects. For example, consider three sticks (A, B, and C) of differing lengths. A is the longest, B is intermediate in length, and C is the shortest. Does the child understand that if A is longer than B, and B is longer than C, then A is longer than C? In Piaget's theory, concrete operational thinkers do; preoperational thinkers do not.

Formal Operational Stage

So far we have studied the first three of Piaget's stages of cognitive development: sensorimotor, preoperational, and concrete operational. What are the characteristics of the fourth stage?

The **formal operational stage**, which appears between 11 and 15 years of age, is the fourth and final Piagetian stage. In this stage, individuals move beyond concrete experiences and think in abstract and more logical ways. As part of thinking more abstractly, adolescents develop images of ideal circumstances. They might think about what an ideal parent is like and compare their parents to their ideal standards. They begin to entertain possibilities for the future and are fascinated with what they can be. In solving problems, formal operational thinkers are more systematic and use logical reasoning.

Abstract, Idealistic, and Logical Thinking   The abstract quality of the adolescent's thought at the formal operational level is evident in the adolescent's verbal problem-solving ability. The concrete operational thinker needs to see the concrete elements A, B, and C to be able to make the logical inference that if A = B and B = C, then A = C. The formal operational thinker can solve this problem merely through verbal presentation.

Another indication of the abstract quality of adolescents' thought is their increased tendency to think about thought itself. One adolescent commented, "I began thinking about why I was thinking about what I was. Then I began thinking about why I was thinking about what I was thinking about what I was." If this sounds abstract, it is, and it characterizes the adolescent's enhanced focus on thought and its abstract qualities.

Might adolescents' ability to reason hypothetically and to evaluate what is ideal versus what is real lead them to engage in demonstrations, such as this protest related to better ethnic relations? What other causes might be attractive to adolescents' newfound cognitive abilities of hypothetical-deductive reasoning and idealistic thinking?

Accompanying the abstract thought of adolescence is thought full of idealism and possibilities. While children frequently think in concrete ways, or in terms of what is real and limited, adolescents begin to engage in extended speculation about ideal characteristics—qualities they desire in themselves and in others. Such thoughts often lead adolescents to compare themselves with others in regard to ideal standards. And the thoughts of adolescents are often fantasy flights into future possibilities. It is not unusual for the adolescent to become impatient with these newfound ideal standards and to become perplexed over which of many ideal standards to adopt.

As adolescents are learning to think more abstractly and idealistically, they are also learning to think more logically. Children are likely to solve problems in a trial-and-error fashion. Adolescents begin to think more as a scientist thinks, devising plans to solve problems and systematically testing solutions. They use **hypothetical-deductive reasoning**, which means that they develop hypotheses, or best guesses, and systematically deduce, or conclude, which is the best path to follow in solving the problem.

One example of hypothetical-deductive reasoning involves a modification of the familiar game Twenty Questions. Individuals are shown a set of 42 color pictures, displayed in a rectangular array (six rows of seven pictures each) and are asked to determine which picture the experimenter has in mind (that is, which is "correct"). The individuals are allowed to ask only questions to which the experimenter can answer "yes" or "no." The object of the game is to select the correct picture by asking as few questions as possible. Adolescents who are deductive hypothesis testers formulate a plan and test a series of hypotheses, which considerably narrows the field of choices. The most effective plan is a "halving" strategy (*Q:* Is the picture in the right half of the array?).

Assimilation (incorporating new information into existing knowledge) dominates the initial development of formal operational thought, and these thinkers perceive the world subjectively and idealistically. Later in adolescence, as intellectual balance is restored, these individuals accommodate to the cognitive upheaval that has occurred (they adjust to the new information).

Some of Piaget's ideas on formal operational thought are being challenged (Byrnes, 2008). There is much more individual variation in formal operational thought than Piaget envisioned. Only about one in three young adolescents is a formal operational thinker. Many American adults never become formal operational thinkers, and neither do many adults in other cultures.

Adolescent Egocentrism   In addition to thinking more logically, abstractly, and idealistically—characteristics of Piaget's formal operational thought stage—in what other ways do adolescents change cognitively? David Elkind (1978) has described how adolescent egocentrism governs the way that adolescents think about social matters. **Adolescent egocentrism** is the heightened self-consciousness of adolescents, which is reflected in their belief that others are as interested in them as they are in themselves,

hypothetical-deductive reasoning Piaget's formal operational concept that adolescents have the cognitive ability to develop hypotheses about ways to solve problems and can systematically deduce which is the best path to follow in solving the problem.

adolescent egocentrism The heightened self-consciousness of adolescents, which is reflected in adolescents' beliefs that others are as interested in them as they are in themselves, and in adolescents' sense of personal uniqueness and invincibility.

Many adolescent girls spend long hours in front of the mirror, depleting cans of hairspray, tubes of lipstick, and jars of cosmetics. *How might this behavior be related to changes in adolescent cognitive and physical development?*

and in their sense of personal uniqueness and invincibility. Elkind proposes that adolescent egocentrism can be dissected into two types of social thinking—imaginary audience and personal fable.

The **imaginary audience** refers to the aspect of adolescent egocentrism that involves attention-getting behavior—the attempt to be noticed, visible, and "onstage." An adolescent boy might think that others are as aware of a few hairs that are out of place as he is. An adolescent girl walks into her classroom and thinks that all eyes are riveted on her complexion. Adolescents especially sense that they are "onstage" in early adolescence, believing they are the main actors and all others are the audience.

According to Elkind, the **personal fable** is the part of adolescent egocentrism that involves an adolescent's sense of personal uniqueness and invincibility. Adolescents' sense of personal uniqueness makes them feel that no one can understand how they really feel. For example, an adolescent girl thinks that her mother cannot possibly sense the hurt she feels because her boyfriend has broken up with her. As part of their effort to retain a sense of personal uniqueness, adolescents might craft stories about themselves that are filled with fantasy, immersing themselves in a world that is far removed from reality. Personal fables frequently show up in adolescent diaries.

Adolescents also often show a sense of invincibility—feeling that although others might be vulnerable to tragedies, such as a terrible car wreck, these things won't happen to them. Some developmentalists believe that the sense of uniqueness and invincibility that egocentrism generates is responsible for some of the seemingly reckless behavior of adolescents, including drag racing, drug use, suicide, and failure to use contraceptives during intercourse (Alberts, Elkind, & Ginsberg, 2007). For example, one study found that eleventh- and twelfth-grade females who were high in adolescent egocentrism were more likely to say they would not get pregnant from engaging in sex without contraception than were their counterparts who were low in adolescent egocentrism (Arnett, 1990).

A recent study of sixth- through twelfth-graders examined whether aspects of the personal fable were linked to various aspects of adolescent adjustment (Aalsma, Lapsley, & Flannery, 2006). A sense of invulnerability was linked to engaging in risky behaviors, such as smoking cigarettes, drinking alcohol, and delinquency, whereas a sense of personal uniqueness was related to depression and suicidal thoughts.

Review and Reflect: Learning Goal 1

 Discuss the Key Processes and Four Stages in Piaget's Theory

REVIEW

- What are the key processes in Piaget's theory of cognitive development?
- What are the main characteristics of the sensorimotor stage? What revisions of Piaget's sensorimotor stage have been proposed?
- What are the main characteristics of the preoperational stage?
- What are the main characteristics of the concrete operational stage?
- What are the main characteristics of the formal operational stage? How has Piaget's formal operational stage been criticized?

REFLECT

- Do you consider yourself to be a formal operational thinker? Do you still sometimes feel like a concrete operational thinker? Give examples.

imaginary audience The aspect of adolescent egocentrism that involves attention-getting behavior motivated by a desire to be noticed, visible, and "onstage."

personal fable The part of adolescent egocentrism that involves an adolescent's sense of uniqueness and invincibility.

2 APPLYING AND EVALUATING PIAGET'S THEORY

Piaget and Education   **Evaluating Piaget's Theory**

What are some applications of Piaget's theory to education? What are the main contributions and criticisms of Piaget's theory?

Piaget and Education

Piaget was not an educator, but he provided a sound conceptual framework for viewing learning and education. Following are some ideas in Piaget's theory that can be applied to teaching children (Elkind, 1976; Heuwinkel, 1996):

1. *Take a constructivist approach.* Piaget emphasized that children learn best when they are active and seek solutions for themselves. Piaget opposed teaching methods that treat children as passive receptacles. The educational implication of Piaget's view is that, in all subjects, students learn best by making discoveries, reflecting on them, and discussing them, rather than blindly imitating the teacher or doing things by rote.

2. *Facilitate, rather than direct, learning.* Effective teachers design situations that allow students to learn by doing. These situations promote students' thinking and discovery. Effective teachers listen, watch, and question students, to help them gain better understanding. They don't just examine what students think and the product of their learning. Rather, they carefully observe students and find out how they think, relevant questions to stimulate their thinking, and ask them to explain their answers.

3. *Consider the child's knowledge and level of thinking.* Students do not come to class with empty minds. They have many ideas about the physical and natural world. They have concepts of space, time, quantity, and causality. These ideas differ from the ideas of adults. Teachers need to interpret what a student is saying and respond in a way that is not too far from the student's level. Also, Piaget suggested that it is important to examine children's mistakes in thinking, not just what they get correct, to help guide them to a higher level of understanding.

4. *Use ongoing assessment.* Individually constructed meanings cannot be measured by standardized tests. Math and language portfolios (which contain work in progress as well as finished products), individual conferences in which students discuss their thinking strategies, and students' written and verbal explanations of their reasoning can be used to evaluate progress.

5. *Promote the student's intellectual health.* When Piaget came to lecture in the United States, he was asked, "What can I do to get my child to a higher cognitive stage sooner?" He was asked this question so often here compared with other countries that he called it the American question. For Piaget, children's learning should occur naturally. Children should not be pushed and pressured into achieving too much too early in their development, before they are maturationally ready. Some parents spend long hours every day holding up large flash cards with words on them to improve their baby's vocabulary. In the Piagetian view, this is not the best way for infants to learn. It places too much emphasis on speeding up intellectual development, involves passive learning, and will not work.

6. *Turn the classroom into a setting of exploration and discovery.* What do actual classrooms look like when the teachers adopt Piaget's views? Several first-

What are some educational strategies that can be derived from Piaget's theory?

and second-grade math classrooms provide some examples (Kamii, 1985, 1989). The teachers emphasize students' own exploration and discovery. The classrooms are less structured than what we think of as a typical classroom. Workbooks and predetermined assignments are not used. Rather, the teachers observe the students' interests and natural participation in activities to determine the course of learning. For example, a math lesson might be constructed around counting the day's lunch money or dividing supplies among students. Often, games are used to stimulate mathematical thinking. For example, a version of dominoes teaches children about even-numbered combinations; a variation on tic-tac-toe replaces *X*s and *O*s with numbers. Teachers encourage peer interaction during the lessons and games because students' different viewpoints can contribute to advances in thinking.

Evaluating Piaget's Theory

What were Piaget's main contributions? Has his theory withstood the test of time?

Contributions   Piaget was a giant in the field of developmental psychology, the founder of the present field of children's cognitive development (Perret-Clermont & Barrelet, 2007). Psychologists owe him a long list of masterful concepts of enduring power and fascination: assimilation, accommodation, object permanence, egocentrism, conservation, and others (Carpendale, Muller, & Bibok, 2008). Psychologists also owe him the current vision of children as active, constructive thinkers. And they have a debt to him for creating a theory that generated a huge volume of research on children's cognitive development.

Piaget also was a genius when it came to observing children. His careful observations demonstrated inventive ways to discover how children act on and adapt to their world. Piaget showed us some important things to look for in cognitive development, such as the shift from preoperational to concrete operational thinking. He also showed us how children need to make their experiences fit their schemes (cognitive frameworks) yet simultaneously adapt their schemes to experience. Piaget also revealed how cognitive change is likely to occur if the context is structured to allow gradual movement to the next higher level. Concepts do not emerge suddenly, full-blown, but instead develop through a series of partial accomplishments that lead to increasingly comprehensive understanding (Haith & Benson, 1998).

Criticisms   Piaget's theory has not gone unchallenged (Byrnes, 2008). Questions are raised about estimates of children's competence at different developmental levels, stages, the training of children to reason at higher levels, and culture and education.

Estimates of Children's Competence   Some cognitive abilities emerge earlier than Piaget thought (Bauer, 2008; Scholnick, 2008). For example, as previously noted, some aspects of object permanence emerge earlier than he proposed. Even 2-year-olds are nonegocentric in some contexts. When they realize that another person will not see an object, they investigate whether the person is blindfolded or looking in a different direction. Some understanding of the conservation of number has been demonstrated as early as age 3, although Piaget did not think it emerged until 7. Young children are not as uniformly "pre" this and "pre" that (precausal, preoperational) as Piaget thought.

Cognitive abilities also can emerge later than Piaget thought (Brynes, 2008). Many adolescents still think in concrete operational ways or are just beginning to master formal operations. Even many adults are not formal operational thinkers. In sum, recent theoretical revisions highlight more cognitive competencies of infants and young children and more cognitive shortcomings of adolescents and adults (Oakes, 2008).

Jean Piaget, the main architect of the field of cognitive development, at age 27.

Stages   Piaget conceived of stages as unitary structures of thought. Thus, his theory assumes developmental synchrony—that is, various aspects of a stage should emerge at the same time. However, some concrete operational concepts do not appear in synchrony. For example, children do not learn to conserve at the same time they learn to cross-classify. Thus, most contemporary developmentalists agree that children's cognitive development is not as stage-like as Piaget thought (Kuhn & Franklin, 2006).

Effects of Training   Some children who are at one cognitive stage (such as preoperational) can be trained to reason at a higher cognitive stage (such as concrete operational). This poses a problem for Piaget's theory. He argued that such training is only superficial and ineffective, unless the child is at a maturational transition point between the stages (Gelman & Williams, 1998).

Culture and Education   Culture and education exert stronger influences on children's development than Piaget reasoned (Gredler, 2008; Holzman, 2009). For example, the age at which children acquire conservation skills is related to how much practice their culture provides in these skills. Among Wolof children in the West African nation of Senegal, only 50 percent of the 10- to 13-year-olds understood the principle of conservation (Greenfield, 1966). Comparable studies among cultures in central Australia, New Guinea (an island north of Australia), the Amazon jungle region of Brazil, and rural Sardinia (an island off the coast of Italy) yielded similar results (Dasen, 1977). An outstanding teacher and education in the logic of math and science can promote concrete and formal operational thought.

An outstanding teacher and education in the logic of science and mathematics are important cultural experiences that promote the development of operational thought. *Might Piaget have underestimated the roles of culture and schooling in children's cognitive development?*

The Neo-Piagetian Approach   **Neo-Piagetians** argue that Piaget got some things right but that his theory needs considerable revision. They give more emphasis to how children use attention, memory, and strategies to process information (Case, 1987, 1999; Morra & others, 2007). They especially believe that a more accurate portrayal of children's thinking requires attention to children's strategies, the speed at which children process information, the particular task involved, and the division of problems into smaller, more precise steps (Demetriou, 2001). In Chapter 7, we will discuss these aspects of children's thought.

Review and Reflect: Learning Goal 2

2   Apply Piaget's Theory to Education and Evaluate His Theory

REVIEW

- How can Piaget's theory be applied to educating children?
- What are some key contributions and criticisms of Piaget's theory?

REFLECT

- How might thinking in formal operational ways rather than concrete operational ways help students to develop better study skills?

neo-Piagetians Developmentalists who have elaborated on Piaget's theory, believing that children's cognitive development is more specific in many respects than Piaget thought and—giving more emphasis to how children use memory, attention, and strategies to process information.

3 VYGOTSKY'S THEORY OF COGNITIVE DEVELOPMENT

The Zone of Proximal Development

Scaffolding

Language and Thought

Teaching Strategies

Evaluating Vygotsky's Theory

Piaget's theory is a major developmental theory. Another developmental theory that focuses on children's cognition is Vygotsky's theory. Like Piaget, Vygotsky (1962) emphasized that children actively construct their knowledge and understanding. In Piaget's theory, children develop ways of thinking and understanding by their actions and interactions with the physical world. In Vygtosky's theory, children are more often described as social creatures than in Piaget's theory. They develop their ways of thinking and understanding primarily through social interaction (Valsiner, 2006). Their cognitive development depends on the tools provided by society, and their minds are shaped by the cultural context in which they live (Cole & Gajdamaschko, 2007; Holzman, 2009).

We briefly described Vygotsky's theory in Chapter 1. Here we take a closer look at his ideas about how children learn and his view of the role of language in cognitive development.

The Zone of Proximal Development

Vygotsky's belief in the importance of social influences, especially instruction, on children's cognitive development is reflected in his concept of the zone of proximal development. **Zone of proximal development (ZPD)** is Vygotsky's term for the range of tasks that are too difficult for the child to master alone but that can be learned with guidance and assistance of adults or more-skilled children. Thus, the lower limit of the ZPD is the level of skill reached by the child working independently. The upper limit is the level of additional responsibility the child can accept with the assistance of an able instructor (see Figure 6.10). The ZPD captures the child's cognitive skills that are in the process of maturing and can be accomplished only with the assistance of a more-skilled person (Alvarez & del Rio, 2007; Gauvain & Perez, 2007). Vygotsky (1962) called these the "buds" or "flowers" of development, to distinguish them from the "fruits" of development, which the child already can accomplish independently.

Let's consider an example that reflects the zone of proximal development (Frede, 1995, p. 125):

> A 5-year-old child is pushing a small shopping cart through the house area of his preschool. His teacher notices that he is putting fruit in the small basket and all other groceries in the larger section of the cart. She has watched him sort objects over the past few weeks and thinks that he may now be able to classify along two dimensions at the same time, with some help from her. She goes to the cash register to pretend to be the cashier and says, "We need to be careful how we divide your groceries into bags. We want to use one bag for things that go in the refrigerator, and other bags for things that will go in the cabinet." Together they devise a system with one bag for each of the following categores: food in cartons that will go into the refrigerator, loose vegetables and fruit for the refrigerator, food cartons that go in the cabinet, and food cans for the cabinet. In this example, the child's unassisted level of classification was fairly gross—fruit versus non-fruit. With the teacher's help, he was able to apply a more sophisticated form of classification.

Vygotsky's concept of the zone of proximal development—that children learn by interacting with more experienced adults and peers, who help them think beyond the "zone" in which they would be able to perform without assistance—has been applied

Upper limit

Level of additional responsibility child can accept with assistance of an able instructor

Zone of proximal development (ZPD)

Lower limit

Level of problem solving reached on these tasks by child working alone

FIGURE 6.10 Vygotsky's Zone of Proximal Development. Vygotsky's zone of proximal development has a lower limit and an upper limit. Tasks in the ZPD are too difficult for the child to perform alone. They require assistance from an adult or a more-skilled child. As children experience the verbal instruction or demonstration, they organize the information in their existing mental structures, so they can eventually perform the skill or task alone.

zone of proximal development (ZPD) Vygotsky's term for tasks too difficult for children to master alone but that can be mastered with assistance from adults of more-skilled children.

primarily to academic learning. Barbara Rogoff (1990, 2003; Rogoff & others, 2007) argues that many of Vygotsky's ideas, including the zone of proximal development, are important in understanding children's development beyond the classroom in everyday interactions with adults and peers. To read further about Rogoff's ideas, see the *Diversity in Child Development* interlude.

Diversity in Child Development

GUIDED PARTICIPATION AND CULTURAL CONTEXTS

According to Rogoff, children serve a sort of apprenticeship in thinking through *guided participation* in social and cultural activities. Guided participation may occur, for example, when adults and children share activities.

Parents can broaden or limit children's opportunities through their decisions about how much and when to expose children to books, television, and child care. They may give children opportunities to learn about cultural traditions and practices through their routines and play. For example, in the Zambian culture of Chewa, children play numerous games, such as "hide-and-seek, guessing games, complex sand drawing games, imaginative games representing local work and family routines, skill games like jacks and a rule game requiring considerable strategic planning and numerical calculations, and constructing models of wire or clay" (Rogoff, 2003, p. 297). In addition, through observational learning, or as Rogoff calls it, learning by "osmosis," children adopt values, skills, and mannerisms by simply watching and listening to peers and adults.

Guided participation is widely used around the world, but cultures may differ in the goals of development—what content is to be learned—and the means for providing guided participation (Rogoff, 2003; Rogoff & others, 2007). Around the world, caregivers and children arrange children's activities and revise children's responsibilities as they gain skill and knowledge. With guidance, children participate in cultural activities that socialize them into skilled activities. For example, Mayan mothers in Guatemala help their daughters learn to weave through guided participation. Throughout the world, learning occurs, not just by studying or by attending classes, but also through interaction with knowledgeable people.

At about 7 years of age, Mayan girls in Guatemala are assisted in beginning to learn to weave a simple belt, with the loom already set up for them. The young girl shown here is American developmental psychologist Barbara Rogoff's daughter, being taught to weave by a Mayan woman. *What are some other ways that children learn through guided participation?*

Scaffolding

Closely linked to the idea of the ZPD is the concept of scaffolding. **Scaffolding** means changing the level of support. Over the course of a teaching session, a more-skilled person (a teacher or advanced peer) adjusts the amount of guidance to fit the child's current performance (Daniels, 2007). When the student is learning a new task, the skilled person may use direct instruction. As the student's competence increases, less guidance is given.

Dialogue is an important tool of scaffolding in the zone of proximal development (Tappan, 1998). Vygotsky viewed children as having rich but unsystematic, disorganized, and spontaneous concepts. In a dialogue, these concepts meet with the skilled helper's more systematic, logical, and rational concepts. As a result, the child's concepts become more systematic, logical, and rational. For example, a dialogue might take place between a teacher and a child when the teacher uses scaffolding to help a child understand a concept like "transportation."

scaffolding In cognitive development, Vygotsky used this term to describe the changing support over the course of a teaching session, with the more-skilled person adjusting guidance to fit the child's current performance level.

Lev Vygotsky (1896–1934), shown here with his daughter, believed that children's cognitive development is advanced through social interaction with skilled individuals embedded in a sociocultural backdrop.

Language and Thought

The use of dialogue as a tool for scaffolding is only one example of the important role of language in a child's development. According to Vygotsky, children use speech not only for social communication, but also to help them solve tasks. Vygotsky (1962) further concluded that young children use language to plan, guide, and monitor their behavior. This use of language for self-regulation is called *private speech*. For Piaget private speech is egocentric and immature, but for Vygotsky it is an important tool of thought during the early childhood years (John-Steiner, 2007; Wertsch, 2007).

Vygotsky said that language and thought initially develop independently of each other and then merge. He emphasized that all mental functions have external, or social, origins. Children must use language to communicate with others before they can focus inward on their own thoughts. Children also must communicate externally and use language for a long period of time before they can make the transition from external to internal speech. This transition period occurs between 3 and 7 years of age and involves talking to oneself. After a while, the self-talk becomes second nature to children, and they can act without verbalizing. When this occurs, children have internalized their egocentric speech in the form of *inner speech*, which becomes their thoughts.

Vygotsky reasoned that children who use a lot of private speech are more socially competent than those who don't (Santiago-Delefosse & Delefosse, 2002). He argued that private speech represents an early transition in becoming more socially communicative. For Vygotsky, when young children talk to themselves, they are using language to govern their behavior and guide themselves. For example, a child working on a puzzle might say to herself, "Which pieces should I put together first? I'll try those green ones first. Now I need some blue ones. No, that blue one doesn't fit there. I'll try it over here."

Piaget stressed that self-talk is egocentric and reflects immaturity. However, researchers have found support for Vygotsky's view that private speech plays a positive role in children's development (Winsler, Diaz, & Montero, 1997; Winsler, Carlton, & Barry, 2000). Researchers have found that children use private speech more when tasks are difficult, following errors, and when they are not sure how to proceed (Berk, 1994). They also have revealed that children who use private speech are more attentive and improve their performance more than children who do not use private speech (Berk & Spuhl, 1995).

Teaching Strategies

Vygotsky's theory has been embraced by many teachers and has been successfully applied to education (Dainels, 2007; Hyson, Copple, & Jones, 2006). Here are some ways Vygotsky's theory can be incorporated in classrooms:

1. *Assess the child's ZPD.* Like Piaget, Vygotsky did not think that formal, standardized tests are the best way to assess children's learning. Rather, Vygotsky argued that assessment should focus on determining the child's zone of proximal development. The skilled helper presents the child with tasks of varying difficulty to determine the best level at which to begin instruction.

2. *Use the child's ZPD in teaching.* Teaching should begin toward the zone's upper limit, so that the child can reach the goal with help and move to a higher level of skill and knowledge. Offer just enough assistance. You might ask, "What can I do to help you?" Or simply observe the child's intentions and attempts and provide support when needed. When the child hesitates, offer encouragement. And encourage the child to practice the skill. You may watch and appreciate the child's practice or offer support when the child forgets what to do.

3. *Use more-skilled peers as teachers.* Remember that it is not just adults who are important in helping children learn. Children also benefit from the support and guidance of more-skilled children (John-Steiner, 2007).

How can Vygotsky's ideas be applied to educating children?

4. *Monitor and encourage children's use of private speech.* Be aware of the developmental change from externally talking to oneself when solving a problem during the preschool years to privately talking to oneself in the early elementary school years. In the elementary school years, encourage children to internalize and self-regulate their talk to themselves.

5. *Place instruction in a meaningful context.* Educators today are moving away from abstract presentations of material, instead providing students with opportunities to experience learning in real-world settings. For example, instead of just memorizing math formulas, students work on math problems with real-world implications.

6. *Transform the classroom with Vygotskian ideas.* What does a Vygotskian classroom look like? The Kamehameha Elementary Education Program (KEEP) is based on Vygotsky's theory (Tharp, 1994). The ZPD is the key element of instruction in this program. Children might read a story and then interpret its meaning. Many of the learning activities take place in small groups. All children spend at least 20 minutes each morning in a setting called "Center One." In this context, scaffolding is used to improve children's literary skills. The instructor asks questions, responds to students' queries, and builds on the ideas that students generate. Thousands of children from low-income families have attended KEEP public schools—in Hawaii, on an Arizona Navajo Indian reservation, and in Los Angeles. Compared with a control group of non-KEEP children, the KEEP children participated more actively in classroom discussion, were more attentive in class, and had higher reading achievement (Tharp & Gallimore, 1988).

To read about the work of a teacher who applies Vygotsky's theory to her teaching, see the *Careers in Child Development* profile. The *Caring for Children* interlude further explores the implications of Vygotsky's theory for children's education.

Careers in Child Development

Donene Polson, Elementary School Teacher

Donene Polson teaches at Washington Elementary School in Salt Lake City, Utah. Washington is an innovative school that emphasizes the importance of people learning together as a community of learners. Children as well as adults plan learning activities. Throughout the school day, children work in small groups.

Polson says that she loves working in a school in which students, teachers, and parents work together as a community to help children learn.

Before the school year begins, Polson meets with parents at the family's home to prepare for the upcoming year, getting acquainted, and establishing schedules to determine when parents can contribute to class-room instruction. At monthly parent-teacher meetings, Polson and the parents plan the curriculum and discuss how children's learning is progressing. They brainstorm about resources in the community that can be used effectively to promote children's learning.

Caring for Children

TOOLS OF THE MIND

Tools of the Mind is an early childhood education curriculum that emphasizes children's development of self-regulation and the cognitive foundations of literacy (Hyson, Copple, & Jones, 2006). The curriculum was created by Elena Bodrova and Deborah Leong (2007) and has been implemented in more than 200 classrooms. Most of the children in the Tools of the Mind programs are at risk because of their living circumstances, which in many instances involve poverty and other difficult conditions such as being homeless and having parents with drug problems.

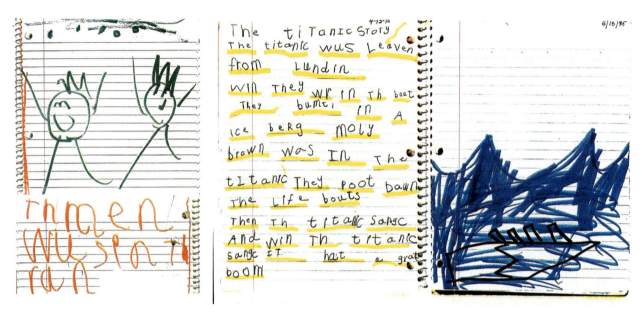

(a) Five-year-old Aaron's independent journal writing prior to the scaffolded writing technique.

(b) Aaron's journal two months after using the scaffolded writing technique.

FIGURE 6.11 Writing Progress of a 5-Year-Old Boy Over Two Months Using the Scaffolding Writing Process in Tools of the Mind

Tools of the Mind is grounded in Vygotsky's (1962) theory with special attention given to cultural tools and developing self-regulation, the zone of proximal development, scaffolding, private speech, shared activity, and play as important activity. In a Tools of the Mind classroom, dramatic play has a central role. Teachers guide children in creating themes that are based on the children's interests, such as treasure hunt, store, hospital, and restaurant. Teachers also incorporate field trips, visitor presentations, videos, and books in the development of children's play. They also help children develop a play plan, which increases the maturity of their play. Play plans describe what the children expect to do in the play period, including the imaginary context, roles, and props to be used. The play plans increase the quality of their play and self-regulation.

Scaffolding writing is another important theme in the Tools of the Mind classroom. Teachers guide children in planning their own message by drawing a line to stand for each word the child says. Children then repeat the message, pointing to each line as they say the word. Then, the child writes on the lines, trying to represent each word with some letters or symbols. Figure 6.11 shows how the scaffolding writing process improved a 5-year-old child's writing over the course of two months.

Research assessments of children's writing in Tools of the Mind classrooms revealed that they have more advanced writing skills than children in other early childhood programs (Bodrova & Leong, 2007) (see Figure 6.11). For example, they write more complex messages, use more words, spell more accurately, show better letter recognition, and have a better understanding of the concept of a sentence.

Evaluating Vygotsky's Theory

Even though their theories were proposed at about the same time, most of the world learned about Vygotsky's theory later than they learned about Piaget's theory, so Vygotsky's theory has not yet been evaluated as thoroughly. Vygotsky's view of the importance of sociocultural influences on children's development fits with the current belief that it is important to evaluate the contextual factors in learning (Daniels, Wertsch, & Cole, 2007; Holzman, 2009).

	Vygotsky	Piaget
Sociocultural Context	Strong emphasis	Little emphasis
Constructivism	Social constructivist	Cognitive constructivist
Stages	No general stages of development proposed	Strong emphasis on stages (sensorimotor, preoperational, concrete operational, and formal operational)
Key Processes	Zone of proximal development, language, dialogue, tools of the culture	Schema, assimilation, accommodation, operations, conservation, classification, hypothetical-deductive reasoning
Role of Language	A major role; language plays a powerful role in shaping thought	Language has a minimal role; cognition primarily directs language
View on Education	Education plays a central role, helping children learn the tools of the culture	Education merely refines the child's cognitive skills that have already emerged
Teaching Implications	Teacher is a facilitator and guide, not a director; establish many opportunities for children to learn with the teacher and more-skilled peers	Also views teacher as a facilitator and guide, not a director; provide support for children to explore their world and discover knowledge

FIGURE 6.12 Comparison of Vygotsky's and Piaget's Theories

We already have mentioned several comparisons of Vygotsky's and Piaget's theories, such as Vygotsky's emphasis on the importance of inner speech in development and Piaget's view that such speech is immature. Although both theories are constructivist, Vygotsky's is a **social constructivist approach**, which emphasizes the social contexts of learning and the construction of knowledge through social interaction.

In moving from Piaget to Vygotsky, the conceptual shift is from the individual to collaboration, social interaction, and sociocultural activity (Halford, 2008). The end point of cognitive development for Piaget is formal operational thought. For Vygotsky, the endpoint can differ, depending on which skills are considered to be the most important in a particular culture. For Piaget, children construct knowledge by transforming, organizing, and reorganizing previous knowledge. For Vygotsky, children construct knowledge through social interaction (Rogoff & others, 2007). The implication of Piaget's theory for teaching is that children need support to explore their world and discover knowledge. The main implication of Vygotsky's theory for teaching is that students need many opportunities to learn with the teacher and more-skilled peers. In both Piaget's and Vygotsky's theories, teachers serve as facilitators and guides, rather than as directors and molders of learning. Figure 6.12 compares Vygotsky's and Piaget's theories.

Criticisms of Vygotsky's theory also have surfaced (Karpov, 2006). Some critics point out that Vygotsky was not specific enough about age-related changes (Gauvain, 2008). Another criticism focuses on Vygotsky not adequately describe how changes in socioemotional capabilities contribute to cognitive development (Gauvain, 2008). Yet another criticism is that he overemphasized the role of language in thinking. Also, his emphasis on collaboration and guidance has potential pitfalls. Might facilitators be too helpful in some cases, as when a parent becomes too overbearing and controlling? Further, some children might become lazy and expect help when they might have done something on their own.

social constructivist approach An emphasis on the social contexts of learning and the construction of knowledge through social interaction. Vygotsky's theory reflects this approach.

Review and Reflect: Learning Goal 3

3 **Identify the Main Concepts in Vygotsky's Theory and Compare It with Piaget's Theory**

REVIEW

- What is the zone of proximal development?
- What is scaffolding?
- How did Vygotsky view language and thought?
- How can Vygotsky's theory be applied to education?
- What are some similarities and differences between Vygotsky's and Piaget's theories? What are some criticisms of Vygotsky's theory?

REFLECT

- Which theory—Piaget's or Vygotsky's—do you think is most effective? Why?

Reach Your Learning Goals

Cognitive Developmental Approaches

1 PIAGET'S THEORY OF COGNITIVE DEVELOPMENT: DISCUSS THE KEY PROCESSES AND FOUR STAGES IN PIAGET'S THEORY

Processes of Development

- In Piaget's theory, children construct their own cognitive worlds, building mental structures to adapt to their world. Schemes are actions or mental representations that organize knowledge. Behavioral schemes (physical activities) characterize infancy, and mental schemes (cognitive activities) develop in childhood. Adaptation involves assimilation and accommodation. Assimilation occurs when children incorporate new information into their existing schemes. Accommodation refers to children's adjustment of their schemes to fit new information and experiences. Through organization, children group isolated behaviors into a higher-order, more smoothly functioning cognitive system. Equilibration is a mechanism Piaget proposed to explain how children shift from one cognitive stage to the next. As children experience cognitive conflict in trying to understand the world, they seek equilibrium. The result is equilibration, which brings the child to a new stage of thought. According to Piaget, there are four qualitatively different stages of thought: sensorimotor, preoperational, concrete operational, and formal operational.

Sensorimotor Stage

- In sensorimotor thought, the first of Piaget's four stages, the infant organizes and coordinates sensory experiences (such as seeing and hearing) with physical movements. The stage lasts from birth to about 2 years of age and is nonsymbolic throughout, according to Piaget. Sensorimotor thought has six substages: simple reflexes; first habits and primary circular reactions; secondary circular reactions; coordination of secondary circular reactions; tertiary circular reactions, novelty, and curiosity; and internalization of schemes. One key aspect of this stage is object permanence, the ability to understand that objects continue to exist even though the infant is no longer observing them. Another aspect involves infants' understanding of cause and effect. In the past two decades, revisions of Piaget's view have been proposed based on research. For example, researchers have found that a stable and differentiated perceptual world is established earlier than Piaget envisioned. However, controversy characterizes how early object permanence emerges.

Preoperational Stage

- Preoperational thought is the beginning of the ability to reconstruct at the level of thought what has been established in behavior. It involves a transition from a primitive to a more sophisticated use of symbols. In preoperational thought, the child does not yet think in an operational way. The symbolic function substage occurs roughly from 2 to 4 years of age and is characterized by symbolic thought, egocentrism, and animism. The intuitive thought substage stretches from about 4 to 7 years of age. It is called intuitive because children seem so sure about their knowledge yet they are unaware of how they know what they know. The preoperational child lacks conservation and asks a barrage of questions.

Concrete Operational Stage

- Concrete operational thought occurs roughly from 7 to 11 years of age. During this stage, children can perform concrete operations, think logically about concrete objects, classify things, and reason about relationships among classes of things. Concrete thought is not as abstract as formal operational thought.

Formal Operational Stage

- Formal operational thought appears between 11 and 15 years of age. Formal operational thought is more abstract, idealistic, and logical than concrete operational thought. Piaget maintains that adolescents become capable of engaging in hypothetical-deductive reasoning. But Piaget did not give adequate attention to individual variation in adolescent thinking. Many young adolescents do not think in hypothetical-deductive ways but rather are consolidating their concrete operational thinking. In addition, adolescents develop a special kind of egocentrism that involves an imaginary audience and a personal fable about being unique and invulnerable.

2   APPLYING AND EVALUATING PIAGET'S THEORY: APPLY PIAGET'S THEORY TO EDUCATION AND EVALUATE HIS THEORY

Piaget and Education

- Piaget was not an educator, but his constructivist views have been applied to teaching. These applications include an emphasis on facilitating rather than directing learning, considering the child's level of knowledge, using ongoing assessment, promoting the student's intellectual health, and turning the classroom into a setting of exploration and discovery.

Evaluating Piaget's Theory

- We owe to Piaget the field of cognitive development. He was a genius at observing children, and he gave us a number of masterful concepts such as assimilation, accommodation, object permanence, and egocentrism. Critics question his estimates of competence at different developmental levels, his stage concept, and other ideas. Neo-Piagetians, who emphasize the importance of information processing, stress that children's cognition is more specific than Piaget thought.

3   VYGOTSKY'S THEORY OF COGNITIVE DEVELOPMENT: IDENTIFY THE MAIN CONCEPTS IN VYGOTSKY'S THEORY AND COMPARE IT WITH PIAGET'S THEORY

The Zone of Proximal Development

- Zone of proximal development (ZPD) is Vygotsky's term for the range of tasks that are too difficult for children to master alone but that can be learned with the guidance and assistance of adults or more-skilled peers.

Scaffolding

- Scaffolding is a teaching technique in which a more-skilled person adjusts the level of guidance to fit the child's current performance level. Dialogue is an important aspect of scaffolding.

Language and Thought

- Vygotsky stressed that language plays a key role in cognition. Language and thought initially develop independently, but then children internalize their egocentric speech in the form of inner speech, which becomes their thoughts. This transition to inner speech occurs from 3 to 7 years of age.

Teaching Strategies

- Applications of Vygotsky's ideas to education include using the child's ZPD and scaffolding, using more-skilled peers as teachers, monitoring and encouraging children's use of private speech, and accurately assessing the ZPD. These practices can transform the classroom and establish a meaningful context for instruction.

Evaluating Vygotsky's Theory

- Like Piaget, Vygotsky emphasized that children actively construct their understanding of the world. Unlike Piaget, he did not propose stages of cognitive development, and he emphasized that children construct knowledge through social interaction. In Vygotsky's theory, children depend on tools provided by the culture, which determines which skills they will develop. Vygotsky's view contrasts with Piaget's view that young children's speech is immature and egocentric. Criticisms of Vygotsky's theory include a lack of specificity about age-related changes and an overemphasis on the role of language in thinking.

KEY TERMS

KEY PEOPLE

Jean Piaget 182
Renée Baillargeon 187

Barbel Inhelder 190
Rochel Gelman 193

David Elkind 195

Lev Vygotsky 200

E-LEARNING TOOLS

To help you master the material in this chapter, you'll find a number of valuable study tools at the Online Learning Center for *Child Development*, twelfth edition (**www.mhhe/santrockcd12**).

Taking It to the Net

Research the answers to these questions:

1. Francesca is surveying *Time* magazine's list of the top 100 people of the twentieth century. She notices that Piaget made the list. Why?

2. Ellen is majoring in interdisciplinary studies. She is preparing a report on famous thinkers who engaged in cross-disciplinary study and teaching and how this influenced their theories. She has heard that Piaget was adept at several disciplines. How can she investigate what they were and how they might have influenced his theory of cognitive development?

3. Theo has to write a comparison and contrast paper for his Early Childhood Education class. He wants to compare Vygotsky and Piaget's theories of cognitive development, focusing on implications from these theories for teachers. Would a paper on how these men believed culture influenced cognitive development be a good choice?

Health and Well-Being, Parenting, and Education Exercises

Build your decision-making skills by trying your hand at the health and well-being, parenting, and education exercises.

Video Clips

The Online Learning Center includes the following videos for this chapter:

- *Categorizing Pictures at Age 4*
A 4-year-old is presented with pictures of a lion, bear, zebra, and wagon and asked which one is different from the others.

- *Lacking Concept of Liquid Conservation at Age 3*
A 3-year-old girl demonstrates that she lacks an understanding of the concept of conservation when she is presented with Piaget's classic liquid test.

- *Lacking Concept of Mass Conservation at Age 4*
A boy demonstrates that he lacks an understanding of the concept of conservation when he is presented with Piaget's classic mass test.

- *Understanding Liquid Conservation at Age 4*
A girl proves she has an understanding of the concept of conservation when presented with Piaget's classic liquid test.

7

The mind is an enchanting thing.

—MARIANNE MOORE
American Poet, 20th Century

LEARNING GOALS

- Explain the information-processing approach.

- Define attention and outline its developmental changes.

- Describe what memory is and how it changes.

- Characterize thinking and its developmental changes.

- Define metacognition and summarize its developmental changes.

INFORMATION PROCESSING

CHAPTER OUTLINE

Images of Child Development
The Story of Laura Bickford

Laura Bickford is a master teacher and chairs the English Department at Nordoff High School in Ojai, California. She recently spoke about how she encourages her students to think:

I believe the call to teach is a call to teach students how to think. In encouraging critical thinking, literature itself does a good bit of work for us but we still have to be guides. We have to ask good questions. We have to show students the value in asking their own questions, in having discussions and conversations. In addition to reading and discussing literature, the best way to move students to think critically is to have them write. We write all the time in a variety of modes: journals, formal essays, letters, factual reports, news articles, speeches, or other formal oral presentations. We have to show students where they merely scratch the surface in their thinking and writing. I call these moments "hits and runs." When I see this "hit and run" effort, I draw a window on the paper. I tell them it is a "window of opportunity" to go deeper, elaborate, and clarify. Many students don't do this kind of thinking until they are prodded to do so.

I also ask them to keep reading logs so they can observe their own thinking as it happens. In addition, I ask students to comment on their own learning by way of grading themselves. This year a student gave me one of the most insightful lines about her growth as a reader I have ever seen from a student. She wrote, "I no longer think in a monotone when I'm reading." I don't know if she grasps the magnitude of that thought or how it came to be that she made that change. It is magic when students see themselves growing like this.

Laura Bickford, working with students writing papers.

PREVIEW

What do children notice in the environment? What do they remember? And how do they think about it? These questions illustrate the information-processing approach. Using this approach, researchers usually do not describe children as being in one stage of cognitive development or another. But they do describe and analyze how the speed of processing information, attention, memory, thinking, and metacognition change over time.

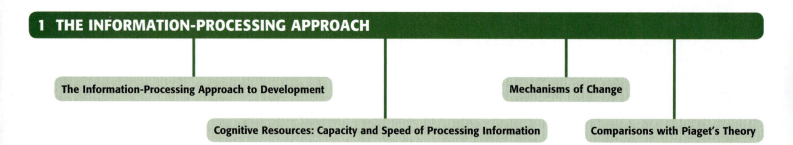

1 THE INFORMATION-PROCESSING APPROACH

The Information-Processing Approach to Development

Mechanisms of Change

Cognitive Resources: Capacity and Speed of Processing Information

Comparisons with Piaget's Theory

What are some of the basic ideas in the information-processing approach? How is it similar to and different from the cognitive developmental approaches we described in Chapter 6?

FIGURE 7.1 A Basic, Simplified Model of Information Processing

The Information-Processing Approach to Development

The information-processing approach shares a basic characteristic with the theories of cognitive development that were discussed in Chapter 6. Like those theories, the information-processing approach rejected the behavioral approach that dominated psychology during the first half of the twentieth century. As we discussed in Chapter 1, the behaviorists argued that to explain behavior it is important to examine associations between stimuli and behavior. In contrast, the theories of Piaget and Vygotsky, which we described in Chapter 6, and the information-processing approach focus on how children think.

The **information-processing approach** analyzes how children manipulate information, monitor it, and create strategies for handling it (Munkata, 2006; Siegler, 2006, 2007). Effective information processing involves attention, memory, and thinking. To see how these processes work, let's examine a student solving an algebraic equation. The sequence begins with an event in the environment. Suppose the event involves a teacher writing an equation on the chalkboard in a mathematics class with the accompanying instruction: "$2x + 10 = 34$. Solve for x." The student looks up and focuses on what the teacher has written (*attention*). The student determines that the teacher has written a series of numbers, letters, and signs, and—at a higher level of identification—two simple statements: (1) "$2x + 10 = 34$" and (2) "Solve for x." The student must preserve the results of this attention by *encoding* the information and storing it over a period of time (*memory*), even if for only the brief time needed to write the problem on a worksheet. Then, the student begins manipulating and transforming the information (*thinking*). The student might think, "Okay, first I have to collect the information on one side of the equation and the known values on the other side. To do this, I'll leave the $2x$ where it is—on the left. This leaves $2x = 24$. Now I have to express the equation as 'x something,' and it's solved. How do I do this? I'll divide each side by 2, and that will leave $1x = 12$. That's the answer." The student writes down the answer (*response*).

Figure 7.1 shows a summary of the basic processes used in solving the algebraic equation. This diagram is a basic, simplified representation of how information processing works, omitting a great deal. In reality, the flow of information takes many routes. For example, the processes may overlap, and they do not always occur in the left-to-right direction indicated. The purpose of the model is to get you to begin thinking in a general way about how people process information. In subsequent sections, we will fill in more of the details about the way children process information and how information processing changes as they develop.

A computer metaphor can illustrate how the information-processing approach can be applied to development. A computer's information processing is *limited* by its hardware and software. The hardware limitations include the amount of data the computer can process—its capacity—and speed. The software limits the kind of data that can be used as input and the ways that data can be manipulated; word processing doesn't handle music, for example. Similarly, children's information processing may be limited by capacity and speed as well as by their ability to manipulate information—in other words, to apply appropriate strategies to acquire and use knowledge. In the information-processing approach, children's cognitive development results from their ability to overcome processing limitations by increasingly

information-processing approach An approach that focuses on the ways children process information about their world—how they manipulate information, monitor it, and create strategies to deal with it.

executing basic operations, expanding information-processing capacity, and acquiring new knowledge and strategies.

Cognitive Resources: Capacity and Speed of Processing Information

Developmental changes in information processing are likely influenced by increases in both capacity and speed of processing (Frye, 2004). These two characteristics are often referred to as *cognitive resources,* which are proposed to have an important influence on memory and problem solving.

Both biology and experience contribute to growth in cognitive resources. Think about how much faster you can process information in your native language than a second language. The changes in the brain we described in Chapter 4 provide a biological foundation for increased cognitive resources. Important biological developments occur both in brain structures, such as changes in the frontal lobes, and at the level of neurons, such as the blooming and pruning of connections between neurons. Also, as we discussed in Chapter 4, myelination (the process that covers the axon with a myelin sheath) increases the speed of electrical impulses in the brain. Myelination continues through childhood and adolescence (Casey, Getz, & Galvan, 2008; Giedd, 2008).

Most information-processing psychologists argue that an increase in capacity also improves processing of information (Keil, 2006; Mayer, 2008). For example, as children's information-processing capacity increases, they likely can hold in mind several dimensions of a topic or problem simultaneously, whereas younger children are more prone to focus on only one dimension.

What is the role of processing speed? How fast children process information often influences what they can do with that information. If an adolescent is trying to add up mentally the cost of items he or she is buying at the grocery store, the adolescent needs to be able to compute the sum before he or she has forgotten the price of the individual items. Children's speed in processing information is linked with their competence in thinking (Bjorklund, 2005; Demetriou & others, 2002). For example, how fast children can articulate a series of words affects how many words they can store and remember. Generally, fast processing is linked with good performance on cognitive tasks. However, some compensation for slower processing speed can be achieved through effective strategies.

Researchers have devised a number of ways for assessing processing speed. For example, it can be assessed through a *reaction-time task* in which individuals are asked to push a button as soon as they see a stimulus such as a light. Or individuals might be asked to match letters or match numbers with symbols on a computer screen.

There is abundant evidence that the speed with which such tasks are completed improves dramatically across the childhood years (Hommel, Li, & Li, 2004; Kail, 2007; Kuhn, 2008). Processing speed continues to improve in early adolescence. For example, in one study, 10-year-olds were approximately 1.8 times slower at processing information than young adults on such tasks as reaction time, letter matching, mental rotation, and abstract matching (Hale, 1990). Twelve-year-olds were approximately 1.5 times slower than young adults, but 15-year-olds processed information on the tasks as fast as the young adults. Also, a recent study of 8- to 13-year-old children revealed that processing speed increased with age, and further that the developmental change in processing speed preceded an increase in working memory capacity (Kail, 2007).

Mechanisms of Change

According to Robert Siegler (1998), three mechanisms work together to create changes in children's cognitive skills: encoding, automaticity, and strategy construction.

How does speed of processing information change during the childhood and adolescent years?

Encoding is the process by which information gets into memory. Changes in children's cognitive skills depend on increased skill at encoding relevant information and ignoring irrelevant information. For example, to a 4-year-old, an *s* in cursive writing is a shape very different from an *s* that is printed. But a 10-year-old has learned to encode the relevant fact that both are the letter *s* and to ignore the irrelevant differences in their shape.

Automaticity refers to the ability to process information with little or no effort. Practice allows children to encode increasing amounts of information automatically. For example, once children have learned to read well, they do not think about each letter in a word as a letter; instead, they encode whole words. Once a task is automatic, it does not require conscious effort. As a result, as information processing becomes more automatic, we can complete tasks more quickly and handle more than one task at a time. If you did not encode words automatically, but instead read this page by focusing your attention on each letter in each word, imagine how long it would take you to read it.

Strategy construction is the creation of new procedures for processing information. For example, children's reading benefits when they develop the strategy of stopping periodically to take stock of what they have read so far (Pressley, 2007).

In addition, Siegler (2007; Siegler & Alibali, 2005) argues that children's information processing is characterized by *self-modification*. That is, children learn to use what they have learned in previous circumstances to adapt their responses to a new situation. Part of this self-modification draws on **metacognition**, which means knowing about knowing (Flavell, 2004). One example of metacognition is what children know about the best ways to remember what they have read. Do they know that they will remember what they have read better if they can relate it to their own lives in some way? Thus, in Siegler's application of the information-processing approach to development, children play an active role in their cognitive development.

What are some important mechanisms of change in the development of children's information processing?

Comparisons with Piaget's Theory

How does the information-processing approach compare with Piaget's theory? According to Piaget, as we discussed in Chapter 6, children actively construct their knowledge and understanding of the world. Their thinking develops in distinct stages. At each stage, the child develops qualitatively different types of mental structures (or schemes) that allow the child to think about the world in new ways.

Like Piaget's theory, some versions of the information-processing approach are constructivist; they see children as directing their own cognitive development. And like Piaget, information-processing psychologists identify cognitive capabilities and limitations at various points in development. They describe ways in which individuals do and do not understand important concepts at different points in life and try to explain how more advanced understanding grows out of a less advanced one. They emphasize the impact that existing understanding has on the ability to acquire a new understanding of something.

Unlike Piaget, however, developmentalists who take an information-processing approach do not see development as occurring abruptly in distinct stages with a brief transition period from one stage to the next. Instead, according to the information-processing approach, individuals develop a gradually increasing capacity for processing information, which allows them to acquire increasingly complex knowledge and skills (Siegler, 2007; Mayer, 2008). Compared with Piaget, the information-processing approach also focuses on more precise analysis of change and on the contributions that ongoing cognitive activity—such as encoding and strategies—make to that change.

encoding The mechanism by which information gets into memory.

automaticity The ability to process information with little or no effort.

strategy construction Creation of new procedures for processing information.

metacognition Cognition about cognition, or "knowing about knowing."

Explain the Information-Processing Approach

REVIEW

- What is the information-processing approach to development?
- How do capacity and processing speed change developmentally?
- What are three important mechanisms of change involved in information processing?
- How can the information-processing approach be compared to Piaget's theory?

REFLECT

- In terms of ability to learn, are there similarities between how children process information and how a computer does? What might be some differences in the way that children and computers process information?

2 ATTENTION

What Is Attention? | **Infancy** | **Childhood**

What are some different ways that children allocate their attention?

attention Concentrating and focusing mental resources.

selective attention Focusing on a specific aspect of experience that is relevant while ignoring others that are irrelevant.

divided attention Concentrating on more than one activity at the same time.

The world holds a lot of information to perceive. Right now, you are perceiving the letters and words that make up this sentence. Now look around you and pick out something to look at other than this book. After that curl up the toes on your right foot. In each of these circumstances, you engaged in the process of paying attention. What is attention, and what effect does it have? How does it change with age?

What Is Attention?

Attention is the focusing of mental resources. Attention improves cognitive processing for many tasks, from grabbing a toy to hitting a baseball or adding numbers. At any one time, though, children, like adults, can pay attention to only a limited amount of information. They allocate their attention in different ways. Psychologists have labeled these types of allocation as selective attention, divided attention, sustained, and executive attention.

- **Selective attention** is focusing on a specific aspect of experience that is relevant while ignoring others that are irrelevant. Focusing on one voice among many in a crowded room or a noisy restaurant is an example of selective attention. When you switched your attention to the toes on your right foot, you were engaging in selective attention.

- **Divided attention** involves concentrating on more than one activity at the same time. If you are listening to music or the television while you are reading this, you are engaging in divided attention.

- **Sustained attention** is the ability to maintain attention to a selected stimulus for a prolonged period of time. Sustained attention is also called *focused attention* and *vigilance*.
- **Executive attention** involves action planning, allocating attention to goals, error detection and compensation, monitoring progress on tasks, and dealing with novel or difficult circumstances.

Infancy

How effectively can infants attend to something? Even newborns can detect a contour and fixate on it. Older infants scan patterns more thoroughly. By 4 months, infants can selectively attend to an object.

Orienting/Investigative Progress
Attention in the first year of life is dominated by an *orienting/investigative process* (Posner & Rothbart, 2007). This process involves directing attention to potentially important locations in the environment (that is, *where*) and recognizing objects and their features (such as color and form) (that is, *what*) (Courage & Richards, 2008). From 3 to 9 months of age, infants can deploy their attention more flexibly and quickly. Another important type of attention is *sustained attention*, also referred to as *focused attention* (Courage & Richards, 2008). New stimuli typically elicit an orienting response followed by sustained attention. It is sustained attention that allows infants to learn about and remember characteristics of a stimulus as it becomes familiar. Researchers have found that infants as young as 3 months of age engage in 5 to 10 seconds of sustained attention. From this age through the second year, the length of sustained attention increases (Courage & Richards, 2008).

Habituation and Dishabituation
Closely linked with attention are the processes of habituation and dishabituation that we discussed in Chapter 5. Recall that if a stimulus—a sight or sound—is presented to infants several times in a row, they usually pay less attention to it each time. This suggests they are bored with it. This is the process of *habituation*—decreased responsiveness to a stimulus after repeated presentations of the stimulus. *Dishabituation* is the recovery of a habituated response after a change in stimulation.

Infants' attention is so strongly governed by novelty and habituation that when an object becomes familiar, attention becomes shorter, making infants more vulnerable to distraction (Amos & Johnson, 2006). One study found that 10-month-olds were more distractible than 26-month-olds (Ruff & Capozzoli, 2003). Another study revealed that infants who were labeled "short lookers" because of the brief time they focused attention had better memory at 1 year of age than were "long lookers," who had more sustained attention (Courage, Howe, & Squires, 2004).

Researchers study habituation to determine the extent to which infants can see, hear, smell, taste, and experience touch (Slater, Field, & Hernandez-Reif, 2007). Studies of habituation can also indicate whether infants recognize something they have previously experienced. Habituation provides a measure of an infant's maturity and well-being. Infants who have brain damage do not habituate well.

Parents can use knowledge of habituation and dishabituation to improve interaction with their infant. If parents keep repeating the same form of stimulation, the infant will stop responding. It is important for parents to do novel things and to repeat them often until the infant stops responding. Wise parents sense when the infant shows interest and know that many repetitions of the stimulus may be necessary for the infant to process the information. The parents stop or change their behavior when the infant redirects attention (Rosenblith, 1992).

Joint Attention
Another aspect of attention that is an important aspect of infant development is **joint attention**, in which individuals focus on the same object or

sustained attention The ability to maintain attention to a selected stimulus for a prolonged period of time. Sustained attention is also called *focused attention* and *vigilance*.

executive attention Involves action planning, allocating attention to goals, error detection and compensation, monitoring progress on tasks, and dealing with novel or difficult circumstances.

joint attention Individuals focusing on the same object or event; requires the ability to track another's behavior, one person directing another's attention, and reciprocal interaction.

A mother and her infant daughter engaging in joint attention. *What about this photograph tells you that joint attention is occurring? Why is joint attention an important aspect of infant development?*

event. Joint attention requires (1) an ability to track another's behavior, such as following someone's gaze; (2) one person directing another's attention; and (3) reciprocal interaction (Butterworth, 2004). Early in infancy, joint attention usually involves a caregiver pointing or using words to direct an infant's attention. Emerging forms of joint attention occur at about 7 to 8 months, but it is not until toward the end of the first year that joint attention skills are frequently observed (Liszkowski, 2007; Meltzoff & Brooks, 2006). In a study conducted by Rechele Brooks and Andrew Meltzoff (2005), at 10 to 11 months of age infants first began engaging in "gaze following," looking where another person has just looked (see Figure 7.2). And by their first birthday, infants have begun to direct adults to objects that capture their interest (Heimann & others, 2006).

Joint attention plays important roles in many aspects of infant development and considerably increases infants' ability to learn from other people (Flom & Pick, 2007; Mundy & Newell, 2007; Tomasello, Carpenter, & Liszkowski, 2007). Nowhere is this more apparent than in observations of interchanges between caregivers and infants as infants are learning language (Poulin-Dubois & Graham, 2007). When caregivers and infants frequently engage in joint attention, infants say their first word earlier and develop a larger vocabulary (Carpenter, Nagell, & Tomasello, 1998; Flom & Pick, 2003). In one study, infants' initiation of joint attention was linked to their receptive and expressive language at 3 years of age (Ulvund & Smith, 1996).

Childhood

Although the infant's attention is related to cognitive development in early childhood, there are some important developmental changes in attention during early childhood (Molholm & others, 2001). The toddler wanders around, shifts attention from one activity to another, and seems to spend little time focused on any one object or event. In contrast, the preschool child might watch television for a half hour at a time (Giavecchio, 2001). One study that observed 99 families in their homes for 4,672 hours found that visual attention to television dramatically increased in the preschool years (Anderson & others, 1985).

Young children especially make advances in two aspects of attention—executive attention and sustained (Courage & Richards, 2008; Rothbart & Gartstein, 2008). Mary Rothbart and Maria Gartstein (2008, p. 332) recently described why advances in executive and sustained attention are so important in early childhood:

> The development of the . . . executive attention system supports the rapid increases in effortful control in the toddler and preschool years. Increases in attention are due, in part, to advances in comprehension and language development. As children are

FIGURE 7.2 Gaze Following in Infancy. Researcher Rechele Brooks shifts her eyes from the infant to a toy in the foreground (*a*). The infant then follows her eye movement to the toy (*b*). Brooks and colleague Andrew Meltzoff (2005) found that infants begin to engage in this kind of behavior called "gaze following" at 10 to 11 months of age. *Why might gaze following be an important accomplishment for an infant?*

(a)

(b)

better able to understand their environment, this increased appreciation of their surroundings helps them to sustain attention for longer periods of time.

In Central European countries, such as Hungary, kindergarten children participate in exercises designed to improve their attention (Mills & Mills, 2000; Posner & Rothbart, 2007). For example, in one eye-contact exercise, the teacher sits in the center of a circle of children, and each child is requred to catch the teacher's eye before being permitted to leave the group. In other exercises created to improve attention, teachers have children participate in stop-go activities during which they have to listen for a specific signal, such as drumbeat or an exact number of rhythmic beats, before stopping the activity.

Control over attention shows important changes during childhood (Posner & Rothbart, 2007). External stimuli are likely to determine the target of the preschooler's attention; what is salient, or obvious, grabs the preschooler's attention. For example, suppose a flashy, attractive clown presents the directions for solving a problem. Preschool children are likely to pay attention to the clown and ignore the directions, because they are influenced strongly by the salient features of the environment. After the age of 6 or 7, children pay more attention to features relevant to performing a task or solving a problem, such as the directions. Thus, instead of being controlled by the most striking stimuli in their environment, older children can direct their attention to more important stimuli. This change reflects a shift to *cognitive control* of attention, so that children act less impulsively and reflect more. Recall from Chapter 4 that the increase in cognitive control during the elementary school years is linked to changes in the brain, especially more focal activation in the prefrontal cortex (Durston & others, 2006).

Preschool children's ability to control and sustain their attention is related to school readiness (Posner & Rothbart, 2007). For example, a study of more than 1,000 children revealed that their ability to sustain their attention at 54 months of age was linked to their school readiness (which included achievement and language skills) (NICHD Early Child Care Research Network, 2005). And a recent study revealed that sustained attention improved from 5 to 6 years to 11 to 12 years of age, and the increased attention was linked to better performance on cognitive tasks (Betts & others, 2006). Another recent study also revealed that attention problems in childhood are linked to information-processing difficulties in late adolescence (Friedman & others, 2007). In the study, 7- to 14-year-old children with attention problems (including inattention, disorganization, impulsivity, and hyperactivity) had difficulty inhibiting responses and working memory difficulties at 17 years of age (Friedman & others, 2007).

What are some changes in attention during childhood and adolescence?

Review and Reflect: Learning Goal 2

2 **Define Attention and Outline Its Developmental Changes**

REVIEW

- What is attention? What are four ways in which children can allocate attention?
- How does attention develop in infancy?
- How does attention develop in childhood?

REFLECT

- Imagine that you are an elementary school teacher. Devise some strategies to help children pay attention in class.

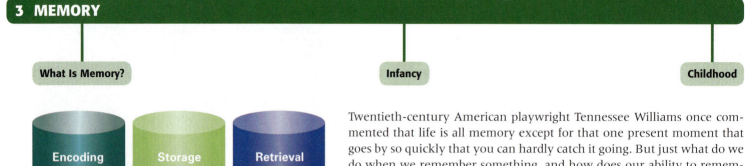

3 MEMORY

What Is Memory?   Infancy   Childhood

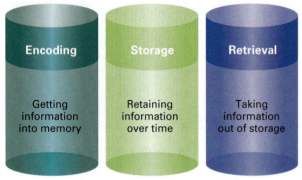

FIGURE 7.3 Processing Information in Memory. As you read about the many aspects of memory in this chapter, think about the organization of memory in terms of these three main activities.

"Can we hurry up and get to the test? My short-term memory is better than my long-term memory."
Copyright © 1999. Reprinted courtesy of Bunny Hoest and *Parade*.

memory Retention of information over time.

short-term memory Limited-capacity memory system in which information is usually retained for up to 15 to 30 seconds, assuming there is no rehearsal of the information. Using rehearsal, individuals can keep the information in short-term memory longer.

long-term memory A relatively permanent and unlimited type of memory.

working memory A mental "workbench" where individuals manipulate and assemble information when making decisions, solving problems, and comprehending written and spoken language.

Twentieth-century American playwright Tennessee Williams once commented that life is all memory except for that one present moment that goes by so quickly that you can hardly catch it going. But just what do we do when we remember something, and how does our ability to remember develop?

What Is Memory?

Memory is the retention of information over time. Without memory you would not be able to connect what happened to you yesterday with what is going on in your life today. Human memory is truly remarkable when you think of how much information we put into our memories and how much we must retrieve to perform all of life's activities.

Processes and Types of Memory   Researchers study how information is initially placed or encoded into memory, how it is retained or stored after being encoded, and how it is found or retrieved for a certain purpose later (see Figure 7.3). Encoding, storage, and retrieval are the basic processes required for memory. Failures can occur in any of these processes. Some part of an event might not be encoded, the mental representation of the event might not be stored, or even if the memory exists, you might not be able to retrieve it.

Examining the storage process led psychologists to classify memories based on their permanence. **Short-term memory** is a memory system with a limited capacity in which information is usually retained for up to 15 to 30 seconds unless strategies are used to retain it longer. **Long-term memory** is a relatively permanent and unlimited type of memory. People are usually referring to long-term memory when they talk about "memory." When you remember the type of games you enjoyed playing as a child or your first date, you are drawing on your long-term memory. But when you remember the word you just read a few seconds ago, you are using short-term memory.

When psychologists first analyzed short-term memory, they described it as if it were a passive storehouse with shelves to store information until it is moved to long-term memory. But we do many things with the information stored in short-term memory. For example, the words in this sentence are part of your short-term memory, and you are manipulating them to form a meaningful whole.

The concept of working memory acknowledges the importance of our manipulations of the information in short-term memory. **Working memory** is a kind of mental "workbench" where individuals manipulate and assemble information when they make decisions, solve problems, and comprehend written and spoken language (Baddeley, 1990, 2001, 2006, 2007a, b). Many psychologists prefer the term working memory over short-term memory to describe how memory works.

Figure 7.4 shows Alan Baddeley's model of working memory. Notice that it includes two short-term stores—one for speech and one for visual and spatial information—as well as a *central executive*. It is the job of the central executive to monitor and control the system—determining what information is stored, relating information from long-term memory to the information in the short-term stores, and moving information into long-term memory.

Working memory is linked to many aspects of children's development (Cowan, 2007; Cowan & Morey, 2007; Imbo & Vandierendonck, 2007). For example, children who have better working memory are more advanced in reading comprehension, math skills, and problem solving than their counterparts with less effective working memory (Andersson & Lyxell, 2007; Demetriou & others, 2002).

Constructing Memories   Memory is not like a tape recorder or a camera or even like computer memory; we don't store and retrieve bits of data in computer-like fashion (Schachter, 2001). Children and adults construct and reconstruct their memories.

Schema Theory   According to **schema theory**, people mold memories to fit information that already exists in their minds. This process is guided by **schemas**, which are mental frameworks that organize concepts and information. Suppose a football fan and a visitor from a country where the sport isn't played are eating at a restaurant and overhear a conversation about last night's game. Because the visitor doesn't have a schema for information about football, he or she is more likely than the fan to mishear what is said. Perhaps the visitor will interpret the conversation in terms of a schema for another sport, constructing a false memory of the conversation.

Schemas influence the way we encode, make inferences about, and retrieve information. We reconstruct the past rather than take an exact photograph of it, and the mind can distort an event as it encodes and stores impressions of it. Often when we retrieve information, we fill in the gaps with fragmented memories.

Fuzzy Trace Theory   Another variation of how individuals reconstruct their memories has been proposed by Charles Brainerd and Valerie Reyna (2004; Reyna & Brainerd, 1995). **Fuzzy trace theory** states that when individuals encode information they create two types of memory representations: (1) a *verbatim memory trace*, which consists of precise details; and (2) a *fuzzy trace*, or *gist*, which is the central idea of the information. For example, consider a child who is presented with information about a pet store that has 10 birds, 6 cats, 8 dogs, and 7 rabbits. Then the child is asked (1) verbatim questions, such as "How many cats are in the pet store, 6 or 8?" and (2) gist questions, such as "Are there more cats or more dogs in the pet store?" Researchers have found that preschool children tend to remember verbatim information more than gist information, but elementary-school-aged children are more likely to remember gist information (Brainerd & Gordon, 1994). The increased use of gist by elementary-school-aged children accounts for their improved memory because fuzzy traces are less likely to be forgotten than verbatim traces (Reyna & Rivers, 2008).

Content Knowledge and Expertise   Our ability to remember new information about a subject does depend considerably on what we already know about it (Mayer, 2008; Schraw, 2006). Much of the research on the role of knowledge in memory has compared experts and novices (Ericsson & others, 2006). *Experts* have acquired extensive knowledge about a particular content area; this knowledge influences what they notice and how they organize, represent, and interpret information. This in turn affects their ability to remember, reason, and solve problems. When individuals have expertise about a particular subject, their memory also tends to be good regarding material related to that subject (Gobet & Charness, 2006).

For example, one study found that 10- and 11-year-olds who were experienced chess players ("experts") were able to remember more information about chess pieces

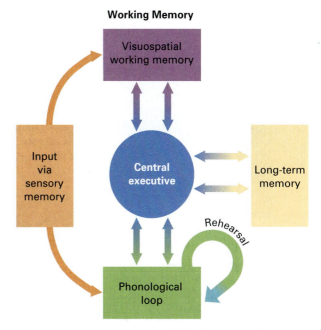

Working Memory

FIGURE 7.4 Working Memory. In Baddeley's working memory model, working memory is like a mental workbench where a great deal of information processing is carried out. Working memory consists of three main components: the phonological loop and visuospatial working memory serve as assistants, helping the central executive do its work. Input from sensory memory goes to the phonological loop, where information about speech is stored and rehearsal takes place, and visuospatial working memory, where visual and spatial information, including imagery, are stored. Working memory is a limited-capacity system, and information is stored there for only a brief time. Working memory interacts with long-term memory, using information from long-term memory in its work and transmitting information to long-term memory for longer storage.

schema theory States that when people reconstruct information, they fit it into information that already exists in their minds.

schemas Mental frameworks that organize concepts and information.

fuzzy trace theory States that memory is best understood by considering two types of memory representations: (1) verbatim memory trace; and (2) fuzzy trace, or gist. In this theory, older children's better memory is attributed to the fuzzy traces created by extracting the gist of information.

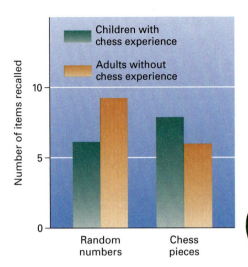

FIGURE 7.5 Memory for Numbers and Chess Pieces

than college students who were not chess players ("novices") (Chi, 1978) (see Figure 7.5). In contrast, when the college students were presented with other stimuli, they were able to remember them better than the children were. Thus, the children's expertise in chess gave them superior memories, but only in chess.

There are developmental changes in expertise. Older children usually have more expertise about a subject than younger children do, which can contribute to their better memory for the subject.

In their study of memory, researchers have not extensively examined the roles that sociocultural factors might play. In the *Diversity in Child Development* interlude, we will explore culture's role in children's memory.

Diversity in Child Development

CULTURE AND CHILDREN'S MEMORY

A culture sensitizes its members to certain objects, events, and strategies, which in turn can influence the nature of memory (Cole, 2006; Fivush, 2007; Greenfield, Suzuki, & Rothstein-Fisch, 2006). In schema theory, a child's background, which is encoded in schemas, is revealed in the way the child reconstructs a story. This effect of cultural background on memory is called the *cultural-specificity hypothesis*. It states that cultural experiences determine what is relevant in a person's life and, thus, what the person is likely to remember. For example, imagine a child living on a remote island in the Pacific Ocean whose parents make their livelihood by fishing. The child's memory about how weather affects fishing is likely to be highly developed. By contrast, a Pacific Islander child might be hard-pressed to encode and recall the details of a major league baseball team.

Cultures may vary in the strategies that children use to remember information, and these cultural variations are usually due to schooling (Cole, 2006). Children in cultures who have experienced schooling are more likely to cluster items together in meaningful ways, which helps them to remember the items. Schooling provides children with specialized information-processing tasks, such as committing large amounts of information to memory in a short time frame and using logical reasoning, that may generate specialized memory strategies. However, there is no evidence that schooling increases memory capacity per se; rather, it influences the strategies for remembering (Cole, 2006).

Scripts are schemas for an event. In one study, adolescents in the United States and Mexico remembered according to script-based knowledge (Harris, Schoen, & Hensley, 1992). In line with common practices in their respective cultures, adolescents in the United States remembered information about a dating script better when no chaperone was present on a date, whereas adolescents in Mexico remembered the information better when a chaperone was present.

American children, especially American girls, describe autobiographical narratives

> that are longer, more detailed, more specific, and more 'personal' (both in terms of mention of self, and mention of internal states), than narratives by children from China and Korea. The pattern is consistent with expectations derived from the finding that in their conversations about past events, American mothers and their children are more elaborative and more focused on autonomous themes . . . and that Korean mothers and their children have less frequent and less detailed conversations about the past. . . . (Bauer, 2006, p. 411)

Possibly the more elaborated content of American children's narratives contributes to the earlier first memories researchers have found in American adults (Han, Leichtman, & Wang, 1998).

Students in a classroom in Nairobi, Kenya. *How might schooling influence memory?*

We have examined a number of basic processes that are important in understanding children's memory. In several places, we have described developmental changes in these processes. Let's now further explore how memory changes from infancy through childhood.

Infancy

Popular child-rearing expert Penelope Leach (1990) told parents that 6- to 8-month-old babies cannot hold in their mind a picture of their mother or father. And historically psychologists stressed that infants cannot store memories until they have language skills. Child development researchers, however, have revealed that infants as young as 3 months of age show a limited type of memory (Courage, Howe, & Squires, 2004).

First Memories   Carolyn Rovee-Collier (1987, 2007) has conducted research that demonstrates that infants can remember perceptual-motor information. In a characteristic experiment, she places a baby in a crib underneath an elaborate mobile and ties one end of a ribbon to the baby's ankle and the other end to the mobile. The baby kicks and makes the mobile move (see Figure 7.6). Weeks later, the baby is returned to the crib, but its foot is not tied to the mobile. The baby kicks, apparently trying to make the mobile move. However, if the mobile's makeup is changed even slightly, the baby doesn't kick. If the mobile is then restored to being exactly as it was when the baby's ankle was originally tied to it, the baby will begin kicking again. According to Rovee-Collier, even by $2\frac{1}{2}$ months the baby's memory is incredibly detailed.

How well can infants remember? Some researchers such as Rovee-Collier have concluded that infants as young as 2 to 6 months of age can remember some experiences through $1\frac{1}{2}$ to 2 years of age (Rovee-Collier, 2007). However, critics such as Jean Mandler (2000), a leading expert on infant cognition, argue that the infants in Rovee-Collier's experiments are displaying only implicit memory. **Implicit memory** refers to memory without conscious recollection—memories of skills and routine procedures that are performed automatically such as riding a bicycle. In contrast, **explicit memory** refers to the conscious memory of facts and experiences.

When people think about memory, they are usually referring to explicit memory. Most researchers find that babies do not show explicit memory until the second half of the first year (Bauer, 2007, 2008). Then, explicit memory improves substantially during the second year of life (Bauer, 2007, 2008). In one longitudinal study, infants were assessed several times during their second year (Bauer & others, 2000). Older infants showed more accurate memory and required fewer prompts to demonstrate their memory than younger infants.

What changes in the brain are linked to infants' memory development? From about 6 to 12 months of age, the maturation of the hippocampus and the surrounding cerebral cortex, especially the frontal lobes, make the emergence of explicit memory possible (de Haan & Martinos, 2008; Nelson, 2008) (see Figure 7.7). Explicit memory continues to improve in the second year, as these brain structures further mature and connections between them increase. Less is known about the areas of the brain involved in implicit memory in infancy.

Infantile Amnesia   Let's examine another aspect of memory. Do you remember your third birthday party? Probably not. Most adults can remember little if anything from the first three years of their life. This is called *infantile*, or *childhood*, *amnesia*. The few reported adult memories of life at age 2 or 3 are at best very sketchy (Neisser, 2004; Newcombe, 2007; Newcombe & others, 2000). Elementary school children also do not remember much of their early child years (Lie & Newcombe, 1999).

What is the cause of infantile amnesia? One reason older children and adults have difficulty recalling events from their infant and early child years is that during these

FIGURE 7.6 The Technique Used in Rovee-Collier's Investigation of Infant Memory. In Rovee-Collier's experiment, operant conditioning was used to demonstrate that infants as young as $2\frac{1}{2}$ months of age can retain information from the experience of being conditioned.

implicit memory Memory without conscious recollection; memory of skills and routine procedures that are performed automatically.

explicit memory Conscious memory of facts and experiences.

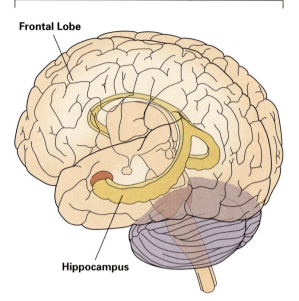

Cerebral Cortex
(tan-colored area with
wrinkles and folds)

Frontal Lobe

Hippocampus

FIGURE 7.7 Key Brain Structures Involved in Memory Development in Infancy

early years the prefrontal lobes of the brain are immature; this area of the brain is believed to play an important role in storing memories for events (Boyer & Diamond, 1992).

In sum, most of young infants' conscious memories appear to be rather fragile and short-lived, although their implicit memory of perceptual-motor actions can be substantial (Bauer, 2007, 2008; Mandler, 2004). By the end of the second year, long-term memory is more substantial and reliable (Bauer, 2007, 2008).

Childhood

Children's memory improves considerably after infancy. Sometimes the long-term memories of preschoolers seem erratic, but young children can remember a great deal of information if they are given appropriate cues and prompts.

One reason children remember less than adults is that they are far less expert in most areas, but their growing knowledge is one likely source of their memory improvement. For example, a child's ability to recount what she has seen on a trip to the library depends greatly on what she already knows about libraries, such as where books on certain topics are located, how to check out books, and so on. If a child knows little about libraries, she will have a much more difficult time recounting what she saw there.

Fuzzy trace theory suggests another way in which memory develops during childhood. Recall from our earlier discussion that young children tend to encode, store, and retrieve verbatim traces, whereas elementary-school-aged children begin to use gist more. The increased use of gist likely produces more enduring memory traces of information. Other sources of improvement in children's memory include changes in memory span and their use of strategies.

Memory Span   Unlike long-term memory, short-term memory has a very limited capacity. One method of assessing that capacity is the *memory-span task*. You simply hear a short list of stimuli—usually digits—presented at a rapid pace (one per second, for example). Then you are asked to repeat the digits.

Research with the memory-span task suggests that short-term memory increases during childhood. For example, in one investigation, memory span increased from about two digits in 2-year-old children to about five digits in 7-year-old children. Between 7 and 12 years of age, memory span increased only by one and a half digits (Dempster, 1981) (see Figure 7.8). Keep in mind, though, that individuals have different memory spans.

Why does memory span change with age? Speed of processing information is important, especially the speed with which memory items can be identified. For example, one study tested children on their speed at repeating words presented orally (Case, Kurland, & Goldberg, 1982). Speed of repetition was a powerful predictor of memory span. Indeed, when the speed of repetition was controlled, the 6-year-olds' memory spans were equal to those of young adults. Rehearsal of information is also important; older children rehearse the digits more than younger children.

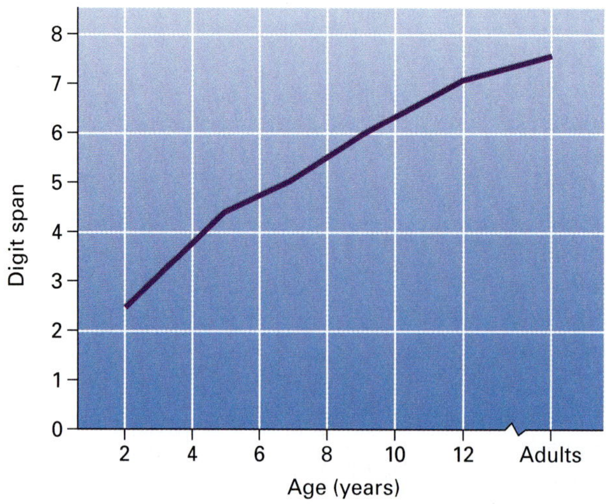

FIGURE 7.8 Developmental Changes in Memory Span. In one study, memory span increased about three digits from 2 years of age to 7 years of age (Dempster, 1981). By 12 years of age, memory span had increased on average another one and a half digits.

Strategies   Rehearsal is just one of the strategies that can sometimes aid memory, although rehearsal is a better strategy for short-term memory than long-term memory. In rehearsal, verbatim information is encoded, and as we have seen in fuzzy trace theory, gist is more likely to produce a longer memory trace. Fuzzy trace theory emphasizes that children's memory improvement is due to an increased use of gist, but children's memory advances also benefit from the use of *strategies*, which involve the use of mental activities to improve the processing of information (Pressley, 2007; Pressley & others, 2007). Important strategies that can improve long-term memory include organization, elaboration, and imagery.

Organization   If children organize information when they encode it, their memory benefits. Consider this demonstration: Recall the 12 months of the year as quickly as you can. How long did it take you? What was the order of your recall? You probably answered something like "a few seconds" and "in chronological order." Now try to remember the months of the year in alphabetical order. Did you make any errors? How long did it take you? It should be obvious that your memory for the months of the year is organized in a particular way.

Organizing is a strategy that older children (and adults) typically use, and it helps them to remember information. Preschool children usually don't use strategies like organization; in middle and late childhood they are more likely to use organization when they need to remember something (Flavell, Miller, & Miller, 2002).

Elaboration   Another important strategy is elaboration, which involves engaging in more extensive processing of information. When individuals engage in elaboration, their memory benefits (Kellogg, 2007). Thinking of examples is a good way to elaborate information. For example, self-reference is an effective way to elaborate information. Thinking about personal associations with information makes the information more meaningful and helps children to remember it.

The use of elaboration changes developmentally (Pressley, 2003; Schneider & Pressley, 1997). Adolescents are more likely than children to use elaboration spontaneously. Elementary school children can be taught to use elaboration strategies on a learning task, but they will be less likely than adolescents to use the strategies on other learning tasks in the future. Nonetheless, verbal elaboration can be an effective strategy even for young elementary school children.

Imagery   Creating mental images is another strategy for improving memory. However, using imagery to remember verbal information works better for older children than for younger children (Schneider, 2004; Schneider & Pressley, 1997). In one study, 20 sentences were presented to first- through sixth-grade children to remember—such as "The angry bird shouted at the white dog" and "The policeman painted the circus tent on a windy day" (Pressley & others, 1987). Children were randomly assigned to an imagery condition (in which they were told to make a picture in their head for each sentence) and a control condition (in which they were told just to try hard). Figure 7.9 shows that the imagery instructions helped older elementary school children (grades 4 through 6) but was not as nearly as helpful to the younger elementary school children (grades 1 through 3). However, mental imagery can help young schoolchildren to remember pictures (Schneider, 2004; Schneider & Pressley, 1997).

Reconstructive Memory and Children as Eyewitnesses   Children's memories, like those of adults, are constructive and reconstructive. Children have schemas for all sorts of information, and these schemas affect how they encode, store, and retrieve memories. If a teacher tells her class a story about two men and two women who were involved in a train crash in France, students won't remember every detail of the story and will reconstruct the story, putting their own individual stamp on it. One student might reconstruct the story by saying the characters died in a plane crash, another might describe three men and three women, another might say the crash was in Germany, and so on.

Reconstruction and distortion are nowhere more apparent than in clashing testimony given by eyewitnesses at trials. A special concern is susceptibility to

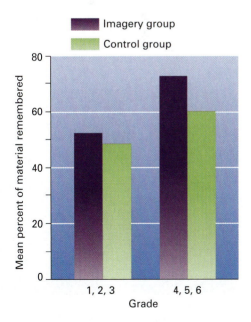

FIGURE 7.9 Imagery and Memory of Verbal Information. Imagery improved older elementary school children's memory for sentences more than younger elementary school children's memory for sentences.

suggestion and how this can alter memory (Bruck, Ceci, & Principe, 2006; Pipe, 2008). Consider a study of individuals who had visited Disneyland (Pickrell & Loftus, 2001). Four groups of participants read ads and answered questionnaires about a trip to Disneyland. One group saw an ad that mentioned no cartoon characters; the second read the same ad and saw a four-foot-tall cardboard figure of Bugs Bunny; the third read a fake ad for Disneyland with Bugs Bunny on it; and the fourth saw the same fake ad along with cardboard Bugs. Participants were asked whether they had ever met Bugs Bunny at Disneyland. Less than 10 percent of those in the first two groups reported having met Bugs Bunny at Disneyland, but approximately 30 to 40 percent of the third and fourth groups remembered meeting Bugs there. People were persuaded they had met Bugs Bunny at Disneyland, even though Bugs is a Warner Brothers character who would never appear at a Disney theme park.

One study found that young children were less likely than older children to reject false claims about events (Ghetti & Alexander, 2004). However, the following conclusions about children as eyewitnesses indicate that a number of factors can influence the accuracy of a young child's memory (Bruck & Ceci, 1999):

- *There are age differences in children's susceptibility to suggestion.* Preschoolers are the most suggestible age group in comparison with older children and adults (Ceci, Papierno, & Kulkofsky, 2007). For example, preschool children are more susceptible to believing misleading or incorrect information given after an event (Ghetti & Alexander, 2004). Despite these age differences, there is still concern about the reaction of older children when they are subjected to suggestive interviews (Poole & Lindsay, 1996).

- *There are individual differences in susceptibility.* Some preschoolers are highly resistant to interviewers' suggestions, whereas others immediately succumb to the slightest suggestion. One study found that children with more advanced verbal abilities and self-control were more likely to resist interviewers' suggestive questions (Clarke-Stewart, Malloy, & Allhusen, 2004). A research review found that the following noncognitive factors were linked to being at risk for suggestibility: low self-concept, low support from parents, and mothers' insecure attachment in romantic relationships (Bruck & Melnyk, 2004).

- *Interviewing techniques can produce substantial distortions in children's reports about highly salient events.* Children are suggestible not just about peripheral details but also about the central aspects of an event (Bruck, Ceci, & Hembrooke, 1998). In some cases, children's false reports can be tinged with sexual connotations. In laboratory studies, young children have made false claims about "silly events" that involved body contact (such as "Did the nurse lick your knee?" or "Did she blow in your ear?"). And these false claims have been found to persist for at least three months (Ornstein & Haden, 2001). A significant number of preschool children have falsely reported that someone touched their private parts, kissed them, and hugged them, when these events clearly did not happen in the research. Nonetheless, young children are capable of recalling much that is relevant about an event (Fivush, 1993; Goodman, Batterman-Faunce, & Kenney, 1992). When children do accurately recall information about an event, the interviewer often has a neutral tone, there is limited use of misleading questions, and there is an absence of any motivation for the child to make a false report (Bruck & Ceci, 1999).

Four-year-old Jennifer Royal was the only eyewitness to one of her playmates being shot to death. She was allowed to testify in open court, and the clarity of her statements helped to convict the gunman. *What are some issues involved in whether young children should be allowed to testify in court?*

To read further about children's suggestibility, see the following *Research in Child Development* interlude.

Research in Child Development

AGE DIFFERENCES IN SUGGESTIBILITY

One study that revealed age differences in suggestibility focused on 329 students in the third/fourth, seventh/eighth, and eleventh/twelfth grades (Lindberg, Keiffer, & Thomas, 2000). Participants saw a short videotape of two boys aged 5 and 11 coming home from school and playing video games. The older boy left to call a friend, at which time the mother came home and dropped a bag of groceries. She asked the younger boy to help her pick them up, but he repeatedly ignored her and continued to play the video game. She then apparently hit him in the head and knocked him to the floor. As he was crying, she picked him up in a rough fashion, dragged him to the kitchen, and apparently hit him again.

The experimenters manipulated a number of factors to determine their effects on the way the children interpreted the video. For example, one question posed to the children was: "How many drops of blood fell from Mark's (the younger boy's) nose?" Actually no drops of blood fell. The children in the third and fourth grades reported more drops of blood than older children did (see Figure 7.10), indicating greater suggestibility in the elementary school children. When the question about drops of blood was used, children at all grade levels were more likely to report seeing blood falling from the boy's nose than when the question was not included.

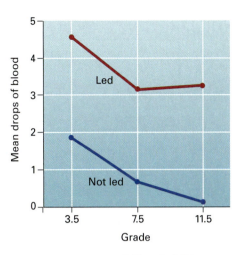

FIGURE 7.10 Suggestibility of Children at Different Grade Levels. The grade levels used in data analysis were combinations of grades (for example, 3.5 = grades 3 and 4 combined). "Led" refers to when the question about drops of blood was used; "Not led" refers to when this question was not used.

In sum, whether a young child's eyewitness testimony is accurate or not may depend on a number of factors such as the type, number, and intensity of the suggestive techniques the child has experienced (Pipe, 2008). It appears that the reliability of young children's reports has as much or more to do with the skills and motivation of the interviewer as with any natural limitations on young children's memory.

According to leading experts who study children's suggestibility, research indicates that these three changes need to be implemented (Bruck, Ceci, & Principe, 2006): (1) interviewers should be required to electronically preserve their interviews with children, (2) a research-validated interview schedule with children needs to be developed, and (3) programs need to be created to teach interviewers how to use interviewing protocols.

Review and Reflect: Learning Goal 3

3 Describe What Memory Is and How It Changes

REVIEW
- What is memory? What are some important processes and types of memory?
- How does memory develop in infancy?
- How does memory change in childhood?

REFLECT
- What is your earliest memory? Why do you think you can remember this particular situation?

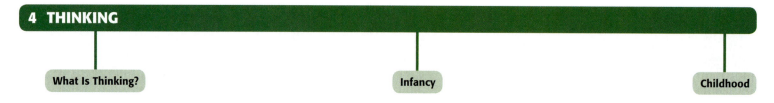

4 THINKING

What Is Thinking? | Infancy | Childhood

"For God's sake, think! Why is he being so nice to you?"

Attention and memory are often steps toward another level of information processing—thinking. What is thinking? How does it change developmentally? What is children's scientific thinking like, and how do they solve problems? Let's explore these questions.

What Is Thinking?

Thinking involves manipulating and transforming information in memory; it is the job of the central executive in Baddeley's model of working memory shown in Figure 7.4. We can think about the concrete (such as a vacation at the beach or how to win at a video game) or we can think in more abstract ways (such as pondering the meaning of freedom or identity). We can think about the past (what happened to us last month) and the future (what our life will be like in the year 2020). We can think about reality (such as how to do better on the next test) and fantasy (what it would be like to meet Elvis Presley or land a spacecraft on Mars). We think in order to reason, reflect, evaluate ideas, solve problems, and make decisions. Let's explore how thinking changes developmentally, beginning with infancy.

Infancy

Interest in thinking during infancy has especially focused on concept formation and categorization (Oakes, 2008; Quinn, Bhatt, & Hayden, 2008). To understand what concepts are, we first have to define *categories*—they group objects, events, and characteristics on the basis of common properties. *Concepts* are ideas about what categories represent, or said another way, the sort of thing we think category members are. Concepts and categories help us to simplify and summarize information (Oakes, 2008). Without concepts, you would see each object and event as unique; you would not be able to make any generalizations.

Do infants have concepts? Yes, they do, although we do not know just how early concept formation begins (Booth, 2006; Mandler, 2004; Quinn, 2007).

Using habituation experiments like those described earlier in the chapter, some researchers have found that infants as young as 3 months of age can group together objects with similar appearances (Quinn, 2007; Quinn, Bhatt, & Hayden, 2008). This research capitalizes on the knowledge that infants are more likely to look at a novel object than a familiar object. For example, in a characteristic study, young infants are shown a series of photographs of different types of cats in pairs (Quinn & Eimas, 1996). As they are shown more pictures of cats, they habituate to the animals, looking at them less and less. Then, after seeing a series of cats paired in photgraphs, when they are shown a photograph of a cat paired with a photogaph of a dog, they look longer at the dog, indicating an ability to group together objects characterized by similar properties.

Jean Mandler (2004) argues that these early categorizations are best described as *perceptual categorization*. That is, the categorizations are based on similar perceptual features of objects, such as size, color, and movement, as well as parts of objects, such as legs for animals. Mandler (2004) concludes that it is not until about 7 to 9 months of age that infants form *conceptual* categories rather than just making perceptual discriminations between different categories. In one study of 9- to 11-month-olds, infants classified birds as animals and airplanes as vehicles even though the objects were perceptually similar—airplanes and birds with their wings spread (Mandler & McDonough, 1993) (see Figure 7.11).

FIGURE 7.11 Categorization in 9- to 11-Month-Olds. These are the stimuli used in the study that indicated 9- to 11-month-old infants categorized birds as animals and airplanes as vehicles even though the objects were perceptually similar (Mandler & McDonough, 1993).

thinking Manipulating and transforming information in memory, usually to form concepts, reason, think critically, and solve problems.

Further advances in categorization occur in the second year of life (Booth, 2006). Many infants' "first concepts are broad and global in nature, such as 'animal' or 'indoor thing.' Gradually, over the first two years these broad concepts become more differentiated into concepts such as 'land animal,' then 'dog,' or to 'furniture,' then 'chair'" (Mandler, 2006, p. 1). Also in the second year, infants often categorize objects on the basis of their shape (Landau, Smith, & Jones, 1998).

Do some very young children develop an intense, passionate interest in a particular category of objects or activities? A recent study of 11-month-old to 6-year-old children confirmed that they do (DeLoache, Simcock, & Macari, 2007). A striking finding was the large gender difference in categories with an extreme intense interest in particular categories stronger for boys than girls. Categorization of boys' intense interests focused on vehicles, trains, machines, dinosaurs, and balls; girls' intense interests were more likely to involve dress-ups and books/reading (see Figure 7.12). By the time your author's grandson Alex was 2 years old, he already had developed an intense, passionate interest in the category of vehicles. He categorized vehicles into such subcategories as cars, trucks, earth-moving equipment, and buses. In addition to common classifications of cars into police cars, jeeps, taxis, and such, and trucks into firetrucks, dump trucks, and the like, his categorical knowledge of earth-moving equipment included bulldozers and excavators, and he categorized buses into school buses, London buses, and funky Malta buses (retro buses on the island of Malta). By 2½ years of age, Alex developed an intense, passionate interest in categorizing dinosaurs.

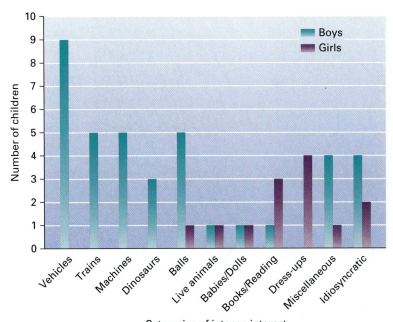

FIGURE 7.12 Categorization of Boys' and Girls' Intense Interests

Childhood

To explore thinking in childhood, we will examine three important types of thinking: critical thinking, scientific thinking, and problem solving.

Currently, there is considerable interest among psychologists and educators in critical thinking (Halpern, 2007; Sternberg, Roediger, & Halpern, 2007). **Critical thinking** involves thinking reflectively and productively, and evaluating evidence. If you think critically, you will do the following:

- Ask not only what happened but how and why.
- Examine supposed "facts" to determine whether there is evidence to support them.
- Argue in a reasoned way rather than through emotions.
- Recognize that there is sometimes more than one good answer or explanation.
- Compare various answers and judge which is the best answer.
- Evaluate what other people say rather than immediately accepting it as the truth.
- Ask questions and speculate beyond what is known to create new ideas and new information.

According to critics such as Jacqueline and Martin Brooks (1993, 2001), few schools teach students to think critically. Schools push students to give a single correct answer rather than encouraging them to come up with new ideas and rethink conclusions. Too

The author's grandson Alex at 2 years of age showing his intense, passionate interest in the category of vehicles while playing with a London taxi and a funky Malta bus.

critical thinking Thinking reflectively and productively, and evaluating the evidence.

What are some examples of children engaging in critical thinking?

Students in a science classroom at Compton-Drew School in St. Louis, one of the locations where Fostering a Community of Learners has been implemented. *What are some themes of Fostering a Community of Learners?*

reciprocal teaching Students take turns leading small-group discussions.

often teachers ask students to recite, define, describe, state, and list rather than to analyze, infer, connect, synthesize, criticize, create, evaluate, think, and rethink. As a result, many schools graduate students who think superficially, staying on the surface of problems rather than becoming deeply engaged in meaningful thinking.

One way to encourage students to think critically is to present them with controversial topics or both sides of an issue to discuss. Some teachers shy away from having students debate issues because arguments supposedly are not "polite" or "nice" (Winn, 2004). But debates can motivate students to delve more deeply into a topic and examine issues, especially if teachers refrain from stating their own views so that students feel free to explore multiple perspectives.

Can schools foster critical thinking among children? Anne Brown and Joe Campione (1996; Brown, 1997, 1998) created an innovative program, Fostering a Community of Learners (FCL), that is appropriate for encouraging critical thinking among 6- to 12-year-old children. The program focuses on literacy and biology and is set in inner-city elementary schools. Reflection and discussion are key dimensions of the program. Constructive commentary, questioning, and criticism are the norm rather than the exception. Three strategies used by FCL that encourage reflection and discussion are as follows:

- *Implementing online consultation.* In FCL classrooms, both children and adults use e-mail as well as face-to-face communication to share expertise and to build community.

- *Having children teach children.* Cross-age teaching, in which older students teach younger students, occurs both face-to-face and via e-mail in FCL. Older students often serve as discussion leaders. Cross-age teaching provides students with invaluable opportunities to talk about learning, gives students responsibility and purpose, and fosters collaboration among peers. FCL also uses **reciprocal teaching**, in which students take turns leading a small-group discussion. Reciprocal teaching requires students to discuss complex passages, collaborate, and share their individual expertise and perspectives.

- *Using adults as role models.* Visiting experts and classroom teachers introduce the big ideas and difficult principles at the beginning of a unit. The adults model how to think and reflect. The adults continually ask students to justify their opinions and then support them with evidence, to think of counterexamples to rules, and so on. Online experts function as role models of thinking. They wonder, query, and make inferences based on incomplete knowledge. Through e-mail, experts also provide coaching, advice, and commentary about what it means to learn and understand.

One example of a teaching theme used in FCL is "changing populations." Outside experts or teachers introduce this lesson and ask students to generate as many questions about it as possible. It is not unusual for students to come up with more than a hundred questions. The teacher and the students categorize the questions into subtopics according to the type of population they refer to, such as extinct, endangered, artificial, and urbanized populations. About six students make up a learning group, and each group takes responsibility for one subtopic.

Research evaluation of the Fostering a Community of Learners approach suggests that it benefits students' understanding and flexible use of content knowledge, resulting in improved achievement in reading, writing, and problem solving. FCL is being increasingly implemented in a number of classrooms (Schoenfeld, 2004; Shulman & Shulman, 2004). In a recent commentary, science education experts Richard Lehrer and Laura Schauble (2006, p. 173) called FCL "A landmark in developmental science education."

Fostering a Community of Learners represents an attempt to apply what is known about children's cognitive development to improving their education (Lehrer & Schauble, 2006). To read about one developmental psychologist who used her training in cognitive development to pursue a career in an applied area, see the *Careers in Child Development* profile.

Careers in Child Development

Helen Schwe, Developmental Psychologist and Toy Designer

Helen Schwe obtained a Ph.D. from Stanford University in developmental psychology but she now spends her days talking with computer engineers and designing "smart" toys for children. Smart toys are designed to improve children's problem-solving and symbolic thinking skills.

When she was a graduate student, Schwe worked part-time for Hasbro toys, testing its children's software on preschoolers. Her first job after graduate school was with Zowie entertainment, which was subsequently bought by LEGO. According to Schwe, "Even in a toy's most primitive stage of development, . . . you see children's creativity in responding to challenges, their satisfaction when a problem is solved or simply their delight when they are having fun" (Schlegel, 2000, p. 50). In addition to conducting experiments and focus groups at different stages of a toy's development, Schwe also assesses the age appropriateness of a toy. Most of her current work focuses on 3- to 5-year-old children. (Source: Schlegel, 2000, pp. 50–51)

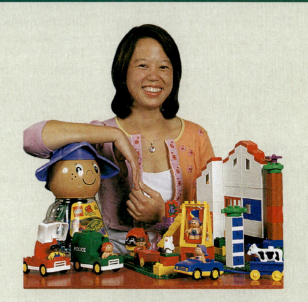

Helen Schwe, a developmental psychologist, with some of the "smart" toys she designed.

Scientific Thinking   Some aspects of thinking are specific to a particular domain, such as mathematics, science, or reading. We will explore reading in Chapter 9, "Language Development." Here we will examine scientific thinking by children.

Like scientists, children ask fundamental questions about reality and seek answers to problems that seem utterly trivial or unanswerable to other people (such as, Why is the sky blue?). Do children generate hypotheses, perform experiments, and reach conclusions about their data in ways resembling those of scientists?

Scientific reasoning often is aimed at identifying causal relations. Like scientists, children place a great deal of emphasis on causal mechanisms (Martin & others, 2005). Their understanding of how events are caused weighs more heavily in their causal inferences than even such strong influences as whether the cause happened immediately before the effect.

There also are important differences between the reasoning of children and the reasoning of scientists (Gallagher, 2007). Children are more influenced by happenstance events than by an overall pattern, and children tend to maintain their old theories regardless of the evidence (Kuhn, Schauble, & Garcia-Mila, 1992). Children might go through mental gymnastics trying to reconcile seemingly contradictory new information with their existing beliefs. For example, after learning about the solar system, children sometimes conclude that there are two Earths, the seemingly flat world in which they live and the round ball floating in space that their teacher described.

Children also have difficulty designing experiments that can distinguish among alternative causes. Instead, they tend to bias the experiments in favor of whatever hypothesis they began with. Sometimes they see the results as supporting their original hypothesis even when the results directly contradict it (Schauble, 1996). Thus, although there are important similarities between children and scientists, in their basic curiosity and in the kinds of questions they ask, there are also important differences in the degree to which they can separate theory and evidence and in their ability to design conclusive experiments (Lehrer & Schauble, 2006).

Too often, the skills scientists use, such as careful observation, graphing, self-regulatory thinking, and knowing when and how to apply one's knowledge to solve problems, are not routinely taught in schools (Bass, Contant, & Carin, 2009; Bybee, Powell, & Trowbridge, 2008). Children have many concepts that are incompatible with science and reality. Good teachers perceive and understand a child's underlying scientific concepts, then use the concepts as a scaffold for learning (Magnusson & Palinscar, 2005). Effective science teaching helps children distinguish between fruitful errors and misconceptions, and detect plainly wrong ideas that need to be replaced by more accurate conceptions (Victor, Kellough, & Tai, 2008).

Many science teachers help their students construct their knowledge of science through discovery and hands-on laboratory investigations (Martin & others, 2009; Victor, Kellough, & Tai, 2008). Constructivist teaching emphasizes that children have to build their own scientific knowledge and understanding. At each step in science learning, they need to interpret new knowledge in the context of what they already understand. Rather than putting fully formed knowledge into children's minds, in the constructivist approach teachers help children construct scientifically valid interpretations of the world and guide them in altering their scientific misconceptions (Peters & Stout, 2006).

Keep in mind, though, that it is important that students not be left completely on their own to construct scientific knowledge independent of *science content.* Students' inquiry should be guided (Moyer, Hackett, & Everett, 2007). It is important for teachers, at a minimum, initially to scaffold students' science learning, extensively monitor their progress, and ensure that they are learning science content. Thus, in pursuing science investigations, students need to learn inquiry skills *and* science content (Gallagher, 2007).

How might family, economic, and cultural experiences be linked to children's science achievement? A recent study of more than 107,000 students in 41 countries examined this question (Chiu, 2007). Students had higher science achievement scores when they lived in two-parent families, experienced more family involvement, lived with fewer siblings, their schools had more resources, they lived in wealthier countries, or they lived in countries with more equal distribution of household income.

Pete Karpyk, who teaches chemistry in Weirton, West Virginia, uses an extensive array of activities that bring science alive for students. Here he has shrink-wrapped himself to demonstrate the effects of air pressure. He has some students give chemistry demonstrations at elementary schools and has discovered that in some cases students who don't do well on tests excel when they teach children. He also adapts his teaching based on feedback from former students and incorporates questions from their college chemistry tests as bonus questions on the tests he gives his high school students (Source: Briggs, 2005. p. 6D).

Solving Problems   Children face many problems, both in school and out of school. *Problem solving* involves finding an appropriate way to attain a goal. Let's examine two ways children solve problems—by applying rules and by using analogies—and then consider some ways to help children learn effective strategies for solving problems.

Using Rules to Solve Problems   During early childhood, the relatively stimulus-driven toddler is transformed into a child capable of flexible, goal-directed problem solving (Zelazo & Muller, 2004). One element in this change is children's developing ability to form representations of reality.

For example, because they lack a concept of perspectives, 3- to 4-year-olds cannot understand that a single stimulus can be redescribed in a different, incompatible way (Perner & others, 2002). Consider a problem in which children must sort stimuli

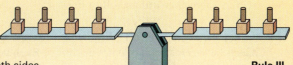

Rule I. If the weight is the same on both sides, predict that the scale will balance. If the weight differs, predict that the side with more weight will go down.

Rule II. If the weight is greater on one side, say that that side will go down. If the weights on the two sides are equal, choose the side on which the weight is farther from the fulcrum.

Balance scale apparatus

Rule III. Act as in Rule II, except that if one side has more weight and the weight on the other side is farther from the fulcrum, then guess.

Rule IV. Proceed as in Rule III, unless one side has more weight and the other more distance. In that case, calculate torques by multiplying weight times distance on each side. Then predict that the side with the greater torque will go down.

FIGURE 7.13 The Type of Balance Scale Used by Siegler (1976). Weights could be placed on pegs on each side of the fulcrum; the torque (the weight on each side times the distance of that weight from the fulcrum) determined which side would go down.

using the rule of *color*. In the course of the color sorting, a child may describe a red rabbit as a *red one* to solve the problem. However, in a subsequent task, the child may need to discover a rule that describes the rabbit as just a *rabbit* to solve the problem. If 3- to 4-year-olds fail to understand that it is possible to provide multiple descriptions of the same stimulus, they persist in describing the stimulus as a red rabbit. In other words, the 3- to 4-year-olds show representational inflexibility. Researchers have found that at about 4 years of age, children acquire the concept of perspectives, which allows them to appreciate that a single thing can be described in different ways (Frye, 1999).

With age, children also learn better rules to apply to problems. Figure 7.13 provides an example; it shows the balance scale problem that has been used to examine children's use of rules in solving problems. The scale includes a fulcrum and an arm that can rotate around it. The arm can tip left or right or remain level, depending on how weights (metal disks with holes in the center) are arranged on the pegs on each side of the fulcrum. The child's task is to look at the configuration of weights on the pegs on each problem and then predict whether the left side will go down, the right side will go down, or the arm will balance.

Robert Siegler (1976) hypothesized that children would use one of the four rules listed in Figure 7.13. He reasoned that presenting problems on which different rules would generate different outcomes would allow assessment of each child's rules. Through a child's pattern of correct answers and errors on a set of such problems, that child's underlying rule could be inferred.

What were the results? Almost all 5-year-olds used Rule I, in which the child considers only the weight on the scales. Almost all 9-year-olds used either Rule II or Rule III, which takes both weight and distance into account, or Rule III, which calls for guessing when the weight and distance dimensions would give conflicting information. Both 13-year-olds and 17-year-olds generally used Rule III.

In other words, the older children performed better at solving the problems because they used a better rule. But even 5-year-old children can be trained to use Rule III if they are taught to pay attention to differences in distance. As children learn more about what is relevant to a problem, and learn to encode the relevant information, their ability to use rules in problem solving improves.

Interestingly, despite the 17-year-olds' having studied balance scales in their physics course, almost none of them used the only rule that generated consistently correct answers, Rule IV. Discussions with their teachers revealed why: The balance scale the students had studied was a pan balance, on which small pans could be hung from various locations along the arm, rather than an arm balance, with pegs extending upward. Retesting the children showed that most could consistently solve the problems when the familiar pan balance was used. This example illustrates a set of lessons that frequently emerge from studies of problem solving—learning is often quite narrow, generalization beyond one's existing knowledge is difficult, and even analogies that seem straightforward are often missed.

Using Analogies to Solve Problems   An *analogy* involves correspondence in some respects between things that are dissimilar. Even very young children can draw reasonable analogies under some circumstances and use them to solve problems (Freeman & Gehl, 1995). Under other circumstances, even college students fail to draw seemingly obvious analogies (as in the high school students' difficulty in extrapolating from the familiar pan balance to the unfamiliar arm balance).

Anne Brown and her collaborators (Brown, 1990; Brown, Kane, & Echols, 1986) have demonstrated that even 1- and 2-year-olds can use analogical reasoning. When 1- and 2-year-olds are shown that a curved stick can be used as a tool to pull in a toy that is too far away to be reached unaided, they draw the correct analogy in choosing which stick to use the next time. They do not choose sticks on the basis of their being the same color or looking exactly like the stick they saw used before. Instead they identify the essential property and will choose whichever objects have it; for example, they will choose a straight rake as well as the curved cane. The 2-year-olds were more likely than the 1-year-olds to learn the initial task without any help, but once they learned the task, both 1- and 2-year-olds drew the right analogy to new problems.

Analogical problem solving often involves tools more abstract than curved sticks for hauling in objects. Maps and verbal descriptions of routes, for example, often help us to figure out how to get where we want to go (DeLoache, Miller, & Pierroutsakos, 1998). Similarly, Judy DeLoache (1989) showed that young children can use scale models to guide their problem-solving activities.

DeLoache (1989) created a situation in which $2\frac{1}{2}$- and 3-year-olds were shown a small toy hidden within a scale model of a room. The child was then asked to find the toy in a real room that was a bigger version of the scale model. If the toy was hidden under the armchair in the scale model, it was also hidden under the armchair in the real room. Considerable development occurred between $2\frac{1}{2}$ and 3 years of age on this task. Thirty-month-old children rarely could solve the problem, but most 36-month-old children could.

Why was the task so difficult for the $2\frac{1}{2}$-year-olds? Their problem was not an inability to understand that a symbol can represent another situation. Shown line drawings or photographs of the larger room, $2\frac{1}{2}$-year-olds had no difficulty finding the object. Instead, the difficulty seemed to come from the toddlers' simultaneously viewing the scale model as a symbol of the larger room and as an object in itself. When children were allowed to play with the scale model before using it as a symbol, their performance worsened, presumably because playing with it made them think of it more as an object in itself. Conversely, when the scale model was placed in a glass case, where the children could not handle it at all, more children used it successfully to find the object hidden in the larger room. The general lesson is that young children can use a variety of tools to draw analogies, but they easily can forget that an object is being used as a symbol of something else and instead treat it as an object in its own right (DeLoache, 2004).

Using Strategies to Solve Problems   Good thinkers routinely use strategies and effective planning to solve problems (Pressley, 2007; Pressley & others, 2007). Do children use one strategy or multiple strategies in problem solving? They often use more than one strategy (Siegler, 2006, 2007).

Most children benefit from generating a variety of alternative strategies and experimenting with different approaches to a problem, discovering what works well, when, and where. This is especially true for children from the middle elementary school grades on, although some cognitive psychologists stress that even young children should be encouraged to practice varying strategies (Siegler & Alibali, 2005). To read further about guiding children to learn effective strategies, see the *Caring for Children* interlude.

Judy DeLoache (*left*) has conducted research that focuses on young children's developing cognitive abilities. She has demonstrated that children's symbolic representation between $2\frac{1}{2}$ and 3 years of age enables them to find a toy in a real room that is a much bigger version of the scale model.

Caring for Children

HELPING CHILDREN LEARN STRATEGIES

In Michael Pressley's view (Pressley, 2003, 2007; Pressley & Hilden, 2006), the key to education is helping students learn a rich repertoire of strategies for solving problems. Pressley argues that when children are given instruction about effective strategies, they often can apply strategies that they had not used on their own. Pressley emphasizes that children benefit when the teacher (1) models the appropriate strategy, (2) verbalizes the steps in the strategy, and (3) guides the children to practice the strategy and supports their practice with feedback. "Practice" means that children use the strategy over and over until they perform it automatically. To execute strategies effectively, they need to have the strategies in long-term memory, and extensive practice makes this possible.

Just having children learn a new strategy is usually not enough for them to continue to use it and to transfer the strategy to new situations. Children need to be motivated to learn and to use the strategies. For effective maintenance and transfer, children should be encouraged to monitor the effectiveness of the new strategy by comparing their performance on tests and other assessments.

Let's examine an example of effective strategy instruction. Good readers extract the main ideas from text and summarize them. In contrast, novice readers (for example, most children) usually don't store the main ideas of what they read. One intervention based on what is known about the summarizing strategies of good readers consisted of instructing children to (1) skim over trivial information, (2) ignore redundant information, (3) replace less inclusive terms with more inclusive ones, (4) use a more inclusive action term to combine a series of events, (5) choose a topic sentence, and (6) create a topic sentence if none is given (Brown & Day, 1983). Instructing elementary school students to use these summarizing strategies improves their reading performance (Rinehart, Stahl, & Erickson, 1986).

Pressley and his colleagues (Pressley & Harris, 2006; Pressley & Hilden, 2006; Pressley & others, 2001, 2003, 2004; 2007) have spent considerable time in recent years observing the use of strategy instruction by teachers and strategy use by students in elementary and secondary school classrooms. They conclude that teachers' use of strategy instruction is far less complete and intense than what is needed for students to learn how to use strategies effectively. They argue that education needs to be restructured so that students are provided with more opportunities to become competent strategic learners.

Review and Reflect: Learning Goal 4

4 **Characterize Thinking and Its Developmental Changes**

REVIEW
- What is thinking?
- How does thinking develop in infancy?
- Can children engage in critical and scientific thinking? What are some ways that children solve problems?

REFLECT
- Some experts lament that few schools teach students to think critically. Does your own experience support this view? If you agree with the experts, why is critical thinking not more widely or effectively taught?

5 METACOGNITION

| What Is Metacognition? | The Child's Theory of Mind | Metacognition in Childhood |

As you read about earlier in this chapter, *metacognition* is cognition about cognition, or "knowing about knowing" (Flavell, 2004). It is a function of the central executive in Baddeley's model (see Figure 7.4).

What Is Metacognition?

Metacognition helps children to perform many cognitive tasks more effectively (Doherty, 2008; Flavell, 2004). In one study, students were taught metacognitive skills to help them solve math problems (Cardelle-Elawar, 1992). In each of 30 daily lessons involving math story problems, a teacher guided low-achieving students to recognize when they did not know the meaning of a word, did not have all of the information necessary to solve a problem, did not know how to subdivide the problem into specific steps, or did not know how to carry out a computation. After the 30 daily lessons, the students who were given this metacognitive training had better math achievement and attitudes toward math.

Metacognition can take many forms. It includes knowledge about when and where to use particular strategies for learning or for solving problems. **Metamemory**, individuals' knowledge about memory, is an especially important form of metacognition. Metamemory includes general knowledge about memory, such as knowing that recognition tests (such as multiple-choice questions) are easier than recall tests (such as essay questions). It also encompasses knowledge about one's own memory, such as knowing whether you have studied enough for an upcoming test.

Cognitive developmentalist John Flavell (*left*) is a pioneer in providing insights about children's thinking. Among his many contributions are establishing the field of metacognition and conducting numerous studies in this area, including matamemory and theory of mind studies.

The Child's Theory of Mind

Even young children are curious about the nature of the human mind. They have a **theory of mind**, which refers to awareness of one's own mental processes and the mental processes of others. Studies of theory of mind view the child as "a thinker who is trying to explain, predict, and understand people's thoughts, feelings, and utterances" (Harris, 2006, p. 847). Researchers are increasingly discovering that children's theory of mind is linked to cognitive processes (Wellman & others, 2008). For example, theory of mind competence at age 3 is related to a higher level of metamemory at age 5 (Lockl & Schneider, 2007).

Developmental Changes   Children's theory of mind changes as they develop through childhood (Astington & Dack, 2008; Doherty, 2008). Some changes occur quite early in development, as we see next.

18 Months to 3 Years of Age   In this time frame, children begin to understand three mental states:

- *Perceptions.* By 2 years of age, children recognize that another person will see what's in front of her own eyes instead of what's in front of the child's eyes (Lempers, Flavell, & Flavell, 1977), and by 3 years of age, they realize that looking leads to knowing what's inside a container (Pratt & Bryant, 1990).

- *Emotions.* The child can distinguish between positive (for example, happy) and negative (sad, for example) emotions. A child might say, "Tommy feels bad."

metamemory Knowledge about memory.

theory of mind Awareness of one's own mental processes and the mental processes of others.

• *Desires.* All humans have some sort of desires. But when do children begin to recognize that someone else's desires may differ from their own? Toddlers recognize that if people want something, they will try to get it. For instance, a child might say, "I want my mommy."

Two- to three-year-olds understand the way that desires are related to actions and to simple emotions. For example, they understand that people will search for what they want, and that if they obtain it, they are likely to feel happy, but if they don't they will keep searching for it and are likely to feel sad or angry (Wellman & Woolley, 1990). Children also refer to desires earlier and more frequently than they refer to cognitive states such as thinking and knowing (Bartsch & Wellman, 1995).

One of the landmark developments in understanding others' desires is recognizing that someone else may have different desires from one's own. Eighteen-month-olds understand that their own food preferences may not match the preferences of others: They will give an adult the food to which she says "Yummy!", even if the food is something that the infants detest (Repacholi & Gopnik, 1997). As they get older, they can verbalize that they themselves do not like something but an adult might (Flavell & others, 1992).

3 to 5 Years of Age   Between the ages of 3 to 5, children come to understand that the mind can represent objects and events accurately or inaccurately. The realization that people can have *false beliefs*—beliefs that are not true—develops in a majority of children by the time they are 5 years old (Wellman, Cross, & Watson, 2001) (see Figure 7.14). This point is often described as a pivotal one in understanding the mind—recognizing that beliefs are not just mapped directly into the mind from the surrounding world, but also that different people can have different, and sometimes incorrect, beliefs (Liu & others, 2008). In a classic false-belief task, young children were shown a Band-Aids box and asked what was inside (Jenkins & Astington, 1996). To the children's surprise, the box actually contained pencils. When asked what a child who had never seen the box would think was inside, 3-year-olds typically responded, "Pencils." However, the 4- and 5-year-olds, grinning at the anticipation of the false beliefs of other children who had not seen what was inside the box, were more likely to say "Band-Aids."

In a similar task, children are told a story about Sally and Ann: Sally places a toy in a basket and then leaves the room (see Figure 7.15). In her absence, Ann takes the toy from the basket and places it in a box. Children are asked where Sally will look for the toy when she returns. The major finding is that 3-year-olds tend to fail false-belief tasks, saying that Sally will look in the box (even though Sally could not know that the toy has moved to this new location). Four-year-olds and older children tend to pass the task, correctly saying that Sally will have a "false belief"—she will think the object is in the basket, even though that belief is now false. The conclusion from these studies is that children younger than 4 years old do not understand that it is possible to have a false belief.

However, there are many reasons to question the focus on this one supposedly pivotal moment in the development of a theory of mind (Mills, 2007). For example, the false-belief task is a complicated one that involves a number of factors such as the characters in the story and all of their individual actions (Bloom & German, 2000). Children also have to disregard their own knowledge in making predictions about what others would think, which is difficult for young children (Birch & Bloom, 2003).

Another important issue is that there is more to understanding the minds of others than this false-belief task would indicate. Indeed, there are signs of understanding the minds of others before children pass the false-belief task (Bloom & German, 2000). Recent research revealed that 15-month-old infants may expect that people will try to find objects based on where they last saw the objects, not where the objects are now, suggesting some sort of primitive understanding of false belief (Onishi & Baillargeon, 2005). And in general, this kind of task has only two possible outcomes: knowledge or ignorance (Miller, 2000). Someone either has the right information to make a judgment of the contents of a box, or someone does not. Even two-and-a-half-year-olds

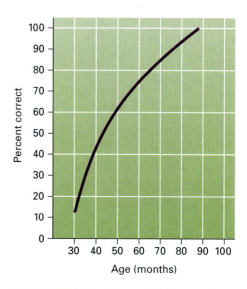

FIGURE 7.14 Developmental Changes in False-Belief Performance. False-belief performance dramatically increases from 2½ years of age through the middle of the elementary school years. In a summary of the results of many studies, 2½-year-olds gave incorrect responses about 80 percent of the time (Wellman, Cross, & Watson, 2001). At 3 years, 8 months, they were correct about 50 percent of the time, and after that, gave increasingly correct responses.

FIGURE 7.15 The Sally and Anne False-Belief Task. In the false-belief task, the skit above in which Sally has a basket and Anne has a box is shown to children. Sally places a toy in her basket and then leaves. While Sally is gone and can't watch, Anne removes the toy from Sally's basket and places it in her box. Sally then comes back and the children are asked where they think Sally will look for her toy. Children are said to "pass" the false-belief task if they understand that Sally looks in her basket first before realizing the toy isn't there.

can recognize when someone is ignorant of information: Toddlers gesture toward a toy placed on a top shelf far more often if their parent was not present when the toy was hidden than if the parent had been in the room (O'Neill, 1996). There is much more to understanding knowledge in the minds of others than understanding that others may be ignorant or knowledgeable of a certain fact. So while passing the false-belief task is important, there is much development in understanding the mind both earlier and later in development.

One example of a limitation in 3- to 5-year-olds' understanding the mind is how they think about thinking. Preschoolers often underestimate when mental activity is likely occurring. For example, they sometimes think that a person who is sitting quietly or reading is not actually thinking very much (Flavell, Green & Flavell, 1995). Their understanding of their own thinking is also limited. One study revealed that even 5-year-olds have difficulty reporting their thoughts (Flavell, Green, & Flavell, 1995). Children were asked to think quietly about the room in their home where they kept their toothbrushes. Shortly after this, many children denied they had been thinking at all and failed to mention either a toothbrush or a bathroom. In another study, when 5-year-olds were asked to try to have no thoughts at all for about 20 seconds, they reported that they were successful at doing this (Flavell, Green, & Flavell, 2000). By contrast, most of the 8-year-olds said they engaged in mental activity during the 20 seconds and reported specific thoughts.

5 to 7 Years of Age It is only beyond the preschool years that children have a deepening appreciation of the mind itself rather than just an understanding of mental states. For example, they begin to recognize that people's behaviors do not necessarily reflect their thoughts and feelings (Flavell, Green, & Flavell, 1993). Not until middle and late childhood do children see the mind as an active constructor of knowledge or processing center (Flavell, Green, & Flavell, 1998) and move from understanding that beliefs can be false to realizing that the same event can be open to multiple interpretations (Carpendale & Chandler, 1996). For example, in one study, children saw an ambiguous line drawing (for example, a drawing that could be seen as either a duck or a rabbit); one puppet told the child she believed the drawing was a duck, while another puppet told the child he believed the drawing was a rabbit (see Figure 7.16). Before the age of 7, children said that there was one right answer, and it was not okay for both puppets to have different opinions.

Five- and six-year olds understand that human sources may have different experiences, but they still think there is an objective truth (Kuhn & others, 2000). They reason that if others have misinformation or misunderstand something, they must be inaccurately perceiving reality. By age 7, children are able to recognize that reality is not directly knowable, that knowledge is subjective, and that people may have different interpretations of the same event due to differing interpretive processes (Mills, 2007).

7 Years and Beyond Although most research on children's theory of mind focuses on children around or before their preschool years, there are important developments in the ability to understand the beliefs and thoughts of others. While understanding that people may have different interpretations is important, it is also important to recognize that some interpretations and beliefs may still be evaluated on the basis of the merits of arguments and evidence (Kuhn, 2000). In early adolescence, children begin to understand that people can have ambivalent feelings (Flavell & Miller, 1998; Whitesell & Harter, 1989). They start to recognize that the same person can feel both happy and sad about the same event. They also engage in more recursive thinking: thinking about what other people are thinking about.

Individual Differences As in other developmental research, there are individual differences in when children reach certain milestones in their theory of mind. For

FIGURE 7.16 Ambiguous Line Drawing

example, preschoolers who have more siblings perform better on theory of mind tasks than preschoolers with fewer siblings, especially if they have older siblings (McAlister & Peterson, 2007; Ruffman & others, 1998). Children who talk with their parents about feelings frequently as 2-year-olds show better performance on theory of mind tasks (Ruffman, Slade, & Crowe, 2002), as do children who frequently engage in pretend play (Harris, 2000). Children who are deaf but have hearing parents perform more poorly on theory of mind tasks than deaf children raised by deaf parents, presumably because they have fewer opportunities to engage in communication with their parents about mental states (Courtin, 2000; Peterson & Siegal, 1999).

Executive function, which describes several functions (such as inhibition and planning) that are important for flexible, future-oriented behavior, also may be connected to theory of mind development (Astington & Dack, 2008; Doherty, 2008). For example, in one executive function task, children are asked to say the word "night" when they see a picture of a sun, and the word "day" when they see a picture of a moon and stars. Children who perform better at executive function tasks seem also to have a better understanding of theory of mind (Carlson & Moses, 2001; Sabbagh & others, 2006).

There may also be some gender differences in talking about the mind. Parents tend to discuss emotions more with their daughters than with their sons, and that could influence children's understanding of other people's feelings and desires (Adams & others, 1995). Some researchers have suggested that females understand false beliefs slightly earlier than males, but other individual differences (such as overall language ability) may be more important in developing a more advanced understanding of theory of mind (Charman, Ruffman, & Clements, 2002).

Theory of Mind and Autism   Another individual difference in understanding the mind involves autism (Doherty, 2008). Approximately 2 to 6 out 1,000 children are estimated to have some sort of autism spectrum disorder (National Institute of Mental Health, 2007). Autism can usually be diagnosed by the age of 3 years, and sometimes earlier. Children with autism show a number of behaviors different from children their age, including deficits in social interaction and communication as well as repetitive behaviors or interests. They often show indifference toward others, in many instances preferring to be alone and showing more interest in objects than people. It now is accepted that autism is linked to genetic and brain abnormalities (Iacoboni & Dapretto, 2006).

Children and adults with autism have difficulty in social interactions, often described as huge deficits in theory of mind (Fernyhough, 2008). These deficits are generally greater than deficits in children the same mental age with mental retardation (Baron-Cohen, 1995). Researchers have found that autistic children have difficulty in developing a theory of mind, especially in understanding others' beliefs and emotions (Harris, 2006). Although children with autism tend to do poorly reasoning in false-belief tasks (Baron-Cohen, Leslie, & Frith, 1985; Peterson, 2005), they can perform much better on reasoning asks requiring an understanding of physical causality.

However, it is important to consider individual variations in autistic children and particular aspects of theory of mind (Harris, 2006). Autistic children are not a homogeneous group, and some have less severe social and communication problems than others. Thus, it is not surprising that children who have less severe forms of autism do better than those who have more severe forms of the disorder on some theory of mind tasks. For example, higher-functioning autistic children show reasonable progress in understanding others' desires (Harris, 2006). A further important consideration in thinking about autism and theory of mind is that autistic children's difficulty in understanding other's beliefs and emotions might not be due solely to theory of mind deficits but to other aspects of cognition, such as problems in focusing attention or some general intellectual impairment (Renner, Grofer Klinger, & Klinger, 2006). Some recent theories of autism suggest that weaknesses in executive functioning may relate to the problems those with autism have on theory of mind tasks. Other theories have pointed out that typically developing individuals process information by

The child sitting on the sofa is autistic. *What are some characteristics of autistic children? What are some deficits in autistic children's theory of mind?*

extracting the big picture, whereas those with autism process information in a very detailed, almost obsessive way. It may be that in autism, a number of different but related deficits lead to the social cognitive deficits (Rajendran & Mitchell, 2007).

Metacognition in Childhood

By 5 or 6 years of age, children usually know that familiar items are easier to learn than unfamiliar ones, that short lists are easier than long ones, that recognition is easier than recall, and that forgetting becomes more likely over time (Lyon & Flavell, 1993). However, in other ways young children's metamemory is limited. They don't understand that related items are easier to remember than unrelated ones or that remembering the gist of a story is easier than remembering information verbatim (Kretuzer & Flavell, 1975). By fifth grade, students understand that gist recall is easier than verbatim recall.

Preschool children also have an inflated opinion of their memory abilities. For example, in one study, a majority of preschool children predicted that they would be able to recall all 10 items of a list of 10 items. When tested, none of the young children managed this feat (Flavell, Friedrichs, & Hoyt, 1970). As they move through the elementary school years, children give more realistic evaluations of their memory skills (Schneider & Pressley, 1997).

Preschool children also have little appreciation for the importance of cues to memory, such as "It helps when you can think of an example of it." By 7 or 8 years of age, children better appreciate the importance of cueing for memory. In general, children's understanding of their memory abilities and their skill in evaluating their performance on memory tasks is relatively poor at the beginning of the elementary school years but improves considerably by 11 to 12 years of age (Bjorklund & Rosenbaum, 2000).

Review and Reflect: Learning Goal 5

5 **Define Metacognition and Summarize Its Developmental Changes**

REVIEW

- What is metacognition?
- What is theory of mind? How does children's theory of mind change developmentally?
- How does metacognition change during childhood?

REFLECT

- How do you think metacognition might be linked to our discussion of strategies in solving problems earlier in the chapter?

Reach Your Learning Goals

Information Processing

1 THE INFORMATION-PROCESSING APPROACH: EXPLAIN THE INFORMATION-PROCESSING APPROACH

The Information-Processing Approach to Development

- The information-processing approach analyzes how individuals manipulate information, monitor it, and create strategies for handling it. Attention, memory, and thinking are involved in effective information processing. The computer has served as a model for how humans process information. In the information-processing approach, children's cognitive development results from their ability to overcome processing limitations by increasingly executing basic operations, expanding information-processing capacity, and acquiring new knowledge and strategies.

Cognitive Resources: Capacity and Speed of Processing Information

- Capacity and speed of processing speed, often referred to as cognitive resources, increase across childhood and adolescence. Changes in the brain serve as biological foundations for developmental changes in cognitive resources. In terms of capacity, the increase is reflected in older children being able to hold in mind several dimensions of a topic simultaneously. A reaction-time task has often been used to assess speed of processing. Processing speed continues to improve in early adolescence.

Mechanisms of Change

- According to Siegler, three important mechanisms of change are encoding (how information gets into memory), automaticity (ability to process information with little or no effort), and strategy construction (creation of new procedures for processing information). Children's information processing is characterized by self-modification and an important aspect of this self-modification involves metacognition, that is, knowing about knowing.

Comparisons with Piaget's Theory

- Unlike Piaget, the information-processing approach does not see development as occurring in distinct stages. Instead, this approach holds that individuals develop a gradually increasing capacity for processing information, which allows them to develop increasingly complex knowledge and skills. Like Piaget's theory, some versions of the information-processing approach are constructivist—they see children directing their own cognitive development.

2 ATTENTION: DEFINE ATTENTION AND OUTLINE ITS DEVELOPMENTAL CHANGES

What Is Attention?

- Attention is the focusing of mental resources. Four ways that children can allocate their attention are selective attention (focusing on a specific aspect of experience that is relevant while ignoring others that are irrelevant); divided attention (concentrating on more than one activity at the same time); sustained attention (the ability to maintain attention to a selected stimulus for a prolonged period of time; also referred to as focused attention and vigilance); and executive attention (involves action planning, allocating attention to goals, error detection and compensation, monitoring progress on tasks, and dealing with novel or difficult tasks).

Infancy

- Even newborns can fixate on a contour but as they get older they scan a pattern more thoroughly. Attention in the first year of life is dominated by the orienting/investigative process. Attention in infancy is often studied through habituation and dishabituation. Habituation can provide a measure of an infant's maturity and well-being. Joint attention increases an infant's ability to learn from others.

Childhood

- Salient stimuli tend to capture the attention of the preschooler. After 6 or 7 years of age, there is a shift to more cognitive control of attention. Young children especially make advances in executive and sustained attention. Selective attention also improves through childhood. Children's attentional skills are increasingly being found to predict later cognitive competencies, such as school readiness.

3   MEMORY: DESCRIBE WHAT MEMORY IS AND HOW IT CHANGES

What Is Memory?

- Memory is the retention of information over time. Psychologists study the processes of memory: how information is initially placed or encoded into memory, how it is retained or stored, and how it is found or retrieved for a certain purpose later. Short-term memory involves the retention of information for up to 15 to 30 seconds, assuming there is no rehearsal of the information. Long-term memory is a relatively permanent and unlimited type of memory. Working memory is a kind of "mental workbench" where individuals manipulate and assemble information when they make decisions, solve problems, and comprehend written and spoken language. Many contemporary psychologists prefer the term working memory over short-term memory. Working memory is linked to children's reading comprehension and problem solving. People construct and reconstruct their memories. Schema theory states that people mold memories to fit the information that already exists in their minds. Fuzzy trace theory states that memory is best understood by considering two types of memory representation: (1) verbatim memory trace and (2) fuzzy trace, or gist. In this theory, older children's better memory is attributed to the fuzzy traces created by extracting the gist of information. Children's ability to remember new information about a subject depends extensively on what they already know about it. The contribution of content knowledge is especially relevant in the memory of experts. Experts have a number of characteristics that can explain why they solve problems better than novices do.

Infancy

- Infants as young as 2 to 3 months of age display implicit memory, which is memory without conscious recollection as in memory of perceptual-motor skills. However, many experts stress that explicit memory, which is the conscious memory of facts and experiences, does not emerge until the second half of the first year of life. Older children and adults remember little if anything from the first three years of their lives.

Childhood

- Young children can remember a great deal of information if they are given appropriate cues and prompts. One method of assessing short-term memory is with a memory-span task, on which there are substantial developmental changes through the childhood years. Children's memory improves in the elementary school years as they begin to use gist more, acquire more content knowledge and expertise, develop large memory spans, and use more effective strategies. Organization, elaboration, and imagery are important memory strategies. A current interest focuses on how accurate children's long-term memories are and the implications of this accuracy for children as eyewitnesses.

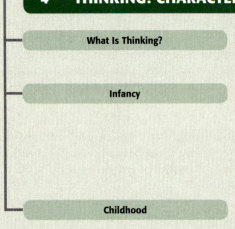

4   THINKING: CHARACTERIZE THINKING AND ITS DEVELOPMENTAL CHANGES

What Is Thinking?

- Thinking involves manipulating and transforming information in memory. We can think about the past, reality, and fantasy. Thinking helps us reason, reflect, evaluate, problem solve, and make decisions.

Infancy

- Studies of thinking in infancy focus on concept formation and categorization. Concepts are categories that group objects, events, and characteristics on the basis of common properties. Infants form concepts early in their development, with perceptual categorization appearing as early as 3 months of age. Mandler argues that it is not until about 7 to 9 months of age that infants form conceptual categories. Infants' first concepts are broad. Over the first two years of life, these broad concepts gradually become more differentiated.

Childhood

- Critical thinking involves thinking reflectively and productively, and evaluating the evidence. A lack of emphasis on critical thinking in schools is a special concern. Children and scientists think alike in some ways, but not alike in others. Three important aspects of solving problems involve using strategies, using rules, and using analogies. Even young children can use analogies to solve problems in some circumstances.

5   METACOGNITION: DEFINE METACOGNITION AND SUMMARIZE ITS DEVELOPMENTAL CHANGES

What Is Metacognition?

- Metacognition is cognition about cognition, or knowing about knowing.

The Child's Theory of Mind

- Theory of mind refers to a child's awareness of his or her own mental processes and the mental processes of others. Young children are curious about the human mind, and this has been studied under the topic of theory of mind. A number of developmental changes characterize children's theory of mind—for example, by 5 years of age most children realize that people can have false beliefs—beliefs that are untrue. Individual variations also are involved in theory mind. For example, autistic children have difficulty in developing a theory of mind.

Metacognition in Childhood

- Metamemory improves in middle and late childhood. As they progress through the elementary school years, children make more realistic judgments about their memory skills and increasingly understand the importance of memory cues.

KEY TERMS

information-processing approach 213
encoding 215
automaticity 215
strategy construction 215
metacognition 215
attention 216

selective attention 216
divided attention 216
sustained attention 217
executive attention 217
joint attention 217
memory 220
short-term memory 220

long-term memory 220
working memory 220
schema theory 221
schemas 221
fuzzy trace theory 221
implicit memory 223
explicit memory 223

thinking 228
critical thinking 229
reciprocal teaching 230
metamemory 236
theory of mind 236

KEY PEOPLE

Robert Siegler 214
Mary Rothbart and Maria Gartstein 218
Alan Baddeley 220

Charles Brainerd and Valerie Reyna 221
Carolyn Rovee-Collier 223
Jean Mandler 228

Jacqueline and Martin Brooks 229
Anne Brown and Joe Campione 230

Judy DeLoache 234
Michael Pressley 235

E-LEARNING TOOLS

To help you master the material in this chapter, you'll find a number of valuable study tools at the Online Learning Center for *Child Development,* twelfth edition (**www.mhhe.com/santrockcd12**).

Taking It to the Net

Research the answers to these questions:

1. Six-year-old Matthew is in the habit of asking his parents to repeat every comment or question. They know he doesn't have a hearing problem—they think he just doesn't pay attention and listen. How can they teach Matthew to pay attention and listen?

2. Fourteen-year-old Nancy, who lives with her grandparents, already has a history of sexual abuse, acting-out, substance abuse, and arrests for petty crimes. Her grandmother knows that Nancy's parents physically and sexually abused Nancy before she came to live with her at the age of 5. Might Nancy recall or otherwise be affected by those early traumatic experiences?

3. Bill Harris, grandfather to fourth-grader Kevin and sixth-grader Jocelyn, is looking for a volunteer opportunity at the children's school. A retired chemical engineer, Bill would like to help the school beef up its science education program. How could he help?

Health and Well-Being, Parenting, and Education Exercises

Build your decision-making skills by trying your hand at the health and well-being, parenting, and education exercises.

Video Clips

The Online Learning Center includes the following videos for this chapter:

- *Memory Ability at Age 4*
  Here a 4-year-old girl is presented with a sequence of numbers and asked to repeat them back. She recalls the numbers successfully and then smiles at her accomplishment.

- *Memory Ability at Age 7*
  A boy is presented with five numbers which are then removed from his view. He recalls all five numbers but is slightly off in sequence. He states "2-6-1-4-5." Same numbers, but in a different pattern.

- *Children's Eyewitness Testimony*
  Stephen Ceci, Cornell University, describes his research on children's eyewitness testimony.

8

As many people, as many minds, each in his own way.

—TERENCE
Roman Playwright, 2nd Century B.C.

LEARNING GOALS

- Explain the concept of intelligence.

- Discuss the development of intelligence.

- Describe the characteristics of mental retardation, giftedness, and creativity.

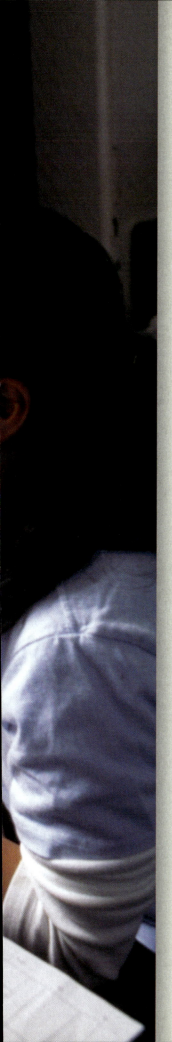

INTELLIGENCE

CHAPTER OUTLINE

Images of Child Development
The Story of Shiffy Landa

Shiffy Landa, a first-grade teacher at H. F. Epstein Hebrew Academy in St. Louis, Missouri, uses the multiple-intelligences approach of Howard Gardner (1983, 1993) in her classroom. Gardner argues that there is not just one general type of intelligence but at least eight specific types.

Landa (2000, pp. 6–8) believes that the multiple-intelligences approach is the best way to reach children because they have many different kinds of abilities. In Landa's words,

> My role as a teacher is quite different from the way it was just a few years ago. No longer do I stand in front of the room and lecture to my students. I consider my role to be one of a facilitator rather than a frontal teacher. The desks in my room are not all neatly lined up in straight rows . . . students are busily working in centers in cooperative learning groups, which gives them the opportunity to develop their interpersonal intelligences.

Students use their "body-kinesthetic intelligence to form the shapes of the letters as they learn to write. . . . They also use this intelligence to move the sounds of the vowels that they are learning, blending them together with letters, as they begin to read."

Landa believes that "intrapersonal intelligence is an intelligence that often is neglected in the traditional classroom." In her classroom, students "complete their own evaluation sheets after they have concluded their work at the centers. They evaluate their work and create their own portfolios," in which they keep their work so they can see their progress.

As she was implementing the multiple-intelligences approach in her classroom, Landa recognized that she needed to educate parents about it. She created "a parent education class called The Parent-Teacher Connection," which meets periodically to view videos, talk about multiple intelligences, and discuss how they are being introduced in the classroom. She also sends a weekly newsletter to parents, informing them about the week's multiple-intelligences activities and students' progress.

PREVIEW

Shiffy Landa's classroom techniques build on Howard Gardner's multiple-intelligence theory, one of theories of intelligence that we will explore in this chapter. You will see that there is spirited debate about whether people have a general intelligence or a number of specific intelligences. The concept of intelligence also has generated other controversies, including whether intelligence is more strongly influenced by heredity or by environment, whether there is cultural bias in intelligence testing, and whether intelligence tests are misused. We will explore these controversies in this chapter, as well as these topics: the development of intelligence from infancy through adolescence and the extremes of intelligence and creativity.

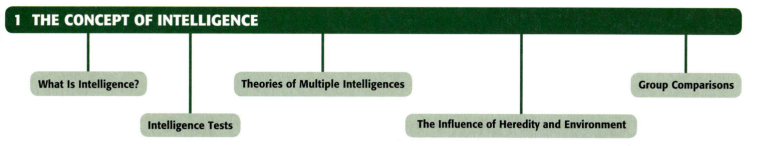

1 THE CONCEPT OF INTELLIGENCE

- What Is Intelligence?
- Intelligence Tests
- Theories of Multiple Intelligences
- The Influence of Heredity and Environment
- Group Comparisons

Intelligence is one of our most prized attributes. However, even the most intelligent people do not agree on how to define it and how to measure it.

What Is Intelligence?

What does the term *intelligence* mean to psychologists? Some experts describe intelligence as the ability to solve problems. Others describe it as the capacity to adapt and learn from experience. Still others argue that intelligence includes characteristics such as creativity and interpersonal skills.

The problem with intelligence is that, unlike height, weight, and age, intelligence cannot be directly measured. We can't peel back a person's scalp and see how much intelligence he or she has. We can evaluate intelligence only *indirectly* by studying and comparing the intelligent acts that people perform.

The primary components of intelligence are similar to the cognitive processes of memory and thinking that we discussed in Chapter 7. The differences in how these cognitive processes are described, and how we will discuss intelligence, lie in the concepts of individual differences and assessment. *Individual differences* are the stable, consistent ways in which people are different from one another. Individual differences in intelligence generally have been measured by intelligence tests designed to tell us whether a person can reason better than others who have taken the test.

We will use as our definition of **intelligence** the ability to solve problems and to adapt and learn from experiences. But even this broad definition doesn't satisfy everyone. As you will see shortly, Howard Gardner proposes that musical skills should be considered part of intelligence. Also, a definition of intelligence based on a theory such as Vygotsky's, which we discussed in Chapter 6, would have to include the ability to use the tools of the culture with help from more-skilled individuals. Because intelligence is such an abstract, broad concept, it is not surprising that there are so many different ways to define it.

Intelligence Tests

Robert Sternberg (1997) had considerable childhood anxieties about intelligence tests. Because he got so stressed out about taking the tests, he did very poorly on them. Fortunately, a fourth-grade teacher worked with Robert and helped instill the confidence in him to overcome his anxieties. He not only began performing better on them, but when he was 13, he devised his own intelligence test and began using it to assess classmates—until the school principal found out and scolded him. Sternberg became so fascinated by intelligence that he made its study a lifelong pursuit, and later in this chapter we will discuss his theory of intelligence.

The two main intelligence tests that are administered to children on an individual basis today are the Stanford Binet test and the Wechsler scales. As you will see next, an early version of the Binet was the first intelligence test that was devised.

The Binet Tests In 1904, the French Ministry of Education asked psychologist Alfred Binet to devise a method of identifying children who were unable to learn in

Alfred Binet constructed the first intelligence test after being asked to create a measure to determine which children could benefit from instruction in France's schools and which could not.

intelligence The ability to solve problems and to adapt to and learn from experiences.

FIGURE 8.1 **The Normal Curve and Standard-Binet IQ Scores.** The distribution of IQ scores approximates a normal curve. Most of the population falls in the middle range of scores. Notice that extremely high and extremely low scores are very rare. Slightly more than two-thirds of the scores fall between 84 and 116. Only about 1 in 50 individuals has an IQ of more than 132, and only about 1 in 50 individuals has an IQ of less than 68.

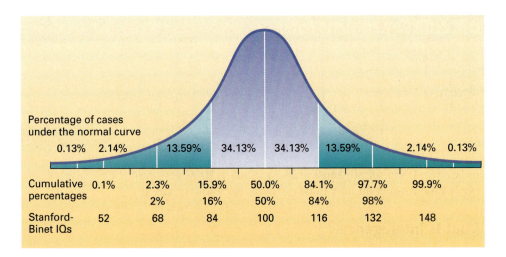

school. School officials wanted to reduce crowding by placing in special schools students who did not benefit from regular classroom teaching. Binet and his student Theophile Simon developed an intelligence test to meet this request. The test is called the 1905 Scale. It consisted of 30 questions, ranging from the ability to touch one's ear to the abilities to draw designs from memory and define abstract concepts.

Binet developed the concept of **mental age (MA)**, an individual's level of mental development relative to others. In 1912, William Stern created the concept of **intelligence quotient (IQ)**, which refers to a person's mental age divided by chronological age (CA), multiplied by 100. That is, MA/CA × 100.

If mental age is the same as chronological age, then the person's IQ is 100. If mental age is above chronological age, then IQ is more than 100. For example, a 6-year-old with a mental age of 8 would have an IQ of 133. If mental age is below chronological age, then IQ is less than 100. For example, a 6-year-old with a mental age of 5 would have an IQ of 83.

The Binet test has been revised many times to incorporate advances in the understanding of intelligence and intelligence testing. These revisions are called the *Stanford-Binet tests* (because the revisions were made at Stanford University). By administering the test to large numbers of people of different ages from different backgrounds, researchers have found that scores on a Stanford-Binet test approximate a normal distribution (see Figure 8.1). A **normal distribution** is symmetrical, with a majority of the scores falling in the middle of the possible range of scores and few scores appearing toward the extremes of the range.

The current Stanford-Binet test is administered individually to people aged 2 through adult. It includes a variety of items, some of which require verbal responses, others nonverbal responses. For example, items that reflect a typical 6-year-old's level of performance on the test include the verbal ability to define at least six words, such as *orange* and *envelope*, as well as the nonverbal ability to trace a path through a maze. Items that reflect an average adult's level of performance include defining such words as *disproportionate* and *regard*, explaining a proverb, and comparing idleness and laziness.

The fourth edition of the Stanford-Binet was published in 1985. One important addition to this version was the analysis of the individual's responses in terms of four functions: verbal reasoning, quantitative reasoning, abstract visual reasoning, and short-term memory. A general composite score is still obtained to reflect overall intelligence. The Stanford-Binet continues to be one of the most widely used tests to assess students' intelligence (Aiken, 2006).

The Wechsler Scales   Another set of tests widely used to assess students' intelligence is called the *Wechsler scales,* developed by psychologist David Wechsler. They

mental age (MA) An individual's level of mental development relative to others.

intelligence quotient (IQ) An individual's mental age divided by chronological age multiplied by 100; devised in 1912 by William Stern.

normal distribution A symmetrical distribution with a majority of the cases falling in the middle of the possible range of scores and few scores appearing toward the extremes of the range.

include the Wechsler Preschool and Primary Scale of Intelligence–Third Edition (WPPSI-III) to test children from 2 years 6 months to 7 years 3 months of age; the Wechsler Intelligence Scale for Children–Fourth Edition (WISC-IV) for children and adolescents 6 to 16 years of age; and the Wechsler Adult Intelligence Scale–Third Edition (WAIS-III).

The Wechsler scales not only provide an overall IQ score and scores on a number of subtests but also yield several composite indexes (for example, the Verbal Comprehension Index, the Working Memory Index, and the Processing Speed Index). The subtest and composite scores allows the examiner to quickly determine the areas in which the child is strong or weak. Three of the Wechsler subscales are shown in Figure 8.2.

Intelligence tests such as the Stanford-Binet and Wechsler are given on an individual basis. A psychologist approaches an individual assessment of intelligence as a structured interaction between the examiner and the child. This provides the psychologist with an opportunity to sample the child's behavior. During the testing, the examiner observes the ease with which rapport is established, the child's enthusiasm and interest, whether anxiety interferes with the child's performance, and the child's degree of tolerance for frustration.

The Use and Misuse of Intelligence Tests Psychological tests are tools. Like all tools, their effectiveness depends on the knowledge, skill, and integrity of the user. A hammer can be used to build a beautiful kitchen cabinet, or it can be used as a weapon of assault. Like a hammer, psychological tests can be used for positive purposes, or they can be abused.

Intelligence tests have real-world applications as predictors of school and job success (Brody, 2007). For example, scores on tests of general intelligence are substantially correlated with school grades and achievement test performance, both at the time of the test and years later (Brody, 2007). IQ in the sixth grade correlates about .60 with the number of years of education the individual will eventually obtain (Jencks, 1979). Intelligence tests also are moderately correlated with work performance (Lubinski, 2000).

Despite the links between IQ and academic achievement and occupational success, it is important to keep in mind that many other factors contribute to success in school and work. These include the motivation to succeed, physical and mental health, and social skills (Sternberg, 2006).

The single number provided by many IQ tests can easily lead to false expectations about an individual (Rosnow & Rosenthal, 1996). Sweeping generalizations are too often made on the basis of an IQ score. For example, imagine you are a teacher in the teacher's lounge the day after a new school year has just started. You mention a student—Johnny Jones—and a fellow teacher remarks that she had Johnny in class last year; she comments that he was a real dunce and points out that his IQ is 78. You cannot help but remember this information, and it might lead to thoughts that Johnny Jones is not very bright, so it is useless to spend much time teaching him. In this way, IQ scores are misused and can become self-fulfilling prophecies (Weinstein, 2004).

Even though they have limitations, tests of intelligence are among psychology's most widely used tools. To be effective, they should be used in conjunction with other information about an individual. For example, an intelligence test alone should not determine whether a child is placed in a special education or gifted class. The child's developmental history, medical background, performance in school, social competencies, and family experiences should be taken into account, too.

Despite their limitations, when used judiciously, intelligence tests provide valuable information. There are not many alternatives to these tests. Subjective judgments about individuals simply reintroduce the bias that the tests were designed to eliminate.

Verbal Subscales

Similarities

A child must think logically and abstractly to answer a number of questions about how things might be similar.

Example: "In what way are a lion and a tiger alike?"

Comprehension

This subscale is designed to measure an individual's judgment and common sense.

Example: "What is the advantage of keeping money in a bank?"

Nonverbal Subscales

Block Design

A child must assemble a set of multicolored blocks to match designs that the examiner shows. Visual-motor coordination, perceptual organization, and the ability to visualize spatially are assessed.

Example: "Use the four blocks on the left to make the pattern on the right."

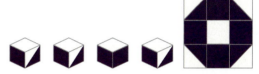

FIGURE 8.2 Sample Subscales of the Wechsler Intelligence Scale for Children–Fourth Edition (WISC-IV). Simulated items similar to those in the Wechsler Intelligence Scale for Children–Fourth Edition. The Wechsler includes 11 subscales, 6 verbal and 5 nonverbal. Three of the subscales are shown here. *Wechsler Intelligence Scale for Children.* Copyright © 2003 by NCS Pearson, Inc. Reproduced with permission. All rights reserved. *"Wechsler Intelligence Scale for Children," "WISC," and Wechsler"* are trademarks, in the US and/or other countries, of Pearson Education, Inc. or its affiliates.

"How are her scores?"
The New Yorker Collection 1987
Edward Koren from cartoonbank.com.
All Rights Reserved.

Robert J. Sternberg, who developed the triarchic theory of intelligence.

"You're wise, but you lack tree smarts."
© The New Yorker Collection, 1988, by Donald Reilly from cartoonbank.com. All Rights Reserved.

triarchic theory of intelligence Sternberg's theory that intelligence comes in three forms: analytical, creative, and practical.

Theories of Multiple Intelligences

Is it more appropriate to think of a child's intelligence as a general ability or as a number of specific abilities? Psychologists have thought about this question since early in the twentieth century and continue to debate the issue.

Sternberg's Triarchic Theory   According to Robert J. Sternberg's (1986, 2004, 2006, 2007a, b; 2008a, b; 2009a, b, e) **triarchic theory of intelligence**, intelligence comes in three forms: analytical, creative, and practical. Analytical intelligence involves the ability to analyze, judge, evaluate, compare, and contrast. Creative intelligence consists of the ability to create, design, invent, originate, and imagine. Practical intelligence focuses on the ability to use, apply, implement, and put into practice. To understand what analytical, creative, and practical intelligence mean, let's look at examples of people who reflect these three types of intelligence:

- Consider Latisha, who scores high on traditional intelligence tests such as the Stanford-Binet and is a star analytical thinker. Latisha's *analytical intelligence* approximates what has traditionally been called intelligence and what is commonly assessed by intelligence tests. In Sternberg's view, analytical intelligence consists of several components: the ability to acquire or store information; to retain or retrieve information; to transfer information; to plan, make decisions, and solve problems; and to translate thoughts into performance.

- Todd does not have the best test scores but has an insightful and creative mind. Sternberg calls the type of thinking at which Todd excels *creative intelligence*. According to Sternberg, creative people have the ability to solve new problems quickly, but they also learn how to solve familiar problems in an automatic way so their minds are free to handle other problems that require insight and creativity.

- Finally, consider Emanuel, whose scores on traditional IQ tests are low but who quickly grasps real-life problems. He easily picks up knowledge about how the world works. Emanuel's "street smarts" and practical know-how are what Sternberg calls *practical intelligence*. Practical intelligence includes the ability to get out of trouble and a knack for getting along with people. Sternberg describes practical intelligence as all of the important information about getting along in the world that you are not taught in school.

Sternberg (2002; Sternberg & Grigorenko, 2007; Sternberg, Jarvin, & Grigorenko, 2008; Sternberg, Kaufman, & Grigorenko, 2008; Sternberg & others, 2007) says that students with different triarchic patterns look different in school. Students with high analytic ability tend to be favored in conventional schools. They often do well in classes in which the teacher lectures and gives objective tests. These students typically get good grades, do well on traditional IQ tests and the SAT, and later gain admission to competitive colleges.

Students high in creative intelligence often are not in the top rung of their class. Creatively intelligent students might not conform to teachers' expectations about how assignments should be done. They give unique answers, for which they might get reprimanded or marked down.

Like students high in creative intelligence, students who are practically intelligent often do not relate well to the demands of school. However, these students frequently do well outside the classroom's walls. Their social skills and common sense may allow them to become successful managers or entrepreneurs, despite undistinguished school records.

Sternberg (2004, 2008a, b; 2009a) stresses that few tasks are purely analytic, creative, or practical. Most tasks require some combination of these skills. For example, when students write a book report, they might analyze the book's main themes, generate new ideas about how the book could have been written better, and think about how the book's themes can be applied to people's lives. Sternberg argues that it is important for classroom instruction to give students opportunities to learn through all three types of intelligence.

Sternberg (1993; Sternberg & others, 2001a) developed the Sternberg Triarchic Abilities Test (STAT) to assess analytical, creative, and practical intelligence. The three kinds of abilities are examined through verbal items and essays, quantitative items, and drawings with multiple-choice items. The goal is to obtain a more complete assessment of intelligence than is possible with a conventional test.

The analytical section of STAT is much like a conventional test, with individuals required to provide the meanings of words, complete number series, and complete matrices. The creative and practical sections are different from conventional tests. For example, in the creative section, individuals write an essay on designing an ideal school. The practical section has individuals solve practical everyday problems such as planning routes and purchasing tickets to an event.

Recently, Sternberg and the Rainbow Project Collaborators (2006) modified the STAT in an attempt to develop an assessment to augment the SAT in predicting college achievement. The results indicated that the Rainbow assessment that reflects Sternberg's triarchic intelligence concept enhanced the prediction of college students' grade-point average beyond the SAT.

Sternberg (1998, 2008c, 2009b) argues that wisdom is linked to both practical and academic intelligence. In his view, academic intelligence is a necessary but in many cases insufficient requirement for wisdom. Practical knowledge about the realities of life also is needed for wisdom. For Sternberg, balance between self-interest, the interests of others, and contexts produces a common good. Thus, wise individuals don't just look out for themselves—they also need to consider others' needs and perspectives, as well as the particular context involved. Sternberg assesses wisdom by presenting problems that require solutions which highlight various intrapersonal, interpersonal, and contextual interests. He also emphasizes that such aspects of wisdom should be taught in schools (Sternberg, 2008c, 2009b; Sternberg, Jarvin, & Reznitskaya, 2009).

Gardner's Eight Frames of Mind   As we indicated in the *Images of Child Development* introduction to this chapter, Howard Gardner (1983, 1993, 2002) says there are many specific types of intelligence, or frames of mind. They are described here along with examples of the occupations in which they are reflected as strengths (Campbell, Campbell, & Dickinson, 2004):

- *Verbal skills:* The ability to think in words and to use language to express meaning
  Occupations: Authors, journalists, speakers
- *Mathematical skills:* The ability to carry out mathematical operations
  Occupations: Scientists, engineers, accountants
- *Spatial skills:* The ability to think three-dimensionally
  Occupations: Architects, artists, sailors
- *Bodily-kinesthetic skills:* The ability to manipulate objects and be physically adept
  Occupations: Surgeons, craftspeople, dancers, athletes
- *Musical skills:* A sensitivity to pitch, melody, rhythm, and tone
  Occupations: Composers, musicians, and music therapists
- *Intrapersonal skills:* The ability to understand oneself and effectively direct one's life
  Occupations: Theologians, psychologists
- *Interpersonal skills:* The ability to understand and effectively interact with others
  Occupations: Successful teachers, mental health professionals
- *Naturalist skills:* The ability to observe patterns in nature and understand natural and human-made systems
  Occupations: Farmers, botanists, ecologists, landscapers

Howard Gardner, here working with a young child, developed the view that intelligence comes in the forms of these eight kinds of skills: verbal, mathematical, spatial, bodily-kinesthetic, musical, intrapersonal, interpersonal, and naturalist.

Children in the Key School form "pods," in which they pursue activities of special interest to them. Every day, each child can choose from activities that draw on Gardner's eight frames of mind. The school has pods that range from gardening to architecture to gliding to dancing.

Gardner argues that each form of intelligence can be destroyed by a different pattern of brain damage, that each involves unique cognitive skills, and that each shows up in unique ways in both the gifted and idiot savants (individuals who have mental retardation but have an exceptional talent in a particular domain, such as drawing, music, or numerical computation).

Let's look at a school that used Gardner's multiple intelligences as a foundation of its instruction. The Key School, a K–6 elementary school in Indianapolis, immerses students in activities that involve a range of skills that closely correlate with Gardner's eight frames of mind (Goleman, Kaufman, & Ray, 1993). Each day every student is exposed to materials designed to stimulate a range of human abilities, including art, music, language skills, math skills, and physical games. In addition, students devote attention to understanding themselves and others.

The Key School's goal is to allow students to discover their natural curiosity and talent, then let them explore these domains. Gardner underscores that if teachers give students the opportunities to use their bodies, imaginations, and different senses, almost every student finds that he or she is good at something. Even students who are not outstanding in any single area will still find that they have relative strengths.

Emotional Intelligence   Both Gardner's and Sternberg's theories include one or more categories related to the ability to understand one's self and others and to get along in the world. In Gardner's theory, the categories are interpersonal intelligence and intrapersonal intelligence; in Sternberg's theory, practical intelligence. Other theorists who emphasize interpersonal, intrapersonal, and practical aspects of intelligence focus on what is called *emotional intelligence,* which was popularized by Daniel Goleman (1995) in his book *Emotional Intelligence.* There is increasing interest in emotional intelligence (Alkhadher, 2007; Kilgore & Yurgelun-Todd, 2007; Mestre & others, 2007).

The concept of emotional intelligence was initially developed by Peter Salovey and John Mayer (1990). They conceptualize **emotional intelligence** as the ability to perceive and express emotion accurately and adaptively (such as taking the perspective of others), to understand emotion and emotional knowledge (such as understanding the roles that emotions play in friendship and other relationships), to use feelings to facilitate thought (such as being in a positive mood, which is linked to creative thinking), and to manage emotions in oneself and others (such as being able to control one's anger).

The Mayer-Salovey-Caruso Emotional Intelligence Test (MSCEIT) measures the four aspects of emotional intelligence just described: perceiving emotions, understanding emotions, facilitating thought, and managing emotions (Mayer, Salovey, & Caruso, 2002, 2004, 2007). The test consists of 141 items, can be given to individuals 17 years of age and older, and takes about 30 to 45 minutes to administer. In one recent study, the MSCEIT predicted high school students' final grades in their courses (Gil-Olarte Marquez, Palomera Martin, & Brackett, 2007).

There continues to be considerable interest in the concept of emotional intelligence (Alkhadher, 2007; Cox & Nelson, 2008; Kilgore & Yurgelun-Todd, 2007; Mestre & others, 2007; Rode & others, 2008). Critics argue that emotional intelligence broadens the concept of intelligence too far and has not been adequately assessed and researched (Matthews, Zeidner, & Roberts, 2006).

Sternberg	Gardner	Salovey/Mayer
Analytical	Verbal Mathematical	
Creative	Spatial Movement Musical	
Practical	Interpersonal Intrapersonal	Emotional
	Naturalistic	

FIGURE 8.3   Comparing Sternberg's, Gardner's, and Salovey/Mayer's Intelligences

emotional intelligence The ability to perceive and express emotion accurately and adaptively, to understand emotion and emotional knowledge, to use feelings to facilitate thought, and to manage emotions in oneself and others.

Do Children Have One Intelligence or Many Intelligences?   Figure 8.3 provides a comparison of Gardner's, Sternberg's, and Salovey/Mayer's views. Notice that Gardner includes a number of types of intelligence not addressed by the other views, and that Sternberg is unique in emphasizing creative intelligence. These theories of multiple intelligence have much to offer. They have stimulated us to think more broadly about what makes up people's intelligence and competence (Moran & Gardner, 2006). And they have motivated educators to develop programs that instruct students in different domains (Winner, 2006).

Theories of multiple intelligences have their critics (Jensen, 2008). They conclude that the research base to support these theories has not yet developed. In particular, some argue that Gardner's classification seems arbitrary. For example, if musical skills represent a type of intelligence, why don't we also refer to chess intelligence, prize-fighter intelligence, and so on?

A number of psychologists still support the concept *of g* (general intelligence) (Jensen, 2008; Johnson, te Nijenhuis, & Bouchard, 2008; Reeve & Lam, 2007). For example, one expert on intelligence, Nathan Brody (2007), argues that people who excel at one type of intellectual task are likely to excel at other intellectual tasks. Thus, individuals who do well at memorizing lists of digits are also likely to be good at solving verbal problems and spatial layout problems. This general intelligence includes abstract reasoning or thinking, the capacity to acquire knowledge, and problem-solving ability (Brody, 2007; Carroll, 1993).

Advocates of the concept of general intelligence point to its success in predicting school and job success (Deary & others, 2007; Watkins, Lee, & Canivez, 2007). For example, scores on tests of general intelligence are substantially correlated with school grades and achievement test performance, both at the time of the test and years later (Brody, 2007; Colomb & Flores-Mendoza, 2007; Strenze, 2007).

As we saw earlier, intelligence tests are moderately correlated with job performance (Lubinski, 2000). Individuals with higher scores on tests designed to measure general intelligence tend to get higher-paying, more prestigious jobs (Strenze, 2007; Zagorsky, 2007). However, general IQ tests predict only about one-fourth of the variation in job success, with most variation being attributable to other factors such as motivation and education (Wagner & Sternberg, 1986). Further, the correlations between IQ and achievement decrease the longer people work at a job, presumably because as they gain more job experience they perform better (Hunt, 1995).

Some experts who argue for the existence of general intelligence conclude that individuals also have specific intellectual abilities (Brody, 2007; Chiappe & MacDonald, 2005). In sum, controversy still characterizes whether it is more accurate to conceptualize intelligence as a general ability, specific abilities, or both (Brody, 2007; Horn, 2007; Sternberg, 2007a, b; 2008a, b). Sternberg (2007a, 2008a, b, 2009a) actually accepts that there is a *g* for the kinds of analytical tasks that traditional IQ tests assess but thinks that the range of tasks those tests measure is far too narrow.

The Influence of Heredity and Environment

We have seen that intelligence is a slippery concept with competing definitions, tests, and theories. It is not surprising, therefore, that attempts to understand the concept of intelligence are filled with controversy. One of the most controversial areas in the study of intelligence centers on the extent to which intelligence is influenced by genetics and the extent to which it is influenced by environment (Davis, Arden, & Plomin, 2008; Sternberg 2009a). In Chapter 2, we indicated how difficult it is to tease apart these influences, but that has not kept psychologists from trying to unravel them.

Genetic Influences   To what degree do our genes make us smart? A research review found that the difference in the average correlations for identical and fraternal twins was not very high, only .15, (Grigorenko, 2000) (see Figure 8.4).

Adoption studies are also used in attempts to analyze the relative importance of heredity in intelligence (Plomin, DeFries, & Fulker, 2007). In most *adoption studies,* researchers determine whether the behavior of adopted children is more like that of their biological parents or their adoptive parents. In two studies, the educational levels attained by biological parents were better predictors of children's IQ scores than were the IQs of

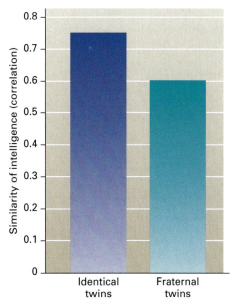

FIGURE 8.4   Correlation Between Intelligence Test Scores and Twin Status. The graph represents a summary of research findings that have compared the intelligence test scores of identical and fraternal twins. An approximate .15 difference has been found with a higher correlation for identical twins (.75) and a lower correlation for fraternal twins (.60).

the children's adoptive parents (Petrill & Deater-Deckard, 2004; Scarr & Weinberg, 1983). But studies of adoption also document the influence of environments. For example, moving children into an adoptive family with a better environment than the child had in the past increased the children's IQs by an average of 12 points (Lucurto, 1990).

How strong is the effect of heredity on intelligence? The concept of heritability attempts to tease apart the effects of heredity and environment in a population. **Heritability** is the fraction of the variance within a population that is attributed to genetics. The heritability index is computed using correlational techniques. Thus, the highest degree of heritabilty is 1.00 and correlations of .70 and above suggest a strong genetic influence. A committee of respected researchers convened by the American Psychological Association concluded that by late adolescence, the heritability of intelligence is about .75, which reflects a strong genetic influence (Neisser & others, 1996).

A key point to keep in mind about heritability is that it refers to a specific group (population), *not* to individuals (Okagaki, 2000). Researchers use the concept of heritability to try to describe why people differ. Heritability says nothing about why a single individual, like yourself, has a certain intelligence. Nor does heritability say anything about differences *between* groups.

Most research on heredity and environment does not include environments that differ radically. Thus, it is not surprising that many genetic studies show environment to be a fairly weak influence on intelligence (Fraser, 1995).

Interestingly, researchers have revealed that the heritability of intelligence increases from as low as .45 in infancy to as high as .80 in late adulthood (Petrill, 2003; Plomin & others, 1997). Why might hereditary influences on intelligence increase with age? Possibly as we grow older, our interactions with the environment are shaped less by the influence of others and the environment on us and more by our ability to choose our environments to allow the expression of genetic tendencies (Neisser & others, 1996). For example, sometimes children's parents push them into environments that are not compatible with their genetic inheritance (wanting to be a doctor or an engineer, for example), but as adults these individuals may select their own career environments.

The heritability index has several flaws. It is only as good as the data that are entered into its analysis and the interpretations made from it. The data are virtually all from traditional IQ tests, which some experts believe are not always the best indicator of intelligence (Gardner, 2002; Sternberg, 2004). Also, the heritability index assumes that we can treat genetic and environmental influences as factors that can be separated, with each part contributing a distinct amount of influence. As we discussed in Chapter 2, genes and the environment always work together. Genes always exist in an environment, and the environment shapes their activity.

Environmental Influences   Most experts today agree that the environment also plays an important role in intelligence (Campbell, 2007; Sternberg, Kaufman, & Grigorenko, 2008). This means that improving children's environments can raise their intelligence (Ramey, Ramey, & Lanzi, 2006; Tong & others, 2007). One argument for the importance of environment in intelligence involves the increasing scores on IQ tests around the world. Scores on these tests have been increasing so fast that a high percentage of people regarded as having average intelligence in the early 1900s would be considered below average in intelligence today (Flynn, 1999, 2007a, b) (see Figure 8.5). If a representative sample of today's children took the Stanford-Binet test used in 1932, about one-fourth would be defined as very superior, a label usually accorded to fewer than 3 percent of the population. Because the increase has taken place in a relatively short period of time, it can't be due to heredity—but, rather, might result from such environmental factors as the explosion in information people are exposed to and the much higher percentage of the population receiving education. This worldwide increase in intelligence test scores over a short time frame is called the *Flynn effect*, after the researcher who discovered it—James Flynn (1999, 2007a, b).

Studies of schooling also reveal effects on intelligence (Ceci & Gilstrap, 2000; Gustafsson, 2007). The biggest effects occurred when large groups of children were deprived of

heritability The fraction of the variance in a population that is attributed to genetics.

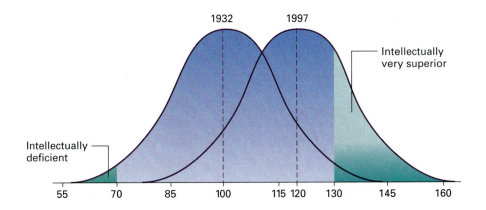

FIGURE 8.5 **The Increase in IQ Scores from 1932 to 1997.** As measured by the Stanford-Binet intelligence test, American children seem to be getting smarter. Scores of a group tested in 1932 fell along a bell-shaped curve with half below 100 and half above. Studies show that if children took that same test today, half would score above 120 on the 1932 scale. Very few of them would score in the "intellectually deficient" end, on the left side, and about one-fourth would rank in the "very superior" range.

formal education for an extended period, resulting in lower intelligence. In one study, the intellectual functioning of ethnic Indian children in South Africa, whose schooling was delayed by four years because of the unavailability of teachers, was investigated (Ramphal, 1962). Compared with children in nearby villages who had teachers, the Indian children whose entry into school was delayed by four years experienced a drop of 5 IQ points for each year of delay.

One analysis of studies on schooling and intelligence concluded that schooling and intelligence influence each other (Ceci & Williams, 1997). For example, individuals who finish high school are more intelligent than those who drop out of school. This might be because brighter individuals stay in school longer, or because the environmental influence of schooling contributes to their intelligence.

Further, intelligence test scores tend to rise during the school year and decline during the summer months (Ceci & Gilstrap, 2000). Also, children whose birthdays just make the cutoff point for school entrance temporarily have higher intelligence scores than those born just slightly later, who are a year behind them in school (Ceci & Gilstrap, 2000).

As we indicated earlier, it is extremely difficult to tease apart the effects of nature or nurture. We still do not know what, if any, specific genes actually promote or restrict a general level of intelligence. If such genes exist, they certainly are found both in children whose families and environments appear to promote the development of children's abilities and in children whose families and environments do not appear to be as supportive. Regardless of one's genetic background, growing up "with all the advantages" does not guarantee high intelligence or success, especially if those advantages are taken for granted. Nor does the absence of such advantages guarantee low intelligence or failure, especially if the family and child can make the most of whatever opportunities are accessible to them.

Researchers increasingly are interested in manipulating the early environment of children who are at risk for impoverished intelligence (Campbell, 2007; Ramey, Ramey, & Lanzi, 2006; Sternberg, 2008b). The emphasis is on prevention rather than remediation. Many low-income parents have difficulty providing an intellectually stimulating environment for their children. Programs that educate parents to be more sensitive caregivers and better teachers, as well as support services such as quality child-care programs, can make a difference in a child's intellectual development.

A review of the research on early interventions concluded the following (Brooks-Gunn, 2003):

- High-quality center-based interventions are associated with increases in children's intelligence and school achievement.

- The interventions are most successful with poor children and children whose parents have little education.

- The positive benefits continue through adolescence but are not as strong as in early childhood or the beginning of elementary school.

Students in an elementary school in South Africa. *How might schooling influence the development of children's intelligence?*

• The programs that are continued into middle and late childhood have the best long-term results.

To read further about environmental influences on intelligence, see the *Research in Child Development* interlude.

Research in Child Development

THE ABECEDARIAN PROJECT

Each morning a young mother waited with her child for the bus that would take the child to school. The child was only 2 months old, and "school" was an experimental program at the University of North Carolina at Chapel Hill. There the child experienced a number of interventions designed to improve her intellectual development—everything from bright objects dangled in front of her eyes while she was a baby to language instruction and counting activities when she was a toddler (Wickelgren, 1999). The child's mother had an IQ of 40 and could not read signs or determine how much change she should receive from a cashier. Her grandmother had a similarly low IQ.

Today, at age 20, the child's IQ measures 80 points higher than her mother's did when the child was 2 months old. Not everyone agrees that IQ can be affected this extensively, but environment can make a substantial difference in a child's intelligence. As behavior geneticist Robert Plomin (1999) says, even something that is heritable (like intelligence) may be malleable to some degree through interventions.

The child we just described was part of the Abecedarian Intervention program at the University of North Carolina at Chapel Hill, conducted by Craig Ramey and his associates (Ramey & Campbell, 1984; Ramey & Ramey, 1998; Ramey, Ramey, & Lanzi, 2006). They randomly assigned 111 young children from low-income, poorly educated families to either an intervention group, which received full-time, year-round child care along with medical and social work services, or a control group, which received medical and social benefits but no child care. The child-care program included gamelike learning activities aimed at improving language, motor, social, and cognitive skills.

The success of the program in improving IQ was evident by the time the children were 3 years of age. At that age, the experimental group showed normal IQs averaging 101, a 17-point advantage over the control group. Recent follow-up results suggest that the effects are long-lasting. More than a decade later at 15, children from the intervention group still maintained an IQ advantage of 5 points over the control-group children (97.7 to 92.6) (Campbell & others, 2001; Ramey, Ramey, & Lanzi, 2001). They also did better on standardized tests of reading and math and were less likely to be held back a year in school. Also, the greatest IQ gains were made by the children whose mothers had especially low IQs—below 70. At age 15, these children showed a 10-point IQ advantage over a group of children whose mothers' IQs were below 70 but did not experience the child-care intervention.

*T*he highest-risk children often benefit the most cognitively when they experience early interventions.

—CRAIG RAMEY
Contemporary Psychologist, Georgetown University

Group Comparisons

For decades, many controversies surrounding intelligence tests have grown from the tendency to compare one group with another. Many people keep asking whether their culture or ethnic group or gender is more intelligent than others.

Cross-Cultural Comparisons   Cultures vary in the way they describe what it means to be intelligent (Sternberg & Grigorenko, 2008a, b). People in Western cultures tend to view intelligence in terms of reasoning and thinking skills, whereas

The intelligence of the Latmul people of Papua New Guinea involves the ability to remember the names of many clans.

On the 680 Caroline Islands in the Pacific Ocean east of the Philippines, the intelligence of their inhabitants includes the ability to navigate by the stars. *Why might it be difficult to create a culture-fair intelligence test for the Latmul children, Caroline Islands children, and U.S. children?*

people in Eastern cultures see intelligence as a way for members of a community to successfully engage in social roles (Nisbett, 2003). One study found that Taiwanese-Chinese conceptions of intelligence emphasize understanding and relating to others, including when to show and when not to show one's intelligence (Yang & Sternberg, 1997).

Robert Serpell (1974, 1982, 2000) has studied concepts of intelligence in rural African communities since the 1970s. He has found that people in rural African communities, especially those in which Western schooling is not common, tend to blur the distinction between being intelligent and being socially competent. In rural Zambia, for example, the concept of intelligence involves being both clever and responsible. Elena Grigorenko and her colleagues (2001) have also studied the concept of intelligence among rural Africans. They found that people in the Luo culture of rural Kenya view intelligence as consisting of four domains: (1) academic intelligence; (2) social qualities such as respect, responsibility, and consideration; (3) practical thinking; and (4) comprehension. In another study in the same culture, children who scored highly on a test of knowledge about medicinal herbs—a measure of practical intelligence—tended to score poorly on tests of academic intelligence (Sternberg & others, 2001b). These results indicated that practical and academic intelligence can develop independently and may even conflict with each other. They also suggest that the values of a culture may influence the direction in which a child develops. In a cross-cultural context, then, intelligence depends a great deal on environment (Matsumoto & Juang, 2008; Shiraev & Levy, 2007).

Cultural Bias in Testing   Many of the early intelligence tests were culturally biased, favoring people who were from urban rather than rural environments, middle socioeconomic status rather than low socioeconomic status, and White rather than African American (Miller-Jones, 1989; Provenzo, 2002). For example, one question on an early test asked what you should do if you find a 3-year-old child in the street. The correct answer was "call the police." But children from inner-city families who perceive the police as adversaries are unlikely to choose this answer. Similarly, children from rural areas might not choose this answer if there is no police force nearby. Such questions clearly do not measure the knowledge necessary to adapt to one's environment or to be "intelligent" in an inner-city neighborhood or in rural America (Scarr, 1984). Also, members of minority groups who do not speak English or who speak nonstandard English are at a disadvantage in trying to understand questions framed in standard English (Gibbs & Huang, 1989).

The *Diversity in Child Development* interlude examines some of the ways intelligence testing can be culturally biased.

Diversity in Child Development

LARRY P.: INTELLIGENT, BUT NOT ON INTELLIGENCE TESTS

Larry P. is African American and poor. When he was 6 years old, he was placed in a class for the "educable mentally retarded" (EMR), which to school psychologists means that Larry learned much more slowly than average children. The primary reason Larry was placed in the EMR class was his very low score of 64 on an intelligence test.

Is there a possibility that the intelligence test Larry was given was culturally biased? Psychologists still debate this issue. A major class-action suit challenged the use of standardized IQ tests to place African American elementary school students in EMR classes. The initial lawsuit, filed on behalf of Larry P., claimed that the IQ test he took underestimated his true learning ability. The lawyers for Larry P. argued that IQ tests place too much emphasis on verbal skills and fail to account for the backgrounds of African American children. Therefore, it was argued, Larry was incorrectly labeled mentally retarded and might forever be saddled with that stigma.

As part of the lengthy court battle involving Larry P., six African American EMR students were independently retested by members of the Bay Association of Black Psychologists in California. The psychologists made sure they established good rapport with the students and made special efforts to overcome the students' defeatism and distraction. For example, items were reworded in terms more consistent with the children's social background, and recognition was given to nonstandard answers that showed a logical, intelligent approach to problems. This testing approach produced scores of 79 to 104—17 to 38 points higher than the scores the students received when initially tested by school psychologists. In every case, the retest scores were above the ceiling for placement in an EMR class.

What was the state's argument for using intelligence tests as one criterion for placing children in EMR classes? Testimony by intelligence-testing experts supported the *predictive validity* (using a measure, such as an intelligence test, to predict performance on another measure, such as grades in school) of IQ for different ethnic groups. In Larry's case, the judge ruled that IQ tests are biased and that their use discriminates against ethnic minorities. IQ tests cannot be used now in California to place children in EMR classes. The decision in favor of Larry P. was upheld by an appeals panel. However, in another court case, *Pace v. Hannon* in Illinois, a judge ruled that IQ tests are not culturally biased.

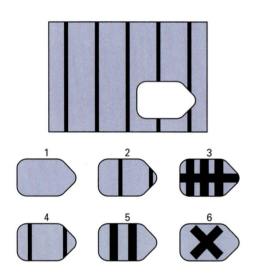

FIGURE 8.6 Sample Item from the Raven's Progressive Matrices Test. Individuals are presented with a matrix arrangement of symbols, such as the one at the top of this figure, and must then complete the matrix by selecting the appropriate missing symbol from a group of symbols, such as the ones at the bottom. Simulated items similar to those in *Raven's Progressive Matrices (Coloured, Sets A, AB, B)*. From *Raven's Progressive Matrices*, Item A5. Raven's. Copyright © 1998 by NCS Pearson, Inc. Reproduced by permission. All rights reserved.

culture-fair tests Intelligence tests that aim to avoid cultural bias.

Psychologists have developed **culture-fair tests**, which are intelligence tests that aim to avoid cultural bias. Two types of culture-fair tests have been developed. The first includes questions that are familiar to people from all socioeconomic and ethnic backgrounds. For example, a child might be asked how a bird and a dog are different, on the assumption that virtually all children are familiar with birds and dogs. The second type of culture-fair test contains no verbal questions. Figure 8.6 shows a sample question from the Raven's Progressive Matrices Test. Even though tests such as the Raven's Progressive Matrices are designed to be culture-fair, people with more education still score higher than those with less education do (Greenfield, 2003).

Why is it so hard to create culture-fair tests? Most tests tend to reflect what the dominant culture thinks is important (Gregory, 2007; Matsumoto & Juang, 2008). If tests have time limits, that will bias the test against groups not concerned with time. If languages differ, the same words might have different meanings for different language groups. Even pictures can produce bias because some cultures have less experience with drawings and photographs (Anastasi & Urbina, 1997). Within the same culture, different groups could have different attitudes, values, and motivation, and this could affect their performance on intelligence tests. Items that ask why buildings should be made of brick are biased against children with little or no experience with brick houses. Questions about railroads, furnaces, seasons of the year, distances between cities, and so on can be biased against groups who have less experience than others with these contexts. Because of such difficulties in creating culture-fair tests, Robert Sternberg and his colleagues (Sternberg, 2008d, 2009d; Sternberg & Grigorenko, 2008b; Zhang & Sternberg, 2008) conclude that there are no culture-fair tests only *culture-reduced tests.*

Ethnic Comparisons In the United States, children from African American and Latino families score below children from White families on standardized intelligence tests. On the average, African American schoolchildren score 10 to 15 points lower on standardized intelligence tests than White American schoolchildren do (Brody, 2000; Lynn, 1996). These are *average scores,* however. About 15 to 25 percent of African American schoolchildren score higher than half of White schoolchildren do, and many Whites score lower than most African Americans. The reason is that the distribution of scores for African Americans and Whites overlap.

How might stereotype threat be involved in ethnic minority students' performance on standardized tests?

As African Americans have gained social, economic, and educational opportunities, the gap between African Americans and Whites on standardized intelligence tests has begun to narrow (Ogbu & Stern, 2001). This gap especially narrows in college, where African American and White students often experience more similar environments than in the elementary and high school years (Myerson & others, 1998). Also, when children from disadvantaged African American families are adopted into more-advantaged middle-socioeconomic-status families, their scores on intelligence tests more closely resemble national averages for middle-socioeconomic-status children than for lower-socioeconomic-status children (Scarr & Weinberg, 1983).

One potential influence on intelligence test performance is **stereotype threat**, the anxiety that one's behavior might confirm a negative stereotype about one's group (Hollis-Sawyer & Sawyer, 2008; Marx & Stapel, 2006; Steele & Aronson, 2004). For example, when African Americans take an intelligence test, they may experience anxiety about confirming the old stereotype that Blacks are "intellectually inferior." Some studies have confirmed the existence of stereotype threat (Beilock, Rydell, & McConnell, 2007; Kellow & Jones, 2008; Rosenthal & Crisp, 2006; Steele & Aronson, 2004). For example, African American students do more poorly on standardized tests if they perceive that they are being evaluated. If they think the test doesn't count, they perform as well as White students (Aronson, 2002). However, critics argue that the extent to which stereotype threat explains the testing gap has been exaggerated (Sackett, Hardison, & Cullen, 2004, 2005).

Gender Comparisons The average scores of males and females do not differ on intelligence tests, but variability in their scores does differ (Brody, 2000). For example, males are more likely than females to have extremely high or extremely low scores.

There also are gender differences in specific intellectual abilities (Reynolds & others, 2008; van der Sluis & others, 2008). Males score better than females in some nonverbal areas, such as spatial reasoning, and females score better than males in some verbal areas, such as the ability to find synonyms for words and verbal memory (Jorm & others, 2004; Lynn & others, 2004). However, there often is extensive overlap in the scores of females and males in these areas, and there is debate about how strong the differences are (Hyde, 2005, 2007). There also is debate about the degree to which the differences are due to heredity or to socialization experiences and bias.

stereotype threat Anxiexy that one's behavior might confirm a stereotype about one's groups.

Review and Reflect: Learning Goal 1

1 Explain the Concept of Intelligence

REVIEW

- What is intelligence?
- What are the main individual tests of intelligence?
- What theories of multiple intelligences have been developed? Do people have one intelligence or many intelligences?
- What evidence indicates that heredity influences IQ scores? What evidence indicates that environment influences IQ scores?
- What is known about the intelligence of people from different cultures and ethnic groups? To what extent are there differences in the intelligence of females and males?

REFLECT

- A CD-ROM is being sold to parents for testing their child's IQ. What are some potential problems with parents giving their child an IQ test and interpreting the results?

2 THE DEVELOPMENT OF INTELLIGENCE

| Tests of Infant Intelligence | Stability and Change in Intelligence Through Adolescence |

How can the intelligence of infants be assessed? Is intelligence stable through childhood? These are some of the questions we will explore as we examine the development of intelligence.

Tests of Infant Intelligence

The infant-testing movement grew out of the tradition of IQ testing. However, tests that assess infants are necessarily less verbal than IQ tests for older children. Tests for infants contain far more items related to perceptual-motor development. They also include measures of social interaction. To read about the work of one infant assessment specialist, see the *Careers in Child Development* profile.

The most important early contributor to the testing of infants was Arnold Gesell (1934). He developed a measure that helped sort out potentially normal babies from abnormal ones. This was especially useful to adoption agencies, which had large numbers of babies awaiting placement. Gesell's examination was used widely for many years and still is frequently employed by pediatricians to distinguish normal and abnormal infants. The current version of the Gesell test has four categories of behavior: motor, language, adaptive, and personal-social. The **developmental quotient (DQ)** combines subscores in these categories to provide an overall score.

The widely used **Bayley Scales of Infant Development** were developed by Nancy Bayley (1969) in order to assess infant behavior and predict later development. The current version, Bayley-III, has five scales: cognitive, language, motor, socioemotional, and adaptive (Bayley, 2006). The first three scales are administered directly to the infant; the latter two are questionnaires given to the caregiver. The Bayley-III also

developmental quotient (DQ) An overall developmental score that combines subscores on motor, language, adaptive, and personal-social domains in the Gesell assessment of infants.

Bayley Scales of Infant Development Initially creates by Nancy Bayley, these scales are widely used in assessing infant development. The current version has five scales: cognitive, language, motor, socioemotional, and adaptive.

Careers in Child Development

Toosje Thyssen Van Beveren, Infant Assessment Specialist

Toosje Thyssen Van Beveren is a developmental psychologist at the University of Texas Medical Center in Dallas. She has a master's degree in child clinical psychology and a Ph.D, in human development.

Her main current work is in a program called New Connections. This 12-week program is a comprehensive intervention for young children (0 to 6 years of age) who were affected by substance abuse prenatally and for their caregivers.

In the New Connections program Van Beveren conducts assessments of infants developmental status and progress, identifying delays and deficits. She might refer the infants to a speech, physical, or occupational therapist and monitor the infants' therapeutic services and developmental progress. Van Beveren trains the program staff and encourages them to use the exercises she recommends. She also discusses the child's problems with the primary caregivers, suggests activities they can carry out with their children, and assists them in enrolling their infants in appropriate programs.

During her graduate work at the University of Texas at Dallas, Van Beveren was author John Santrock's teaching assistant for four years in his undergraduate course on development. As a teaching assistant, she attended classes, graded exams, counseled students, and occasionally gave lectures. Each semester, Van Beveren returns to give a lecture on prenatal development and infancy. Van Beveren

also teaches part-time in the psychology department at UT-Dallas. She teaches an undergraduate course. "The Child in Society," and a graduate course, "Infant Development."

In Van Beveren's words, "My days are busy and full. The work is often challenging. There are some disappointments but mostly the work is enormously gratifying."

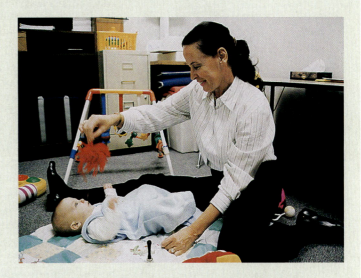

Toosje Thyssen Van Beveren conducting an infant assessment.

---

is more appropriate for use in clinical settings than the two previous editions (Lennon & others, 2008).

How should a 6-month-old perform on the Bayley cognitive scale? The 6-month-old infant should be able to vocalize pleasure and displeasure, persistently search for objects that are just out of immediate reach, and approach a mirror that is placed in front of the infant by the examiner. By 12 months of age, the infant should be able to inhibit behavior when commanded to do so, imitate words the examiner says (such as *Mama*), and respond to simple requests (such as "Take a drink").

The explosion of interest in infant development has produced many new measures, especially tasks that evaluate the ways infants process information (Fagan, Holland, & Wheeler, 2007; Rose, Feldman, & Wallace, 1992). The Fagan Test of Infant Intelligence is increasingly being used (Fagan, 1992). This test focuses on the infant's ability to process information in such ways as encoding the attributes of objects, detecting similarities and differences between objects, forming mental representations, and retrieving these representations. For example, it uses the amount of time babies look at a new object compared with the amount of time they spend looking at a familiar object to estimate their intelligence.

The Fagan test elicits similar performances from infants in different cultures and, unlike the Gesell and Bayley scales, is correlated with measures of intelligence in older children. In fact, evidence is accumulating that measures of habituation and dishabituation predict intelligence in childhood and adolescence (Bornstein & Sigman, 1986; DiLalla, 2000; Sigman, Cohen, & Beckwith, 2000). Recall from our discussion in

Items used in the Bayley Scales of Infant Development.

Chapter 5 that *habituation* is reduced responsiveness to a stimulus after repeated presentations of the stimuli, and *dishabituation* is recovery of a habituated response after a change in stimulation. Quicker habituation and greater amounts of looking in dishabituation reflect more efficient information processing. A research review concluded that when measured between 3 and 12 months, both habituation and dishabituation are related to higher IQ scores on tests given at various times between infancy and adolescence (average correlation .37) (Kavšek, 2004).

Stability and Change in Intelligence Through Adolescence

One study examined correlations between IQ at a number of different ages (Honzik, MacFarlane, & Allen, 1948). There was a strong relation between IQ scores obtained at the ages of 6, 8, and 9 and IQ scores obtained at the age of 10. For example, the correlation between IQ at the age of 8 and IQ at the age of 10 was .88. The correlation between IQ at the age of 9 and IQ at the age of 10 was .90. These figures show a very high relation between IQ scores obtained in these years. The correlation between IQ in the preadolescent years and IQ at the age of 18 was slightly less but still statistically significant. For example, the correlation between IQ at the age of 10 and IQ at the age of 18 was .70.

What has been said so far about the stability of intelligence has been based on measures of groups of individuals. The stability of intelligence also can be evaluated through studies of individuals. Robert McCall and his associates (McCall, Applebaum, & Hogarty, 1973) studied 140 children between the ages of $2\frac{1}{2}$ and 17. They found that the average range of IQ scores was more than 28 points. The scores of one out of three children changed by as much as 40 points.

What can we conclude about the stability and change of intelligence in childhood? Intelligence test scores can fluctuate dramatically across the childhood years. Intelligence is not as stable as the original intelligence theorists envisioned. Children are adaptive beings. They have the capacity for intellectual change, but they do not become entirely new intelligent beings. In a sense, children's intelligence changes but has connections to early points in development.

Review and Reflect: Learning Goal 2

2 **Discuss the Development of Intelligence**

REVIEW

- How is intelligence assessed during infancy?
- How much does intelligence change through childhood and adolescence?

REFLECT

- As a parent, would you want your infant's intelligence tested? Why or why not?

---

3 THE EXTREMES OF INTELLIGENCE AND CREATIVITY

Mental Retardation   **Giftedness**   **Creativity**

Mental retardation and intellectual giftedness are the extremes of intelligence. Often intelligence tests are used to identify exceptional individuals. Let's explore the nature of mental retardation and giftedness. Then, we'll explore how creativity differs from intelligence.

Mental Retardation

The most distinctive feature of mental retardation is inadequate intellectual functioning. Long before formal tests were developed to assess intelligence, individuals with mental retardation were identified by a lack of age-appropriate skills in learning and caring for themselves. Once intelligence tests were developed, they were used to identify degrees of mental retardation. But of two individuals with mental retardation having the same low IQ, one might be married, employed, and involved in the community and the other require constant supervision in an institution. Such differences in social competence led psychologists to include deficits in adaptive behavior in their definition of mental retardation.

Mental retardation is a condition of limited mental ability in which the individual (1) has a low IQ, usually below 70 on a traditional intelligence test; (2) has difficulty adapting to everyday life; and (3) first exhibits these characteristics by age 18. The age limit is included in the definition of mental retardation because, for example, we don't usually think of a college student who suffers massive brain damage in a car accident, resulting in an IQ of 60, as being "mentally retarded." The low IQ and low adaptiveness should be evident in childhood, not after normal functioning is interrupted by damage of some form. About 5 million Americans fit this definition of mental retardation.

Mental retardation can be classified in several ways (Hallahan, Kaufmann, & Pullen, 2009; Hodapp & Dykens, 2006). Most school systems use the classifications shown in Figure 8.7. It uses IQ scores to categorize retardation as mild, moderate, severe, or profound.

Note that a large majority of individuals diagnosed with mental retardation fit into the mild category. However, these categories are not perfect predictors of functioning. The American Association on Mental Retardation (1992) developed a different classification based on the degree of support required for a person with mental retardation to function at the highest level. As shown in Figure 8.8, these categories of support are intermittent, limited, extensive, and pervasive.

Some cases of mental retardation have an organic cause (Hardman, Drew, & Egan, 2006). *Organic retardation* is mental retardation caused by a genetic disorder or by brain damage. Down syndrome is one form of organic mental retardation. As discussed in Chapter 2, it occurs when an extra chromosome is present.

Other causes of organic retardation include fragile X syndrome, an abnormality in the X chromosome that was discussed in Chapter 2; prenatal malformation; metabolic disorders; and diseases that affect the brain. Most people who suffer from organic retardation have IQs between 0 and 50.

Type of Mental Retardation	IQ Range	Percentage
Mild	55–70	89
Moderate	40–54	6
Severe	25–39	4
Profound	Below 25	1

FIGURE 8.7 Classification of Mental Retardation Based on IQ

This young boy has Down syndrome. *What causes a child to develop Down syndrome? In what major classification of mental retardation does the condition fall?*

Intermittent	Supports are provided "as needed." The individual may need episodic or short-term support during life-span transitions (such as job loss or acute medical crisis). Intermittent supports may be low or high intensity when provided.
Limited	Supports are intense and relatively consistent over time. They are time-limited but not intermittent. Require fewer staff members and cost less than more intense supports. These supports likely will be needed for adaptation to the changes involved in the school-to-adult period.
Extensive	Supports are characterized by regular involvement (for example, daily) in at least some setting (such as home or work) and are not time-limited (for example, extended home-living support).
Pervasive	Supports are constant, very intense, and are provided across settings. They may be of a life-sustaining nature. These supports typically involve more staff members and intrusiveness than the other support categories.

FIGURE 8.8 Classification of Mental Retardation Based on Levels of Support Needed

mental retardation A condition of limited mental ability in which the individual (1) has a low IQ, usually below 70 on a traditional intelligence test; (2) has difficulty adapting to everyday life; and (3) has an onset of these characteristics by age 18.

At 2 years of age, art prodigy Alexandra Nechita colored in coloring books for hours and also took up pen and ink. She had no interest in dolls or friends. By age 5 she was using watercolors. Once she started school, she would start painting as soon as she got home. At the age of 8, in 1994, she saw the first public exhibit of her work. In succeeding years, working quickly and impulsively on canvases as large as 5 feet by 9 feet, she has completed hundreds of paintings, some of which sell for close to $100,000 apiece. As a teenager, she continues to paint—relentlessly and passionately. It is, she says, what she loves to do. *What are some characteristics of children who are gifted?*

gifted Having above-average intelligence (an IQ of 130 or higher) and/or superior talent for something.

creativity The ability to think in novel and unusual ways and come up with unique solutions to problems.

When no evidence of organic brain damage can be found, cases of mental retardation are labeled *cultural-familial retardation*. Individuals with this type of retardation have IQs between 55 and 70. Psychologists suspect that these mental deficits often result from growing up in a below-average intellectual environment. Children who are familially retarded can be identified in schools, where they often fail, need tangible rewards (candy rather than praise), and are highly sensitive to what others expect of them. However, as adults, individuals who are familially retarded are usually invisible, perhaps because adult settings don't tax their cognitive skills as sorely. It may also be that individuals who are familially retarded increase their intelligence as they move toward adulthood.

Giftedness

There have always been people whose abilities and accomplishments outshine others'—the whiz kid in class, the star athlete, the natural musician. People who are **gifted** have above-average intelligence (an IQ of 130 or higher) and/or superior talent for something. When it comes to programs for the gifted, most school systems select children who have intellectual superiority and academic aptitude, whereas children who are talented in the visual and performing arts (arts, drama, dance), athletics, or other special aptitudes tend to be overlooked (Clark, 2008; Karnes & Stephens, 2008; Liben, 2009; Winner, 2009).

What are the characteristics of children who are gifted? Despite speculation that giftedness is linked with having a mental disorder, no relation between giftedness and mental disorder has been found. Similarly, the idea that gifted children are maladjusted is a myth, as Lewis Terman (1925) found when he conducted an extensive study of 1,500 children whose Stanford-Binet IQs averaged 150. The children in Terman's study were socially well adjusted, and many went on to become successful doctors, lawyers, professors, and scientists. Studies support the conclusion that gifted people tend to be more mature than others, have fewer emotional problems than others, and grow up in a positive family climate (Davidson, 2000; Feldman, 2001).

Ellen Winner (1996) described three criteria that characterize gifted children, whether in art, music, or academic domains:

1. *Precocity.* Gifted children are precocious. They begin to master an area earlier than their peers. Learning in their domain is more effortless for them than for ordinary children. In most instances, these gifted children are precocious because they have an inborn high ability in a particular domain or domains.

2. *Marching to their own drummer.* Gifted children learn in a qualitatively different way than ordinary children. One way that they march to a different drummer is that they need minimal help, or scaffolding, from adults to learn. In many instances, they resist any kind of explicit instruction. They often make discoveries on their own and solve problems in unique ways.

3. *A passion to master.* Gifted children are driven to understand the domain in which they have high ability. They display an intense, obsessive interest and an ability to focus. They motivate themselves, says Winner, and do not need to be "pushed" by their parents.

Is giftedness a product of heredity or environment? Likely both (Sternberg, 2009e). Individuals who are gifted recall that they had signs of high ability in a particular area at a very young age, prior to or at the beginning of formal training (Howe & others, 1995). This suggests the importance of innate ability in giftedness. However, researchers have also found that individuals with world-class status in the arts, mathematics, science, and sports all report strong family support and years of training and practice (Bloom, 1985). Deliberate practice is an important characteristic of individuals who become experts in a particular domain. For example, in one study, the best musicians engaged in twice as much deliberate practice over their lives as did the least successful ones (Ericsson, Krampe, & Tesch, 1993).

An increasing number of experts argue that the education of children who are gifted in the United States requires a significant overhaul (Jarvin & others, 2008; Kaufman & Sternberg, 2008). Consider the titles of books and reports such as *Genius Denied: How to Stop Wasting Our Brightest Young Minds* (Davidson & Davidson, 2004) and *A Nation Deceived: How Schools Hold Back America's Brightest Students* (Colangelo, Assouline, & Gross, 2004).

Underchallenged gifted children can become disruptive, skip classes, and lose interest in achieving. Sometimes these children just disappear into the woodwork, becoming passive and apathetic toward school. It is extremely important for teachers to challenge children who are gifted to reach high expectations (Webb & others, 2007; Winner, 2006).

Some educators conclude that the inadequate education of children who are gifted has been compounded by the federal government's No Child Left Behind policy that seeks to raise the achievement level of students who are not doing well in school at the expense of enriching the education of children who are gifted (Clark, 2008; Cloud, 2007). Ellen Winner (1996, 2006) argues that too often children who are gifted are socially isolated and underchallenged in the classroom. It is not unusual for them to be ostracized and labeled "nerds" or "geeks." A child who is truly gifted often is the only such child in the room who does not have the opportunity to learn with students of like ability. Many eminent adults report that school was a negative experience for them, that they were bored and sometimes knew more than their teachers (Bloom, 1985). Winner argues that American education will benefit when standards are raised for all children. When some children are still underchallenged, she recommends that they be allowed to attend advanced classes in their domain of exceptional ability such as allowing some especially precocious middle school students to take college classes in their area of expertise. For example, Bill Gates, founder of Microsoft, took college math classes and hacked a computer security system at 13; Yo-Yo Ma, famous cellist, graduated from high school at 15 and attended Juilliard School of Music in New York City.

A number of individuals work with children who are gifted in various capacities in school systems. To read about the work of gifted children specialist Sterling Jones, see the *Careers in Child Development* profile.

Creativity

We brought up the term "creative" on several occasions in our discussion of giftedness. What does it mean to be creative? **Creativity** is the ability to think about something in novel and unusual ways and come up with unique solutions to problems.

Intelligence and creativity are not the same thing (Sternberg, 2009f). Most creative people are quite intelligent, but the reverse is not necessarily true. Many highly intelligent people (as measured by high scores on conventional tests of intelligence) are not very creative (Sternberg & O'Hara, 2000). Many highly intelligent people produce large numbers of products but they are not necessarily novel.

Margaret (Peg) Cagle with some of the gifted seventh- and eighth-grade math students she teaches at Lawrence Middle School in Chatsworth, California. Cagle especially advocates challenging students who are gifted to take intellectual risks. To encourage collaboration, she often has students work together in groups of four, and frequently tutors students during lunch hour. As 13-year-old Madeline Lewis commented, "If I don't get it one way, she'll explain it another and talked to you about it and show you until you do get it." Cagle says it is important to be passionate about teaching math and open up a world for students that shows them how beautiful learning math can be (Wong Briggs, 2007, p. 6D).

A young Bill Gates, founder of Microsoft and now the world's richest person. Like many highly gifted students, Gates was not especially fond of school. He hacked a computer security system when he was 13 and as a high school student, he was allowed to take some college math classes. He dropped out of Harvard University and began developing a plan for what was to become Microsoft Corporation. *What are some ways that schools can enrich the education of such highly talented students as Gates to make it a more challenging, interesting, and meaningful experience?*

Careers in Child Development

Sterling Jones, Supervisor of Gifted and Talented Education

Sterling Jones is program supervisor for gifted and telented children in the Detroit Public School System. Jones has been working for more than three decades with children who are gifted. He believes that students' mastery of skills mainly depends on the amount of time devoted to instruction and the length of time allowed for learning. Thus, he believes that many basic strategies for challenging children who are gifted to develop their skills can be applied to a wider range of students than once believed. He has rewritten several pamphlets for use by teachers and parents, including *How to Help Your Child Succeed* and *Gifted and Talented Education for Everyone.*

Jones has undergraduate and graduate degrees from Wayne State University and taught English for a number of years before becoming involved in the program for gifted children. He also has written materials on African Americans, such as *Voices from the Black Experience,* that are used in the Detroit schools.

Sterling Jones with some of the children in the gifted program in the Detroit Public School System.

Why don't IQ scores predict creativity? Creativity requires divergent thinking (Guilford, 1967). **Divergent thinking** produces many answers to the same question. In contrast, conventional intelligence tests require **convergent thinking.** For example, a typical item on a conventional intelligence test is, "How many quarters will you get in return for 60 dimes?" There is only one correct answer to this question. In contrast, a question such as "What image comes to mind when you hear the phrase 'sitting alone in a dark room'?" has many possible answers; it calls for divergent thinking.

Individuals show creativity in some domains more than others (Runco, 2004). For example, a child who shows creativity in mathematics might not be as creative in art. To read about some strategies for helping children become more creative, see the following *Caring for Children* interlude.

 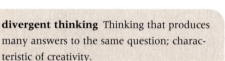

Caring for Children

divergent thinking Thinking that produces many answers to the same question; characteristic of creativity.

convergent thinking Thinking that produces one correct answer; characteristic of the kind of thinking required on conventional intelligence tests.

brainstorming A technique in which children are encouraged to come up with creative ideas in a group, play off one another's ideas, and say practically whatever comes to mind.

GUIDING CHILDREN'S CREATIVITY

An important goal is to help children become more creative (Beghetto & Kaufman, 2009; Sternberg, 2009f; Sternberg, Kaufman, & Grigorenko, 2008). What are the best strategies for accomplishing this goal? We examine some of these strategies next.

Encourage Creative Thinking on a Group and Individual Basis

Brainstorming is is a technique in which children are encouraged to come up with creative ideas in a group, play off each other's ideas, and say practically whatever comes to mind that seems relevant to a particular issue. Participants are usually told to hold off from criticizing others' ideas at least until the end of the brainstorming session.

Provide Environments That Stimulate Creativity

Some environments nourish creativity, others inhibit it (Bereiter & Scardamalia, 2006; Piggot, 2007). Parents and teachers who encourage creativity often rely on children's natural curiosity. They provide exercises and activities that stimulate children to find insightful solutions to problems, rather than ask a lot of questions that require rote answers. Teachers also encourage creativity by taking students on field trips to locations where creativity is valued. Howard Gardner (1993) emphasizes that science, discovery, and children's museums offer rich opportunities to stimulate creativity.

Don't Overcontrol Students

Teresa Amabile (1993) says that telling children exactly how to do things leaves them feeling that originality is a mistake and exploration is a waste of time. If, instead of dictating which activities they should engage in, you let children select their interests and you support their inclinations, you will be less likely to destroy their natural curiosity. Amabile also emphasizes that when parents and teachers hover over students all of the time, they make them feel that they are constantly being watched while they are working. When children are under constant surveillance, their creative risk taking and adventurous spirit diminish. Children's creativity also is diminished when adults have grandiose expectations for children's performance and expect perfection from them, according to Amabile.

Encourage Internal Motivation

Excessive use of prizes, such as gold stars, money, or toys, can stifle creativity by undermining the intrinsic pleasure students derive from creative activities. Creative children's motivation is the satisfaction generated by the work itself. Competition for prizes and formal evaluations often undermine intrinsic motivation and creativity (Amabile & Hennesey, 1992). However, this is not to rule out material rewards altogether.

Guide Children to Help Them Think in Flexible Ways

Creative thinkers are flexible in the way they approach problems in many different ways rather than getting locked into rigid patterns of thought. Give children opportunities to exercise this flexibility in their thinking.

Build Children's Confidence

To expand children's creativity, encourage children to believe in their own ability to create something innovative and worthwhile. Building children's confidence in their creative skills aligns with Bandura's (2008, 2009) concept of *self-efficacy*, the belief that one can master a situation and produce positive outcomes.

Guide Children to Be Persistent and Delay Gratification

Most highly successful creative products take years to develop. Most creative individuals work on ideas and projects for months and years without being rewarded for their efforts (Sternberg & Williams, 1996). As we discussed in Chapter 7, children don't become experts at sports, music, or art overnight. It usually takes many years working at something to become an expert at it; so it is with being a creative thinker who produces a unique, worthwhile product.

Encourage Children to Take Intellectual Risks

Creative individuals take intellectual risks and seek to discover or invent something never before discovered or invented (Sternberg & Williams, 1996). They risk spending a lot of time on an idea or project that may not work. Creative individuals are not afraid of failing or getting something wrong (Sternberg, Kaufman, & Pretz, 2004). They often see failure as an opportunity to learn. They might go down twenty dead-end streets before they come up with an innovative idea.

What are some good strategies teachers can use to guide children in thinking more creatively?

Review and Reflect: Learning Goal 3

3 **Describe the Characteristics of Mental Retardation, Giftedness, and Creativity**

REVIEW

- What is mental retardation, and what are its causes?
- What makes individuals gifted?
- What makes individuals creative?

REFLECT

- If you were an elementary school teacher, what would you do to encourage students' creativity?

Reach Your Learning Goals

Intelligence

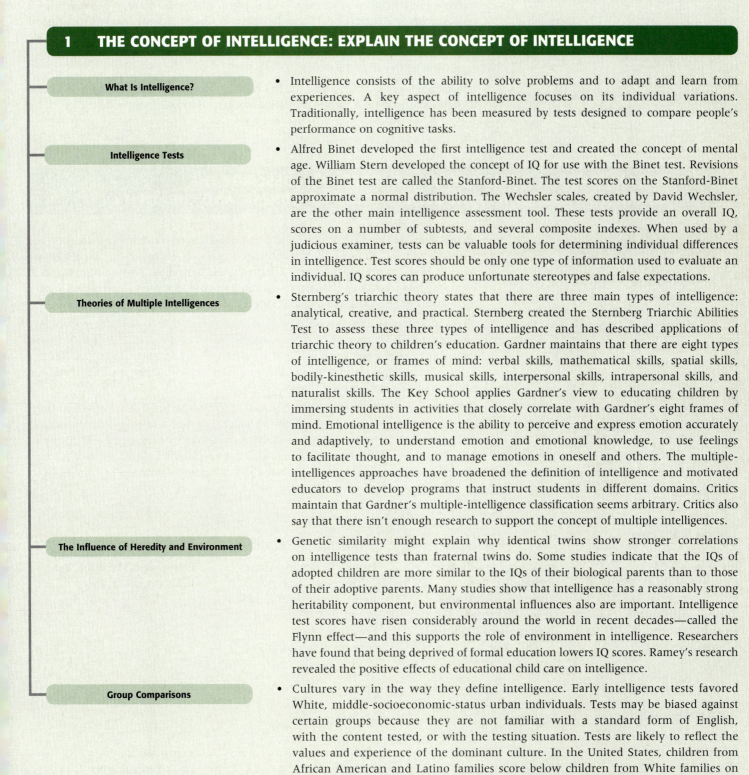

1 THE CONCEPT OF INTELLIGENCE: EXPLAIN THE CONCEPT OF INTELLIGENCE

What Is Intelligence?

- Intelligence consists of the ability to solve problems and to adapt and learn from experiences. A key aspect of intelligence focuses on its individual variations. Traditionally, intelligence has been measured by tests designed to compare people's performance on cognitive tasks.

Intelligence Tests

- Alfred Binet developed the first intelligence test and created the concept of mental age. William Stern developed the concept of IQ for use with the Binet test. Revisions of the Binet test are called the Stanford-Binet. The test scores on the Stanford-Binet approximate a normal distribution. The Wechsler scales, created by David Wechsler, are the other main intelligence assessment tool. These tests provide an overall IQ, scores on a number of subtests, and several composite indexes. When used by a judicious examiner, tests can be valuable tools for determining individual differences in intelligence. Test scores should be only one type of information used to evaluate an individual. IQ scores can produce unfortunate stereotypes and false expectations.

Theories of Multiple Intelligences

- Sternberg's triarchic theory states that there are three main types of intelligence: analytical, creative, and practical. Sternberg created the Sternberg Triarchic Abilities Test to assess these three types of intelligence and has described applications of triarchic theory to children's education. Gardner maintains that there are eight types of intelligence, or frames of mind: verbal skills, mathematical skills, spatial skills, bodily-kinesthetic skills, musical skills, interpersonal skills, intrapersonal skills, and naturalist skills. The Key School applies Gardner's view to educating children by immersing students in activities that closely correlate with Gardner's eight frames of mind. Emotional intelligence is the ability to perceive and express emotion accurately and adaptively, to understand emotion and emotional knowledge, to use feelings to facilitate thought, and to manage emotions in oneself and others. The multiple-intelligences approaches have broadened the definition of intelligence and motivated educators to develop programs that instruct students in different domains. Critics maintain that Gardner's multiple-intelligence classification seems arbitrary. Critics also say that there isn't enough research to support the concept of multiple intelligences.

The Influence of Heredity and Environment

- Genetic similarity might explain why identical twins show stronger correlations on intelligence tests than fraternal twins do. Some studies indicate that the IQs of adopted children are more similar to the IQs of their biological parents than to those of their adoptive parents. Many studies show that intelligence has a reasonably strong heritability component, but environmental influences also are important. Intelligence test scores have risen considerably around the world in recent decades—called the Flynn effect—and this supports the role of environment in intelligence. Researchers have found that being deprived of formal education lowers IQ scores. Ramey's research revealed the positive effects of educational child care on intelligence.

Group Comparisons

- Cultures vary in the way they define intelligence. Early intelligence tests favored White, middle-socioeconomic-status urban individuals. Tests may be biased against certain groups because they are not familiar with a standard form of English, with the content tested, or with the testing situation. Tests are likely to reflect the values and experience of the dominant culture. In the United States, children from African American and Latino families score below children from White families on standardized intelligence tests. Males are more likely than females to have extremely high or extremely low IQ scores. There also are gender differences in specific intellectual abilities.

2   THE DEVELOPMENT OF INTELLIGENCE: DISCUSS THE DEVELOPMENT OF INTELLIGENCE

Tests of Infant Intelligence

- A test developed by Gesell was an important early contributor to the developmental testing of infants. Tests designed to assess infant intelligence include the widely used Bayley scales. The Fagan Test of Infant Intelligence, which assesses how effectively infants process information, is increasingly being used. Infant information-processing tasks that involve attention—especially habituation and dishabituation—are related to standardized scores of intelligence in childhood.

Stability and Change in Intelligence Through Adolescence

- Intelligence is not as stable across the child and adolescent years as the original theorists thought. Many children's scores on intelligence tests fluctuate considerably.

3   THE EXTREMES OF INTELLIGENCE AND CREATIVITY: DESCRIBE THE CHARACTERISTICS OF MENTAL RETARDATION, GIFTEDNESS, AND CREATIVITY

Mental Retardation

- Mental retardation is a condition of limited mental ability in which the individual (1) has a low IQ, usually below 70; (2) has difficulty adapting to everyday life; and (3) has an onset of these characteristics by age 18. Most affected individuals have an IQ in the 55 to 70 range (mild retardation). Mental retardation can have an organic cause (called organic retardation) or be social and cultural in origin (called cultural-familial retardation).

Giftedness

- Individuals who are gifted have above-average intelligence (an IQ of 130 or higher) and/or superior talent for something. Three characteristics of gifted children are precocity, marching to their own drummer, and a passion to master their domain. Giftedness is likely a consequence of both heredity and environment. Concerns exist about the education of children who are gifted.

Creativity

- Creativity is the ability to think about something in novel and unusual ways and come up with unique solutions to problems. Although most creative people are intelligent, individuals with high IQs are not necessarily creative. Creative people tend to be divergent thinkers; traditional intelligence tests measure convergent thinking. Parents and teachers can use a number of strategies to increase children's creative thinking.

KEY TERMS

intelligence 247
mental age (MA) 248
intelligence quotient (IQ) 248
normal distribution 248
triarchic theory of
   intelligence 250

emotional intelligence 252
heritability 254
culture-fair tests 258
stereotype threat 259
developmental quotient
   (DQ) 260

Bayley Scales of Infant
   Development 260
mental retardation 263
gifted 264
creativity 265
divergent thinking 266

convergent thinking 266
brainstorming 266

KEY PEOPLE

Alfred Binet 247
Theophile Simon 248
David Wechsler 248
Robert J. Sternberg 250
Howard Gardner 251

Daniel Goleman 252
Peter Salovey and John
   Mayer 252
James Flynn 254
Robert Plomin 256

Craig Ramey 256
Robert Serpell 257
Elena Grigorenko 257
Arnold Gesell 260
Nancy Bayley 260

Robert McCall 262
Lewis Terman 264
Ellen Winner 264

E-LEARNING TOOLS

To help you master the material in this chapter, you'll find a number of valuable study tools at the Online Learning Center for *Child Development*, twelfth edition (**www.mhhe.com/santrockcd12**).

Taking It to the Net

Research the answers to these questions:

1. Terry and Lauren are on a debating team. They have to argue for the proposition, "Intelligence is hereditary." Another pair of members will argue for the opposite proposition, "Intelligence is not related to heredity." What facts do Terry and Lauren need to know as they prepare for the debate?

2. Motabi is from the Congo. He is arguing with his developmental psychology classmates about the meaning of intelligence. Motabi insists that different cultures construct their own paradigms of intelligence and that intelligence in the Congo is a very different concept from intelligence in Illinois. Is there any evidence to support Motabi's argument?

3. Maureen and Harry received a letter from the elementary school principal suggesting that they enroll their daughter, Jasmine, in the gifted program. They know what Jasmine's IQ score is—125—certainly not in the genius category. Is there more to giftedness than IQ score? What talents might Jasmine's teachers have noticed in her that may qualify her as being gifted?

Health and Well-Being, Parenting, and Education Exercises

Build your decision-making skills by trying your hand at the health and well-being, parenting, and education exercises.

Video Clips

The Online Learning Center includes the following video for this chapter:

- *Intelligence Testing*

Intelligence tests are pervasive in our culture—"they are the gatekeepers" to opportunities in our society. Dr. Stephen Ceci gives examples of how these tests can underpredict an individual's true abilities.

9

LEARNING GOALS

- Define language and describe its rule systems.

- Describe how language develops.

- Discuss the biological and environmental contributions to language development.

- Evaluate how language and cognition are linked.

LANGUAGE DEVELOPMENT

CHAPTER OUTLINE

Images of Child Development
The Story of Helen Keller

One of the most stunning portrayals of children isolated from the mainstream of language is the case of Helen Keller (1880–1968). At 18 months of age, Helen was an intelligent toddler in the process of learning her first words. Then she developed an illness that left her both deaf and blind, suffering the double affliction of sudden darkness and silence. For the next five years, she lived in a world she learned to fear because she could not see or hear.

Even with her fears, Helen spontaneously invented a number of gestures to reflect her wants and needs. For example, when she wanted ice cream, she turned toward the freezer and shivered. When she wanted bread and butter, she imitated the motions of cutting and spreading. But this homemade language system severely limited her ability to communicate with the surrounding community, which did not understand her idiosyncratic gestures.

Alexander Graham Bell, the famous inventor of the telephone, suggested to her parents that they hire a tutor named Anne Sullivan to help Helen overcome her fears. By using sign language, Anne was able to teach Helen to communicate. Anne realized that language learning needs to occur naturally, so she did not force Helen to memorize words out of context as in the drill methods that were in vogue at the time. Sullivan's success depended not only on the child's natural ability to organize language according to form and meaning but also on introducing language in the context of communicating about objects, events, and feelings about others.

Helen Keller eventually graduated from Radcliffe with honors, became a very successful educator, and crafted books about her life and experiences. She had this to say about language: "Whatever the process, the result is wonderful. Gradually from naming an object we advance step by step until we have traversed the vast distance between our first stammered syllable and the sweep of thought in a line of Shakespeare."

PREVIEW

In this chapter, we will tell the remarkable story of language and how it develops. The questions we will explore include these: What is language? What is the developmental course of language? What does biology contribute to language? How does experience influence language? How are language and cognition linked?

1 WHAT IS LANGUAGE?

Defining Language

Language's Rule Systems

In 1799, a nude boy was observed running through the woods in France. The boy was captured when he was 11 years old. He was called the Wild Boy of Aveyron and was believed to have lived in the woods alone for six years (Lane, 1976). When found, he made no effort to communicate. He never learned to communicate effectively. Sadly, a modern-day wild child named Genie was discovered in Los Angeles in 1970. Despite intensive intervention, Genie has acquired only a limited form of spoken language.

Both cases—the Wild Boy of Aveyron and Genie—raise questions about the biological and environmental determinants of language, topics that we will examine later in the chapter. First, though, we need to define language.

Defining Language

Language is a form of communication—whether spoken, written, or signed—that is based on a system of symbols. Language consists of the words used by a community and the rules for varying and combining them.

Think how important language is in our everyday lives. It is difficult to imagine what Helen Keller's life would have been like if she had never learned language. We need language to speak with others, listen to others, read, and write. Our language enables us to describe past events in detail and to plan for the future. Language lets us pass down information from one generation to the next and create a rich cultural heritage.

All human languages have some common characteristics (Owens, 2008). These include infinite generativity and organizational rules. **Infinite generativity** is the ability to produce an endless number of meaningful sentences using a finite set of words and rules. When we say "rules," we mean that language is orderly and that rules describe the way language works. Let's further explore what these rules involve.

Language's Rule Systems

When nineteenth-century American writer Ralph Waldo Emerson said, "The world was built in order and the atoms march in tune," he must have had language in mind. Language is highly ordered and organized (Berko Gleason, 2009; Colombo, McCardle, & Freund, 2009). The organization involves five systems of rules: phonology, morphology, syntax, semantics, and pragmatics.

Phonology   Every language is made up of basic sounds. **Phonology** is the sound system of a language, including the sounds that are used and how they may be combined (Menn & Stoel-Gammon, 2009; Stoel-Gammon & Sosa, 2007). For example, English has the sounds *sp, ba,* and *ar,* but the sound sequences *zx* and *qp* do not occur. A *phoneme* is the basic unit of sound in a language; it is the smallest unit of sound that affects meaning. A good example of a phoneme in English is /k/, the sound represented by the letter *k* in the word *ski* and the letter *c* in the word *cat.* The /k/ sound is slightly different in these two words, and in some languages such as Arabic these two sounds are separate phonemes. However, this variation is not distinguished in English, and the /k/ sound is therefore a single phoneme.

Morphology   **Morphology** is the rule system that governs how words are formed in a language. A *morpheme* is a minimal unit of meaning; it is a word or a part of a word that cannot be broken into smaller meaningful parts. Every word in the English language is made up of one or more morphemes. Some words consist of a single morpheme (for example, *help*), whereas others are made up of more than one morpheme (for example, *helper,* which has two morphemes, *help er,* with the morpheme *-er* meaning "one who," in this case "one who helps"). Thus, not all morphemes are words by themselves; for example, *-pre, -tion,* and *-ing* are morphemes.

Just as the rules that govern phonology describe the sound sequences that can occur in a language, the rules of morphology describe the way meaningful units (morphemes) can be combined in words (Tager-Flusberg, & Zukowski, 2009). Morphemes have many jobs in grammar, such as marking tense (for example, she *walks* versus she *walked*) and number (*she* walks versus *they* walk).

Syntax   **Syntax** involves the way words are combined to form acceptable phrases and sentences. The term syntax is often used interchangeably with the term grammar. If someone says to you, "Bob slugged Tom" or "Bob was slugged by Tom," you know

---

language A form of communication, whether spoken, written, or signed, that is based on a systems of symbols.

infinite generativity The ability to produce an endless number of meaningful sentences using a finite set of words and rules.

phonology The sound system of a language—includes the sounds used and rules about how they may be combined.

morphology The rule system that governs how words are formed in a language.

syntax The ways words are combined to form acceptable phrases and sentences.

FRANK & ERNEST © Thaves. Distributed by Newspaper Enterprise Association, Inc.

who did the slugging and who was slugged in each case because you have a syntactic understanding of these sentence structures. You also understand that the sentence, "You didn't stay, did you?" is a grammatical sentence but that "You didn't stay, didn't you?" is unacceptable and ambiguous.

If you learn another language, English syntax will not get you very far. For example, in English an adjective usually precedes a noun (as in *blue sky*), whereas in Spanish the adjective usually follows the noun (*cielo azul*). Despite the differences in their syntactic structures, however, the world's languages have much in common (Tager-Flusberg & Zukowski, 2009). For example, consider the following short sentences:

The cat killed the mouse.

The mouse ate the cheese.

The farmer chased the cat.

In many languages, it is possible to combine these sentences into more complex sentences. For example:

The farmer chased the cat that killed the mouse.

The mouse the cat killed ate the cheese.

However, no language we know of permits sentences like the following one:

The mouse the cat the farmer chased killed ate the cheese.

Can you make sense of this sentence? If you can, you probably can do it only after wrestling with it for several minutes. You likely could not understand it at all if someone uttered it during a conversation. It appears that language users cannot process subjects and objects arranged in too complex a fashion in a sentence. That is good news for language learners, because it means that all syntactic systems have some common ground. Such findings are also considered important by researchers who are interested in the universal properties of syntax (Tager-Flusberg, 2005).

Semantics   **Semantics** refers to the meaning of words and sentences. Every word has a set of semantic features, or required attributes related to meaning. *Girl* and *women*, for example, share many semantic features but they differ semantically in regard to age.

Words have semantic restrictions on how they can be used in sentences (Naigles & Swensen, 2007; Pan & Uccelli, 2009). The sentence *The bicycle talked the boy into buying a candy bar* is syntactically correct but semantically incorrect. The sentence violates our semantic knowledge that bicycles don't talk.

Pragmatics   A final set of language rules involves **pragmatics**, the appropriate use of language in different contexts. Pragmatics covers a lot of territory. When you take turns speaking in a discussion or use a question to convey a command ("Why is it so noisy in here?" "What is this, Grand Central Station?"), you are demonstrating knowledge of pragmatics. You also apply the pragmatics of English when you use polite language in appropriate situations (for example, when talking to one's teacher) or tell

semantics The meaning of words and sentences.

pragmatics The appropriate use of language in different contexts.

Rule System	Description	Examples
Phonology	The sound system of a language. A phoneme is the smallest sound unit in a language.	The word *chat* has three phonemes or sounds: /ch/ /a/ /t/. An example of phonological rule in the English language is while the phoneme /r/ can follow the phonemes /t/ or /d/ in an English consonant cluster (such as *track* or *drab*), the phoneme /l/ cannot follow these letters.
Morphology	The system of meaningful units involved in word formation.	The smallest sound units that have a meaning are called morphemes, or meaning units. The word *girl* is one morpheme, or meaning unit; it cannot be broken down any further and still have meaning. When the suffix *s* is added, the word becomes *girls* and has two morphemes because the *s* changed the meaning of the word, indicating that there is more than one girl.
Syntax	The system that involves the way words are combined to form acceptable phrases and sentences.	Word order is very important in determining meaning in the English language. For example, the sentence, "Sebastian pushed the bike" has a different meaning than "The bike pushed Sebastian."
Semantics	The system that involves the meaning of words and sentences.	Knowing the meaning of individual words—that is, vocabulary. For example, semantics includes knowing the meaning of such words as *orange*, *transportation*, and *intelligent*.
Pragmatics	The system of using appropriate conversation and knowledge of how to effectively use language in context.	An example is using polite language in appropriate situations, such as being mannerly when talking with one's teacher. Taking turns in a conversation involves pragmatics.

FIGURE 9.1 The Rule Systems of Language

stories that are interesting, jokes that are funny, and lies that convince. In each of these cases, you are demonstrating that you understand the rules of your culture for adjusting language to suit the context.

Pragmatic rules can be complex and differ from one culture to another (Bryant, 2009; Levinson, 2009). If you were to study the Japanese language, you would come face-to-face with countless pragmatic rules about conversing with individuals of various social levels and with various relationships to you. Some of these pragmatic rules concern the ways of saying thank you. Indeed, the pragmatics of saying *thank you* are complex even in our own culture. Preschoolers' use of the phrase thank you varies with sex, socioeconomic status, and the age of the individual they are addressing.

At this point, we have discussed five important rule systems involved in language. An overview of these rule systems is presented in Figure 9.1

Review and Reflect: Learning Goal 1

1 Define Language and Describe Its Rule Systems

REVIEW

- What is language?
- What are language's five main rule systems?

REFLECT

- How good are your family members and friends at the pragmatics of language? Describe an example in which one of the individuals showed pragmatic skills and another in which he or she did not.

2 HOW LANGUAGE DEVELOPS

| Infancy | Early Childhood | Middle and Late Childhood | Adolescence |

Long before infants speak recognizable words, they communicate by producing a number of vocalizations and gestures. *At approximately what ages do infants begin to produce different types of vocalization and gestures?*

FIGURE 9.2 From Universal Linguist to Language-Specific Listener. In Patricia Kuhl's research laboratory, babies listen to tape-recorded voices that repeat syllables. When the sounds of the syllables change, the babies quickly learn to look at the bear. Using this technique, Kuhl has demonstrated that babies are universal linguists until about 6 months of age, but in the next six months become language-specific listeners. *Does Kuhl's research give support to the view that either "nature" or "nurture" is the source of language acquisition?*

According to an ancient historian, in the thirteenth century, the emperor of Germany, Frederick II, had a cruel idea. He wanted to know what language children would speak if no one talked to them. He selected several newborns and threatened their caregivers with death if they ever talked to the infants. Frederick never found out what language the children spoke because they all died. As we move forward in the twenty-first century, we are still curious about infants' development of language, although our experiments and observations are, to say the least, far more humane than the evil Frederick's.

Infancy

Whatever language they learn, infants all over the world follow a similar path in language development. What are some key milestones in this development?

Babbling and Other Vocalizations   Long before infants speak recognizable words, they produce a number of vocalizations (Jaswal & Fernald, 2007; Sachs, 2009). The functions of these early vocalizations are to practice making sounds, to communicate, and to attract attention (Lock, 2004). Babies' sounds go through this sequence during the first year:

- *Crying.* Babies cry even at birth. Crying can signal distress, but as we will discuss in Chapter 10, there are different types of cries that signal different things.
- *Cooing.* Babies first coo at about 1 to 2 months. These are gurgling sounds that are made in the back of the throat and usually express pleasure during interaction with the caregiver.
- *Babbling.* In the middle of the first year babies babble—that is, they produce strings of consonant-vowel combinations, such as *ba, ba, ba, ba.*

Those deaf infants who are born to deaf parents who use sign language, babble with their hands and fingers at about the same age as hearing children babble vocally (Bloom, 1998). Such similarities in timing and structure between manual and vocal babbling indicate that a unified language capacity underlies signed and spoken language.

Gestures   Infants start using gestures, such as showing and pointing, at about 8 to 12 months of age. They may wave bye-bye, nod to mean "yes," show an empty cup to want more milk, and point to a dog to draw attention to it. Some early gestures are symbolic, as when an infant smacks her lips to indicate food/drink. Pointing is considered by language experts as an important index of the social aspects of language, and it follows this developmental sequence: From pointing without checking on adult gaze to pointing while looking back and forth between an object and the adult. Lack of pointing is a significant indicator of problems in the infant's communication system. For example, failure to engage in pointing characterizes many autistic children.

Recognizing Language Sounds   Long before they begin to learn words, infants can make fine distinctions among the sounds of the language (Hollich & Houston, 2007; Menn & Stoel-Gammon, 2009). In Patricia Kuhl's (1993, 2000, 2007, 2009; Kuhl & others, 2006) research, phonemes from languages all over the world are piped through a speaker for infants to hear (see Figure 9.2). A box with a toy bear in it is placed where the infant can see it. A string of identical syllables is played; then the syllables are changed (for example, *ba ba ba ba*, and then *pa pa pa pa*). If the infant turns its head when the syllables change, the box lights up and the bear dances and drums, rewarding the infant for noticing the change.

Kuhl's (2007) research has demonstrated that from birth up to about 6 months of age, infants are "citizens of the world": They recognize when sounds change most of the time no matter what language the syllables come from. But over the next six months, infants get even better at perceiving the changes in sounds from their "own" language, the one their parents speak, and gradually lose the ability to recognize differences that are not important in their own language.

An example involves the English *r* and *l* sounds, which distinguish words such as *rake* and *lake* (Iverson & Kuhl, 1996; Iverson & others, 2003). In the United States, infants from English-speaking homes detect the changes from *ra* to *la* when they are 6 months old and get better at detecting the change by 12 months of age. However, in Japanese there is no such *r* or *l*. In Japan, 6-month-old infants perform as well as their American counterparts in recognizing the *r* and *l* distinction, but by 12 months of age they lose this ability.

Infants must fish out individual words from the nonstop stream of sound that makes up ordinary speech (Menn & Stoel-Gammon, 2009). To do so, they must find the boundaries between words, which is very difficult for infants because adults don't pause between words when they speak. Still, infants begin to detect word boundaries by 8 months of age. For example, in one study, 8-month-old infants listened to recorded stories that contained unusual words, such as *hornbill* and *python* (Jusczyk & Hohne, 1997). Two weeks later, the researchers tested the infants with two lists of words, one made up of words in the stories, the other of new, unusual words that did not appear in the stories. The infants listened to the familiar words for a second longer, on average, than to new words.

What characterizes the infant's early word learning?

First Words Infants understand words before they can produce or speak them. For example, many infants recognize their name when someone says it as early as 5 months of age. However, the infant's first spoken word, a milestone eagerly anticipated by every parent, usually doesn't occur until 10 to 15 months of age and at an average of about 13 months. Yet long before babies say their first words, they have been communicating with their parents, often by gesturing and using their own special sounds. The appearance of first words is a continuation of this communication process (Berko Gleason, 2009).

A child's first words include those that name important people (*dada*), familiar animals (*kitty*), vehicles (*car*), toys (*ball*), food (*milk*), body parts (*eye*), clothes (*hat*), household items (*clock*), and greeting terms (*bye*). These were the first words of babies 50 years ago. They are the first words of babies today. Children often express various intentions with their single words, so that "cookie" might mean, "That's a cookie" or "I want a cookie."

As indicated earlier, children understand their first words earlier than they speak them. On the average, infants understand about 50 words at about 13 months, but they can't say this many words until about 18 months (Menyuk, Liebergott, & Schultz, 1995). Thus, in infancy *receptive vocabulary* (words the child understands) considerably exceeds *spoken vocabulary* (words the child uses).

The infant's spoken vocabulary rapidly increases once the first word is spoken (Pan & Uccelli, 2009; Waxman, 2009). The average 18-month-old can speak about 50 words, but by the age of 2 years can speak about 200 words. This rapid increase in vocabulary that begins at approximately 18 months is called the *vocabulary spurt* (Bloom, Lifter, & Broughton, 1985).

Like the timing of a child's first word, the timing of the vocabulary spurt varies. Figure 9.3 shows the range for these two language milestones in 14 children. On average, these children said their first word at 13 months and had a vocabulary spurt at 19 months. However, the ages for the first word of individual children varied from 10 to 17 months and for their vocabulary spurt from 13 to 25 months.

There are some interesting cross-linguistic differences in word learning. Children learning Mandarin Chinese, Korean, and Japanese acquire more verbs earlier in their

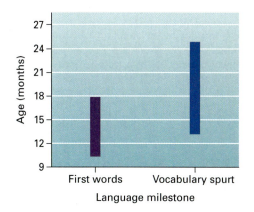

FIGURE 9.3 Variation in Language Milestones

What is a difference in the way children learn Chinese Mandarin and English?

Typical Age	Language Milestones
Birth	Crying
1 to 2 months	Cooing begins
6 months	Babbling begins
5 months	Comprehension of first word
6 to 12 months	Change from universal linguist to language-specific listener
8 to 12 months	Use gestures, such as showing and pointing Comprehension of words appears
13 months	First word spoken
18 months	Vocabulary spurt starts
18 to 24 months	Uses two-word utterances Rapid expansion of understanding of words

FIGURE 9.4 Some Language Milestones in Infancy. Despite great variations in the language input received by infants, around the world they follow a similar path in learning to speak.

telegraphic speech The use of short, precise words without grammatical markers such as articles, auxiliary verbs, and other connectives.

development than do children learning English. This cross-linguistic difference reflects the greater use of verbs in the language input to children in these Asian languages.

Some children use a referential style, others an expressive style, in learning words. A *referential style* refers to more frequently using words that refer to objects, whereas an *expressive style* indicates a greater use of pronouns and socially linked words. Examples of the referential style include words that describe events, people, animals, and food; examples of the expressive style are "hello," "bye-bye," and "thank you." Another example of individual variations is that some children use whole phrases, such as "gimme," "lemme see," and "help me," early in their word learning, whereas other children don't use these whole phrases early on.

Children sometimes overextend or underextend the meanings of the words they use (Woodward & Markman, 1998). *Overextension* is the tendency to apply a word to objects that are inappropriate for the word's meaning. For example, children at first may say "*dada*" not only for "father" but also for other men, strangers, or boys. Children may overextend word meanings because they don't know the appropriate word or can't recall it. With time, overextensions decrease and eventually disappear. *Underextension* is the tendency to apply a word too narrowly; it occurs when children fail to use a word to name a relevant event or object. For example, a child might use the word *boy* to describe a 5-year-old neighbor but not apply the word to a male infant or to a 9-year-old male. The most common explanation of underextension is that children have heard a name used in reference to a small, unrepresentative sample.

Two-Word Utterances   By the time children are 18 to 24 months of age, they usually utter two-word utterances. To convey meaning with just two words, the child relies heavily on gesture, tone, and context. The wealth of meaning children can communicate with a two-word utterance includes the following (Slobin, 1972):

- Identification: "See doggie."
- Location: "Book there."
- Repetition: "More milk."
- Nonexistence: "All gone thing."
- Possession: "My candy."
- Attribution: "Big car."
- Agent-action: "Mama walk."
- Question: "Where ball?"

These examples are from children whose first language is English, German, Russian, Finnish, Turkish, or Samoan.

Notice that the two-word utterances omit many parts of speech and are remarkably succinct. In fact, in every language, a child's first combinations of words have this economical quality; they are telegraphic. **Telegraphic speech** is the use of short and precise words without grammatical markers such as articles, auxiliary verbs, and other connectives. Telegraphic speech is not limited to two words. "Mommy give ice cream" and "Mommy give Tommy ice cream" also are examples of telegraphic speech.

We have discussed a number of language milestones in infancy. Figure 9.4 summarizes the time at which infants typically reach these milestones.

Around the world, most young children learn to speak in two-word utterances, at about 18 to 24 months of age. *What implications does this have for the biological basis of language?*

Early Childhood

Toddlers move rather quickly from producing two-word utterances to creating three-, four-, and five-word combinations. Between 2 and 3 years of age they begin the transition from saying simple sentences that express a single proposition to saying complex sentences (Bloom, 1998).

Young children's understanding sometimes gets way ahead of their speech. One 3-year-old, laughing with delight as an abrupt summer breeze stirred his hair and tickled his skin, commented, "I got breezed!" Many of the oddities of young children's language sound like mistakes to adult listeners. However, from the children's point of view, they are not mistakes. They represent the way young children perceive and understand their world. As children go through their early childhood years, their grasp of the rule systems that govern language increase.

As young children learn the special features of their own language, there are extensive regularities in how they acquire that particular language (Berko Gleason, 2009). For example, all children learn the prepositions *on* and *in* before other prepositions. Children learning other languages, such as Russian or Chinese, also acquire the particular features of those languages in a consistent order.

However, some children develop language problems, including speech and hearing problems. To read about the work of one individual who works with children who have speech/language and hearing problems, see the *Careers in Child Development* profile.

Careers in Child Development

Sharla Peltier, Speech Pathologist

A speech pathologist is a health professional who works with individuals who have a communication disorder. Sharla Peltier is a speech pathologist in Manitoulin, Ontario, Canada. Peltier works with Native American children in the First Nations Schools. She conducts screening for speech/language and hearing problems and assesses infants as young as 6 months of age as well as school-aged children. She works closely with community health nurses to identify hearing problems.

Diagnosing problems is only about half of what Peltier does in her work. She especially enjoys treating speech/language and hearing problems. She conducts parent training sessions to help parents understand and help with their children's language problem. As part of this training, she guides parents in improving their communication skills with their children.

Speech therapist Sharla Peltier, helping a young child improve her language and communication skills.

Understanding Phonology and Morphology During the preschool years, most children gradually become more sensitive to the sounds of spoken words and become increasingly capable of producing all the sounds of their language (National Research Council, 1999). By the time, children are 3 years of age, they can produce all the vowel sounds and most of the consonant sounds (Menn & Stoel-Gammon, 2009).

Young children can even produce complex consonant clusters such as *str-* and *-mpt-*. They notice rhymes, enjoy poems, make up silly names for things by substituting one sound for another (such as *bubblegum, bubblebum, bubbleyum*), and clap along with each syllable in a phrase.

This is a wug.

Now there is another one.
There are two of them.
There are two _____.

FIGURE 9.5 Stimuli in Berko's Study of Young Children's Understanding of Morphological Rules. In Jean Berko's (1958) study, young children were presented cards, such as this one with a "wug" on it. Then the children were asked to supply the missing word; in supplying the missing word, they had to say it correctly too. "Wugs" is the correct response here.

How do children's language abilities develop during early childhood?

fast mapping A process that helps to explain how young children learn the connection between a word and its referent so quickly.

By the time children move beyond two-word utterances, they demonstrate a knowledge of morphology rules (Berko Gleason, 2009; Tager-Flusberg & Zukowski, 2009). Children begin using the plural and possessive forms of nouns (such as *dogs* and *dog's*). They put appropriate endings on verbs (such as *-s* when the subject is third-person singular and *-ed* for the past tense). They use prepositions (such as *in* and *on*), articles (such as *a* and *the*), and various forms of the verb *to be* (such as "I *was* going to the store"). Some of the best evidence for changes in children's use of morphological rules occurs in their overgeneralization of the rules, as when a preschool child say "foots" instead of "feet," or "goed" instead of "went."

In a classic experiment that was designed to study children's knowledge of morphological rules, such as how to make a plural, Jean Berko (1958) presented preschool children and first-grade children with cards such as the one shown in Figure 9.5. Children were asked to look at the card while the experimenter read aloud the words on the card. Then the children were asked to supply the missing word. This might sound easy, but Berko was interested in the children's ability to apply the appropriate morphological rule, in this case to say "wugs" with the *z* sound that indicates the plural.

Although the children's answers were not perfect, they were much better than chance. What makes Berko's study impressive is that most of the words were made up for the experiment. Thus, the children could not base their responses on remembering past instances of hearing the words. Since they could make the plurals or past tenses of words they had never heard before, this was proof that they knew the morphological rules.

Changes in Syntax and Semantics   Preschool children also learn and apply rules of syntax (Lieven, 2008; Tager-Flusberg & Zukowski, 2009). They show a growing mastery of complex rules for how words should be ordered.

Consider *wh-* questions, such as "Where is Daddy going?" or "What is that boy doing?" To ask these questions properly, the child must know two important differences between *wh-* questions and affirmative statements (for instance, "Daddy is going to work" and "That boy is waiting on the school bus"). First, a *wh-* word must be added at the beginning of the sentence. Second, the auxiliary verb must be inverted—that is, exchanged with the subject of the sentence. Young children learn quite early where to put the *wh-* word, but they take much longer to learn the auxiliary-inversion rule. Thus, preschool children might ask, "Where Daddy is going?" and "What that boy is doing?"

Gains in semantics also characterize early childhood. Vocabulary development is dramatic (Lieven, 2008; Pan & Uccelli, 2009). Some experts have concluded that between 18 months and 6 years of age, young children learn about one new word every waking hour (Carey, 1977; Gelman & Kalish, 2006)! By the time they enter first grade, it is estimated that children know about 14,000 words (Clark, 1993). Children who enter elementary school with a small vocabulary are at risk for developing reading problems (Berko Gleason, 2005; Berninger, 2006).

Why can children learn so many new words so quickly? One possibility is **fast mapping**, which involves children's ability to make an initial connection between a word and its referent after only limited exposure to the word (Woodward, Markman, & Fitzimmons, 1994). Researchers have found that exposure to words on multiple occasions over several days results in more successful word learning than the same number of exposures in a single day (Childers & Tomasello, 2002).

Language researchers have proposed that young children may use a number of working hypotheses to accomplish their fast mapping (Pan & Uccelli, 2009). One working hypothesis children use is to give a novel label to a novel object. Parents can be especially helpful in aiding children's learning of novel labels for novel objects. As a mother looks at a picture book with her young child, she knows that the child understands the referent for car but not bus, so she says, "That's a *bus*, not a *car*. A bus is bigger than a car." Another working hypothesis children use is that a word refers to a whole object rather than parts of an object, such as labeling a tiger a tiger instead of tail or paw. Yet another working hypothesis children invoke is *mutual exclusivity*, in which they give only one name to one object. For example, in the case of a child's dog named Rufus, the child is likely to discard Rufus as a potential referent for *bone* because Rufus already possesses a name. Sometimes children's initial mappings are incorrect. In such cases, they benefit from hearing the words mature speakers use to test and revise their word-referent connections (Gershkoff-Stowe & Hahn, 2007).

Researchers have found that the nature of the talk parents direct to their children is linked with the children's vocabulary growth and the socioeconomic status of families. To read about this link, see the *Research in Child Development* interlude.

Research in Child Development

FAMILY ENVIRONMENT AND YOUNG CHILDREN'S LANGUAGE DEVELOPMENT

What characteristics of a family make a difference to a child's language development? Socioeconomic status has been linked with how much parents talk to their children and with young children's vocabulary. Betty Hart and Todd Risley (1995) observed the language environments of children whose parents were professionals and children whose parents were on welfare. Compared with the professional parents, the parents on welfare talked much less to their young children, talked less about past events, and provided less elaboration. As indicated in Figure 9.6, the children of the professional parents had a much larger vocabulary at 36 months of age than the children of the welfare parents.

Other research has linked how much mothers speak to their infants and the infants' vocabularies. For example, in one study by Janellen Huttenlocher and her colleagues (1991), infants whose mothers spoke more often to them had markedly higher vocabularies. By the second birthday, vocabulary differences were substantial.

However, a recent study of 1- to 3-year-old children living in low-income families found that the sheer amount of maternal talk was not the best predictor of a child's vocabulary growth (Pan & others, 2005). Rather, it was maternal language and literacy skills that were positive related to the children's vocabulary development. For example, when mothers used a more diverse vocabulary when talking with their children, their children's vocabulary benefited, but their children's vocabulary was not related to the total amount of their talkativeness with their children. Also, mothers who frequently used pointing gestures had children with a greater vocabulary. Pointing usually occurs in concert with speech, and it may enhance the meaning of mothers' verbal input to their children.

These research studies and others (NICHD Early Child Care Research Network, 2005) demonstrate the important effect that early speech input and poverty can have on the development of a child's language skills.

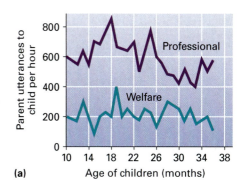

(a)

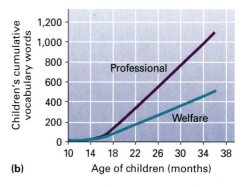

(b)

FIGURE 9.6 Language Input in Professional and Welfare Families and Young Children's Vocabulary Development. (*a*) In this study (Hart & Risley, 1995), parents from professional families talked with their young children more than parents from welfare families. (*b*) All of the children learned to talk, but children from professional families developed vocabularies that were twice as large as those from welfare families. Thus, by the time children go to preschool, they already have experienced considerable differences in language input in their families and developed different levels of vocabulary that are linked to their socioeconomic context. *Does this study indicate that poverty caused deficiencies in vocabulary development?*

Advances in Pragmatics   Changes in pragmatics also characterize young children's language development (Aktar & Herold, 2008; Bryant, 2009). A 6-year-old is simply a much better conversationalist than a 2-year-old is (Lieven, 2008). What are some of the improvements in pragmatics during the preschool years?

Young children begin to engage in extended discourse (Aktar & Herold, 2008, p. 581). For example, they learn culturally specific rules of conversation and politeness, and become sensitive to the need to adapt their speech in different settings. Their developing linguistic skills and increasing ability to take the perspective of others contribute to their generation of more competent narratives.

As children get older, they become increasingly able to talk about things that are not here (grandma's house, for example) and not now (what happened to them yesterday

What characterizes advances in pragmatics during early childhood?

or might happen tomorrow, for example). A preschool child can tell you what she wants for lunch tomorrow, something that would not have been possible at the two-word stage of language development.

At about 4 years of age, children develop a remarkable sensitivity to the needs of others in conversation. One way in which they show such sensitivity is through their use of the articles *the* and *an* (or *a*). When adults tell a story or describe an event, they generally use *an* (or *a*) when they first refer to an animal or an object, and then use *the* when referring to it later. (For example, "Two boys were walking through the jungle when *a* fierce lion appeared. *The* lion lunged at one boy while the other ran for cover.") Even 3-year-olds follow part of this rule; they consistently use the word *the* when referring to previously mentioned things. However, the use of the word *a* when something is initially mentioned develops more slowly. Although 5-year-old children follow this rule on some occasions, they fail to follow it on others.

Around 4 to 5 years of age, children learn to change their speech style to suit the situation. For example, even 4-year-old children speak differently to a 2-year-old than to a same-aged peer; they use shorter sentences with the 2-year-old. They also speak differently to an adult than to a same-aged peer, using more polite and formal language with the adult (Shatz & Gelman, 1973).

Early Literacy   The concern about the ability of U.S. children to read and write has led to a careful examination of preschool and kindergarten children's experiences, with the hope that a positive orientation toward reading and writing can be developed early in life (Giorgis & Glazer, 2009; Morrow, 2009). What should a literacy program for preschool children be like? Instruction should be built on what children already know about oral language, reading, and writing. Further, early precursors of literacy and academic success include language skills, phonological and syntactic knowledge, letter identification, and conceptual knowledge about print and its conventions and functions (Jalongo, 2007; Otto, 2008). A longitudinal study found that phonological awareness, letter name and sound knowledge, and naming speed in kindergarten were linked to reading success in the first and second grade (Schattschneider & others, 2004). In another longitudinal study, the number of letters children knew in kindergarten was highly correlated (.52) with their reading achievement in high school (Stevenson & Newman, 1986).

Middle and Late Childhood

Children gain new skills as they enter school that make it possible to learn to read and write, or to advance the reading and writing skills they have developed in early childhood. These new skills include increasingly using language to talk about things that are not physically present, learning what a word is, and learning how to recognize and talk about sounds (Berko Gleason, 2005). They have to learn the *alphabetic principle*, that the letters of the alphabet represent sounds of the language. As children develop during middle and late childhood, changes in their vocabulary and grammar also take place (Snow, 2007; Vukelich, Christie, & Enz, 2008).

What are some important aspects of young children's literacy?

Vocabulary, Grammar, and Metalinguistic Awareness   During middle and late childhood, changes occur in the way children's mental vocabulary is organized. When asked to say the first word that comes to mind when they hear a word, young children typically provide a word that often follows the word in a sentence. For example, when asked to respond to *dog* the young child may say "barks," or to the word *eat* say "lunch." At about 7 years of age, children begin to respond with a word that is the same part of speech as the stimulus word. For example, a child may now respond to the word *dog* with "cat" or "horse." To *eat*, they now might say "drink." This is evidence that children now have begun to categorize their vocabulary by parts of speech (Berko Gleason, 2003).

The process of categorizing becomes easier as children increase their vocabulary. Children's vocabulary increases from an average of about 14,000 words at 6 years of age to an average of about 40,000 words by 11 years of age.

Children make similar advances in grammar. During the elementary school years, children's improvement in logical reasoning and analytical skills helps them understand such constructions as the appropriate use of comparatives (*shorter, deeper*) and subjectives ("If you were president . . ."). During the elementary school years, children become increasingly able to understand and use complex grammar, such as the following sentence: *The boy who kissed his mother wore a hat.* They also learn to use language in a more connected way, producing connected discourse. They become able to relate sentences to one another to produce descriptions, definitions, and narratives that make sense. Children must be able to do these things orally before they can be expected to deal with them in written assignments.

These advances in vocabulary and grammar during the elementary school years are accompanied by the development of **metalinguistic awareness**, which is knowledge about language, such as knowing what a preposition is or the ability to discuss the sounds of a language. Metalinguistic awareness allows children "to think about their language, understand what words are, and even define them" (Berko Gleason, 2005, p. 4). It improves considerably during the elementary school years (Pan & Uccelli, 2009). Defining words becomes a regular part of classroom discourse, and children increase their knowledge of syntax as they study and talk about the components of sentences such as subjects and verbs (Meltzi & Ely, 2009).

Children also make progress in understanding how to use language in culturally appropriate ways—pragmatics (Bryant, 2009). By the time they enter adolescence, most children know the rules for the use of language in everyday contexts—that is, what is appropriate to say and what is inappropriate to say.

Reading   One model describes the development of reading skills as occurring in five stages (Chall, 1979) (see Figure 9.7). The age boundaries are approximate and do not apply to every child, but the stages convey a sense of the developmental changes involved in learning to read.

Before learning to read, children learn to use language to talk about things that are not present; they learn what a word is; and they learn how to recognize sounds

> *Children pick up words as pigeons peas.*
>
> —JOHN RAY
> *English Naturalist, 17th Century*

metalinguistic awareness Knowledge about language.

Stage	Age range/Grade level	Descripton
0	Birth to first grade	Children master several prerequisites for reading. Many learn the left-to-right progression and order of reading, how to identify letters of the alphabet, and how to write their names. Some learn to read words that appear on signs. As a result of TV shows like *Sesame Street* and attending preschool and kindergarten programs, many young children today develop greater knowledge about reading earlier than in the past.
1	First and second grades	Many children learn to read at this time. In doing so, they acquire the ability to sound out words (that is, translate letters into sounds and blend sounds into words). They also complete their learning of letter names and sounds.
2	Second and third grades	Children become more fluent at retrieving individual words and other reading skills. However, at this stage reading is still not used much for learning. The demands of reading are so taxing for children at this stage that they have few resources left over to process the content.
3	Fourth through eighth grades	In fourth through eighth grade, children become increasingly able to obtain new information from print. In other words, they read to learn. They still have difficulty understanding information presented from multiple perspectives within the same story. When children don't learn to read, a downward spiral unfolds that leads to serious difficulties in many academic subjects.
4	High school	Many students become fully competent readers. They develop the ability to understand material told from many perspectives. This allows them to engage in sometimes more sophisticated discussions of literature, history, economics, and politics.

FIGURE 9.7 A Model of Developmental Stages in Reading

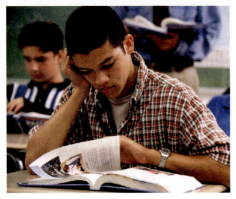

What are some developmental changes in reading?

This teacher is helping a student sound out words. Researchers have found that phonics instruction is a key aspect of teaching students to read, especially beginning readers and students with weak reading skills.

phonics approach An approach that emphasizes that reading instruction should focus on phonics and its basic rules for translating written symbols into sounds.

whole-language approach An approach that stresses that reading instruction should parallel children's natural language learning. Reading materials should be whole and meaningful.

and talk about them (Berko Gleason, 2003). If they develop a large vocabulary, their path to reading is eased. Children who begin elementary school with a small vocabulary are at risk when it comes to learning to read (Berko Gleason, 2003).

Vocabulary development plays an important role in reading comprehension (Cunningham, 2009; O'Hara & Pritchard, 2009). For example, a recent study revealed that a good vocabulary was linked with reading comprehension in second-grade students (Berninger & Abbott, 2005). Having a good vocabulary helps readers access word meaning effortlessly.

Recent analyses by Rich Mayer (2004, 2008) focused on the cognitive processes a child needs to go through in order to read a printed word. In his view, the three processes are (1) *being aware of sound units in words*, which consists of recognizing phonemes; (2) *decoding words*, which involves converting printed words into sounds; and (3) *accessing word meaning*, which consists of finding a mental representation of a word's meaning.

What are some approaches to teaching children how to read? Education and language experts continue to debate how children should be taught to read. Currently, debate focuses on the phonics approach versus the whole-language approach (Reutzel & Cooter, 2008).

The **phonics approach** emphasizes that reading instruction should focus on phonics and basic rules for translating written symbols into sounds. Early reading instruction should involve simplified materials. Only after they have learned the correspondence rules that relate spoken phonemes to the alphabet letters that represent them should children be given complex reading materials, such as books and poems (Cunningham & Hall, 2009; Rasinski & Padak, 2008).

By contrast, the **whole-language approach** stresses that reading instruction should parallel children's natural language learning. Reading materials should be whole and meaningful. That is, children should be given material in its complete form, such as stories and poems, so that they learn to understand language's communicative function. Reading should be connected with listening and writing skills. Although there are variations in whole-language programs, most share the premise that reading should be integrated with other skills and subjects, such as science and social studies, and that it should focus on real-world material. Thus, a class might read newspapers, magazines, or books, and then write about and discuss them. In some whole-language classes, beginning readers are taught to recognize whole words or even entire sentences, and to use the context of what they are reading to guess at unfamiliar words.

Which approach is better? Children can benefit from both approaches, but direct instruction in phonics needs to be emphasized especially in kindergarten and the first grade (Mayer, 2008; Mraz, Padak, & Rasinski, 2008). A recent study revealed that in a school in which students showed high achievement in reading both phonics and whole language were emphasized (Pressley & others, 2007a). In this study, intensive instruction in phonics improved the reading achievement of students with weak reading skills, whereas more holistic instruction was linked with higher achievement for students with stronger reading skills.

At the beginning of our discussion of reading, we described Mayer's (2004, 2008) view that decoding words is a key cognitive process in learning to read. Important in this regard are certain metacognitive skills and increasing automaticity that is characterized by fluency (Allington, 2009; Kuhn, 2009).

Metacognition, which we discussed in Chapter 7, is involved in reading in the sense that good readers develop control of their own reading skills and understand how reading works. For example, good readers know that it is important to comprehend the "gist" of what an author is saying. Teachers can help students develop good metacognitive strategies for reading by getting them to monitor their own reading, especially when they run into difficulties in their reading (Boulware-Gooden & others, 2007; Israel, 2007).

When students process information automatically, they do so with little or no conscious effort. When word recognition occurs rapidly, meaning also often follows in a rapid fashion. Many beginning or poor readers do not recognize words automatically. Their processing capacity is consumed by the demands of word recognition, so they have less capacity to devote to comprehension of groupings of words as phrases or sentences. As their processing of words and passages become more automatic, it is said that their reading becomes more fluent (Hiebert, 2008; Kuhn, 2009). Children's fluency often improves when they (1) hear others read a passage before and after they read it, which is called assisted practice; and (2) spend considerable time at reading various passages (Mayer, 2008).

Reading, like other important skills, takes time and effort (Pressley & others, 2007a). In a national assessment, children in the fourth grade had higher scores on a national reading test when they read 11 or more pages daily for school and homework (National Assessment of Educational Progress, 2000) (see Figure 9.8). Teachers who required students to read a great deal on a daily basis had students who were more proficient at reading than teachers who required little reading by their students.

Writing Children's writing emerges out of their early scribbles, which appear at around 2 to 3 years of age. In early childhood, children's motor skills usually develop to the point that they can begin printing letters. Most 4-year-olds can print their first name. Five-year-olds can reproduce letters and copy several short words. They gradually learn to distinguish the distinctive characteristics of letters, such as whether the lines are curved or straight, open or closed. Through the early elementary grades, many children continue to reverse letters such as *b* and *d* and *p* and *q* (Temple & others, 1993). At this age, if other aspects of the child's development are normal, letter reversals do not predict literacy problems.

As they begin to write, children often invent spellings. Usually they base these spellings on the sounds of words they hear (Spandel, 2009). Parents and teachers should encourage children's early writing but not be overly concerned about the formation of letters or spelling.

Like becoming a good reader, becoming a good writer takes many years and lots of practice (Jalongo, 2007). Children should be given many writing opportunities in the elementary and secondary school years (Graham, 2009; Graham & Olinghouse, 2009). As their language and cognitive skills improve with good instruction, so will their writing skills. For example, developing a more sophisticated understanding of syntax and grammar serves as an underpinning for better writing (Irvin, Buehl, & Kiemp, 2007).

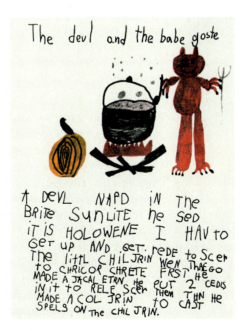

Anna Mudd is the 6-year-old author of "The Devl and the Babe Goste." Anna has been writing stories for at least two years. Her story includes poetic images, sophisticated syntax, and vocabulary that reflect advances in language development.

> *Children most at risk for reading difficulties in the first grade are those who began school with less verbal skill, less phonological awareness, less letter knowledge, and less familiarity with the basic purposes and mechanisms of reading.*
>
> —CATHERINE SNOW
> *Harvard University*

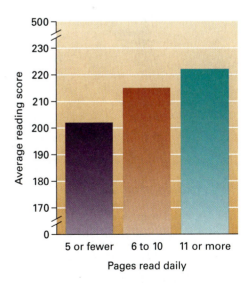

FIGURE 9.8 The Relation of Reading Achievement to Number of Pages Read Daily. In the recent analysis of reading in the fourth grade in the National Assessment of Educational Progress (2000), reading more pages daily in school and as part of homework assignments was related to higher scores on a reading test in which scores ranged from 0 to 500.

PEANUTS © United Features Syndicate, Inc.

So do such cognitive skills as organization and logical reasoning (Deshler & Hock, 2007; Perin, 2007). Through elementary, middle, and high school, students develop increasingly sophisticated methods of organizing their ideas. In early elementary school, they narrate and describe or write short poems. In late elementary and middle school, they move to projects such as book reports that combine narration with more reflection and analysis. In high school, they become more skilled at forms of exposition that do not depend on narrative structure (Conley, 2007; 2008; McKeough & others, 2007). A recent meta-analysis (use of statistical techniques to combine the results of studies) revealed that the following interventions were the most effective in improving fourth-through twelfth-grade students' writing quality: (1) strategy instruction, (2) summarization, (3) peer assistance, and (4) setting goals (Graham & Perin, 2007).

Major concerns about students' writing competence are increasingly being voiced (Graham, 2009; Harris & others, 2008). One study revealed that 70 to 75 percent of U.S. students in grades 4 through 12 are low-achieving writers (Persky, Dane, & Jin, 2003). College instructors report that 50 percent of high school graduates are not prepared for college-level writing (Achieve, Inc., 2005).

As with reading, teachers play a critical role in students' development of writing skills (Graham & Olinghouse, 2009; Smith & Read, 2009). The observations of classrooms made by Michael Pressley and his colleagues indicate that (2007b) students become good writers when teachers spend considerable time on writing instruction and are passionate about teaching students to write. Their observations also indicate that classrooms with students who score high on writing assessments have walls that overflow with examples of effective writing, whereas it is much harder to find such examples on the walls of classrooms that have many students who score low on writing assessments.

Beverly Gallagher, a third-grade teacher in Princeton, New Jersey, working with students to stimulate their interest in writing. She created the Imagine the Possibilities program, which brings nationally known poets and authors to her school. She phones each student's parents periodically to describe their child's progress and new interests. She invites students from higher grades to work with small groups in her class so that she can spend more one-on-one time with students. Each of her students keeps a writer's notebook to record thoughts, inspirations, and special words that intrigue them. Students get special opportunities to sit in an author's chair, where they read their writing to the class. (*Source: USA Today,* 2000)

Bilingualism and Second-Language Learning Are there sensitive periods in learning a second language? That is, if individuals want to learn a second language, how important is the age at which they begin to learn it? For many years, it was claimed that if individuals did not learn a second language prior to puberty, they would never reach native-language-learners' proficiency in the second language (Johnson & Newport, 1991). However, recent research indicates a more complex conclusion: Sensitive periods likely vary across different language systems (Thomas & Johnson, 2008). Thus, for late language learners, such as adolescents and adults, new vocabulary is easier to learn than new sounds or new grammar (Neville, 2006; Werker & Tees, 2005). For example, children's ability to pronounce words with a nativelike accent in a second language typically decreases with age, with an especially sharp drop occurring after the age of about 10 to 12. Also, adults tend to learn a second language faster than children, but their final level of second-language attainment is not as high as children's. And the way children and adults learn a second language differs somewhat. Compared with adults, children are less sensitive to feedback, less likely to use explicit strategies, and more likely to learn a second language from large amount of input (Thomas & Johnson, 2008).

Some aspects of children's ability to learn a second langue are transferred more easily to the second language than others (Pena & Bedore, 2009). A recent research review indicated that in learning to read, phonolological awareness is rooted in general cognitive processes and thus transfers easily across languages; however, decoding is more language-specific and needs to be relearned with each language (Bialystok, 2007, 2009).

Students in the United States are far behind their counterparts in many developed countries in learning a second language. For example, in Russia, schools have 10 grades, called *forms*, which roughly correspond to the 12 grades in American schools. Children begin school at age 7 in Russia and begin learning English in the third form. Because of this emphasis on teaching English, most Russian citizens under the age of 40 today are able to speak at least some English. The United States is the only technologically advanced Western nation that does not require foreign language study in high school, even for students in rigorous academic programs.

U.S. students may be missing more than the chance to acquire a skill by not learning to speak a second language (Garcia, 2008; Quicho & Ulanhoff, 2009). *Bilingualism*—the ability to speak two languages—has a positive effect on children's cognitive development (Gibbons & Ng, 2004). Children who are fluent in two languages perform better than their single-language counterparts on tests of control of attention, concept formation, analytical reasoning, cognitive flexibility, and cognitive complexity (Bialystok, 2001, 2009). They also are more conscious of the structure of spoken and written language and better at noticing errors of grammar and meaning, skills that benefit their reading ability (Bialystok, 1997).

In the United States, many immigrant children go from being monolingual in their home language to bilingual in that language and in English, only to end up monolingual speakers of English. This is called *subtractive bilingualism* and it can have negative effects on children, who often become ashamed of their home language.

A current controversy related to bilingualism involves the most effective way of teaching children whose primary language is not English (Diaz-Rico, 2008; Gozales, 2009; Lessow-Hurley, 2009). To read about the work of one bilingual education teacher, see the *Careers in Child Development* profile, and for a discussion of the debate about bilingual education, read the *Diversity in Child Development* interlude that follows.

Careers in Child Development

Salvador Tamayo, Bilingual Education Teacher

Salvador Tamayo teaches bilingual education in the fifth grade at Turner Elementary School in West Chicago. He recently was given a National Educator Award by the Milken Family Foundation for his work in bilingual education. Tamayo especially is adept at integrating technology into his bilingual education classes. He and his students have created several award-winning Web sites about the West Chicago City Museum, the local Latino community, and the history of West Chicago. His students also developed an "I Want to Be an American Citizen" Web site to assist family and community members in preparing for the U.S. Citizenship Test. Tamayo also teaches a bilingual education class at Wheaton College.

Salvador Tamayo working with bilingual education students.

Diversity in Child Development

BILINGUAL EDUCATION

What is the best way to teach children whose primary language is not English? For the last two decades, the preferred strategy has been *bilingual education,* which teaches academic subjects to immigrant children in their native language while slowly teaching English (Diaz-Rico, 2008; Quiocho & Ulanoff, 2009). Advocates of bilingual education programs argue that if children who do not know English are taught only in English, they will fall behind in academic subjects. How, they ask, can 7-year-olds learn arithmetic or history taught only in English when they do not speak the language?

Some critics of bilingual programs argue that too often it is thought that immigrant children need only one year of bilingual education. However, in general it takes immigrant children approximately three to five years to develop speaking proficiency and seven years to develop reading proficiency in English (Hakuta, Butler, & Witt, 2001). Also, immigrant children of course vary in their ability to learn English (Lessow-Hurley, 2009; Levine & McClosky, 2009). Children who come from lower socioeconomic backgrounds have more difficulty than those from higher socioeconomic backgrounds (Hakuta, 2001). Thus, especially for immigrant children from low socioeconomic backgrounds, more years of bilingual education may be needed than they currently are receiving.

Critics who oppose bilingual education argue that as a result of these programs, the children of immigrants are not learning English, which puts them at a permanent disadvantage in U.S. society. California, Arizona, and Massachusetts have significantly reduced the number of bilingual education programs. Some states continue to endorse bilingual education, but the emphasis that test scores be reported separately for English-language learners (students whose main language is not English) in the No Child Left Behind state assessments has shifted attention to literacy in English (Rivera & Collum, 2006; Snow & Yang, 2006).

What have researchers found regarding outcomes of bilingual education programs? Drawing conclusions about the effectiveness of bilingual education programs is difficult because of variations across programs in the number of years they are in effect, type of instruction, qualities of schooling other than bilingual education, teachers, children, and other factors. Further, no effectively conducted experiments that compare bilingual education with English-only education in the United States have been conducted (Snow & Yang, 2006). Some experts have concluded that the quality of instruction is more important in determining outcomes than the language in which it is delivered (Lesaux & Siegel, 2003).

Research supports bilingual education in that (1) children have difficulty learning a subject when it is taught in a language they do not understand; and (2) when both languages are integrated in the classroom, children learn the second language more readily and participate more actively (Gonzales, Yawkey, & Minaya-Rowe, 2006; Hakuta, 2005). However, many of the research results report only modest rather than strong support for bilingual education, and some supporters of bilingual education now acknowledge that English-only instruction can produce positive outcomes for English-language learners (Lesaux & Siegel, 2003).

A first- and second-grade bilingual English-Cantonese teacher instructing students in Chinese in Oakland, California. *What is the nature of bilingual education?*

Adolescence

Language development during adolescence includes increased sophistication in the use of words. With an increase in abstract thinking, adolescents are much better than children at analyzing the function a word plays in a sentence.

Adolescents also develop more subtle abilities with words. They make strides in understanding **metaphor**, which is an implied comparison between unlike things. For example, individuals "draw a line in the sand" to indicate a nonnegotiable position; a political campaign is said to be a marathon, not a sprint; a person's faith is shattered. And adolescents become better able to understand and to use **satire**, which is the use of irony, derision, or wit to expose folly or wickedness. Caricatures are an example of satire. More advanced logical thinking also allows adolescents, from about 15 to 20 years of age, to understand complex literary works.

Most adolescents are also much better writers than children are. They are better at organizing ideas before they write, at distinguishing between general and specific points as they write, at stringing together sentences that make sense, and at organizing their writing into an introduction, body, and concluding remarks.

Everyday speech changes during adolescence "and part of being a successful teenager is being able to talk like one" (Berko Gleason, 2005, p. 9). Young adolescents often speak a **dialect** with their peers that is characterized by jargon and slang (Cave, 2002). A dialect is a variety of language that is distinguished by its vocabulary, grammar, or pronunciation. For example, when meeting a friend, instead of saying hello, a young adolescent might say, "Give me five." Nicknames that are satirical and derisive ("Stilt," "Refrigerator," "Spaz") also characterize the dialect of young adolescents. Such labels might be used to show that one belongs to the group and to reduce the seriousness of a situation (Cave, 2002).

What are some changes in language development in adolescence?

Review and Reflect: Learning Goal 2

 2 **Describe How Language Develops**

REVIEW

- What are some key milestones of language development during infancy?
- How do language skills change during early childhood?
- How does language develop in middle and late childhood?
- How does language develop in adolescence?

REFLECT

- Should children in the United States be required to learn more than one language? Explain.

3 BIOLOGICAL AND ENVIRONMENTAL INFLUENCES

Biological Influences   **Environmental Influences**   **An Interactionist View of Language**

We have described how language develops, but we have not explained what makes this amazing development possible. Everyone who uses language in some way "knows" its rules and has the ability to create an infinite number of words and sentences. Where does this knowledge come from? Is it the product of biology? Or is language learned and influenced by experiences?

metaphor An implied comparison between two unlike things.

satire The use of irony, derision, or wit to expose folly or wickedness.

dialect A variety of language that is distinguished by its vocabulary, grammar, or pronunciation.

In the wild, chimps communicate through calls, gestures, and expressions, which evolutionary psychologists believe might be the roots of true language.

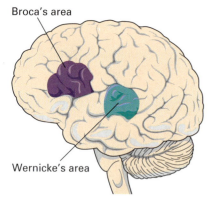

Broca's area

Wernicke's area

FIGURE 9.9 Broca's Area and Wernicke's Area. Broca's area is located in the frontal lobe of the brain's left hemisphere, and it is involved in the control of speech. Individuals with damage to Broca's area have problems saying words correctly. Also shown is Wernicke's area, a portion of the left hemisphere's temporal lobe that is involved in understanding language. Individuals with damage to this area cannot comprehend words; that is, they hear the words but don't know what they mean.

Broca's area An area of the brain's left frontal lobe that is involved in speech production and grammatical processing

Wernicke's area An area of the brain's left hemisphere that is involved in language comprehension.

aphasia A disorder resulting from brain damage to Broca's area or Wernicke's area that involves a loss or impairment of the ability to use or comprehend words.

language acquisition device (LAD) Chomsky's term that describes a biological endowment that enables the child to detect the features and rules of language, including phonology, syntax, and semantics.

Biological Influences

Some language scholars view the remarkable similarities in how children acquire language all over the world, despite the vast variation in language input they receive, as strong evidence that language has a biological basis. What role did evolution play in the biological foundations of language?

Evolution and the Brain's Role in Language

The ability to speak and understand language requires a certain vocal apparatus as well as a nervous system with certain capabilities. The nervous system and vocal apparatus of humanity's predecessors changed over hundreds of thousands or millions of years (Fisher & Marcus, 2006). With advances in the nervous system and vocal structures, *Homo sapiens* went beyond the grunting and shrieking of other animals to develop speech. Although estimates vary, many experts believe that humans acquired language about 100,000 years ago, which in evolutionary time represents a very recent acquisition. It gave humans an enormous edge over other animals and increased the chances of human survival (Lachlan & Feldman, 2003; Pinker, 1994).

There is evidence that particular regions of the brain are predisposed to be used for language (Berko Gleason, 2009; Schwartz & Trooper, 2009). Two regions involved in language were first discovered in studies of brain-damaged individuals: **Broca's area**, an area in the left frontal lobe of the brain involved in speech production and grammatical processing, and **Wernicke's area**, a region of the brain's left hemisphere involved in language comprehension (see Figure 9.9). Damage to either of these areas produces types of **aphasia**, which is a loss or impairment of language processing. Individuals with damage to Broca's area have difficulty producing words correctly; individuals with damage to Wernicke's area have poor comprehension and often produce fluent but incomprehensible speech.

Chomsky's Language Acquisition Device (LAD)

Linguist Noam Chomsky (1957) proposed that humans are biologically prewired to learn language at a certain time and in a certain way. He said that children are born into the world with a **language acquisition device (LAD)**, a biological endowment that enables the child to detect certain features and rules of language, including phonology, syntax, and semantics. Children are prepared by nature with the ability to detect the sounds of language, for example, and follow rules such as how to form plurals and ask questions.

MIT linguist Noam Chomsky. *What is Chomsky's view of language?*

Chomsky's LAD is a theoretical construct, not a physical part of the brain. Is there evidence for the existence of a LAD? Supporters of the LAD concept cite the uniformity of language milestones across languages and cultures, evidence that children create language even in the absence of well-formed input, and biological substrates of language But as we will see, critics argue that even if infants have something like a LAD, it cannot explain the whole story of language acquisition.

Environmental Influences

Decades ago, behaviorists opposed Chomsky's hypothesis and argued that language represents nothing more than chains of responses acquired through reinforcement (Skinner, 1957). A baby happens to babble "Ma-ma"; Mama rewards the baby with hugs and smiles; the baby says "Mama" more and more. Bit by bit, said the behaviorists, the baby's language is built up. According to behaviorists, language is a complex learned skill, much like playing the piano or dancing.

The behaviorial view of language learning has several problems. First, it does not explain how people create novel sentences—sentences that people have never heard or spoken before. Second, children learn the syntax of their native language even if they are not reinforced for doing so. Social psychologist Roger Brown (1973) spent long hours observing parents and their young children. He found that parents did not directly or explicitly reward or correct the syntax of most children's utterances. That is, parents did not say "good," "correct," "right," "wrong," and so on. Also, parents did not offer direct corrections such as "You should say two shoes, not two shoe." However, as we will see shortly, many parents do expand on their young children's grammatically incorrect utterances and recast many of those that have grammatical errors (Bonvillian, 2005).

The behavioral view is no longer considered a viable explanation of how children acquire language. But a great deal of research describes ways in which children's environmental experiences influence their language skills. Many language experts argue that a child's experiences, the particular language to be learned, and the context in which learning takes place can strongly influence language acquisition (Snow & Yang, 2006; Tomasello, 2006).

Language is not learned in a social vacuum. Most children are bathed in language from a very early age (Meltzoff & Brooks, 2009). The Wild Boy of Aveyron, who never learned to communicate effectively, had lived in social isolation for years. The support and involvement of caregivers and teachers greatly facilitate a child's language learning (Pan & others, 2005; Snow & Yang, 2006). For example, one study found that when mothers immediately smiled and touched their 8-month-old infants' after they babbled, the infants subsequently made more complex speechlike sounds than when mothers responded to their infants in a random manner (Goldstein, King, & West, 2003) (see Figure 9.10).

Michael Tomasello (2002, 2003, 2006) stresses that young children are intensely interested in their social world and that early in their development they can understand the intentions of other people. His *interaction view* of language emphasizes that children learn language in specific contexts. For example, when a toddler and a father are jointly focused on a book, the father might say, "See the birdie." In this case, even a toddler understands that the father intends to name something and knows to look in the direction of the pointing. Through this kind of joint attention, early in their development children are able to use their social skills to acquire language (Tomasello & Carpenter, 2007; Tomasello, Carpenter, & Liszkowski, 2007).

One intriguing component of the young child's linguistic environment is **child-directed speech**, language spoken in a higher pitch than normal with simple words and sentences (Zangl & Mills, 2007). It is hard to use child-directed speech when not in the presence of a baby. As soon as you start talking to a baby, though, you shift into child-directed speech. Much of this is automatic and something most parents are not aware they are doing. Even 4-year-olds speak in simpler ways to 2-year-olds than to their 4-year-old friends. Child-directed speech has the important function of capturing the infant's attention and maintaining communication (Jaswal & Fernald, 2007).

Adults often use strategies other than child-directed speech to enhance the child's acquisition of language, including recasting, expanding, and labeling:

- **Recasting** is rephrasing something the child has said, perhaps turning it into a question or restating the child's immature utterance in the form of a fully grammatical sentence. For example, if the child says, "The dog was barking," the

FIGURE 9.10 Social Interaction and Babbling. One study focused on two groups of mothers and their 8-month-old infants (Goldstein, King, & West, 2003). One group of mothers was instructed to smile and touch their infants immediately after the babies cooed and babbled; the other group was also told to smile and touch their infants but in a random manner, unconnected to sounds the infants made. The infants whose mothers immediately responded in positive ways to their babbling subsequently made more complex, speechlike sounds, such as "*da*" and "*gu*." The research setting for this study, which underscores how important caregivers are in the early development of language, is shown here.

child-directed speech Language spoken in a higher pitch than normal with simple words and sentences.

recasting Rephrasing a statement that a child has said, perhaps turning it into a question, or restating a child's immature utterance in the form of a fully grammatical utterance.

adult can respond by asking, "When was the dog barking?" Effective recasting lets the child indicate an interest and then elaborates on that interest.

- **Expanding** is restating, in a linguistically sophisticated form, what a child has said. For example, a child says, "Doggie eat," and the parent replies, "Yes, the doggie is eating."

- **Labeling** is identifying the names of objects. Young children are forever being asked to identify the names of objects. Roger Brown (1958) called this "the original word game" and claimed that much of a child's early vocabulary is motivated by this adult pressure to identify the words associated with objects.

Parents use these strategies naturally and in meaningful conversations. Parents do not (and should not) use any deliberate method to teach their children to talk, even for children who are slow in learning language. Children usually benefit when parents guide their children's discovery of language rather than overloading them with language; "following in order to lead" helps a child learn language. If children are not ready to take in some information, they are likely to tell you (perhaps by turning away). Thus, giving the child more information is not always better.

Remember, the encouragement of language development, not drill and practice, is the key. Language development is not a simple matter of imitation and reinforcement. To read further about ways that parents can facilitate children's language development, see the *Caring for Children* interlude.

Caring for Children

HOW PARENTS CAN FACILITATE INFANTS' AND TODDLERS' LANGUAGE DEVELOPMENT

In *Growing Up with Language,* linguist Naomi Baron (1992) provided ideas to help parents facilitate their child's language development. A summary of her ideas follows:

Infants

- ***Be an active conversational partner.*** Initiate conversation with the infant. If the infant is in a daylong child-care program, ensure that the baby receives adequate language stimulation from adults.

- ***Talk as if the infant understands what you are saying.*** Parents can generate self-fulfilling prophecies by addressing their young children as if they understand what is being said. The process may take four to five years, but children gradually rise to match the language model presented to them.

- ***Use a language style with which you feel comfortable.*** Don't worry about how you sound to other adults when you talk with your child. Your affect, not your content, is more important when talking with an infant. Use whatever type of baby talk with which you feel comfortable.

Toddlers

- ***Continue to be an active conversational partner.*** Engaging toddlers in conversation, even one-sided conversation, is the most important thing a parent can do to nourish a child linguistically.

- ***Remember to listen.*** Since toddlers' speech is often slow and laborious, parents are often tempted to supply words and thoughts for them. Be patient and let toddlers express themselves, no matter how painstaking the process is or how great a hurry you are in.

expanding Restating, in a linguistically sophisticated form, what a child has said.

labeling Identifying the names of objects.

- *Use a language style with which you are comfortable, but consider ways of expanding your child's language abilities and horizons.* For example, using long sentences need not be problematic. Use rhymes. Ask questions that encourage answers other than "yes" and "no." Actively repeat, expand, and recast the child's utterances. Introduce new topics. And use humor in your conversation.

- *Adjust to your child's idiosyncrasies instead of working against them.* Many toddlers have difficulty pronouncing words and making themselves understood. Whenever possible, make toddlers feel that they are being understood.

- *Avoid sexual stereotypes.* Don't let the toddler's sex determine your amount or style of conversation. Many American mothers are more linguistically supportive of girls than of boys, and many fathers talk less with their children than mothers do. Cognitively enriching initiatives from both mothers and fathers benefit both boys and girls.

- *Resist making normative comparisons.* Be aware of the ages at which your child reaches specific milestones (such as the first word, first 50 words), but do not measure this development rigidly against that of other children. Such social comparisons can bring about unnecessary anxiety.

It is a good idea for parents to begin talking to their babies at the start. The best language teaching occurs when the talking is begun before the infant becomes capable of intelligible speech. *What are some other guidelines for parents to follow in helping their infants and toddlers develop their language?*

An Interactionist View of Language

If language acquisition depended only on biology, then Genie and the Wild Boy of Aveyron (discussed earlier in the chapter) should have talked without difficulty. A child's experiences influence language acquisition. But we have seen that language does have strong biological foundations. No matter how much you converse with a dog, it won't learn to talk. In contrast, children are biologically prepared to learn language. Children all over the world acquire language milestones at about the same time and in about the same order. An interactionist view emphasizes that both biology and experience contribute to language development (Bohannon & Bonvillian, 2009).

This interaction of biology and experience can be seen in the variations in the acquisition of language. Children vary in their ability to acquire language, and this variation cannot be readily explained by differences in environmental input alone. For children who are slow in developing language skills, however, opportunities to talk and be talked with are important. Children whose parents provide them with a rich verbal environment show many positive benefits. Parents who pay attention to what their children are trying to say, expand their children's utterances, read to them, and label things in the environment, are providing valuable, if unintentional, benefits (Berko Gleason, 2009).

American psychologist Jerome Bruner (1983, 1996) proposed that the sociocultural context is extremely important in understanding children's language development. His view has some similarities with the ideas of Lev Vygotsky that were described in Chapter 2 and Chapter 6. Bruner stresses the role of parents and teachers in constructing what he called a *language acquisition support system (LASS).*

Today, most language acquisition researchers maintain that children from a wide variety of cultural contexts acquire their native language without explicit teaching. In some cases, they do so even without encouragement. However, caregivers greatly facilitate a child's language learning (Berko Gleason, 2009; Goldfield & Snow, 2009).

4 LANGUAGE AND COGNITION

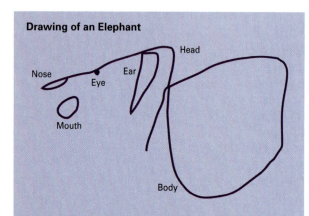

Drawing of an Elephant

Head
Nose
Ear
Eye
Mouth
Body

Verbal Description of an Elephant

And what an elephant is, it is one of the animals. And what the elephant does, it lives in the jungle. It can also live in the zoo. And what it has, it has long gray ears, fan ears, ears that can blow in the wind. It has a long trunk that can pick up grass, or pick up hay. . . . If they're in a bad mood it can be terrible. . . . If the elephant gets mad it could stomp; it could charge. Sometimes elephants can charge. They have big long tusks. They can damage a car. . . . It could be dangerous. When they're in a pinch, when they're in a bad mood it can be terrible. You don't want an elephant as a pet. You want a cat or a dog or a bird. . . .

FIGURE 9.11 Disparity in the Verbal and Motor Skills of an Individual with Williams Syndrome

As a teenager, Wendy Verougstraete felt that she was on the road to becoming a professional author. "You are looking at a professional author," she said. "My books will be filled with drama, action, and excitement. And everyone will want to read them. I am going to write books, page after page, stack after stack."

Overhearing her remarks, you might have been impressed not only by Wendy's optimism and determination, but also by her expressive verbal skills. In fact, at a young age Wendy showed a flair for writing and telling stories. Wendy has a rich vocabulary, creates lyrics for love songs, and enjoys telling stories. You probably would not be able to immediately guess that she has an IQ of only 49, and cannot tie her shoes, cross the street by herself, read or print words beyond the first-grade level, and do even simple arithmetic.

Wendy Verougstraete has Williams syndrome, a genetic birth disorder that was first described in 1961 and affects about 1 in 20,000 births (Mervis & Becerra, 2007). The most noticeable features of the syndrome include a unique combination of expressive verbal skills with an extremely low IQ and limited visuospatial skills and motor control (Jarrold, Baddeley, & Phillips, 2007; Paterson & Schultz, 2007). Children with Williams syndrome are natural-born storytellers who provide highly expressive narratives (Reilly & others, 2005). Figure 9.11 shows the great disparity in the verbal and motor skills of one person with Williams syndrome. Individuals with Williams syndrome often have good musical skills and interpersonal skills (Lincoln & others, 2007). A recent study indicated that children with Williams syndrome in the United States and Japan were more sociable than normally developing children in their respective countries, reflecting a genetic predisposition for sociability in children with Williams syndrome (Zitzer-Comfort & others, 2007). However, normally developing U.S. children were as sociable as Japanese children with Williams syndrome, reflecting different cultural expectations in the two countries. The syndrome also includes a number of physical characteristics as well, such as heart defects and a pixielike facial appearance. Despite having excellent verbal skills and competent interpersonal skills, most individuals with Williams syndrome cannot live independent lives (American Academy of Pediatrics, 2001). For example, Wendy Verougstraete lives in a group home for adults who are mentally retarded.

The verbal abilities of individuals with Williams syndrome are very distinct from those shown by individuals with Down syndrome, a type of mental retardation that we discussed in Chapters 2 and 8 (Brock, 2007). On vocabulary tests, children with Williams syndrome show a liking for unusual words. When asked to name as many animals as they can think of in one minute, Williams children come up with creatures like ibex, chihuahua, saber-toothed tiger, weasel, crane, and newt. Children with Down syndrome give simple examples like dog, cat, and mouse. When children with Williams syndrome tell stories, their voices come alive with drama and emotion, punctuating the dialogue with audience attention-grabbers like "gadzooks" or "lo and behold!" By contrast, children with Down syndrome tell very simple stories with little emotion.

Aside from being an interesting genetic disorder, Williams syndrome offers insights into the normal development of thinking and language. In our society, verbal ability is generally associated with high intelligence. But Williams syndrome raises the possibility that thinking and language might not be so closely related. Williams disorder is due to a defective gene that seems to protect expressive verbal ability but not reading and many other cognitive skills. Thus, cases like Wendy Verougstraete's cast some doubt on the general categorization of intelligence as verbal ability and prompts the question, "What is the relation between thinking and language?"

There are essentially two basic and separate issues involved in exploring connections between language and cognition. The first is this: Is cognition necessary for language? Although some researchers have noted that certain aspects of language development typically follow mastery of selected cognitive skills in both normally developing children and children with mental retardation, it is not clear that language development depends on any specific aspect of cognitive abilities (Lenneberg, 1967). Some experts argue that it is more likely that language and cognitive development occur in parallel but dissociated fashions (Cromer, 1987). Thus, according to research and experts' judgments, cognition is not necessary for language development.

The second issue is this: Is language necessary for (or important to) cognition? This issue is addressed by studies of deaf children. On a variety of thinking and problem-solving skills, deaf children perform at the same level as children of the same age who have no hearing problems. Some of the deaf children in these studies do not even have command of written or sign language (Furth, 1973). Thus, based on studies of deaf children, language is not necessary for cognitive development.

There is, however, some evidence of related activity in the cognitive and language worlds of children (Goldin-Meadow, 2000; Oates & Grayson, 2004). Piaget's concept of object permanence has been the focus of some research that links cognitive and language development. Piaget emphasized that children come to learn about the world first and then they learn to label what they know. Infants may need a concept of object permanence before they start to use words for disappearance, such as *all gone* (Gopnik & Meltzoff, 1997).

In sum, thought likely can influence language, and language can influence thought. However, there is increasing evidence that language and thought are not part of a single, automated cognitive system, but rather evolved as separate modular, biologically prepared components of the mind.

Review and Reflect: Learning Goal 4

4 **Evaluate How Language and Cognition Are Linked**

REVIEW

• What characterizes children with Williams syndrome? To what extent are language and cognition linked? Are they part of a single, automated cognitive system?

REFLECT

• Do children always think in words? Explain.

Reach Your Learning Goals

Language Development

1 WHAT IS LANGUAGE?: DEFINE LANGUAGE AND DESCRIBE ITS RULE SYSTEMS

Defining Language

- Language is a form of communication, whether spoken, written, or signed, that is based on a system of symbols. Language consists of all the words used by a community and the rules for varying and combining them. Infinite generativity is the ability to produce an endless number of meaningful sentences using a finite set of words and rules.

Language's Rule Systems

- The five main five rule systems of language are phonology, morphology, syntax, semantics, and pragmatics. Phonology is the sound system of a language, including the sounds used and which sound sequences may occur in the language. Morphology refers to how words are formed. Syntax is the way words are combined to form acceptable phrases and sentences. Semantics involves the meaning of words and sentences. Pragmatics is the appropriate use of language in different contexts.

2 HOW LANGUAGE DEVELOPS: DESCRIBE HOW LANGUAGE DEVELOPS

Infancy

- Among the milestones in infant language development are crying (birth), cooing (1 to 2 months), babbling (6 months), making the transition from universal linguist to language-specific listener (6 to 12 months), using gestures (8 to 12 months), recognition of their name (as early as 5 months), first word spoken (10 to 15 months), vocabulary spurt (18 months), rapid expansion of understanding words (18 to 24 months), and two-word utterances (18 to 24 months).

Early Childhood

- Advances in phonology, morphology, syntax, semantics, and pragmatics continue in early childhood. The transition to complex sentences begins at 2 or 3 years and continues through the elementary school years. Currently, there is considerable interest in the early literacy of children.

Middle and Late Childhood

- In middle and late childhood, children become more analytical and logical in their approach to words and grammar. Chall's model proposes five stages in reading, ranging from birth/first grade to high school. Current debate involving how to teach children to read focuses on the phonics approach versus the whole-language approach. Researchers have found strong evidence that the phonics approach should be used in teaching children to read, especially in kindergarten and the first grade, and with struggling readers, but that children also benefit from the whole-language approach. Children's writing emerges out of scribbling. Advances in children's language and cognitive development provide the underpinnings for improved writing. Strategy instruction is especially effective in improving children's writing. Bilingual education aims to teach academic subjects to immigrant children in their native languages, while gradually adding English instruction. Researchers have found that bilingualism does not interfere with performance in either language. Success in learning a second language is greater in childhood than in adolescence.

Adolescence

- In adolescence, language changes include more effective use of words; improvements in the ability to understand metaphor, satire, and adult literary works; and improvements in writing. Young adolescents often speak a dialect with their peers, using jargon and slang.

3 BIOLOGICAL AND ENVIRONMENTAL INFLUENCES: DISCUSS THE BIOLOGICAL AND ENVIRONMENTAL CONTRIBUTIONS TO LANGUAGE DEVELOPMENT

Biological Influences

- In evolution, language clearly gave humans an enormous edge over other animals and increased their chance of survival. A substantial portion of language processing occurs in the brain's left hemisphere, with Broca's area and Wernicke's area being important left-hemisphere locations. Chomsky argues that children are born with the ability to detect basic features and rules of language. In other words, they are biologically prepared to learn language with a prewired language acquisition device (LAD).

Environmental Influences

- The behavioral view—that children acquire language as a result of reinforcement—is no longer supported. Adults help children acquire language through child-directed speech, recasting, expanding, and labeling. Environmental influences are demonstrated by differences in the language development of children as a consequence of being exposed to different language environments in the home. Parents should talk extensively with an infant, especially about what the baby is attending to.

An Interactionist View of Language

- An interactionist view emphasizes the contributions of both biology and experience in language. One interactionist view is that both Chomsky's LAD and Bruner's LASS are involved in language acquisition.

4 LANGUAGE AND COGNITION: EVALUATE HOW LANGUAGE AND COGNITION ARE LINKED

- Children with Williams syndrome have a unique combination of expressive verbal skills with an extremely low IQ and limited visuospatial skills and motor control. These children offer insights into the normal development of thinking and language. Two basic and separate issues are these: (1) Is cognition necessary for language? (2) Is language necessary for cognition? At an extreme, the answer likely is no to these questions, but there is evidence of linkages between language and cognition. There is increasing evidence that language and thought are not part of a single, automated cognitive system, but rather evolved as separate, modular, biologically prepared components of the mind. The disorder of Williams syndrome supports this modular view.

KEY TERMS

language 275
infinite generativity 275
phonology 275
morphology 275
syntax 275
semantics 276
pragmatics 276

telegraphic speech 280
fast mapping 282
metalinguistic
   awareness 285
phonics approach 286
whole-language
   approach 286

metaphor 291
satire 291
dialect 291
aphasia 292
Broca's area 292
Wernicke's area 292

language acquisition device
   (LAD) 293
child-directed speech 293
recasting 293
expanding 294
labeling 294

KEY PEOPLE

Helen Keller 274
Patricia Kuhl 278
Jean Berko 282

Betty Hart and Todd Risley 283
Janellen Huttenlocher 283

Noam Chomsky 292
Roger Brown 293

Naomi Baron 294
Jerome Bruner 295

E-LEARNING TOOLS

To help you master the material in this chapter, you'll find a number of valuable study tools at the Online Learning Center for *Child Development*, twelfth edition (**www.mhhe.com/santrockcd12**).

Taking It to the Net

Research the answers to these questions:

1. Clarissa wants to be a speech therapist. In her child development class, she learned that Vygotsky believed that linguistic and cognitive development go hand in hand after a certain age. How can she learn more about his theory, so that it might give her some helpful insight in understanding children's language problems?

2. Todd is working in a child-care center after school. He notices that there is a wide range in the children's use of language, even within age groups. Are there any guidelines that Todd can obtain that could help determine if a child is delayed in language development?

3. Jared is concerned because his 7-year-old son, Damion, does not like to read. His second-grade teacher says he is about average for his age, but she has to prod him to do his reading assignments at school. What can Jared do to help Damion become a better reader?

Health and Well-Being, Parenting, and Education Exercises

Build your decision-making skills by trying your hand at the health and well-being, parenting, and education exercises.

Video Clips

The Online Learning Center includes the following videos for this chapter:

- *Crying at 10 Weeks*
  Here a 10-week-old baby boy cries and waves his arms and legs around as his mother attempts to soothe him.

- *Motherese with a 4-Month Old*
  In this clip, we hear the verbal interactions between mother and infant. A nice demonstration of motherese.

- *Babbling at 7.5 Months*
  In this clip we see a tired infant babbling to her mother. The mother tries to engage her in play, but the infant is uninterested.

- *Language Ability at Age 2*
  While engaging in a pretend tea party with her mother, 2-year-old Abby demonstrates her advancing language ability.

FOUR

SOCIOEMOTIONAL DEVELOPMENT

I am what I hope and give.

—ERIK ERIKSON
*European-Born American
Psychotherapist, 20th Century*

As children develop, they need the meeting eyes of love. They split the universe into two halves: "me" and "not me." They juggle the need to curb their own will with becoming what they can will freely. They also want to fly but discover that first they have to learn to stand and walk and climb and dance. As they become adolescents, they try on one face after another, looking for a face of their own. In Section 4, you will read four chapters: "Emotional Development" (Chapter 10), "The Self and Identity" (Chapter 11), "Gender" (Chapter 12), and "Moral Development" (Chapter 13).

10

LEARNING GOALS

◆ Discuss basic aspects of emotion.

◆ Describe the development of emotion.

◆ Characterize variations in temperament and their significance.

◆ Explain the early development of social orientation/understanding, attachment, and child care.

EMOTIONAL DEVELOPMENT

CHAPTER OUTLINE

Many fathers are spending more time with their infants today than in the past.

Images of Child Development
The Story of Tom's Fathering

An increasing number of fathers are staying home to care for their children (Rochlen & others, 2007; Wong & Rochlen, 2008). Consider Tom, a 1-year-old boy whose father cares for him during the day. His mother works full time at a job away from home, and his father is a writer who works at home. Tom's father is doing a great job of caring for him. He keeps Tom nearby while he is writing and spends lots of time talking to him and playing with him. They genuinely enjoy each other.

Tom's father looks to the future and imagines the Little League games Tom will play and the many other activities he can enjoy with Tom. His own father matched the stereotype of 1950s fathers, which portrayed men as emotionally distant, preoccupied with their jobs, and not involved in their children's lives. Remembering how little time his own father spent with him, Tom's father is dedicated to making sure that Tom has an involved, nurturing experience with his father.

When Tom's mother comes home in the evening, she spends considerable time with him. Tom shows a positive attachment to both his mother and his father. His parents have cooperated and have successfully juggled their careers and work schedules to provide 1-year-old Tom with excellent child care.

PREVIEW

For many years, emotion was neglected in the study of children's development. Today, emotion is increasingly important in conceptualizations of development. Even infants show different emotional styles, display varying temperaments, and begin to form emotional bonds with their caregivers. In this chapter, we will study the roles of temperament and attachment in development. But first we will examine emotion itself, exploring the functions of emotions in children's lives and the development of emotion from infancy through middle and late childhood.

1 EXPLORING EMOTION

| What Are Emotions? | A Functionalist View of Emotions | Regulation of Emotion | Emotional Competence |

Imagine your life without emotion. Emotion is the color and music of life, as well as the tie that binds people together. How do psychologists define and classify emotions, and why are they important to development?

What Are Emotions?

Defining *emotion* is difficult because it is not easy to tell when a child or an adult is in an emotional state (Izard, 2009; Kagan, 2007). For example, facial expressions can be misleading, individuals' self-reports of their emotions can be unreliable, and physiological markers (such as increased respiration rate) aren't necessarily linked to specific emotional states. For our purposes, we will adopt Joseph Campos' (2005) definition of **emotion** as feeling, or affect, that occurs when a person is engaged in an interaction that is important to him or her, especially to his or her well-being. Emotion is characterized by behavior

emotion Feeling, or affect, that occurs when a person is engaged in an interaction that is important to him or her, especially to his or her well-being.

306

that reflects (expresses) the pleasantness or unpleasantness of the state individuals are in, or the transactions they are experiencing. Emotions also can be more specific and take the form of joy, fear, anger, and so on, depending on how a transaction affects the person (for example, is the transaction a threat, a frustration, a relief, something to be rejected, something unexpected, and so on). And emotions can vary in how intense they are. For example, an infant may show intense fear or only mild fear in a particular situation.

When we think about emotions, a few dramatic feelings such as rage or glorious joy spring to mind. But emotions can be subtle as well, such as uneasiness in a new situation or the feeling of joy a mother has when she holds her baby. Psychologists classify the broad range of emotions in many ways, but almost all classifications designate an emotion as either positive or negative. Positive emotions include enthusiasm, joy, and love. Negative emotions include anxiety, anger, guilt, and sadness.

Emotions are influenced by biological foundations and experience (Hastings & others, 2008). In *The Expression of Emotions in Man and Animals,* Charles Darwin (1872/1965) stated that the facial expressions of humans are innate, not learned; are the same in all cultures around the world; and evolved from the emotions of animals. Darwin compared human snarls of anger with the growls of dogs and the hisses of cats. Today, psychologists still stress that the emotions, especially facial expressions of emotions, have a strong biological foundation (Goldsmith, 2002). Children who are blind from birth and have never observed the smile or frown on another person's face smile and frown in the same way that children with normal vision do. Researchers also have found that facial expressions of basic emotions such as happiness, surprise, anger, and fear are the same across cultures.

How do Japanese mothers handle their infants' and children's emotional development differently than non-Latino White mothers?

However, display rules—when, where, and how emotions should be expressed—are not culturally universal (Shiraev & Levy, 2007; Triandis, 1994). For example, in cultures that are characterized by individuality—such as North America, Western Europe, and Australia—emotional displays tend to be long and intense. In contrast, Asians tend to conceal their emotions when in the presence of others. In Asian and other cultures that emphasize social connections, displays of emotions such as sympathy, respect, and shame are more common than in Western countries, whereas negative emotions that might disrupt communication in a close-knit group are rarely displayed. Also, researchers have found that East Asian infants display less frequent and less intense positive and negative emotions than non-Latino White infants (Camras & others, 1998; Cole & Tan, 2007). Throughout childhood, East Asian parents encourage their children to show emotional reserve rather than emotional expressivity (Chen & others, 1998; Cole & Tan, 2007). Further, Japanese parents try to prevent their children from experiencing negative emotions, whereas non-Latino White mothers are more likely to respond after their children become distressed and then help them cope (Cole & Tan, 2007; Rothbaum & Trommsdorff, 2007).

The biological foundations of emotion involve the development of the nervous system (Kagan, 2007). Emotions are linked with early developing regions of the human nervous system, including structures of the limbic system and the brain stem (Lewis & Steiben, 2004; Thompson, Easterbrooks, & Walker, 2003). The capacity of infants to show distress, excitement, and rage reflects the early emergence of these biologically rooted emotional brain systems. Significant advances in emotional responding occur during infancy and childhood as a result of changes in neurobiological systems (including the frontal regions of the cerebral cortex) that can exert control over the more primitive limbic system (Porges, Doussard-Roosevelt, & Maiti, 1994). As children develop, maturation of the cerebral cortex allows a decrease in unpredictable mood swings and an increase in the self-regulation of emotion.

Caregivers play a role in the infant's neurobiological regulation of emotions (Repetti, Taylor, & Saxbe, 2007; Thompson, 2006). For example, by soothing the infant when the infant cries and shows distress, caregivers help infants to modulate their emotion and reduce the level of stress hormones (Gunnar & Quevado, 2007).

In sum, biological evolution has endowed human beings to be emotional, but culture and relationships with others provide diversity in emotional experiences (Beaulieu & Bugental, 2007; Saarni & others, 2006). As we see next, this emphasis on the role of relationships in emotion is at the core of the functionalist view of emotion.

A Functionalist View of Emotions

Developmentalists today tend to view emotions as the result of individuals' attempts to adapt to specific contextual demands (Saarni & others, 2006). Thus, a person's emotional responses cannot be separated from the situations in which they are evoked. In many instances, emotions are elicited in interpersonal contexts. For example, emotional expressions serve the important functions of signaling to others how one feels, regulating one's own behavior, and playing pivotal roles in social exchange.

One implication of the functionalist view is that emotions are relational rather than strictly internal, intrapsychic phenomena (Saarni & others, 2006). Consider just some of the roles of emotion in parent-child relationships. The beginnings of an emotional bond between parents and an infant are based on affectively toned interchanges, as when an infant cries and the caregiver sensitively responds. By the end of the first year, a parent's facial expression—either smiling or fearful—influences whether an infant will explore an unfamiliar environment. And when children hear their parents quarreling, they often react with distressed facial expressions and inhibited play (Cummings, 1987). Well-functioning families often include humor in their interactions, sometimes making each other laugh and creating a light mood state to defuse conflict. When a positive mood has been induced in a child, the child is more likely to comply with a parent's directions.

A second implication of the functionalist view is that emotions are linked with an individual's goals in a variety of ways (Saarni & others, 2006). Regardless of what the goal is, an individual who overcomes an obstacle to attain a goal experiences happiness. By contrast, a person who must relinquish a goal as unattainable experiences sadness. And a person who faces difficult obstacles in pursuing a goal often experiences frustration, which can become anger when the obstacles are perceived as unfair or intentionally put in the way to hinder the individual's goal attainment.

The specific nature of the goal can affect the experience of a given emotion. For example, the avoidance of threat is linked with fear, the desire to atone is related to guilt, and the wish to avoid the scrutiny of others is associated with shame.

Regulation of Emotion

The ability to control one's emotions is a key dimension of development (Kopp, 2008; Thompson, Meyer, & Jochem, 2008). Emotional regulation consists of effectively managing arousal to adapt and reach a goal. Arousal involves a state of alertness or activation, which can reach levels that are too high for effective functioning. Anger, for example, often requires regulation.

Here are some developmental trends in regulating emotion during childhood (Eisenberg, 1998, 2001):

- *External and internal resources.* With increasing age in infancy and early childhood, regulation of emotion shifts gradually from external sources in the world (for example, parents) to self-initiated, internal resources. Caregivers soothe young children, manage young children's emotion by choosing the contexts in which they behave, and provide children with information (facial cues, narratives, and so on) to help them interpret events. With age and advances in cognitive development, children are better equipped to manage emotion themselves. For example, older children might minimize the escalation of negative emotion in an interpersonal conflict by monitoring their facial expressions (for example, avoiding sneering or looks of contempt).

- *Cognitive strategies.* Cognitive strategies for regulating emotions, such as thinking about situations in a positive light, cognitive avoidance, and the ability to shift the focus of one's attention, increase with age.

- *Self-regulation of arousal.* With greater maturity, children develop greater capacity to modulate their emotional arousal (such as controlling angry outbursts).

- *Situations and relationships.* With age, individuals become more adept at selecting and managing situations and relationships in ways that minimize negative emotion.

- *Coping with stress.* With age, children become more capable of selecting effective ways to cope with stress.

Of course, there are wide variations in children's ability to modulate their emotions. Indeed, a prominent feature of adolescents with problems is that they often have difficulty managing their emotions.

Parents can help children learn to regulate their emotions (Coplan, Arbeau, & Armer, 2008; Denham, Bassett, & Wyatt, 2007). Depending on how they talk with their children about emotion, parents can be described as taking an emotion-coaching or an emotion-dismissing approach (Gottman, 2008). *Emotion-coaching parents* monitor their children's emotions, view their children's negative emotions as opportunities for teaching, assist them in labeling emotions, and coach them in how to deal effectively with emotions. For example, consider a girl who reports to her father that her best friend rejected her bid to play with her on the playground at school. If he is an emotion-coaching parent, he might ask her how it felt to be ignored and discuss age-appropriate strategies for handling that situation in the future. In contrast, *emotion-dismissing parents* view their role as to deny, ignore, or change negative emotions. If the father just mentioned is an emotion-dismissing parent, he might tell his daughter not to worry about being rejected by her friend, or that being ignored by this friend didn't matter much. Researchers have found that when interacting with their children, emotion-coaching parents were less rejecting, used more scaffolding and praise, and were more nurturant than emotion-dismissing parents (Gottman & DeClaire, 1997). The children of emotion-coaching parents were better at physiologically soothing themselves when they got upset, were better at regulating their negative affect, could focus their attention better, and had fewer behavior problems than the children of emotion-dismissing parents. A recent study revealed that having emotion-dismissing parents was linked with children's poor emotion regulation (Lunkenheimer, Shields, & Cortina, 2007).

An emotion-coaching parent. *What are some differences in emotion-coaching and emotion-dismissing parents?*

Emotional Competence

In Chapter 8, we briefly described the concept of emotional intelligence. Here we will examine a closely related concept, emotional competence, that focuses on the adaptive nature of emotional experience. Carolyn Saarni (1999; Saarni & others, 2006) argues that becoming emotionally competent involves developing a number of skills in social contexts. Figure 10.1 describes these skills and examples of them.

As children acquire these emotional competence skills in a variety of contexts, they are more likely to effectively manage their emotions, become resilient in the face of stressful circumstances, and develop more positive relationships (Denham, Bassett, & Wyatt, 2007; Saarni & others, 2006).

Skill	Example
Awareness of one's emotional states	Being able to differentiate whether sad or anxious
Detecting others' emotions	Understanding when another person is sad rather than afraid
Using the vocabulary of emotion terms in socially and culturally appropriate ways	Appropriately describing a social situation in one culture's when a person is feeling distress
Empathic and sympathetic sensitivity to others' emotional experiences	Being sensitive to others when they are feeling distressed
Recognizing that inner emotional states do not have to correspond to outer expressions	Recognizing that one can feel very angry yet manage one's emotional expression so that it appears more neutral
Adaptively coping with negative emotions by using self-regulatory strategies that reduce the intensity or duration of such emotional states	Reducing anger by walking away from an aversive situation and engaging in an activity that takes one's mind off of the aversive situation
Awareness that the expression of emotions plays a major role in relationship	Knowing that expressing anger toward a friend on a regular basis is likely to harm the friendship
Viewing oneself overall as feeling the way one wants to feel	Feeling like one can cope effectively with the stress in one's life and feeling that one is doing this successfully

FIGURE 10.1 Emotional Competence Skills

Review and Reflect: Learning Goal 1

1 **Discuss Basic Aspects of Emotion**

REVIEW

- How is emotion defined?
- What characterizes functionalism in emotion?
- What are some developmental changes in the regulation of emotion?
- What constitutes emotional competence, according to Saarni?

REFLECT

- Think back to your childhood and adolescent years. How effective were you in regulating your emotion? Give some examples. Has your ability to regulate your emotions changed as you have grown older? Explain.

2   DEVELOPMENT OF EMOTION

Joy

Sadness

Fear

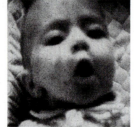

Surprise

FIGURE 10.2 Expression of Different Emotions in Infants

primary emotions Emotions that are present in humans and other animals, and emerge early in life; examples are joy, anger, sadness, fear, and disgust.

self-conscious emotions Emotions that require self-awareness, especially consciousness and a sense of "me"; examples include jealousy, empathy, and embarrassment.

Infancy **Early Childhood** **Middle and Late Childhood**

Does an older child's emotional life differ from a younger child's? Does a young child's emotional life differ from an infant's? Does an infant even have an emotional life? In this section, we will sketch an overview of the changes in emotion from infancy through middle childhood, looking not only at changes in emotional experience but also at the development of emotional competence.

Infancy

What are some early developmental changes in emotions? What functions do infants' cries serve? When do infants begin to smile?

Early Emotions   Leading expert on infant emotional development, Michael Lewis (2007, 2008) distinguishes between primary emotions and self-conscious emotions. **Primary emotions** are emotions that are present in humans and other animals; these emotions appear in the first six months of the human infant's development. Primary emotions include surprise, interest, joy, anger, sadness, fear, and disgust (see Figure 10.2 for infants' facial expressions of some of these early emotions). In Lewis' classification, **self-conscious emotions** require self-awareness that involves consciousness and a sense of "me." Self-conscious emotions include jealousy, empathy, embarrassment, pride, shame, and guilt, most of these occurring for the first time at some point in the second half of the first year through the second year. Some experts on emotion call self-conscious emotions such as embarrassment, shame, guilt, and pride *other-conscious emotions* because they involve the emotional reactions of others when they are generated (Saarni & others, 2006). For example, approval from parents is linked to toddlers beginning to show pride when they successfully complete a task.

Leading researchers such as Joseph Campos (2005, 2008) and Michael Lewis (2007; Campos, Anderson & Barbu-Roth, 2009) debate how early in the infant and toddler years the emotions that we have described first appear and their sequence. As an indication of the controversy regarding when certain emotions first are displayed by infants, consider jealousy. Some researchers argue that jealousy does not emerge until approximately 18 months of age (Lewis, 2007), whereas others emphasize that it is displayed much earlier (Draghi-Lorenz, Reddy, & Costall, 2001). Consider a research study in which 6-month-old infants observed their mothers giving attention either to a lifelike baby doll (hugging or gently rocking it, for example) or to a book (Hart & Carrington, 2002). When mothers directed their attention to the doll, the infants were more likely to display negative emotions, such as anger and sadness, which may have indicated their jealousy (see Figure 10.3). On the other hand, their expressions of anger and sadness may have reflected frustration in not being able to have the novel doll to play with. Debate about the onset of an emotion such as jealousy illustrates the complexity and difficulty in indexing early emotions.

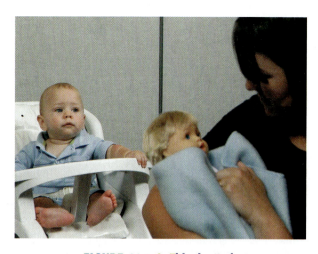

FIGURE 10.3 Is This the Early Appearance of Jealousy? In Sybil Hart's view, the infant here became distressed when his mother gave attention to a lifelike baby doll. However, some experts on emotional development conclude that determining whether an infant is displaying jealousy is a complex and difficult task. *For example, what are some other possible interpretations of the infant's behavior in the photograph?*

Emotional Expression and Social Relationships   Emotional expressions are involved in infants' first relationships. The ability of infants to communicate emotions permits coordinated interactions with their caregivers and the beginning of an emotional bond between them (Thompson & Newton, 2009). Not only do parents change their emotional expressions in response to infants' emotional expressions, but infants also modify their emotional expressions in response to their parents' emotional expressions. In other words, these interactions are mutually regulated. Because of this coordination, the interactions are described as *reciprocal*, or *synchronous*, when all is going well. Sensitive, responsive parents help their infants grow emotionally, whether the infants respond in distressed or happy ways (Thompson, 2009a, b; Thompson, Meyer, & Jochem, 2008).

Cries and smiles are two emotional expressions that infants display when interacting with parents. These are babies' first forms of emotional communication.

Crying   Crying is the most important mechanism newborns have for communicating with their world. The first cry verifies that the baby's lungs have filled with air. Cries also may provide information about the health of the newborn's central nervous system (Zeskind, 2009). Newborns even tend to respond with cries and negative facial expressions when they hear other newborns cry (Dondi, Simion, & Caltran).

Babies have at least three types of cries:

What are some different types of cries?

- **Basic cry:** A rhythmic pattern that usually consists of a cry, followed by a briefer silence, then a shorter whistle that is somewhat higher in pitch than the main cry, then another brief rest before the next cry. Some infancy experts argue that hunger is one of the conditions that incite the basic cry.

- **Anger cry:** A variation of the basic cry in which more excess air is forced through the vocal cords.

- **Pain cry:** A sudden long, initial loud cry followed by breath holding; no preliminary moaning is present. The pain cry is stimulated by a high-intensity stimulus.

Most adults can determine whether an infant's cries signify anger or pain (Zeskind, Klein, & Marshall, 1992). Parents can distinguish the cries of their own baby better than those of another baby.

Smiling   The power of the infant's smiles was appropriately captured by British theorist John Bowlby (1969):

> Can we doubt that the more and better an infant smiles the better he is loved and cared for? It is fortunate for their survival that babies are so designed by nature that they beguile and enslave mothers.

basic cry A rhythmic pattern usually consisting of a cry, a briefer silence, a shorter inspiratory whistle that is higher pitched than the main cry, and then a brief rest before the next cry.

anger cry A cry similar to the basic cry but with more excess air forced through the vocal cords.

pain cry A sudden appearance of loud crying without preliminary moaning and a long initial cry followed by an extended period of breath holding.

FIGURE 10.4 A 6-Month-Old's Strong Smile. This strong smile reflects the Duchenne marker (eye constriction) and mouth opening.

*H*e who binds himself to joy
Does the winged life destroy;
But he who kisses the joy as it flies;
Lives in eternity's sun rise.

—WILLIAM BLAKE
English Poet, 19th Century

reflexive smile A smile that does not occur in response to external stimuli. It happens during the month after birth, usually during sleep.

social smile A smile in response to an external stimulus, which, early in development, typically is a face.

stranger anxiety An infant's fear of and wariness toward strangers; it tends to appear in the second half of the first year of life.

separation protest Occurs when infants experience a fear of being separated from a caregiver, which results in crying when the caregiver leaves.

Two types of smiling can be distinguished in infants:

- **Reflexive smile:** A smile that does not occur in response to external stimuli and appears during the first month after birth, usually during sleep.
- **Social smile:** A smile that occurs in response to an external stimulus, typically a face in the case of the young infant. Social smiling occurs as early as 4 to 6 weeks of age in response to a caregiver's voice (Campos, 2005).

Daniel Messinger (2008) recently described the developmental course of infant smiling. From two to six months after birth, infants' social smiling increases considerably, both in self-initiated smiles and smiles in response to others' smiles. At 6 to 12 months of age, smiles that couple what is called the Duchenne marker (eye constriction) and mouth opening occur in the midst of highly enjoyable interactions and play with parents (see Figure 10.4). In the second year, smiling continues to occur in such positive circumstances with parents, and in many cases an increase in smiling occurs when interacting with peers. Also in the second year, toddlers become increasingly aware of the social meaning of smiles, especially in their relationship with parents.

Fear   One of a baby's earliest emotions is fear, which typically first appears at about 6 months of age and peaks at about 18 months. However, abused and neglected infants can show fear as early as 3 months (Campos, 2005). Researchers have found that infant fear is linked to guilt, empathy, and low aggression at 6 to 7 years of age (Rothbart, 2007).

The most frequent expression of an infant's fear involves **stranger anxiety**, in which an infant shows a fear and wariness of strangers. Stranger anxiety usually emerges gradually. It first appears at about 6 months of age in the form of wary reactions. By age 9 months, the fear of strangers is often more intense, and it continues to escalate through the infant's first birthday (Scher & Harel, 2008).

Not all infants show distress when they encounter a stranger. Besides individual variations, whether an infant shows stranger anxiety also depends on the social context and the characteristics of the stranger (Kagan, 2008).

Infants show less stranger anxiety when they are in familiar settings. For example, in one study, 10-month-olds showed little stranger anxiety when they met a stranger in their own home but much greater fear when they encountered a stranger in a research laboratory (Sroufe, Waters, & Matas, 1974). Also, infants show less stranger anxiety when they are sitting on their mothers' laps than when placed in an infant seat several feet away from their mothers (Bohlin & Hagekull, 1993). Thus, it appears that, when infants feel secure, they are less likely to show stranger anxiety.

Who the stranger is and how the stranger behaves also influence stranger anxiety in infants. Infants are less fearful of child strangers than adult strangers. They also are less fearful of friendly, outgoing, smiling strangers than of passive, unsmiling strangers (Bretherton, Stolberg, & Kreye, 1981).

In addition to stranger anxiety, infants experience fear of being separated from their caregivers (Scher & Harel, 2008). The result is **separation protest**—crying when the caregiver leaves. Separation protest tends to peak at about 15 months among U.S. infants (Kagan, 2008). In fact, one study found that separation protest peaked at about 13 to 15 months in four different cultures (Kagan, Kearsley, & Zelazo, 1978). As indicated in Figure 10.5, the percentage of infants who engaged in separation protest varied across cultures, but the infants reached a peak of protest at about the same age—just before the middle of the second year of life.

Emotional Regulation and Coping   Earlier, we described some general developmental changes in emotional regulation across the childhood years. Here we examine in more detail how infants develop emotional regulation and coping skills.

During the first year of life, the infant gradually develops an ability to inhibit, or minimize, the intensity and duration of emotional reactions (Eisenberg, Spinrad, &

Smith, 2004). From early in infancy, babies put their thumbs in their mouths to soothe themselves. But at first, infants mainly depend on caregivers to help them soothe their emotions, as when a caregiver rocks an infant to sleep, sings lullabyes to the infant, gently strokes the infant, and so on.

The caregivers' actions influence the infant's neurobiological regulation of emotions (Saarni & others, 2006; Thompson, 2006; Thompson, Easterbrooks, & Walker, 2003). By soothing the infant, caregivers help infants to modulate their emotion and reduce the level of stress hormones (Gunnar & Quevado, 2007). Many developmentalists stress that it is a good strategy for a caregiver to soothe an infant before the infant gets into an intense, agitated, uncontrolled state (Thompson, 1994).

Later in infancy, when they become aroused, infants sometimes redirect their attention or distract themselves in order to reduce their arousal (Grolnick, Bridges, & Connell, 1996). By 2 years of age, toddlers can use language to define their feeling states and the context that is upsetting them (Kopp & Neufeld, 2002). A toddler might say, "Feel bad. Dog scare." This type of communication may help caregivers to help the child in regulating emotion.

Contexts can influence emotional regulation (Kopp & Neufeld, 2002; Saarni & others, 2006; Thompson, 2009a, b). Infants are often affected by fatigue, hunger, time of day, which people are around them, and where they are. Infants must learn to adapt to different contexts that require emotional regulation. Further, new demands appear as the infant becomes older and parents modify their expectations. For example, a parent may take it in stride if a 6-month-old infant screams in a grocery store but may react very differently if a 2-year-old starts screaming.

To soothe or not to soothe—should a crying baby be given attention and soothed, or does this spoil the infant? Many years ago, the behaviorist John Watson (1928) argued that parents spend too much time responding to infant crying. As a consequence, he said, parents reward crying and increase its incidence. Some researchers have found that a caregiver's quick, soothing response to crying increased crying (Gewirtz, 1977). However, infancy experts Mary Ainsworth (1979) and John Bowlby (1989) stress that you can't respond too much to infant crying in the first year of life. They argue that a quick, comforting response to the infant's cries is an important ingredient in the development of a strong bond between the infant and caregiver. In one of Ainsworth's studies, infants whose mothers responded quickly when they cried at 3 months of age cried less later in the first year of life (Bell & Ainsworth, 1972).

Controversy still characterizes the question of whether or how parents should respond to an infant's cries (Lewis & Ramsay, 1999). However, developmentalists increasingly argue that an infant cannot be spoiled in the first year of life, which suggests that parents should soothe a crying infant. This reaction should help infants develop a sense of trust and secure attachment to the caregiver.

Another technique for calming young infants is *swaddling,* which involves wrapping a young baby in a blanket. Swaddling is popular in many Middle Eastern countries and in the Navajo nation in the United States (Whiting, 1981). However, in the United States swaddling has generally been unpopular because it restricts freedom of movement and is thought to make babies passive (Chisolm, 1989; Saarni & others, 2006). Nonetheless, an increasing number of pediatricians recommend swaddling. Some recent research studies have shown positive outcomes for swaddling. In one study, newborns with brain injuries were randomly assigned to a swaddling condition (wrapping the baby in a blanket) or a massage therapy condition (Ohgi & others, 2004). Swaddling reduced the infants' crying more than the massage therapy. A

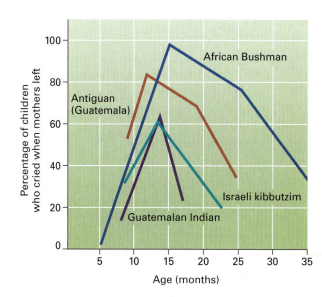

FIGURE 10.5 Separation Protest in Four Cultures. Note that separation protest peaked at about the same time in all four cultures in this study (13 to 15 months of age) (Kagan, Kearsley, & Zelazo, 1978). However, a higher percentage (100 percent) of infants in an African Bushman culture engaged in separation protest compared to only about 60 percent of infants in Guatemalan Indian and Israeli kibbutzim cultures. *What might explain the fact that separation protest peaks at about the same time in these cultures?*

Should a baby be given attention and soothed, or does this spoil the infant? Should the infant's age, the type of cry, and the circumstances be considered?

A young child expressing the emotion of shame. *Why is shame called a "self-conscious emotion"?*

recent research review concluded that swaddled infants arouse less and sleep longer (van Sleuwen & others, 2007).

Pediatricians and nurses who recommend swaddling stress that it stops the baby's uncontrolled arm and leg movements that can lead to frenzied crying (Huang & others, 2004; Karp, 2002). They also recommend tucking the baby tightly in the blanket so it does not become loose and become wrapped around the baby's face. An excellent book on how to calm a crying baby, including specific instructions on swaddling, is *The Happiest Baby on the Block* (Karp, 2002).

Early Childhood

The young child's growing awareness of self is linked to the ability to feel an expanding range of emotions. Young children, like adults, experience many emotions during the course of a day. At times, they also try to make sense of other people's emotional reactions and to control their own emotions.

Self-Conscious Emotions   Recall from our earlier discussion that even young infants experience emotions such as joy and fear, but to experience *self-conscious emotions,* children must be able to refer to themselves and be aware of themselves as distinct from others (Lewis, 2007, 2008). Pride, shame, embarrassment, and guilt are examples of self-conscious emotions. Self-conscious emotions do not appear to develop until self-awareness appears in the last half of the second year of life.

During the early childhood years, emotions such as pride and guilt become more common. They are especially influenced by parents' responses to children's behavior. For example, a young child may experience shame when a parent says, "You should feel bad about biting your sister."

The development of self-conscious emotions reflects the importance of connections between emotional development and cognitive development (Dragi-Lorenz, 2007; Lewis, 2007, 2008). We will have much more to say about these connections as they pertain to the development of the self in Chapter 11.

Young Children's Emotion Language and Understanding of Emotion   Among the most important changes in emotional development in early childhood are an increased ability to talk about their own and others' emotions and an increased understanding of emotion (Kuebli, 1994). Between 2 and 4 years of age, children considerably increase the number of terms they use to describe emotions (Ridgeway, Waters, & Kuczaj, 1985). They also are learning about the causes and consequences of feelings (Denham, 1998; Denham, Bassett, & Wyatt, 2007).

When they are 4 to 5 years of age, children show an increased ability to reflect on emotions. They also begin to understand that the same event can elicit different feelings in different people. Moreover, they show a growing awareness that they need to manage their emotions to meet social standards (Bruce, Olen, & Jensen, 1999).

Middle and Late Childhood

During middle and late childhood, many children show marked improvement in understanding and managing their emotions. However, in some instances, as when they experience stressful circumstances, their coping abilities can be challenged.

Developmental Changes in Emotion   Here are some important developmental changes in emotions during these years (Kuebli, 1994; Thompson & Goodvin, 2005; Wintre & Vallance, 1994):

- *Improved emotional understanding.* Children in elementary school develop an increased ability to understand such complex emotions as pride and shame. These emotions become less tied to the reactions of other people; they become more self-generated and integrated with a sense of personal responsibility. A child may feel a sense of pride about developing new reading skills or shame after hurting a friend's feelings.

- *Marked improvements in the ability to suppress or conceal negative emotional reactions.* Children now sometimes intentionally hide their emotions. Although a boy may feel sad that a friend does not want to play with him, he may decide not to share those feelings with his parents.

- *The use of self-initiated strategies for redirecting feelings.* In the elementary school years, children reflect more about emotional experiences and develop strategies to cope with their emotional lives. Children can more effectively manage their emotions by cognitive means, such as using distracting thoughts. A boy may be excited about his birthday party later in the afternoon, but still be able to concentrate on his schoolwork during the day.

- *An increased tendency to take into fuller account the events leading to emotional reactions.*

- *Development of a capacity for genuine empathy.* Two girls see another child in distress on the playground and run to the child and ask if they can help.

Coping with Stress   An important aspect of children's lives is learning how to cope with stress (Coplan & Arbeau, 2008; Findlay, Coplan, & Bowker, 2008). As children get older, they are able to more accurately appraise a stressful situation and determine how much control they have over it. Older children generate more coping alternatives to stressful conditions and use more cognitive coping strategies (Saarni & others, 2006). For example, older children are better than younger children at intentionally shifting their thoughts to something that is less stressful. Older children are also better at reframing, or changing one's perception of a stressful situation. For example, younger children may be very disappointed that their teacher did not say hello to them when they arrived at school. Older children may reframe this type of situation and think, "She may have been busy with other things and just forgot to say hello."

By 10 years of age, most children are able to use these cognitive strategies to cope with stress (Saarni & others, 2006). However, in families that have not been supportive and are characterized by turmoil or trauma, children may be so overwhelmed by stress that they do not use such strategies (Field & others, 2008; Klingman, 2006).

The terrorist attacks on the World Trade Center in New York City and the Pentagon in Washington, D.C., on September 11, 2001, and Hurricanes Katrina and Rita in August and September 2005, raised special concerns about how to help children cope with such stressful events. Children who have a number of coping techniques have the best chance of adapting and functioning competently in the face of traumatic events. Here are some recommendations for helping children cope with the stress of these types of events (Gurwitch & others, 2001, pp. 4–11):

- *Reassure children of their safety and security.* This may need to be done numerous times.

- *Allow children to retell events and be patient in listening to them.*

- *Encourage children to talk about any disturbing or confusing feelings.* Tell them that these are normal feelings after a stressful event.

- *Help children make sense of what happened.* Children may misunderstand what took place. For example, young children "may blame themselves, believe things happened that did not happen, believe that terrorists are in the school, etc. Gently help children develop a realistic understanding of the event" (p. 10).

- *Protect children from reexposure to frightening situations and reminders of the trauma.* This includes limiting conversations about the event in front of the children.

What are some effective strategies to help children cope with traumatic events such as Hurricane Katrina in August 2005?

3 TEMPERAMENT

"Oh, he's cute, all right, but he's got the temperament of a car alarm."
© The New Yorker Collection 1999. Barbara Smaller from cartoonbank.com. All rights reserved. Reprinted with permission.

Describing and Classifying Temperament

Biological Foundations and Experience

Goodness of Fit and Parenting

Do you get upset a lot? Does it take much to get you angry, or to make you laugh? Even at birth, babies seem to have different emotional styles. One infant is cheerful and happy much of the time; another baby seems to cry constantly. These tendencies reflect **temperament**, which is an individual's behavioral style and characteristic way of responding.

Describing and Classifying Temperament

How would you describe your temperament or the temperament of a friend? Researchers have described and classified the temperament of individuals in different ways. Here we will examine three of those ways.

Chess and Thomas' Classification Psychiatrists Alexander Chess and Stella Thomas (Chess & Thomas, 1977; Thomas & Chess, 1991) identified three basic types, or clusters, of temperament:

- An **easy child** is generally in a positive mood, quickly establishes regular routines in infancy, and adapts easily to new experiences.
- A **difficult child** reacts negatively and cries frequently, engages in irregular daily routines, and is slow to accept change.
- A **slow-to-warm-up child** has a low activity level, is somewhat negative, and displays a low intensity of mood.

In their longitudinal investigation, Chess and Thomas found that 40 percent of the children they studied could be classified as easy, 10 percent as difficult, and 15 percent as slow to warm up. Notice that 35 percent did not fit any of the three patterns. Researchers have found that these three basic clusters of temperament are moderately stable across the childhood years.

temperament An individual's behavioral style and characteristic emotional response.

easy child A temperament style in which the child is generally in a positive mood, quickly establishes regular routines, and adapts easily to new experiences.

difficult child A temperament style in which the child tends to react negatively and cry frequently, engages in irregular daily routines, and is slow to accept new experiences.

slow-to-warm-up child A temperament style in which the child has a low activity level, is somewhat negative, and displays a low intensity of mood.

Kagan's Behavioral Inhibition Another way of classifying temperament focuses on the differences between a shy, subdued, timid child and a sociable, extraverted, bold child (Asendorph, 2008; Jerome Kagan (2000, 2002, 2007, 2008, 2009) regards shyness with strangers (peers or adults) as one feature of a broad temperament category called *inhibition to the unfamiliar.* Inhibited children react to many aspects of unfamiliarity with initial avoidance, distress, or subdued affect, beginning about 7 to 9 months of age.

Kagan has found that inhibition shows considerable stability from infancy through early childhood. One study classified toddlers into extremely inhibited, extremely uninhibited, and intermediate groups (Pfeifer & others, 2002). Follow-up assessments occurred at 4 and 7 years of age. Continuity was demonstrated for both inhibition and lack of inhibition, although a substantial number of the inhibited children moved into the intermediate groups at 7 years of age.

Rothbart and Bates' Classification New classifications of temperament continue to be forged. Mary Rothbart and John Bates (2006) argue that three broad dimensions best represent what researchers have found to characterize the structure of temperament: extraversion/surgency, negative affectivity, and effortful control (self-regulation):

What are some ways that developmentalists have classified infants' temperaments? Which classification makes the most sense to you based on your observations of infants?

- *Extraversion/surgency* includes "positive anticipation, impulsivity, activity level, and sensation seeking" (Rothbart, 2004, p. 495). Kagan's uninhibited children fit into this category.

- *Negative affectivity* includes "fear, frustration, sadness, and discomfort" (Rothbart, 2004, p. 495). These children are easily distressed; they may fret and cry often. Kagan's inhibited children fit this category. Negative emotional reactivity or irritability reflect the core of Chess and Thomas' category of the difficult child (Bates & Pettit, 2007).

- *Effortful control (self-regulation)* includes "attentional focusing and shifting, inhibitory control, perceptual sensitivity, and low-intensity pleasure" (Rothbart, 2004, p. 495). Infants who are high on effortful control show an ability to keep their arousal from getting too high and have strategies for soothing themselves. By contrast, children low on effortful control are often unable to control their arousal; they become easily agitated and intensely emotional (Rothbart & Sheese, 2007).

In Rothbart's (2004, p. 497) view, "early theoretical models of temperament stressed the way we are moved by our positive and negative emotions or level of arousal, with our actions driven by these tendencies." The more recent emphasis on effortful control, however, advocates that individuals can engage in a more cognitive, flexible approach to stressful circumstances.

Rothbart and Maria Gartstein (2008, p. 323) recently described the following developmental changes in temperament during infancy. During early infancy, smiling and laughter are emerging as part of the positive affectivity dimension of temperament. Also, by 2 months of age, infants show anger and frustration when their actions don't produce an interesting outcome. During this time, infants often are susceptible to distress and overstimulation. From 4 to 12 months of age, fear and irritability become more differentiated with inhibition (fear) increasingly linked to new and unpredictable experiences. Not all temperament characteristics are in place by the first birthday. Positive emotionality becomes more stable later in infancy, and the characteristics of extraversion/surgency can be determined in the toddler period. Improved attention skills in the toddler and preschool years are related to an increase in effortful control, which serves as a foundation for improved self-regulation (Rothbart, 2009).

Biological Foundations and Experience

How does a child acquire a certain temperament? Kagan (2002, 2003, 2007, 2009) argues that children inherit a physiology that biases them to have a particular type of temperament. However, through experience they may learn to modify their temperament to some degree. For example, children may inherit a physiology that biases them to be fearful and inhibited, but they learn to reduce their fear and inhibition to some degree.

Biological Influences

Physiological characteristics have been linked with different temperaments (Asendorph, 2008; Rothbart & Bates, 2006). In particular, an inhibited temperament is associated with a unique physiological pattern that includes high and stable heart rate, high level of the hormone cortisol, and high activity in the right frontal lobe of the brain (Kagan, 2003, 2007, 2008, 2009). This pattern may be tied to the excitability of the amygdala, a structure of the brain that plays an important role in fear and inhibition (Kagan, 2003, 2007, 2008, 2009; LeDoux, 1998, 2002). An inhibited temperament or negative affectivity may also be linked to low levels of the neurotransmitter serotonin, which may increase an individual's vulnerability to fear and frustration (Kramer, 1993).

What is heredity's role in the biological foundations of temperament? Twin and adoption studies suggest that heredity has a moderate influence on differences in temperament within a group of people (Plomin & others, 1994). The contemporary view is that temperament is a biologically based but evolving aspect of behavior; it evolves as the child's experiences are incorporated into a network of self-perceptions and behavioral preferences that characterize the child's personality (Thompson & Goodvin, 2005).

Developmental Connections

Do young adults show the same behavioral style and characteristic emotional responses as they did when they were infants or young children? Activity level is an important dimension of temperament. Are children's activity levels linked to their personality in early adulthood? In one longitudinal study, children who were highly active at age 4 were likely to be very outgoing at age 23, which reflects continuity (Franz, 1996). From adolescence into early adulthood, most individuals show fewer emotional mood swings, become more responsible, and engage in less risk-taking behavior, which reflects discontinuity (Caspi, 1998).

Is temperament in childhood linked with adjustment in adulthood? Here is what we know based on the few longitudinal studies that have been conducted on this topic (Caspi, 1998). In one longitudinal study, children who had an easy temperament at 3 to 5 years of age were likely to be well adjusted as young adults (Chess & Thomas, 1977). In contrast, many children who had a difficult temperament at 3 to 5 years of age were not well adjusted as young adults. Also, other researchers have found that boys with a difficult temperament in childhood are less likely as adults to continue their formal education, whereas girls with a difficult temperament in childhood are more likely to experience marital conflict as adults (Wachs, 2000).

Inhibition is another temperament characteristic that has been studied extensively (Asendorph, 2008; Kagan, 2008, 2009). Researchers have found that individuals with an inhibited temperament in childhood are less likely as adults to be assertive or to experience social support, and more likely to delay entering a stable job track (Wachs, 2000). A recent study revealed that infants classified as highly reactive (vigorous motor activity and frequent crying) to unfamiliar stimuli were likely to avoid unfamiliar events in infancy and often were subdued, cautious, and wary of new situations in adolescence (Kagan & others, 2007). By contrast, low-reactive infants were unlikely to approach unfamiliar events in infancy and be emotionally spontaneous and sociable in adolescence.

Yet another aspect of temperament involves emotionality and the ability to control one's emotions. In one longitudinal study, when 3-year-old children showed good control of their emotions and were resilient in the face of stress, they were likely to continue to handle emotions effectively as adults (Block, 1993). By contrast, when 3-year-olds had low emotional control and were not very resilient, they were likely to show problems in these areas as young adults.

Initial Temperament Trait: Inhibition

	Child A	Child B
	Intervening Context	
Caregivers	Caregivers (parents) who are sensitive and accepting, and let the child set his or her own pace.	Caregivers who use inappropriate "low level control" and attempt to force the child into new situations.
Physical Environment	Presence of "stimulus shelters" or "defensible spaces" that the children can retreat to when there is too much stimulation.	The child continually encounters noisy, chaotic environments that allow no escape from stimulation.
Peers	Peer groups with other inhibited children with common interests, so the child feels accepted.	Peer groups consist of athletic extraverts, so the child feels rejected.
Schools	School is "undermanned" so inhibited children are more likely to be tolerated and feel they can make a contribution.	School is "overmanned" so inhibited children are less likely to be tolerated and more likely to feel undervalued.
	Personality Outcomes	
	As an adult, individual is closer to extraversion (outgoing, sociable) and is emotionally stable.	As an adult, individual is closer to introversion and has more emotional problems.

FIGURE 10.6 Temperament in Childhood, Personality in Adulthood, and Intervening Contexts. Varying experiences with caregivers, the physical environment, peers, and schools may modify links between temperament in childhood and personality in adulthood. The example given here is for inhibition.

In sum, these studies reveal some continuity between certain aspects of temperament in childhood and adjustment in early adulthood. However, keep in mind that these connections between childhood temperament and adult adjustment are based on only a small number of studies; more research is needed to verify these linkages.

Developmental Contexts What accounts for the continuities and discontinuities between a child's temperament and an adult's personality? Physiological and hereditary factors likely are involved in continuity (Kagan, 2008, 2009). Theodore Wachs (1994, 2000) proposed ways that linkages between temperament in childhood and personality in adulthood might vary depending on the contexts in individuals' experience. Figure 10.6 summarizes how one characteristic might develop in different ways, depending on the context.

Gender can be an important factor shaping the context that influences the fate of temperament. Parents might react differently to a child's temperament, depending on whether the child is a boy or a girl and on the culture in which they live (Kerr, 2001). For example, in one study, mothers were more responsive to the crying of irritable girls than to the crying of irritable boys (Crockenberg, 1986).

Similarly, the reaction to an infant's temperament may depend, in part, on culture (Austin & Chorpita, 2004; Cole & Tan, 2007). For example, an active temperament might be valued in some cultures (such as the United States) but not in other cultures (such as China). Indeed, children's temperament can vary across cultures (Cole & Tan, 2007; Putnam, Sanson, & Rothbart, 2002). Behavioral inhibition is more highly valued in China than in North America, and researchers have found that Chinese infants are more inhibited than Canadian infants (Chen & others, 1998). The cultural differences in temperament were linked to parental attitudes and behaviors. Canadian mothers of inhibited 2-year-olds were less accepting of their infants' inhibited temperament, whereas Chinese mothers were more accepting.

In short, many aspects of a child's environment can encourage or discourage the persistence of temperament characteristics (Rothbart, 2009; Rothbart & Garstein, 2008). One useful way of thinking about these relationships applies the concept of goodness of fit, which we examine next.

Goodness of Fit and Parenting

Goodness of fit refers to the match between a child's temperament and the environmental demands the child must cope with (Bates & Pettit, 2007; Schoppe-Sullivan & others, 2007). Suppose Jason is an active toddler who is made to sit still for long periods of time and Jack is a slow-to-warm-up toddler who is abruptly pushed into new situations on a regular basis. Both Jason and Jack face a lack of fit between their temperament and environmental demands. Lack of fit can produce adjustment problems (Rothbart, 2009; Rothbart & Bates, 2006).

Some temperament characteristics pose more parenting challenges than others, at least in modern Western societies (Bates & Pettit, 2007; Rothbart & Garstein, 2008). When children are prone to distress, as exhibited by frequent crying and irritability, their parents may eventually respond by ignoring the child's distress or trying to force the child to "behave." In one research study, though, extra support and training for mothers of distress-prone infants improved the quality of mother-infant interaction (van den Boom, 1989). The training led the mothers to alter their demands on the child, improving the fit between the child and the environment. Also, in a longitudinal study, researchers found that a high level of fearlessness on the part of infants, when combined with harsh parenting, was linked with persistent conduct problems at age 8 (Shaw & others, 2003).

Many parents don't become believers in temperament's importance until the birth of their second child. They viewed their first child's behavior as a result of how they treated the child. But then they find that some strategies that worked with their first child are not as effective with the second child. Some problems experienced with the first child (such as those involved in feeding, sleeping, and coping with strangers) do not exist with the second child, but new problems arise. Such experiences strongly suggest that children differ from each other very early in life, and that these differences have important implications for parent-child interaction (Kwak & others, 1999; Rothbart & Putnam, 2002).

To read further about some positive strategies for parenting that take into account the child's temperament, see the *Caring for Children* interlude.

Caring for Children

PARENTING AND THE CHILD'S TEMPERAMENT

What are the implications of temperamental variations for parenting? Although answers to this question necessarily are speculative, these conclusions regarding the best parenting strategies to use in relation to children's temperament were reached by temperament experts Ann Sanson and Mary Rothbart (1995):

- *Attention to and respect for individuality.* One implication is that it is difficult to generate general prescriptions for "good parenting." A goal might be accomplished in one way with one child and in another way with another child, depending on the child's temperament. Parents need to be sensitive and flexible to the infant's signals and needs.

- *Structuring the child's environment.* Crowded, noisy environments can pose greater problems for some children (such as a "difficult child" than others (such as an "easy child"). We might also expect that a fearful, withdrawing child would benefit from slower entry into new contexts.

- *The "difficult child" and packaged parenting programs.* Programs for parents often focus on dealing with children who have "difficult" temperaments. In some cases, "difficult child" refers to Thomas and Chess' description of a child who reacts negatively, cries frequently, engages in irregular daily routines, and is slow to accept change. In others, the concept might be used to describe a child who is

What are some good strategies for parents to adopt when responding to their infant's temperament?

goodness of fit The match between a child's temperament and the environmental demands the child must cope with.

irritable, displays anger frequently, does not follow directions well, or has some other negative characteristic. Acknowledging that some children are harder than others to parent is often helpful, and advice on how to handle particular difficult characteristics can be useful. However, whether a particular characteristic is difficult depends on its fit with the environment. To label a child "difficult" has the danger of becoming a self-fulfilling prophecy. If a child is identified as difficult, people may treat the child in a way that actually elicits difficult behavior. One recent study did find that having access to experiences that encourage coping and build self-regulatory skills was beneficial to children with a difficult temperament (Bradley & Corwyn, 2008).

Too often, we pigeonhole children into categories without examining the context (Rothbart & Bates, 2006; Wachs, 2000). Nonetheless, caregivers need to take children's temperament into account. Research does not yet allow for many highly specific recommendations, but, in general, caregivers should (1) be sensitive to the individual characteristics of the child, (2) be flexible in responding to these characteristics, and (3) avoid applying negative labels to the child.

Review and Reflect: Learning Goal 3

3 Characterize Variations in Temperament and Their Significance

REVIEW

- How can temperament be described and classified?
- How is temperament influenced by biological foundations and experience?
- What is goodness of fit? What are some positive parenting strategies for dealing with a child's temperament?

REFLECT

- Consider your own temperament. We described a number of temperament categories. Which one best describes your temperament? Has your temperament changed as you have gotten older? If your temperament has changed, what factors contributed to the changes?

---

4 SOCIAL ORIENTATION/UNDERSTANDING, ATTACHMENT, AND CHILD CARE

| Social Orientation/Understanding | Attachment | Child Care |

So far, we have discussed how emotions and emotional competence change as children develop. We have also examined the role of emotional style; in effect, we have seen how emotions set the tone of our experiences in life. But emotions also write the lyrics because they are at the core of our interest in the social world and our relationships with others.

A mother and her baby engaging in face-to-face play. *At what age does face-to-face play usually begin, and when does it typically start decreasing in frequency?*

Social Orientation/Understanding

As socioemotional beings, infants show a strong interest in the social world and are motivated to orient to it and understand it. In earlier chapters, we described many of the biological and cognitive foundations that contribute to the infant's development of social orientation and understanding. We will call attention to relevant biological and cognitive factors as we explore social orientation; locomotion; intention, goal-directed behavior, and cooperation; and social referencing. Discussing biological, cognitive, and social processes together reminds us of an important aspect of development that was pointed out in Chapter 1: These processes are intricately intertwined (Diamond, 2007).

Social Orientation   From early in their development, infants are captivated by the social world. As we discussed in our coverage of infant perception in Chapter 5, young infants stare intently at faces and are attuned to the sounds of human voices, especially their caregiver's (Ramsay-Rennels & Langlois, 2007; Saffran, Werker, & Werner, 2006). Later, they become adept at interpreting the meaning of facial expressions.

Face-to-face play often begins to characterize caregiver-infant interactions when the infant is about 2 to 3 months of age. The focused social interaction of face-to-face play may include vocalizations, touch, and gestures (Leppanen & others, 2007). Such play is part of many mothers' motivation to create a positive emotional state in their infants (Laible & Thompson, 2007; Thompson, 2006).

In part because of such positive social interchanges between caregivers and infants, by 2 to 3 months of age, infants respond differently to people than objects, showing more positive emotion to people than inanimate objects, such as puppets (Legerstee, 1997). At this age, most infants expect people to react positively when the infants initiate a behavior, such as a smile or a vocalization. This finding has been discovered using a method called the *still-face paradigm*, in which the caregiver alternates between engaging in face-to-face interaction with the infant and remaining still and unresponsive. As early as 2 to 3 months of age, infants show more withdrawal, negative emotions, and self-directed behavior when their caregivers are still and unresponsive (Adamson & Frick, 2003). The frequency of face-to-face play decreases after 7 months of age as infants become more mobile (Thompson, 2006).

Infants also learn about the social world through contexts other than face-to-face play with a caregiver (Field, 2007; Thompson & Newton, 2009). Even though infants as young as 6 months of age show an interest in each other, their interaction with peers increases considerably in the last half of the second year. Between 18 to 24 months of age, children markedly increase their imitative and reciprocal play, such as imitating nonverbal actions like jumping and running (Eckerman & Whitehead, 1999). One recent study involved presenting 1- and 2-year-olds with a simple cooperative task that consisted of pulling a lever to get an attractive toy (Brownell, Ramani, & Zerwas, 2006) (see Figure 10.7). Any coordinated actions of the 1-year-olds appeared to be more coincidental rather than cooperative, whereas the 2-year-olds' behavior was characterized as more active cooperation to reach a goal. As increasing numbers of U.S. infants experience child care outside the home, they are spending more time in social play with other peers (Field, 2007). Later in the chapter, we will further discuss child care.

FIGURE 10.7 The Cooperation Task. The cooperation on task consisted of two handles on a box, atop which was an animated musical toy, surreptitiously activated by remote control when both handles were pulled. The handles were placed far enough apart that one child could not pull both handles. The experimenter demonstrated the task, saying, "Watch! If you pull the handles, the doggie will sing" (Brownell, Ramani, & Zerwas, 2006).

Locomotion   Recall from earlier in the chapter how important independence is for infants, especially in the second year of life. As infants develop the ability to crawl, walk, and run, they are able to explore and expand their social world. These newly developed self-produced locomotor skills allow the infant to independently initiate social interchanges on a more frequent basis (Laible & Thompson, 2007; Thompson, 2006). Remember from Chapter 5 that the development of these gross motor skills is the result of a number of factors including the development of the nervous system, the goal the infant is motivated to reach, and environmental support for the skill (Adolph & Joh, 2007, 2008; Thelen & Smith, 2006).

Locomotion is also important for its motivational implications (Thompson, 2008). Once infants have the ability to move in goal-directed pursuits, the reward from these pursuits leads to further efforts to explore and develop skills.

Intention, Goal-Directed Behavior, and Cooperation   Perceiving people as engaging in intentional and goal-directed behavior is an important social cognitive accomplishment, and this initially occurs toward the end of the first year (Laible & Thompson, 2007; Thompson, 2006). Joint attention and gaze following help the infant to understand that other people have intentions (Meltzoff, 2007; Mundy & Newell, 2007; Mundy & others, 2007; Tomasello & Carpenter, 2007). Recall from Chapter 7 that *joint attention* occurs when the caregiver and infant focus on the same object or event. We indicated that emerging aspects of joint attention occur at about 7 to 8 months, but at about 10 to 11 months of age joint attention intensifies and infants begin to follow the caregiver's gaze. By their first birthday, infants have begun to direct the caregiver's attention to objects that capture their interest (Heimann & others, 2006).

In the study on cooperating to reach a goal that was discussed earlier, 1- and 2-year-olds also were assessed with two social understanding tasks, observation of children's behavior in a joint attention task, and the parents' perceptions of the language the children use about the self and others (Brownell, Ramani, & Zerwas, 2006). Those with more advanced social understanding were more likely to cooperate. To cooperate, the children had to connect their own intentions with the peer's intentions and put this understanding to use in interacting with the peer to reach a goal. Further, a recent study revealed that initiating and responding to joint attention at 12 months of age were linked to being socially competent (for example, not aggressive or defiant, showing empathy, and engaging in sustained attention) at 30 months of age (Vaughn, Van Hecke & others, 2007).

Social Referencing   Another important social cognitive accomplishment in infancy is developing the ability to "read" the emotions of other people. **Social referencing** is the term used to describe "reading" emotional cues in others to help determine how to act in a particular situation. The development of social referencing helps infants to interpret ambiguous situations more accurately, as when they encounter a stranger and need to know whether to fear the person (de Rosnay & others, 2006; Thompson, 2006). By the end of the first year, a mother's facial expression—either smiling or fearful—influences whether an infant will explore an unfamiliar environment.

Infants become better at social referencing in the second year of life. At this age, they tend to "check" with their mother before they act; they look at her to see if she is happy, angry, or fearful. For example, in one study, 14- to 22-month-old infants were more likely to look at their mother's face as a source of information for how to act in a situation than were 6 to 9-month-old infants (Walden, 1991).

Infants' Social Sophistication and Insight   In sum, researchers are discovering that infants are more socially sophisticated and insightful at younger ages than previously envisioned (Hamlin, Hallinan, & Woodward, 2008; Thompson, 2008, 2009a, b). This sophistication and insight is reflected in infants perceptions of others' actions as intentionally motivated and goal-directed (Brune & Woodward, 2007) and their motivation to share and participate in that intentionality by their first birthday (Tomasello & Carpenter, 2007). The more advanced social cognitive skills of infants could be expected to influence their understanding and awareness of attachment to a caregiver.

social referencing "Reading" emotional cues in others to help determine how to act in a particular situation.

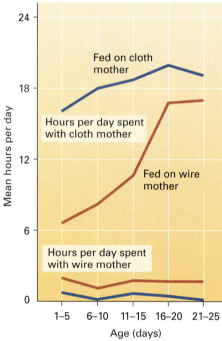

FIGURE 10.8 Contact Time with Wire and Cloth Surrogate Mothers. Regardless of whether the infant monkeys were fed by a wire or a cloth mother, they overwhelmingly preferred to spend contact time with the cloth mother. *How do these results compare with what Freud's theory and Erikson's theory would predict about human infants?*

attachment A close emotional bond between two people.

Attachment

A small curly-haired girl named Danielle, age 11 months, begins to whimper. After a few seconds, she begins to wail. Soon her mother comes into the room, and Danielle's crying ceases. Quickly, Danielle crawls over to where her mother is seated and reaches out to be held. Danielle has just demonstrated *attachment* to her mother. **Attachment** is a close emotional bond between two people.

Theories of Attachment There is no shortage of theories about why infants like Danielle become attached to a caregiver. Three theorists discussed in Chapter 1—Freud, Erikson, and Bowlby—proposed influential views.

Freud reasoned that infants become attached to the person or object that provides oral satisfaction. For most infants, this is the mother, since she is most likely to feed the infant. Is feeding as important as Freud thought? A classic study by Harry Harlow (1958) reveals that the answer is no (see Figure 10.8).

Harlow removed infant monkeys from their mothers at birth; for six months they were reared by surrogate (substitute) "mothers." One surrogate mother was made of wire, the other of cloth. Half of the infant monkeys were fed by the wire mother, half by the cloth mother. Periodically, the amount of time the infant monkeys spent with either the wire or the cloth mother was computed. Regardless of which mother fed them, the infant monkeys spent far more time with the cloth mother. Even if the wire mother but not the cloth mother provided nourishment, the infant monkeys spent more time with the cloth mother. And when Harlow frightened the monkeys, those "raised" by the cloth mother ran to the mother and clung to it; those raised by the wire mother did not. Whether the mother provided comfort seemed to determine whether the monkeys associated the mother with security. This study clearly demonstrated that feeding is not the crucial element in the attachment process, and that contact comfort is important.

Physical comfort also plays a role in Erik Erikson's (1968) view of the infant's development. Recall Erikson's proposal that the first year of life represents the stage of trust versus mistrust. Physical comfort and sensitive care, according to Erikson (1968), are key to establishing a basic trust in infants. The infant's sense of trust, in turn, is the foundation for attachment and sets the stage for a lifelong expectation that the world will be a good and pleasant place to be.

The ethological perspective of British psychiatrist John Bowlby (1969, 1989) also stresses the importance of attachment in the first year of life and the responsiveness of the caregiver. Bowlby points out that both infants and their primary caregivers are biologically predisposed to form attachments. He argues that the newborn is biologically equipped to elicit attachment behavior. The baby cries, clings, coos, and smiles. Later, the infant crawls, walks, and follows the mother. The immediate result is to keep the primary caregiver nearby; the long-term effect is to increase the infant's chances of survival.

Attachment does not emerge suddenly but rather develops in a series of phases, moving from a baby's general preference for human beings to a partnership with primary caregivers. Following are four such phases based on Bowlby's conceptualization of attachment (Schaffer, 1996):

- *Phase 1: From birth to 2 months.* Infants instinctively direct their attachment to human figures. Strangers, siblings, and parents are equally likely to elicit smiling or crying from the infant.

- *Phase 2: From 2 to 7 months.* Attachment becomes focused on one figure, usually the primary caregiver, as the baby gradually learns to distinguish familiar from unfamiliar people.

- *Phase 3: From 7 to 24 months.* Specific attachments develop. With increased locomotor skills, babies actively seek contact with regular caregivers, such as the mother or father.

- *Phase 4: From 24 months on.* Children become aware of others' feelings, goals, and plans and begin to take these into account in forming their own actions. Researchers' recent findings that infants are more socially sophisticated and insightful than previously envisioned suggests that some of the characteristics of Bowlby's phase 4, such as understanding the goals and intentions of the attachment figure, appear to be developing in phase 3 as attachment security is taking shape (Thompson, 2008).

Bowlby argued that infants develop an *internal working model* of attachment, a simple mental model of the caregiver, their relationship, and the self as deserving of nurturant care. The infant's internal working model of attachment with the caregiver influences the infant's and later the child's subsequent responses to other people (Bretherton & Munholland, 2009; Posada, 2008). The internal model of attachment also has played a pivotal role in the discovery of links between attachment and subsequent emotion understanding, conscious development, and self-concept (Thompson, 2006, 2009c).

In sum, attachment emerges from the social cognitive advances that allow infants to develop expectations for the caregiver's behavior and to determine the affective quality of their relationship (Laible & Thompson, 2007; Thompson, 2006, 2009c). These social cognitive advances include recognizing the caregiver's face, voice, and other features, as well as developing an internal working model of expecting the caregiver to provide pleasure in social interaction and relief from distress.

Individual Differences in Attachment   Although attachment to a caregiver intensifies midway through the first year, isn't it likely that the quality of babies' attachment experiences varies? Mary Ainsworth (1979) thought so. Ainsworth created the **Strange Situation**, an observational measure of infant attachment in which the infant experiences a series of introductions, separations, and reunions with the caregiver and an adult stranger in a prescribed order. In using the Strange Situation, researchers hope that their observations will provide information about the infant's motivation to be near the caregiver and the degree to which the caregiver's presence provides the infant with security and confidence.

Based on how babies respond in the Strange Situation, they are described as being securely attached or insecurely attached (in one of three ways) to the caregiver:

What is the nature of secure and insecure attachment?

- **Securely attached babies** use the caregiver as a secure base from which to explore the environment. When in the presence of their caregiver, securely attached infants explore the room and examine toys that have been placed in it. When the caregiver departs, securely attached infants might mildly protest, and when the caregiver returns these infants reestablish positive interaction with her, perhaps by smiling or climbing on her lap. Subsequently, they often resume playing with the toys in the room.

- **Insecure avoidant babies** show insecurity by avoiding the mother. In the Strange Situation, these babies engage in little interaction with the caregiver, are not distressed when she leaves the room, usually do not reestablish contact with her on her return, and may even turn their back on her. If contact is established, the infant usually leans away or looks away.

- **Insecure resistant babies** often cling to the caregiver and then resist her by fighting against the closeness, perhaps by kicking or pushing away. In the Strange Situation, these babies often cling anxiously to the caregiver and don't explore the playroom. When the caregiver leaves, they often cry loudly and push away if she tries to comfort them on her return.

- **Insecure disorganized babies** are disorganized and disoriented. In the Strange Situation, these babies might appear dazed, confused, and fearful. To be classified as disorganized, babies must show strong patterns of avoidance and resistance or display certain specified behaviors, such as extreme fearfulness around the caregiver.

Strange Situation Ainsworth's observational measure of infant attachment to a caregiver that requires the infant to move through a series of introductions, separations, and reunions with the caregiver and an adult stranger in a prescribed order.

securely attached babies Babies who use the caregiver as a secure base from which to explore the environment.

insecure avoidant babies Babies who show insecurity by avoiding the mother.

insecure resistant babies Babies who might cling to the caregiver, then resist her by fighting against the closeness, perhaps by kicking or pushing away.

insecure disorganized babies Babies who show insecurity by being disorganized and disoriented.

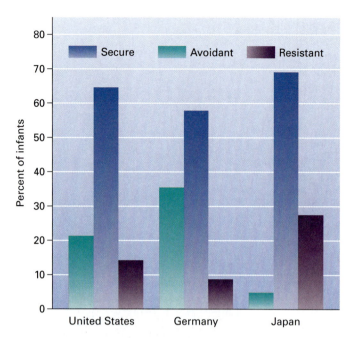

FIGURE 10.9 Cross-Cultural Comparison of Attachment. In one study, infant attachment in three countries—the United States, Germany, and Japan—was measured in the Ainsworth Strange Situation (van IJzendoorn & Kroonenberg, 1988). The dominant attachment pattern in all three countries was secure attachment. However, German infants were more avoidant and Japanese infants were less avoidant and more resistant than U.S. infants. *What are some explanations for differences in how German, Japanese, and U.S. infants respond to the Strange Situation?*

Evaluating the Strange Situation   Does the Strange Situation capture important differences among infants? As a measure of attachment, it may be culturally biased (Grossman & Grossman, 2009; van IJzendoorn & Sagi-Schwartz, 2009). For example, German and Japanese babies often show different patterns of attachment than American infants. As illustrated in Figure 10.9, German infants are more likely to show an avoidant attachment pattern and Japanese infants are less likely to display this pattern than U.S. infants (van IJzendoorn & Kroonenberg, 1988). The avoidant pattern in German babies likely occurs because their caregivers encourage them to be independent (Grossmann & others, 1985). Also as shown in Figure 10.9, Japanese babies are more likely than American babies to be categorized as resistant. This may have more to do with the Strange Situation as a measure of attachment than with attachment insecurity itself. Japanese mothers rarely let anyone unfamiliar with their babies care for them. Thus, the Strange Situation might create considerably more stress for Japanese infants than for American infants, who are more accustomed to separation from their mothers (Miyake, Chen, & Campos, 1985). Even though there are cultural variations in attachment classification, the most frequent classification in every culture studied so far is secure attachment (Thompson, 2006; van IJzendoorn & Kroonenberg, 1988).

Some critics stress that behavior in the Strange Situation—like other laboratory assessments—might not indicate what infants do in a natural environment. But researchers have found that infants' behaviors in the Strange Situation are closely related to how they behave at home in response to separation and reunion with their mothers (Pederson & Moran, 1996). Thus, many infant researchers conclude that the Strange Situation continues to show merit as a measure of infant attachment.

Interpreting Differences in Attachment   Do individual differences in attachment matter? Ainsworth observes that secure attachment in the first year of life provides an important foundation for psychological development later in life. The securely attached infant moves freely away from the mother but keeps track of where she is through periodic glances. The securely attached infant responds positively to being picked up by others and, when put back down, freely moves away to play. An insecurely attached infant, by contrast, avoids the mother or is ambivalent toward her, fears strangers, and is upset by minor, everyday separations.

If early attachment to a caregiver is important, it should relate to a child's social behavior later in development. For some children, early attachments seem to foreshadow later functioning (Benolt, 2009; Egeland, 2009; Sroufe & others, 2005a, b; Steele & others, 2007). In the extensive longitudinal study conducted by Alan Sroufe and his colleagues (2005a, b), early secure attachment (assessed by the Strange Situation at 12 and 18 months) was linked with positive emotional health, high self-esteem, self-confidence, and socially competent interaction with peers, teachers, camp counselors, and romantic partners through adolescence. Another study found that infants who were securely attached at 15 months of age were more cognitively and socioemotionally competent at 4 years of age than their counterparts who were insecurely attached at 15 months of age (Fish, 2004). Yet another study revealed that being classified as insecure ambivalent in infancy was a negative predictor of cognitive development in elementary school (O'Connor & McCartney, 2007).

For some children, though, there is little continuity (Thompson & Goodvin, 2005). Not all research reveals the power of infant attachment to predict subsequent development. In one longitudinal study, attachment classification in infancy did not predict attachment classification at 18 years of age (Lewis, Feiring, & Rosenthal, 2000). In this study, the best predictor of an insecure attachment classification at 18 was the occurrence of parental divorce in the intervening years. Consistently positive caregiving over a number of years is likely an important factor in connecting early attachment and the child's functioning later in development. Indeed, researchers have found that early secure attachment *and* subsequent experiences, especially maternal care and life stresses, are linked with children's later behavior and adjustment (Cassidy, 2009; Thompson, 2006).

Some developmentalists suggest that too much emphasis has been placed on the attachment bond in infancy, especially exclusive care of the child by the mother (Newcombe, 2007). Jerome Kagan (1987, 2000), for example, observes that infants are highly resilient and adaptive; he argues that they are evolutionarily equipped to stay on a positive developmental course, even in the face of wide variations in parenting. Kagan and others stress that genetic characteristics and temperament play more important roles in a child's social competence than the attachment theorists, such as Bowlby and Ainsworth, are willing to acknowledge (Bakermans-Kranenburg & others, 2007; Chaudhuri & Williams, 1999). For example, if some infants inherit a low tolerance for stress, this, rather than an insecure attachment bond, may be responsible for an inability to get along with peers.

Another criticism of attachment theory is that it ignores the diversity of socializing agents and contexts that exists in an infant's world. A culture's value system can influence the nature of attachment (Cole & Tan, 2007; Kagitcibasi, 2007; Saarni & others, 2006). Mothers' expectations for infants to be independent are high in northern Germany, whereas Japanese mothers are more strongly motivated to keep their infants close to them (Grossman & others, 1985; Rothbaum & Trommsdorff, 2007). Not surprisingly, northern German infants tend to show less distress than Japanese infants when separated from their mother. Also, in some cultures, infants show attachments to many people. Among the Hausa (who live in Nigeria), both grandmothers and siblings provide a significant amount of care for infants (Harkness & Super, 1995). Infants in agricultural societies tend to form attachments to older siblings, who are assigned a major responsibility for younger siblings' care. Researchers recognize the importance of competent, nurturant caregivers in an infant's development (Bornstein, 2006; Parke & Buriel, 2006). At issue, though, is whether or not secure attachment, especially to a single caregiver, is critical (Lamb, 2005; Thompson, 2006).

Despite such criticisms, there is ample evidence that security of attachment is important to development (Cassidy, 2009; Egeland, 2009; Thompson & Newton, 2009). Secure attachment in infancy is important because it reflects a positive parent-infant relationship and provides the foundation that supports healthy socioemotional development in the years that follow.

In the Hausa culture, siblings and grandmothers provide a significant amount of care for infants. *How might this practice affect attachment?*

Caregiving Styles and Attachment   Is the style of caregiving linked with the quality of the infant's attachment? Securely attached babies have caregivers who are sensitive to their signals and are consistently available to respond to their infants' needs (Cassidy, 2009; Main, 2000). These caregivers often let their babies have an active part in determining the onset and pacing of interaction in the first year of life. One study found that maternal sensitivity in parenting was linked with secure attachment in infants in two different cultures: the United States and Columbia (Carbonell & others, 2002).

How do the caregivers of insecurely attached babies interact with them? Caregivers of avoidant babies tend to be unavailable or rejecting (Berlin & Cassidy, 2000). They often don't respond to their babies' signals and have little physical contact with them. When they do interact with their babies, they may behave in an angry and irritable way. Caregivers of resistant babies tend to be inconsistent; sometimes they respond to their babies' needs, and sometimes they don't. In general, they tend not to be very affectionate with their babies and show little synchrony

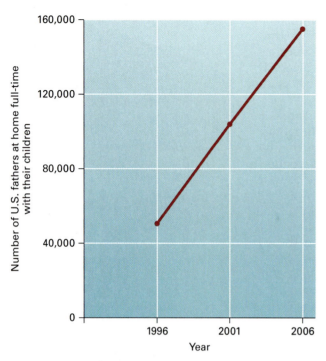

FIGURE 10.10 The Increase in the Number of U.S. Fathers Staying at Home Full-Time with Their Children

when interacting with them. Caregivers of disorganized babies often neglect or physically abuse them (Toth, 2009). In some cases, these caregivers are depressed.

Mothers and Fathers as Caregivers An increasing number of U.S. fathers stay home full time with their children (Wong & Rochlen, 2008). As indicated in Figure 10.10, there was a 300-plus percent increase in stay-at-home fathers in the United States from 1996 to 2006. A large portion of the full-time fathers have career-focused wives who provide the main family income. A recent study revealed that the stay-at-home fathers were as satisfied with their marriage as traditional parents, although they indicated that they missed their daily life in the workplace (Rochlen & others, 2007). In this study, the stay-at-home fathers reported that they tended to be ostracized when they took their children to playgrounds and often were excluded from parent groups.

Can fathers take care of infants as competently as mothers can? Observations of fathers and their infants suggest that fathers have the ability to act as sensitively and responsively as mothers with their infants (Parke & Buriel, 2006; Parke & others, 2008). Perhaps the caregiving behavior of male humans resembles that of other male primates, who show notoriously low interest in their offspring. However, when forced to live with infants whose female caregivers are absent, the males can competently rear the infants. Remember, however, that although fathers can be active, nurturant, involved caregivers with their infants, many do not choose to follow this pattern (Lamb, 2005).

Do fathers behave differently toward infants than mothers do? Maternal interactions usually center on child-care activities—feeding, changing diapers, and bathing. Paternal interactions are more likely to include play (Parke, 2002; Parke & Buriel, 2006). Fathers engage in more rough-and-tumble play. They bounce infants, throw them up in the air, tickle them, and so on (Lamb, 1986, 2000). Mothers do play with infants, but their play is less physical and arousing than that of fathers.

In one study, fathers were interviewed about their caregiving responsibilities when their children were 6, 15, 24, and 36 months of age (NICHD Early Child Care Research Network, 2000). Some of the fathers were videotaped while playing with their children at 6 and 36 months. Fathers were more involved in caregiving—bathing, feeding, dressing the child, taking the child to child care, and so on—when they worked fewer hours and mothers worked more hours, when mothers and fathers were younger, when mothers reported greater marital intimacy, and when the children were boys.

Child Care

Many U.S. children today experience multiple caregivers. Most do not have a parent staying home to care for them; instead, the children have some type of care provided by others—"child care." Many parents worry that child care will reduce their infants' emotional attachment to them, retard the infants' cognitive development, fail to teach them how to control anger, and allow them to be unduly influenced by their peers. How extensive is child care? Are the worries of these parents justified?

Parental Leave Today far more young children are in child care than at any other time in history. About 2 million children in the United States currently receive formal, licensed child care, and uncounted millions of children are cared for by unlicensed babysitters. In part, these numbers reflect the fact that U.S. adults cannot receive paid leave from their jobs to care for their young children. However, as described in the *Diversity in Child Development* interlude, many countries provide extensive parental leave policies.

How do most fathers and mothers interact differently with infants?

Diversity in Child Development

CHILD-CARE POLICIES AROUND THE WORLD

Child care policies around the world vary in elgibility criteria, leave duration, benefit level, and the extent to which parents take advantage of the policies (Kamerman, 2009, Lero, 2009; Tolani & Brooks-Gunn, 2008). There are five types of parental leave from employment (Kammerman, 1989, 2000a, b):

*   ***Maternity leave.*** In some countries, the prebirth leave is compulsory as is a six- to ten-week leave following birth.

*   ***Paternity leave.*** This is usually much briefer than maternity leave. It may be especially important when a second child is born and the first child requires care.

*   ***Parental leave.*** This gender-neutral leave usually follows a maternity leave and allows either women or men to share the leave policy or choose which of them will use it. In 1998, the European Union mandated a three-month parental leave.

*   ***Child-rearing leave.*** In some countries, this is a supplement to a maternity leave or a variation on a parental leave. A child-rearing leave is usually longer than a maternity leave and is typically paid at a much lower level.

*   ***Family leave.*** This covers reasons other than the birth of a new baby and can allow time off from employment to care for an ill child or other family members, time to accompany a child to school for the first time, or time to visit a child's school.

Europe led the way in creating new standards of parental leave: The European Union (EU) mandated a paid 14-week maternity leave in 1992. In most European countries today, working parents on leave receive from 70 percent of the worker's prior wage to the full wage and paid leave averages about 16 weeks (Tolani & Brooks-Gunn, 2008). The United States currently allows up to 12 weeks of unpaid leave for caring for a newborn.

Most countries restrict eligible benefits to women employed for a minimum time prior to childbirth (Belsky, 2009; Howes, 2009; Owen, 2009). In Denmark, even unemployed mothers are eligible for extended parental leave related to childbirth. In Germany, child-rearing leave is available to almost all parents. The Nordic countries (Denmark, Norway, and Sweden) have extensive gender-equity family leave policies for childbirth that emphasize the contributions of both women and men (Tolani & Brooks-Gunn, 2008). For example, in Sweden, parents can take an 18-month job-protected parental leave with benefits allowed to be shared by parents and applied to full-time or part-time work.

How are child-care policies in many European countries, such as Sweden, different than those in the United States?

Variations in Child Care   Because the United States does not have a policy of paid leave for child care, child care in the United States has become a major national concern (Tolani & Brooks-Gunn, 2008). Many factors influence the effects of child care, including the age of the child, the type of child care, and the quality of the program.

The type of child care varies extensively (Ahnert & Lamb, 2009; McCartney, 2009). Child care is provided in large centers with elaborate facilities and in private homes. Some child-care centers are commercial operations; others are nonprofit centers run by churches, civic groups, and employers. Some child-care providers are professionals; others are untrained adults who want to earn extra money. Figure 10.11 presents the primary care arrangement for children under 5 years of age with employed mothers (Clarke-Stewart & Miner, 2008).

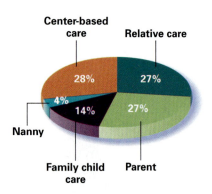

Center-based care
Relative care

28% | 27%

4%

14% | 27%

Nanny

Family child care | **Parent**

FIGURE 10.11 Primary Care Arrangements in the United States for Children Under 5 Years of Age with Employed Mothers

Use of different types of child care varies by ethnicity (Johnson & others, 2003). For example, Latino families are far less likely than non-Latino White and African American families to have children in child-care centers (11 percent, 20 percent, and 21 percent, respectively, in one study (Smith, 2002). Despite indicating a preference for center-based care, African American and Latino families often rely on family-based care, especially by grandmothers. However, there has been a substantial increase in the use of center-based care by African American mothers.

Child-care quality makes a difference. What constitutes a high-quality child-care program for infants? In high-quality child care (Clarke-Stewart & Miner, 2008, p. 273):

caregivers encourage the children to be actively engaged in a variety of activities, have frequent, positive interactions that include smiling, touching, holding, and speaking at the child's eye level, respond properly to the child's questions or requests, and encourage children to talk about their experiences, feelings, and ideas.

High-quality child care also involves providing children with a safe environment, access to age-appropriate toys and participation in age-appropriate activities, and a low caregiver-child ratio that allows caregivers to spend considerable time with children on an individual basis.

Children are more likely to experience poor-quality child care if they come from families with few resources (psychological, social, and economic) (Cabrera, Hutchens, & Peters, 2006). Many researchers have examined the role of poverty in quality of child care (Lucas & others, 2008). One study found that extensive child care was harmful to low-income children only when the care was of low quality (Votrub-Drzal & others, 2004). Even if the child was in child care more than 45 hours a week, high-quality care was linked with fewer internalizing problems (anxiety, for example) and externalizing problems (aggressive and destructive behaviors, for example). A recent study revealed that children from low-income families benefited in terms of school readiness and language development when their parents selected higher-quality child care (McCartney & others, 2007).

To read about one individual who provides quality child care to individuals from impoverished backgrounds, see the *Careers in Child Development* profile. And to learn more about the effects of child care on children's development, see the *Research in Child Development* interlude.

Careers in Child Development

Rashmi Nakhre, Child-Care Director

Rashmi Nakhre has two master's degrees—one in psychology the other in child development—and is director of the Hattie Daniels Day Care Center in Wilson, North Carolina. At a "Celebrating a Century of Women" ceremony, Nakhre received the Distinguished Women of North Carolina Award for 1999–2000.

Nakhre first worked at the child-care center soon after she arrived in the United States 25 years ago. She says that she took the job initially because she needed the money but "ended up falling in love with my job." Nakhre has turned the Wilson, North Carolina, child-care center into a model for other centers. The Hattie Daniels center almost closed several years after she began working there because of financial difficulties. Dr. Nakhre played a major role in raising funds not only to keep it open but to improve it. The center provides quality child care for the children of many Latino migrant workers.

Rashmi Nakhre, child-care director, working with some of the children at her center.

Research in Child Development

A NATIONAL LONGITUDINAL STUDY OF CHILD CARE

A major, ongoing longitudinal study of U.S. child care was initiated by the National Institute of Child Health and Human Development (NICHD) in 1991. Data are being collected on a diverse sample of almost 1,400 children and their families at ten locations across the United States over more than a decade. Researchers used multiple methods (trained observers, interviews, questionnaires, and testing), and they measured many facets of children's development, including physical health, cognitive development, and socioemotional development. Following are some of the results of what is now referred to as the NICHD Study of Early Child and Youth Development, or NICHD SECCYD (NICHD Early Child Care Research Network, 2001, 2002, 2003, 2004, 2005, 2006).

- *Patterns of use.* Many families placed their infants in child care very soon after the child's birth, and there was considerable instability in the child-care arrangements. By 4 months of age, nearly three-fourths of the infants had entered some form of nonmaternal child care. Almost half of the infants were cared for by a relative when they first entered care; only 12 percent were enrolled in child-care centers. Socioeconomic factors were linked to the amount and type of care. For example, mothers who believed that maternal employment has positive effects on children were more likely than other mothers to place their infant in nonmaternal care for more hours. Low-income families were more likely than more affluent families to use child care. In the preschool years, mothers who were single, those with more education, and families with higher incomes used more hours of center care than other families. Minority families and mothers with less education used more hours of care by relatives.

- *Quality of care.* Evaluations of quality of care were based on such characteristics as group size, child-adult ratio, physical environment, caregiver characteristics (such as formal education, specialized training, and child-care experience), and caregiver behavior (such as sensitivity to children). An alarming conclusion is that a majority of the child care in the first three years of life was of unacceptable low quality. Positive caregiving by nonparents in child-care settings was infrequent—only 12 percent of the children studied experienced positive nonparental child care (such as positive exchanges, warm and expressive involvement, and appropriate language stimulation)! Further, infants from low-income families experienced lower quality of child care than infants from higher-income families. When quality of caregivers' care was high, children performed better on cognitive and language tasks, were more cooperative with their mothers during play, showed more positive and skilled interaction with peers, and had fewer behavior problems. Caregiver training and good child-staff ratios were linked with higher cognitive and social competence when children were 54 months of age. Using data collected as part of the NICHD early child care longitudinal study, a recent analysis indicated that higher-quality early child care, especially at 27 months of age, was linked to children's higher vocabulary scores in the fifth grade (Belsky & others, 2007).

Higher-quality child care was also related to higher-quality mother-child interaction among the families that used nonmaternal care. Further, poor-quality

What are some important findings from the National Longitudinal Study of Child Care conducted by the National Institute of Child Health and Human Development?

care was related to an increase of insecure attachment to the mother among infants who were 15 months of age, but only when the mother was low in sensitivity and responsiveness. However, child-care quality was not linked to attachment security at 36 months of age.

- *Amount of child care.* The quantity of child care predicted some child outcomes. When children spent extensive amounts of time in child care beginning in infancy, they experienced less sensitive interactions with their mother, showed more behavior problems, and had higher rates of illness (Vandell, 2004). Many of these comparisons involved children in child care for less than 30 hours a week versus those in child care for more than 45 hours a week. In general, though, when children spent 30 hours or more per week in child care, their development was less than optimal (Ramey, 2005).

- *Family and parenting influences.* The influence of families and parenting was not weakened by extensive child care. Parents played a significant role in helping children to regulate their emotions. Especially important parenting influences were being sensitive to children's needs, being involved with children, and cognitively stimulating them.

We have all the knowledge necessary to provide absolutely first-rate child care in the United States. What is missing is the commitment and the will.

—**EDWARD ZIGLER**
Contemporary Developmental Psychologist, Yale University

What are some strategies parents can follow in regard to child care? Child-care expert Kathleen McCartney (2003, p. 4) offered this advice:

- *Recognize that the quality of your parenting is a key factor in your child's development.*

- *Make decisions that will improve the likelihood you will be good parents.* "For some this will mean working full-time"—for personal fulfillment, income, or both. "For others, this will mean working part-time or not working outside the home."

- *Monitor your child's development.* "Parents should observe for themselves whether their children seems to be having behavior problems." They need to talk with child-care providers and their pediatrician about their child's behavior.

- *Take some time to find the best child care.* Observe different child-care facilities and be certain that you like what you see. Quality child care costs money, and not all parents can afford the child care they want. However, state subsidies, and other programs like Head Start, are available for families in need.

Review and Reflect: Learning Goal 4

4   Explain the Early Development of Social Orientation/ Understanding, Attachment, and Child Care

REVIEW

- What characterizes the early development of social orientation and social understanding?
- How does attachment develop in infancy?
- What is the nature of child care?

REFLECT

- Imagine that a friend of yours is getting ready to put her baby in child care. What advice would you give to her? Do you think she should stay home with the baby? Why or why not? What type of child care would you recommend?

Reach Your Learning Goals

Emotional Development

1   EXPLORING EMOTION: DISCUSS BASIC ASPECTS OF EMOTION

What Are Emotions?

- Emotion is feeling, or affect, that occurs when a person is engaged in an interaction that is important to him or her, especially to his or her well-being. Emotions can be classified as positive or negative. Darwin described the evolutionary basis of emotions, and today psychologists stress that emotions, especially facial expressions of emotions, have a biological foundation. Facial expressions of emotion are similar across cultures, but display rules are not culturally universal. Biological evolution endowed humans to be emotional, but culture and relationships with others provide diversity in emotional experiences.

A Functionalist View of Emotions

- The functionalist view of emotion emphasizes the importance of contexts and relationships in emotion. For example, when parents induce a positive mood in their child, the child is more likely to follow the parents' directions. In this view, goals are involved in emotions in a variety of ways, and the goal's specific nature can affect the individual's experience of a given emotion.

Regulation of Emotion

- The ability to control one's emotions is a key dimension of development. Emotional regulation consists of effectively managing arousal to adapt and reach a goal. In infancy and early childhood, regulation of emotion gradually shifts from external sources to self-initiated, internal sources. Also with increasing age, children are more likely to increase their use of cognitive strategies for regulating emotion, modulate their emotional arousal, become more adept at managing situations to minimize negative emotion, and choose effective ways to cope with stress. Emotion-coaching parents have children who engage in more effective self-regulation of their emotions than do emotion-dismissing parents.

Emotional Competence

- Saarni argues that becoming emotionally competent involves developing a number of skills such as being aware of one's emotional states, discerning others' emotions, adaptively coping with negative emotions, and understanding the role of emotions in relationships.

2   DEVELOPMENT OF EMOTION: DESCRIBE THE DEVELOPMENT OF EMOTION

Infancy

- Infants display a number of emotions early in their development, although researchers debate the onset and sequence of these emotions. Lewis distinguishes between primary emotions and self-conscious emotions. Primary emotions include joy, anger, and fear, self-conscious emotions include pride, shame, and guilt. Crying is the most important mechanism newborns have for communicating with their world. Babies have at least three types of cries—basic, anger, and pain cries. Social smiling in response to a caregiver's voice occurs as early as 4 to 6 weeks of age. Two fears that infants develop are stranger anxiety and separation from a caregiver (which is reflected in separation protest). Controversy swirls about whether babies should be soothed when they cry, although increasingly experts recommend immediately responding in a caring way in the first year. Infants gradually develop an ability to inhibit the duration and intensity of their emotional reactions.

Early Childhood

- Young children's range of emotions expands during early childhood as they increasingly experience self-conscious emotions such as pride, shame, and guilt. Two- and three-year-olds use an increasing number of terms to describe emotion and learn more about the causes and consequences of feelings. At 4 to 5 years of age, children show an increased ability to reflect on emotions and understand that a single event can elicit different emotions in different people.

Middle and Late Childhood

- In middle and late childhood, children show a growing awareness about controlling and managing emotions to meet social standards. Also in this age period, they show improved emotional understanding, markedly improve their ability to suppress or conceal negative emotions, use self-initiated strategies for redirecting feelings, have an increased tendency to take into fuller account the events that lead to emotional reactions, and develop a capacity for genuine empathy.

---

3 TEMPERAMENT: CHARACTERIZE VARIATIONS IN TEMPERAMENT AND THEIR SIGNIFICANCE

Describing and Classifying Temperament

- Temperament is an individual's behavioral style and characteristic way of responding. Developmentalists are especially interested in the temperament of infants. Chess and Thomas classified infants as (1) easy, (2) difficult, or (3) slow to warm up. Kagan argues that inhibition to the unfamiliar is an important temperament category. Rothbart and Bates' view of temperament emphasizes this classification: (1) extraversion/surgency, (2) negative affectivity, and (3) effortful control (self-regulation).

Biological Foundations and Experience

- Physiological characteristics are associated with different temperaments, and a moderate influence of heredity has been found in twin and adoption studies of the heritability of temperament. Children inherit a physiology that biases them to have a particular type of temperament, but through experience they learn to modify their temperament style to some degree. Very active young children are likely to become outgoing adults. In some cases, a difficult temperament is linked with adjustment problems in early adulthood. The link between childhood temperament and adult personality depends in part on context, which helps shape the reaction to a child and thus the child's experiences. For example, the reaction to a child's temperament depends in part on the child's gender and on the culture.

Goodness of Fit and Parenting

- Goodness of fit refers to the match between a child's temperament and the environmental demands the child must cope with. Goodness of fit can be an important aspect of a child's adjustment. Although research evidence is sketchy at this point in time, some general recommendations are that caregivers should (1) be sensitive to the individual characteristics of the child, (2) be flexible in responding to these characteristics, and (3) avoid negative labeling of the child.

---

4 SOCIAL ORIENTATION/UNDERSTANDING, ATTACHMENT, AND CHILD CARE: EXPLAIN THE EARLY DEVELOPMENT OF SOCIAL ORIENTATION/UNDERSTANDING, ATTACHMENT, AND CHILD CARE

Social Orientation/Understanding

- Infants show a strong interest in the social world and are motivated to understand it. Infants orient to the social world early in their development. Face-to-face play with a caregiver begins to occur at 2 to 3 months of age. Newly developed self-produced locomotion skills significantly expand the infant's ability to initiate social interchanges and explore their social world more independently. Perceiving people as engaging in intentional and goal-directed behavior is an important social cognitive accomplishment, and this occurs toward the end of the first year. Social referencing increases in the second year of life.

Attachment

- Attachment is a close emotional bond between two people. In infancy, contact comfort and trust are important in the development of attachment. Bowlby's ethological theory stresses that the caregiver and the infant are biologically predisposed to form an attachment. Attachment develops in four phases during infancy. Securely attached babies use the caregiver, usually the mother, as a secure base from which to explore the environment. Three types of insecure attachment are avoidant, resistant, and disorganized. Ainsworth created the Strange Situation, an observational measure of attachment. Ainsworth points out that secure attachment in the first year of life provides an important foundation for psychological development later in life. The strength of the link between early attachment and later development has varied somewhat across studies. Some critics argue that attachment theorists have not given adequate attention to genetics and temperament. Other critics stress that they have not adequately taken into account the diversity of social agents and contexts. Cultural variations in attachment have been found, but in all cultures studied to date secure attachment is the most common classification. Caregivers of secure babies are sensitive to the babies' signals and are consistently available to meet their needs. Caregivers of avoidant babies tend to be unavailable or rejecting. Caregivers of resistant babies tend to be inconsistently available to their babies and usually are not very affectionate. Caregivers of disorganized babies often neglect or physically abuse their babies. The mother's primary role when interacting with the infant is caregiving; the father's is playful interaction.

Child Care

- More U.S. children are in child care now than at any earlier point in history. The quality of child care is uneven, and child care remains a controversial topic. Quality child care can be achieved and seems to have few adverse effects on children. In the NICHD child-care study, infants from low-income families were more likely to receive the lowest quality of care. Also, higher quality of child care was linked with fewer child problems.

KEY TERMS

emotion 306
primary emotions 310
self-conscious emotions 310
basic cry 311
anger cry 311
pain cry 311

reflexive smile 312
social smile 312
stranger anxiety 312
separation protest 312
temperament 316
easy child 316

difficult child 316
slow-to-warm-up child 316
goodness of fit 320
social referencing 323
attachment 324
Strange Situation 325

securely attached babies 325
insecure avoidant
  babies 325
insecure resistant babies 325
insecure disorganized
  babies 325

KEY PEOPLE

Joseph Campos 306
Carolyn Saarni 309
Michael Lewis 310
John Watson 313
Mary Ainsworth 313

John Bowlby 313
Daniel Messinger 313
Alexander Chess and Stella
  Thomas 316
Jerome Kagan 317

Mary Rothbart 317
Theodore Wachs 319
Harry Harlow 324

Erik Erikson 324
Alan Sroufe 326
Kathleen McCartney 332

E-LEARNING TOOLS

To help you master the material in this chapter, you'll find a number of valuable study tools at the Online Learning Center for *Child Development*, twelfth edition (**www.mhhe.com/santrockcd12**).

Taking It to the Net

Research the answers to these questions:

1. Catherine is conducting a class for new parents at a local clinic. What advice should Catherine give the parents about how parenting practices can affect a child's inborn temperament?

2. Peter and Rachel are adopting a 3-month-old infant. What are some practical things they can do to help ensure that their child develops a healthy attachment bond with them in the first few months of life?

3. Veronica is anxious about choosing the best child-care center for her child. What are the main things she should consider as she visits the facilities on her list?

Health and Well-Being, Parenting, and Education Exercises

Build your decision-making skills by trying your hand at the health and well-being, parenting, and education exercises.

Video Clips

The Online Learning Center includes the following videos for this chapter:

- *Adolescent and Parent Emotions*
Dr. Reed Larson describes adolescents' and parents' emotional behavior, how they differ, and how they can clash.

- *Adolescent Loneliness*
Dr. Larson discusses the significance of time alone on adolescent emotions.

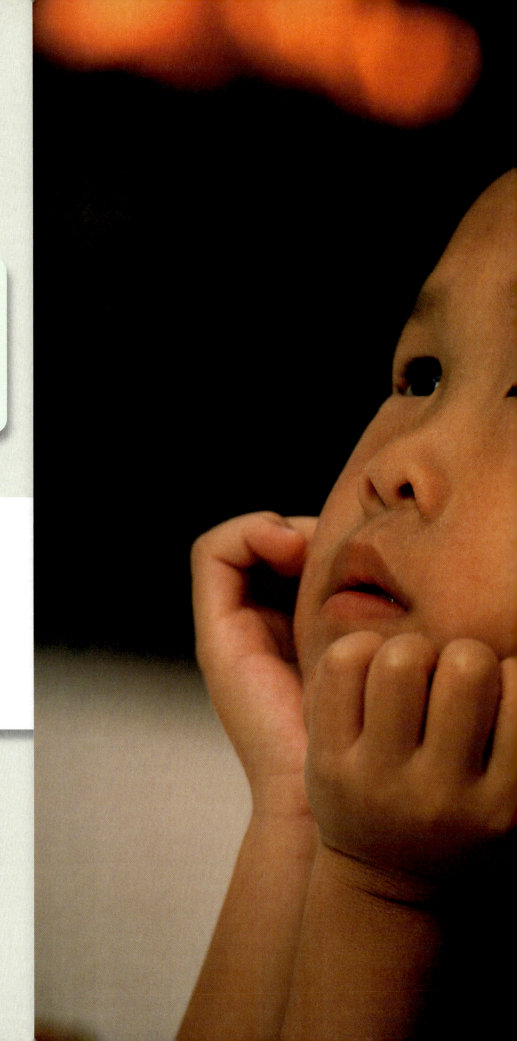

11

When I say "I," I mean something absolutely unique, not to be confused with any other.

—Ugo Betti
Italian Playwright, 20th Century

LEARNING GOALS

◆ Discuss the development of self-understanding and understanding others.

◆ Explain self-esteem and self-concept.

◆ Describe identity and its development.

THE SELF AND IDENTITY

CHAPTER OUTLINE

Images of Child Development
The Story of Maxine Hong Kingston: Bridging Cultural Worlds

Maxine Hong Kingston as a young girl and as an adult.

Maxine Hong Kingston's vivid portrayals of her Chinese ancestry and struggles of Chinese immigrants have made her one of the world's leading Asian American writers. Kingston's parents were both Chinese immigrants. Born in California in 1940, she spent many hours working with her parents and five brothers and sisters in the family's laundry. As a youth, Kingston was profoundly influenced by her parents' struggle to adapt to American culture and by their descriptions of their Chinese heritage.

Growing up as she did, Kingston felt the pull of two very different cultures. She was especially intrigued by stories about Chinese women who were perceived as either privileged or degraded.

Her first book is titled *The Woman Warrior: Memoirs of a Girlhood Among Ghosts* (Kingston, 1976). In *The Woman Warrior,* Kingston described her aunt, who gave birth to an illegitimate child. Because having a child outside of wedlock was taboo and perceived as a threat to the community's stability, the entire Chinese village condemned her, pushing her to kill herself and her child. From then on, even mentioning her name was forbidden.

In 1980, Kingston published *China Men,* which won the American Book Award for nonfiction and was runner-up for the Pulitzer Prize. Based on the experiences of her father and several generations of other male relatives, the book examines the lives of Chinese men who left their homeland to settle in the United States. It contains stories of loneliness and discrimination as well as determination and strength. Kingston currently teaches at the University of California at Berkeley. She says that she doesn't want to be viewed as an exotic writer but as someone who writes and teaches about Americans and what it means to be human. Kingston says she likes to guide people in how to find meaning in their lives, especially by exploring their cultural backgrounds.

PREVIEW

Maxine Hong Kingston's life and writings reflect important aspects of each of our lives as we grew up: our efforts to understand ourselves and to develop an identity that reflects our cultural heritage. This chapter is about these topics: the self and identity. As we examine these topics, reflect on how much you understood yourself at different points in your life as you were growing up, and think about how you acquired the stamp of your identity.

1 SELF-UNDERSTANDING AND UNDERSTANDING OTHERS

Self-Understanding

Understanding Others

Recent research studies have revealed that young children are more pychologically aware—of themselves and others—than used to be thought (Harris, 2006; Laible & Thompson, 2007). This increased psychological awareness reflects young children's expanding psychological sophistication.

Self-Understanding

Self-understanding is a child's cognitive representation of the self, the substance and content of the child's self-conceptions. For example, an 11-year-old boy understands that he is a student, a boy, a football player, a family member, a video game lover, and a rock music fan. A 13-year-old girl understands that she is a middle school student, in the midst of puberty, a girl, a cheerleader, a student council member, and a movie fan. A child's self-understanding is based, in part, on the various roles and membership categories that define who children are (Harter, 1999, 2006). Though not the whole of personal identity, self-understanding provides its rational underpinnings.

Developmental Changes   Children are not just given a self by their parents or culture; rather, they find and construct selves. As children develop, their self-understanding changes. First, let's examine self-understanding in infants.

Infancy   According to leading expert Ross Thompson (2007), studying the self in infancy is difficult mainly because infants cannot tell us how they experience themselves. Infants cannot verbally express their views of the self. They also cannot understand complex instructions from researchers.

A rudimentary form of self-recognition—being attentive and positive toward one's image in a mirror—appears as early as 3 months of age (Mascolo & Fischer, 2007; Pipp, Fischer, & Jennings, 1987). However, a central, more complete index of self-recognition—the ability to recognize one's physical features—does not emerge until the second year (Thompson, 2006).

One ingenious strategy to test infants' visual self-recognition is the use of a mirror technique, in which an infant's mother first puts a dot of rouge on the infant's nose. Then an observer watches to see how often the infant touches its nose. Next, the infant is placed in front of a mirror, and observers detect whether nose touching increases. Why does this matter? The idea is that increased nose touching indicates that the infant recognizes the self in the mirror and is trying to touch or rub off the rouge because the rouge violates the infant's view of the self. Increased touching indicates that the infant realizes that it is the self in the mirror but that something is not right since the real self does not have a dot of rouge on it.

Figure 11.1 displays the results of two investigations that used the mirror technique. The researchers found that before they were 1 year old, infants did not recognize themselves in the mirror (Amsterdam, 1968; Lewis & Brooks-Gunn, 1979). Signs of self-recognition began to appear among some infants when they were 15 to 18 months old. By the time they were 2 years old, most children recognized themselves in the mirror. In sum, infants begin to develop a self-understanding called self-recognition at approximately 18 months of age (Hart & Karmel, 1996; Lewis & others, 1989).

In one study, biweekly assessments from 15 to 23 months of age were conducted (Courage, Edison, & Howe, 2004). Self-recognition gradually emerged over this time, first appearing in the form of mirror recognition, followed by use of the personal pronoun and then by recognizing a photo of themselves. These aspects of self-recognition are often referred to as the first indications of toddlers' understanding of the mental state of "me," "that they are objects in their own mental representation of the world" (Lewis, 2005, p. 363).

Late in the second year and early in the third year, toddlers show other emerging forms of self-awareness that reflect a sense of "me" (Laible &Thompson, 2007). For example, they refer to themselves such as by saying "Me big"; they label their internal experiences such as emotions; they monitor themselves as when a toddler says, "Do it myself"; and say that things are theirs (Bullock & Lutkenhaus, 1990; Fasig, 2000).

Early Childhood   Because children can verbally communicate, research on self-understanding in childhood is not limited to visual self-recognition, as it is during infancy. Mainly through interviews, researchers have probed many aspects of children's

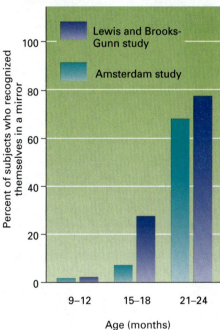

FIGURE 11.1   The Development of Self-Recognition in Infancy. The graph shows the findings of two studies in which infants less than 1 year of age did not recognize themselves in the mirror. A slight increase in the percentage of infant self-recognition occurred around 15 to 18 months of age. By 2 years of age, a majority of children recognized themselves. *Why do researchers study whether infants recognize themselves in a mirror?*

self-understanding A child's cognitive representation of the self; the substance and content of a child's self-conceptions.

self-understanding. Here are five main characteristics of self-understanding in young children:

- *Confusion of self, mind, and body.* Young children generally confuse self, mind, and body. Most young children conceive of the self as part of the body, which usually means the head. For them, the self can be described along many material dimensions, such as size, shape, and color.

- *Concrete descriptions.* Preschool children mainly think of themselves and define themselves in concrete terms. A young child might say, "I know my ABC's," "I can count," and "I live in a big house" (Harter, 2006). Although young children mainly describe themselves in terms of concrete, observable features and action tendencies, at about 4 to 5 years of age, as they hear others use psychological trait and emotion terms, they begin to include these in their own self-descriptions (Thompson, 2006). Thus, in a self-description, a 4-year-old might say, "I'm not scared. I'm always happy."

- *Physical descriptions.* Young children also distinguish themselves from others through many physical and material attributes. Says 4-year-old Sandra, "I'm different from Jennifer because I have brown hair and she has blond hair." Says 4-year-old Ralph, "I am different from Hank because I am taller, and I am different from my sister because I have a bicycle."

- *Active descriptions.* The *active dimension* is a central component of the self in early childhood. For example, preschool children often describe themselves in terms of activities such as play.

- *Unrealistic positive overestimations.* Self-evaluations during early childhood are often unrealistically positive and represent an overestimation of personal attributes (Harter, 2006). These unrealistic positive overestimations of the self occur because young children (1) have difficulty in differentiating their desired and actual competence, (2) cannot yet generate an ideal self that is distinguished from a real self, and (3) rarely engage in *social comparison*—how they compare with others. Perhaps as adults we should all be so optimistic about our abilities! (Thompson, 2008).

Middle and Late Childhood   Children's self-evaluation becomes more complex during middle and late childhood. Five key changes characterize the increased complexity:

- *Psychological characteristics and traits.* In middle and late childhood, especially from 8 to 11 years of age, children increasingly describe themselves with psychological characteristics and traits in contrast to the more concrete self-descriptions of younger children. Older children are more likely to describe themselves as *"popular, nice, helpful, mean, smart,* and *dumb"* (Harter, 2006, p. 526).

- *Social descriptions.* In middle and late childhood, children begin to include *social aspects* such as references to social groups in their self-descriptions (Harter, 2006; Livesly & Bromley, 1973). For example, children might describe themselves as Girl Scouts, as Catholics, or as someone who has two close friends.

- *Social comparison.* Children's self-understanding in middle and late childhood includes increasing reference to social comparison (Harter, 2006). At this point in development, children are more likely to distinguish themselves from others in comparative rather than in absolute terms. That is, elementary-school-age children are likely to think about what they can do *in comparison with others.* For example, Diane Ruble (1983) gave children a difficult task and then offered feedback on their performance, as well as information about the performances of other children their age. The children were then asked for self-evaluations. Children younger than 7 made virtually no reference to the information about other children's performances. However, many children older than 7 included socially comparative information in their self-descriptions.

- *Real self and ideal self.* In middle and late childhood, children begin to distinguish between their real and ideal selves (Harter, 2006). This involves differentiating their actual competencies from those they aspire to have and think are the most important.

- *Realistic.* In middle and late childhood, children's self-evaluations become more realistic (Harter, 2006). This may occur because of increased social comparison and perspective taking.

Adolescence   The development of self-understanding in adolescence is complex and involves a number of aspects of the self (Harter, 2006; Nurmi, 2004). The tendency to compare themselves with others continues to increase in the adolescent years. However, when asked whether they engage in social comparison, most adolescents deny it because they are aware that it is somewhat socially undesirable to do so. Let's examine other ways in which the adolescent's self-understanding differs from the child's:

- *Abstract and idealistic.* Remember from our discussion of Piaget's theory of cognitive development in Chapter 6 that many adolescents begin to think in more *abstract* and *idealistic* ways. When asked to describe themselves, adolescents are more likely than children to use abstract and idealistic labels. Consider 14-year-old Laurie's abstract description of herself: "I am a human being. I am indecisive. I don't know who I am." Also consider her idealistic description of herself: "I am a naturally sensitive person who really cares about people's feelings. I think I'm pretty good looking." Not all adolescents describe themselves in idealistic ways, but most adolescents distinguish between the real self and the ideal self.

- *Self-consciousness.* Adolescents are more likely than children to be *self-conscious* about and *preoccupied* with their self-understanding. This self-consciousness and self-preoccupation reflect adolescent egocentrism, which we discussed in Chapter 6.

- *Contradictions within the self.* As adolescents begin to differentiate their concept of the self into multiple roles in different relationship contexts, they sense potential contradictions between their differentiated selves (Harter, 2006). An adolescent might use this self-description: "I'm moody *and* understanding, ugly *and* attractive, bored *and* inquisitive, caring *and* uncaring, and introverted *and* fun-loving (Harter, 1986). Young adolescents tend to view these opposing characteristics as contradictory, which can cause internal conflict. However, older adolescents and emerging adults begin to understand why an individual can possess opposing characteristics, view this opposition as more adaptive than when they were younger, and integrate these opposing self-labels into their emerging identity (Fischer & Bidell, 2006; Harter, 2006).

- *The fluctuating self.* The adolescent's self-understanding fluctuates across situations and across time (Harter, 2006). The adolescent's self continues to be characterized by instability until the adolescent constructs a more unified theory of self, usually not until late adolescence or even early adulthood.

- *Real and ideal selves.* The adolescent's emerging ability to construct ideal selves in addition to actual ones can be perplexing and agonizing to the adolescent. In one view, an important aspect of the ideal or imagined self is the possible self—what individuals might become, what they would like to become, and what they are afraid of (Markus & Nurius, 1986). Thus, adolescents' **possible selves** include both what adolescents hope to be as well as what they dread they will become (Dunkel & Kerpelman, 2004). The attributes of future positive selves (getting into a good college, being admired, having a successful career) can direct future positive states. The attributes of future negative selves (being unemployed, being lonely, not getting into a good college) can identify what is to be avoided.

To read further about the important concept of multiple selves and culture in adolescence, see the *Diversity in Child Development* interlude.

*K*now thyself, for once we know ourselves, we may learn how to care for ourselves, but otherwise we never shall.

—SOCRATES
Greek Philosopher, 5th Century B.C.

How does self-understanding change in adolescence?

possible self   What an individual might become, what the person would like to become, and what the person is afraid of becoming.

Diversity in Child Development

MULTIPLE SELVES AND SOCIOCULTURAL CONTEXTS

Differentiation of the self increases across the childhood and adolescent periods of development (Harter, 2006). Adolescents' portraits of themselves can change depending on whether they describe themselves when they are with their mother, father, close friend, romantic partner, or peer. They also can change depending on whether they describe themselves in the role of student, athlete, or employee. And adolescents might create different selves depending on their ethnic and cultural background and experiences.

The multiple selves of ethnically diverse youth reflect their experiences in navigating their multiple worlds of family, peers, school, and community (Cooper & others, 1995). Research with American youth of African, Chinese, Filipino, Latino, European, Japanese, and Vietnamese descent, as well as Japanese youth, shows that as youth move across cultural worlds, they can encounter barriers related to language, racism, gender, immigration, and poverty. In each of their different worlds, they might also find resources in other people, in institutions, and in themselves. Youth who find it too difficult to move between worlds can become alienated from their school, family, and peers. However, youth who effectively navigate their various worlds can develop bicultural or multicultural selves and become "culture brokers" for others.

Hazel Markus and her colleagues (1999) point out that it is important to understand how multiple selves emerge through participation in cultural practices. They argue that all selves are culture-specific selves that emerge as individuals adapt to their cultural environments. Markus and her colleagues recognize that cultural groups are characterized by diversity, but nonetheless they conclude that it is helpful to understand the dominant aspects of multiple selves within a culture. Mainstream North American culture promotes and maintains individuality. North Americans, when given the opportunity to describe themselves, often provide not only portraits of their current selves but also notions of their future selves. They also frequently show a need to have multiple selves that are stable and consistent. In Japan, multiple selves are often described in terms of relatedness to others. Self-improvement also is an important aspect of the multiple selves of many Japanese.

How might sociocultural contexts be involved in adolescents' multiple selves?

- *Self-integration.* In late adolescence and emerging adulthood, self-understanding becomes more *integrative,* with the disparate parts of the self more systematically pieced together (Harter, 2006). Older adolescents are more likely to detect inconsistencies in their earlier self-descriptions as they attempt to construct a general theory of self, an integrated sense of identity.

Understanding Others

As we indicated earlier, young children are more sophisticated at understanding not only themselves, but others, than used to be thought. The term **social cognition** refers to the processes involved in understanding the world around us, especially how we think and reason about other people. Developmental psychologists are increasingly studying how children develop this understanding of others.

In Chapter 10, "Emotional Development," we described the development of social understanding in infancy. Recall that perceiving people as engaging in intentional and goal-directed behavior is an important social cognitive accomplishment, and this occurs toward the end of the first year. Social referencing, which involves "reading" emotional

social cognition The processes involved in understanding the world around us, especially how we think and reason about other people.

cues in others to help determine how to act in a particular situation, increases in the second year of life. Here we will describe further changes in social understanding that occur during the childhood years.

Early Childhood   Children also make advances in their understanding of others in early childhood (Gelman, Heyman, Legare, 2007). As we saw in Chapter 7, "Information Processing," young children's theory of mind includes understanding that other people have emotions and desires. And at about 4 to 5 years, children not only start describing themselves in terms of psychological traits but they also begin to perceive others in terms of psychological traits. Thus, a 4-year-old might say, "My teacher is nice."

Something important for children to develop is an understanding that people don't always give accurate reports of their beliefs (Gee & Heyman, 2007). Researchers have found that even 4-year-olds understand that people may make statements that aren't true to obtain what they want or to avoid trouble (Lee & others, 2002). For example, one recent study revealed that 4- and 5-year-olds were increasingly skeptical of another child's claim to be sick when the children were informed that the child was motivated to avoid having to go to camp (Gee & Heyman, 2007). Another recent study found that at 3 years of age, children mistrusted people who made a single error, but it wasn't until 4 years of age that children took into account the relative frequency of errors informants made when deciding whom to trust (Pasquini & others, 2007).

While in some ways children can be fairly sophisticated in determining what sources to doubt, they also show signs of gullibility. In one study, preschoolers were introduced to a new fantasy character called the "Candy Witch," who could visit the houses of children, after Halloween, who were interested in trading their candy for a toy. Preschoolers sometimes believed that the Candy Witch was real after only hearing about her a few times. Children's level of belief in other fantasy beings, such as Santa Claus, was highly related to their belief in the Candy Witch, suggesting that perhaps an understanding of different kinds of fantasy beings is connected (Woolley, Boerger, & Markman, 2004).

Even though children do sometimes believe things that are false, it may be adaptive to believe most things that people say, given that it is impossible to learn everything about the world through firsthand experience (Harris & Koenig, 2006). If we made decisions based only on our own perceptions, for instance, we might think the world is flat, perhaps with a dome-shaped roof. By being able to talk with others who are more knowledgeable than we are, we can learn that the world is indeed spherical. Figuring out what information to trust and what information to discount is an important aspect of developing an effective understanding of others.

Individual differences characterize young children's social understanding (Laible & Thompson, 2007; Thompson, 2006). Some young children are better than others at understanding what people are feeling and what they desire, for example. To some degree, these individual differences are linked to conversations caregivers have with young children about other people's feelings and desires, and children's opportunities to observe others talking about people's feelings and desires. For example, a mother might say to a 3-year-old, "You should think about Raphael's feelings next time before you hit him."

Middle and Late Childhood   In middle and late childhood, children show an increase in **perspective taking**, the ability to assume other people's perspectives and understand their thoughts and feelings. In Robert Selman's view (1980), at about 6 to 8 years of age, children begin to understand that others may have a perspective because some people have more access to information. Then, he says, in the next several years, children become aware that each individual is aware of the other's perspective and that putting one's self in the other's place is a way of judging the other person's intentions, purposes, and actions.

Young children are more psychologically aware of themselves and others than used to be thought. Some children are better than others at understanding people's feelings and desires—and, to some degree, these individual differences are influenced by conversations caregivers have with young children about feelings and desires.

perspective taking The ability to assume others' perspective and understand their thoughts or feelings.

What are some changes in children's understanding of others in middle and late childhood?

Perspective taking is especially thought to be important in whether children develop prosocial or antisocial attitudes and behavior. In terms of prosocial behavior, taking another's perspective improves children's likelihood of understanding and sympathizing with others when they are distressed or in need (Eisenberg, Fabes, & Spinrad, 2006). In terms of antisocial behavior, some researchers have found that children who have a low level of perspective-taking skills engage in more antisocial behavior than children at higher levels (Chandler, 1973).

In middle and late childhood, children also become more skeptical of others' claims. Earlier we indicated that even 4-year-old children show some skepticism of others' claims. In middle and late childhood, children become increasingly skeptical of some sources of information about psychological traits. For example, in one study, 10- to 11-year-olds were more likely to reject other children's self-reports that they were *smart* and *honest* than were 6- to 7-year-olds (Heyman & Legare, 2005). The more psychologically sophisticated 10- to 11-year-olds also showed a better understanding that others' self-reports may involve socially desirable tendencies than the 6- to 7-year-olds. In a recent cross-cultural comparison of 6- to 11-year-olds from the United States and China, older children showed increased skepticism of others' self-reports concerning value-laden traits, such as *honest, smart,* and *nice,* but did not show increased skepticism about less value-laden characteristics such as *outgoing, likes salty food,* and *likes the color red* (Heyman, Fu, & Lee, 2007). Older Chinese children were more likely to expect others to show modesty when talking about themselves than were their U.S. counterparts.

Elementary-school-aged children also begin to understand other motivations. For example, they understand that a desire to win a prize may tarnish someone's judgment (Mills & Keil, 2005).

Review and Reflect: Learning Goal 1

1 Discuss the Development of Self-Understanding and Understanding Others

REVIEW

- What is self-understanding? How does self-understanding change from infancy through adolescence?
- How does the understanding of others develop?

REFLECT

- If a psychologist had interviewed you at 10 and at 16 years of age, how would your self-understanding have been different?

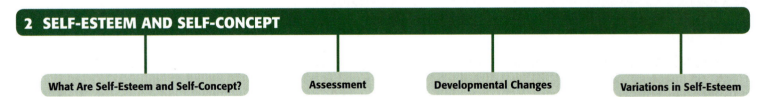

2 SELF-ESTEEM AND SELF-CONCEPT

| What Are Self-Esteem and Self-Concept? | Assessment | Developmental Changes | Variations in Self-Esteem |

Self-conception involves more than self-understanding. Not only do children try to define and describe attributes of the self (self-understanding), but they also evaluate these attributes. These evaluations create self-esteem and self-concept, and they have far-reaching implications for children's development.

FIGURE 11.2 **Evaluating Self-Esteem**

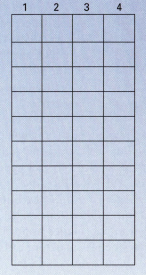

These items are from a widely used measure of self-esteem, the Rosenberg Scale of Self-Esteem. The items deal with your general feelings about yourself. Place a check mark in the column that best describes your feelings about yourself:
1 = strongly agree, 2 = agree, 3 = disagree, 4 = strongly disagree.

	1	2	3	4
1. I feel that I am a person of worth, at least on an equal plane with others.				
2. I feel that I have a number of good qualities.				
3. All in all, I am inclined to feel that I am a failure.				
4. I am able to do things as well as most other people.				
5. I feel I do not have much to be proud of.				
6. I take a positive attitude toward myself.				
7. On the whole, I am satisfied with myself.				
8. I wish I could have more respect for myself.				
9. I certainly feel useless at times.				
10. At times I think I am no good at all.				

To obtain your self-esteem score, reverse your scores for items 3, 5, 8, 9, and 10. (That is, on item 3 if you gave yourself a 1, instead give yourself a 4.) Add those scores to your scores for items 1, 2, 4, 6, and 7 for your overall self-esteem score. Scores can range from 10 to 40. If you scored below 20, consider contacting the counseling center at your college or university for help in improving your self-esteem.

What Are Self-Esteem and Self-Concept?

Sometimes the terms self-esteem and self-concept are used interchangeably, or they are not precisely defined (Harter, 2006). Here we use **self-esteem** to refer to a person's self-worth or self-image, a person's global evaluation of the self. For example, a child might perceive that she is not merely a person but a good person. (To evaluate your self-esteem, see Figure 11.2.) We use the term **self-concept** to refer to domain-specific evaluations of the self. Children can make self-evaluations in many domains of their lives—academic, athletic, physical appearance, and so on. In sum, self-esteem refers to global self-evaluations, self-concept to more domain-specific evaluations.

Self-esteem reflects perceptions that do not always match reality (Baumeister & others, 2003). A child's self-esteem might reflect a belief about whether he or she is intelligent and attractive, for example, but that belief is not necessarily accurate. Thus, high self-esteem may refer to accurate, justified perceptions of one's worth as a person and one's successes and accomplishments, but it can also refer to an arrogant, grandiose, unwarranted sense of superiority over others. In the same manner, low self-esteem may reflect either an accurate perception of one's shortcomings or a distorted, even pathological insecurity and inferiority.

Assessment

Measuring self-esteem and self-concept hasn't always been easy (Dusek & McIntyre, 2003). An example of a useful measure developed to assess self-evaluations by children is Susan Harter's (1985) Self-Perception Profile for Children. It taps general self-worth plus self-concept for five specific domains—scholastic competence, athletic competence, social acceptance, physical appearance, and behavioral conduct.

The Self-Perception Profile for Children is designed to be used with third-grade through sixth-grade children. Harter also developed a separate scale for adolescents, the Self-Perception Profile for Adolescents (Harter, 1989). It assesses global self-worth

self-esteem The global evaluative dimension of the self; also called self-worth or self-image.

self-concept Domain-specific self-evaluations.

Domain	Harter's U.S. Samples	Other Countries
Physical appearance	.65	.62
Scholastic competence	.48	.41
Social acceptance	.46	.40
Behavioral conduct	.45	.45
Athletic competence	.33	.30

FIGURE 11.3 Correlations Between Global Self-Esteem and Self-Evaluations of Domains of Competence. *Note:* The correlations shown are the average correlations computed across a number of studies. The other countries in this evaluation were England, Ireland, Australia, Canada, Germany, Italy, Greece, the Netherlands, and Japan. Recall from Chapter 1 that correlation coefficients can range from −1.00 to +1.00. The correlations between physical appearance and global self-esteem (.65 and .62) are moderately high.

and the five domains tested for children plus three additional domains—close friendship, romantic appeal, and job competence.

Harter's measures can separate self-evaluations in different domains in one's life. How are these specific self-evaluations related to their general self-esteem? Even children have both a general level of self-esteem and varying levels of self-conceptions in particular domains of their lives (Harter, 1998; Ward, 2004). For example, a child might have a moderately high level of general self-esteem but have these self-conceptions in specific areas: high in athletic competence, high in social acceptance, high in physical appearance, high in behavioral conduct, but low in scholastic competence.

Self-esteem appears to have an especially strong tie with self-perception in one domain in particular: physical appearance. For example, researchers have found that among adolescents, global self-esteem is correlated more strongly with perceived physical appearance than with scholastic competence, social acceptance, behavioral conduct, or athletic competence (Harter, 1999, 2006; Maeda, 1999) (see Figure 11.3). Notice in Figure 11.3 that the link between perceived physical appearance and self-esteem has been made in many countries. This association between physical appearance and self-esteem is not confined only to adolescence; it holds across the life span from early childhood through middle age (Harter, 1999, 2006).

Developmental Changes

Researchers disagree about the extent to which self-esteem varies with age. One study found that self-esteem is high in childhood, declines in adolescence, and increases in adulthood until late adulthood, when it declines again (Robins & others, 2002) (see Figure 11.4). Some researchers argue that although there may be a decrease in self-esteem during adolescence, the drop is actually very slight and not nearly as pronounced as presented in the media (Harter, 2002; Hyde, 2005, 2007; Kling & others, 1999). A recent study revealed that self-esteem increased during emerging adulthood (18 to 25 years of age) (Galambos, Barker, & Krahn, 2006).

Notice in Figure 11.4 that the self-esteem of males was higher than that of females through most of the life span. During adolescence, the self-esteem of girls declined more than that of boys. Another recent study also found that female adolescents had lower self-esteem than male adolescents, and their lower self-esteem was associated with less healthy adjustment (Raty & others, 2005). One explanation for this gender

FIGURE 11.4 Self-Esteem Across the Life Span. One large-scale study asked more than 300,000 individuals to rate the extent to which they have high self-esteem on a 5-point scale, 5 being "Strongly Agree" and 1 being "Strongly Disagree." Self-esteem dropped in adolescence and late adulthood. Self-esteem of females was lower than self-esteem of males through most of the life span.

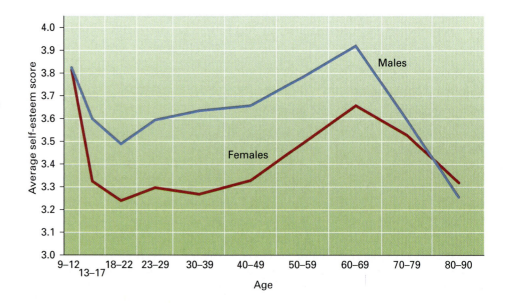

difference holds that the drop in self-esteem is driven by a negative body image and that girls have more negative body images during pubertal change compared with boys. Another explanation emphasizes the greater interest that adolescent girls take in social relationships and society's failure to reward that interest (Crawford & Unger, 2004; Impett, & others, 2008). But also note in Figure 11.4 that despite the drop in self-esteem among adolescent girls, their average self-esteem score (3.3) was still higher than the neutral point on the scale (3.0). A recent study examined why some adolescent girls recover and develop healthy self-esteem but others don't (Impett & others, 2008). In this study, both self-esteem and relationship authenticity (a consistency between what one thinks and feels, and what one says and does in relational contexts) increased from the eighth through the twelfth grade. Also, the self-esteem of girls who scored high on relationship authenticity in the eighth grade increased over the course of adolescence more than that of girls who scored low on this measure in the eighth grade. To read further about self-esteem in adolescence, see the *Research in Child Development* interlude.

Research in Child Development

ADOLESCENTS' SELF-IMAGES

One recent study examined the self-image of 675 adolescents (289 males and 386 females) from 13 to 19 years of age in Naples, Italy (Bacchini & Magliulo, 2003). Self-image was assessed using the Offer Self-Image Questionnaire, which consists of 130 items grouped into 11 scales that define five different aspects of self-image:

- The *psychological self* (made up of scales that assess impulse control, emotional tone, and body image)
- The *social self* (consists of scales that evaluate social relationships, morals, and vocational and educational aspirations)
- The *coping self* (composed of scales to measure mastery of the world, psychological problems, and adjustment)
- The *familial self* (made up of only one scale that evaluates how adolescents feel about their parents)
- The *sexual self* (composed of only one scale that examines adolescents' feelings and attitudes about sexual matters)

The adolescents had positive self-images with their scores being above a neutral score (3.5) on all 11 scales. For example, the adolescents' average body self-image score was 4.2. The aspect of their lives in which adolescents had the most positive self-image involved their educational and vocational aspirations (average score of 4.8). The lowest self-image score was for impulse control (average score of 3.9). These results support the view that adolescents have a more positive perception of themselves than is commonly believed.

Gender differences were found on a number of the self-image scales, with boys consistently having more positive self-images than did girls. Keep in mind, though, that as we indicated earlier, even though girls reported lower self-images than boys, their self-images still were mainly in the positive range.

Might adolescents' self-esteem be influenced by cohort effects? (*Cohort effects* are effects that are due to a person's time of birth or generation but not to actual age.) One analysis of studies conducted from the 1960s into the 1990s found that the self-esteem of college students was higher in the 1990s than it was in the 1960s (Twenge & Campbell, 2001).

What are some issues involved in understanding children's self-esteem in school?

The living self has one purpose only: to come into its own fullness of being, as a tree comes into full blossom, or a bird into spring beauty, or a tiger into lustre.

—**D. H. LAWRENCE**
English Author, 20th Century

The explanation given for this increase in self-esteem involves the self-esteem movement and the active encouragement of self-esteem in schools.

Variations in Self-Esteem

Variations in self-esteem have been linked with many aspects of children's development. However, much of the research is *correlational* rather than *experimental*. Recall from Chapter 1 that correlation does not equal causation. Thus, if a correlational study finds an association between children's low self-esteem and low academic achievement, low academic achievement could cause the low self-esteem as much as low self-esteem causes low academic achievement (Bowles, 1999). In fact, there are only moderate correlations between school performance and self-esteem, and these correlations do not suggest that high self-esteem produces better school performance (Baumeister & others, 2003). Efforts to increase students' self-esteem have not always led to improved school performance (Davies & Brember, 1999).

Children with high self-esteem show greater initiative, but this can produce positive or negative outcomes (Baumeister & others, 2003). High-self-esteem children are prone to both prosocial and antisocial actions. For example, they are more likely than children with low self-esteem to defend victims against bullies, but they are also more likely to be bullies.

Researchers have also found strong links between self-esteem and happiness (Baumeister & others, 2003). For example, the two were strongly related in an international study of 13,000 college students from 49 universities in 31 countries (Diener & Diener, 1995). It seems likely that high self-esteem increases happiness (Baumeister & others, 2003).

Many studies have found that individuals with low self-esteem report that they feel more depressed than individuals with high self-esteem (Harter, 2006). Low self-esteem has also been linked to suicide attempts and to anorexia nervosa (Osvath, Voros, & Fekete, 2004). One recent study found that adolescents who had low self-esteem had lower levels of mental health, physical health, and economic prospects as adults than adolescents with high self-esteem (Trzesniewski & others, 2006). Another recent study found that low self-esteem in childhood was linked with depression in adolescence and early adulthood (Orth & others, 2008).

Are a parent's characteristics and behavior linked to a child's self-esteem? In the most extensive investigation of parent-child relationships and self-esteem, these parenting attributes were associated with boys' high self-esteem (Coopersmith, 1967): expression of affection; concern about the child's problems; harmony in the home; participation in joint family activities; availability to give competent, organized help to the boys when they need it; setting clear and fair rules; abiding by these rules; and allowing the children freedom within well-prescribed limits. Remember that these findings are correlational, and so we cannot say that these parenting attributes cause children's high self-esteem. Such factors as parental acceptance and allowing children freedom within well-prescribed limits probably are important determinants of children's self-esteem, but we still must say that they are related to, rather than that they cause, children's self-esteem, based on the available research data. To explore ways that children's low self-esteem might be increased, see the *Caring for Children* interlude.

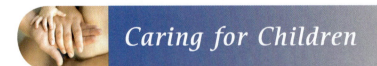

Caring for Children

INCREASING CHILDREN'S SELF-ESTEEM

A current concern is that too many of today's children and adolescents grow up receiving empty praise and as a consequence have inflated self-esteem (Graham, 2005; Stipek, 2005). Too often they are given praise for performance that is mediocre or even poor. They may have difficulty handling competition and criticism. The title of a book, *Dumbing Down Our Kids: Why American Children Feel Good About Themselves But Can't Read, Write, or Add* (Sykes, 1995) vividly captures the theme that the academic problems of many U.S. children, adolescents, and college students stem from unmerited praise aimed at propping up their self-esteem. But it is possible to raise children's self-esteem by (1) identifying the domains of competence important to the child, (2) providing emotional support and social approval, (3) praising achievement, and (4) encouraging coping.

Harter (1999) argues that intervention must occur at the level of the causes of self-esteem if the individual's self-esteem is to improve significantly. Children have the highest self-esteem when they perform competently in domains that are important to them. Therefore, children should be encouraged to identify and to value areas in which they are competent.

Emotional support and social approval also powerfully influence children's self-esteem. Some children with low self-esteem come from conflicted families or experienced abuse or neglect—situations in which emotional support was unavailable. For some children, formal programs such as Big Brothers and Big Sisters can provide alternative sources of emotional support and social approval; for others, support can come informally through the encouragement of a teacher, a coach, or another significant adult. Peer approval becomes increasingly important during adolescence, but adult as well as peer support continues to be an important influence on self-esteem through adolescence.

Achievement also can improve children's self-esteem. The straightforward teaching of real skills to children often results in increased achievement and enhanced self-esteem. When children know what tasks are necessary to achieve goals and have experience performing these or similar tasks, their self-esteem improves.

Self-esteem also is often increased when children face a problem and try to cope with it, rather than avoid it (Compas, 2004; Folkman & Moskowitz, 2004). If coping rather than avoidance prevails, children often face problems realistically, honestly, and nondefensively. This produces favorable self-evaluative thoughts, which lead to the self-generated approval that raises self-esteem. The converse is true of low self-esteem. Unfavorable self-evaluations trigger denial, deception, and avoidance, which lead to self-generated disapproval.

How can parents help children develop higher self-esteem?

Review and Reflect: Learning Goal 2

 Explain Self-Esteem and Self-Concept

REVIEW

- What are self-esteem and self-concept?
- What are two measures for assessing self-esteem and self-concept?
- How is self-esteem linked with age?
- What are some variations in self-esteem, and how are they linked to children's development? What role do parent-child relationships play in self-esteem?

REFLECT

- What behaviors would you look for when observing a child to give you an indication that a child has low or high self-esteem?

3 IDENTITY

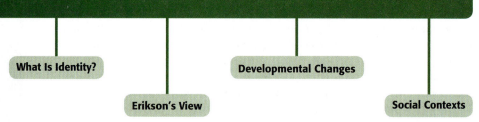

What Is Identity?

Erikson's View

Developmental Changes

Social Contexts

What are some important dimensions of identity?

Who am I? What am I all about? What am I going to do with my life? What is different about me? How can I make it on my own? These questions reflect the search for an identity. By far the most comprehensive and provocative theory of identity development is Erik Erikson's. In this section, we examine his views on identity. We also discuss contemporary research on how identity develops and how social contexts influence that development.

What Is Identity?

Identity is a self-portrait composed of many pieces, including these:

- The career and work path the person wants to follow (vocational/career identity)
- Whether the person is conservative, liberal, or middle of the road (political identity)
- The person's spiritual beliefs (religious identity)
- Whether the person is single, married, divorced, and so on (relationship identity)
- The extent to which the person is motivated to achieve and is intellectual (achievement, intellectual identity)
- Whether the person is heterosexual, homosexual, or bisexual (sexual identity)
- Which part of the world or country a person is from and how intensely the person identifies with his or her cultural heritage (cultural/ethnic identity)
- The kind of things a person likes to do, which can include sports, music, hobbies, and so on (interests)
- The individual's personality characteristics (such as being introverted or extraverted, anxious or calm, friendly or hostile, and so on) (personality)
- The individual's body image (physical identity)

At the bare minimum, identity involves commitment to a vocational direction, an ideological stance, and a sexual orientation. We put these pieces together to form a sense of ourselves continuing through time within a social world. Synthesizing the identity components can be a long and drawn-out process, with many negations and affirmations of various roles and faces. Identity development gets done in bits and pieces. Decisions are not made once and for all, but have to be made again and again. Identity development does not happen neatly, and it does not happen cataclysmically (Kroger, 2007).

"Who are you?" said the caterpillar. Alice replied rather shyly, "I—I hardly know, sir, just at present—at least I know who I was when I got up this morning, but I must have changed several times since then."

—LEWIS CARROLL
English Writer, 19th Century

Erikson's View

Questions about identity surface as common, virtually universal, concerns during adolescence. It was Erik Erikson (1950, 1968) who first understood how central such questions are to understanding adolescent development. That identity is now believed to be a key aspect of adolescent development is a result of Erikson's masterful thinking and analysis. His ideas reveal rich insights into adolescents' thoughts and feelings, and reading one or more of his books is worthwhile. A good starting point is *Identity: Youth and Crisis* (1968). Other works that portray identity development are *Young Man Luther* (1962) and *Gandhi's Truth* (1969). Erikson's theory was introduced in Chapter 1. Recall that his fifth developmental stage, which individuals experience during adolescence, is **identity versus identity confusion**. During this time, said Erikson, adolescents are faced with deciding who they are, what they are all about, and where they are going in life.

These questions about identity occur throughout life, but they become especially important for adolescents. Erikson points out that adolescents face an overwhelming number of choices. As they gradually come to realize that they will be responsible for themselves and their own lives, adolescents search for what those lives are going to be.

The search for an identity during adolescence is aided by a **psychosocial moratorium**, which is Erikson's term for the gap between childhood security and adult autonomy. During this period, society leaves adolescents relatively free of responsibilities and free to try out different identities. Adolescents in effect search their culture's identity files, experimenting with different roles and personalities. They may want to pursue one career one month (lawyer, for example) and another career the next month (doctor, actor, teacher, social worker, or astronaut, for example). They may dress neatly one day, sloppily the next. This experimentation is a deliberate effort on the part of adolescents to find out where they fit in the world.

Many parents and other adults, accustomed to having children go along with what they say, may be bewildered or incensed by the wisecracks, the rebelliousness, and the rapid mood changes that accompany adolescence. It is important for these adults to give adolescents the time and opportunity to explore different roles and personalities. Most adolescents eventually discard undesirable roles.

Youth who successfully cope with these conflicting identities emerge with a new sense of self that is both refreshing and acceptable. Adolescents who do not successfully resolve this identity crisis suffer what Erikson calls *identity confusion*. The confusion takes one of two courses: individuals withdraw, isolating themselves from peers and family, or they immerse themselves in the world of peers and lose their identity in the crowd.

There are hundreds of roles for adolescents to try out, and probably just as many ways to pursue each role. Erikson stresses that, by late adolescence, vocational roles are central to identity development, especially in a highly technological society like the United States. Youth who have been well trained to enter a workforce that offers the potential of reasonably high self-esteem will experience the least stress during this phase of identity development.

Some youth reject jobs offering good pay and high social status in order to work in jobs that help people directly, such as in the Peace Corps, in mental health clinics, or in schools in low-income neighborhoods. Some youth prefer unemployment to the prospect of working at a job they feel they could not perform well or would make them feel useless. To Erikson, these choices reflect the desire to achieve a meaningful identity by being true to oneself, instead of burying one's identity in the larger society.

Erik Erikson.

Developmental Changes

Although questions about identity may especially begin to emerge during adolescence, identity formation neither begins nor ends during these years. It begins with the appearance of attachment, the development of the sense of self, and the emergence of independence in infancy; the process reaches its final phase with a life review and integration in old age. What is important about identity development in adolescence, especially late adolescence, is that for the first time, physical development, cognitive development, and socioemotional development advance to the point at which the individual can begin to sort through and synthesize childhood identities and identifications to construct a viable path toward adult maturity.

Some decisions made during adolescence might seem trivial: whom to date, whether or not to break up, which major to study, whether to study or play, whether or not to be politically active, and so on. Over the years of adolescence, however, such decisions begin to form the core of what the individual is all about as a human being—what is called his or her identity.

identity versus identity confusion Erikson's fifth developmental stage, which individuals experience during the adolescent years. At this time, adolescents examine who they are, what they are all about, and where they are going in life.

psychosocial moratorium Erikson's term for the gap between childhood security and adult autonomy that adolescents experience as part of their identity exploration.

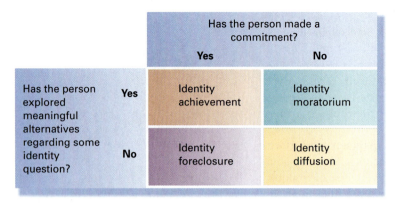

FIGURE 11.5 Marcia's Four Statuses of Identity

Identity Statuses   How do individual adolescents go about the process of forming an identity? Eriksonian researcher James Marcia (1980, 1994) proposes that Erikson's theory of identity development contains four statuses of identity, or ways of resolving the identity crisis: identity diffusion, identity foreclosure, identity moratorium, and identity achievement. What determines an individual's identity status? Marcia classifies individuals based on the existence or extent of their crisis or commitment (see Figure 11.5). **Crisis** is defined as a period of identity development during which the individual is exploring alternatives. Most researchers use the term *exploration* rather than crisis. **Commitment** is personal investment in identity.

The four statuses of identity are as follows:

- **Identity diffusion** is the status of individuals who have not yet experienced a crisis or made any commitments. Not only are they undecided about occupational and ideological choices, they are also likely to show little interest in such matters.

- **Identity foreclosure** is the status of individuals who have made a commitment but not experienced a crisis. This occurs most often when parents hand down commitments to their adolescents, usually in an authoritarian way, before adolescents have had a chance to explore different approaches, ideologies, and vocations on their own.

- **Identity moratorium** is the status of individuals who are in the midst of a crisis but whose commitments are either absent or are only vaguely defined.

- **Identity achievement** is the status of individuals who have undergone a crisis and made a commitment.

To evaluate your identity in different areas of development, see Figure 11.6. Let's explore some examples of Marcia's identity statuses. Thirteen-year-old Mia has

crisis A period of identity development during which the adolescent is choosing among meaningful alternatives.

commitment Personal investment in identity.

identity diffusion Marcia's term for the status of individuals who have not yet experienced a crisis (that is, they have not yet explored meaningful alternatives) or made any commitments.

identity foreclosure Marcia's term the status of individuals who have made a commitment but have not experienced a crisis.

identity moratorium Marcia's term for the status of individuals who are in the midst of a crisis, but whose commitments either are absent or are only vaguely defined.

identity achievement Marcia's term for the status of individuals who have undergone a crisis and made a commitment.

Think deeply about your exploration and commitment in the areas listed here. For each area, check whether your identity status is diffused, foreclosed, moratorium, or achieved.

Identity Component	Identity Status			
	Diffused	Foreclosed	Moratorium	Achieved
Vocational (career)				
Political				
Religious				
Relationships				
Achievement				
Sexual				
Gender				
Ethnic/Cultural				
Interests				
Personality				
Physical				

FIGURE 11.6   Exploring Your Identity.   If you checked diffused or foreclosed for any areas, take some time to think about what you need to do to move into a moratorium identity status in those areas. *How much has your identity in each of the areas changed in recent years?*

neither begun to explore her identity in any meaningful way nor made an identity commitment; she is identity diffused. Eighteen-year-old Oliver's parents want him to be a medical doctor, so he is planning on majoring in premedicine in college and has not explored other options; he is identity foreclosed. Nineteen-year-old Sasha is not quite sure what life paths she wants to follow, but she recently went to the counseling center at her college to find out about different careers; she is in identity moratorium status. Twenty-one-year-old Marcelo extensively explored several career options in college, eventually getting his degree in science education, and is looking forward to his first year of teaching high school students; he is identity achieved. These examples focused on the career dimension, but remember that identity has a number of dimensions.

In Marcia's terms, young adolescents are primarily in the identity statuses of diffusion, foreclosure, or moratorium. To move to the status of identity achievement, young adolescents need three things (Marcia, 1987, 1996): (1) they must be confident that they have parental support, (2) they must have an established sense of industry, and (3) they must be able to adopt a self-reflective stance toward the future.

The identity status approach has been sharply criticized by some researchers and theoreticians (Kroger, 2007; Lapsley & Power, 1988). They maintain that the identity status approach distorts and trivializes Erikson's notions of crisis and commitment. For example, Erikson's idea of commitment loses the meaning of investing oneself in certain lifelong projects and is interpreted simply as having made a firm decision or not. Others still argue that the identity status approach is a valuable contribution to understanding identity (Marcia, 2002; Waterman, 1992).

Beyond Erikson   Some researchers observe that the most important identity changes take place during *emerging adulthood,* the period from about 18 to 25 years of age (Arnett, 2007; Kroger, 2007; Luycks & others, 2008a, g; Orbe, 2008). For example, Alan Waterman (1985, 1989, 1992) has found that from the years preceding high school through the last few years of college, the number of individuals who are identity achieved increases, whereas the number of who are identity diffused decreases. Many young adolescents are identity diffused. College upperclassmen are more likely than high school students or college freshmen to be identity achieved.

The timing of changes in identity status may depend on the particular area of life involved. For example, for religious beliefs and political ideology, many college students have identity-foreclosure and identity-moratorium status. Many college students are still wrestling with ideological commitments (Kroger, 2007).

One of emerging adulthood's themes is not having many social commitments, which gives individuals considerable independence in developing a life path (Arnett, 2006, 2007). James Cote (2006) argues that because of this freedom, developing a positive identity in emerging adulthood requires considerable self-discipline and planning. Without this self-discipline and planning, emerging adults are likely to drift and not follow any particular direction. Cote also stresses that emerging adults who obtain a higher education are more likely to be on a positive identity path. Those who don't obtain a higher education, he says, tend to experience frequent job changes, not because they are searching for an identity but rather because they are just trying to earn a living in a society that rewards higher education.

Resolution of the identity issue during adolescence or emerging adulthood does not mean that identity will be stable through the remainder of life (Kroger, 2007; Pals, 2006). Many individuals who develop positive identities follow what are called "MAMA" cycles—that is, their identity status changes from *m*oratorium to *a*chievement to *m*oratorium to *a*chievement (Archer, 1989). These cycles may be

How does identity change in emerging adulthood?

> *As long as one keeps searching, the answers come.*
>
> —JOAN BAEZ
> *American Folk Singer, 20th Century*

How is an adolescent's identity development influenced by parents?

individuality Consists of two dimensions: self-assertion, the ability to have and communicate a point of view; and separateness, the use of communication patterns to express how one is different from others.

connectedness Consists of two dimensions: mutuality, sensitivity to and respect for others' views; and permeability, openness to others' views.

repeated throughout life (Francis, Fraser, & Marcia, 1989). Marcia (2002) reasons that the first identity is just that—it is not, and should not be expected to be, the final product.

In short, questions about identity come up throughout life. An individual who develops a healthy identity is flexible and adaptive, open to changes in society, in relationships, and in careers (Adams, Gulotta, & Montemayor, 1992). This openness assures numerous reorganizations of identity throughout the individual's life.

Consider Maxine Hong Kingston's life. When she was 9 years old, she began writing. "All of a sudden," she told an interviewer, "this poem started coming out of me. On and on I went, oblivious to everything. . . . It is a bad habit that doesn't go away." Still, when Kingston enrolled at the University of California, she began an engineering program. Eventually, she changed her major to English literature, became a teacher, and then published her award-winning books. In 1991, however, Kingston's identity was threatened by a catastrophe. Kingston rushed from her father's funeral to a house in flames. Nothing was left of the novel she had been writing. "After the fire," she said, "I just wanted to take care of myself. . . . I had lost my writing" (Alegre & Welsch, 2003). Several years later, however, Kingston reclaimed her identity as an author, again writing fiction for publication.

Social Contexts

Social contexts play important roles in identity. Let's examine how family, culture, and ethnicity are linked to identity development.

Family Influences Parents are important figures in the adolescent's development of identity (Luyckx & others, 2006, 2008c; Schacter & Ventura, 2008). Do parenting styles influence identity development? Democratic parents, who encourage adolescents to participate in family decision making, foster identity achievement. Autocratic parents, who control the adolescent's behavior without giving the adolescent an opportunity to express opinions, encourage identity foreclosure. Permissive parents, who provide little guidance to adolescents and allow them to make their own decisions, promote identity diffusion (Enright & others, 1980). One study found that poor communication between mothers and adolescents and persistent conflicts with friends were linked to less positive identity development (Reis & Youniss, 2004).

It is during adolescence that the search for balance between the need for autonomy and the need for connectedness becomes especially important to identity. Developmentalist Catherine Cooper and her colleagues (Carlson, Cooper, & Hsu, 1990; Cooper & Grotevant, 1989; Grotevant & Cooper, 1985, 1998) found that the presence of a family atmosphere that promotes both individuality and connectedness are important in the adolescent's identity development:

- **Individuality** consists of two dimensions: self-assertion—the ability to have and communicate a point of view—and separateness—the use of communication patterns to express how one is different from others.
- **Connectedness** also consists of two dimensions: mutuality—which involves sensitivity to and respect for others' views—and permeability—which involves openness to others' views.

In general, Cooper's research indicates that identity formation is enhanced by family relationships that are both individuated, which encourages adolescents to develop their own point of view, and connected, which provides a secure base from which to explore the widening social worlds of adolescence. When connectedness is strong and individuation weak, adolescents often have an identity-foreclosure status. When connectedness is weak, adolescents often reveal identity confusion (Archer & Waterman, 1994).

Culture and Ethnicity   "I feel that I have had to translate a whole Eastern culture and bring it to the West," Maxine Hong Kingston told one interviewer, "then bring the two cultures together seamlessly . . ." (Alegre & Welsch, 2003). For Kingston, this melding is "how one makes the Asian American culture." Her efforts illustrate one way of developing an **ethnic identity**, which is an enduring aspect of the self that includes a sense of membership in an ethnic group, along with the attitudes and feelings related to that membership (Phinney, 1996).

Throughout the world, ethnic minority groups have struggled to maintain their ethnic identities while blending in with the dominant culture (Erikson, 1968). Erikson thought this struggle for a separate identity within the larger culture has been the driving force in the founding of churches, empires, and revolutions throughout history.

Many aspects of sociocultural contexts may influence ethnic identity (Phinney, 2008; Phinney & Ong, 2007; Phinney & others, 2006; Umana-Taylor & others, 2008). Ethnic identity tends to be stronger among members of minority groups than among members of mainstream groups. For example, in one study, the exploration of ethnic identity was higher among ethnic minority college students than among White non-Latino college students (Phinney & Alipuria, 1990).

Time is another aspect of the context that influences ethnic identity. The indicators of identity often differ for each succeeding generation of immigrants (Phinney, 2003; Phinney & Ong, 2007). First-generation immigrants are likely to be secure in their identities and unlikely to change much; they may or may not develop a new identity. The degree to which they begin to feel "American" appears to be related to whether or not they learn English, develop social networks beyond their ethnic group, and become culturally competent in their new country. Second-generation immigrants are more likely to think of themselves as "American" possibly because citizenship is granted at birth. Maxine Hong Kingston noted, "I have been in America all of my life; Chinese is a foreign culture to me" (Alegre & Welsch, 2003). For second-generation immigrants, ethnic identity is likely to be linked to retention of their ethnic language and social networks. In the third and later generations, the issues become more complex. Broad social factors may affect the extent to which members of this generation retain their ethnic identities. For example, media images may either discourage or encourage members of an ethnic group from identifying with their group or retaining parts of its culture. Discrimination may force people to see themselves as cut off from the majority group and encourage them to seek the support of their own ethnic culture.

The immediate contexts in which ethnic minority youth live also influence their identity development (Cooper, Behrens, & Trinh, 2008; Spencer, 2006; Way & others, 2008). In the United States, many ethnic minority youth live in pockets of poverty, are exposed to drugs, gangs, and crime, and interact with youth and adults who have dropped out of school or are unemployed. Support for developing a positive identity is scarce. In such settings, programs for youth can make an important contribution to identity development.

Researchers are increasingly finding that a positive ethnic identity is linked to positive outcomes for ethnic minority adolescents. Consider these four studies:

- Ethnic identity was related to higher school engagement and lower aggression (Van Buren & Graham, 2003).

Michelle Chin, age 16: "Parents do not understand that teenagers need to find out who they are, which means a lot of experimenting, a lot of mood swings, a lot of emotions and awkwardness. Like any teenager, I am facing an identity crisis I am still trying to figure out whether I am a Chinese American or an American with Asian eyes."

Researcher Margaret Beale Spencer, shown here talking with adolescents, stresses that adolescence is often a critical juncture in the identity development of ethnic minority individuals. Most ethnic minority individuals consciously confront their ethnicity for the first time in adolescence.

ethnic identity An enduring aspect of the self that includes a sense of membership in an ethnic group, along with the attitudes and feelings related to that membership.

- A stronger ethnic identity was associated with higher self-esteem in African American, Latino, and Asian American youth (Bracey, Bamaca, & Umana-Taylor, 2004).

- Navajo adolescents' positive ethnic heritage was linked to higher self-esteem, school connectedness, and social functioning (Jones & Galliher, 2007).

- The strength of ninth-grade students' ethnic identification was a better predictor of their academic success than the specific ethnic labels they used to describe themselves (Fuligni, Witkow, & Garcia, 2005). In this study, the ethnic groups most likely to incorporate more of their family's national origin and cultural background into their ethnic identification were Mexican and Chinese immigrants.

To read about one individual who guides Latino adolescents in developing a positive identity, see the *Careers in Child Development* profile.

Careers in Child Development

Armando Ronquillo, High School Counselor

Armando Ronquillo is a high school counselor and admissions advisor at Pueblo High School in a low-income area of Tuson, Arizona. More than 85 percent of the students have a Latino background. Ronquillo was named the top high school counselor in the state of Arizona for the year 2000.

Ronquillo especially works with Latino students to guide them in developing a positive identity. He talks with them about their Latino background and what it's like to have a bicultural identity—preserving important aspects of their Latino heritage but also pursuing what is important to be successful in the contemporary culture of the United States.

He believes that helping them stay in school and getting them to think about the lifelong opportunities provided by a college education will benefit their identity development. Ronquillo also works with parents to help them understand that their child going to college is doable and affordable.

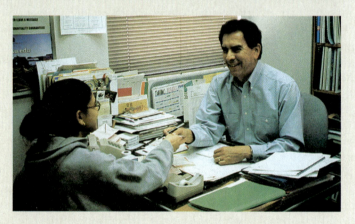

Armando Ronquillo, counseling a Latina high school student about college.

Jean Phinney (2006) recently described how ethnic identity may change in emerging adulthood, especially highlighting how certain experiences of ethnic minority individuals may shorten or lengthen emerging adulthood. For ethnic minority individuals who have to take on family responsibilities and do not go to college, identity formation may occur earlier. By contrast, especially for ethnic minority individuals who go to college, identity formation may take longer because of the complexity of exploring and understanding a bicultural identity. The cognitive challenges of higher education likely stimulate ethnic minority individuals to reflect on their identity and examine changes in the way they want to identify themselves. This increased reflection may focus on integrating parts of one's ethnic minority culture and the mainstream non-Latino White culture. For example, some emerging adults have to come to grips with resolving a conflict between family loyalty and interdependence emphasized in one's ethnic minority culture and the values of independence and self-assertion emphasized by the mainstream non-Latino White culture (Arnett, 2006). One recent study of Mexican American and Asian American college students found that they identified both with the American mainstream culture and their culture of origin (Devos, 2006).

Review and Reflect: Learning Goal 3

 Describe Identity and Its Development

REVIEW

- What is identity?
- What is Erikson's view of identity?
- How do individuals develop their identity? What are the identity statuses that can be used to classify individuals?
- How do the social contexts of family, culture, and ethnicity influence identity?

REFLECT

- Do you think that your parents influenced your identity development? If so, how?

Reach Your Learning Goals

The Self and Identity

1 SELF-UNDERSTANDING AND UNDERSTANDING OTHERS: DISCUSS THE DEVELOPMENT OF SELF-UNDERSTANDING AND UNDERSTANDING OTHERS

Self-Understanding

- Self-understanding is a child's cognitive representation of the self, the substance and content of the child's self-conceptions. It provides the rational underpinnings for personal identity. Infants develop a rudimentary form of self-recognition as early as 3 months of age, and a more complete form of self-understanding at approximately 18 months of age. Self-understanding in early childhood is characterized by confusion of self, mind, and body; concrete, physical, and active descriptions; and unrealistic positive overestimations. Self-understanding in middle and late childhood involves an increase in the use of psychological characteristics and traits, social descriptions, and social comparison; distinction between the real and ideal self; and an increase in realistic self-evaluations. Adolescents tend to engage in more social comparison, to develop abstract and idealistic conceptions of themselves, and to become self-conscious about their self-understanding. Their self-understanding often fluctuates, and they construct multiple selves, including possible selves.

Understanding Others

- Young children display more sophisticated self-understanding and understanding of others than previously thought. Even 4-year-olds understand that people make statements that aren't true to obtain what they want or to avoid trouble. Children increase their perspective taking in middle and late childhood, and they become even more skeptical of others' claims.

2 SELF-ESTEEM AND SELF-CONCEPT: EXPLAIN SELF-ESTEEM AND SELF-CONCEPT

What Are Self-Esteem and Self-Concept?

- Self-esteem, also referred to as self-worth or self-image, is the global, evaluative dimension of the self. Self-concept refers to domain-specific evaluations of the self.

Assessment

- Harter's Self-Perception Profile for Children is used with third-grade through sixth-grade children to assess general self-worth and self-concept in five skill domains. Harter's Self-Perception Profile for Adolescents assesses global self-worth in five skill domains, plus additional domains dealing with friendship, romance, and job competence.

Developmental Changes

- Some researchers have found that self-esteem drops in adolescence, more so for girls than boys, but there is controversy about how extensively self-esteem varies with age.

Variations in Self-Esteem

- Researchers have found only moderate correlations between self-esteem and school performance. Individuals with high self-esteem have greater initiative than those with low self-esteem, and this can produce positive or negative outcomes. Self-esteem is related to perceived physical appearance and happiness. Low self-esteem is linked with depression, suicide attempts, and anorexia nervosa. In Coopersmith's study, children's self-esteem was associated with parental acceptance and allowing children freedom within well-prescribed limits.

3 IDENTITY: DESCRIBE IDENTITY AND ITS DEVELOPMENT

What Is Identity?

- Identity development is complex and is done in bits and pieces. At a bare minimum, identity involves commitment to a vocational direction, an ideological stance, and a sexual orientation. Synthesizing identity components can be a long, drawn-out process.

Erikson's View

- Erikson argues that identity versus identity confusion is the fifth stage of the human life span, which individuals experience during adolescence. This stage involves entering a psychosocial moratorium between the security of childhood and the autonomy of adulthood. Personality and role experimentation are important aspects of identity development. In technological societies like those in North America, the vocational role is especially important.

- Identity development begins during infancy and continues through old age. James Marcia proposed four identity statuses—identity diffusion, foreclosure, moratorium, and achievement—that are based on crisis (exploration) and commitment. Some experts argue the main changes in identity occur in emerging adulthood rather than adolescence. Individuals often follow *moratorium-achievement-moratorium-achievement* (MAMA) cycles in their lives.

- Parents are important figures in adolescents' identity development. Democratic parenting facilitates identity development; autocratic and permissive parenting do not. Both individuality and connectedness in family relations are related to identity development. Throughout the world, ethnic minority groups have struggled to maintain their identities while blending into the majority culture. A positive ethnic identity is linked to positive outcomes for ethnic minority adolescents.

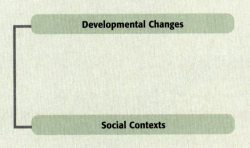

Developmental Changes

Social Contexts

KEY TERMS

self-understanding 339
possible self 341
social cognition 342
perspective taking 343
self-esteem 345

self-concept 345
identity versus identity confusion 351
psychosocial moratorium 351

crisis 352
commitment 352
identity diffusion 352
identity foreclosure 352
identity moratorium 352

identity achievement 352
individuality 354
connectedness 354
ethnic identity 355

KEY PEOPLE

Diane Ruble 340
Hazel Markus 342
Robert Selman 343

Susan Harter 345
Erik Erikson 350

James Marcia 352
Alan Waterman 353

Catherine Cooper 354
Jean Phinney 356

E-LEARNING TOOLS

To help you master the material in this chapter, you'll find a number of valuable study tools at the Online Learning Center for *Child Development,* twelvth edition (**www.mhhe.com/santrockcd12**).

Taking It to the Net

Research the answers to these questions:

1. Rita's child development teacher wants each student to depict some aspect of child development from infancy to age 6 as a chronological timeline represented by descriptions or illustrations. Rita has chosen the development of the self. What behaviors at 6, 12, and 18 months, and at 2, 3, 4, 5, and 6 years of age represent milestones in self-awareness, self-concept, self-understanding, and self-esteem?

2. Margie's psychology professor returned a draft of her class paper on self-esteem, indicating that she needed to add more information on how to enhance self-esteem in children. What suggestions can she add to build this part of her paper in accordance with her professor's comments?

3. Thirteen-year-old Amy was adopted out of a Korean orphanage when she was 4 years old. She is now struggling with an identity crisis. Is she Korean or American? She doesn't feel that she is either. How can Amy best resolve this ethnic identity crisis?

Health and Well-Being, Parenting, and Education Exercises

Build your decision-making skills by trying your hand at the health and well-being, parenting, and education exercises.

Video Clips

The Online Learning Center includes the following videos for this chapter:

- *Parents and Adolescent Self-Esteem*
Susan Harter offers lessons for parents and teachers on how to help adolescents reconcile the challenges of multiple selves.

- *Self-Perception at 10 Years and 8 Years of Age*
Two Latino siblings, Laura and Jared, are asked to describe themselves. Laura responds that she works hard, tries her best, and talks too much. Jared, however, responds only that he does not talk that much.

12

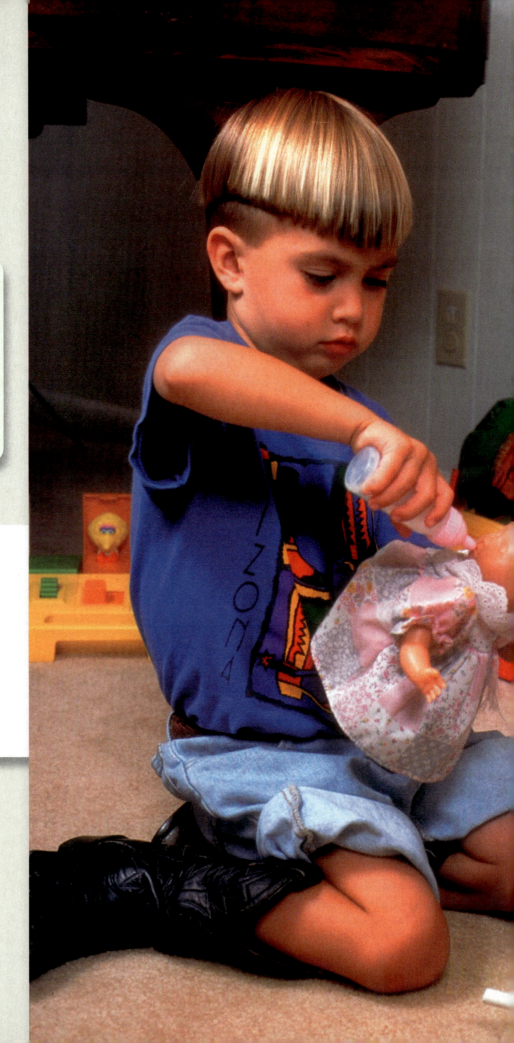

> *To be meek, patient, tactful, modest, honorable, brave, is not to be either manly or womanly, but is to be humane.*
>
> —JANE HARRISON
> *English Writer, 20th Century*

LEARNING GOALS

- ◆ Discuss the main biological, social, and cognitive influences on gender.

- ◆ Describe gender stereotypes, similarities, and differences.

- ◆ Identify how gender roles can be classified.

GENDER

CHAPTER OUTLINE

Images of Child Development
The Story of Jerry Maguire: Gender, Emotion, and Caring

How are gender, emotion, and caring portrayed in the movie Jerry Maguire?

Gender and emotion researcher Stephanie Shields (1998) analyzed the movie *Jerry Maguire* in terms of how it reflects the role of gender in emotions and relationships. In brief, the movie is a "buddy" picture with sports agent Jerry Maguire (played by Tom Cruise) paired with two buddies: the too-short Arizona Cardinals wide receiver Rod Tidwell (played by Cuba Gooding, Jr.) and 6-year-old Ray, son of Jerry's love interest, the accountant Dorothy Boyd (played by Renee Zellweger). Through his buddies, the thinking-but-not-feeling Jerry discovers the right path by connecting to Ray's emotional honesty and Rod's devotion to his family.

The image of nurturing and nurtured males is woven throughout the movie. Through discovering a caring relationship with Ray, Jerry makes his first genuine move toward emotional maturity. The boy is the guide to the man. Chad, Ray's baby-sitter, is another good example in the movie of appropriate caring by a male.

Males are shown crying in the movie. Jerry sheds tears while writing his mission statement, when thinking about Dorothy's possible move to another city (which also means he would lose Ray), and at the success of his lone client (Rod). Rod is brought to tears when he speaks of his family. Historically, weeping, more than any emotional expression, has been associated with feminine emotion. However, it has increasingly taken on a more prominent role in the male's emotional makeup.

The movie *Jerry Maguire* reflects changes in gender roles as an increasing number of males show an interest in improving their social relationships and achieving emotional maturity. However, as we will see later in this chapter, experts on gender argue that overall females are more competent in their social relationships than males, and that large numbers of males still have a lot of room for improvement in dealing better with their emotions.

gender The characteristics of people as males and females.

gender role A set of expectations that prescribes how females and males should think, act, and feel.

gender typing The process by which children acquire the thoughts, feelings, and behaviors that are considered appropriate for their gender in their culture.

PREVIEW

What exactly do we mean by gender? Gender refers to the characteristics of people as males and females. A gender role is a set of expectations that prescribes how females and males should act, think, and feel. Gender typing is the process by which children acquire the thoughts, feelings, and behaviors that are considered appropriate for their gender in a particular culture. We will begin this chapter by examining various influences on gender development and then turn our attention to gender stereotypes, similarities, and differences. Next, we will discuss how gender roles are classified.

1 INFLUENCES ON GENDER DEVELOPMENT

Biological Influences   **Social Influences**   **Cognitive Influences**

How is gender influenced by biology? By children's social experiences? By cognitive factors?

Biological Influences

It was not until the 1920s that researchers confirmed the existence of human sex chromosomes, the genetic material that determines our sex. Humans normally have 46 chromosomes, arranged in pairs. A 23rd pair with two X-shaped chromosomes produces a female. A 23rd pair with an X chromosome and a Y chromosome produces a male.

Hormones In Chapter 4, we discussed the two classes of hormones that have the most influence on gender: estrogens and androgens. Both estrogens and androgens occur in both females and males, but in very different concentrations.

Estrogens primarily influence the development of female physical sex characteristics and help regulate the menstrual cycle. Estrogens are a general class of hormones. An example of an important estrogen is estradiol. In females, estrogens are produced mainly by the ovaries.

Androgens primarily promote the development of male genitals and secondary sex characteristics. One important androgen is testosterone. Androgens are produced by the adrenal glands in males and females, and by the testes in males.

In the first few weeks of gestation, female and male embryos look alike. Male sex organs start to differ from female sex organs when a gene on the Y chromosome directs a small piece of tissue in the embryo to turn into testes. In females, there is no Y chromosome so the tissue turns into ovaries. Once the tissue has turned into testes, they begin to secrete testosterone.

To explore biological influences on gender, researchers have studied individuals who are exposed to unusual levels of sex hormones early in development (Berenbaum & Korman Bryk, 2008; Blakemore, Berenbaum, & Liben, 2009). Here are four examples of the problems that may occur as a result (Lippa, 2005, pp. 122–124, 136–137):

- *Congenital adrenal hyperplasia (CAH).* Some girls have this condition, which is caused by a genetic defect. Their adrenal glands enlarge, resulting in abnormally high levels of androgens. Although CAH girls are XX females, they vary in how much their genitals look like male or female genitals. Their genitals may be surgically altered to look more like those of a typical female. Although CAH girls usually grow up to think of themselves as girls and women, they are less content with being a female and show a stronger interest in being a male than non-CAH girls (Berenbaum & Bailey, 2003; Ehrhardt & Baker, 1974; Hall & others, 2004). They like sports and enjoy playing with boys and boys' toys more than non-CAH girls. CAH girls usually don't like typical girl activities such as playing with dolls and wearing makeup.

- *Androgen-insensitive males.* Due to a genetic error, a small number of XY males don't have androgen cells in their bodies. Their bodies look female, they develop a female gender identity, and they usually are sexually attracted to males.

- *Pelvic field defect.* A small number of newborns have a disorder called pelvic field defect, which in boys involves a missing penis. These XY boys have normal

estrogens Hormones, the most important of which is estradiol, that influence the development of female physical sex characteristics and help regulate the menstrual cycle.

androgens Hormones, the most important of which is testosterone, that promote the development of male genitals and secondary sex characteristics.

"How is it gendered?"

amounts of testosterone prenatally but usually have been castrated just after being born and raised as females. One study revealed that despite the efforts by parents to rear them as girls, most of the XY children insisted that they were boys (Reiner, 2001). Apparently, normal exposure to androgens prenatally had a stronger influence on their gender identity than being castrated and raised as girls.

• In another intriguing case, one of two identical twin boys lost his penis due to an errant circumcision. The twin who lost his penis was surgically reassigned to be a girl and reared as a girl. Bruce (the real name of the boy) became "Brenda." Early indications were that the sex reassignment had positive outcomes (Money, 1975), but later it was concluded that "Brenda" wasn't adjusted well as a girl (Diamond & Sigmundson, 1997). As a young adult, Brenda became Bruce once again and lived as a man with a wife and adopted children (Colapinto, 2000). Tragically in 2004, when Bruce was 38 years old, he committed suicide.

Although sex hormones alone, of course, do not determine behavior, researchers have found links between sex hormone levels and certain behaviors. The most established effects of testosterone on humans involve aggressive behavior and sexual behavior (Hyde, 2007a). Levels of testosterone are correlated with sexual behavior in boys during puberty (Udry & others, 1985). Violent male criminals have above-average levels of testosterone (Dabbs & others, 1987), and professional football players have higher levels of testosterone than ministers do (Dabbs & Morris, 1990).

The Evolutionary Psychology View In Chapter 2 we described the approach of evolutionary psychology, which emphasizes that adaptation during the evolution of humans produced psychological differences between males and females (Buss, 1995, 2000, 2004, 2007, 2008). Evolutionary psychologists argue that primarily because of their differing roles in reproduction, males and females faced different pressures in primeval environments when the human species was evolving. In particular, because having multiple sexual liaisons improves the likelihood that males will pass on their genes, natural selection favored males who adopted short-term mating strategies. These males competed with other males to acquire more resources in order to access females. Therefore, say evolutionary psychologists, males evolved dispositions that favor violence, competition, and risk taking.

In contrast, according to evolutionary psychologists, females' contributions to the gene pool was improved by securing resources for their offspring, which was promoted by obtaining long-term mates who could support a family. As a consequence, natural selection favored females who devoted effort to parenting and chose mates who could provide their offspring with resources and protection. Females developed preferences for successful, ambitious men who could provide these resources (Geher & Miller, 2007).

Critics of evolutionary psychology argue that its hypotheses are backed by speculations about prehistory, not evidence, and that in any event people are not locked into behavior that was adaptive in the evolutionary past. Critics also claim that the evolutionary view pays little attention to cultural and individual variations in gender differences (Matlin, 2008; Smith, 2007).

Social Influences

Many social scientists do not locate the cause of psychological gender differences in biological dispositions. Rather, they argue that these differences are due to social experiences. Three theories that reflect this view have been influential.

Alice Eagly (2001, 2008, 2009) proposed **social role theory**, which states that gender differences result from the contrasting roles of women and men. In most cultures

social role theory A theory stating that gender differences result from the contrasting roles of women and men—social hierarchy and division of labor strongly influence gender differences in power, assertiveness, and nuture.

Theory	Processes	Outcome
Psychoanalytic theory	Sexual attraction to opposite-sex parent at 3 to 5 years of age; anxiety about sexual attraction and subsequent identification with same-sex parent at 5 to 6 years of age	Gender behavior similar to that of same-sex parent
Social cognitive theory	Rewards and punishments of gender-appropriate and -inappropriate behavior by adults and peers; observation and imitation of models' masculine and feminine behavior	Gender behavior

FIGURE 12.1 Parents Influence Their Children's Gender Development by Action and Example

FIGURE 12.2 Expectations for Boys and Girls. First imagine that this is a photograph of a baby girl. *What expectations would you have for her?* Then imagine that this is a photograph of a baby boy. *What expectations would you have for him?*

around the world, women have less power and status than men have and they control fewer resources (Wood & Eagly, 2007). Compared with men, women perform more domestic work, spend fewer hours in paid employment, receive lower pay, and are more thinly represented in the highest levels of organizations. In Eagly's view, as women adapted to roles with less power and less status in society, they showed more cooperative, less dominant profiles than men. Thus, the social hierarchy and division of labor are important causes of gender differences in power, assertiveness, and nurture (Eagly, 2009).

The **psychoanalytic theory of gender** stems from Freud's view that the preschool child develops erotic feelings toward the opposite-sex parent. Eventually, these feelings arouse anxiety, so that at 5 or 6 years of age, the child renounces these feelings and identifies with the same-sex parent, unconsciously adopting the same-sex parent's characteristics. However, developmentalists do not believe gender development proceeds as Freud proposed (Callan, 2001).

The social cognitive approach discussed in Chapter 1 provides an alternative explanation of how children develop gender-typed behavior (see Figure 12.1). According to the **social cognitive theory of gender**, children's gender development occurs through observation and imitation, and through the rewards and punishments children experience for gender-appropriate and gender-inappropriate behavior (Bussey & Bandura, 1999).

Parents, by action and example, influence their children's and adolescents' gender development (Blakemore, Berenbaum, & Liben, 2009). Once the label girl or boy is assigned, virtually everyone, from parents to siblings to strangers, begins treating the infant differently (see Figure 12.2). Parents often use rewards and punishments to teach their daughters to be feminine ("Karen, you are such a good mommy with your dolls") and their sons to be masculine ("C'mon now, Keith, big boys don't cry").

Mothers and fathers often interact differently with sons and daughters, and these gendered interactions that begin in infancy usually continue through childhood and adolescence. In reviewing research on this topic, Phyllis Bronstein (2006) recently provided these conclusions:

- *Mothers' socialization strategies.* In many cultures mothers socialize their daughters to be more obedient and responsible than their sons. They also place more restrictions on daughters' autonomy.

- *Fathers' socialization strategies.* Fathers show more attention to sons than daughters, engage in more activities with sons, and put forth more effort to promote sons' intellectual development.

Thus, according to Bronstein (2006, pp. 269–270), "Despite an increased awareness in the United States and other Western cultures of the detrimental effects of gender stereotyping, many parents continue to foster behaviors and perceptions that are consonant with traditional gender role norms."

Children also learn about gender from observing other adults in the neighborhood and in the media (Fagot, Rodgers, & Leinbach, 2000). As children get older,

psychoanalytic theory of gender A theory that stems from Freud's view that preschool children develop erotic feelings toward the opposite-sex parent. Eventually these feeling cause anxiety, so that at 5 or 6 years of age, children renounce these feelings and identify with the same-sex parent, unconsciously adopting the same-sex parent's characteristics.

social cognitive theory of gender This theory emphasizes that children's gender development occurs through observation and imitation of gender behavior, and through rewards and punishments they experience for gender-appropriate and gender-inappropriate behavior.

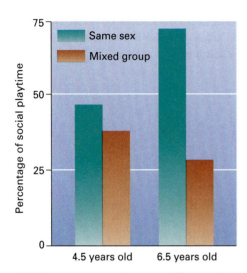

FIGURE 12.3 Developmental Changes in Percentage of Time Spent in Same-Sex and Mixed-Group Settings. Observations of children show that they are more likely to play in same-sex than mixed-sex groups. This tendency increases between 4 and 6 years of age.

cognitive developmental theory of gender In this view, children's gender typing occurs after they have developed a concept of gender. Once they begin to consistently conceive of themselves as male or female, children prefer activities, objects, and attitudes consistent with this gender label.

gender schema theory According to this theory, gender typing emerges as children gradually develop schemas of what is gender-appropriate and gender-inappropriate in their culture.

peers become increasingly important. Peers extensively reward and punish gender behavior (Leaper & Friedman, 2007). For example, when children play in ways that the culture says are sex-appropriate, they tend to be rewarded by their peers. Those who engage in activities that are considered inappropriate tend to be criticized or abandoned by their peers.

Children show a clear preference for being with and liking same-sex peers, and this tendency usually becomes stronger during the middle and late childhood years (Maccoby, 2002) (see Figure 12.3). What kind of socialization takes place in these same-sex play groups? In one study, researchers observed preschoolers over six months (Martin & Fabes, 2001). The more time boys spent interacting with other boys, the more their activity level, rough-and-tumble play, and sex-typed choice of toys and games increased, and the less time boys spent near adults. By contrast, the more time the preschool girls spent interacting with other girls, the more their activity level and aggression decreased, and the more their girl-type play activities and time spent near adults increased. After watching elementary school children repeatedly play in same-sex groups, two researchers characterized the playground as "gender school" (Luria & Herzog, 1985).

Cognitive Influences

Observation, imitation, rewards, and punishment—these are the mechanisms by which gender develops according to social cognitive theory. Interactions between the child and the social environment are the main keys to gender development in this view. Some critics argue that this explanation pays too little attention to the child's own mind and understanding, and portrays the child as passively acquiring gender roles (Martin, Ruble, & Szkrybalo, 2002). Two cognitive theories—cognitive developmental theory and gender schema theory—stress that individuals actively construct their gender world:

- The **cognitive developmental theory of gender** states that children's gender typing occurs *after* children think of themselves as boys and girls. Once they consistently conceive of themselves as male or female, children prefer activities, objects, and attitudes consistent with this label.

- **Gender schema theory** states that gender typing emerges as children gradually develop gender schemas of what is gender-appropriate and gender-inappropriate in their culture. A *schema* is a cognitive structure, a network of associations that guide an individual's perceptions. A *gender schema* organizes the world in terms of female and male. Children are internally motivated to perceive the world and to act in accordance with their developing schemas.

Initially proposed by Lawrence Kohlberg (1966), the cognitive developmental theory of gender holds that gender development depends on cognition, and it applies the ideas of Piaget that we discussed in Chapter 6. As young children develop the conservation and categorization skills described by Piaget, said Kohlberg, they develop a concept of gender. What's more, they come to see that they will always be male or female. As a result, they begin to select models of their own sex to imitate. The little girl acts as if she is thinking, "I'm a girl, so I want to do girl things. Therefore, the opportunity to do girl things is rewarding."

Notice that in this view gender-typed behavior occurs only after children develop *gender constancy,* which is the understanding that sex remains the same, even though activities, clothing, and hair style might change (Ruble, 2000). However, researchers have found that children do not develop gender constancy until they are about 6 or 7 years old. Even before this time, however, most little girls prefer girlish toys and clothes and games, and most little boys prefer boyish toys and games. Thus, contrary to Kohlberg's description of cognitive developmental theory, gender typing does not appear to depend on gender constancy.

Theory	Processes	Emphasis
Cognitive developmental theory	Development of gender constancy, especially around 6 to 7 years of age, when conservation skills develop; after children develop ability to consistently conceive of themselves as male or female, children often organize their world on the basis of gender, such as selecting same-sex models to imitate	Cognitive readiness facilitates gender identity
Gender schema theory	Sociocultural emphasis on gender-based standards and stereotypes; children's attention and behavior are guided by an internal motivation to conform to these gender-based standards and stereotypes, allowing children to interpret the world through a network of gender-organized thoughts	Gender schemas reinforce gender behavior

FIGURE 12.4 **The Development of Gender-Typed Behavior According to the Cognitive Developmental and Gender Schema Theories of Gender Development**

Unlike cognitive developmental theory, gender schema theory does not require children to perceive gender constancy before they begin gender typing (see Figure 12.4). Instead, gender schema theory states that gender typing occurs when children are ready to encode and organize information along the lines of what is considered appropriate for females and males in their society (Blakemore, Berenbaum, & Liben, 2009; Zosuls, Lurye, & Ruble, 2008). Bit by bit, children pick up what is gender-appropriate and gender-inappropriate in their culture, and develop gender schemas that shape how they perceive the world and what they remember (Martin & Dinella, 2001). Children are motivated to act in ways that conform with these gender schemas. Thus, gender schemas fuel gender typing. To read about how gender schemas extend to young children's judgments about occupations, see the *Research in Child Development* interlude.

Research in Child Development

YOUNG CHILDREN'S GENDER SCHEMAS OF OCCUPATIONS

In one study, researchers interviewed children 3 to 7 years old about ten traditionally masculine occupations (airplane pilot, car mechanic) and feminine occupations (clothes designer, secretary), using questions such as these (Levy, Sadovsky, & Troseth, 2000):

- *Example of a traditionally masculine occupation item:* An airplane pilot is a person who "flies airplanes for people." Who do you think would do the best job as an airplane pilot, a man or a woman?

- *Example of a traditionally feminine occupation item:* A clothes designer is a person "who draws up and makes clothes for people." Who do you think would do the best job as a clothes designer, a man or a woman?

As indicated in Figure 12.5, the children had well-developed gender schemas, in this case reflected in stereotypes, of occupations. They "viewed men as more competent than women in masculine occupations, and rated women as more competent than men in feminine occupations" (p. 993). Also, "girls' ratings of women's competence at feminine occupations were substantially higher than their ratings of men's competence at masculine occupations. Conversely, boys' ratings of men's

FIGURE 12.5 **Children's Judgments About the Competence of Men and Women in Gender-Stereotyped Occupations**

	Boy	Girl
"Masculine Occupations"		
Percentage who judged men more competent	87	70
Percentage who judged women more competent	13	30
"Feminine Occupations"		
Percentage who judged men more competent	35	8
Percentage who judged women more competent	64	92

competence at masculine occupations were considerably greater than their ratings of women's competence at feminine occupations" (p. 1002). These findings demonstrate that most children as young as 3 to 4 years of age tend to have strong gender schemas regarding the perceived competencies of men and women in gender-typed occupations.

The researchers also asked the children to select from a list of emotions how they would feel if they grew up to have each of the ten occupations. Girls said they would be happy with the feminine occupations and angry or disgusted with the masculine occupations. As expected, boys reversed their choices, saying they would be happy if they grew up to have the masculine occupations but angry and disgusted with the feminine occupations. However, the boys' emotions were more intense (more angry and disgusted) in desiring to avoid the feminine occupations than girls wanting to avoid the masculine occupations. This finding supports other research that indicates gender roles tend to constrict boys more than girls (Hyde, 2007a; Matlin, 2008).

It is important to note that the children in this study were at the height of gender stereotyping, a topic that will be discussed shortly. Most older children, adolescents, and adults become more flexible about occupational roles (Hyde, 2007a; Leaper & Friedman, 2007).

In sum, cognitive factors contribute to the way children think and act as males and females. Through biological, social, and cognitive processes, children develop their gender attitudes and behaviors (Blakemore, Berenbaum, & Liben, 2009; Lippa, 2005).

Review and Reflect: Learning Goal 1

 Discuss the Main Biological, Social, and Cognitive Influences on Gender

REVIEW
- What are some ways that biology may influence gender?
- What are three social theories of gender?
- What are two cognitive views of gender?

REFLECT
- Does any theory of gender development explain everything you know about differences between men and women? What might an eclectic view of gender development be like? (You might want to review the discussion of an eclectic theoretical orientation in Chapter 1.)

Gender Stereotyping

Gender Similarities and Differences

How pervasive is gender stereotyping? What are the real differences between boys and girls?

Gender Stereotyping

Gender stereotypes are general impressions and beliefs about females and males. For example, men are powerful; women are weak. Men make good mechanics; women make good nurses. Men are good with numbers; women are good with words. Women are emotional; men are not. All of these are stereotypes. They are generalizations about a group that reflect widely held beliefs (Matlin, 2008).

Traditional Masculinity and Femininity   A classic study in the early 1970s assessed which traits and behaviors college students believed were characteristic of females and which they believed were characteristic of males (Broverman & others, 1972). The traits associated with males were labeled *instrumental:* They included characteristics such as being independent, aggressive, and power oriented. The traits associated with females were labeled *expressive:* They included characteristics such as being warm and sensitive.

Thus, the instrumental traits associated with males suited them for the traditional masculine role of going out into the world as the breadwinner. The expressive traits associated with females paralleled the traditional feminine role of being the sensitive, nurturing caregiver in the home. These roles and traits, however, are not just different; they also are unequal in terms of social status and power. The traditional feminine characteristics are childlike, suitable for someone who is dependent and subordinate to others. The traditional masculine characteristics suit one to deal competently with the wider world and to wield authority.

Stereotyping and Culture   How widespread is gender stereotyping? In a far-ranging study of college students in 30 countries, stereotyping of females and males was pervasive (Williams & Best, 1982). Males were widely believed to be dominant, independent, aggressive, achievement oriented, and enduring. Females were widely believed to be nurturant, affiliative, less esteemed, and more helpful in times of distress.

Of course, in the decades since this study was conducted, traditional gender stereotypes and gender roles have been challenged in many societies, and social inequalities between men and women have diminished. Do gender stereotypes change when the relationship between men and women changes? In a subsequent study, women and men who lived in relatively wealthy, industrialized countries perceived themselves as more similar than did women and men who lived in less developed countries (Williams & Best, 1989). In the more developed countries, the women were more likely to attend college and be gainfully employed. Thus, as sexual equality increases, gender stereotypes may diminish.

However, recent research continues to find that gender stereotyping is pervasive (Blakemore, Berenbaum, & Liben, 2009; Zosuls, Lurye, & Ruble, 2008). For example, a recent study found extensive differences in the stereotyping of females' and males' emotions (Durik & others, 2006). Females were stereotyped as expressing more fear, guilt, love, sadness, shame, surprise, and sympathy than their male counterparts. Males were stereotyped as expressing more anger and pride than their female counterparts.

Developmental Changes in Gender Stereotyping   Earlier we described how young children stereotype occupations as being "masculine" or "feminine." When do children

If you are going to generalize about women, you will find yourself up to here in exceptions.

—**Dolores Hitchens**
American Mystery Writer, 20th Century

gender stereotypes Broad categories that reflect impressions and widely held beliefs about what behavior is appropriate for females and males.

begin to engage in gender stereotyping? A recent study examined the extent to which children and their mothers engage in gender stereotyping (Gelman, Taylor, & Nguyen, 2004). The researchers videotaped mothers and their 2-, 4-, and 6-year-old sons and daughters as they discussed a picture book with stereotyped (a boy playing football, for example) and nonstereotyped (a female race car driver, for example) gender activities. Children engaged in more gender stereotyping than did their mothers. However, mothers expressed gender concepts to their children by referencing categories of gender ("Why do you think only *men* can be firefighters?" for example), labeling gender ('That looks like a daddy," for example), and contrasting males and females ("Is that a girl job or a boy job?" for example). Gender stereotyping by children was present even in the 2-year-olds, but increased considerably by 4 years of age. This study demonstrated that even when adults don't explicitly engage in gender stereotyping when talking with children, they provide children with information about gender by categorizing gender, labeling gender, and contrasting males and females. Children use these cues to construct an understanding of gender and to guide their behavior (Leaper & Bigler, 2004).

Gender stereotyping continues to change during middle and late childhood and adolescence (Ruble, Martin, & Berenbaum, 2006). By the time children enter elementary school, they have considerable knowledge about which activities are linked with being male or female. Until about 7 to 8 years of age, gender stereotyping is extensive because young children don't recognize individual variations in masculinity and femininity. By 5 years of age, both boys and girls stereotype boys as powerful and in more negative terms, such as mean, and girls in more positive terms, such as nice (Miller & Ruble, 2005). Across the elementary school years, children become more flexible in their gender attitudes (Trautner & others, 2005). In early adolescence, gender stereotyping might increase again, a topic we will address shortly. By late adolescence, gender attitudes become more flexible.

Gender Similarities and Differences

What is the reality behind gender stereotypes? Let's examine some of the differences between the sexes, keeping in mind that (1) the differences are averages and do not apply to all females or all males; (2) even when gender differences occur, there often is considerable overlap between males and females; and (3) the differences may be due primarily to biological factors, sociocultural factors, or both.

First, we will examine physical similarities and differences, and then we will turn to cognitive and socioemotional similarities and differences.

Physical Similarities and Differences We could devote pages to describing physical differences between the average man and woman. For example, women have about twice the body fat of men, most concentrated around breasts and hips. In males, fat is more likely to go to the abdomen. On the average, males grow to be 10 percent taller than females. Androgens (the "male" hormones) promote the growth of long bones; estrogens (the "female" hormones) stop such growth at puberty.

What are some developmental changes in children's gender stereotyping?

Many physical differences between men and women are tied to health. From conception on, females have a longer life expectancy than males, and females are less likely than males to develop physical or mental disorders. Females are more resistant to infection, and their blood vessels are more elastic than males'. Males have higher levels of stress hormones, which cause faster clotting and higher blood pressure. For example, a recent study of emerging adults found that the hypothalamic-pituitary-adrenal (HPA) axis responses of males were greater than females following a psychological stress test (Uhart & others, 2006). This greater response of the HPA axis in males was reflected in elevated levels of such stress-related hormones as cortisol.

Does gender matter when it comes to brain structure and activity? Human brains are much alike, whether the brain belongs to a male or a female (Hwang & others, 2004; Hyde, 2007a). However, researchers have found some differences (Goldstein & others, 2001; Hofer & others, 2006, 2007). Among the differences that have been discovered are as follows:

- Female brains are smaller than male brains, but female brains have more folds; the larger folds (called *convolutions*) allow more surface brain tissue within the skulls of females than in males (Luders & others, 2004).

- One part of the hypothalamus involved in sexual behavior tends to be larger in men than in women (Swaab & others, 2001).

- Portions of the corpus callosum—the band of tissues through which the brain's two hemispheres communicate—may be larger in females than in males, although some studies have found this not to be the case (Bishop & Wahlsten, 1997; Driesen & Raz, 1995; LeVay, 1994).

- An area of the parietal lobe that functions in visuospatial skills tends to be larger in males than in females (Frederikse & others, 2000).

- The areas of the brain involved in emotional expression tend to show more metabolic activity in females than in males (Gur & others, 1995).

Similarities and differences in the brains of males and females could be due to evolution and heredity, as well as social experiences (Hyde, 2007b).

Cognitive Similarities and Differences

Many years ago, Eleanor Maccoby and Carol Jacklin (1974) concluded that males have better math and visuospatial skills (the kinds of skills an architect needs to design a building's angles and dimensions) than females, whereas females have better verbal abilities than males. Subsequently, Maccoby (1987) concluded that the verbal differences between females and males had virtually disappeared but that the math and visuospatial differences persisted. Today, some experts in gender, such as Janet Shibley Hyde (2005; 2007a, b; Hyde & others, 2008), stress that the cognitive differences between females and males have been exaggerated. For example, Hyde points out that there is considerable overlap in the distributions of female and male scores on visuospatial tasks (see Figure 12.6). However, some researchers have found that boys have better visuospatial skills than girls (Blakemore, Berenbaum, & Liben, 2009; Halpern & others, 2007; Ruble, Martin, & Berenbaum, 2006). Despite equal participation in the National Geography Bee, in most years all ten finalists have been boys (Liben, 1995).

In the most recent National Assessment of Educational Progress (2005, 2007) reports, girls scored significantly higher than boys in literacy skills, although boys scored slightly higher than girls in math and science. For example, in reading skills, 41 percent of girls reached the proficient level (compared with 29 percent of boys) and in writing skills, 32 percent of girls were proficient (compared with 16 percent of boys). In math, 25 percent of males were proficient (compared with 21 percent of females) and in science, 21 percent of males were proficient (compared with 16 percent of females). Clearly, both U.S. boys and girls have room to make considerable improvement in their academic skills.

Keep in mind, though, that measures of achievement in school or scores on standardized tests may reflect many factors besides cognitive ability. For example, some test scores may reflect stereotype threat (as discussed in Chapter 8). Performance in school may in part reflect attempts to conform to gender roles or differences in motivation, self-regulation, or other socioemotional characteristics (Watt, 2008; Watt & Eccles, 2008).

With regard to school achievement, females earn better grades and complete high school at a higher rate than boys (Halpern, 2006). Males are more likely than females to be assigned to special/remedial education classes. Females are more likely to be engaged with academic material, be attentive in class, put forth more academic effort, and participate more in class than boys are (DeZolt & Hull, 2001).

Might same-sex education be better for children than coed education? The research evidence related to this question is mixed (Ruble, Martin, & Berenbaum, 2006).

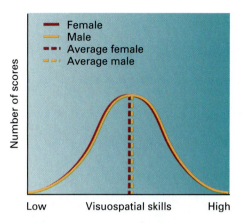

FIGURE 12.6 Visuospatial Skills of Males and Females. Notice that, although an average male's visuospatial skills are higher than an average female's, scores for the two sexes almost entirely overlap. Not all males have better visuospatial skills than all females—the overlap indicates that, although the average male score is higher, many females outperform most males on such tasks.

"So according to the stereotype, you can put two and two together, but I can read the handwriting on the wall."

What are some gender differences in communication?

Some research indicates that same-sex education has positive outcomes for girls' achievement, whereas other research does not show any improvements in achievement for girls or boys in same-sex education (Mael, 1998; Warrington & Younger, 2003).

Socioemotional Similarities and Differences   Are males and females so dramatically different that "men are from Mars" and "women are from Venus" as was proposed in a popular trade book (Gray, 1992). Perhaps the gender differences that most fascinate people are those in how males and females relate to each other as people. For just about every imaginable socioemotional characteristic, researchers have examined whether there are differences between males and females. Here we will examine five areas of socioemotional development in which gender has been studied: relationships, aggression, emotion, prosocial behavior, and achievement.

Relationships   Sociolinguist Deborah Tannen (1990) distinguishes between rapport talk and report talk:

- **Rapport talk** is the language of conversation and a way of establishing connections and negotiating relationships. Girls enjoy rapport talk and conversation that is relationship oriented more than boys do.
- **Report talk** is talk that gives information. Public speaking is an example of report talk. Males hold center stage through report talk with such verbal performances as storytelling, joking, and lecturing with information.

Tannen says that boys and girls grow up in different worlds of talk—parents, siblings, peers, teachers, and others talk to boys and girls differently. The play of boys and girls is also different. Boys tend to play in large groups that are hierarchically structured, and their groups usually have a leader who tells the others what to do and how to do it. Boys' games have winners and losers and often are the subject of arguments. And boys often boast of their skill and argue about who is best at what. In contrast, girls are more likely to play in small groups or pairs, and at the center of a girl's world is often a best friend. In girls' friendships and peer groups, intimacy is pervasive. Turn taking is more characteristic of girls' games than of boys' games. And much of the time, girls simply like to sit and talk with each other, concerned more about being liked by others than jockeying for status in some obvious way.

In sum, Tannen concludes that females are more relationship oriented than males—and that this relationship orientation should be prized as a skill in our culture more than it currently is. Note, however, that some researchers criticize Tannen's ideas as being overly simplified and that communication between males and females is more complex than Tannen indicates (Edwards & Hamilton, 2004). Further, some researchers have found similarities in males' and females' relationship communication strategies (Hyde, 2007a, b). In one study, in their talk men and women described and responded to relationship problems in ways that were more similar than different (MacGeorge, 2004).

Further modification of Tannen's view is suggested by a recent *meta-analytic* review of gender differences in talkativeness (general communicative competence), affiliative speech (language used to establish or maintain connections with others, such as showing support or expanding on a person's prior remarks), and self-assertive speech (language used to influence others, such as directive statements or disagreements) (Leaper & Smith, 2004). This review confirms the criticism that Tannen overemphasizes the size of the gender difference in communication. Gender differences did occur, with girls slightly more talkative and engaging in more affiliative speech than boys, and boys being more likely to use self-assertive speech. But the gender differences were small. Perhaps the most important message from this review is that gender differences in communication often depended on the context:

- *Group size.* The gender difference in talkativeness (girls being more competent in communicating) occurred more in large groups than in dyads.

rapport talk The language of conversation and a way of establishing connections and negotiating relationships; more characteristic of females than of males.

report talk Talk that conveys information; more characteristic of males than females.

- *Speaking with peers or adults.* No average differences in talk with peers occurred, but girls talked more with adults than boys.
- *Familiarity.* The gender difference in self-assertive speech (boys using it more) was more likely to occur when talking with strangers than with familiar individuals.
- *Age.* The gender difference in affiliative speech was largest in adolescence. This may be due to adolescent girls' increased interest in socioemotional behavior traditionally prescribed for females.

What are some gender differences in aggression?

Aggression   One of the most consistent gender differences is that boys are more physically aggressive than girls (Keenan, 2009; Tremblay, 2009). The difference occurs in all cultures and appears very early in children's development (Baillargeon & others, 2007). The difference in physical aggression is especially pronounced when children are provoked.

Although boys are consistently more physically aggressive than girls, might girls show as much or more verbal aggression, such as yelling, than boys? When verbal aggression is examined, gender differences typically either disappear or are sometimes even more pronounced in girls (Eagly & Steffen, 1986).

Recently, increased interest has been shown in *relational aggression,* which involves harming someone by manipulating a relationship (Coyne & others, 2008). Relational aggression includes such behaviors as trying to make others dislike a certain individual by spreading malicious rumors about the person (Underwood, 2004). Researchers have found mixed results regarding gender and relational aggression, with some studies showing girls engaging in more relational aggression and others revealing no differences between boys and girls (Young, Boye, & Nelson, 2006). One consistency in findings is that relational aggression comprises a greater percentage of girls' overall aggression than is the case for boys (Putallaz & others, 2007).

Emotion and Its Regulation   Beginning in the elementary school years, boys are more likely to hide their negative emotions, such as sadness, and girls are less likely to express emotions such as disappointment that might hurt others' feelings (Eisenberg, Martin, & Fabes, 1996). Beginning in early adolescence, girls say they experience more sadness, shame, and guilt, and report more intense emotions, whereas boys are more likely to deny that they experience these emotions (Ruble, Martin, & Berenbaum, 2006).

An important skill is to be able to regulate and control one's emotions and behavior. Boys usually show less self-regulation than girls (Eisenberg, Spinrad, & Smith, 2004). This low self-control can translate into behavior problems. In one study, children's low self-regulation was linked with greater aggression, teasing of others, overreaction to frustration, low cooperation, and inability to delay gratification (Block & Block, 1980).

Prosocial Behavior   Are there gender differences in prosocial behavior? Females view themselves as more prosocial and empathic, and they also engage in more prosocial behavior than males (Eisenberg, Fabes, & Spinrad, 2006). For example, a review of research found that across childhood and adolescence, females engaged in more prosocial behavior (Eisenberg & Fabes, 1998). The biggest gender difference occurred for kind and considerate behavior, with a smaller difference in sharing.

Achievement   Although women have made considerable progress in attaining high status in many fields, they still are underrepresented in many areas of technology, math, and science (Wigfield & others, 2006). However, some measures of achievement-related behaviors do not reveal gender differences. For example, girls and boys show similar persistence at tasks.

With regard to school achievement, females earn better grades. For example, evidence suggests that boys predominate in the academic bottom half of high school classes (DeZolt & Hull, 2001). That is, although many boys perform at the average or advanced level, the bottom 50 percent academically is made up mainly of boys. Males are more likely than females to be assigned to special/remedial education classes. Females are more likely to be engaged with academic material, be attentive in class, put forth more academic effort, and participate more in class than boys are (DeZolt & Hull, 2001).

Gender Controversy   Controversy continues about the extent of gender differences and what might cause them (Blakemore, Berenbaum, & Liben, 2009). As we saw earlier, evolutionary psychologists such as David Buss (2008) argue that gender differences are extensive and caused by the adaptive problems they have faced across their evolutionary history. Alice Eagly (2001, 2008, 2009) also concludes that gender differences are substantial but reaches a very different conclusion about their cause. She emphasizes that gender differences are due to social conditions that have resulted in women having less power and controlling fewer resources than men.

By contrast, Janet Shibley Hyde (2005, 2007a, b; Hyde & others, 2008) concludes that gender differences have been greatly exaggerated, especially fueled by popular books such as John Gray's (1992) *Men Are from Mars, Women Are from Venus* and Deborah Tannen's (1990) *You Just Don't Understand.* She argues that the research indicates females and males are similar on most psychological factors. In a recent review, Hyde (2005) summarized the results of 44 meta-analyses of gender differences and similarities. A *meta-analysis* is a statistical analysis that combines the results of many different studies. In most areas, gender differences either were nonexistent or small, including math ability and communication. Gender differences in physical aggression were moderate. The largest difference occurred on motor skills (favoring males), followed by sexuality (males masturbate more and are more likely to endorse sex in a casual, uncommitted relationship) and physical aggression (males are more physically aggressive than are females).

Hyde's recent summary of meta-analyses is still not likely to quiet the controversy about gender differences and similarities, but further research should continue to provide a basis for more accurate judgments about this controversy.

At this point, we have discussed many aspects of stereotypes, similarities, differences, and controversies in children's development. The following *Caring for Children* interlude provides some recommendations for parents and teachers related to children's gender.

Caring for Children

GUIDING CHILDREN'S GENDER DEVELOPMENT

Boys

1. ***Encourage boys to be sensitive in relationships and engage in more prosocial behavior.*** An important socialization task is to help boys become more interested in having positive close relationships and become more caring. Fathers can play an especially important role for boys in this regard by being a model who is sensitive and caring.

2. ***Encourage boys to be less physically aggressive.*** Too often, boys are encouraged to be tough and physically aggressive. A positive strategy is to encourage them to be self-assertive but not physically aggressive.

3. ***Encourage boys to handle their emotions more effectively.*** This involves helping boys not only to regulate their emotions, as in controlling their anger, but also to learn to express their anxieties and concerns rather than keeping them bottled up.

4. ***Work with boys to improve their school performance.*** Girls get better grades, put forth more academic effort, and are less likely than boys to be assigned to special/remedial classes. Parents and teachers can help boys by emphasizing the importance of school and expecting better academic effort.

Girls

1. ***Encourage girls to be proud of their relationship skills and caring.*** The strong interest that girls show in relationships and caring should be supported by parents and teachers.

2. ***Encourage girls to develop their self-competencies.*** While guiding girls to retain their relationship strengths, adults can help girls to develop their ambition and achievement.

3. ***Encourage girls to be more self-assertive.*** Girls tend to be more passive than boys and can benefit from being encouraged to be more self-assertive.

4. ***Encourage girls' achievement.*** This can involve encouraging girls to have higher academic expectations and exposing them to a greater range of career options.

Boys and Girls

1. ***Help children to reduce gender stereotyping and discrimination.*** Don't engage in gender stereotyping and discrimination yourself; otherwise, you will be providing a model of gender stereotyping and discrimination for children.

Review and Reflect: Learning Goal 2

 Describe Gender Stereotypes, Similarities, and Differences

REVIEW

- What are gender stereotypes? How extensive is gender stereotyping?
- What are some gender similarities and differences in the areas of biological, cognitive, and socioemotional development?

REFLECT

- How is your gender behavior and thinking similar to or different from your mother's and grandmothers' if you are a female? How is your gender behavior and thinking different from your father's and grandfathers' if you are a male?

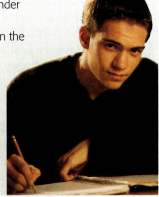

---

3 GENDER-ROLE CLASSIFICATION

| What Is Gender-Role Classification? | Masculinity in Childhood and Adolescence | Gender-Role Transcendence | Gender in Context |

Not very long ago, it was accepted that boys should grow up to be masculine and girls to be feminine, that boys are made of "frogs and snails" and girls are made of "sugar and spice and all that's nice." Let's further explore such gender classifications of boys and girls as "masculine" and "feminine."

What Is Gender-Role Classification?

In the past, a well-adjusted boy was supposed to be independent, aggressive, and powerful. A well-adjusted girl was supposed to be dependent, nurturant, and uninterested in power. The masculine characteristics were considered to be healthy and good by society; the feminine characteristics were considered undesirable.

FIGURE 12.7 **The Bem Sex-Role Inventory: Are You Androgynous?**

The following items are from the Bem Sex-Role Inventory. When taking the BSRI, a person is asked to indicate on a 7-point scale how well each of the 60 characteristics describes herself or himself. The scale ranges from 1 (never or almost never true) to 7 (always or almost always true).

EXAMPLES OF MASCULINE ITEMS	EXAMPLES OF FEMININE ITEMS
Defends open beliefs	Does not use harsh language
Forceful	Affectionate
Willing to take risks	Loves children
Dominant	Understanding
Aggressive	Gentle

Scoring: The items are scored on independent dimensions of masculinity and femininity as well as androgyny and undifferentiated classifications.

In the 1970s, as both females and males became dissatisfied with the burdens imposed by their stereotypic roles, alternatives to femininity and masculinity were proposed. Instead of describing masculinity and femininity as a continuum in which more of one means less of the other, it was proposed that individuals could have both masculine and feminine traits. This thinking led to the development of the concept of **androgyny**, the presence of masculine and feminine characteristics in the same person (Bem, 1977; Spence & Helmreich, 1978). The androgynous boy might be assertive (masculine) and nurturant (feminine). The androgynous girl might be powerful (masculine) and sensitive to others' feelings (feminine). In one study, it was confirmed that societal changes are leading females to be more assertive (Spence & Buckner, 2000).

Measures have been developed to assess androgyny. One of the most widely used measures is the Bem Sex-Role Inventory. To see whether your gender-role classification is masculine, feminine, or androgynous, see Figure 12.7.

Gender experts, such as Sandra Bem, argue that androgynous individuals are more flexible, competent, and mentally healthy than their masculine or feminine counterparts. To some degree, though, deciding on which gender-role classification is best depends on the context involved (Woodhill & Samuels, 2004). For example, in close relationships, feminine and androgynous orientations might be more desirable because of the expressive nature of close relationships. However, masculine and androgynous orientations might be more desirable in traditional academic and work settings because of the achievement demands in these contexts. For example, one study found that masculine and androgynous individuals had higher expectations for being able to control the outcomes of their academic efforts than feminine or undifferentiated individuals (Choi, 2004).

Masculinity in Childhood and Adolescence

Concern about the ways boys have been brought up in traditional ways has been called a "national crisis of boyhood" by William Pollack (1999) in his book *Real Boys.* Pollack says that although there has been considerable talk about the "sensitive male," little has been done to change what he calls the "boy code." He says that this code tells boys they should show little if any emotion as they are growing up. Too often boys are socialized to not show their feelings and act tough, says Pollack. Boys learn the boy code in many different contexts—sandboxes, playgrounds, schoolrooms, camps, hangouts—and are taught the code by parents, peers, coaches, teachers, and other adults. Pollack, as well as many others, argues that boys would benefit from being socialized to express their anxieties and concerns rather than keep them bottled up as well as to learn how to better regulate their aggression.

There also is a special concern about boys who adopt a strong masculine role in adolescence, because this is associated with problem behaviors. Joseph Pleck (1995)

androgyny The presence of masculine and feminine characteristics in the same person.

points out that what defines traditional masculinity in many Western cultures includes behaviors that do not have social approval but nonetheless validate the adolescent boy's masculinity. That is, in the male adolescent culture, male adolescents perceive that they will be thought of as more masculine if they engage in premarital sex, drink alcohol, take drugs, and participate in illegal delinquent activities.

Gender-Role Transcendence

Some critics of androgyny say enough is enough and that there is too much talk about gender. They say that androgyny is less of a panacea than originally envisioned. An alternative is gender-role transcendence, the view that when an individual's competence is at issue, it should be conceptualized on a personal basis rather than on the basis of masculinity, femininity, or androgyny (Pleck, 1983). That is, we should think about ourselves as people, not as masculine, feminine, or androgynous. Parents should rear their children to be competent boys and girls, not masculine, feminine, or androgynous, say the gender-role critics. They stress that such gender-role classification leads to too much stereotyping.

Gender in Context

The concept of gender-role classification involves a personality trait–like categorization of a person. However, it may be helpful to think of personality in terms of person-situation interaction rather than personality traits alone. Thus, in our discussion of gender-role classification, we described how different gender roles might be more appropriate, depending on the context, or setting, involved.

To see the importance of considering gender in context, let's examine helping behavior and emotion. The stereotype is that females are better than males at helping. However, it depends on the situation. Females are more likely than males to volunteer their time to help children with personal problems and to engage in caregiving behavior (Taylor, 2002). However, in situations in which males feel a sense of competence and involve danger, males are more likely than females to help (Eagly & Crowley, 1986). For example, a male is more likely than a female to stop and help a person stranded by the roadside with a flat tire.

"She is emotional; he is not"—that is the master emotional stereotype. However, like differences in helping behavior, emotional differences in males and females depend on the particular emotion involved and the context in which it is displayed (Shields, 1998). Males are more likely to show anger toward strangers, especially male strangers, when they feel they have been challenged. Males also are more likely to turn their anger into aggressive action. Emotional differences between females and males often show up in contexts that highlight social roles and relationships. For example, females are more likely to discuss emotions in terms of relationships, and they are more likely to express fear and sadness.

The importance of considering gender in context is nowhere more apparent than when examining what is culturally prescribed behavior for females and males in different countries around the world (Shiraev & Levy, 2007). To read further about cross-cultural variations in gender, see the *Diversity in Child Development* interlude.

Diversity in Child Development

GENDER ROLES ACROSS CULTURES

In recent decades, roles assumed by males and females in the United States have become increasingly similar—that is, androgynous. In many countries, though, gender roles have remained more gender-specific (UNICEF, 2007). For example, in a number of Middle

Although access to education for girls has improved, boys still receive approximately 4.4 years more education around the world than girls do. Shown here is a private school for boys in Africa.

Eastern countries, the division of labor between males and females is dramatic: males are socialized to work in the public sphere, females in the private world of home and child rearing; a man's duty is to provide for his family, the woman's to care for her family and household. Any deviations from this traditional gender-role orientation are severely disapproved of.

Access to education for girls has improved somewhat around the world, but girls' education still lags behind boys' education. For example, according to a UNICEF (2003) analysis of education around the world, by age 18, girls have received, on average, 4.4 years less education than boys have. This lack of education reduces their chances of developing their potential. Noticeable exceptions to lower participation and completion rates in education for girls occur in Western nations, Japan, and the Philippines (Brown & Larson, 2002). In most countries, more men than women gain advanced training or advanced degrees (Fussell & Greene, 2002).

Although most countries still have gender gaps that favor males, evidence of increasing gender equality is appearing (Brown & Larson, 2002). For example, among upper-socioeconomic-status families in India and Japan, fathers are assuming more child-rearing responsibilities (Stevenson & Zusho, 2002; Verma & Saraswathi, 2002). Rates of employment and career opportunities are expanding in many countries for women. Control over adolescent girls' social relationships, especially sexual and romantic relationships, is decreasing in some countries.

Cultural and ethnic backgrounds also influence how boys and girls are socialized in the United States. One study revealed that Latino and Latina adolescents were socialized differently as they were growing up (Raffaelli & Ontai, 2004). Latinas experienced far greater restrictions than Latinos in curfews, interacting with members of the other sex, getting a driver's license, getting a job, and involvement in after-school activities.

Review and Reflect: Learning Goal 3

3 Identify How Gender Roles Can Be Classified

REVIEW

- What is gender-role classification?
- What are some risks of masculinity in childhood and adolescence?
- What is gender-role transcendence?
- How can gender be conceptualized in terms of context?

REFLECT

- Several decades ago, the word *dependency* was used to describe the relational orientation of femininity. Dependency took on a negative connotation; for instance, it suggested that females can't take care of themselves whereas males can. Today, the term *dependency* is being replaced by *relational abilities*, which has more positive connotations (Caplan & Caplan, 1999). Rather than being thought of as dependent, women are now more often described as skilled in forming and maintaining relationships. Make up a list of words that you associate with masculinity and femininity. Do these words have any negative connotations for males and females? For the words that do have negative connotations, think about replacements that have more positive connotations.

Reach Your Learning Goals

Gender

1 INFLUENCES ON GENDER DEVELOPMENT: DISCUSS THE MAIN BIOLOGICAL, SOCIAL, AND COGNITIVE INFLUENCES ON GENDER

Biological Influences

- The 23rd pair of chromosomes determines our sex. Ordinarily, females have two X chromosomes, males one X and one Y. Males and females also produce different concentrations of the hormones known as androgens and estrogens. Early hormonal production is linked with later gender development. In the evolutionary psychology view, evolutionary adaptations produced psychological sex differences that are especially present in sexual behavior and mating strategies. Chromosomes determine anatomical sex differences, but culture and society strongly influence gender.

Social Influences

- In the social role theory, gender differences result from men and women's contrasting roles; in most culture, women have less power and status than men and control fewer resources—this gender hierarchy and sexual division of labor are important causes of sex-differentiated behavior. Psychoanalytic theory of gender emphasizes sexual attraction to the same-sex parent, anxiety about the attraction, and subsequent adoption of the same-sex parent's gender characteristics. Social cognitive theory emphasizes rewards and punishments for gender-appropriate and gender-inappropriate behavior. Parents and other adults also might assign gender roles to children and reward or punish behavior along gender lines. Peers are especially adept at rewarding gender-appropriate behavior.

Cognitive Influences

- Both cognitive developmental and gender schema theories emphasize the role of cognition in gender development. In gender schema theory, gender typing emerges gradually as children develop gender schemas of what their culture considers to be gender-appropriate and gender-inappropriate. According to cognitive developmental theory, gender typing emerges after children think of themselves as boys or girls.

2 GENDER STEREOTYPES, SIMILARITIES, AND DIFFERENCES: DESCRIBE GENDER STEREOTYPES, SIMILARITIES, AND DIFFERENCES

Gender Stereotyping

- Gender stereotypes are general impressions and beliefs about males and females. Gender stereotypes are widespread. Gender stereotyping changes developmentally; it is present even at 2 years of age but increases considerably in early childhood. In middle and late childhood, children become more flexible in their gender attitudes, but gender stereotyping may increase again in early adolescence. By late adolescence, gender attitudes are often more flexible.

Gender Similarities and Differences

- Physical and biological differences between males and females are substantial. Women have about twice the body fat as men, are less likely to develop physical or mental disorders, and have a longer life expectancy. Males are often better at math and visuospatial skills. However, some experts, such as Hyde, argue that cognitive differences between males and females have been exaggerated. Males are more physically aggressive and active than females, while females engage in more prosocial behavior, have a stronger interest in social relationships, and are more achievement oriented in school than males. There is considerable controversy about how similar or different females and males are in a number of areas.

3   GENDER-ROLE CLASSIFICATION: IDENTIFY HOW GENDER ROLES CAN BE CLASSIFIED

What Is Gender-Role Classification?

- In the past, the well-adjusted male was supposed to show masculine traits; the well-adjusted female, feminine traits. In the 1970s, alternatives to traditional gender roles were introduced. It was proposed that competent individuals could show both masculine and feminine traits. This thinking led to the development of the concept of androgyny, the presence of masculine and feminine traits in one individual. Gender-role measures often categorize individuals as masculine, feminine, androgynous, or undifferentiated. Most androgynous individuals are flexible and mentally healthy, although the particular context and the individual's culture also determine the adaptiveness of a gender-role orientation.

Masculinity in Childhood and Adolescence

- A special concern is that boys raised in a traditional manner are socialized to conceal their emotions. Researchers have found that problem behaviors often characterize highly masculine adolescents.

Gender-Role Transcendence

- One alternative to androgyny is gender-role transcendence, which states that there has been too much emphasis on gender and that a better strategy is to think about competence in terms of people rather than gender.

Gender in Context

- In thinking about gender, it is important to keep in mind the context in which gender behavior is displayed. In many countries, traditional gender roles are still dominant.

KEY TERMS

gender 362
gender role 362
gender typing 362
estrogens 363
androgens 363

social role theory 364
psychoanalytic theory of
  gender 365
social cognitive theory of
  gender 365

cognitive developmental
  theory of gender 366
gender schema theory 366
gender stereotypes 369
rapport talk 372

report talk 372
androgyny 376

KEY PEOPLE

Stephanie Shields 362
Alice Eagly 364
Sigmund Freud 365
Phyllis Bronstein 365

Lawrence Kohlberg 366
Eleanor Maccoby 371
Carol Jacklin 371

Janet Shibley Hyde 371
Deborah Tannen 372
David Buss 374

Sandra Bem 376
William Pollack 376
Joseph Pleck 376

E-LEARNING TOOLS

To help you master the material in this chapter, you'll find a number of valuable study tools at the Online Learning Center for *Child Development*, twelfth edition (**www.mhhe.com/ santrockcd12**).

Taking It to the Net

Research the answers to these questions:

1. Ellen is taking a class in gender psychology. She wants to test the theory of androgyny among her peers in her large geology lecture. She has heard that there is an online version of the test, and thinks people will feel more comfortable taking it online.

What conclusions can Ellen draw on the androgyny theory after taking this test?

2. Derek is the program chair for the Men's Focus Group on campus. He is planning a program on the social barriers to men being fully involved fathers. He thinks it has something to do with gender stereotyping that suggests that women are the best nurturers and caregivers. Is there some research Derek ought to share with the group?

3. Professor Lombard told the child development class to find out what the current thinking was on how to treat infants who are born without fully developed male or female genitalia. She said

that the old line of thinking was that these children should be surgically altered during infancy so as to be genitally correct females. Are other alternatives being considered today?

Health and Well-Being, Parenting, and Education Exercises

Build your decision-making skills by trying your hand at the health and well-being, parenting, and education exercises.

Video Clips

The Online Learning Center includes the following videos for this chapter:

- *Sex-Typed Play at Age 1*

A 1-year-old girl is shown in a room surrounded by an assortment of toys. She shows interest only in the Barbie dolls, which she examines carefully from every angle.

- *Lacking Gender Consistency at Age 4*

A boy is asked to identify the gender of a male doll placed in front of him.

- *Sex-Typed Play*

Early sex-typed behavior is demonstrated as we watch a boy and girl make toy selections.

- *Girls Engaging in Sex-Typed Play*

Two girls show their preference for a non-sex-typed toy as they enthusiastically play with a remote control truck, ignoring the elaborate, colorful dollhouse that sits inches away.

- *Developing a Sexual Identity*

Ramona Oswald, University of Illinois, talks about the development of sexual identity.

13

> *It is one of the beautiful compensations of this life that no one can sincerely try to help another without helping himself.*
>
> —CHARLES DUDLEY WARNER
> *American Essayist, 19th Century*

LEARNING GOALS

◆ Discuss theory and research on the four domains of moral development.

◆ Explain how parenting and schools influence moral development.

◆ Describe the development of prosocial and antisocial behavior.

◆ Summarize the nature of children's and adolescents' religious and spiritual development.

MORAL DEVELOPMENT

CHAPTER OUTLINE

Images of Child Development
The Story of Jewel Cash, Teen Dynamo

Jewel Cash, seated next to her mother, participating in a crime watch meeting at a community center.

The mayor of the city says that she is "everywhere." She recently persuaded the city's school committee to consider ending the practice of locking tardy students out of their classrooms. She also swayed a neighborhood group to support her proposal for a winter jobs program. According to one city councilman, "People are just impressed with the power of her arguments and the sophistication of the argument" (Silva, 2005, pp. B1, B4). She is Jewel E. Cash, and she is just 16 years old.

A junior at Boston Latin Academy, Jewel was raised in one of Boston's housing projects by her mother, a single parent. Today she is a member of the Boston Student Advisory Council, mentors children, volunteers at a women's shelter, manages and dances in two troupes, and is a member of a neighborhood watch group—among other activities. Jewel told an interviewer from the *Boston Globe,* "I see a problem and I say, 'How can I make a difference?' . . . I can't take on the world, even though I can try. . . . I'm moving forward but I want to make sure I'm bringing people with me" (Silva, 2005, pp. B1, B4). Jewel is far from typical, but her motivation to help others illustrates the positive side of moral development.

> ### PREVIEW
>
> **Moral development is one of the oldest topics of interest to those who are curious about human nature. In prescientific periods, philosophers and theologians debated children's moral status at birth, which they believed had implications for how children should be reared. Today, most people have strong opinions not only about moral and immoral behavior but also about how moral behavior should be fostered in children. We will begin our coverage of moral development by exploring its main domains and then examine some important contexts that influence moral development. Next, we discuss children's prosocial and antisocial behavior. The chapter concludes with an overview of children's religious and spiritual development.**

1 DOMAINS OF MORAL DEVELOPMENT

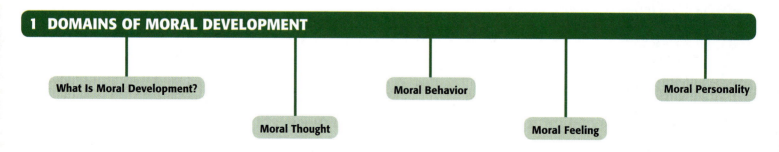

What Is Moral Development?

Moral Thought

Moral Behavior

Moral Feeling

Moral Personality

What is moral development? What are its main domains?

What Is Moral Development?

Moral development involves changes in thoughts, feelings, and behaviors regarding standards of right and wrong. Moral development has an *intrapersonal* dimension, which regulates a person's activities when she or he is not engaged in social interaction, and an *interpersonal* dimension, which regulates social interactions and arbitrates conflict (Walker, 2006). To understand moral development, we need to consider four basic questions:

First, how do individuals *reason* or *think* about moral decisions?

Second, how do individuals actually *behave* in moral circumstances?

Third, how do individuals *feel* about moral matters?

Fourth, what characterizes an individual's moral *personality*?

As we consider these four domains in the following sections, keep in mind that thoughts, behaviors, feelings, and personality often are interrelated. For example, if the focus is on an individual's behavior, it is still important to evaluate the person's reasoning. Also, emotions can distort moral reasoning. And moral personality encompasses thoughts, behavior, and feeling.

Piaget extensively observed and interviewed 4- to 12-year-old children as they played games to learn how they used and thought about the games' rules.

Moral Thought

How do individuals think about what is right and wrong? Are children able to evaluate moral questions in the same way that adults can? Piaget had some thoughts about these questions. So did Lawrence Kohlberg.

Piaget's Theory Interest in how children think about moral issues was stimulated by Piaget (1932), who extensively observed and interviewed children from the ages of 4 through 12. Piaget watched children play marbles to learn how they used and thought about the game's rules. He also asked children about ethical issues—theft, lies, punishment, and justice, for example. Piaget concluded that children go through two distinct stages, separated by a transition period, in how they think about morality.

- From 4 to 7 years of age, children display **heteronomous morality**, the first stage of moral development in Piaget's theory. Children think of justice and rules as unchangeable properties of the world, removed from the control of people.
- From 7 to 10 years of age, children are in a transition showing some features of the first stage of moral reasoning and some stages of the second stage, autonomous morality.
- From about 10 years of age and older, children show **autonomous morality**, Piaget's second stage of moral development. They become aware that rules and laws are created by people, and in judging an action, they consider the actor's intentions as well as the consequences.

Because young children are heteronomous moralists, they judge the rightness or goodness of behavior by considering its consequences, not the intentions of the actor. For example, to the heteronomous moralist, breaking twelve cups accidentally is worse than breaking one cup intentionally. As children develop into moral autonomists, intentions assume paramount importance.

The heteronomous thinker also believes that rules are unchangeable and are handed down by all-powerful authorities. When Piaget suggested to young children that they use new rules in a game of marbles, they resisted. By contrast, older children—moral autonomists—accept change and recognize that rules are merely convenient conventions, subject to change.

The heteronomous thinker also believes in **immanent justice**, the concept that if a rule is broken, punishment will be meted out immediately. The young child

moral development Changes in thoughts, feelings, and behaviors regarding standards of right and wrong.

heteronomous morality (Piaget) The first stage of moral development in Piaget's theory, occurring from 4 to 7 years of age. Justice and rules are conceived of as unchangeable properties of the world, removed from the control of people.

autonomous morality The second stage of moral development in Piaget's theory, displayed by older children (about 10 years of age and older). The child becomes aware that rules and laws are created by people and that, in judging an action, one should consider the actor's intentions as well as the consequences.

immanent justice Piaget's concept that if a rule is broken, punishment will be meted out immediately.

How is this child's moral thinking likely to be different about stealing a cookie depending on whether he is in Piaget's heteronomous or autonomous stage?

Lawrence Kohlberg is the architect of a provocative cognitive developmental theory of moral development. *What is the nature of his theory?*

preconventional reasoning The lowest level in Kohlberg's theory of moral development. The individual's moral reasoning is controlled primarily by external rewards and punishment.

heteronomous morality (Kohlberg) Kohlberg's first stage of preconventional reasoning, in which moral thinking is tied to punishment.

believes that a violation is connected automatically to its punishment. Thus, young children often look around worriedly after doing something wrong, expecting inevitable punishment. Immanent justice also implies that if something unfortunate happens to someone, the person must have transgressed earlier. Older children, who are moral autonomists, recognize that punishment occurs only if someone witnesses the wrongdoing and that, even then, punishment is not inevitable.

How do these changes in moral reasoning occur? Piaget argued that, as children develop, they become more sophisticated in thinking about social matters, especially about the possibilities and conditions of cooperation. Piaget reasoned that this social understanding comes about through the mutual give-and-take of peer relations. In the peer group, where others have power and status similar to the child's, plans are negotiated and coordinated, and disagreements are reasoned about and eventually settled. Parent-child relations, in which parents have the power and children do not, are less likely to advance moral reasoning, because rules are often handed down in an authoritarian way.

Kohlberg's Theory A second major perspective on moral development was proposed by Lawrence Kohlberg (1958, 1986). Piaget's cognitive stages of development serve as the underpinnings for Kohlberg's theory, but Kohlberg suggested that there are six stages of moral development. These stages, he argued, are universal. Development from one stage to another, said Kohlberg, is fostered by opportunities to take the perspective of others and to experience conflict between one's current stage of moral thinking and the reasoning of someone at a higher stage.

Kohlberg arrived at his view after 20 years of using a unique interview with children. In the interview, children are presented with a series of stories in which characters face moral dilemmas. The following is the most popular Kohlberg dilemma:

> In Europe a woman was near death from a special kind of cancer. There was one drug that the doctors thought might save her. It was a form of radium that a druggist in the same town had recently discovered. The drug was expensive to make, but the druggist was charging ten times what the drug cost him to make. He paid $200 for the radium and charged $2,000 for a small dose of the drug. The sick woman's husband, Heinz, went to everyone he knew to borrow the money, but he could only get together $1,000 which is half of what it cost. He told the druggist that his wife was dying and asked him to sell it cheaper or let him pay later. But the druggist said, "No, I discovered the drug, and I am going to make money from it." So Heinz got desperate and broke into the man's store to steal the drug for his wife. (Kohlberg, 1969, p. 379)

This story is one of 11 that Kohlberg devised to investigate the nature of moral thought. After reading the story, the interviewee answers a series of questions about the moral dilemma. Should Heinz have stolen the drug? Was stealing it right or wrong? Why? Is it a husband's duty to steal the drug for his wife if he can get it no other way? Would a good husband steal? Did the druggist have the right to charge that much when there was no law setting a limit on the price? Why or why not?

The Kohlberg Stages Based on the answers interviewees gave for this and other moral dilemmas, Kohlberg described three levels of moral thinking, each of which is characterized by two stages (see Figure 13.1).

Preconventional reasoning is the lowest level of moral reasoning, said Kohlberg. At this level, good and bad are interpreted in terms of external rewards and punishments.

• *Stage 1.* **Heteronomous morality** is the first stage in preconventional reasoning. At this stage, moral thinking is tied to punishment. For example, children think that they must obey because they fear punishment for disobedience.

LEVEL 1	LEVEL 2	LEVEL 3
Preconventional Level No Internalization	**Conventional Level** Intermediate Internalization	**Postconventional Level** Full Internalization
Stage 1 Heteronomous Morality *Children obey because adults tell them to obey. People base their moral decisions on fear of punishment.*	**Stage 3** Mutual Interpersonal Expectations, Relationships, and Interpersonal Conformity *Individuals value trust, caring, and loyalty to others as a basis for moral judgments.*	**Stage 5** Social Contract or Utility and Individual Rights *Individuals reason that values, rights, and principles undergird or transcend the law.*
Stage 2 Individualism, Purpose, and Exchange *Individuals pursue their own interests but let others do the same. What is right involves equal exchange.*	**Stage 4** Social Systems Morality *Moral judgments are based on understanding of the social order, law, justice, and duty.*	**Stage 6** Universal Ethical Principles *The person has developed moral judgments that are based on universal human rights. When faced with a dilemma between law and conscience, a personal, individualized conscience is followed.*

FIGURE 13.1 Kohlberg's Three Levels and Six Stages of Moral Development

- *Stage 2.* **Individualism, instrumental purpose, and exchange** is the second stage of preconventional reasoning. At this stage, individuals reason that pursuing their own interests is the right thing to do but they let others do the same. Thus, they think that what is right involves an equal exchange. They reason that if they are nice to others, others will be nice to them in return.

Conventional reasoning is the second, or intermediate, level in Kohlberg's theory of moral development. At this level, individuals apply certain standards, but they are the standards set by others, such as parents or the government.

- *Stage 3.* **Mutual interpersonal expectations, relationships, and interpersonal conformity** is Kohlberg's third stage of moral development. At this stage, individuals value trust, caring, and loyalty to others as a basis of moral judgments. Children and adolescents often adopt their parents' moral standards at this stage, seeking to be thought of by their parents as a "good girl" or a "good boy."
- *Stage 4.* **Social systems morality** is the fourth stage in Kohlberg's theory of moral development. At this stage, moral judgments are based on understanding the social order, law, justice, and duty. For example, adolescents may reason that in order for a community to work effectively, it needs to be protected by laws that are adhered to by its members.

Postconventional reasoning is the highest level in Kohlberg's theory of moral development. At this level, the individual recognizes alternative moral courses, explores the options, and then decides on a personal moral code.

- *Stage 5.* **Social contract or utility and individual rights** is the fifth Kohlberg stage. At this stage, individuals reason that values, rights, and principles undergird or transcend the law. A person evaluates the validity of actual laws, and social systems can be examined in terms of the degree to which they preserve and protect fundamental human rights and values.
- *Stage 6.* **Universal ethical principles** is the sixth and highest stage in Kohlberg's theory of moral development. At this stage, the person has developed a moral standard based on universal human rights. When faced with a conflict between law and conscience, the person reasons that conscience should be followed, even though the decision might bring risk.

individualism, instrumental purpose, and exchange The second Kohlberg stage of moral development. At this stage, individuals pursue their own interests but also let others do the same.

conventional reasoning The second, or intermediate, level in Kohlberg's theory of moral development. At this level, individuals abide by certain standards, but they are the standards of others such as parents or the laws of society.

mutual interpersonal expectations, relationships, and interpersonal conformity Kohlberg's third stage of moral development. At this stage, individuals value trust, caring, and loyalty to others as a basis of moral judgments.

social systems morality The fourth stage in Kohlberg's theory of moral development. Moral judgments are based on understanding the social order, law, justice, and duty.

postconventional reasoning The highest level in Kohlberg's theory of moral development. At this level, the individual recognizes alternative moral courses, explores the options, and then decides on a personal moral code.

social contract or utility and individual rights The fifth Kohlberg stage. At this stage, individuals reason that values, rights, and principles undergird or transcend the law.

universal ethical principles The sixth and highest stage in Kohlberg's theory of moral development. Individuals develop a moral standard based on universal human rights.

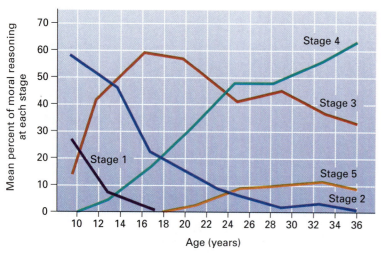

FIGURE 13.2 Age and the Percentage of Individuals at Each Kohlberg Stage. In one longitudinal study of males from 10 to 36 years of age, at age 10 most moral reasoning was at stage 2 (Colby & others, 1983). At 16 to 18 years of age, stage 3 became the most frequent type of moral reasoning, and it was not until the mid-twenties that stage 4 became the most frequent. Stage 5 did not appear until 20 to 22 years of age and it never characterized more than 10 percent of the individuals. In this study, the moral stages appeared somewhat later than Kohlberg envisioned, and stage 6 was absent.

Kohlberg observed that these levels and stages occur in a sequence and are age related: Before age 9, most children use level 1, preconventional reasoning based on external rewards and punishments, when they consider moral choices. By early adolescence, their moral reasoning is increasingly based on the application of standards set by others. Most adolescents reason at stage 3, with some signs of stages 2 and 4. By early adulthood, a small number of individuals reason in postconventional ways.

What evidence supports this description of development? A 20-year longitudinal investigation found that use of stages 1 and 2 decreased with age (Colby & others, 1983) (see Figure 13.2). Stage 4, which did not appear at all in the moral reasoning of 10-year-olds, was reflected in the moral thinking of 62 percent of the 36-year-olds. Stage 5 did not appear until age 20 to 22 and never characterized more than 10 percent of the individuals.

Thus, the moral stages appeared somewhat later than Kohlberg initially envisioned, and reasoning at the higher stages, especially stage 6, was rare. Although stage 6 has been removed from the Kohlberg moral judgment scoring manual, it still is considered to be theoretically important in the Kohlberg scheme of moral development.

Influences on the Kohlberg Stages What factors influence movement through Kohlberg's stages? Although moral reasoning at each stage presupposes a certain level of cognitive development, Kohlberg argued that advances in children's cognitive development did not ensure development of moral reasoning. Instead, moral reasoning also reflects children's experiences in dealing with moral questions and moral conflict.

Several investigators have tried to advance individuals' levels of moral development by having a model present arguments that reflect moral thinking one stage above the individuals' established levels. This approach applies the concepts of equilibrium and conflict that Piaget used to explain cognitive development. By presenting arguments slightly beyond the children' level of moral reasoning, the researchers created a disequilibrium that motivated the children to restructure their moral thought. The upshot of studies using this approach is that virtually any plus-stage discussion, for any length of time, seems to promote more advanced moral reasoning (Walker, 1982).

Kohlberg emphasized that peer interaction and perspective taking are critical aspects of the social stimulation that challenges children to change their moral reasoning. Whereas adults characteristically impose rules and regulations on children, the give-and-take among peers gives children an opportunity to take the perspective of another person and to generate rules democratically. Kohlberg stressed that in principle, encounters with any peers can produce perspective-taking opportunities that may advance a child's moral reasoning. A recent research review of cross-cultural studies involving Kohlberg's theory revealed strong support for a link between perspective-taking skills and more advanced moral judgments (Gibbs & others, 2007).

Kohlberg's Critics Kohlberg's theory has provoked debate, research, and criticism (Gibbs, 2008; Narvaez & Lapsley, 2009; Nucci & Narvaez, 2008; Power & Higgins-D'Allesandro, 2008). Key criticisms involve the link between moral thought and moral behavior, the roles of culture and the family in moral development, and the significance of concern for others.

Moral Thought and Moral Behavior Kohlberg's theory has been criticized for placing too much emphasis on moral thought and not enough emphasis on moral behavior (Walker, 2004). Moral reasons can sometimes be a shelter for immoral behavior. Corrupt CEOs and politicians endorse the loftiest of moral virtues in public before

Both Piaget and Kohlberg reasoned that peer relations are a critical part of the social stimulation that challenges children to advance their moral reasoning. The mutual give-and-take of peer relations provides children with role-taking opportunities that give them a sense that rules are generated democratically.

their own behavior is exposed. Whatever the latest public scandal, you will probably find that the culprits displayed virtuous thoughts but engaged in immoral behavior. No one wants a nation of cheaters and thieves who can reason at the postconventional level. The cheaters and thieves may know what is right yet still do what is wrong. Heinous actions can be cloaked in a mantle of moral virtue.

Culture and Moral Reasoning Kohlberg emphasized that his stages of moral reasoning are universal, but some critics claim his theory is culturally biased (Miller, 2006, 2007; Wainryb, 2006). Both Kohlberg and his critics may be partially correct.

One review of 45 studies in 27 cultures around the world, mostly non-European, provided support for the universality of Kohlberg's first four stages (Snarey, 1987). Individuals in diverse cultures developed through these four stages in sequence as Kohlberg predicted. A more recent research study revealed support for the qualitative shift from Stage 2 to Stage 3 across cultures (Gibbs & others, 2007).

Stages 5 and 6, however, have not been found in all cultures (Gibbs & others, 2007; Snarey, 1987). Furthermore, Kohlberg's scoring system does not recognize the higher-level moral reasoning of certain cultures—thus, moral reasoning is more culture-specific that Kohlberg envisioned (Snarey, 1987).

In particular, researchers have heard moral judgments based on the principles of communal equity and collective happiness in Israel, the unity and sacredness of all life-forms in India, and collective moral responsibility in New Guinea (Snarey, 1987). These examples of moral reasoning would not be scored at the highest level in Kohlberg's system because they are not based on principles of justice. Similar results occurred in a study that assessed the moral development of 20 adolescent male Buddhist monks in Nepal (Huebner & Garrod, 1993). Justice, a basic theme in Kohlberg's theory, was not of paramount importance in the monks' moral views, and their concerns about the prevention of suffering and the role of compassion are not captured by Kohlberg's theory.

In sum, although Kohlberg's approach does capture much of the moral reasoning voiced in various cultures around the world, his approach misses or miscontrues some important moral concepts in particular cultures (Miller, 2006, 2007; Wainryb, 2006). To read further about cultural variations in moral reasoning, see the *Diversity in Child Development* interlude.

Diversity in Child Development

MORAL REASONING IN THE UNITED STATES AND INDIA

Cultural meaning systems vary around the world, and these systems shape children's morality (Miller, 2007; Shiraez & Levy, 2007; Shweder & others, 2006). Consider a comparison of American and Indian Hindu Brahman children (Shweder, Mahapatra, & Miller, 1987). Like people in many other non-Western societies, Indians view moral rules as part of the natural world order. This means that Indians do not distinguish between physical, moral, and social regulation, as Americans do. For example, in India, violations of food taboos and marital restrictions can be just as serious as acts intended to cause harm to others. In India, social rules are seen as inevitable, much like the law of gravity.

According to William Damon (1988), where culturally specific practices take on profound moral and religious significance, as in India, the moral development of children focuses extensively on their adherence to custom and convention. In contrast, Western moral doctrine tends to elevate abstract principles, such as justice and welfare, to a higher moral status than customs or conventions. As in India, socialization practices in many Third World countries actively instill in children a great respect for their culture's traditional codes and practices.

How might Asian Indian children and American children reason differently about moral issues?

Carol Gilligan is shown with some of the students she has interviewed about the importance of relationships in a female's development. *What is Gilligan's view of moral development?*

Families and Moral Development Kohlberg argued that family processes are essentially unimportant in children's moral development. As noted earlier, he argued that parent-child relationships usually provide children with little opportunity for give-and-take or perspective taking. Rather, Kohlberg said that such opportunities are more likely to be provided by children's peer relations.

Did Kohlberg underestimate the contribution of family relationships to moral development? A number of developmentalists emphasize that *inductive discipline*—which uses reasoning and focuses children's attention on the consequences of their actions for others—positively influences moral development (Hoffman, 1970). They also stress that parents' moral values influence children's developing moral thoughts (Gibbs, 2008). Nonetheless, most developmentalists agree with Kohlberg, and Piaget, that peers play an important role in the development of moral reasoning.

Gender and the Care Perspective Perhaps the most publicized criticism of Kohlberg's theory has come from Carol Gilligan (1982, 1992, 1996), who argues that Kohlberg's theory reflects a gender bias. According to Gilligan, Kohlberg's theory is based on a male norm that puts abstract principles above relationships and concern for others and sees the individual as standing alone and independently making moral decisions. It puts justice at the heart of morality. In contrast to Kohlberg's **justice perspective**, which focuses on the rights of the individual, Gilligan argues for a **care perspective**, which is a moral perspective that views people in terms of their connectedness with others and emphasizes interpersonal communication, relationships with others, and concern for others. According to Gilligan, Kohlberg greatly underplayed the care perspective, perhaps because he was a male, because most of his research was with males rather than females, and because he used male responses as a model for his theory.

A meta-analysis (a statistical analysis that combines the results of many different studies) casts doubt on Gilligan's claim of substantial gender differences in moral judgment (Jaffe & Hyde, 2000). In this study, overall, only a small sex difference in care-based reasoning favored females, but this sex difference was greater in adolescence than childhood. When differences occurred, they were better explained by the nature of the dilemma than by gender (for example, both males and females tended to use care-based reasoning to deal with interpersonal dilemmas and justice reasoning to handle societal dilemmas). In sum, experts have now concluded that there is no evidence to support Gilligan's claim that Kohlberg downplayed females' moral thinking (Hyde, 2005, 2007; Walker, 2006).

Assessment of Moral Reasoning Some developmentalists fault the quality of Kohlberg's research and stress that more attention should be paid to the way moral development is assessed (Thoma, 2006). For example, James Rest (1986; Rest & others, 1999) argued that alternative methods should be used to collect information about moral thinking instead of relying on a single method that requires individuals to reason about hypothetical moral dilemmas. Rest developed his own measure of moral development, called the Defining Issues Test (DIT). Unlike Kohlberg's procedure, the DIT attempts to determine which moral issues individuals feel are crucial in a given situation by presenting a series of dilemmas and a list of potential considerations in making a decision. Rest argued that this method provides a more valid and reliable way to assess moral thinking than Kohlberg's method (Rest & others, 1999).

Social Conventional Reasoning Some theorists and researchers argue that Kohlberg did not adequately distinguish between moral reasoning and social conventional reasoning (Smetana, 2006; Turiel, 2006). **Social conventional reasoning** focuses on conventional rules that have been established by social consensus in order to control behavior and maintain the social system. The rules themselves are arbitrary, such as using a fork at meals and raising your hand in class before speaking.

justice perspective A moral perspective that focuses on the rights of the individual; individuals independently make moral decisions.

care perspective The moral perspective of Carol Gilligan; views people in terms of their connectedness with others and emphasizes interpersonal communication, relationships with others, and concern for others.

social conventional reasoning Focuses on conventional rules established by social consensus, as opposed to moral reasoning that stresses ethical issues.

In contrast, moral reasoning focuses on ethical issues and rules of morality. Unlike conventional rules, moral rules are not arbitrary. They are obligatory, widely accepted, and somewhat impersonal (Turiel, 2006). Rules pertaining to lying, cheating, stealing, and physically harming another person are moral rules because violation of these rules affronts ethical standards that exist apart from social consensus and convention. Moral judgments involve concepts of justice, whereas social conventional judgments are concepts of social organization.

Recently, a distinction also has been made between moral and conventional issues, which are viewed as legitimately subject to adult social regulation, and personal issues, which are more likely subject to the child's or adolescent's independent decision making and personal discretion (Smetana, 2006; Turiel, 2006). Personal issues include control over one's body, privacy, and choice of friends and activities. Thus, some actions belong to a *personal* domain, not governed by moral strictures or social norms.

Moral Behavior

What are the basic processes responsible for moral behavior? What is the nature of self-control and resistance to temptation? How does social cognitive theory view moral development?

Basic Processes   The processes of reinforcement, punishment, and imitation have been invoked to explain how individuals learn certain responses and why their responses differ from one another (Grusec, 2006). When individuals are reinforced for behavior that is consistent with laws and social conventions, they are likely to repeat that behavior. When provided with models who behave morally, individuals are likely to adopt their actions. Finally, when individuals are punished for immoral behaviors, those behaviors can be eliminated, but at the expense of sanctioning punishment by its very use and of causing emotional side effects for the individual.

These general conclusions come with some important qualifiers. The effectiveness of reward and punishment depends on the consistency and timing with which they are administered. For example, it is generally more effective to reward moral behavior soon after the event occurs than later. The effectiveness of modeling depends on the characteristics of the model and the cognitive skills of the observer. For example, if a parent models giving a donation to a charity, her child must be old enough to understand this behavior in order for these actions to have an impact on the child's moral development.

Behavior is situationally dependent. Thus, individuals do not consistently display moral behavior in different situations. How consistent is moral behavior? In a classic investigation of moral behavior, one of the most extensive ever conducted, Hugh Hartshorne and Mark May (1928–1930) observed the moral responses of 11,000 children who were given the opportunity to lie, cheat, and steal in a variety of circumstances—at home, at school, at social events, and in athletics. A completely honest or a completely dishonest child was difficult to find. Situation-specific behavior was the rule. Children were more likely to cheat when their friends put pressure on them to do so and when the chance of being caught was slim. However, other analyses suggest that although moral behavior is influenced by situational determinants, some children are more likely than others to cheat, lie, and steal (Burton, 1984).

Social Cognitive Theory   The **social cognitive theory of morality** emphasizes a distinction between an individual's moral competence (the ability to perform moral

How does social conventional reasoning differ from moral reasoning? What are some examples of social conventional reasoning?

social cognitive theory of morality The theory that distinguishes between moral competence—the ability to produce moral behaviors—and moral performance—those behaviors in specific situations.

behaviors) and moral performance (performing those behaviors in specific situations) (Mischel & Mischel, 1975). *Moral competencies* include what individuals are capable of doing, what they know, their skills, their awareness of moral rules and regulations, and their cognitive ability to construct behaviors. Moral competence is the outgrowth of cognitive-sensory processes. *Moral performance*, or behavior, however, is determined by motivation and the rewards and incentives to act in a specific moral way.

Albert Bandura (1991, 2002) also stresses that moral development is best understood by considering a combination of social and cognitive factors, especially those involving self-control. He proposes that in developing a moral self, individuals adopt standards of right and wrong that serve as guides and deterrents for conduct. In this self-regulatory process, people monitor their conduct and the conditions under which it occurs, judge it in relation to moral standards, and regulate their actions by the consequences they apply to themselves. They do things that provide them satisfaction and a sense of self-worth. They refrain from behaving in ways that violate their moral standards because such conduct will bring self-condemnation. Self-sanctions keep conduct in line with internal standards (Bandura, 2002, p. 102). Thus, in Bandura's view, self-regulation rather than abstract reasoning is the key to positive moral development.

Moral Feeling

Think about when you do something you sense is wrong. Does it affect you emotionally? Maybe you get a twinge of guilt. And when you give someone a gift, you might feel joy. What role do emotions play in moral development, and how do these emotions develop?

Psychoanalytic Theory   According to Sigmund Freud, guilt and the desire to avoid feeling guilty are the foundation of moral behavior. In Freud's theory, as we discussed in Chapter 1, the *superego* is the moral branch of personality. According to Freud, children fear losing their parents' love and being punished for their unacceptable sexual wishes toward the opposite-sex parent. To reduce anxiety, avoid punishment, and maintain parental affection, children identify with the same-sex parent. Through this identification, children *internalize* the parents' standards of right and wrong, which reflect societal prohibitions, and hence develop the superego. In the psychoanalytic account of moral development, children conform to societal standards to avoid guilt. In this way, self-control replaces parental control.

Freud's claims regarding the formation of the ego ideal and conscience cannot be verified. However, researchers can examine the extent to which children feel guilty when they misbehave. Grazyna Kochanska and her colleagues (Kochanska & Askan, 2007; Kochanska & others, 2002, 2005, 2008) have conducted a number of studies that explore children's conscience development. In a recent research review of children's conscience, she concluded that young children are aware of right and wrong, have the capacity to show empathy toward others, experience guilt, indicate discomfort following a transgression, and are sensitive to violating rules (Kochanska & Aksan, 2007). In one study, Kochanska and her colleagues (2002) observed 106 preschool children in laboratory situations in which they were led to believe that they had damaged valuable objects. In these mishaps, the behavioral indicators of guilt that were coded by observers included avoiding gaze (looking away or down), body tension (squirming, backing away, hanging head down, covering face with hands), and distress (looking uncomfortable, crying). Girls expressed more guilt than boys did. Children with a more fearful temperament expressed more guilt. Children of mothers who used power-oriented discipline (such as spanking, slapping, and yelling) displayed less guilt.

What characterizes a child's conscience?

Empathy   Positive feelings, such as empathy, contribute to the child's moral development (Eisenberg, Spinrad, & Sadovsky, 2006; Hastings, Utendale, & Sullivan, 2007). Feeling **empathy** means reacting to another's feelings with an emotional response that is similar to the other's feelings (Damon, 1988). To empathize is not just to sympathize; it is to put oneself in another's place emotionally.

Although empathy is an emotional state, it has a cognitive component—the ability to discern another's inner psychological states, or what we have previously called *perspective taking* (Eisenberg & others, 2002). Infants have the capacity for some purely empathic responses, but for effective moral action, children must learn to identify a wide range of emotional states in others and to anticipate what kinds of action will improve another person's emotional state.

What are the milestones in children's development of empathy? According to an analysis by child developmentalist William Damon (1988), changes in empathy take place in early infancy, at 1 to 2 years of age, in early childhood, and at 10 to 12 years of age.

Global empathy is the young infant's empathic response in which clear boundaries between the feelings and needs of the self and those of another have not yet been established. For example, one 11-month-old infant fought off her own tears, sucked her thumb, and buried her head in her mother's lap after she had seen another child fall and hurt himself. Not all infants cry every time someone else is hurt, though. Many times, an infant will stare at another's pain with curiosity. Although global empathy is observed in some infants, it does not consistently characterize all infants' behavior.

When they are 1 to 2 years of age, infants may feel genuine concern for the distress of other people, but only when they reach early childhood can they respond appropriately to another person's distress. This ability depends on children's new awareness that people have different reactions to situations. By late childhood, they may begin to feel empathy for the unfortunate. To read further about Damon's description of the developmental changes in empathy from infancy through adolescence, see Figure 13.3.

The Contemporary Perspective on the Role of Emotion in Moral Development
We have seen that classical psychoanalytic theory emphasizes the power of unconscious guilt in moral development but that other theorists, such as Damon, emphasize the role of empathy. Today, many child developmentalists believe that both positive feelings—such as empathy, sympathy, admiration, and self-esteem—and negative feelings—such as anger, outrage, shame, and guilt—contribute to children's moral development (Damon, 1988; Eisenberg, Fabes, & Spinrad, 2006; Thompson, 2009a, c). When strongly experienced, these emotions influence children to act in accord with standards of right and wrong.

Moral Personality

So far we have examined three key dimensions of moral development: thoughts, behavior, and feelings. Recently, there has been a surge of interest in a fourth dimension: personality (Lapsley & Narvaez, 2006; Walker & Frimer, 2008a, b). Three aspects of moral personality that have recently been emphasized are (1) moral identity, (2) moral character, and (3) moral exemplars.

Moral Identity
A central aspect of the recent interest in the role of personality in moral development focuses on **moral identity**. Individuals have a moral identity when moral notions and commitments are central to one's life (Blasi, 2005). In this view, behaving in a manner that violates this moral commitment places the integrity of the self at risk (Lapsley & Narvaez, 2006; Narvaez & Lapsley, 2009).

Age Period	Nature of Empathy
Early infancy	Characterized by global empathy, the young infant's empathic response does not distinguish between feelings and needs of self and others.
1 to 2 years of age	Undifferentiated feelings of discomfort at another's distress grow into more genuine feelings of concern, but infants cannot translate realization of other's unhappy feelings into effective action.
Early childhood	Children become aware that every person's perspective is unique and that someone else may have a different reaction to a situation. This awareness allows the child to respond more appropriately to another person's distress.
10 to 12 years of age	Children develop an emergent orientation of empathy for people who live in unfortunate circumstances—the poor, the handicapped, and the socially outcast. In adolescence, this newfound sensitivity may give a humanitarian flavor to the individual's ideological and political views.

FIGURE 13.3 Damon's Description of Developmental Changes in Empathy

empathy Reacting to another's feelings with an emotional response that is similar to the other's feelings.

moral identity The aspect of personality that is present when individuals have moral notions and commitments that are central to their lives.

Rosa Parks (*top photo*, sitting in the front of a bus after the U.S. Supreme Court ruled that segregation was illegal on her city's bus system) and Andrei Sakharov (*bottom photo*) are moral exemplars. Parks (1913–2005), an African American seamstress in Montgomery, Alabama, became famous for her quiet, revolutionary act of not giving up her bus seat to a non-Latino White man in 1955. Her heroic act is cited by many historians as the beginning of the modern civil rights movement in the United States. Across the next four decades, Parks continued to work for progress in civil rights. Sakharov (1921–1989) was a Soviet physicist who spent several decades designing nuclear weapons for the Soviet Union and came to be known as the father of the Soviet hydrogen bomb. However, later in his life he became one of the Soviet Union's most outspoken critics and worked relentlessly to promote human rights and democracy.

moral exemplars People who have lived extraordinary lives. Emphasizes the development of personality, identity, character, and virtue that reflect moral excellence and commitment.

Moral Character In James Rest's (1995) view, *moral character* involves having the strength of your convictions, persisting, and overcoming distractions and obstacles. If individuals don't have moral character, they may wilt under pressure or fatigue, fail to follow through, or become distracted and discouraged, and fail to behave morally. Moral character presupposes that the person has set moral goals and that achieving those goals involves the commitment to act in accord with those goals.

Lawrence Walker (2002; Walker & Pitts, 1998) has studied moral character by examining people's conceptions of moral excellence. Among the moral virtues people emphasize are "honesty, truthfulness, and trustworthiness, as well as those of care, compassion, thoughtfulness, and considerateness. Other salient traits revolve around virtues of dependability, loyalty, and conscientiousness" (Walker, 2002, p. 74).

Moral Exemplars **Moral exemplars** are people who have lived exemplary lives. Moral exemplars have a moral personality, identity, character, and set of virtues that reflect moral excellence and commitment.

In one study, three different exemplars of morality were examined—brave, caring, and just (Walker & Hennig, 2004). Different personality profiles emerged for the three exemplars. The brave exemplar was characterized by being dominant and extraverted, the caring exemplar by being nurturant and agreeable, and the just exemplar by being conscientious and open to experience. However, a number of traits characterized all three moral exemplars, considered by the researchers to reflect a possible core of moral functioning. This core included being honest and dependable.

Review and Reflect: Learning Goal 1

1 **Discuss Theory and Research on the Four Domains of Moral Development**

REVIEW

- What is moral development?
- What are Piaget's and Kohlberg's theories of moral development? What are some criticisms of Kohlberg's theory? What is social conventional reasoning?
- What processes are involved in moral behavior? What is the social cognitive theory of moral development?
- How are moral feelings related to moral development?
- What characterizes moral personality?

REFLECT

- What do you think about these circumstances? (1) A man who had been sentenced to serve 10 years for selling a small amount of marijuana walked away from a prison camp after serving only six months of his sentence. Twenty-five years later he was caught. He is now in his fifties and is a model citizen. Should he be sent back to prison? Why or why not? At which Kohlberg stage should your response be placed? (2) A young woman who had been in a tragic accident is "brain dead" and has been kept on life-support systems for four years without ever regaining consciousness. Should the life-support systems be removed? Explain your response. At which Kohlberg stage should your response be placed?

2 CONTEXTS OF MORAL DEVELOPMENT

Parenting

Schools

So far, we have examined four key domains of moral development—thoughts, behaviors, feelings, and personality. We noted that both Piaget and Kohlberg stressed that peer relations exert an important influence on moral development. What other contexts play a role in moral development? In particular, what are the roles of parents and schools?

Parenting

Both Piaget and Kohlberg held that parents do not provide unique or essential inputs to children's moral development. Parents, in their view, are responsible for providing role-taking opportunities and cognitive conflict, but peers play the primary role in moral development. Research reveals that both parents and peers contribute to children's moral maturity (Walker, Hennig, & Krettenauer, 2000).

In Ross Thompson's (2006, 2009c; Laible & Thompson, 2007) view, young children are moral apprentices, striving to understand what is moral. They can be assisted in this quest by the "sensitive guidance of adult mentors in the home who provide lessons about morality in everyday experiences" (Thompson, McGinley, & Meyer, 2006). Among the most important aspects of the relationship between parents and children that contribute to children's moral development are relational quality, parental discipline, proactive strategies, and conversational dialogue.

Relational Quality　Parent-child relationships introduce children to the mutual obligations of close relationships (Laible & Thompson, 2007; Thompson, 2006, 2009c). Parents' obligations include engaging in positive caregiving and guiding children to become competent human beings. Children's obligations include responding appropriately to parents' initiatives and maintaining a positive relationship with parents. A recent study revealed that an early mutually responsive orientation between parents and their infant and a decrease in parents' use of power assertion in disciplining a young child were linked to an increase in the child's internalization and self-regulation (Kochanska & others, 2008). Thus, warmth and responsibility in the mutual obligations of parent-child relationships are important foundations for the positive moral growth in the child.

In terms of relationship quality, secure attachment may play an important role in children's moral development (Thompson, 2009c). A secure attachment can place the child on a positive path for internalizing parents' socializing goals and family values (Waters & others, 1990). In one study, secure attachment in infancy was linked to early conscience development (Laible & Thompson, 2000). And in a longitudinal study, secure attachment at 14 months of age served as a precursor for a link between positive parenting and the child's conscience during early childhood (Kochanska & others, 2004).

Parental Discipline　Discipline techniques used by parents can be classified as love withdrawal, power assertion, and induction (Hoffman, 1970, 1988):

- **Love withdrawal** is a discipline technique in which a parent withholds attention or love from the child, as when the parent refuses to talk to the child or states a dislike for the child. For example, the parent might say, "I'm going to leave you if you do that again" or "I don't like you when you do that."
- **Power assertion** is a discipline technique in which a parent attempts to gain control over the child or the child's resources. Examples include spanking, threatening, or removing privileges.
- **Induction** is the discipline technique in which a parent uses reasoning and explains the consequences for others of the child's actions. Examples of induction

love withdrawal A discipline technique in which a parent withholds attention or love from the child.

power assertion A discipline technique in which a parent attempts to gain control over the child or the child's resources.

induction A discipline technique in which a parent uses reasoning and explains the consequences for others of the child's actions.

How are parents' discipline techniques linked to children's moral development?

include, "Don't hit him. He was only trying to help" and "Why are you yelling at her? She didn't mean to trip you."

How are these techniques likely to affect moral development? Moral development theorist and researcher Martin Hoffman (1970) points out that any discipline produces arousal on the child's part. Love withdrawal and power assertion are likely to evoke a very high level of arousal, with love withdrawal generating considerable anxiety and power assertion considerable hostility.

When a parent uses power assertion or love withdrawal, the child may be so aroused that even if the parent explains the consequences of the child's actions for others, the child might not pay attention. Also, power assertion presents parents as weak models of self-control—as individuals who cannot control their feelings. Accordingly, children may imitate this model of poor self-control when they face stressful circumstances.

In contrast to love withdrawal and power assertion, induction is more likely to produce a moderate level of arousal in children, a level that permits them to attend to the cognitive rationale parents offer. Furthermore, induction focuses the child's attention on the action's consequences for others, not on the child's own shortcomings. For these reasons, Hoffman (1988) suggests that parents should use induction to encourage children's moral development.

Proactive Strategies An important parenting strategy is to proactively avert potential misbehavior by children before it takes place (Thompson, 2009c; Thompson, McGinley, & Meyer, 2006). With younger children, being proactive means using diversion, such as distracting their attention or moving them to alternative activities. With older children, being proactive may involve talking with them about values that the parents deem important. Transmitting these values can help older children and adolescents to resist the temptations that inevitably emerge in such contexts as peer relations and the media that can be outside the scope of direct parental monitoring.

Conversational Dialogue Conversations related to moral development can benefit children whether they occur as part of a discipline encounter or outside the encounter in the everyday stream of parent-child interaction (Laible & Thompson, 2007; Thompson, McGinley, & Meyer, 2006; Thompson, 2009c). Even when they are not intended to teach a moral lesson or explicitly encourage better moral judgment, such conversations can contribute to children's moral development.

To read further about strategies parents can adopt to promote their children's moral development, see the *Caring for Children* interlude.

> *B*oth theory and empirical data support the conclusion that parents play an important role in children's moral development.
>
> —NANCY EISENBERG
> *Contemporary Psychologist,*
> *Arizona State University*

Caring for Children

PARENTING RECOMMENDATIONS FOR RAISING A MORAL CHILD

A research review concluded that, in general, children who behave morally tend to have parents who (Eisenberg & Valiente, 2002, p. 134):

- "are warm and supportive rather than punitive;
- use inductive discipline;
- provide opportunities for the children to learn about others' perspectives and feelings;

- involve children in family decision making and in the process of thinking about moral decisions;
- model moral behaviors and thinking themselves, and provide opportunities for their children to do so;
- provide information about what behaviors are expected and why; and
- foster an internal rather than an external sense of morality."

Parents who show this configuration of behaviors likely foster concern and caring about others in their children, and create a positive parent-child relationship.

In addition, parenting recommendations based on Ross Thompson's (2006; Thompson, McGinley, & Meyer, 2006) analysis of parent-child relations suggest that children's moral development is likely to benefit when there are mutual parent-child obligations involving warmth and responsibility, when parents use proactive strategies, and when parents engage children in conversational dialogue.

What are some good strategies parents can adopt to foster their child's moral development?

Schools

However parents treat their children at home, they may feel that they have little control over a great deal of their children's moral education. Children spend extensive time away from their parents at school, and the time spent can influence children's moral development (Lapsley, 2008; Narvaez, 2008; Narvaez & Lapsley, 2009; Nucci, 2008; Power & others, 2008; Snarey, 2008).

The Hidden Curriculum   More than 60 years ago, educator John Dewey (1933) recognized that even when schools do not have specific programs in moral education, they provide moral education through a "hidden curriculum." The **hidden curriculum** is conveyed by the moral atmosphere that is a part of every school. The moral atmosphere is created by school and classroom rules, the moral orientation of teachers and school administrators, and text materials. Teachers serve as models of ethical or unethical behavior. Classroom rules and peer relations at school transmit attitudes about cheating, lying, stealing, and consideration of others. And through its rules and regulations, the school administration infuses the school with a value system.

Character Education   Yet another approach to moral education is **character education**, a direct education approach that involves teaching students a basic "moral literacy" to prevent them from engaging in immoral behavior and doing harm to themselves or others (Arthur, 2008; Carr, 2008; Narvaez & Lapsley, 2009; Nucci & Narvaez, 2008). The argument is that such behaviors as lying, stealing, and cheating are wrong, and students should be taught this throughout their education (Berkowitz, Battistich, & Bier, 2008; Davidson, Lickona, & Khmelkov, 2008).

Every school should have an explicit moral code that is clearly communicated to students. Any violations of the code should be met with sanctions. Instruction in specified moral concepts, such as cheating, can take the form of example and definition, class discussions and role playing, or rewarding students for proper behavior. More recently, an emphasis on the importance of encouraging students to develop a care perspective has been accepted as a relevant aspect of character education (Noddings, 2008; Sherblom, 2008). Rather than just instructing adolescents in refraining from engaging in morally deviant behavior, a care perspective advocates educating students in the importance of engaging in prosocial behaviors, such as considering others' feelings, being sensitive to others, and helping others in a semester-long course to discuss a number of moral issues. The instructor acts as a facilitator rather than as a director of the class. The hope is that students will develop more advanced

hidden curriculum The pervasive moral atmosphere that characterizes schools.

character education A direct moral education approach that involves teaching students a basic "moral literacy" to prevent them from engaging in immoral behavior or doing harm to themselves or others.

More than just about anything else, 12-year-old Katie Bell (*at bottom*) wanted a playground in her New Jersey town. She knew that other kids also wanted one so she put together a group, which generated fund-raising ideas for the playground. They presented their ideas to the town council. Her group got more youth involved. They helped raise money by selling candy and sandwiches door-to-door. Katie says, "We learned to work as a community. This will be an important place for people to go and have picnics and make new friends." Katie's advice: "You won't get anywhere if you don't try."

values clarification Helping people clarify what their lives are for and what is worth working for. Students are encouraged to define their own values and understand others' values.

cognitive moral education Education based on the belief that students should learn to value things like democracy and justice as their moral reasoning develops; Kohlberg's theory has been the basis for many of the cognitive moral education approaches.

service learning A form of education that promotes social responsibility and service to the community.

notions of such concepts as cooperation, trust, responsibility, and community (Enright & others, 2008; Power & Higgins-D'Alessandro, 2008). Currently, 40 of 50 states have mandates to include character education in children's education (Nucci & Narvaez, 2008).

Values Clarification One approach to providing moral education is **values clarification**, which means helping people to clarify what their lives are for and what is worth working for. Unlike character education, which tells students what their values should be, values clarification encourages students to define their own values and understand the values of others (Williams & others, 2003).

Advocates of values clarification say it is value-free. However, critics argue that its content offends community standards and that the values-clarification exercises fail to stress right behavior.

Cognitive Moral Education Another approach to moral education, **cognitive moral education**, is based on the belief that students should learn to value such things as democracy and justice as their moral reasoning develops. Kohlberg's theory has served as the foundation for a number of cognitive moral education programs. In a typical program, high school students meet in a semester-long course to discuss a number of moral issues. The instructor acts as a facilitator rather than as a director of the class. The hope is that students will develop more advanced notions of such concepts as cooperation, trust, responsibility, and community (Enright & others, 2008; Power & Higgins-D'Alessandro, 2008).

Service Learning **Service Learning** is a form of education that promotes social responsibility and service to the community. In service learning, adolescents engage in activities such as tutoring, helping older adults, working in a hospital, assisting at a child-care center, or cleaning up a vacant lot to make a play area. An important goal of service learning is for adolescents to become less self-centered and more strongly motivated to help others (Catalano, Hawkins, & Toumbourou, 2008; Hart, Matsuba, & Atkins, 2008). Service learning is often more effective when two conditions are met (Nucci, 2006): (1) giving students some degree of choice in the service activities in which they participate, and (2) providing students opportunities to reflect about their participation.

Service learning takes education out into the community (Enfield & Collins, 2008; Nelson & Eckstein, 2008). Adolescent volunteers tend to be extraverted, committed to others, and have a high level of self-understanding (Eisenberg & Morris, 2004). Also, a recent study revealed that adolescent girls participated in service learning more than adolescent boys (Webster & Worrell, 2008).

Researchers have found that service learning benefits adolescents in a number of ways (Hart, Matsuba, & Atkins, 2008; Reinders & Youniss, 2006). These improvements in adolescent development related to service learning include higher grades in school, increased goal setting, higher self-esteem, an improved sense of being able to make a difference for others, and an increased likelihood that they will serve as volunteers in the future. A recent study of more than 4,000 high school students revealed that those who worked directly with individuals in need were better adjusted academically, whereas those who worked for organizations had better civic outcomes (Schmidt, Shumow, & Kackar, 2007).

One analysis revealed that 26 percent of U.S. public high schools require students to participate in service learning (Metz & Youniss, 2005). The benefits of service learning, both for the volunteer and the recipient, suggest that more adolescents should be required to participate in such programs (Enfield & Collins, 2008; Nelson & Eckstein, 2008).

Cheating A moral education concern is whether students cheat and how to handle the cheating if they discover it (Anderman & Murdock, 2007; Narvaez & others,

2008). Academic cheating can take many forms including plagiarism, using "cheat sheets" during an exam, copying from a neighbor during a test, purchasing papers, and falsifying lab results. A 2006 survey revealed that 60 percent of secondary school students said they had cheated on a test in school during the past year, and one-third of the students reported that they had plagiarized information from the Internet in the past year (Josephson Institute of Ethics, 2006).

Why do students cheat? Among the reasons students give for cheating include the pressure for getting high grades, time pressures, poor teaching, and lack of interest (Stephens, 2008). In terms of poor teaching, "students are more likely to cheat when they perceive their teacher to be incompetent, unfair, and uncaring" (Stephens, 2008, p. 140).

A long history of research also implicates the power of the situation in determining whether students cheat or not (Hartshorne & May, 1928–1930; Murdock, Miller, & Kohlhardt, 2004; Vandehey, Diekhoff, & LaBeff, 2007). For example, students are more likely to cheat when they are not being closely monitored during a test, when they know their peers are cheating, whether they know if another student has been caught cheating, and when student scores are to be made public (Anderman & Murdock, 2007; Carrell, Malmstrom, & West, 2008; Harmon, Lambrinos, & Kennedy, 2008).

Among the strategies for decreasing academic cheating—in addition to closely monitoring students' behavior while they are taking tests—are preventive measures such as making sure students are aware of what constitutes cheating; what the consequences will be if they cheat; and the importance of being a moral, responsible individual who engages in academic integrity. In promoting academic integrity, many colleges have instituted an honor code policy that emphasizes self-responsibility, fairness, trust, and scholarship. However, few secondary schools have developed honor code policies. The Center for Academic Integrity (www.academicintegrity.org/) has extensive materials available to help schools develop academic integrity policies.

An Integrative Approach Darcia Narvaez (2006) emphasizes an *integrative approach* to moral education that encompasses both the reflective moral thinking and commitment to justice advocated in Kohlberg's approach, and developing a particular moral character as advocated in the character education approach. She highlights the Child Development Project as an excellent example of an integrative moral education approach. In the Child Development Project, students are given multiple opportunities to discuss other students' experiences, which encourages empathy and perspective taking, and they participate in exercises that encourage them to reflect on their own behaviors in terms of such values as fairness and social responsibility (Solomon & others, 2002). Adults coach students in ethical decision making and guide them in becoming more caring individuals. Students experience a caring community, not only in the classroom, but also in after-school activities and through parental involvement in the program. Research evaluations of the Child Development Project indicate that it is related to an improved sense of community, an increase in prosocial behavior, better interpersonal understanding, and an increase in social problem solving (Battisich, 2008; Solomon & others, 1990).

Another integrative moral education program that is being implemented is called *integrative ethical education* (Holter & Narvaez, 2008; Narvaez, 2006, 2008; Narvaez & others, 2004). This program builds on the concept of expertise that we discussed in Chapter 7. The goal is to turn moral novices into moral experts by educating students about four ethical skills that moral experts possess: ethical sensitivity, ethical judgment, ethical focus, and ethical action. Figure 13.4 describes the types of skills reflected in these categories.

Why do students cheat? What are some strategies teachers can adopt to prevent cheating?

Ethical Sensitivity

Understanding emotional expression
Taking the perspective of others
Connecting to others
Responding to diversity
Controlling social bias
Interpreting situations
Communicating effectively

Ethical Judgment

Understanding ethical problems
Using codes and identifying judgment criteria
Reasoning generally
Reasoning ethically
Understanding consequences
Reflecting on the process and outcome
Coping and resiliency

Ethical Focus

Respecting others
Cultivating conscience
Acting responsibly
Helping others
Finding meaning in life
Valuing traditions and institutions
Developing ethical identity and integrity

Ethical Action

Resolving conflicts and problems
Asserting respectfully
Taking initiative as a leader
Implementing decisions
Cultivating courage
Persevering
Working hard

FIGURE 13.4 Ethical Skills in Integrative Ethical Education

Review and Reflect: Learning Goal 2

2 **Explain How Parenting and Schools Influence Moral Development**

REVIEW

- How does parental discipline affect moral development? What are some effective parenting strategies for advancing children's moral development?
- What is the hidden curriculum? What are some contemporary approaches to moral education?

REFLECT

- What type of discipline did your parents use with you? What effect do you think this has on your moral development?

3 PROSOCIAL AND ANTISOCIAL BEHAVIOR

Prosocial Behavior

Antisocial Behavior

Service learning encourages positive moral behavior. This behavior is not just moral behavior but behavior that is intended to benefit other people, and psychologists call it *prosocial behavior* (Carlo, 2006; Eisenberg, Spinrad, & Sadovsky, 2006). Jewel Cash, whose story we described at the beginning of the chapter, is an exemplary model of someone committed to engage in prosocial behavior. Of course, people have always engaged in antisocial behavior as well. In this section, we will take a closer look at prosocial and antisocial behavior, focusing on how they develop.

Prosocial Behavior

Caring about the welfare and rights of others, feeling concern and empathy for them, and acting in a way that benefits others are all components of prosocial behavior. The purist forms of prosocial behavior are motivated by **altruism**, an unselfish interest in helping another person (Eisenberg, Fabes, & Spinrad, 2006; Hastings, Utendale, & Sullivan, 2007). As we see next, learning to share is an important aspect of prosocial behavior.

William Damon (1988) described a developmental sequence by which sharing develops in children. Most sharing during the first three years of life is done for nonempathic reasons, such as for the fun of the social play ritual or out of imitation. Then, at about 4 years of age, a combination of empathic awareness and adult encouragement produces a sense of obligation on the part of the child to share with others. Most 4-year-olds are not selfless saints, however. Children believe they have an obligation to share but do not necessarily think they should be as generous to others as they are to themselves. Neither do their actions always support their beliefs, especially when they covet an object. What is important developmentally is that the child has developed a belief that sharing is an obligatory part of a social relationship and involves a question of right and wrong. These early ideas about sharing set the stage for giant strides that children make in the years that follow.

altruism An unselfish interest in helping another person.

By the start of the elementary school years, children begin to express more complicated notions of what is fair. Throughout history, varied definitions of fairness have been used as the basis for distributing goods and resolving conflicts. These definitions involve the principles of equality, merit, and benevolence: *Equality* means that everyone is treated the same; *merit* means giving extra rewards for hard work, a talented performance, or other laudatory behavior; *benevolence* means giving special consideration to individuals in a disadvantaged condition.

Equality is the first of these principles used regularly by elementary school children. It is common to hear 6-year-old children use the word *fair* as synonymous with *equal* or *same*. By the mid- to late elementary school years, children also believe that equity means special treatment for those who deserve it—a belief that applies the principles of merit and benevolence.

Missing from the factors that guide children's sharing is one that many adults might expect to be the most influential: the motivation to obey adult authority figures. Surprisingly, a number of studies have shown that adult authority has only a small influence on children's sharing. For example, when Nancy Eisenberg (1982) asked children to explain their own spontaneous acts of sharing, they mainly gave empathic and pragmatic reasons. Not one of the children referred to the demands of adult authority.

Parental advice and prodding certainly foster standards of sharing, but the give-and-take of peer requests and arguments provide the most immediate stimulation of sharing. Parents can set examples that children carry into their interactions and communication with peers, but parents are not present during all of their children's peer exchanges. The day-to-day construction of fairness standards is done by children in collaboration and negotiation with each other. Over the course of many years and thousands of encounters, children's understanding of such notions as equality, merit, benevolence, and compromise deepens. With this understanding comes a greater consistency and generosity in children's sharing (Damon, 1988).

How does prosocial behavior change through childhood and adolescence? Prosocial behavior occurs more often in adolescence than in childhood, although examples of caring for others and comforting someone in distress occur even during the preschool years (Eisenberg, Spinrad, & Sadovsky, 2006).

Also, keep in mind the gender differences in prosocial behavior we described in Chapter 12. Recall that females view themselves as more prosocial and empathic, and they also engage in more prosocial behavior than males (Eisenberg, Fabes, & Spinrad, 2006).

How does children's sharing change from the preschool to the elementary school years?

Antisocial Behavior

Most children and adolescents at one time or another act out or do things that are destructive or troublesome for themselves or others. If these behaviors occur often, psychiatrists diagnose them as conduct disorders. If these behaviors result in illegal acts by juveniles, society labels them *delinquents*. Both problems are much more common in males than in females.

Conduct Disorder   **Conduct disorder** refers to age-inappropriate actions and attitudes that violate family expectations, society's norms, and the personal or property rights of others. Children with conduct problems show a wide range of rule-violating behaviors, from swearing and temper tantrums to severe vandalism, theft, and assault (Sterzer & others, 2005). Conduct disorder is much more common among boys than girls (McCabe & others, 2004).

Consider 4-year-old Andy, who threw his booster seat in his mother's face and thought it was funny. He was acting up even though he had already received one time-out for yelling and screaming at the table. Then he picked up a fork and threw it at his sister, barely missing her eye. Consider also 10-year-old Nick, who, when he

conduct disorder Age-inappropriate actions and attitudes that violate family expectations, society's norms, and the personal or property rights of others.

What are some characteristics of conduct disorder?

was only 2 years old, put two unopened cans of cat food on the stove and lit the burner. One of the cans exploded. Over the next 10 years, Nick killed several family pets, set fires, beat up classmates, stole money, and regularly terrorized his younger sister. Both of these children's behaviors suggest that they have a conduct disorder (Mash & Wolfe, 2007).

As part of growing up, most children and youth break the rules from time to time—they fight, skip school, break curfew, steal, and so on. As many as 50 percent of the parents of 4- to 6-year-old children report that their children steal, lie, disobey, or destroy property at least some of the time (Achenbach, 1997). Most of these children show a decrease in antisocial behavior from 4 to 18 years of age, but adolescents who are referred to psychological clinics for therapy still show high rates of antisocial behavior (Achenbach, 1997).

An estimated 5 percent of children show serious conduct problems, like those of Nick. These children are often described as showing an *externalizing,* or *undercontrolled,* pattern of behavior. Children who show this pattern often are impulsive, overactive, and aggressive and engage in delinquent actions.

Conduct problems in children are best explained by a confluence of causes, or risk factors, operating over time (Dodge & Pettit, 2003). These include possible genetic inheritance of a difficult temperament, ineffective parenting, and living in a neighborhood where violence is the norm.

Despite considerable efforts to help children with conduct problems, there is a lack of consensus on what works (Mash & Wolfe, 2007). A multisystem treatment is sometimes recommended, which is carried out with all family members, school personnel, juvenile justice staff, and other individuals in the child's life (Farmer & others, 2002).

Juvenile Delinquency   Closely linked with conduct disorder is **juvenile delinquency**, which refers to an adolescent who breaks the law or engages in behavior that is considered illegal. Like other categories of disorders, juvenile delinquency is a broad concept; legal infractions range from littering to murder. Because the adolescent technically becomes a juvenile delinquent only after being judged guilty of a crime by a court of law, official records do not accurately reflect the number of illegal acts juvenile delinquents commit. Estimates of the number of juvenile delinquents in the United States are sketchy, but FBI statistics indicate that at least 2 percent of all youth are involved in juvenile court cases.

U.S. government statistics reveal that 8 of 10 cases of juvenile delinquency involve males (Snyder & Sickmund, 1999). In the last two decades, however, there has been a greater increase in female delinquency than in male delinquency (Snyder & Sickmund, 1999). For both male and female delinquents, rates for property offenses are higher than for other rates of offenses (such as offenses against persons, drug offenses, and public order offenses). Arrests of adolescent males for delinquency still are much higher than for adolescent females.

A distinction is made between early-onset—before age 11—and late-onset—after 11—antisocial behavior. Early-onset antisocial behavior is associated with more negative developmental outcomes than late-onset antisocial behavior (Schulenberg & Zarrett, 2006). Early-onset antisocial behavior is more likely to persist into emerging adulthood and is associated with more mental health and relationship problems (Stouthamer-Loeber & others, 2004).

Delinquency rates among minority groups and lower-socioeconomic-status youth are especially high in proportion to the overall population of these groups. However, such groups have less influence over the judicial decision-making process in the United States and, therefore, may be judged delinquent more readily than their White, middle-socioeconomic-status counterparts.

juvenile delinquency Refers to a great variety of behaviors by an adolescent, ranging from unacceptable behavior to breaking the law.

In the Pittsburgh Youth Study, a longitudinal study focused on more than 1,500 inner-city boys, three developmental pathways to delinquency were (Loeber & Farrington, 2001; Loeber & others, 1998; Stoutheimer-Loeber & others, 2002):

- *Authority conflict.* Youth on this pathway showed stubbornness prior to age 12, then moved on to defiance and avoidance of authority.
- *Covert.* This pathway included minor covert acts, such as lying, followed by property damage and moderately serious delinquency, then serious delinquency.
- *Overt.* This pathway included minor aggression followed by fighting and violence.

Causes of Delinquency Although delinquency is less exclusively a phenomenon of lower socioeconomic status than it was in the past, some characteristics of lower-class culture might promote delinquency. The norms of many lower-SES peer groups and gangs are antisocial, or counterproductive, to the goals and norms of society at large. Getting into and staying out of trouble are prominent features of life for some adolescents in low-income neighborhoods (Flannery & others, 2003; Loeber, Burke, & Pardini, 2009). Adolescents from low-income backgrounds may sense that they can gain attention and status by performing antisocial actions. Being "tough" and "masculine" are high-status traits for lower-SES boys, and these traits are often measured by the adolescent's success in performing and getting away with delinquent acts. Furthermore, adolescents in communities with high crime rates observe many models who engage in criminal activities. These communities may be characterized by poverty, unemployment, and feelings of alienation toward the middle class. Quality schooling, educational funding, and organized neighborhood activities may be lacking in these communities (Sabol, Coulton, & Korbin, 2004).

Certain characteristics of family support systems are also associated with delinquency (Cavell & others, 2007; Feinberg & others, 2007; Loeber, Burke, & Pardini, 2009). Parents of delinquents are less skilled in discouraging antisocial behavior and in encouraging skilled behavior than are parents of nondelinquents. Parental monitoring of adolescents is especially important in determining whether an adolescent becomes a delinquent (Laird & others, 2008). For example, a recent study revealed that maternal monitoring was linked to a lower incidence of delinquency in Latino girls (Loukas, Suizzo, & Prelow, 2007). Family discord and inconsistent and inappropriate discipline are also associated with delinquency (Granic & Patterson, 2006). A recent study revealed that being physically abused in the first five years of life was linked to a greater risk of delinquency in adolescence (Lansford & others, 2007). And an increasing number of studies have found that siblings can have a strong influence on delinquency (Bank, Burraston, & Snyder, 2004). In one study, high levels of hostile sibling relationships and older sibling delinquency were linked with younger sibling delinquency in both brother and sister pairs (Slomkowski & others, 2001).

Having delinquent peers and friends greatly increases the risk of becoming delinquent (Bukowski, Brendgen, & Vitaro, 2007; Dishion, Piehler, & Myers, 2008). For example, a recent study found that peer rejection and having deviant friends at 7 to 13 years of age were linked with increased delinquency at 14 to 15 years of age (Vitaro, Pedersen, & Brendgen, 2007). Also, another recent study revealed that association with deviant peers was linked to a higher incidence of delinquency in male African American adolescents (Bowman, Prelow, & Weaver, 2007).

Cognitive factors, such as low self-control, low intelligence, and lack of sustained attention, also were implicated in delinquency. For example, a recent study revealed that low-IQ serious delinquents were characterized by low self-control (Koolhof & others, 2007). Another recent study found that at age 16 nondelinquents were more

What are some factors that influence whether adolescents will become delinquents?

likely to have a higher verbal IQ and engage in sustained attention than delinquents (Loeber & others, 2007). One individual whose goal is to reduce juvenile delinquency and cope more effectively with their lives is Rodney Hammond. To read about his work, see the *Careers in Child Development* profile. The following *Research in Child Development* interlude describes a program that seeks to intervene in the lives of children who show early conduct problems with the goal of reducing their delinquency risk in adolescence.

Careers in Child Development

Rodney Hammond, Health Psychologist

Rodney Hammond described his college experiences: "When I started as an undergraduate at the University of Illinois Champaign-Urbana, I hadn't decided on my major. But to help finance my education, I took a part-time job in a child development research program sponsored by the psychology department. There, I observed inner-city children in settings designed to enhance their learning. I saw first-hand the contribution psychology can make, and I knew I wanted to be a psychologist" (American Psychological Association, 2003, p. 26).

Rodney Hammond went on to obtain a doctorate in school and community college with a focus on children's development. For a number of years, he trained clinical psychologists at Wright State University in Ohio and directed a program to reduce violence in ethnic minority youth. There, he and his associates taught at-risk youth how to use social skills to effectively manage conflict and to recognize situations that could lead to violence. Today, Hammond is Director of Violence Prevention at the Centers for Disease Control and Prevention in Atlanta. Hammond says that if you are interested in people and problem solving, psychology is a wonderful way to put these together. (Source: American Psychological Association, 2003, pp. 26–27)

Rodney Hammond, talking with an adolescent about strategies for coping with stress and avoiding risk-taking behaviors.

Research in Child Development

FAST TRACK

Fast Track is an intervention that attempts to lower the risk of juvenile delinquency and other problems (Conduct Problems Prevention Research Group, 2007; Dodge & the Conduct Problems Prevention Research Group, 2007; Lochman & the Conduct Problems Prevention Research Group, 2007; Slough, McMahon, & the Conduct Problems Prevention Research Group, 2008). Schools in four areas (Durham, North Carolina; Nashville, Tennessee; Seattle, Washington; and rural central Pennsylvania) were identified as high-risk based on neighborhood crime and poverty data. Researchers screened more than 9,000 kindergarten children in the four schools and randomly assigned 891 of the highest-risk and moderate-risk children to intervention or control conditions. The average age of the children when the intervention began was 6.5 years of age.

The 10-year intervention consisted of parent behavior management training, child social cognitive skills training, reading tutoring, home visitations, mentoring, and a revised classroom curriculum that was designed to increase socioemotional competence and decrease aggression. Outcomes were assessed in the third-, sixth-, and ninth grades for conduct disorder (multiple instances of behaviors such as truancy, running away, fire setting, cruelty to animals, breaking and entering, and excessive fighting across a six-month period); oppositional defiant disorder (an ongoing pattern of disobedient, hostile, and defiant behavior toward authority figures); attention deficit hyperactivity disorder having one or more of these characteristics over a period of time: inattention, hyperactivity, and impulsivity); any externalizing disorder (presence of any of the three disorders previously described); and self-reported antisocial behavior (a list of 34 behaviors, such as skipping school, stealing, and attacking someone with an intent to hurt them).

The extensive intervention was successful only for children and adolescents who were identified as the highest risk in kindergarten, lowering their incidence of conduct disorder, attention deficit hyperactivity disorder, any externalized disorder, and antisocial behavior. Positive outcomes for the intervention occurred as early as the third grade and continued through the ninth grade. For example, in the ninth grade the intervention reduced the likelihood that the highest-risk kindergarten children would develop conduct disorder by 75 percent, attention deficit hyperactivity disorder by 53 percent, and any externalized disorder by 43 percent.

Review and Reflect: Learning Goal 3

 3

Describe the Development of Prosocial and Antisocial Behavior

REVIEW

- How is altruism defined? How does prosocial behavior develop?
- What is conduct disorder? What are key factors in the development of juvenile delinquency?

REFLECT

- As the head of a major government agency responsible for reducing delinquency in the United States, what programs would you try to implement?

---

4 RELIGIOUS AND SPIRITUAL DEVELOPMENT

Childhood   **Adolescence**

Earlier in the chapter, we described the many positive benefits of service learning. A number of studies have found that that adolescents who are involved in religious institutions are more likely to engage in service learning than their counterparts who don't participate in religious institutions (Oser, Scarlett, & Bucher, 2006). Let's explore children's and adolescents' concepts of religion and spirituality, as well as their religious and spiritual experiences.

Childhood

Can children understand religious ideas? How do parents influence children's religious thought and behavior?

Applying Piaget's Stages to Religious Thought

The cognitive developmental theory of Jean Piaget (1952) provides a theoretical backdrop for understanding religious development in children and adolescents. For example, in one study children were asked about their understanding of certain religious pictures and Bible stories

(Goldman, 1964). The children's responses fell into three stages closely related to Piaget's theory.

In the first stage (up to 7 or 8 years of age)—*preoperational intuitive religious thought*— children's religious thoughts were unsystematic and fragmented. The children often either did not fully understand the stories or did not consider all of the evidence. For example, asked "Why was Moses afraid to look at God?" (Exodus 3:6) one child answered, "Because God had a funny face!"

In the second stage (from 7 or 8 to 13 or 14 years of age)—*concrete operational religious thought*—children focused on particular details of pictures and stories. For example, in response to the question about why Moses was afraid to look at God, one child said, "Because it was a ball of fire. He thought he might burn him." Another child replied, "It was a bright light and to look at it might blind him."

In the third stage (age 14 through the remainder of adolescence)—*formal operational religious thought*—adolescents revealed a more abstract religious understanding. For example, one adolescent said that Moses was afraid to look at God because "God is holy and the world is sinful." Another youth responded, "The awesomeness and almightiness of God would make Moses feel like a worm in comparison."

Other researchers have found similar developmental changes in children and adolescents. For example, in one study, at about 17 or 18 years of age, adolescents increasingly commented about freedom, meaning, and hope—abstract concepts—when making religious judgments (Oser & Gmünder, 1991).

Parenting and Religion

Societies use many methods—such as Sunday schools, parochial education, and parental teaching—to ensure that people will carry on a religious tradition. In a recent national study, 63 percent of parents with children at home said they pray or read Scripture with their children, and 60 percent reported that they send their children to religious education programs (Pew Research Center, 2008). Does this religious socialization work? In many cases it does (Paloutzian, 2000).

In general, individuals tend to adopt the religious teachings of their upbringing. However, it is important to consider the quality of the parent-adolescent relationship (Ream & Savin-Williams, 2003). Adolescents who have a positive relationship with their parents or are securely attached to them are likely to adopt the religious orientation of their parents (Dudley, 1999). Adolescents who have a negative relationship with their parents or are insecurely attached to them may turn away from religion or seek religion-based attachments that are missing in their family system (Streib, 1999).

How do religious thought and behavior change as children and adolescents develop? How are children's and adolescents' religious conceptions influenced by their cognitive development?

Adolescence

Religious issues are important to many adolescents, but in the twenty-first century, a downtrend in religious interest among adolescents has occurred. In a national study of American freshmen, in 2007, 78 percent said they attended a religious service frequently or occasionally during their senior year in high school, down from a high of 85 percent in 1997 (Pryor & others, 2007). Further, in 2007, more than twice as many first-year students (19 percent) reported that they don't have a religious preference than in 1978 (8 percent).

A recent developmental study revealed that religiousness declined from 14 to 20 years of age in the United States (Koenig, McGue, & Iacono, 2008) (see Figure 13.5). In this study, religiousness was assessed with items such as frequency of prayer, frequency of discussing religious teachings, frequency of deciding moral actions for religious reasons, and the overall importance of religion in everyday life. As indicated in Figure 13.5, more change in religiousness occurred from 14 to 18 years of age than from 20 to 25 years of age. Also, attending religious services was highest at 14 years of age, declining from 14 to 18 years of age and increasing at 20 years of age. More change occurred in attending religious services than in religiousness.

Analysis of the World Values Survey of 18- to 24-year-olds revealed that emerging adults in less developed countries were more likely to be religious than their counterparts in more developed countries (Lippman & Keith, 2006). For example, emerging adults' reports of religion being very important in their lives ranged from a low of 0 in Japan to 93 percent in Nigeria, and belief in God ranged from a low of 40 percent in Sweden to a high of 100 percent in Pakistan.

Religion and Identity Development
During adolescence and emerging adulthood, especially emerging adulthood, identity development becomes a central focus (Erikson, 1968; Kroger, 2007; Templeton & Eccles, 2006). Adolescents and emerging adults want to know answers to questions like these: "Who am I?" "What am I all about as a person?" "What kind of life do I want to lead?" As part of their search for identity, adolescents and emerging adults begin to grapple in more sophisticated, logical ways with such questions as "Why am I on this planet?" "Is there really a God or higher spiritual being, or have I just been believing what my parents and the church imprinted in my mind?" "What really are my religious views?" A recent analysis of the link between identity and spirituality concluded that adolescence and adulthood can serve as gateways to a spiritual identity that "transcends, but not necessarily excludes, the assigned religious identity in childhood" (Templeton & Eccles, 2006, p. 261).

The Positive Role of Religion in Adolescents' Lives
Researchers have found that various aspects of religion are linked with positive outcomes for adolescents (Lerner, Roeser, & Phelps, 2009; Oser, Scarlett, & Butcher, 2006). Religion also plays a role in adolescents' health and whether they engage in problem behaviors (Cotton & others, 2006). For example, in a recent national random sample of more than 2,000 11- to 18-year-olds, those who were higher in religiosity were less likely to smoke, drink alcohol, use marijuana, be truant from school, engage in delinquent activities, and be depressed than their low-religiosity counterparts (Sinha, Cnaan, & Gelles, 2007). A recent study of Indonesian Muslim 13-year-olds revealed that their religiousness involvement was linked to their social competence, including positive peer relations, academic achievement, emotional regulation, prosocial behavior, and self-esteem (French & others, 2008).

Many religious adolescents also internalize their religion's message about caring and concern for people (Ream & Savin-Williams, 2003). For example, in one survey, religious youth were almost three times as likely to engage in community service as nonreligious youth (Youniss, McLellan, & Yates, 1999).

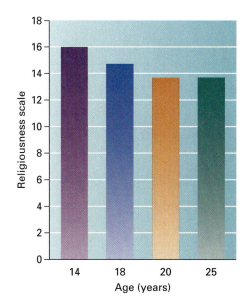

FIGURE 13.5 Developmental Changes in Religiousness from 14 to 25 Years of Age. *Note:* The religiousness scale ranged from 0 to 32 with higher scores indicating stronger religiousness.

Adolescents participating in a youth church group. *What are some positive aspects of religion in adolescents' lives?*

Review and Reflect: Learning Goal 4

4 **Summarize the Nature of Children's and Adolescents' Religious and Spiritual Development**

REVIEW

- How does religious and spiritual interest and understanding develop in childhood?
- What characterizes religious and spiritual development in adolescence?

REFLECT

- What do you think are the most positive aspects of exposing children to religion?

Reach Your Learning Goals

Moral Development

1 DOMAINS OF MORAL DEVELOPMENT: DISCUSS THEORY AND RESEARCH ON THE FOUR DOMAINS OF MORAL DEVELOPMENT

What Is Moral Development?

- Moral development involves changes in thoughts, feelings, and behaviors regarding right and wrong. Moral development consists of intrapersonal and interpersonal dimensions.

Moral Thought

- Piaget distinguished between the heteronomous morality of younger children and the autonomous morality of older children. Kohlberg developed a provocative theory of moral reasoning. He argued that development of moral reasoning consists of three levels—preconventional, conventional, and postconventional—and six stages (two at each level). Kohlberg reasoned that these stages were age related. Influences on the Kohlberg stages include cognitive development, dealing with moral questions and moral conflict, peer relations, and perspective taking. Criticisms of Kohlberg's theory have been made, especially by Gilligan, who advocates a stronger care perspective. Other criticisms focus on the inadequacy of moral reasoning to predict moral behavior, and culture and family influences, and the assessment of moral reasoning. A distinction can be made between moral reasoning and social conventional reasoning, which concerns social consensus and conventions to control behavior and maintain the social system.

Moral Behavior

- The processes of reinforcement, punishment, and imitation have been used to explain the acquisition of moral behavior, but they provide only a partial explanation. Situational variability is stressed by behaviorists. Social cognitive theory emphasizes a distinction between moral competence and moral performance.

Moral Feeling

- In Freud's theory, the superego is the moral branch of personality. According to Freud, guilt is the foundation of children's moral behavior. Empathy is an important aspect of moral feelings, and it changes developmentally. In the contemporary perspective, both positive and negative feelings contribute to moral development.

Moral Personality

- Recently, there has been a surge of interest in studying moral personality. This interest has focused on moral identity, moral character, and moral exemplars. Blasi points out that individuals have a moral identity when notions and commitment are central to the individual's life. Moral character involves having the strength of your convictions, persisting, and overcoming distractions and obstacles. Moral character consists of having certain virtues, such as honesty, truthfulness, loyalty, and compassion. Moral exemplars have a moral character, identity, personality and a set of virtues reflecting excellence and commitment; they are honest and dependable.

2 CONTEXTS OF MORAL DEVELOPMENT: EXPLAIN HOW PARENTING AND SCHOOLS INFLUENCE MORAL DEVELOPMENT

Parenting

- Warmth and responsibility in mutual obligations of parent-child relationships provide important foundations for the child's positive moral growth. Love withdrawal, power assertion, and induction are discipline techniques. Induction is most likely to be linked with positive moral development. Moral development can be advanced by these parenting strategies: being warm and supportive rather than punitive; using inductive discipline; providing opportunities to learn about others' perspectives and feelings; involving children in family decision making; modeling moral behaviors; averting misbehavior before it takes place; and engaging in conversational dialogue related to moral development.

Schools

- The hidden curriculum, initially described by Dewey, is the moral atmosphere of every school. Contemporary approaches to moral education include character education, values clarification, cognitive moral education, service learning, and integrative ethical education. Cheating is a moral education concern and can take many forms. Various aspects of the situation influence whether students will cheat or not.

3 PROSOCIAL AND ANTISOCIAL BEHAVIOR: DESCRIBE THE DEVELOPMENT OF PROSOCIAL AND ANTISOCIAL BEHAVIOR

Prosocial Behavior

- An important aspect of prosocial behavior is altruism, an unselfish interest in helping another person. Damon described a sequence by which children develop their understanding of fairness and come to share more consistently. Peers play a key role in this development.

Antisocial Behavior

- Conduct disorder involves age-inappropriate actions and attitudes that violate family expectations, society's norms, and the personal or property rights of others. The disorder is more common in boys than in girls. Juvenile delinquency refers to an adolescent who breaks the law or engages in behaviors considered illegal. In the Pittsburgh Youth Study, pathways to delinquency included conflict with authority, minor covert acts followed by property damage and more serious acts, and overt acts including minor aggression followed by fighting and violence. Associating with peers and friends who are delinquents; low parental monitoring; ineffective discipline; having an older sibling who is a delinquent; living in an urban, high-crime area, having low self-control; and having low intelligence are also linked with delinquency.

4 RELIGIOUS AND SPIRITUAL DEVELOPMENT: SUMMARIZE THE NATURE OF CHILDREN'S AND ADOLESCENTS' RELIGIOUS AND SPIRITUAL DEVELOPMENT

Childhood

- Piaget's theory provides a foundation for understanding developmental changes in children's and adolescents' conceptions of religion. Many children and adolescents show an interest in religion. Many children adopt their parents' religious beliefs.

Adolescence

- The twenty-first century has shown a downtrend in adolescents' religious interest. Emerging adults from less developed countries were more likely to be religious than those from more developed countries. As part of their search for identity, many adolescents and emerging adults begin to grapple with more complex aspects of religion. When adolescents have a positive relationship with parents or are securely attached to them, they often adopt their parents' religious beliefs. Various aspects of religion are linked with positive outcomes in adolescent development. Religious youth were less likely to smoke, drink alcohol, or use marijuana, and more likely to engage in community service than nonreligious youth.

KEY TERMS

moral development 385
heteronomous morality (Piaget) 385
autonomous morality 385
immanent justice 385
preconventional reasoning 386
heteronomous morality (Kohlberg) 386

individualism, instrumental purpose, and exchange 387
conventional reasoning 387
mutual interpersonal expectations, relationships, and interpersonal conformity 387
social systems morality 387

postconventional reasoning 387
social contract or utility and individual rights 387
universal ethical principles 387
justice perspective 390
care perspective 390
social conventional reasoning 390

social cognitive theory of morality 391
empathy 393
moral identity 393
moral exemplars 394
love withdrawal 395
power assertion 395
induction 395
hidden curriculum 397

character education 397	cognitive moral	service learning 398	conduct disorder 401
values clarification 398	education 398	altruism 400	juvenile delinquency 402

KEY PEOPLE

Jean Piaget 385	Hugh Hartshorne and Mark	William Damon 394	Darcia Narvaez 399
Lawrence	May 391	Lawrence Walker 395	Nancy Eisenberg 401
Kohlberg 386	Albert Bandura 392	Ross Thompson 396	
Carol Gilligan 390	Sigmund Freud 392	Martin Hoffman 396	
James Rest 390	Grazyna Kochanska 393	John Dewey 397	

E-LEARNING TOOLS

To help you master the material in this chapter, you'll find a number of valuable study tools at the Online Learning Center for *Child Development*, twelfth edition **(www.mhhe.com/ santrockcd12)**.

Taking It to the Net

Research the answers to these questions:

1. Geraldine is giving a report on Kohlberg's theory of moral development. She is having a hard time thinking of an example of moral reasoning that would demonstrate each of Kohlberg's six stages of moral development. What examples would best demonstrate each of the six stages of moral development?

2. Kirk is planning to be a fifth-grade teacher. He is interested in the new approach to disciplining students that is designed to strengthen a child's character and impart moral values. How can Kirk begin to use this approach in the classroom?

3. Justin was having a heated discussion with his dad over the factors that may have contributed to a young boy's shooting and killing a schoolmate. Justin thinks that the boy may have witnessed, or been a victim of, violence in his home. His father says that if everyone who saw violence was violent we would all be locked up. How should Justin respond?

Health and Well-Being, Parenting, and Education Exercises

Build your decision-making skills by trying your hand at the health and well-being, parenting, and education exercises.

Video Clip

The Online Learning Center includes the following video for this chapter:

- *Juvenile Offenders*

Laurence Steinberg, Temple University, discusses juvenile offenders.

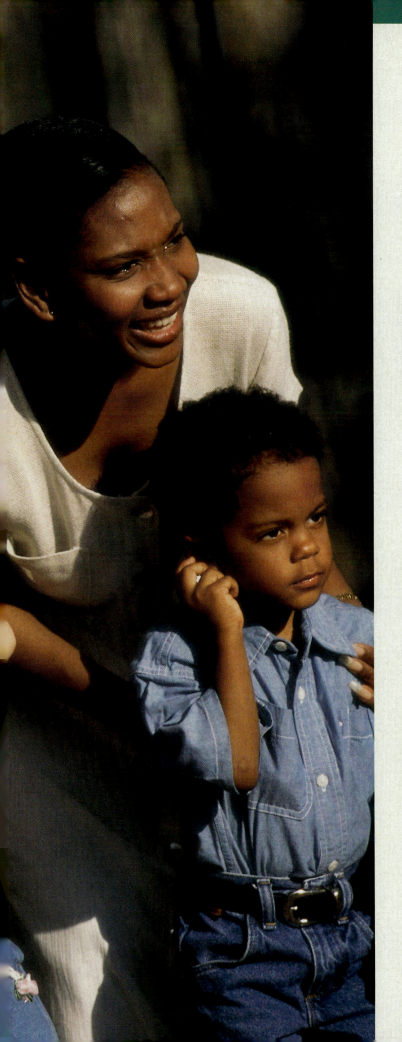

FIVE

SOCIAL CONTEXTS OF DEVELOPMENT

It is not enough for parents to understand children. They must also accord children the privilege of understanding them.

—MILTON SAPIRSTEIN
*American Psychiatrist and Writer,
20th Century*

Parents cradle children's lives, but children's growth is also shaped by successive choirs of siblings, peers, friends, and teachers. Children's small worlds widen as they discover new refuges and new people. In the end, there are but two lasting bequests that parents can leave children: one being roots, the other wings. In this section, we will study four chapters: "Families" (Chapter 14), "Peers" (Chapter 15), "Schools and Achievement" (Chapter 16), and "Culture and Diversity" (Chapter 17).

14

There's no vocabulary for love within a family, love that's lived in but not looked at, love within the light of which all else is seen, the love within which all other love finds speech. That love is silent.

—T. S. Eliot
*American-Born English Poet,
20th Century*

LEARNING GOALS

◆ Discuss family processes.

◆ Explain how parenting is linked to children's and adolescents' development.

◆ Identify how siblings influence children's development.

◆ Characterize the changing family in a changing social world.

FAMILIES

CHAPTER OUTLINE

1 **FAMILY PROCESSES**
Interactions in the Family System
Cognition and Emotion in Family Processes
Sociocultural and Historical Changes

2 **PARENTING**
Adapting Parenting to Developmental Changes in Children
Parents as Managers of Children's Lives
Parenting Styles and Discipline
Parent-Adolescent Relationships

3 **SIBLINGS**
Sibling Relationships
Birth Order

4 **THE CHANGING FAMILY IN A CHANGING SOCIAL WORLD**
Working Parents
Children in Divorced Families
Stepfamilies
Gay Male and Lesbian Parents
Cultural, Ethnic, and Socioeconomic Variations in Families

Images of Child Development
The Story of a Mother with Multiple Sclerosis

When Shelley Peterman Schwarz (2004) and her husband, David, had been married four years, they decided to have children. They had two children, Andrew and Jamie. When they were 3 and 5 years old, Shelley was diagnosed with multiple sclerosis. Two years later, she had to quit her job as a teacher of hearing-impaired children because of her worsening condition.

By the time the children were 7 and 9 years old, it was more difficult for Shelley to prepare meals for the family by herself, so David began taking over that responsibility. They also enlisted the children's help in preparing meals.

Despite her multiple sclerosis, Shelley participated in parenting classes and workshops at her children's school. She even initiated a "Mothers-of-10-Year-Olds" support group. But parenting with multiple sclerosis had its frustrations for Shelley. In her words,

attending school functions, teacher's conferences, and athletic events often presented problems because the facilities weren't always easily wheelchair accessible. I felt guilty if I didn't at least "try" to attend. I didn't want my children to think I didn't care enough to try. . . .

When Jamie was 19 and Andrew was 17, I started to relax a little. I could see how capable and independent they were becoming. My having a disability hadn't ruined their lives. In fact, in some ways, they are better off because of it. They learned to trust themselves and to face personal challenges head-on. When the time came for them to leave the nest and head off to college, I knew they were ready.

As for me, I now understand that having a disability wasn't the worst thing in the world that could happen to a parent. What would be a tragedy is letting your disability cripple your ability to stay in your children's lives. Parenting is so much more than driving car pools, attending gymnastic meets, or baking cookies for an open house. It's loving, caring, listening, guiding, and supporting your child. It's consoling a child crying because her friends thought her haircut was ugly. It's counseling a child worried because his 12-year-old friend is drinking. It's helping a child understand relationships and what it's like to "be in love." (Schwarz, 2004, p. 5)

Shelley Peterman Schwarz (*left*) with her family.

PREVIEW

This chapter is about the many aspects of children's development in families. We will explore the best ways to parent children, relationships among siblings, and the changing family in a changing social world. Along the way, we will examine such topics as child maltreatment, working parents, children in divorced families, stepfamilies, and many others.

1 FAMILY PROCESSES

| Interactions in the Family System | Cognition and Emotion in Family Processes | Sociocultural and Historical Changes |

As we examine the family and other social contexts of development, keep in mind Urie Bronfenbrenner's (1995, 2000, 2004; Bronfenbrenner & Morris, 2006) ecological theory, which we discussed in Chapter 1. Recall that Bronfenbrenner analyzes the social contexts of development in terms of five environmental systems:

- The microsystem or the setting in which the individual lives, such as a family, the world of peers, schools, work, and so on
- The mesosystem, which consists of links between microsystems, such as the connection between family processes and peer relations
- The exosystem, which consists of influences from another setting that the individual does not experience directly, such as how parents' experiences at work might affect their parenting at home
- The macrosystem or the culture in which the individual lives, such as a nation or an ethnic group
- The chronosystem or sociohistorical circumstances, such as the increase in the numbers of working mothers, divorced parents, and stepparent families in the United States in the last 30 to 40 years

Let's begin our examination of the family at the level of the microsystem.

Interactions in the Family System

Every family is a *system*—a complex whole made up of interrelated and interacting parts. The relationships never go in just one direction. For example, the interaction of mothers and their infants is sometimes symbolized as a dance in which successive actions of the partners are closely coordinated. This coordinated dance can assume the form of *mutual synchrony,* which means that each person's behavior depends on the partner's previous behavior. Or the interaction can be *reciprocal* in a precise sense, which means that the actions of the partners can be matched, as when one partner imitates the other or when there is mutual smiling (Cohn & Tronick, 1988).

An important example of early synchronized interaction is mutual gaze or eye contact. In one investigation, the mother and infant engaged in a variety of behaviors while they looked at each other; by contrast, when they looked away from each other, the rate of such behaviors dropped considerably (Stern & others, 1977). In one investigation, synchrony in parent-child relationships was positively related to children's social competence (Harrist, 1993).

Another example of synchronization occurs in **scaffolding**, which means adjusting the level of guidance to fit the child's performance, as we discussed in Chapter 6. The parent responds to the child's behavior with scaffolding, which in turn affects the child's behavior. Scaffolding can be used to support children's efforts at any age. For example, in the game peek-a-boo, parents initially cover their babies, then remove the covering, and finally register "surprise" at the babies' reappearance. As infants become more skilled at peek-a-boo, infants gradually do some of the covering and uncovering. Parents try to time their actions in such a way that the infant takes turns with the parent.

How does the game of peek-a-boo reflect the concept of scaffolding?

scaffolding Adjusting the level of parental guidance to fit the child's efforts, allowing children to be more skillful than they would be if they relied only on their own abilities.

Children socialize parents just as parents socialize children.

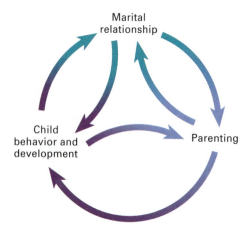

FIGURE 14.1 Interaction Between Children and Their Parents: Direct and Indirect Effects

In addition to peek-a-boo, patty-cake and so-big are other caregiver games that exemplify scaffolding and turn-taking sequences. In one investigation, infants who had more extensive scaffolding experiences with their parents, especially in the form of turn taking, were more likely to engage in turn taking as they interacted with their peers (Vandell & Wilson, 1988). Engaging in turn taking and games like peek-a-boo reflect the development of joint attention by the caregiver and infant, which we discussed in Chapter 7, "Information Processing" (Tomasello & Carpenter, 2007).

The mutual influence that parents and children exert on each other goes beyond specific interactions in games such as peek-a-boo; it extends to the whole process of socialization. Socialization between parents and children is not a one-way process Parents do socialize children, but socialization in families is reciprocal (Kuczynski & Parkin, 2007; Parke & others, 2008). **Reciprocal socialization** is socialization that is bidirectional; children socialize parents just as parents socialize children.

Of course, while parents are interacting with their children, they are also interacting with each other. To understand these interactions and relationships, it helps to think of the family as a constellation of subsystems defined in terms of generation, gender, and role. Each family member is a participant in several subsystems—some *dyadic* (involving two people), some *polyadic* (involving more than two people). The father and child represent one dyadic subsystem, the mother and father another; the mother-father-child represent one polyadic subsystem, the mother and two siblings another (Parke & others, 2008).

These subsystems interact and influence one another (Cox & others, 2008). Thus, as Figure 14.1 illustrates, marital relations, parenting, and infant/child behavior can have both direct and indirect effects on one another (Belsky, 1981). The link between marital relationships and parenting has received increased attention. The most consistent findings are that compared with unhappily married parents, happily married parents are more sensitive, responsive, warm, and affectionate toward their children (Grych, 2002).

Researchers have found that promoting marital satisfaction often leads to good parenting. The marital relationship provides an important support for parenting (Cox & others, 2008; Schoppe-Sullivan & others, 2007). When parents report more intimacy and better communication in their marriage, they are more affectionate to their children (Grych, 2002). Thus, marriage-enhancement programs may end up improving parenting and helping children. Programs that focus on parenting skills might also benefit from including attention to the participants' marriages.

Cognition and Emotion in Family Processes

Both cognition and emotion are increasingly thought to be central to understanding how family processes work (Grusec, 2009; Parke & Buriel, 2006). The role of cognition in family socialization comes in many forms, including parents' cognitions, beliefs, and values about their parental role, as well as how parents perceive, organize, and understand their children's behaviors and beliefs. For example, one study found a link between mothers' beliefs and their preschool children's social problem-solving skills (Rubin, Mills, & Rose-Krasnor, 1989). Mothers who placed a higher value on such skills as making friends, sharing with others, and leading or influencing other children had children who were more assertive, prosocial, and competent problem solvers than mothers who valued these skills less.

Children's social competence is also linked to the emotional lives of their parents (Denham, Bassett, & Wyatt, 2007). For example, one study found that parents who expressed positive emotions had children who were high in competence (Boyum & Parke, 1995). Through interaction with parents, children learn to express their emotions in appropriate ways.

Researchers are also finding that parental sensitivity to children's emotions is related to children's ability to manage their emotions in positive ways (Calkins & Hill, 2007; Grusec & Davidov, 2007; Lagattuta & Thompson, 2007; Thompson, 2009a).

reciprocal socialization The bidirectional process by which children socialize parents just as parents socialize them.

Recall from Chapter 10, "Emotional Development," the distinction that was made between emotion-coaching and emotion-dismissing parents (Gottman, 2002). *Emotion-coaching parents* monitor their children's emotions, view their children's negative emotions as opportunities for teaching, assist them in labeling emotions, and coach them in how to deal effectively with emotions. In contrast, *emotion-dismissing parents* view their role as to deny, ignore, or change negative emotions. One study found that the children of emotion-coaching parents were better at physiologically soothing themselves when they got upset, were better at regulating their negative affect, could focus their attention better, and had fewer behavior problems than the children of emotion-dismissing parents (Gottman & DeClaire, 1997).

A recent study conducted by Maayan Davidov and Joan Grusec (2006) found some specific outcomes for children's emotional development, depending on which aspect of parenting was expressed. In the study, parent's responses to children's distress (such as responding with empathy), but not parents' warmth, was linked to children's capacity to regulate their negative emotions (such as expressing appropriate affect in response to aggression by peers); in contrast, the mother's warmth, but not her response to her child's distress, was related to children's regulation of positive emotions (such as being cheerful) (Davidov & Grusec, 2006). This study underscores an important point about parenting. Many studies take a global approach to parenting, rather than examining specific components. For example, parents' responses to a child's distress and parents' warmth are often lumped together in a broad positive parenting category. However, in the Davidov and Grusec study, parents' responses to a child's distress and parents' warmth predicted different outcomes for children. Other developmentalists also argue that in many cases distinctive parenting responses should be activated, depending on the domain involved (Beaulieu & Bugental, 2007). For example, if a child becomes distressed, a sensitive parent soothes the child, whereas an insensitive parent might try to distract the child's attention by asking the child to play a game or become power assertive; however, when a child is angrily defiant, a more assertive response, rather than soothing, might be required by the parent (Maccoby, 2007).

How is parents' sensitivity to children's emotions linked to children's ability to manage their emotions?

Sociocultural and Historical Changes

Family development does not occur in a social vacuum. Important sociocultural and historical influences affect family processes, which reflect Bronfenbrenner's concepts of the macrosystem and chronosystem (Bronfenbrenner & Morris, 2006). Both great upheavals such as war, famine, or massive immigration and subtle transitions in ways of life may stimulate changes in families (Berry, 2007; Elder & Shanahan, 2006). One example is the effect on U.S. families of the Great Depression of the 1930s. During its height, the Depression produced economic deprivation, adult discontent, and depression about living conditions. It also increased marital conflict, inconsistent child rearing, and unhealthy lifestyles—heavy drinking, demoralized attitudes, and health disabilities—especially in fathers (Elder & Shanahan, 2006).

Subtle changes in a culture have significant influences on the family (Morelli & Rothbaum, 2007; Parke & others, 2008). Such changes include the longevity of older adults, movement to urban and suburban areas, television, and a general dissatisfaction and restlessness (Mead, 1978).

In the first part of the twentieth century, individuals who survived were usually hearty and still closely linked to the family, often helping to maintain the family's existence. Today, individuals live longer, which means that their middle-aged children are often pressed into a caregiving role for their parents, or the elderly parents may be placed in a nursing home (Holden & Hatcher, 2006). Older parents may have lost some of their socializing role in the family during the twentieth century as many of their children moved great distances away. However, in the twenty-first century, an increasing number of grandparents are raising their grandchildren (Hughes & others, 2007).

Two important changes in families are the increased mobility of families and the increase in television viewing. *What are some other changes?*

Many of the family moves in the last 75 years have been away from farms and small towns to urban and suburban settings. In the small towns and farms, individuals were surrounded by lifelong neighbors, relatives, and friends. Today, neighborhood and extended-family support systems are not nearly as prevalent. Families now move all over the country, often uprooting children from a school and peer group they have known for a considerable length of time. And it is not unusual for this type of move to occur every several years, as one or both parents are transferred from job to job.

The media and technology also play a major role in the changing family (Murray & Murray, 2008; Wartella, 2007). Many children who watch television find that parents are too busy working to share this experience with them. Children increasingly experience a world in which their parents are not participants. Instead of interacting in neighborhood peer groups, children come home after school and watch television or log on to a computer.

Another change in families has been an increase in general dissatisfaction and restlessness. The result of such restlessness and the tendency to divorce and remarry has been a hodgepodge of family structures, with far greater numbers of divorced and remarried families than ever before in history (Ahrons, 2007).

Many of the changes we have described in this section not only apply to U.S. families, but also to families in many countries around the world. Later in the chapter, we discuss such aspects of the changing social world of the child and the family in greater detail.

Review and Reflect: Learning Goal 1

1   Discuss Family Processes

REVIEW

- How can the family be viewed as a system? What is reciprocal socialization?
- How are cognition and emotion involved in family processes?
- What are some sociocultural and historical changes that have influenced the family?

REFLECT

- What do you predict will be some major changes in families by the end of the twenty-first century?

2   PARENTING

Adapting Parenting to Developmental Changes in Children

Parents as Managers of Children's Lives

Parenting Styles and Discipline

Parent-Adolescent Relationships

Parenting calls on a number of interpersonal skills and makes intense emotional demands, yet there is little in the way of formal education for this task. Most parents learn parenting practices from their own parents. Some of these practices they accept, some they discard. Husbands and wives may bring different views of parenting to the marriage.

Unfortunately, when parents' methods are passed on from one generation to the next, both desirable and undesirable practices are perpetuated. What have developmentalists learned about parenting? How should parents adapt their practices to developmental changes in their children? How important is it for parents to be effective managers of their children's lives? And how do different parenting styles and discipline influence children's development?

Adapting Parenting to Developmental Changes in Children

Children change as they grow from infancy to early childhood and on through middle and late childhood and adolescence. The 5-year-old and the 2-year-old have different needs and abilities. A competent parent adapts to the child's developmental changes (Maccoby, 1984). As we see next, though, considerable adaptation also is required in making the transition to parenting.

The Transition to Parenting   Whether people become parents through pregnancy, adoption, or stepparenting, they face disequilibrium and must adapt (Claxton & Perry-Jenkins, 2008). Parents want to develop a strong attachment with their infant, but they still want to maintain strong attachments to their spouse and friends, and possibly continue their careers. Parents ask themselves how this new being will change their lives. A baby places new restrictions on partners; no longer will they be able to rush out to a movie on a moment's notice, and money may not be readily available for vacations and other luxuries. Dual-career parents ask, "Will it harm the baby to place her in child care? Will we be able to find responsible baby-sitters?"

In a longitudinal investigation of couples from late pregnancy until $3\frac{1}{2}$ years after the baby was born, couples enjoyed more positive marital relations before the baby was born than after (Cowan & Cowan, 2000; Cowan & others, 2005). Still, almost one-third showed an increase in marital satisfaction. Some couples said that the baby had both brought them closer together and moved them farther apart; being parents enhanced their sense of themselves and gave them a new, more stable identity as a couple. Babies opened men up to a concern with intimate relationships, and the demands of juggling work and family roles stimulated women to manage family tasks more efficiently and pay attention to their own personal growth.

The Bringing Home Baby project is a workshop for new parents that emphasizes strengthening the couples' relationship, understanding and becoming acquainted with the baby, resolving conflict, and developing parenting skills. Evaluations of the project revealed that parents who participated improved in their ability to work together as parents, fathers were more involved with their baby and sensitive to the baby's behavior, mothers had a lower incidence of postpartum depression symptoms, and their baby showed better overall development than participants in a control group (Gottman, 2008; Shapiro & Gottman, 2005).

Infancy and Early Childhood   In the first year, parent-child interaction moves from a heavy focus on routine caregiving—feeding, changing diapers, bathing, and soothing—to later include more noncaregiving activities, such as play and visual-vocal exchanges (Bornstein, 2002). During the child's second and third years, parents often handle disciplinary matters by physical manipulation: They carry the child away from a mischievous activity to the place they want the child to go to; they put fragile and dangerous objects out of reach; they sometimes spank. As the child grows older, however, parents increasingly turn to reasoning, moral exhortation, and giving or withholding special privileges. As children move toward the elementary school years, parents show them less physical affection.

Parent-child interactions during early childhood focus on such matters as modesty, bedtime regularities, control of temper, fighting with siblings and peers, eating behavior and manners, autonomy in dressing, and attention seeking (Edwards & Liu, 2002). Although some of these issues—fighting and reaction to discipline, for example—are carried forward into the elementary school years, many new issues appear by the age of 7. These include whether children should be made to perform chores and, if so,

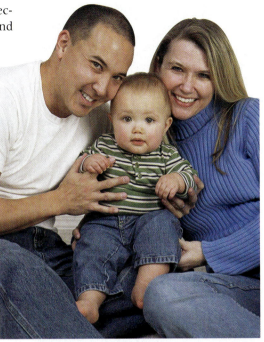

What characterizes the transition to parenting?

What are some changes in the focus of parent-child relationships in middle and late childhood?

whether they should be paid for them, how to help children learn to entertain themselves rather than relying on parents for everything, and how to monitor children's lives outside the family in school and peer settings.

Middle and Late Childhood   As children move into the middle and late childhood years, parents spend less time with them. In one study, parents spent less than half as much time with their children aged 5 to 12 in caregiving, instruction, reading, talking, and playing as when the children were younger (Hill & Stafford, 1980). Although parents spend less time with their children in middle and late childhood than in early childhood, parents continue to be extremely important in their children's lives. In a recent analysis of the contributions of parents in middle and late childhood, the following conclusion was reached: "Parents serve as gatekeepers and provide scaffolding as children assume more responsibility for themselves and . . . regulate their own lives" (Huston & Ripke, 2006, p. 422).

Parents especially play an important role in supporting and stimulating children's academic achievement in middle and late childhood (Huston & Ripke, 2006). The value parents place on education can mean the difference in whether children do well in school. Parents not only influence children's in-school achievement, but they also make decisions about children's out-of-school activities. Whether children participate in sports, music, and other activities is heavily influenced by the extent to which parents sign up children for such activities and encourage their participation (Simpkins & others, 2006).

Elementary school children tend to receive less physical discipline than they did as preschoolers. Instead of spanking or coercive holding, their parents are more likely to use deprivation of privileges, appeals to the child's self-esteem, comments designed to increase the child's sense of guilt, and statements that the child is responsible for his or her actions.

During middle and late childhood, some control is transferred from parent to child. The process is gradual, and it produces *coregulation* rather than control by either the child or the parent alone. Parents continue to exercise general supervision and control, and children are allowed to engage in moment-to-moment self-regulation. The major shift to autonomy does not occur until about the age of 12 or later. A key developmental task as children move toward autonomy is learning to relate to adults outside the family on a regular basis—adults who interact with the child much differently than parents, such as teachers.

In sum, considerable adaptation in parenting is required as children develop. Later in the chapter, we will further examine adaptations in parenting when discussing family influences on adolescents' development.

Parents as Managers of Children's Lives

Parents can play important roles as managers of children's opportunities, as monitors of their lives, and as social initiators and arrangers (Parke & Buriel, 2006; Parke & others, 2008). An important developmental task of childhood and adolescence is to develop the ability to make competent decisions in an increasingly independent manner (Mortimer & Larson, 2002). To help children and adolescents reach their full potential, an important parental role is to be an effective manager, one who finds information, makes contacts, helps structure choices, and provides guidance (Gauvain & Perez, 2007; Youniss & Ruth, 2002). Parents who fulfill this important managerial role help children and adolescents to avoid pitfalls and to work their way through a myriad of choices and decisions they face (Furstenberg & others, 1999). Mothers are more likely than fathers to engage in a managerial role in parenting.

From infancy through adolescence, parents can serve important roles in managing their children's experiences and opportunities. In infancy, this might involve taking a child to a doctor and arranging for child care; in early childhood, it might involve a decision about which preschool the child should attend; in middle and late childhood, it might include directing the child to take a bath, to match their clothes and wear clean clothes, and to put away toys; in adolescence, it could involve participating in a parent-teacher conference and subsequently managing the adolescent's homework activity.

A key aspect of the managerial role of parenting is effective monitoring, which is especially important as children move into the adolescent years. Monitoring includes supervising an adolescent's choice of social settings, activities, and friends. As we saw in Chapter 13, a lack of adequate parental monitoring is the parental factor that is related to juvenile delinquency more than any other (Patterson & Stouthamer-Loeber, 1984). To read about one individual who helps parents become more effective in managing children's lives, see the *Careers in Child Development* profile.

Careers in Child Development

Janis Keyser, Parent Educator

Janis Keyser is a parent educator and teaches in the Department of Early Childhood Education at Cabrillo College in California. In addition to teaching college classes and conducting parenting workshops, she also has coauthored a book with Laura Davis (1997), *Becoming the Parent You Want to Be: A Source-Book of Strategies for the First Five Years.*

Janis also writes as an expert on the iVillage Web site (www.parentsplace.com). And she also coauthors a nationally syndicated parenting column, "Growing Up, Growing Together."

Janis Keyser (*right*), conducting a parenting workshop.

Researchers also have found that family management practices are positively related to students' grades and self-responsibility, and negatively to school-related problems (Eccles, 2007; Taylor & Lopez, 2005). Among the most important family management practices in this regard are maintaining a structured and organized family environment, such as establishing routines for homework, chores, bedtime, and so on, and effectively monitoring the child's behavior. A recent research review of family functioning in African American students' academic achievement found that when African American parents monitored their son's academic achievement by ensuring that homework was completed, restricted time spent on nonproductive distractions (such as video games and TV), and participated in a consistent, positive dialogue with teachers and school officials, their son's academic achievement benefited (Mandara, 2006).

Parenting Styles and Discipline

A few years ago, there was considerable interest in Mozart CDs that were marketed with the promise that playing them would enrich infants' and young children's brains. Some of the parents who bought them probably thought, "I don't have enough time to spend with my children so I'll just play these intellectual CDs and then they won't need me as much." Similarly, one-minute bedtime stories are being marketed for parents to read to their children (Walsh, 2000). There are one-minute bedtime bear books, puppy books, and so on. Parents who buy them know it is good for them to read with their children, but they don't want to spend a lot of time doing it. Behind

*P*arenting is a very important profession, but no test of fitness for it is ever imposed in the interest of children.

—GEORGE BERNARD SHAW
Irish Playwright, 20th Century

the popularity of these products is an unfortunate theme which suggests that parenting can be done quickly, with little or no inconvenience (Sroufe, 2000).

What is wrong with these quick-fix approaches to parenting? Good parenting takes time and effort (Bornstein, 2006; Powell, 2005, 2006). You can't do it in a minute here and a minute there. You can't do it with CDs.

Of course, it's not just the quantity of time parents spend with children that is important for children's development—the quality of the parenting is clearly important (Bornstein & Zlotnik, 2008). To understand variations in parenting, let's consider the styles parents use when they interact with their children, how they discipline their children, and coparenting.

Baumrind's Parenting Styles Diana Baumrind (1971) points out that parents should be neither punitive nor aloof. Rather, they should develop rules for their children and be affectionate with them. She has described four types of parenting styles:

- **Authoritarian parenting** is a restrictive, punitive style in which parents exhort the child to follow their directions and respect their work and effort. The authoritarian parent places firm limits and controls on the child and allows little verbal exchange. For example, an authoritarian parent might say, "You do it my way or else." Authoritarian parents also might spank the child frequently, enforce rules rigidly but not explain them, and show rage toward the child. Children of authoritarian parents are often unhappy, fearful, and anxious about comparing themselves with others, fail to initiate activity, and have weak communication skills. Sons of authoritarian parents may behave aggressively (Hart & others, 2003).

- **Authoritative parenting** encourages children to be independent but still places limits and controls on their actions. Extensive verbal give-and-take is allowed, and parents are warm and nurturant toward the child. An authoritative parent might put his arm around the child in a comforting way and say, "You know you should not have done that. Let's talk about how you can handle the situation better next time." Authoritative parents show pleasure and support in response to children's constructive behavior. They also expect mature, independent, and age-appropriate behavior by children. Children whose parents are authoritative are often cheerful, self-controlled and self-reliant, and achievement oriented; they tend to maintain friendly relations with peers, cooperate with adults, and cope well with stress.

- **Neglectful parenting** is a style in which the parent is very uninvolved in the child's life. Children whose parents are neglectful develop the sense that other

authoritarian parenting This is a restrictive, punitive style in which the parent exhorts the child to follow the parent's directions and to respect their work and effort. Firm limits and controls are placed on the child, and little verbal exchange is allowed. This style is associated with children's social incompetence, including a lack of initiative and weak communication skills.

authoritative parenting This style encourages children to be independent but still places limits and controls on their actions. Extensive verbal give-and-take is allowed, and parents are warm and nurturant toward the child. This style is associated with children's social competence, including being achievement oriented and self-reliant.

Calvin and Hobbes   by Bill Watterson

WHAT ASSURANCE DO I HAVE THAT YOUR PARENTING ISN'T SCREWING ME UP?

CALVIN AND HOBBES Copyright © Watterson. Distributed by UNIVERSAL PRESS SYNDICATE. Reprinted with permission. All rights reserved.

aspects of the parents' lives are more important than they are. These children tend to be socially incompetent. Many have poor self-control and don't handle independence well. They frequently have low self-esteem, are immature, and may be alienated from the family. In adolescence, they may show patterns of truancy and delinquency.

- **Indulgent parenting** is a style in which parents are highly involved with their children but place few demands or controls on them. Such parents let their children do what they want. The result is that the children never learn to control their own behavior and always expect to get their way. Some parents deliberately rear their children in this way because they believe the combination of warm involvement and few restraints will produce a creative, confident child. However, children whose parents are indulgent rarely learn respect for others and have difficulty controlling their behavior. They might be domineering, egocentric, noncompliant, and have difficulties in peer relations.

These four classifications of parenting involve combinations of acceptance and responsiveness on the one hand and demand and control on the other (Maccoby & Martin, 1983). How these dimensions combine to produce authoritarian, authoritative, neglectful, and indulgent parenting is shown in Figure 14.2.

Parenting Styles in Context Do the benefits of authoritative parenting transcend the boundaries of ethnicity, socioeconomic status, and household composition? Although some exceptions have been found, evidence linking authoritative parenting with competence on the part of the child occurs in research across a wide range of ethnic groups, social strata, cultures, and family structures (Steinberg, Blatt-Eisengart, & Cauffman, 2006; Steinberg & Silk, 2002). A recent study of more than 1,300 14- to 18-year-olds who had been adjudicated because of serious delinquent acts found that the juvenile offenders who had authoritative parents were more psychosocially mature and academically competent than those who had neglectful parents (Steinberg, Blatt-Eisengart, & Cauffman, 2006). The juvenile offenders whose parents were authoritarian or indulgent tended to score between the extremes of those whose parents were authoritative and neglectful, although those with authoritarian parents consistently functioned better than those with indulgent parents. Most of these youth came from poor, ethnic minority backgrounds.

Other research with ethnic groups suggests that some aspects of the authoritarian style may be associated with positive child outcomes (Parke & Buriel, 2006). Elements of the authoritarian style may take on different meanings and have different effects, depending on the context.

For example, Asian American parents often continue aspects of traditional Asian child-rearing practices that have sometimes been described as authoritarian. The parents exert considerable control over their children's lives. However, Ruth Chao (2001, 2005, 2007) argues that the style of parenting used by many Asian American parents is distinct from the domineering control of the authoritarian style. Instead, Chao argues that the control reflects concern and involvement in their children's lives and is best conceptualized as a type of training. The high academic achievement of Asian American children may be a consequence of their "training" parents (Stevenson & Zusho, 2002).

An emphasis on requiring respect and obedience is also associated with the authoritarian style, but in Latino child rearing this focus may be positive rather than punitive. Rather than suppressing the child's development, it may encourage the development of a different type of self. Latino child-rearing practices encourage the

	Accepting, responsive	Rejecting, unresponsive
Demanding, controlling	Authoritative	Authoritarian
Undemanding, uncontrolling	Indulgent	Neglectful

FIGURE 14.2 Classification of Parenting Styles. The four types of parenting styles (authoritative, authoritarian, indulgent, and neglectful) involve the dimensions of acceptance and responsiveness, on the one hand, and demand and control on the other. For example, authoritative parenting involves being both accepting/responsive and demanding/controlling.

neglectful parenting A style in which the parent is very uninvolved in the child's life. It is associated with children's social incompetence, especially a lack of self-control and poor self-esteem.

indulgent parenting A style in which parents are highly involved with their children but place few demands or controls on them. This is associated with children's social incompetence, especially a lack of self-control and a lack of respect for others.

According to Ruth Chao, what type of parenting style do many Asian American parents use?

development of a self and identity that is embedded in the family and requires respect and obedience (Dixon, Graber, & Brooks-Gunn, 2008). Furthermore, many Latino families have several generations living together and helping each other (Zinn & Wells, 2000). In these circumstances, emphasizing respect and obedience by children may be part of maintaining a harmonious home and may be important in the formation of the child's identity.

Even physical punishment, another characteristic of the authoritarian style, may have varying effects in different contexts. African American parents are more likely than non-Latino White parents to use physical punishment (Deater-Deckard & Dodge, 1997). However, the use of physical punishment has been linked with increased externalized child problems (such as acting out and high levels of aggression) in non-Latino White families but not in African American families. One explanation of this finding points to the need for African American parents to enforce rules in the dangerous environments in which they are more likely to live (Harrison-Hale, McLoyd, & Smedley, 2004). In this context, requiring obedience to parental authority may be an adaptive strategy to keep children from engaging in antisocial behavior that can have serious consequences for the victim or the perpetrator. As we see next, though, overall, the use of physical punishment in disciplining children raises many concerns.

Punishment   For centuries, corporal (physical) punishment, such as spanking, has been considered a necessary and even desirable method of disciplining children. Use of corporal punishment is legal in every state in America. A recent national survey of U.S. parents with 3- and 4-year-old children found that 26 percent of parents reported spanking their children frequently, and 67 percent of the parents reported yelling at their children frequently (Regaldo & others, 2004). A cross-cultural comparison found that individuals in South Korea and the United States were among those with the most favorable attitudes toward corporal punishment and were the most likely to remember it being used by their parents (Curran & others, 2001) (see Figure 14.3).

Despite the widespread use of corporal punishment, there have been surprisingly few research studies on physical punishment, and those that have been conducted are correlational (Baumrind, Larzelere, & Cowan, 2002; Kazdin & Benjet, 2003). Clearly, it would be highly unethical to randomly assign parents to either spank or not spank their children in an experimental study. Recall that cause and effect cannot be determined in a correlational study. In one correlational study, spanking by parents was linked with children's antisocial behavior, including cheating, telling lies, being mean to others, bullying, getting into fights, and being disobedient (Strauss, Sugarman, & Giles-Sims, 1997).

A research review concluded that corporal punishment by parents is associated with higher levels of immediate compliance and aggression by the children (Gershoff, 2002). The review also found that corporal punishment is associated with lower levels of moral internalization and mental health (Gershoff, 2002). A longitudinal study found that spanking before age 2 was related to behavioral problems in middle and late childhood (Slade & Wissow, 2004). A recent study found a link between the use of physical punishment by parents and children's negative behavioral adjustment at 36 months and in the first grade (Mulvaney & Mebert, 2007). Another recent study revealed that a history of harsh physical discipline was linked to adolescent depression and externalized problems, such as juvenile delinquency (Bender & others, 2007). Some critics, though, argue that the research evidence is not yet sound enough to warrant a blanket injunction against corporal punishment, especially mild corporal punishment (Baumrind, Larzelere, & Cowan, 2002; Kazdin & Benjet, 2003).

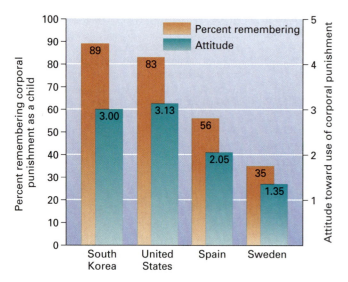

FIGURE 14.3 Corporal Punishment in Different Countries. A 5-point scale was used to assess attitudes toward corporal punishment with scores closer to 1 indicating an attitude against its use and scores closer to 5 suggesting an attitude favoring its use. *Why are studies of corporal punishment correlational studies, and how does that affect their interpretation?*

What are some reasons for avoiding spanking or similar punishments? The reasons include the following:

- When adults punish a child by yelling, screaming, or spanking, they are presenting children with out-of-control models for handling stressful situations. Children may imitate this aggressive, out-of-control behavior (Sim & Ong, 2005).

- Punishment can instill fear, rage, or avoidance. For example, spanking the child may cause the child to avoid being around the parent and to fear the parent.

- Punishment tells children what not to do rather than what to do. Children should be given feedback, such as "Why don't you try this?"

- Punishment can be abusive. Parents might unintentionally become so aroused when they are punishing the child that they become abusive (Ateah, 2005).

Because of reasons such as these, Sweden passed a law in 1979 forbidding parents to physically punish (spank or slap, for example) children. Since the law was enacted, youth rates of delinquency, alcohol abuse, rape, and suicide have dropped in Sweden (Durrant, 2000). These improvements may have occurred for other reasons, such as changing attitudes and opportunities for youth. Nonetheless, the Swedish experience suggests that physical punishment of children may be unnecessary (Durrant, 2008). Many other countries also have passed antispanking laws (Gracia & Herrero, 2008).

Most child psychologists recommend handling misbehavior by reasoning with the child, especially explaining the consequences of the child's actions for others. *Time out,* in which the child is removed from a setting that offers positive reinforcement, can also be effective. For example, when the child has misbehaved, a parent might take away TV viewing for a specified time.

Earlier in this chapter, we described the family as a system and discussed possible links between marital relationships and parenting practices (Cox & others, 2004). To read about a recent family systems study involving marital conflict and the use of physical punishment, see the *Research in Child Development* interlude.

How do most child psychologists recommend handling a child's misbehavior?

Research in Child Development

MARITAL CONFLICT, INDIVIDUAL HOSTILITY, AND THE USE OF PHYSICAL PUNISHMENT

A longitudinal study assessed couples across the transition to parenting to investigate possible links between marital conflict, individual adult hostility, and the use of physical punishment with young children (Kanoy & others, 2003). Before the birth of the first child, the level of marital conflict was observed in a marital problem-solving discussion; answers to questionnaires regarding individual characteristics were also obtained. Thus, these characteristics of the couples were not influenced by characteristics of the child. When the children were 2 and 5 years old, the couples were interviewed about the frequency and intensity of their physical punishment of the children. At both ages, the parents' level of marital conflict was again observed in a marital problem-solving discussion.

The researchers found that both hostility and marital conflict were linked with the use of physical punishment. Individuals with high rates of hostility on the prenatal measures used more frequent and more severe physical punishment with their children. The same was evident for marital conflict—when marital conflict was high, both mothers and fathers were more likely to use physical punishment in disciplining their young children.

What characterizes coparenting?

If parents who have a greater likelihood of using physical punishment can be identified in prenatal classes, these families could be encouraged to use other forms of discipline before they get into a pattern of physically punishing their children.

Coparenting   The relationship between marital conflict and the use of punishment highlights the importance of **coparenting**, which is the support that parents provide one another in jointly raising a child. Poor coordination between parents, undermining of the other parent, lack of cooperation and warmth, and disconnection by one parent are conditions that place children at risk for problems (Feinberg & Kan, 2008; McHale & Sullivan, 2008). For example, a recent study revealed that coparenting influenced young children's effortful control above and beyond maternal and paternal parenting by themselves (Karreman & others, 2008).

Parents who do not spend enough time with their children or who have problems in child rearing can benefit from counseling and therapy. To read about the work of marriage and family counselor Darla Botkin, see the *Careers in Child Development* interlude.

Careers in Child Development

Darla Botkin, Marriage and Family Therapist

Darla Botkin is a marriage and family therapist who teaches, conducts research, and engages in marriage and family therapy. She is on the faculty of the University of Kentucky. Botkin obtained a bachelor's degree in elementary education with a concentration in special education and then went on to receive a master's degree in early childhood education. She spent the next six years working with children and their families in a variety of settings, including child care, elementary school, and Head Start. These experiences led Botkin to recognize the interdependence of the developmental settings that children and their parents experience (such as home, school, and work). She returned to graduate school and obtained a Ph.D. in family studies from the University of Tennessee. She then became a faculty member in the Family Studies program at the University of Kentucky. Completing further coursework and clinical training in marriage and family therapy, she became certified as a marriage and family therapist.

Botkin's current interests include working with young children in family therapy, gender and ethnic issues in family therapy, and the role of spirituality in family wellness.

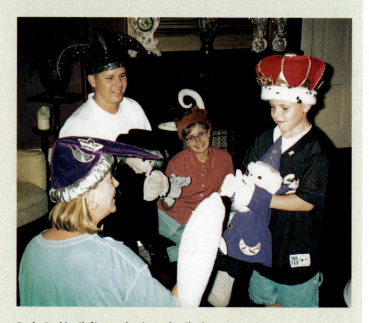

Darla Botkin (*left*), conducting a family therapy session.

coparenting The amount of support parents provide for each other in jointly raising children.

Child Maltreatment   Unfortunately, punishment sometimes leads to the abuse of infants and children (Newton & Vandeven, 2008; Oates, 2009; Stanley & Appleton, 2008; Toth & Cicchetti, 2009). In 2002, approximately 896,000 U.S. children were found to be victims of child abuse (U.S. Department of Health and Human Services, 2003). Eighty-four percent of these children were abused by a parent or parents. Laws in many states now require doctors and teachers to report suspected cases of child abuse, yet many cases go unreported, especially those of battered infants.

Whereas the public and many professionals use the term *child abuse* to refer to both abuse and neglect, developmentalists increasingly use the term *child maltreatment* (Cicchetti & Toth, 2006; Toth & Cicchetti, 2009). This term does not have quite the emotional impact of the term *abuse* and acknowledges that maltreatment includes diverse conditions.

Types of Child Maltreatment   The four main types of child maltreatment are physical abuse, child neglect, sexual abuse, and emotional abuse (National Clearinghouse on Child Abuse and Neglect, 2004):

- *Physical abuse* is characterized by the infliction of physical injury as result of punching, beating, kicking, biting, burning, shaking, or otherwise harming a child. The parent or other person may not have intended to hurt the child; the injury may have resulted from excessive physical punishment (Hornor, 2005).

- *Child neglect* is characterized by failure to provide for the child's basic needs (Sedlak & others, 2006). Neglect can be physical (abandonment, for example), educational (allowing chronic truancy, for example), or emotional (marked inattention to the child's needs, for example). Child neglect is by far the most common form of child maltreatment. In every country where relevant data have been collected, neglect occurs up to three times as often as abuse (Benoit, Coolbear, & Crawford, 2008).

- *Sexual abuse* includes fondling a child's genitals, intercourse, incest, rape, sodomy, exhibitionism, and commercial exploitation through prostitution or the production of pornographic materials (Fitzgerald & others, 2008; Johnson, 2008).

- *Emotional abuse (psychological/verbal abuse/mental injury)* includes acts or omissions by parents or other caregivers that have caused, or could cause, serious behavioral, cognitive, or emotional problems (Gelles & Cavanaugh, 2005).

Although any of these forms of child maltreatment may be found separately, they often occur in combination. Emotional abuse is almost always present when other forms are identified.

The Context of Abuse   No single factor causes child maltreatment (Cicchetti & Toth, 2006; Cicchetti & others, 2008; Toth & Cicchetti, 2009). A combination of factors, including the culture, family, and development, likely contribute to child maltreatment.

The extensive violence that takes place in American culture is reflected in the occurrence of violence in the family (Freisthler, Merritt, & LaScala, 2006; Kitzmann, 2009). A regular diet of violence appears on television screens, and parents often resort to power assertion as a disciplinary technique. In China, where physical punishment is rarely used to discipline children, the incidence of child abuse is reported to be very low.

The family itself is obviously a key part of the context of abuse (MacMillan, 2009). The interactions of all family members need to be considered, regardless of who performs the violent acts against the child (Kim & Cicchetti, 2004). For example, even though the father may be the one who physically abuses the child, contributions by the mother, the child, and siblings also should be evaluated.

Were parents who abuse children abused by their own parents? About one-third of parents who were abused themselves when they were young abuse their own children (Cicchetti & Toth, 2005, 2006; Cicchetti & others, 2008; Toth & Cicchetti, 2009). Thus, some, but not a majority, of parents are locked into an intergenerational transmission of abuse (Dixon, Browne, & Hamilton-Giachritsis, 2005). Mothers who break out of the intergenerational transmission of abuse often have at least one warm, caring adult in their background; have a close, positive marital relationship; and have received therapy (Egeland, Jacobvitz, & Sroufe, 1988).

Developmental Consequences of Abuse   Among the developmental consequences of child maltreatment are poor emotion regulation, attachment problems, problems in

> *C*hild maltreatment involves grossly inadequate and destructive aspects of parenting.
>
> —**Dante Cicchetti**
> *Contemporary Developmental Psychologist, University of Minnesota*

This print ad was created by Prevent Child Abuse America to make people aware of its national blue wristband campaign. The campaign's goal is to educate people about child abuse prevention and encourage them to support the organization. *Source: Prevent Child Abuse America*

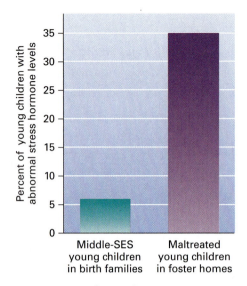

FIGURE 14.4 Abnormal Stress Hormone Levels in Young Children in Different Types of Rearing Conditions

What are strategies that parents can use to guide adolescents in effectively handling their increased motivation for autonomy?

peer relations, difficulty in adapting to school, and other psychological problems (Cicchetti & Toth, 2006; Cicchetti & others, 2008; Pollack, 2009; Toth & Cicchetti, 2009).

Among the consequences of child maltreatment in childhood and adolescence are poor emotion regulation, attachment problems, problems in peer relations, difficulty in adapting to school, and other psychological problems such as depression and delinquency (Cicchetti & Toth, 2006; Cicchetti & others, 2008; Toth & Cicchetti, 2009). As shown in Figure 14.4, maltreated young children in foster care were more likely to show abnormal stress hormone levels than middle-SES young children living with their birth family (Gunnar, Fisher, & the Early Experience, Stress, and Prevention Network, 2006). In this study, the abnormal stress hormone levels were mainly present in the foster children who were neglected, best described as "institutional neglect" (Fisher, 2005). Abuse also may have this effect on young children (Gunnar, Fisher, & the Early Experience, Stress, and Prevention Network, 2006). Later, during the adult years, individuals who were maltreated as children often have difficulty in establishing and maintaining healthy intimate relationships (Minzenberg, Poole, & Vinogradov, 2006). As adolescents and adults, maltreated children are also at higher risk for violent behavior toward others—especially dating partners and marital partners—as well as for substance abuse, anxiety, and depression (Maas, Herrenkohl, & Sousa, 2008; Stewart, Livingston, & Dennison, 2008). In sum, maltreated children are at risk for developing a wide range of problems and disorders (Haugaard & Hazen, 2004).

An important strategy is to prevent child maltreatment (Cicchetti & Toth, 2006; Lyons, Henly, & Schuerman, 2005). In one study of maltreating mothers and their 1-year-olds, two treatments were effective in reducing child maltreatment: (1) home visitation that emphasized improved parenting, coping with stress, and increasing support for the mother; and (2) parent-infant psychotherapy that focused on improving maternal-infant attachment (Cicchetti, Toth, and Rogosch, 2005).

Parent-Adolescent Relationships

Even the best parents may find their relationship with their child strained during adolescence. Important aspects of parent-adolescent relationships include autonomy/attachment and conflict.

Autonomy and Attachment The adolescent's push for autonomy and responsibility puzzles and angers many parents. Parents see their teenager slipping from their grasp. They may have an urge to take stronger control as the adolescent seeks autonomy and responsibility. Heated emotional exchanges may ensue, with either side calling names, making threats, and doing whatever seems necessary to gain control. Most parents anticipate that their teenager will have some difficulty adjusting to the changes that adolescence brings, but few parents can imagine and predict just how strong an adolescent's desires will be to spend time with peers or how much adolescents will want to show that it is they—not their parents—who are responsible for their successes and failures.

The ability to attain autonomy and gain control over one's behavior in adolescence is acquired through appropriate adult reactions to the adolescent's desire for control. At the onset of adolescence, the average individual does not have the knowledge to make mature decisions in all areas of life. As the adolescent pushes for autonomy, the wise adult relinquishes control in those areas in which the adolescent can make reasonable decisions but continues to guide the adolescent to make reasonable decisions in areas in which the adolescent's knowledge is more limited. Gradually, adolescents acquire the ability to make mature decisions on their own (Collins & Steinberg, 2006; Harold, Colarossi, & Mercier, 2007).

Gender differences characterize autonomy-granting in adolescence, with boys being given more independence than girls are. In one study, this was especially true in those U.S. families with a traditional gender-role orientation (Bumpus, Crouter, & McHale, 2001).

Cultural differences also characterize adolescent autonomy (Rothbaum & Trommsdorff, 2007). In one study, U.S. adolescents sought autonomy earlier than Japanese adolescents (Rothbaum & others, 2000). In the transition to adulthood, Japanese youth are less likely to live outside the home than Americans are (Hendry, 1999).

Even while adolescents seek autonomy, parent-child attachment remains important. Researchers have linked adolescents' secure attachment to their parents with the adolescents' well-being (Furman, 2007; Zimmerman, 2007). For example, Joseph Allen and his colleagues (Allen, 2007, 2008; Allen & others, 2003) have found that securely attached adolescents are less likely than those who were insecurely attached to engage in problem behaviors, such as juvenile delinquency and drug abuse. In other research, securely attached adolescents had better peer relations than their insecurely attached counterparts (Laible, Carlo, & Raffaeli, 2000). A recent study also revealed that securely attached adolescents in the senior year of high school had a greater capacity for romantic intimacy four years later (Mayseless & Scharf, 2007).

Conflict with parents increases in early adolescence. *What is the nature of this conflict in a majority of American families?*

Parent-Adolescent Conflict   Although attachment to parents may remain strong during adolescence, the connectedness is not always smooth (Crean, 2008; Eisenberg & others, 2008; Harold, Colarossi, & Mercier, 2007). Early adolescence is a time when conflict with parents escalates (Collins & Steinberg, 2006; Smetana, 2008; Smetana, Campione-Barr, & Metzger, 2006). Much of the conflict involves the everyday events of family life, such as keeping a bedroom clean, dressing neatly, getting home by a certain time, and large cell-phone bills. The conflicts rarely involve major dilemmas, such as drugs and delinquency.

The increased conflict in early adolescence may be due to a number of factors: the biological changes of puberty, cognitive changes involving increased idealism and logical reasoning, social changes focused on independence and identity, maturational changes in parents, and expectations that are violated by parents and adolescents (Collins & Steinberg, 2006). Adolescents compare their parents with an ideal standard and then criticize their flaws. Many parents see their adolescent changing from a compliant child to someone who is noncompliant, oppositional, and resistant to parental standards. Also, early-maturing adolescents experience more conflict with their parents than adolescents who mature late or on time (Collins & Steinberg, 2006).

It is not unusual to hear parents of young adolescents ask, "Is it ever going to get better?" Things usually do get better as adolescents move from early to late adolescence. Conflict with parents often escalates during early adolescence, remains somewhat stable during the high school years, and then lessens as the adolescent reaches 17 to 20 years of age. Parent-adolescent relationships become more positive if adolescents go away to college than if they stay at home and go to college (Sullivan & Sullivan, 1980).

The everyday conflicts that characterize parent-adolescent relationships may serve a positive function. These minor disputes and negotiations facilitate the adolescent's transition from being dependent on parents to becoming an autonomous individual. For example, in one study, adolescents who expressed disagreement with their parents explored identity development more actively than did adolescents who did not express disagreement with their parents (Cooper & others, 1982). One way for parents to cope with the adolescent's push for independence and identity is to recognize that adolescence is a 10- to 15-year transitional period in the journey to adulthood, rather than an overnight accomplishment. Recognizing that conflict and negotiation can serve a positive developmental function can tone down parental

Old Model	New Model
Autonomy, detachment from parents; parent and peer worlds are isolated	Attachment and autonomy; parents are important support systems and attachment figures; adolescent-parent and adolescent-peer worlds have some important connections
Intense, stressful conflict throughout adolescence; parent-adolescent relationships are filled with storm and stress on virtually a daily basis	Moderate parent-adolescent conflict common and can serve a positive developmental function; conflict greater in early adolescence, especially during the apex of puberty

FIGURE 14.5 Old and New Models of Parent-Adolescent Relationships

hostility too. Understanding parent-adolescent conflict, though, is not simple (Riesch & others, 2003).

In sum, the old model of parent-adolescent relationships suggested that parent-adolescent conflict is intense and stressful throughout adolescence. The new model emphasizes that most parent-adolescent conflict is moderate rather than intense and that the moderate conflict can serve a positive function. Figure 14.5 summarizes the old and new models of parent-adolescent relationships, which include changes in thinking about attachment and autonomy.

Still, a high degree of conflict characterizes some parent-adolescent relationships. According to one estimate, parents and adolescents engage in prolonged, intense, repeated, unhealthy conflict in about one in five families (Montemayor, 1982). In other words, 4 to 5 million American families encounter serious, highly stressful parent-adolescent conflict. And this prolonged, intense conflict is associated with a number of adolescent problems—movement out of the home, juvenile delinquency, school dropout, pregnancy and early marriage, membership in religious cults, and drug abuse (Brook & others, 1990).

Some cultures are marked by less parent-adolescent conflict than others. American psychologist Reed Larson (1999) studied middle-socioeconomic-status adolescents and their families in India. He observed that in India there seems to be little parent-adolescent conflict and that many families likely would be described as "authoritarian" in Baumrind's categorization. Larson also observed that in India adolescents do not go through a process of breaking away from their parents and that parents choose their youths' marital partners. Researchers have also found considerably less conflict between parents and adolescents in Japan than in the United States (Rothbaum & others, 2000).

Conclusions We have seen that parents play very important roles in adolescent development. Although adolescents are moving toward independence, they still need to stay connected with families (Collins & Steinberg, 2006). In the National Longitudinal Study on Adolescent Health (Council of Economic Advisors, 2000) of more than 12,000 adolescents, those who did not eat dinner with a parent five or more days a week had dramatically higher rates of smoking, drinking, marijuana use, getting into fights, and initiation of sexual activity. In another study, parents who played an active role in monitoring and guiding their adolescents' development were more likely to have adolescents

Stacey Christensen, age 16: "I am lucky enough to have open communication with my parents. Whenever I am in need or just need to talk, my parents are there for me. My advice to parents is to let your teens grow at their own pace, be open with them so that you can be there for them. We need guidance; our parents need to help but not be too overwhelming."

with positive peer relations and lower drug use than parents who had a less active role (Mounts, 2002).

Competent adolescent development is most likely when adolescents have parents who (Small, 1990) show them warmth and mutual respect; demonstrate sustained interest in their lives; recognize and adapt to their cognitive and socioemotional development; communicate expectations for high standards of conduct and achievement; and display constructive ways of dealing with problems and conflict. These ideas coincide with Diana Baumrind's (1971, 1991) authoritative parenting style.

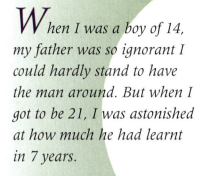

When I was a boy of 14, my father was so ignorant I could hardly stand to have the man around. But when I got to be 21, I was astonished at how much he had learnt in 7 years.

—MARK TWAIN
American Writer and Humorist, 19th Century

Review and Reflect: Learning Goal 2

2 Explain How Parenting Is Linked to Children's and Adolescents' Development

REVIEW
- What adaptations do parents need to make to developmental changes in their children?
- How can parents be effective managers of children's lives?
- What are the main parenting styles and variations in discipline?
- What are some important aspects of parenting adolescents?

REFLECT
- What was the nature of your relationship with your parents during middle school and high school? Has your relationship with your parents changed since then? Does it involve less conflict? What do you think are the most important characteristics of a competent parent of adolescents?

3 SIBLINGS

Sibling Relationships   Birth Order

What are sibling relationships like? How extensively does birth order influence behavior?

Sibling Relationships

Approximately 80 percent of American children have one or more siblings—that is, sisters and brothers (Dunn, 2007). Any of you who have grown up with siblings probably have a rich memory of aggressive, hostile interchanges. Siblings in the presence of each other when they are 2 to 4 years of age, on average, have a conflict once every 10 minutes and then the conflicts go down somewhat from 5 to 7 years of age (Kramer, 2006). One recent study revealed that an increase in sibling conflict was linked to an increase in children's depressive symptoms, whereas an increase in sibling intimacy was related to an increase in children's peer competence (Kim & others, 2007).

What are some characteristics of sibling relationships?

What do parents do when they encounter siblings having a verbal or physical confrontation? One study revealed that they do one of three things: (1) intervene and try to help them resolve the conflict, (2) admonish or threaten them, or (3) do nothing at all (Kramer & Perozynski, 1999). Of interest is that in families with two siblings 2 to 5 years of age, the most frequent parental reaction is to do nothing at all.

Laurie Kramer (2006), who had conducted a number of research studies on siblings, says that not intervening and letting sibling conflict escalate is not a good strategy. She developed a program titled "More Fun with Sisters and Brothers" that teaches 4- to 8-year-old siblings social skills for developing positive interactions (Kramer & Radey, 1997). Among the social skills taught in the program are how to appropriately initiate play, how to accept and refuse invitations to play, perspective taking, how to deal with angry feelings, and how to manage conflict. A recent study of 5- to 10-year-old siblings and their parents found that training parents to mediate sibling disputes increased children's understanding of conflicts and reduced sibling conflict (Smith & Ross, 2007).

However, conflict is only one of the many dimensions of sibling relations (Howe & Recchia, 2009). Sibling relations include helping, sharing, teaching, fighting, and playing, and siblings can act as emotional supports, rivals, and communication partners (Pomery & others, 2006).

Judy Dunn (2007), a leading expert on sibling relationships, recently described three important characteristics of sibling relationships:

- *Emotional quality of the relationship.* Both intensive positive and negative emotions are often expressed by siblings toward each other. Many children and adolescents have mixed feelings toward their siblings.

- *Familiarity and intimacy of the relationship.* Siblings typically know each other very well, and this intimacy suggests that they can either provide support or tease and undermine each other, depending on the situation.

- *Variation in sibling relationships.* Some siblings describe their relationships more positively than others. Thus, there is considerable variation in sibling relationships. We previously indicated that many siblings have mixed feelings about each other, but some children and adolescents mainly describe their sibling in warm, affectionate ways, whereas others primarily talk about how irritating and mean a sibling is.

Birth Order

Whether a child has older or younger siblings has been linked to development of certain personality characteristics. For example, a recent review concluded that "firstborns are the most intelligent, achieving, and conscientious, while later-borns are the most rebellious, liberal, and agreeable" (Paulhus, 2008, p. 210). Compared with later-born children, firstborn children have also been described as more adult oriented, helpful, conforming, and self-controlled. However, when such birth order differences are reported, they often are small.

What accounts for such differences related to birth order? Proposed explanations usually point to variations in interactions with parents and siblings associated with being in a particular position in the family. This is especially true in the case of the firstborn child (Teti, 2001). The oldest child is the only one who does not have to share parental love and affection with other siblings—until another sibling comes along. An infant requires more attention than an older child; this means that the firstborn sibling receives less attention after the newborn arrives. Does this result in conflict between parents and the firstborn? In one research study, mothers became more negative, coercive, and restraining and played less with the firstborn following the birth of a second child (Dunn & Kendrick, 1982).

What is the only child like? The popular conception is that the only child is a "spoiled brat," with such undesirable characteristics as dependency, lack of self-control, and self-centered behavior. But researchers present a more positive portrayal of the only child. Only children often are achievement oriented and display a desirable personality, especially in comparison with later-borns and children from large families (Falbo & Poston, 1993; Jiao, Ji, & Jing, 1996).

So far, our discussion suggests that birth order might be a strong predictor of behavior. However, an increasing number of family researchers stress that when all of the factors that influence behavior are considered, birth order itself shows limited ability to predict behavior.

Think about some of the other important factors in children's lives that influence their behavior beyond birth order. They include heredity, models of competency or incompetency that parents present to children on a daily basis, peer influences, school influences, socioeconomic factors, sociohistorical factors, and cultural variations. When someone says firstborns are always like this but last-borns are always like that, the person is making overly simplistic statements that do not adequately take into account the complexity of influences on a child's development.

The one-child family is becoming much more common in China because of the strong motivation to limit the population growth in the People's Republic of China. The effects of this policy have not been fully examined. *In general, what have researchers found the only child to be like?*

Review and Reflect: Learning Goal 3

3 Identify How Siblings Influence Children's Development

REVIEW

- How can sibling relationships be characterized?
- What role does birth order play in children's development?

REFLECT

- If you grew up with a sibling, you likely showed some jealousy of your sibling and vice versa. What can parents do to help children reduce their jealousy toward a sibling?

4 THE CHANGING FAMILY IN A CHANGING SOCIAL WORLD

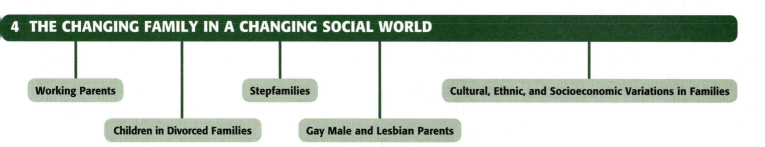

Working Parents — Stepfamilies — Cultural, Ethnic, and Socioeconomic Variations in Families

Children in Divorced Families — Gay Male and Lesbian Parents

U.S. children are growing up in a greater variety of family contexts than ever before. As we discussed in Chapter 10, "Emotional Development," U.S. children are experiencing many sorts of caregiving—not only from stay-at-home mothers but also from stay-at-home fathers, from different types of child-care programs, and from after-school programs. The structure of American families also varies. As shown in Figure 14.6, the United States has a higher percentage of single-parent

FIGURE 14.6 Single-Parent Families in Different Countries

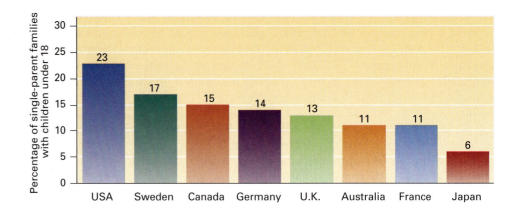

families than other countries with similar levels of economic and technological development. And many U.S. children are being raised in stepfamilies formed after a divorce and by gay male or lesbian parents. How are these and other variations in family life affecting children?

Working Parents

The increased number of mothers in the labor force represents one source of change in U.S. families and U.S. society (Burchinal & Clarke-Stewart, 2007; Heidi, 2006). Many mothers spend the greatest part of their day away from their children, even their infants. More than one of every two mothers with a child under the age of 5 is in the labor force; more than two of every three with a child from 6 to 17 years of age is. How have these changes influenced children's development?

Recall that in Bronfenbrenner's ecological theory, the exosystem is an environmental system where experiences in another social context—in which the individual does not have an active role—influence what the individual experiences in an immediate social context. The link between the social context of parents' work and the social context of the family illustrates the concept of exosystem.

Work can produce positive and negative effects on parenting (Crouter & McHale, 2005). Recent research indicates that what matters for children's development is the nature of parents' work rather than whether one or both parents works outside the home (Clarke-Stewart, 2006). Ann Crouter (2006) recently described how parents bring their experiences at work into their homes. She concluded that parents who have poor working conditions, such as long hours, overtime work, stressful work, and lack of autonomy at work, are likely to be more irritable at home and engage in less effective parenting than their counterparts who have better work conditions in their jobs. A consistent finding is the children (especially girls) of working mothers engage in less gender stereotyping and have more egalitarian views of gender (Goldberg & Lucas-Thompson, 2008).

Many children of working parents participate in out-of-school care (before- and after-school programs, extracurricular activities, father care, and nonadult care—usually an older sibling). These settings were examined in one study to determine their possible link with children's academic achievement toward the end of the first grade (NICHD Early Child Care Research Network, 2004). "Children who consistently participated in extracurricular activities during kindergarten and first grade obtained higher standardized math test scores than children who did not consistently participate in these activities. Participation in other types of out-of-school care was not related to child functioning in the first grade" (p. 280). Parents who enroll their children in extracurricular activities may be more achievement oriented and have higher achievement expectations for their children than parents who don't place their children in these activities.

A recent research review found a positive link between participation of 5- to 18-year-olds in organized activities and a number of indicators of positive development, including academic achievement, psychological adjustment, and positive interaction with parents (Mahoney, Harris, & Eccles, 2006). Some critics argue that too many parents overschedule their children and youth. However, in the research review just described, even when youth participated 20 hours a week or more in organized activities, their psychological adjustment was better than youth who did not participate in organized activities.

Children in Divorced Families

Divorce rates changed rather dramatically in the United States and many countries around the world in the late twentieth century (Amato & Irving, 2006). The U.S. divorce rate increased dramatically in the 1960s and 1970s but has declined since the 1980s. However, the divorce rate in the United States is still much higher than in most other countries.

It is estimated that 40 percent of children born to married parents in the United States will experience their parents' divorce (Hetherington & Stanley-Hagan, 2002). Let's examine some important questions about children in divorced families:

- *Are children better adjusted in intact, never-divorced families than in divorced families?* Most researchers agree that children from divorced families show poorer adjustment than their counterparts in nondivorced families (Clarke-Stewart & Brentano, 2006; Hetherington, 2005, 2006; Kelly, 2007; Wallerstein, 2008) (see Figure 14.7). Those who have experienced multiple divorces are at greater risk. Children in divorced families are more likely than children in nondivorced families to have academic problems, to show externalized problems (such as acting out and delinquency) and internalized problems (such as anxiety and depression), to be less socially responsible, to have less competent intimate relationships, to drop out of school, to become sexually active at an early age, to take drugs, to associate with antisocial peers, to have low self-esteem, and to be less securely attached as young adults (Conger & Chao, 1996). A recent study revealed that adolescent girls with divorced parents were especially vulnerable to developing depressive symptoms (Oldehinkel & others, 2008). Another study found that experiencing a divorce in childhood was associated with insecure attachment in early adulthood (Brockmeyer, Treboux, & Crowell, 2005). Yet another study revealed that when individuals experienced the divorce of their parents in childhood and adolescence, it was linked to having unstable romantic and marital relationships and low levels of education in adulthood (Amato, 2006). Nonetheless, keep in mind that a majority of children (75 percent) in divorced families do not have significant adjustment problems (Barber & Demo, 2006).

- *Should parents stay together for the sake of the children?* Whether parents should stay in an unhappy or conflicted marriage for the sake of their children is one of the most commonly asked questions about divorce (Hetherington, 2005, 2006). If the stresses and disruptions in family relationships associated with an unhappy, conflictual marriage that erode the well-being of children are reduced by the move to a divorced, single-parent family, divorce can be advantageous. However, if the diminished resources and increased risks associated with divorce also are accompanied by inept parenting and sustained or increased conflict, not only between the divorced

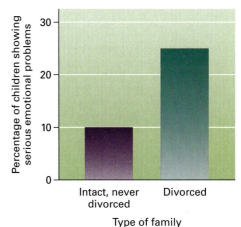

FIGURE 14.7 Divorce and Children's Emotional Problems. In Hetherington's research, 25 percent of children from divorced families showed serious emotional problems compared with only 10 percent of children from intact, never-divorced families. However, keep in mind that a substantial majority (75 percent) of the children from divorced families did not show serious emotional problems.

What concerns are involved in whether parents should stay together for the sake of the children or become divorced?

couple but also among the parents, children, and siblings, the best choice for the children would be for an unhappy marriage to be retained (Hetherington & Stanley-Hagan, 2002). It is difficult to determine how these "ifs" will play out when parents either remain together in an acrimonious marriage or become divorced.

Note that marital conflict may have negative consequences for children in the context of marriage or divorce (McDonald & Grych, 2006). A longitudinal study revealed that conflict in nondivorced families was associated with emotional problems in children (Amato, 2006). Indeed, many of the problems children from divorced homes experience begin during the predivorce period, a time when parents are often in active conflict with each other. Thus, when children from divorced homes show problems, the problems may not be due only to the divorce, but also to the marital conflict that led to it (Thompson, 2008).

- *How much do family processes matter in divorced families?* Family processes matter a great deal (Clarke-Stewart & Brentano, 2006; Walper & Beckh, 2006). When divorced parents' relationship with each other is harmonious, and when they use authoritative parenting, the adjustment of children improves (Hetherington, 2005, 2006). A number of researchers have shown that a disequilibrium, which includes diminished parenting skills, occurs in the year following the divorce—but by two years after the divorce, restabilization has occurred and parenting skills have improved (Hetherington, 1989).

- *What factors influence an individual child's vulnerability to suffering negative consequences as a result of living in a divorced family?* Among the factors involved in the child's risk and vulnerability are the child's adjustment prior to the divorce, as well as the child's personality and temperament, gender, and custody situation (Hetherington, 2005, 2006). Children whose parents later divorce show poorer adjustment before the breakup (Amato & Booth, 1996). Children who are socially mature and responsible, who show few behavioral problems, and who have an easy temperament are better able to cope with their parents' divorce. Children with a difficult temperament often have problems in coping with their parents' divorce (Hetherington, 2005).

  Earlier studies reported gender differences in response to divorce, with divorce being more negative for girls than boys in mother-custody families. However, more recent studies have shown that gender differences are less pronounced and consistent than was previously believed. Some of the inconsistency may be due to the increase in father custody, joint custody, and increased involvement of noncustodial fathers, especially in their sons' lives (Palmer, 2004). One analysis of studies found that children in joint-custody families were better adjusted than children in sole-custody families (Bauserman, 2002). Some studies have shown that boys adjust better in father-custody families, girls in mother-custody families, whereas other studies have not (Maccoby & Mnookin, 1992; Santrock & Warshak, 1979).

- *What role does socioeconomic status play in the lives of children in divorced families?* Custodial mothers experience the loss of about one-fourth to one-half of their predivorce income, in comparison with a loss of only one-tenth by custodial fathers (Emery, 1994). This income loss for divorced mothers is accompanied by increased workloads, high rates of job instability, and residential moves to less desirable neighborhoods with inferior schools (Sayer, 2006).

In sum, many factors are involved in determining how divorce influences a child's development (Clarke-Stewart & Brentano, 2006; Hetherington, 2006). To read about some strategies for helping children cope with the divorce of their parents, see the *Caring for Children* interlude.

Caring for Children

COMMUNICATING WITH CHILDREN ABOUT DIVORCE

Ellen Galinsky and Judy David (1988) developed a number of guidelines for communicating with children about divorce.

Explain the Separation

As soon as daily activities in the home make it obvious that one parent is leaving, tell the children. If possible, both parents should be present when children are told about the separation to come. The reasons for the separation are very difficult for young children to understand. No matter what parents tell children, children can find reasons to argue against the separation. It is extremely important for parents to tell the children who will take care of them and to describe the specific arrangements for seeing the other parent.

Explain That the Separation Is Not the Child's Fault

Young children often believe their parents' separation or divorce is their own fault. Therefore, it is important to tell children that they are not the cause of the separation. Parents need to repeat this a number of times.

Explain That It May Take Time to Feel Better

Tell young children that it's normal to not feel good about what is happening and that many other children feel this way when their parents become separated. It is also okay for divorced parents to share some of their emotions with children, by saying something like "I'm having a hard time since the separation just like you, but I know it's going to get better after a while." Such statements are best kept brief and should not criticize the other parent.

Keep the Door Open for Further Discussion

Tell your children to come to you anytime they want to talk about the separation. It is healthy for children to express their pent-up emotions in discussions with their parents and to learn that the parents are willing to listen to their feelings and fears.

Provide as Much Continuity as Possible

The less children's worlds are disrupted by the separation, the easier their transition to a single-parent family will be. This means maintaining the rules already in place as much as possible. Children need parents who care enough to not only give them warmth and nurturance but also set reasonable limits.

Provide Support for Your Children and Yourself

After a divorce or separation, parents are as important to children as before the divorce or separation. Divorced parents need to provide children with as much support as possible. Parents function best when other people are available to give them support as adults and as parents. Divorced parents can find people who provide practical help and with whom they can talk about their problems.

Stepfamilies

Not only has divorce become commonplace in the United States, so has getting remarried (Hetherington, 2006). It takes time for parents to marry, have children, get divorced, and then remarry. Consequently, there are far more elementary and secondary school children than infant or preschool children living in stepfamilies.

How does living in a stepfamily influence a child's development?

The number of remarriages involving children has grown steadily in recent years. Also, divorces occur at a 10 percent higher rate in remarriages than in first marriages (Cherlin & Furstenberg, 1994). About half of all children whose parents divorce will have a stepparent within four years of the separation.

Remarried parents face some unique tasks. The couple must define and strengthen their marriage and at the same time renegotiate the biological parent-child relationships and establish stepparent-stepchild and stepsibling relationships (Ganong, Coleman, & Hans, 2006). The complex histories and multiple relationships make adjustment difficult in a stepfamily (Goldscheider & Sassler, 2006). Only one-third of stepfamily couples stay remarried.

In some cases, the stepfamily may have been preceded by the death of a spouse. However, by far the largest number of stepfamilies are preceded by divorce rather than death (Pasley & Moorefield, 2004). Three common types of stepfamily structure are (1) stepfather, (2) stepmother, and (3) blended or complex. In stepfather families, the mother typically had custody of the children and remarried, introducing a stepfather into her children's lives. In stepmother families, the father usually had custody and remarried, introducing a stepmother into his children's lives. In a blended or complex stepfamily, both parents bring children from previous marriages to live in the newly formed stepfamily.

In E. Mavis Hetherington's (2006) most recent longitudinal analyses, children and adolescents who had been in a simple stepfamily (stepfather or stepmother) for a number of years were adjusting better than in the early years of the remarried family and were functioning well in comparison to children and adolescents in conflicted nondivorced families and children and adolescents in complex (blended) stepfamilies. More than 75 percent of the adolescents in long-established simple stepfamilies described their relationships with their stepparents as "close" or "very close." Hetherington (2006) concluded that in long-established simple stepfamilies adolescents seem to eventually benefit from the presence of a stepparent and the resources provided by the stepparent.

Children often have better relationships with their custodial parents (mothers in stepfather families, fathers in stepmother families) than with stepparents (Santrock, Sitterle, & Warshak, 1988). Also, children in simple families (stepmother, stepfather) often show better adjustment than their counterparts in complex (blended) families (Anderson & others, 1999; Hetherington & Kelly, 2002).

As in divorced families, children in stepfamilies show more adjustment problems than children in nondivorced families (Hetherington, 2006). The adjustment problems are similar to those found among children of divorced parents—academic problems and lower self-esteem, for example (Anderson & others, 1999). However, it is important to recognize that a majority of children in stepfamilies do not have problems. In one analysis, 25 percent of children from stepfamilies showed adjustment problems compared with 10 percent in intact, never-divorced families (Hetherington & Kelly, 2002).

Adolescence is an especially difficult time for the formation of a stepfamily (Anderson & others, 1999). This may occur because becoming part of a stepfamily exacerbates normal adolescent concerns about identity, sexuality, and autonomy.

Gay Male and Lesbian Parents

Increasingly, gay male and lesbian couples are creating families that include children (Goldberg & Sayer, 2006) (see Figure 14.8). Approximately 33 percent of lesbian couples and 22 percent of gay male couples are parents (Patterson, 2004). There may be more than 1 million gay and lesbian parents in the United States today.

Like heterosexual couples, gay male and lesbian parents vary greatly. They may be single or they may have same-gender partners. Many lesbian mothers and gay

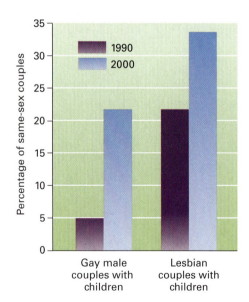

FIGURE 14.8 Percentage of Gay Male and Lesbian Couples with Children: 1990 and 2000. *Why do you think more lesbian couples have children than gay male couples?*

fathers are noncustodial parents because they lost custody of their children to heterosexual spouses after a divorce.

Most children of gay and lesbian parents were born in a heterosexual relationship that ended in a divorce: In most cases, it was probably a relationship in which one or both parents only later identified themselves as gay male or lesbian. In other cases, lesbians and gay men became parents as a result of donor insemination and surrogates, or through adoption.

Parenthood among lesbians and gay men is controversial. Opponents claim that being raised by male or lesbian parents harms the child's development. But researchers have found few differences in children growing up with lesbian mothers or gay fathers and children growing up with heterosexual parents (Patterson, 2004; Patterson & Hastings, 2007). For example, children growing up in gay or lesbian families are just as popular with their peers, and there are no differences in the adjustment and mental health of children living in these families when they are compared with children in heterosexual families (Hyde, 2007). Also, the overwhelming majority of children growing up in a gay or lesbian family have a heterosexual orientation (Tasker & Golombok, 1997).

Cultural, Ethnic, and Socioeconomic Variations in Families

Parenting can be influenced by culture, ethnicity, and socioeconomic status. In Bronfenbrenner's theory (introduced in Chapter 1), these influences are described as part of the macrosystem.

What are the research findings regarding the development and psychological well-being of children raised by gay male and lesbian couples?

Cross-Cultural Studies   Different cultures often give different answers to such basic questions as what the father's role in the family should be, what support systems are available to families, and how children should be disciplined (Shiraev & Levy, 2007). There are important cross-cultural variations in parenting (Kagitcibasi, 2007). In some countries, authoritarian parenting is widespread. For example, in the Arab world, many families today are very authoritarian, dominated by the father's rule, and children are taught strict codes of conduct and family loyalty (Booth, 2002). In one study, Chinese mothers of preschool children reported that they used more physical coercion, more encouragement of modesty, more shaming and love withdrawal, less warmth, and less democratic participation than U.S. mothers of preschool children (Wu & others, 2002).

What type of parenting is most frequent? In one study of parenting behavior in 186 cultures around the world, the most common pattern was a warm and controlling style, one that was neither permissive nor restrictive (Rohner & Rohner, 1981). The investigators commented that the majority of cultures have discovered, over many centuries, that children's healthy social development is most effectively promoted by love and at least some moderate parental control.

Cultural change is coming to families in many countries around the world (Berry, 2007; Bornstein & Cote, 2006). There are trends toward greater family mobility, migration to urban areas, separation as some family members work in cities or countries far from their homes, smaller families, fewer extended-family households, and increases in maternal employment (Brown & Larson, 2002). These trends can change the resources that are available to children. For example, when several generations no longer live close by, children may lose support and guidance from grandparents, aunts, and uncles. Also, smaller families may produce more openness and communication between parents and children.

Ethnicity   Families within different ethnic groups in the United States differ in their typical size, structure, composition, reliance on kinships networks, and levels of income and education (Harwood & Feng, 2006; Hernandez, 2007). Large and

What are some characteristics of families within different ethnic groups?

extended families are more common among minority groups than among the White majority. For example, 19 percent of Latino families have three or more children, compared with 14 percent of African American and 10 percent of White families. African American and Latino children interact more with grandparents, aunts, uncles, cousins, and more-distant relatives than do White children.

Single-parent families are more common among African Americans and Latinos than among White Americans (Harris & Graham, 2007; McAdoo, 2006). In comparison with two-parent households, single parents often have more limited resources of time, money, and energy (Ryan, Fauth, & Brooks-Gunn, 2006). Ethnic minority parents also are less educated and more likely to live in low-income circumstances than their White counterparts. Still, many impoverished ethnic minority families manage to find ways to raise competent children (Huston & Ripke, 2006).

Some aspects of home life can help protect ethnic minority children from injustice. The family can filter out destructive racist messages, and parents can present alternative frames of reference to those presented by the majority. For example, TV shows may tell the 10-year-old boy that he will grow up to be either a star athlete or a bum; his parents can show him that his life holds many possibilities other than these. The extended family also can serve as an important buffer to stress (McAdoo, 2006).

Of course, individual families vary, and how ethnic minority families deal with stress depends on many factors (McLoyd, Aikens, & Burton, 2006). Whether the parents are native-born or immigrants, how long the family has been in this country, their socioeoncomic status, and their national origin all make a difference (Berry, 2007; Fuligni & Fuligni, 2007). The characteristics of the family's social context also influence its adaptation. What are the attitudes toward the family's ethnic group within its neighborhood or city? Can the family's children attend good schools? Are there community groups that welcome people from the family's ethnic group? Do members of the family's ethnic group form community groups of their own? To read further about ethnic minority parenting, see the *Diversity in Child Development* interlude.

Diversity in Child Development

ACCULTURATION AND ETHNIC MINORITY PARENTING

Ethnic minority children and their parents "are expected to transcend their own cultural background and to incorporate aspects of the dominant culture" into children's development. They undergo varying degrees of **acculturation**, which refers to cultural changes that occur when one culture comes in contact with another. Asian American parents, for example, may feel pressed to modify the traditional training style of parental control discussed earlier as they encounter the more permissive parenting typical of the dominant culture.

The level of family acculturation can affect parenting style by influencing expectations for children's development, parent-child interactions, and the role of the extended family (Ishii-Kuntz, 2004). For example, in one study, the level of acculturation and maternal education were the strongest predictors of maternal-infant interaction patterns in Latino families (Perez-Febles, 1992).

The family's level of acculturation also influences important decisions about child care and early childhood education. For example, "an African American mother might

acculturation Cultural changes that occur when one culture comes in contact with another culture.

prefer to leave her children with extended family while she is at work because the kinship network is seen as a natural way to cope with maternal absence. This well-intentioned, culturally appropriate decision might, however, put the child at an educational and social disadvantage relative to other children of similar age who have the benefit of important preschool experiences that may ease the transition into early school years." Less acculturated and more acculturated family members may disagree about the appropriateness of various caregiving practices, possibly creating conflict or confusion.

The opportunities for acculturation that young children experience depend mainly on their parents and extended family. If they send the children to a child-care center, school, church, or other community setting, the children are likely to learn about the values and behaviors of the dominant culture, and they may be expected to adapt to that culture's norms. Thus, Latino children raised in a traditional family in which the family's good is considered more important than the individual's interests may attend a preschool in which children are rewarded for asserting themselves. Chinese American children, whose traditional parents value behavioral inhibition (as discussed in Chapter 10), may be rewarded outside the home for being active and emotionally expressive. Over time, the differences in the level of acculturation experienced by children and by their parents and extended family may grow. (Source: Garcia Coll & Pachter, 2002, pp. 7–8)

How is acculturation involved in ethnic minority parenting?

Socioeconomic Status Low-income families have less access to resources than higher-income families (Conger & Dogan, 2007; Patterson & Hastings, 2007). The differential in access to resources includes nutrition, health care, protection from danger, and enriching educational and socialization opportunities, such as tutoring and lessons in various activities. These differences are compounded in low-income families characterized by long-term poverty (McLoyd, Aikens, & Burton, 2006; Philipsen, Johnson & Brooks-Gunn, 2009).

In America and most Western cultures, differences also have been found in child rearing among different socioeconomic-status (SES) groups (Hoff, Laursen, & Tardif, 2002, p. 246):

- "Lower-SES parents (1) are more concerned that their children conform to society's expectations, (2) create a home atmosphere in which it is clear that parents have authority over children," (3) use physical punishment more in disciplining their children, and (4) are more directive and less conversational with their children.

- "Higher-SES parents (1) are more concerned with developing children's initiative" and delay of gratification, "(2) create a home atmosphere in which children are more nearly equal participants and in which rules are discussed as opposed to being laid down" in an authoritarian manner, (3) are less likely to use physical punishment, and (4) "are less directive and more conversational" with their children.

Parents in different socioeconomic groups also tend to think differently about education (Huston & Ripke, 2006). Middle- and upper-income parents more often think of education as something that should be mutually encouraged by parents and teachers. By contrast, low-income parents are more likely to view education as the teacher's job. Thus, increased school-family linkages especially can benefit students from low-income families. We will have much more to say about socioeconomic variations in families, especially the negative ramifications of poverty for children's development, as well as other aspects of culture and its role in parenting and children's development in Chapter 17, "Culture and Diversity."

Review and Reflect: Learning Goal 4

4 **Characterize the Changing Family in a Changing Social World**

REVIEW

- How are children influenced by working parents?
- How does divorce affect children's development?
- How does living in a stepfamily influence children's development?
- How do lesbian mothers and gay fathers influence children's development?
- How do culture, ethnicity, and socioeconomic status influence children's development in a family?

REFLECT

- Now that you have studied many aspects of families in this chapter, imagine that you have decided to write a book on some aspect of families. What specific aspect of families would you mainly focus on? What would be the title of your book? What would be the major theme of the book?

Reach Your Learning Goals

Families

1 FAMILY PROCESSES: DISCUSS FAMILY PROCESSES

Interactions in the Family System

- The family is a system of interrelated and interacting individuals with different subsystems—some dyadic, some polyadic. The subsystems have both direct and indirect effects on one another. Positive marital relations can have a positive influence on parenting. Reciprocal socialization is the bidirectional process by which children socialize parents just as parents socialize them.

Cognition and Emotion in Family Processes

- Cognition and emotion are central to understanding how family processes work. The role of cognition includes parents' cognitions, beliefs, and values about their parental role, as well as the way they perceive, organize, and understand their children's behaviors and beliefs. The role of emotion includes the regulation of emotion in children, understanding emotion in children, and emotion in carrying out the parenting role. Children learn to express and manage emotions appropriately through interaction with emotion-coaching parents and have fewer behavior problems than children of emotion-dismissing parents.

Sociocultural and Historical Changes

- Changes in families may be due to great upheavals, such as war, or more subtle changes, such as television and the mobility of families. Increased restlessness and dissatisfaction in families has resulted in more divorced and remarried families than at any other point in history.

2 PARENTING: EXPLAIN HOW PARENTING IS LINKED TO CHILDREN'S AND ADOLESCENTS' DEVELOPMENT

Adapting Parenting to Developmental Changes in Children

- The transition to parenthood requires considerable adaptation and adjustment on the part of parents. Discipline with younger children is often handled by physical manipulation, such as carrying a 2-year-old away from mischief. As children grow older, parents increasingly turn to reasoning or withholding privileges in disciplining children. Parents spend less time with children in middle and late childhood, a time when parents play an especially important role in their children's academic achievement. Control is more coregulatory in middle and late childhood.

Parents as Managers of Children's Lives

- An increased trend is to conceptualize parents as managers of children's lives. Parents play important roles as managers of children's opportunities, in effectively monitoring children's relationships, and as social initiators and arrangers. Parental monitoring is linked to lower levels of juvenile delinquency, and effective parental management is related to children's higher academic achievement.

Parenting Styles and Discipline

- Authoritarian, authoritative, neglectful, and indulgent are the four main categories of parenting styles. Authoritative parenting is associated with socially competent child behavior more than the other styles. However, ethnic variations in parenting styles indicate that in African American and Asian American families, some aspects of control may benefit children. Latino parents often emphasize connectedness with the family and respect and obedience in their child rearing. There are a number of reasons not to use physical punishment in disciplining children, and in Sweden physical punishment of children has been outlawed. Intense punishment presents the child with an out-of-control model. Punishment can instill fear, rage, or avoidance in children. Punishment tells children what not to do rather than what to do. Punishment can be abusive. Coparenting has positive outcomes for children. Child maltreatment is a multifaceted problem. Understanding child maltreatment requires information about the cultural context and family influences. Child maltreatment places the child at risk for a number of developmental problems.

Parent-Adolescent Relationships

- Many parents have a difficult time handling the adolescent's push for autonomy. Secure attachment to parents increases the likelihood that the adolescent will be socially competent. Conflict with parents often increases in early adolescence, but this conflict is often moderate rather than severe. The increase in conflict probably serves the positive developmental functions of increasing adolescent autonomy and identity. A subset of adolescents experience high parent-adolescent conflict, and this is linked with negative outcomes for adolescents.

3 SIBLINGS: IDENTIFY HOW SIBLINGS INFLUENCE CHILDREN'S DEVELOPMENT

Sibling Relationships

- Three important aspects of sibling relationships involve (1) emotional quality of the relationship, (2) familiarity and intimacy of the relationship, and (3) variation. Sibling relationships include not only conflict and fighting but also helping, teaching, sharing, and playing—and siblings can function as rivals, emotional supports, and communication partners.

Birth Order

- Birth order is related in certain ways to child characteristics. Firstborn children are more self-controlled, conforming, have more guilt and anxiety, argue and excel academically and professionally compared with later-born children. However, some critics argue that birth order has been overestimated as a predictor of child behavior.

4 THE CHANGING FAMILY IN A CHANGING SOCIAL WORLD: CHARACTERIZE THE CHANGING FAMILY IN A CHANGING SOCIAL WORLD

Working Parents

- In general, having both parents employed full-time outside the home has not been shown to have negative effects on children. However, depending on the circumstances, work can produce positive or negative effects on parenting. If parents experience poor work conditions, they frequently become inattentive to their children, who show more behavioral problems and do more poorly at school. There is a positive link between participation in extracurricular activities and academic achievement, psychological adjustment, and positive interaction with parents.

Children in Divorced Families

- Children in divorced families show more adjustment problems than their counterparts in nondivorced families. Whether parents should stay in an unhappy or conflicted marriage for the sake of the children is difficult to determine. Children show better adjustment in divorced families when parents' relationships with each other are harmonious and authoritative parenting is used. Factors to be considered in the adjustment of children in divorced families are adjustment prior to the divorce, personality and temperament, developmental status, gender, and custody. Income loss for divorced mothers may be linked with a number of stresses that can affect the child's adjustment.

Stepfamilies

- Like in divorced families, children in stepfamilies have more problems than their counterparts in nondivorced families. Restabilization often takes longer in stepfamilies than in divorced families. Children often have better relationships with their biological parents than with their stepparents and show more problems in complex, blended families than simple ones. Adolescence is an especially difficult time to experience the remarriage of parents.

Gay Male and Lesbian Parents

- Approximately 33 percent of lesbians and 22 percent of gay men are parents. There is considerable diversity among lesbian mothers, gay fathers, and their children. Researchers have found few differences between children growing up in gay male or lesbian families and children growing up in heterosexual families.

Cultural, Ethnic, and Socioeconomic Variations in Families

- Cultures vary on a number of issues regarding families. African American and Latino children are more likely than White American children to live in single-parent families, larger families, and families with extended connections. Higher-SES families are less likely to use physical discipline, create a home atmosphere in which rules are discussed, and are concerned with developing children's initiative and delay of gratification. Lower-SES families are more likely to use physical punishment in disciplining their children, are more directive and less conversational, and want their children to conform to society's expectations.

KEY TERMS

scaffolding 417
reciprocal socialization 418

authoritarian parenting 424
authoritative parenting 424

neglectful parenting 424
indulgent parenting 425

coparenting 428
acculturation 442

KEY PEOPLE

Urie Bronfenbrenner 417
Maayan Davidov and Joan
   Grusec 419

Diana Baumrind 424
Ruth Chao 425
Joseph Allen 431

Reed Larson 432
Laurie Kramer 434
Judy Dunn 434

Ann Crouter 436
E. Mavis Hetherington 437

E-LEARNING TOOLS

To help you master the material in this chapter, you'll find a number of valuable study tools at the Online Learning Center for *Child Development*, twelfth edition (**www.mhhe.com/santrockcd12**).

Taking It to the Net

Research the answers to these questions:

1. Frieda is the middle child in a family with five siblings. She is interested in what sibling researchers have to say about the effect of birth order on sibling relationships. How does being a middle child contribute to the dynamics between Frieda and her brothers and sisters?

2. Mary and Peter are the parents of 13-year-old Cameron and 15-year-old Suzanne. They had heard that the adolescent years could be difficult, but they were not prepared for the constant conflicts and bickering. They don't feel that they are doing a very good job as parents. Are there some guidelines that will help them restore some peace and sanity to their family?

3. Bruce and Caitlin are planning to separate and divorce. Both are miserable, and the household is like an armed camp. They have three children, ages 6, 8, and 12. What should they tell the children, and how and when should they do so?

Health and Well-Being, Parenting, and Education Exercises

Build your decision-making skills by trying your hand at the health and well-being, parenting, and education exercises.

Video Clips

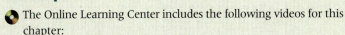 The Online Learning Center includes the following videos for this chapter:

- *Children and Divorce*
Robert Emery, University of Virginia, offers advice on how parents can help children cope with divorce.

- *Children's Feelings About Work and Family*
Two siblings discuss their feelings about their dad working.

- *Social Worker's View on Children's Abuse and Neglect*
An elementary school social worker describes the prevalence of abuse and neglect among children and how, unfortunately, it is difficult to identify until it is too late.

15

You are troubled at seeing him spend his early years in doing nothing. What! Is it nothing to be happy? Is it nothing to skip, to play, to run about all day long? Never in his life will he be so busy as now.

—Jean-Jacques Rousseau
*Swiss-Born French Philosopher,
18th Century*

LEARNING GOALS

◆ Discuss peer relations in childhood.

◆ Describe children's play.

◆ Explain friendship.

◆ Characterize peer relations in adolescence.

PEERS

CHAPTER OUTLINE

Images of Child Development
The Stories of Young Adolescent Girls' Friends and Relational Worlds

Lynn Brown and Carol Gilligan (1992) conducted in-depth interviews of one hundred 10- to 13-year-old girls who were making the transition to adolescence. They listened to what these girls were saying.

A number of the girls talked about how many girls say nice things to be polite but often don't really mean them. The girls know the benefits of being perceived as the perfect, happy girl. Judy spoke about her interest in romantic relationships. Although she and her girlfriends were only 13, they wanted to be romantic, and she talked about her lengthy private conversations with her girlfriends about boys. Noura said that she learned how very painful it is to be the person everyone doesn't like.

Cliques figured largely in these girls' lives. They provided emotional support for girls who were striving to be perfect but knew they were not. Victoria commented that some girls like her, who weren't very popular, nonetheless were accepted into a "club" with three other girls. Now when she was sad or depressed she could count on the "club" for support. Though they were "leftovers" and did not get into the most popular cliques, these four girls knew they were liked.

Through these interviews, we see the girls' curiosity about the human world they lived in. They kept track of what was happening to their peers and friends. The girls spoke at length about the pleasure they derived from the intimacy and fun of human connection, about the potential for hurt in relationships, and about the importance of friends.

> ## PREVIEW
>
> This chapter is about peers, who clearly are very important in the lives of the adolescent girls just described. They also are very important in the lives of children. We begin this chapter by examining a number of ideas about children's peer relations, including their functions and variations. Then we turn to children's play and the roles of friends in children's development. We conclude by discussing peer relationships in adolescence.

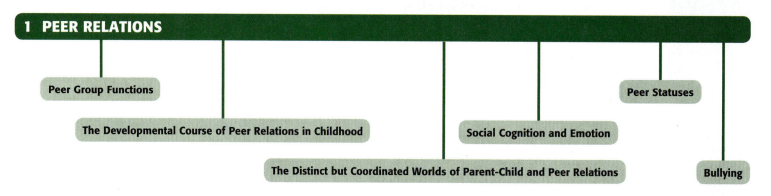

1 PEER RELATIONS

- Peer Group Functions
- The Developmental Course of Peer Relations in Childhood
- The Distinct but Coordinated Worlds of Parent-Child and Peer Relations
- Social Cognition and Emotion
- Peer Statuses
- Bullying

As children grow up, they spend increasing amounts of time with their peers. What is the function of a child's peer group?

Peer Group Functions

Peers are children of about the same age or maturity level. They fill a unique role in the child's development. One of their most important functions is to provide a source of information and comparison about the world outside the family. Children receive feedback about their abilities from their peer group. They evaluate what they do in terms of whether it is better than, as good as, or worse than what other children do. It is hard to do this at home because siblings are usually older or younger.

Are Peers Necessary for Development?
Good peer relations might be necessary for normal social development in adolescence (Brown & others, 2008). Social isolation, or the inability to "plug in" to a social network, is linked with many different forms of problems and disorders, ranging from delinquency and problem drinking to depression (Snyder & others, 2008).

Positive and Negative Peer Relations
Peer influences can be both positive and negative (Blanton & Burkley, 2008; Brown & others, 2008). Both Jean Piaget (1932) and Harry Stack Sullivan (1953) were influential theorists who stressed that it is through peer interaction that children and adolescents learn important aspects of relationships. They also learn to be keen observers of peers' interests and perspectives in order to smoothly integrate themselves into ongoing peer activities. In addition, Sullivan argued that adolescents learn to be skilled and sensitive partners in intimate relationships by forging close friendships with selected peers. These intimacy skills are carried forward to help form the foundation of later dating and marital relationships, according to Sullivan.

We discussed yet another function of peers in Chapter 13: According to Piaget and Lawrence Kohlberg, through the give-and-take of peer relations, children develop their social understanding and moral reasoning. Children explore the principles of fairness and justice by working through disagreements with peers.

Consider the results of these two longitudinal studies that illustrate the positive long-term influence that peer relations in childhood can have:

- Competence in peer relations during middle and late childhood was linked to work success and satisfaction in romantic relationships in early adulthood (Collins & van Dulmen, 2006). Competence in peer relations was assessed by teacher ratings of children's social contact with peers, popularity, friendship, and social skills and leadership.
- Popularity with peers and a low level of aggression at age 8 foreshadowed a higher occupational status at age 48 (Huesmann & others, 2006).

In contrast, some theorists have emphasized the negative influences of peers on adolescents' development. Being rejected or overlooked by peers leads some adolescents to feel lonely or hostile. Further, such rejection and neglect by peers are related to an individual's subsequent mental health and criminal problems (Bukowski, Velasquez, & Brendgen, 2008). Some theorists have also described the adolescent peer culture as a corrupt influence that undermines parental values and control. Further, peer relations are linked to adolescents' patterns of drug use, delinquency, and depression. Consider the results of these three recent studies:

- Time spent hanging out with antisocial peers in adolescence was a stronger predictor of substance abuse than time spent with parents (Nation & Heflinger, 2006).
- Higher levels of antisocial peer involvement in early adolescence (13 to 16 years of age) were linked with higher rates of delinquent behavior in late adolescence (17 to 18 years of age) (Laird & others, 2005).
- Deviant peer affiliation was related to adolescents' depressive symptoms (Connell & Dishion, 2006).

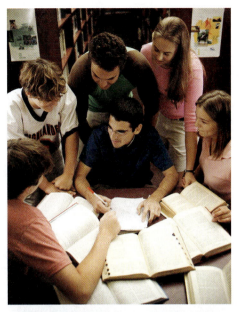

In what ways can peer relations be positive and negative?

peers Children of about the same age or maturity level.

As you read further about peers, keep in mind that findings about the influence of peers vary according to the way peer experience is measured, the outcomes specified, and the developmental trajectories traversed (Hartup & Laursen, 1999). "Peers" and "peer group" are global concepts. A "peer group" of an adolescent might refer to a neighborhood crowd, reference crowd, church crowd, sports team, friendship group, and friend (Brown, 1999). The influence of peers or peer groups depends on their specific setting or context.

In terms of contexts, peers play an important role in the development of individuals in all cultures. However, as indicated in the *Diversity in Child Development* interlude, cultures vary in how strong the socializing role of peers is.

Diversity in Child Development

CROSS-CULTURAL COMPARISONS OF PEER RELATIONS

In some countries, adults restrict adolescents' access to peers. For example, in many areas of rural India and in Arab countries, opportunities for peer relations in adolescence are severely restricted, especially for girls (Brown & Larson, 2002). If girls attend school in these regions of the world, it is usually in sex-segregated schools. In these countries, interaction with the other sex or opportunities for romantic relationships are restricted (Booth, 2002).

In Chapter 14, we indicated that Japanese adolescents seek autonomy from their parents later and have less conflict with them than American adolescents do (Rothbaum & Trommsdorff, 2007). In a cross-cultural analysis, the peer group was more important to U.S. adolescents than to Japanese adolescents (Rothbaum & others, 2000). Japanese adolescents spend less time outside the home, have less recreational leisure time, and engage in fewer extracurricular activities with peers than U.S. adolescents (White, 1993). Also, U.S. adolescents are more likely to put pressure on their peers to resist parental influence than Japanese adolescents are (Rothbaum & others, 2000).

A trend, though, is that in societies in which adolescents' access to peers has been restricted, adolescents are engaging in more peer interaction during school and in shared leisure activities, especially in middle-SES contexts (Brown & Larson, 2002). For example, in Southeast Asia and some Arab regions, adolescents are starting to rely more on peers for advice and share interests with them (Booth, 2002; Santa Maria, 2002).

In many countries and regions, though, peers play more prominent roles in adolescents' lives (Brown & Larson, 2002). For example, in sub-Saharan Africa, the peer group is a pervasive aspect of adolescents' lives (Nsamenang, 2002); similar results have been observed throughout Europe and North America (Arnett, 2002).

In some cultures, children are placed in peer groups for much greater lengths of time at an earlier age than they are in the United States. For example, in the Murian culture of eastern India, both male and female children live in a dormitory from the age of 6 until they get married (Barnouw, 1975). The dormitory is a religious haven where members are devoted to work and spiritual harmony. Children work for their parents, and the parents arrange the children's marriages.

In some cultural settings, peers even assume responsibilities usually assumed by parents. For example, street youth in South America rely on networks of peers to help them negotiate survival in urban environments (Welti, 2002).

Street youth in Rio de Janeiro.

The Developmental Course of Peer Relations in Childhood

Some researchers argue that the quality of peer interaction in infancy provides valuable information about socioemotional development (Hughes & Dunn, 2007; Vandell,

1985). For example, in one investigation, positive affect in infant peer relations was related to easy access to peer play groups and to peer popularity in early childhood (Howes, 1985). As increasing numbers of children attend child care, peer interaction in infancy takes on a more important developmental role.

Around the age of 3, children already prefer to spend time with same-sex rather than opposite-sex playmates, and this preference increases in early childhood. During these same years the frequency of peer interaction, both positive and negative, picks up considerably (Hartup, 1983). Although aggressive interaction and rough-and-tumble play increase, the proportion of aggressive exchanges, compared with friendly exchanges, decreases. Many preschool children spend considerable time in peer interaction just conversing with playmates about such matters as "negotiating roles and rules in play, arguing, and agreeing" (Rubin, Bukowski, & Parker, 2006).

As children enter the elementary school years, reciprocity becomes especially important in peer interchanges. Children play games, function in groups, and cultivate friendships. The amount of time children spend in peer interaction also rises during middle and late childhood and adolescence. Researchers estimate that the percentage of time spent in social interaction with peers increases from approximately 10 percent at 2 years of age to more than 30 percent in middle and late childhood (Rubin, Bukowski, & Parker, 2006). In one early study, children interacted with peers 10 percent of their day at age 2, 20 percent at age 4, and more than 40 percent between the ages of 7 and 11. A typical school day included 299 episodes with peers (Barker & Wright, 1951). Other changes in peer relations as children move through middle and late childhood involve an increase in the size of their peer group and peer interaction that is less closely supervised by adults (Rubin, Bukowski, & Parker, 2006).

These many interactions take varied forms—cooperative and competitive, boisterous and quiet, joyous and humiliating. There is increasing evidence that gender plays an important role in these interactions (McDougall & Hymel, 2007; Underwood, 2007). Gender influences not only the composition of children's groups but also their size and interactions within them (Maccoby, 2002). From about 5 years of age onward, boys tend to associate in large clusters more than girls do; girls are more likely than boys to play in groups of two or three. As discussed in Chapter 12, "Gender," boys' groups and girls' groups also tend to favor certain types of activities. Boys' groups are more likely to engage in rough-and-tumble play, competition, conflict, ego displays, risk taking, and dominance seeking. By contrast, girls' groups are more likely to engage in collaborative discourse (Leman, Ahmed, & Ozarow, 2005). Let's now examine these factors that may influence children's relations with peers: parents, social cognition, and emotion.

The Distinct but Coordinated Worlds of Parent-Child and Peer Relations

Parents may influence their children's peer relations in many ways, both directly and indirectly. For one thing, they may coach their children in ways of relating to peers. In one investigation, parents indicated that they recommended specific strategies to their children regarding peer relations (Rubin & Sloman, 1984). For example, parents told their children how to mediate disputes or how to become less shy with others. They also encouraged them to be tolerant and to resist peer pressure.

Parents also influence their children's peer relations by how they manage their children's lives and their opportunities for interacting with peers, which we discussed in Chapter 14 (Collins & Steinberg, 2006). One study found that parents who frequently initiated peer contacts for their preschool children had children who were more accepted by their peers and had higher levels of prosocial behavior (Ladd & Hart, 1992). Furthermore, basic lifestyle decisions by parents—their choices of neighborhoods, churches, schools, and their own friends—largely determine the pool from which their children select possible friends (Cooper & Ayers-Lopez, 1985). For example, the chosen schools can lead to particular academic and extracurricular activities,

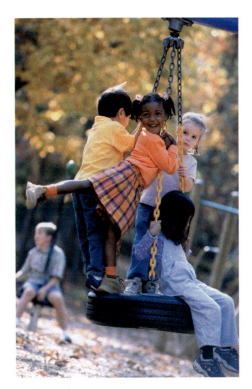

What are some characteristics of peer relations in early childhood?

What are some links between relationships with parents and relationships with peers?

which in turn affect which students their children meet, their purpose in interacting, and eventually which children become their friends. The chosen schools may also have policies that influence children's peer relations. For example, classrooms in which teachers encourage cooperative peer interchanges tend to have fewer isolated children.

Researchers also have found that children's peer relations are linked to attachment security, parents' marital quality, and parents' mental health (Allen & Antonishak, 2008; Cummings, Goerke-Morey, & Raymond, 2004). For example, a recent longitudinal study revealed that a more secure attachment with the mother and a more emotionally intimate marital relationship between parents were related to children's positive interactions with a close friend (Lucas-Thompson & Clarke-Stewart, 2007).

Do these results indicate that children's peer relations are wedded to parent-child relationships (Hartup & Laursen, 1999)? Although parent-child relationships influence children's subsequent peer relations, children also learn other modes of relating through their relationships with peers, as our discussion of Piaget and Sullivan indicated.

In sum, parent-child and peer worlds are coordinated and connected (Ladd & Pettit, 2002; Maccoby, 1996). However, they also are distinct. Rough-and-tumble play occurs mainly with other children, not in parent-child interaction. And, in times of stress, children often turn to parents, not peers, for support. In parent-child relationships, children learn how to relate to authority figures. With their peers, children are likely to interact on a much more equal basis and to learn a mode of relating based on mutual influence.

Social Cognition and Emotion

Mariana expects all her playmates to let her play with their toys whenever she asks. When Josh isn't picked for a team on the playground, he thinks his friends have turned against him. These are examples of social cognitions, which involve thoughts about social matters (Peets, Hodges, & Salmivalli, 2008). How might children's social cognitions contribute to their peer relations? Three possibilities are through their perspective-taking ability, social information-processing skills, and emotional regulation.

Perspective Taking   As children enter the elementary school years, both their peer interaction and their perspective-taking ability increase. As we discussed in Chapter 13, "Moral Development," **perspective taking** involves taking another's point of view. Researchers have documented a link between perspective-taking skills and the quality of peer relations, especially in the elementary school years (LeMare & Rubin, 1987).

Perspective taking is important in part because it helps children communicate effectively. In one investigation, the communication exchanges among peers at kindergarten, first-, third-, and fifth-grade levels were evaluated (Krauss & Glucksberg, 1969). Children were asked to instruct a peer in how to stack a set of blocks. The peer sat behind a screen with blocks similar to those the other child was stacking (see Figure 15.1). The kindergarten children made numerous errors in telling the peer how to duplicate the novel block stack. The older children, especially the fifth-graders, were much more efficient in communicating to a peer how to stack the blocks. They were far superior at perspective taking and figuring out how to talk to a peer so that the peer could understand them. In elementary school, children also become more efficient at understanding complex messages, so the listening skills of the peer in this experiment probably helped the communicating peer as well.

Social Information-Processing Skills   How children process information about peer relationships also influences those relationships (Bibok, Carpendale, & Lewis, 2008; Mueller & others, 2008; Rah & Parke, 2008). For example, suppose Andrew

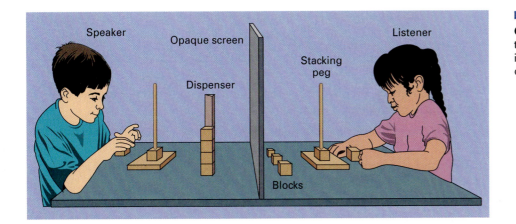

FIGURE 15.1 The Development of Communication Skills. This is an experimental arrangement of speaker and listener in the investigation of the development of communication skills.

accidentally trips and knocks Alex's soft drink out of his hand. Alex misinterprets the encounter as hostile, which leads him to retaliate aggressively against Andrew. Through repeated encounters of this kind, other peers come to perceive Alex as habitually acting inappropriately.

Peer relations researcher Kenneth Dodge (1993) argues that children go through five steps in processing information about their social world: decoding social cues, interpreting, searching for a response, selecting an optimal response, and enacting it. Dodge has found that aggressive boys are more likely to perceive another child's actions as hostile when the child's intention is ambiguous—and when aggressive boys search for clues to determine a peer's intention, they respond more rapidly, less efficiently, and less reflectively than nonaggressive children.

Emotional Regulation   Not only does cognition play an important role in peer relations, so does emotion. For example, the ability to regulate emotion is linked to successful peer relations (Orobio de Castro & others, 2005; Rubin, Bukowski, & Parker, 2006). Moody and emotionally negative individuals experience greater rejection by peers, whereas emotionally positive individuals are more popular (Saarni & others, 2006). Children who have effective self-regulatory skills can modulate their emotional expressiveness in contexts that evoke intense emotions, as when a peer says something negative (Orobio de Castro & others, 2005). In one study, rejected children were more likely than popular children to use negative gestures in a provoking situation (Underwood & Hurley, 1997).

A recent study focused on the emotional aspects of social information processing in aggressive boys (Orobio de Castro & others, 2005). Highly aggressive boys and a control group of less aggressive boys listened to vignettes involving provocations involving peers. The highly aggressive boys expressed less guilt, attributed more hostile intent, and generated less adaptive emotion-regulation strategies than the comparison group of boys.

Peer Statuses

Which children are likely to be popular with their peers, and which ones are disliked? Developmentalists address this and similar questions by examining *sociometric status*, a term that describes the extent to which children are liked or disliked by their peer group (McElhaney, Antonishak, & Allen, 2008; Rubin, Bukowski, & Parker, 2006). Sociometric status is typically assessed by asking children to rate how much they like or dislike each of their classmates. Or it may be assessed by asking children to nominate the children they like the most and those they like the least.

What role does emotion play in peer relations? How do aggressive boys process information about their social world?

What are some statuses that children have with their peers?

Developmentalists have distinguished five peer statuses (Wentzel & Asher, 1995):

- **Popular children** are frequently nominated as a best friend and are rarely disliked by their peers.
- **Average children** receive an average number of both positive and negative nominations from their peers.
- **Neglected children** are infrequently nominated as a best friend but are not disliked by their peers.
- **Rejected children** are infrequently nominated as someone's best friend and are actively disliked by their peers.
- **Controversial children** are frequently nominated both as someone's best friend and as being disliked.

Popular children have a number of social skills that contribute to their being well liked. Researchers have found that popular children give out reinforcements, listen carefully, maintain open lines of communication with peers, are happy, control their negative emotions, act like themselves, show enthusiasm and concern for others, and are self-confident without being conceited (Hartup, 1983; Rubin, Bukowski, & Parker, 2006).

Neglected children engage in low rates of interaction with their peers and are often described as shy by peers. Rejected children often have more serious adjustment problems than those who are neglected (Rubin, Bukowski, & Parker, 2006; Sandstrom & Zakriski, 2004). One study found that in kindergarten, children who were rejected by their peers were less likely to engage in classroom participation, more likely to express a desire to avoid school, and more likely to report being lonely than children who were accepted by their peers (Buhs & Ladd, 2001).

Peer Rejection and Aggression The combination of being rejected by peers and being aggressive forecasts problems (Bukowski, Brendgen, & Vitaro, 2007; Rubin, Bukowski, & Parker, 2006). For example, one study found that when third-grade boys were highly aggressive and rejected by their peers, they showed markedly higher levels of delinquency as adolescents and young adults than other boys (Miller-Johnson, Coie, & Malone, 2003).

An analysis by John Coie (2004, pp. 252–253) provided three reasons why aggressive peer-rejected boys have problems in social relationships:

- First, the rejected, aggressive boys are more impulsive and have problems sustaining attention. As a result, they are more likely to be disruptive of ongoing activities in the classroom and in focused group play.
- Second, rejected, aggressive boys are more emotionally reactive. They are aroused to anger more easily and probably have more difficulty calming down once aroused. Because of this they are more prone to become angry at peers and attack them verbally and physically.
- Third, rejected children have fewer social skills in making friends and maintaining positive relationships with peers.

Not all rejected children are aggressive (Hymel, McDougall, & Renshaw, 2004). Although aggression and its related characteristics of impulsiveness and disruptiveness underlie rejection about half the time, approximately 10 to 20 percent of rejected children are shy.

What are the antecedents of peer rejection? According to Gerald Patterson, Tom Dishion, and their colleagues (Patterson, DeBaryshe, & Ramsay, 1989; Patterson, Reid, & Dishion, 1992; Shaw & others, 2006), poor parenting skills are at the root of children becoming rejected by their peers. They especially argue that inadequate monitoring and harsh punishment, in some instances being reactions to a child's

popular children Children who are frequently nominated as a best friend and are rarely disliked by their peers.

average children Children who receive an average number of both positive and negative nominations from their peers.

neglected children Children who are infrequently nominated as a best friend but are not disliked by their peers.

rejected children Children who are infrequently nominated as a best friend and are actively disliked by their peers.

controversial children Children who are frequently nominated both as someone's best friend and as being disliked.

difficult temperament, produce a child with aggressive, antisocial tendencies. The child carries these tendencies to the world of peers, where the child becomes rejected by better-adjusted peers who have a more positive temperament (such as "easy" or "effortful control") and have experienced more positive parenting (such as authoritative parenting).

Social-Skills Training Programs How can neglected children and rejected children be trained to interact more effectively with their peers? The goal of many training programs for neglected children is to help them attract attention from their peers in positive ways and to hold their attention by asking questions, by listening in a warm and friendly way, and by saying things about themselves that relate to the peers' interests. They also are taught to enter groups more effectively.

For rejected children, training programs may teach how to more accurately assess whether the intentions of their peers are negative. Rejected children also may be asked to engage in role-playing or to discuss hypothetical situations involving negative encounters with peers, such as when a peer cuts into line ahead of them. In some programs, children are shown videotapes of appropriate peer interaction; then they are asked to comment on them and to draw lessons from what they have seen (Ladd, Buhs, & Troop, 2004).

One recent social-skills intervention program was successful in increasing social acceptance and self-esteem and decreasing depression and anxiety in peer-rejected children (DeRosier & Marcus, 2005). Students participated in the program once a week (50 to 60 minutes) for eight weeks. The program included instruction in how to manage emotions, how to improve prosocial skills, how to become better communicators, and how to compromise and negotiate.

Despite the positive outcomes of some programs that attempt to improve the social skills of adolescents, researchers have often found it difficult to improve the social skills of adolescents who are actively disliked and rejected. Many of these adolescents are rejected because they are aggressive or impulsive and lack the self-control to keep these behaviors in check. Still, some intervention programs have been successful in reducing the aggressive and impulsive behaviors of these adolescents (Ladd, Buhs, & Troop, 2004).

Social-skills training programs have generally been more successful with children 10 years of age or younger than with adolescents (Malik & Furman, 1993). Peer reputations become more fixed as cliques and peer groups become more salient in adolescence. Once an adolescent gains a negative reputation among peers as being "mean," "weird," or a "loner," the peer group's attitude is often slow to change, even after the adolescent's problem behavior has been corrected. Thus, researchers have found that skills interventions may need to be supplemented by efforts to change the minds of peers.

Bullying

Significant numbers of students are victimized by bullies (Juvonen & Galvan, 2008; Pepler & others, 2008). In a national survey of more than 15,000 sixth- through tenth-grade students, nearly one of every three students said that they had experienced occasional or frequent involvement as a victim or perpetrator in bullying (Nansel & others, 2001). In this study, bullying was defined as verbal or physical behavior intended to disturb someone less powerful. As shown in Figure 15.2, being belittled about looks or speech was the most frequent type of bullying. A recent study revealed that bullying decreased as students went from the fall of the sixth grade (20 percent were bullied extensively) through the spring of the eighth grade (6 percent were bullied extensively) (Nylund & others, 2007).

Who is likely to be bullied? In the study just described, boys and younger middle school students were most likely to be affected (Nansel & others, 2001). Children who said they were bullied reported more loneliness and difficulty in making friends,

*P*eer rejection contributes to subsequent problems of adaptation, including antisocial behavior.

—John Coie
Contemporary Psychologist, Duke University

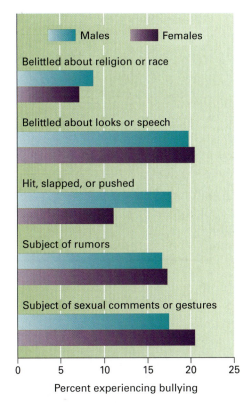

FIGURE 15.2 Bullying Behaviors Among U.S. Youth. This graph shows the type of bullying most often experienced by U.S. youth (Nansel & others, 2001). The percentages reflect the extent to which bullied students said that they had experienced a particular type of bullying. In terms of gender, note that when they were bullied, boys were more likely to be hit, slapped, or pushed than girls were.

whereas those who did the bullying were more likely to have low grades and to smoke and drink alcohol. Researchers have found that anxious, socially withdrawn, and aggressive children are often the victims of bullying (Hannish & Guerra, 2004). Anxious and socially withdrawn children may be victimized because they are nonthreatening and unlikely to retaliate if bullied, whereas aggressive children may be the targets of bullying because their behavior is irritating to bullies (Rubin, Bukowski, & Parker, 2006).

What are the outcomes of bullying? In one study, 9- to 12-year-old children who were the victims of bullies had a much higher incidence of headaches, sleeping problems, abdominal pain, feeling tired, and depression than children not involved in bullying behavior (Fekkes, Pijpers, & Verloove-Vanhorick, 2004). A recent study also indicated that bullies and their victims in adolescence were more likely to experience depression and engage in suicide ideation and attempt suicide than their counterparts who were not involved in bullying (Brunstein Klomek & others, 2007). Another recent study revealed that bullies, victims, or those who were both bullies and victims had more health problems (such as headaches, dizziness, sleep problems, and anxiety) than their counterparts who were not involved in bullying (Srabstein & others, 2006). And a study of U.S. sixth-grade students also examined the three groups of bullies, victims, and bully-victims (Juvonen, Graham, & Schuster, 2003). Bully-victims were the most troubled group, displaying the highest level of conduct, school, and relationship problems. Despite increased conduct problems, bullies enjoyed the highest standing of the three groups among their classmates. To read further about bullying, see the *Research in Child Development* interlude.

Research in Child Development

AGGRESSIVE VICTIMS, PASSIVE VICTIMS, AND BULLIES

One study examined the extent to which aggressive victims (who provoke their peers and respond to threats or attacks with reactive aggression), passive victims (who submit to aggressors' demands), and bullies (who aggress against peers but are rarely attacked in return) showed different developmental pathways (Hanish & Guerra, 2004). The children were assessed initially in the fourth grade and then again in the sixth grade.

Peer sociometric ratings were used to identify aggressive victim, passive victim, bully, uninvolved, and average children. Each child received a booklet containing randomized lists (separated by gender) of the names of all children in the class. The children were asked to mark all peers' names that were applicable to certain questions, which included items that assessed aggression (for example, "Who starts a fight over nothing?") and victimization (for example, "Who are the children who are getting picked on?").

The results indicated that "aggressive victims became less prevalent and passive victims and bullies became more prevalent with age. Although it was common for aggressive victims and bullies to move from one group to the other across time, there was little overlap with the passive victim group" (p. 17).

How can bullying be reduced? A recent research review revealed mixed results for school-based intervention (Vreeman & Carroll, 2007). School-based interventions vary greatly, ranging from involving the whole school in an antibullying campaign to individualized social-skills training. Following are three of the most promising bullying intervention programs and where you can obtain information about them:

- *Olweus Bullying Prevention*. Created by Dan Olweus, this program focuses on 6- to 15-year-olds, with the goal of decreasing opportunities and rewards for bullying. School staff are instructed in ways to improve peer relations and make schools safer. When properly implemented, the program reduces bullying by 30 to 70 percent (Ericson, 2001; Olweus, 2003). Information on how to implement the program can be obtained from the Center for the Study and Prevention of Violence at the University of Colorado: www.colorado.edu/cspv/blueprints.

- *Bully-Proofing Your School*. This program is tailored for students in kindergarten through the eighth grade and offers a school-wide approach and a teacher curriculum for reducing bullying. It emphasizes how to recognize bullying behavior and quickly respond to it and how to develop students' communication skills in conflict situations. Intervention methods are provided, school posters related to bullying are available, and a parent's guide helps involve parents in effective ways to reduce bullying. Recent research indicates that this program is effective in reducing bullying (Beran & Tutty, 2002; Plog, Epstein, & Porter, 2004). Information about the Bully-Proofing Your School program is available at www.sopriswest.com.

- *Steps to Respect*. This bullying program consists of three steps: (1) establishing a school-wide approach, such as creating antibullying policies and determining consequences for bullying; (2) training staff and parents to deal with bullying; and (3) teaching students to recognize, not tolerate, and handle bullying. In this third step, teachers provide skills training, such as how to be assertive, and information about bullying to students in grades 3 through 6. The skills training by teachers occurs over a 12- to 14-week period. A recent study found that Steps to Respect was successful in reducing bullying and argumentativeness in third- through sixth-grade students (Frey & others, 2005). For more information about Steps to Respect, consult this Web site: www.cfchildren.org.

What are some strategies to reduce bullying?

Review and Reflect: Learning Goal 1

1 **Discuss Peer Relations in Childhood**

REVIEW

- What are peers, and what the functions of peer groups?
- What is the developmental course of peer relations in childhood?
- How are the worlds of parents and peers distinct but coordinated?
- How is social cognition involved in peer relations? How is emotion involved in peer relations?
- What are five peer statuses of children?
- What is the nature of bullying?

REFLECT

- Think back to your middle school/junior high and high school years. What was your relationship with your parents like? Were you securely attached or insecurely attached to them? How do you think your relationship with your parents affected your friendship and peer relations?

2 PLAY

Play's Functions   **Parten's Classic Study of Play**   **Types of Play**

*A*nd *that park grew up with me; that small world widened as I learned its secrets and boundaries, as I discovered new refuges in its woods and jungles: hidden homes and lairs for the multitudes of imagination, for cowboys and Indians. . . . I used to dawdle on half holidays along the bent and Devon-facing seashore, hoping for gold watches or the skull of a sheep or a message in a bottle to be washed up with the tide.*

—DYLAN THOMAS
Welsh Poet, 20th Century

play A pleasurable activity that is engaged in for its own sake.

play therapy Therapy that allows the child to work off frustrations and is a medium through which the therapist can analyze the child's conflicts and ways of coping with them. Children may feel less threatened and be more likely to express their true feelings in the context of play.

Much of the time when children, especially young children, are interacting with their peers, they are playing. **Play** is a pleasurable activity that is engaged in for its own sake, and social play is just one type of play.

Play's Functions

Many of the key theorists discussed in early chapters have written about the functions of play in the child's development. According to Freud and Erikson, play helps the child master anxieties and conflicts. Because tensions are relieved in play, the child can cope with life's problems. Play permits the child to work off excess physical energy and to release pent-up emotions, which increases the child's ability to cope with problems. In part, these functions of play inspired the development of **play therapy**, in which therapists use play to allow children to work off frustrations and to provide an opportunity for analyzing children's conflicts and ways of coping. Children may feel less threatened and be more likely to express their true feelings in the context of play.

Piaget (1962) saw that play is both an activity constrained by a child's cognitive development and a medium that advances cognitive development. Play permits children to practice their competencies and skills in a relaxed, pleasurable way. Piaget stressed that cognitive structures need to be exercised, and play provides the perfect setting for this exercise. For example, children who have just learned to add or multiply begin to play with numbers in different ways as they perfect these operations, laughing as they do so.

Vygotsky (1962) also pointed out that play is an excellent setting for cognitive development. He was especially interested in the symbolic and make-believe aspects of play, as when a child rides a stick as if it were a horse. For young children, the imaginary situation is real. Parents should encourage such imaginary play because it advances the child's cognitive development, especially creative thought.

Daniel Berlyne (1960) described play as exciting and pleasurable in itself because it satisfies the exploratory drive each of us possesses. This drive involves curiosity and a desire for information about something new or unusual. Play is a means whereby children can safely explore and seek out new information—something they might not otherwise do. Play encourages this exploratory behavior by offering children the possibilities of novelty, complexity, uncertainty, surprise, and incongruity.

Play also teaches children about gender roles. One study found that over the course of six months, the more time boys spent playing with other boys, their activity level, rough-and-tumble play, and sex-typed choices of toys and games increased, and the less time they spent near adults (Martin & Fabes, 2001). By contrast, the more time girls spent playing with girls, the lower was their aggression and activity level, the higher their choices of girl-type play and activities, and the more time they spent near adults.

In short, theorists and researchers paint a convincing portrait of the importance of play to development (Bornstein & Tamis-Lemonda, 2007; Roscos & Christie, 2007). Play is essential to a young child's health. Play releases tension, advances cognitive development, and increases exploration. Play also increases affiliation with peers; it raises the probability that children will interact and converse with each other. During this interaction, children practice the roles that they will assume later in life.

An increasing concern is that the large number of hours children spend with electronic media, such as television and computers, takes time away from play (Linn,

2008). An important agenda for parents is to include ample time for play in their children's lives.

Parten's Classic Study of Play

Many years ago, Mildred Parten (1932) developed an elaborate classification of children's play. Based on observations of children in free play at nursery school, Parten proposed the following types of play:

Mildred Parten classified play into six categories. *Study this photograph—which of Parten's categories are reflected in the behavior of the children?*

- **Unoccupied play** is not play as it is commonly understood. The child may stand in one spot or perform random movements that do not seem to have a goal. In most nursery schools, unoccupied play is less frequent than other forms of play.

- **Solitary play** happens when the child plays alone and independently of others. The child seems engrossed in the activity and does not care much about anything else that is happening. Two- and three-year-olds engage more frequently in solitary play than older preschoolers do.

- **Onlooker play** takes place when the child watches other children play. The child may talk with other children and ask questions but does not enter into their play behavior. The child's active interest in other children's play distinguishes onlooker play from unoccupied play.

- **Parallel play** occurs when the child plays separately from others but with toys like those the others are using or in a manner that mimics their play. The older children are, the less frequently they engage in this type of play. However, even older preschool children engage in parallel play quite often.

- **Associative play** involves social interaction with little or no organization. In this type of play, children seem to be more interested in each other than in the tasks they are performing. Borrowing or lending toys and following or leading one another in line are examples of associative play.

- **Cooperative play** consists of social interaction in a group with a sense of group identity and organized activity. Children's formal games, competitions aimed at winning, and groups formed by a teacher for doing things together are examples of cooperative play. Cooperative play is the prototype for the games of middle childhood. Little cooperative play is seen in the preschool years.

Types of Play

Parten's categories represent one way of thinking about the different types of play, but they omit some types of play that are important in children's development. Whereas Parten's categories emphasize the role of play in the child's social world, the contemporary perspective on play emphasizes both the cognitive and the social aspects of play (Sumaroka & Bornstein, 2008). Among the most widely studied types of children's play today are sensorimotor and practice play, pretense/symbolic play, social play, constructive play, and games (Bergen, 1988).

Sensorimotor and Practice Play   **Sensorimotor play** is behavior by infants to derive pleasure from exercising their sensorimotor schemes. The development of sensorimotor play follows Piaget's description of sensorimotor thought, which we discussed in Chapter 6. Infants initially engage in exploratory and playful visual and motor transactions in the second quarter of the first year of life. At 9 months of age, infants begin to select novel objects for exploration and play, especially those that are responsive, such as toys that make noise or bounce. At 12 months of age, infants enjoy making things work and exploring cause and effect.

Practice play involves the repetition of behavior when new skills are being learned or when physical or mental mastery and coordination of skills are required

unoccupied play Play in which the child is not engaging in play as it is commonly understood and might stand in one spot, look around the room, or perform random movements that do not seem to have a goal.

solitary play Play in which the child plays alone and independently of others.

onlooker play Play in which the child watches other children play.

parallel play Play in which the child plays separately from others, but with toys like those the others are using or in a manner that mimics their play.

associative play Play that involves social interaction with little or no organization.

cooperative play Play that involves social interaction in a group with a sense of group identity and organized activity.

sensorimotor play Behavior engaged in by infants to derive pleasure from exercising their existing sensorimotor schemes.

practice play Play that involves repetition of behavior when new skills are being learned or when physical or mental mastery and coordination of skills are required for games or sports. Sensorimotor play, which often involves practice play, is primarily confined to infancy, while practice play can be engaged in throughout life.

A preschool "superhero" at play.

In the elementary school years, children increasingly play games, such as those playing hoptscotch here on a school playground.

for games or sports. Sensorimotor play, which often involves practice play, is primarily confined to infancy, whereas practice play can be engaged in throughout life. During the preschool years, children often engage in play that involves practicing various skills. Although practice play declines in the elementary school years, practice play activities such as running, jumping, sliding, twirling, and throwing balls or other objects are frequently observed on the playgrounds at elementary schools.

Pretense/Symbolic Play   **Pretense/symbolic play** occurs when the child transforms the physical environment into a symbol. Between 9 and 30 months of age, children increase their use of objects in symbolic play (Lillard, 2007). They learn to transform objects—substituting them for other objects and acting toward them as if they were these other objects (Smith, 2007). For example, a preschool child treats a table as if it were a car and says, "I'm fixing the car," as he grabs a leg of the table.

Many experts on play consider the preschool years the "golden age" of symbolic/pretense play that is dramatic or sociodramatic in nature (Fein, 1986; Rubin, Bukowski, & Parker, 2006). This type of make-believe play often appears at about 18 months of age and reaches a peak at 4 to 5 years of age, then gradually declines.

Some child psychologists conclude that pretend play is an important aspect of young children's development and often reflects advances in their cognitive development, especially as an indication of symbolic understanding. For example, Catherine Garvey (2000) and Angeline Lillard (2007) emphasize that hidden in young children's pretend play narratives are remarkable capacities for role-taking, balancing of social roles, metacognition (thinking about thinking), testing of the reality-pretense distinction, and numerous nonegocentric capacities that reveal the remarkable cognitive skills of young children.

Social Play   **Social play** is play that involves interaction with peers. Social play increases dramatically during the preschool years. Parten's categories, described earlier, are oriented toward social play. Social play includes varied interchanges such as turn taking, conversations about numerous topics, social games and routines, and physical play (Sumaroka & Bornstein, 2008). Social play often involves a high degree of pleasure on the part of the participants (Sumaroka & Bornstein, 2008).

Constructive Play   **Constructive play** combines sensorimotor/practice play with symbolic representation of ideas. Constructive play occurs when children engage in the self-regulated creation of a product or a solution. Constructive play increases in the preschool years as symbolic play increases and sensorimotor play decreases. In the preschool years, some practice play is replaced by constructive play. For example, instead of moving their fingers around and around in finger paint (practice play), children are more likely to draw the outline of a house or a person in the paint (constructive play). Constructive play is also a frequent form of play in the elementary school years, both in and out of the classroom. Constructive play is one of the few playlike activities allowed in work-centered classrooms. For example, if children create a play about a social studies topic, they are engaging in constructive play.

Games   **Games** are activities that are engaged in for pleasure and have rules. Often they involve competition with one or more individuals. Preschool children may begin to participate in social game play that involves simple rules of reciprocity and turn taking. However, games take on a much stronger role in the lives of elementary school children. In one study, the highest incidence of game playing occurred

pretense/symbolic play Play that occurs when a child transforms the physical environment into a symbol.

social play Play that involves interactions with peers.

constructive play Play that combines sensorimotor/practice play with symbolic representation of ideas. Constructive play occurs when children engage in self-regulated creation or construction of a product or a solution.

games Activities engaged in for pleasure that include rules and often competition with one or more individuals.

between 10 and 12 years of age (Eiferman, 1971). After age 12, games decline in popularity (Bergen, 1988).

In sum, play ranges from an infant's simple exercise of a new sensorimotor talent to a preschool child's riding a tricycle to an older child's participation in organized games. It is also important to note that children's play can involve a combination of the play categories we have described. For example, social play can be sensorimotor (rough-and-tumble), symbolic, or constructive.

Review and Reflect: Learning Goal 2

 Describe Children's Play

REVIEW

- What are the functions of play?
- How would you describe Parten's classic study of play?
- What are the different types of play?

REFLECT

- Do you think most young children's lives today are too structured? Do young children have too little time to play? Explain.

---

3 FRIENDSHIP

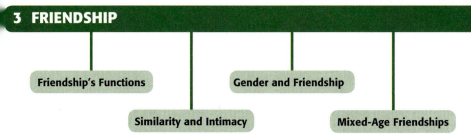

Friendship's Functions   Gender and Friendship

Similarity and Intimacy   Mixed-Age Friendships

Children play with varying acquaintances. They interact with some children they barely know, and with others they know well, for hours every day. It is to the latter type—friends—that we now turn.

Friendship's Functions

Friendships serve six functions (Gottman & Parker, 1987):

1. *Companionship.* Friendship provides children with a familiar partner, someone who is willing to spend time with them and join in collaborative activities.

2. *Stimulation.* Friendship provides children with interesting information, excitement, and amusement.

3. *Physical support.* Friendship provides resources and assistance.

4. *Ego support.* Friendship provides the expectation of support, encouragement, and feedback that helps children to maintain an impression of themselves as competent, attractive, and worthwhile individuals.

5. *Social comparison.* Friendship provides information about where children stand vis-à-vis others and whether children are doing okay.

6. *Intimacy/affection.* Friendship provides children with a warm, close, trusting relationship with another individual, a relationship that involves self-disclosure.

What are some characteristics of children's friendships?

What changes take place in friendship during the adolescent years?

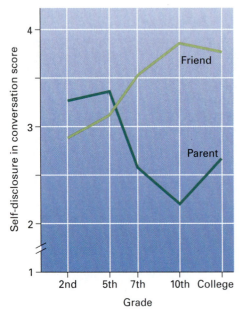

FIGURE 15.3 Developmental Changes in Self-Disclosing Conversations. Self-disclosing conversations with friends increased dramatically in adolescence while declining in an equally dramatic fashion with parents. However, self-disclosing conversations with parents began to pick up somewhat during the college years. The measure of self-disclosure involved a 5-point rating scale completed by the children and youth with a higher score representing greater self-disclosure. The data shown represent the means for each age group.

Although having friends can be a developmental advantage, not all friendships are alike (Rubin, Fredstrom, & Bowker, 2008). People differ in the company they keep—that is, who their friends are. Developmental advantages occur when children have friends who are socially skilled, supportive, and oriented toward academic achievement (Crosnoe & others, 2008). However, it is not developmentally advantageous to have coercive, conflict-ridden, and poor-quality friendships (Snyder & others, 2008; Waldrip, Malcolm, & Jensen-Campbell, 2008).

Not only does the quality of friendships have important influences on adolescents, but the friend's character, interests, and attitudes also matter (Brown, 2004). For example, researchers have found that delinquent adolescents often have delinquent friends, and they reinforce each other's delinquent behavior (Dishion, Andrews, & Crosby, 1995). Other research has indicated that nonsmoking adolescents who become friends with smoking adolescents are more likely to start smoking themselves (Urberg, 1992). Also, a recent study of more than 2,400 adolescents over 9 to 18 months revealed that adolescents whose friends were sexually experienced were more likely to initiate sexual intercourse than those whose friends were sexually inexperienced (Sieving & others, 2006). By the same token, having friends who are into school, sports, or religion is likely to have a positive influence on the adolescent.

The importance of friendship was underscored in a two-year longitudinal study (Wentzel, Barry, & Caldwell, 2004). Sixth-grade students who did not have a friend engaged in less prosocial behavior (cooperation, sharing, helping others), had lower grades, and were more emotionally distressed (depression, low well-being) than their counterparts who had one or more friends. Two years later, in the eighth grade, the students who did not have a friend in the sixth grade were still more emotionally distressed. Why are friendships so significant?

Harry Stack Sullivan (1953) was the most influential theorist to discuss the importance of friendships. In contrast to other psychoanalytic theorists' narrow emphasis on the importance of parent-child relationships, Sullivan contended that friends also play important roles in shaping children's and adolescents' well-being and development.

According to Sullivan, all people have a number of basic social needs, including the need for tenderness (secure attachment), playful companionship, social acceptance, intimacy, and sexual relations. Whether or not these needs are fulfilled largely determines our emotional well-being. For example, if the need for playful companionship goes unmet, then we become bored and depressed; if the need for social acceptance is not met, we suffer a lowered sense of self-worth. Sullivan stressed that the need for intimacy intensifies during early adolescence, motivating teenagers to seek out close friends.

Research findings support many of Sullivan's ideas. For example, adolescents report disclosing intimate and personal information to their friends more often than do younger children (Buhrmester, 1990; Buhrmester & Furman, 1987) (see Figure 15.3). Adolescents also say they depend more on friends than on parents to satisfy their needs for companionship, reassurance of worth, and intimacy (Furman & Buhrmester, 1992). In one study, daily interviews with 13- to 16-year-old adolescents over a five-day period were conducted to find out how much time they spent engaged in meaningful interactions with friends and parents (Buhrmester & Carbery, 1992). Adolescents spent an average of 103 minutes per day in meaningful interactions with friends, compared with just 28 minutes per day with parents. In addition, the quality of friendship is more strongly linked to feelings of well-being during adolescence than during childhood. Teenagers with superficial friendships, or no close friendships at all, report feeling lonelier and more depressed, and they have a lower sense of self-esteem than do teenagers with intimate friendships (Yin, Buhrmester, & Hibbard, 1996). In another study, friendship in early adolescence was a significant predictor of self-worth in early adulthood (Bagwell, Newcomb, & Bukowski, 1994).

Friendship relationships are often important sources of support (Berndt, 1999). Sullivan described how adolescent friends support one another's sense of personal worth. When close friends disclose their mutual insecurities and fears about themselves, they discover that they are not "abnormal" and that they have nothing to be ashamed of. Friends also act as important confidants who help children and adolescents work through upsetting problems (such as difficulties with parents or the breakup of romance) by providing both emotional support and informational advice. Friends can also protect "at-risk" adolescents from victimization by peers (Bukowski, Sippola, & Boivin, 1995). In addition, friends can become active partners in building a sense of identity. During countless hours of conversation, friends act as sounding boards as teenagers explore issues ranging from future plans to stances on religious and moral issues.

Willard Hartup (1996, 2000), who has studied peer relations across four decades, has concluded that children often use friends as cognitive and social resources on a regular basis. Hartup also commented that normative transitions, such as moving from elementary to middle school, are negotiated more competently by children who have friends than by those who don't.

To read about appropriate and inappropriate strategies for making friends, see the *Caring for Children* interlude.

Caring for Children

APPROPRIATE AND INAPPROPRIATE STRATEGIES FOR MAKING FRIENDS

Here are some strategies that adults can recommend to children and adolescents for making friends (Wentzel, 1997):

- *Initiate interaction.* Learn about a friend: Ask for his or her name, age, favorite activities. Use these prosocial overtures: Introduce yourself, start a conversation, and invite him or her to do things.

- *Be nice.* Show kindness, be considerate, and compliment the other person.

- *Engage in prosocial behavior.* Be honest and trustworthy: Tell the truth, keep promises. Be generous, share, and be cooperative.

- *Show respect for yourself and others.* Have good manners, be polite and courteous, and listen to what others have to say. Have a positive attitude and personality.

- *Provide social support.* Show you care.

What are some appropriate and inappropriate strategies for making friends?

And here are some inappropriate strategies for making friends that adults can recommend that children and adolescents avoid using (Wentzel, 1997):

- *Be psychologically aggressive.* Show disrespect and have bad manners. Use others, be uncooperative, don't share, ignore others, gossip, and spread rumors.

- *Present yourself negatively.* Be self-centered, snobby, conceited, and jealous; show off, care only about yourself. Be mean, have a bad attitude, be angry, throw temper tantrums, and start trouble.

- *Behave antisocially.* Be physically aggressive, yell at others, pick on them, make fun of them, be dishonest, tell secrets, and break promises.

What are some differences in the friendships of females and males?

intimacy in friendship Self-disclosure or the sharing of private thoughts.

Similarity and Intimacy

What characteristics do children and adolescents look for in their friends? The answers change somewhat as children grow up, but one characteristic of friends is found throughout the childhood and adolescent years: Friends are generally similar—in terms of age, sex, ethnicity, and many other factors (Prinstein & Dodge, 2008; Rubin, Fredstrom & Bowker, 2008). Friends often have similar attitudes toward school, similar educational aspirations, and closely aligned achievement orientations. Friends like the same music, wear the same kind of clothes, and prefer the same leisure activities (Berndt, 1982). Differences may lead to conflicts that weaken the friendship. For example, if two friends have differing attitudes toward school, one may repeatedly want to play basketball or go to the mall while the other insists on completing homework, and the two may drift apart.

Priorities change as the child reaches adolescence (Collins & Steinberg, 2006). The most consistent finding in the last two decades of research on adolescent friendships is that intimacy is an important feature of friendship (Berndt & Perry, 1990; Bukowski, Newcomb, & Hoza, 1987). In most research studies, **intimacy in friendship** is defined narrowly as self-disclosure or sharing of private thoughts; private or personal knowledge about a friend has been used as an index of intimacy (Selman, 1980; Sullivan, 1953). When young adolescents are asked what they want from a friend or how they can tell someone is their best friend, they frequently say that a best friend will share problems with them, understand them, and listen when they talk about their own thoughts or feelings. When young children talk about their friendships, they rarely comment about intimate self-disclosure or mutual understanding. In one investigation, friendship intimacy was more prominent in 13- to 16-year-olds than in 10- to 13-year-olds (Buhrmester, 1990).

Gender and Friendship

Are the friendships of girls different from the friendships of boys? An increasing number of studies indicate that they are different (Bukowski & Saldarriaga Mesa, 2007). For example, the influence of friendship, both positive and negative, may be stronger for girls. Also, issues of control and intimacy likely play a more powerful role in girls' friendships. For example, a recent study revealed that girls reported intimacy was more important in their friendship, whereas boys indicated that doing things together, such as engaging in common activities like sports or playing computer games, was more important in their friendship (McDougall & Hymel, 2007).

Let's further examine gender differences in the intimacy aspect of friendship. When asked to describe their best friends, girls refer to intimate conversations and faithfulness more than boys do (Collins & Steinberg, 2006; Ruble, Martin, & Berenbaum, 2006). For example, girls are more likely to describe their best friend as "sensitive just like me" or "trustworthy just like me" (Duck, 1975). When conflict is present, girls place a higher priority on relationship goals such as being patient until the relationship improves, whereas boys are more likely to seek control over a friend (Rose & Asher, 1999; Ruble, Martin, & Berenbaum, 2006). Although girls' friendships in adolescence are more likely to focus on intimacy, boys' friendships tend to emphasize power and excitement (Ruble, Martin, & Berenbaum, 2006). Boys may discourage one another from openly disclosing their problems because self-disclosure is not masculine (Maccoby, 1996). Boys make themselves vulnerable to being called "wimps" if they can't handle their own problems and insecurities. These gender differences are generally assumed to reflect a greater orientation toward interpersonal relationships among girls than boys.

As indicated in the *Caring for Children* interlude, friendship often provides social support. A recent study of third- through ninth-graders, though, revealed that one aspect of girls' social support in friendship may have costs as well as benefits (Rose, Carlson, & Waller, 2007). In the study, girls' co-rumination (as reflected in excessively discussing problems) predicted not only an increase in positive friendship quality but also an increase in further co-rumination as well as an increase in depressive and anxiety symptoms. One implication of the research is that some girls who are vulnerable to developing internalized problems may go undetected because they have supportive friendships.

The study just described indicates that the characteristics of an adolescents' friends can influence whether the friends have a positive or negative influence on the adolescent. Consider a recent study which revealed that friends' grade-point average was an important positive attribute (Cook, Deng, & Morgano, 2007). Friends' grade-point average was a consistent predictor of positive school achievement and also was linked to a lower level of negative behavior in areas such as drug abuse and acting out. Another recent study found that taking math courses in high school, especially for girls, was strongly linked to the achievement of their best friends (Crosnoe & others, 2008). And as we saw in Chapter 13, having delinquent peers and friends greatly increases the risk of becoming delinquent (Brown & others, 2008; Dishion, Piehler, & Myers, 2008).

Mixed-Age Friendships

Although most adolescents develop friendships with individuals who are close to their own age, some adolescents become best friends with younger or older individuals. A common fear, especially among parents, is that adolescents who have older friends will be encouraged to engage in delinquent behavior or early sexual behavior. Researchers have found that adolescents who interact with older youth do engage in these behaviors more frequently, but it is not known whether the older youth guide younger adolescents toward deviant behavior or whether the younger adolescents were already prone to deviant behavior before they developed the friendship with the older youth (Billy, Rodgers, & Udry, 1984). A recent study also revealed that over time, from the sixth through tenth grades, girls were more likely to have older male friends, which places some girls on a developmental trajectory for engaging in problem behavior (Poulin & Pedersen, 2007).

Review and Reflect: Learning Goal 3

 3 Explain Friendship

REVIEW

- What are six functions of friendship? What is Sullivan's view of friendship?
- What role do similarity and intimacy play in friendship?
- How does gender impact friendship?
- What is the developmental outcome of mixed-age friendship?

REFLECT

- Examine the list of six functions of friendships at the beginning of this section. Rank order the six functions from most (1) to least (6) important as you were growing up.

4 PEER RELATIONS IN ADOLESCENCE

What characterizes peer pressure in adolescence?

Peer Pressure and Conformity   **Adolescent Groups Versus Child Groups**

Cliques and Crowds

We already have discussed a number of changes in adolescents' peer relations, including the increasing importance of friendships. Peer relations play such a powerful role in the lives of adolescents that we further consider additional aspects in this section.

When you think back to your adolescent years, many of your most enjoyable moments probably were spent with peers—on the telephone, in school activities, in the neighborhood, at dances, or just hanging out. Peer relations undergo important changes in adolescence. In childhood, the focus of peer relations is on being liked by classmates and being included in games or lunchroom conversations. Being overlooked or, worse yet, being rejected can have damaging effects on children's development that sometimes are carried forward to adolescence. Beginning in early adolescence, teenagers typically prefer to have a smaller number of friendships that are more intense and intimate than those of young children. Cliques are formed and shape the social lives of adolescents as they begin to "hang out" together.

Peer Pressure and Conformity

Young adolescents conform more to peer standards than children do. Around the eighth and ninth grades, conformity to peers—especially to their antisocial standards—peaks (Brown & others, 2008). At this point, adolescents are most likely to go along with a peer to steal hubcaps off a car, draw graffiti on a wall, or steal cosmetics from a store counter. A recent study revealed that 14 to 18 years of age is an especially important time for developing the ability to stand up for what one believes and resist peer pressure to do otherwise (Steinberg & Monahan, 2007). One study also found that U.S. adolescents are more likely than Japanese adolescents to put pressure on their peers to resist parental influence (Rothbaum & others, 2000).

Which adolescents are most likely to conform to peers? Adolescents who are uncertain about their social identity, which can appear in the form of low self-esteem and high social anxiety, are most likely to conform to peers (Prinstein, 2007; Prinstein & Dodge, 2008). This uncertainty often increases during times of transitions, such as school and family transitions. Also peers are more likely to conform when they are in the presence of someone they perceive to have higher status than themselves.

I didn't belong as a kid, and that always bothered me. If only I'd known that one day my differentness would be an asset, then my early life would have been much easier.

—BETTE MIDLER
Contemporary American Actress

cliques Small groups that range from 2 to about 12 individuals and average about 5 to 6 individuals. Cliques can form because of friendship or because individuals engage in similar activities, and members usually are of the same sex and about the same age.

Cliques and Crowds

Cliques and crowds assume more important roles in the lives of adolescents than children (Brown, 2003, 2004; Brown & others, 2008). **Cliques** are small groups that range from 2 to about 12 individuals and average about 5 to 6 individuals. The clique members are usually of the same sex and about the same age. Cliques can form because adolescents engage in similar activities, such as being in a club or on a sports team. Some cliques also form because of friendship. Several adolescents may form a clique because they have spent time with each other and enjoy each other's company. Not necessarily friends, they often develop a friendship if they stay in the clique. What do adolescents do in cliques? They share ideas, hang out together, and often develop an in-group identity in which they believe that their clique is better than other cliques.

Crowds are a larger group structure than cliques. Adolescents are usually members of a crowd based on reputation and may or may not spend much time together. Crowds are less personal than cliques. Many crowds are defined by the activities adolescents engage in (such as "jocks," who are good at sports, or "druggies," who take drugs). Reputation-based crowds often appear for the first time in early adolescence and usually become less prominent in late adolescence (Collins & Steinberg, 2006).

In one study, crowd membership was associated with adolescent self-esteem (Brown & Lohr, 1987). The crowds included jocks (athletically oriented), populars (well-known students who led social activities), normals (middle-of-the-road students who made up the masses), druggies or toughs (known for illicit drug use or other delinquent activities), and nobodies (low in social skills or intellectual abilities). The self-esteem of the jocks and the populars was highest, whereas that of the nobodies was lowest. One group of adolescents not in a crowd had self-esteem equivalent to that of the jocks and the populars; this group was the independents, who indicated that crowd membership was not important to them. Keep in mind that these data are correlational; self-esteem could increase an adolescent's probability of becoming a crowd member, just as crowd membership could increase the adolescent's self-esteem.

Adolescent Groups Versus Child Groups

Adolescent groups differ from child groups in at least three important ways. First, during the adolescent years, groups tend to include a broader array of members than they did during childhood. The members of child groups often are friends or neighborhood acquaintances; in contrast, many adolescent groups include members who are neither friends nor neighborhood acquaintances. Try to recall the student council, honor society, or football team at your junior high school. If you were a member of any of these organizations, you probably remember that they were made up of many people you had not met before and that they were a more heterogeneous group than your childhood peer groups. For example, peer groups in adolescence are more likely to have a mixture of individuals from different ethnic groups than are peer groups in childhood.

Second, in adolescent peer groups, rules and regulations are usually defined more precisely than in children's peer groups. Childhood groups are usually not as formalized as many adolescent groups. For example, captains or leaders are often formally elected or appointed in adolescent peer groups.

Third, during adolescence mixed-sex participation in groups increases (Collins & Steinberg, 2006). Dexter Dunphy (1963) documented this increase in mixed-sex groups in a well-known observational study. Figure 15.4 outlines his view of how these mixed-sex groups develop. In late childhood, boys and girls participate in small, same-sex cliques. As they move into the early adolescent years, the same-sex cliques begin to interact with each other. Gradually, the leaders and high-status members form further cliques based on mixed-sex relationships. Eventually, the newly created mixed-sex cliques replace the same-sex cliques. The mixed-sex cliques interact with each other in large crowd activities, too—at dances and athletic events, for example. In late adolescence, the crowd begins to dissolve as couples develop more-serious relationships and make long-range plans that may include engagement and marriage.

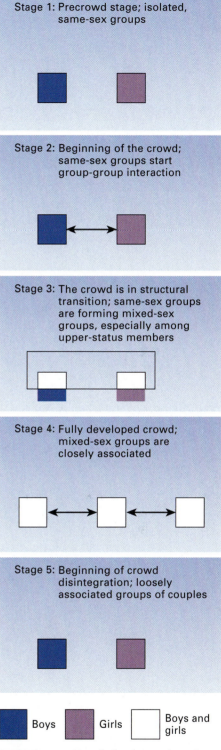

FIGURE 15.4 Dunphy's Progression of Peer Group Relations in Adolescence

crowds The crowd is a larger group structure than a clique. Adolescents usually are members of a crowd based on reputation and may or may not spend much time together. Many crowds are defined by the activities adolescents engage in.

Review and Reflect: Learning Goal 4

4 Characterize Peer Relations in Adolescence

REVIEW

- What is peer pressure and conformity like in adolescence?
- How are cliques and crowds involved in adolescent development?
- How do adolescents' groups differ from children's groups?

REFLECT

- What were your peer relationships like during adolescence? What peer groups were you involved in? How did they influence your development? If you could change anything about the way you experienced peer relations in adolescence, what would it be?

Reach Your Learning Goals

Peers

1 PEER RELATIONS: DISCUSS PEER RELATIONS IN CHILDHOOD

Peer Group Functions

- Peers are children who are at about the same age or maturity level. Peers provide a means of social comparison and a source of information about the world outside the family. Good peer relations may be necessary for normal social development. The inability to "plug in" to a social network is associated with a number of problems. Peer relations can be both positive and negative. Piaget and Sullivan stressed that peer relations provide the context for learning important aspects of relationships, such as observing others' interests and perspectives and exploring fairness and justice by working through disagreements. Peer relations vary according to the way peer experience is measured, the outcomes specified, and the developmental trajectories traversed.

The Developmental Course of Peer Relations in Childhood

- Some researchers argue that the quality of social interaction with peers in infancy provides valuable information about socioemotional development. As increasing numbers of infants have attended child care, infant peer relations have increased. The frequency of peer interaction, both positive and negative, increases in the preschool years. Children spend even more time with peers in the elementary and secondary school years, and their preference for same-sex groups increases. Boys' groups are larger than girls', and they participate in more organized games than girls. Girls engage in more collaborative discourse in peer groups than boys.

The Distinct but Coordinated Worlds of Parent-Child and Peer Relations

- Healthy family relations usually promote healthy peer relations. Parents can model or coach their children in ways of relating to peers. Parents' choices of neighborhoods, churches, schools, and their own friends influence the pool from which their children might select possible friends. Rough-and-tumble play occurs mainly in peer relations rather than in parent-child relations. In times of stress, children usually turn to parents rather than peers. Peer relations have a more equal basis than parent-child relations.

Social Cognition and Emotion

- Perspective taking and social information-processing skills are important dimensions of social cognition in peer relations. Perspective taking helps children communicate effectively. Self-regulation of emotion is associated with positive peer relations.

Peer Statuses

- Popular children are frequently nominated as a best friend and are rarely disliked by their peers. Average children receive an average number of both positive and negative nominations from their peers. Neglected children are infrequently nominated as a best friend but are not disliked by their peers. Rejected children are infrequently nominated as a best friend and are disliked by their peers. Rejected children often have more serious adjustment problems than neglected children. Controversial children are frequently nominated both as one's best friend and as being disliked by peers.

Bullying

- Bullying is physical or verbal behavior meant to disturb a less powerful individual. Significant numbers of students are bullied, and this is linked to adjustment problems for the victim, the bully, or the individual who is both a bully and a victim.

2 PLAY: DESCRIBE CHILDREN'S PLAY

Play's Functions

- The functions of play include affiliation with peers, tension release, advances in cognitive development, and exploration.

Parten's Classic Study of Play

- Parten examined these categories of social play: unoccupied, solitary, onlooker, parallel, associative, and cooperative. Parten's categories emphasize the role of play in the child's social world.

Types of Play

- The contemporary perspective emphasizes both social and cognitive aspects of play. The most widely studied types of play include sensorimotor and practice play, pretense/symbolic play, social play, constructive play, and games.

3   FRIENDSHIP: EXPLAIN FRIENDSHIP

Friendship's Functions

- The functions of friendship include companionship, stimulation, physical support, ego support, social comparison, and intimacy/affection. Sullivan points out that whether or not these functions of friendship are fulfilled largely determines our emotional well-being. Sullivan argued that there is a dramatic increase in the psychological importance and intimacy of close friends in early adolescence. Research findings support his view.

Similarity and Intimacy

- Similarity and intimacy are two of the most common characteristics of friendships. Friends often have similar attitudes toward school, similar educational aspirations, and so on. Intimacy in friendship is much more common in adolescents than children.

Gender and Friendship

- An increasing number of studies indicate that the friendships of girls are different from the friendships of boys. The influence of friendship, both positive and negative, may be stronger for girls, and the issue of intimacy plays a powerful role in girls' friendships, and power and excitement and control play important roles in boys' friendships.

Mixed-Age Frienships

- Children and adolescents who become friends with older individuals engage in more deviant behaviors than their counterparts with same-age friends. Girls in grades 6 through 10, who often have older male friends, may be more likely to engage in problem behavior.

4   PEER RELATIONS IN ADOLESCENCE: CHARACTERIZE PEER RELATIONS IN ADOLESCENCE

Peer Pressure and Conformity

- The pressure to conform to peers is strong during adolescence, especially in eighth and ninth grade, and can be positive or negative.

Cliques and Crowds

- Cliques and crowds assume more importance in the lives of adolescents than children. Membership in certain crowds—especially jocks and populars—is associated with increased self-esteem. Independents also show high self-esteem.

Adolescent Groups Versus Child Groups

- Children's groups are less formal, less heterogeneous, and have less mixed-sex participation than adolescents' groups.

KEY TERMS

peers 451
perspective taking 454
popular children 456
average children 456
neglected children 456
rejected children 456

controversial children 456
play 460
play therapy 460
unoccupied play 461
solitary play 461
onlooker play 461

parallel play 461
associative play 461
cooperative play 461
sensorimotor play 461
practice play 461
pretense/symbolic play 462

social play 462
constructive play 462
games 462
intimacy in friendship 466
cliques 468
crowds 469

KEY PEOPLE

Kenneth Dodge 455
Erik Erikson 460
Sigmund Freud 460

Jean Piaget 460
Lev Vygotsky 460
Daniel Berlyne 460

Mildred Parten 461
Catherine Garvey and Angeline
   Lillard 462

Harry Stack Sullivan 464
Willard Hartup 465
Dexter Dunphy 469

E-LEARNING TOOLS

To help you master the material in this chapter, you'll find a number of valuable study tools at the Online Learning Center for *Child Development*, twelfth edition (**www.mhhe.com/santrockcd12**).

Taking It to the Net

Research the answers to these questions:

1. Barbara is going to lead a discussion in her child development class about peer relationships and friendships in early childhood. What should Barbara tell the class about how peer relationships develop between the ages of 3 and 6 years?

2. Darla, 13, has been living in foster homes since she was 4. As a result of being abandoned by her parents and moved from foster home to foster home, she doesn't trust anyone. She is in counseling to help her adjust to her latest home and new middle school. Her therapist brings up the importance of making and having friends, a concept alien to Darla. Why does Darla need to learn to have friends and to be one?

3. Kristin is getting intense pressure from her friends at school to go out and drink with them. She wants to spend time with them, but has no interest in drinking. Since she can't turn to her friends to help her, she hopes her mother can give her some pointers for dealing with this pressure. How can Kristin's mother help?

Health and Well-Being, Parenting, and Education Exercises

Build your decision-making skills by trying your hand at the health and well-being, parenting, and education exercises.

Video Clips

The Online Learning Center includes the following videos for this chapter:

- *Describing Friends at Age 5*
Tara states that she has two special friends. She explains that these friends are special because they play together.

- *Describing Friendships at Age 8*
In this clip, a boy describes his two best friends and what they like to do together. When asked if he has any girlfriends, he quickly responds, "No." But then he adds that his sisters are his friends.

- *15-Year-Old Girls' Relationships with Boys*
In this clip, we hear three high school students talk about how their relationships with boys have changed since middle school.

- *Talking About Cliques at Age 15*
Three high school girls describe the cliques in their school and what makes someone popular. They describe physical appearance as important but personality too.

16

> *The whole art of teaching is the art of awakening the natural curiosity of young minds.*
>
> —ANATOLE FRANCE
> *French Novelist, 20th Century*

LEARNING GOALS

- ◆ Discuss approaches to schooling and development.

- ◆ Describe the roles of socioeconomic status and ethnicity in schools.

- ◆ Characterize children with disabilities and their schooling.

- ◆ Explain the development of achievement in children.

SCHOOLS AND ACHIEVEMENT

Images of Child Development
The Story of Reggio Emilia's Children

A Reggio Emilia classroom in which young children explore topics that interest them.

The Reggio Emilia approach is an educational program for young children that was developed in the northern Italian city of Reggio Emilia. Children of single parents and children with disabilities have priority in admission; other children are admitted according to a scale of needs. Parents pay on a sliding scale based on income.

The children are encouraged to learn by investigating and exploring topics that interest them. A wide range of stimulating media and materials is available for children to use as they learn—music, movement, drawing, painting, sculpting, collages, puppets and disguises, and photography, for example (Strong-Wilson & Ellis, 2007).

In this program, children often explore topics in a group, which fosters a sense of community, respect for diversity, and a collaborative approach to problem solving (Hyson, Copple, & Jones, 2006). Two co-teachers are present to serve as guides for children. The Reggio Emilia teachers consider a project as an adventure, which can start from an adult's suggestion, from a child's idea, or from an event, such as a snowfall or something else unexpected. Every project is based on what the children say and do. The teachers allow children enough time to think and craft a project.

At the core of the Reggio Emilia approach is the image of children who are competent and have rights, especially the right to outstanding care and education. Parent participation is considered essential, and cooperation is a major theme in the schools. Many early childhood education experts believe the Reggio Emilia approach provides a supportive, stimulating context in which children are motivated to explore their world in a competent and confident manner (New, 2005, 2007).

PREVIEW

This chapter is about becoming educated and achieving. We will explore such topics as contemporary approaches to student learning, school transitions, the roles that socioeconomic status and ethnicity play in schools, educational issues involving children with disabilities, and becoming motivated to achieve goals.

1 EXPLORING CHILDREN'S SCHOOLING

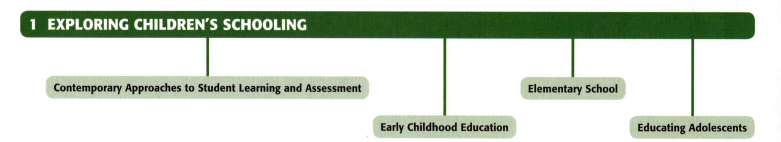

Contemporary Approaches to Student Learning and Assessment

Early Childhood Education

Elementary School

Educating Adolescents

We have discussed many aspects of schools throughout this book but especially in Section 3, "Cognition and Language." Recall our coverage of applications of Piaget's and Vygotsky's theories to education in Chapter 6, strategies for encouraging children's critical thinking in schools in Chapter 7, applications of Gardner's and Sternberg's theories of intelligence to education in Chapter 8, and bilingual education in Chapter 9. Here we take a closer look at contemporary approaches to student learning in U.S.

schools and at how schooling varies from early childhood education through high school.

Contemporary Approaches to Student Learning and Assessment

Controversy swirls about the best way to teach children and how to hold schools and teachers accountable for whether children are learning (Johnson & others, 2008; Stiggins, 2008).

Constructivist and Direct Instruction Approaches

The **constructivist approach** is a learner-centered approach that emphasizes the importance of individuals actively constructing their knowledge and understanding with guidance from the teacher. In the constructivist view, teachers should not attempt to simply pour information into children's minds. Rather, children should be encouraged to explore their world, discover knowledge, reflect, and think critically with careful monitoring and meaningful guidance from the teacher (Eby, Herrell, & Jordan, 2009; Morrison, 2009). The constructivist belief is that for too long in American education children have been required to sit still, be passive learners, and rotely memorize irrelevant as well as relevant information (Armstrong, Henson, & Savage, 2009).

Today, constructivism may include an emphasis on collaboration—children working with each other in their efforts to know and understand (Bodrova & Leong, 2007). A teacher with a constructivist instructional philosophy would not have children memorize information rotely but would give them opportunities to meaningfully construct the knowledge and understand the material while guiding their learning (Kellough & Carjuzaa, 2009).

Consider an elementary school classroom that is investigating a school bus (Katz & Chard, 1989). The children write to the district's school superintendent and ask if they can have a bus parked at their school for a few days. They study the bus, discover the functions of its parts, and discuss traffic rules. Then, in the classroom, they build their own bus out of cardboard. The children are having fun, but they also are practicing writing, problem solving, and even some arithmetic. When the class has their parents' night, all that the parents want to see is the bus because their children have been talking about it at home for weeks. Many education experts emphasize that this is the kind of education all children deserve. That is, they argue that children should be active, constructivist learners and taught through concrete, hands-on experience.

By contrast, the **direct instruction approach** is a structured, teacher-centered approach that is characterized by teacher direction and control, high teacher expectations for students' progress, maximum time spent by students on academic tasks, and efforts by the teacher to keep negative affect to a minimum. An important goal in the direct instruction approach is maximizing student learning time.

Advocates of the constructivist approach argue that the direct instruction approach turns children into passive learners and does not adequately

Is this classroom more likely constructivist or direct instruction? **Explain.**

*E*ducation is the transmission of civilization.

—**ARIEL AND WILL DURANT**
American Authors and Philosophers, 20th Century

constructivist approach A learner-centered approach that emphasizes the importance of individuals actively constructing their knowledge and understanding with guidance from the teacher.

direct instruction approach A teacher-centered approach characterized by teacher direction and control, mastery of academic material, high expectations for students' progress, and maximum time spent on learning tasks.

challenge them to think in critical and creative ways (Oakes & Lipton, 2007). The direct instruction enthusiasts say that the constructivist approaches do not give enough attention to the content of a discipline, such as history or science. They also point out that the constructivist approaches are too relativistic and vague.

Some experts in educational psychology observe that many effective teachers use both a constructivist *and* a direct instruction approach rather than either exclusively (Bransford & others, 2006; Darling-Hammond & Bransford, 2005). Further, some circumstances may call more for a constructivist approach, others for a direction instruction approach. For example, experts increasingly recommend an explicit, intellectually engaging direct instruction approach when teaching students with a reading or a writing disability (Berninger, 2006).

Accountability   Since the 1990s, the U.S. public and governments at every level have demanded increased accountability from schools. One result was the spread of state-mandated tests to measure just what students had or had not learned (Gronlund & Waugh, 2009; Oosterhof, 2009). Many states identified objectives for students in their state and created tests to measure whether students were meeting those objectives. This approach became national policy in 2002 when the No Child Left Behind (NCLB) legislation was signed into law.

Advocates argue that state-wide standardized testing will have a number of positive effects. These include improved student performance; more time teaching the subjects that are tested; high expectations for all students; identification of poorly performing schools, teachers, and administrators; and improved confidence in schools as test scores rise.

Most educators support high expectations and high standards for students. At issue, however, is whether the tests and procedures mandated by NCLB are the best ones for achieving high standards (Yell & Drasgow, 2009).

Critics argue that the NCLB legislation will do more harm than good (Stiggins, 2008). One criticism stresses that using a single test as the sole indicator of students' progress and competence presents a very narrow view of students' skills (Lewis, 2007). This criticism is similar to the one leveled at IQ tests, which we described in Chapter 8. To assess student progress and achievement, many psychologists and educators emphasize that a number of measures should be used, including tests, quizzes, projects, portfolios, classroom observations, and so on. Also, the tests used as part of NCLB don't measure creativity, motivation, persistence, flexible thinking, and social skills (Clark, 2008; Cloud, 2007). Critics point out that teachers end up spending far too much class time "teaching to the test" by drilling students and having them memorize isolated facts at the expense of teaching that focuses on thinking skills, which students need for success in life. Despite such criticisms, most U.S. schools are making accommodations to meet the requirements of NCLB.

Let's now explore how schools work at different developmental levels of students. We will begin with early childhood education.

Early Childhood Education

To the teachers at a Reggio-Emilia program (described in the chapter opening), preschool children are active learners, exploring the world with their peers, constructing their knowledge of the world in collaboration with their community, aided but not directed by the teachers. In many ways, the Reggio Emilia approach applies ideas consistent with the views of Piaget and Vygotsky discussed in Chapter 6. Does it matter to the children? How do other early education programs treat children, and how do the children fare? Our exploration of early childhood education focuses on variations in programs, education for children who are disadvantaged, and some controversies in early childhood education.

What are some of the most important purposes of standardized tests?

Variations in Early Childhood Education   There are many variations in the way young children are educated (Henninger, 2009; Morrison, 2009; Schweinhart, 2009). The foundation of early childhood education has been the child-centered kindergarten.

The Child-Centered Kindergarten   Nurturing is a key aspect of the **child-centered kindergarten**, which emphasizes the education of the whole child and concern for his or her physical, cognitive, and socio-emotional development (Driscoll & Nagel, 2008). Instruction is organized around the child's needs, interests, and learning styles. Emphasis is on the process of learning, rather than what is learned (Morrison, 2009). The child-centered kindergarten honors three principles: Each child follows a unique developmental pattern; young children learn best through first-hand experiences with people and materials; and play is extremely important in the child's total development.

The Montessori Approach   Montessori schools are patterned after the educational philosophy of Maria Montessori (1870–1952), an Italian physician-turned-educator, who crafted a revolutionary approach to young children's education at the beginning of the twentieth century. The **Montessori approach** is a philosophy of education in which children are given considerable freedom and spontaneity in choosing activities. They are allowed to move from one activity to another as they desire. The teacher acts as a facilitator rather than a director. The teacher shows the child how to perform intellectual activities, demonstrates interesting ways to explore curriculum materials, and offers help when the child requests it. "By encouraging children to make decisions from an early age, Montessori programs seek to develop self-regulated problem solvers who can make choices and manage their time effectively" (Hyson, Copple, & Jones, 2006, p. 14). The number of Montessori schools in the United States has expanded dramatically in recent years, from one school in 1959 to 355 schools in 1970 to approximately 4,000 in 2005 (Whitescarver, 2006).

Some developmentalists favor the Montessori approach, but others maintain that it neglects children's socioemotional development. For example, while Montessori fosters independence and the development of cognitive skills, it deemphasizes verbal interaction between the teacher and child and peer interaction. Montessori's critics also argue that it restricts imaginative play and that its heavy reliance on self-corrective materials may not adequately allow for creativity and for a variety of learning styles (Goffin & Wilson, 2001).

Developmentally Appropriate and Inappropriate Education   A growing number of educators and psychologists argue that preschool and young elementary school children learn best through active, hands-on teaching methods such as games and dramatic play. They know that children develop at varying rates and that schools need to allow for these individual differences (Brewer, 2007; Kostelnik, Soderman, & Whiren, 2007). They also observe that schools should focus on improving children's socioemotional development, as well as their cognitive development (Morrison, 2009). Educators refer to this type of schooling as **developmentally appropriate practice**, which is based on knowledge of the typical development of children within an age span (age-appropriateness) as well as the uniqueness of the child (individual-appropriateness) (NAEYC, 1997). In contrast, developmentally inappropriate practice for young child relies on abstract paper-and-pencil activities presented to large groups.

One study compared 182 children from five developmentally appropriate kindergarten classrooms (with hands-on activities and integrated curriculum tailored to meet age group, cultural, and individual learning styles) and five developmentally inappropriate kindergarten classrooms (which had an academic, direct instruction emphasis with extensive use of workbooks/worksheets, seatwork, and rote drill/practice activities) in a Louisiana school system (Hart & others, 2003). Children from the two types of classrooms did not differ in pre-kindergarten readiness, and the classrooms were balanced in terms of sex

Larry Page and Sergey Brin, founders of the highly successful Internet search engine, Google, recently said that their early years at Montessori schools were a major factor in their success (International Montessori Council, 2006). During an interview with Barbara Walters, they said they learned how to be self-directed and self-starters at Montessori (ABC News, 2005). They commented that Montessori experiences encouraged them to think for themselves and allowed them the freedom to develop their own interests.

child-centered kindergarten Education that involves the whole child by considering both the child's physical, cognitive, and socioemotional development and the child's needs, interests, and learning styles.

Montessori approach An educational philosophy in which children are given considerable freedom and spontaneity in choosing activities and are allowed to move from one activity to another as they desire.

developmentally appropriate practice Education that focuses on the typical developmental patterns of children (age-appropriateness) and the uniqueness of each child (individual-appropriateness). Such practice contrasts with developmentally inappropriate practice, which relies on abstract paper-and-pencil activities presented to large groups of young children.

and socioeconomic status. Teacher ratings of child behavior and scores on the California Achievement Test were obtained through the third grade. Children taught in developmentally inappropriate classrooms had slower growth in vocabulary, math application, and math computation.

However, not all studies show significant positive benefits for developmentally appropriate education (Hyson, 2007; Hyson, Copple, & Jones, 2006). Among the reasons it is difficult to generalize about research on developmentally appropriate education is that individual programs often vary, and developmentally appropriate education is an evolving concept. Recent changes in the concept have given more attention to sociocultural factors, the teacher's active involvement and implementation of systematic intentions, as well as how strong academic skills should be emphasized and how they should be taught.

Education for Young Children Who Are Disadvantaged

For many years, U.S. children from low-income families did not receive any education before they entered the first grade. As a result, they began first grade already several steps behind their classmates who had attended kindergarten and possibly preschool. In the summer of 1965, the federal government began an effort to break the cycle of poverty and poor education for young children in the United States through **Project Head Start**. It is a compensatory program designed to provide children from low-income families the opportunity to acquire the skills and experiences important for success in school. Project Head Start is the largest federally funded program for U.S. children (Hagen & Lamb-Parker, 2008).

The goals and methods of Head Start programs vary greatly around the country. The U.S. Congress is considering whether to infuse Head Start programs with a stronger academic focus. Some worry that the emphasis on academic skills will come at the expense of reduced health services and decreased emphasis on socioemotional skills (Stipek, 2004).

Head Start programs are not all created equal (Hustedt & Barnett, 2009; Zigler, 2009). One estimate is that 40 percent of the 1,400 Head Start programs are of questionable quality (Zigler & Styfco, 1994). More attention needs to be given to developing consistently high-quality Head Start programs. One individual who is strongly motivated to make Head Start a valuable learning experience for young children from disadvantaged backgrounds is Yolanda Garcia. To read about her work, see the *Careers in Child Development* profile.

Project Head Start Compensatory education designed to provide children from low-income families the opportunity to acquire the skills and experiences important for school success.

Careers in Child Development

Yolanda Garcia, Director of Children's Services/Head Start

Yolanda Garcia has worked in the field of early childhood education and family support for three decades. She has been the Director of the Children's Services Department for the Santa Clara, California, County Office of Education since 1980. As director, she is responsible for managing child development programs for 2,500 3- to 5-year-old children in 127 classrooms. Her training includes two master's degrees, one in public policy and child welfare from the University of Chicago and another in educational administration from San Jose State University.

Garcia has served on many national advisory committees that have resulted in improvements in the staffing of Head Start programs. Most notably, she served on the Head Start Quality Committee that recommended the development of Early Head Start and revised performance standards for Head Start programs. Garcia currently is a member of the American Academy of Science Committee on the Integration of Science and Early Childhood Education.

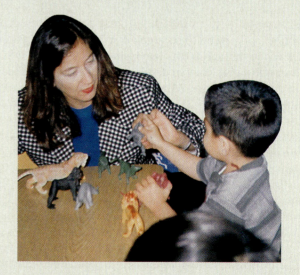

Yolanda Garcia, Director of Children's Services/Head Start, working with some Head Start children in Santa Clara, California.

Evaluations support the positive influence of quality early childhood programs on both the cognitive and social worlds of disadvantaged young children (Chambers, Chung, & Slavin, 2006; Ryan, Fauth, & Brooks-Gunn, 2006). One high-quality early childhood education program (although not a Head Start program) is the Perry Preschool program in Ypsilanti, Michigan, a two-year preschool program that includes weekly home visits from program personnel. In analyses of the long-term effects of the program, adults who had been in the Perry Preschool program were compared with a control group of adults from the same background who did not receive the enriched early childhood education (Schweinhart & others, 2005; Weikart, 1993). Those who had been in the Perry Preschool program had fewer teen pregnancies and higher high school graduation rates and at age 40 more were in the workforce, owned their own homes, had a savings account, and had fewer arrests.

Controversies in Early Childhood Education   Currently there is controversy about what the curriculum of U.S. early childhood education should be (Henninger, 2009; Hyson, 2007; Kagan & Kauerz, 2009). On one side are those who advocate a child-centered, constructivist approach much like that emphasized by the National Association for the Education of Young Children (NAEYC) along the lines of developmentally appropriate practice. On the other side are those who advocate an academic, direct instruction approach.

In reality, many high-quality early childhood education programs include both academic and constructivist approaches. Many education experts like Lillian Katz (1999), though, worry about academic approaches that place too much pressure on young children to achieve and don't provide any opportunities to actively construct knowledge. Competent early childhood programs also should focus on cognitive development *and* socioemotional development, not exclusively on cognitive development (Kagan & Kauerz, 2009; Kagan & Scott-Little, 2004).

Early childhood education should encourage adequate preparation for learning, varied learning activities, trusting relationships between adults and children, and increased parental involvement (Brewer, 2007). Too many young children go to substandard early childhood programs (Morrison, 2008).

Especially because so many young children do not experience an environment that approximates a good early childhood program, there are increasing calls for instituting preschool education for all U.S. 4-year-old children (Zigler, Gilliam, & Jones, 2006). Attending preschool is rapidly becoming the norm for U.S. children. In 2002, 43 states funded pre-kindergarten programs, and 55 percent of U.S. 3- and 4-year-old children attended center-based programs (NAEYC, 2005). Many other 3- and 4-year-old children attend private preschool programs.

Edward Zigler and his colleagues (2006) recently argued that the United States should have universal preschool education. They emphasize that quality preschools prepare children for school readiness and academic success. Zigler and his colleagues (2006) cite research that shows quality preschool programs increase the likelihood that once children go to elementary and secondary school they will be less likely to be retained in a grade or drop out of school. They also point to analyses indicating that universal preschool would bring considerable cost savings on the order of billions of dollars because of a diminished need for remedial and justice services (Karoly & Bigelow, 2005). A number of early childhood education experts agree with Zigler and his colleagues that U.S. 4-year-olds would benefit from universal preschool education (Finn-Stevenson, 2006; Styfco, 2006).

Critics of universal preschool education argue that the gains attributed to preschool and kindergarten

What are two controversies in early childhood education?

education are often overstated. They especially stress that research has not proven that nondisadvantaged children improve as a result of attending a preschool. Thus, the critics say it is more important to improve preschool education for young children who are disadvantaged rather than funding preschool education for all 4-year-old children. Some critics, especially home schooling advocates, emphasize that young children should be educated by their parents, not by schools. Thus, controversy continues to characterize whether universal preschool education should be implemented.

In Japan and many developing countries, some of the goals of early childhood education are quite different from those of American programs. To read about the differences, see the *Diversity in Child Development* interlude.

Diversity in Child Development

EARLY CHILDHOOD EDUCATION IN JAPAN AND DEVELOPING COUNTRIES

As in America, there is diversity in Japanese early childhood education. Some Japanese kindergartens have specific aims, such as early musical training or the practice of Montessori strategies. In large cities, some kindergartens are attached to universities that have elementary and secondary schools. In most Japanese preschools, however, little emphasis is put on academic instruction.

In one study, 300 Japanese and 210 American preschool teachers, child development specialists, and parents were asked about various aspects of early childhood education (Tobin, Wu, & Davidson, 1989). Only 2 percent of the Japanese respondents listed "to give children a good start academically" as one of their top three reasons for a society to have preschools. In contrast, over half the American respondents chose this as one of their top three choices. Japanese schools do not teach reading, writing, and mathematics but rather skills like persistence, concentration, and the ability to function as a member of a group. The vast majority of young Japanese children are taught to read at home by their parents.

In the comparison of Japanese and American parents, more than 60 percent of the Japanese parents said that the purpose of preschool is to give children experience being a member of the group compared with about only 20 percent of the U.S. parents (Tobin, Wu, & Davidson, 1989) (see Figure 16.1). Lessons in living and working together grow naturally out of the Japanese culture. In many Japanese kindergartens, children wear the same uniforms, including caps, which are of different colors to indicate the classrooms to which they belong. They have identical sets of equipment, kept in identical drawers and shelves. This is not intended to turn the young children into robots, as some Americans have observed, but to impress on them that other people, just like themselves, have needs and desires that are equally important (Hendry, 1995).

Japan is a highly advanced industrialized country. What about developing countries—how do they compare to the United States in educating young children? The wide range of programs and emphasis on the education of the whole child—physically, cognitively, and socioemotionally—that characterize U.S. early childhood education do not exist in many developing countries (Roopnarine & Metindogan, 2006). Economic pressures and parents' belief that education should be academically rigorous have produced teacher-centered rather child-centered early childhood education programs in most developing countries. Among the countries in which this type of early childhood education has been observed are Jamaica, China, Thailand, Kenya, and Turkey. In these countries, young children are usually given few choices and are educated in highly structured settings. Emphasis is on learning academic skills through rote memory

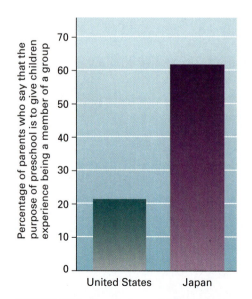

FIGURE 16.1 Comparison of Japanese and U.S. Parents' Views on the Purpose of Preschool

What characterizes early childhood education in Japan?

A kindergarten class in Kingston, Jamaica. *What characterizes kindergarten in many developing countries like Jamaica?*

and recitation (Lin, Johnson, & Johnson, 2003). Programs in Mexico, Singapore, Korea, and Hong Kong have been observed to be closer to those in the United States in their emphasis on curriculum flexibility and play-based methods (Cisneros-Cohernour, Moreno, & Cisneros, 2000).

Elementary School

For many children, entering the first grade signals a change from being a "home-child" to being a "school-child"—a situation in which new roles and obligations are experienced. Children take up the new role of being a student, interact, develop new relationships, adopt new reference groups, and develop new standards by which to judge themselves. School provides children with a rich source of new ideas to shape their sense of self.

Too often early schooling proceeds mainly on the basis of negative feedback. For example, children's self-esteem in the latter part of elementary school is lower than it is in the earlier part, and older children rate themselves as less smart, less good, and less hardworking than do younger ones (Blumenfeld & others, 1981; Eccles, 2003; Eccles, Wigfield, & Byrnes, 2003).

Educating Adolescents

What is the transition from elementary to middle or junior high school like? What are the characteristics of effective schools for young adolescents? How can adolescents be encouraged to stay in school?

The Transition to Middle or Junior High School The first year of middle school or junior high school can be difficult for many students (Anderman & Mueller, 2009; Cook & others, 2008). For example, in one study of the transition from sixth grade in an elementary school to the seventh grade in a junior high school, adolescents' perceptions of the quality of their school life plunged in the seventh grade (Hirsch & Rapkin, 1987). Compared with their earlier feelings as sixth-graders, the seventh-graders were less satisfied with school, were less committed to school, and liked their teachers less. The drop in school satisfaction occurred regardless of how academically successful the students were.

The transition to middle or junior high school takes place at a time when many changes—in the individual, in the family, and in school—are occurring simultaneously. These changes include puberty and related concerns about body image; the

As children make the transition to elementary school, they interact and develop relationships with new and significant others. School provides them with a rich source of new ideas to shape their sense of self.

The transition from elementary to middle or junior high school occurs at the same time as a number of other developmental changes. *What are some of these other developmental changes?*

emergence of at least some aspects of formal operational thought, including accompanying changes in social cognition; increased responsibility and decreased dependency on parents; change to a larger, more impersonal school structure; change from one teacher to many teachers and from a small, homogeneous set of peers to a larger, more heterogeneous set of peers; and an increased focus on achievement and performance. Moreover, when students make the transition to middle or junior high school, they experience the **top-dog phenomenon**, moving from being the oldest, biggest, and most powerful students in the elementary school to being the youngest, smallest, and least powerful students in the middle or junior high school. A recent study in North Carolina schools revealed that sixth-grade students attending middle schools were far more likely to be cited for discipline problems than their counterparts who were attending elementary schools (Cook & others, 2008).

There can also be positive aspects to the transition to middle or junior high school. Students are more likely to feel grown up, have more subjects from which to select, have more opportunities to spend time with peers and locate compatible friends, and enjoy increased independence from direct parental monitoring. They also may be more challenged intellectually by academic work.

Effective Schools for Young Adolescents Educators and psychologists worry that junior high and middle schools have become watered-down versions of high schools, mimicking their curricular and extracurricular schedules. Critics argue that these schools should offer activities that reflect a wide range of individual differences in biological and psychological development among young adolescents. In 1989, the Carnegie Corporation issued an extremely negative evaluation of our nation's middle schools. It concluded that most young adolescents attended massive, impersonal schools; were taught from irrelevant curricula; trusted few adults in school; and lacked access to health care and counseling. It recommended that the nation should develop smaller "communities" or "houses" to lessen the impersonal nature of large middle schools, have lower student-to-counselor ratios (10 to 1 instead of several-hundred-to-1), involve parents and community leaders in schools, develop new curricula, have teachers team teach in more flexibly designed curriculum blocks that integrate several disciplines, boost students' health and fitness with more in-school programs, and help students who need public health care to get it. Twenty-five years later, experts are still finding that middle schools throughout the nation need a major redesign if they are to be effective in educating adolescents (Eccles, 2004, 2007).

High School Just as there are concerns about U.S. middle school education, so are there concerns about U.S. high school education. Critics stress that in many high schools expectations for success and standards for learning are too low. Critics also argue that too often high schools foster passivity and that schools should create a variety of pathways for students to achieve an identity. Many students graduate from high school with inadequate reading, writing, and mathematical skills—including many who go on to college and have to enroll in remediation classes there. Other students drop out of high school and do not have skills that will allow them to obtain decent jobs, much less to be informed citizens.

In the last half of the twentieth century and the first several years of the twenty-first century, U.S. high school dropout rates declined (National Center for Education Statistics, 2008a) (see Figure 16.2). In the 1940s, more than half of U.S. 16- to 24-year-olds had dropped out of school; by 2006, this figure had decreased to 9.3 percent. The dropout rate of Latino adolescents remains high, although it is decreasing in the twenty-first century (from 28 percent in 2000 to 22.1 percent in 2006). The

top-dog phenomenon The circumstance of moving from the top position in elementary school to the lowest position in middle or junior high school.

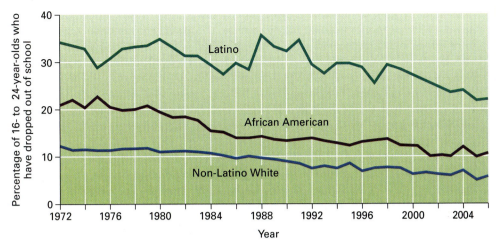

FIGURE 16.2 Trends in High School Dropout Rates. From 1972 through 2006, the school dropout rate for Latinos remained very high (22.1 percent of 16- to 24-year-olds in 2006). The African American dropout rate was still higher (10.7 percent) than the White non-Latino rate (5.8 percent) in 2004. (*Source:* National Center for Education Statistics, 2008a).

highest dropout rate in the United States, though, likely occurs for Native American youth—less than 50 percent finish their high school education.

Students drop out of schools for many reasons (Christensen & Thurlow, 2004). In one study, almost 50 percent of the dropouts cited school-related reasons for leaving school, such as not liking school or being expelled or suspended (Rumberger, 1995). Twenty percent of the dropouts (but 40 percent of the Latino students) cited economic reasons for leaving school. One-third of the female students dropped out for personal reasons such as pregnancy or marriage.

According to one review, the most effective programs to discourage dropping out of high school provide early reading programs, tutoring, counseling, and mentoring (Lehr & others, 2003). They also emphasize the creation of caring environments and relationships, use block scheduling, and offer community-service opportunities.

Early detection of children's school-related difficulties, and getting children engaged with school in positive ways, are important strategies for reducing the dropout rate. Recently the Bill and Melinda Gates Foundation (2006, 2008) has funded efforts to reduce the dropout rate in schools where dropout rates are high. One strategy that is being emphasized in the Gates' funding is keeping students at risk for dropping out of school with the same teachers through their high school years. The hope is that the teachers will get to know these students much better, their relationship with the students will improve, and they will be able to monitor and guide the students toward graduating from high school. To read about one program that attempts to reduce the school dropout rate, see the *Caring for Children* interlude.

Students in the technology training center at Wellpint Elementary/High School located on the Spokane Indian Reservation in Washington. An important educational goal is to increase the high school graduation rate of Native American adolescents.

Caring for Children

"I HAVE A DREAM"

"I Have a Dream" (IHAD) is an innovative comprehensive, long-term dropout prevention program administered by the national "I Have a Dream" Foundation in New York. Since the national IHAD Foundation was created in 1986, it has grown to number over 180 projects in 64 cities and 27 states, serving more than 12,000 children ("I Have a Dream"

These adolescents participate in the "I Have a Dream" (IHAD) program, a comprehensive, long-term dropout prevention program that has been very successful.

Foundation, 2008). Local IHAD projects around the country "adopt" entire grades (usually the third or fourth) from public elementary schools, or corresponding age cohorts from public housing developments. These children—"Dreamers"—are then provided with a program of academic, social, cultural, and recreational activities throughout their elementary, middle school, and high school years. An important part of this program is that it is personal rather than institutional: IHAD sponsors and staff develop close long-term relationships with the children. When participants complete high school, IHAD provides the tuition assistance necessary for them to attend a state or local college or vocational school.

The IHAD program was created in 1981, when philanthropist Eugene Lang made an impromptu offer of college tuition to a class of graduating sixth-graders at P.S. 121 in East Harlem. Evaluations of IHAD programs have found dramatic improvements in grades, test scores, and school attendance, as well as a reduction of behavioral problems of Dreamers. In a recent analysis of the "I Have a Dream" program in Houston, 91 percent of the participants received passing grades in reading/English, 83 percent said they liked school, 98 percent said getting good grades is important to them, 100 percent said they plan to graduate from high school, and 94 percent reported they plan to go to college ("I Have a Dream" Foundation, 2008).

Review and Reflect: Learning Goal 1

 Discuss Approaches to Schooling and Development

REVIEW

- What are some contemporary approaches to student learning?
- What are some variations in early childhood education?
- What are some characteristics of elementary education?
- How are U.S. adolescents educated, and what are the challenges in educating adolescents?

REFLECT

- How would you characterize the approach of the schools that you attended as a child and as an adolescent? Do you think your schools were effective? Explain.

2 SOCIOECONOMIC STATUS AND ETHNICITY IN SCHOOLS

Educating Students from Low-Income Backgrounds   **Ethnicity in Schools**

Children from low-income, ethnic minority backgrounds have more difficulties in school than do their middle-socioeconomic-status, White counterparts (Hutson, 2008). Why? Critics argue that schools are not doing a good job of educating low-income or ethnic minority students (Gollnick & Chinn, 2009; Taylor & Whittaker, 2009). Let's further explore the roles of socioeconomic status and ethnicity in schools.

Educating Students from Low-Income Backgrounds

Many children in poverty face problems that present barriers to their learning (Hutson, 2008; Leon-Guerrero, 2009). They might have parents who don't set high educational standards for them, who are incapable of reading to them, and who don't have enough money to pay for educational materials and experiences, such as books and trips to zoos and museums. They might live in a crowded, noisy apartment where it is difficult to find a quiet place to do homework or even to sleep. They might be malnourished; they might live in a dangerous neighborhood where crime, violence, and fear are a way of life.

Compared with schools in higher-income areas, schools in low-income areas are more likely to have more students with low achievement test scores, low graduation rates, and small percentages of students going to college; they are more likely to have young teachers with less experience; and they are more likely to encourage rote learning (Manning & Baruth, 2009; Spring, 2008). Too few schools in low-income neighborhoods provide students with environments that are conducive to learning (Ballentine & Hammock, 2009; Bennett, 2007). Many of the schools' buildings and classrooms are old and crumbling. These are the types of undesirable conditions Jonathan Kozol (2005) observed in many inner-city schools, including the South Bronx in New York City.

Jill Nakamura, teaching in her first-grade classroom. Jill teaches in a school located in a high-poverty area. She visits students at home early in the school year in an effort to connect with them and develop a partnership with their parents. "She holds a daily afternoon reading club for students reading below grade level . . . In one school year (2004), she raised the percent of students reading at or above grade level from 29 percent to 76 percent" (Briggs, 2004, p. 6D).

Ethnicity in Schools

More than one-third of all African American and almost one-third of all Latino students attend schools in the 47 largest city school districts in the United States, compared with only 5 percent of all White and 22 percent of all Asian American students. Many of these inner-city schools are grossly underfunded, do not provide adequate opportunities for children to learn effectively, and are still segregated despite integration measures that have been in place for decades. Even outside of inner-city schools, school segregation remains a factor in U.S. education. Almost one-third of all African American and Latino students attend schools in which 90 percent or more of the students are from minority groups (Banks, 2008). Thus, the effects of SES and the effects of ethnicity are often intertwined.

The school experiences of students from different ethnic groups vary considerably (Coltrane & others, 2008; Healey, 2009; Liu & others, 2008; Rowley, Kurtz-Costes, & Cooper, 2009). African American students are twice as likely as Latinos, Native Americans, or Whites to be suspended from school. African American and Latino students are much more likely than non-Latino White or Asian American students to be enrolled in remedial and special education programs, and much less likely to be enrolled in college preparatory programs. Asian American students are far more likely than other ethnic minority groups to take advanced math and science courses in high school.

Some experts charge that a form of institutional racism, by which teachers accept a low level of performance from children of color, permeates many American schools (Ogbu & Stern, 2001; Spencer, 1999). American anthropologist John Ogbu (1989) proposed that ethnic minority students are placed in a position of subordination and exploitation in the American educational system. He points out that students of color, especially African Americans and Latinos, have inferior educational opportunities, are exposed to teachers and school administrators who have low academic expectations for them, and encounter negative stereotypes (Ogbu & Stern, 2001). In one study of middle schools in predominantly Latino areas of

Miami, Latino and White teachers rated African American students as having more behavioral problems than African American teachers rated the same students as having (Zimmerman & others, 1995).

Following are some strategies for improving relationships among ethnically diverse students:

What are some features of a jigsaw classroom?

- *Turn the class into a jigsaw classroom.* When Elliot Aronson was a professor at the University of Texas at Austin, the school system contacted him for ideas on how to reduce the increasing racial tension in classrooms. Aronson (1986) developed the concept of "jigsaw classroom," in which students from different cultural backgrounds are placed in a cooperative group in which they have to construct different parts of a project to reach a common goal. Aronson used the term *jigsaw* because he saw the technique as much like a group of students cooperating to put different pieces together to complete a jigsaw puzzle. How might this work? Team sports, drama productions, and music performances are examples of contexts in which students participate cooperatively to reach a common goal; however, the jigsaw technique also lends itself to group science projects, history reports, and other learning experiences with a variety of subject matter.

- *Encourage students to have positive personal contact with diverse other students.* Mere contact does not do the job of improving relationships with diverse others. For example, busing ethnic minority students to predominantly White schools, or vice versa, has not reduced prejudice or improved interethnic relations (Minuchin & Shapiro, 1983). What matters is what happens after children get to school. Especially beneficial in improving interethnic relations is sharing one's worries, successes, failures, coping strategies, interests, and other personal information with people of other ethnicities. When this happens, people tend to look at others as individuals rather than as members of a homogeneous group.

- *Reduce bias.* Teachers can reduce bias by displaying images of children from diverse ethnic and cultural groups, selecting play materials and classroom activities that encourage cultural understanding, helping students resist stereotyping, and working with parents to reduce children's exposure to bias and prejudice at home.

- *View the school and community as a team.* James Comer (1988, 2004, 2006) advocates a community, team approach as the best way to educate children. Three important aspects of the Comer Project for Change are (1) a governance and management team that develops a comprehensive school plan, assessment strategy, and staff development plan; (2) a mental health or school support team; and (3) a parent's program. Comer suggests that the entire school community should have a cooperative rather than an adversarial attitude. The Comer program is currently operating in more than 600 schools in 26 states. Read further about James Comer's work in the *Careers in Child Development* profile.

- *Be a competent cultural mediator.* Teachers can play a powerful role as cultural mediators by being sensitive to biased content in materials and classroom interactions, learning more about different ethnic groups, being sensitive to children's ethnic attitudes, viewing students of color positively, and thinking of positive ways to get parents of color more involved as partners with teachers in educating children.

Careers in Child Development

James Comer, Child Psychiatrist

James Comer grew up in a low-income neighborhood in East Chicago, Indiana, and credits his parents with leaving no doubt about the importance of education. He obtained a B.A. degree from Indiana University. He went on to obtain a medical degree from Howard University College of Medicine, a Master of Public Health degree from the University of Michigan School of Public Health, and psychiatry training at the Yale University School of Medicine's Child Study Center. He currently is the Maurice Falk Professor of Child Psychiatry at the Yale University Child Study Center and an Associate Dean at the Yale University Medical School. During his years at Yale, Comer has concentrated his career on promoting a focus on child development as a way of improving schools. His efforts in support of healthy development of young people are known internationally.

Dr. Comer, perhaps, is best known for the founding of the School Development program in 1968, which promotes the collaboration of parents, educators, and community to improve social, emotional, and academic outcomes for children. His concept of teamwork is currently improving the educational environment in more than 600 schools throughout America.

James Comer (*left*) is shown with some of the inner-city African American children who attend a school that became a better learning environment because of Comer's intervention.

Review and Reflect: Learning Goal 2

 2 Describe the Roles of Socioeconomic Status and Ethnicity in Schools

REVIEW

- How do socioeconomic status and poverty influence children's schooling?
- How is ethnicity involved in children's schooling?

REFLECT

- In the context of education, are ethnic differences always negative? Come up with some differences that might be positive in U.S. classrooms.

3 CHILDREN WITH DISABILITIES

| Learning Disabilities | Attention Deficit Hyperactivity Disorder (ADHD) | Autism Spectrum Disorders (ASDs) | Educational Issues |

So far we have discussed schools as they are experienced by the majority of U.S. students. But 13.5 percent of all children from 3 to 21 years of age in the United States receive special education or related services (National Center for Education Statistics,

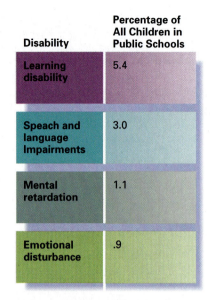

Disability	Percentage of All Children in Public Schools
Learning disability	5.4
Speach and language Impairments	3.0
Mental retardation	1.1
Emotional disturbance	.9

FIGURE 16.3 **U.S. Children with a Disability Who Receive Special Education Services.** Figures are for the 2006–2007 school year and represent the four categories with the highest number and percentage of children. Both learning disability and attention deficit hyperactivity disorder are combined in the learning disabilities category (National Center for Education Statistics, 2008b).

learning disabilities Disabilities that involve understanding or using spoken or written language, and the difficulty can appear in listening, thinking, reading, writing, and spelling. A learning disability also may involve difficulty in doing mathematics. To be classified as a learning disability, the learning problem is not primarily the result of visual, hearing, or motor disabilities; mental retardation; emotional disorders; or due to environmental, cultural, or economic disadvantage.

dyslexia A category of learning disabilities involving a severe impairment in the ability to read and spell.

2008b). Figure 16.3 shows the four largest groups of students with a disability who were served by federal programs in the 2006–2007 school year (National Center for Education Statistics, 2008b). As indicated in Figure 16.3, students with a learning disability were by far the largest group of students with a disability to be given special education, followed by children with speech and language impairments, mental retardation, and emotional disturbance.

Learning Disabilities

A child with a **learning disability** has difficulty in learning that involves understanding or using spoken or written language, and the difficulty can appear in listening, thinking, reading, writing, and spelling. A learning disability also may involve difficulty in doing mathematics. To be classified as a learning disability, the learning problem is not primarily the result of visual, hearing, or motor disabilities; mental retardation; emotional disorders; or due to environmental, cultural, or economic disadvantage.

From the mid-1970s through the mid-1990s, there was a dramatic increase in the percentage of U.S. students receiving special education services for a learning disability (from 1.8 percent in 1976–1977 to 5.8 percent in 1995–1996), although in the twenty-first century there has been a slight decrease in this percentage (6.1 percent in 2000 to 5.4 percent in 2006–2007) (National Center for Education Statistics, 2008b). Some experts say that the dramatic increase reflected poor diagnostic practices and overidentification. They argue that teachers sometimes are too quick to label children with the slightest learning problem as having a learning disability, instead of recognizing that the problem may rest in their ineffective teaching. Other experts say the increase in the number of children being labeled with a "learning disability" is justified (Bender, 2008; Hallahan, Kaufmann, & Pullen, 2009).

About three times as many boys as girls are classified as having a learning disability. Among the explanations for this gender difference are a greater biological vulnerability among boys and *referral bias.* That is, boys are more likely to be referred by teachers for treatment because of their behavior.

Diagnosing whether a child has a learning disability is often a difficult task (Bender, 2008; Fritschmann & Solari, 2008). Because federal guidelines are just that, guidelines, it is up to each state, or in some cases school systems within a state, to determine how to define and implement diagnosis of learning disabilities. The same child might be diagnosed as having a learning disability in one school system and receive services but not be diagnosed and not receive services in another school system. In such cases, parents sometimes will move to either to obtain or avoid the diagnosis.

The most common problem that characterizes children with a learning disability involves reading, which affects approximately 80 percent of children with a learning disability (Fletcher & others, 2007; Shaywitz, Gruen, & Shaywitz, 2007). Such children have difficulty with phonological skills, which involve being able to understand how sounds and letters match up to make words. **Dyslexia** is a category reserved for individuals with a severe impairment in their ability to read and spell (Reid & others, 2009; Shastry, 2007).

The precise causes of learning disabilities have not yet been determined. However, some possible causes have been proposed (Bender, 2008). Learning disabilities tend to run in families with one parent having a disability such as dyslexia, although the specific genetic transmission of learning disabilities has not been discovered (Petrill & others, 2006). Some leading researchers argue that some reading disabilities are likely due to genetics but that majority are the result of environmental influences (Shaywitz, Lyon, & Shaywitz, 2006).

Researchers also use brain-imaging techniques, such as magnetic resonance imaging, to reveal any regions of the brain that might be involved in learning disabilities (Shaywitz, Morris & Shaywitz, 2008) (see Figure 16.4). This research indicates that it is unlikely learning disabilities reside in a single, specific brain location. More likely learning disabilities are due to problems in integrating information from multiple brain regions or subtle difficulties in brain structures and functions (National Institutes of Health, 1993).

Many interventions have focused on improving the child's reading ability (Bender, 2008; Lyytinen & Erskine, 2009). Intensive instruction over a period of time by a competent teacher can help many children (Berninger, 2006). For example, a recent brain-imaging study of 15 children with severe reading difficulties who had not shown adequate progress in response to reading instruction in the first grade were given an intensive eight weeks of instruction in phonological decoding skills and then another intensive eight weeks of word recognition skills (Simos & others, 2007). Significant improvement in a majority of the children's reading skills and changes in brain regions involved in reading occurred as a result of the intensive instruction.

Attention Deficit Hyperactivity Disorder (ADHD)

Attention deficit hyperactivity disorder (ADHD) is a disability in which children consistently show one or more of these characteristics over a period of time: (1) inattention, (2) hyperactivity, and (3) hyperactivity/impulsivity. Children who are inattentive have such difficulty focusing on any one thing that they may get bored with a task after only a few minutes—or even seconds. Children who are hyperactive show high levels of physical activity, seeming to be almost constantly in motion. Children who are impulsive have difficulty curbing their reactions; they do not do a good job of thinking before they act. Depending on the characteristics that children with ADHD display, they can be diagnosed as (1) ADHD with predominantly inattention, (2) ADHD with predominantly hyperactivity/impulsivity, or (3) ADHD with both inattention and hyperactivity/impulsivity.

The number of children diagnosed and treated for ADHD has increased substantially in recent decades, by some estimates doubling in the 1990s. The disorder occurs as much as four to nine times more in boys than in girls. There is controversy, however, about the increased diagnosis of ADHD (Gargiulo, 2009). Some experts attribute the increase mainly to heightened awareness of the disorder. Others are concerned that many children are being incorrectly diagnosed.

Unlike learning disabilities, ADHD is not supposed to be diagnosed by school teams because ADHD is a disorder that appears in the classification of psychiatric disorders called DSM-IV with specific diagnosis criteria (Bender, 2008). Although some school teams may diagnose a child as having ADHD, this is incorrectly done and can lead to legal problems for schools and teachers. One reason that is given as to why a school team should not do the diagnosis for ADHD is that ADHD is difficult to differentiate from other childhood disorders, and accurate diagnosis requires the evaluation by a specialist in the disorder, such as a child psychiatrist.

Definitive causes of ADHD have not been found. However, a number of causes have been proposed (Biederman, 2007; Stein & others, 2007). Some children likely inherit a tendency to develop ADHD from their parents (Goos, Ezzatian, & Schachar, 2007; Lasky-Su & others, 2007). Other children likely develop ADHD because of damage to their brain during prenatal or postnatal development (Banerjee, Middleton, & Faraone, 2007; Thompson, Moore, & Symons, 2007). Among early possible contributors to ADHD are cigarette and alcohol exposure during prenatal development and low birth weight (Greydanus, Pratt, & Patel, 2007; Neuman & others, 2007).

As with learning disabilities, the development of brain-imaging techniques is leading to a better understanding of the brain's role in ADHD (Shaw & others, 2007). A recent study revealed that peak thickness of the cerebral cortex occurred three years later (10.5 years) in children with ADHD than in children without ADHD (peak at 7.5 years) (Shaw & others, 2007). The delay was more prominent in the prefrontal regions of the brain that especially are important in attention and planning (see Figure 16.5).

Stimulant medication such as Ritalin or Adderall (which has fewer side effects than Ritalin) is effective in improving the attention of many children with ADHD, but it usually does not improve their attention to the same level as children who do not

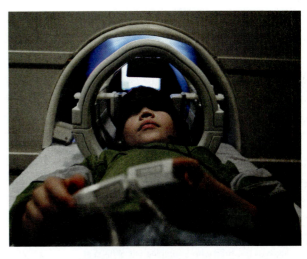

FIGURE 16.4 Brain Scans and Learning Disabilities. An increasing number of studies are using MRI brain scans to examine the brain pathways involved in learning disabilities. Shown here is 9-year-old Patrick Price, who has dyslexia. Patrick is going through an MRI scanner disguised by drapes to look like a child-friendly castle. Inside the scanner, children must lie virtually motionless as words and symbols flash on a screen, and they are asked to identify them by clicking different buttons.

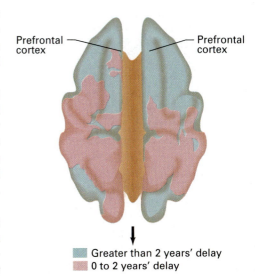

Prefrontal cortex — Prefrontal cortex

■ Greater than 2 years' delay
■ 0 to 2 years' delay

FIGURE 16.5 Regions of the Brain in Which Children with ADHD Had a Delayed Peak in the Thickness of the Cerebral Cortex. *Note:* The greatest delays occurred in the prefrontal cortex.

attention deficit hyperactivity disorder (ADHD) A disability in which children consistently show one or more of the following characteristics: (1) inattention, (2) hyperactivity, and (3) hyperactivity/impulsivity.

Many children with ADHD show impulsive behavior, such as this child who is jumping out of his seat and throwing a paper airplane at other children. *How would you handle this situation if you were a teacher and this were to happen in your classroom?*

What characterizes autism spectrum disorders?

autism spectrum disorders (ASDs) Also called pervasive developmental disorders, they range from the severe disorder labeled autistic disorder to the milder disorder called Asperger syndrome. Children with these disorders are characterized by problems in social interaction, verbal and nonverbal communication, and repetitive behaviors.

autistic disorder A severe developmental autism spectrum disorder that has its onset in the first three years of life and includes deficiencies in social relationships; abnormalities in communication; and restricted, repetitive, and stereotyped patterns of behavior.

Asperger syndrome A relatively mild autism spectrum disorder in which the child has relatively good verbal language, milder nonverbal language problems, and a restricted range of interests and relationships.

have ADHD (Barbaresi & others, 2006; Pliszka, 2007). Researchers have often found that a combination of medication (such as Ritalin) and behavior management improves the behavior of children with ADHD better than medication alone or behavior management alone, although not in all cases (Chronis & others, 2004; Jensen & others, 2007). Other drugs, such as the stimulant called mixed amphetamine salts extended release (MAS XR) and the nonstimulant Strattera are currently being studied in the treatment of children with ADHD, and early findings involving these drugs are promising (Bhatara & Aparasu, 2007; Faraone, 2007).

Teachers play an important role in monitoring whether ADHD medication has been prescribed at the right dosage level. For example, it is not unusual for a student on ADHD medication to complete academic tasks in the morning, but later, when the dosage has worn off, to be inattentive or hyperactive in the afternoon (Thompson, Moore, & Symons, 2007).

Critics argue that many physicians are too quick to prescribe stimulants for children with milder forms of ADHD (Marcovitch, 2004). Also, in 2006, the U.S. government issued a warning about the cardiovascular risks of stimulant medication to treat ADHD.

Recent studies have also focused on the possibility that exercise might reduce ADHD (Tantillo & others, 2006). Some mental health experts now recommend that children with ADHD exercise several times a day and speculate that the increase in rates of ADHD have coincided with the decline in U.S. children's exercise (Ratey, 2006).

Autism Spectrum Disorders (ASDs)

Autism spectrum disorders (ASDs), also called pervasive developmental disorders, range from the severe disorder labeled *autistic disorder* to the milder disorder called *Asperger syndrome*. Autism spectrum disorders are characterized by problems in social interaction, problems in verbal and nonverbal communication, and repetitive behaviors (Charman, 2009; Hall, 2009; Simpson & LaCava, 2008). Children with these disorders may also show atypical responses to sensory experiences (National Institute of Mental Health, 2008). Autism spectrum disorders can often be detected in children as early as 1 to 3 years of age.

Autistic disorder is a severe developmental autism spectrum disorder that has its onset in the first three years of life and includes deficiencies in social relationships; abnormalities in communication; and restricted, repetitive, and stereotyped patterns of behavior. Estimates indicate that approximately two to five of every 10,000 young children in the United States have an autistic disorder. Boys are about four times more likely to have an autistic disorder than girls.

Asperger syndrome is a relatively mild autism spectrum disorder in which the child has relatively good verbal language, milder nonverbal language problems, and a restricted range of interests and relationships (Bennett & others, 2008). Children with Asperger syndrome often engage in obsessive repetitive routines and preoccupations with a particular subject. For example, a child may be obsessed with baseball scores or railroad timetables.

What causes the autism spectrum disorders? The current consensus is that autism is a brain dysfunction with abnormalities in brain structure and neurotransmitters (Lainhart, 2006). Genetic factors likely play a role in the development of the autism spectrum disorders (Katzov, 2007). A recent study revealed that mutations—missing or duplicated pieces of DNA on chromosome 16, can raise a child's risk of developing autism 100-fold (Weiss & others, 2008). Estimates are that approximately 1 million U.S. children have an autistic disorder, so about 10,000 of them have this genetic mutation. There is no evidence that family socialization causes autism. Mental retardation is present in some children with autism; others show average or above-average intelligence (McCarthy, 2007).

Children with autism benefit from a well-structured classroom, individualized instruction, and small-group instruction. As with children who are mentally retarded, behavior modification techniques are sometimes effective in helping autistic children learn (Hall, 2009).

Educational Issues

Until the 1970s, most U.S. public schools either refused enrollment to children with disabilities or inadequately served them. This changed in 1975, when *Public Law 94-142,* the Education for All Handicapped Children Act, required that all students with disabilities be given a free, appropriate public education. In 1990, Public Law 94-142 was recast as the *Individuals with Disabilities Education Act* (IDEA). IDEA was amended in 1997 and then reauthorized in 2004 and renamed the Individuals with Disabilities Education Improvement Act (Turnbull, Huerta, & Stowe, 2009).

IDEA spells out broad mandates for services to children with disabilities of all kinds (Carter, Prater, & Dyches, 2009; Smith & others, 2008). These services include evaluation and eligibility determination, appropriate education and an individualized education plan (IEP), and education in the least restrictive environment (LRE).

An **individualized education plan (IEP)** is a written statement that spells out a program that is specifically tailored for the student with a disability (Gargiulo, 2009). The **least restrictive environment (LRE)** is a setting that is as similar as possible to the one in which children who do not have a disability are educated. This provision of the IDEA has given a legal basis to efforts to educate children with a disability in the regular classroom (Hisk & Thomas, 2009; Smith & others, 2008). The term **inclusion** describes educating a child with special education needs full-time in the regular classroom (Bryant, Smith, & Bryant, 2008). Figure 16.6 indicates that in a recent school year that slightly more than 50 percent of U.S. students with a disability spent more than 80 percent of their school day in a general classroom.

A major aspect of the 2004 reauthorization of IDEA involved aligning it with the government's No Child Left Behind (NCLB) legislation, which mandates general assessments of educational progress that include students with disabilities. This alignment includes requiring most students with disabilities "to take standard tests of academic achievement and to achieve at a level equal to that of students without disabilities. Whether this expectation is reasonable is an open question" (Hallahan & Kauffman, 2006, pp. 28–29).

FIGURE 16.6 Percentage of U.S. Students with Disabilities 6 to 21 Years of Age Receiving Special Services in the General Classroom. *Note:* Data for 2004–2005 School Year; National Center for Education Statistics, 2007.

Increasingly, children with disabilities are being taught in the regular classroom, as is this child with mild mental retardation.

Review and Reflect: Learning Goal 3

3 **Characterize Children with Disabilities and Their Schooling**

REVIEW

- Who are children with disabilities, and what characterizes children with learning disabilities?
- How would you describe children with attention deficit hyperactivity disorder? What kind of treatment are they typically given?
- What characterizes autism spectrum disorders?
- What are some issues in educating children with disabilities?

REFLECT

- Think back to your own schooling and how children with learning disabilities or ADHD either were or were not diagnosed. Were you aware of such individuals in your classes? Were they helped by specialists? You may know one or more individuals with a learning disability or ADHD. Ask them about their educational experiences and whether they believe schools could have done a better job of helping them.

individualized education plan (IEP) A written statement that spells out a program tailored to a child with a disability.

least restrictive environment (LRE) The concept that a child with a disability must be educated in a setting that is as similar as possible to the one in which children who do not have a disability are educated.

inclusion Educating a child with special education needs full-time in the regular classroom.

4 ACHIEVEMENT

- Extrinsic and Intrinsic Motivation
- Mastery Motivation and Mindset
- Self-Efficacy
- Expectations
- Goal Setting, Planning, and Self-Monitoring
- Ethnicity and Culture

In any classroom, whoever the teacher is and whatever approach is used, some children achieve more than others. Why? The reasons for variations in achievement include the motivation, expectations, goals, and other characteristics of the child as well as sociocultural contexts.

Extrinsic and Intrinsic Motivation

Extrinsic motivation involves external incentives such as rewards and punishments. **Intrinsic motivation** is based on internal factors such as self-determination, curiosity, challenge, and effort. Cognitive approaches stress the importance of intrinsic motivation in achievement. Some students study hard because they want to make good grades or avoid parental disapproval (extrinsic motivation). Other students work hard because they are internally motivated to achieve high standards in their work (intrinsic motivation).

Current evidence strongly favors establishing a classroom climate in which students are intrinsically motivated to learn (Blumenfeld, Kempler, & Krajcik, 2006; Blumenfeld, Marx, & Harris, 2006; Wigfield & others, 2006). For example, one recent study of third- through eighth-grade students found that intrinsic motivation was positively linked with grades and standardized test scores, whereas extrinsic motivation was negatively related to achievement outcomes (Lepper, Corpus, & Iyengar, 2005).

Students are more motivated to learn when they are given choices, become absorbed in challenges that match their skills, and receive rewards that have informational value but are not used for control. Praise also can enhance students' intrinsic motivation. To see why these things are so, let's first explore three views of intrinsic motivation: (1) self-determination and personal choice, (2) interest, and (3) cognitive engagement and self-responsibility. Then we'll discuss how external rewards can either enhance or undermine intrinsic motivation. Finally, we will offer some concluding thoughts about intrinsic and extrinsic motivation.

These students were given an opportunity to write and perform their own play. These kinds of self-determining opportunities can enhance students' motivation to achieve.

extrinsic motivation Response to external incentives such as rewards and punishments.

intrinsic motivation Internal motivational factors such as self-determination, curiosity, challenge, and effort.

Self-Determination and Personal Choice One view of intrinsic motivation emphasizes self-determination (Deci, Koestner, & Ryan, 2001; Deci & Ryan, 1994). In this view, children have control over what they doing because of their own will, not because of external success or rewards.

Researchers have found that giving children some choice and providing opportunities for personal responsibility increases their internal motivation and intrinsic interest in school tasks (Anderman & Wolters, 2006; Blumenfeld, Kempler, & Krajcik, 2006). For example, one study found that high school science students who were encouraged to organize their own experiments demonstrated more care and interest in laboratory work than their counterparts who were given detailed instructions and directions (Rainey, 1965). In another study that included mainly African American students from low-SES backgrounds, teachers were encouraged to give them more responsibility for their school program (deCharms, 1984). This consisted of opportunities to set their own goals, plan how to reach the goals, and monitor their progress toward the goals. Students were given some choice in the

Calvin and Hobbes   by Bill Watterson

activities they wanted to engage in and when they would do them. They also were encouraged to take personal responsibility for their behavior, including reaching the goals they had set. Compared with a control group, students in the intrinsic motivation/self-determination group had higher achievement gains and were more likely to graduate from high school.

Interest   Educational psychologists also have examined the concept of *interest*, which has been proposed as more specific than intrinsic motivation (Wigfield & others, 2006). A distinction has been made between individual interest, which is thought to be relatively stable, and situational interest, which is believed to be generated by specific aspects of a task activity. Research on interest has focused mainly on how interest is related to learning. Interest is especially linked to measures of deep learning, such as recall of main ideas and responses to more difficult comprehension questions than to surface learning, such as responses to simple questions and verbatim recall of text (Schiefele, 1996; Wigfield & others, 2006).

Cognitive Engagement and Self-Responsibility   Another variation on intrinsic motivation emphasizes the importance of creating learning environments that encourage students to become cognitively engaged and take responsibility for their learning (Blumenfeld, Kempler, & Krajcik, 2006). The goal is to get students to become motivated to expend the effort to persist and master ideas rather than simply doing enough work to just get by and make passing grades. Especially important in encouraging students to become cognitively engaged and responsible for their learning is to embed subject matter content and skills learning within meaningful contexts, especially real-world situations that mesh with students' interests (Eccles, 2007; National Research Council, 2004).

Some Final Thoughts About Intrinsic and Extrinsic Motivation   An overwhelming conclusion is that it is important for parents and teachers to encourage students to become intrinsically motivated and to create learning environments that promote students' cognitive engagement and self-responsibility for learning (Blumenfeld, Marx, & Harris, 2006). That said, the real world is not just one of intrinsic motivation, and too often intrinsic and extrinsic motivation have been pitted against each other as polar opposites. In many aspects of students' lives, both intrinsic and extrinsic motivation are at work (Cameron & Pierce, 2008; Schunk, 2008). Keep in mind, though, that many psychologists recommend that extrinsic motivation by itself is not a good strategy.

The student:

- Says "I can't"
- Doesn't pay attention to teacher's instructions
- Doesn't ask for help, even when it is needed
- Does nothing (for example, stares out the window)
- Guesses or answers randomly without really trying
- Doesn't show pride in successes
- Appears bored, uninterested
- Is unresponsive to teacher's exhortations to try
- Is easily discouraged
- Doesn't volunteer answers to teacher's questions
- Maneuvers to get out of or to avoid work (for example, has to go to the nurse's office)

FIGURE 16.7 Behaviors That Suggest a Helpless Orientation

Carol Dweck, who developed the concepts of mastery motivation and mindset.

mastery orientation An orientation in which one is task oriented; instead of focusing on one's ability is concerned with learning strategies and the achievement process rather than the outcome.

helpless orientation An orientation in which one seems trapped by the experience of difficulty and attributes one's difficulty to a lack of ability.

performance orientation An orientation in which one focuses on winning rather than achievement outcomes, and happiness is thought to result from winning.

Our discussion of extrinsic and intrinsic motivation sets the stage for introducing other cognitive processes involved in motivating students to learn. As we explore these additional cognitive processes, notice how intrinsic and extrinsic motivation continue to be important. The processes are (1) mastery motivation and mindset; (2) self-efficacy; (3) expectations; and (4) goal, setting, planning, and self-monitoring.

Mastery Motivation and Mindset

Becoming cognitively engaged and self-motivated to improve are reflected in adolescents with a mastery motivation. These children also have a growth mindset that they can produce positive outcomes if they put forth the effort.

Mastery Motivation   Developmental psychologists Valanne Henderson and Carol Dweck (1990) have found that children often show two distinct responses to difficult or challenging circumstances. Children who display **mastery motivation** are task oriented; instead of focusing on their ability, they concentrate on learning strategies and the process of achievement rather than the outcome. Those with a **helpless orientation** seem trapped by the experience of difficulty, and they attribute their difficulty to lack of ability. They frequently say such things as "I'm not very good at this," even though they might earlier have demonstrated their ability through many successes. And, once they view their behavior as failure, they often feel anxious, and their performance worsens even further. Figure 16.7 describes some behaviors that might reflect helplessness (Stipek, 2002).

In contrast, mastery-oriented children often instruct themselves to pay attention, to think carefully, and to remember strategies that have worked for them in previous situations. They frequently report feeling challenged and excited by difficult tasks, rather than being threatened by them (Anderman & Wolters, 2006; Dweck, Mangels, & Good, 2004).

Another issue in motivation involves whether to adopt a mastery or a performance orientation. Children with a **performance orientation** are focused on winning, rather than on achievement outcome, and believe that happiness results from winning. Does this mean that mastery-oriented children do not like to win and that performance-oriented children are not motivated to experience the self-efficacy that comes from being able to take credit for one's accomplishments? No. A matter of emphasis or degree is involved, though. For mastery-oriented individuals, winning isn't everything; for performance-oriented individuals, skill development and self-efficacy take a back seat to winning. One recent study of seventh-grade students found that girls were more likely than boys to have mastery rather than performance goals in their approach to math achievement (Kenny-Benson & others, 2006).

The U.S. government's No Child Left Behind (NCLB) Act emphasizes testing and accountability. Although NCLB may motivate some teachers and students to work harder, motivation experts worry that it encourages a performance rather than a mastery motivation orientation on the part of students (Schunk, Pintrich, & Meece, 2008).

A final point needs to be made about mastery and performance goals: They are not always mutually exclusive. Students can be both mastery and performance oriented, and researchers have found that mastery goals combined with performance goals often benefit students' success (Schunk, Pintrich, & Meece, 2008).

Mindset   Carol Dweck's (2006, 2007) most recent analysis of motivation for achievement stresses the importance of children developing a **mindset**, which she defines as the cognitive view individuals develop for themselves. She concludes that individuals have one of two mindsets: (1) *fixed mindset,* in which they believe that their qualities are carved in stone and cannot change; or (2) *growth mindset,* in which they believe their qualities can change and improve through their effort. A fixed mindset is similar to a helpless orientation, a growth mindset in much like having mastery motivation (Dweck, 2007).

In her recent book, *Mindset,* Dweck (2006) argued that individuals' mindsets influence whether they will be optimistic or pessimistic, shapes their goals and how hard they will strive to reach those goals, and affects many aspect of their lives, including achievement and success in school and sports. Dweck says that mindsets begin to be shaped as children interact with parents, teachers, and coaches, who themselves have either a fixed mindset or a growth mindset. She described the growth mindset of Patricia Miranda:

Patricia Miranda (*in blue*) winning the bronze medal in the 2004 Olympics. *What characterizes her growth mindset and how is it different from someone with a fixed mindset?*

> [She] was a chubby, unathletic school kid who wanted to wrestle. After a bad beating on the mat, she was told, "You're a joke." First she cried, then she felt: "That really set my resolve . . . I had to keep going and had to know if effort and focus and belief and training could somehow legitimize me as a wrestler." Where did she get this resolve?
>
> Miranda was raised in a life devoid of challenge. But when her mother died of an aneurysm at age forty, ten-year-old Miranda . . . [thought] "If you only go through life doing stuff that's easy, shame on you." So when wrestling presented a challenge, she was ready to take it on. Her effort paid off. At twenty-four, Miranda was having the last laugh. She won a spot on the U.S. Olympic team and came home from Athens with a bronze medal. And what was next? Yale Law School. People urged her to stay where she was already on top, but Miranda felt it was more exciting to start at the bottom again and see what she could grow into this time. (Dweck, 2006, pp. 22–23)

Self-Efficacy

Like having a growth mindset, **self-efficacy**, the belief that one can master a situation and produce favorable outcomes, is an important cognitive view for children to develop. Albert Bandura (1997, 2000, 2004, 2006, 2007, 2008, 2009), whose social cognitive theory we described in Chapter 1, argues that self-efficacy is a critical factor in whether or not children achieve. Self-efficacy has much in common with mastery motivation. Self-efficacy is the belief that "I can"; helplessness is the belief that "I cannot" (Stipek, 2002). Children with high self-efficacy endorse such statements as "I know that I will be able to learn the material in this class" and "I expect to be able to do well at this activity."

Dale Schunk (2004, 2008; Schunck, Pintrich, & Meece, 2008) has applied the concept of self-efficacy to many aspects of students' achievement. In his view, self-efficacy influences a student's choice of activities. Students with low self-efficacy for learning might avoid many learning tasks, especially those that are challenging. In contrast, their high-self-efficacy counterparts eagerly work at learning tasks. High-self-efficacy students are more likely to expend effort and persist longer at a learning task than low-self-efficacy students. High-self-efficacy students are more likely to have confidence in exploring challenging career options (Betz, 2004).

Expectations

Children's motivation, and likely their performance, are influenced by the expectations that their parents, teachers, and other adults have for their achievement. Children benefit when both parents and teachers have high expectations for them and provide the necessary support for them to meet those expectations. An especially

> *They can because they think they can.*
>
> —VIRGIL
> **Roman Poet, 1st Century** B.C.

mindset Dweck's concept that refers to the cognitive view individuals develop for themselves; individuals have either a fixed or growth mindset.

self-efficacy The belief that one can master a situation and produce favorable outcomes.

How do parents' and teachers' expectations influence childrens' expectations for achievement?

A student and teacher at Langston Hughes Elementary School in Chicago, a school whose teachers have high expectations for students. *How do teachers' expectations influence students' achievement?*

*L*ife is a gift . . . Accept it.
Life is an adventure . . . Dare it.
Life is a mystery . . . Unfold it.
Life is a struggle . . . Face it
Life is a puzzle . . . Solve it.
Life is an opportunity . . .
Take it.
Life is a mission . . . Fulfill it.
Life is a goal . . . Achieve it.

—Author Unknown

important factor in the lower achievement of students from low-income families is lack of adequate resources, such as an up-to-date computer in the home (or even a computer at all) to support students' learning (Schunk, Pintrich, & Meece, 2008).

Teachers' expectations influence students' motivation and performance (National Research Council, 2004; Pressley & others, 2007a, b). "When teachers hold high generalized expectations for student achievement and students perceive these expectations, students achieve more, experience a greater sense of self-esteem and competence as learners, and resist involvement in problem behaviors both during childhood and adolescence" (Wigfield & others, 2006, p. 976). In a recent observational study of twelve classrooms, teachers with high expectations spent more time providing a framework for students' learning, asked higher-level questions, and were more effective in managing students' behavior than teachers with average and low expectations (Rubie-Davis, 2007).

In thinking about teachers' expectations, it also is important to examine these expecations in concert with parents' expectations. For example, a recent study revealed that mothers' and teachers' high expectations had a positive effect on urban youths' achievement outcomes, and further that mothers' high achievement expectations for their youth had a buffering effect in the face of low teacher expectations (Benner & Mistry, 2007). Interestingly, in another recent study, teachers' positive expectations for students' achievement tended to protect students from the negative influence of low parental expectations (Wood, Kaplan, & McLoyd, 2007).

Teachers often have more positive expectations for high-ability than for low-ability students, and these expectations are likely to influence their behavior toward them. For example, teachers require high-ability students to work harder, wait longer for them to respond to questions, respond to them with more information and in a more elaborate fashion, criticize them less often, praise them more often, are more friendly to them, call on them more often, seat them closer to the teachers' desks, and are more likely to give them the benefit of the doubt on close calls in grading than they are for students with low ability (Brophy, 2004). An important teaching strategy is to monitor your expectations and be sure to have positive expectations for students with low abilities. Fortunately, researchers have found that with support teachers can adapt and raise their expectations for students with low abilities (National Research Council, 2004).

Goal Setting, Planning, and Self-Monitoring

Goal setting, planning, and self-monitoring are important aspects of children's and adolescents' achievement (Anderman & Wolters, 2006; Schunk, Pintrich, & Meece, 2008; Wigfield & others, 2006). Researchers have found that self-efficacy and achievement improve when individuals set goals that are specific, proximal, and challenging (Bandura, 1997). A nonspecific, fuzzy goal is "I want to be successful." A more concrete, specific goal is "I want to make the honor roll at the end of this semester."

Individuals can set both long-term (distal) and short-term (proximal) goals. It is okay to set some long-term goals, such as "I want to graduate from high school" or "I want to go to college," but it also is important to create short-term goals, which are steps along the way. "Getting an A on the next math test" is an example of a short-term, proximal goal. So is "Doing all of my homework by 4 P.M. Sunday."

Another good strategy is to set challenging goals. A challenging goal is a commitment to self-improvement. Strong interest and involvement in activities is sparked by challenges. Goals that are easy to reach generate little interest or effort. However, goals should be optimally matched to the adolescent's skill level. If goals are unrealistically high, the result will be repeated failures that lower self-efficacy.

It is not enough to simply set goals. It also is important to plan how to reach the goals (Schunk, 2008). Being a good planner means managing time effectively, setting priorities, and being organized.

Researchers have found that high-achieving individuals often are self-regulatory learners (Boekaerts, 2006; Schunk, Pintrich, & Meece, 2008). For example, high-achieving students self-monitor their learning more and systematically evaluate their progress toward a goal more than low-achieving students do. When parents and teachers encourage students to self-monitor their learning, they give them the message that they are responsible for their own behavior and that learning requires their active, dedicated participation (Zimmerman, Bonner, & Kovach, 1996).

Ethnicity and Culture

How do ethnicity and culture influence children's achievement? Of course, diversity exists within every group in terms of achievement. But Americans have been especially concerned about two questions related to ethnicity and culture. First, does their ethnicity deter ethnic minority children from high achievement in school? And second, is there something about American culture that accounts for the poor performance of U.S. children in math and science?

Ethnicity   Sandra Graham (1986, 1990) has conducted a number of studies that reveal stronger socioeconomic status than ethnic differences in achievement. She is struck by how consistently middle-income African American students, like their White middle-income counterparts, have high achievement expectations and understand that failure is usually due to a lack of effort.

A special challenge for many ethnic minority students is dealing with negative stereotypes and discrimination. Many ethnic minority students living in poverty must also deal with conflict between the values of their neighborhood and those of the majority culture, a lack of high-achieving role models, and as we discussed earlier, poor schools (McLoyd, 2000). Even students who are motivated to learn and achieve may find it difficult to perform effectively in such contexts.

Cross-Cultural Comparisons   Since the early 1990s, the poor performance of American children and adolescents in math and science has become well publicized (Peak, 1996). However, although U.S. children and adolescents still score below their counterparts in some countries, especially Asian countries, recent comparisons indicate that U.S. children's and adolescents' math and science skills are improving (Gonzales & others, 2004). Despite improvents, U.S. children and adolescents still lag behind many countries in math and achievement. In the *Research in Child Development* interlude, you can read about Harold Stevenson's efforts to find out why American students fare so poorly in mathematics.

UCLA educational psychologist Sandra Graham is shown talking with adolescent boys about motivation. She has conducted a number of studies which reveal that middle-socioeconomic-status African American students—like their White counterparts—have high achievement expectations and attribute success to internal factors such as effort rather than external factors such as luck.

Research in Child Development

CROSS-CULTURAL COMPARISONS IN LEARNING MATH AND MATH INSTRUCTION

Harold Stevenson conducted research on children's learning for five decades. The research explored the reasons for the poor performance of American students. Stevenson and his colleagues (Stevenson, 1995; Stevenson & others, 1990) completed five cross-cultural comparisons of students in the United States, China, Taiwan, and Japan. In these studies, Asian students consistently outperformed American students. And, the longer the students were in school, the wider the gap became between Asian and American students—the lowest difference was in the first grade, the highest in the eleventh grade (the highest grade studied).

To learn more about the reasons for these large cross-cultural differences, Stevenson and his colleagues spent thousands of hours observing in classrooms, as well as interviewing and surveying teachers, students, and parents. They found that the Asian

Asian grade schools intersperse studying with frequent periods of activities. This approach helps children maintain their attention and likely makes learning more enjoyable. Shown here are Japanese fourth-graders making wearable masks. *What are some differences in the way children in many Asian countries are taught compared with children in the United States?*

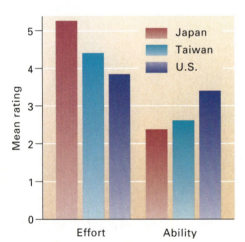

FIGURE 16.8 Mother's Beliefs About the Factors Responsible for Children's Math Achievement in Three Countries. In one study, mothers in Japan and Taiwan were more likely to believe that their children's math achievement was due to effort rather than innate ability, while U.S. mothers were more likely to believe their children's math achievement was due to innate ability (Stevenson, Lee, & Stigler, 1986). If parents believe that their children's math achievement is due to innate ability and their children are not doing well in math, the implication is that they are less Likely to think their children will benefit from putting forth more effort.

teachers spent more of their time teaching math than did the American teachers. For example, more than one-fourth of total classroom time in the first grade was spent on math instruction in Japan, compared with only one-tenth of the time in the U.S. first-grade classrooms. Also, the Asian students were in school an average of 240 days a year, compared with 178 days in the United States.

In addition, differences were found between the Asian and American parents. The American parents had much lower expectations for their children's education and achievement than did the Asian parents. Also, the American parents were more likely to state that their children's math achievement was due to innate ability; the Asian parents were more likely to say that their children's math achievement was the consequence of effort and training (see Figure 16.8). The Asian students were more likely to do math homework than were the American students, and the Asian parents were far more likely to help their children with their math homework than were the American parents (Chen & Stevenson, 1989).

Review and Reflect: Learning Goal 4

4 Explain the Development of Achievement in Children

REVIEW

- What are intrinsic and extrinsic motivation? How are they related to achievement?
- What role do mastery motivation and mindset play in children's achievement?
- What is self-efficacy, and how is it related to achievement?
- How are expectations involved in children's achievement?
- Why are goal setting, planning, and self-monitoring important in achievement?
- How do cultural, ethnic, and socioeconomic variations influence achievement?

REFLECT

- Think about several of your own past schoolmates who showed low motivation in school. Why do you think they behaved that way? What teaching strategies may have helped them?

Reach Your Learning Goals

Schools and Achievement

---

1 EXPLORING CHILDREN'S SCHOOLING: DISCUSS APPROACHES TO SCHOOLING AND DEVELOPMENT

Contemporary Approaches to Student Learning and Assessment

- Contemporary approaches to student learning include direct instruction, which is a teacher-centered approach, and constructivist, which is learner-centered. Some experts recommend that both a constructivist and direct instruction approach be used, depending on circumstances. Increased concern by the public and government in the United States has produced extensive state-mandated testing, which has both strengths and weaknesses, and is controversial. The most visible example of the increased state-mandated testing is the No Child Left Behind federal legislation.

Early Childhood Education

- The child-centered kindergarten emphasizes the education of the whole child, with particular attention to individual variation, the process of learning, and the importance of play in development. The Montessori approach is an increasingly popular early childhood education choice. Developmentally appropriate practice focuses on the typical patterns of children (age-appropriateness) and the uniqueness of each child (individual-appropriateness). Such practice contrasts with developmentally inappropriate practice, which relies on pencil-and-paper activities. The U.S. government has tried to break the poverty cycle with programs such as Head Start. Model programs have been shown to have positive effects on children who live in poverty. Controversy characterizes early childhood education curricula. On the one side are the child-centered, constructivist advocates, on the other are those who advocate an instructivist, academic approach. Another controversy focuses on whether universal preschool education should be implemented.

Elementary School

- Children take up the new role of student, interact, develop new relationships, and discover rich sources of new ideas in elementary school. A special concern is that early elementary school education proceeds too much on the basis of negative feedback to children.

Educating Adolescents

- The transition to middle or junior high school coincides with many social, familial, and individual changes in the adolescent's life, and this transition is often stressful. One source of stress is the move from the top-dog to the lowest position in school. Some critics argue that a major redesign of U.S. middle schools is needed. Critics say that U.S. high schools foster passivity and do not develop students' academic skills adequately. A number of strategies have been proposed for improving U.S. high schools, including higher expectations and better support. The overall high school dropout rate declined considerably in the last half of the twentieth century, but the dropout rates of Latino and Native American youth remain very high.

---

2 SOCIOECONOMIC STATUS AND ETHNICITY IN SCHOOLS: DESCRIBE THE ROLES OF SOCIOECONOMIC STATUS AND ETHNICITY IN SCHOOLS

Educating Students from Low-Income Backgrounds

- Children in poverty face problems at home and at school that present barriers to learning. Neighborhoods are dangerous and fear may be a way of life. Many schools' buildings are crumbling with age. Teachers are likely to encourage rote learning, and parents often don't set high educational standards.

Ethnicity in Schools

- The school experiences of children from different ethnic groups vary considerably. Teachers often have low expectations for children of color. A number of strategies can be adopted to improve relationships with diverse others.

3 CHILDREN WITH DISABILITIES: CHARACTERIZE CHILDREN WITH DISABILITIES AND THEIR SCHOOLING

Learning Disabilities

- Learning disabilities are disabilities in which children have difficulty in learning that involves understanding or using spoken or written language, and the difficulty can appear in listening, thinking, reading, writing, and spelling. A learning disability also may involve difficulty in doing mathematics. To be classified as a learning disability, the learning problem is not primarily the result of visual, hearing, or motor disabilities; mental retardation; emotional disorders; or due to environmental, cultural, or economic disadvantage. Dyslexia is a category of learning disabilities that involves a severe impairment in the ability to read and spell.

Attention Deficit Hyperactivity Disorder (ADHD)

- Attention deficit hyperactivity disorder (ADHD) is a disability in which individuals consistently show problems in one or more of these areas: (1) inattention, (2) hyperactivity, and (3) hyperactivity/impulsivity. ADHD has been increasingly diagnosed. Treatment can involve stimulant medication such as Ritalin or Adderall and may include behavior management therapy.

Autism Spectrum Disorders (ASDs)

- Autism spectrum disorders (ASDs), also called pervasive developmental disorders, range from the severe developmental autistic disorder to the relatively mild Asperger syndrome. These disorders are characterized by problems in social interaction, repetitive behaviors, and problems in both verbal and nonverbal communication. Current consensus is that they are caused by abnormalities in brain structure and neurotransmitters, and genetic factors likely play a role.

Educational Issues

- In 1975, Public Law 94-142, the Education for All Handicapped Children Act, required that all children with disabilities be given a free, appropriate public education. This law was renamed the Individuals with Disabilities Education Act (IDEA) in 1990 and updated in 2004. IDEA includes requirements that children with disabilities receive an individual education plan (IEP), which is a written plan that spells out a program tailored to the child. The least restrictive environment (LRE) is an educational setting for children with disabilities that is as similar as possible to the one in which children without disabilities are educated. The trend is toward the use of inclusion, although some aspects of inclusion have recently been criticized.

4 ACHIEVEMENT: EXPLAIN THE DEVELOPMENT OF ACHIEVEMENT IN CHILDREN

Extrinsic and Intrinsic Motivation

- Extrinsic motivation involves external incentives such as rewards and punishment. Intrinsic motivation is based on internal factors such as self-determination, curiosity, challenge, and effort. One view is that giving students some choice and providing opportunities for personal responsibility increase intrinsic motivation. Interest is conceptualized as more specific than intrinsic motivation, and interest is positively linked to learning. It is important for teachers to create learning environments that encourage students to become cognitively engaged and develop a responsibility for their learning. Overall, the overwhelming conclusion is that it is a wise strategy to create learning environments that encourage students to become intrinsically motivated. However, in many real-world situations, both intrinsic and extrinsic motivation are involved, and too often intrinsic and extrinsic motivation have been pitted against each other as polar opposites.

Mastery Motivation and Mindset

- A mastery orientation is preferred over helpless or performance orientations in achievement situations. Mindset is the cognitive view, either fixed or growth, that individuals develop for themselves. Dweck argues that a key aspect of adolescents' development is to guide them in developing a growth mindset.

Self-Efficacy

- Self-efficacy is the belief that one can master a situation and produce positive outcomes. Bandura points out that self-efficacy is a critical factor in whether students will achieve. Schunk argues that self-efficacy influences a student's choice of tasks, with low-efficacy students avoiding many learning tasks.

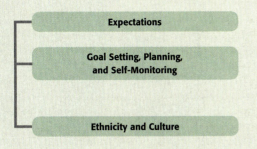

- Students' expectations for success influence their motivation. Children benefit when their parents, teachers, and other adults have high expectations for their achievement.

- Setting specific, proximal (short-term), and challenging goals benefits students' self-efficacy and achievement. Being a good planner means managing time effectively, setting priorities, and being organized. Self-monitoring is a key aspect of self-regulation and benefits student learning.

- In most investigations, socioeconomic status predicts achievement better than ethnicity. U.S. children do more poorly on math and science achievement tests than children in Asian countries such as China and Japan.

KEY TERMS

constructivist approach 477
direct instruction
  approach 477
child-centered
  kindergarten 479
Montessori approach 479
developmentally
  appropriate practice 479

Project Head Start 480
top-dog phenomenon 484
learning disabilities 490
dyslexia 490
attention deficit hyperactivity
  disorder (ADHD) 491
autism spectrum disorders
  (ASDs) 492

autistic disorder 492
Asperger syndrome 492
individualized education
  plan (IEP) 493
least restrictive
  environment (LRE) 493
inclusion 493
extrinsic motivation 494

intrinsic motivation 494
mastery orientation 496
helpless orientation 496
performance
  orientation 496
mindset 497
self-efficacy 497

KEY PEOPLE

Maria Montessori 479
Lillian Katz 481
Edward Zigler 481
Jonathan Kozol 487

John Ogbu 487
Elliot Aronson 488
James Comer 488

Valanne Henderson and Carol
  Dweck 496
Albert Bandura 497

Dale Schunk 497
Sandra Graham 499
Harold Stevenson 499

E-LEARNING TOOLS

To help you master the material in this chapter, you'll find a number of valuable study tools at the Online Learning Center for *Child Development*, twelfth edition (**www.mhhe.com/santrockcd12**).

Taking It to the Net

Reach the answers to these questions:

1. Mark is going to teach high school mathematics. He has read that parents' involvement in their children's education is virtually nonexistent by the time their kids reach high school. What can Mark do as a teacher to encourage parental involvement?

2. Eight-year-old Grace has just been diagnosed with dyslexia. Her parents do not know what causes the disorder or how to help her. What causes dyslexia? And what can be done to help Grace?

3. Karen is on a school board committee studying how the transition to middle school may decrease student motivation and lead to social and academic problems that may continue into high school. She wants to present an overview of the psychological research on this issue. What have psychologists found to be the negative effects that middle schools have on achievement and motivation?

Health and Well-Being, Parenting, and Education Exercises

Build your decision-making skills by trying your hand at the health and well-being, parenting, and education exercises.

Video Clips

The Online Learning Center includes the following videos for this chapter:

- *Philosophy of Preschool Teaching*
A head teacher of a 4-year-old classroom describes her "whole child" philosophy to teaching young children.

- *Schools and Public Policy*
Dr. Eccles describes how her research on gender and school transitions has influenced public policy.

- *Non-College-Bound Adolescents*
A discussion of the unique problems faced by non-college-bound adolescents.

- *Sex Differences and School*
Why are there achievement differences between boys and girls? The research is unclear, according to Dr. Eccles. She states most likely it is a two-way interaction between biological and cultural factors.

17

Our most basic common link is that we all inhabit this planet. We all breathe the same air. We all cherish our children's future.

—JOHN F. KENNEDY
United States President, 20th Century

LEARNING GOALS

◆ Discuss the role of culture in children's development.

◆ Describe how socioeconomic status and poverty impact children's lives.

◆ Explain how ethnicity is linked to children's development.

◆ Summarize the influence of technology on children's development.

CULTURE AND DIVERSITY

CHAPTER OUTLINE

Images of Child Development
The Stories of Sonya's and Michael's Cultural Conflicts

Sonya, a 16-year-old Japanese American girl, was upset over her family's reaction to her White American boyfriend. "Her parents refused to meet him and on several occasions threatened to disown her" (Sue & Morishima, 1982, p. 142). Her older brothers also reacted angrily to Sonya's dating a White American, warning that they were going to beat him up. Her parents were also disturbed that Sonya's grades, above average in middle school, were beginning to drop.

Generational issues contributed to the conflict between Sonya and her family (Nagata, 1989). Her parents had experienced strong sanctions against dating Whites when they were growing up and were legally prevented from marrying anyone but a Japanese. As Sonya's older brothers were growing up, they valued ethnic pride and solidarity. The brothers saw her dating a White as "selling out" her own ethnic group. Sonya and the other members of her family obviously had different cultural values.

Michael, a 17-year-old Chinese American high school student, was referred to a therapist by the school counselor because he was depressed and had suicidal tendencies (Huang & Ying, 1989). Michael was failing several classes and frequently was absent from school. Michael's parents, successful professionals, expected Michael to excel in school and go on to become a doctor. They were angered by Michael's school failures, especially since he was the firstborn son, who in Chinese families is expected to achieve the highest standards.

The therapist encouraged the parents to put less academic pressure on Michael and to have more realistic expectations for Michael (who had no interest in becoming a doctor). Michael's school attendance changed, and his parents noticed his improved attitude toward school. Michael's case illustrates how expectations that Asian American youth will be "whiz kids" can become destructive.

> ### PREVIEW
> Culture had a strong influence on the conflict Sonya and Michael experienced in their families and on their behavior outside of the family—in Sonya's case, dating; in Michael's case, school. Of course, a family's cultural background does not always produce conflict between children and other family members, but these two cases underscore the importance of culture in children's development. In this chapter, we will explore many aspects of culture, including cross-cultural comparisons of children's development, the harmful effects of poverty, the role of ethnicity, and the benefits and dangers that technology can bring to children's lives.

1 CULTURE AND CHILDREN'S DEVELOPMENT

The Relevance of Culture to the Study of Children   Cross-Cultural Comparisons

culture The behavior, patterns, beliefs, and all other products of a particular group of people that are passed on from generation to generation.

In Chapter 1, we defined **culture** as the behavior, patterns, beliefs, and all other products of a particular group of people that are passed on from generation to generation. The products result from the interaction between groups of people and their environment over many years. Here we examine the role of culture in children's development.

The Relevance of Culture to the Study of Children

A key aspect of the relevance of culture to the study of children is that culture is reflected in attitudes that people have and the way they interact with children. For example, culture is manifested in parents' beliefs, values, and goals that they have for their children and these in turn influence the contexts in which children develop (Hughes, 2007; Kim & others, 2009).

Culture includes many components and can be analyzed in many ways (Berry, 2007; Matsumoto & Juang, 2008; Tewari & Alvarez, 2009). Cross-cultural expert Richard Brislin (1993) described a number of characteristics of culture:

- Culture is made up of ideals, values, and assumptions about life that guide people's behavior.
- Culture consists of those aspects of the environment that people make.
- Culture is transmitted from generation to generation, with the responsibility for the transmission resting on the shoulders of parents, teachers, and community leaders.
- Culture's influence becomes noticed the most in well-meaning clashes between people from very different cultural backgrounds.
- Despite compromises, cultural values still remain.
- When their cultural values are violated, or their cultural expectations are ignored, people react emotionally.
- It is not unusual for people to accept a cultural value at one point in their lives and reject it at another point. For example, rebellious adolescents and emerging adults might accept a culture's values and expectations after having children of their own.

Despite all the differences among cultures, research by American psychologist Donald Campbell and his colleagues (Brewer & Campbell, 1976) revealed that people in all cultures tend to believe that what happens in their culture is "natural" and "correct" and that what happens in other cultures is "unnatural" and "incorrect"; perceive their cultural customs as universally valid—that is, they believe that what is good for them is good for everyone; and behave in ways that favor their cultural group and feel hostile toward other cultural groups. In other words, people in all cultures tend to be *ethnocentric*—favoring their own group over others.

The future will bring extensive contact between people from varied cultural and ethnic backgrounds (Matsumoto & Juang, 2008; Suyemoto, 2009). If the study of child development is to be a relevant discipline in the remainder of the twenty-first century, increased attention will need to be given to culture and ethnicity. Global interdependence is no longer a matter of belief or choice. It is an inescapable reality. Children and their parents are not just citizens of the United States, or Canada, or another country. They are citizens of the world—a world that, through advances in transportation and technology, has become increasingly interactive. By better understanding the behavior and values of cultures around the world, we may be able to interact more effectively with each other and make this planet a more hospitable, peaceful place in which to live (Kim & others, 2009).

Copyright © Sidney Harris. Used by permission.

Cross-Cultural Comparisons

As we described in Chapter 1, **cross-cultural studies**, which involve the comparison of a culture with one or more other cultures, provide information about other cultures,

cross-cultural studies Studies that compare a culture with one or more other cultures. Such studies provide information about the degree to which children's development is similar, or universal, across cultures or about the degree to which it is culture-specific.

Individualistic	Collectivistic
Focuses on individual	Focuses on groups
Self is determined by personal traits independent of groups; self is stable across contexts	Self is defined by in-group terms; self can change with context
Private self is more important	Public self is most important
Personal achievement, competition, power are important	Achievement is for the benefit of the in-group; cooperation is stressed
Cognitive dissonance is frequent	Cognitive dissonance is infrequent
Emotions (such as anger) are self-focused	Emotions (such as anger) are often relationship based
People who are the most liked are self-assured	People who are the most liked are modest, self-effacing
Values: pleasure, achievement, competition, freedom	Values: security, obedience, in-group harmony, personalized relationships
Many casual relationships	*Few close* relationships
Save own face	Save own and other's face
Independent behaviors: swimming, sleeping alone in room, privacy	Interdependent behaviors: co-bathing, co-sleeping
Relatively rare mother-child physical contact	Frequent mother-child physical contact (such as hugging, holding)

FIGURE 17.1 **Characteristics of Individualistic and Collectivistic Cultures**

Cross-cultural studies involve the comparison of a culture with one or more other cultures. Shown here is a 14-year-old !Kung girl who has added flowers to her beadwork during the brief rainy season in the Kalahari desert in Botswana, Africa. Delinquency and violence occur much less frequently in the peaceful !Kung culture than in most other cultures around the world.

and examine the role of culture in children's development. This comparison provides information about the degree to which children's development is similar, or universal, across cultures, or the degree to which it is culture-specific (Chiu & Hong, 2007; Kagitcibasi, 2007). In terms of gender, for example, the experiences of male and female children and adolescents continue to be worlds apart in some cultures (Larson & Wilson, 2004). In many countries, males have far greater access to educational opportunities, more freedom to pursue a variety of careers, and fewer restrictions on sexual activity than females (UNICEF, 2007).

Individualism and Collectivism

In cross-cultural research, the search for basic traits has focused on the dichotomy between individualism and collectivism (Triandis, 2001, 2007):

- **Individualism** involves giving priority to personal goals rather than to group goals; it emphasizes values that serve the self, such as feeling good, personal distinction and achievement, and independence.
- **Collectivism** emphasizes values that serve the group by subordinating personal goals to preserve group integrity, interdependence of the members, and harmonious relationships.

Figure 17.1 summarizes some of the main characteristics of individualistic and collectivistic cultures. Many Western cultures, such as the United States, Canada, Great Britain, and the Netherlands, are described as individualistic; many Eastern cultures, such as China, Japan, India, and Thailand, are described as collectivistic. So is Mexican culture.

Many of psychology's basic tenets have been developed in individualistic cultures like the United States. Consider the flurry of self-terms in psychology that have an individualistic focus—for example, self-actualization, self-awareness, self-efficacy, self-reinforcement, self-criticism, self-serving, selfishness, and self-doubt (Lonner, 1988).

Researchers have found that self-conceptions are related to culture. In one study, American and Chinese college students completed 20 sentences beginning with "I am _____" (Trafimow, Triandis, & Goto, 1991). As indicated in Figure 17.2, the American college students were much more likely to describe themselves with personal traits ("I am assertive"), whereas the Chinese students were more likely to identify themselves by their group affiliations ("I am a member of the math club"). A recent study also revealed the lack of a group orientation in the United States (Mejia-Arauz & others, 2007). The study focused on the interaction of 6- to 10-year-old children from three different cultures while they worked on a task. The children were observed in a group of three (triad). Triads of children whose families had immigrated to the United from indigenous regions of Mexico, and whose mothers averaged only seven years of schooling, were more likely to coordinate their work on the task as an ensemble; in contrast, the triads of European heritage children who had more extensive schooling more frequently engaged dyadically (in twos) or individually. Mexican

individualism Giving priority to personal goals rather than to group goals; emphasizing values that serve the self, such as feeling good, personal distinction and achievement, and independence.

collectivism Emphasizing values that serve the group by subordinating personal goals to preserve group integrity, interdependence of members, and harmonious relationships.

heritage U.S. triads whose mothers had extensive schooling showed an intermediate pattern or more closely resembled the European heritage children.

Human beings have always lived in groups, whether large or small, and have always needed one another for survival. Critics of the Western notion of psychology argue that the Western emphasis on individualism may undermine our basic species need for relatedness (Kagitcibasi, 2007). Some social scientists argue that many problems in Western cultures are intensified by their emphasis on individualism. Compared with collectivist cultures, individualistic cultures have higher rates of suicide, drug abuse, crime, teenage pregnancy, divorce, child abuse, and mental disorders.

A recent analysis proposed four values that reflect parents' beliefs in individualistic cultures about what is required for children's effective development of autonomy: (1) *personal choice*; (2) *intrinsic motivation*; (3) *self-esteem*; and (4) *self-maximization*, which consists of achieving one's full potential (Tamis-LeMonda & others, 2008). The analysis also proposed that three values reflect parents' beliefs in collectivistic cultures: (1) *connectedness to the family and other close relationships*, (2) *orientation to the larger group*, and (3) *respect and obedience*.

Critics of the individualistic and collectivistic cultures concept argue that these terms are too broad and simplistic, especially with globalization increasing (Kagitcibasi, 2007; Rothbaum & Trommsdorff, 2007). Regardless of their cultural background, people need both a positive sense of self and connectedness to others to develop fully as human beings. The analysis by Catherine Tamis-LeMonda and her colleagues (2008) emphasizes that in many families, children are not reared in environments that uniformly endorse individualistic or collectivistic values, thoughts, and actions. Rather, in many families, children are

expected to be quiet, assertive, respectful, curious, humble, self-assured, independent, dependent, affectionate, or reserved depending on the situation, people present, children's age, and social-political and economic circles.

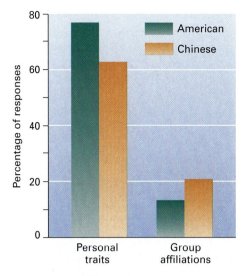

FIGURE 17.2 American and Chinese Self-Conceptions. College students from the United States and China completed 20 "I am _____" sentences. Both groups filled in personal traits more than group affiliations. However, the U.S. college students more often filled in the blank with personal traits, the Chinese with group affiliations.

Review and Reflect: Learning Goal 1

1 Discuss the Role of Culture in Children's Development

REVIEW

- What is the relevance of culture to the study of children?
- What are cross-cultural comparisons? What characterizes individualistic and collectivistic cultures? What are some criticisms of the individualistic and collectivistic cultures concept?

REFLECT

- What was the achievement orientation in your family as you grew up? How did the cultural background of your parents influence this orientation?

---

2 SOCIOECONOMIC STATUS AND POVERTY

| What Is Socioeconomic Status? | Socioeconomic Variations in Families, Neighborhoods, and Schools | Poverty |

Many subcultures exist within countries. For example, Sonya's family, discussed in the opening of the chapter, had beliefs and patterns different from Michael's family. Some, but not all, subcultures are tied to ethnicity or socioeconomic characteristics or both. For example, the values and attitudes of children growing up in an urban ghetto or

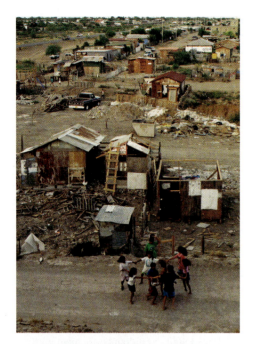

(*Top*) Children playing in Nueva Era, a low-income area on the outskirts of Nuevo Laredo, Mexico. (*Bottom*) Two boys who live in a poverty section of the South Bronx in New York City. *How might socioeconomic status affect the lives of children like these?*

socioeconomic status (SES) A grouping of people with similar occupational, educational, and economic characteristics.

rural Appalachia may differ from those of children growing up in a wealthy suburb. In any event, children growing up in these different contexts are likely to have different socioeconomic statuses, and this inequality may influence their development.

What Is Socioeconomic Status?

In Chapter 1, we defined **socioeconomic status (SES)** as the grouping of people with similar occupational, educational, and economic characteristics. Socioeconomic status implies certain inequalities. Generally, members of a society have (1) occupations that vary in prestige, and some individuals have more access than others to higher-status occupations; (2) different levels of educational attainment, and some individuals have more access than others to better education; (3) different economic resources; and (4) different levels of power to influence a community's institutions. These differences in the ability to control resources and to participate in society's rewards produce unequal opportunities (Conger & Conger, 2008; Liu & Hernandez, 2008). Socioeconomic differences are a "proxy for material, human, and social capital within and beyond the family" (Huston & Ripke, 2006, p. 425).

The number of significantly different socioeconomic statuses depends on the community's size and complexity. Most research on socioeconomic status delineates two categories, low and middle, but some research delineates as many as six categories. Sometimes low socioeconomic status is described as low-income, working class, or blue collar; sometimes the middle category is described as middle-income, managerial, or white collar. Examples of low-SES occupations are factory worker, manual laborer, and maintenance worker. Examples of middle-SES occupations include skilled worker, manager, and professional (doctor, lawyer, teacher, accountant, and so on).

Socioeconomic Variations in Families, Neighborhoods, and Schools

The families, neighborhoods, and schools of children have socioeconomic characteristics. A parent's SES is likely linked to the neighborhoods and schools in which children live and the schools they attend (Coltrane & others, 2008; Hutson, 2008). Such variations in neighborhood settings can influence children's adjustment (Conger & Conger, 2008; Fauth & Brooks-Gunn, 2008). For example, a recent study revealed that neighborhood disadvantage (involving such characteristics as low neighborhood income and unemployment), was linked to less consistent, less stimulating, and more punitive parenting, and ultimately to negative child outcomes (low verbal ability and behavioral problems) (Kohen & others, 2008). Schools in low-income areas not only have fewer resources than those in higher-income areas but also tend to have more students with lower achievement test scores, lower rates of graduation, and smaller percentages of students going to college (Wigfield & others, 2006).

Let's further examine socioeconomic differences in family life (Coltrane & others, 2008; Conger & Conger, 2008). In chapter 14, "Families," we described socioeconomic differences in child rearing (Hoff, Laursen, & Tardif, 2002). Recall that lower-SES parents are more concerned that their children conform to society's expectations, have an authoritarian parenting style, use physical punishment more in disciplining their children, and are more directive and less conversational with their children. By contrast, higher-SES parents tend to be more concerned with developing children's initiative, create a home atmosphere in which children are more nearly equal participants, are less likely to use physical punishment, and are less directive and more conversational with their children.

Like their parents, children from low-SES backgrounds are at high risk for experiencing mental health problems (McLoyd, Aikens, & Burton, 2006). Problems such as depression, low self-confidence, peer conflict, and juvenile delinquency are more prevalent among children living in low-SES families than among economically advantaged children (Gibbs & Huang, 1989).

Of course, children from low-SES backgrounds vary considerably in intellectual and psychological functioning. For example, a sizable portion of children from low-SES backgrounds perform well in school; some perform better than many middle-SES students. One study found that when low-income parents had high educational aspirations it was linked to more positive educational outcomes in youth (Schoon, Parsons, & Sacker, 2004). When children from low-SES backgrounds are achieving well in school, it is not unusual to find a parent or parents making special sacrifices to provide the living conditions and support that contribute to school success.

Poverty

When sixth-graders in a poverty-stricken area of St. Louis were asked to describe a perfect day, one boy said he would erase the world, then he would sit and think (Children's Defense Fund, 1992). Asked if he wouldn't rather go outside and play, the boy responded, "Are you kidding, out there?"

The world is a dangerous and unwelcoming place for too many of America's youth, especially those whose families, neighborhoods, and schools are in low-income contexts (Leventhal, Brooks-Gunn, & Kamerman, 2008). Some children are resilient and cope with the challenges of poverty without any major setbacks, but too many struggle unsuccessfully (Spencer, 2006). Each child of poverty who reaches adulthood unhealthy, unskilled, or alienated keeps our nation from being as competent and productive as it can be (Children's Defense Fund, 2008).

In 2006, 17 percent of children under 18 years of age were living in families below the poverty line (Federal Interagency Forum on Child and Family Statistics, 2008). This is an increase from 2001 (16.2 percent) but down from a peak of 22.7 percent in 1993. The U.S. figure of 17 percent of children living in poverty is much higher than those from other industrialized nations. For example, Canada has a child poverty rate of 9 percent and Sweden has a rate of 2 percent. Especially problematic is when poverty persists in children's lives over a number of years (Hutson, 2008). For example, a recent study also revealed that the more years children spent living in poverty, the more their physiological indices of stress were elevated (Evans & Kim, 2007).

Poverty in the United States is demarcated along family structure and ethnic lines (Fauth, Leventhall & Brooks-Gunn, 2008; Federal Interagency Forum on Child and Family Statistics, 2008). In 2006, 42 percent of female-headed families lived in poverty compared with only 8 percent of married-couple families. In 2006, 33 percent of African American families and 27 percent of Latino families lived in poverty, compared with only 10 percent of non-Latino White families. Compared with White children, ethnic minority children are more likely to experience persistent poverty over many years and live in isolated poor neighborhoods where social supports are minimal and threats to positive development abundant (Jarrett, 1995) (see Figure 17.3).

Psychological Ramifications of Poverty Living in poverty has many psychological effects on both adults and children (Engle & Black, 2008; Healey 2009; Leon-Guerrero, 2009). First, the poor are often powerless. In occupations, they rarely are the decision makers. Rules are handed down to them in an authoritarian manner. Second, the poor are often vulnerable to disaster. They are not likely to be given notice before they are laid off from work and usually do not have financial resources to fall back on when problems arise. Third, their range of alternatives is often restricted. Only a limited number of jobs are open to them. Even when alternatives are available, the poor might not know about them or be prepared to make a wise decision, because of inadequate education and inability to read well. Fourth, being poor means having less prestige. This lack of prestige is transmitted to children early in their lives. The child in poverty observes that many other children wear nicer clothes and live in more attractive houses.

Although positive times occur in the lives of children growing up in poverty, many of their negative experiences are worse than those of their middle-SES counterparts

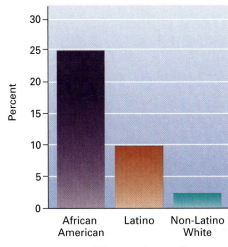

FIGURE 17.3 Percentages of Youth Under 18 Who Are Living in Distressed Neighborhoods. *Note:* A distressed neighborhood is defined by high levels (at least one standard deviation above the mean) of (1) poverty, (2) female-headed families, (3) high school dropouts, (4) unemployment, and (5) reliance on welfare.

(Barajas, Philipsen, & Brooks-Gunn, 2007). These adversities involve physical punishment and lack of structure at home, violence in the neighborhood, and domestic violence in their buildings. A research review concluded that compared with their economically more advantaged counterparts, poor children experience widespread environmental inequities that include the following (Evans, 2004, p. 77):

- Exposure "to more family turmoil, violence, separation from their families, instability, and chaotic households" (Emery & Laumann-Billings, 1998)

- "Less social support, and their parents are less responsive and more authoritarian" (Bo, 1994)

- "Read to relatively infrequently, watch more TV, and have less access to books and computers" (Bradley & others, 2001)

- Schools and child-care facilities that are inferior and parents who "are less involved in their children's school activities" (Benveniste, Carnoy, & Rothstein, 2003)

- Air and water that are more polluted and homes that "are more crowded, more noisy, and of lower quality" (Myers, Baer, & Choi, 1996)

- More dangerous and physically deteriorating neighborhoods with less adequate municipal services (Brody & others, 2001)

To read further about the risks that children living in poverty face, see the *Research in Child Development* interlude.

Research in Child Development

MULTIPLE RISKS OF CHILDREN LIVING IN POVERTY

In Chapter 1, we briefly described the results of one study that explored multiple risks in the lives of children from poverty and middle-income backgrounds (Evans & English, 2002). Here we provide more details about this study. Six multiple risks were examined in 287 8- to 10-year-old non-Latino White children living in rural areas of upstate New York: family turmoil, child separation (a close family member being away from home often), exposure to violence, crowding, noise level, and housing quality. Family turmoil, child separation, and exposure to violence were assessed by maternal reports of the life events their children had experienced. Crowding was determined by the number of people per room, and noise level was measured by the decibel level in the home. Housing quality (based on structural quality, cleanliness, clutter, resources for children, safety hazards, and climatic conditions) was rated by observers who visited the homes. Each of the six factors was defined as presenting a risk or no risk. Thus, the multiple stressor exposure for children could range from 0 to 6. Families were defined as poor if the household lived at or below the federally defined poverty line.

Children in poor families experienced greater risks than their middle-income counterparts. As shown in Figure 17.4, a higher percentage of children in poor families were exposed to each of the six risk factors (family turmoil, child separation, exposure to violence, crowding, noise level, and poor quality of housing).

Were there differences in the children's adjustment that might reflect these differences in exposure to risk factors? The researchers assessed the children's levels of psychological stress through reports by the children and their mothers. Problems in self-regulation of behavior were determined by whether

Risk factor (stressor)	Poor children exposed (%)	Middle-income children exposed (%)
Family turmoil	45	12
Child separation	45	14
Exposure to violence	73	49
Crowding	16	7
Excessive noise	32	21
Poor housing quality	24	3

FIGURE 17.4 Percentage of Poor and Middle-Income Children Exposed to Each of Six Stressors

children chose immediate rather than delayed gratification on a task. Resting blood pressure and overnight neuroendocrine hormones were measured to indicate children's levels of psychophysiological stress.

The researchers found that compared with children from middle-income backgrounds, poor children had higher levels of psychological stress, more problems in self-regulation of behavior, and elevated psychophysiological stress. Analysis indicated that cumulative exposure to stressors may contribute to difficulties in socioemotional development for children living in poverty.

When poverty is persistent and long-standing, it can have especially damaging effects on children (Philipsen, Johnson, & Brooks-Gunn, 2008; Wilson, 2007). In one study, the longer children lived in families with income below the poverty line, the lower was the quality of their home environments (Garrett, Ng'andu, & Ferron, 1994). Also in this study, improvements in family income had their strongest effects on the home environments of chronically poor children. Further, a study of more than 30,000 individuals from birth into the adult years found that the greater risk for developmental outcomes took place with persistent and accumulating socioeconomic disadvantage throughout childhood and adolescence (Schoon & others, 2002).

A special concern is the high percentage of single mothers in poverty, more than one-third of whom are in poverty, compared with only 10 percent of single fathers. Vonnie McLoyd (1998) concluded that because poor, single mothers are more distressed than their middle-SES counterparts are, they often show low support, nurturance, and involvement with their children. Among the reasons for the high poverty rate of single mothers are women's low pay, infrequent awarding of alimony payments, and poorly enforced child support by fathers.

Vonnie McLoyd (*right*) has conducted a number of important investigations of the roles of poverty, ethnicity, and unemployment in children's and adolescents' development. She has found that economic stressors often diminish children's and adolescents' belief in the utility of education and their achievement strivings.

Countering Poverty's Effects   Some studies show that benefits provided to parents may have important effects on children as well. One study showed that work-based antipoverty programs for parents were linked to enhanced school performance and social behavior of children (Huston & others, 2001). In this study, wage supplements sufficient to raise family income above the poverty threshold and subsidies for child care and health insurance were given to adults who worked full-time. Positive effects were found for boys' academic achievement, classroom behavior skills, problem behaviors, and educational and occupational aspirations. The effects were more positive for boys than girls, perhaps because boys have more behavioral and school-related problems to begin with.

One trend in antipoverty programs is to conduct two-generation interventions (McLoyd, 1998). That is, the programs provide both services for children (such as educational child care or preschool education) and services for parents (such as adult education, literacy training, and job-skill training). Evaluations suggest that two-generation programs have more positive effects on parents than they do on children (St. Pierre, Layzer, & Barnes, 1996). Also, when the two-generation programs do show benefits for children, these are more likely to be health benefits than cognitive gains. Some studies have shown that poverty interventions are more effective with young children than older children and adolescents (Duncan & Magnuson, 2008; Magnuson, Duncan, & Kalil, 2006). However, a downward trajectory is not inevitable for older children and youth living in poverty, and the success of poverty interventions likely depends on the quality and type of intervention.

In a recent experimental study, Aletha Huston and her colleagues (2006; Gupta, Thornton, & Huston, 2007) evaluated the effects of New Hope, a program designed to increase parental employment and reduce family poverty, on adolescent development.

They randomly assigned families with 6- to 10-year-old children living in poverty to the New Hope program and a control group. New Hope offered poor adults who were employed 30 or more hours a week benefits that were designed to increase family income (a wage supplement that ensured that net income increased as parents earned more), to provide work supports through subsidized child care (for any child under age 13), and health insurance. Management services were provided to New Hope participants to assist them in job searches and other needs. The New Hope program was available to the experimental group families for three years (until the children were 9 to 13 years old). Five years after the program began and two years after it had ended, the program's effects on the children were examined when they were 11 to 16 years old. Compared with adolescents in the control group, New Hope adolescents were more competent at reading, had better school performance, were less likely to be in special education classes, had more positive social skills, and were more likely to be in formal after-school arrangements. New Hope parents reported better psychological well-being and a greater sense of self-efficacy in managing their adolescents than control parents did. To read about another program that benefited youth living in poverty, see the *Caring for Children* interlude.

Caring for Children

THE QUANTUM OPPORTUNITIES PROGRAM

A downward trajectory is not inevitable for youth living in poverty (Carnegie Council on Adolescent Development, 1995). One potential positive path for such youth is to become involved with a caring mentor. The Quantum Opportunities program, funded by the Ford Foundation, was a four-year, year-round mentoring effort (Carnegie Council on Adolescent Development, 1995). The students were entering the ninth grade at a high school with high rates of poverty, were minorities, and came from families that received public assistance. Each day for four years, mentors provided sustained support, guidance, and concrete assistance to their students.

The Quantum program required students to participate in (1) academic-related activities outside school hours, including reading, writing, math, science, and social studies, peer tutoring, and computer skills training; (2) community service projects, including tutoring elementary school students, cleaning up the neighborhood, and volunteering in hospitals, nursing homes, and libraries; and (3) cultural enrichment and personal development activities, including life skills training, and college and job planning. In exchange for their commitment to the program, students were offered financial incentives that encouraged participation, completion, and long-range planning. A stipend of $1.33 was given to students for each hour they participated in these activities. For every 100 hours of education, service, or development activities, students received a bonus of $100. The average cost per participant was $10,600 for the four years, which is one-half the cost of one year in prison.

An evaluation of the Quantum project compared the mentored students with a nonmentored control group. Sixty-three percent of the mentored students graduated from high school, but only 42 percent of the control group did; 42 percent of the mentored students are currently enrolled in college, but only 16 percent of the control group are. Furthermore, control-group students were twice as likely as the mentored students to receive food stamps or welfare, and they had more arrests. Such programs clearly have the potential to overcome the intergenerational transmission of poverty and its negative outcomes.

The original Quantum Opportunities program no longer exists but the Eisenhower Foundation (2008) recently began replicating the Quantum program in Alabama, South Carolina, New Hampshire, Virginia, Misssssipi, Oregon, Maryland, and Washington, DC.

Review and Reflect: Learning Goal 2

2 Describe How Socioeconomic Status and Poverty Impact Children's Lives

REVIEW

- What is socioeconomic status?
- What are some socioeconomic variations in families, neighborhoods, and schools?
- What characterizes children living in poverty?

REFLECT

- What would you label the socioeconomic status of your family as you grew up? How do you think the SES status of your family influenced your development?

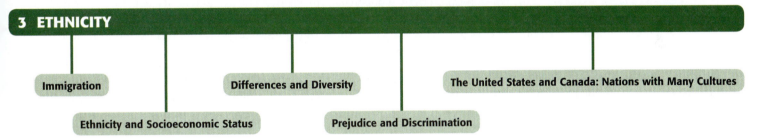

3 ETHNICITY

Immigration

Ethnicity and Socioeconomic Status

Differences and Diversity

Prejudice and Discrimination

The United States and Canada: Nations with Many Cultures

Nowhere are cultural changes in the United States more dramatic than in the increasing ethnic diversity of America's children. Recall from Chapter 1 that **ethnicity** refers to characteristics rooted in cultural heritage, including nationality, race, religion, and language. Ninety-three languages are spoken in Los Angeles alone! With increased diversity have come conflict and concerns about the future.

Immigration

Relatively high rates of minority immigration have contributed to the growth in the proportion of ethnic minorities in the U.S. population (Banks, 2008; Suyemoto, 2009). And this growth of ethnic minorities is expected to continue throughout the twenty-first century. Asian Americans are expected to be the fastest-growing ethnic group of adolescents, with a growth rate of almost 600 percent by 2100. Latino adolescents are projected to increase almost 400 percent by 2100. Figure 17.5 shows the actual numbers of adolescents in different ethnic groups in the year 2000, as well as the numbers projected through 2100. Notice that by 2100, Latino adolescents are expected to outnumber non-Latino White adolescents.

Immigrants often experience special stressors (Liu & others, 2009). These include language barriers, separations from support networks, changes in SES, and the struggle both to preserve ethnic identity and to adapt to the majority culture (Banks, 2008; Wong, Kinzie, & Kinzie, 2009).

Recent research increasingly shows links between acculturation and adolescent problems (Gonzales & others, 2006, 2007). For example, more-acculturated Latino youth in the United States experience higher rates of conduct problems, substance abuse, depression, and risky sexual behavior than their less-acculturated counterparts

ethnicity A dimension of culture based on cultural heritage, nationality, race, religion, and language.

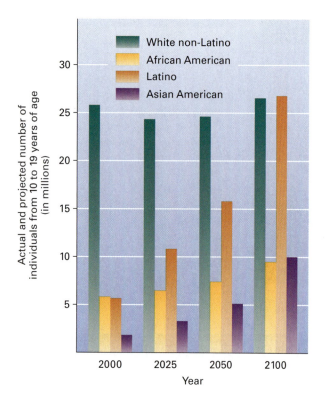

FIGURE 17.5 Actual and Projected Number of U.S. Adolescents Aged 10 to 19, 2000 to 2100. In 2000, there were more than 25 million White non-Latino adolescents 10 to 19 years of age in the United States, whereas the numbers for ethnic minority groups were substantially lower. However, projections for 2025 through 2100 reveal dramatic increases in the number of Latino and Asian American adolescents to the point at which in 2100 it is projected that there will be more Latino than non-Latino Whites in the United States and more Asian American than African American adolescents.

Latino immigrants in the Rio Grande Valley, Texas. *What are some characteristics of the families who have recently immigrated to the United States?*

(Gonzales & others, 2006, 2007). Conflict between parents and adolescents that results from the cultural shifts that have taken place in immigrant families is likely responsible for the link between acculturation and adolescent problems (Gonzales & others, 2006, 2007). The conflict is often greatest when adolescents have acculturated more quickly than their parents.

Many of the families that have immigrated in recent decades to the United States, such as Mexican Americans and Asian Americans, come from collective cultures in which family obligation and duty to one's family is strong (Hayashino & Chopra, 2009; Fuligni & Fuligni, 2007). This family obligation and duty may take the form of assisting parents in their occupations and contributing to the family's welfare (Parke & Buriel, 2006). This often occurs in service and manual labor jobs, such as those in construction, gardening, cleaning, and restaurants.

Asian American and Latino families place a greater emphasis on family duty and obligation than do non-Latino White families (Fuligni & Fuligni, 2007). In one study of 18- to 25-year-olds, Asian Americans said family interdependence was more important to them than did non-Latino Whites (Tseng, 2004). Researchers have found that Asian American and Latino adolescents believe that they should spend more time taking care of their siblings, helping around the house, assisting their parents at work, and being with their family than adolescents with a European heritage (Fuligni, Tseng, & Lamb, 1999)

Of course, individual families vary, and how ethnic minority families deal with stress depends on many factors (Tewari & Alvarez, 2009). Whether the parents are native-born or immigrants, how long the family has been in this country, their socioeconomic status, and their national origin all make a difference (Kagiticibasi, 2006, 2007). The characteristics of the family's social context also influence its adaptation. What are the attitudes toward the family's ethnic group within its neighborhood or city? Can the family's children attend good schools? Are there community groups that welcome people from the family's ethnic group? Do members of the family's ethnic group form community groups of their own? To read about the work of one individual who studies immigrant adolescents, see the *Careers in Child Development* profile.

Ethnicity and Socioeconomic Status

As we indicated in Chapter 16, much of the research on ethnic minority children has failed to tease apart the influences of ethnicity and socioeconomic status (SES). Ethnicity and SES can interact in ways that exaggerate the negative influence of ethnicity because ethnic minority individuals are overrepresented in the lower socioeconomic levels of American society (Greder & Allen, 2007; Wilson, 2007). Ethnicity has often defined who will enjoy the privileges of citizenship and to what degree and in what ways. In many instances, an individual's ethnic background has determined whether the individual will be alienated or disadvantaged.

Too often researchers have given ethnic explanations of child development that were largely based on socioeconomic status rather than on ethnicity. For example, decades of research on group differences in self-esteem failed to consider the socioeconomic status of African American and White American children (Hare & Castenell, 1985). When the self-esteem of African American children from low-income backgrounds is compared with that of White American children from middle-class backgrounds, the differences

Careers in Child Development

Carola Suárez-Orozco, Immigration Studies Researcher and Professor

Carola Suárez-Orozco currently is Chair and Professor of Applied Psychology and Co-Director Immigration Studies at New York University. She formerly was Co-Director of the Harvard University Immigration Projects. Carola obtained her undergraduate degree (in development studies) and doctoral degree (in clinical psychology) at the University of California at Berkeley.

She has worked both in clinical and public school settings in California and Massachusetts. While at Harvard, Suárez-Orozco conducted a five-year longitudinal study of immigrant adolescents' (coming from Central America, China, and the Dominican Republic) adaptation to schools and society. She especially advocates more research at the intersection of cultural and psychological factors in the adaptation of immigrant and ethnic minority youth (Suárez-Orozco, 2007; Suárez-Orozco & Qin, 2006).

Carola Suárez-Orozco, with her husband, Marcelo, who also studies the adaptation of immigrants.

are often large but not informative because of the confounding of ethnicity and SES (Scott-Jones, 1995).

Even ethnic minority children from middle-SES backgrounds do not entirely escape the problems of minority status (Banks, 2008; McAdoo, 2007). Middle-SES ethnic minority children still encounter much of the prejudice, discrimination, and bias associated with being a member of an ethnic minority group.

Although not all ethnic minority families are poor, poverty contributes to the stressful life experiences of many ethnic minority children (Clark & King, 2008). Vonnie McLoyd and her colleagues (McLoyd, 1998; McLoyd, Aikens, & Burton, 2006) conclude that ethnic minority children experience a disproportionate share of the adverse effects of poverty and unemployment in America today. Thus, many ethnic minority children experience a double disadvantage: (1) prejudice, discrimination, and bias because of their ethnic minority status; and (2) the stressful effects of poverty.

Differences and Diversity

Historical, economic, and social experiences produce differences between various ethnic minority groups, and between ethnic minority groups and the majority White group (Hattery & Smith, 2007). Individuals living in a particular ethnic or cultural group adapt to the values, attitudes, and stresses of that culture. Recognizing and respecting these differences is an important aspect of getting along with others in a diverse, multicultural world. Children, like all of us, need to take the perspective of individuals from ethnic and cultural groups that are different from their own and think, "If I were in their shoes, what kind of experiences might I have had?" "How would I feel if I were a member of their ethnic or cultural group?" "How would I think and behave if I had grown up in their world?" Such perspective taking often increases empathy and understanding of individuals from ethnic and cultural groups different from one's own.

For too long, differences between any ethnic minority group and Whites were conceptualized as deficits or inferior characteristics on the part of the ethnic

Consider the flowers of a garden: Though differing in kind, color, form, and shape, yet, in as much as they are refreshed by the waters of one spring, revived by the breath of one wind, invigorated by the rays of one sun, this diversity increases their charm and adds to their beauty. . . . How unpleasing to the eye if all the flowers and plants, the leaves and blossoms, the fruits, the branches, and the trees of that garden were all of the same shape and color! Diversity of hues, form, and shape enriches and adorns the garden and heightens its effect.

—ABDU'L BAHA
Persian Baha'i Religious Leader, 19th/20th Century

Jason Leonard, age 15: "I want America to know that most of us black teens are not troubled people from broken homes and headed to jail. . . . In my relationships with my parents, we show respect for each other and we have values in our house. We have traditions we celebrate together, including Christmas and Kwanzaa."

minority group. Indeed, research on ethnic minority groups often focused only on a group's negative, stressful aspects. For example, research on African American adolescent girls invariably examined such topics as poverty, unwed mothers, and dropping out of school; research on the psychological strengths of African American adolescent girls was sorely needed. The self-esteem, achievement, motivation, and self-control of children from different ethnic minority groups deserve considerable study.

The current, long-overdue emphasis of research on ethnic groups underscores the strengths of various minority groups (Hayashino & Chopra, 2009). For example, the extended-family support system that characterizes many ethnic minority groups is now recognized as an important factor in coping. And researchers are finding that African American males are better than Anglo-American males at detecting and using nonverbal cues such as body language in communication, at communicating with people from different cultures, and at solving unexpected problems (Evans & Whitfield, 1988).

As we noted in Chapter 1, there is considerable diversity within each ethnic group (Banks, 2008; Harris & Graham, 2007). Ethnic minority groups have different social, historical, and economic backgrounds (Tewari & Alvarez, 2009). For example, Mexican, Cuban, and Puerto Rican immigrants are Latinos, but they had different reasons for migrating, came from varying socioeconomic backgrounds in their native countries, and experience different rates and types of employment in the United States (Coll & others, 1995). The U.S. federal government now recognizes the existence of 511 different Native American tribes, each having a unique ancestral background with differing values and characteristics. Asian Americans include the Chinese, Japanese, Filipinos, Koreans, and Southeast Asians, each group having a distinct ancestry and language. The diversity of Asian Americans is reflected in their educational attainment: Some achieve a high level of education; many others have little education (Lee & Wong, 2009). For example, 90 percent of Korean American males graduate from high school, but only 71 percent of Vietnamese American males do.

Diversity also exists within each of these groups (Suyemoto, 2009). No group is homogeneous. Sometimes, well-meaning individuals fail to recognize the diversity within an ethnic group (Sue, 1990). For example, a sixth-grade teacher had two Mexican American adolescents in her class. She asked them to be prepared to demonstrate to the class on the following Monday how they danced at home. The first boy got up in front of the class and began dancing in a typical American fashion. The teacher said, "No, I want you to dance like you and your family do at home, like you do when you have Mexican American celebrations." The boy informed the teacher that his family did not dance that way. The second boy demonstrated a Mexican folk dance to the class. Failing to recognize diversity within ethnic groups reinforces stereotypes and encourages prejudice.

Prejudice and Discrimination

Prejudice is an unjustified negative attitude toward an individual because of the individual's membership in a group. The group toward which the prejudice is directed can be made up of people of a particular ethnic group, sex, age, religion, or other detectable difference (Brewer, 2007). Our concern here is prejudice against ethnic minority groups.

Research studies provide insight into the discrimination experienced by ethnic minority adolescents (Chavous & others, 2007; Qin, Way, & Pandy, 2008; Smalls & others, 2007; Way & others, 2008). In one study, African American and Latino adolescents experienced discrimination at school and in shopping malls (Fajardo & others, 2003). In another study, discrimination of seventh- to tenth-grade African American students was related—to their lower level of psychological functioning, including perceived stress, symptoms of depression, and lower perceived well-being;

prejudice An unjustified negative attitude toward an individual because of her or his membership in a group.

more positive attitudes toward African Americans were associated with more positive psychological functioning in adolescents (Sellers & others, 2006). Figure 17.6 shows the percentage of African American adolescents who reported experiencing different types of racial hassles in the past year. Also, in a study of Latino youth, discrimination was negatively linked—and social and parental support were positively related—to their academic success (DeGarmo & Martinez, 2006). A recent study of sixth-grade students in the United States revealed that Chinese American children experienced discrimination from their peers that was comparable to discrimination faced by African American children (Rivas, Hughes, & Way, 2007).

Progress has been made in ethnic minority relations, but discrimination and prejudice still exist, and equality has not been achieved. Much remains to be accomplished (Alvarez, 2009; Banks, 2008; Lee & Wong, 2009).

The United States and Canada: Nations with Many Cultures

The United States has been and continues to be a great receiver of ethnic groups. It has embraced new ingredients from many cultures (Clark & King, 2008). The cultures often collide and cross-pollinate, mixing their ideologies and identities. Some of the culture of origin is retained, some of it is lost, some of it is mixed with the American culture.

Other nations have also experienced the immigration of varied ethnic groups. Possibly we can learn more about the potential benefits, problems, and varied responses by examining their experiences. Canada is a prominent example. Canada comprises a mixture of cultures that are loosely organized along the lines of economic power. The Canadian cultures include these (Siegel & Wiener, 1993):

- Native peoples, or First Nations, who were Canada's original inhabitants
- Descendants of French settlers who came to Canada during the seventeenth and eighteenth centuries
- Descendants of British settlers who came to Canada during and after the seventeenth century, or from the United States after the American Revolution in the latter part of the eighteenth century
- Descendants of immigrants from Asia, mainly China, who settled on the west coast of Canada in the latter part of the nineteenth and early twentieth centuries
- Descendants of nineteenth-century immigrants from various European countries, who came to central Canada and the prairie provinces
- Twentieth-century and current immigrants from countries in economic and political turmoil (in Latin America, the Caribbean, Asia, Africa, the Indian subcontinent, the former Soviet Union, and the Middle East), who have settled in many parts of Canada

Canada has two official languages—English and French. Primarily French-speaking individuals reside mainly in the province of Quebec; primarily English-speaking individuals reside mainly in other Canadian provinces. In addition to its English- and French-speaking populations, Canada has a large multicultural community. In three large Canadian cities—Toronto, Montreal, and Vancouver—more than 50 percent of the children and adolescents come from homes in which neither English nor French is the native language (Siegel & Wiener, 1993).

Type of racial hassle	Percent of adolescents who reported the racial hassle in the past year
Being accused of something or treated suspiciously	71.0
Being treated as if you were "stupid," being "talked down to"	70.7
Others reacting to you as if they were afraid of intimidated	70.1
Being observed or followed while in public places	69.1
Being treated rudely or disrespectfully	56.4
Being ignored, overlooked, not given service	56.4
Others expecting your work to be inferior	54.1
Being insulted, called a name or harassed	52.2

FIGURE 17.6 **African American Adolescents' Reports of Racial Hassles in the Past Year**

Review and Reflect: Learning Goal 3

3 Explain How Ethnicity Is Linked to Children's Development

REVIEW

- How does immigration influence children's development?
- How are ethnicity and socioeconomic status related?
- What is important to know about differences and diversity?
- How are prejudice and discrimination involved in children's development?
- How are the United States and Canada nations of blended cultures?

REFLECT

- No matter how well intentioned children are, their life circumstances likely have given them some prejudices. If they don't have prejudices toward people with different cultural and ethnic backgrounds, other kinds of people may bring out prejudices in them. For example, prejudices can be developed about people who have certain religious or political conventions, people who are unattractive or too attractive, people with a disability, and people in a nearby town. As a parent or teacher, how would you attempt to reduce children's prejudices?

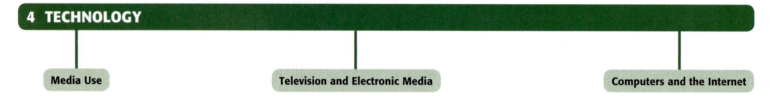

4 TECHNOLOGY

Media Use **Television and Electronic Media** **Computers and the Internet**

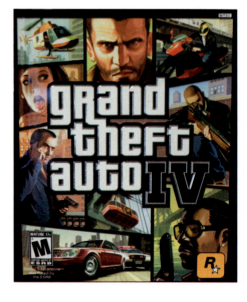

A major change in children's and adolescents' lives involves the dramatic increase in the use of media and technology by children and adolescents (Murray & Murray, 2008). "Unlike their parents, they have never known anything but a world dominated by technology. Even their social lives revolve around the Web, iPods, and cellphones" (Jayson, 2006, p. 1D).

There likely are both positive and negative aspects to how the technology revolution is affecting children and adolescents. Technology can provide an expansive, rich set of knowledge and used in a constructive way can improve children's and adolescents' education (Egbert, 2009; Forcier & Descy, 2009). However, the possible downside of technology was captured in a recent book, *The Dumbest Generation: How the Digital Age Stupefies Young Americans and Jeopardizes Our Future (Or, Don't Trust Anyone Under 30)*, written by Emory University English Professor Mark Bauerlein (2008). Among the book's themes are that many of today's youth are more interested in information retrieval than information formation, don't read books and aren't motivated to read them, can't spell without spellcheck, and have become encapsulated in a world of cell phones, iPods, text messaging, YouTube, MySpace, *Grand Theft Auto* (the video game's introduction in 2008 had first week sales of $500 million, dwarfing other movie and video sales), and other technology contexts. In terms of retaining general information and historical facts, Bauerlein may be correct. And in terms of some skills, such as adolescents' reading and writing, there is considerable concern as evidenced by U.S. employers spending 1.3 billion dollars a year to teach writing skills to employees (Begley & Interlandi, 2008). However, in terms of cognitive skills, such as thinking and reasoning, he likely is wrong given that IQ scores have been rising significantly since the 1930s (Flynn, 2007). Further, there is no research evidence that being immersed in a technological world of iPods and YouTube impairs thinking skills (Begley & Interlandi, 2008).

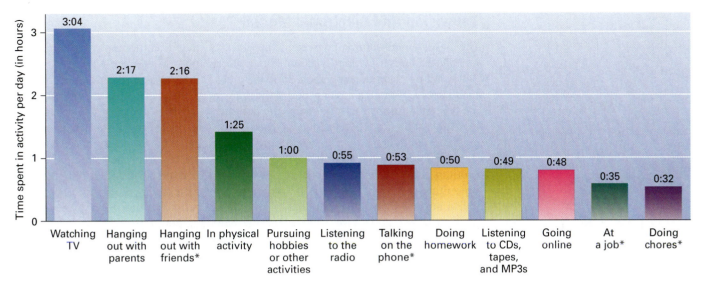

*Data collected among 7th- to 12th-graders only. All other results are among all 8- to 18-year-olds.

FIGURE 17.7 **Amount of Time U.S. 8- to 18-Year-Olds Spend per Day in Different Activities**

A major trend in the use of technology is the dramatic increase in media multitasking (Roberts & Foehr, 2008). It is not unusual for children and youth to simultaneously watch TV while text messaging their friends, for example. In some cases, media multitasking—such as text messaging, listening to an iPod, and updating a YouTube site—is engaged in at the same time as doing homework. It is hard to imagine how that can be a good thing for doing homework efficiently, although there is little research on such media multitasking.

Media Use

If the amount of time spent in an activity is any indication of its importance, then there is no doubt that the mass media play important roles in the lives of U.S. children and adolescents (Brooks-Gunn & Donahue, 2008; Murray & Murray, 2008). A national study that surveyed more than 2,000 children and adolescents from 8 through 18 years of age confirmed that they use media heavily (Rideout, Roberts, & Foehr, 2005). The average child and adolescent in the study spent almost 6 hours a day using media compared with approximately $2\frac{1}{4}$ hours with parents, about $1\frac{1}{4}$ hours in physical activity, and 50 minutes in homework (see Figure 17.7). As shown in the figure, the children and adolescents spent the most time watching TV (just over 3 hours a day). A recent estimate indicates that when media multitasking is taken into account, 8- through 18-year-olds use media an average of 8 hours per day rather than just 6 hours per day (Roberts & Foehr, 2008).

A recent study revealed that parents who reported their children who watched TV two or more hours a day at $2\frac{1}{2}$ years of age but had reduced TV watching at $5\frac{1}{2}$ years of age did not have significant social or behavioral problems (Mistry & others, 2007). However, children who infrequently watched TV as toddlers but watched two or more hours a day at $5\frac{1}{2}$ years of age were having problems in social skills. Children who were sustained, heavy TV watchers from $2\frac{1}{2}$ to $5\frac{1}{2}$ years of age had problems in social skills, attention, and aggression.

Media use by children and adolescents varies greatly not only with age but also with gender, ethnicity, socioeconomic status, and intelligence. For example, a national survey found that 8- to 18-year-old boys spent more time watching television than girls do but that girls spent considerably more time listening to music (Roberts & Foehr, 2003). Boys use computers and video games more than girls do (Roberts & others, 1999). African American and Latino children and adolescents spend significantly more time using media—especially television—than non-Latino White children do (Roberts, Henriksen, & Foehr, 2004; Roberts & others, 1999). Media exposure among African American 8- to 18-year-olds averages just over 9 hours daily, among Latino youth more than 8 hours, and among non-Latino White youth about 7 hours (Roberts, Henriksen, & Foehr, 2004).

"Mrs. Horton, could you stop by school today?"
Copyright © 1981 Martha F. Campbell. Used by permission of Martha F. Campbell.

Television and Electronic Media

Few developments during the second half of the twentieth century had a greater impact on children than television (Asamen, Ellis, & Berry, 2008; Strasburger, Wilson, & Jordan, 2008). Many children spend more time in front of the television set than they do with their parents. Although it is only one of the many mass media that affect children's behavior, television is the most influential. The persuasive capabilities of television are staggering. The 20,000 hours of television watched by the time the average American adolescent graduates from high school are greater than the number of hours spent in the classroom.

Television can have positive or negative effects on children's development (Preiss & others, 2007). Television can have a positive influence on children's development by presenting motivating educational programs, increasing their information about the world beyond their immediate environment, and providing models of prosocial behavior (Bryant, 2007; Fisch, 2007; Mares & Woodard, 2007). However, television can have a negative influence on children by making them passive learners, distracting them from doing homework, teaching them stereotypes, providing them with violent models of aggression, and presenting them with unrealistic views of the world (Dubow, Huesmann, & Greenwood, 2007; Murray, 2007).

Television, Violent Video Games, and Aggression What role does televised violence likely play in aggression among children and adolescents? Does television merely stimulate a child to go out and buy a Star Wars ray gun, or can it trigger an attack on a playmate? When children grow up, can television violence increase the likelihood that they will violently attack someone?

In one longitudinal investigation, the amount of violence viewed on television at age 8 was significantly related to the seriousness of criminal acts performed as an adult (Huesmann, & others, 2003). In another investigation, long-term exposure to television violence was significantly related to the likelihood of aggression in 1,565 boys 12 to 17 years old (Belson, 1978). Boys who watched the most aggression on television were the most likely to commit a violent crime, swear, be aggressive in sports, threaten violence toward another boy, write slogans on walls, or break windows. A recent study revealed that when 2- to 5-year-old boys regularly watched violent TV shows they were at risk for engaging in antisocial behavior at 7 to 10 years of age; no link was found for girls (Christakis & Zimmerman, 2007). These investigations are correlational, so we can't conclude from them that television violence causes children to be more aggressive, only that watching television violence is associated with aggressive behavior.

In one experiment, children were randomly assigned to one of two groups: One group watched television shows taken directly from violent Saturday-morning cartoons on 11 different days; the second group watched television cartoon shows with all of the violence removed (Steur, Applefield, & Smith, 1971). The children were then observed during play at their preschool. The preschool children who saw the TV cartoon shows with violence kicked, choked, and pushed their playmates more than the preschool children who watched nonviolent TV cartoon shows did. Because children were randomly assigned to the two conditions (TV cartoons with violence versus with no violence), we can conclude that exposure to TV violence caused the increased aggression in children in this investigation.

Some critics have argued that research results do not warrant the conclusion that TV violence causes aggression (Freedman, 1984). However, many experts insist that TV violence can cause aggressive or antisocial behavior in children (Comstock & Scharrer, 2006; Dubow, Heussman, & Greenwood, 2007). Of course, television violence is not the only cause of aggression. There is no one cause of any social behavior. Aggression, like all other social behaviors, has multiple determinants (Donnerstein, 2001). The link between TV violence and aggression in children is influenced by children's aggressive tendencies and by their attitudes toward violence and their exposure to it.

One study implemented a year-long intervention with the goal of reducing the harmful effects of violent TV on children's behavior (Rosenkoetter & others, 2004). The classroom-based intervention consisted of 31 brief lessons with first- through

How is television violence linked to children's aggression?

third-grade children that focused on the many ways that television distorts violence. The intervention reduced the frequency that children watched violent TV and decreased their identification with violent TV characters.

Violent video games, especially those that are highly realistic, also raise concerns about their effects on children and adolescents (Anderson, Gentile, & Buckley, 2007; Escobar & Anderson, 2008). One difference between television and violent video games is that the games can engage children and adolescents so intensely that they experience an altered state of consciousness in "which rational thought is suspended and highly arousing aggressive scripts are increasingly likely to be learned" (Roberts, Henriksen, & Foehr, 2004, p. 498). Another difference involves the direct rewards ("winning points") that game players receive for their behavior. Research indicates that children and adolescents who extensively play violent electronic games are more aggressive, less sensitive to real-life violence, and more likely to engage in delinquent acts than their counterparts who spend less time playing the games or do not play them at all (Anderson & Bushman, 2001; Anderson, Gentile, & Buckley, 2007; Carnagey, Anderson, & Bushman, 2007). Are there any positive outcomes when children play video games? Some evidence points to video games improving children's visuospatial skills (Schmidt & Vandewater, 2008).

Prosocial Behavior Television and electronic media also can teach children that it is better to behave in positive, prosocial ways than in negative, antisocial ways (Bryant, 2007). Aimee Leifer (1973) demonstrated that television is associated with prosocial behavior in young children. She selected a number of episodes from the television show *Sesame Street* that reflected positive social interchanges. She was especially interested in situations that taught children how to use their social skills. For example, in one interchange, two men were fighting over the amount of space available to them. They gradually began to cooperate and to share the space. Children who watched these episodes copied these behaviors, and in later social situations they applied the prosocial lessons they had learned. More recent research has documented that electronic media programs designed to promote prosocial behavior are effective in increasing children's altruism, cooperation, and tolerance of others (Wilson, 2008).

Electronic Media, Learning, and Achievement The effects of electronic media on children depends on how old children are and the type of media. A recent research review concluded the following about infants and young children (Kirkorian, Anderson, & Wartella, 2008):

- *Infancy*. Learning from electronic media is difficult for infants and toddlers, and they learn much more easily from direct experiences with people.
- *Early childhood*. At about 3 years of age, children can learn from electronic media with educational material if the media use effective strategies, such as repeating concepts a number of times, using images and sounds that get young children's attention, and use child rather than adult voices. However, the vast majority of media young children experience is entertainment rather than education oriented.

Several important cognitive shifts take place between early childhood and middle and late childhood, and these shifts influence the effects of electronic media. Children bring varied cognitive skills and abilities to their television viewing. Preschool children often focus on the most striking perceptual features of a TV program and are likely to have difficulty in distinguishing reality from fantasy in the portrayals. As children enter elementary school, they are better able to link scenes together and draw causal conclusions from narratives. Judgments about what is reality and what is fantasy also become more accurate as children grow up.

How does television influence children's attention, creativity, and mental ability? Media use has not been found to cause attention deficit hyperactivity disorder but a small link between heavy television and nonclinical attention levels in children (Schmidt & Vanderwater, 2008). In general, television has not been shown to influence children's creativity but is negatively related to their mental ability (Comstock &

How might playing violent video games be linked to adolescent aggression?

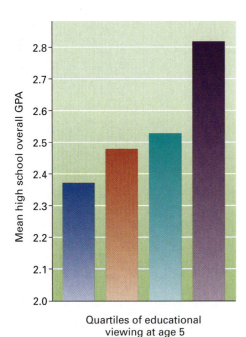

FIGURE 17.8 Educational TV Viewing in Early Childhood and High School Grade-Point Average for Boys. When boys watched more educational television (especially *Sesame Street*) as preschoolers, they had higher grade-point averages in high school. The graph displays the boys' early TV viewing patterns in quartiles and the means of their grade-point averages. The bar on the left is for the lowest 25 percent of boys who viewed educational TV programs, the next bar the next 25 percent, and so on, with the bar on the right for the 25 percent of the boys who watched the most educational TV shows as preschoolers.

Internet Worldwide computer-mediated communication system that provides an incredible array of information.

Scharrer, 2006). Exposure to aural and printed media does more than television to enhance children's verbal skills, especially their expressive language (Williams, 1986).

The more children watch TV, the lower their school achievement is (Comstock & Scharrer, 2006). Why might TV watching be negatively linked to children's achievement? Three possibilities involve interference, displacement, and self-defeating tastes/preferences (Comstock & Scharrer, 2006). In terms of interference, having a television on while doing homework can distract children while they are doing cognitive tasks, such as homework. In terms of displacement, television can take away time and attention from engaging in achievement-related tasks, such as homework, reading, writing, and mathematics. Researchers have found that children's reading achievement is negatively linked with the amount of time they watch TV (Comstock & Scharrer, 2006). In terms of self-defeating tastes and preferences, television attracts children to entertainment, sports, commercials, and other activities that capture their interest more than school achievement. Children who are heavy TV watchers tend to view books as dull and boring (Comstock & Scharrer, 2006).

However, some types of television content—such as educational programming for young children—may enhance achievement. In one longitudinal study, viewing educational programs, such as *Sesame Street* and *Mr. Roger's Neighborhood,* as preschoolers was related to a number of positive outcomes through high school, including higher grades, reading more books, and enhanced creativity (Anderson & others, 2001) (see Figure 17.8). Newer technologies, especially interactive television, hold promise for motivating children to learn and become more exploratory in solving problems.

Computers and the Internet

Culture involves change, and nowhere is that change greater than in the technological revolution today's children and adolescents are experiencing with increased use of computers and the Internet. Today's children and adolescents are using computers to communicate the way their parents used pens, postage stamps, and telephones.

The Internet The **Internet** is the core of computer-mediated communication. The Internet system is worldwide and connects thousands of computer networks, providing an incredible array of information adolescents can access.

Internet Use by Children and Adolescents Youth throughout the world are increasingly using the Internet, despite substantial variation in use in different countries around the world and in socioeconomic groups (Brookshear, 2009; Reed, 2009; Subrahmanyam & Greenfield, 2008). In 2005, 75 percent of U.S. 8- to 18-year-olds lived in a home with an Internet connection and almost one-third had a computer in their bedroom and 20 percent had an Internet connection there (Rideout, Roberts, & Foehr, 2005). Among 15- to 17-year-olds, one-third use the Internet for six hours a week or more, 24 percent use it for three to five hours a week, and 20 percent use it for one hour a week or less (Woodard, 2000). In a typical day, about half of 8- to 18-year-olds go online from home, and their most frequent online recreational activities are playing games and communicating via instant messaging (Rideout, Roberts, & Foehr, 2005).

Special concerns have emerged about children's and adolescents' access to information on the Internet, which has been largely unregulated. Youth can access adult sexual material, instructions for making bombs, and other information that is inappropriate for them.

In one study, about half of parents said that being online is more positive than watching TV for adolescents (Tarpley, 2001). However, an analysis of content suggests they might be wise to be more concerned about children's and adolescents' use of the Internet. One study found that 12 percent of adolescents have visited a Web site where they can obtain information about how to buy a gun (Donnerstein, 2002). A recent national study revealed that 42 percent of U.S. 10- to 17-year-olds had been exposed to Internet pornography in the past year with 66 percent of the exposure being unwanted (Wolak, Mitchell, & Finkelhor, 2007).

The Online Social Environment of Children and Adolescents   The social environment of children and adolescents on the Internet includes chat rooms, e-mail, instant messaging, blogs, and the highly popular Web sites of MySpace and Facebook. Chat room conversations are mainly public and often involve multiple participants and simultaneous conversations. Instant messaging is used to communicate with friends from school primarily about gossip and friends.

One recent study examined the content of 583 participants in online teen chat rooms (Subrahmanyam, Smahel, & Greenfield, 2006). More than 50 percent of the participants provided identity information, usually their gender. Younger participants (self-described as 10 to 13 years of age) were the most self-disclosing about their identity, older ones the least (self-described as 18 to 24 years of age). Sexual themes comprised 5 percent of the utterances (one sexual comment per minute) and bad/obscene language occurred in 3 percent of the utterances. Females discussed sex in more implicit ways, males in a more explicit manner. Older participants discussed sex more explicitly than younger participants.

MySpace and Facebook provide opportunities on the Internet for adolescents to communicate with others who share their interests. MySpace has become the most popular online hangout for adolescents, and Facebook fulfills this role for college students.

Research on the social aspects of the Internet is just beginning, but early indications suggest that youth use the Internet to enhance their communication and relationships with people they know (Subrahmanyam & Greenfield, 2008). However, some youth do communicate with strangers in chat rooms and on bulletin boards. Also, there has been a substantial increase in youth harassment on the Internet and cyberbullying.

Clearly, the Internet is a technology that needs parents to monitor and regulate adolescents' use of it (Willoughby, 2008; Wolak, Mitchell, & Finkelhor, 2008). Consider Bonita Williams, who began to worry about how obsessed her 15-year-old daughter, Jade, had become with MySpace (Kornblum, 2006). She became even more concerned when she discovered that Jade was posting suggestive photos of herself and gave her cell phone number out to people in different parts of the United States. She grounded her daughter, blocked MySpace at home, and moved Jade's computer out of her bedroom and into the family room.

To read about sociocultural diversity and technology, see the *Diversity in Child Development* interlude.

What characterizes the online social environment of adolescents?

 ## Diversity in Child Development

COMPUTERS, THE INTERNET, AND SOCIOCULTURAL DIVERSITY

Traditionally, students have learned within the walls of their classroom and interacted with their teacher and the students in their class. With advances in telecommunications, students can learn with and from teachers and students from around the world.

Students in a Research Center for Educational Technology's AT&T classroom at Kent State University studying plant biology with students at the Instituto Thomas Jefferson in Mexico City.

What are some important concerns about sociocultural diversity and technology?

At the Research Center for Educational Psychology (RCET) at Kent State University, elementary school students and their teachers collaborate with their peers at the Instituto Thomas Jefferson in Mexico City on a variety of projects, including studies of plant biology, climate, and biography using both videoconferencing and e-mail (Swan & others, 2006). Biogeography researchers have found that projects that share common understandings but highlight local differences are especially productive (Swan & others, 2006).

An increasing number of schools are using Internet-based videoconferencing for foreign language instruction. Instead of simulating a French café in a typical French language class, American students might talk with French students in a real café in France.

Such global technology projects can go a long way toward reducing American students' ethnocentric beliefs. The active building of connections around the world through telecommunications gives students the opportunity to experience others' perspectives, better understand other cultures, and reduce prejudice.

Technology brings with it certain social issues related to different groups within the United States (Comstock & Scharrer, 2006). For example, will schools' increased use of technology, especially computers, widen the learning gap between rich and poor students or between male and female students? In 2003, 96 percent of schools with the lowest poverty concentration had a school Web site, whereas only 72 percent of schools with the highest poverty concentration had a school Web site (National Center for Education Statistics, 2005). The problem of computer access and use also is compounded by the far greater presence of computers in the homes of middle- and upper-income families. There are gaps in computer availability across ethnic groups as well (Gorski, 2005). A recent study found that 80 percent of non-Latino White children and adolescents have Internet access at home, but only 67 percent of Latino children and 61 percent of African American children and adolescents do (Rideout, Roberts, & Foehr, 2005). Another recent study revealed that access to and use of a home computer, presence of a computer area in classrooms, lower child/computer ratio in school, and frequent use of software for literacy and math were linked to higher academic achievement in African American kindergarten and first-grade students (Judge, 2005). And yet another recent study revealed that 10- to 18-year-olds from low-income families who used the Internet at home more had higher reading achievement scores and higher grades in school than their counterparts who used it less (Jackson & others, 2006).

Review and Reflect: Learning Goal 4

4 **Summarize the Influence of Technology on Children's Development**

REVIEW

- What role do mass media play in the lives of children and adolescents?
- How do television and electronic media influence children's development?
- What roles do computers and the Internet play in children's development?

REFLECT

- How much television did you watch as a child? What effect do you believe it has had on your development?

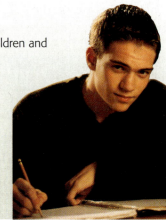

Reach Your Learning Goals

Culture and Diversity

1 CULTURE AND CHILDREN'S DEVELOPMENT: DISCUSS THE ROLE OF CULTURE IN CHILDREN'S DEVELOPMENT

The Relevance of Culture to the Study of Children

- Culture refers to the behavior patterns, beliefs, and all other products of a particular group of people that are passed on from generation to generation. If the study of children is to be a relevant discipline in the twenty-first century, there will have to be increased attention to culture. In future years, children will be citizens of the world, and by understanding the values of other cultures and others' cultural behaviors, the more effectively we may be able to interact.

Cross-Cultural Comparisons

- Cross-cultural comparisons compare one culture with one or more other cultures, which provides information about the degree to which characteristics are universal or culture-specific. The social contexts in which children develop—gender, family, and school—display important differences from one culture to another. One analysis of cross-cultural comparisons suggests that children raised in individualistic cultures are taught different values and conceptions of the self than those raised in collectivistic cultures. However, critics argue that individualistic and collectivistic analyses of cultures are too broad and simplistic, and further that in many families, parents expect their children to think and act in ways that reflect both individualistic and collectivistic values.

2 SOCIOECONOMIC STATUS AND POVERTY: DESCRIBE HOW SOCIOECONOMIC STATUS AND POVERTY IMPACT CHILDREN'S LIVES

What Is Socioeconomic Status?

- Socioeconomic status (SES) is the grouping of people with similar occupational, educational, and economic characteristics. SES implies inequalities.

Socioeconomic Variations in Families, Neighborhoods, and Schools

- The families, neighborhoods, and schools of children have SES characteristics that are related to the child's development. Parents from low-SES families are more likely to value conformity and to use physical punishment more than their middle-SES counterparts. High-SES children live in more attractive homes and in safer neighborhoods than low-SES children. Low-SES children are more apt to experience problems such as depression, low-self esteem, and delinquency. When low-SES children do well in school, it often is because parents have made sacrifices to improve conditions and provide support that contribute to school success.

Poverty

- Poverty is defined by economic hardship. The poor often face not only economic hardship but also social and psychological difficulties. Poor children are exposed to more family violence, have less access to books and computers, attend inferior child care and schools, and receive less social support. When poverty is persistent and long-lasting, it especially has adverse effects on children's development.

3 ETHNICITY: EXPLAIN HOW ETHNICITY IS LINKED TO CHILDREN'S DEVELOPMENT

Immigration

- Ethnicity is based on cultural heritage, nationality characteristics, race, religion, and language. The immigration of families to the United States brings about a number of challenges for helping children adapt to their new culture. Immigrant children often experience language barriers, changes in SES, and separation from support networks in addition to struggling to preserve both their ethnic identity and adapt to the majority culture. Parents and children may be at different stages of acculturation.

527

Ethnicity and Socioeconomic Status

- Too often researchers have not teased apart the influence of ethnic and socioeconomic status when studying ethnic minority children. Many ethnic minority children experience prejudice and discrimination, along with the difficulties caused by poverty. Although not all ethnic minority families are poor, poverty contributes to the stress of many ethnic minority families and to differences between ethnic minority groups and the White majority.

Differences and Diversity

- Recognizing and respecting differences in ethnicity is an important aspect of getting along with others in a diverse, multicultural world. Too often differences have been described as deficits on the part of ethnic minority individuals. Ethnic minority groups are not homogeneous. Failure to recognize this diversity results in stereotyping.

Prejudice and Discrimination

- Prejudice is an unjustified negative attitude toward an individual because of the individual's membership in a group. Despite progress in the treatment of minority groups, children who are members of these groups still often face prejudice and discrimination.

The United States and Canada: Nations with Many Cultures

- The United States and Canada have been, and continue to be, great receivers of ethnic immigrants. This has resulted in the United States and Canada being nations with many cultures.

4 TECHNOLOGY: SUMMARIZE THE INFLUENCE OF TECHNOLOGY ON CHILDREN'S DEVELOPMENT

Media Use

- In terms of exposure, the average U.S. 8- to 18-year-old spends almost 6 hours a day using electronic media, with the most time spent watching television (if media multitasking is taken into account, they use electronic media 8 hours per day). However, children and adolescents are rapidly increasing the time they spend online. Boys reduce their TV viewing and increase time playing video games and using computers. Girls increase their music listening and computer use. Adolescents also use the print media more than children do. There are large individual variations in adolescent media use.

Television and Electronic Media

- One negative aspect of television is that it involves passive learning. Special concerns are the ways ethnic minorities, sex, and aggression are portrayed on television. TV violence is not the only cause of adolescents' aggression, but most experts agree that it can induce aggression and antisocial behavior. Prosocial behavior on TV is associated with increased positive behavior by children. There also is concern about adolescents playing violent video games. Children's cognitive skills and abilities influence their TV viewing experiences. TV viewing is negatively related to children's mental ability and achievement. However, educational TV programming can enhance achievement.

Computers and the Internet

- Today's children and adolescents are experiencing a technology revolution through computers and the Internet. Children's and adolescents' online time can have positive or negative outcomes. Large numbers of adolescents and college students engage in social networking on MySpace and Facebook. A special concern is the difficulty parents have monitoring the information their children are accessing. Another concern is whether increased use of technology will widen the learning gap between rich and poor, and between different ethnic groups.

KEY TERMS

culture 506	collectivism 508	ethnicity 515
cross-cultural studies 507	socioeconomic status	prejudice 518
individualism 508	(SES) 510	Internet 524

KEY PEOPLE

Richard Brislin 507	Catherine Tamis-LeMonda 509	Aletha Huston 513
Donald Campbell 507	Vonnie McLoyd 513	Aimee Leifer 523

E-LEARNING TOOLS

To help you master the material in this chapter, you'll find a number of valuable study tools at the Online Learning Center for *Child Development*, twelfth edition (**www.mhhe.com/santrockcd12**).

Taking It to the Net

Research the answers to these questions:

1. Jeremy is attending college in California, where he is majoring in political science. For his senior thesis, he is required to choose an area of social policy and develop a legislative agenda. Based upon recent news reports about the increasing number of low- and middle-income wage earners who don't make enough money for decent housing, food, and health care for their children, he decides to make the needs of these children his priority. What types of programs should he propose for the children of these families?

2. Mrs. Bernstein thinks that she ought to involve her fourth-grade students in a dialogue about racism and prejudice, since there are several ethnic groups represented in her class. But a colleague warned her that talking to kids about racism could backfire and actually cause prejudice. What are the possible reactions of students to a discussion of racism?

3. Denise has heard about the "digital divide," the concept that ethnic minorities and economically deprived populations are not participating in the Internet explosion. Since Denise is about to begin teaching third grade in an inner-city school, she wonders if the school will be as well equipped technologically as a school in a better neighborhood. What are the facts?

Health and Well-Being, Parenting, and Education Exercises

Build your decision-making skills by trying your hand at the health and well-being, parenting, and education exercises.

Video Clips

The Online Learning Center includes the following videos for this chapter:

- *Ethnic and Racial Identity in Adolescence*

Two African-American girls discuss candidly their feelings about being African American.

- *Talking About Ethnic Identity in Adolescence*

Three adolescent girls talk about their own ethnicities, and that of their friends.

- *Impact of Media on Children*

Dr. Sandra Calvert defines the three ways in which the media impact children.

GLOSSARY

A

accommodation Piagetian concept of adjusting schemes to fit new information and experiences.

acculturation Cultural changes that occur when one culture comes in contact with another culture.

active (niche-picking) genotype-environment correlations Correlations that exist when children seek out environments they find compatible and stimulating.

adolescence The developmental period of transition from childhood to early adulthood, entered at approximately 10 to 12 years of age and ending at 18 to 19 years of age.

adolescent egocentrism The heightened self-consciousness of adolescents, which is reflected in adolescents' beliefs that others are as interested in them as they are in themselves, and in adolescents' sense of personal uniqueness and invincibility.

adoption study A study in which investigators seek to discover whether the behavior and psychological characteristics of adopted children are more like their adoptive parents, who provided a home environment, or more like their biological parents, who contributed their heredity. Another form of the adoption study is to compare adoptive and biological siblings.

affordances Opportunities for interaction offered by objects that are necessary to perform activities.

altruism An unselfish interest in helping another person.

amnion The life-support system that is like a bag or envelope and contains a clear fluid in which the developing embryo floats.

amygdala The seat of emotions in the brain.

androgens Hormones, the most important of which is testosterone, that promote the development of male genitals and secondary sex characteristics.

androgens The main class of male sex hormones.

androgyny The presence of masculine and feminine characteristics in the same person.

anger cry A cry similar to the basic cry but with more excess air forced through the vocal cords.

animism A facet of preoperational thought; the belief that inanimate objects have lifelike qualities and are capable of action.

A-not-B error Also called $A\overline{B}$ error, this occurs when infants make the mistake of selecting the familiar hiding place (A) rather than the new hiding place (B) as they progress into substage 4 in Piaget's sensorimotor stage.

Apgar Scale A widely used method to assess the health of newborns at one and five minutes after birth. The Apgar Scale evaluates infants' heart rate, respiratory effort, muscle tone, body color, and reflex irritability.

aphasia A disorder resulting from brain damage to Broca's area or Wernicke's area that involves a loss or impairment of the ability to use or comprehend words.

Asperger syndrome A relativity mild autism spectrum disorder in which the child has relatively verbal language, milder nonverbal language problems, and a restricted range of interests and relationships.

assimilation Piagetian concept of the incorporation of new information into existing knowledge (schemes).

associative play Play that involves social interaction with little or no organization.

attachment A close emotional bond between two people.

attention Concentrating and focusing mental resources.

attention deficit hyperactivity disorder (ADHD) A disability in which children consistently show one or more of the following characteristics: (1) inattention, (2) hyperactivity, and (3) hyperactivity/impulsivity.

authoritarian parenting This is a restrictive, punitive style in which the parent exhorts the child to follow the parent's directions and to respect their work and effort. Firm limits and controls are placed on the child, and little verbal exchange is allowed. This style is associated with children's social incompetence, including a lack of initiative and weak communication skills.

authoritative parenting This style encourages children to be independent but still places limits and controls on their actions. Extensive verbal give-and-take is allowed, and parents are warm and nurturant toward the child. This style is associated with children's social competence, including being achievement oriented and self-reliant.

autism spectrum disorders (ASDs) Also called pervasive development disorders, they range from the severe disorder labeled autistic disorder to the milder disorder called Asperger syndrome. Children with these disorders are characterized by problems in social interaction, verbal and nonverbal communication, and repetitive behaviors.

autistic disorder A severe developmental autism spectrum disorder that has its onset in the first three years of life and includes deficiencies in social relationships; abnormalities in communication; and restricted, repetitive, and stereotyped patterns of behavior.

automaticity The ability to process information with little or no effort.

autonomous morality The second stage of moral development in Piaget's theory, displayed by older children (about 10 years of age and older). The child becomes aware that rules and laws are created by people and that, in judging an action, one should consider the actor's intentions as well as the consequences.

average children Children who receive an average number of both positive and negative nominations from their peers.

B

basic cry A rhythmic pattern usually consisting of a cry, a briefer silence, a shorter inspiratory whistle that is higher pitched than the main cry, and then a brief rest before the next cry.

Bayley Scales of Infant Development Initially created by Nancy Bayley, these scales are widely used in assessing infant development. The current version has five scales: cognitive, language, motor, socio-emotional, and adaptive.

behavior genetics The field that seeks to discover the influence of heredity and environment on individual differences in human traits and development.

biological processes Changes in an individual's body.

blastocyst The inner layer of cells that develops during the germinal period. These cells later develop into the embryo.

bonding The formation of a close connection, especially a physical bond, between parents and their newborn in the period shortly after birth.

brainstorming A technique in which children are encouraged to come up with creative ideas in a group, play off one another's ideas, and say practically whatever comes to mind.

Brazelton Neonatal Behavioral Assessment Scale (NBAS) A test given within 24 to 36 hours after birth to assess newborns' neurological development, reflexes, and reactions to people.

breech position The baby's position in the uterus that causes the buttocks to be the first part to emerge from the vagina.

Broca's area An area of the brain's left frontal lobe that is involved in speech production and grammatical processing.

Bronfenbrenner's ecological theory An environmental systems theory that focuses on five environmental systems: microsystem, mesosystem, exosystem, macrosystem, and chronosystem.

C

care perspective The moral perspective of Carol Gilligan; views people in terms of their connectedness with others and emphasizes interpersonal communication, relationships with others, and concern for others.

case study An in-depth look at a single individual.

centration The focusing of attention on one characteristic to the exclusion of all others.

cephalocaudal pattern The sequence in which the fastest growth occurs at the top—the head—with physical growth in size, weight, and feature differentiation gradually working from top to bottom.

cesarean delivery The baby is removed from the mother's uterus through an incision made in her abdomen.

character education A direct moral education approach that involves teaching students a basic "moral literacy" to prevent them from engaging in immoral behavior or doing harm to themselves or others.

child-centered kindergarten Education that involves the whole child by considering both the child's physical, cognitive, and socioemotional development and the child's needs, interests, and learning styles.

child-directed speech Language spoken in a higher pitch than normal with simple words and sentences.

chromosomes Threadlike structures that come in 23 pairs, one member of each pair coming from each parent. Chromosomes contain the genetic substance DNA.

cliques Small groups that range from 2 to about 12 individuals and average about 5 to 6 individuals. Cliques can form because of friendship or because individuals engage in similar activities, and members usually are of the same sex and about the same age.

cognitive developmental theory of gender In this view, children's gender typing occurs after they have developed a concept of gender. Once they begin to consistently conceive of themselves as male or female, children prefer activities, objects, and attitudes consistent with this gender label.

cognitive moral education Education based on the belief that students should learn to value things like democracy and justice as their moral reasoning develops; Kohlberg's theory has been the basis for many of the cognitive moral education approaches.

cognitive processes Changes in an individual's thought, intelligence, and language.

collectivism Emphasizing values that serve the group by subordinating personal goals to preserve group integrity, interdependence of members, and harmonious relationships.

commitment Personal investment in identity.

concrete operational stage Piaget's third stage, which lasts from approximately 7 to 11 years of age; children can perform concrete operations, and logical reasoning replaces intuitive reasoning as long as the reasoning can be applied to specific or concrete examples.

conduct disorder Age-inappropriate actions and attitudes that violate family expectations, society's norms, and the personal or property rights of others.

connectedness Consists of two dimensions: mutuality, sensitivity to and respect for others' views; and permeability, openness to others' views.

conservation The idea that altering an object's or substance's appearance does not change its basic properties.

constructive play Play that combines sensorimotor/practice play with symbolic representation of ideas. Constructive play occurs when children engage in self-regulated creation or construction of a product or a solution.

constructivist approach A learner-centered approach that emphasizes the importance of individuals actively constructing their knowledge and understanding with guidance from the teacher.

context The settings, influenced by historical, economic, social, and cultural factors, in which development occurs.

continuity-discontinuity issue The issue regarding whether development involves gradual, cumulative change (continuity) or distinct stages (discontinuity).

controversial children Children who are frequently nominated both as someone's best friend and as being disliked.

conventional reasoning The second, or intermediate, level in Kohlberg's theory of moral development. At this level, individuals abide by certain standards, but they are the standards of others such as parents or the laws of society.

convergent thinking Thinking that produces one correct answer; characteristic of the kind of thinking required on conventional intelligence tests.

cooperative play Play that involves social interaction in a group with a sense of group identity and organized activity.

coparenting The amount of support parents provide for each other in jointly raising children.

corpus callosum Where fibers connect the brain's left and right hemispheres.

correlation coefficient A number based on statistical analysis that is used to describe the degree of association between two variables.

correlational research The goal is to describe the strength of the relationship between two or more events or characteristics.

creativity The ability to think in novel and unusual ways and come up with unique solutions to problems.

crisis A period of identity development during which the adolescent is choosing among meaningful alternatives.

critical thinking Thinking reflectively and productively, and evaluating the evidence.

cross-cultural studies Comparisons of one culture with one or more other cultures. These provide information about the degree to which children's development is similar, or universal, across cultures, and to the degree to which it is culture-specific.

cross-sectional approach A research strategy in which individuals of different ages are compared at one time.

crowds The crowd is a larger group structure than a clique. Adolescents usually are members of a crowd based on reputation and may or may not spend much time together. Many crowds are defined by the activities adolescents engage in.

culture The behavior, patterns, beliefs, and all other products of a particular group of people that are passed on from generation to generation.

culture-fair tests Intelligence tests that aim to avoid cultural bias.

D

descriptive research Has the purpose of observing and recording behavior.

development The pattern of movement or change that begins at conception and continues through the life span.

developmental quotient (DQ) An overall developmental score that combines subscores on motor, language, adaptive, and personal-social domains in the Gesell assessment of infants.

developmentally appropriate practice Education that focuses on the typical developmental patterns of children (age-appropriateness) and the uniqueness of each child (individual-appropriateness). Such practice contrasts with developmentally inappropriate practice, which relies on abstract paper-and-pencil activities presented to large groups of young children.

dialect A variety of language that is distinguished by its vocabulary, grammar, or pronunciation.

difficult child A temperament style in which the child tends to react negatively and cry frequently, engages in irregular daily routines, and is slow to accept new experiences.

direct instruction approach A teacher-centered approach characterized by teacher direction and control, mastery of academic material, high expectations for students' progress, and maximum time spent on learning tasks.

dishabituation The recovery of a habituated response after a change in stimulation.

divergent thinking Thinking that produces many answers to the same question; characteristic of creativity.

divided attention Concentrating on more than one activity at the same time.

DNA A complex molecule with a double helix shape that contains genetic information.

doula A caregiver who provides continuous physical, emotional, and educational support for the mother before, during, and after childbirth.

Down syndrome A chromosomally transmitted form of mental retardation, caused by the presence of an extra copy of chromosome 21.

dynamic systems theory A theory, proposed by Esther Thelen, that seeks to explain how motor behaviors are assembled for perceiving and acting.

dyslexia A category of learning disabilities involving a severe impairment in the ability to read and spell.

E

early childhood The developmental period that extends from the end of infancy to about 5 to 6 years of age, sometimes called the preschool years.

early-later experience issue The issue of the degree to which early experiences (especially infancy) or later experiences are the key determinants of the child's development.

easy child A temperament style in which the child is generally in a positive mood, quickly establishes regular routines, and adapts easily to new experiences.

eclectic theoretical orientation An orientation that does not follow any one theoretical approach, but rather selects from each theory whatever is considered the best in it.

ecological view The view, proposed by the Gibsons, that people directly perceive information in the world around them. Perception brings people in contact with the environment in order to interact with it and adapt to it.

egocentrism An important feature of preoperational thought, the inability to distinguish between one's own and someone else's perspective.

embryonic period The period of prenatal development two to eight weeks after conception. During the embryonic period, the rate of cell differentiation intensifies, support systems for the cells form, and organs appear.

emotion Feeling, or affect, that occurs when a person is engaged in an interaction that is important to him or her, especially to his or her well-being.

emotional intelligence The ability to perceive and express emotion accurately and adaptively, to understand emotion and emotional knowledge, to use feelings to facilitate thought, and to manage emotions in oneself and others.

empathy Reacting to another's feelings with an emotional response that is similar to the other's feelings.

encoding The mechanism by which information gets into memory.

epigenetic view Emphasizes that development is the result of an ongoing, bidirectional interchange between heredity and environment.

equilibration A mechanism that Piaget proposed to explain how children shift from one stage of thought to the next. The shift occurs as children experience cognitive conflict, or disequilibrium, in trying to understand the world. Eventually, they resolve the conflict and reach a balance, or equilibrium, of thought.

Erikson's theory Includes eight stages of human development. Each stage consists of a unique developmental task that confronts individuals with a crisis that must be resolved.

estradiol An estrogen that is a key hormone in girls' pubertal development.

estrogens Hormones, the most important of which is estradiol, that influence the development of female physical sex characteristics and help regulate the menstrual cycle.

estrogens The main class of female sex hormones.

ethnic gloss Using an ethnic label such as African American or Latino in a superficial way that portrays an ethnic group as being more homogeneous than it really is.

ethnic identity An enduring aspect of the self that includes a sense of membership in an ethnic group, along with the attitudes and feelings related to that membership.

ethnicity A dimension of culture based on cultural heritage, nationality, race, religion, and language.

ethology Stresses that behavior is strongly influenced by biology, is tied to evolution, and is characterized by critical or sensitive periods.

evocative genotype-environment correlations Correlations that exist when the child's genotype elicits certain types of physical and social environments.

evolutionary psychology Emphasizes the importance of adaptation, reproduction, and "survival of the fittest" in shaping behavior.

executive attention Involves action planning, allocating attention to goals, error detection and compensation, monitoring progress on tasks, and dealing with novel or difficult circumstances.

expanding Restating, in a linguistically sophisticated form, what a child has said.

experiment A carefully regulated procedure in which one or more of the factors believed to influence the behavior being studied are manipulated while all other factors are held constant.

explicit memory Conscious memory of facts and experiences.

extrinsic motivation Response to external incentives such as rewards and punishments.

F

fast mapping A process that helps to explain how young children learn the connection between a word and its referent so quickly.

fertilization A stage in reproduction whereby an egg and a sperm fuse to create a single cell, called a zygote.

fetal alcohol spectrum disorders (FASD) A cluster of abnormalities that appears in the offspring of mothers who drink alcohol heavily during pregnancy.

fetal period The prenatal period of development that begins two months after conception and lasts for seven months, on the average.

fine motor skills Motor skills that involve more finely tuned movements, such as finger dexterity.

formal operational stage Piaget's fourth and final stage, which occurs between the ages of 11 and 15; individuals move beyond concrete experiences and think in more abstract and logical ways.

fragile X syndrome A chromosomal disorder involving an abnormality in the X chromosome, which becomes constricted and often breaks.

fuzzy trace theory States that memory is best understood by considering two types of memory representations: (1) verbatim memory trace; and (2) fuzzy trace, or gist. In this theory, older children's better memory is attributed to the fuzzy traces created by extracting the gist of information.

G

games Activities engaged in for pleasure that include rules and often competition with one or more individuals.

gender The characteristics of people as males and females.

gender role A set of expectations that prescribes how females and males should think, act, and feel.

gender schema theory According to this theory, gender typing emerges as children gradually develop schemas of what is gender-appropriate and gender-inappropriate in their culture.

gender stereotypes Broad categories that reflect impressions and widely held beliefs about what behavior is appropriate for females and males.

gender typing The process by which children acquire the thoughts, feelings, and behaviors that are considered appropriate for their gender in their culture.

genes Units of hereditary information composed of short segments of DNA. Genes direct cells to reproduce themselves and manufacture the proteins that maintain life.

genotype A person's genetic heritage; the actual genetic material.

germinal period The period of prenatal development that takes place in the first two weeks after conception. It includes the creation of the zygote, continued cell division, and the attachment of the zygote to the uterine wall.

gifted Having above-average intelligence (an IQ of 130 or higher) and/or superior talent for something.

goodness of fit The match between a child's temperament and the environmental demands the child must cope with.

grasping reflex A neonatal reflex that occurs when something touches the infant's palms. The infant responds by grasping tightly.

gross motor skills Motor skills that involve large-muscle activities, such as moving one's arms and walking.

H

habituation Decreased responsiveness to a stimulus after repeated presentations of the stimulus.

helpless orientation An orientation in which one seems trapped by the experience of difficulty and attributes one's difficulty to a lack of ability.

heritability The fraction of the variance in a population that is attributed to genetics.

heteronomous morality (Kohlberg) Kohlberg's first stage of preconventional reasoning, in which moral thinking is tied to punishment.

heteronomous morality (Piaget) The first stage of moral development in Piaget's theory, occurring from 4 to 7 years of age. Justice and rules are conceived of as unchangeable properties of the world, removed from the control of people.

hidden curriculum The pervasive moral atmosphere that characterizes schools.

horizontal décalage Piaget's concept that similar abilities do not appear at the same time within a stage of development.

hormones Powerful chemical substances secreted by the endocrine glands and carried through the body by the bloodstream.

hypotheses Specific assumptions and predictions that can be tested to determine their accuracy.

hypothetical-deductive reasoning Piaget's formal operational concept that adolescents have the cognitive ability to develop hypotheses about ways to solve problems and can systematically deduce which is the best path to follow in solving the problem.

I

identity achievement Marcia's term for the status of individuals who have undergone a crisis and made a commitment.

identity diffusion Marcia's term for the status of individuals who have not yet experienced a crisis (that is, they have not yet explored meaningful alternatives) or made any commitments.

identity foreclosure Marcia's term for the status of individuals who have made a commitment but have not experienced a crisis.

identity moratorium Marcia's term for the status of individuals who are in the midst of a crisis, but whose commitments either are absent or are only vaguely defined.

identity versus identity confusion Erikson's fifth developmental stage, which individuals experience during the adolescent years. At this time, adolescents examine who they are, what they are all about, and where they are going in life.

imaginary audience The aspect of adolescent egocentrism that involves attention-getting behavior motivated by a desire to be noticed, visible, and "onstage."

immanent justice Piaget's concept that if a rule is broken, punishment will be meted out immediately.

implicit memory Memory without conscious recollection; memory of skills and routine procedures that are performed automatically.

inclusion Educating a child with special education needs full-time in the regular classroom.

individualism Giving priority to personal goals rather than to group goals; emphasizing values that serve the self, such as feeling good, personal distinction and achievement, and independence.

individualism, instrumental purpose, and exchange The second Kohlberg stage of moral development. At this stage, individuals pursue their own interests but also let others do the same.

individuality Consists of two dimensions: self-assertion, the ability to have and communicate a point of view; and separateness, the use of communication patterns to express how one is different from others.

individualized education plan (IEP) A written statement that spells out a program tailored to a child with a disability.

induction A discipline technique in which a parent uses reasoning and explains the consequences for others of the child's actions.

indulgent parenting A style in which parents are highly involved with their children but place few demands or controls on them. This is associated with children's social incompetence, especially a lack of self-control and a lack of respect for others.

infancy The developmental period that extends from birth to about 18 to 24 months.

infinite generativity The ability to produce an endless number of meaningful sentences using a finite set of words and rules.

information-processing approach An approach that focuses on the ways children process information about their world—how they manipulate information, monitor it, and create strategies to deal with it.

information-processing theory Emphasizes that individuals manipulate information, monitor it, and strategize about it. Central to this theory are the processes of memory and thinking.

innate goodness view The idea, presented by Swiss-born French philosopher Jean-Jacques Rousseau, that children are inherently good.

insecure avoidant babies Babies who show insecurity by avoiding the mother.

insecure disorganized babies Babies who show insecurity by being disorganized and disoriented.

insecure resistant babies Babies who might cling to the caregiver, then resist her by fighting against the closeness, perhaps by kicking or pushing away.

intelligence The ability to solve problems and to adapt to and learn from experiences.

intelligence quotient (IQ) An individual's mental age divided by chronological age multiplied by 100; devised in 1912 by William Stern.

intermodal perception The ability to relate and integrate information about two or more sensory modalities, such as vision and hearing.

Internet Worldwide computer-mediated communication system that provides an incredible array of information.

intimacy in friendship Self-disclosure or the sharing of private thoughts.

intrinsic motivation Internal motivational factors such as self-determination, curiosity, challenge, and effort.

intuitive thought substage The second substage of preoperational thought, occurring between approximately 4 and 7 years of age. Children begin to use primitive reasoning and want to know the answers to all sorts of questions.

J

joint attention Individuals focusing on the same object or event; requires the ability to track another's behavior, one person directing another's attention, and reciprocal interaction.

justice perspective A moral perspective that focuses on the rights of the individual; individuals independently make moral decisions.

juvenile delinquency Refers to a great variety of behaviors by an adolescent, ranging from unacceptable behavior to breaking the law.

K

kangaroo care A way of holding a preterm infant so that there is skin-to-skin contact.

Klinefelter syndrome A chromosomal disorder in which males have an extra X chromosome, making them XXY instead of XY.

kwashiokor Severe malnutrition caused by a protein-deficient diet, causing the feet and abdomen to swell with water.

L

labeling Identifying the names of objects.

laboratory A controlled setting in which many of the complex factors of the "real world" are removed.

language A form of communication, whether spoken, written, or signed, that is based on a systems of symbols.

language acquisition device (LAD) Chomsky's term that describes a biological endowment that enables the child to detect the features and rules of language, including phonology, syntax, and semantics.

lateralization Specialization of function in one hemisphere of the cerebral cortex or the other.

learning disabilities Disabilities that involve understanding or using spoken or written language, and the difficulty can appear in listening, thinking, reading, writing, and spelling. A learning disability also may involve difficulty in doing mathematics. To be classified as a learning disability, the learning problem is not primarily the result of visual, hearing, or motor disabilities; mental retardation; emotional disorders; or due to environmental, cultural, or economic disadvantage.

least restrictive environment (LRE) The concept that a child with a disability must be educated in a setting that is as similar as possible to the one in which children who do not have a disability are educated.

long-term memory A relatively permanent and unlimited type of memory.

longitudinal approach A research strategy in which the same individuals are studied over a period of time, usually several years or more.

love withdrawal A discipline technique in which a parent withholds attention or love from the child.

low birth weight infants An infant that weighs less than $5\frac{1}{2}$ pounds at birth.

M

marasmus Severe malnutrition caused by an insufficient protein-calorie intake, resulting in a shrunken, elderly appearance.

mastery orientation An orientation in which one is task oriented; instead of focusing on one's ability is concerned with learning strategies and the achievement process rather than the outcome.

meiosis A specialized form of cell division that occurs to form eggs and sperm (or gametes), each of which contains only half of the parent cell's genetic material.

memory Retention of information over time.

menarche A girl's first menstruation.

mental age (MA) An individual's level of mental development relative to others.

mental retardation A condition of limited mental ability in which the individual (1) has a low IQ, usually below 70 on a traditional intelligence test; (2) has difficulty adapting to everyday life; and (3) has an onset of these characteristics by age 18.

metacognition Cognition about cognition, or "knowing about knowing."

metalinguistic awareness Knowledge about language.

metamemory Knowledge about memory.

metaphor An implied comparison between two unlike things.

middle and late childhood The developmental period that extends from about 6 to 11 years of age, sometimes called the elementary school years.

mindset Dweck's concept that refers to the cognitive view individuals develop for themselves; individuals have either a fixed or growth mindset.

mitosis Cellular reproduction in which the cell's nucleus duplicates itself with two new cells being formed, each containing the same DNA as the parent cell, arranged in the same 23 pairs of chromosomes.

Montessori approach An educational philosophy in which children are given considerable freedom and spontaneity in choosing activities and are allowed to move from one activity to another as they desire.

moral development Changes in thoughts, feelings, and behaviors regarding standards of right and wrong.

moral exemplars People who have lived extraordinary lives. Emphasizes the development of personality, identity, character, and virtue that reflect moral excellence and commitment.

moral identity The aspect of personality that is present when individuals have moral notions and commitments that are central to their lives.

Moro reflex A neonatal startle response that occurs in reaction to a sudden, intense noise or movement. When startled, the newborn arches its back, throws its head back, and flings out its arms and legs. Then the newborn rapidly closes its arms and legs to the center of the body.

morphology The rule system that governs how words are formed in a language.

mutual interpersonal expectations, relationships, and interpersonal conformity Kohlberg's third stage of moral development. At this stage, individuals value trust, caring, and loyalty to others as a basis of moral judgments.

myelination The process of encasing axons with a myelin sheath that increases the speed of processing information.

N

natural childbirth Developed in 1914 by Dick-Read, this method attempts to reduce the mother's pain by decreasing her fear through education about childbirth and relaxation techniques during delivery.

naturalistic observation Observing behavior in real-world settings.

nature-nurture issue Involves the debate about whether development is primarily influenced by nature or nurture. The "nature" proponents claim biological inheritance is the most important influence on development; the "nurture" proponents claim that environmental experiences are the most important.

neglected children Children who are infrequently nominated as a best friend but are not disliked by their peers.

neglectful parenting A style in which the parent is very uninvolved in the child's life. It is associated with children's social incompetence, especially a lack of self-control and poor self-esteem.

Neonatal Intensive Care Unit Neurobehavioral Scale (NNNS) An "offspring" of the NBAS, the NNNS provides a more comprehensive analysis of the newborn's behavior, neurological and stress responses, and regulatory capacities.

neo-Piagetians Developmentalists who have elaborated on Piaget's theory, believing that children's cognitive development is more specific in many respects than Piaget thought and giving more emphasis to how children use memory, attention, and strategies to process information.

neurons Nerve cells, which handle information processing at the cellular level in the brain.

nonshared environmental experiences The child's own unique experiences, both within the family and outside the family, that are not shared by another sibling. Thus, experiences occurring within the family can be part of the "nonshared environment."

normal distribution A symmetrical distribution with a majority of the cases falling in the middle of the possible range of scores and few scores appearing toward the extremes of the range.

O

object permanence The Piagetian term for one of an infant's most important accomplishments: understanding that objects and events continue to exist even when they cannot directly be seen, heard, or touched.

onlooker play Play in which the child watches other children play.

operations Internalized actions that allow children to do mentally what before they had done only physically. Operations also are reversible mental actions.

organization Piaget's concept of grouping isolated behaviors into a higher-order, more smoothly functioning cognitive system; the grouping or arranging of items into categories.

organogenesis Organ formation that takes place during the first two months of prenatal development.

original sin view Advocated during the Middle Ages, the belief that children were born into the world as evil beings and were basically bad.

P

pain cry A sudden appearance of loud crying without preliminary moaning and a long initial cry followed by an extended period of breath holding.

parallel play Play in which the child plays separately from others, but with toys like those the others are using or in a manner that mimics their play.

passive genotype-environment correlations Correlations that exist when the biological parents, who are genetically related to the child, provide a rearing environment for the child.

peers Children of about the same age or maturity level.

perception The interpretation of sensation.

performance orientation An orientation in which one focuses on winning rather than achievement outcomes, and happiness is thought to result from winning.

personal fable The part of adolescent egocentrism that involves an adolescent's sense of uniqueness and invincibility.

perspective taking The ability to assume others' perspective and understand their thoughts or feelings.

phenotype The way an individual's genotype is expressed in observed and measurable characteristics.

phenylketonuria (PKU) A genetic disorder in which the individual cannot properly metabolize phenylalanine, an amino acid. PKU is now easily detected—but, if left untreated, results in mental retardation and hyperactivity.

phonics approach An approach that emphasizes that reading instruction should focus on phonics and its basic rules for translating written symbols into sounds.

phonology The sound system of a language—includes the sounds used and rules about how they may be combined.

Piaget's theory States that children actively construct their understanding of the world and go through four stages of cognitive development.

placenta The life-support system that consists of a disk-shaped group of tissues in which small blood vessels from the mother and offspring intertwine but do not join.

play A pleasurable activity that is engaged in for its own sake.

play therapy Therapy that allows the child to work off frustrations and is a medium through which the therapist can analyze the child's conflicts and ways of coping with them. Children may feel less threatened and be more likely to express their true feelings in the context of play.

popular children Children who are frequently nominated as a best friend and are rarely disliked by their peers.

possible self What an individual might become, what the person would like to become, and what the person is afraid of becoming.

postconventional reasoning The highest level in Kohlberg's theory of moral development. At this level, the individual recognizes alternative moral courses, explores the options, and then decides on a personal moral code.

postpartum depression Characteristic of women who have such strong feelings or sadness, anxiety, or despair that they have trouble coping with daily tasks in the postpartum period.

postpartum period The period after childbirth when the mother adjusts, both physically and psychologically, to the process of childbirth. This period lasts for about six weeks or until her body has completed its adjustment and returned to a near-prepregnant state.

power assertion A discipline technique in which a parent attempts to gain control over the child or the child's resources.

practice play Play that involves repetition of behavior when new skills are being learned or when physical or mental mastery and coordination of skills are required for games or sports. Sensorimotor play, which often involves practice play, is primarily confined to infancy, while practice play can be engaged in throughout life.

pragmatics The appropriate use of language in different contexts.

preconventional reasoning The lowest level in Kohlberg's theory of moral development. The individual's moral reasoning is controlled primarily by external rewards and punishment.

prefrontal cortex The highest level of the frontal lobes that is involved in reasoning, decision making, and self-control.

prejudice An unjustified negative attitude toward an individual because of her or his membership in a group.

prenatal period The time from conception to birth.

preoperational stage The second Piagetian developmental stage, which lasts from about 2 to 7 years of age; children begin to represent the world with words, images, and drawings.

prepared childbirth Developed by French obstetrician Ferdinand Lamaze, this childbirth strategy is similar to natural childbirth but includes a special breathing technique to control pushing in the final stages of labor and a more detailed anatomy and physiology course.

pretense/symbolic play Play that occurs when a child transforms the physical environment into a symbol.

preterm infants Those born three weeks or more before the pregnancy has reached its full term.

primary emotions Emotions that are present in humans and other animals, and emerge early in life; examples are joy, anger, sadness, fear, and disgust.

Project Head Start Compensatory education designed to provide children from low-income families the opportunity to acquire the skills and experiences important for school success.

proximodistal pattern The sequence in which growth starts at the center of the body and moves toward the extremities.

psychoanalytic theories Describe development as primarily unconscious and heavily colored by emotion. Behavior is merely a surface characteristic, and the symbolic workings of the mind have to be analyzed to understand behavior. Early experiences with parents are emphasized.

psychoanalytic theory of gender A theory that stems from Freud's view that preschool children develop erotic feelings toward the opposite-sex parent. Eventually these feelings cause anxiety, so that at 5 or 6 years of age, children renounce these feelings and identify with the same-sex parent, unconsciously adopting the same-sex parent's characteristics.

psychosocial moratorium Erikson's term for the gap between childhood security and adult autonomy that adolescents experience as part of their identity exploration.

puberty A period of rapid physical maturation involving hormonal and bodily changes that take place primarily in early adolescence.

R

rapport talk The language of conversation and a way of establishing connections and negotiating relationships; more characteristic of females than of males.

recasting Rephrasing a statement that a child has said, perhaps turning it into a question, or restating a child's immature utterance in the form of a fully grammatical utterance.

reciprocal socialization The bidirectional process by which children socialize parents just as parents socialize them.

reciprocal teaching Students take turns leading small-group discussions.

reflexive smile A smile that does not occur in response to external stimuli. It happens during the month after birth, usually during sleep.

rejected children Children who are infrequently nominated as a best friend and are actively disliked by their peers.

report talk Talk that conveys information; more characteristic of males than females.

rooting reflex A newborn's built-in reaction that occurs when the infant's cheek is stroked or the side of the mouth is touched. In response, the infant turns its head toward the side that was touched, in an apparent effort to find something to suck.

S

satire The use of irony, derision, or wit to expose folly or wickedness.

semantics The meaning of words and sentences.

scaffolding Adjusting the level of parental guidance to fit the child's efforts, allowing children to be more skillful than they would be if they relied only on their own abilities.

scaffolding In cognitive development, Vygotsky used this term to describe the changing support over the course of a teaching session, with the more-skilled person adjusting guidance to fit the child's current performance level.

schema theory States that when people reconstruct information, they fit it into information that already exists in their minds.

schemas Mental frameworks that organize concepts and information.

schemes In Piaget's theory, actions or mental representations that organize knowledge.

scientific method An approach that can be used to obtain accurate information. It includes these steps: (1) conceptualize the problem, (2) collect data, (3) draw conclusions, and (4) revise research conclusions and theory.

securely attached babies Babies who use the caregiver as a secure base from which to explore the environment.

selective attention Focusing on a specific aspect of experience that is relevant while ignoring others that are irrelevant.

self-concept Domain-specific self-evaluations.

self-conscious emotions Emotions that require self-awareness, especially consciousness and a sense of "me"; examples include jealousy, empathy, and embarrassment.

self-efficacy The belief that one can master a situation and produce favorable outcomes.

self-esteem The global evaluative dimension of the self; also called self-worth or self-image.

self-regulatory learning Generating and monitoring thoughts, feelings, and behaviors to reach a goal.

self-understanding A child's cognitive representation of the self; the substance and content of a child's self-conceptions.

sensation Reaction that occurs when information contacts sensory receptors—the eyes, ears, tongue, nostrils, and skin.

sensorimotor play Behavior engaged in by infants to derive pleasure from exercising their existing sensorimotor schemes.

sensorimotor stage The first of Piaget's stages, which lasts from birth to about 2 years of age; infants construct an understanding of the world by coordinating sensory experiences (such as seeing and hearing) with motoric actions.

separation protest Occurs when infants experience a fear of being separated from a caregiver, which results in crying when the caregiver leaves.

seriation The concrete operation that involves ordering stimuli along a quantitative dimension (such as length).

service learning A form of education that promotes social responsibility and service to the community.

shape constancy Recognition that an object remains the same even though its orientation to us changes.

shared environmental experiences Siblings' common environmental experiences, such as their parents' personalities and intellectual orientation, the family's socioeconomic status, and the neighborhood in which they live.

short-term memory Limited-capacity memory system in which information is usually retained for up to 15 to 30 seconds, assuming there is no rehearsal of the information. Using rehearsal, individuals can keep the information in short-term memory longer.

sickle-cell anemia A genetic disorder that affects the red blood cells and occurs most often in African Americans.

size constancy Recognition that an object remains the same even though the retinal image of the object changes.

slow-to-warm-up child A temperament style in which the child has a low activity level, is somewhat negative, and displays a low intensity of mood.

small for date infants Also called small for gestational age infants, these infants' birth weights are below normal when the length of pregnancy is considered. Small for date infants may be preterm or full term.

social cognition The processes involved in understanding the world around us, especially how we think and reason about other people.

social cognitive theory The view of psychologists who emphasize behavior, environment, and cognition as the key factors in development.

social cognitive theory of gender This theory emphasizes that children's gender development occurs through observation and imitation of gender behavior, and through rewards and punishments they experience for gender-appropriate and gender-inappropriate behavior.

social cognitive theory of morality The theory that distinguishes between moral competence—the ability to produce moral behaviors—and moral performance—those behaviors in specific situations.

social constructivist approach An emphasis on the social contexts of learning and the construction of knowledge through social interaction. Vygotsky's theory reflects this approach.

social contract or utility and individual rights The fifth Kohlberg stage. At this stage, individuals reason that values, rights, and principles undergird or transcend the law.

social conventional reasoning Focuses on conventional rules established by social consensus, as opposed to moral reasoning that stresses ethical issues.

social play Play that involves interactions with peers.

social policy A government's course of action designed to promote the welfare of its citizens.

social referencing "Reading" emotional cues in others to help determine how to act in a particular situation.

social role theory A theory stating that gender differences result from the contrasting roles of women and men—social hierarchy and division of labor strongly influence gender differences in power, assertiveness, and nature.

social smile A smile in response to an external stimulus, which, early in development, typically is a face.

social systems morality The fourth stage in Kohlberg's theory of moral development. Moral judgments are based on understanding the social order, law, justice, and duty.

socioeconomic status (SES) A grouping of people with similar occupational, educational, and economic characteristics.

socioemotional processes Changes in an individual's relationships with other people, emotions, and personality.

solitary play Play in which the child plays alone and independently of others.

standardized test A test with uniform procedures for administration and scoring. Many standardized tests allow a person's performance to be compared with the performance of other individuals.

stereotype threat Anxiety that one's behavior might confirm a stereotype about one's group.

Strange Situation Ainsworth's observational measure of infant attachment to a caregiver that requires the infant to move through a series of introductions, separations, and reunions with the caregiver and an adult stranger in a prescribed order.

stranger anxiety An infant's fear of and wariness toward strangers; it tends to appear in the second half of the first year of life.

strategy construction Creation of new procedures for processing information.

sucking reflex A newborn's built-in reaction of automatically sucking an object placed in its mouth. The sucking reflex enables the infant to get nourishment before it has associated a nipple with food.

sudden infant death syndrome (SIDS) A condition that occurs when an infant stops breathing, usually during the night, and suddenly dies without an apparent cause.

sustained attention The ability to maintain attention to a selected stimulus for a prolonged period of time. Sustained attention is also called *focused attention* and *vigilance*.

symbolic function substage The first substage of preoperational thought, occurring roughly between the ages of 2 and 4. In this substage, the young child gains the ability to represent mentally an object that is not present.

syntax The ways words are combined to form acceptable phrases and sentences.

T

tabula rasa view The idea, proposed by John Locke, that children are like a "blank tablet."

telegraphic speech The use of short, precise words without grammatical markers such as articles, auxiliary verbs, and other connectives.

temperament An individual's behavioral style and characteristic emotional response.

teratogen From the Greek word *tera*, meaning "monster." A teratogen is any agent that potentially can cause a birth defect or negatively alters cognitive and behavioral outcomes. The field of study that investigates the causes of birth defects is called teratology.

testosterone An androgen that is a key hormone in boys' pubertal development.

theory An interrelated, coherent set of ideas that helps to explain and make predictions.

theory of mind Awareness of one's own mental processes and the mental processes of others.

thinking Manipulating and transforming information in memory, usually to form concepts, reason, think critically, and solve problems.

top-dog phenomenon The circumstance of moving from the top position in elementary school to the lowest position in middle or junior high school.

transitivity If a relation holds between a first object and a second object, and holds between the second object and a third object, then it holds between the first object and the third object. Piaget argued that an understanding of transitivity is characteristic of concrete operational thought.

triarchic theory of intelligence Sternberg's theory that intelligence comes in three forms: analytical, creative, and practical.

trophoblast The outer layer of cells that develops in the germinal period. These cells provide nutrition and support for the embryo.

Turner syndrome A chromosomal disorder in females in which either an X chromosome is missing, making the person XO instead of XX, or the second X chromosome is partially deleted.

twin study A study in which the behavioral similarity of identical twins is compared with the behavioral similarity of fraternal twins.

U

umbilical cord The life-support system containing two arteries and one vein and connects the baby to the placenta.

universal ethical principles The sixth and highest stage in Kohlberg's theory of moral development. Individuals develop a moral standard based on universal human rights.

unoccupied play Play in which the child is not engaging in play as it is commonly understood and might stand in one spot, look around the room, or perform random movements that do not seem to have a goal.

V

values clarification Helping people clarify what their lives are for and what is worth working for. Students are encouraged to define their own values and understand others' values.

visual preference method A method developed by Fantz to determine whether infants can distinguish one stimulus from another by measuring the length of time they attend to different stimuli.

Vygotsky's theory A sociocultural cognitive theory that emphasizes how culture and social interaction guide cognitive development.

W

Wernicke's area An area of the brain's left hemisphere that is involved in language comprehension.

whole-language approach An approach that stresses that reading instruction should parallel children's natural language learning. Reading materials should be whole and meaningful.

working memory A mental "workbench" where individuals manipulate and assemble information when making decisions, solving problems, and comprehending written and spoken language.

X

XYY syndrome A chromosomal disorder in which males have an extra Y chromosome.

Z

zone of proximal development (ZPD) Vygotsky's term for tasks too difficult for children to master alone but that can be mastered with assistance from adults or more-skilled children.

zygote A single cell formed through fertilization.

REFERENCES

A

Aalsma, M., Lapsley, D. K., & Flannery, D. (2006). Narcissism, personal fables, and adolescent adjustment. *Psychology in the Schools, 43,* 481–491

ABC News. (2005, December 12). Larry Page and Sergey Brim. Retrieved October 10, 2006, from http: //abcnews.go.com?Entertainment/ 12/8/05

Accornero, V. H., Anthony, J. C., Morrow, C. E., Xue, L., & Bandstra, E. S. (2006). Prenatal cocaine exposure: An examination of childhood externalizing and internalizing - behavior problems at age 7 years. *Epidemiology, Psychiatry, and Society, 15,* 20–29.

Achenbach, T. M. (1997). What is normal? What is abnormal? Developmental perspectives on behavioral and emotional problems. In S. S. Luthar, J. A. Burack, D. Cicchetti, & J. R. Weisz (Eds.), *Developmental psychopathology: Perspectives on adjustment, risk, and disorder.* New York: Cambridge University Press.

Achieve, Inc. (2005). *An Action agenda for improving America's high Schools.* Washington, DC: Author.

Acredolo, L. P., & Hake, J. L. (1982). Infant perception. In B. B. Wolman (Ed.). *Handbook of developmental psychology.* Englewood Cliffs, NJ: Prentice Hall.

Adams, G. R., Gulotta, T. P., & Montemayor, R. (Eds.). (1992). *Adolescent identity formation.* Newbury Park, CA: Sage.

Adams, S., Kuebli, J., Boyle, P. A., Fivush, R. (1995). Gender differences in parent-child conversations about past emotions: A longitudinal investigation. *Sex Roles, 33,* 309–323.

Adamson, L., & Frick, J. (2003). The still face: A history of a shared experimental paradigm. *Infancy, 4,* 451–473.

Adolph, K. E. (1997). Learning in the development of infant locomotion. *Monographs of the Society for Research in Child Development, 62* (3, Serial No. 251).

Adolph, K. E. (2008). Motor and physical development: Locomotion. In M. M. Haith & J. B. Benson (Eds.), *Encyclopedia of infant and early childhood development.* Oxford, UK: Elsevier.

Adolph, K. E. (2009, in press). The growing body in action: What infant locomotion tells us about perceptually guided action. In R. Klatsky, M. Behrmann, & B. McWhinney (Eds.), *Embodiment, ego-space, and action.* Clifton, NJ: Psychology Press.

Adolph, K. E., & Avolio, A. M. (2000). Walking infants adapt locomotion to changing body dimensions. *Journal of Experimental Psychology: Human Perception and Performance, 26,* 1148–1166.

Adolph, K. E., & Berger, S. E. (2005). Physical and motor development. In M. H. Bornstein & M. E. Lamb (Eds.), *Developmental psychology* (5th ed.). Mahwah, NJ: Erlbaum.

Adolph, K. E., & Joh, A. S. (2007). Motor development: How infants get into the act. In A. Slater & M. Lewis (Eds.), *Introduction to infant development* (2nd ed.), New York: Oxford University Press.

Adolph, K. E., & Joh, A. S. (2008, in press). Multiple learning mechanisms in the development of action. In A. Woodward and A. Needham (Eds.), *Learning and the infant mind.* New York: Oxford University Press.

Adolph, K. E., Joh, A. S., Franchak, J. M., Ishak, S., & Gill-Alvarez, S. V. (2009, in press). Flexibility in the development of action. In J. Bargh, P. Gollwitzer, & E. Morsella (Eds.), *The psychology of action* (Vol. 2). Oxford, UK: Oxford University Press.

Adolph, K. E., Karasik, L., & Tamis-LeMonda, C. S. (2009, in press). Moving between cultures: cross-cultural research on motor development. In M. Bornstein (Ed.), *Handbook of cross-cultural developmental science* (Vol. 1). Clifton, NJ: Psychology Press.

Adolph, K. E., Tamis-LeMonda, C. S., Ishak, S., Karasik, L. B., & Lobo, S. A. (2008, in press). Locomotor experience and use of social information are posture specific. *Developmental Psychology.*

Adolph, K. E., Vereijken, B., & Shrout, P. E. (2003). What changes in infant walking and why. *Child Development, 74,* 475–497.

Agency for Healthcare Research and Quality. (2007). *Evidence report/Technology assessment Number 153: Breastfeeding and maternal and health outcomes in developed countries.* Rockville, MD: U.S. Department of Health and Human Services.

Agras, W. S., Hammer, L. D., McNicholas, F., & Kraemer, H. C. (2004). Risk factors for childhood overweight: A prospective study from birth to 9.5 years. *Journal of Pediatrics, 145,* 20–25.

Aguiar, A., & Baillargeon, R. (2002). Developments in young infants' reasoning about occluded objects. *Cognitive Psychology, 45,* 263–336.

Ahluwalia, I. B., Tessaro, I., Grumer-Strawn, L. M., MacGowan, C., & Benton-Davis, S. (2000). Georgia's breastfeeding promotion program for low-income women. *Pediatrics, 105,* e85–e87.

Ahnert, L., & Lamb, M. E. (2009, in press). Child care and its impact on young children (2–5). In R. E. Tremblay, R. deV Peters, M. Boivan, & R. G. Barr (Eds.), *Encyclopedia on early childhood development.* Montreal: Center of Excellence for Early Childhood Development.

Ahrons, C. R. (2007). Family ties after divorce: Long-term implications for children. *Family Processes, 46,* 53–65.

Aiken, L. R. (2006). *Psychological testing and assessment* (10 th ed.). Boston: Allyn & Bacon.

Ainsworth, M. D. S. (1979). Infant-mother attachment. *American Psychologist, 34,* 932–937.

Aktar, N., & Herold, K. (2008). Pragmatic development. In M. M. Haith & J. B. Benson (Eds.), *Encyclopedia of infant and early childhood development.* Oxford, UK: Elsevier.

Alario, A., & Birnkrant, J. (2008). *Practical guide to the care of the pediatric patient* (2nd ed.). Oxford, UK: Elsevier.

Alberts, A., Elkind, D., & Ginsberg, S. (2007). The personal fable and risk-taking in early adolescence. *Journal of Youth and Adolescence, 36,* 71–76.

Alegre, M., & Welsch, D. (2003). *Maxine Hong Kingston after the fire.* Retrieved January 26, 2003, from www.powers.com/authors

Alexander, R. T., & Radisch, D. (2005). Sudden infant death syndrome risk factors with regards to sleep position, sleep surface, and co-sleeping. *Journal of Forensic Science, 50,* 147–151.

Alkhadher, O. (2007). Emotional intelligence and psychological health in a sample of Kuwaiti college students. *Perceptual and Motor Skills, 104,* 923–936.

Allen, J. P. (2007, March). *A transformational perspective on the attachment system in adolescence.* Paper presented at the meeting of the Society for Research in Child Development, Boston.

Allen, J. P. (2008). The attachment system in adolescence. In J. Cassidy & P. R. Shaver (Eds.), *Handbook of attachment* (2nd ed.). New York: Guilford.

Allen, J. P., & Antonishak, J. (2008). Adolescent peer influences: Beyond the dark side. In M. J. Prinstein & K. A. Dodge (Eds.), *Understanding peer influence in children and adolescents.* New York: Guilford.

Allen, J. P., McElhaney, K. B., Land, D. J., Kumperminc, G. P., Moore, C. W., O'Beirne-Kelly, H., & Kilmer, S. L. (2003). A secure base in adolescence: Markers of attachment security in the mother-adolescent relationship. *Child Development, 74,* 292–307.

Allen, M., Brown, P., & Finlay, B. (1992). *Helping children by strengthening families.* Washington, DC: Children's Defense Fund.

Allen, M. C. (2008). Neurodevelopmental outcomes of preterm infants. *Current Opinion in Neurology, 21,* 123–128.

Allington, R. L. (2009). *What really matters in fluency.* Boston: Allyn & Bacon.

Alm, B., Lagercrantz, H., & Wennergren, G. (2006). Stop SIDS—sleeping solitary supine, sucking smoother, stopping smoking substitutes. *Acta Pediatrica, 95,* 260–262.

Als, H., & Butler, S. C. (2008). Screening, newborn, and maternal well-being. In M. M. Haith & J. B. Benson (Eds.), *Encyclopedia of infancy and early childhood development.* Oxford, UK: Elsevier.

Altarac, M., & Saroha, E. (2007). Lifetime prevalence of learning disability among U.S. children. *Pediatrics, 119* (Suppl. 1), S77–S83.

Altimer, L. (2008). Shaken baby syndrome. *Journal of Perinatal and Neonatal Nursing, 22,* 68–76.

Alvarez, A. (2009). Racism: "It isn't fair." In N. Tewari & A. Alvarez (Eds.), *Asian American psychology.* Clifton, NJ: Psychology Press.

Alvarez, A., & del Rio, P. (2007). Inside and outside the zone of proximal development: An eco-functional reading of Vygotsky. In H. Daniels, J. Wertsch, & M. Cole (Eds.), *The Cambridge companion to Vygotsky.* New York: Cambridge University Press.

Alvik, A., Haldorsen, T., Groholt, B., & Lindemann, R. (2006). Alcohol consumption before and during pregnancy comparing concurrent and retrospective reports. *Alcohol: Clinical and Experimental Research, 30,* 510–515.

Amabile, T. M. (1993). Commentary. In D. Goleman, P. Kaufman, & M. Ray, *The creative spirit.* New York: Plume.

Amabile, T. M., & Hennesey, B. A. (1992). The motivation for creativity in children. In A. K. Boggiano & T. S. Pittman (Eds.), *Achievement and motivation.* New York: Cambridge University Press.

Amato, P. R. (2006). Marital discord, divorce, and children's well-being: Results from a 20-year longitudinal study of two generations. In A. Clarke-Stewart & J. Dunn (Eds.), *Families count.* New York: Cambridge University Press.

Amato, P. R., & Booth, A. (1996). A prospective study of divorce and parent-child relationships. *Journal of Marriage and the Family, 58,* 356–365.

Amato, P. R., & Irving, S. (2006). Historical trends in divorce and dissolution. In M. A. Fine & J. H. Harvey (Eds.), *Handbook of divorce and relationship dissolution.* Mahwah, NJ: Erlbaum.

American Academy of Pediatrics. (2001). Health care supervision for children with Williams syndrome. *Pediatrics, 107,* 1192–1204.

American Academy of Pediatrics (AAP) Task Force on Infant Positioning and SIDS. (2000). Changing concepts of sudden infant death syndrome. *Pediatrics, 105,* 650–656.

American Academy of Pediatrics (AAP) Work Group on Breastfeeding. (1997). Breastfeeding and the use of human milk. *Pediatrics, 100,* 1035–1039.

American Academy of Pediatrics Council on Sports Medicine and Fitness, McCambrige, T. M., & Stricker, P. R. (2008). Strength training by children and adolescents. *Pediatrics, 121,* 835–840.

American Association on Mental Retardation, Ad Hoc Committee on Terminology and Classification. (1992). *Mental retardation* (9th ed.). Washington, DC: Author.

American Psychological Association. (2003). *Psychology: Scientific problem solvers.* Washington, DC: Author.

American Public Health Association. (2006). *Understanding the health culture of recent immigrants to the United States.* Retrieved February 10, 2006, from www.apha.org/ppp/red/Intro.htm

Amos, D., & Johnson, S. P. (2006). Learning by selection: Visual search and object perception in young infants. *Developmental Psychology, 42,* 1236–1245.

Amsterdam, B. K. (1968). *Mirror behavior in children under two years of age.* Unpublished doctoral dissertation, University of North Carolina, Chapel Hill.

Anastasi, A., & Urbina, S. (1997). *Psychological testing* (7th ed.). Upper Saddle River, NJ: Prentice Hall.

Anderman, E. M., & Mueller, C. E. (2009, in press). Middle school transitions and adolescent development: Disentangling psychological, social, and biological effects. In J. Meece & J. Eccles (Eds.), *Handbook of research on schools, schooling, and human development.* Clifton, NJ: Psychology Press.

Anderman, E. M., & Murdock, T. B. (Eds.). (2007). *Psychology of academic cheating.* San Diego: Academic Press.

Anderman, E. M., & Wolters, C. A. (2006). Goals, values, and affect: Influences on student motivation. In P. A. Alexander & P. H. Winne (Eds.), *Handbook of educational psychology* (2nd ed.). Mahwah, NJ: Erlbaum.

Anderson, C. A., & Bushman, B. J. (2001). Effects of violent video games on aggressive behavior, aggressive cognition, aggressive affect, physiological arousal, and prosocial behavior: A meta-analytic review of the scientific literature. *Psychological Science, 12,* 353–359.

Anderson, C. A., Gentile, D. A., & Buckley, K. E. (2007). *Violent video game effects on children and adolescents.* New York: Oxford University Press.

Anderson, D. R., Huston, A. C., Schmitt, K., Linebarger, D. L., & Wright, J. C. (2001). Early childhood viewing and adolescent behavior: The recontact study. *Monographs of the Society for Research in Child Development, 66* (Serial No. 264).

Anderson, D. R., Lorch, E. P., Field, D. E., Collins, P. A., & Nathan, J. G. (1985, April). *Television viewing at home: Age trends in visual attention and time with TV.* Paper presented at the biennial meeting of the Society for Research in Child Development, Toronto.

Anderson, E., Greene, S. M., Hetherington, E. M., & Clingempeel, W. G. (1999). The dynamics of parental remarriage. In E. M. Hetherington (Ed.), *Coping with divorce, single parenting, and remarriage.* Mahwah, NJ: Erlbaum.

Andersson, J. L., Waller, D. K., Canfield, M. A., Shaw, G. M., Watkins, M. L., & Werler, M. M. (2005). Maternal obesity, gestational diabetes, and central nervous system birth defects. *Epidemiology, 16,* 87–92.

Andersson, U., & Lyxell, B. (2007). Working memory deficit in children with mathematical difficulties: A general or specific deficit? *Journal of Experimental Child Psychology, 96,* 197–228.

Andrews, K. M., Brouilette, D. B., & Brouilette, R. T. (2008). Mortality, infant. In M. M. Haith & J. B. Benson (Eds.), *Encyclopedia of infant and early childhood development.* Oxford, UK: Elsevier.

Ang, S. & van Dyne, L. (2009, in press). *Handbook on cultural intelligence.* New York: M.E. Sharpe.

Ara, I., Vicente-Rodrigquez, G., Jimenez-Ramirez, J., Dorado, C., Serrano-Sanchez, J. A., & Calbet, J. A. (2004). Regular participation in sports is associated with enhanced physical fitness and lower body mass in prepubertal boys. *International Journal of Obesity and Related Metabolic Disorders, 28,* 1585–1593.

Archer, S. L. (1989). The status of identity: Reflections on the need for intervention. *Journal of Adolescence, 12,* 345–359.

Archer, S. L., & Waterman, A. S. (1994). Adolescent identity development: Contextual perspectives. In C. B. Fisher & R. M. Lerner (Eds.), *Applied developmental psychology.* New York: McGraw-Hill.

Archibald, A. B., Graber, J. A., & Brooks-Gunn, J. (2003). Pubertal processes and physical growth in adolescence. In G. R. Adam & M. Berzonsky (Eds.), *Handbook on adolescence.* Malden, MA: Blackwell.

Ariagno, R. L., van Liempt, S., & Mirmiran,M. (2006). Fewer spontaneous arousals during prone sleep in preterm infants at 1 and 3 months corrected age. *Journal of Perinatology, 26,* 306–312.

Ariès, P. (1962). *Centuries of childhood* (R. Baldrick, Trans.). New York: Knopf.

Armstrong, D. G., Henson, K. T., & Savage, T. V. (2009). *Teaching today* (8th ed.). Boston: Allyn & Bacon.

Arnett, J. (1990). Contraceptive use, sensation seeking, and adolescent egocentrism. *Journal of Youth and Adolescence, 19,* 171–180.

Arnett, J. J. (2002). Adolescents in Western countries in the 21st century: Vast opportunities—for all? In B. B. Brown, R. W. Larson, & T.S. Saraswathi (Eds.), *The world's youth.* New York: Cambridge University Press.

Arnett, J. J. (2006). Emerging adulthood: Understanding the new way of coming of age. In J. J. Arnett & J. L. Tanner (Eds.), *Emerging adults in America.* Washington, DC: American Psychological Association.

Arnett, J. J. (2007). Socialization in emerging adulthood. In J. E. Grusec & P. D. Hastings (Eds.), *Handbook of socialization.* New York: Guilford.

Aron, A., Aron, E., & Coupos, E. (2008). *Statistics for the behavioral and social sciences.* Upper Saddle River, NJ: Prentice Hall.

Aronson, E. (1986, August). *Teaching students things they think they already know about: The case of prejudice and desegregation.* Paper presented at the meeting of the American Psychological Association, Washington, DC.

Aronson, J. (2002). Stereotype threat: Contending and coping with unnerving expectations. In J. Aronson (Ed.), *Improving academic achievement.* San Diego: Academic Press.

Arredondo, E. M., Elder, J. P., Ayala, G. X., Campbell, N., Baquero, B., & Duerksen, S. (2006). Is parenting style related to children's healthy eating and physical activity in Latino families? *Health Education Research, 21,* 862–871.

Arria, A. M., & others. (2006). Methamphetamine and other substance use during pregnancy: Preliminary estimates from the Infant Development, Environment, and Lifestyle (IDEAL) Study. *Maternal and Child Health Journal, 5,* 1–10.

Arterberry, M. E. (2008). Perceptual development. In M. M. Haith & J. B. Benson (Eds.), *Encyclopedia of infant and early childhood development.* Oxford, UK: Elsevier.

Arthur, J. (2008). Traditional approaches to character education in Britain and America. In L. Nucci & D. Narvaez (Eds.), *Handbook of moral and character education.* Clifton NJ: Psychology Press.

Asamen, J. K., Ellis, M. L., & Berry, G. L. (Eds.). (2008). *The SAGE handbook of child development, multiculturalism, and media.* Thousand Oaks, CA: Sage.

Asendorph, J. B. (2008). Shyness. In M. M. Haith & J. B. Benson (Eds.), *Encyclopedia of infant*

and early childhood development. Oxford, UK: Elsevier.

Ash, P. (2006). Adolescents in adult court: Does the punishment fit the criminal? *The Journal of the American Academy of Psychiatry and the Law, 34,* 145–149.

Ashmead, D. H., Wall, R. S., Ebinger, K. A., Hill, M.-M., Yang, X., and Eaton, S. (1998). Spatial hearing in children with visual disabilities. *Perception, 27,* 105–122.

Ashton, D. (2006). Prematurity—infant mortality: The scourge remains. *Ethnicity and Disease, 16 (Suppl.),* S3–S58.

Aslin, R. N. (1987). Visual and auditory development in infancy. In J. Osofsky (Ed.), *Handbook of infant development* (2nd ed.). New York: Wiley.

Aslin, R. N., Clayards, M. A., & Bardhan, N. P. (2008, in press). Mechanisms of auditory reorganization during development: From sounds to words. In C. A. Nelson & M. Luciana (Eds.), *Handbook of developmental cognitive science* (2nd ed.). Cambridge, MA: MIT Press.

Aslin, R. N., & Lathrop, A. L. (2008). Visual perception. In M. M. Haith & J. B. Benson (Eds.), *Encyclopedia of infant and early childhood development.* Oxford, UK: Elsevier.

Aslin, R. N., Jusczyk, P. W., & Pisoni, D. B. (1998). Speech and auditory processing during infancy: Constraints on and precursors to language. In W. Damon (Ed.), *Handbook of child psychology* (5th ed., Vol.2). New York: Wiley.

Assanand, S., dias, M., Richardson, E., & Waxler-Morrison, N. (1990). The South Asians. In N. Waxler-Morrison, J. M. Anderson, & E. Richardson (Eds.), *Cross-cultural caring.* Vancouver, BC: UBC Press.

Astington, J. W., & Dack, L. A. (2008). Theory of mind. In M. M. Haith & J. B. Benson (Eds.), *Encyclopedia of infant and early childhood development.* Oxford, UK: Elsevier.

Ateah, C. A. (2005). Maternal use of physical punishment in response to child misbehavior: Implications for child abuse prevention. *Child Abuse and Neglect, 29,* 169–185.

Aucoin, K. J., Frick, P. J., & Bodin, S. D. (2006). Corporal punishment and child adjustment. *Journal of Applied Developmental Psychology, 27,* 527–541.

Austin, A. A., & Chorpita, B. F. (2004). Temperament, anxiety, and depression: Comparisons across five ethnic groups of children. *Journal of Clinical Child and Adolescent Psychology, 33,* 216–226.

Avent, N. D., Plummer, Z. E., Madgett, T.E., Maddocks, D. G., & Soothill, P. W. (2008). Post-genomic studies and their application to non-invasive prenatal diagnosis. *Seminars in Fetal and Neonatal Medicine, 13,* 91–98.

Avgil, M., & Ornoy, A. (2006). Herpes simplex virus and Epstein-Barr virus infections in pregnancy: Consequences of neonatal or intrauter-

ine infection. *Reproductive Toxicology, 21,* 436–445.

Axelrad, D. A., Bellinger, D. C., Ryan, L. M., & Woodruff, T. J. (2007). Dose-response relationship of prenatal mercury exposure and IQ: An integrative analysis of epidemiologic data. *Environmental Health Perspectives, 115,* 609–615.

Ayala, G. X., Mickens, L., Galindo, P., & Elder, J. P. (2007). Acculturation and body image perception among Latino youth. *Ethnicity and Health, 12,* 21–41.

Aylott, M. (2006). The neonatal energy triangle. Part 1: Metabolic adaptation. *Pediatric Nursing 18,* 38–42.

B

Bacchini, D., & Magliulo, F. (2003). Self-image and perceived self-efficacy during adolescence. *Journal of Youth and Adolescence, 32,* 337–349.

Badaly, D., & Adolph, K. E. (2008, in press). Beyond the average: Infants take steps longer than their leg length: *Infant Behavior and Development.*

Baddeley, A. D. (1990). *Human memory: Theory and practice.* Boston: Allyn & Bacon.

Baddeley, A. D. (2001). *Is working memory still working?* Paper presented at the meeting of the American Psychological Association, San Francisco.

Baddeley, A. D. (2006) Working memory: An overview. In S. Pickering, (Ed.), *Working memory and education.* New York: Academic Press.

Baddeley, A. D. (2007a). *Working memory, thought, and action.* New York: Oxford University Press.

Baddeley, A. D. (2007b). Working memory. In H. L. Roediger, Y. Dudai, & S. M. Fitzpatrick (Eds.), *Science of memory.* New York: Oxford University Press.

Baddock, S. A., Galland, B. C., Taylor, B. J., & Bolton, D. P. (2007). Sleep arrangements and behavior of bed-sharing families in the home setting. *Pediatrics, 119,* e200–e2007.

Bagwell, C. L., Newcomb, A. F., & Bukowski, W. M. (1994, February). *Early adolescent friendship as a predictor of adult adjustment: A twelve year follow-up investigation.* Paper presented at the biennial meeting of the Society for Research on Adolescence, San Diego.

Bahrick, L. E., & Hollich, G. (2008). Intermodal perception. In M. Haith & J. Benson (Eds.), *Encyclopedia of infant and early childhood development.* London: Elsevier.

Bailit, J. L., Love, T. E., & Dawson, N. V. (2006). Quality of obstetric care and risk-adjusted primary cesarean delivery rates. *American Journal of Obstetrics and Gynecology, 194,* 402–407.

Baillargeon, R. H., (1995). The object concept revisited: New directions in the investigation of infants' physical knowledge, In C. E. Granrud (Ed.), *Visual perception and cognition in infancy.* Hillsdale, NJ: Erlbaum.

Baillargeon, R. H., (2004). The acquisition of physical knowledge in infancy: A summary in eight lessons. In U. Goswami (Ed.), *Blackwell handbook of childhood cognitive development.* Malden, MA: Blackwell.

Baillargeon, R. H., & Devoe, J. (1991). Object permanence in young children: Further evidence. *Child Development, 62,* 1227–1246.

Baillargeon, R. H., Zoccolillo, M., Keenna, K., Cote, S., Perusse, D., Wu, H-X., Boivin, M., & Tremblay, R. E. (2007). Gender differences in physical aggression: A prospective population-based survey of children before and after two years of age. *Developmental Psychology, 43,* 13–26.

Bajanowski, T., Brinkmann, B., Mitchell, E.A., Vennemann, M. M., Leukel, H. W., Larsch, K. P., Beike, J., & the GeSID Group. (2008). Nicotine and cotinine in infants dying from sudden infant death syndrome. *International Journal of Legal Medicine, 122,* 23–28.

Bakeman, R., & Brown, J. V. (1980). Early interaction: Consequences for social and mental development at three years. *Child Development, 51,* 437–447.

Baker, D. A. (2007). Consequences of herpes simplex virus in pregnancy and their prevention. *Current Opinions in Infectious Diseases, 20,* |73–76.

Bakermans-Kranenburg, M. J., Breddels-Van Bardewijk, F., Juffer, M. K., Velderman, M. H., & van IJzendoorn, M. H. (2007). Insecure mothers with temperamentally reactive infants. In F. Juffer, M. J. Bakermans-Kranenburg, & M. H. van IJzendoorn (Eds.), *Promoting positive parenting.* Mahwah, NJ: Erlbaum.

Balasubramanian, A., Koontz, J., & Reynolds, C. A. (2008). Genetics and inheritance. In M. M. Haith & J. B. Benson (Eds.), *Encyclopedia of infancy and early childhood development.* Oxford, UK: Elsevier.

Ballentine, J. H., & Hammock, J. H. (2009). *The sociology of education* (6th ed.). Upper Saddle River, NJ: Prentice Hall.

Baltes, P. B., Lindenberger, U., & Staudinger, U. (2006). Life span theory in developmental psychology. In W. Damon & R. Lerner (Eds.), *Handbook of child psychology* (6th ed.). New York: Wiley.

Bandura, A. (1991). Social cognitive theory of moral thought and action. In W. M. Kurtines & J. L. Gewirtz (Eds.), *Handbook of moral behavior and development* (Vol. 1). Hillsdale, NJ: Erlbaum.

Bandura, A. (1997). *Self-efficacy.* New York: W. H. Freeman.

Bandura, A. (1998, August). *Swimming against the mainstream: Accentuating the positive aspects of humanity.* Paper presented at the meeting of the American Psychological Association, San Francisco.

Bandura, A. (2000). Self-efficacy. In A. Kazdin (Ed.), *Encyclopedia of psychology.* Washington, DC, and New York: American Psychological Association and Oxford University Press.

Bandura, A. (2001). Social cognitive theory. *Annual Review of Psychology* (Vol. 52). Palo Alto, CA: Annual Reviews.

Bandura, A. (2002). Selective moral disengagement in the exercise of moral agency. *Journal of Moral Education, 31,* 101–119.

Bandura, A. (2004, May). *Toward a psychology of human agency.* Paper presented at the meeting of the American Psychological Society, Chicago.

Bandura, A. (2005). Evolution of social cognitive theory. In K. G. Smith & M. A. Hitt (Eds.), *Great minds in management* (pp. 9–35). Oxford, UK: Oxford University Press.

Bandura, A. (2006). Going global with social cognitive theory: From prospect to paydirt. In S. I. Donaldson, D. E. Berger, & K. Pezdek (Eds.). *The rise of applied psychology: New frontiers and rewarding careers.* Mahwah, NJ: Erlbaum.

Bandura, A. (2007a). Self-efficacy in health functioning. In S. Ayers & others (Eds.), *Cambridge handbook of psychology, health, and medicine,* (2nd ed.). New York: Cambridge University Press.

Bandura, A. (2007b). Social cognitive theory. In W. Donsbach (Ed.), *International encyclopedia of communication.* Thousand Oaks, CA: Sage.

Bandura, A. (2008). Reconstrual of free will from the agentic perspective of social cognitive theory. In J. Baer, J. C. Kaufman, & R. F. Baumeister (Eds.), *Are we free? Psychology and free will.* Oxford, UK: Oxford University Press.

Bandura, A. (2009, in press). Social and policy impact of social cognitive theory. In M. Mark, S. Donaldson & B. Campell (Eds.), *Social psychology and program/policy evaluation.* New York: Guilford.

Banerjee, T. D., Middleton, F., & Faraone, S. V. (2007). Environmental risk factors for -attention-deficit hyperactivity disorder. *Acta Pediatrica, 96,* 1269–1274.

Bank, L., Burraston, B., & Snyder, J. (2004). Sibling conflict and ineffective parenting as predictors of adolescent boys' antisocial behavior and peer difficulties: Additive and interactive effects. *Journal of Research on Adolescence, 14,* 99–125.

Banks, J. A. (2008). *Introduction to multicultural education* (4th ed.). Boston: Allyn & Bacon.

Banks, M. S. (2005). The benefits and costs of combining information between and within the senses. In J. J. Reiser, J. J. Lockman, & C. A. Nelson (Eds.), *The role of action in learning and development.* Mahwah, NJ: Erlbaum.

Barabasz, A., & Perez, N. (2007). Salient findings: Hypnotizability as core construct and the clinical utility of hypnosis. *International Journal of Clinical Hypnosis, 55,* 372–379.

Barajas, R. G., Philipsen, N., & Brooks-Gunn, J. (2007). Cognitive and emotional outcomes for children in poverty. In D. R. Crane & T. B. Heaton (Eds.), *Handbook of families and poverty.* Thousand Oaks, CA: Sage.

Barbaresi, W. J., Katusic, S. K., Colligan, R. C., Weaver, A. L., Leibson, C. L., & Jacobsen, S. J. (2006). Long-term stimulant medication treatment of attention-deficit/hyperactivity disorder: Results from a population-based study. *Journal of Developmental and Behavioral Pediatrics, 27,* 1–10.

Barber, B. L., & Demo, D. (2006). The kids are alright (at least most of them): Links to divorce and dissolution. In M. A. Fine & J. H. Harvey (Eds.), *Handbook of divorce and relationship dissolution.* Mahwah, NJ: Erlbaum.

Barker, R., & Wright, H. F. (1951). *One boy's day.* New York: Harper & Row.

Barnouw, V. (1975). *An introduction to anthropology: Vol. 2. Ethnology.* Homewood, IL: Dorsey Press.

Baron, N. S. (1992). *Growing up with language.* Reading, MA: Addison-Wesley.

Baron-Cohen, S. (1995). *Mindblindness: An essay on autism and theory of mind.* Cambridge, MA: MIT Press.

Baron-Cohen, S., Leslie, A. M., & Frith, U. (1985). Does the autistic child have a "theory of mind"? *Cognition, 21,* 37–46.

Barrett, T. M., & Needham, A. (2008). Developmental differences in infants' use of an object's shape to grasp it securely. *Developmental Psychobiology, 50,* 97–106.

Barrett, T. M., Davis, E. F., & Needham, A. (2007). Learning about tools in infancy. *Developmental Psychology, 43,* 352–368.

Barrett, T. M., Traupman, E., & Needham, A. (2008). Infants' visual anticipation of object structure in grasp planning. *Infant Behavior and Development, 31,* 1–9.

Barron, J., Petrilli, F., Strath, L., & McCaffrey, R. (2007). Successful interventions for smoking cessation in pregnancy. *MCN American Journal of Maternal Child Nursing, 32,* 42–47.

Bartle, C. (2007). Developing a service for children with iron deficiency anemia. *Nursing Standard, 21,* 44–49.

Bartsch, K., & Wellman, H. M. (1995). *Children talk about the mind.* Oxford University Press.

Basaran, A. (2007). Progesterone to prevent preterm delivery: Enigma or ready? *American Journal of Obstetric and Gynecology, 197,* 686.

Bass, J. E., Contant, T. L., & Carin, A. A. (2009). *Activities for teaching science as inquiry* (7th ed.). Boston: Allyn & Bacon.

Bateman, B. T., & Simpson, L. L. (2006). Higher rate of stillbirth at the extremes of reproductive age: A large nationwide sample of deliveries in the United States. *American Journal of Obstetrics and Gynecology, 194,* 840–845.

Bates, A. S., Fitzgerald, J. F., Dittus, R. S., & Wollinsky, F. D. (1994). Risk factors for under-immunization in poor urban infants. *Journal of the American Medical Association, 272,* 1105–1109.

Bates, J. E., & Pettit, G. S. (2007). Temperament, parenting, and socialization. In J. E. Grusec & P. D. Hastings (Eds.), *Handbook of socialization.* New York: Guilford.

Bates, J. E., Viken, R. J., Alexander, D. B. Beyers, J., & Stockton, L. (2002). Sleep and adjustment in preschool children: Sleep diary reports by mothers relate to behavior reports by teachers. *Child Development, 73,* 62–74.

Battistich, V. A. (2008). The Child Development Project: Creating caring school communities. In L. Nucci & D. Narvaez (Eds.), *Handbook of moral and character education.* Clifton, NJ: Psychology Press.

Bauer, P. J. (2006). Event memory. In W. Damon & R. Lerner (Eds.), *Handbook of child psychology* (6th ed.). New York: Wiley.

Bauer, P. J. (2007). *Remembering the times of our lives.* Mahwah, NJ: Erlbaum.

Bauer, P. J. (2008, in press). Learning and memory: Like a horse and Carriage. In A. Needham & A. Woodward (Eds.), *Learning and the infant mind.* New York: Oxford University Press.

Bauer, P. J., Wenner, J. A., Dropik, P. I., & Wewerka, S. S. (2000). Parameters of remembering and forgetting in the transition from infancy to early childhood. *Monographs of the Society for Research in child Development, 65* (4, Serial No. 263).

Baumeister, R. F., Campbell, J. D., Krueger, J. I., & Vohs, K. D. (2003). Does high self-esteem cause better performance, interpersonal success, happiness, or healthier lifestyles? *Psychological Science in the Public Interest, 4* (No. 1). 1–44.

Baumrind, D. (1971). Current patterns of parental authority. *Developmental Psychology Monographs, 4* (1, Pt. 2).

Baumrind, D. (1991). Effective parenting during the early adolescent transition. In P. A. Cowan & E. M. Hetherington (Eds.), *Advances in family research* (Vol. 2). Hillsdale, NJ: Erlbaum.

Baumrind, D. (1999, November). Unpublished review of J. W. Santrock's *Child development,* 9thed. (New York: McGraw-Hill).

Baumrind, D., Larzelere, R. E., & Cowan, P. A. (2002). Ordinary physical punishment: Is it harmful? Comment on Gershoff. *Psychological Bulletin, 128,* 590–595.

Bauerlein, M. (2008). *The dumbest generation: How the digital age stupefies young Americans and jeopardizes our future (Or, don't trust anyone under 30).* New York: Tarcher.

Bauserman, R. (2002). Child adjustment in joint-custody versus sole-custody arrangements: A meta-analytic review. *Journal of Family Psychology, 16,* 91–102.

Bavelier, D., & Neville, H. J. (2002). Cross-modal plasticity: Where and how? *Nature Reviews: Neuroscience, 3,* 443–452.

Bayley, N. (1969). *Manual for the Bayley Scales of Infant Development.* New York: Psychological Corporation.

Bayley, N. (2006). *Bayley Scales of Infant and Toddler Development* (3rd ed.). San Antonio: Harcourt Assessment.

Bearman, S. K., Presnall, K., Martinez, E., & Stice, E. (2006). The skinny on body dissatisfaction: A longitudinal study of adolescent girls and boys. *Journal of Youth and Adolescence, 35,* 217–229.

Beaulieu, D. A., & Bugental, D. B. (2007). An evolutionary approach to socialization. In J. E. Grusec & P. D. Hastings (Eds.), *Handbook of socialization.* New York: Guilford.

Bech, B. H., Obel, C., Henriksen, T. B., & Olsen, J. (2007). Effect of reducing caffeine intake on birth weight and length of gestation: Randomized controlled trial. *British Medical Journal, 334,* 409.

Bechtold, A. G., Busnell, E. W., & Salapatek, P. (1979, April.) *Infants' visual localization of visual and auditory targets.* Paper presented at the meeting of the Society for Research in Child Development, San Francisco.

Beck, C. T. (2002). Theoretical perspectives of postpartum depression and their treatment implications. *American Journal of Maternal/Child Nursing, 27,* 282–287.

Beck, C. T. (2006). Postpartum depression: It isn't just the blues. *American Journal of Nursing, 106,* 40–50.

Beckmann, M. M., & Garrett, A. J. (2006). Antenatal perineal massage for reducing perineal trauma. *Cochrane Database of Systematic Reviews, 1,* CD005123.

Beeghly, M., Martin, B., Rose-Jacobs, R., Cahral, H., Heeren, T., Augustyn, M., Bellinger, D., & Frank, D. A. (2006). Prenatal cocaine exposure and children's language functioning at 6 and 9.5 years: Moderating effects of child age, birthweight, and gender. *Journal of Pediatric Psychology, 31,* 98–115.

Beets, M. W., & Foley, J. T. (2008). Association of father involvement and neighborhood quality with kindergartners' physical activity: A multilevel structural equation model. *American Journal of Health Promotion, 22,* 195–203.

Beghetto, R. A., & Kaufman, J. C. (2009, in press). *Nurturing creativity in the classroom.* New York: Cambridge University Press.

Begley, S., & Interlandi, J. (2008, July 2). The dumbest generation? Don't be dumb.

Newsweek, retrieved July 15, 2008, from www.newsweek.com/id/138536

Beilock, S. L., Rydell, R. J., & McConnell, A. R. (2007). Stereotype threat and working memory: mechanisms, alleviation, and spillover. *Journal of Experimental Psychology: General, 136,* 256–276.

Bell, S. M., & Ainsworth, M. D. S. (1972). Infant crying and maternal responsiveness. *Child Development, 43,* 1171–1190.

Bellinger, D., Leviton, A, Waternaux, C., Needleman, H., & Rabinowitz, M. (1987). Longitudinal analysis of prenatal and postnatal lead exposure and early cognitive development. *New England Journal of Medicine, 316,* 1037–1043.

Belsky, J. (1981). Early human experience: A family perspective. *Developmental Psychology, 17,* 3–23.

Belsky, J. (2009a, in press). Social-contextual determinants of parenting. In R. E. Tremblay, R. deV Peters, M. Boivan, & R. G. Barr (Eds.), *Encyclopedia on early childhood development.* Montreal: Centre of Excellence for Early Childhood Development.

Belsky, J. (2009b, in press). Child care and its impact on young children (0–2). In R. E. Tremblay, R. deV Peters, M. Boivan, & R. G. Barr (Eds.), *Encyclopedia on early childhood development.* Montreal: Centre of Excellence for Early Childhood Development.

Belsky, J., Vandell, D. L., Burchinal, M., Clarke-Stewart, A., McCartney, K., Owen, M. T., & the NICHD Early Child Care Research Network. (2007). Are there long-term effects of early child care. *Child Development, 78,* 681–701.

Belson, W. (1978). *Television violence and the adolescent boy.* London: Saxon House.

Bem, S. (1997). On the utility of alternative procedures for assessing psychological androgyny. *Journal of Consulting and Clinical Psychology, 45,* 196–205.

Bender, H. L., Allen, J. P., McElhaney, K. B., Antonishak, J., Moore, C. M., Kello, H. O., & Davis, S. M. (2007). Use of harsh physical discipline and developmental outcomes in adolescence. *Development and Psychopathology, 19,* 227–242.

Bender, W. N. (2008). *Learning disabilities* (6thed.). Boston: Allyn & Bacon.

Bendersky, M., & Sullivan, M. W. (2007). Basic methods in infant research. In A. Slater & M. Lewis (Eds.), *Infant development,* (2nd ed.). New York: Oxford University Press.

Benner, A. D., & Mistry, R. S. (2007). Congruence of mother and teacher educational expectations and low-income youth's academic competence. *Journal of Educational Psychology, 99,* 140–153.

Bennett, C. I. (2007). *Comprehensive multicultural education* (6th ed.). Boston: Allyn & Bacon.

Bennett, T., Szatmari, P., Bryson, S., Volden, J., Zwaigenbaum, L., Vaccarella, L., Duku, E., & Boyle, M. (2008). Differentiating autism and Asperger syndrome on the basis of language delay or impairment. *Journal of Autism and Developmental Disorders, 38,* 616–625.

Benoit, D. (2009, in press). Efficacy of attachment-based interventions. In R. E. Tremblay, R. deV Peters, M. Boivin, & R. G. Barr (Eds.), *Encyclopedia on early childhood development.* Montreal: Centre of Excellence for Early Childhood Development.

Benoit, D., Coolbear, J., & Crawford, A. (2008). Abuse, neglect, and maltreatment of infants. In M. M. Haith & J. B. Benson (Eds.), *Encyclopedia of infant and early childhood development.* Oxford, UK: Elsevier.

Benson, A. C., Torode, M. E., & Fiatarone Singh, M. A. (2008, in press). The effects of high-intensity progressive resistance training on adiposity in children: A randomized controlled trial. *International Journal of Obesity.*

Benveniste, L., Carnoy, M., & Rothstein, R. (2003). *All else equal.* New York: Routledge-Farmer.

Beran, T. N., & Tutty, L. (2002). *An evaluation of the Bully Proofing Your School, School Program,* Unpublished manuscript, Calgary: RESOLVE, Alberta, CAN.

Bereiter, C., & Scaramalia, M. (2006). Education for the knowledge age: Design-centered models of teaching and instruction. In P. A. Alexander & P. H. Winner (Eds.), *Handbook of educational psychology* (2nd ed.). Mahwah, NJ: Erlbaum.

Berenbaum, S. A., & Bailey, J. M. (2003). Effects on gender identity of prenatal androgens and genital appearance: Evidence from girls with congenital adrenal hyperplasia. *Journal of Clinical Endocrinology and Metabolism, 88,* 1102–1106.

Berenbaum, S. A., & Korman Bryk, K. L. (2008). Biological contributions to gendered occupational outcome: Prenatal androgen effects on predictors of outcomes. In H. M. G. Watt & J. S. Eccles (Eds.), *Gender and occupational outcomes.* Washington, DC: American Psychological Association.

Bergen, D. (1988). Stages of play development. In D. Bergen (Ed.), *Play as a medium for learning and development.* Portsmouth, NH: Heinemann.

Berk, L. E. (1994). Why children talk to themselves. *Scientific American, 271* (5), 78–83.

Berk, L. E., & Spuhl, S. T. (1995). Maternal interaction, private speech, and task performance in preschool children. *Early Childhood Research Quarterly, 10,* 145–169.

Berko, J. (1958). The child's learning of English morphology. *Word, 14,* 15–177.

Berko Gleason, J. (2003). Unpublished review of J. W. Santrock's *Life-span development,* 9th ed. (New York: McGraw-Hill).

Berko Gleason, J. (2005). The development of language: An overview and a preview. In J. Berko Gleason (Ed.), *The development of language* (6th ed.). Boston: Allyn & Bacon.

Berko Gleason, J. (2009). The development of language: An overview. In J. Berko Gleason & N. Ratner (Eds.), *The development of language* (7th ed.). Boston: Allyn & Bacon.

Berkowitz, M. W., Battistich, V. A., & Bier, M. (2008). What works in character education: What is known and what needs to be known. In L. Nucci & D Narvaez (Eds.), *Handbook of moral and character education.* Clifton, NJ: Psychology Press.

Berlin, L., & Cassidy, J. (2000). Understanding parenting: Contributions of attachment theory and research. In J. D. Osofsky & H. E. Fitzgerald (Eds.), *WAIMH handbook of infant mental health* (Vol. 3). New York: Wiley.

Berlyne, D. E. (1960). *Conflict, arousal, and curiosity.* New York: McGraw-Hill.

Bern, S. L. (1977). On the utility of alternative procedures for assessing psychological androgyny. *Journal of Consulting and Clinical Psychology, 45,* 196–205.

Bernard, K., & Dozier, M. (2008). Adoption and foster placement. In M. M. Haith & J. B. Benson (Eds.), *Encyclopedia of infant and early childhood development.* Oxford, UK: Elsevier.

Berndt, T. J. (1982). The features and effects of friendships in early adolescence. *Child Development, 53,* 1447–1460.

Berndt, T. J. (1999). Friends' influence on children's adjustment. In W. A. Collins & B. Laursen (Eds.), *Relationships as developmental contexts.* Mahwah, NJ: Erlbaum.

Berndt, T. J., & Perry, T. B. (1990). Distinctive features and effects of early adolescent friendships. In R. Montemayor (Ed.), *Advances in adolescent research.* Greenwich, CT: JAI Press.

Berninger, V. W. (2006). Learning disabilities. In W. Damon & R. Lerner (Eds.), *Handbook of child psychology* (6th ed.). New York: Wiley.

Berninger, V. W., & Abbott, R. (2005, April). *Paths leading to reading comprehension in at-risk and normally developing second-grade readers.* Paper presented at the meeting of the Society for Research in Child Development, Atlanta.

Berry, J. W. (2007). Acculturation. In J. E. Grusec & P. D. Hastings (Eds.), *Handbook of socialization.* New York: Guilford.

Bertenthal, B. L. (2008). Perception and action. In M. M. Haith & J. B. Benson (Eds.), *Encyclopedia of infant and early childhood development.* Oxford, UK: Elsevier.

Betts, J., McKay, J., Maruff, P., & Anderson, V. (2006). The development of sustained attention in children: The effect of age and task load. *Child Neuropsychology, 12,* 205–221.

Betz, N. E. (2004). Contributions of self—efficacy theory to career counseling: A personal perspective. *Career Development Quarterly, 52,* 340–353.

Bhatara, V. S., & Aparasu, R. R. (2007). Pharmacotherapy with atomoxetine for U.S. children and adolescents. *Annals of Clinical Psychiatry, 19,* 175–180.

Bialystok, E. (1997). Effects of bilingualism and biliteracy on children's emerging concepts of print. *Developmental Psychology, 33,* 429–440.

Bialystok, E. (2001). *Bilingualism in development: Language, literacy, and cognition.* New York: Cambridge University Press.

Bialystok, E. (2007). Acquisition of literacy in preschool children: A framework for research. *Language Learning, 57,* 45–77.

Bialystok, E. (2009, in press). Second-language acquisition and bilingualism at an early age and the impact on early cognitive development. In R. E. Tremblay, R. deV Peters, M. Boivin, & R. G. Barr (Eds.), *Encyclopedia on early childhood development.* Montreal: Centre of Excellence for Early Childhood Development.

Bianco, I. H., Carl, M., Russell, C., Clarke, J.D., & Wilson, S. W. (2008). Brain asymmetry is encoded at the level of axon terminal morphology. *Neural Development, 3,* 9.

Bibok, M. B., Carpendale, J. I. M., & Lewis, C. (2008). Social knowledge and social skill: An action-based view of social understanding. In U.Mueller, J. I. M. Carpendale, N. Budwig, & B. W. Sokol (Eds.), *Social life and social knowledge.* Philadelphia: Psychology Press.

Biederman, J. (2007). Advances in the neurobiology of ADHD. *CNS Spectrums, 12* (Suppl. 4), S6–S7.

Biehl, M. C., Natsuaki, M. N., & Ge, X. (2007). The influence of pubertal timing on alcohol use and heavy drinking trajectories. *Journal of Youth and Adolescence, 36,* 153–167.

Bill and Melinda Gates Foundation. (2006). *The silent epidemic: Perspectives on high school dropouts.* Seattle: Author.

Bill and Melinda Gates Foundation. (2008). *Report gives voice to dropouts.* Retrieved July 5, 2008, from www.gatesfoundation.org/UnitedStates/Education/TransformingHighSchools/Related...

Billson, F. A., Fitzgerald, B. A., & Provis, J.M. (1985). Visual deprivation in infancy and childhood: Clinical aspects. *Australian and New Zealand Journal of Ophthalmology, 13,* 279–286.

Billy, J. O. G., Rodgers, J. L., & Udry, J. R. (1984). Adolescent sexual behavior and friendship choice. *Social Forces, 62,* 653–678.

Binder, T., & Vavrinkova, B. (2008). Prospective randomized comparative study of the effect of buprenorphine, methadone, and heroin on the course of pregnancy, birthweight of newborns, early postpartum adaptation, and the course of neonatal abstinence syndrome (NAS). *Neuroendocrinology Letters, 29,* 80–86.

Birch, E. E., Morale, S. E., Jeffrey, B. G., O'Connor, A. R., & Fawcett, S. L. (2005).

Measurement of stereoacuity outcomes at ages 1 to 24 months: Random stereocards. *Journal of AAPOS, 9,* 31–36.

Birch, S., & Bloom, P. (2003). Children are cursed: An asymmetric bias in mental state attribution. *Psychological Science, 14,* 283–286.

Birnbach, D. J., & Ranasinghe, J. S. (2008). Anesthesia complications in the birthplace: Is the neuraxial block always to blame? *Clinical Perinatology, 35,* 35–52.

Birren, J. E. (Ed.). (2007). *Encyclopedia of gerontology* (2nd ed.). Oxford, UK: Elsevier.

Bishop, K. M., & Wahlsten, D. (1997). Sex differences in the human corpus callosum: Myth or reality? *Neuroscience and Biobehavioral Reviews, 21,* 581–601.

Bjorklund, D. F. (2005). *Children's thinking* (4th ed.). Belmont, CA: Wadsworth.

Bjorklund, D. F. (2006). Mother knows best: Epigenetic inheritance, maternal effects, and the evolution of human intelligence. *Developmental Review, 26,* 213–242.

Bjorklund, D. F. (2007). *Why youth is not wasted on the young.* Malden, MA: Blackwell.

Bjorklund, D. F., & Pellegrini, A. D. (2002). *The origins of human nature.* New York: Oxford University Press.

Bjorklund, D. F., & Rosenbaum, K. (2000). Middle childhood: Cognitive development. In A. Kazdin (Ed.), *Encyclopedia of psychology.* Washington, DC, & New York: American Psychological Association and Oxford University Press.

Black, M. M., & Hurley, K. M. (2007). Helping children develop healthy eating habits. In Tremblay, R. E., Barr, R. G., Peters, R. D., & Boivin, M. (Eds.), *Encyclopedia on early childhood development.* Retrieved March 19, 2008, from www.child-encyclopedia.com/documents/BlackHurleyANGxp_rev-Eating.pdf

Black, M. M., & Hurley, K. M. (2009, in press). Helping children develop healthy eating habits. In R. E. Tremblay, R. deV Peters, M. Boivin, & R. G. Barr (Eds.), *Encyclopedia on early childhood development.* Montreal: Centre of Excellence for Early Childhood Development.

Black, M. M., & Lozoff, B. (2008). Nutrition and diet. In M. M. Haith & J. B. Benson (Eds.), *Encyclopedia of infant and early childhood development.* Oxford, UK: Elsevier.

Blaine, S. M., & others. (2008, in press). Interactive genetic counseling role-play: A novel educational strategy for family physicians. *Journal of Genetic Counseling.*

Blakemore, J. E. O., Berenbaum, S. A., & Liben, L. S. (2009). *Gender development.* Clifton, NJ: Psychology Press.

Blanton, H., & Burkley, M. (2008). Deviance regulation theory: Applications to adolescent social influence. In M. J. Prinstein & K. A. Dodge (Eds.), *Understanding peer influence in children and adolescents.* New York: Guilford.

Blasi, A. (2005). Moral character: A psychological approach. In D. K. Lapsley & F. C. Power (Eds.), *Character psychology and character education.* Notre Dame, IN: University of Notre Dame Press.

Blass, E. (2008). Suckling. In M. M. Haith & J. B. Benson (Eds.), *Encyclopedia of infant and early childhood development.* Oxford, UK: Elsevier.

Block, J. (1993). Studying personality the long way. In D. Funder, R. D. Parke, C. Tomlinson-Keasey, & K. Widaman (Ed.), *Studying lives through time.* Washington, DC: American Psychological Association.

Block, J. H., & Block, J. (1980). The role of ego-control and ego-resiliency in the organization of behavior. In W. A. Collins (Ed.), *Minnesota symposium on child psychology* (Vol. 13). Minneapolis: University of Minnesota Press.

Bloom, B. (1985). *Developing talent in young people.* New York: Ballentine.

Bloom, L. (1998). Language acquisition in its developmental context. In W. Damon (Ed.), *Handbook of child psychology* (5th ed., Vol. 2). New York: Wiley.

Bloom, L., Lifter, K., & Broughton, J. (1985). The convergence of early cognition and language in the second year of life: Problems in conceptualization and measurement. In M. Barrett (Ed.), *Single word speech.* London: Wiley.

Bloom, P., & German, T. P. (2000). Two reasons to abandon the false belief task as a test of theory of mind. *Cognition, 77,* B25–B31.

Blum, J. W., Beaudoin, C. M., & Caton-Lemos, L. (2005). Physical activity patterns and maternal well-being in postpartum women. *Maternal and Child Health Journal, 8,* 163–169.

Blumenfeld, P. C., Kempler, T. M., & Krajcik, J. S. (2006). Motivation and cognitive engagement in learning environments. In R. K. Sawyer (Ed.), *The Cambridge handbook of the learning sciences.* New York: Cambridge University Press.

Blumenfeld, P. C., Marx, R. W., & Harris, C. J. (2006). Learning environments. In W. Damon & R. Lerner (Eds.), *Handbook of child psychology* (6th ed.). New York: Wiley.

Blumenfeld, P. C., Pintrich, P. R., Wessles, K., & Meece, J. (1981, April). *Age and sex differences in the impact of classroom experiences on self-perceptions.* Paper presented at the biennial meeting of the Society of Research in Child Development, Boston.

Bo, I. (1994). The sociocultural environment as a source of support. In F. Nestmann & K. Hurrelmann (Eds.), *Social networks and social support in childhood and adolescence.* New York: Walter de Gruyter.

Bodrova, E., & Leong, D. J. (2007). *Tools of the mind* (2nd ed.). Geneva, Switzerland: International Bureau of Education. UNESCO.

Boekaerts, M. (2006). Self-regulation and effort investment. In W. Damon & R. Lerner (Eds.), *Handbook of child psychology* (6th ed.). New York: Wiley.

Boer, K., Nellen, J. F., Patel, D., Timmermans, S., Tempelman, C., Wibaut, M. Sluman, M. A., van der Ende, M. E., & Godfried, M. H. (2007). The AmRo study: Pregnancy outcomes in HIV-1-infected women under effective highly active antiretroviral therapy and a policy of vaginal delivery. *British Journal of Obstetrics and Gynecology, 114,* 148–155.

Boeving, C. A., & Forsyth, B. (2008). AIDS and HIV. In M. M. Haith & J. B. Benson (Eds.), *Encyclopedia of infant and early childhood development.* London, UK: Elsevier.

Bohannon, J. N., & Bonvillian, J. D. (2009). Theoretical approaches to language acquisition. In J. Berko Gleason & N. B. Ratner (Eds.), *The development of language.* Boston: Allyn & Bacon.

Bohlin, G., & Hagekull, B. (1993). Stranger wariness and sociability in the early years. *Infant Behavior and Development, 16,* 53–67.

Bolling, C. F., & Daniel, S. R. (2008). Obesity. In M. M. Haith & J. B. Benson (Eds.), *Encyclopedia of infant and early childhood development.* Oxford, UK: Elsevier.

Bonvillian, J. (2005). Unpublished review of J. W. Santrock's *Topical life-span development,* 3rd ed. (New York: McGraw-Hill).

Booth, A. (2006). Object function and categorization in infancy: Two mechanisms of facilitation. *Infancy, 10,* 145–169.

Booth, M. (2002). Arab adolescents facing the future: Enduring ideals and pressures to change. In B. B. Brown, R. W. Larson, & T. S. Saraswathi (Eds.), *The world's youth.* New York: Cambridge University Press.

Bornstein, M. H. (1975). Qualities of color vision in infancy. *Journal of Experimental Child Psychology, 19,* 401–409.

Bornstein, M. H. (2002). Parenting infants. In M. H. Bornstein (Ed.), *Handbook of parenting* (2nd ed., Vol. 1). Mahwah, NJ: Erlbaum.

Bornstein, M. H. (2006). Parenting: Science and practice. In W. Damon & R. Lerner (Eds.), *Handbook of child psychology* (6th ed.). New York: Wiley.

Bornstein, M. H., & Cote, L. R. (Eds.). (2006). *Acculturation and parent-child relationships.* Mahwah, NJ: Erlbaum.

Bornstein, M. H., & Sigman, M. D. (1986). Continuity in mental development from infancy. *Child Development, 57,* 251–274.

Bornstein, M. H., & Tamis-Lemonda, S. (2007). Infants at play: Development, functions, and partners. In A. Slater & M. Lewis (Eds.), *Introduction to infant development* (2nd ed.). New York: Oxford University Press.

Bornstein, M. H., & Zlotnik, D. (2008). Parenting styles and their effects. In M. M. Haith & J. B. Benson (Ed.), *Encyclopedia of infant and early childhood development.* Oxford, UK: Elsevier.

Borowski, K., & Niebyl, J. R. (2008). Drugs in pregnancy. In J. Studd, S. L. Tan, & F. A. Cherenak (Eds.), *Progress in obstetrics and gynecology.* London: Elsevier.

Bouchard, T. J., Lykken, D. T., McGue, M., Segal, N. L., & Tellegen, A. (1990). Source of human psychological differences. The Minnesota Study of Twins Reared Apart. *Science, 250,* 223–228.

Boukydis, C. F. Z., & Lester, B. (2008). Mother-infant consultation during drug treatment: Research and innovative clinical practice. *Harm Reduction Journal, 5,* 6.

Boulware-Gooden, R., Carreker, S., Thornill, A., & Joshi, R. M. (2007). Instruction of metacognitive strategies enhances reading comprehension and vocabulary achievement of third-grade students. *Reading Teacher, 61,* 70–77.

Bower, J. K., Hales, D. P., Tate, D. F., Rubin, D. A., Benjamin, S. E., & Ward, D. S. (2008). The childcare environment and children's physical activity. *American Journal of Preventive Medicine, 34,* 23–29.

Bower, T. G. R. (1966). Slant perception and shape constancy in infants. *Science, 151,* 832–834.

Bower, T. G. R. (2002). Space and Objects. In A. Slater & M. Lewis (Eds.), *Introduction to infant development.* New York: Oxford University Press.

Bowlby, J. (1969). *Attachment and loss* (Vol. 1). London: Hogarth Press.

Bowlby, J. (1989). *Secure and insecure attachment.* New York: Basic Books.

Bowles, T. (1999). Focusing on time orientation to explain adolescent self concept and academic achievement: Part II. Testing a model. *Journal of Applied Health Behavior, 1,* 1–8.

Bowman, M. A., Prelow, H. M., & Weaver, S. R. (2007). Parenting behaviors, association with deviant peers, and delinquency in African American adolescents: A mediated-moderation model. *Journal of Youth and Adolescence, 36,* 517–527.

Boyer, K., & Diamond, A. (1992). Development of memory for temporal order in infants and young children. In A. Diamond (Ed.), *Development and neural bases of higher cognitive function.* New York: New York Academy of Sciences.

Boyum, L., & Parke, R. D. (1995). Family emotional expressiveness and children's social competence. *Journal of Marriage and the Family, 57,* 593–608.

Bracey, J. R., Bamaca, M. Y., & Umana-Taylor, A. J. (2004). Examining ethnic identity among biracial and monoracial adolescents. *Journal of Youth and Adolescence, 33,* 123–132.

Bracken, M. B., Eskenazi, B., Sachse, K., McSharry, J., Hellenbrand, K., & Leo-Summers, L. (1990). Association of cocaine use with sperm concentration, motility, and morphology. *Fertility and Sterility, 53,* 315–322.

Bradley, R. H., & Corwyn, R. F. (2008). Infant temperament, parenting, and externalizing behavior in first grade: A test of the differential susceptibility hypothesis. *Journal of Child Psychology and Psychiatry, 49,* 124–131.

Bradley, R. H., Corwyn, R. F., McAdoo, H., & Coll, C. (2001). The home environments of children in the United States: Part I. Variations by age, ethnicity, and poverty status. *Child Development, 72,* 1844–1867.

Brainerd, C. J., & Gordon, L. L. (1994). Development of verbatim and gist memory for numbers. *Developmental Psychology, 30,* 163–177.

Brainerd, C. J., & Reyna, V. F. (2004). Fuzzytrace theory and memory development. *Developmental Review, 24,* 396–439.

Bransford, J., & others (2006). Learning theories in education. In P. A. Alexander & P. H. Winne (Eds.), *Handbook of educational psychology* (2nd ed.). Mahwah, NJ: Erlbaum.

Brazelton, T. B. (1956). Sucking in infancy. *Pediatrics, 17,* 400–404.

Brazelton, T. B., (2004). Preface: The Neonatal Intensive Care Unit Network Neurobehavioral Scale. *Pediatrics; 113* (Suppl.), S632–S633.

Bremner, G. (2007). Perception and knowledge of the world. In A. Slater & M. Lewis (Eds.), *Introduction to infant development* (2nded.). Malden, MA: Blackwell.

Brent, R. L. (2008). Environmental causes of human congenital malformations. In J. Studd, S. L. Tan, & F. A. Cherenak (Eds.), *Progress in obstetrics and gynecology.* London: Elsevier.

Breslau, N., Paneth, N. S., & Lucia, V. C. (2004). The lingering academic deficits of low birth weight children. *Pediatrics, 114,* 1035–1040.

Bretherton, I., & Munholland, K. A. (2009). Internal working models in attachment relationships: Elaborating a central construct in attachment theory. In J. Cassidy & P. R. Shaver (Eds.), *Handbook of attachment* (2nd Ed.). New York: Guilford.

Bretherton, I., Stolberg, U., & Kreye, M. (1981). Engaging strangers in proximal interaction: Infants' social initiative. *Developmental Psychology, 17,* 746–755.

Brewer, J. A. (2007). *Introduction to early childhood education* (6th ed.). Boston: Allyn & Bacon.

Brewer, M. (2007). The social psychology of intergroup relations: Social categorization, in group bias, and outgroup prejudice. In A. W. Kruglanski & E. T. Higgins (Eds.), *Social psychology: handbook of basic principles* (2nd ed.). New York: Guilford.

Brewer, M. B., & Campbell, D. T. (1976). *Ethnocentrism and intergroup attitudes.* New York: Wiley.

Briggs, T. W. (2004, October 14). *USA Today's* 2004 all-USA teacher team. *USA Today,* p. 6D.

Briggs, T. W. (2005, October 13). *USA Today's* 2005 all-USA teacher team. *USA Today,* p. 6D.

Bril, B. (1999). Dires sur l'enfant selon les cultures. Etat des lieux et perspectives. In B. Bril, P.R. Dasen, C. Sabatier, & B. Krewer (Eds.), *Propos sur l'enfant et l'adolescent. Quels enfants pour quelles cultures?* Paris: L'Harmattan.

Brislin, R. (1993). *Understanding culture's influence on behavior.* Fort Worth, TX: Harcourt Brace.

Brock, J. (2007). Language abilities in Williams syndrome: A critical review. *Developmental Psychopathology, 19,* 97–127.

Brockmeyer, S., Treboux, D., & Crowell, J. A. (2005, April). *Parental divorce and adult children's attachment status and marital relationships.* Paper presented at the meeting of the Society for Research in Child Development. Atlanta.

Brody, G. H., Ge, X., Conger, R. D., Gibbons, F., Murry, V., Gerrard, M., & Simons, R. (2001). The influence of neighborhood disadvantage, collective socialization, and parenting on African American children's affiliation with deviant peers. *Child Development, 72,* 1231–1246.

Brody, N. (2000). Intelligence. In A. Kazdin (Ed.), *Encyclopedia of psychology.* Washington, DC, & New York: American Psychological Association and Oxford University Press.

Brody, N. (2007). Does education influence intelligence? In P. C. Kyllonen, R. D. Roberts, & L. Stankov (Eds.), *Extending intelligence.* Mahwah, NJ: Erlbaum.

Brodzinsky, D. M., & Pinderhughes, E. (2002). Parenting and child development in adoptive families. In M. H. Bornstein (Ed.), *Handbook of parenting* (Vol. 1). Mahwah, NJ: Erlbaum.

Brodzinsky, D. M., Lang, R., & Smith, D. W. (1995). Parenting adopted children. In M. H. Bornstein (Ed.). *Handbook of parenting* (Vol. 3). Hillsdale, NJ: Erlbaum.

Bromage, D. I. (2006). Prenatal diagnosis and selective abortion: A result of the cultural turn. *Medical Humanities, 32,* 38-42.

Bronfenbrenner, U. (1986). Ecology of the family as a context for human development: Research perspectives. *Developmental Psychology, 22,* 723–742.

Bronfenbrenner, U. (1995). Developmental ecology through space and time: A future perspective. In P. Moen, G. H. Elder, & K. Lüscher (Eds.), *Examining lives in context.* Washington, DC: American Psychological Association.

Bronfenbrenner, U. (2000). Ecological theory. In A. Kazdin (Ed.), *Encyclopedia of psychology.* Washington, DC, & New York: American Psychological Association and Oxford University Press.

Bronfenbrenner, U. (2004). *Making human beings human.* Thousand Oaks, CA: Sage.

Bronfenbrenner, U., & Morris, P. (1998). The ecology of developmental processes. In W. Damon (Ed.), *Handbook of child psychology* (5th ed., Vol. 1). New York: Wiley.

Bronfenbrenner, U., & Morris, P. A. (2006). The ecology of developmental processes. In

W. Damon & R. Lerner (Eds.), *Handbook of child psychology* (6th ed.). New York: Wiley.

Bronstein, P. (2006). The family environment: Where gender role socialization begins. In J. Worell & C. D. Goodheart (Eds.), *Handbook of girl's and women's psychological health.* New York: Oxford University Press.

Brook, J. S., Brook, D. W., Gordon, A. S., Whiteman, M., & Cohen, P. (1990). The psychological etiology of adolescent drug use: A family interactional approach. *Genetic, Social, and General Psychology Monographs, 116,* 110–267.

Brooker, R. J. (2009). *Genetics* (3rd ed.). New York: McGraw-Hill.

Brooks, J. G., & Brooks, M. G. (1993). *The case for constructivist classrooms.* Alexandria, VA: Association for Supervision and Curriculum.

Brooks, J. G., & Brooks, M. G. (2001). *The case for constructivist classrooms* (2nd ed.). Upper Saddle River, NJ: Erlbaum.

Brooks, R., & Meltzoff, A. N. (2005). The development of gaze following and its relation to language. *Developmental Science, 8,* 535–543.

Brooks-Gunn, J. (2003). Do you believe in magic?: What we can expect from early childhood programs. *Social Policy Report, Society for Research in Child Development, XVII* (No. 1), 1–13.

Brooks-Gunn, J., & Donahue, E. H. (2008). Introducing the issue. *Future of Children, 18* (No.1), 3–10.

Brooks-Gunn, J., & Warren, M. P. (1989). The psychological significance of secondary sexual characteristics in 9- to 11-year-old girls. *Child Development, 59,* 161–169.

Brookshear, J. G. (2009). *Computer science* (10th ed.). Upper Saddle River, NJ: Addison-Wesley.

Brophy, J. (2004). *Motivating students to learn* (2nd ed.). Mahwah, NJ: Erlbaum.

Brosco, J. P., Mattingly, M., & Sanders, L. M. (2006). Impact of specific medical interventions on reducing the prevalence of mental retardation. *Archives of Pediatric and Adolescent Medicine, 160,* 302–309.

Broverman, L., Vogel. S., Broverman, D., Clarkson, F., & Rosenkranz, P. (1972). Sex-role stereotypes: A current appraisal. *Journal of Social Issues, 28,* 59–78.

Brown, A. L. (1990). Domain-specific principles affect learning and transfer in children. *Cognitive Science, 14,* 107–133.

Brown, A. L. (1997). Transforming schools into communities of learners. *American Psychologist, 52,* 399–409.

Brown, A. L. (1998, April). *Reciprocal teaching.* Paper presented at the meeting of the American Educational Research Association, San Diego.

Brown, A. L., & Campione, J. C. (1996). Psychological learning theory and the design of innovative environments. In L. Schauble & R. Glaser (Eds.), *Contributions of instructional innovation to understanding learning.* Mahwah, NJ: Erlbaum.

Brown, A. L., & Day, J. D. (1983). Macrorules for summarizing texts: The development of expertise. *Journal of Verbal Learning and Verbal Behavior, 22,* 1–14.

Brown, A. L., Kane, M. J., & Echols, K. (1986). Young children's mental models determine analogical transfer across problems with a common goal structure. *Cognitive Development, 1,* 103–122.

Brown, B. B. (1999). Measuring the peer environment of American adolescents. In S. L. Friedman & T. D. Wachs (Eds.), *Measuring environment across the life span.* Washington, DC: American Psychological Association.

Brown, B. B. (2003). Crowds, cliques, & friendships. In G. Adams & M. Berzonsky (Eds.), *Blackwell handbook of adolescence.* Malden, MA: Blackwell.

Brown, B. B. (2004). Adolescents' relationships with peers. In R. Lerner & L. Steinberg (Eds.), *Handbook of adolescent Psychology* (2nd ed.). New York: Wiley.

Brown, B. B., & Larson, R. W. (2002). The kaleidoscope of adolescence: Experiences of the world's youth at the beginning of the 21st century. In B. B. Brown, R. W. Larson, & T. S. Saraswathi (Eds.), *The world's youth.* New York: Cambridge University Press.

Brown, B. B., & Lohr, M. J. (1987). Peer-group affiliation and adolescent self-esteem: An integration of ego-identity and symbolic-interaction theories. *Journal of Personality and Social Psychology, 52,* 47–55.

Brown, B. B., Bakken, J. P., Ameringer, S.W., & Mahon, S. D. (2008). A comprehensive conceptualization of the peer influence process in adolescence. In M. J. Prinstein & K.A. Dodge (Eds.), *Understanding peer influence in children and adolescents.* New York: Guilford.

Brown, L. M., & Gilligan, C. (1992). *Meeting at the crossroads: Women's and girls' development.* Cambridge, MA: Harvard University Press.

Brown, M., Keynes, R., & Lumsden, A. (2001). *The developing brain.* New York: Oxford University Press.

Brown, R. (1958). *Words and things.* Glencoe, IL: Free Press.

Brown, R. (1973). *A first language: The early stages.* Cambridge, MA: Harvard University Press.

Brownell, C. A., Ramani, G. B., & Zerwas, S. (2006). Becoming a social partner with peers: Cooperation and social understanding in one- and two-year-olds. *Child Development, 77,* 803–821.

Bruce, J. M., Olen, K., & Jensen, S. J. (1999, April). *The role of emotion and regulation in social competence.* Paper presented at the meeting of the Society in Research in Child Development, Albuquerque, NM.

Bruck, M., & Ceci, S. J. (1999). The suggestibility of children's memory. *Annual Review of Psychology, 50,* 419–439.

Bruck, M., Ceci, S. J., & Hembrooke, H. (1998). Reliability and credibility of young children's reports: From research to policy and practice. *American Psychologist, 53*(2), 136–151.

Bruck, M., Ceci, S. J., & Principe, G. F. (2006). The child and the law. In W. Damon & R. Lerner (Eds.), *Handbook of child psychology* (6th ed.). New York: Wiley.

Bruck, M., & Melnyk, L. (2004). Individual differences in children's suggestibility: A review and a synthesis. *Applied Cognitive Psychology, 18,* 947–996.

Brune, C. W., & Woodward, A. L. (2007). Social cognition and social responsiveness in 10-month-old infants. *Journal of Cognition and Development, 2,* 3–27.

Bruner, J. S. (1983). *Child Talk.* New York: W. W. Norton.

Bruner, J. S. (1996). *The culture of education.* Cambridge, MA: Harvard University Press.

Bruni, O., Ferri, R., Novelli, L., Finotti, E., Miano, S., & Guilleminault, C. (2008, in press). NREM sleep instability in children with sleep terrors: The role of slow wave activity interruptions. *Clinical Neuropsychology.*

Brunstein Klomek, A., Marrocco, F., Kleinman, M., Schofeld, I. S., & Gould, M. S. (2007). Bullying, depression, and suicidality in adolescents. *Journal of the American Academy of Child and Adolescent Psychiatry, 46,* 40–49.

Bryant, D. P., Smith, D. D., & Bryant, B. R. (2008). *Teaching students with special needs in inclusive classrooms.* Boston: Allyn & Bacon.

Bryant, J. A. (Ed.). (2007). *The children's television community.* Mahwah, NJ: Erlbaum.

Bryant, J. B. (2009). Language in social contexts. In J. Berko Gleason & N. B. Ratner (Eds.), *The development of language* (7th ed.). Boston: Allyn & Bacon.

Bryce, J., Coitinho, D., Darnton-Hill, I., Pelletier, D., Pinstrup-Andersen, P., & the Maternal and Child Undernutrition Study Group. (2008). Maternal and child undernutrition: Effective action at the national level. *Lancet, 371,* 510–526.

Bugental, D., & Grusec, J. (2006). Socialization processes. In W. Damon & R. Lerner (Eds.), *Handbook of child psychology* (6thed.). New York: Wiley.

Buhrmester, D. (1990). Friendship, interpersonal competence, and adjustment in preadolescence and adolescence. *Child Development, 61,* 1101–1111.

Buhrmester, D., & Carbery, J. (1992, March). *Daily patterns of self-disclosure and adolescent adjustment.* Paper presented at the biennial meeting of the Society for Research on Adolescence, Washington, DC.

Buhrmester, D., & Furman, W. (1987). The development of companionship and intimacy. *Child Development, 58,* 1101–1113.

Buhs, E. S., & Ladd, G. W. (2001). Peer rejection as an antecedent of young children's school adjustment: An examination of mediating processes. *Developmental Psychology, 37,* 550–560.

Bukowski, R., & others. (2008, January). *Folic acid and preterm birth.* Paper presented at the meeting of the Society for Maternal-Fetal Medicine, Dallas.

Bukowski, W. M., & Saldarriaga Mesa, L. N. (2007). The study of sex, gender, and relationships with peers: A full or empty experience? *Merrill-Palmer Quarterly, 53,* 507–519.

Bukowski, W. M., Brendgen, M., & Vitaro, F. (2007). Peers and socialization: Effects on externalizing and internalizing problems. In J. E. Grusec & P.D. Hastings (Eds.), *Handbook of socialization.* New York; Guilford.

Bukowski, W. M., Newcomb, A. F., & Hoza, B. (1987). Friendship conceptions among early adolescents: A longitudinal study of stability and change. *Journal of Early Adolescence, 7,* 143–152.

Bukowski, W. M., Sippola, L. K., & Boivin, M. (1995, March). *Friendship protects "at risk" children from victimization by peers.* Paper presented at the meeting of the Society for Research in Child Development, Indianapolis.

Bukowski, W. M., Velasquez, A. M., & Brendgen, M. (2008). Variations in patterns of peer influence: Considerations of self and other. In M. J. Prinstein & K. A. Dodge (Eds.), *Understanding peer influence in children and adolescents.* New York: Guilford.

Buller, D. J. (2005). Evolutionary psychology: The emperor's new paradigm. *Trends in Cognitive Science, 9,* 277–283.

Bullock, M., & Lutkenhaus, P. (1990). Who am I? Self-understanding in toddlers. *Merrill-Palmer Quarterly, 36,* 217–238.

Bumpus, M. F., Crouter, A. C., & McHale, S. M. (2001). Parental autonomy granting during adolescence: Exploring gender differences in context. *Developmental Psychology, 37,* 161–173.

Burchinal, M. R., & Clarke-Stewart, K. A. (2007). Maternal employment and child cognitive outcomes: The importance of analytic approach. *Developmental Psychology, 43,* 1140–1155.

Burns, C., Dunn, A., Brady, M., Starr, N. B., & Blosser, C. (2009). *Pediatric primary care.* Oxford, UK: Elsevier.

Burns, L., Mattick, R. P., Lim, K., & Wallace, C. (2007). Methadone in pregnancy: Treatment retention and neonatal outcomes. *Addiction, 102,* 264–270.

Burton, R. V. (1984). A paradox in theories and research in moral development. In W. M. Kurtines & J. L. Gewirtz (Eds.), *Morality, moral behavior, and moral development.* New York: Wiley.

Bushnell, I. W. R. (2003). Newborn face recognition. In O. Pascalis & A. Slater (Eds.), *The development of face processing in infancy and early childhood.* New York: NOVA Science.

Buss, D. M. (1995). Psychological sex differences: Origins through sexual selection. *American Psychologist, 50,* 164–168.

Buss, D. M. (2000). Evolutionary psychology. In A. Kazdin (Ed.), *Encyclopedia of psychology.* Washington, DC, & New York: American Psychological Association and Oxford University Press.

Buss, D. M. (2004). *Evolutionary psychology* (2nd ed.). Boston: Allyn & Bacon.

Buss, D. M. (2007). Foreward. In G. Geher & G. Miller (Eds.), *Mating intelligence.* Mahwah, NJ: Erlbaum.

Buss, D. M. (2008). *Evolutionary psychology* (3rd ed.). Boston: Allyn & Bacon.

Bussey, K., & Bandura, A. (1999). Social cognitive theory of gender development and differentiation. *Psychological Review, 106,* 676–713.

Butcher, K., Sallis, J. F., Mayer, J. A., & Woodruff, S. (2008). Correlates of physical activity guideline compliance for adolescents in 100 cities. *Journal of Adolescent Health, 42,* 360–368.

Butterworth, G. (2004). Joint visual attention in infancy. In G. Bremner & A. Slater (Eds.), *Theories of infant development.* Malden, MA: Blackwell.

Bybee, R. W., Powell, J. C., & Trowbridge, L. W. (2008). *Teaching secondary science* (9th ed.). Upper Saddle River, NJ: Prentice Hall.

Byrd-Williams, C. E., Shaibi, G. Q., Sun, P., Lane, C. J., Ventura, E. E., Davis, J. N., Kelly, L. A., & Goran, M. I. (2008, in press). Cardiorespiratory fitness predicts change in adiposity in overweight Hispanic boys. *Obesity.*

Byrnes, J. P. (2008). Piaget's cognitive developmental theory. In M. M. Haith & J. B. Benson (Eds.), *Encyclopedia of infant and early childhood development.* Oxford, UK: Elsevier.

C

Cabrera, N., Hutchens, R., & Peters, H. E. (Eds.). (2006). *From welfare to childcare.* Mahwah, NJ: Erlbaum.

Cairns, R.B., & Cairns, B.D. (2006). The making of developmental psychology. In W. Damon & R. Lerner (Eds.), *Handbook of child psychology* (6th ed.). New York: Wiley.

Caley, L., Syms, C., Robinson, L., Cederbaum, J., Henry, M., & Shipkey, N. (2008). What human service professionals know and want to know about fetal alcohol syndrome. *Canadian Journal of Clinical Pharmacology, 15,* e117-e123.

Calkins, S. D., & Hill, A. (2007). Caregiver influences on emerging emotion regulation: Biological and environmental transactions in early development. In J. J. Gross (Ed.), *Handbook of emotion regulation.* New York: Guilford.

Callan, J. E. (2001). Gender development: Psychoanalytic perspectives. In J. Worell (Ed.), *Encyclopedia of women and gender.* San Diego: Academic Press.

Callaway, L. K., Lust, K., & McIntyre, H. D. (2005). Pregnancy outcomes in woman of very advanced maternal age. *Obstetric and Gynecology Survey, 60,* 562–563.

Cameron, J., & Pierce, D. (2008). Intrinsic versus extrinsic motivation. In N. J. Salkind (Ed.), *Encyclopedia of educational psychology.* Thousand Oaks, CA: Sage.

Campbell, D. A., Lake, M. F., Falk, M., & Backstrand, J. R. (2006). A randomized controlled trial of continuous support by a lay doula. *Journal of Obstetrics and Gynecology: Neonatal Nursing, 35,* 456–464.

Campbell, F. A. (2007). The malleability of the cognitive development of children of low-income African American families: Intellectual test performance over twenty-one years. In P. C. Kyllonen, R. D. Roberts, & L. Stankov (Eds.), *Extending intelligence.* Mahwah, NJ: Erlbaum.

Campbell, F. A., Pungello, E. P., Miller-Johnson, S., Burchinal, M., & Ramey, C. T. (2001). The development of cognitive and academic abilities: Growth curves from an early childhood educational experiment. *Developmental Psychology, 37,* 231–243.

Campbell, L., Campbell, B., & Dickinson, D. (2004). *Teaching and learning through multiple intelligence* (3rd ed.). Boston: Allyn & Bacon.

Campbell, M. K., & Mottola, M. F. (2001). Recreational exercise and occupational safety during pregnancy and birth weight: A case-control study. *American Journal of Obstetrics and Gynecology, 184,* 403–408.

Campos, J. J., Anderson, D., & Barbu-Roth, M. (2009, in press). Human infancy: What we know, what we don't know, and where do we go from here? *Annual Review of Psychology, Vol. 60.* Palo Alto, CA: Annual Reviews.

Campos, J. J., Langer, A., & Krowitz, A. (1970). Cardiac responses on the visual cliff in prelocomotor human infants. *Science, 170,* 196–197.

Camras L. A., Oster H., Campos J., Campos R., Ujiie T., Miyake K., & others. (1998). Production of emotional facial expressions in European American, Japanese, and Chinese infants. *Developmental Psychology, 34,* 616–628.

Canfield, R. L., & Haith, M. M. (1991). Young infants' visual expectations for symmetric and asymmetric stimulus sequences. *Developmental Psychology, 27,* 198–208.

Canfield, R. L., & Jusko, T. A. (2008). Lead poisoning. In M. M. Haith & J. B. Benson (Eds.), *Encyclopedia of infancy and early childhood development.* London, UK: Elsevier.

Canterino, J. C., Ananth, C. V., Smulian, J., Harrigan, J. T., & Vintzileos, A. M. (2004). Maternal age and risk of fetal death in Singleton gestations: United States, 1995–2000. *Obstetrics and Gynecology Survey, 59,* 649–650.

Caplan, P. J., & Caplan, J. B. (1999). *Thinking critically about research on sex and gender* (2nd ed.). New York: HarperCollins.

Carbonell, O. A., Alzte, G., Bustamante, M. R., & Quiceno, J. (2002). Maternal caregiving and infant security in two cultures. *Developmental Psychology, 38,* 67–78.

Cardelle-Elawar, M. (1992). Effects of teaching metacognitive skills to students with low mathematics ability. *Teaching and Teacher Education, 8,* (No. 2), 109–121.

Carey, S. (1977). The child as word learner. In M. Halle, J. Bresman, & G. Miller (Eds.), *Linguistic theory and psychological reality.* Cambridge, MA: MIT Press.

Carlo, G. (2006). Care-based and altruistically-based morality. In M. Killen & J. Smetana (Eds.), *Handbook of moral development.* Mahwah, NJ: Erlbaum.

Carlsen, K. H., & Carlsen, K. C. (2008). Respiratory effects of tobacco smoking on infants and young children. *Pediatric Respiratory Reviews, 9,* 11–20.

Carlson, C., Cooper, C., & Hsu, J. (1990, March). *Predicting school achievement in early adolescence: The role of family process.* Paper presented at the meeting of the Society for Research in Adolescence, Atlanta.

Carlson, S. M., & Moses, L. J. (2001). Individual differences in inhibitory control and children's theory of mind. *Child Development, 72,* 1032–1053.

Carlson, S. M., & Zelazo, P. D. (2008). Symbolic thought. In M. M. Haith & J. B. Benson (Eds.), *Encyclopedia of infant and early childhood development.* Oxford, UK: Elsevier.

Carnagey, N. L., Anderson, C. A., & Bushman, B. J. (2007). The effect of video game violence on physiological desensitization to real-life violence. *Journal of Experimental Social Psychology, 43,* 489–460.

Carnegie Council on Adolescent Development. (1995). *Great transitions.* New York: Carnegie Foundation.

Carnegie Foundation. (1989). *Turning points: Preparing youth for the 21st century.* New York: Author.

Carnethon, M. R., Gulati, M., & Greenland,P. (2005). Prevalence of cardio-vascular disease correlates of low cardiorespiratory fitness in adolescents and adults. *Journal of the American Medical Association, 294,* 2981–2988.

Carpendale, J. I. M., Muller, U., & Bibok, M.B. (2008). Piaget's theory of cognitive development. In N. J. Salkind (Ed.), *Encyclopedia of educational psychology.* Thousand Oaks, CA: Sage.

Carpendale, J. I., & Chandler, M. J. (1996). On the distinction between false belief understanding and subscribing to an interpretive theory of mind. *Child Development, 67,* 1686–1706.

Carpenter, J., Nagell, K., & Tomasello, M. (1998). Social cognition, joint attention, and communicative competence from 9 to 15 months of age. *Monographs of the Society for Research in Child Development, 70* (1, Serial No. 279).

Carr, D. (2008). Character education as the cultivation of virtue. In L. Nucci & D. Narvaez (Eds.), *Handbook of moral and character education.* Clifton, NJ: Psychology Press.

Carrell, S. E., Malmstrom, F. V., & West, J. E. (2008). Peer effects in academic cheating. *Journal of Human Resources, 43,* 173–207.

Carroll, J. (1993). *Human cognitive abilities.* Cambridge: Cambridge University Press.

Carskadon, M. A. (Ed.). (2002). *Adolescent sleep patterns.* New York: Cambridge University Press.

Carskadon, M. A. (2004). Sleep difficulties in young people. *Archives of Pediatric and Adolescent Medicine, 158,* 597–598.

Carskadon, M. A. (2005). Sleep and circadian rhythms in children and adolescents: Relevance for athletic performance of young people. *Clinical Sports Medicine, 24,* 319–328.

Carskadon, M. A. (2006, March). *Too little, too late: Sleep bioregulatory process across adolescence.* Paper presented at the meeting of the Society for Research on Adolescence, San Francisco.

Carskadon, M. A., Acebo, C., & Jenni, O. G. (2004). Regulation of adolescent sleep: Implications for behavior. *Annals of the New York Academy of Sciences, 102,* 276–291.

Carter, N., Prater, M. A., & Dyches, T. T. (2009). *What every teacher should know about: Adaptations and accommodations for students with mild to moderate disabilities.* Upper Saddle River, NJ: Prentice Hall.

Cartwright, R., Agargun, M. Y., Kirkby, J., & Friedman, J. K. (2006). Relation of dreams to waking concerns. *Psychiatry Research, 141,* 261–270.

Carvalho Bos, S., & others. (2008, in press). Sleep and behavioral/emotional problems in children: A population-based study. *Sleep Medicine.*

Carver, A. C., Livesey, D. J., & Charles, M. (2001). Age related changes in inhibitory control as measured by stop signal task performance. *The International Journal of Neuroscience. 107,* 43–61.

Case, R. (1987). Neo-Piagetian theory: Retrospect and prospect. *International Journal of Psychology, 22,* 773–791.

Case, R. (1999). Conceptual development in the child and the field: A personal view of the Piagetian legacy. In E. K. Skolnick, K. Nelson, S.A. Gelman, & P. H. Miller (Eds.), *Conceptual development.* Mahwah, NJ: Erlbaum.

Case, R., Kurland, D. M., & Goldberg, J. (1982). Operational efficiency and the growth of short-term memory span. *Journal of Experimental Child Psychology, 33,* 386–404.

Case, R., & Mueller, M. P. (2001). Differentiation, integration, and covariance mapping as fundamental processes in cognitive and neurological growth. In J. L. McClelland & R. S. Siegler (Eds.), *Mechanisms of cognitive development.* Mahwah, NJ: Erlbaum.

Casey, B. J., Getz, S., & Galvan, A. (2008). The adolescent brain. *Developmental Review, 28,* 78–106.

Casey, B. J., Jones, R. M., & Hare, T. A. (2008). The adolescent brain. *Annals of the New York Academy of Sciences, 1124,* 111–126.

Casey, P. H. (2008). Growth of low birth weight preterm children. *Seminars in Perinatology, 32,* 20–27.

Caspi, A. (1998). Personality development across the life course. In W. Damon (Ed.), *Handbook of child psychology* (Vol. 3). New York: Wiley.

Cassidy, J. (2009, in press). The nature of the child's ties. In J. Cassidy & P. R. Shaver (Eds.), *Handbook of attachment* (2nd Ed.). New York: Guilford.

Casson, I. F. (2006) Pregnancy in women with diabetes—after the CEMACH report, what now? *Diabetic Medicine, 23,* 481–484.

Catalano, R. F., Hawkins, J. D., & Toumbourou, J. W. (2008). Positive youth development in the United States: History, efficacy, and links to moral and character education. In L. Nucci & D. Narvaez (Eds.), *Handbook of moral and character education.* Clifton, NJ: Psychology Press.

Caughey, A. B., Hopkins, L. M., & Norton, M. E. (2006). Chorionic villus sampling compared with amniocentesis and the difference in the rate of pregnancy loss. *Obstetrics and Gynecology, 108,* 612–616.

Cave, R. K. (2002, August). *Early adolescent language: A content analysis of child development and educational psychology textbooks.* Unpublished doctoral dissertation, University of Nevada-Reno, Reno.

Cavell, T. A., Hymel, S., Malcolm, K. T., & Seay, A. (2007). Socialization and interventions for antisocial youth. In J. E. Grusec & P. D. Hastings (Eds.), *Handbook of socialization.* New York: Guilford.

Ceci, S. J., & Gilstrap, L. L. (2000). Determinants of intelligence: Schooling and intelligence. In A. Kazdin (Ed.), *Encyclopedia of psychology.* Washington, DC, & New York: American Psychological Association and Oxford University Press.

Ceci, S. J., Papierno, P. B., & Kulkovsky, S. (2007). Representational constraints on children's suggestibility. *Psychological Science, 18,* 503–509.

Ceci, S. J., & Williams, W. M. (1997). Schooling, intelligence, and income. *American Psychologist, 52,* 1051–1058.

Centers for Disease Control and Prevention. (2006, December). Assisted reproductive technology success rates. Atlanta: Author.

Centers for Disease Control and Prevention. (2008). *SIDS.* Retrieved April 26, 2008, from www.cdc.gov/SIDS/index.htm

Centers for Disease Control and Prevention. (2008). *Body mass index for children and teens.* Atlanta: Author.

Cepeda, M. S., Carr, D. B., Lau, J., & Alvarez, H. (2006). Music for pain relief. *Cochrane Database of Systematic Reviews, 2,* CD004843.

Chaillet, N., & Dumont, A. (2007). Evidence-based strategies for reducing cesarean section rates: A meta-analysis. *Birth, 34,* 53–64.

Chall, J. S. (1979). The great debate: Ten years later with a modest proposal for reading stages. In L. B. Resnick & P. A. Weaver (Eds.), *Theory and practice of early reading.* Hillsdale, NJ: Erlbaum.

Chambers, B., Cheung, A. C. K., & Slavin, R.F. (2006). Effective preschool programs for children at risk of school failure: A best-evidence synthesis. In B. Spodek & O. N. Saracho (Eds.), *Handbook of research on the education of young children.* Mahwah, NJ: Erlbaum.

Chan, C. (2008). Childhood obesity and -adverse health effects in Hong Kong. *Obesity Reviews, 9* (Suppl. 1), S87–S90.

Chan, W. S. (1963). *A source book in Chinese philosophy.* Princeton, NJ: Princeton University Press.

Chandler, M. (1973). Egocentrism and antisocial behavior: The assessment and training of social perspective-taking skills. *Developmental Psychology, 9,* 326–332.

Chang, M. Y., Chen, C. H., & Huang, K. F. (2006). A comparison of massage effects on labor pain using the McGill Pain Questionnaire. *Journal of Nursing Research, 14,* 190–197.

Chang, S. C., & Chen, C. H. (2004). The application of music therapy in maternal nursing. *Hu Li Za Zhi, 51,* 61–66. (Article in Chinese).

Chang, S. C., O'Brien, K. O., Nathanson, M.S., Mancini, J., & Witter, F. R. (2003). Characteristics and risk factors for adverse birth outcomes in pregnant black adolescents. *Journal of Obstetrics and Gynecology Canada, 25,* 751–759.

Chao, R. K. (2001). Extending research on the consequences of parenting style for Chinese Americans and European Americans. *Child Development, 72,* 1832–1843.

Chao, R. K. (2005, April). *The importance of Guan in describing control of immigrant Chinese.* Paper presented at the meeting of the Society for Research in Child Development, Atlanta.

Chao, R. K. (2007, March). *Research with Asian Americans: Looking back and moving forward.* Paper presented at the meeting of the Society for Research in Child Development, Boston.

Charman, T. (2009, in press). Autism and its impact on child development. In R. E. Tremblay, R. deV Peters, M. Boivin, & R. G. Barr (Eds.), *Encyclopedia on early childhood development.* Montreal: Centre of Excellence for Early Childhood Development.

Charman, T., Ruffman, T., & Clements, W. (2002). Is there a gender difference in false belief development? *Social Development, 11,* 1–10.

Chatzimichael, A., Tsalkidis, A., Cassimos,D., Gardikis, S., Tripsianis, G., Deftereos, S., Ktenidou-Kartali, S., & Tsanaksas, I. (2007). The role of breastfeeding and passive smoking on the development of severe bronchiolitis in infants. *Minerva Pediatrica, 59,* 199–2006.

Chauhuri, J. H., & Williams, P. H. (1999, April). *The contribution of infant temperament and parent emotional availability to toddler attachment.* Paper presented at the meeting of the Society for Research in Child Development, Albuquerque.

Chavous, T., Branch, L., Cogburn, C., Griffin, T., Maddox, J., & Sellers, R. M. (2007, in press). Achievement motivation among African American college students at predominantly White institutions: Risk and protective processes related to group identity and contextual experiences. Manuscript accepted for publication in F. Salili & R. Hoosain (Eds.), *Culture, motivation and learning: A multicultural perspective.* Information Age Publishing.

Chen, C., & Stevenson, H. W. (1989). Homework: A cross-cultural examination. *Child Development, 60,* 551–561.

Chen, M. Y., Wang, E. K., & Jeng, Y. J. (2006). Adequate sleep among adolescents is positively associated with health status and health-related behaviors. *BMC Public Health, 6,* 59.

Chen, X., Hastings, P. D., Rubin, K. H., Chen, H., Cen, G., & Stewart, S. L. (1998). Child-rearing attitudes and behavioral inhibition in Chinese and Canadian toddlers: A cross-cultural study. *Developmental Psychology, 34,* 677–686.

Chen, X. K., Wen, S. W., Fleming, N., Demissie, K., Rhoads, G. G., & Walker, M. C. (2007a). Teenage pregnancy and adverse birth outcomes: A large population based retrospective cohort study. *International Journal of Epidemiology, 2007,* 368–373.

Chen, X. K., Wen, S. W., Yang, Q., & Walker, M. C. (2007b). Adequacy of prenatal care and neonatal mortality in infants born to mothers with and without antenatal high-risk conditions. *Australian and New Zealand Journal of Obstetrics and Gynecology, 47,* 122–127.

Chersich,M. F., Luchters, S. M., Othigo, M. J., Yard, E., Mandaliya, K., & Temmerman, M. (2008). HIV testing and counseling for women attending child health clinics: An opportunity for entry to prevent mother-to-child transmission and HIV treatment. *International Journal of STD and AIDS, 19,* 42–46.

Cherlin, A. J., & Furstenberg, F. F. (1994). Stepfamilies in the United States: A reconsideration. In J. Blake & J. Hagen (Eds.), *Annual review of sociology.* Palo Alto, CA: Annual Reviews.

Chess, S., & Thomas, A. (1977). Temperamental individuality from childhood to adolescence. *Journal of Child Psychiatry, 16,* 218–226.

Chi, M. T. (1978). Knowledge structures and memory development. In R. S. Siegler (Ed.), *Children's thinking: What develops?* Hillsdale, NJ: Erlbaum.

Chia, P., Sellick, K., & Gan, S. (2006). The attitudes and practices of neonatal nurses in the use of kangaroo care. *Australian Journal of Advanced Nursing, 23,* 20–27.

Chiappe, D., & MacDonald, K. (2005). The evolution of domain-general mechanisms in intelligence and learning. *Journal of General Psychology, 132,* 5–40.

Childers, J. B., & Tomasello, M. (2002). Two-year-olds learn novel nouns, verbs, and conventional actions from massed or distributed exposures. *Developmental Psychology, 38,* 967–978.

Children's Defense Fund. (1992). *The state of America's children, 1992.* Washington, DC: Author.

Children's Defense Fund. (2007). *Children's welfare and mental health.* Retrieved January 6, 2007, from www.childrensdefense.org

Children's Defense Fund. (2008). *Children's welfare and mental health.* Retrieved June 4th, 2008, from www.childrensdefense. org

Chisholm, J. S. (1989). Biology, culture and the development of temperament: A Navajo example. In J. K. Nugent, B. Lester, & T. B. Brazelton (Eds.), *The cultural context of infancy: Vol. 1. Biology, culture, and infant development* (pp. 341–364). Norwood, NJ: Ablex.

Chiu, C., & Hong, Y. (2007). Cultural processes: Basic principles. In A. W. Kruglanski & E. T. Higgins (Eds.), *Social psychology: Handbook of basic principles* (2nd ed.). New York: Guilford.

Chiu, M. M. (2007). Families, economies, cultures, and science achievements in 41 countries: Country-, school-, and student-level analyses. *Journal of Family Psychology, 21,* 510–519.

Choi, N. (2004). Sex role group differences in specific, academic, and general self-efficacy. *Journal of Psychology, 138,* 149–159.

Chomsky, N. (1957). *Syntactic structures*. The Hague: Mouton.

Christensen, L. B. (2007). *Experimental methodology* (10th ed.). Boston: Allyn & Bacon.

Christensen, S. L., & Thurlow, M. L. (2004). School dropouts: Prevention, considerations, interventions, and challenges. *Current Directions in Psychological Science, 13*, 36–39.

Chronis, A. M., Chacko, A., Fabiano, G. A., Wymbs, B. T., & Pelham, W. E. (2004). Enhancements to the behavioral parent training paradigm for families of children with ADHD: Review and future directions. *Clinical Child and Family Psychology Review, 7*, 1–27.

Cicchetti, D., & Toth, S. L. (2006). Developmental psychopathology and preventive intervention. In W. Damon & R. Lerner (Eds.), *Handbook of child psychology* (6th ed.). New York: Wiley.

Cicchetti, D., Toth, S. L., Nilsen, W. J., & Manly, J. T. (2008, in press). What do we know and why does it matter? The dissemination of evidence-based interventions for child maltreatment. In H. R. Schaffer & K. Durkin (Eds.), *Blackwell handbook of developmental psychology in action*. Oxford, UK: Blackwell.

Cicchetti, D., Toth, S. L., & Rogosch, F. A. (2005). *A prevention program for child maltreatment*. Unpublished manuscript, University of Rochester, Rochester, NY.

Cipriano, L. E., Rupar, C. A., & Zaric, G. S. (2007). The cost effectiveness of expanding newborn screening for up to 21 inherited metabolic disorders using tandem mass spectrometry: Results from a decision-analytic model. *Value Health, 10*, 83–97.

Cisneros-Cohernour, E. J., Moreno, R. P., & Cisneros, A. A. (2000). Curriculum reform in Mexico: Kindergarten teachers' challenges and dilemmas. Proceedings of the Lilian Katz Symposium. In D. Rothenberg (Ed.), *Issues in early childhood education: Curriculum reform, teacher education, and dissemination of information*. Urbana-Champaign: University of Illinois.

Clark, B. (2008). *Growing up gifted* (7th ed.). Upper Saddle River, NJ: Prentice Hall.

Clark, E. (1993). *The lexicon in acquisition*. New York: Cambridge University Press.

Clark, R. L., & King, R. B. (2008). Social and economic aspects of immigration. *Annals of the New York Academy of Sciences, 1136*, 289–297.

Clarke-Stewart, K. A. (2006). What have we learned: Proof that families matter, policies for families and children, prospects for future research. In A. Clarke-Stewart & J. Dunn (Eds.), *Families count*. New York: Cambridge University Press.

Clarke-Stewart, K. A., & Brentano, C. (2006). Divorce: Causes and consequences. *New Haven, CT: Yale University Press.*

Clarke-Stewart, K. A., & Dunn, J. (Eds.). (2006). *Families count*. New York: Cambridge University Press.

Clarke-Stewart, K. A., Malloy, L. C., & Allhusen, V. D. (2004). Verbal ability, self-control, and close relationships with parents protect children against misleading statements. *Applied Cognitive Psychology, 18*, 1037–1058.

Clarke-Stewart, K. A., & Miner, J. L. (2008). Child and day care, effects of. In M. M. Haith & J. B. Benson (Eds.), *Encyclopedia of infant and early childhood development*. Oxford, UK: Elsevier.

Claxton, A., & Perry-Jenkins, M. (2008). No fun anymore: Leisure and marital quality across the transition to parenthood. *Journal of Marriage and the Family, 70*, 28–43.

Clearfield, M. W., Diedrich, F. J., Smith, L. B., & Thelen, E. (2006). Young infants reach correctly in A-not-B tasks: On the development of stability and perseveration. *Infant Behavior and Development, 29*, 435–444.

Clifton, R. K., Morrongiello, B. A., Kulig, J. W., & Dowd, J. M. (1981). Developmental changes in auditory localization in infancy. In R.N. Aslin, J. R. Alberts, & M. R. Petersen (Eds.), *Development of perception* (Vol. 1). Orlando, FL: Academic Press.

Clifton, R. K., Muir, D. W., Ashmead, D. H., & Clarkson, M. G. (1993). Is visually guided reaching in early infancy a myth? *Child Development, 64*, 1099–1110.

Cloud, J. (2007, August 27). Failing our geniuses. *Time*, pp. 40–47.

Cohen, N. J., Lojkasek, M., Zadeh, Z. Y., Pugliese, M., & Kiefer, H. (2008, in press). Children adopted in China: A prospective study of their growth and development. *Journal of Child Psychology and Psychiatry.*

Cohn, J. F., & Tronick, E. Z. (1988). Mother-infant face-to-face interaction. Influence is bidirectional and unrelated to periodic cycles in either partner's behavior. *Developmental Psychology, 24*, 396–397.

Coie, J. (2004). The impact of negative social Experiences on the development of antisocial behavior. In J. B. Kupersmidt & K. A. Dodge (Eds.), *Children's peer relations: From development to intervention*. Washington, DC: American Psychological Association.

Colangelo, N. C., Assouline, S. G., Gross, M. U. M. (2004). *A nation deceived: How schools hold back America's brightest students*. Retrieved February 15, 2004, http://nationdeceived.org/

Colapinto, J. (2000). *As nature made him*. New York: Simon & Schuster.

Colby, A., Kohlberg, L., Gibbs, J., & Lieberman, M. (1983). A longitudinal study of moral judgment. *Monographs of the Society for Research in Child Development, 48* (21, Serial No. 201).

Cole, M. (2006). Culture and cognitive development in phylogenetic, historical, and ontogenetic perspective. In W. Damon & R. Lerner (Eds.), *Handbook of child psychology* (6th ed.). New York: Wiley.

Cole, M., & Gajdamaschko, N. (2007). Vygotsky and culture. In H. Daniels, J. Wertsch, & M. Cole (Eds.), *The Cambridge companion to Vygotsky*. New York: Cambridge University Press.

Cole, P. M., & Tan, P. Z. (2007). Emotion socialization from a cultural perspective. In J. E. Grusec & P. D. Hastings (Eds.), *Handbook of socialization*. New York: Guilford.

Coleman, V. H., Erickson, K., Schulkin, J., Zinberg, S., & Sachs, B. P. (2005). Vaginal birth after cesarean delivery: Practice patterns of obstetricians-gynecologists. *Journal of Reproductive Medicine, 50*, 261–266.

Coll, C. T. G., Erkut, S., Alarcon, O., Garcia, H. A. V., & Tropp, L. (1995, March). *Puerto Rican adolescents and families: Lessons in construct and instrument development*. Paper presented at the meeting of the Society for Research in Child Development, Indianapolis.

Collins, W. A., & Steinberg, L. (2006). Adolescent development in interpersonal context. In W. Damon & R. Lerner (Eds.). *Handbook of child psychology* (6th ed.). New York: Wiley.

Collins, W. A., & van Dulmen, M. (2006). The significance of middle childhood peer competence for work and relationships in early adulthood. In A. C. Huston & M. N. Ripke (Eds.), *Developmental contexts in middle childhood*. New York: Cambridge University Press.

Colom, R., & Flores-Mendoza, C. E. (2007). Intelligence predicts scholastic achievement irrespective of SES factors: Evidence from Brazil. *Intelligence, 35*, 243–251.

Colombo, J., McCardle, P., & Freund, L. (Eds.), (2009). *Infant pathways to language*. Clifton, NJ: Psychology Press.

Coltrane, S. L., Parke, R. D., Schofield, T. J., Tsuha, S. J., Chavez, M., & Lio, S. (2008). Mexican American families and poverty. In D. R. Crane & T. B. Heaton (Eds.), *Handbook of families and poverty*. Thousand Oaks, CA: Sage.

Comer, J. P. (1988). Educating poor minority children. *Scientific American, 259*, 42–48.

Comer, J. P. (2004). *Leave no child behind*. New Haven, CT: Yale University Press.

Comer, J. P. (2006). Child development: The under-weighted aspect of intelligence. In P. C. Kyllonen, R. D. Roberts, & L. Stankov (Eds.), *Extending intelligence*. Mahwah, NJ: Erlbaum.

Commoner, B. (2002). Unraveling the DNA myth: The spurious foundation of genetic engineering. *Harper's Magazine, 304*, 39–47.

Compas, B. E. (2004). Processes of risk and resilience during adolescence: Linking contexts and individuals. In R. Lerner & L. Steinberg (Eds.), *Handbook of adolescent psychology*. New York: Wiley.

Comstock, G., & Scharrer, E. (2006). Media and popular culture. In W. Damon & R. Lerner (Eds.). *Handbook of child psychology* (6th ed.). New York: Wiley.

Conduct Problems Prevention Research Group. (2007). The Fast Track randomized controlled trial to prevent externalizing psychiatric disorders: Findings from grades 3 to 9. *Journal of the American Academy of Child and Adolescent Psychiatry 46*, 1250–1262.

Conger, R. D., & Chao, W. (1996). Adolescent depressed mood. In R. L. Simons (Ed.), *Understanding differences between divorced and intact families: Stress, interaction, and child outcome.* Thousand Oaks, CA: Sage.

Conger, R. D., & Conger, K. J. (2008). Understanding the processes through which economic hardship influences rural families and children. In D. R. Crane & T. B. Heaton (Eds.), *Handbook of families and poverty.* Thousand Oaks, CA: Sage.

Conger, R. D., & Dogan, S. J. (2007). Social class and socialization in families. In J. E. Grusec & P. D. Hastings (Eds.), *Handbook of socialization.* New York: Guilford.

Conley, M. W. (2007). Reconsidering adolescent literacy: From competing agendas to shared commitment. In M. Pressley, A. K. Billman, K. H. Perry, K. E. Reffitt, & J. M. Reynolds (Eds.), *Shaping literacy achievement.* New York: Guilford.

Conley, M. W. (2008). *Content area literacy: Learners in context.* Boston: Allyn & Bacon.

Connell, A. M., & Dishion, T. J. (2006). The contribution of peers to monthly variation in adolescent depressed mood: A short-term longitudinal study with time-varying predictors. *Developmental Psychopathology, 18,* 139–154.

Cook, M., & Birch, R. (1984). Infant perception of the shapes of tilted plane forms. *Infant Behavior and Development, 7,* 389–402.

Cook, P. J., MacCoun, R., Muschkin, C., & Vigor, J. (2008). The negative impacts of starting middle school in the sixth grade. *Journal of Policy Analysis and Management, 27,* 104–121.

Cook, T. D., Deng, Y., & Morgano, E. (2007). Friendship influences during early adolescence: The special role of friends' grade point average. *Journal of Research on Adolescence, 17,* 325–356.

Cooper, A. R., & Moley, K. H. (2008). Maternal tobacco use and its preimplantation effects on fertility: More reasons to stop smoking. *Seminars in Reproductive Medicine, 26,* 204–212.

Cooper, C. R., & Ayers-Lopez, S. (1985). Family and peer systems in early adolescence: New models of the role of relationships in development. *Journal of Early Adolescence, 5,* 9–22.

Cooper, C. R., Behrens, R., & Trinh, N. (2008, in press). Identity development. In R. A. Shweder, T. R. Bidell, A. C. Daily, S. D. Dixon, P. J. Miller, & J. Model (Eds.), *The Chicago companion to the child.* Chicago: University of Chicago Press.

Cooper, C. R., & Grotevant, H. D. (1989, April). *Individuality and connectedness in the family and adolescent's self and relational competence.* Paper presented at the meeting of the Society for Research in Child Development, Kansas City.

Cooper, C. R., Grotevant, H. D., Moore, M. S., & Condon, S. M. (1982, August). *Family support and conflict: Both foster adolescent identity and role taking.* Paper presented at the meeting of American Psychological Association, Washington, DC.

Cooper, C. R., Jackson, J. F., Azmitia, M., Lopez, E., & Dunbar, N. (1995). Bridging students' multiple worlds: African American and Latino youth in academic outreach programs. In R. F. Macias & R. G. Garcia-Ramos (Eds.), *Changing schools for changing students.* Santa Barbara: University of California Linguistic Minority Research Institute.

Cooper, C., Harvey, N., Javaid, K., Hanson, M., & Dennison, E. (2008). Growth and bone development. *Nestle Nutrition Workshop Series, 61,* 53–68.

Coopersmith, S. (1967). *The antecedents of self-esteem.* San Francisco: W. H. Freeman.

Coplan, R. J., & Arbeau, K. A. (2008, in press). The stresses of a brave new world: Shyness and adjustment in kindergarten. *Journal of Research in Childhood Education.*

Coplan, R. J., Arbeau, K. A., & Armer, M. (2008). Don't fret, be supportive! Maternal characteristics linking child shyness to psychosocial and school adjustment in kindergarten. *Journal of Abnormal Child Psychology, 36,* 359–371.

Corbett, T. (2007). Social indicators as policy tool: Welfare reform as a case study. In B. Brown (Ed.), *Key indicators of child and youth well-being.* Mahwah, NJ: Erlbaum.

Costello, E. J., Sung, M., Worthman, C., & Angold, A. (2007). Pubertal maturation and the development of alcohol use and abuse. *Dung and Alcohol Dependence, 88* (Suppl.). S50–S59.

Cotton, S., Zebracki, M. A., Rosenthal, S. L., Tsevat, J., & Drotar, D. (2006). Religion/spirituality and adolescent health outcomes: A review. *Journal of Adolescent Health, 38,* 472–480.

Council of Economic Advisors. (2000). *Teens and their parents in the 21st century: An examination of trends in teen behavior and the role of parent involvement.* Washington, DC: Author.

Couperus, J. W., & Nelson, C. A. (2006). Early brain development and plasticity. In K. McCartney & D. Phillips (Eds.), *Blackwell handbook of early childhood development.* Malden, MA: Blackwell.

Courage, M. L., Edison, S. C., & Howe, M. L. (2004). Variability in the early development of visual self-recognition. *Infant Behavior and Development, 27,* 509–532.

Courage, M. L., Howe, M. L., & Squires, S. E. (2004). Individual differences in 3.5 month olds' visual attention: What do they predict at 1 year? *Infant Behavior and Development, 127,* 19–30.

Courage, M. L., & Richards, J. E. (2008). Attention. In M. M. Haith & J. B. Benson (Eds.), *Encyclopedia of infant and early childhood development.* Oxford, UK: Elsevier.

Courtin, C. (2000). The impact of sign language on the cognitive development of deaf children: The case of theories of mind. *Journal of Deaf Studies and Deaf Education, 5,* 201–219.

Cowan, N. (2007). The development of working memory. In N. Cowan & M. Courage (Eds.), *The development of memory in childhood.* Philadelphia: Psychology Press.

Cowan, N., & Morey, C. C. (2007). How can dual-task working memory retention limits be investigated? *Psychological Science, 18,* 686–888.

Cowan, P., & Cowan, C. (2000). *When partners become parents: The big life change for couples.* Mahwah, NJ: Erlbaum.

Cowan, P., Cowan, C., Ablow, J., Johnson, V. K., & Measelle, J. (2005). *The family context of parenting in children's adaptation to elementary school.* Mahwah, NJ: Erlbaum.

Cox, J. (2006). Postnatal depression in fathers. *Lancet, 366,* 982.

Cox, J. E., & Nelson, D. (2008). The relationship between thinking patterns and emotional skills. *Journal of Humanistic Counseling, Education, and Development, 47,* (No. 1) 1–9.

Cox, M. J., Burchinal, M., Taylor, L. C., Frosch, B., Goldman, B., & Kanoy, K. (2004). The transition to parenting: Continuity and change in early parenting behavior and attitudes. In R. D. Conger, F. O. Lorenz, & K. A. S. Wickrama (Eds.), *Continuity and change in family relations.* Mahwah, NJ: Erlbaum.

Cox, M. J., Neilbron, N., Mills-Koonce, W. R., Pressel, A., Oppenheimer, C. W., & Szwedo, D. E. (2008). Marital relationship. In M. M. Haith & J. B. Benson (Eds.), *Encyclopedia of infant and early childhood development.* Oxford, UK: Elsevier.

Cox, R. H. (2007). *Sport psychology* (6th ed.). New York: McGraw-Hill.

Coyne, S. M., Archer, J., Eslea, M., & Liechty, T. (2008, in press). Adolescent perceptions of indirect forms of relational aggression: Sex of perpetrator effects. *Aggressive Behavior.*

Crane, D. R., & Heaton, T. B., (Eds.). (2008). *Handbook of families and poverty.* Thousand Oaks, CA: Sage.

Crawford, M., & Unger, R. (2004). *The psychology of women* (3rd ed.). New York: McGraw-Hill.

Crean, H. F. (2008). Conflict in the Latino parent-youth dyad: The role of emotional support from the opposite parent. *Journal of Family Psychology, 22,* 484–493.

Creswell, J. W. (2008). *Educational research* (3rded.). Upper Saddle River, NJ: Prentice Hall.

Cristakis, D. A., & Zimmerman, F. J. (2007). Violent television viewing during preschool is associated with antisocial behavior during school age. *Pediatrics, 120,* 993–999.

Crockenberg, S. B. (1986). Are temperamental differences in babies associated with predictable differences in caregiving? In J. V. Lerner &

R. M. Lerner (Eds.), *Temperament and social interaction during infancy and childhood.* San Francisco: Jossey-Bass.

Cromer, R. (1987). Receptive language in the mentally retarded: Processes and diagnostic distinctions. In R. Schiefelbusch & L. Lloyd (Eds.), *Language perspectives: Acquisition, retardation, and intervention.* Baltimore: University Park Press.

Crosnoe, R., Riegle-Crumb, C., Field, S., Frank, K., & Muller, C. (2008). Peer group contexts of girls' and boys' academic experiences. *Child Development, 79,* 139–155.

Crouter, A. C. (2006). Mothers and fathers at work. In A. Clarke-Stewart & J. Dunn (Eds.), *Families count.* New York: Cambridge University Press.

Crouter, A. C., & McHale, S. (2005). The long arm of the job revisited: Parenting in dual-earner families. In T. Luster & L. Okagaki (Eds.), *Parenting.* Mahwah, NJ: Erlbaum.

Crowley, K., Callahan, M. A., Tenenbaum, H. R., & Allen, E. (2001). Parents explain more to boys than to girls during shared scientific thinking. *Psychological Science, 12,* 258–261.

Csaba, A., Bush, M. C., & Saphier, C. (2006). How painful are amniocentesis and chorionic villus sampling? *Prenatal Diagnosis, 26,* 35–38.

Cullen, K. (2001). *Context and eating behavior in children.* Unpublished research, Children's Nutrition Research Center, Baylor School of Medicine, Houston.

Cummings, E. M. (1987). Coping with background anger in early childhood. *Child Development, 58,* 976–984.

Cummings, E. M., Goeke-Morey, M. C., & Raymond, J. (2004). Fathers in family context: Effects of marital quality and marital conflict. In. M. Lamb (Ed.), *The role of the father in child development* (4th ed.). New York: Wiley.

Cummings, M. (2006). *Human heredity* (7thed.). Pacific Grove, CA: Brooks Cole.

Cunningham, P. M. (2009). *What really matters in vocabulary.* Boston: Allyn & Bacon.

Cunningham, P. M., & Hall, D. P. (2009). *Making words first grade.* Boston: Allyn & Bacon.

Cunningham-Sabo, L., Bauer, M., Pareo, S., Phillips-Benally, S. Roanhorse, J., & Garcia,L. (2008, in press). Qualitative investigation of factors contributing to effective nutrition education for Navajo families. *Maternal and Child Health Journal.*

Curran, K., DuCette, J., Eisenstein, J., & Hyman, I. A. (2001, August). *Statistical analysis of the cross-cultural data: The third year.* Paper presented at the meeting of the American Psychological Association, San Francisco.

Cuzon, V. C., Yeh, P. W., Yanagawa, Y., Obata, K., & Yeh, H. H. (2008). Ethanol consumption during early pregnancy alters the disposition of tangentially migrating GABA ergic interneurons in the fetal cortex. *Journal of Neuroscience, 28,* 1854–1864.

Cyna, A. M., McAuliffe, G. L., & Andrew, M. I. (2004). Hypnosis for pain relief in labor and childbirth: A systematic review. *British Journal of Anesthesia, 93,* 505–511.

Czeizel, A. E., & Puho, E. (2005). Maternal use of nutritional supplements during the first month of pregnancy and decreased risk of Down's syndrome: Case-control study. *Nutrition, 21,* 698–704.

D

D'Onofrio, B. M. (2008). Nature vs. nurture. In M. M. Haith & J. B. Benson (Eds.), *Encyclopedia of infancy and early childhood development.* Oxford, UK: Elsevier.

Dabbs, J. M., Jr., & Morris, R. (1990). Testosterone, social class, and antisocial behavior in a sample of 4,462 men. *Psychological Science, 1,* 209–211.

Dabbs, J. M., Jr., Frady, R. I., Carr, T. S., & Besch, M. F. (1987). Saliva, testosterone, and criminal violence in young adult prison inmates. *Psychosomatic Medicine, 49,* 174–182.

Dahl, R. E. (2004). Adolescent brain development: A period of vulnerabilities and opportunities. *Annals of the New York Academy of Sciences, 1021,* 1–22.

Dahl, R. E., & Lewin, D. S. (2002). Pathways to adolescent health sleep regulation and behavior. *Journal of Adolescent Health, 31* (Suppl.), 175–184.

Daley, A. J., Macarthur, C., & Winter, H. (2007). The role of exercise in treating postpartum depression: A review of the literature. *Journal of Midwifery and Women's Health, 52,* 56–62.

Dalton, T. C., & Bergenn, V. W. (2007). *Early experience, the brain, and consciousness.* Mahwah, NJ: Erlbaum.

Damon, W. (1988). *The moral child.* New York: Free Press.

Daniels, H. (2007). Pedagogy. In H. Daniels, J.Wertsch, & M. Cole (Eds.), *The Cambridge companion to Vygotsky.* New York: Cambridge University Press.

Daniels, H., Wertsch, J., & Cole, M. (eds.). (2007). *The Cambridge companion to Vygotsky.* New York: Cambridge University Press.

Daniels, P., Noe, G. F., & Mayberry, R. (2006). Barriers to prenatal care among Black women of low socioeconomic status. *American Journal of Health Behavior, 30,* 188–198.

Darling-Hammond, L., & Bransdford, J. (Eds.). (2005). *Preparing teachers for a changing world.* San Francisco: Jossey-Bass.

Darwin, C. (1859). *On the origin of species.* London: John Murray.

Darwin, C. (1965). *The expression of the emotions in man and animals.* Chicago: University of Chicago Press. (Original work published 1872)

Dasen, P. R. (1977). Are cognitive processes universal? A contribution to cross-cultural

Piagetian psychology. In N. Warran (Ed.), *Studies in cross-cultural psychology* (Vol. 1). London: Academic Press.

Datar, A., & Sturm, R. (2004). Childhood overweight and parent- and teacher-reported behavior problems: Evidence from a prospective study of kindergartners. *Archives of Pediatric and Adolescent Medicine, 158,* 804–810.

Davidov, M., & Grusec, J. E. (2006). Untangling the links of parental responsiveness to distress and warmth to child outcomes. *Child Development, 77,* 44–58.

Davids, T., Gordon, K. A., Clutton, D., & Papsin, B. C. (2007). Bone-anchored hearing aids in infants and children younger than 5 years. *Archives of Otolaryngology: Head and Neck Surgery, 133,* 51–55.

Davidson, J. (2000). Giftedness. In A. Kazdin (Ed.), *Encyclopedia of psychology.* Washington, DC, & New York: American Psychological Association and Oxford University Press.

Davidson, J., & Davidson, B. (2004). *Genius denied: How to stop wasting our brightest young minds.* New York: Simon & Schuster.

Davidson, M., Lickona, T., & Khmelkov, V. (2008). A new paradigm for high school character education. In L. Nucci & D. Narvaez (Eds.), *Handbook of moral and character education.* Clifton, NJ: Psychology Press.

Davidson, M. R., London, M. L., & Ladewig, P. A. (2008). *Olds' maternal-newborn nursing and women's health across the lifespan* (8th ed.). Upper Saddle River, NJ: Prentice Hall.

Davies, J., & Brember, I. (1999). Reading and mathematics attainments and self-esteem in years 2 and 6—an eight-year cross-sectional study. *Educational Studies, 25,* 145–157.

Davis, B. E., Moon, R. Y., Sachs, H. C., & Ottolini, M. C. (1998). Effects of sleep position on infant motor development. *Pediatrics, 102,* 1135–1140.

Davis, C. L., Tomporowski, P. D., Boyle, C.A., Waller, J. L., Miller, P. H., Nagieri, J. A., & Gregoski, M. (2007). Effects of aerobic exercise on overweight children's cognitive functioning: A randomized controlled trial. *Research Quarterly for Exercise and Sport, 78,* 510–519.

Davis, D. K. (2005). Leading the midwifery renaissance. *RCM Midwives, 8,* 264–268.

Davis, L., & Keyser, J. (1997). *Becoming the parent you want to be.* New York: Broadway Books.

Davis, O. S. P., Arden, R., & Plomin, R. (2008). *g* in middle childhood: Moderate genetic and shared environmental influence diverse measures of general cognitive ability at 7, 9, and 10 years in large population sample of twins. *Intelligence, 36,* 68–80.

Day, N. L., Goldschmidt, L., & Thomas, C. A. (2006). Prenatal marijuana exposure contributes to the prediction of marijuana use at age 14. *Addiction, 101,* 1313–1322.

Day, N. L., Leech, S. L., Richardson, G. A., Cornelius, M. D., Robles, N., & Larkby, C. (2002). Prenatal alcohol exposure predicts continued deficits in offspring size at 14 years of age. *Alcohol: Clinical and Experimental Research, 26,* 1584–1591.

Day, R. H., & McKenzie, B. E. (1973). Perceptual shape constancy in early infancy. *Perception, 2,* 315–320.

De Baets, A. J., Bulterys, M., Abrams, E. J., Kankassa, C., & Pazvakavambwa, I. E. (2007). Care and treatment of HIV-infected children in Africa: Issues and challenges at the district hospital level. *Pediatric Infectious Disease Journal, 26,* 163–173.

de Haan, M., & Martinos, M. (2008). Brain function. In M. M. Haith & J. B. Benson (Eds.), *Encyclopedia of infant and early childhood development.* Oxford, UK: Elsevier.

de la Rochebrochard, E., & Thonneau, P. (2002). Paternal age and maternal age are risk factors for miscarriage: Results of a multicentre European study. *Human Reproduction, 17,* 1649–1656.

de Moraes Barros, M. C., Guinsburg, R., de Araujo Peres, C., Mitsuhiro, S., Chalem, E., & Laranjeira, R. R. (2006). Exposure to marijuana during pregnancy alters neurobehavior in the early neonatal period. *Journal of Pediatrics, 149,* 781–787.

de Rosnay, M., Cooper, P. J., Tsigaras, N., & Murray, L. (2006). Transmission of social anxiety from mother to infant: An experimental study using a social referencing paradigm. *Behavior Research and Therapy, 44,* 1165–1175.

Deary, I. J., Strand, S., Smith, P., & Fernandes, C. (2007). Intelligence and educational achievement. *Intelligence, 35,* 13–21.

Deater-Deckard, K., & Dodge K. (1997). Externalizing behavior problems and discipline revisited: Non-linear effects and variation by culture, context and gender. *Psychological Inquiry, 8,* 161–175.

DeCasper, A. J., & Spence, M. J. (1986). Prenatal maternal speech influences newborn's perception of speech sounds. *Infant Behavior and Development, 9,* 133–150.

deCharms, R. (1984). Motivation enhancement in educational settings. In R. Ames & C. Ames (Eds.), *Research on motivation in education* (Vol. 1). Orlando: Academic Press.

Deci, E. L., Koestner, R., & Ryan, R. M. (2001). Extrinsic rewards and intrinsic motivation in education: Reconsidered once again. *Review of Educational Research, 71,* 1–28.

Deci, E., & Ryan, R. (1994). Promoting self-determined education. *Scandinavian Journal of Educational Research, 38,* 3–14.

Declercq, E., Cunningham, D. K., Johnson, C., & Sakala, C. (2008). Mothers' reports of postpartum pain associated with vaginal and cesarean deliveries: Results of a national survey. *Birth, 35,* 16–24.

DeGarmo, D. S., & Martinez, C. R. (2006). A culturally informed model of academic well-being for Latino youth: The importance of discriminatory experiences and social support. *Family Relations, 55,* 267–278.

Delbaere, I., Verstraelen, H., Goetgeluk, S., Martens, G., De Backer, G., & Temmerman,M. (2007). Pregnancy outcome in primipare of advanced maternal age. *European Journal of Obstetrics, Gynecology, and Reproductive Biology, 135,* 41–46.

DeLeon, C. W., & Karraker, K. H. (2007). Intrinsic and extrinsic factors associated with night waking in 9-month-old infants. *Infant Behavior and Development, 30,* 596–605.

DeLoache, J. S. (1989). The development of representation in young children. In H. W. Reese (Ed.), *Advances in child development and behavior.* New York: Academic Press.

DeLoache, J. S. (2004). Early development of the understanding and use of symbolic artifacts. In U. Goswami (Ed.), *Blackwell handbook of childhood cognitive development.* Malden, MA: Blackwell.

DeLoache, J. S., Miller, K. F., & Pierroutsakos, S. L. (1998). Reasoning and problem solving. In D. Kuhn & R. S. Siegler (Eds.), *Handbook of child psychology* (5th ed., Vol. 2). New York: Wiley.

DeLoache, J. S., Simcock, G., & Macari, S. (2007). Planes, trains, automobiles—and tea-sets: Extremely intense interests in very young children. *Developmental Psychology, 43,* 1579–1586.

Delpisheh, A., Attia, E., Drammond, S., & Brabin, B. J. (2006). Adolescent smoking in pregnancy and birth outcomes. *European Journal of Public Health, 16,* 168–172.

Dement, W. C. (2005). History of sleep medicine. *Neurologic Clinics, 23,* 964–965.

Demetriou, A. (2001, April). Towards a comprehensive theory of intellectual development: Integrating psychometric and post-Piagetian theories. Paper presented at the meeting of the Society for Research in Child Development, Minneapolis.

Demetriou, A., Christou, C., Spanoudis, G., & Platsidou, M. (2002). The development of mental processing: Efficiency, working memory, and thinking. *Monographs of the Society for Research in Child Development, 67* (1, Serial No. 268).

Dempster, F. N. (1981). Memory span: Sources of individual and developmental differences. *Psychological Bulletin, 80,* 63–100.

Denham, S. A. (1998). *Emotional development in young children.* New York: Guilford.

Denham, S. A., Bassett, H. H., & Wyatt, T. (2007). The socialization of emotional competence. In J. E. Grusec & P. D. Hastings (Eds.), *Handbook of Socialization.* New York: Guilford.

Denmark, F. L., Russo, N. F., Frieze, I. H., & Eschuzur, J. (1988). Guidelines for avoiding sexism in psychological research: A report of the ad hoc committee on nonsexist research. *American Psychologist, 43,* 582–585.

Derbyshire, E. (2007a). Nutrition in pregnant teenagers: How nurses can help. *British Journal of Nursing, 16,* 144–145.

Derbyshire, E. (2007b). The importance of adequate fluid and fiber intake during pregnancy. *Nursing Standard, 21,* 40–43.

Derks, E. M., Hudziak, J. J., Dolan, C. V., van Beijsterveldt, T. C., Verhulst, F. C., & Boomsma, D. I. (2008). Genetic and environmental influences on the relation between attention problems and attention deficit hyperactivity disorder. *Behavior Genetics, 38,* 11–23.

DeRosier, M. E., & Marcus, S. R. (2005). Building friendships and combating bullying: Effectiveness of S.S.GRIN at one-year follow-up. *Journal of Clinical Child and Adolescent Psychology, 34,* 140–150.

DeSantis, L. (1998). Building healthy communities with immigrants and refugees. *Journal of Transcultural Nursing, 9,* 20–31.

Deshler, D. D., & Hock, M. F. (2007). Adolescent literacy: Where we are, where we need to go. In M. Pressley, A. K. Billman, K. H. Perry, K. E. Reffitt, & J. M. Reynolds (Eds.), *Shaping literacy achievement.* New York: Guilford.

Devos, T. (2006). Implicit bicultural identity among Mexican American and Asian American college students. *Cultural Diversity and Ethnic Minority Psychology, 12,* 381–402.

Dewey, J. (1933). *How we think.* Lexington, MA: D. C. Heath.

DeZolt, D. M., & Hull, S. H. (2001). Classroom and school climate. In J. Worell (Ed.), *Encyclopedia of women and gender.* San Diego: Academic Press.

Diamond, A. D. (1985). Development of the ability to use recall to guide action, as indicated by infants' performance on A–B. *Child Development, 56,* 868–883.

Diamond, A. D. (2001). A model system for studying the role of dopamine in the prefrontal cortex during early development in humans: Early and continuously treated phenylketonuria. In C. Nelson & M. Luciana (Eds.), *Handbook of developmental cognitive neuroscience.* Cambridge, MA: MIT Press.

Diamond, A. D. (2007). Interrelated and interdependent. *Developmental Science, 10,* 152–158.

Diamond, M., & Sigmundson, H. K. (1997). Sex reassignment at birth: Long-term review and clinical implications. *Archives of Pediatric and Adolescent Medicine, 151,* 298–304.

Diaz-Rico, L. T. (2008). *A course for teaching English learners.* Boston: Allyn & Bacon.

Diener, E., & Diener, M. (1995). Cross-cultural correlates of life satisfaction and self-esteem. *Journal of Personality and Social Psychology, 68,* 653–663.

Dietrich, R. S., & Cohen, I. (2006). Fetal MR imaging. *Magnetic Resonance Imaging Clinics of North America, 14,* 503–522.

DiLalla, L. F. (2000). Development of intelligence: Current research and theories. *Journal of School Psychology, 38,* 3–8.

DiPietro, J. A. (2008). Prenatal development. In M. M. Haith & J. B. Benson (Eds.), *Encyclopedia of infancy and early childhood development.* London, UK: Elsevier.

Dishion, T. J., Andrews, D. W., & Crosby, L. (1995). Antisocial boys and their friends in adolescence: Relationship characteristics, quality, and interactional process. *Child Development, 66,* 139–151.

Dishion, T. J., Piehler, T. F., & Myers, M. W. (2008). Dynamics and ecology of adolescent peer influence. In M. J. Prinstein & K. A. Dodge (Eds.), *Understanding peer influence in children and adolescents.* New York: Guilford.

Divall, S. A., & Radovick, S. (2008). Pubertal development and menarche. *Annals of the New York Academy of Sciences, 1135,* 19-28.

Dixon, L., Browne, K., & Hamilton-Giachritsis, C. (2005). Risk factors of parents abused as children: A mediational analysis of the intergenerational continuity of child maltreatment (Part I). *Journal of Child Psychology and Psychiatry and Allied Disciplines, 46,* 47–57.

Dixon, S. V., Graber, J. A., & Brooks-Gunn, J. (2008). The roles of respect for parental authority and parenting practices in parent-child conflict among African American, Latino, and European American families. *Journal of Family Psychology, 22,* 1–10.

Doblado, M., & Moley, K. H. (2007). Glucose metabolism in pregnancy and embryogensis. *Current Opinion in Endocrinology, Diabetes, and Obesity, 14,* 488–493.

Dodge, K. A. (1993). Social cognitive mechanisms in the development of conduct disorder and depression. *Annual Review of Psychology, 44,* 559–584.

Dodge, K. A., & the Conduct Problems Prevention Research Group. (2007, March). *The impact of Fast Track on adolescent conduct disorder.* Paper presented at the meeting of the Society for Research in Child Development, Boston.

Dodge, K. A., & Pettit, G. S. (2003). A biopsychosocial model of the development of chronic conduct problems in adolescence. *Developmental Psychology, 39,* 349–371.

Doherty, M. (2008). *Theory of mind.* Philadelphia: Psychology Press.

Dondi, M., Simion, F., & Caltran, G. (1999). Can newborns discriminate between their own cry and the cry of another newborn infant? *Developmental Psychology, 35*(2), 418–426.

Dong, G. H., May, Y. N., Ding, H. L., Cao, Y., Zhao, Y. D., & He, Q. C. (2008, in press). Effects of housing characteristics and home environmental factors on respiratory symptoms in 10,784 elementary school children from northeast China. *Respiration.*

Donnerstein, E. (2001). Media violence. In J. Worell (Ed.), *Encyclopedia of gender and women.* San Diego: Academic Press.

Donnerstein, E. (2002). The Internet. In V. C. Strasburger & B. J. Wilson (Eds.), *Children, adolescents, and the media.* Newbury Park, CA: Sage.

Dontigny, L., & others. (2008). Rubella in pregnancy. *Journal of Obstetrics and Gynecology Canada, 30,* 152–168.

Dorn, L. D., Dahl, R. E., Wooward, H. R., & Biro, F. (2006). Defining the boundaries of early adolescence: A user's guide to assessing pubertal status and pubertal timing in research with adolescents. *Applied Developmental Science, 10,* 30–56.

Doty, R. L., & Shah, M. (2008). Taste and smell. In M. M. Haith & J. B. Benson (Eds.), *Encyclopedia of infant and early childhood development.* Oxford, UK: Elsevier.

Dowker, A. (2006). What can functional brain imaging studies tell us about typical and atypical cognitive development in children. *Journal of Physiology, Paris, 99,* 333–341.

Downe, S. (Ed.). (2008). *Normal childbirth (*2nd ed.*).* Oxford, UK: Elsevier.

Dragi-Lorenz, R. (2007, July). *Self-conscious emotions in young infants and the direct perception of self and others in interaction.* Paper presented at the meeting of the International Society for Research on Emotions, Sunshine Coast, Australia.

Draghi-Lorenz, R., Reddy, V., & Costall, A. (2001). Rethinking the development of "nonbasic" emotions: A critical review of existing theories. *Developmental Review, 21,* 263–304.

Driesen, N. R., & Raz, N. (1995) The influence of sex, age, and handedness on corpus callosum morphology: A meta-analysis. *Psychology, 23,* 240–247.

Driscoll, A., & Nagel, N. G. (2008). *Early childhood education* (4th ed.). Boston: Allyn & Bacon.

Dube, S., Boily, M. C., Mugurungi, O., Mahomva, A., Chikhata, F., & Gregson, F. (2008, in press). Estimating vertically acquired HIV infections and the impact of the prevention of mother-to-child transmission program in Zimbabwe. *Journal of Acquired Immune Deficiency Syndrome.*

Dubois, J., & others. (2008). Microstructural correlates of infant functional development: Example of the visual pathways. *Journal of Neuroscience, 28,* 1943–1948.

Dubow, E. F., Huesmann, L. R., & Greenwood, D. (2007). Media and youth socialization. In J. E. Grusec & P. D. Hastings (Eds.), *Handbook of socialization.* New York: Guilford.

Duck, S. W. (1975). Personality similarity and friendship choices by adolescents. *European Journal of Social Psychology, 5,* 351–365.

Dudley, R. L. (1999). Youth religious commitment over time: Longitudinal study of retention. *Review of Religious Research, 41,* 110–121.

Duke, K., & Don, M. (2005). Acupuncture use for prebirth treatment. *Complementary Therapy in Clinical Practice, 11,* 121–126.

Duncan, G., & Magnuson, K. (2008, in press). Can society profit from investing in early education programs? In A. Tarlov (Ed.), *Nurturing the national treasure: Childhood education and development before kindergarten.* New York: Palgrave Macmillan.

Dundek, L. H. (2006). Establishment of a Somali doula program at a large metropolitan hospital. *Journal of Perinatal and Neonatal Nursing, 20,* 128–137.

Dunkel, C., & Kerpelman, J. (Eds.). (2004). *Possible selves: Theory, research, and application.* Huntington, NY: Nova.

Dunn, J. (2007). Siblings and socialization. In J. E. Grusec & P. D. Hastings (Eds.), *Handbook of socialization.* New York: Guilford.

Dunn, J., & Kendrick, C. (1982). *Siblings.* Cambridge, MA: Harvard University Press.

Dunn, N. F., Miller, R., Griffioen, A., & Lee, C. A. (2008, in press). Carrier testing in haemophilia A and B: Adult carriers' and their partners' experiences and their views on the testing of young females. *Haemophilia.*

Dunphy, D. C. (1963). The social structure of urban adolescent peer groups. *Society, 26,* 230–246.

Dunson, D. B., Baird, D. D., & Columbo, B. (2004). Increased fertility with age in men and women. *Obstetrics and Gynecology, 103,* 51–56.

Durieux-Smith, A., Fitzpatrick, E., & Whittingham, J. (2008). Universal newborn hearing screening: A question of evidence. *International Journal of Audiology, 47,* 1–10.

Durik, A. M., Hyde, J. S., Marks, A. C., Roy, A. L., Anaya, D., & Schultz, G. (2006). Ethnicity and gender stereotypes of emotions. *Sex Roles, 54,* 429–445.

Durrant, J. E. (2000). Trends in youth crime and well-being since the abolition of corporal punishment in Sweden. *Youth and Society, 3,* 437–455.

Durrant, J. E. (2008). Physical punishment, culture, and rights: Current issues for professionals. *Journal of Developmental and Behavioral Pediatrics, 29,* 55–66.

Durston, S., & Casey, B. J. (2006). What have we learned about cognitive development from neuroimaging? *Neuropsychologia, 44,* 2149–2157.

Durston, S., Davidson, M. C., Tottenham, N. T., Galvan, A., Spicer, J., Fossella, J. A., & Casey, B. J. (2006). A shift from diffuse to focal cortical activity with development. *Developmental Science, 9,* 1–8.

Dusek, J. B., & McIntyre, J. G. (2003). Self-concept and self-esteem development. In G. Adams & M. Berzonsky (Eds.), *Blackwell handbook of adolescence*. Malden, MA: Blackwell.

Dweck, C. S. (2006). *Mindset*. New York: Random House.

Dweck, C. S. (2007). Boosting achievement with messages that motivate. *Education Canada*, *47*, 6–10.

Dweck, C. S., Mangels, J. A., & Good, C. (2004). Motivational effects on attention, cognition, and performance. In D. Yun Dai & R. J. Sternberg (Eds.), *Motivation, emotion, and cognition*. Mahwah, NJ: Erlbaum.

Dyl, J., Kittler, J., Phillips, K. A., & Hunt, J. I. (2006). Body dysmorphic disorder and other clinically significant body image concerns in adolescent psychiatric inpatients: Prevalence and clinical characteristics. *Child Psychiatry and Human Development, 36*, 369–382.

E

Eagly, A. H. (2001). Social role theory of sex differences and similarities. In J. Worell (Ed.), *Encyclopedia of women and gender*. San Diego: Academic Press.

Eagly, A. H. (2008, in press). Gender roles. In J. Levine & M. Hogg (Eds.), *Encyclopedia of group processes and intergroup relations*. Thousand Oaks, CA: Sage

Eagly, A. H., & Crowley, M. (1986). Gender and helping behavior: A meta-analytic review of the social psychological literature. *Psychological Bulletin, 100*, 283–308.

Ebbeling, C. A., & Luding, D. S. (2008). Tracking pediatric obesity. *Journal of the American Medical Association, 299*, 2442–2443.

Eby, J. W., Herrell, A. L., & Jordan, M. L. (2009). *Teaching in elementary school: A reflective approach* (5th ed.). Boston: Allyn & Bacon.

Eccles, J. (2003). Education: Junior and high school. In G. Adams & M. Berzonsky (Eds.), *Blackwell handbook of adolescence*. Malden, MA: Blackwell.

Eccles, J. S. (2004). Schools, academic motivation, and stage-environment fit. In R. Lerner & L. Steinberg (Eds.), *Handbook of adolescent psychology*. New York: Wiley.

Eccles, J. S. (2007). Families, schools, and developing achievement-related motivations and engagement. In J. E. Grusec & P. D. Hastings (Eds.), *Handbook of socialization*. New York: Guilford.

Eccles, J., Wigfield, A., & Byrnes, J. (2003). Cognitive development in adolescence. In I. B. Weiner (Ed.), *Handbook of psychology* (Vol. VI). New York: Wiley.

Eckerman, C., & Whitehead, H. (1999). How toddler peers generate coordinated action: A cross-cultural exploration. *Early Education and Development, 10*, 241–266.

Eckstein, K. C., Mikhail, L. M., Ariza, A. J., Thomson, J. S., Millard, S. C., Binns, H. J., & the Pediatric Practice Research Group. (2006). Parents' perceptions of their child's weight and health. *Pediatrics, 117*, 681–190.

Edwards, C. P., & Liu, W. (2002). Parenting toddlers. In M. H. Bornstein (Ed.), *Handbook of parenting* (2nd ed., Vol. 1). Mahwah, NJ: Erlbaum.

Edwards, R., & Hamilton, M. A. (2004). You need to understand my gender role: An empirical test of Tannen's model of gender and communication. *Sex Roles, 50*, 491–504.

Egbert, J. L. (2009). *Supporting learning with technology*. Boston: Allyn & Bacon.

Egeland, B. (2009, in press). Attachment-based interventions on the quality of attachment among infants and young children. In R. E. Tremblay, R. deV Peters, M. Boivin, & R. G. Barr (Eds.), *Encyclopedia on early childhood development*. Montreal: Centre of Excellence for Early Childhood Development.

Egeland, B., Jacobvitz, D., & Sroufe, L. A. (1988). Breaking the cycle of abuse. *New Directions for Child Development, 11*, 77–92.

Ehrhardt, A. A., & Baker, S. W. (1974). Fetal androgens, human central nervous system differentiation, and behavior sex differences. In R. C. Friedman, R. M. Richart, & R. L. Vande Wiele (Eds.), *Sex differences in behavior*. New York: Wiley.

Eiferman, R. R. (1971). Social play in childhood. In R. Herron & B. Sutton-Smith (Eds.), *Child's play*. New York: Wiley.

Einarson, A., & Ito, S. (2007). Re: Use of contemporary antidepressants during breast-feeding: A proposal for a specific safety index. *Drug Safety, 30*, 643.

Eisenberg, N. (Ed.). (1982). *The development of prosocial behavior*. New York: Wiley.

Eisenberg, N. (1998). Introduction. In N. Eisenberg (Ed.), *Handbook of child psychology* (5th ed., Vol 3). New York: Wiley.

Eisenberg, N. (2001). Emotion-regulated regulation and its relation to quality of social functioning. In W. W. Hartup & R. A. Weinberg (Eds.), *Child psychology in retrospect and prospect*. Mahwah, NJ: Erlbaum.

Eisenberg, N., & Fabes, R. A. (1998). Prosocial development. In N. Eisenberg (Ed.), *Handbook of child psychology* (5th ed., Vol. 3). New York: Wiley.

Eisenberg, N., Fabes, R. A., Guthrie, I. K., & Reiser, M. (2002). The role of emotionality and regulation in children's social competence and adjustment. In L. Pulkkinen & A. Caspi (Eds.), *Paths to successful development*. New York: Cambridge University Press.

Eisenberg, N., Fabes, R. A., & Spinrad, T. L. (2006). Prosocial development. In W. Damon &

R. Lerner (Eds.), *Handbook of child psychology* (6th ed.). New York: Wiley.

Eisenberg, N., Martin, C. L., & Fabes, R. A. (1996). Gender development and gender effects. In D. C. Berliner & R. C. Calfee (Eds.), *Handbook of educational psychology*. New York: Macmillan.

Eisenberg, N., & Morris, A. S. (2004). Moral cognitions and prosocial responding in adolescence. In R. Lerner & L. Steinberg (Eds.), *Handbook of adolescent psychology* (2nd ed.). New York: Wiley.

Eisenberg, N., & others. (2008). Understanding mother-adolescent conflict discussions: Concurrent and across-time prediction from youths' dispositions and parenting. *Monographs of the Society for Research in Child Development, 73* (2), 1–160.

Eisenberg, N., Spinrad, T., & Sadovsky, A. (2006). Empathy-related responding in children. In M. Killen & J. Smetana (Eds.), *Handbook of moral development*. Mahwah, NJ: Erlbaum.

Eisenberg, N., Spinard, T. L., & Smith, C. L. (2004). Emotion-related regulation: Its conceptualization, relations to social functioning, and socialization. In P. Philippot & R. S. Feldman (Eds.), *The regulation of emotion*. Mahwah, NJ: Erlbaum.

Eisenberg, N., & Valiente, C. (2002). Parenting and children's prosocial and moral development. In M. H. Bornstein (Ed.), *Handbook of parenting* (2nd ed.). Mahwah, NJ: Erlbaum.

Eisenhower Foundation. (2008). *Quantum Opportunities Program*. Retrieved June 4, 2008, from www.eisenhowerfoundation.org/qop.php

Elder, G. H., & Shanahan, M. J. (2006). The life course and human development. In W. Damon & R. Lerner (Eds.), *Handbook of child psychology* (6th ed.). New York: Wiley.

Elkind, D. (1976). *Child development and education. A Piagetian perspective*. New York: Oxford University Press.

Elkind, D. (1978). Understanding the young adolescent. *Adolescence, 13*, 127–134.

Elliott, V. S. (2004). Methamphetamine use increasing. Retrieved October 12, 2005, from: www.amaassn.org/amednews/2004/07/26/hlsc0726.htm

El-Sheikh, M., Buckhalt, J. A., Mize, J., & Acebo, C. (2006). Marital conflict and disruption of children's sleep. *Child Development, 77*, 31–43.

El-Toukhy, T., Khalaf, Y., & Braude, P. (2006). IVF results: Optimize not maximize. *American Journal of Obstetrics and Gynecology, 194*, 322–331.

Emery, R. E. (1994). *Renegotiating family relationships*. New York: Guilford.

Emery, R. E., & Laumann-Billings, L. (1998). An overview of the nature, causes, and consequences of abusive family relationships. *American Psychologist, 53,* 121–135.

Enfield, A., & Collins, D. (2008). The relationship of service-learning, social justice, multicultural competence, and civic engagement. *Journal of College Student Development, 49,* 95–109.

Enger, E. (2007). *Concepts in biology* (12th ed.). New York: McGraw-Hill.

Enger, E., Ross, F. C., & Bailey, D. (2009). *Concepts in biology* (13th ed.). New York: McGraw-Hill.

Engle, P. L., & Black, M. M. (2008). The effect of poverty on child development and educational outcomes. *Annals of the New York Academy of Sciences, 1136,* 243–256.

Engler, A. J., Ludington-Hoe, S. M., Cusson, R. M., Adams, R., Bahnsen, M., Brumbaugh, E., Coates, P., Grief, J., McHargue, D., Ryan, D. L., Settle, M., & Williams, D. (2002). Kangaroo care: National survey of practice, knowledge, barriers, and perceptions. *American Journal of Maternal/Child Nursing, 27,* 146–153.

Enright , M. S., Schaefer, L. V., Schaefer, P., & Schaefer, K. A. (2008). Building a just adolescent community. *Montessori Life, 20,* 36–42.

Enright, R. D., Lapsley, D. K., Dricas, A. S., & Fehr, L. A. (1980). Parental influence on the development of adolescent autonomy and identity. *Journal of Youth and Adolescence, 9,* 529–546.

Ensembl Human. (2008). *Explore the Homo sapiens genome.* Retrieved June 22, 2008, from www.ensembl.org/Homo_sapiens/index.html

Eogan, M., Daly, L., & O'Herlihy, C. (2006). The effect of regular antenatal perineal massage on postnatal pain and anal sphincter injury: A prospective observational study. *Journal of Maternal-Fetal and Neonatal Medicine, 19,* 225–229.

Ericson, N. (2001, June). *Addressing the problem of juvenile bullying.* Washington, DC: Office of Juvenile Justice and Delinquency Prevention, Office of Justice Programs, U.S. Department of Justice.

Ericsson, K. A., Charness, N., Feltovich, P. J., Hoffman, & R. R., (Eds.). (2006). *The Cambridge handbook of expertise and expert performance.* New York: Cambridge University Press.

Ericsson, K. A., Krampe, R., & Tesch-Romer, C. (1993). The role of deliberate practice in the acquisition of expert performance. *Psychological Review, 100,* 363–406.

Erikson, E. H. (1950). *Childhood and society.* New York: W. W. Norton.

Erikson, E. H. (1962). *Young man Luther.* New York: W. W. Norton.

Erikson, E. H. (1968). *Identity: Youth and crisis.* New York: W. W. Norton.

Erikson, E. H. (1969). *Gandhi's truth.* New York: W. W. Norton.

Ernst, M., & Mueller, S. C. (2008). The adolescent brain: Insights from functional neuroimaging research. *Developmental Neuroscience, 68,* 729–743.

Eschevarria, J., Vogt, M., & Short, D. J. (2008). *Making content comprehensible for English learners* (3rd ed.). Boston: Allyn & Bacon.

Escorbar-Chaves, S. L., & Anderson, C. A. (2008). Media and risky behavior. *Future of Children, 18* (No. 1), 147–180.

Eshel, N., Nelson, E. E., Blair, R. J., Pine, D. S., & Ernst, M. (2007). Neural substrates of choice selection in adults and adolescents: Development of the ventrolateral prefrontal and anterior cingulated cortices. *Neuropsychologia, 45,* 1270–1279.

Evans, B. J., & Whitfield, J. R. (Eds.). (1988). *Black males in the United States: An annotated bibliography from 1967 to 1987.* Washington, DC: American Psychological Association.

Evans, G. W. (2004). The environment of childhood poverty. *American Psychologist, 59,* 77–92.

Evans, G. W., & English, K. (2002). The environment of poverty: Multiple stressor exposure, psychophysiological stress, and socioemotional adjustment. *Child Development, 73,* 1238–1248.

Evans, G. W., & Kim, P. (2007). Childhood poverty and health: Cumulative risk exposure and stress dysregulation. *Psychological Science, 18,* 953–957.

F

Fagan, J. F. (1992). Intelligence: A theoretical viewpoint. *Current Directions in Psychological Science, 1,* 82–86.

Fagan, J. F., Holland, C. R., & Wheeler, K. (2007). The prediction, from infancy, of adult IQ and achievement. *Intelligence, 35,* 225–231.

Fagot, B. J., Rodgers, C. S., & Leinbach, M. D. (2000). Theories of gender socialization. In T. Eckes & H. M. Trautner (Eds.), *The developmental social psychology of gender.* Mahwah, NJ: Erlbaum.

Fahey, T. D., Insel, P. M., & Roth, W. T. (2009). *Fit and well* (8th ed.). New York: McGraw-Hill.

Fair, D., & Schlaggar, B. L. (2008). Brain development. In M. M. Haith & J. B. Benson (Eds.), *Encyclopedia of infant and early childhood development.* London, UK: Elsevier.

Fajardo, G., Wakefield, W. D., Godinez, M., & Simental, J. F. (2003, April). Latino and African American adolescents' experiences with discrimination. Paper presented at the meeting of the Society for Research in Child Development, Tampa.

Falbo, T., & Poston, D. L. (1993). The academic, personality, and physical outcomes of only children in China. *Child Development, 64,* 18–35.

Fantz, R. L. (1963). Pattern vision in newborn infants. *Science, 140,* 296–297.

Faraone, S. V. (2007). Stimulant therapy in the management of ADHD: Mixed amphetamine salts (extended release). *Expert Opinion on Pharmacotherapy, 8,* 2127–2134.

Farmer, E. M., Compton, S. N., Bums, B. J., & Robertson, E. (2002). Reviews of the evidence for treatment of childhood psychopathology: Externalizing disorders. *Journal of Consulting and Clinical Psychology, 70,* 1267–1302.

Fasig, L. (2000). Toddlers' understanding of ownership: Implications for self-concept development. *Social Development, 9,* 370–382.

Fassler, D. (2004, May 8). Commentary in Teen brains on trial. *Science News Online,* p. 1.

Fauth, R. C., & Brooks-Gunn, J. (2008). Are some neighborhoods better for child health than others? In R. F. Schoeni, J. S. House, G. A. Kaplan, & H. Pollack (Eds.), *Making Americans healthier: Social and economic policy as health policy.* New York: Russell Sage Foundation.

Fauth, R. C., Leventhal, T., & Brooks-Gunn, J. (2008, in press). Seven years later: Effects of a neighborhood mobility program on poor Black and Latino adults' well-being. *Journal of Health and Social Behavior.*

Fear, N. T., Hey, K., Vincent, T., & Murphy, M. (2007). Paternal occupation and neural tube defects: A case-control study based on the Oxford Record Linkage Study register. *Pediatric and Perinatal Epidemiology, 21,* 163–168.

Federal Interagency Forum on Child and Family Statistics. (2002). *Key national indicators of well-being.* Washington, DC: U.S. Government Printing Office.

Federal Interagency Forum on Child and Family Statistics. (2007). *American's children: Key indicators of well-being 2007.* Washington, DC: U.S. Government Printing Office.

Federal Interagency Forum on Child and Family Statistics. (2008). *America's children in brief: Key national indicators of well-being, 2008.* Retrieved July 31, 2008, from http://www. childstats.gov/

Fein, G. G. (1986). Pretend play. In D. Görlitz & J. F. Wohlwill (Eds.), *Curiosity, imagination, and play.* Hillsdale, NJ: Erlbaum.

Feinberg, M. E., Button, T. M., Neiderhiser, J. M., Reiss, D., & Hetherington, E. M. (2007). Parenting and antisocial behavior and depression: Evidence of genotype 3 parenting environment interaction. *Archives of General Psychiatry, 64,* 457–465.

Feinberg, M. E., & Kan, M. L. (2008). Establishing family foundations: Intervention effects on coparenting, parent/infant well-being, and parent-child relations. *Journal of Family Psychology, 22,* 253–263.

Fekkes, M., Pijpers, F. I., & Verloove-Vanhorick, S. P. (2004). Bullying behavior and associations with psychosomatic complaints and depression in victims. *Journal of Pediatrics, 144,* 17–22.

Feldman, H. D. (2001, April). *Contemporary developmental theories and the concept of talent.* Paper presented at the meeting of the Society for Research in Child Development, Minneapolis.

Feldman, R., & Eidelman, A. I. (2007). Maternal postpartum behavior and the emergence of infant-mother and infant-father synchrony in preterm and full-term infants: The role of neonatal vagal tone. *Developmental Psychobiology, 49,* 290–302.

Feldman, R., Weller, A., Sirota, L., & Eidelman, A. I. (2002). Skin-to-skin contact (Kangaroo care) promotes self-regulation in premature infants: Sleep-wake cyclicity, arousal modulation, and sustained exploration. *Developmental Psychology, 38,* 194–207.

Feldman, R., Weller, A., Sirota, L., & Eidelman, A. I. (2003). Testing a family intervention hypothesis: The contribution of mother-infant skin-to-skin (kangaroo care) to family interaction, proximity, and touch. *Journal of Family Psychology, 17,* 94–107.

Ferber, S. G., & Makhoul, I. R. (2008). Neurobehavioral assessment of skin-to-skin effects on reaction to pain in preterm infants: A randomized, controlled within-subject trial. *Acta Pediatrica, 97,* 171–176.

Ferguson, D. M., Harwood, L. J., & Shannon, F. T. (1987). Breastfeeding and subsequent social adjustment in 6-to 8-year-old children. *Journal of Child Psychology and Psychiatry, 28,* 378–386.

Fernandez, O., Sabharwal, M., Smiley, T., Pastuszak, A., Koren, G., & Einarson, T. (1998). Moderate to heavy caffeine consumption during pregnancy and relationship to spontaneous abortion and abnormal fetal growth: A meta-analysis. *Reproductive Toxicology, 12,* 435–444.

Fernyhough, C. (2008). Getting Vygotskian about theory of mind: Mediation, dialogue, and the development of social understanding. *Developmental Review, 28,* 225–262.

Ferrarra, M., Coppola, L., Coppola, A., & Capozzi, L. (2006). Iron deficiency in childhood and adolescence: Retrospective review. *Hematology, 11,* 183–186.

Fidler, D. J. (2008). Down syndrome. In M. M. Haith & J. B. Benson (Eds.), *Encyclopedia of infancy and early childhood development.* Oxford, UK: Elsevier.

Field, A., Cartwright-Hatton, S., Reynolds, S., & Creswell, C. (Eds.). (2008). Child Anxiety theory and treatment. Clifton, NJ: Psychology Press.

Field, T. M. (1998). Massage therapy effects. *American Psychologist, 53,* 1270–1281.

Field, T. M. (2001). Massage therapy facilitates weight gain in preterm infants. *Current Directions in Psychological Science, 10,* 51–55.

Field, T. M. (2003). Stimulation of preterm infants. *Pediatrics Review, 24,* 4–11.

Field, T. M. (2007). *The amazing infant.* Malden, MA: Blackwell.

Field, T. M. (2008, in press). Breastfeeding and antidepressants. *Infant Behavior and Development.*

Field, T. M., & Diego, T. M. (2008, in press). Vagal activity, early growth, and emotional development. *Infant Behavior and Development.*

Field, T. M., Diego, M., & Hernandez-Reif, M. (2007). Massage therapy research. *Developmental Review, 27,* 75–89.

Field, T. M., Diego, M., & Hernandez-Reif, M. (2008). *Prematurity and Potential Predictors. International Journal of Neuroscience, 118,* 277–289.

Field, T. M., Grizzle, N., Scafidi, F., & Schanberg, S. (1996). Massage and relaxation therapies' effects on depressed adolescent mothers. *Adolescence, 31,* 903–911.

Field, T. M., Henteleff, T., Hernandez-Reif, M., Martines, E., Mavunda, K., Kuhn, C., & Schanberg, S. (1998). Children with asthma have improved pulmonary functions after message therapy. *Journal of Pediatrics, 132,* 854–858.

Field, T., & Hernandez-Reif, M. (2008). Touch and pain. In M. M. Haith & J. B. Benson (Eds.), *Encyclopedia of infant and early childhood development.* Oxford, UK: Elsevier.

Field, T. M., Hernandez-Reif, M., Feijo, L., & Freedman, J. (2006). Prenatal, perinatal, and neonatal stimulation. *Infant Behavior and Development, 29,* 24–31.

Field, T. M., Hernandez-Reif, M., & Freedman, J. (2004, Fall). Stimulation programs for preterm infants. *SRCD Social Policy Reports, XVIII* (No. 1), 1–20.

Field, T. M., Hernandez-Reif, M., Seligman, S., Krasnegor, J., & Sunshine, W. (1997). Juvenile rheumatoid arthritis: Benefits from massage therapy. *Journal of Pediatric Psychology, 22,* 607–617.

Field, T. M., Hernandez-Reif, M., Taylor, S., Quinitino, O., & Burman, I. (1997). Labor pain is reduced by massage therapy. *Journal of Psychosomatic Obstetrics and Gynecology, 18,* 286–291.

Field, T. M., Lasko, D., Mundy, P., Henteleff, T., Kabat, S., Talpins, S., & Dowling, M. (1997). Brief report: Autistic children's attentiveness and responsivity improve after touch therapy. *Journal of Autism and Developmental Disorders, 27,* 333–338.

Field, T. M., Quintino, O., Hernandez-Reif, M., & Koslosky, G. (1998). Adolescents with attention deficit hyperactivity disorder benefit from massage therapy. *Adolescence, 33,* 103–108.

Fiese, B. H., & Winter, M. A. (2008). Family influences. In M. M. Haith & J. B. Benson (Eds.), *Encyclopedia of infancy and early childhood development.* Oxford, UK: Elsevier.

Findlay, L. C., Coplan, R. J., & Bowker, A. (2008, in press). Keeping it all inside: Shyness, internalizing coping strategies and socio-emotional adjustment in middle childhood. *International Journal of Behavioural Development.*

Finning, K. M., & Chitty, L. S. (2008). Non-invasive fetal sex determination: Impact on clinical practice. *Seminars in Fetal and Neonatal Medicine, 13,* 69–75.

Finn-Stevenson, M. (2006). What the school of the 21st century can teach us about universal preschool. In E. Zigler, W. S. Gilliam, & S. M. Jones (Eds.), *A vision for universal preschool education.* New York: Cambridge University Press.

Fisch, S. M. (2007). Peeking behind the scenes: Varied approaches to the production of educational television. In J. A. Bryant (Ed.), *The children's television community.* Mahwah, NJ: Erlbaum.

Fischer, K. W. (2008). Dynamic cycles of cognitive and brain development: Measuring growth in mind, brain, and education. In A. M. Battro, K. W. Fischer & P. Léna (Eds.), *The educated brain.* Cambridge UK: Cambridge University Press.

Fischer, K. W., & Bidell, T. R. (2006). Dynamic development of action and thought. In W. Damon & R. Lerner (Eds.), *Handbook of child psychology* (6th ed.). New York: Wiley.

Fischer, K. W., & Immordino- Yang, M. H. (2008, in press). The fundamental importance of the brain and learning for education. *The Jossey-Bass reader on the brain and learning.* San Francisco: Jossey-Bass.

Fischer, K. W., & Rose, S. P. (1995, Fall) Concurrent cycles in the dynamic development of brain and behavior. *SRCD Newsletter,* pp. 3–4, 15–16.

Fish, M. (2004). Attachment in infancy and preschool in low socioeconomic status rural Appalachian children: Stability and change and relations to preschool and kindergarten competence. *Developmental Psychopathology, 16,* 293–312.

Fisher, P. A. (2005, April). *Translational research on underlying mechanisms of risk among foster children: Implications for prevention science.* Paper presented at the meeting of the Society for Research in Child Development, Washington, DC.

Fisher, S. E., & Marcus, G. F. (2006). The eloquent ape: Genes, brains, and the evolution of language. *Nature Review: Genetics, 7,* 9–20.

Fitzgerald, E. F., Hwang, S. A., Lannguth, K., Cayo, M., Yang, B. Z., Bush, S.,

Worswick, P., & Lauzon, T. (2004). Fish consumption and other environmental exposures and their associations with serum PCB concentrations among Mohawk women at Akwesasne. *Environmental Research, 94,* 160–170.

Fitzgerald, M. M. J., Schneider, R. A., Salstrom, S., Zinzow, H. M., Jackson, J., & Fossel, R. V. (2008). Child sexual abuse, early family risk, and childhood parentification: Pathways to current psychosocial adjustment. *Journal of Family Psychology, 22,* 320–324.

Fivush, R. (1993). Developmental perspectives on autobiographical recall. In G. S. Goodman, & B. Bottoms (Eds.), *Child victims and child witnesses: Understanding and improving testimony.* New York: Guilford.

Fivush, R. (2007). Memory development in sociocultural contexts. In N. Cowan & M. Courage (Eds.), *The development of memory in childhood.* Philadelphia: Psychology Press.

Flannery, D. J., Hussey, D., Biebelhausen, L., & Wester, K. (2003). Crime, delinquency, and youth gangs. In G. Adams & M. Berzonsky (Eds.), *Blackwell handbook of adolescence.* Malden, MA: Blackwell.

Flavell, J. H. (2004). Theory-of-mind development: Retrospect and prospect. *Merrill-Palmer Quarterly, 50,* 274–290.

Flavell, J. H., Friedrichs, A., & Hoyt, J. (1970). Developmental changes in memorization processes. *Cognitive Psychology, 1,* 324–340.

Flavell, J. H., Green, F. L., & Flavell, E. R. (1993). Children's understanding of the stream of consciousness. *Child Development, 64,* 95–120.

Flavell, J. H., Green, F. L., & Flavell, E. R. (1995). The development of children's knowledge about attentional focus. *Developmental Psychology, 31,* 706–712.

Flavell, J. H., Green, F. L., & Flavell, E. R. (1998). The mind has a mind of its own: Developing knowledge about mental uncontrollability. *Cognitive Development, 13,* 127–138.

Flavell, J. H., Green, F. L., & Flavell, E. R. (2000). Development of children's awareness of their own thoughts. *Journal of Cognition and Development, 1,* 97–112.

Flavell, J. H., & Miller, P. H. (1998). Social cognition. In W. Damon (Ed.), *Handbook of child psychology.* (5th ed.). New York: Wiley.

Flavell, J. H., Miller, P. H., & Miller, S. (2002). *Cognitive development* (4th ed.). Upper Saddle River, NJ: Prentice Hall.

Flavell, J., Mumme, D., Green, F., and Flavell E. (1992). Young children's understanding of different types of beliefs. *Child Development, 63,* 960–977.

Flegal, W. A. (2007). Blood group genotyping in Germany. *Transfusion, 47* (Suppl. 1), S47–S53.

Fletcher, J. M., Lyon, G. R., Fuchs, L. S., & Barnes, M. A. (2007). *Learning disabilities.* New York: Guilford.

Flint, M. S., Baum, A., Chambers, W. H., & Jenkins, F. J. (2007). Induction of DNA damage, alteration of DNA repair and transcriptional activation by stress hormones. *Psychoneuroendocrinology, 32,* 470–479.

Flohr, J. W., Atkins, D. H., Bower, T. G. R., & Aldridge, M. A. (2001, April). *Infant music preferences.* Paper presented at the meeting of the Society for Research in Child Development, Minneapolis.

Flom, R., & Pick, A. D. (2003). Verbal encouragement and joint attention in 18-month-old infants. *Infant Behavior and Development, 26,* 121–134.

Flom, R., & Pick, A. D. (2007). Increasing specificity and the development of joint visual attention. In R. Flom, K. Lee, & D. Muir (Eds.), *Gaze-following.* Mahwah, NJ: Erlbaum.

Floriani, V., & Kennedy, C. (2008). Promotion of physical activity in children. *Current Opinion in Pediatrics, 20,* 90–95.

Flynn, J. R. (1999). Searching for justice: The discovery of IQ gains over time. *American Psychologist, 54,* 5–20.

Flynn, J. R. (2007a). The history of the American mind in the 20th century: A scenario to explain gains over time and a case for the irrelevance of *g*. In P. C. Kyllonen, R. D. Roberts, & L. Stankov (Eds.), *Extending intelligence.* Mahwah, NJ: Erlbaum.

Flynn, J. R. (2007b). *What is intelligence? Beyond the Flynn effect.* New York: Cambridge University Press.

Flynn, L., Budd, M., & Modelski, J. (2008). Enhancing resource utilization among pregnant adolescents. *Public Health Nursing, 25,* 140–148.

Fogelholm, M. (2008). How physical activity can work? *International Journal of Pediatric Obesity, 3* (Suppl. 1), S10–S14.

Folkman, S., & Moskowitz, J. T. (2004). Coping: Pitfalls and promises. *Annual Review of Psychology* (Vol. 55). Palo Alto, CA: Annual Reviews.

Fonseca, E. B., Celik, E., Parra, M., Singh, M., Nicolaides, K. H., & the Fetal Medicine Foundation Second Trimester Screening Group. (2007). Progesterone and the risk of preterm birth among Women with a short cervix. *New England Journal of Medicine. 357,* 462–469.

Fontenot, H. B. (2007). Transition and adaptation to adoptive motherhood. *Journal of Obstetrics, Gynecologic, and Neonatal Nursing, 36,* 175–182.

Forcier, R. C., & Descy, D. E. (2008). *Computer as an educational tool* (5th ed.). Boston: Allyn & Bacon.

Forrester, M. B., & Merz, R. D. (2007). Genetic counseling utilization by families with offspring affected by birth defects, Hawaii, 1986–2003. *American Journal of Medical Genetics A, 143,* 1045–1052.

Forster, B., Eardley, A. F., & Eimer, M. (2007). Altered tactile spatial attention in the early blind. *Brain Research, 113,* 149–154.

Foster, H., & Brooks-Gunn, J. (2008, in press). Role strain in the transition to adolescence: Pubertal timing associations with behavior problems by gender and race/ethnicity. *Developmental Psychology.*

Foster-Cohen, S., Edgin, J. O., Champion, P. R., & Woodward, L. J. (2007). Early delayed language development in very preterm infants: Evidence from the MacArthur-Bates CDI. *Journal of Child Language, 34,* 655–675.

Fowden, A. L., Forhead, A. J., Coan, P. M., & Burton, G. J. (2008, in press). The placenta and intrauterine programming. *Journal of Neuroendocrinology.*

Fox, M. K., Pac, S., Devaney, B., & Jankowski, L. (2004). Feeding infants and toddlers study: What foods are infants and toddlers eating? *American Dietetic Association Journal 104,* (Suppl.), S22–S30.

Fraga, C. G., Motchnik, P. A., Shigenaga, M. K., Helbock, H. J., Jacob, R. A., & Ames, B. N. (1991). Ascorbic acid protects against endogenous oxidative DNA damage in human sperm. *Proceedings of the National Academy of Sciences of the USA, 88,* 11003–11006.

Francis, J., Fraser, G., & Marcia, J. E. (1989). *Cognitive and experimental factors in moratorium-achievement (MAMA) cycles.* Unpublished manuscript, Department of Psychology, Simon Fraser University, Burnaby, British Columbia.

Franz, C. E. (1996). The implications of preschool tempo and motoric activity level for personality decades later. Reported in Caspi, A. (1998). Personality development across the life course. In W. Damon (Ed.), *Handbook of child psychology* (Vol 3). New York: Wiley, p. 337.

Fraser, S. (Ed.). (1995). *The bell curve wars: Race, intelligence, and the future of America New York:* Basic Books.

Fratelli, N., Papageorghiou, A. T., Prefumo, F., Bakalis, S., Homfray, T., & Thilaganathan, B. (2007). Outcome of prenatally diagnosed agenesis of the corpus callosum. *Prenatal Diagnosis, 27,* 512–517.

Frede, E. C. (1995). The role of program quality in producing early childhood program benefits. *The Future of Children, 5* (No. 3), 115–132.

Frederick, I. O., Williams, M. A., Sales, A.E., Martin, D. P., & Killien, M. (2007, in press). Pre-pregnancy body mass index, gestational weight gain, and other maternal characteristics in relation to infant birth weight. *Maternal Child Health Journal.*

Frederiske, M., Lu, A., Aylward, E., Barta, P., Sharma, T., & Pearlson, G. (2000). Sex differences in inferior lobule volume in schizophrenia. *American Journal of Psychiatry, 157,* 422–427.

Fredrikson, K., Rhodes, J., Reddy, R., & Way, N. (2004). Sleepless in Chicago: Tracking the effects of sleep loss during middle school years. *Child Development, 75,* 84–95.

Freedman, D. S., Mei, Z., Srinivasan, S. R., Berenson, G. S., & Dietz, W. H. (2007). Cardiovascular risk factors and excess adiposity among overweight children and adolescents in the Bogalusa Heart Study. *Journal of Pediatrics, 150,* 12–17.

Freedman, J. L. (1984). Effects of television violence on aggressiveness. *Psychological Bulletin, 96,* 227–246.

Freeman, K. E., & Gehl, K. S. (1995, March). *Beginnings, middles, and ends: 24-month-olds' understanding of analogy.* Paper presented at the meeting of the Society for Research in Child Development, Indianapolis.

Freisthler, B., Merritt, D. H., & LaScala, E.A. (2006). Understanding the ecology of child maltreatment: A review of the literature and directions for future research. *Child Maltreatment, 11* (3), 263–280.

French, D. C., Eisenberg, N., Vaughan, J., Purwono, U., & Suryanti, T. A. (2008). Religious involvement and the social competence and adjustment of Indonesian Muslim adolescents. *Developmental Psychology, 44,* 597–611.

Fretts, R. C., Zera, C., & Heffner, C. Z. (2008). Maternal age and pregnancy. In M. M. Haith & J. B. Benson (Eds.), *Encyclopedia of infancy and early childhood development.* London, UK: Elsevier.

Freud, S. (1917). *A general introduction to psychoanalysis.* New York: Washington Square Press.

Frey, K. S., Hirschstein, M. K., Snell, J. L., Edstrom, L. V. S., & Broderick, C. J. (2005). Reducing playground bullying and supporting beliefs: An experimental trial of the Steps to Respect program. *Developmental Psychology, 41,* 479–490.

Friedman, N. P., Haberstick, B. C., Willcutt, E. G., Miyake, A., Young, S. E., Corley, R. P., & Hewitt, J. K. (2007). Greater attention problems during childhood predict poorer executive functioning in late adolescence. *Psychological Science, 18,* 893–900.

Fritschmann, N. S., & Solari, E. J. (2008). Learning disabilities. In N. J. Salkind (Ed.), *Encyclopedia of educational psychology.* Thousand Oaks, CA: Sage.

Frye, D. (1999). Development of intention: The relation of executive function to theory of mind. in P. D. Zelazo, J. W. Astington, & D. R. Olson (Eds.), *Developing theories of intention: Social understanding and self-control.* Mahwah, NJ: Erlbaum.

Frye, D. (2004). Unpublished review of J. W. Santrock's. *Child development,* 11th ed. (New York: McGraw-Hill).

Fuligni, A. J., & Fuligni, A. S. (2007). Immigrant families and the educational development of their children. In J. E. Lansford, K. Deater-Deckard, & M. H. Bornstein (Eds.), *Immigrant families in contemporary society.* New York: Guilford.

Fuligni, A. J., Tseng, V., & Lamb, M. (1999). Attitudes toward family obligations among American adolescents from Asian, Latin American, and European backgrounds. *Child Development, 70,* 1030–1044.

Fuligni, A. J., Witkow, M., & Garcia, C. (2005, April). *Ethnic identity and the academic adjustment of adolescents from Mexican, Chinese, and European backgrounds.* Paper presented at the meeting of the Society for Research in Child Development, Atlanta.

Funai, E. F., Evans, M., & Lockwood, C. J. (2008). *High risk obstetrics.* Oxford, UK: Elsevier.

Furman, W. C. (2007, March). *The conceptualization of attachment in adolescents' relationships.* Paper presented at the meeting of the Society for Research in Child Development, Boston.

Furman, W., & Buhrmester, D. (1992). Age and sex differences in perceptions of networks of personal relationships. *Child Development, 63,* 103–115.

Furnival, R. A., Street, K. A., & Schunk, J. E. (1999). Too many pediatric trampoline injuries. *Pediatrics, 103,* e57.

Furstenberg, F. F., Cook, T. D., Eccles, J., Elder, G. H., & Sameroff, A. (1999). *Managing to make it: Urban families and adolescent success.* Chicago: University of Chicago Press.

Furth, H. G. (1973). *Deafness and learning: A psychosocial approach.* Belmont, CA: Wadsworth.

Furth, H. G., & Wachs, H. (1975). *Thinking goes to school.* New York: Oxford University Press.

Fussell, E., & Greene, M. E. (2002). Demographic trends affecting youth around the world. In B. B. Brown. R. W. Larson, & T. S. Saraswathi (Eds.), *The world's youth.* New York: Cambridge University Press.

G

Gable, S., Chang, Y., & Krull, J. L. (2007). Television watching and frequency of family meals are predictive of overweight onset and persistence in a national sample of preschool children. *Journal of the American Dietetic Association, 107,* 53–61.

Gaff, C. L., Williams, J. K., & McInerney, J.D. (2008, in press). Genetics in health practice and education special issue. *Journal of Genetic Counseling.*

Galambos, N. L., Barker, E. T., & Krahn, H. J. (2006). Depression, self-esteem, and anger in emerging adulthood: Seven-year trajectories. *Developmental Psychology, 42,* 350–365.

Galinsky, E., & David, J. (1988). *The preschool years: Family strategies that work—from experts and parents.* New York: Times Books.

Gallagher, J. J. (2007). *Teaching science for understanding.* Upper Saddle River, NJ: Prentice Hall.

Galloway, J. C., & Thelen, E. (2004). Feet first: Object exploration in young infants. *Infant Behavior & Development, 27,* 107–112.

Ganong, L., Coleman, M., & Hans, J. (2006). Divorce as prelude to stepfamily living and the consequences of re-divorce. In M. A. Fine & J. H. Harvey (Eds.), *Handbook of divorce and relationship dissolution.* Mahwah, NJ: Erlbaum.

Garcia Coll, C., & Pachter, L. M. (2002). Ethnic and minority parenting. In M. H. Bornstein (Ed.), *Handbook of parenting* (2nd ed., Vol. 4). Mahwah, NJ: Erlbaum.

Garcia, E. E. (2008). Bilingual education in the United Sates. In J. Altarriba & R. R. Heredia (Eds.), *An introduction to bilingualism.* Philadelphia: Psychology Press.

Garcia-Bournissen, F., & others. (2008). Fetal exposure to isotretinoin—an international problem. *Reproductive Toxicology, 25,* 124–128.

Gardner, H. (1983). *Frames of mind.* New York: Basic Books.

Gardner, H. (1993). *Multiple intelligences.* New York: Basic Books.

Gardner, H. (2002). The pursuit of excellence through education. In M. Ferrari (Ed.), *Learning from extraordinary minds.* Mahwah, NJ: Erlbaum.

Garel, C. (2008). Fetal MRI: What is the future? *Ultrasound in Obstetrics and Gynecology, 31,* 123–128.

Gargiulo, R. M. (2009). *Special education in contemporary society.* Thousand Oaks, CA: Sage.

Garrett, P., Ng'andu, N., & Ferron, J. (1994). Poverty experiences of young children and the quality of their home environments. *Child Development, 65,* 331–345.

Garvey, C. (2000). *Play* (enlarged ed.). Cambridge, MA: Harvard University Press.

Gathwala, G., Singh, B., & Balhara, B. (2008). KMG facilitates mother baby attachment in low birth weight infants. *Indian Journal of Pediatrics, 75,* 43–47.

Gaudernack, L. C., Forbord, S., & Hole, E. (2006). Acupuncture administered after spontaneous rupture of membranes at term significantly reduces the length of birth and use of oxytocin. *Acta Obstetricia et Gynecologica Scandinavica, 85,* 1348–1353.

Gauvain, M. (2008). Vygotsky's sociocultural theory. In M. M. Haith & J. B. Benson (Eds.), *Encyclopedia of infant and early childhood development.* Oxford, UK: Elsevier.

Gauvain, M., & Perez, S. M. (2007). The socialization of cognition. In J. E. Grusec & P. D. Hastings (Eds.), *Handbook of socialization.* New York: Guilford.

Gee, C. L., & Heyman, G. D. (2007). Children's evaluations of other people's self-descriptions. *Social Development, 16,* 800–818.

Geher, G., & Miller, G. (Eds.). (2007). *Mating intelligence*. Mahwah, NJ: Erlbaum.

Geissbuehler, V., Stein, S., & Eberhard, J. (2004). Waterbirths compared to landbirths: An observational study of nine years. *Journal of Perinatal Medicine, 32*, 308–314.

Gelles, R. J., & Cavanaugh, M. M. (2005). Violence, abuse, and neglect in families and intimate relationships. In P. C. McKenry & S. J. Price (Eds.), *Families and change* (3rd ed.). Thousand Oaks, CA: Sage.

Gelman, R. (1969). Conservation acquisition: A problem of learning to attend to relevant attributes. *Journal of Experimental Child Psychology, 7*, 67–87.

Gelman, R., & Williams, E. M. (1998). Enabling constraints for cognitive development and learning. In W. Damon (Ed.). *Handbook of child psychology* (5th ed., Vol. 4). New York: Wiley.

Gelman, S. A., Heyman, G. D., & Legare, C. H. (2007). Developmental changes in the coherence of essentialist beliefs about psychological characteristics. *Child Development, 78*, 757–774.

Gelman, S. A., & Kalish, C. W. (2006). Conceptual development. In W. Damon & R. Lerner (Eds.), *Handbook of child psychology* (6th ed.). New York: Wiley.

Gelman, S. A., & Opfer, J. E. (2004). Development of the animate-inanimate distinction. In U. Goswami (Ed.), *Blackwell handbook of childhood cognitive development*. Malden, MA: Blackwell.

Gelman, S. A., Taylor, M. G., & Nguyen, S. P. (2004). Mother-child conversations about gender. *Monographs of the Society for Research in Child Development.* 69 (1, Serial No. 275).

Gennetian, L. A., & Miller, C. (2002). Children and welfare reform: A view from an experimental welfare reform program in Minnesota. *Child Development, 73*, 601–620.

Gerards, F. A., Twisk, J. W., Fetter, W. P., Wijnaendts, L. C., & van Vugt, J. M. (2008). Predicting pulmonary hypoplasia with 2- or 3-dimensional ultrasonography in complicated pregnancies. *American Journal of Gynecology and Obstetrics. 198*, e1–e6.

Gershkoff-Stowe, L., & Hahn, E. R. (2007). Fast mapping skills in the developing lexicon. *Journal of Speech, Language, and Hearing, 50*, 682–697.

Gershoff, E. T. (2002). Corporal punishment by parents and associated child behaviors and experiences: A meta-analysis and theoretical review. *Psychological Bulletin, 128*, 539–579.

Gesell, A. L. (1928). *Infancy and human growth*. New York: Macmillan.

Gesell, A. L. (1934). *Infancy and human growth*. New York: Macmillan.

Gewirtz, J. (1977). Maternal responding and the conditioning of infant crying: Directions of influence within the attachment-acquisition process. In B. C. Etzel, J. M. LeBlanc, & D. M. Baer (Eds.), *New developments in behavioral research*. Hillsdale, NJ: Erlbaum.

Ghetti, S., & Alexander, K. W. (2004). "If it happened, I would remember it": Strategic use of event memorability in the rejection of false autobiographical events. *Child Development, 75*, 542–561.

Ghi, T., Pilu, G., Falco, P., Segata, M., Carletti, A., Cocchi, G., Santini, D., Bonasoni, P., Tani, G., & Rizzo, N. (2006). Prenatal diagnosis of open and closed spina bifida. *Ultrasound in Obstetrics and Gynecology, 28*, 899–903.

Giavecchio, L. (2001, April). *Sustained attention and receptive language in preschool Head Start story time.* Paper presented at the meeting of the Society for Research in Child Development, Minneapolis.

Gibbons, J., & Ng, S. H. (2004). Acting bilingual and thinking bilingual. *Journal of Language and Social Psychology, 23*, 4–6.

Gibbs, J. C. (2008, in press). Moral development. In S. J. Lopez & A. Bevchamp (Eds.), *Encyclopedia of positive psychology*. Washington, DC: American Psychological Association.

Gibbs, J. C., Basinger, K. S., Grime, R. L., & Snarey, J. R. (2007). Moral judgment development across cultures: Revisiting Kohlberg's universality claims. *Developmental Review, 27*, 443–500.

Gibbs, J. T., & Huang, L. N. (1989). A conceptual framework for assessing and treating minority youth. In J. T. Gibbs & L. N. Huang (Eds.), *Children of color*. San Francisco: Jossey-Bass.

Gibson, E. J. (1969). *Principles of perceptual learning and development*. New York: Appleton-Century-Crofts.

Gibson, E. J. (1989). Exploratory behavior in the development of perceiving, acting, and the acquiring of knowledge. *Annual Review of Psychology*, (Vol. 39). Palo Alto, CA: Annual Reviews.

Gibson, E. J. (2001). *Perceiving the affordances*. Mahwah, NJ: Erlbaum.

Gibson, E. J., & Walk, R. D. (1960). The "visual cliff." *Scientific American, 202*, 64–71.

Gibson, E. J., Riccio, G., Schmuckler, M. A., Stoffregen, T. A., Rosenberg, D., & Taormina, J. (1987). Detection of the traversability of surfaces by crawling and walking infants. *Journal of Experimental Psychology: Human Perception and Performance, 13*, 533–544.

Gibson, J. J. (1966). *The senses considered as perceptual systems*. Boston: Houghton Mifflin.

Gibson, J. J. (1979). *The ecological approach to visual perception*. Boston: Houghton Mifflin.

Gibson, L. Y., Bryne, S. M., Blair, E., Davis, E. A., Jacoby, P., & Zubrick, S. R. (2008). Clustering of psychological symptoms in overweight children. *Australian and New Zealand Journal of Psychiatry, 42*, 118–125.

Giedd, J. N. (2008). The teen brain: InSights from neuroimaging. *Journal of Adolescent medicine, 42*, 335–343.

Giedd, J. N., & others. (2006). Puberty—related influences on brain development. *Molecular and Cellular Endocrinology, 25*, 154–162.

Giglia, R. C., & Binns, C. W. (2007). Alcohol and breastfeeding: What do Australian mothers know? *Asia Pacific Journal of Clinical Nutrition, 16*, (Suppl. 1), S473–S477.

Gillen, M. M., Lefkowitz, E. S., & Shearer, C. L. (2006). Does body image play a role in risky sexual behavior and attitudes? *Journal of Youth and Adolescence, 35*, 230–242.

Gilligan, C. (1982). *In a different voice*. Cambridge, MA: Harvard University Press.

Gilligan, C. (1992, May). *Joining the resistance: Girls' development in adolescence*. Paper presented at the symposium on development and vulnerability in close relationships, Montreal, Quebec.

Gilligan, C. (1996). The centrality of relationships in psychological development: A puzzle, some evidence, and a theory. In G. G. Noam & K. W. Fischer (Eds.), *Development and vulnerability in close relationships*. Hillsdale, NJ: Erlbaum.

Gilmore, J. H., & others. (2007). Regional gray matter growth, sexual dimorphism, cerebral -dimorphism, and cerebral asymmetry in the neonatal brain. *Journal of Neuroscience, 27*, 1255–1260.

Gil-Olarte Marquez, P., Palomera, M. R., & Brackett, M. A. (2007). Relating emotional intelligence to social competence and academic achievement in high school students. *Psicothema, 18 (Suppl.)*, S118–S123.

Giorgis, C., & Glazer, J. I. (2009). *Literature for young children* (6th ed.). Upper Saddle River, NJ: Prentice Hall.

Girling, A. (2006). The benefits of using the Neonatal Behavioral Assessment Scale in health visiting practice. *Community Practice, 79*, 118–120.

Given, L. M. (2008). Qualitative research methods. In N. J. Salkind (Ed.), *Encyclopedia of educational psychology*. Thousand Oaks, CA: Sage.

Gjerdingen, D., Katon, W., & Rich, D. E. (2008). Stepped care treatment of postpartum depression: A primary care-based management model. *Women's Health Issues, 18*, 44–52.

Glantz, J. C. (2005). Elective induction vs. spontaneous labor associations and outcomes. *Journal of Reproductive Medicine, 50*, 235–240.

Gliori, G., Imm, P., Anderson, H. A., & Knobeloch, L. (2006). Fish consumption and advisory awareness among expectant women. *Wisconsin Medicine Journal, 105*, 41–44.

Glynn, L. M., Schetter, C. D., Hobel, C. J., & Sandman, C. A. (2008). Pattern of perceived stress and anxiety in pregnancy predicts preterm birth. *Health Psychology, 27*, 43–51.

Gobet, F., & Charness, N. (2006). In K. A. Ericsson, N. Charness, P. J. Feltovich, & R. R. Hoffman (Eds.), *The Cambridge handbook of expertise and expert performance.* New York: Cambridge University Press.

Godding, V., Bonnier, C., Fiasse, L., Michel, M., Longueville, E., Lebecque, P., Robert, A., & Galanti, L. (2004). Does in utero exposure to heavy maternal smoking induce nicotine withdrawal symptoms in neonates? *Pediatric Research, 55,* 645–651.

Goffin, S. G., & Wilson, C. S. (2001). *Curriculum models and early childhood education. Appraising the relationship* (2nd ed.). Upper Saddle River, NJ: Prentice Hall.

Goh, V. I., & Koren, G. (2008). Folic acid in pregnancy and fetal outcomes. *Journal of Obstetrics and Gynecology, 28,* 3–13.

Goldberg, A. E., & Sayer, A. (2006). Lesbian couples' relationship quality across the transition to parenthood. *Journal of Marriage and the Family, 68,* 87–100.

Goldberg, W. A., & Lucas-Thompson, R. (2008). Maternal and paternal employment, effects of. In M. M. Haith & J. B. Benson (Eds.), *Encyclopedia of infant and early childhood development.* Oxford, UK: Elsevier.

Goldenberg, R. L., & Culhane, J. F. (2007). Low birth weight in the United States. *American Journal of Clinical Nutrition, 85* (Suppl.), S584–S590.

Goldenberg, R. L., & Nagahawatte, N. T. (2008). Poverty, maternal health, and adverse pregnancy outcomes. In S. G. Kahler & O. M. Rennert (Eds.), *Annals of the New York Academy of Sciences, Vol. 1136.*

Goldfield, B. A., & Snow, C. E. (2009). Individual differences: Implications for the study of language acquisition. In J. Berko Gleason & N. B. Ratner (Eds.), *The development of language.* Boston: Allyn & Bacon.

Goldin-Meadow, S. (2000). Language: Language development, syntax, and communication. In A. Kazdin (Ed.), *Encyclopedia of psychology.* Washington, DC, & New York: American Psychological Association and Oxford University Press.

Goldman, R. (1964). *Religious thinking from childhood to adolescence.* London: Routledge & Kegan Paul.

Goldscheider, F., & Sassler, S. (2006). Creating stepfamilies: Integrating children into the study of union formation. *Journal of Marriage and the Family, 68,* 275–291.

Goldschmidt, L., Richardson, G. A., Willford, J., & Day, N. L. (2008, in press). Prenatal marijuana exposure and intelligence test performance at age 6. *Journal of the American Academy of Child and Adolescent Psychiatry.*

Goldsmith, H. H. (2002). Genetics of emotional development. In R. J. Davidson, K. R. Scherer, & H. H. Goldsmith (Eds.), *Handbook of affective sciences.* New York: Oxford University Press.

Goldstein, J. M., Seidman, L. J., Horton, N. J., Makris, N., Kennedy, D. N., Caviness, V. S. Faraone, S. V., & Tsuang, M. T. (2001). Normal sexual dimorphism of the adult human brain assessed by in vivo magnetic resonance imaging. *Cerebral Cortex, 11,* 490–497.

Goldstein, M. H., King, A. P., & West, M. J. (2003). Social interaction shapes babbling: Testing parallels between birdsong and speech. *Proceedings of the National Academy of Sciences, 100,* 8030–8035.

Goleman, D. (1995). *Emotional intelligence.* New York: Basic Books.

Goleman, D., Kaufman, P., & Ray, M. (1993). *The creative spirit.* New York: Plume.

Gollnick, D. M., & Chinn, P. C. (2009). *Multicultural education in a pluralistic society* (8th ed.). Boston: Allyn & Bacon.

Golombok, S., MacCallum, F., & Goodman, E. (2001). The "test-tube" generation: Parent-child relationships and the psychological well-being of in vitro fertilization children at adolescence. *Child Developmental, 72,* 599–608.

Gonzales, N. A., Deardorff, J., Formoso, D., Barr, A., & Barrera, M. (2006). Family mediators of the relation between acculturation and adolescent mental health. *Family Relations, 55,* 318–330.

Gonzales, N. A., Dumka, L. E., Murarico, A. M., & German, M. (2007). Building bridges: Strategies to promote academic and psychological resilience for adolescents of Mexican origin. In J. E. Lansford, K. Deater Deckhard, & M. H. Bornstein (Eds.), *Immigrant families in contemporary society.* New York: Guilford.

Gonzales, P., Buzman, J. C., Partelow, L., Pahlke, E., Jocelyn, L., Kastberg, D., & Williams, T. (2004). *Highlights from the Trends in International Mathematics and Science Study (TIMSS) 2003* (NCES 2005-005). Washington, DC: U.S. Department of Education, National Center for Education Statistics.

Gonzalez, J. M. (Ed.) (2009). *Encyclopedia on bilingual education.* Thousand Oaks, CA: Sage.

Gonzalez, V., Yawkey, T. D., & Minaya-Rowe, L. (2006). *English-as-a-second-language (ESL) teaching and learning.* Boston: Allyn & Bacon.

Goodman, G. S., Batterman-Faunce, J. M., & Kenney, R. (1992). Optimizing children's testimony: Research and social policy issues Concerning allegations of child sexual abuse. In D. Cicchetti & S. Toth (Eds.), *Child abuse, child development and social policy.* Norwood, NJ: Ablex.

Goos, L. M., Ezzatian, P., & Schachar, R. (2007). Parent-of-origin effects in attention-deficit hyperactivity disorder. *Psychiatry Research, 149,* 1–9.

Gopnik, A., & Meltzoff, A. (1997). *Words, thoughts, and theories.* Cambridge, MA: MIT Press.

Gorski, P. (2005). *Multicultural education and the Internet* (2nd ed.). New York: McGraw-Hill.

Gottliéb, G. (2005). Unpublished review of J. W. Santrock's *Topical approach to life span development,* 3rded. (New York: McGraw-Hill).

Gottleib, G., Wahlsten, D., & Lickliter, R. (2006). The significance of biology for human development: A developmental psychobiological systems view. In W. Damon & R. Lerner (Eds.), *Handbook of child psychology* (6th ed.). New York: Wiley.

Gottlieb, G. (2007). Probabilistic epigenesis. *Developmental Science, 10,* 1–11.

Gottman, J. M. (2002). *Four parenting styles: The emotion-coaching parent.* Seattle: Talaris Research Institute.

Gottman, J. M. (2008). *Research on parenting.* Retrieved March 25, 2008, from www.gottman.com/parenting/research

Gottman, J. M., & DeClaire, J. (1997). *The heart of parenting: Raising an emotionally intelligent child.* New York: Simon & Schuster.

Gottman, J. M., & Parker, J. G. (Eds.). (1987). *Conversations of friends.* New York: Cambridge University Press.

Gould, S. J. (1981). *The mismeasure of man.* New York: W. W. Norton.

Graber, J. A. (2008, in press). Pubertal and neuroendocrine development and risk for depressive disorders. In N. B. Allen, & L. Sheeber (Eds.), *Adolescent emotional development and the emergence of depressive disorders.* New York: Cambridge University Press.

Graber, J. A., & Brooks-Gunn, J. (2002). Adolescent girls' sexual development. In G. M. Wingood & R. J. DiClemente (Eds.), *Handbook of sexual and reproductive health.* New York: Plenum.

Gracia, E., & Herrero, J. (2008). Is it considered violence? The acceptability of physical punishment of children in Europe. *Journal of Marriage and the Family, 70,* 210–217.

Graham, J. M., & Shaw, G. M. (2006). Gene-environment interactions in rare diseases that include common birth defects. *Birth Defects Research, 73,* 865–867.

Graham, S. (1986, August). *Can attribution theory tell us something about motivation in blacks?* Paper presented at the meeting of the American Psychological Association, Washington, DC.

Graham, S. (1990). Motivation in Afro-Americans. In G. L. Berry & J. K. Asamen (Eds.), *Black students: Psychosocial issues and academic achievement.* Newbury Park, CA: Sage.

Graham, S. (1992). Most of the subjects were white and middle class. *American Psychologist, 47,* 629–637.

Graham, S. (2005, February 16). Commentary in *USA Today,* p. 2D.

Graham, S. (2009). Teaching writing. P. Hogan (Ed.), *Cambridge encyclopedia of language sciences.* Cambridge, UK: Cambridge University Press.

Graham, S. (Ed.). (2006). Our children too: A history of the first 25 years of the Society for Research in Child Development. *Monographs of*

the Society for Research in Child Development, 71(No.1), 1–227.

Graham, S., & Olinghouse, N. (2009). Learning and teaching writing. In E. Anderman & L. Anderman (Eds.), *Psychology of classroom learning.* Farmington Hills, MI: Thomas Gale.

Graham, S., & Perin, D. (2007). A meta-analysis of writing instruction for adolescent students. *Journal of Educational Psychology, 99,* 445–476.

Granic, L., & Patterson, G. R. (2006). Toward a comprehensive model of antisocial development: A dynamic systems approach. *Psychological Review, 113,* 101–131.

Grant, J. (1993). *The state of the world's children.* New York: UNICEF and Oxford University Press.

Graven, S. (2006). Sleep and brain development. *Clinical Perinatology, 33,* 693–706.

Gray, J. (1992). *Men are from Mars, women are from Venus.* New York: HarperCollins.

Gray, K. A., Day, N. L., Leech, S., & Richardson, G. A. (2005). Prenatal marijuana exposure: Effect on child depressive symptoms at ten years of age. *Neurotoxicology and Teratology, 27,* 439–448.

Graziano, A. M., & Raulin, M. L. (2007). *Research methods* (6th ed). Boston: Allyn & Bacon.

Greder, K. A., & Allen, W. D. (2007). Parenting in color: Culturally diverse perspectives on parenting. In B. S. Trask & R. R. Hamon (Eds.), *Cultural diversity and families.* Thousand Oaks, CA: Sage.

Gredler, M. E. (2008). Vygotsky's cultural historical theory of development. In N. J. Salkind (Ed.), *Encyclopedia of educational psychology.* Thousand Oaks, CA: Sage.

Greenfield, P. M. (1966). On culture and conservation. In J. S. Bruner, R. P. Oliver, & P. M. Greenfield (Eds.), *Studies in cognitive growth.* New York: Wiley.

Greenfield, P. M. (2003, February). Commentary. *Monitor on Psychology, 34,* (No. 2), p. 58.

Greenfield, P. M., Suzuki, L. K., & Rothstein-Fisch, C. (2006). Cultural pathways through human development. In W. Damon & R. Lerner (Eds.), *Handbook of child psychology* (6th ed.). New York: Wiley.

Greenough, A. (2007). Late respiratory outcomes after preterm birth. *Early Human Development, 83,* 785–788.

Greenough, W. T. (1997, April 21). Commentary in article, "Politics of biology." *U.S. News & World Report,* p. 79.

Greenough, W. T. (1999, April). *Experience, brain development, and links to mental retardation.* Paper presented at the meeting of the Society for Research in Child Development, Albuquerque.

Greenough, W. T., Klintsova, A. Y., Irvan, S. A., Galvez, R., Bates, K. E., & Weiler, I. J. (2001). Synaptic regulation of protein synthesis and the fragile X protein. *Proceedings of the National Academy of Sciences, USA, 98,* 7101–7106.

Greer, F. R., Sicherer, S. H., Burks, A. W., & the Committee on Nutrition and Section on Allergy and Immunology. (2008). Effects of early nutritional interventions on the development of atopic disease in infants and children: The role of maternal dietary restriction, breast feeding, timing of introduction of complementary foods, and hydrolyzed formulas. *Pediatrics, 121,* 183–191.

Gregory, R. J. (2007). *Psychological testing* (5th ed.). Boston: Allyn & Bacon.

Greydanus, D. E., Pratt, H. D., & Patel, D. R. (2007). Attention deficit hyperactivity disorder across the lifespan: The child, adolescent, and adult. *Disease-A-Month, 53,* 70–131.

Grigorenko, E. (2000). Heritability and intelligence. In R. J. Sternberg (Ed.), *Handbook of intelligence.* New York: Cambridge University Press.

Grigorenko, E. L., Geissler, P., Prince, R., Okatcha, F., Nokes, C., Kenney, D. A., Bundy, D. A., & Sternberg, R. J. (2001). The organization of Luo conceptions of intelligence: A study of implicit theories in a Kenyan village. *International Journal of Behavioral Development, 25,* 368–378.

Grigoriadis, S., & Kennedy, S. H. (2002). Role of estrogen in the treatment of depression. *American Journal of Therapy, 9,* 503–509.

Groer, M. W., & Morgan, K. (2007). Immune, health, and endocrine characteristics of -depressed postpartum mothers. *Psychoneuroimmunology, 32,* 133–138.

Grolnick, W. S., Bridges, L. J., & Connell, J. P. (1996). Emotion regulation in two-year-olds: Strategies and emotional expression in four contexts. *Child Development, 67,* 928–941.

Gronlund, N. E., & Waugh, C. K. (2009). *Assessment of student achievement* (9th ed.). Upper Saddle River, NJ: Prentice Hall.

Gropman, A. L., & Adams, D. R. (2007). Atypical patterns of inheritance. *Seminars in Pediatric Neurology, 14,* 34–45.

Gross, E. F. (2004). Adolescent Internet use: What we expect, what teens report. *Journal of Applied Developmental Psychology, 24,* 633–649.

Grossman, K., & Grossman, K. E. (2009, in press). The impact of attachment to mother and father at an early age on children's psychosocial development through early adulthood. In R. E. Tremblay, R. deV Peters, M. Boivin, & R. G. Barr (Eds.), *Encyclopedia on early childhood development.* Montreal: Centre of Excellence for Early Childhood Development.

Grossmann, K., Grossmann, K. E., Spangler, G., Suess, G., & Unzner, L. (1985). Maternal sensitivity and newborns' orientation responses as related to quality of attachment in northern Germany. In I. Bretherton & E. Waters (Eds.), Growing points of attachment theory and research. *Monographs of the Society for Research in Child Development, 50* (1–2, Serial No. 209).

Grotevant, H. D., & Cooper, C. R. (1985). Patterns of interaction in family relationships and the development of identity exploration in adolescence. *Child Development, 56,* 415–428.

Grotevant, H. D., & Cooper, C. R. (1998). Individuality and connectedness in adolescent development: Review and prospects for research on identity, relationships, and context. In E. Skoe & A. von der Lippe (Eds.), *Personality development in adolescence: A cross-national and life-span perspective.* London: Routledge.

Grotevant, H. D., van Dulmen, M. H. M., Dunbar, N., Nelson-Christinedaughter, J., Christensen, M., Fan, X., & Miller, B. C. (2006). Antisocial behavior of adoptees and nonadoptees: Prediction from early history and adolescent relationships. *Journal of Research on Adolescence, 16,* 105–131.

Grusec, J. (2006). Development of moral behavior and a conscience from a socialization perspective. In M. Killen & J. G. Smetana (Eds.), *Handbook of moral development.* Mahwah, NJ: Erlbaum.

Grusec, J. E. (2009, in press). Parents' attitudes and beliefs: Their impact on children's development. In R. E. Tremblay, R. deV Peters, M. Boivin, & R. G. Barr (Eds.), *Encyclopedia on early childhood development.* Montreal: Centre of Excellence for Early Childhood Development.

Grusec, J. E., Almas, A., & Willoughby, K. (2008). Discipline and compliance. In M. M. Haith & J. B. Benson (Eds.), *Encyclopedia of infancy and early childhood development.* Oxford, UK: Elsevier.

Grusec, J. E., & Davidov, M. (2007). Socialization in the family: The roles of parents. In J. E. Grusec & P. D. Hastings (Eds.), *Handbook of socialization.* New York: Guilford.

Grusec, J. E., & Hastings, P. D. (Eds.). (2007). *Handbook of socialization.* New York: Guilford.

Grych, J. H. (2002). Marital relationships and parenting. In M. H. Bornstein (Ed.), *Handbook of parenting.* Mahwah, NJ: Erlbaum.

Guilford, J. P. (1967). *The structure of intellect.* New York: McGraw-Hill.

Gunderson, E. P., Rifas-Shiman, S. L., Oken, E., Rich-Edwards, J. W., Kleinman, K. P., Taveras, E. M., & Gilman, M. W. (2008). Association of fewer hours of sleep at 6 months postpartum with substantial weight retention at 1 year postpartum. *American Journal of Epidemiology, 167,* 178–187.

Gunnar, M. R., & Quevado, K. (2007). The neurobiology of stress and development. *Annual Review of Psychology* (Vol. 58). Palo Alto, CA: Annual Reviews.

Gunnar, M. R., Fisher, P. A., & the Early Experience, Stress, and Prevention Network. (2006). Bringing basic research on early experience and stress neurobiology to bear on preventive interventions for neglected and maltreated children. *Development and Psychopathology, 18,* 651–677.

Gunnar, M. R., Malone, S., & Fisch, R. O. (1987). The psychobiology of stress and coping in the human neonate: Studies of the adreno-cortical activity in response to stress in the first week of life. In T. Field, P. McCabe, & N. Scheiderman (Eds.). *Stress and coping.* Hillsdale, NJ: Erlbaum.

Guo, S. S., Wu, W., Chumlea, W. C., & Roche, A. F. (2002). Predicting overweight and obesity in adulthood from body mass index values in childhood and adolescence. *American Journal of Clinical Nutrition, 76,* 653–658.

Gupta, A., Thornton, J. W., & Huston, A. C. (2007). Working families should not be poor—the New Hope project. In D. R. Crane & T. B. Heaton (Eds.), *Handbook of families and poverty.* Thousand Oaks, CA: Sage.

Gur, R. C., Mozley, L. H., Mozley, P. D., Resnick, S. M., Karp, J. S., Alavi, A., Arnold, S. E., & Gur, R. E. (1995). Sex differences in regional cerebral glucose metabolism during a resting state. *Science, 267,* 528–531.

Gurgan, T., & Demirol, A. (2007). Unresolved issues regarding assisted reproduction technology. *Reproductive Biomedicine Online, 14* (Suppl.1), S40–S43.

Gurwitch, R. H., Silovsky, J. F., Schultz, S., Kees, M., & Burlingame, S. (2001). *Reactions and guidelines for children following trauma/disaster.* Norman, OK: Department of Pediatrics, University of Oklahoma Health Sciences Center.

Gustafsson, J-E. (2007). Schooling and intelligence: Effects of track of study on level and profile of cognitive abilities. In P. C. Kyllonen, R. D. Roberts, & L. Stankov (Eds.), *Extending intelligence.* Mahwah, NJ: Erlbaum.

Gutman, L. M. (2008). Risk and resilience. In M. M. Haith & J. B. Benson (Eds.), *Encyclopedia of infancy and early childhood development.* Oxford, UK: Elsevier.

H

Haga, M. (2008). The relationship between physical fitness and motor competence in children. *Child: Child Care and Health Development, 34,* 329–334.

Hagen, J. W., & Lamb-Parker, F. G. (2008). Head Start. In M. M. Haith & J. B. Benson (Eds.), *Encyclopedia of infant and early childhood development.* Oxford, UK: Elsevier.

Hahn, C. S., & DiPietro, J. A. (2001). In vitro fertilization and the family: Quality of parenting, family functioning, and child psychosocial adjustment. *Development Psychology, 37,* 37–48.

Hahn, D. B., Payne, W. A., & Lucas, E. B. (2009). *Focus on health* (9th ed.). New York: McGraw-Hill.

Hahn, S., Zhong, X. Y., & Holzgreve, W. (2008). Recent progress in non-invasive prenatal diagnosis. *Seminars in Fetal and Neonatal Medicine, 13,* 57–62.

Haith, M. M., & Benson, J. B. (1998). Infant cognition. In W. Damon (Ed.), *Handbook of child psychology* (5th ed., Vol. 2). New York: Wiley.

Haith, M. M., Hazen, C., & Goodman, G. S. (1988). Expectation and anticipation of dynamic visual events by 3.5 month old babies. *Child Development, 59,* 467–479.

Hakuta, K. (2001, April 5). *Key policy milestones and directions in the education of English language learners.* Paper prepared for the Rockefeller Foundation Symposium, Leveraging change: An emerging framework for educational equity, Washington, DC.

Hakuta, K. (2005, April). *Bilingualism at the intersection of research and public policy.* Paper presented at the meeting of the Society for Research in Child Development, Atlanta.

Hakuta, K., Butler, Y. G., & Witt, D. (2001). *How long does it take English learners to attain proficiency?* Berkeley, CA: The University of California Linguistic Minority Research Institute Policy Report 2000–1.

Hale, S. (1990). A global developmental trend in cognitive processing speed. *Child Development, 61,* 653–663.

Halford, G. S. (2008). Cognitive developmental theories. In M. M. Haith & J. B. Benson (Eds.), *Encyclopedia of infant and early childhood development.* Oxford, UK: Elsevier.

Hall, C. M., Jones, J. A., Meyer-Bahlburg, H. F., Dolezal, C., Coleman, M., Foster, P., Price, D. A., & Clayton, P. E. (2004). Behavioral and physical masculinization are related to genotype in girls with congenital adrenal hyperplasia. *Journal of Clinical Endocrinology and Metabolism, 89,* 419–424.

Hall, G. S. (1904). *Adolescence* (Vols. 1 & 2). Englewood Cliffs, NJ: Prentice Hall.

Hall, L., (2009). *Autism spectrum disorders: From therapy to practice.* Boston: Allyn & Bacon.

Hallahan, D. P., & Kauffman, J. M. (2006). *Exceptional learners* (10th ed.). Boston: Allyn & Bacon.

Hallahan, D. P., Kaufmann, J. M., & Pullen, P. C. (2009). *Exceptional learners* (11th ed.). Boston: Allyn & Bacon.

Halpern, D. F. (2006). Girls and academic success: Changing patterns of academic achievement. In J. Worell & C. D. Goodheart (Eds.), *Handbook of girls' and women's psychological health.* New York: Oxford University Press.

Halpern, D. F. (2007). The nature and nurture of critical thinking. In R. J. Sternberg, H. Roediger, & D. Halpern (Eds.), *Critical thinking in psychology.* New York: Cambridge University Press.

Halpern, D. F., Benbow, C. P., Geary, D. C., Gur, R. C. & Hyde, J. S. (2007). The science of sex differences in science and mathematics. *Psychological Science in the Public Interest, 8,* 1–51.

Hamlin, J. K., Hallinan, E. V., & Woodward, A. L. (2008, in press). Do as I do: 7-month-old infants selectively reproduce others' goals. *Developmental Science.*

Hampton, T. (2008). Scientists build map of imprinted genes. *Journal of the American Medical Association, 299,* 161.

Han, J. J., Leichtman, M. D., & Wang, Q. (1998). Autobiographical memory in Korean, Chinese, and American children. *Developmental Psychology, 34,* 701–713.

Hancox, R. J., Milne, B. J., & Poulton, R. (2004). Association between child and adolescent television viewing and adult health: A longitudinal birth cohort study. *Lancet, 364,* 257–262.

Hankins, G. D., & Longo, M. (2006). The role of stillbirth prevention and late preterm (near-term) births. *Seminars in Perinatology, 30,* 20–23.

Hannish, L. D., & Guerra, N. G. (2004). Aggressive victims, passive victims, and bullies: Developmental continuity or developmental change? *Merrill-Palmer Quarterly, 50,* 17–38.

Hansen, M., Janssen, I., Schiff, A., Zee, P.C., & Dubocovich, M. L. (2005). The impact of school daily schedule on adolescent sleep. *Pediatrics, 115,* 1555–1561.

Hardman, M. L., Drew, C. J., & Egan, M. W. (2006). *Human exceptionality* (8th ed., Update). Boston: Allyn & Bacon.

Hare, B. R., & Castenell, L. A. (1995). No place to run, no place to hide: Comparative statistics and future prospects of black boys. In M.B., Spencer, G.K. Brookins, & W.R. Allen (Eds.), *Beginnings: The social and affective development of black children.* Hillsdale, NJ: Erlbaum.

Harkness, S., & Super, E. M. (1995). Culture and parenting. In M. H. Bornstein (Ed.), *Handbook of parenting* (Vol. 3). Hillsdale, NJ: Erlbaum.

Harlow, H. F. (1958). The nature of love. *American Psychologist, 13,* 673–685.

Harmon, O. R., Lambrinos, J., & Kennedy, P. (2008). Are online exams an invitation to cheat? *Journal of Economic Education, 39,* 116–125.

Harold, R. D., Colarossi, L. G., & Mercier, L. R. (2007). *Smooth sailing or stormy waters: Family transitions through adolescence and their implications for practice and policy.* Mahwah, NJ: Erlbaum.

Harris, J. B. (1998). *The nurture assumption: Why children turn out the way they do: Parents matter less than you think and peers matter more.* New York: Free Press.

Harris, K. R., Graham, S., Mason, L., & Friedlander, B. (2008). *Powerful writing strategies for all students.* Baltimore, MD: Brookes.

Harris, L. (1997). *A national poll of children and exercise.* Washington, DC: Lou Harris & Associates.

Harris, P. L. (2000). *The work of the imagination.* Oxford University Press.

Harris, P. L. (2006). Social cognition. In W. Damon & R. Lerner (Eds.), *Handbook of child psychology* (6th ed.). New York: Wiley.

Harris, P. L., & Koenig, M. A. (2006). Trust in testimony: How children learn about science and religion. *Child Development. 77,* 505–524.

Harris, R. J., Schoen, L. M., & Hensley, D. L., (1992). A cross-cultural study of story memory. *Journal of Cross-Cultural Psychology, 23,* 133–147.

Harris, Y. R., & Graham, J. A. C. (2007). *The African American child.* New York: Springer.

Harrison-Hale, A. O., McLoyd, V. C., & Smedley, B. (2004). Racial and ethnic status: Risk and protective processes among African-American families. In K. L. Maton, C. J. Schellenbach, B. J. Leadbetter, & A. L. Solarz (Eds.), *Investing in children, families, and communities.* Washington, DC: American Psychological Association.

Harrist, A. W. (1993, March). *Family interaction styles as predictors of children's competence: The role of synchrony and nonsynchrony.* Paper presented at the biennial meeting of the Society for Research in Child Development, New Orleans.

Hart, B., & Risley, T. R. (1995). *Meaningful differences.* Baltimore, MD: Paul Brookes.

Hart, C. H., Yang, C., Charlesworth, R., & Burts, D. C. (2003, April). *Early childhood teachers' curriculum beliefs, classroom practices, and children's' outcomes: What are the connections?* Paper presented at the biennial meeting of the Society for Research in Child Development, Tampa, FL.

Hart, D., & Karmel, M. P. (1996). Self-awareness and self-knowledge in humans, great apes, and monkeys. In A. Russon, K. Bard, & S. Parker (Eds.), *Reaching into thought.* New York: Cambridge University Press.

Hart, D., Burock, D., London, B., & Atkins, R. (2003). Prosocial development, antisocial development, and moral development. In A. M. Slater & G. Bremner (Eds.), *An introduction to developmental psychology.* Malden, MA: Blackwell.

Hart, D., Matsuba, M. K., & Atkins, R. (2008). The moral and civic effects of learning to serve. In L. Nucci & D. Narvaez (Eds.), *Handbook of moral and character education.* Clifton, NJ: Psychology Press.

Hart, S., & Carrington, H. (2002). Jealousy in 6-month-old infants. *Infancy, 3,* 395–402.

Harter, S. (1985). *Self-Perception Profile for Children.* Denver: University of Denver, Department of Psychology.

Harter, S. (1986). Processes underlying the construction, maintenance, and enhancement of the self-concept of children. In J. Suls & A. Greenwald (Eds.), *Psychological perspective on the self* (Vol. 3). Hillsdale, NJ: Erlbaum.

Harter, S. (1989). *Self-Perception Profile for Adolescents.* Denver: University of Denver, Department of Psychology.

Harter, S. (1998). The development of self-representations. In W. Damon (Ed.), *Handbook of child psychology* (5th ed., Vol. 3). New York: Wiley.

Harter, S. (1999). *The construction of the self.* New York: Guilford.

Harter, S. (2002). Unpublished review of J. W. Santrock's *Child development,* 10th ed. (New York: McGraw-Hill).

Harter, S. (2006). The self. In W. Damon & R. Lerner (Eds.), *Handbook of child psychology* (6th ed.). New York: Wiley.

Hartshorne, H., & May, M. S. (1928–1930). *Moral studies in the nature of character: Studies in deceit* (Vol. 1); *Studies in self-control* (Vol. 2); *Studies in the organization of character* (Vol. 3). New York: Macmillan.

Hartup, W. W. (1983). The peer system. In P. H. Mussen (Ed.), *Handbook of child psychology* (4th ed., Vol. 4). New York: Wiley.

Hartup, W. W. (1996). The company they keep: Friendships and their development significance. *Child Development, 67,* 1–13.

Hartup, W. W. (1999, April). *Peer relations and the growth of the individual child.* Paper presented at the meeting of the Society for Research in Child Development Albuquerque.

Hartup, W. W. (2000). Middle childhood: Socialization and social context. In A. Kazdin (Ed.), *Encyclopedia of psychology.* Washington, DC, & New York: American Psychological Association and Oxford University Press.

Hartup, W. W., & Laursen, B. (1999). Relationships as developmental contexts: Retrospective themes and contemporary issues. In W. Andrew Collins & B. Laursen (Eds.), *Relationships as developmental contexts.* Mahwah, NJ: Erlbaum.

Hartwell, L. (2008). *Genetics* (3rd ed.). New York: McGraw-Hill.

Harwood, R. L., & Feng, X. (2006). Studying acculturation among Latinos in the United States. In M. H. Bornstein & L. R. Cote (Eds.), *Acculturation and parent-child relationships.* Mahwah, NJ: Erlbaum.

Hastings, P. D., Sullivan, C., McShane, K. E., Coplan, R. J., Utendale, W. T., & Vyncke, J. D. (2008). Parental socialization, vagal regulation and preschoolers' anxious difficulties. Direct mothers and moderated fathers. *Child Development, 79,* 45–64.

Hastings, P. D., Utendale, W. T., & Sullivan, C. (2007). The socialization of prosocial development. In J. E. Grusec & P. D. Hastings (Eds.), *Handbook of socialization.* New York: Guilford.

Hattery, A. J., & Smith, E. (2007). *African American families.* Thousand Oaks, CA: Sage.

Hauck, F. R., Omojokun, O. O., & Siadaty, M. S. (2005). Do pacifiers reduce the risk of sudden infant death syndrome? A meta—analysis. *Pediatrics, 116,* e717–e723.

Haugaard, J. J., & Hazan, C. (2004). Adoption as a natural experiment. *Developmental Psychopathology, 15,* 909–926.

Haugaard, J. J., & Hazan, C. (2004). Recognizing and treating uncommon behavioral and emotional disorders in children and adolescents who have been severely maltreated: Reactive attachment disorder. *Child Maltreatment, 9,* 154–160.

Hausman, B. L. (2005). Risky business: framing childbirth in hospital settings. *Journal of Medical Ethics, 26,* 23–38.

Hayashino, D., & Chopra, S. B. (2009). Parenting and raising families. In N. Tewari & A. Alvarez (Eds.), *Asian American psychology.* Clifton, NJ: Psychology Press.

Healey, J. F. (2009). *Race, ethnicity, and class* (5th ed.). Thousand Oaks, CA: Sage.

Health Management Resources. (2001). *Child health and fitness.* Boston: Author.

Heck, K. E., Braveman, P., Cubbin, C., Chavez, G. F., & Kiely, J. L. (2006). Socioeconomic status and breastfeeding initiation among California mothers. *Public Health Reports, 121,* 51–59.

Hegaard, H. K., Hedegaard, M., Damm, P., Ottesen, B., Petersson, K., & Henriksen, T. B. (2008). Leisure time physical activity is associated with a reduced risk of preterm delivery. *American Journal of Obstetrics and Gynecology, 198,* e1–e5.

Heidi, R. R. (2006). The adaptive response of families to maternal employment: An introduction. In H. R. Riggio & D. F. Halpern (Eds.), *Changes at the intersection of work and family* (Vol. 2). Thousand Oaks, CA: Sage.

Heimann, M., Strid, K., Smith, L., Tjus, T., Ulvund, S. E., & Melzoff, A. N. (2006). Exploring the relation between memory, gestural communication, and the emergence of language in infancy: A longitudinal study. *Infant and Child Development, 15,* 233–249.

Henderson, V. L., & Dweck, C. S. (1990). Motivation and achievement. In S. S. Feldman & G. R. Elliott (Eds.), *At the threshold: The developing adolescent.* Cambridge, MA: Harvard University Press.

Hendry, J. (1995). *Understanding Japanese society.* London: Routledge.

Hendry, J. (1999). *Social anthropology.* New York: Macmillan.

Henninger, M. L. (2009). *Teaching young children* (4th ed.). Upper Saddle River, NJ: Prentice Hall.

Henriksen, T. B., Hjollund, N. H., Jensen, T. K., Bonde, J. P., Andersson, A. M.,

Kolstad, H., Ernst, E., Giwereman, A., Skakkebaek, N. E., & Olsen, J. (2004). Alcohol consumption at the time of conception and spontaneous abortion. *American Journal of Epidemiology, 160,* 661–667.

Hepper, P. (2007). The foundations of development. In A. Slater & M. Lewis (Eds.), *Introduction to infant development* (2nd ed.). New York: Oxford University Press.

Herbison, A. E., Porteus, R., Paper, J. R., Mora, J. M., & Hurst, P. R. (2008). Gonadotropin-releasing hormone neuron requirements for puberty, ovulation, and fertility. *Endocrinology, 149,* 597–604.

Herbst, M. A., Mercer, B. M., Beasley, D., Meyer, N., & Carr, T. (2003). Relationship of prenatal care and perinatal morbidity in low-birth-weight infants. *American Journal of Obstetrics and Gynecology, 189,* 930–933.

Herman, D. R., Harrison, G. G., Afifi, A. A., & Jenks, E. (2008). Effect of a target subsidy on intake of fruits and vegetables among low-income women in the Special Supplemental Nutrition Program for Women, Infants, and Children. *American Journal of Public Health, 98,* 98–105.

Herman-Giddens, M. E. (2007). The decline in the age of menarche in the United States: Should we be concerned? *Journal of Adolescent Health, 40,* 201–203.

Hermann, M., King, K., & Weitzman, M. (2008). Prenatal tobacco smoke and postnatal secondhand smoke exposure and child neurodevelopment. *Current Opinion in Pediatrics, 20,* 184–190.

Hernandez, D. H. (2007, March). *Children in immigrant families in the 21st century.* Paper presented at the meeting of the Society for Research in Child Development, Boston.

Hernandez-Reif, M., Diego, M., & Field, T. (2007). Preterm infants show reduced stress behaviors and activity after 5 days of massage therapy. *Infant Behavior and Development, 30,* 557–561.

Hertz-Picciotto, I., Park, H. Y., Dostal, M., Kocan, A., Trnovec, T., & Sram, R. (2008). Prenatal exposure to persistent and non-persistent organic compounds, and effects on immune system development. *Basic and Clinical Pharmacology and Toxicology, 102,* 146–154.

Hesmet, S., & Lo, K. C. (2006). Evaluation and treatment of ejaculatory duct obstruction in infertile men. *Canadian Journal of Urology, 13* (Suppl. 1), 18–21.

Hetherington, E. M. (1989). Coping with family transitions: Winners, losers, and survivors. *Child Development, 60,* 1–14.

Hetherington, E. M. (1993). An overview of the Virginia Longitudinal Study of Divorce and Remarriage with a focus on early adolescence. *Journal of Family Psychology, 7,* 39–56.

Hetherington, E. M. (2005). Divorce and the adjustment of children. *Pediatrics in Review, 26,* 163–169.

Hetherington, E. M. (2006). The influence of conflict, marital problem solving, and parenting on children's adjustment in nondivorced, divorced, and remarried families. In A.Clarke-Stewart & J. Dunn (Eds.), *Families count.* New York: Oxford University Press.

Hetherington, E. M., & Kelly, J. (2002). *For better or for worse: Divorce reconsidered.* New York: Norton.

Hetherington, E. M., Reiss, D., & Plomin, R. (Eds.). (1994). *Separate social worlds of siblings: The impact of nonshared environment on development.* Hillsdale, NJ: Erlbaum.

Hetherington, E. M., & Stanley-Hagan, M. (2002). Parenting in divorced and remarried families. In M. H. Bornstein (Ed.), *Handbook of parenting* (2nd ed., Vol. 3). Mahwah, NJ: Erlbaum.

Heuwinkel, M. K. (1996). New ways of learning: 5 new ways of teaching. *Childhood Education, 72,* 27–31.

Heyman, G. D., & Legare, C. H. (2005). Children's evaluation of sources of information about traits. *Developmental Psychology, 41,* 636–647.

Heyman, G. D., Fu, G., & Lee, K. (2007). Evaluating claims people make about themselves: The development of skepticism. *Child Development, 78,* 367–375.

Hick, P., & Thomas, G. (Eds.). (2009). *Inclusion and diversity in education.* Thousand Oaks, CA: Sage.

Hiebert, E. H. (2008). The word zone fluency curriculum: An alternative approach. In M. R. Kuhn & P. J. Schwanenflugel (Eds.), *Fluency in the classroom.* New York: Guilford.

Hill, C. R., & Stafford, F. P. (1980). Parental care of children: Time diary estimate of quantity, predictability, and variety. *Journal of Human Resources, 15,* 219–239.

Hill, M. A. (2007). Early human development. *Clinical Obstetrics and Gynecology, 50,* 2–9.

Hirsch, B. J., & Rapkin, B. D. (1987). The transition to junior high school: A longitudinal study of self-esteem, psychological symptomatology, school life, and social support. *Child Development, 58,* 1235–1243.

Hockenberry, M., & Wilson, D. (2009). *Wong's essentials of pediatric nursing.* Oxford, UK: Elsevier.

Hodapp, R. M., & Dykens, E. M. (2006). Mental retardation. In W. Damon & R. Lerner (Eds.), *Handbook of child psychology.* Mahwah, NJ: Erlbaum.

Hoefnagels, M. (2009). *Biology.* New York: McGraw-Hill.

Hofer, A., Seidentopf, C. M., Ischebeck, A., Rettenbacher, M. A., Verius, M., Felber, S., & Fleischhacker, W. (2006). Gender differences in regional cerebral activity during the perception of emotion: A functional MRI study. *Neuroimage, 32,* 854–862.

Hofer, A., Siedentopf, C. M., Ischebeck, A., Rettenbacher, M. A., Verius, M., Felber, S., & Fleischhacker, W. (2007). Sex differences in brain activation patterns during processing of positively and negatively valenced emotional stimuli. *Psychological Medicine, 37,* 109–119.

Hofer, S. M., & Sliwinski, M. J. (2006). Design and analysis of longitudinal studies on aging. In J. E. Birren & K. W. Schaie (Eds.), *Handbook of the psychology of aging* (6th ed.). San Diego: Academic Press.

Hoff, E., & Shatz, M. (Eds.). (2007). *Blackwell handbook of language development.* Malden, MA: Blackwell.

Hoff, E., Laursen, B., & Tardif, T. (2002). Socioeconomic status and parenting. In M. H. Bornstein (Ed.), *Handbook of parenting* (2nd ed.). Mahwah, NJ: Erlbaum.

Hoffman, M. L. (1970). Moral development. In P. H. Mussen (Ed.), *Manual of child psychology* (3rd ed., Vol. 2). New York: Wiley.

Hoffman, M. L. (1988). Moral development. In M. H. Bornstein & E. Lamb (Eds.), *Developmental psychology: An advanced textbook* (2nd ed.). Hillsdale, NJ: Erlbaum.

Hofheimer, J. A., & Lester, B. M. (2008). Neuropsychological assessment. In M. M. Haith & J. B. Benson (Eds.), *Encyclopedia of infancy and early childhood development.* Oxford, UK: Elsevier.

Hogan, M. A., Glazebrook, R., Brancato, V., & Rogers, J. (2007). *Maternal-newborn nursing: Review and rationales* (2nd ed.). Upper Saddle River, NJ: Prentice Hall.

Holden, K., & Hatcher, C. (2006). Economic status of the aged. In R. H. Binstock and L. K. George (Eds.), *Handbook of aging and the social sciences.* San Diego: Academic Press.

Hollich, G. J. (2007). Language development: From speech perception to first words. In A. Slater & M. Lewis (Eds.), *Introduction to infant development.* New York: Oxford University Press.

Hollich, G. J., & Houston, D. M. (2007). Language development: From speech to first words. In A. Slater & M. Lewis (Eds.), *Introduction to infant development* (2nd ed.). New York: Oxford University Press.

Hollich, G. J., Newman, R. S., & Jusczyk, P. W. (2005). Infants' use of synchronized visual information to separate streams of speech. *Child Development, 76,* 598–613.

Hollier, L., & Wendel, G. (2008). Third trimester antiviral prophylaxis for preventing maternal genital herpes simplex virus (HSV) recurrences and neonatal infection. *Cochrane Database of Systematic Reviews, 1,* CD004946.

Hollis-Sawyer, L. A., & Sawyer, T. P. (2008). Potential stereotypes threat and face validity effects on cognitive-based test performance in the classroom. *Educational Psychology, 28,* 291–304.

Holter, A., & Narvaez, D. (2008, in press). Moral education. In E. Anderman & L. Anderman (Eds.), *Psychology of classroom* *learning: An encyclopedia.* Farmington Hills, MI: Thomson Gale.

Holzman, L. (2009). *Vygotsky at work and play.* Oxford, UK: Routledge.

Hommel, B., Li, K. Z. H., & Li, S. C. (2004). Visual search across the life span. *Developmental Psychology, 40,* 545–558.

Honzik, M. P., MacFarlane, I. W., & Allen, L. (1948). The stability of mental test performance between two and eighteen years. *Journal of Experimental Education, 17,* 309–324.

Hood, B. M. (1995). Gravity rules for 2- to 4-year-olds? *Cognitive Development, 10,* 577–598.

Hooper, S. R., & others. (2008). Executive functions in young males with fragile X syndrome in comparison to mental age-matched controls: Baseline findings from a longitudinal study. *Neuropsychology, 22,* 36–47.

Hopkins, B. (1991). Facilitating early motor development: An intracultural study of West Indian mothers and their infants living in Britain. In J. K. Nugent, B. M. Lester, & T. B. Brazelton (Eds.), *The cultural context of infancy: Vol. 2. Multicultural and interdisciplinary approaches to parent-infant relations.* Norwood, NJ: Ablex.

Hopkins, B., & Westra, T. (1988). Maternal handling and motor development: An intracultural study. *Genetic Psychology Monographs, 14,* 377–420.

Hopkins, B., & Westra, T. (1990). Motor development, maternal expectations, and the role of handling. *Infant Behavior and Development, 13,* 117–122.

Horn, J. (2007). Spearman, *g*, expertise, and the nature of human cognitive capacity. In P. C. Kyllonen, R. D. Roberts, & L. Stankov (Eds.), *Extending intelligence.* Mahwah, NJ: Erlbaum.

Horne, R. S., Franco, P., Adamson, T. M., Groswasser, J., & Kahn, A. (2002). Effects of body position on sleep and arousal characteristics in infants. *Early Human Development, 69,* 25–33.

Hornor, G. (2005). Physical abuse: Recognition and reporting. *Journal of Pediatric Health Care, 19,* 4–11.

Horowitz, J. A., & Cousins, A. (2006). Postpartum depression treatment rates for at-risk women. *Nursing Research, 55* (Suppl. 2), S23-S27.

Horsthemke, B., & Buiting, K. (2008). Genomic imprinting and imprinting defects in humans. *Advances in Genetics, 61,* 225–246.

Horton, R. (2006). The coming decade for global action on child health. *Lancet, 367,* 3–5.

Hosea Blewett, H. J., Cicalo, M. C., Holland, C. D., & Field, C. J. (2008). The immunological components of human milk. *Advances in Food and Nutrition Research, 54,* 45–80.

Howe, L. D., Hutley, S. R., & Abramsky, T. (2006). Risk factors for injuries in young children in four developing countries: The Young Lives Study. *Tropic Medicine and International Health, 11,* 1557–1566.

Howe, M. J. A., Davidson, J. W., Moore, D. G., & Sloboda, J. A. (1995). Are there early childhood signs of musical ability? *Psychology of Music, 23,* 162–176.

Howe, N., & Recchia, H. E. (2008). Siblings and sibling rivalry. In M. M. Haith & J. B. Benson (Eds.), *Encyclopedia of infant and early childhood development.* Oxford, UK: Elsevier.

Howe, N., & Recchia, H. E. (2009, in press). Sibling relations and their impact on children's development. In R. E. Tremblay, R. deV Peters, M. Boivin, & R. G. Barr (Eds.), *Encyclopedia on early childhood development.* Montreal: Centre of Excellence for Early Childhood Development.

Howes, C. (1985, April). *Predicting preschool sociometric status from toddler peer interaction.* Paper presented at the meeting of the Society for Research in Child Development, Toronto.

Howes, C. (2009, in press). The impact of child care on young children (0–2). In R. E. Tremblay, R. deV Peters, M. Boivan, & R. G. Barr (Eds.), *Encyclopedia on early childhood development.* Montreal: Centre of Excellence for Early Childhood Development.

Hoyert, D. L., Mathews, T. J., Menacker, F., Strobino, D. M., & Guyer, B. (2006). Annual summary of vital statistics: 2004. *Pediatrics, 117,* 168–183.

Hu, H., & others. (2007). Fetal lead exposure at each stage of pregnancy as a predictor of infant mental development. *Environmental Health Perspectives, 114,* 1730–1735.

Huang, C. M., Tung, W. S., Kuo, L. L., & Ying-Ju, C. (2004). Comparison of pain responses of premature infants to the heelstick between containment and swaddling. *Journal of Nursing Research, 12,* 31–40.

Huang, L. N., Ying, Y. (1989). Chinese American children & adolescents. In J. T. Gibbs & L. N. Huang, (Eds.), *Children of color.* San Francisco: Jossey-Bass.

Huebner, A. M., & Garrod, A. C. (1993). Moral reasoning among Tibetan monks: A study of Buddhist adolescents and young adults in Nepal. *Journal of Cross-Cultural Psychology, 24,* 167–185.

Huesmann, L. R., Dubow, E. F., Eron, L.D., & Boxer, P. (2006). Middle childhood family-contextual and personal factors as predictors of adult outcomes. In A. C. Huston & M. N. Ripke (Eds.), *Developmental contexts in middle childhood.* New York: Cambridge University Press.

Huesmann, L. R., Moise-Titus, J., Podolski, C., & Eron, L. D. (2003). Longitudinal relations between children's exposure to TV violence and their aggressive and violent behavior in young adulthood: 1977–1992. *Developmental Psychology, 39,* 201–221.

Hueston, W. J., Geesey, M. E., & Diaz, V. (2008). Prenatal care initiation among pregnant teens in the United States: An analysis over 25 years. *Journal of Adolescent Health, 42,* 243–248.

Hughes, C., & Dunn, J. (2007). Children's relationships with other children. In C. A. Brownell & C. B. Kopp (Eds.), *Socioemotional development in the toddler years.* New York: Guilford.

Hughes, D. (2007). Unpublished review of J.W. Santrock's *Child development,* 12th ed. (New York: McGraw-Hill).

Hughes, M. E., Waite, L. J., LaPierre, T. A., & Luo, Y. (2007). All in the family: The impact of caring for grandchildren on grandparents' health. *Journals of Gerontology B: Psychological Sciences and Social Sciences, 62,* S108–S119.

Huizink, A. C., & Mulder, E. J. (2006). Maternal smoking, drinking, or cannibis use during pregnancy and neurobehavioral and cognitive functioning in human offspring. *Neuroscience and Biobehavioral Research, 30,* 24–41.

Hunt, E. (1995). *Will we be smart enough? A cognitive analysis of the coming work force.* New York: Russell Sage.

Hurt, H., Brodsky, N. L., Roth, H., Malmud, F., & Giannetta, J. M. (2005). School performance of children with gestational cocaine exposure. *Neurotoxicology and Teratology, 27,* 203–211.

Hurwitz, L. M., & others. (2006). Radiation dose to the fetus from body MDCT during early gestation. *American Journal of Roentgenology, 186,* 871–876.

Hustedt, J. T., & Barnett, W. S. (2009, in press). Head Start policy. In R. E. Tremblay, R. deV Peters, M. Boivin, & R. G. Barr (Eds.), *Encyclopedia on early childhood development.* Montreal: Centre of Excellence for Early Childhood Development.

Huston, A. C., & Ripke, N. N. (2006). Experiences in middle and late childhood and children's development. In A. C. Huston & M. N. Ripke (Eds.), *Developmental contexts in middle childhood.* New York: Cambridge University Press.

Huston, A. C., Duncan, G. J., Grander, R., Bos, J., McLoyd, V., Mistry, R., Crosby, D., Gibson, C., Magnuson, K., Romich, J., & Ventura, A. (2001). Work-based antipoverty programs for parents can enhance the school performance and social behavior of children. *Child Development, 72,* 318–336.

Huston, A. C., Epps, S. R., Shim, M. S., Duncan, G. J., Crosby, D. A., & Ripke, M.N. (2006). Effects of a family poverty intervention program last from middle childhood to adolescence. In A. C. Huston, & M. N. Ripke, (Eds.), *Developmental contexts of middle childhood: Bridges to adolescence and adulthood.* New York: Cambridge University Press.

Hutson, R. A. (2008). Poverty. In N. J. Salkind (Ed.), *Encyclopedia of educational psychology.* Thousand Oaks, CA: Sage.

Huttenlocher, J., Haight, W., Bruk, A., Seltzer, M., & Lyons, T. (1991). Early vocabulary growth: Relation to language input and gender. *Developmental Psychology, 27,* 236–248.

Huttenlocher, P. R., & Dabholkar, A. S. (1997). Regional differences in synaptogenesis in human cerebral cortex. *Journal of Comparative Neurology, 37* (2), 167–178.

Hvas, A. M., Nexos, E., & Nielsen, J. B. (2006). Vitamin B(12) and vitamin B(6) supplementation is needed among adults with phenylketonuria (PKU). *Journal of Inherited Metabolic Disorders, 29,* 47–53.

Hwang, S. J., Ji, E. K., Kim, Y. M., Shinn, Y., Cheon, Y. H., & Rhyu, I. J. (2004). Gender differences in the corpus collosum of neonates. *Neuroreport, 29,* 1029–1032.

Hyde, D. R. (2009). *Introduction to genetic principles.* New York: McGraw-Hill.

Hyde, J. S. (2005). The gender similarities hypothesis. *American Psychologist, 60,* 581–592.

Hyde, J. S. (2007a). *Half the human experience* (7th ed.). Boston: Houghton Mifflin.

Hyde, J. S. (2007b). New directions in the study of gender similarities and differences. *Current Directions in Psychological Science, 16,* 259–263.

Hyde, J. S., Lindberg, S. M., Linn, M. C., Ellis, A. B., & Williams, C. C. (2008). Gender similarities characterize math performance. *Science, 321,* 494–495.

Hymel, S., McDougall, P., & Renshaw, P. (2004). Peer acceptance/rejection. In P. K. Smith & C. H. Hart (Eds.), *Blackwell handbook of childhood social development.* Malden, MA: Blackwell.

Hyson, M. (2007). Curriculum. In R. New & M.Cochran (Eds.), *Early childhood education: An international encyclopedia of early childhood education.* New York: Greenwood.

Hyson, M. C., Copple, C., & Jones, J. (2006). Early childhood development and education. In W. Damon & R. Lerner (Eds.), *Handbook of child psychology* (6th ed.). New York: Wiley.

I

"I Have a Dream" Foundation. (2008). *About us.* Retrieved July 5, 2008, from http://www. ihad.org

Iacoboni, M., & Dapretto, M. (2006). The mirror neuron system and the consequences of its dysfunction. *Nature Reviews: Neuroscience, 7,* 942–951.

Ige, F., & Shelton, D. (2004). Reducing the risk of sudden infant death syndrome (SIDS) in African-American communities. *Journal of Pediatric Nursing. 19,* 290–292.

Imada, T., Zhang, Y., Cheour, M., Taulu, S., Ahonen, A., & Kuhl, P. K. (2007). Infant speech perception activates Broca's area: A developmental magnetoencephalography study. *Neuroreport, 17,* 957–962.

Imbo, I., & Vandierendonck, A. (2007). The development of strategy use in elementary school children: Working memory and individual differences. *Journal of Experimental Child Psychology, 96,* 284–309.

Immordino-Yang, M. H., & Fischer, K. W. (2007). Dynamic development of hemispheric biases in three cases: Cognitive/hemispheric cycles, music, and hemispherectomy. In D.Coch, G. Dawson, & K. W. Fischer (Eds.), *Human behavior, learning, and the developing brain.* New York: Guilford.

Impett, E. A., Schoolder, D., Tolman, L., Sorsoli, L., & Henson, J. M. (2008). Girls' relationship authenticity and self-esteem across adolescence. *Developmental Psychology, 44,* 722–733.

International Montessori Council. (2006). Much of their success on prime-time television. Retrieved November 15, 2006, from www. Montessori.org/enews/barbara_walters.html

Ip, S., Chung, M., Raman, G., Chew, P., Magula, N., Devine, D., Trikalinos, T., & Lau, J. (2007). Breastfeeding and maternal and infant health outcomes in developed countries. *Evidence Report/Technology Assessment, 153,* 1–86.

Irvin, J. L., Buehl, D. R., & Kiemp, R. M. (2007). *Reading and the high school student* (2nd ed.). Boston: Allyn & Bacon.

Isen, J., & Baker, L. A. (2008). Genetic disorders: Sex-linked. In M. M. Haith & J. B. Benson (Eds.), *Encyclopedia of infant and early childhood development.* Oxford, UK: Elsevier.

Ishii-Kuntz, M. (2004). Asian American families. In M. Coleman & L. Ganong (Eds.), *Handbook of contemporary families.* Thousand Oaks, CA: Sage.

Israel, S. E. (2007). *Using metacognitive assessments to create individualized reading instruction.* Newark, DE: International Reading Association.

Ito, A., Honmna, Y., Inamori, E., Yada, Y., Momoi, M. Y., & Nakamura, Y. (2006). Developmental outcome of very low birth weight twins conceived by assisted reproduction techniques. *Journal of Perinatology, 26,* 130–136.

Itti, E., Gaw Gonzalo, I. T., Pawlikowska-Haddal, A., Boone, K. B., Mlikotic, A., Itti, L., Mishkin, F. S., & Swerdloff, R. S. (2006). The structural brain correlates of cognitive deficits in adults with Klinefelter's syndrome. *Journal of Clinical Endocrinology and Metabolism, 91,* 1423–1427.

Iverson, P., & Kuhl, P. K. (1996). Influences of phonetic identification and category goodness on American listeners' perceptions of /r/ and /l/. *Journal of the Acoustical Society of America, 99,* 1130–1140.

Iverson, P., Kuhl, P. K., Akahane-Yamada, R., Diesch, E., Tohkura, Y., Ketterman, A., & Siebert, C. (2003). A perceptual interference account of acquisition difficulties in non-native phonemes. *Cognition, 87,* B47–B57.

Izard, C. E. (2009, in press). Emotion theory and research: Highlights, unanswered questions, and emerging issues. *Annual Review of Psychology, Vol. 60.* Palo Alto, CA: Annual Reviews.

J

Jackson, L. A., Eye, A., Biocca, F. A., Barbatsis, G., Zhao, G., & Fitzgerald, H. E. (2006). Does home Internet use influence the academic performance of low-income children? *Developmental Psychology, 42,* 429–435.

Jackson, S. L. (2008). *Research methods.* Belmont, CA: Wadsworth.

Jacobson, J. L., & Jacobson, S. W. (2002). Association of prenatal exposure to an environmental contaminant with intellectual function in childhood. *Journal of Toxicology—Clinical Toxicology, 40,* 467–475.

Jacobson, J. L., & Jacobson, S. W. (2003). Prenatal exposure to polychlorinated biphenyls and attention at school age. *Journal of Pediatrics, 143,* 780–788.

Jacobson, J. L., Jocobson, S. W., Fein, G. G., Schwartz, P. M., & Dowler, J. (1984). Prenatal exposure to an environmental toxin: A test of the multiple-effects model. *Developmental Psychology, 20,* 523–532.

Jaddoe, V. W., Troe, E. J., Hofman, A., Mackenbach, J. P., Moll, H. A., Steegers, E. A., & Witteman, J. C. (2008). Active and passive smoking during pregnancy and the risks of low birthweight and preterm birth: The Generation R Study. *Pediatric and Perinatal Epidemiology, 22,* 162–171.

Jaffee, S., & Hyde, J. S. (2000). Gender differences in moral orientation: A meta-analysis. *Psychological Bulletin, 126,* 703–726.

Jalongo, M. R. (2007). *Early childhood language arts* (4th ed.). Boston: Allyn & Bacon.

James, A. H., Brancazio, L. R., & Price, T. (2008). Aspirin and reproductive outcomes. *Obstetrical and Gynecological Survey, 63,* 49–57.

James, D. C., & Dobson, B. (2005). Position of the American Dietetic Association: Promoting and supporting breastfeeding. *Journal of the American Dietetic Association, 105,* 810–818.

James, W. (1890/1950). *The principles of psychology.* New York: Dover.

Jansen, I. (2006). Decision making in childbirth: The influence of traditional structures in a Ghanaian village. *International Nursing Review, 53,* 41–46.

Jarrett, R. L. (1995). Growing up poor: The family experiences of socially mobile youth in low-income African-American neighborhoods. *Journal of Adolescent Research, 10,* 111–135.

Jarrold, C., Baddeley, A. D., & Phillips, C. (2007). Long-term memory for verbal and visual information in Down syndrome and

Williams syndrome: Performance on the Doors and People test. *Cortex, 43,* 233–247.

Jarvin, L., Newman, T., Randi, J., Sternberg, R. J., & Grigorenko, E. L. (2008). Matching instruction and assessment. In J. A. Plucker & C. M. Callahan (Eds.), *Critical issues and practices in gifted education* (pp. 345–365). Waco, TX: Prufrock.

Jaswal, V. K., & Fernald, A. (2007). Learning to communicate. In A. Slater & M. Lewis (Eds.), *Introduction to infant development* (2nd ed.). New York: Oxford University Press.

Jayson, S. (2006, June 29). The "millenials" come of age. *USA Today,* pp. 1–2D.

Jencks, C. (1979). *Who gets ahead? The determinants of economic success in America.* New York: Basic Books.

Jenkins, J. M., & Astington, J. W. (1996). Cognitive factors and family structure associated with theory of mind development in young children. *Developmental Psychology, 32,* 70–78.

Jenni, O. G., & Lebourgeois, M. K. (2006). Understanding sleep-wake behavior and disorders in children: The value of a model. *Current Opinions in Psychiatry, 19,* 282–287.

Jensen, A. R. (2008). Book review. *Intelligence, 36,* 96–97.

Jensen, P. S., & others. (2007). 3-year follow-up of the NIMH MTA study. *Journal of the American Academy of Child and Adolescent Psychiatry, 46,* 989–1002.

Ji, B. T., Shu, X. O., Linet, M. S., Zheng, W., Wacholde, S., Gao, Y. T., Ying, D. M., & Jin, E. (1997). Paternal cigarette smoking and the risk of childhood cancer among offspring of nonsmoking mothers. *Journal of the National Cancer Institute, 89,* 238–244.

Jiao, S., Ji, G., & Jing, Q. (1996). Cognitive development of Chinese urban only children and children with siblings. *Child Development, 67,* 387–395.

Johnson, A. N. (2005). Kangaroo holding beyond the NICU. *Pediatric Nursing, 31,* 53–56.

Johnson, A. N. (2007). Factors influencing implementation of kangaroo holding in a special care nursery. *MCN American Journal of Maternal Child Nursing, 32,* 25–29.

Johnson, D. J., Jaeger, E., Randolph, S. M., Cauce, A., Ward, J., & National Institute of Child Health and Human Development Early Child Care Research Network (2003). Studying the effects of early child care experiences on the development of children of color in the United States. *Child Development, 74,* 1227–1244.

Johnson, G. B. (2008). *The living world* (5th ed.). New York: McGraw-Hill.

Johnson, H. L., Erbelding, E. J., & Ghanem, K. G. (2007). Sexually transmitted infections during pregnancy. *Current Infectious Disease Reports, 9,* 125–133.

Johnson, J. A., Musial, D. L., Hall, G. E., Gollnick, D. M., & Dupuis, V. L. (2008). *Foundations of American education* (14th ed.). Boston: Allyn & Bacon.

Johnson, J. S., & Newport, E. L. (1991). Critical period effects on universal properties of language: The status of subjacency in the acquisition of a second language. *Cognition, 39,* 215–258.

Johnson, R. J. (2008). Advances in understanding and treating childhood sexual abuse: Implications for research and policy. *Family and Community Health, 31* (Suppl. 1), S24–S31.

Johnson, S. (2007). Cognitive and behavioral outcomes following very preterm birth. *Seminars in Fetal and Neonatal Medicine, 12,* 363–373.

Johnson, W., te Nijenhuis, J., & Bouchard, T. J. (2008). Still just 1 *g*: Consistent results from five test batteries. *Intelligence, 36,* 81–95.

John-Steiner, V. (2007). Vygotsky on thinking and speaking. In H. Daniels, J. Wertsch, & M. Cole (Eds.), *The Cambridge companion to Vygotsky.* New York: Cambridge University Press.

Johnston, A. D., Tarrant, K., & Brooks-Gunn, J. (2008). Early childhood education and care: An opportunity to enhance the lives of poor children. In D. R. Crane & T. B. Heaton (Eds.), *Handbook of families and poverty.* Thousand Oaks, CA: Sage.

Johnston, B. B. (2008). Will increasing folic acid in fortified grain products further reduce neural tube defects without causing harm?: Consideration of the evidence. *Pediatric Research, 63,* 2–8.

Jolley, S. N., Ellmore, S., Barnard, K. E., & Carr, D. B. (2007). Dysregulation of the hypothalamic-pituitary-adrenal axis in postpartum depression. *Biological Research for Nursing, 8,* 210–222.

Jones, D. C., Bain, N., & King, S. (2008). Weight and muscularity concerns as longitudinal predictors of body image among early adolescent boys: a test of the dual path model. *Body Image, 5,* 195–204.

Jones, H. W. (2007). Iatrogenic multiple births: A 2003 checkup. *Fertility and Sterility, 87,* 453–455.

Jones, M. C. (1965). Psychological correlates of somatic development. *Child Development, 36,* 899–911.

Jones, M. D. & Galliher, R. V. (2007). Navajo ethnic identity: Predictors of psychosocial outcomes in Navajo adolescents. *Journal of Research on Adolescence, 17,* 683–696.

Jordan, S. J., & Others. (2008, in press). Serious ovarian, fallopian tube, and primary peritoneal cancers: A comprehensive epidemiological analysis. *International Journal of Cancer.*

Jorm, A. F., Anstey, K. J., Christensen, H., & Rodgers, B. (2004). Gender differences in cognitive abilities: The mediating role of health state and health habits. *Intelligence, 32,* 7–23.

Joseph, J. (2006). *The missing gene.* New York: Algora.

Josephson Institute of Ethics. (2006). *2006 Josephson Institute report card on the ethics of American youth. Part one—integrity.* Los Angeles: Josephson Institute.

Joshi, S., & Kotecha, S. (2007). Lung growth and development. *Early Human Development, 83,* 789–794.

Judge, S. (2005, April). *Impact of computer technology on the academic achievement of young African American children.* Paper presented at the meeting of the Society for Research in Child Development, Atlanta.

Juffer, F., & van IJzendoorn, M. H. (2005). Behavior problems and mental health referrals of international adoptees: A meta-analysis. *Journal of the American Medical Association, 293,* 2501–2513.

Juffer, F., & van IJzendoorn, M. H. (2007). Adoptees do not lack self-esteem: A meta-analysis of studies on self-esteem of transracial, international, and domestic adoptees. *Psychological Bulletin, 133,* 1067–1083.

Juhl, M., Andersen, P. K., Olsen, J., Madsen, M., Jorgensen, T., Nohr, E. A., & Andersen, A. M. (2008, in press). Physical exercise during pregnancy and the risk of preterm birth: A study within the Danish National Birth Cohort. *American Journal of Epidemiology.*

Jusczyk, P. W. (2002). Language development: From speech perception to words. In A. Slater & M. Lewis (Eds.), *Introduction to infant development.* New York: Oxford University Press.

Jusczyk, P. W., & Hohne, E. A. (1997). Infants' memory for spoken words. *Science, 277,* 1984–1986.

Juvonen, J., & Galvan, A. (2008). Peer influence in involuntary groups: Lessons from research on bullying. In M. J. Prinstein & K. A. Dodge (Eds.), *Understanding peer influence in children and adolescents.* New York: Guilford.

Juvonen, J., Graham, S., & Schuster, M. A. (2003). Bullying among young adolescents. *Pediatrics, 112,* 1231–1237.

K

Kagan, J. (1987). Perspectives on infancy. In J. D. Osofsky (Eds.), *Handbook on infant development* (2nd ed.). New York: Wiley.

Kagan, J. (1992). Yesterday's promises, tomorrow's promises. *Developmental Psychology, 28,* 990–997.

Kagan, J. (2000). Temperament. In A. Kazdin (Ed.), *Encyclopedia of psychology.* Washington, DC, & New York: American Psychological Association and Oxford University Press.

Kagan, J. (2002). Behavioral inhibition as a temperamental category. In R. J. Davidson, K. R. Scherer, & H. H. Goldsmith (Eds.), *Handbook of affective sciences.* New York: Oxford University Press.

Kagan, J. (2003). Biology, context, and development. *Annual Review of Psychology* (Vol. 54). Palo Alto, CA: Annual Reviews.

Kagan, J. (2004, May 8). Commentary in Teen brains on trial. *Science News Online*, p. 2.

Kagan, J. (2007). *What is emotion?* New Haven, CT: Yale University Press.

Kagan, J. (2008). Fear and wariness. In M. M. Haith & J. B. Benson (Eds.), *Encyclopedia of infant and early childhood development.* Oxford, UK: Elsevier.

Kagan, J. (2009, in press). Temperament. In R. E. Tremblay, deV Peters, M. Boivan, & R. G. Barr (Eds.), *Encyclopedia on early childhood development.* Montreal: Center of Excellence for Early Childhood Development.

Kagan, J., Kearsley, R. B., & Zelazo, P. R. (1978). *Infancy: Its place in human development.* Cambridge, MA: Harvard University Press.

Kagan, J., & Snidman, N. (1991). Infant predictors of inhibited and uninhibited behavioral profiles. *Psychological Science, 2,* 40–44.

Kagan, J., Snidman, N., Kahn, V., & Towsley, S. (2007). The preservation of two infant temperaments into adolescence. *Monographs of the Society for Research in Child Development, 72* (No. 2), 1–75.

Kagan, S. L., & Kauerz, K. (2009, in press). Preschool programs: Effective curricula. In R. G. Tremblay, R. deV Peters, M. Boivin, & R. G. Barr (Eds.), *Encyclopedia on early childhood development.* Montreal: Centre for Early Childhood Development.

Kagan, S. L., & Scott-Little, C. (2004). Early learning standards. *Phi Delta Kappan, 82,* 388–395.

Kagitcibasi, C. (2006). An overview of acculturation and parent-child relationships. In M. H. Bornstein & L. R. Cote (Eds.), *Acculturation and parent-child relationships.* Mahwah, NJ: Erlbaum.

Kagitcibasi, C. (2007). *Family, self, and human development across cultures.* Mahwah, NJ: Erlbaum.

Kail, R. V. (2007). Longitudinal evidence that increases in processing speed and working memory enhance children's reasoning. *Psychological Science, 18,* 312–313.

Kalant, H. (2004). Adverse effects of cannabis on health: An update of the literature since 1996. *Progress in Neuropsychopharmacology and Biological Psychiatry, 28,* 849–863.

Kalichman, S. C., Simbayi, L. C., Jooste, S., Cherry, C., & Cain, D. (2005). Poverty related stressors and HIV AIDS transmission risks in two South African communities. *Journal of Urban Health, 82,* 237–249.

Kammerman, S. B. (1989). Child care, women, work, and the family: An international overview of child-care services and related policies. In J. S. Lande, S. Scarr, & N. Gunzenhauser (Eds.), *Caring for children: Challenge to America.* Hillsdale, NJ: Erlbaum.

Kammerman, S. B. (2000a). Parental leave policies. *Social Policy Report of the Society for Research in Child Development, XIV* (No. 2), 1–15.

Kammerman, S. B. (2000b). From maternity to paternity child leave policies. *Journal of the Medical Women's Association, 55,* 98–99.

Kammerman, S. B. (2009, in press). Maternity, paternity, and parental leave policies. In R. E. Tremblay, deV Peters, M. Boivan, & R. G. Barr (Eds.), *Encyclopedia on early childhood development.* Montreal: Center of Excellence for Early Childhood Development.

Kamii, C. (1985). *Young children reinvent arithmetic: Implications of Piaget's theory.* New York: Teachers College Press.

Kamii, C. (1989). *Young children continue to reinvent arithmetic.* New York: Teachers College Press.

Kanoy, K., Ulku-Steiner, B., Cox, M., & Burchinal, M. (2003). Marital relationship and individual psychological characteristics that predict physical punishment of children. *Journal of Family Psychology, 17,* 20–28.

Karnes, F. A., & Stephens, K. R. (2008). *Achieving excellence: Educating the gifted and talented.* Upper Saddle River, NJ: Prentice Hall.

Karoly, L. A. & Bigelow, J. A. (2005). *The economics of investing in universal preschool education in California.* Santa Monica, CA: The RAND Corporation.

Karp, H. (2002). *The happiest baby on the block.* New York: Bantam.

Karpov, Y. V. (2006). *The neo-Vygotskian - approach to child development.* New York: Cambridge University Press.

Karreman, A., van Tuijl, C., van Aken, M. A. G., & Dekovic, M. (2008). Parenting, coparenting, and effortful control in preschoolers. *Journal of Family Psychology, 22,* 30–40.

Katz, L. (1999). Curriculum disputes in early childhood education. *ERIC Clearinghouse on Elementary and Early Childhood Education,* Document EDO-PS-99-13.

Katz, L., & Chard, S. (1989). *Engaging the minds of young children: The project approach.* Norwood, NJ: Ablex.

Katzov, H. (2007). New insights into autism from a comprehensive genetic map. *Clinical Genetics, 72,* 186–187.

Kaufman, S. B., & Sternberg, R. J. (2008). Conceptions of giftedness. In S. Pfeiffer (Ed.), *Handbook of giftedness.* New York: Springer.

Kavsek, M. (2004). Predicting IQ from infant visual habituation and dishabituation: A meta-analysis. *Journal of Applied Developmental Psychology, 25,* 369–393.

Kazdin, A. E., & Benjet, C. (2003). Spanking children: Evidence and issues. *Current Directions in Psychological Science, 12,* 99–103.

Keen, R. (2005). Unpublished review of J. W. Santrock's *Topical life-span development* (3rd ed.), (New York: McGraw-Hill).

Keenan, K. (2009, in press). The development and socialization of aggression in the first five years of life. In R. E. Tremblay, R. deV Peters, M. Boivin, & R. G. Barr (Eds.), *Encyclopedia on early childhood development.* Montreal: Centre of Excellence for Early Childhood Development.

Keens, T. G., & Gemmill, D. R. (2008). SIDS. In M. M. Haith & J. B. Benson (Eds.), *Encyclopedia of infant and early childhood development.* Oxford, UK: Elsevier.

Keil, F. (2006). Cognitive science and cognitive development. In W. Damon & R. Lerner (Eds.), *Handbook of child psychology* (6th ed.). New York: Wiley.

Kellman, P. J., & Arterberry, M. E. (2006). Infant visual perception. In W. Damon & R. Lerner (Eds.), *Handbook of child psychology* (6thed.). New York: Wiley.

Kellman, P. J., & Banks, M. S. (1998). Infant visual perception. In W. Damon (Eds.), *Handbook of child psychology* (5th ed., Vol. 2). New York: Wiley.

Kellogg, R. T. (2007). *Fundamentals of cognitive psychology.* Thousand Oaks, CA: Sage.

Kellough, R. D., & Carjuzaa, J. D. (2009). *Teaching in the middle and secondary schools* (9thed.). Boston: Allyn & Bacon.

Kellow, J. T., & & Jones, B. D. (2008). The effects of stereotypes on the achievement gap: Reexamining the academic performance of African American high school students. *Journal of Black Psychology, 34,* 94–120.

Kelly, D. J., & others. (2007a). Cross-race preferences for same-race faces extend beyond the African versus Caucasian contrast in 3-month-old infants. *Infancy, 11,* 87–95.

Kelly, D. J., & others. (2007b). Three-month-olds, but not newborns, prefer own-race faces. *Developmental Science, 8,* F31–F36.

Kelly, J. B. (2007). Children's living arrangements following separation and divorce: Insights from empirical and clinical research. *Family Process, 46,* 35–52.

Kelly, J. P., Borchert, J., & Teller, D. Y. (1997). The development of chromatic and achromatic sensitivity in infancy as tested with the sweep VEP. *Vision Research, 37,* 2057–2072.

Kennedy, R. D., & D'Andrea, A. D. (2006). DNA repair pathways in clinical practice: Lessons from pediatric cancer susceptibility syndromes. *Journal of Clinical Oncology, 24,* 3799–3808.

Kennell, J. H. (2006). Randomized controlled trial of skin-to-skin contact from birth versus conventional incubator for physiological stabilization in 1200 g to 2199 g newborns. *Acta Paediatica (Sweden), 95,* 15–16.

Kennell, J. H., & McGrath, S. K. (1999). Commentary: Practical and humanistic lessons from the third world for perinatal caregivers everywhere. *Birth, 26,* 9–10.

Kenney-Benson, G. A., Pomerantz, E. M., Ryan, A. M., & Patrick, H. (2006). Sex differences in math performance: The role of children's approach to schoolwork. *Developmental Psychology, 42*, 11–26.

Kerr, M. (2001). Culture as a context for temperament. In T. D. Wachs & G. A. Kohnstamm (Eds.), *Temperament in context.* Mahwah, NJ: Erlbaum.

Kessen, W., Haith, M. M., & Salapatek, P. (1970). Human infancy. In P. H. Mussen (Eds.), *Manual of child psychology* (3rd ed., Vol. 1). New York: Wiley.

Killgore, W. D., & Yurgelun-Todd, D. A. (2007). Neural correlates of emotional intelligence in adolescent children. *Cognitive, Affective, and Behavioral Neuroscience, 7*, 140–151.

Kim, J., & Cicchetti, D. (2004). A longitudinal study of child maltreatment, mother-child relationship quality and maladjustment: The role of self-esteem and social competence. *Journal of Abnormal Child Psychology, 32*, 341–354.

Kim, J., Peterson, K. E., Scanlon, K. S., Fitzmaurice, G. M., Must, A., Oken, E., Rifas-Shiman, S. L., Rich-Edwards, J. W., & Gillman, M. W. (2006). Trends in overweight from 1980 through 2001 among preschool-aged children enrolled in a health maintenance organization. *Obesity, 14*, 1107–1112.

Kim, J-K., McHale, S. M., Crouter, A. C., & Osgood, D. W. (2007). Longitudinal linkages between sibling relationships and adjustment from middle childhood through adolescence. *Developmental Psychology, 43*, 960–973.

Kim, S. Y., Su, J., Yancura, L., & Yee, B. (2009). Asian American and Pacific Islander families. In N. Tewari & A. Alvarez (Eds.), *Asian American psychology.* Clifton, NJ: Psychology Press.

Kimber, L., McNabb, M., McCourt, C., Haines, A., & Brocklehurst, P. (2008, in press). Massage or music for pain relief in labor: A pilot randomized placebo controlled trial. *European Journal of Pain.*

King, A. A., DeBraun, M. R., & White, D. A. (2008). Need for cognitive rehabilitation for children with sickle-cell disease and strokes. *Expert Review of Neurotherapeutics, 8*, 291–296.

Kingston, M. K. (1976). *The woman warrior: Memoirs of a girlhood among ghosts.* New York: Vintage Books.

Kingston, M. K. (1980). *China men.* New York: Knopf.

Kirkorian, H. L., Wartella, E. A., & Anderson, D. A. (2008). Media and young children's learning. *Future of Children, 18* (No. 1), 39–61.

Kisilevsky, S., Hains, S. M., Jacquet, A. Y., Granier-Deferre, C., & Lecanuet, J. P. (2004). Maturation of fetal responses to music. *Developmental Science, 7*, 550–559.

Kitzmann, K. M. (2009, in press). Domestic violence and its impact on the social and emotional development of young children. In R. E. Tremblay, R. deV Peters, M. Boivin, & R. G. Barr (Eds.), *Encyclopedia on early childhood development.* Montreal: Centre of Excellence for Early Childhood Development.

Klaus, M., & Kennell, H. H. (1976). *Maternal-infant bonding.* St. Louis: Mosby.

Klieger, C., Pollex, E., & Koren, G. (2008). Treating the mother—protecting the newborn: The safety of hypoglycemic drugs in pregnancy. *Journal of Maternal-Fetal and Neonatal Medicine, 21*, 191–196.

Kliegman, R. M., Behrman, R. E., Jenson, H. B., & Stanton, B. F. (2007). *Nelson textbook of pediatrics* (18th ed.). London: Elsevier.

Kling, K. C., Hyde, J. S., Showers, C. J., & Buswell, B. N. (1999). Gender differences in self-esteem: A meta-analysis. *Psychological Bulletin, 125*, 470–500.

Klingman, A. (2006). Children and war trauma. In W. Damon & R. Lerner (Eds.), *Handbook of child psychology* (6th ed.). New York: Wiley.

Knowles, R. (2004). *Alzheimer's disease.* Upper Saddle River, NJ: Prentice Hall.

Kobayashi, K., Tajima, M., Toishi, S., Fujimori, K. Suzuki, Y., & Udagama, H. (2005). Fetal growth restriction associated with measles virus infection during pregnancy. *Journal of Perinatal Medicine, 33*, 67–68.

Kochanska, G., & Aksan, N. (2007). Conscience in childhood: Past, present, and future. *Merrill-Palmer Quarterly, 50*, 299–310.

Kochanska, G., Aksan, N., Knaack, A., & Rhines, H. M. (2004). Maternal parenting and children's conscience: Early security as a moderator. *Child Development, 75*, 1229–1242.

Kochanska, G., Aksan, N., Prisco, T. R., & Adams, E. E. (2008). Mother-child and father-child mutually responsive orientation in the first two years and children's outcomes at preschool age: Mechanisms of influence. *Child Development, 79*, 30–44.

Kochanska, G., Forman, D. R., Aksan, N., & Dunbar, S. B. (2005). Pathways to conscience: Early mother-child mutually responsive orientation and children's moral emotion, conduct, and cognition. *Journal of Child Psychology and Psychiatry, 46*, 19–34.

Kochanska, G., Gross, J. N., Lin, M., & Nichols, K. E. (2002). Guilt in young children: Development, determinants, and relations with a broader set of standards. *Child Development, 73*, 461–482.

Koenig, L. B., McGue, M., & Iacono, W. G. (2008). Stability and change in religousness during emerging adulthood. *Developmental Psychology, 44*, 523–543.

Kohen, D. E., Leventhal, T., Dahinten, V.S., & McIntosh, C. N. (2008). Neighborhood disadvantage: Pathways of effects for young children. *Child Development, 79*, 156–169.

Kohlberg, L. (1958). *The development of modes of moral thinking and choice in the years 10 to 16.* Unpublished doctoral dissertation, University of Chicago.

Kohlberg, L. (1966). A cognitive—developmental analysis of children's sex-role concepts and attitudes. In E. E. Maccoby (Ed.), *The development of sex differences.* Palo Alto, CA: Stanford University Press.

Kohlberg, L. (1969). Stage and sequence: The cognitive-developmental approach to socialization. In D. A. Goslin (Ed.), *Handbook of socialization theory and research.* Chicago: Rand McNally.

Kohlberg, L. (1986). A current statement on some theoretical issues. In S. Modgil & C. Modgil (Eds.), *Lawrence Kohlberg.* Philadelphia: Falmer.

Koolhof, R., Loeber, R., Wei, E. H., Pardini, D., & D'escury, A. C. (2007). Inhibition deficits of serious delinquent boys of low intelligence. *Criminal Behavior and Mental Health, 17*, 274–292.

Kopp, C. B. (2008). Self-regulatory processes. In M. M. Haith & J. B. Benson (Eds.), *Encyclopedia of infant and early childhood development.* Oxford, UK: Elsevier.

Kopp, C. B., & Neufeld, S. J. (2002). Emotional development in infancy. In R. Davidson & K. Scherer (Eds.), *Handbook of affective sciences.* New York: Oxford University Press.

Kornblum, J. (2006, March 9). How to monitor the kids? *USA Today, 1D*, p. 1.

Korres, S., & others. (2008, in press). Outcomes of efficacy of newborn hearing screening: Strengths and weaknesses (success or failure?). *Laryngoscope.*

Korrick, S. A., & Sagiv, S. K. (2008). Polychlorinated biphenyls, organopesticides, and neurodevelopment. *Current Opinion in Pediatrics, 20*, 198–204.

Kostelnik, M. J., Soderman, A. K., & Whiren, A. P. (2007). *Developmentally appropriate curriculum* (4th ed.). Upper Saddle River, NJ: Prentice Hall.

Kotovsky, L., & Baillargeon, R. (1994). Calibration-based reasoning about collision events in 11-month-old infants. *Cognition, 51*, 107–129.

Kottak, C. P., & Kozaitis, K. A. (2008). *On being different: Diversity and multiculturalism in theUnited States* (3rd ed.). New York: McGraw-Hill.

Koukoura, O., Sifakis, S., Stratoudakis, G., Manta, N., Kaminopetros, P., & Koumantakis, E. (2006). A case report of recurrent anencephaly and literature review. *Clinical and Experimental Obstetrics and Gynecology, 33*, 185–189.

Koulougiolti, C., Cole, R., & Kitzman, H. (2008). Inadequate sleep and unintentional injuries in young children. *Public Health Nursing, 25*, 106–114.

Kozol, J. (2005). *The shame of the nation.* New York: Crown.

Kramer, L. (2006, July 10). Commentary in "How your siblings make you who you are" by J. Kluger. *Time,* pp. 46–55.

Kramer, L., & Perozynski, L. (1999). Parental beliefs about managing sibling conflict. *Developmental Psychology, 35,* 489–499.

Kramer, L., & Radey, C. (1997). Improving sibling relationships among young children: A social skills training model. *Family Relations, 46,* 237–246.

Kramer, P. (1993). *Listening to Prozac.* New York: Penguin Books.

Kranz, S., Lin, P. J., & Wagstaff, D. A. (2007). Children's dairy intake in the United States: Too little, too fat? *Journal of Pediatrics, 151,* 642–646.

Kraska, M. (2008). Quantitative research methods. In N. J. Salkind (Ed.), *Encyclopedia of educational psychology.* Thousand Oaks, CA: Sage.

Krauss, R. A., & Glucksberg, S. (1969). The development of communication: Competence as a function of age. *Child Development, 40,* 255–266.

Kretuzer, L. C., & Flavell, J. H. (1975). An interview study of children's knowledge about memory. *Monographs of the Society for Research in Child Development, 40* (1, Serial No. 159).

Krimel, L. S., & Goldman-Rakic, P. S. (2001). Prefrontal microcircuits. *Journal of Neuroscience, 21,* 3788–3796.

Kroger, J. (2007). *Identity development: Adolescence through adulthood* (2nd ed.). Thousand Oaks, CA: Sage.

Krogh, D. (2007). *Brief guide to biology.* Upper Saddle River, NJ: Prentice Hall.

Kuczynski, L., & Parkin, C. N. (2007). Agency and bidirectionality in socialization: Interactions, transactions, and relational dialectics. In J. E. Grusec & P. D. Hastings (Eds.), *Handbook of socialization.* New York: Guilford.

Kuebli, J. (1994, March). Young children's understanding of everyday emotions. *Young Children,* pp. 36–48.

Kuhl, P. K. (1993). Infant speech perception: A window on psycholinguistic development. *International Journal of Psycholinguistics, 9,* 33–56.

Kuhl, P. K. (2000). A new view of language acquisition. *Proceedings of the National Academy of Sciences, 97* (22), 11850–11857.

Kuhl, P. K. (2007). Is speech learning "gated" by the social brain? *Developmental Science, 10,* 110–120.

Kuhl, P. K. (2009). Linking infant speech perception to language acquisition: Phonetic learning predicts language growth. In J. Colombo, P. McCardle, & L. Freund (Eds.), *Infant pathways to language.* Clifton, NJ: Psychology Press.

Kuhl, P. K., Stevens, E., Hayashi, A., Deguchi, T., Kiritani, S., & Iverson, P. (2006). Infants show a facilitation for native language phonetic perception between 6 and 12 months. *Developmental Science, 9,* F13–F21.

Kuhn, D. (1998). Afterword to Volume 2: Cognition, perception, and language. In W. Damon (Ed.), *Handbook of child psychology* (5th ed., Vol. 2). New York: Wiley.

Kuhn, D. (2008). Formal operations in the twenty-first century. *Human Development, 51,* 48–55.

Kuhn, D., Cheney, R., & Weinstock, M. (2000). The development of epistemological understanding. *Cognitive Development, 15,* 309–328.

Kuhn, D., & Franklin, S. (2006). The second decade: What develops (and how)? In W. Damon & R. Lerner (Eds.), *Handbook of child psychology* (6th ed.). New York: Wiley.

Kuhn, D., Schauble, L., & Garcia-Mila, M. (1992). Cross-domain development of scientific reasoning. *Cognition and Instruction, 9,* 285–327.

Kuhn, M. R. (2009). *The hows and whys of fluency instruction.* Boston: Allyn & Bacon.

Kukulu, K., & Demirok, H. (2008). Effects of epidural anesthesia on labor progress. *Pain Management Nursing, 9,* 10–16.

Kumar, R., Gautam, G., Gupta, N. P., Aron, M., Dada, R., Kucheria, K., Gupta, S. K., & Mitra, A. (2006). Role of testicular fine-needle aspiration cytology in infertile men with clinical obstructive azoospermia. *National Medical Journal of India, 19,* 18–20.

Kwak, H. K., Kim, M., Cho, B. H., & Ham, Y. M. (1999, April). *The relationship between children's temperament, maternal control strategies, and children's compliance.* Paper presented at the meeting of the Society for Research in Child Development, Albuquerque.

L

Lachlan, R. F., & Feldman, M. W. (2003). Evolution of cultural communication systems. *Journal of Evolutionary Biology, 16,* 1084–1095.

Ladd, G. W., Buhs, E., & Troop, W. (2004). School adjustment and social skills training. In P. K. Smith & C. H. Hart (Eds.), *Blackwell handbook of childhood social development.* Malden, MA: Blackwell.

Ladd, G. W., & Hart, C. H. (1992). Creating informal play opportunities: Are parents' and preschoolers' initiations related to children's competence with peers? *Cognitive Psychology, 28,* 1179–1187.

Ladd, G. W., & Pettit, G. S. (2002). Parenting and the development of children's peer relationships. In M. H. Bornstein (ed.), *Handbook of parenting* (2nd ed., Vol. 5). Mahwah, NJ: Erlbaum.

Lagattuta, K. H., & Thompson, R. A. (2007). The development of self-conscious emotions. In J. L. Tracy, R. W. Robins, & J. P. Tangney (Eds.), *The self-conscious emotions.* New York: Guilford.

Laible, D. J., Carlo, G., & Raffaeli, M. (2000). The differential relations of parent and peer attachment to adolescent adjustment. *Journal of Youth and Adolescence, 29,* 45–53.

Laible, D. J., & Thompson, R. A. (2000). Mother-child discourse, attachment security, shared positive affect, and early conscience development. *Child Development, 71,* 1424–1440.

Laible, D., & Thompson, R. A. (2007). Early socialization: A relationship perspective. In J. E. Grusec & P. D. Hastings (Eds.), *Handbook of socialization.* New York: Guilford.

Laifer-Narin, S., Budorick, N. E., Simpson, L. L., & Platt, L. D. (2007). Fetal magnetic resonance imaging: A review. *Current Opinion in Obstetrics and Gynecology, 19,* 151–156.

Lainhart, J. E. (2006). Advances in autism neuroimaging research for the clinician and geneticist. *American Journal of Medical Genetics, C: Seminars in Medical Genetics, 142,* 33–39.

Laird, R. D., Criss, M. M., Pettit, G. S., Dodge, K. A., & Bates, J. E. (2008, in press). Parents' monitoring knowledge attenuates the link between antisocial friends and adolescent delinquent behavior. *Journal of Abnormal Child Psychology.*

Laird, R. D., Pettit, G. S., Dodge, K. A., & Bates, J. E. (2005). Peer relationship antecedents of delinquent behavior in late adolescence: Is there evidence of demographic group differences in developmental processes? *Development and Psychopathology, 17,* 127–144.

Lajunen, H. R., Keski-Rahkonen, A., Pulkkinen, L., Rose, R. J., Rissanen, A., & Kaprio, J. (2007). Are computer and cell phone use associated with body mass index and overweight? A population study among twin adolescents. *BMC Public Health, 26,* 24.

Lamb, M. E. (1986). *The father's role: Applied perspectives.* New York: Wiley.

Lamb, M. E. (1994). Infant care practices and the application of knowledge. In C. B. Fisher & R. M. Lerner (Eds.), *Applied developmental psychology.* New York: McGraw-Hill.

Lamb, M. E. (2000). The history of research on father involvement: An overview. *Marriage and Family Review, 29,* 23–42.

Lamb, M. E. (2005). Attachments, social networks, and developmental contexts. *Human Development, 48,* 108–112.

Lamb, M. E., Bornstein, M. H., & Teti, D. M. (2002). *Development in infancy* (4th ed.). Mahwah, NJ: Erlbaum.

Lamb, M. E., & Sternberg, K. J. (1992). Sociocultural perspectives in nonparental child-care. In M. E. Lamb, K. J. Sternberg, C. Hwang,

& A. G. Broberg (Eds.), *Child care in context.* Hillsdale, NJ: Erlbaum.

Lamont, R. F., & Jaggat, A. N. (2007). Emerging drug therapies for preventing spontaneous labor and preterm birth. *Expert Opinion on Investigational Drugs, 16,* 337–345.

Lampl, M. (2008). Physical growth. In M. M. Haith & J. B. Benson (Eds.), *Encyclopedia of infant and early childhood development.* Oxford, UK: Elsevier.

Landa, S. (2000, Fall). If you can't make waves, make ripples. *Intelligence Connections Newsletter of the ASCD, X* (No. 1), 6–8.

Landau, B., Smith, L., & Jones, S. (1998). Object perception and object naming in early development. *Trends in Cognitive Science, 2,* 19–24.

Lane, H. (1976). *The wild boy of Aveyron.* Cambridge, MA: Harvard University Press.

Langer, O. (2008a). Type 2 diabetes in pregnancy: Exposing deception appearances. *Journal of Maternal-Fetal and Neonatal Medicine, 21,* 181–189.

Langer, O. (2008b). Management of obesity in GDM: Old habits die hard. *Journal of Maternal-Fetal and Neonatal Medicine, 21,* 165–171.

Lansford, J. E., Miller-Johnson, S., Berlin, L. J., Dodge, K. A., Bates, J. E., & Pettit, G. S. (2007). Early physical abuse and later violent delinquency: A prospective longitudinal study. *Child Maltreatment, 12,* 233–245.

Lapsley, D. K. (2008). Moral self-identity as the aim of education. In L. Nucci & D. Narvaez (Eds.), *Handbook of moral and character education.* Clifton, NJ: Psychology Press.

Lapsley, D. K., & Narvaez, D. (2006). Character education. In W. Damon & R. Lerner (Eds.), *Handbook of child psychology* (6th ed.). New York: Wiley.

Lapsley, D. K., & Power, F. C. (Eds.). (1988). *Self, ego, and identity.* New York: Springer-Verlag.

Larson, K., Russ, S. A., Crall, J. J., & Halfon, N. (2008). Influence of multiple social risks on children's health. *Pediatrics, 121,* 337–344.

Larson, R. W. (1999, September). Unpublished review of J. W. Santrock's *Adolescence,* 8th ed. (New York: McGraw-Hill).

Larson, R. W., & Wilson, S. (2004). Adolescence across place and time: Globalization and the changing pathways to adulthood. In R. Lerner & L. Steinberg (Eds.), *Handbook of adolescent psychology.* New York: Wiley.

Lasiuk, G. C., & Ferguson, L. M. (2005). From practice to midrange theory and back again: Beck's theory of postpartum depression. *Advanced Nursing Science, 28,* 127–136.

Lasker, J. N., Coyle, B., Li, K., & Ortynsky, M. (2005). Assessment of risk factors for low birth weight deliveries. *Health Care for Women International, 26,* 262–280.

Lasky-Su, J., Biederman, J., Laird, N., Tsuang, M., Doyle, A. E., Smoller, J. W., Lange, C., & Faraone, S. V. (2007). Evidence for an association of the dopamine D5 receptor gene on age at onset of attention deficit hyperactivity disorder. *Annals of Human Genetics, 71,* 648–659.

Latimer, J. (2007). Becoming informed: Genetic counseling, ambiguity, and choice. *Health Care Analysis, 15,* 13–23.

Lawrence, L., Shaha, S., & Lillis, K. (2008). Observational study of helmet use among children skiing and skateboarding. *Pediatric Emergency Care, 24,* 219–221.

Lawrence, R. A. (2008). Breastfeeding. In M. M. Haith & J. B. Benson (Eds.), *Encyclopedia of infant and early childhood development.* Oxford; UK: Elsevier.

LeVay, S. (1994). *The sexual brain.* Cambridge, MA: MIT Press.

Leach, P. (1990). *Your baby and child: From birth to age five.* New York: Knopf.

Leaper, C., & Bigler, R. S. (2004). Commentary: Gender language and sexist thought. *Monographs of the Society for Research in Child Development. 69* (1, Serial No. 275), 128–142.

Leaper, C., & Friedman, C. K. (2007). The socialization of gender. In J. E. Grusec & P. D. Hastings (Eds.), *Handbook of socialization.* New York: Guilford.

Leaper, C., & Smith, T. E. (2004). A meta-analytic review of gender variations in children's language use: Talkativeness, affiliative speech, and assertive speech. *Developmental Psychology, 40,* 993–1027.

LeDoux, J. E. (1998). *The emotional brain: The mysterious underpinnings of emotional life.* New York: Simon & Schuster.

LeDoux, J. E. (2002). *The synaptic self.* New York: Viking.

Lee, A., & Chan, S. (2006). Acupuncture and anesthesia. *Best Practices in Research and Clinical Anesthesia, 20,* 303–314.

Lee, H. C., El-Sayed, Y. Y., & Gould, J. B. (2008, in press). Population trends in cesarean delivery for breech presentation in the United States, 1997–2003. *American Journal of Obstetrics and Gynecology.*

Lee, H., & others. (2007). Anatomical traces of vocabulary acquisition in adolescent brain. *Journal of Neuroscience, 27,* 1184–1189.

Lee, K. C., Shults, R. A., Greenspan, A. I., Haileyesus, T., & Dellinger, A. M. (2008). Child passenger restraint use and emergency department-reported injuries: A special study using the National Electronic Injury Surveillance System—All Injury Program, 2004. *Journal of Safety Research, 39,* 25–31.

Lee, K., Cameron, C. A., Doucette, J., & Talwar, V. (2002). Phantoms and fabrications: Young children's detection of implausible lies. *Child Development, 73,* 1688–1702.

Lee, S. J., & Wong, A. N. (2009). The model minority and the perceptual foreigner: Stereotypes of Asian Americans. In N. Tewari & A. Alvarez (Eds.), *Asian American psychology.* Clifton, NJ: Psychology Press.

Legerstee, M. (1997). Contingency effects of people and objects on subsequent cognitive functioning in 3-month-old infants. *Social Development, 6,* 307–321.

Lehr, C. A., Hanson, A., Sinclair, M. F., & Christensen, S. L. (2003). Moving beyond dropout prevention towards school completion. *School Psychology Review, 32,* 342–364.

Lehrer, R., & Schauble, L. (2006). Scientific thinking and scientific literacy. In W. Damon & R. Lerner (Eds.), *Handbook of child psychology* (6th ed.). New York: Wiley.

Leifer, A. D. (1973). *Television and the development of social behavior.* Paper presented at the meeting of the International Society for the Study of Behavioral Development, Ann Arbor, Michigan.

Leman, P. J., Ahmed, S., & Ozarow, L. (2005). Gender, gender relations, and the social dynamics of children's conversations. *Developmental Psychology, 41,* 64–74.

LeMare, L. J., & Rubin, K. H. (1987). Perspective taking and peer interaction: Structural and developmental analyses. *Child Development, 58,* 306–315.

Lempers, J. D., Flavell, E. R., & Flavell, J. H. (1977). The development in very young children of tacit knowledge concerning visual perception. *Genetic Psychology Monographs, 95,* 3–53.

Lenders, C. M., McElrath, T. F., Scholl, T. O. (2000). Nutrition in pregnancy. *Current Opinions in Pediatrics, 12,* 291–296.

Lenneberg, E. (1967). *The biological foundations of language.* New York: Wiley.

Lennon, E. M., Gardner, J. M., Karmel, B. Z., & Flory, M. J. (2008). Bayley Scales of Infant Development. In M. M. Haith & J. B. Benson (Eds.), *Encyclopedia of infant and early childhood development.* Oxford, UK: Elsevier.

Lenoir, C. P., Mallet, E. & Calenda, E. (2000). Siblings of sudden infant death syndrome and near miss in about 30 families: Is there a genetic link? *Medical Hypotheses, 54,* 408–411.

Lenzi, T. A., & Johnson, T. R. B. (2008). Screening, prenatal. In M. M. Haith & J. B. Benson (Eds.), *Encyclopedia of infant and early childhood development.* Oxford, UK: Elsevier.

Leonardi-Bee, J. A., Smyth, A. R., Britton, J., & Coleman, T. (2008, in press). Environmental tobacco smoke on fetal health: Systematic review and analysis. *Archives of Disease in Childhood: Fetal and Neonatal Edition.*

Leon-Guerrero, A. (2009). *Social problems* (2nd ed.). Thousand Oaks, CA: Sage.

Leppanen, J. M., Moulson, M., Vogel-Farley, V. K., & Nelson, C. A. (2007). An ERP study of emotional face processing in the adult and infant brain. *Child Development, 78,* 232–245.

Lepper, M. R., Corpus, J. H., & Iyengar, S.S. (2005). Intrinsic and extrinsic orientations in the classroom: Age differences and academic correlates. *Journal of Educational Psychology, 97,* 184–196.

Lerner, R. M., Boyd, M., & Du, D. (2008, in press). Adolescent development. In I. B. Weiner & C. B. Craighead (Eds.), *Encyclopedia of Psychology* (4th ed.). Hoboken, NJ: Wiley.

Lerner, R. M., Roeser, R. W., & Phelps, E. (Eds.). (2009, in press). *Positive youth development and spirituality: From theory to research.* West Conshohocken, PA: Templeton Foundation.

Lero, D. S. (2009, in press). Research on parental leave policies and children's development: Implications for policy makers and service providers. In R. E. Tremblay, R. deV Peters, M. Boivan, & R. G. Barr (Eds.), *Encyclopedia on early childhood development.* Montreal: Center of Excellence for Early Childhood Development.

Lesaux, N. K., & Siegel, L. S. (2003). The development of reading in children who speak English as a second language. *Developmental Psychology, 39,* 1005–1019.

Lessow-Hurley, J. (2009). *The foundations of dual language instruction* (5th Ed.). Boston: Allyn & Bacon.

Lester, B. M., Tronick, E. Z., & Brazelton, T.B. (2004). The Neonatal Intensive Care Unit Network Neurobehavioral Scale procedures. *Pediatrics, 113* (Suppl.), S641–S667.

Lester, B. M., Tronick, E. Z., LaGasse, L., Seifer, R., Bauer, C. R., Shankaran, S., Bada, H. S., Wright, L. L., Smeriglio, V. L., Lu, J., Finnegan, L. P., & Maza, P. L. (2002). The maternal lifestyle study: Effects of substance exposure during pregnancy on neuordevelopmental outcome in 1-month-old infants. *Pediatrics, 110,* 1182–1192.

Leventhal, T., Brooks-Gunn, J., & Kamerman, S. B. (2008). Communities as place, face, and space: Provision of services to poor urban children and their families. In J. DeFilippis & S. Saegert (Eds.), *The community development reader.* New York: Routledge.

Levine, L. N., & McCloskey, M. L. (2009). *Teaching learners of English in mainstream.* Boston: Allyn & Bacon.

Levinson, S. (2009). Pragmatics, universals in. In P. Hogan (Ed.), *The Cambridge encyclopedia of language sciences.* Cambridge, UK: Cambridge University Press.

Levy, G. D., Sadovsky, A. L., & Troseth, G. L. (2000). Aspects of young children's perceptions of gender-typed occupations. *Sex Roles, 42,* 993–1006.

Lewis, A. C. (2007). Looking beyond NCLB. *Phi Delta Kappan, 88,* 483–484.

Lewis, B. A., Kirchner, H. L., Short, E. J., Minnes, S., Weishampel, P., Satayathum, S., & Singer, L. T. (2007). Prenatal cocaine and tobacco effects on children's language trajectories. *Pediatrics, 120,* e78–e85.

Lewis, M. (2005). Selfhood. In B. Hopkins (Ed.), *The Cambridge encyclopedia of child development.* Cambridge, UK: Cambridge University Press.

Lewis, M. (2008). The emergence of human emotions. In M. Lewis, J. M. Haviland Jones, & L. Feldman Barrett (Eds.), *Handbook of emotions* (3rd Ed.). New York: Guilford.

Lewis, M., & Brooks-Gunn, J. (1979). *Social cognition and the acquisition of the self.* New York: Plenum.

Lewis, M., Feiring, C., & Rosenthal, S. (2000). Attachment over time. *Child Development, 71,* 707–720.

Lewis, M., & Ramsay, D. S. (1999). Effect of maternal soothing and infant stress response. *Child Development, 70,* 11–20.

Lewis, M. D., & Steiben, J. (2004). Emotion regulation in the brain: Conceptual issues and directions for developmental research. *Child Development, 75,* 371–376.

Lewis, M., Sullivan, M. W., Sanger, C., & Weiss, M. (1989). Self-development and self-conscious emotions. *Child Development, 60,* 146–156.

Lewis, R. (2007). *Human genetics* (7th ed.). New York: McGraw-Hill.

Li, C., Goran, M. I., Kaur, H., Nollen, N., & Ahluwalia, J. S. (2007). Developmental trajectories of overweight during childhood: Role of early life factors. *Obesity, 15,* 760–761.

Li, D. K., Willinger, M., Petitti, D. B., Odulil, R. K., Liu, L., & Hoffman, H. J. (2006). Use of a dummy (pacifier) during sleep and risk of sudden infant death syndrome (SIDS); Population based case-control study. *British Medical Journal, 332,* 18–22.

Li, Y., Yang, X., Zhai, F., Piao, J., Zhao, W.,Zhang, J., & Ma, G. (2008). Childhood obesity and its health consequence in China. *Obesity Reviews, 9* (Suppl. 1), S82–S86.

Liben, L. S. (1995). Psychology meets geography: Exploring the gender gap on the national geography bee. *Psychological Science Agenda, 8,* 8–9.

Liben, L. S. (2009). Giftedness during childhood: The spatial-graphic domain. In F. D. Horowitz, R. F. Subotnik, & D. J. Matthews (Eds.), *The development of giftedness and talent across the life span.* Washington, DC: American Psychological Association.

Lidral, A. C., & Murray, J. C. (2005). Genetic approaches to identify disease genes for birth defects with cleft lip/palate as a model. *Birth Defects Research, 70,* 893–901.

Lie, E., & Newcombe, N. (1999). Elementary school children's explicit and implicit memory for faces of preschool classmates. *Developmental Psychology, 35,* 102–112.

Lieberman, E., Davidson, K., Lee-Parritz, A., & Shearer, E. (2005). Changes in fetal position during labor and their association with epidural analgesia. *Obstetrics and Gynecology, 105,* 974–982.

Liegois, F., Connelly, A., Baldeweg, T., & Vargha-Khadem, F. (2008, in press). Speaking with a single cerebral hemisphere: fMRI language organization after hemispherectomy in childhood. *Brain and Language.*

Lieven, E. (2008). Language development: overview. In M. M. Haith & J. B. Benson (Eds.), *Encyclopedia of infant and early childhood development.* Oxford, UK: Elsevier.

Lillard, A. (2007). Pretend play in toddlers. In C. A. Brownell & C. B. Kopp (Eds.), *Socioemotional development in the toddler years.* New York: Guilford.

Lin, M., Johnson, J. E., & Johnson, K. M. (2003). Dramatic play in Montessori kindergartens in Taiwan and Mainland China. Unpublished manuscript, Department of Curriculum and Instruction, Pennsylvania State University, University Park, PA.

Lincoln, A. J., Searcy, Y. M., Jones, W., & Lord, C. (2007). Social interaction behaviors discriminate young children with autism and Williams syndrome. *Journal of the American Academy of Child and Adolescent Psychiatry, 46,* 323–331.

Lindberg, M. A., Keiffer, J., & Thomas, S. W. (2000). Eyewitness testimony for physical abuse as a function of personal experience, development, and focus of study. *Journal of Applied Developmental Psychology, 21,* 555–591.

Linn, S. (2008). *The case for make believe: Saving play in a commercialized world.* New York: The New Press.

Lippa, R. A. (2005). *Gender, nature, and nurture* (2nd ed.). Mahwah, NJ: Erlbaum.

Lippman, L. A., & Keith, J. D. (2006). The demographics of spirituality among youth: International perspectives. In E. Roehlkepartain, P. E. King, L. Wagener, & P. L. Benson (Eds.), *The handbook of spirituality in childhood and adolescence.* Thousand Oaks, CA: Sage.

Liszkowski, U. (2007, March). *A new look at infant pointing.* Paper presented at the meeting of the Society for Research in Child Development, Boston.

Litovsky, R. Y., & Ashmead, D. H. (1997). Development of binaural and spatial hearing in infants and children. In R. H. Gilkey & T. R. Anderson (Eds.), *Binaural and spatial hearing in real and virtual environments.* Mahwah, NJ: Erlbaum.

Liu, A., Hu, X., Ma, G., Cui, Z., Pan, Y., Chang, S., Zhao, W., & Chen, C. (2008). Evaluations of a classroom-based physical activity promoting program. *Obesity Reviews, 9* (Suppl.1), S130–S134.

Liu, C. H., Murakami, J., Eap, S., & Nagayama, Hall, G. C. (2009). Who are Asian Americans? An overview of history, immigration, and communities. In N. Tewari & A. Alvarez (Eds.), *Asian American psychology.* Clifton, NJ: Psychology Press.

Liu, D., Wellman, H. M., Tardif, T., & Sabbagh, M. A. (2008). Theory of mind development in Chinese children: A meta-analysis of false-belief understanding across cultures and languages. *Developmental Psychology, 44,* 523–531.

Liu, W. M., & Hernandez, J. (2008). Social class and classism. In N. J. Salkind (Ed.), *Encyclopedia of educational psychology.* Thousand Oaks, CA: Sage.

Livesly, W., & Bromley, D. (1973). *Person perception in childhood and adolescence.* New York: Wiley.

Lochman, J., & the Conduct Problems Prevention Research Group. (2007, March). *Fast Track intervention outcomes in the middle school years.* Paper presented at the meeting of the Society for Research in Child Development.

Lock, A. (2004). Preverbal communication. In U. Goswami (Ed.), *Blackwell handbook of childhood cognitive development.* Malden, MA: Blackwell.

Lockl, K., & Schneider, W. (2007). Knowledge about the mind: Links between theory of mind and later metamemory. *Child Development, 78,* 147–167.

Loebel, M., & Yali, A. M. (1999, August). *Effects of positive expectancies on adjustments to pregnancy.* Paper presented at the meeting of the American Psychological Association, Boston.

Loeber, R., Burke, J., & Pardini, D. (2009, in press). The etiology and development of antisocial and delinquent behavior. *Annual Review of Psychology* (Vol. 60). Palo Alto, CA: Annual Reviews.

Loeber, R., DeLamatre, M., Keenan, K., & Zhang, Q. (1998). A prospective replication of developmental pathways in disruptive and delinquent behavior. In R. Cairns, L. Bergman, & J. Kagan (Eds.), *Methods and models for studying the individual.* Thousand Oaks, CA: Sage.

Loeber, R. & Farrington, D. P. (Eds.), (2001). *Child delinquents: Development, intervention and service needs.* Thousand Oaks, CA: Sage.

Loeber, R., Pardini, D. A., Stouthamer-Loeber, M., & Raine, A. (2007). Do cognitive, physiological, and psychosocial risk and promotive factors predict desistance from delinquency in males? *Development and Psychopathology, 19,* 867–887.

Loehlin, J. C., Horn, J. M., & Ernst, J. L. (2007). Genetic and environmental influences on adult life outcomes: Evidence from the Texas adoption project. *Behavior Genetics, 37,* 463–476.

London, M. L., Ladewig, P. A., Ball, J. W., & Bindler, R. A. (2007). *Maternal and child nursing care* (2nd ed.). Upper Saddle River, NJ: Prentice Hall.

Longo-Mbenza, B., Lukoki, L. E, & M'buyambia-Kabangu, J. R. (2007). Nutritional status, socioeconomic status, heart rate, and blood pressure in African school children and adolescents. *International Journal of Cardiology, 121,* 171–177.

Lonner, W. J. (1988, October). *The introductory psychology text and cross-cultural psychology: A survey of cross-cultural psychologists.* Bellingham: Western Washington University, Center for Cross-cultural Research.

Lopez Alvarez, M. J. (2007). Proteins in human milk. *Breastfeeding Review, 15,* 5–16.

Lorenz, K. Z. (1965). *Evolution and the modification of behavior.* Chicago: University of Chicago Press.

Loughlin, K. R. (2007). Urologic radiology during pregnancy. *Urology Clinics of North America, 34,* 23–26.

Loukas, A., Suizzo, M-A., & Prelow, H. M. (2007). Examining resource and protective factors in the adjustment of Latino youth in low income families: What role does maternal acculturation play? *Journal of Youth and Adolescence, 36,* 489–501.

Lozoff, B., Corapci, F., Burden, M. J., Kaciroti, N., Angulo-Baaroso, R., Sazawal, S., & Black, M. (2007). Preschool-aged children with iron deficiency anemia show altered affect and behavior. *Journal of Nutrition, 137,* 683–689.

Lu, M. C., & Lu, J. S. (2008). Prenatal care. In M. M. Haith & J. B. Benson (Eds.), *Encyclopedia of infancy and early childhood development.* Oxford, UK: Elsevier.

Lubinski, D. (2000). Measures of intelligence: Intelligence tests. In A. Kazdin (Ed.), *Encyclopedia of Psychology.* Washington, DC, & New York: American Psychological Association and Oxford University Press.

Lucas, P. J., McIntosh, K., Petticrew, M., Roberts, H., & Shiell, A. (2008). Financial benefits for child health and well-being in low income or socially disadvantaged families in developed world countries. *Cochrane Database of Systematic Reviews, 16,* CD006358.

Lucas-Thompson, R., & Clarke-Stewart, A.K. (2007). Forecasting friendship: How marital quality, maternal mood, and attachment security are linked to children's friendships. *Journal of Applied Developmental Psychology, 28,* 499–514.

Lucurto, C. (1990). The malleability of IQ as judged from adoption studies. Intelligence, 14, 275–292.

Luders, E., Narr, K. L., Thompson, P. M., Rex, D. E., Uancke, L., Steinmetz, H., & Toga, A. W. (2004). Gender differences in cortical complexity. *Nature Neuroscience, 7,* 799–800.

Ludington-Hoe, S. M., Lewis, T., Morgan,K., Cong, X., Anderson, L., & Reese, S. (2006). Breast and infant temperatures with twins during kangaroo care. *Journal of Obstetric, Gynecologic, and Neonatal Nursing, 35,* 223–231.

Lunkenheimer, E. S., Shields, A. M., & Cortina, K. S. (2007). Parental coaching and dismissing of children's emotions in family interaction. *Social Development, 16,* 232–248.

Lunney, K. M., & others. (2008). HIV-positive poor women may stop breast-feeding early to protect their infants from HIV infection -although available replacement diets are grossly inadequate. *Journal of Nutrition, 138,* 351–357.

Luria, A., & Herzog, E. (1985, April). *Gender segregation across and within settings.* Paper presented at the biennial meeting of the Society for Research in Child Development, Toronto.

Luyckx, K., Schwartz, S. J., Goossens, L., Soenens, B., & Beyers, W. (2008a, in press). Developmental typologies of identity formation and adjustment in emerging adulthood: A latent class growth analysis approach. *Journal of Research on Adolescence.*

Luyckx, K., Schwarz, S. J., Soenens, B., Vansteenkiste, M., & Goossens, L. (2008b, in press). The path from identity commitments to adjustment: Motivational underpinnings and mediating mechanisms. *Journal of Counseling and Development.*

Luyckx, K., Soenens, B., Goosens, L., & Berzonsky, M. D. (2006). Parent psychological control and dimensions of identity formation in emerging adulthood. *Journal of Family Psychology, 42,* 305–318.

Luyckx, K., Soenens, B., Vansteenkiste, M., Goossens, L., & Berzonsky, M. D. (2008c, in press). Parental psychological control and dimensions of identity formation in emerging adulthood. *Journal of Family Psychology.*

Lykken, D. (2001). *Happiness: What studies on twins show us about nature, nurture, and the happiness set point.* New York: Golden Books.

Lynn, R. (1996). Racial and ethnic differences in intelligence in the U. S. on the Differential Ability Scale. *Personality and Individual Differences, 26,* 271–273.

Lynn, R., Allik, J., Pullman, H., & Laidra, K. (2004). Sex differences on the progressive matrices among adolescents: Some data from Estonia. *Personality and Individual Differences, 36,* 1249–1255.

Lyon, T. D., & Flavell, J. H. (1993). Young children's understanding of forgetting over time. *Child Development, 64,* 789–800.

Lyons, S. J., Henly, J. R., & Schuerman, J. R. (2005). Informal support in maltreating families: Its effects on parenting practices. *Children and Youth Services Review, 27,* 21–38.

Lyytinen, H., & Erskine, J. (2009, in press). Early identification and prevention of reading problems. In R. E. Tremblay, R. deV Peters, M. Boivin, & R. G. Barr (Eds.), *Encyclopedia on early childhood development.* Montreal: Centre of Excellence for Early Childhood Development.

M

Maas, C., Herrenkohl, T. I., & Sousa, C. (2008). Review of research on child maltreatment and violence in youth. *Trauma, Violence, and Abuse, 9,* 56–67.

Maccoby, E. E. (1984). Middle childhood in the context of the family. In W. A. Collins (Ed.), *Development during middle childhood.* Washington, DC: National Academy Press.

Maccoby, E. E. (1987, November). Interview with Elizabeth Hall: All in the family. *Psychology Today,* pp. 54–60.

Maccoby, E. E. (1996). Peer conflict and intrafamily conflict: Are there conceptual bridges? *Merrill-Palmer Quarterly, 42,* 165–176.

Maccoby, E. E. (2002). Gender and group process: A developmental perspective. *Current Directions in Psychological Science, 11,* 54–57.

Maccoby, E. E. (2002). Gender and group processes. *Current Directions in Psychological Science, 11,* 54–58.

Maccoby, E. E. (2007). Historical overview of socialization theory and research. In J. E. Grusec & P. D. Hastings (Eds.), *Handbook of socialization.* New York: Guilford.

Maccoby, E. E., & Jacklin, C. N. (1974). *The psychology of sex differences.* Palo Alto, CA: Stanford University Press.

Maccoby, E. E., & Martin, J. A. (1983). Socialization in the context of the family: Parent-child interaction. In P. H. Mussen (Ed.), *Handbook of child psychology* (4th ed., Vol. 4). New York: Wiley.

Maccoby, E. E., & Mnookin, R. H. (1992). *Dividing the child: Social and legal dilemmas of custody.* Cambridge, MA: Harvard University Press.

MacDorman, M. F., Declercq, E., Menacker, F., & Malloy, M. H. (2008). Neonatal mortality for primary cesarean and vaginal births to low-risk women: Application of a "intention-to-treat" model. *Birth, 35,* 3–8.

MacFarlane, J. A. (1975). Olfaction in the development of social preferences in the human neonate. In *Parent-infant interaction.* Ciba Foundation Symposium No. 33. Amsterdam: Elsevier.

MacGeorge, E. L. (2004). The myth of gender cultures: Similarities outweigh differences in men's and women's provisions of and responses to supportive communication. *Sex Roles, 50,* 143–175.

Machaalani, R., & Waters, K. A. (2008). Neuronal cell death in the sudden infant death syndrome brainstem and associations with risk factors. *Brain, 131,* 218–228.

MacMillan, H. L. (2009, in press). Preventing child maltreatment. In R. E. Tremblay, R. deV Peters, & R. G. Barr (Eds.), *Encyclopedia on early childhood development.* Montreal: Centre of Excellence for Early Childhood Development.

Maconochie, N., Doyle, P., Prior, S., & Simmons, R. (2007). Risk factors for first trimester miscarriage—results from a UK-population-based case control study. *British Journal of Obstetrics and Gynecology, 114,* 170–176.

Madan, A., Palaniappan, L., Urizar, G., Wang, Y., Fortmann, S. P., & Gould, J. B. (2006). Sociocultural factors that affect pregnancy outcomes in two dissimilar immigrant groups in the United States. *Journal of Pediatrics, 148,* 341–346.

Mader, S. M. (2009). *Concepts of biology.* New York: McGraw-Hill.

Maeda, K. (1999). *The Self-Perception Profile for Children administered to a Japanese sample.* Unpublished data, Ibaraki Prefectural University of Health Sciences, Ibaraki, Japan.

Mael, F. A. (1998). Single-sex and coeducational schooling: Relationships to socioemotional and academic development. *Review of Educational Research. 68* (2), 101–129.

Magnuson, K., Duncan, G. J., & Kalil, A. (2006). The contribution of middle childhood contexts to adolescent achievement and behavior. In A. C. Huston & M. N. Ripke (Eds.), *Developmental contexts in middle childhood.* New York: Cambridge University Press.

Magnusson, S. J., & Palinscar, A. S. (2005). Teaching to promote the development of scientific knowledge and reasoning about light at the elementary school level. In *How people learn.* Washington, DC: National Academies Press.

Magriples, U., Kershaw, T. S., Rising, S. S., Massey, Z., & Ickovics, J. R. (2008). Prenatal health care beyond the obstetrics service: Utilization and predictors of unscheduled care. *American Journal of Obstetrics and Gynecology, 198,* e1–e7.

Mahoney, J. L., Harris, A. L., & Eccles, J. S. (2006). Organized activity participation, positive youth development, and the overscheduling hypothesis. *Social Policy Report, Society for Research in Child Development, XX,* 1–30.

Main, M. (2000). Attachment theory. In A. Kazdin (Ed.), *Encyclopedia of psychology.* Washington, DC, & New York: American Psychological Association and Oxford University Press.

Malamitsi—Puchner, A., & Boutsikou, T. (2006). Adolescent pregnancy and perinatal outcome. *Pediatric Endocrinology Reviews, 3* (Suppl. 1), 170–171.

Malik, N. M., & Furman, W. (1993). Practitioner review: Problems in children's peer relations: What can the clinician do? *Journal of Child Psychology and Psychiatry, 34,* 1303–1326.

Mamtani, M., Patel, A., & Kulkarni, H. (2008). Association of the pattern of transition between arousal states in neonates with the cord blood lead level. *Early Human Development, 84,* 231–235.

Mandara, J. (2006). The impact of family functioning on African American males' academic achievement: A review and clarification of the empirical literature. *Teachers College Record, 108,* 206–233.

Mandler, J. M. (2000). Unpublished review of J. W. Santrock's *Life-span development,* 8th ed. (New York: McGraw-Hill).

Mandler, J. M. (2004). *The foundations of mind.* New York: Oxford University Press.

Mandler, J. M. (2006). *Jean Mandler.* Retrieved May 6, 2006, from http://cogsci.ucsd.edu/~jean/

Mandler, J. M., & McDonough, L. (1993). Concept formation in infancy. *Cognitive Development, 8,* 291–318.

Manning, M. L., & Baruth, L. G. (2009). *Multicultural education of children and adolescents* (5th ed.). Boston: Allyn & Bacon.

Marcia, J. E. (1980). Ego identity development. In J. Adelson (Ed.), *Handbook of adolescent psychology.* New York: Wiley.

Marcia, J. E. (1987). The identity status approach to the study of ego identity development. In T. Honess & K. Yardley (Eds.), *Self and identity: Perspectives across the lifespan.* London: Routledge & Kegan Paul.

Marcia, J. E. (1994). The empirical study of ego identity. In H. A. Bosma, T. L. G. Graafsma, H. D. Grotevant, & D. J. De Levita (Eds.), *Identity and development.* Newbury Park, CA: Sage.

Marcia, J. E. (1996). Unpublished review of J. W. Santrock's *Adolescence,* 7th ed. (Dubuque, IA: Brown & Benchmark).

Marcia, J. E. (2002). Identity and psychosocial development in adulthood. *Identity, 2,* 7–28.

Marcovitch, H. (2004). Use of stimulants for attention deficit hyperactivity disorder: AGAINST. *British Medical Journal, 329,* 908–909.

Mares, M-L., & Woodard, E. H. (2007). Positive effects of television on children's social interaction. In P. R. Press, B. M. Gayle, N. Burrell M. Allen, & J. Bryant (Eds.), *Mass media effects research.* Mahwah, NJ: Erlbaum.

Markus, H. R., & Nurius, P. (1986). Possible selves. *American Psychologist, 41,* 954–969.

Markus, H. R., Mullally, P. R., & Kitayama, S. (1999). *Selfways: Diversity in modes of cultural participation.* Unpublished manuscript, Department of Psychology, University of Michigan.

Martin, C. L., & Dinella, L. (2001). Gender development: Gender schema theory. In J. Worell (Ed.), *Encyclopedia of women and gender.* San Diego: Academic Press.

Martin, C. L., & Fabes, R. A. (2001). The stability and consequences of young children's same-sex peer interactions. *Developmental Psychology, 37,* 431–446.

Martin, C. L., Ruble, D. N., & Szkrybalo, J. (2002). Cognitive theories of early gender development. *Psychological Bulletin, 128,* 903–933.

Martin, D. W. (2008). *Doing psychology experiments* (7th ed.). Belmont, CA: Wadsworth.

Martin, J. A., Hamilton, B. E., Menacker, F., Sutton, P. D., & Matthews, T. J. (2005, November 15). Preliminary births for 2004: Infant and maternal health. *Health E-Stats.* Atlanta: National Center for Health Statistics.

Martin, R., Sexton, C., Franklin, T., & Gerlovich, J. (2005). *Teaching science for all children* (4th ed.). Boston: Allyn & Bacon.

Martin, R., Sexton, C., Franklin, T., Gerlovich, J., & McElroy, D. (2009). *Teaching science for all children* (5th ed.). Boston: Allyn & Bacon.

Maruthy, S., & Mannarukrishnaiah, J. (2008). Effect of early onset otitis media on brainstem and cortical auditory processing. *Behavioral and Brain Functions, 4,* 17.

Marx, D. M., & Stapel, D. A. (2006). Distinguishing stereotype threat from priming effects: On the role of the social self and threat-based concerns. *Journal of Personality and Social Psychology, 91,* 243–254.

Mascolo, M. F., & Fischer, K. (2007). The co-development of self and socio-moral emotions during the toddler years. In C. A. Brownell & C. B. Kopp (Eds.), *Transitions in early development.* New York: Guilford.

Mash, E. J., & Wolfe, D. A. (2007). *Abnormal child psychology* (3rd ed.). Belmont, CA: Wadsworth.

Mason, J. A., & Hermann, K. R. (1998). Universal infant hearing screening by automated auditory brainstem response measurement. *Pediatrics, 101,* 221–228.

Mass, J. (2008, March 4). Commentary in L. Szabo, "Parents with babies need time to reset inner clock." *USA Today,* p. 4D.

Massey, Z., Rising, S. S., & Ickovics, J. (2006). Centering Pregnancy group prenatal care: Promoting relationship-centered care. *Journal of Obstetric, Gynecologic, and Neonatal Nursing, 35,* 286–294.

Masten, A. S. (2004). Regulatory processes, risk, and resilience in adolescent development. *Annals of the New York Academy of Science, 102,* 310–319.

Masten, A. S. (2006). Developmental psychopathology: Pathways to the future. *International Journal of Behavioral Development, 31,* 46–53.

Masten, A. S. (2007). Resilience in developing systems: Progress and promise as the fourth wave rises. *Development and Psychopathology, 19,* 921–930.

Masten, A. S., Burt, K., & Coatsworth, J. D. (2006). Competence and psychopathology in development. In D. Cicchetti & D. Cohen (Eds.), *Developmental psychopathology* (Vol. 3) *Risk, disorder and psychopathology* (2nd ed.) New York: Wiley.

Matlin, M. W. (2008). *The psychology of women* (6th ed.). Belmont, CA: Wadsworth.

Matsumoto, D., & Juang, L. (2008). *Culture and psychology* (4th ed.). Belmont, CA: Wadsworth.

Matthews, G., Zeidner, M., & Roberts, R. D. (2006). Models of personality and affect for education: A review and synthesis. In P. A. Alexander & P. H. Wynne (Eds.), *Handbook of educational psychology* (2nd ed.). Mahwah, NJ: Erlbaum.

Matthews, J. D., & Cramer, E. P. (2006). Envisioning the adoption process to strengthen gay- and lesbian-headed families: Recommendations for adoption professionals. *Child Welfare, 85,* 317–340.

Maurer, D., & Salapatek, P. (1976). Developmental changes in the scanning of faces by young infants. *Child Development, 47,* 523–527.

Mayer, J. D., Salovey, P. R., & Caruso, D. R. (2007). What is emotional intelligence and what does it predict? In P. C. Kyllonen, R. D. Roberts, & L. Stankov (Eds.), *Extending intelligence.* Mahwah, NJ: Erlbaum.

Mayer, J. D., Salovey, P. R., & Caruso, D. R. (2002). *Mayer–Salovey–Caruso Emotional Intelligence Test (MSCEIT): User's manual.* Toronto, Ontario: Multi-Health Systems.

Mayer, J. D., Salovey, P. R., & Caruso, D. R. (2004). Emotional intelligence: Theory, findings, and implications. *Psychological Inquiry, 15,* 197–215.

Mayer, R. E. (2004). Teaching of subject matter. *Annual Review of Psychology* (Vol. 55). Palo Alto, CA: Annual Reviews.

Mayer, R. E. (2008). *Learning and instruction* (2nd ed.). Upper Saddle River, NJ: Prentice Hall.

Mayes, L. (2003). Unpublished review of J. W. Santrock's *Tropical life-span development,* 2nd ed. (New York: McGraw Hill).

Mayseless, O., & Scharf, M. (2007). Adolescents' attachment representations and their capacity for intimacy in close relationships. *Journal of Research in Adolescence, 17,* 23–50.

Mbonye, A. K., Neema, S., & Magnussen, P. (2006). Treatment-seeking practices for malaria in pregnancy among rural women in Mukono district, Uganda. *Journal of Biosocial Science, 38,* 221–237.

McAdoo, H. P. (2006). *Black families* (4th ed.). Thousand Oaks, CA: Sage.

McAlister, A., & Peterson, C. (2007). A longitudinal study of child siblings and theory of mind development. *Cognitive Development, 22,* 258–270.

McAnarney, E. R. (2008). Adolescent brain development: Forging new links? *Journal of Adolescent Health, 42,* 321–323.

McCabe, K. M., Rodgers, C., Yeh, M., & Hough, R. (2004). Gender differences in childhood onset conduct disorder. *Development and Psychopathology, 16,* 179–192.

McCall, R. B., Applebaum, M. I., & Hogarty, P. S. (1973). Developmental changes in mental performance. *Monographs of the Society for Research in Child Development, 38* (Serial No. 150).

McCarthy, J. (2007). Children with autism spectrum disorders and intellectual disability. *Current Opinion in Psychiatry, 20,* 472–476.

McCartney, K. (2003, July 16). Interview with Kathleen McCartney in A. Bucuvalas, "Child care and behavior." *HGSE News,* pp. 1–4. Cambridge, MA: Harvard Graduate School of Education.

McCartney, K. (2009, in press). Current research on childcare effects. In R. E. Tremblay, R. deV Peters, M. Boivan, & R. G. Barr (Eds.), *Encyclopedia on early childhood development.* Montreal: Center of Excellence for Early Childhood Development.

McCartney, K., Dearing, E., Taylor, B. A., & Bub, K. L. (2007). Quality child care supports the achievement of low-income children: Direct and indirect pathways through caregiving and the home environment. *Journal of Applied Developmental Psychology, 28,* 411–426.

McDonald, R., & Grych, J. H. (2006). Young children's appraisals of interparental conflict: Measurement and links with adjustment problems. *Journal of Family Psychology, 20,* 88–99.

McDougall, P., & Hymel, S. (2007). Same-gender versus cross-gender friendship conceptions. *Merrill-Palmer Quarterly, 53,* 347–380.

McElhaney, K. B., Antonishak, J., & Allen, J. P. (2008). "They like me, they like me not": Popularity and adolescents' perceptions of acceptance predicting social functioning over time. *Child Development, 79,* 720–731.

McGarvey, C., McDonnell, M., Hamilton, K., O'Regan, M., & Matthews, T. (2006). An 8year study of risk factors for SIDS: Bed—sharing versus non-bed-sharing. *Archives of Disease in Childhood, 91,* 318–323.

McHale, J., & Sullivan, M. (2008). Family systems. In M. Hersen & A. Gross (Eds.), *Handbook of clinical psychology, Vol. II: Children and adolescents.* New York: Wiley.

McKenna, J. J., & McDade, T. (2005). Why babies should never sleep alone: A review of the co-sleeping controversy in relation to SIDS, bedsharing, and breastfeeding. *Pediatric Respiratory Reviews, 6,* 134–152.

McKeough, A., Palmer, J., Jarvey, M., & Bird, S. (2007). Best narrative writing practices when teaching from a developmental perspective. In S. Graham, C. A. MacArthur, & J. Fitzgerald (Eds.), *Best practices in writing instruction.* New York: Guilford.

McLoyd, V. C. (1998). Children in poverty. In I. E. Siegel & K. A. Renninger (Eds.), *Handbook of child psychology* (5th ed., Vol. 4). New York: Wiley.

McLoyd, V. C. (2000). Poverty. In A. Kazdin (Ed.), *Encyclopedia of psychology*. Washington, DC, and New York: American Psychological Association and Oxford University Press.

McLoyd, V. C., Aikens, N. L., & Burton, L. M. (2006). Childhood poverty, policy, and practice. In W. Damon & R. Lerner (Eds.), *Handbook of child psychology* (6th ed.). New York: Wiley.

McMillen, I. C., MacLaughlin, S. M., Muhlhausler, B. S., Gentili, S., Duffield, J. L., & Morrison, J. L. (2008). Developmental origins of adult health and disease: The role of periconceptional and fetal nutrition. *Basic and Clinical Pharmacology and Toxicology 102,* 82–89.

McNamara, F., & Sullivan, C. E. (2000). Obstructive sleep apnea in infants. *Journal of Pediatrics, 136,* 318–323.

Mead, M. (1978, Dec. 30–Jan. 5). The American family: An endangered species. *TV Guide,* pp. 21–24.

Meerlo, P., Sgoifo, A., & Suchecki, D. (2008, in press). Restricted and disrupted sleep: Effects on autonomic function, neuroendocrine stress systems, and stress responsivity. *Sleep Medicine Review.*

Meis, P. J., & Peaceman, A. M. (2003). Prevention of recurrent preterm delivery by 17-alpha-hydroxyprogesterone caproate. *New England Journal of Medicine, 348,* 2379–2385.

Mejia-Arauz, R., Rogoff, B., Dexter, A., & Najafi, B. (2007). Cultural variation in children's social organization. *Child Development, 78,* 1001–1014.

Melgar-Quinonez, H. R., & Kaiser, L. L. (2004). Relationship of child-feeding practices to overweight in low-income Mexican-American preschool-aged children. *Journal of the American Dietetic Association, 104,* 1110–1119.

Meltzi, G., & Ely, R. (2009). Language development in the school years. In J. B. Gleason & N. Ratner (Eds.), *The development of language* (7th ed.). Boston: Allyn & Bacon.

Meltzoff, A. N. (2007). "Like me": A foundation for social cognition. *Developmental Science, 10,* 126–134.

Meltzoff, A. N. (2008). Unpublished review of J. W. Santrock's *Life-Span development,* 12th ed. (New York: McGraw-Hill).

Meltzoff, A. N., & Brooks, R. (2006). Eyes wide shut: The importance of eyes in infant gaze following and understanding of other minds. In R. Flom, K. Lee, & D. Muir (Eds.), *Gaze-following.* Mahwah, NJ: Erlbaum.

Meltzoff, A. N., & Brooks, R. (2009). Social cognition: The role of gaze following in early word learning. In J. Colombo, P. McCardle, &

L. Freund (Eds.), *Infant pathways to language.* Clifton, NJ: Psychology Press.

Mendle, J., Turkheimer, E., & Emery, R. E. (2007). Detrimental psychological outcomes associated with early pubertal timing in adolescent girls. *Developmental Review, 27,* 151–171.

Menias, C. O., Elsayes, K. M., Peterson, C. M., Huete, A., Gratz, B. I., & Bhalla, S. (2007). CT of pregnancy-related complications. *Emergency Radiology, 13,* 299–306.

Menn, L., & Stoel-Gammon, C. (2005). Phonological development: Learning sounds and sound patterns. In J. Berko Gleason (Ed.), *The development of language* (6th ed.). Boston: Allyn & Bacon.

Menn, L., & Stoel-Gammon, C. (2009). Phonological development: Learning sounds and sound patterns. In J. Berko Gleason & N. Ratner (Eds.), *The development of language* (7th ed.). Boston: Allyn & Bacon.

Mennuti, M. T. (2008). Genetic screening in reproductive health care. *Clinical Obstetrics and Gynecology, 51,* 3–23.

Menyuk, P., Liebergott, J., & Schultz, M. (1995). *Early language development in full-term and premature infants.* Hillsdale, NJ: Erlbaum.

Meredith, N. V. (1978). Research between 1960 and 1970 on the standing height of young children in different parts of the world. In H. W. Reece & L. P. Lipsitt (Eds.), *Advances in child development and behavior* (Vol. 12). New York: Academic Press.

Merewood, A., Patel, B., Newton, K. N., MacAuley, L. P., Chamberlin, L. B., Francisco, P., & Mehta, S. D. (2007). Breastfeeding duration rates and factors affecting continued breastfeeding among infants born at an inner-city U.S. baby-friendly hospital. *Journal of Human Lactation, 23,* 157–164.

Merrick, J., Morad, M., Halperin, I., & Kandel, I. (2005). Physical fitness and adolescence. *International Journal of Adolescent Medicine, 17,* 89–91.

Mervis, C. B., & Becerra, A. M. (2007). Language and communicative development in Williams syndrome. *Mental Retardation and Developmental Disabilities Research Review, 13,* 3–15.

Messinger, D. (2008). Smiling. In M. M. Haith & J. B. Benson (Eds.), *Encyclopedia of infant and early childhood development.* Oxford, UK: Elsevier.

Mestre, J. M., Guil, R., Lopes, P. N., Salovey, P., & Gil-Olarte, P. (2007). Emotional intelligence and social and academic adaptation to school. *Psicothema, 18 (Suppl.),* S112–S117.

Metz, E. C., & Youniss, J. (2005). Longitudinal gains in civic development through school-based required service. *Political Psychology, 26,* 413–437.

Mikkelsson, L., Kaprio, J., Kautianinen, H., Kujala, U., Mikkelsson, M., & Nupponen,H. (2006). School fitness tests as predictors of adult health-related fitness. *American Journal of Human Biology, 18,* 342–349.

Miller, B. C., Fan, X., Christensen, M., Grotevant, H. D., & von Dulmen, M. (2000). Comparisons of adopted and nonadopted adolescents in a large, nationally representative sample. *Child Development, 71,* 1458–1473.

Miller, C. F., & Ruble, D. N. (2005). *Development changes in the accessibility of gender stereotypes.* Unpublished manuscript, Department of Psychology. New York University.

Miller, J. G. (2006). Insights into moral development from cultural psychology. In M. Killen & J. G. Smetana (Eds.), *Handbook of moral development.* Mahwah, NJ: Erlbaum.

Miller, J. G. (2007). Cultural psychology of moral development. In S. Kitayama & D. Cohen (Eds.), *Handbook of cultural psychology.* New York: Guilford.

Miller, S. A. (2000). Children's understanding of preexisting differences in knowledge and belief. *Developmental Review, 20,* 227–282.

Miller-Johnson, S., Coie, J., & Malone, P. S. (2003, April). *Do aggression and peer rejection in childhood predict early adult outcomes?* Paper to be presented at the biennial meeting of the Society for Research in Child Development, Tampa, FL.

Miller-Jones, D. (1989). Culture and testing. *American Psychologist, 44,* 360–366.

Mills, C. M. (2007). *Theory of mind.* Unpublished manuscript, University of Texas at Dallas, School of Behavioral and Brain Sciences, Richardson, TX.

Mills, C. M., & Keil, F. C. (2005). The development of cynicism. *Psychological Science, 16,* 385–390.

Mills, D., & Mills, C. (2000). *Hungarian kindergarten curriculum translation.* London: Mills Production.

Minde, K., & Zelkowitz, P. (2008). Premature babies. In M. M. Haith & J. B. Benson (Eds.), *Encyclopedia of infancy and early childhood development.* Oxford, UK: Elsevier.

Minuchin, P. O., & Shapiro, E. K. (1983). The school as a context for social development. In P. H. Mussen (Ed.), *Handbook of child psychology* (4th ed., Vol. 4). New York: Wiley.

Minzenberg, M. J., Poole, J. H., & Vinogradov, S. (2006). Adult social attachment disturbance is related to childhood maltreatment and current symptoms in borderline personality disorder. *Journal of Nervous and Mental Disorders, 194,* 341–348.

Mischel, W., & Mischel, H. (1975, April). *A cognitive social-learning analysis of moral development.* Paper presented at the meeting of the Society for Research in Child Development, Denver.

Mistry, K. B., Minkovitz, C. S., Strobino, D. M., & Borzekowski, D. L. G. (2007). Children's television exposure and behavioral and social outcomes at 5.5 years: Does timing of exposure matter? *Pediatrics, 120,* 762–769.

Mitchell, E. A. (2007). Sudden infant death syndrome: Should bed sharing be discouraged? *Archives of Pediatric and Adolescent Medicine, 161,* 305–316.

Mitchell, E. A., Blair, P. S., & L'Hoir, M. P. (2006). Should pacifiers be recommended to prevent sudden infant death syndrome? *Pediatrics, 117,* 1811–1812.

Mitchell, E. A., Hutchinson, L., & Stewart, A. W. (2007). The continuing decline in SIDS mortality. *Archives of Disease in Childhood, 92,* 625–626.

Mitchell, E. A., Stewart, A. W., Crampton, P., & Salmond, C. (2000). Deprivation and sudden infant death syndrome. *Social Science and Medicine, 51,* 147–150.

Miyake, K., Chen, S., & Campos, J. (1985). Infants' temperament, mothers' mode of inter- action and attachment in Japan: An interim report. In I. Bretherton & F. Waters (Eds.), Growing points of attachment theory and re- search, *Monographs of the Society for Research in Child Development, 50* (1–2, Serial N. 109), 276–297.

MMMR. (2006, June 9). *Youth risk behavior surveillance—United States, 2005.* Atlanta: Centers for Disease Control and prevention.

Moise, K. J. (2005). Fetal RhD typing with free DNA I maternal plasma. *American Journal of Obstetrics and Gynecology, 192,* 663–665

Molholm, S., Christodoulou, C., Ritter, W., & Cowan, N. (2001). *The development of auditory attention in children.* Unpublished manuscript, Department of Psychology, City College of the City University of New York.

Money, J. (1975). Ablato penis: Normal male infant sex-reassigned as a girl. *Archives of Sexual Behavior, 4,* 65–71.

Montan, S. (2007). Increased risk in the elderly parturient. *Current Opinion in Obstetrics and Gynecology, 19,* 110–112.

Montemayor, R. (1982). The relationship between parent-adolescent conflict and the amount of time adolescents spend with par- ents, peers, and alone. *Child Development, 53,* 1512–1519.

Moore, D. (2001). *The dependent gene.* New York: W. H. Freeman.

Moore, M. K., & Meltzoff, A. N. (2008). Factors affecting infants' manual search for occluded objects and the genesis of object permanence. *Infant Behavior and Development, 31,* 168–180.

Moos, M. K. (2006). Prenatal care: Limitations and opportunities. *Journal of Obstetric, Gynecologic, and Neonatal Nursing, 35,* 278–285.

Moran, S., & Gardner, H. (2006). Extraordinary achievements. In W. Damon &

R. Lerner (Eds.), *Handbook of child psychology* (6th ed.). New York: Wiley.

Morelli, G. A., & Rothbaum, F. (2007). Situating the child in context: Attachment relationships and self-regulation in different cultures. In S. Kitayama & D. Cohen (Eds.), *Handbook of cultural psychology.* New York: Guilford.

Morelli, G. A., Rogoff, B., Oppenheim, D., & Goldsmith, D. (1992). Cultural variation in infants' sleeping arrangements: Questions of independence. *Developmental Psychology, 28,* 604–613.

Morokuma, S., & others. (2008, in press). Developmental change in fetal response to repeated low-intensity sound. *Developmental Science.*

Morra, S., Gobbo, C., Marini, Z., & Sheese, R. (2007). *Cognitive development: Neo-Piagetian perspectives.* Mahwah, NJ: Erlbaum.

Morris, D. S., Tenkku, L. E., Salas, J., Xaverius, P. K., & Mengel, M. B. (2008). Exploring pregnancy-related changes in alcohol consumption between Black and White women. *Alcoholism: Clinical and Experimental Research, 32,* 505–512.

Morrison, G. S. (2008). *Fundamentals of early childhood education* (5th ed.). Upper Saddle River, NJ: Prentice Hall.

Morrison, G. S. (2009). *Early childhood educa- tion today* (11th ed.). Upper Saddle River, NJ: Prentice Hall.

Morrissey, M. V. (2007). Suffer no more in silence: Challenging the myths of women's mental health in childbearing. *International Journal of Psychiatric Nursing Research, 12,* 1429–1438.

Morrongiello, B. A., Fenwick, K. D., & Chance, G. (1990). Sound localization acuity in very young infants: An observer-based testing procedure. *Developmental Psychology, 26,* 75–84.

Morrow, C. E., Cullbertson, J. L., Accornero, V. H., Xue, L., Anthony, J. C., & Bandstra, E. S. (2006). Learning disabilities and intellectual functioning in school-aged children with prenatal cocaine exposure. *Developmental Neuropsychology, 30,* 905–931.

Morrow, L. (2009). *Literacy development in the early years* (6th ed.). Boston: Allyn & Bacon.

Mortimer, J. T., & Larson, R. W. (Eds.). (2002). *The changing adolescent experience.* New York: Cambridge University Press.

Moschonis, G., Grammatikaki, E., & Manios, Y. (2008, in press). Perinatal predictors of overweight at infancy and preschool child- hood: The GENESIS study. *International Journal of Obesity.*

Mottershead, N. (2006). Hypnosis: Removing labor from birth. *Practicing Midwife, 9,* 26–27, 29.

Moulson, M. C., & Nelson, C. A. (2008). Neurological development. In M. M. Haith & J. B. Benson (Eds.), *Encyclopedia of infancy and early childhood.* Oxford, UK: Elsevier.

Mounts, N. S. (2002). Parental management of adolescent peer relationships in context: The role of parenting style. *Journal of Family Psychology, 16,* 58–69.

Moyer, R. H., Hackett, J. K., & Everett, S. A. (2007). *Teaching science as investigations.* Upper Saddle River, NJ: Prentice Hall.

Mozingo, J. N., Davis, M. W., Droppleman, P. G., & Merideth, A. (2000), "It wasn't work- ing." Women's experiences with short-term breast feeding. *American Maternal Journal of Nursing, 25,* 120–126.

Mraz, M., Padak, N. D., & Rasinski, T. V. (2008). *Evidence-based instruction in reading.* Boston: Allyn & Bacon.

Mueller, U., Carpendale, J. I. M., Budwig, N., & Sokol, B. W. (Eds.). (2008). *Social life and social knowledge.* Philadelphia: Psychology Press.

Muhler, M. R., Hartmann, C., Werner, W., Meyer, O., Bollmann, R., & Klingebiel, R. (2007). Fetal MRI demonstrates glioependymal cyst in a case of sonographic unilateral ventricu- lomegaly. *Pediatric Radiology, 37,* 391–395.

Mullis, P. E., & Tonella, P. (2008). Regulation of fetal growth: Consequences and impact of being born small. *Best Practice Research: Clinical Endocrinology and Metabolism, 22,* 173–190.

Mulvaney, M. K., & Mebert, C. J. (2007). Parental corporal punishment predicts behav- ioral problems in early childhood. *Journal of Family Psychology, 21,* 389–397.

Munakata, Y. (2006). Information processing approaches to development. In W. Damon & R. Lerner (Eds.), *Handbook of child psychology* (6thed.). New York: Wiley.

Mundy, P., & Newell, L. (2007). Attention, joint attention, and social cognition. *Current Directions in Psychological Science, 16,* 269–274.

Mundy, P., Block, J., Vaughan Van Hecke, A., Delgado, C., Parlade, M., & Pomares, Y. (2007). Individual differences in the develop- ment of joint attention in infancy. *Child Development, 78,* 938–954.

Murdock, T. B., Miller, A., & Kohylardt, J. (2004). Effects of classroom context variables on high school students' judgments of the accept- ability and likelihood of cheating. *Journal of Educational Psychology, 96,* 765–777.

Murnane, R. J. (2007). Improving the educa- tion of children living in poverty. *Future of Children, 17,* 161–182.

Murphy, M. M., & Mazzocco, M. M. (2008). Mathematics learning disabilities in girls with fragile X or Turner syndrome during late - elementary school. *Journal of Learning Disabilities, 41,* 29–46.

Murray, J. P. (2007). TV violence: Research and controversy. In N. Pecora, J. P. Murray, & E. A. Wartella (Eds.), *Children and*

Murray, J. P., & Murray, A. D. (2008). *Television: Uses and effects. In M. M. Haith & J.B. Benson (Eds.),* Encyclopedia of infant and early childhood development. *Oxford, UK: Elsevier.*

Myers, A., & Hansen, C. (2006). *Experimental psychology* (6th ed.). Belmont, CA: Wadsworth.

Myers, D., Baer, W., & Choi, S. (1996). The changing problem of overcrowded housing. *Journal of the American Planning Association, 62,* 66–84.

Myerson, J., Rank, M. R., Raines, F. Q., & Schnitzler, M. A. (1998). Race and general cognitive ability: The myth of diminishing returns in education. *Psychological Science, 9,* 139–142.

N

NAEYC. (1997). *Developmentally appropriate practice in early childhood education programs serving children from birth through age 8.* Washington, DC: Author.

NAEYC. (2005). *Critical facts about young children and early childhood in the United States.* Washington, DC: Author.

Nagata, D. K. (1989). Japanese American children and adolescents. In J. T. Gibbs & L. N. Huang (Eds.), *Children of color.* San Francisco: Jossey-Bass.

Nagel, H. T., Kneght, A. C., Kloosterman, M. D., Wildschut, H. I., Leschot, N. J., & Vandenbussche, F. P. (2007). Prenatal diagnosis in the Netherlands, 1991–2000: Number of invasive procedures, indications, abnormal results, and terminations of pregnancies. *Prenatal Diagnosis, 27,* 251–257.

Naigles, L. R., & Swensen, L. D. (2007). Syntactic supports for word learning. In E. Hoff & M. Shatz (Eds.), *Blackwell handbook of language development.* Malden, MA: Blackwell.

Nakamura, K., Sheps, S., & Clara Arck, P. (2008, in press). Stress and reproductive failure: Past nations, present insights, and future directions. *Journal of Assisted Reproduction and Genetics.*

Nanovskaya, T. N., Nekhayeva, I. A., Hankins, G. D., & Ahmed, M. S. (2008). Transfer of methadone across the dually perfused preterm human placental lobule. *American Journal of Obstetrics and Gynecology, 198,* e1–e4.

Nansel, T. R., Overpeck, M., Pilla, R., Ruan, W., Simons-Morton, B., & Scheidt, P. (2001). Bullying behaviors among U.S. youth. *Journal of the American Medical Association, 285,* 2094–2100.

Narberhaus, A., Segarra, D., Caldu, X., Gimenez, M., Pueyo, R., Botet, F., & Junque, C. (2008). Corpus collosum and prefrontal functions in adolescents with history of very preterm birth. *Neuropsychologia, 46,* 111–116.

Nardi, P. M. (2006). *Doing survey research* (2nded.). Boston: Allyn & Bacon.

Narvaez, D. (2006). Integrative ethical education. In M. Killen & J. Smetana (Eds.), *Handbook of moral development.* Mahwah, NJ: Erlbaum.

Narvaez, D. (2008). Four component model. In F. C. Power, R. J. Nuzzi, D. Narvaez, D. K. Lapsley, & T. C. Hunt (Eds.), *Moral education: A handbook.* Westport, CT: Greenwood.

Narvaez, D., Bock, T., Endicott, L., & Lies, J. (2004). Minnesota's Community Voices and Character Education Project. *Journal of Research in Character Education, 2,* 89–112.

Narvaez, D., & Lapsley, D. (Eds.). (2009, in press). Moral personality, identity, and character: An interdisciplinary future. New York: Cambridge University Press.

Narvaez, D., Lynchard, N., Vaydich, J., & Mattan, B. (2008, March). *Cheating: Explicit recognition, implicit evaluation, moral judgment and honor code training.* Annual Meeting of the Society for Research in Adolescence.

Nation, M., & Heflinger, C. A. (2006). Risk factors for serious alcohol and drug use: The role of psychosocial variables in predicting the frequency of substance abuse among adolescents. *American Journal of Alcohol Abuse, 32,* 415–433.

National Assessment of Educational Progress. (2000). *Reading achievement.* Washington, DC: National Center for Education Statistics.

National Assessment of Educational Progress. (2005). *The nation's report card: 2005.* Washington, DC: U.S. Department of Education.

National Assessment of Educational Progress. (2007). *The nation's report card: 2007.* Washington, DC: U.S. Department of Education.

National Association for Sport and Physical Education. (2002). *Active start: A statement of physical activity guidelines for children birth to five years.* Reston, VA: Author.

National Center for Education Statistics. (2003). *Digest of Education Statistics.* Washington, DC: Author.

National Center for Education Statistics. (2005). *Internet access in U.S. public schools.* Washington, DC: U.S. Department of Education.

National Center for Education Statistics. (2007). *Students with disabilities. Indicator 31,* (p.68). Washington, DC: U.S. Department of Education.

National Center for Education Statistics. (2008a). *School dropout rates.* Washington, DC: U. S. Department of Education.

National Center for Education Statistics. (2008b). *The condition of education 2008. Indicator 8. Children and youth with disabilities in public schools.* Washington, DC: U.S. Department of Education.

National Center for Health Statistics. (2000). *Health United States, 1999.* Atlanta: Centers for Disease Control and Prevention.

National Center for Health Statistics. (2007). *Births.* Atlanta: Centers for Disease Control and Prevention.

National Clearing House on Child Abuse and Neglect. (2004). *What is child abuse and neglect?* Washington, DC: U.S. Department of Health and Human Services.

National Institute of Mental Health. (2004). *Autism spectrum disorders.* Bethesda, MD: Author.

National Institute of Mental Health. (2008). *Autism spectrum disorders (pervasive developmental disorders).* Retrieved January 6, 2008, from http://www.nimh.nih.gov/Publicat/autism.cfm

National Institute of Neurological Disorders and Stroke. (2008). *Brain basics: Understanding sleep.* Retrieved June 30, 2008, from www.ninds.nih.gov/disorders/brain_basics/understanding_sleep.htm

National Institutes of Health. (1993). *Learning disabilities* (NIH publication No. 93–3611). Bethesda, MD: Author.

National Institutes of Health. (2008). *Clinical trial.gov* Retrieved April 22, 2008, from http://clinicaltrials.gov/ct2/show/NCT00059293?cond=%22Intracranial1Embolism%22&r...

National Research Council. (1999). *Starting out right: A guide to promoting children's reading success.* Washington, DC: National Academy Press.

National Research Council. (2004). *Engaging schools: Fostering high school students' motivation to learn.* Washington, DC: National Academic Press.

National Sleep Foundation. (2005). *Sleep in American Poll: Children and sleep.* Washington, DC: Author.

National Sleep Foundation. (2006). *2006 Sleep in America Poll.* Washington, DC: Author.

National Sleep Foundation. (2007). *Sleep in America poll 2007.* Washington, DC: Author.

National Sleep Foundation. (2008). *Children and sleep.* Retrieved April 26, 2008, from www.sleepfoundation.org/site/c.huIXKjM0IxF/b.2418873/k.B9AD/ Children_and_SI...

National Vital Statistics Report. (2004, March 7). Deaths: Leading causes for 2002. Atlanta: Center for Disease Control and Prevention.

Nava-Campo, A.A., & Koren, G. (2007). Human teratogens and evidence-based teratogen risk counseling: The Motherisk approach. *Clinical Obstetrics and Gynecology, 50,* 123-131.

Needham, A. (2008, in press). Learning in infants' object perception, object-directed action, and tool use. In A. Woodward & A. Needham (Eds.), *Learning and the infant mind.* New York: Oxford University Press.

Needham, A., Barrett, T., & Peterman, K. (2002) A pick-me-up for infants' exploratory skills: Early simulated experiences reaching for objects using 'sticky mittens' enhances young infants' object exploration skills. *Infant Behavior and Development, 25,* 279–295.

Neisser, U. (2004). Memory development: New questions and old. *Developmental Review, 24,* 154–158.

Neisser, U., Boodoo, G., Bouchard, T. J., Boykin, A. W., Brody, N., Ceci, S. J., Halpern, D. F., Loehlin, J. C., Perloff, R. J., Sternberg, R., & Urbina, S. (1996). Intelligence: Knowns and unknowns. *American Psychologist, 51,* 77–101.

Nelson, C. A. (2003). Neural development and lifelong plasticity. In R. M. Lerner, F. Jacobs, & D. Wertlieb (Eds.), *Handbook of applied developmental science* (Vol. 1). Thousand Oaks, CA: Sage.

Nelson, C. A. (2007). A developmental cognitive neuroscience approach to the study of atypical development: A model system involving infants of diabetic mothers. In D. Coch, G. Dawson, & K. W. Fischer (Eds.), *Human behavior, learning, and the developing brain.* New York: Guilford.

Nelson, C. A. (2008, in press). Brain development and behavior. In A. M. Rudolph, C. Rudolph, L. First, G. Lister, & A. A. Gershon (Eds.), *Rudolph's pediatrics* (22nd ed.). New York: McGraw-Hill.

Nelson, C. A., Thomas, K. M., & de Haan, M. (2006). Neural bases of cognitive development. In W. Damon, R. Lerner. D. Kuhn, & R. Siegler (Eds.), *Handbook of child psychology* (6th ed., Vol. 2). New York: Wiley.

Nelson, C. A., Zeanah, C., & Fox, N. A. (2007). The effects of early deprivation on brain-behavioral development: The Bucharest Early Intervention Project. In D. Romer & E. Walker (Eds.), *Adolescent psychopathology and the developing brain: Integrating brain and prevention science.* New York: Oxford University Press.

Nelson, J. A., & Eckstein, D. (2008). A service-learning model for at-risk adolescents. *Education and Treatment of Children, 31,* 223–237.

Nelson, K. (1999). Levels and modes of representation: Issues for the theory of conceptual change and development. In E. K. Skolnick, K. Nelson, S. A. Gelman, & P. H. Miller (Eds.), *Conceptual development.* Mahwah, NJ: Erlbaum.

Ness, A., Dias, T., Damus, K., Burd, I., & Berghella, V. (2006). Impact of recent randomized trials on the use of progesterone to prevent preterm birth: A 2005 follow-up survey. *American Journal of Obstetrics and Gynecology, 195,* 1174–1179.

Neuman, R. J., Lobos, E., Reich, W., Henderson, C. A., Sun, L. W., & Todd, R. D. (2007). Prenatal smoking exposure and dopaminergic genotypes interact to cause a severe ADHD subtype. *Biological Psychiatry, 61,* 1320–1328.

Neumark-Sztainer, D., Paxton, S. J., Hannan, P. J., Haines, J., & Story, M. (2006). Does body satisfaction matter? Five-year longitudinal association between body satisfaction and health behaviors in adolescent females and males. *Journal of Adolescent Health, 39,* 244–251.

Neville, H. J. (2006). Different profiles of plasticity within human cognition. In Y. Munakata & M. H. Johnson (Eds.), *Attention and Performance XXI: Processes of change in brain and cognitive development.* Oxford. UK: Oxford University Press.

New, R. (2005). The Reggio Emilia approach: Provocations and partnerships with U.S. early childhood educators. In J. I. Roopnarine & J. E. Johnson (Eds.), *Approaches to early childhood education* (4th ed.). Columbus, OH: Merrill/Prentice Hall.

New, R. (2007). Reggio Emilia as cultural activity. *Theory Into Practice, 46,* 5–13.

Newburg, D. S., & Walker, W. A. (2007). Protection of the neonate by the innate immune system of developing gut and of human milk. *Pediatric Research, 61,* 2–8.

Newcombe, N. S. (2007). The development of implicit and explicit memory. In N. Cowan & M. Courage (Eds.), *The development of memory in childhood.* Philadelphia: Psychology Press.

Newcombe, N. S., Drummey, A. B., Fox, N. A., Lile, E., & Ottinger-Alberts, W. (2000). Remembering early childhood: How much, how, and why (or why not)? *Current Directions in Psychological Science, 9,* 55–58.

Newell, K., Scully, D. M., McDonald, P. V., & Baillargeon, R. (1989). Task constraints and infant grip configurations. *Developmental Psychobiology, 22,* 817–832.

Newman, B. M., & Newman, P. R. (2007). *Theories of human development.* Mahwah, NJ: Erlbaum.

Newson, A. J. (2008). Ethical aspects arising from non-invasive fetal diagnosis. *Seminars in Fetal and Neonatal Medicine, 13,* 103–108.

Newton, A. W., & Vandeven, A. M. (2006). Unexplained infant death: A reviews of sudden infant death syndrome, sudden unexplained infant death, and child maltreatment facilities in shaken baby syndrome. *Current Opinions in Pediatrics, 18,* 196–200.

Newton, A. W., & Vandeven, A. M. (2008). Update on child maltreatment. *Current Opinion in Pediatrics, 20,* 205–212.

Ney, D. M., Hull, A. K., van Calcar, S. C., Liu, X., & Etzel, M. R. (2008). Dietary glycomacropeptide supports growth and reduces the concentrations of phenylalanine in plasma and brain in a murine model of phenylketonuria. *Journal of Nutrition, 138,* 316–322.

NICHD Early Child Care Research Network. (2000). Factors associated with fathers' caregiving activities and sensitivity with young children. *Developmental Psychology, 14,* 200–219.

NICHD Early Child Care Research Network. (2001). Nonmaternal care and family factors in early development: An overview of the NICHD study of early child care. *Journal of Applied Developmental Psychology, 22,* 457–492.

NICHD Early Child Care Research Network. (2002). Structure n Process n Outcome: Direct and indirect effects of child care quality on young children's development. *Psychological Science, 13,* 199–206.

NICHD Early Child Care Research Network. (2003). Does amount of time spent in child care predict socioemotional adjustment during the transition to kindergarten? *Child Development, 74,* 976–1005.

NICHD Early Child Care Research Network. (2004). Are child developmental outcomes related to before- and after-school care arrangement? *Child Development, 75,* 280–295.

NICHD Early Child Care Research Network. (2004). Type of child care and children's development at 54 months. *Early Childhood Research Quarterly, 19,* 203–230.

NICHD Early Child Care Research Network. (2005). *Child care and development.* New York: Guilford.

NICHD Early Child Care Research Network. (2005). Duration and developmental timing of poverty and children's cognitive and social development from birth through third grade. *Child Development, 76,* 795–810.

NICHD Early Child Care Research Network. (2005). Predicting individual differences in attention, memory, and planning in first graders from experiences at home, child care, and school. *Developmental Psychology, 41,* 99–114.

NICHD Early Child Care Research. (2006). Infant-mother attachment classification: Risk and protection in relation to changing maternal caregiving quality. *Developmental Psychology, 42,* 38–58.

Nieto, S., & Bode, P. (2008). *Affirming diversity* (5th ed.). Boston: Allyn & Bacon.

Nisbett, R. (2003). *The geography of thought.* New York: Free Press.

Nixon, G. M., & others. (2008). Short sleep duration in middle childhood: Risk factors and consequences. *Sleep, 31,* 71–78.

Noddings, N. (2008). Caring and moral education. In L. Nucci & D. Narvaez (Eds.), *Handbook of moral and character education.* Clifton, NJ: Psychology Press.

Nohr, E. A., Bech, B. H., Davies, M. J., Fryenberg, M., Henriksen, T. B., & Olsen, J. (2005). Prepregnancy obesity and fetal death: A study with the Danish National Birth Cohort. *Obstetrics and Gynecology, 106,* 250–259.

Noland, J. S., Singer, L. T., Short, E. J., Minnes, S., Arendt, R. E., Kirchner, H. L., & Bearer, C. (2005). Prenatal drug exposure and selective attention in preschoolers. *Neurotoxicology, and Teratology, 27,* 429–438.

Norbury, G., & Norbury, C. J. (2008). Non-invasive prenatal diagnosis of single gene disorders: How close are we? *Seminars in Fetal and Neonatal Medicine, 13,* 76–83.

Norgard, B., Puho, E., Czeizel, A. E., Skriver, M. V., & Sorensen, H. T. (2005). Aspirin use during early pregnancy and the risk of congenital abnormalities. *American Journal of Obstetrics & Gynecology, 192,* 922–923.

Nottelmann, F. D., Susman, E. J., Blue, J. H., Inoff-Germain, G., Dorn, L. D., Loriaux, D. L., Cutler, G. B., & Chrousos, G.P. (1987). Gonadal and adrenal hormone correlates of adjustment in early adolescence. In R. M. Leiner & T. T. Foch (Eds.), *Biological-psychological interactions in early adolescence.* Hillsdale, NJ: Erlbaum.

Nsamenang, A. B. (2002). Adolescence in sub-Saharan Africa: An image constructed from Africa's triple heritage. In B. B. Brown, R. W. Larson, & T. S. Saraswathi (Eds.), *The world's youth.* New York: Cambridge University Press.

Nucci, L. (2006). Education in the moral domain. In M. Killen & J. G. Smetana (Eds.), *Handbook of moral development.* Mahwah, NJ: Erlbaum.

Nucci, L. (2008). Moral education and domain theory. In L. Nucci & D. Narvaez (Eds.), *Handbook of moral and character education.* Clifton, NJ: Psychology Press.

Nucci, L., & Narvaez, D. (2008). Introduction and overview. In L. Nucci & D. Narvaez (Eds.), *Handbook of moral and character education.* Clifton, NJ: Psychology Press.

Nugent, K., & Brazelton, T. B. (2000). Preventive infant mental health: Uses of the Brazelton scale. In J. D. Osofsky & H. E. Fitzgerald (Eds.), *WAIMH Handbook of infant mental health* (Vol. 2). New York: Wiley.

Nurmi, J. (2004). Socialization and self-development: Channeling, selection, adjustment, and reflection. In R. Lerner & L. Steinberg, (Eds.), *Handbook of adolescent psychology.* New York: Wiley.

Nylund, K., Bellmore, A., Nishina, A., & Graham, S. (2007). Subtypes, severity, and structural stability of peer victimization: What does latent class analysis say? *Child Development, 78,* 1706–1722.

O

O'Connor, A. B., & Roy, C. (2008). Electric power plant emissions and public health. *American Journal of Nursing, 108,* 62–70.

O'Connor, E., & McCartney, K. (2007). Attachment and cognitive skills: An investiga-tion of mediating mechanisms. *Journal of Applied Developmental Psychology, 28,* 458–476.

O'Hara, S., & Prichard, R. (2009). *Teaching vocabulary with hypermedia, 6–12.* Boston: Allyn & Bacon.

O'Neill, D. (1996). Two-year-old children's sensitivity to a parent's knowledge state when making requests. *Child Development, 67,* 659–677.

Oakes, J., & Lipton, M. (2007). *Teaching to change the world* (3rd ed.). New York: McGraw-Hill.

Oakes, L. M. (2008). Categorization skills and concepts. In M. M. Haith & J. B. Benson (Eds.), *Encyclopedia of infant and early childhood develop-ment.* Oxford UK: Elsevier.

Oakley, G. P. (2007). When will we eliminate folic acid–preventable spina bifida? *Epidemiology, 18,* 367–368.

Oates, J., & Grayson, A. (2004). *Cognitive and language development in children.* Malden, MA: Blackwell.

Obel, C., & others. (2008, in press). Smoking during pregnancy and hyperactivity-inattention in the offspring—comparing results from three Nordic cohorts. *International Journal of Epidemiology.*

Obenauer, S., & Maestre, L. A. (2008). Fetal MRI of lung hypoplasia: Imaging findings. *Clinical Imaging, 32,* 48–50.

Oberlander, T. F., Bonaguro, R. J., Misri, S., Papsdorf, M., Ross, C. J., & Simpson, E. M. (2008). Infant serotonin transporter (SLC6A4) promoter genotype is associated with adverse neonatal outcomes after prenatal exposure to serotonin reuptake inhibitor medications. *Molecular Psychiatry, 13,* 65–73.

Ogbu, J. U. (1989, April). *Academic socialization of Black children: An inoculation against future failure?* Paper presented at the meeting of the Society for Research in Child Development, Kansas City.

Ogbu, J., & Stern, P. (2001). Caste status and intellectual ability. In R. J. Sternberg & E. L. Grigorento (Eds.), *Environmental effects on cogni-tive abilities.* Mahwah, NJ: Erlbaum.

Ogden, C. L., Carroll, M. D., & Flegal, K. M. (2008). High body mass index for age among U. S. children and adolescents, 2003–2006. *Journal of the American Medical Association, 299,* 2401–2405.

Ohgi, S., Akiyama, T., Arisawa, K., & Shigemori, K. (2004). Randomized controlled trial of swaddling versus massage in the man-agement of excessive crying in infants with cerebral injuries. *Archives of Disease in Childhood, 89,* 212–216.

Ohgi, S., Fukuda, M., Moriuchi, H., Kusumoto, T., Akiyama, T., Nugetn, J. K., Brazelton, T. B., Arisawa, K., Takahashi, T., & Saitoh, H. (2002). Comparison of kangaroo care and standard care: Behavioral organization, development, and temperament in healthy, low birth weight infants through 1 year. *Journal of Perinatology, 22,* 374–379.

Okagaki, L. (2000). Determinants of intelli-gence: Socialization of intelligence.

Oldehinkel, A. J., Ormel, J., Veenstra, R., De Winter, A., & Verhulst, F. C. (2008). Parental divorce and offspring depressive symp-toms: Dutch developmental trends during early adolescence. *Journal of Marriage and the Family, 70,* 284–293.

Olds, D. L., & others. (2004). Effects of home visits by paraprofessionals and nurses: Age four follow-up of a randomized trial. *Pediatrics, 114,* 1560–1568.

Olds, D. L., & others. (2007). Effects of nurse home visiting on maternal and child function-ing: Age-9 follow-up of a randomized trial. *Pediatrics, 120,* e832–e845.

Olson, H. C., King, S., & Jirikowic, T. (2008). Fetal alcohol spectrum disorders. In M. M. Haith & J. B. Benson (Eds.), *Encyclopedia of infancy and early childhood development.* Thousand Oaks, CA: Sage.

Olweus, D. (2003). Prevalence estimation of school bullying with the Olweus bully/victim questionnaire. *Aggressive Behavior, 29* (3), 239–269.

Onishi, K. H., & Baillargeon, R. (2005). Do 15-month-old infants understand false beliefs? *Science, 308,* 255–258.

Ono, M. Y., Farzin, F., & Hagerman, R. J. (2008). Fragile X syndrome. In M. M. Haith & J.B. Benson (Eds.), *Encyclopedia of infant and early childhood development.* Oxford, UK: Elsevier.

Oosterhof, A. (2009). *Developing and using classroom assessments* (4th ed.). Upper Saddle River, NJ: Prentice Hall.

Orbe, M. P. (2008). Theorizing multidimen-sional identity negotiation: Reflections on the lived experiences of first-generation college students. In M. Azmitia, M. Syed, & K. Radmacher (Eds.), *The intersections of personal and social identities. New Directions for Child and Adolescent Development, 120,* 81–95.

Orecchia, R., Lucignani, G., & Tosi, G. (2008). Prenatal irradiation and pregnancy: The effects of diagnostic imaging and radiation therapy. *Recent Results in Cancer Research, 178,* 3–20.

Ornstein, P. A., & Haden, C. A. (2001). False childhood memories and eyewitness suggestibil-ity. In M. L. Eisen, J. A. Quas, & G. S. Goodman (Eds.), *Memory and suggestibility in the forensic interview.* Mahwah, NJ: Erlbaum.

Orobio de Castro, B., Merk, W., Koops, W., Veerman, J. W., & Bosch, J. D. (2005). Emotions in social information processing and their relations with reactive and proactive aggression in referred aggressive boys. *Journal of Clinical Child and Adolescent Psychology, 34,* 105–116.

Orth, U., Robins, R. W., & Roberts, B. W. (2008, in press). Low self-esteem prospectively predicts depression in adolescence and young adulthood. *Journal of Personality and Social Psychology.*

Oscarsson, M. E., Amer-Wahlin, I., Rydhstroem, H., & Kallen, K. (2006). Outcome in obstetric care related to oxytocin use: A population-based study. *Acta Obstetricia et Gynecologica Scandinavica, 85,* 1094–1098.

Oser, F. K., & Gmünder, P. (1991). *Religious judgment: A developmental perspective.* Birmingham, AL: Religious Education Press.

Oser, F. K., Scarlett, W. G., & Bucher, A. (2006). Religious and spiritual development throughout the life span. In W. Damon & R. Lerner (Eds.), *Handbook of child psychology* (4th ed.). New York: Wiley.

Osvath, P., Voros, V., & Fekete, S. (2004). Life events and psychopathology in a group of suicide attempters. *Psychopathology, 37,* 36–40.

Otto, B. W. (2008). *Literacy development in early childhood.* Upper Saddle River, NJ: Prentice Hall.

Owen, M. T. (2009, in press). Child care and the development of young children (0–2). In R. E. Tremblay, R. deV Peters, M. Boivan, & R. G. Barr (Eds.), *Encyclopedia on early childhood development.* Montreal: Centre of Excellence for Early Childhood Development.

Owens, J. A., Stahl, J., Patton, A., Reddy, U., & Crouch, M. (2006). Sleep practices, attitudes, and beliefs in inner city middle school children: A mixed-methods study. *Behavioral Sleep Medicine, 4,* 114–134.

Owens, R. E. (2008). *Language development* (7th ed.). Boston: Allyn & Bacon.

P

Palmer, S. E. (2004). Custody and access issues with children whose parents are separated or divorced. *Canadian Journal of Community Mental Health, 4* (Suppl.) 25–38.

Palomaki, G. E., Steinort, K., Knight, G. J., & Haddow, J. E. (2006). Comparing three screening strategies for combining first-and second-trimester Down syndrome markers. *Obstetrics and Gynecology, 107,* 1170.

Paloutzian, R. F. (2000). *Invitation to the psychology of religion* (3rd ed.). Needham Heights, MA: Allyn & Bacon.

Pals, J. L. (2006). Constructing the "springboard effect": Causal connections, self-making, and growth within the life story. In D. P. McAdams, R. Josselson, & A. Lieblich (Eds.), *Identity and story.* Washington, DC: American Psychological Association.

Pan, B. A., Rowe, M. L., Singer, J. D., & Snow, C. E. (2005). Maternal correlates of growth in toddler vocabulary production in low-income families. *Child Development, 76,* 763–782.

Pan, B. A., & Uccelli, P. (2009). Semantic development. In J. Berko Gleason & N. Ratner (Eds.). *The development of language* (7th ed.). Boston: Allyn & Bacon.

Pang, V. O. (2005). *Multicultural education* (2nded.). New York: McGraw-Hill.

Parazzini, F., Chatenoud, L., Surace, M., Tozzi, L., Salerio, B., Bettoni, G., & Benzi, G. (2003). Moderate alcohol drinking and risk of preterm birth. *European Journal of Clinical Nutrition, 57,* 1345–1349.

Park, T. R., Brooks, J. M., Chrischilles, E.A., & Bergus, G. (2008). Estimating the effect of treatment changes when treatment benefits are heterogeneous: Antibiotics and otitis media. *Value in Health, 11,* 304–314.

Parke, R. D., & Buriel, R. (2006). Socialization in the family: Ethnic and ecological perspectives. In W. Damon & R. Lerner (Eds.), *Handbook of child psychology* (6th ed.). New York: Wiley.

Parke, R. D., Leidy, M. S., Schofield, T. J., Miller, M. A., & Morris, K. L. (2008). Socialization. In M. M. Haith & J. B. Benson (Eds.), *Encyclopedia of infant and early childhood development.* Oxford, UK: Elsevier.

Parten, M. (1932). Social play among preschool children. *Journal of Abnormal Social Psychology, 27,* 243–269.

Pascalis, O., & Kelly, D. J. (2008). Face processing. In M. M. Haith & J. B. Benson (Eds.), *Encyclopedia of infant and early childhood development.* Oxford, UK: Elsevier.

Pasley, K., & Moorefield, B. S. (2004). Stepfamilies. In M. Coleman & L. Ganong (Eds.), *Handbook of contemporary families.* Thousand Oaks, CA: Sage.

Pasquini, E. S., Corriveau, K. H., Koenig, M., & Harris, P. L. (2007). Preschoolers monitor the relative accuracy of informants. *Developmental Psychology, 43,* 1216–1226.

Pate, R. R., Pfeiffer, K. A., Trost, S. G., Ziegler, P., & Dowda, M. (2004). Physical activity among children attending preschools. *Pediatrics, 114,* 1258–1263.

Patel, S. R., & Hu, F. B. (2008). Short sleep duration and weight gain: A systematic review. *Obesity, 16,* 643–653.

Paterson, S. J., & Schultz, R. T. (2007). Neurodevelopmental and behavioral issues in Williams syndrome. *Current Psychiatry Reports, 9,* 165–171.

Patterson, C. J. (2004). What differences does a civil union make? Changing public policies and the experiences of same-sex couples: Comment on Solomon, Rothblum, and Balsam (2004). *Journal of Family Psychology, 18,* 287–289.

Patterson, C. J., & Hastings, P. D. (2007). Socialization in the context of family diversity. In J. E. Grusec & P. D. Hastings (Eds.), *Handbook of socialization.* New York: Guilford.

Patterson, G. R., DeBaryshe, B. D., & Ramsey, E. (1989). A developmental perspective on antisocial behavior. *American Psychologist, 44* (2), 329–335.

Patterson, G. R., Reid, J. B., & Dishion, T. J. (1992). *Antisocial boys: Vol. 4. A social interactional approach.* Eugene, OR: Castalia.

Patterson, G. R., & Stouthamer-Loeber, M. (1984). The correlation of family management practices and delinquency. *Child Development, 55,* 1299–1307.

Paulhus, D. L. (2008). Birth order. In M. M. Haith & J. B. Benson (Eds.), *Encyclopedia of infant and early childhood development.* Oxford, UK: Elsevier.

Paulson, J. F., Dauber, S., & Leiferman, J. A. (2006). Individual and combined effects of postpartum depression in mothers and fathers on parenting behavior. *Pediatrics, 118,* 659–668.

Paus, T., Toro, R., Leonard, G., Lerner, J. V., Lerner, R. M., Perron, M., Pike, G. B., Richer, L., Steinberg, L., Veillete, S., & Pausova, Z. (2008, in press). Morphological properties of the action-observation cortical network in adolescents with low and high resistance to peer influence. *Social Neuroscience.*

Pavlov, I. P. (1927). In G. V. Anrep (Trans.), *Conditioned reflexes.* London: Oxford University Press.

Peak, L. (1996). *Pursuing excellence: A study of U.S. eighth-grade mathematics and science teaching, learning, curriculum, and achievement in international context.* Washington, DC: U.S. Department of Education, National Center for Educational Statistics.

Pederson, D. R., & Moran, G. (1996). Expressions of the attachment relationship outside of the Strange Situation. *Child Development, 67,* 915–927.

Pedroso, F. S. (2008). Reflexes. In M. H. Haith & J. B. Benson (Eds.), *Infant and early childhood development.* Oxford, UK: Elsevier.

Peets, K., Hodges, E. V. E., & Salmivalli, C. (2008). Affect-congruent social cognitive evaluations and behaviors. *Child Development, 79,* 170–185.

Pei, J. R., Rinaldi, C. M., Rasmussen, C., Massey, V., & Massey, D. (2008). Memory patterns of acquisition and retention of verbal and nonverbal information in children with fetal alcohol spectrum disorders. *Canadian Journal of Clinical Pharmacology, 15,* e44-e56.

Pelayo, R., Owens, J., Mindell, J., & Sheldon, S. (2006). Bed sharing with unimpaired parents is not an important risk for sudden infant death syndrome: To the editor, *Pediatrics, 117,* 993–994.

Pena, E., & Bedore, J. A. (2009). Bilingualism. In R. G. Schwartz (Ed.), *Handbook of child language disorders*. Clifton, NJ: Psychology Press.

Penagarikano, O., Mulle, J. G., & Warren, S.T. (2007). The pathophysiology of fragile X syndrome. *Annual Review of Genomics and Human Genetics, 8*, 109–129.

Pennick, V. E., & Young, G. (2007). Interventions for preventing and treating pelvic and back pain in pregnancy. *Cochrane Database of Systematic Reviews, 1*, CD001139.

Pepler, D., Jiang, D. Craig, W., & Connolly, J. (2008). Developmental trajectories of bullying and associated factors. *Child Development, 79*, 325–338.

Perez-Febles, A. M. (1992). *Acculturation and interactional styles of Latina mothers and their infants.* Unpublished honors thesis, Brown University, Providence, RI.

Perin, D. (2007). Best practices in teaching writing to adolescents. In S. Graham, C. A. MacArthur, & J. Fitzgerald (Eds.), *Best practices in writing instruction*. New York: Guilford.

Perner, J., Stummer, S., Sprung, M., & Doherty, M. (2002). Theory of mind finds its Piagetian perspective: Why alternative naming comes with understanding belief. *Cognitive Development, 17*, 1451–1472.

Perret-Clermont, A-N., & Barrelet, J-M. (Eds.). (2007). *Jean Piaget and Neuchatel.* Philadelphia: Psychology Press.

Persky, H. R., Dane, M. C., & Jin, Y. (2003). *The nation's report card: Writing 2002.* Washington, DC: U. S. Department of Education.

Peskin, H. (1967). Pubertal onset and ego functioning. *Journal of Abnormal Psychology, 72*, 1–15.

Peters, J. M., & Stout, D. L. (2006). *Concepts and inquiries for teaching elementary school sciences* (5th ed.). Upper Saddle River, NJ: Prentice Hall.

Petersen, A. C. (1979, January). Can puberty come any faster? *Psychology Today*, pp. 45–56.

Peterson, C. C. (2005). Mind and body: Concepts of human cognition, physiology and false belief in children with autism or typical development. *Journal of Autism and Developmental Disorders, 35*, 487–497.

Peterson, C. C., & Siegal, M. (1999). Representing inner worlds: Theory of mind in autistic, deaf, and normal hearing children. *Psychological Science, 10*, 126–129.

Peterson, M. B., Wang, Q., & Willems, P. J. (2008). Sex-linked deafness. *Clinical Genetics, 73*, 14–23.

Petrill, S. A. (2003). The development of intelligence: Behavioral genetic approaches. In R. J. Sternberg, J. Lautrey, & T. I. Lubert (Eds.), *Models of intelligence: International perspectives.*

Washington, DC: American Psychological Association.

Petrill, S. A., & Deater-Deckard, K. (2004). The heritability of general cognitive ability: A within-family adoption design. *Intelligence, 32*, 403–409.

Petrill, S. A., Deater-Deckherd, K., Thompson, L. A., Dethorne, L. S., & Schatschneider, C. (2006). Reading skills in early readers: Genetic and shared environmental influences. *Journal of Learning Disabilities, 39*, 48–55.

Pew Research Center. (2008). *Pew forum on religion and public life: U.S. Religious Landscape Survey.* Washington, DC: Author.

Pfeifer, M., Goldsmith, H. H., Davidson, R. J., & Rickman, M. (2002). Continuity and change in inhibited and uninhibited children. *Child Development, 73*, 1474–1485.

Philipsen, N. M., Johnson, A. D., & Brooks-Gunn, J. (2008, in press). Poverty, effects on social and emotional development. *International encyclopedia of education* (3rd ed.). St. Louis, MO: Elsevier.

Phillips, D. (2006). Child care as risk or protection in the context of welfare reform. In N. Cabrera, R. Hutchens, & H. E. Peters (Eds.), *From welfare to childcare*. Mahwah, NJ: Erlbaum.

Phinney, J. S. (1996). When we talk about American ethnic groups, what do we mean? *American Psychologist, 51*, 918–927.

Phinney, J. S. (2003). Identity and acculturation. In K. M. Chun, P. B. Organista, & G. Marin (Eds.), *Acculturation*. Washington, DC: American Psychological Association.

Phinney, J. S. (2006). Ethic identity exploration in emerging adulthood. In J. J. Arnett & J. L. Tanner (Eds.), *Emerging adults in America*. Washington, DC: American Psychological Association.

Phinney, J. S. (2008). Bridging identities and disciplines: Advances and challenges in understanding multiple identities. In M. Azmitia, M. Syed, & K. Radmacher (Eds.), *The intersections of personal and social identities. New Directions for Child and Adolescent Development, 120*, 81–95.

Phinney, J. S., & Alipura, L. L. (1990). Ethnic identity in college students from four ethnic groups. *Journal of Adolescence, 13*, 171–183.

Phinney, J. S., Berry, J. W., Vedder, P., & Liebkind, K. (2006). The acculturation experience: Attitudes, identities, and behaviors of immigrant youth. In J. W. Berry, J. S. Phinney, D. L. Sam, & P. Vedder (Eds.), *Immigrant youth in cultural transition*. Mahwah, NJ: Erlbaum.

Phinney, J. S., & Ong, A. D. (2007). Conceptualization and measurement of ethnic identity: Current status and future directions. *Journal of Counseling Psychology, 54*, 271–281.

Piaget, J. (1932). *The moral judgment of the child.* New York: Harcourt Brace Jovanovich.

Piaget, J. (1952). *The origins of intelligence in children.* (M. Cook, Trans.). New York: International Universities Press.

Piaget, J. (1954). *The construction of reality in the child.* New York: Basic Books.

Piaget, J. (1962). *Play, dreams, and imitation in childhood.* New York: W. W. Norton.

Piaget, J., & Inhelder, B. (1969). *The child's conception of space* (F. J. Langdon & J. L. Lunger, Trans.). New York: W. W. Norton.

Pickrell, J., & Loftus, E. F. (2001). *Creating false memories.* Paper presented at the meeting of the American Psychological Society, Toronto.

Pierce, G. F., Lillicrap, D., Pipe, S. W., & Vandenriessche, T. (2007). Gene therapy, bioengineered clotting factors, and novel technologies for hemophilia treatment. *Journal of Thrombosis and Haemostasis, 5*, 901–906.

Piggott, J. (2007). Cultivating creativity. *Mathematics Incorporating Micromath* (No. 202), 3–6.

Pinette, M. G., Wax, J., Blackstone, J., Cartin, A., & McCrann, D. (2004). Timing of early amniocentesis as a function of membrane fusion. *Journal of Clinical Ultrasound, 32*, 8–11.

Pinette, M. G., Wax, J. & Wilson, E. (2004). The risks of underwater birth. *American Journal of Obstetrics and Gynecology, 190*, 1211–15.

Ping, H., & Hagopian, W. (2006). Environmental factors in the development of type 1 diabetes. *Reviews in Endocrine and Metabolic Disorders, 7*, 149–162.

Pinheiro, R. T., Magalhaes, P. V., Horta, B. L., Pinheiro, K. A., da Silva, R. A., & Pinto, R. H. (2006). Is paternal postpartum depression associated with maternal postpartum depression? Population-based study in Brazil. *Acta Psychiatrica Scandinavia, 113*, 230–232.

Pinker, S. (1994). *The language instinct.* New York: HarperCollins.

Pipe, M. (2007). Children as eyewitnesses: Memory in the forensic context. In N. Cowan & M. Courage (Eds.), *The development of memory in childhood*. Philadelphia: Psychology Press.

Pipe, M. (2008). Children as eyewitnesses: Memory in the forensic context. In M. Courage & N. Cowan (Eds.), *The development of memory in infancy and childhood*. Philadelphia: Psychology Press.

Pipp, S. L., Fischer, K. W., & Jennings, S. L. (1987). The acquisition of self and mother knowledge in infancy. *Developmental Psychology, 23*, 86–96.

Plachta-Danielzik, S., Landsberg, B., Johannsen, M., Lange, D., & Muller, D. J. (2008). Association of different obesity indices with blood pressure and blood lipids in children and adolescents. *British Journal of Nutrition, 18,* 1–11.

Pleck, J. H. (1983). The theory of male sex role identity: Its rise and fall, 1936–present. In M. Levin (Ed.), *In the shadow of the past: Psychology portrays the sexes.* New York: Columbia University Press.

Pleck, J. H. (1995). The gender-role strain paradigm. In R. F. Levant & W. S. Pollack (Eds.), *A new psychology of men.* New York: Basic Books.

Pliszka, S. R. (2007). Pharmacologic treatment of attention deficit hyperactivity disorder: Efficacy, safety, and mechanisms of action. *Neuropsychology Review, 17,* 61–72.

Plog, A., Epstein, L., & Porter, W. (2004, April). *Implementation fidelity: Lessons learned from the Bully-Proofing Your School Program.* Paper presented at the meeting of the National School Psychologists Association, Dallas.

Plomin, R. (1999). Genetics and general cognitive ability. *Nature, 402* (Suppl.), C25–C29.

Plomin, R. (2004). Genetics and developmental psychology. *Merrill-Palmer Quarterly, 50,* 341–352.

Plomin, R., DeFries, J. C., Craig, I. W., & McGuffin, P. (Eds.). (2003). *Behavioral genetics in the postgenomic era.* APA Books: Washington, DC.

Plomin, R., DeFries, J. C., & Fulker, D. W. (2007). *Nature and nurture during infancy and early childhood (2nd ed.).* New York: Cambridge University Press.

Plomin, R., Fulker, D. W., Corley, R., & DeFries, J. C. (1997). Nature, nurture, and cognitive development from 1 to 16 years: A parent-offspring adoption study. *Psychological Science, 8,* 442—447.

Plomin, R., Reiss, D., Hetherington, E. M., & Howe, G. W. (1994). Nature and nurture: Contributions to measures of the family environment. *Developmental Psychology, 30,* 32–43.

Pollack, W. (1999). *Real boys.* New York: Owl Books.

Pollak, S. (2009, in press). The impact of child maltreatment on the psychosocial development of young children. In R. E. Tremblay, R. deV Peters, M. Boivin, & R. G. Barr (Eds.), *Encyclopedia on early childhood development.* Montreal: Centre of Excellence for Early Childhood Development.

Pollard, I. (2007). Neuropharmacology of drugs and alcohol in mother and fetus. *Seminars in Fetal and Neonatal Medicine, 12,* 106–113.

Pomery, E. A., Gibbons, F. X., Ferrard, M., Cleveland, M. J., Brody, G. H., & Wills, T. A. (2005). Families and risk: Protective analyses of familial and social influences on adolescent substance abuse. *Journal of Family Psychology, 19,* 560–570.

Poole, D. A., & Lindsey, D. S. (1996). *Effects of parents' suggestions, interviewing techniques, and age on young children's event reports.* Presented at the NATO Advanced Study Institute, Port de Bourgenay, France.

Porges, S. W., Doussard-Roosevelt, J. A., & Maiti, A. K. (1994). Vagal tone and the physiological regulation of emotion. In N. A. Fox (Ed.), *Emotion regulation: Behavioral and biological considerations. Monographs of the Society for Research in Child Development, 59,* (Serial No. 240), 167–196.

Posada, G. (2008). Attachment. In M. M. Haith & J. B. Benson (Eds.), *Encyclopedia of infant and early childhood development.* Oxford, UK: Elsevier.

Posner, M. I., & Rothbart, M. K. (2007). *Educating the human brain.* Washington, DC: American Psychological Association.

Poulin, F., & Pedersen, S. (2007). Developmental changes in gender composition of friendship networks in adolescent girls and boys. *Developmental Psychology, 43,* 1484–1496.

Poulin-Dobois, D., & Graham, S. A. (2007). Cognitive processes in early word learning. In E. Hoff & M. Shatz (Eds.), *Blackwell handbook of language development.* Malden, MA: Blackwell.

Powell, D. R. (2005). Searching for what works in parenting interventions. In T. Luster & L. Okagaki (Eds.), *Parenting* (2nd ed.). Mahwah, NJ: Erlbaum.

Powell, D. R. (2006). Families and early childhood interventions. In W. Damon & R. Lerner (Eds.), *Handbook of child psychology* (6th ed.). New York: Wiley.

Power, F. C., & Higgins-D'Alessandro, A. (2008). The Just Community Approach to moral education and moral atmosphere of the school. In L. Nucci & D. Narvaez (Eds.), *Handbook of moral and character education.* Clifton, NJ: Psychology Press.

Power, F. C., Narvaez, D., Nuzzi, R., Lapsley, D. & Hunt, T. (Eds.). (2008). *Moral education: A handbook.* Westport, CT: Greenwood.

Pratt, C., & Bryant, P. E. (1990). Young children understand that looking leads to knowing (so long as they are looking in a single barrel). *Child Development, 61,* 973–982.

Preiss, R. W., Gayle, B. M., Burrell, N., Allen, M., & Bryant, J. (Eds.). (2007). *Mass media effects research.* Mahwah, NJ: Erlbaum.

Pressley, M. (2003). Psychology of literacy and literacy instruction. In I. B. Weiner (Ed.), *Handbook of psychology* (Vol. 7). New York: Wiley.

Pressley, M. (2007). Achieving best practices. In L. B. Gambrell, L. M. Morrow, & M. Pressley (Eds.), *Best practices in literary instruction.* New York: Guilford.

Pressley, M., Allington, R., Wharton-McDonald, R., Block, C. C., & Morrow, L. M. (2001). *Learning to read: Lessons from exemplary first grades.* New York: Guilford.

Pressley, M., Cariliga-Bull, T., Deane, S., & Schneider, W. (1987). Short-term memory, verbal competence, and age as predictors of imagery instructional effectiveness. *Journal of Experimental Child Psychology, 43,* 194–211.

Pressley, M., Dolezal, S. E., Raphael, L. M., Welsh, L. M., Bogner, K., & Roehrig, A. D. (2003). *Motivating primary-grades teachers.* New York: Guilford.

Pressley, M., & Harris, K. (2006). Cognitive strategies instruction. In P. A. Alexander & P. H. Winne (Eds.), *Handbook of educational psychology* (2nd ed.). Mahwah, NJ: Erlbaum.

Pressley, M., & Hilden, K. (2006). Cognitive strategies. In W. Damon & R. Lerner (Eds.), *Handbook of child psychology* (6th ed.). New York: Wiley.

Pressley, M., Mohan, L., Fingeret, L., Reffitt, K., & Raphael-Bogaert, L. R. (2007b). Writing instruction in engaging and effective elementary settings. In S. Graham, C. A. MacArthur, & J. Fitzgerald (Eds.), *Best practices in writing instruction.* New York: Guilford.

Pressley, M., Mohan, L., Raphael, L. M., & Fingeret, L. (2007). How does Bennett Woods Elementary School produce such high reading and writing achievement? *Journal of Educational Psychology, 99,* 221–240.

Pressley, M., Raphael, L., Gallagher, D., & DiBella, J. (2004). Providence-St. Mel School: How a school that works for African-American students works. *Journal of Educational Psychology, 96,* 216–235.

Presson, J. C. & Jenner, J. C. (2008). *Biology.* New York: McGraw-Hill.

Prinstein, M. J. (2007). Moderators of peer contagion: A longitudinal examination of depression socialization between adolescents and their best friends. *Journal of Clinical Child and Adolescent Psychology, 36,* 159–170.

Prinstein, M. J., & Dodge, K. A. (2008). Current issues in peer influence. In M. J. Prinstein & K. A. Dodge (Eds.), *Understanding peer influence in children and adolescents.* New York: Guilford.

Provenzo, E. F. (2002). *Teaching, learning, and schooling in American culture: A critical perspective.* Boston: Allyn & Bacon.

Pryor, J. H., Hurtado, S., Sharkness, J., & Korn, W. S. (2007). *The American freshman: National norms for fall, 2007.* Los Angeles: Higher Education Research Institute, UCLA.

Pujol, J., Lopez-Sala, A., Sebastian-Galles, N., Deus, J., Cardoner, N., Soriano-Mas, C.,

Moreno, A., & Sans, A. (2004). Delayed myelination in children with developmental delay detected by volumetric MRI. *Neuroimage, 22,* 897–903.

Putallaz, M., Grimes, C. L., Foster, K. J., Kupersmidt, J. B., Coie, J. D., & Dearing, K. (2007). Overt and relational aggression and victimization: Multiple perspectives within the school setting. *Journal of School Psychology, 45,* 523–547.

Putnam, S. P., Sanson, A. V., & Rothbart, M. K. (2002). Child temperament and parenting. In M. H. Bornstein (Ed.), *Handbook of parenting* (2nd ed.). Mahwah, NJ: Erlbaum.

Q

Qin, D., Way, N., & Pandy, P. (2008). The other side of the model minority story: The familial and peer challenges faced by Chinese American adolescents. *Youth and Society, 39,* 480–506.

Quadrelli, R., Quadrelli, A., Mechoso, B., Laufer, M., Jaumandreu, C., & Vaglio, A. (2007). Parental decisions to abort or continue a pregnancy following prenatal diagnosis of chromosomal abnormalities in a setting where termination pregnancy is not legally available. *Prenatal Diagnosis, 27,* 228–232.

Quinn, P. C. (2007). Categorization. In A. Slater & M. Lewis (Eds.), *Introduction to infant development* (2nd ed.). New York: Oxford University Press.

Quinn, P. C., Bhatt, R. S., & Hayden, A. (2008, in press). What goes with what: Development of perceptual grouping in infancy. In B. H. Ross (Ed.), *Motivation,* (Vol. 49). London: Elsevier.

Quinn, P. C., & Eimas, P. D. (1996). Perceptual cues that permit categorical differentiation of animal species by infants. *Journal of Experimental Child Psychology, 63,* 189–211.

Quiocho, A. L., & Ulanoff, S. H. (2009). *Differentiated literacy instruction for English language learners.* Boston: Allyn & Bacon.

R

Raabe, A., & Muller, W. U. (2008, in press). Radiation exposure during pregnancy. *Neurosurgery Review.*

Raffaelli, M., & Ontai, L. L. (2004). Gender socialization in Latino/a families: Results from two retrospective studies. *Sex Roles, 50,* 287–299.

Rafla, N., Nair, M. S., & Kumar, S. (2008). Exercise in pregnancy. In J. Studd, S. L. Tan, & F. A. Cherenak (Eds.), *Progress in obstetrics and gynecology.* Oxford, UK: Elsevier.

Rah, Y., & Parke, R. D. (2008). Pathways between parent-child interactions and peer acceptance: The role of children's social information processing. *Social Development, 17,* 341–357.

Rainey, R. (1965). The effects of directed vs. non-directed laboratory work on high school chemistry achievement. *Journal of Research in Science Teaching, 3,* 286–292.

Rajendran, G., & Mitchell, P. (2007). Cognitive theories of autism. *Developmental Review, 27,* 224–260.

Ram, K. T., Bobby, P., Hailpern, S. M., Lo, J. C., Schocken, M., Skurnick, J., & Santoro, N. (2008). Duration of lactation is associated with lower prevalence of the metabolic syndrome in midlife—SWAN, the study of women's health across the nation. *American Journal of Obstetrics and Gynecology, 198,* e1–e6.

Ramey, C. T., & Campbell, F. A. (1984). Preventive education for high-risk children: Cognitive consequences of the Carolina Abecedarian Project. *American Journal of Mental Deficiency, 88,* 515–523.

Ramey, C. T., & Ramey, S. L. (1998). Early prevention and early experience. *American Psychologist, 53,* 109–120.

Ramey, C. T., Ramey, S. L., & Lanzi, R. G. (2001). Intelligence and experience. In R. J. Sternberg & E. L. Grigorenko (Eds.), *Environmental effects on cognitive abilities.* Mahwah, NJ: Erlbaum.

Ramey, C. T., Ramey, S. L., & Lanzi, R. G. (2006). Children's health and education. In W. Damon & R. Lerner (Eds.), *Handbook of child psychology* (6th ed.). New York: Wiley.

Ramey, S. L. (2005). Human developmental science serving children and families: Contributions of the NICHD study of early child care. In NICHD Early Child Care Network (Eds.), *Child care and development.* New York: Guilford.

Ramphal, C. (1962). *A study of three current problems in education.* Unpublished doctoral dissertation, University of Natal, India.

Ramsey-Rennels, J. L., & Langlois, J. H. (2007). How infants perceive and process faces. In A. Slater & M. Lewis (Eds.), *Introduction to infant development* (2nd ed.). Malden, MA: Blackwell.

Rasinski, T. V., & Padak, N. (2008). *From phonics to fluency* (2nd ed.). Boston: Allyn & Bacon.

Ratcliffe, S. D. (2008). *Family medicine obstetrics* (3rd ed.). Oxford, UK: Elsevier.

Ratey, J. (2006, March 27). Commentary in L. Szabo, "ADHD treatment is getting a workout." *USA Today,* p. 6D.

Raty, L. K., Larsson, G., Soderfeldt, B. A., & Larsson, B. M. (2005). Psychosocial aspects of health in adolescence: The influence of gender and general self-concept. *Journal of Adolescent Health. 36,* 530.

Raven, P. H., Johnson, G. B., Mason, K. A., Losos, J., & Singer, S. (2008). *Biology* (8thed.). New York: McGraw-Hill.

Ream, G. L., & Savin-Williams, R. (2003). Religious development in adolescence. In G. Adams & M. Berzonsky (Eds.), *Blackwell handbook of adolescence.* Malden, MA: Blackwell.

Reddy, U. M., Filly, R. A., & Copel, J. A. (2008). Prenatal imaging: Ultrasonography and magnetic resonance imaging. *Obstetrics and Gynecology, 112,* 145–157.

Reddy, U. M., Wapner, R. J., Rebar, R. W., & Tasca, R. J. (2007). Infertility assisted reproductive technology, and adverse pregnancy outcomes: Executive summary of the National Institute of Child Health and Human Development workshop. *Obstetrics and Gynecology, 109,* 967–977.

Reeb, B. C., Fox, N. A., Nelson, C. A., & Zeanah, C. H. (2008, in press). The effects of early institutionalization on social behavior and underlying neural correlates. In M. de Haan & M. Gunnar (Eds.), *Handbook of social developmental neuroscience.* Malden, MA: Blackwell.

Reece, E. A. (2008). Obesity, diabetes, and links to congenital defects: A review of the evidence and recommendations for intervention. *Journal of Maternal-Fetal and Neonatal Medicine, 21,* 173–180.

Reed, D. (2009). *Balanced introduction to computer science* (2nd ed.). Upper Saddle River, NJ: Prentice Hall.

Reeve, C. L., & Lam, H. (2007). Consideration of *g* as a common antecedent for cognitive ability test performance, test motivation, and perceived fairness. *Intelligence, 35,* 347–358.

Regaldo, M., Sareen, H., Inkelas, M., Wissow, L. S., & Halfon, N. (2004). Parents' discipline of young children: Results from the National Survey of Early Childhood Health. *Pediatrics, 113,* 1952–1958.

Regev, R. H., Lusky, A., Dolfin, T., Litmanovitz, I., Arnon, S., Reichman, B., & the Israel Neonatal Network. (2003). Excess mortality and morbidity among small-for-gestational-age premature infants: A population based study. *Journal of Pediatrics, 143,* 186–191.

Reid, G., Fawcett, A., Manis, F., & Siegel, L. (Eds.) (2009). *The SAGE handbook of dyslexia.* Thousand Oaks, CA: Sage.

Reid, P. T., & Zalk, S. R. (2001). Academic environments: Gender and ethnicity in U.S. higher education. In J. Worrell (Ed.), *Encyclopedia of women and gender.* San Diego: Academic Press.

Reilly, J. J. (2009, in press). Early prevention of obesity. In R. E. Tremblay, R. deV Peters, M. Boivin, & R. G. Barr (Eds.), *Encyclopedia on early childhood development.* Montreal: Centre of Excellence for Early Childhood Development.

Reilly, J., Bernicot, J., Vicari, S., Lacroix, A., & Bellugi, U. (2005). Narratives in children with Williams syndrome: A cross linguistic perspective. In D. Ravid & H. B., Shyldkrot (Eds.), *Perspectives on language and language development in honor of Ruth A. Berman.* Dordrecht, The Netherlands: Kluwer.

Reinders, H., & Youniss, J. (2006). School-based required community service and civic development in adolescence. *Applied Developmental Science, 10,* 2–12.

Reiner, W. G. (2001). Gender identity and sex reassignment. In L. King, B. Belman, & S. Kramer (Eds.), *Clinical pediatric urology* (3rd ed.). London: ISIS Medical.

Reiner, W. G., & Gearhart, J. P. (2004). Discordant sexual identity in some genetic males with cloacal exstrophy assigned to female sex at birth. *New England Journal of Medicine, 350,* 333–341.

Reis, O., & Youniss, J. (2004). Patterns of identity change and development in relationships with mother and friends. *Journal of Adolescent Research, 19,* 31–44.

Renner, P., Grofer Klinger, L., & Klinger, M. R. (2006). Exogenous and endogenous attention orienting in autism spectrum disorders. *Child Neuropsychology, 12,* 361–382.

Repacholi, B. M., & Gopnik, A. (1997). Early reasoning about desires: Evidence from 14- and 18-month-olds. *Developmental Psychology, 33,* 12–21.

Repetti, R., Taylor, S. E., & Saxbe, D. (2007). The influence of early socialization experiences on the development of biological systems. In J. E. Grusec & P. D. Hastings (Eds.), *Handbook of socialization.* New York: Guilford.

Rest, J. R. (1986). *Moral development: Advances in theory and research.* New York: Praeger.

Rest, J. R. (1995). *Concerns for the social—psychological development of youth and educational strategies: Report for the Kaufmann Foundation.* Minneapolis: University of Minnesota, Department of Educational Psychology.

Rest, J. R., Narvaez, D., Bebeau, M., & Thoma, S. (1999). *Postconventional moral thinking: A neo-Kohlbergian approach.* Hillsdale, NJ: Erlbaum.

Reutzel, D. R., & Cooter, R. B. (2008). *Teaching children to read* (5th ed.). Upper Saddle River, NJ: Prentice Hall.

Reyna, V. F., & Brainerd, C. J. (1995). Fuzzytrace theory: An interim synthesis: *Learning and Individual Differences, 7,* 1–75.

Reyna, V. F., & Rivers, S. E. (2008). Current theories of risk and decision making. *Developmental Review, 28,* 1–11.

Reynolds, M. R., Keith, T. Z., Ridley, K. P., & Patel, P. G. (2008). Sex differences in latent general and broad cognitive abilities for children and youth: Evidence from higher-order MG-MACS and MIMIC models. *Intelligence, 36,* 236–260.

Richardson, B. A., Nduati, R., Mbori-Ngacha, D., Overbaugh, J., & John-Stewart, G. C. (2008). Acute HIV infection among Kenyan infants. *Clinical Infectious Diseases, 46,* 289–295.

Richardson, G. A., Goldschmidt, L., & Larkby, C. (2007). Effects of prenatal cocaine exposure on growth: A longitudinal analysis. *Pediatrics, 120,* e1017–e1027.

Richardson, G. A., Goldschmidt, L., & Willford, J. (2008). The effects of prenatal cocaine use on infant development. *Neurotoxicology and Teratology, 30,* 96–106.

Richardson, G. A., Ryan, C., Willford, J., Day, N. L., & Goldschmidt, L. (2002). Prenatal alcohol and marijuana exposure: Effects on neuropsychological outcomes at 10 years. *Neurotoxicology and Teratology, 24,* 309–320.

Richmond, E. J., & Rogol, A. D. (2007). Male pubertal development and the role of androgen therapy. *Nature Clinical Practice: Endocrinology and Metabolism, 3,* 338–344.

Richter, L. (2004). Poverty, underdevelopment, and infant mental health. *Journal of Pediatric and Child Health, 39,* 243–248.

Rideout, V., Roberts, D. F., & Foehr, U. G. (2005). *Generation M: Media in the lives of 8–18 year-olds.* San Francisco: Kaiser Family Foundation.

Ridgeway, D., Waters, E., & Kuczaj, S. A. (1985). Acquisition of emotion-descriptive language: Receptive and productive vocabulary norms for ages 18 months to 6 years. *Developmental Psychology, 21,* 901–908.

Riesch, S. K., Gray, J., Hoefs, M., Keenan, T., Ertil, T., & Mathison, K. (2003). Conflict and conflict resolution: Parent and young teen perceptions. *Journal of Pediatric Health Care, 17,* 22–31.

Rifas-Shiman, S. L., Rich-Edwards, J. W., Willett, W. C., Kleinman, K. P., Oken, E., & Gillman, M. W. (2006). Changes in dietary intake from the first to the second trimester of pregnancy. *Pediatric and Perinatal Epidemiology, 20,* 35–42.

Riley, E. H., Fuentes-Afflick, E., Jackson, R.A., Escobar, G. J., Brawarsky, P., Schreiber, M., & Haas, J. S. (2005). Correlates of prescription drug use during pregnancy. *Journal of Women's Health, 14,* 401–409.

Rinehart, S. D., Stahl, S. A., & Erickson, L. G. (1986). Some effects of summarization training on reading and studying. *Reading Research Quarterly, 21,* 422–438.

Rink, J. E. (2009). *Designing the physical education curriculum.* New York: McGraw-Hill.

Rivas, D., Hughes, D., & Way, N. (2008). A closer look at ethnic discrimination, ethnic identity, and psychological well-being among urban Chinese American sixth graders. *Journal of Youth and Adolescence, 37,* 12–21.

Rivera, C., & Collum, E. (Eds.). *State assessment policy and practice for English language learners.* Mahwah, NJ: Erlbaum.

Rizzo, M. S. (1999, May 8). Genetic counseling combines science with a human touch. *Kansas City Star,* p. 3.

Robbins, G., Powers, D., & Burgess, S. (2008). *A fit way of life.* New York: McGraw-Hill.

Roberts, D. F., & Foehr, U. G. (2003). *Kids and media in America: Patterns of use at the millennium.* New York: Cambridge University Press.

Roberts, D. F., & Foehr, U. G. (2008). Trends in media use. *Future of Children, 18* (No. 1), 11–37.

Roberts, D. F., Foehr, U. G., Rideout, V. J., & Brodie, M. (1999). *Kids and media at the new millennium: A Kaiser Family Foundation Report.* Menlo Park, CA: Henry J. Kaiser Family Foundation.

Roberts, D. F., Henriksen, L., & Foehr, V. G. (2004). Adolescents and the media. In R. Lerner & L. Steinberg (Ed.), *Handbook of adolescent psychology,* (2nd ed.). New York: Wiley.

Roberts, W., & Strayer, J. (1996). Empathy, emotional expressiveness, and prosocial behavior. *Child Development, 67,* 471–489.

Robertson, D. M., & South, M. (2007). *Practical pediatrics* (6th ed.). London: Elsevier.

Robins, R. W., Trzesniewski, K. H., Tracy, J. L., Gosling, S. D., & Potter, J. (2002). Global self-esteem across the life Span. *Psychology and Aging, 17,* 423–434.

Rochlen, A. B., Suizzo, M. A., Scaringi, V., Bredow, A., & McKelley, R. A. (2007, August). *A Paper qualitative study of stay-at-home fathers.* presented at the meeting of the American Psychological Association, San Francisco.

Rode, J. C., Mooney, C. H., Arthaud-Day, M. L., Near, J. P., Rubin, R. S., Baldwin, T., & Bommer, W. H. (2008). An examination of the structural, discriminant, nomological, incremental predictive validity of the MSCEIT. *Intelligence, 36,* 350–366.

Rode, S. S., Chang, P., Fisch, R. O., & Sroufe, I. A. (1981). Attachment patterns of infants separated at birth. *Developmental Psychology, 17,* 188–191.

Rogoff, B. (1990). *Apprenticeship in thinking.* New York: Oxford University Press.

Rogoff, B. (2003). *The cultural nature of human development.* New York: Oxford University Press.

Rogoff, B., Moore, L., Najafi, B., Dexter, A., Correa-Chavez, M., & Solis, J. (2007). Children's development of cultural repertoires through participation in everyday routines and practices. In J. E. Grusec & P. D. Hastings (Eds.), *Handbook of socialization.* New York: Guilford.

Rohner, R. P., & Rohner, E. C. (1981). Parental acceptance-rejection and parental control: Cross-cultural codes. *Ethnology, 20,* 245–260.

Romano, A. M., & Lothian, J. A. (2008). Promoting, Protecting, and supporting normal birth: A look at the evidence. *Journal of Obstetric, Gynecological, and Neonatal Nursing, 37,* 94–104.

Roopnarine, J. L., & Metindogan, A. (2006). Early childhood education research in cross-national perspective. In B. Spodek & O. N. Saracho (Eds.), *Handbook of research on the education of young children.* Mahwah, NJ: Erlbaum.

Rose, A. J., & Asher, S. R. (1999). Children's goals and strategies in response to conflicts within a friendship. *Developmental Psychology, 35,* 69–79.

Rose, A. J., Carlson, W., & Waller, E. M. (2007). Prospective associations of co-rumination with friendship and emotional adjustment: Considering the socioemotional trade-offs of co-rumination. *Developmental Psychology, 43,* 1019–1031.

Rose, M. R., & Rauser, C. L. (2007). Evolution and comparative biology. In J. E. Birren (Ed.), *Encyclopedia of gerontology* (2nd ed.). San Diego: Academic Press.

Rose, S. A., Feldman, J. F., & Wallace, I. F. (1992). Infant information processing in relation to six-year cognitive outcomes. *Child Development, 63,* 1126–1141.

Rosenberg, T. J., Garbers, S., Lipkind, H., & Chiasson, M. A. (2005). Maternal obesity and diabetes as risk factors for adverse pregnancy outcomes: Differences among 4 racial/ethnic groups. *American Journal of Public Health, 95,* 1545–1551.

Rosenblith, J. F. (1992). *In the beginning* (2nd ed.). Newbury Park, CA: Sage.

Rosenheck, R. (2008, in press). Fast food consumption and increased caloric intake: A systematic review of a trajectory towards weight gain and obesity risk. *Obesity Reviews.*

Rosenkoetter, L. I., Rosenkoetter, S. E., Ozretich, R. A., & Acock, A. C. (2004). Mitigating the harmful effects of violent television. *Applied Developmental Psychology, 25,* 25–47.

Rosenstein, D., & Oster, H. (1988). Differential facial responses to four basic tastes in newborns. *Child Development, 59,* 1555–1568.

Rosenthal, H. E., & Crisp, R. J. (2006). Reducing stereotype threat by blurring intergroup boundaries. *Personality and Social Psychology Bulletin, 32,* 501–511.

Roskos, K. A., & Christie, J. F. (Eds.). (2007). *Play and literacy in early childhood.* Mahwah, NJ: Erlbaum.

Rosnow, R. L., & Rosenthal, R. (1996). *Beginning behavioral research* (2nd ed.). Upper Saddle River, NJ: Prentice Hall.

Rosnow, R. L., & Rosenthal, R. (2008). *Beginning behavioral research* (6th ed.). Upper Saddle River, NJ: Prentice Hall.

Ross, C., & Kirby, G. (2006). Welfare-to-work transitions for parents of infants. In N. Cabrera, R. Hutchens, H. E. Peters, & L. Peters (Eds.), *From welfare to childcare.* Mahwah, NJ: Erlbaum.

Ross, J. L., & others. (2008, in press). Cognitive and motor development during childhood in boys with Klinefelter syndrome. *American Journal of Medical Genetics A.*

Rothbart, M. K. (2004). Temperament and the pursuit of an integrated developmental psychology. *Merrill-Palmer Quarterly, 50,* 492–505.

Rothbart, M. K. (2007). Temperament, development, and personality. *Current Directions in Psychological Science, 16,* 207–212.

Rothbart, M. K. (2009, in press). Early temperament and psychosocial development. In R. E. Tremblay, deV Peters, M. Boivan, & R. G. Barr (Eds.), *Encyclopedia on early childhood development.* Montreal: Center of Excellence for Early Childhood Development.

Rothbart, M. K., & Bates, J. E. (2006). Temperament. In W. Damon & R. Lerner (Eds.), *Handbook of child psychology* (6th ed.). New York: Wiley.

Rothbart, M. K., & Garstein, M. A. (2008). Temperament. In M. M. Haith & J. B. Benson (Eds.), *Encyclopedia of infant and early childhood development.* Oxford, UK: Elsevier.

Rothbart, M. K., & Putnam, S. P. (2002). Temperament and socialization. In L. Pulkkinen & A. Caspi (Eds.), *Paths to successful development.* New York: Cambridge University Press.

Rothbart, M. K., & Sheese, B. E. (2007). Temperament and emotion regulation. In J. J. Gross (Ed.), *Handbook of emotion regulation.* New York: Guilford.

Rothbaum, F., Pott, M., Azuma, H., Miyake, K., & Weisz, J. (2000). The development of close relationships in Japan and the United States: Paths of symbiotic harmony and generative tension. *Child Development, 71,* 1121–1142.

Rothbaum, F., & Trommsdorff, G. (2007). Do roots and wings complement or oppose one another?: The socialization of relatedness and autonomy in cultural context. In J. E. Grusec & P. D. Hastings (Eds.), *Handbook of Socialization.* New York: Guilford.

Rouse, D. J., & others. (2007). A trial of 17 alpha-hyroxyprogesterone caproate to prevent prematurity in twins. *New England Journal of Medicine, 357,* 454–461.

Rovee-Collier, C. (1987). Learning and memory in children. In J. D. Osofsky (Ed.), *Handbook of infant development* (2nd ed.). New York: Wiley.

Rovee-Collier, C. (2004). Infant learning and memory. In U. Goswami (Ed.), *Blackwell handbook of childhood cognitive development.* Malden, MA: Blackwell.

Rovee-Collier, C. (2007). The development of infant memory. In N. Cowan & M. Courage (Eds.), *The development of memory in childhood.* Philadelphia: Psychology Press.

Rovers, M. M., de Kok, I. M., & Schilder, A.G. (2006). Risk factors for otitis media: An international perspective. *International Journal of Otorhinoloaryngology, 70,* 1251–1256.

Rowley, S. R., Kurtz-Costas, B., & Cooper, S. M. (2009, in press). The role of schooling in ethnic minority achievement and attainment. In J. Meece & J. Eccles (Eds.), *Handbook of research on schools, schooling, and human development.* Clifton, NJ: Psychology Press.

Roza, S. J., Verburg, B. O., Jaddoe, V. W., Hofman, A., Mackenbach, J. P., Steegers, E. A., Witteman, J. C., Verhulst, F. C., Tiemeir, H. (2007). Effects of maternal smoking in pregnancy on prenatal brain development: The Generation R study. *European Journal of Neuroscience, 25,* 611–627.

Rubenstein, D. (2004). Language games and natural resources. *Journal of the Theory of Social Behavior, 34,* 55–71.

Rubie-Davies, C. M. (2007). Classroom interactions: Exploring the practices of high- and low-expectation teachers. *British Journal of Educational Psychology, 77,* 289–306.

Rubin, D. H., Krasilnikoff, P. A., Leventhal, J. M., Weile, B., & Berget, A. (1986, August 23). Effect of passive smoking on birthweight. *The Lancet,* 415–417.

Rubin, K. H., Bukowski, W., & Parker, J. (2006). Peer interactions, relationships, and groups. In W. Damon & R. Lerner (Eds.), *Handbook of child psychology* (6th ed.). New York: Wiley.

Rubin, K. H., Fredstrom, B., & Bowker, J. (2008, in press). Future directions in . . . friendship in childhood and early adolescence. *Social Development.*

Rubin, K. H., Mills, R. S. L., & Rose-Krasnor, L. (1989). Maternal beliefs and children's competence. In B. Schneider, G. Attili, J. Nadel, & R. Weissberg (Eds.), *Social competence in developmental perspective.* Amsterdam: Kluwer Academic.

Rubin, Z., & Sloman, J. (1984). How parents influence their children's friendships. In M. Lewis (Ed.), *Beyond the dyad.* New York: Plenum.

Ruble, D. (1983). The development of social comparison processes and their role in achievement-related self-socialization. In E. Higgins, D. Ruble, & W. Hartup (Eds.), *Social cognitive development: A social-cultural perspective.* New York: Cambridge University Press.

Ruble, D. N. (2000). Gender constancy. In A. Kazdin (Ed.), *Encyclopedia of psychology.* Washington, DC, & New York: American Psychological Association and Oxford University Press.

Ruble, D. N., Martin, C. L., & Berenbaum, S. A. (2006). Gender development. In

W. Damon & R. Lerner (Eds.), *Handbook of child psychology* (6th ed.). New York: Wiley.

Rubnitz, J. E., Razzouk, B. I., Lensing, S., Pounds, S., Pui, C. H., & Ribeiro, R. C. (2006). Prognostic factors and outcome of recurrence in childhood acute myeloid leukemia. *Cancer, 109,* 157–163.

Ruel, M. T., & others. (2008). Age-based preventive targeting of food assistance and behavior change and communication for reduction of childhood undernutrition in Haiti: A cluster randomized trial. *Lancet, 371,* 588–595.

Ruff, H. A., & Capozzoli, M. C. (2003). Development of attention and distractibility in the first four years of life. *Developmental Psychology, 39,* 877–890.

Ruffman, T., Perner, J., Naito, M., Parkin, L., & Clements, W. A. (1998). Older (but not younger) siblings facilitate false belief understanding. *Developmental Psychology, 34,* 161–174.

Ruffman, T., Slade, L., & Crowe, E. (2002). The relation between children's and mothers' mental state language and theory-of-mind understanding. *Child Development, 73,* 734–751.

Rumberger, R. W. (1995). Dropping out of middle school: A multilevel analysis of students and schools. *American Educational Research Journal, 3,* 583–625.

Runco, M. A. (2004). Creativity. *Annual Review of Psychology (Vol. 55).* Palo Alto, CA: Annual Reviews.

Runquist, J. (2007). Persevering through postpartum fatigue. *Journal of Obstetric, Gynecologic, and Neonatal Nursing, 36,* 28–37.

Rutter, M. (2007). Gene-environment interplay and developmental psychopathology. In A. S. Masten (Ed.), *Multilevel dynamics in developmental psychology.* Mahwah, NJ: Erlbaum.

Ryan, R. M., Fauth, R. C., & Brooks-Gunn, J. (2006). Childhood poverty: Implications for school readiness and early childhood education. In B. Spodek & O. N. Saracho (Eds.), *Handbook of research on the education of young children.* Mahwah, NJ: Erlbaum.

Ryan, S. D., Pearlmutter, S., & Groza, V. (2004). Coming out of the closet: Opening agencies to gay and lesbian adoptive parents. *Social Work, 49,* 85–95.

Ryan-Harshman, M., & Aldoori, W. (2008). Folic acid and prevention of neural tube defects. *Canadian Family Physician, 54,* 36–38.

S

Saarni, C. (1999). *The development of emotional competence.* New York: Guilford.

Saarni, C., Campos, J., Camras, L. A., & Witherington, D. (2006). Emotional development. In W. Damon & R. Lerner (Eds.), *Handbook of child psychology* (6th ed.). New York: Wiley.

Sabbagh, M. A., Xu, F., Carlson, S. M., Moses, L. J., & Lee, K. (2006). The development of executive functioning and theory of mind: A comparison of Chinese and U.S. preschoolers. *Psychological Science, 17,* 74–81.

Sabin, M. A., & Shield, J. P. (2008). Childhood obesity. *Frontiers of Hormone Research, 36,* 85–96.

Sabol, W. J., Coulton, C. J., & Korbin, J. F. (2004). Building community capacity for violence prevention. *Journal of Interpersonal Violence, 19,* 322–340.

Sachs, J. (2009). Communication development in infancy. In J. Berko Gleason & N. B. Ratner (Eds.), *The development of language* (7th ed.). Boston: Allyn & Bacon.

Sackett, P. R., Hardison, C. M., & Cullen, M. J. (2004). On interpreting stereotype threat as accounting for African-American White differences in cognitive tests. *American Psychologist, 59,* 7–13.

Sackett, P. R., Hardison, C. M., & Cullen, M. J. (2005). On interpreting research on stereotype threat and test performance. *American Psychologist, 60,* 271–272.

Sadeh, A. (2008). Sleep. In M. M. Haith & J. B. Benson (Eds.), *Encyclopedia of infant and early childhood development.* Oxford, UK: Elsevier.

Saffran, J. R., Werker, J. F., & Werner, L. A. (2006). The infant's auditory world: Hearing, speech, and the beginnings of language. In W. Damon & R. Lerner (Eds.), *Handbook of child psychology* (6th ed.). New York: Wiley.

Sagi, A., Koren-Karie, N., Gini, M., Ziv, Y., & Joels, T. (2002). Shedding further light on the effects of various types and quality of early child care on infant-mother attachment relationship: The Haifa study of early child care. *Child Development, 73,* 1166–1186.

Salazar-Martinez, E., Allen, B., Fernandez-Ortega, C., Torres-Mejia, G., Galal, O., & Lazcano-Ponce, E. (2006). Overweight and obesity status among adolescents from Mexico and Egypt. *Archives of Medical Research, 37,* 535–542.

Salmon, J., Campbell, K. J., & Crawford, D.A. (2006). Television viewing habits associated with obesity risk factors: A survey of Melbourne schoolchildren. *Medical Journal of Australia, 184,* 64–67.

Salovy, P., & Mayer, J. D. (1990). Emotional intelligence. *Imagination, Cognition, and Personality, 9,* 185–211.

Sandstrom, M. J., & Zakriski, A. L. (2004). Understanding the experience of peer rejection. In J. B. Kupersmidt & K. A. Dodge (Eds.), *Children's peer relations: From development to intervention.* Washington, DC: American Psychological Association.

Sann, C., & Streri, A. (2007). Perception of object shape and texture in human newborns: Evidence from cross-modal tasks. *Developmental Science, 10,* 399–410.

Sanson, A., & Rothbart, M. K. (1995). Child temperament and parenting. In M. H. Bornstein (Ed.), *Handbook of parenting* (Vol. 4). Hillsdale, NJ: Erlbaum.

Santa Maria, M. (2002). Youth in Southeast Asia: Living within the continuity of tradition and the turbulence of change. In B. B. Brown, R. W. Larson, & T. S. Saraswathi (Eds.), *The world's youth.* New York: Cambridge University Press.

Santiago-Delefosse, M. J., & Delefosse, J.M. O. (2002). Three positions on child thought and language. *Theory and Psychology, 12,* 723–747.

Santrock, J. W., Sitterle, K. A., & Warshak, R. A. (1988). Parent-child relationships in stepfather families. In P. Bronstein & C. P. Cowan (Eds.), *Fatherhood today: Men's changing roles in the family.* New York: Wiley.

Santrock, J. W., & Warshak, R. A. (1979). Father custody and social development in boys and girls. *Journal of Social Issues, 35,* 112–125.

Sanz, M. A. (2006). Treatment of acute promyelocytic leukemia. *Hematology,* 147–155.

Sausenthaler, S., Kompauer, I., Mielck, A., Borte, M., Herbarth, O., Schaaf, B., von Berg, A., & Heinrich, J. (2007). Impact of parental education and income equality on children's food intake. *Public Health Nutrition, 10,* 24–33.

Sayal, K., Heron, J., Golding, J., & Emond, A. (2007). Prenatal alcohol exposure and gender differences in childhood mental health problems: a longitudinal population-based study. *Pediatrics, 119,* e426–e434.

Sayer, L. C. (2006). Economic aspects of divorce and relationship dissolution. In M. A. Fine & J. H. Harvey (Eds.), *Handbook of divorce and relationship dissolution.* Mahwah, NJ: Erlbaum.

Scafidi, F., & Field, T. M. (1996). Massage therapy improves behavior in neonates born to HIV-positive mothers. *Journal of Pediatric Psychology, 21,* 889–897.

Scarr, S. (1984, May). Interview. *Psychology Today.* pp. 59–63.

Scarr, S. (1993). Biological and cultural diversity: The legacy of Darwin for development. *Child Development, 64,* 1333–1353.

Scarr, S., & Weinberg, R. A. (1983). The Minnesota adoption studies: Genetic differences and malleability. *Child Development, 54,* 182–259.

Schacter, D. L. (2001). *The seven sins of memory.* Boston: Houghton Mifflin.

Schacter, E. P., & Ventura, J. J. (2008). Identity agents: Parents as active and reflective participants in their children's identity formation. *Journal of Research on Adolescence, 18,* 449–476.

Schaffer, H. R. (1996). *Social development.* Cambridge, MA: Blackwell.

Schaie, K. W. (2007). Generational differences; the age-cohort period model. In J. E. Birren

(Ed.), *Encyclopedia of gerontology* (2nd ed.). Oxford, UK: Elsevier.

Schattschneider, C., Fletcher, J. M., Francis, D. J., Carlson, C. D., & Foorman, B. R. (2004). Kindergarten prediction of reading skills: A longitudinal comparative analysis. *Journal of Educational Psychology, 96,* 265–282.

Schauble, L. (1996). The development of scientific reasoning in knowledge-rich contexts. *Developmental Psychology, 32,* 102–119.

Scher, A., & Harel, J. (2008). Separation and stranger anxiety. In M. M. Haith & J. B. Benson (Eds.), *Encyclopedia of infant and early childhood development.* Oxford, UK: Elsevier.

Schiefele, U. (1996). Topic interest, text representation, and quality of experience. *Contemporary Educational Psychology, 21,* 3–18.

Schiff, W. J. (2009). *Nutrition for healthy living.* New York: McGraw-Hill.

Schindler, S., & others. (2007). The effects of large neutral amino acid supplements in PKU: An MRS and neuropsychological study. *Molecular Genetics and Metabolism, 91,* 48–54.

Schlegel, M. (2000). All work and play. *Monitor on Psychology, 31*(11), 50–51.

Schmidt, J., Shumow, L., & Kackar, H. (2007). Adolescents' participation in service activities and its impact on academic, behavioral, and civic outcomes. *Journal of Youth and Adolescence, 36,* 127–140.

Schmidt, M. E., & Vandewater, E. A. (2008). Media and attention, cognition, and school achievement. *Future of Children, 18* (No. 1), 64–85.

Schneider, W. (2004). Memory development in childhood. In P. Smith & C. Han (Eds.), *Blackwell handbook of childhood cognitive development.* Malden, MA: Blackwell.

Schneider, W., & Pressley, M. (1997). *Memory development between two and twenty.* Mahwah, NJ: Erlbaum.

Schoenfeld, A. H. (2004). Multiple learning communities: Students, teachers, instructional designers, and researchers. *Journal of Curriculum Studies, 36,* 237–255.

Scholnick, E. K. (2008). Reasoning in early development. In M. M. Haith & J. B. Benson (Eds.), *Encyclopedia of infant and early childhood development.* Oxford, UK: Elsevier.

Schoon, I., Bynner, J., Joshi, H., Parsons, S., Wiggins, R. D., & Sacker, A. (2002). The influence of context, timing, and duration of risk experiences for the passage from childhood to midadulthood. *Child Development, 73,* 1486–1504.

Schoon, I., Parsons, S., & Sacker, A. (2004). Socioeconomic adversity, educational resilience, and subsequent levels of adult adaptation. *Journal of Adolescent Research, 19,* 383–404.

Schoppe-Sullivan, S. J., Mangelsdorf, S. C., Brown, G. L., & Sokolowski, M. S. (2007). Goodness-of-fit in family context: Infant temperament, marital quality, and early coparenting behavior. *Infant Behavior and Development, 30,* 82–96.

Schrag, S. G., & Dixon, R. L. (1985). Occupational exposure associated with male reproductive dysfunction. *Annual Review of Pharmacology and Toxicology, 25,* 467–592.

Schraw, G. (2006). Knowledge: Structures and processes. In P. A. Alexander & P. H. Winne (Eds.), *Handbook of educational psychology* (2nd ed.). Mahwah, NJ: Erlbaum.

Schulenberg, J. E., & Zarrett, N. R. (2006). Mental health during emerging adulthood: Continuities and discontinuities in course, content, and meaning. In J. J. Arnett & J. Tanner (Eds.), *Advances in emerging adulthood.* Washington, DC: American Psychological Association.

Schunk, D. H. (2004). *Learning theories: An educational perspective* (4th ed.) Upper Saddle River, NJ: Prentice Hall.

Schunk, D. H. (2008). *Learning theories: An educational perspective* (5th ed.). Upper Saddle River, NJ: Prentice Hall.

Schunk, D. H., Pintrich, P. R., & Meece, J. L. (2008). *Motivation in education: Theory, research, and applications* (3rd ed.). Upper Saddle River, NJ: Prentice Hall.

Schwartz, R. G., & Trooper, B. (2009). Neurobiology. In R. G. Schwartz (Ed.), *Handbook of child language disorders.* Clifton, NJ: Psychology Press.

Schwarz, S. P. (2004). A mother's story. Retrieved January 16, 2004, from www.makinglifeeasier.com

Schwebel, D. C. (2008). Safety and childproofing. In M. M. Haith, & J. B. Benson (Eds.), *Encyclopedia of infant and early childhood development.* Oxford, UK: Elsevier.

Schweinhart, L. J. (2009). Preschool programs. In R. E. Tremblay, R. deV Peters, M. Boivin, & R. G. Barr (Eds.), *Encyclopedia on early childhood development.* Montreal: Centre of Excellence for Early Childhood Development.

Schweinhart, L. J., Montie, J., Xiang, Z., Barnett, W. S., Belfield, C. R., & Nores, M. (2005). *Lifetime effects: The High/Scope Perry Preschool Study Through Age 40.* Ypsilanti, MI: High/Scope Press.

Scott-Jones, D. (1995, March). *Incorporating ethnicity and socioeconomic status in research with children.* Paper presented at the meeting of the Society for Research in Child Development, Indianapolis.

Scourfield, J., Van den Bree, M., Martin, N., & McGuffin, P. (2004). Conduct problems in children and adolescents: A twin study. *Archives of General Psychiatry, 61,* 489–496.

Sedlak, A. J., Schultz, D., Wells, S. J., Lyons, P., Doueck, H. J., & Gragg, F. (2006). Child protection and justice systems processing of serious abuse and neglect cases. *Child Abuse and Neglect, 30,* 657–677.

Sellers, R. M., Linder, N. C., Martin, P. P., & Lewis, R. L. (2006). Racial identity matters: The relationship between racial discrimination and psychological functioning in African American adolescents. *Journal of Research on Adolescence, 16* (2), 187–216.

Selman, R. L. (1980). *The growth of interpersonal understanding: Developmental and clinical analysis.* New York: Academic Press.

Serpell, R. (1974). Aspects of intelligence in a developing country. *African Social Research, 17,* 576–596.

Serpell, R. (1982). Measures of perception, skills, and intelligence. In W. W. Hartup (Ed.), *Review of child development research* (Vol. 6). Chicago: University of Chicago Press.

Serpell, R. (2000). Culture and intelligence. In A. Kazdin (Ed.), *Encyclopedia of psychology.* Washington, DC, & New York: American Psychological Association and Oxford University Press.

Shaibi, G. Q., Ball, G. D., & Goran, M. I. (2006). Aerobic fitness among Caucasian, African-American, and Latino youth. *Ethnicity and Disease, 16,* 120–125.

Shamah, T., & Villalpando, S. (2006). The role of enriched foods in infant and child nutrition. *British Journal of Nutrition, 96,* (Suppl, 1), S73–S77.

Shani, R., Fifer, W. P., & Myers, M. M. (2007). Identifying infants at risk for sudden infant death syndrome. *Current Opinion in Pediatrics, 19,* 145–149.

Shankaran, S., Lester, B. M., Das, A., Bauer, C. R., Bada, H. S., Lagasse, L., & Higgins, R. (2007). Impact of maternal substance use during pregnancy on childhood outcome. *Seminars in Fetal and Neonatal Medicine, 12,* 143–150.

Shapiro, A. F., and Gottman, J. M., (2005). Effects on marriage of a psycho-education intervention with couples undergoing the transition to parenthood, evaluation at 1-year post-intervention. *Journal of Family Communication, 5,* 1–24.

Shapiro-Mendoza, C. K., & others. (2008). Effect of late-term birth and maternal medical conditions on newborn morbidity risk. *Pediatrics, 121,* e223–e232.

Sharma, A. R., McGue, M. K., & Benson, P. L. (1996). The emotional and behavioral adjustment of adopted adolescents: Part I: Age at adoption. *Children and Youth Services Review, 18,* 101–114.

Sharma, B. R. (2007). Sudden infant death syndrome: A subject of medicolegal research. *American Journal of Forensic Medicine and Pathology, 28,* 69–72.

Shastry, B. S. (2007). Developmental dyslexia: An update. *Journal of Human Genetics, 52,* 104–109.

Shatz, M., & Gelman, R. (1973). The development of communication skills: Modifications in the speech of young children as a function of the listener. *Monographs of the Society for Research in Child Development, 38* (Serial No. 152).

Shaw, D. S., Dishion, T. J., Supplee, L., & Gardner, F., & Arnds, K. (2006). Randomized trial of a family-centered approach to the prevention of early conduct problems: 2-year effects of the family check-up in early childhood. *Journal of Consulting and Clinical Psychology, 74,* 1–9.

Shaw, D., Gilliom, M., Ingoldsby, E. M., & Nagin, D. S. (2003). Trajectories leading to school-age conduct problems. *Developmental Psychology, 39,* 189–200.

Shaw, P., Eckstrand, K., Sharp, W., Blumenthal, J., Lerch, J. P., Greenstein, D., Clasen, L., Evans, A., Giedd, J., & Rapoport, J. L. (2007). Attention-deficit/hyperactivity disorder is characterized by a delay in cortical maturation. *Proceedings of the National Academy of Sciences, 104* (No. 49), 19649–19654.

Shaywitz, B. A., Lyon, G. R., & Shaywitz, S. E. (2006). The role of functional magnetic resonance imaging in understanding reading and dyslexia. *Developmental Neuropsychology, 30,* 613–632.

Shaywitz, S. E., Gruen, J. R., & Shaywitz, B. A. (2007). Management of dyslexia, its rationale, and underlying neurobiology. *Pediatric Clinics of North America, 54,* 609–623.

Shaywitz, S. E., Morris, R., & Shaywitz, B. A. (2008). The education of dyslexic children from childhood to young adulthood. *Annual Review of Psychology* (Vol. 59). Palo Alto, CA: Annual Reviews.

Shea, A. K., & Steiner, M. (2008). Cigarette smoking during pregnancy. *Nicotine and Tobacco Research, 10,* 267–278.

Shema, L., Ore, L., Ben-Shachar, M., Haj, M., & Linn, S. (2007). The association between breastfeeding and breast cancer occurrence among Jewish women: A case control study. *Journal of Cancer Research and Clinical Oncology, 133,* 903.

Sherblom, S. (2008). The legacy of the "care challenge": Re-envisioning the outcome of the justice-care debate. *Journal of Moral Education, 37,* 81–98.

Sheridan, M., & Nelson, C. A. (2008, in press). Neurobiology of fetal and infant development: Implications for mental health. In C. H. Zeanah (Ed.), *Handbook of infant mental health* (3rd ed.). New York: Guilford.

Shields, S. A. (1998, August). *What Jerry Maguire can tell us about gender and emotion.* Paper presented at the meeting of the International Society for Research on Emotions, Wurzburg, Germany.

Shiraev, E., & Levy, D. (2007). *Cross-cultural psychology: Critical thinking and critical applications* (3rd ed.). Belmont, CA:

Shiva, F., Nasiri, M., Sadeghi, B., & Padyab, M. (2004). Effects of passive smoking on common respiratory symptoms in young children. *Acta Pediatrics, 92,* 1394–1397.

Shoup, J. A., Gattshall, M., Dandamudi, P., & Estabrooks, P. (2008, in press). Physical activity, quality of life, and weight status in overweight children. *Quality of Life Research.*

Shulman, L. S., & Shulman, J. H. (2004). How and what teachers learn: A shifting perspective. *Journal of Curriculum Studies, 36,* 257–274.

Shweder, R., Goodnow, J., Hatano, G., LeVine, R. A., Markus, H., & Miller, P. (2006). The cultural psychology of development. In W. Damon & R. Lerner (Eds.), *Handbook of child psychology* (6th ed.). New York: Wiley.

Shweder, R., Mahapatra, M., & Miller, J. (1987). Culture and moral development. In J. Kagan & S. Lamb (Eds.), *The emergence of morality in young children.* Chicago: University of Chicago Press.

Siega-Riz, A. M., Kranz, S., Blanchette, D., Haines, P. S., Guilkey. D. K., & Popkin, B. M. (2004). The effect of participation in the WIC program on preschoolers diets. *Journal of Pediatrics, 144,* 229–234.

Siegel, L. S., & Wiener, J. (1993, Spring). Canadian special education policies: Children with disabilities in a bilingual and multicultural society. *Social Policy Report, Society for Research in Child Development, 7,* 1–16.

Siegler, R. S. (1976). Three aspects of cognitive development. *Cognitive Psychology, 8,* 481–520.

Siegler, R. S. (1998). *Children's thinking* (3rd ed.). Upper Saddle River, NJ: Prentice Hall.

Siegler, R. S. (2006). Microgenetic analysis of learning. In W. Damon & R. Lerner (Eds.), *Handbook of child psychology* (6th ed.). New York: Wiley.

Siegler, R. S. (2007). Cognitive variability. *Developmental Science 10,* 104–109.

Siegler, R. S., & Alibali, M. W. (2005). *Children's Thinking.* (4th ed.). Upper Saddle River, NJ: Prentice Hall.

Sieving R. E. Eisenberg M. E., Pettingell, S., & Skay C. (2006). Friends' influence on adolescents' first sexual intercourse. *Perspectives on Sexual and Reproductive Health, 38,* 13–19.

Sigman, M., Cohen, S. E., & Beckwith, L. (2000). Why does infant attention predict adolescent intelligence? In D. Muir & A. Slater (Eds.), *Infant development: Essential readings.* Malden, MA: Blackwell.

Signal, T. L., Gander, P. H., Sangalli, M. R., Travier, N., Firestone, R. T., & Tuohy, J. F. (2007). Sleep duration and quality in healthy nulliparous and multiparous women across pregnancy and post-partum. *Australian and New Zealand Journal of Obstetrics and Gynecology, 47,* 16–22.

Signore, R. J. (2004). Bradley method offers option for natural childbirth. *American Family Physician, 70,* 650.

Silva, C. (2005, October 31). When teen dynamo talks, city listens. *Boston Globe,* pp. 81–84.

Sim, T. N., & Ong, L. P. (2005). Parent punishment and child aggression in a Singapore Chinese preschool sample. *Journal of Marriage and the Family, 67,* 85–99.

Simard, V., Nielsen, T. A., Tremblay, R. E., Boivan, M., & Montplaisir, J. Y. (2008). Longitudinal study of bad dreams in preschool-aged children: Prevalence, demographic correlates, risk, and protective factors. *Sleep, 31,* 62–70.

Simos, P. G., Fletcher, J. M., Sarkari, S., Billingsley, R. L., Denton, C., & Papanicolaou, A. C. (2007). Altering the brain circuits for reading through intervention: A magnetic source imaging study. *Neuropsychology, 21,* 485–496.

Simpkin, P., & Bolding, A. (2004). Update on nonpharmacological approaches to relieve labor pain and prevent suffering. *Journal of Midwifery and Women's Health, 49,* 489–504.

Simpkins, S. D., Fredricks, J. A., Davis-Kean, P. E., & Eccles, J. S. (2006). Healthy mind, healthy habits: The influence of activity involvement in middle childhood. In A. C. Huston & M. N. Ripke (Eds.), *Developmental contexts in middle childhood.* Mahwah, NJ: Erlbaum.

Simpson, R. L., & LaCava, P. G. (2008). Autism spectrum disorders. In N. J. Salkind (Ed.), *Encyclopedia of educational psychology.* Thousand Oaks, CA: Sage.

Singh, S., Smith, G. A., Fields, S. K., & McKenzie, L. B. (2008). Gymnastics-related injuries to children treated in emergency departments in the United States, 1990–2005. *Pediatrics, 121,* e954–e960.

Sinha, J. W., Cnaan, R. A., & Gelles, R. J. (2007). Adolescent risk behaviors and religion: Findings from a national study. *Journal of Adolescence, 30,* 231–249.

Siow, H. M., Cameron, D. B., & Ganley, T. J. (2008). Acute knee injuries in skeletally immature athletes. *Physical Medicine and Rehabilitation Clinics of North America, 19,* 319–345.

Sivell, S., & others. (2008). How risk is perceived, constructed, and interpreted by clients in clinical genetics, and the effects on decision making: A review. *Journal of Genetic Counseling, 17,* 30–63.

Skinner, B. F. (1938). *The behavior of organisms: An experimental analysis.* New York: Appleton-Century-Crofts.

Skinner, B. F. (1957). *Verbal behavior.* New York: Appleton-Century-Crofts.

Slade, E. P., & Wissow, L. S. (2004). Spanking in early childhood and later behavior problems: A prospective study. *Pediatrics, 113,* 1321–1330.

Slater, A. (2004). Visual perception. In A. Fogel & G. Bremner (Eds.), *Blackwell handbook of infant development.* London: Blackwell.

Slater, A., Field, T., & Hernandez-Reif, M. (2007). The development of the senses. In A. Slater & M. Lewis (Eds.), *Introduction to infant development,* (2nd ed.). New York: Oxford University Press.

Slater, A., Morison, V., & Somers, M. (1988). Orientation discrimination and cortical function in the human newborn. *Perception, 17,* 597–602.

Slobin, D. (1972, July). Children and language: They learn the same way around the world. *Psychology Today,* 71–76.

Slomkowski, C., Rende, R., Conger, K. J., Simons, R. L., & Conger, R. D. (2001). Sisters, brothers, and delinquency: Social - influence during early and middle adolescence. *Child Development, 72,* 271–283.

Slough, N. M., McMahon, R. J., & the Conduct Problems Prevention Research Group. (2008). Preventing serious conduct problems in school-age youth: The Fast Track program. *Cognitive and Behavioral Practice, 15,* 3–17.

Smaldone, A., Honig, J. C., & Byrne, M. W. (2007). Sleepless in America: Inadequate sleep and relationships to health and well-being of our nation's children. *Pediatrics, 119, Suppl 1,* S29–S37.

Small, S. A. (1990). *Preventive programs that support families with adolescents.* Washington, DC: Carnegie Council on Adolescent Development.

Smalls, C., White, R., Chavous, T., & Sellers,R. (2007). Racial ideological beliefs and racial discrimination experiences as predictors of academic engagement among African American adolescents. *Journal of Black Psychology, 33,* 299–330.

Smetana, J. (2006). Social domain theory. In M. Killen & J. G. Smetana (Eds.), *Handbook of moral development.* Mahwah, NJ: Erlbaum.

Smetana, J. G. (2008). Commentary: Conflicting views of conflict. *Monographs of the Society for Research in Child Development, 73* (2), 484–493.

Smetana, J., Campione-Barr, N., & Metzger, A. (2006). Adolescent development in interpersonal and societal contexts. *Annual Review of Psychology* (Vol. 57). Palo Alto, CA: Annual Reviews.

Smith, B. (2007). *The psychology of sex and gender.* Boston: Allyn & Bacon.

Smith, C. A., & Crowther, C. A. (2004). Acupuncture for the induction of labor. *Cochrane Database of Systematic Review, 1,* CD0029262.

Smith, C. A., Collins, C. T., Cyna, A. M., & Crowther, C. A. (2006). Complementary and alternative therapies for pain management in labor. *Cochrane Database of Systematic Reviews, 4,* CD003521.

Smith, D. L. (2008). Birth complications and outcomes. In M. M. Haith & J. B. Benson (Eds.), *Encyclopedia of infancy and early childhood development.* Oxford, UK: Elsevier.

Smith, J. A., & Read, S. (2009). *Early literacy instruction* (2nd ed.). Upper Saddle River, NJ: Prentice Hall.

Smith, J., & Ross, H. (2007). Training parents to mediate sibling disputes affects children's negotiation and conflict understanding. *Child Development, 78,* 790–805.

Smith, K. (2002). *Who's minding the kids? Child care arrangements: Spring 1977.* Current Population Reports, P70–86. Washington, DC: U.S. Census Bureau.

Smith, L. B. (1999). Do infants possess innate knowledge structures? The con side. *Developmental Science, 2,* 133–144.

Smith, L. B., & Breazeal, C. (2007). The dynamic lift of developmental processes. *Developmental Science, 10,* 61–68.

Smith, L. M., & others. (2008). Prenatal methamphetamine use and neonatal neurobehavioral outcome. *Neurotoxicology and Teratology, 30,* 20–28.

Smith, L. M., Chang, L., Yonekura, M. L., Gilbride, K., Kuo, J., Poland, R. E., Walot,L., & Ernst, T. (2001). Brain proton magnetic resonance spectroscopy and imaging in children exposed to cocaine in utero. *Pediatrics, 107,* 227.

Smith, P. K. (2007). Pretend play and children's cognitive and literacy development: Sources of evidence and some lessons from the past. In K. A. Roskos & J. F. Christie (Eds.), *Play and literacy in early childhood.* Mahwah, NJ: Erlbaum.

Smith, T. E. C., Polloway, E. A., Patton, J. R., & Dowdy, C. A. (2008). *Teaching students with special needs in inclusive settings* (5th ed.). Boston: Allyn & Bacon.

Snarey, J. (1987, June). A question of morality. *Psychology Today,* pp. 6–8.

Snarey, J. (2008). Moral education in the cognitive developmental tradition. In L. Nucci & D. Narvaez (Eds.), *Handbook of moral and character education.* Clifton, NJ: Psychology Press.

Snijders, B. E., & others. (2007). Breastfeeding duration and infant atopic manifestations, by maternal allergic status, in the first two years of life (KOALA study). *Journal of Pediatrics, 151,* 347–351.

Snow, C. (2007, March). *Socializing children for academic success: The power and limits of language.* Paper presented at the meeting of the Society for Research in Child Development, Boston.

Snow, C. E., & Yang, J. Y. (2006). Becoming bilingual, biliterate, and bicultural. In W. Damon & R. Lerner (Eds.), *Handbook of child psychology* (6th ed.). New York: Wiley.

Snowdon, A. W., Hussein, A., High, L., Millar-Polgar, J., Patriack, L., & Ahmed, E. (2008). The effectiveness of a multimedia intervention on parents' knowledge and use of vehicle safety systems for children. *Journal of Pediatric Nursing, 23,* 126–139.

Snyder, H. N., & Sickmund, M. (1999, October). *Juvenile offenders and victims: 1999 national report.* Washington, DC: National Center for Juvenile Justice.

Snyder, J., Schrepferman, L., McDachern, A., Barner, S., Johnson, K., & Provines, J. (2008). Peer deviancy training and peer coercion: Dual processes associated with early-onset conduct problems. *Child Development, 79,* 252–268.

Snyder, K. A., & Torrence, C. M. (2008). Habituation and novelty. In M. M. Haith & J. B. Benson (Eds.), *Encyclopedia of infant and early childhood development.* Oxford, UK: Elsevier.

Soergel, P., Pruggmayer, M., Schwerdtfeger, R., Mulhaus, K., & Scharf, A. (2006). Screening for trisomy 21 with maternal age, fetal nuchal translucency, and maternal serum biochemistry at 11–14 weeks: A regional experience from Germany. *Fetal Diagnosis and Therapy, 21,* 264–268.

Solomon, D., Watson, M. S., & Battistich, V. A. (2002). Teaching and school effects on moral/prosocial development. In V. Richardson (Ed.), *Handbook for research on teaching.* Washington, DC: American Educational Research Association.

Solomon, D., Watson, P., Schapes, E., Battistich, V., & Solomon, J. (1990). Cooperative learning as part of a comprehensive program designed to promote prosocial development. In S. Sharan (Ed.), *Cooperative learning.* New York: Praeger.

Sophian, C. (1985). Perseveration and infants' search: A comparison of two-and three-location tasks. *Developmental Psychology, 21,* 187–194.

Sorof, J., & Daniels, S. (2002). Obesity hypertension: A problem of epidemic proportions. *Hypertension, 404,* 441–447.

Sowell, E. (2004, July). Commentary in M. Beckman, "Crime, culpability, and the adolescent brain. *Science Magazine, 305,* 599.

Spandel, V. (2009). *Creating 6-trait revisers and editors for grade 2.* Boston: Allyn & Bacon.

Spelke, E. S. (1979). Perceiving bimodally specified events in infancy. *Developmental Psychology, 5,* 626–636.

Spelke, E. S. (1991). Physical knowledge in infancy: Reflections on Piaget's theory. In S. Carey & R. Gelman (Eds.), *The epigenesis of mind: Essays on biology and cognition*. Hillsdale, NJ: Erlbaum.

Spelke, E. S. (2000). Core knowledge. *American Psychologist, 55*, 1233–1243.

Spelke, E. S., Breinlinger, K., Macomber, J., & Jacobson, K. (1992). Origins of knowledge. *Psychological Review, 99*, 605–632.

Spelke, E. S., & Hespos, S. J. (2001). Continuity, competence, and the object concept. In E. Dupoux (Ed.), *Language, brain, and behavior*. Cambridge, MA: Bradford/MIT Press.

Spelke, E. S., & Kinzler, K. D. (2007). Core knowledge. *Developmental Science 10*, 89–96.

Spelke, E. S., & Kinzler, K. D. (2008, in press). Core systems in human cognition. *Progress in Brain Research, 164*.

Spelke, E. S., & Owsley, C. J. (1979). Intermodal exploration and knowledge in infancy. *Infant Behavior and Development, 2*, 13–28.

Spence, J. T., & Buckner, C. E. (2000). Instrumental and expressive traits, trait stereotypes, and sexist attitudes: What do they signify? *Psychology of Women Quarterly, 24*, 44–62.

Spence, J. T., & Helmreich, R. (1978). *Masculinity and feminity: Their psychological dimensions*. Austin: University of Texas Press.

Spencer, M. B. (1999). Social and cultural influences on school adjustment: The application of an identity-focused cultural ecological perspective. *Educational Psychologist, 34*, 43–57.

Spencer, M. B. (2006). Phenomenology and ecological systems theory. In W. Damon & R. Lerner (Eds.), *Handbook of child psychology* (6thed.). New York: Wiley.

Spencer, S. (2005). Giving birth on the beach: Hypnosis and psychology. *Practicing Midwife, 8*, 27–29.

Spironelli, C., & Angrilli, A. (2008, in press). Developmental aspects of automatic word processing: Language lateralization of early ERP components in children, young adults, and middle-aged adults. *Biological Psychology*.

Spohr, H. L., Willms, J., & Steinhausen, H. C. (2007). Fetal alcohol spectrum disorders in young adulthood. *Journal of Pediatrics, 150*, 175–179.

Spring, J. (2008). *American education* (13th ed.). New York: McGraw-Hill.

Sprinthall, R. C. (2007). *Basic statistical analysis* (8th ed.). Boston: Allyn & Bacon.

Squire, W. (2008). Shaken baby syndrome: The quest for evidence. *Developmental Medicine and Child Neurology, 50*, 10–14.

Srabstein, J. C., McCarter, R. J., Shao, C., & Huang, Z. J. (2006). Morbidities associated with bullying behaviors in adolescents: School based study of American adolescents. *International Journal of Adolescent Medicine and Health, 18*, 587–596.

Sroufe, L. A. (2000, Spring). The inside scoop on child development: Interview. *Cutting through the hype*. Minneapolis: College of Education and Human Development, University of Minnesota.

Sroufe, L. A. (2007). Commentary: The place of development in developmental psychology. In A. Masten (Ed.), *Multilevel dynamics in developmental psychology*. Mahwah, NJ: Erlbaum.

Sroufe, L. A., Egeland, B., Carlson, E., & Collins, W. A. (2005b). The place of early attachment in developmental context. In K. E. Grossman, K. Krossman, & E. Waters (Eds.), *The power of longitudinal attachment research: From infancy and childhood to adulthood*. New York: Guilford.

Sroufe, L. A., Waters, E., & Matas, L. (1974). Contextual determinants of infant affectional response. In M. Lewis & L. Rosenblum (Eds.), *Origins of fear*. New York: Wiley.

St. Pierre, R., Layzer, J., & Barnes, H. (1996). *Regenerating two-generation programs*. Cambridge, MA: Abt Associates.

Stanley, N., & Appleton, J. (2008). International perspectives on child harm. *Child Abuse Review, 17*, 75–78.

Steele, C. M., & Aronson, J. A. (2004). Stereotype threat does not live by Steele and Aronson (1995) alone. *American Psychologist, 59*, 47–48.

Steele, M., Hodges, J., Kaniuk, J., Steele, H., D'Agostino, D., Blom, I., Hillman, S., & Henderson, K. (2007). Intervening with maltreated children and their families. In D. Oppenheim & D. F. Goldsmith (Eds.), *Attachment theory in clinical work with children*. New York: Guilford.

Stein, D. J., Fan, J., Fossella, J., & Russell, V. A. (2007). Inattention and hyperactivity-impulsivity: Psychobiological and evolutionary underpinnings. *CNS Spectrum, 12*, 190–196.

Stein, M. T., Kennell, J. H., & Fulcher, A. (2004). Benefits of a doula present at the birth of a child. *Journal of Developmental and Behavioral Pediatrics, 25* (5 Suppl.), S89–S92.

Steinberg, L., Blatt-Eisengart, I., & Cauffman, E. (2006). Patterns of competence and adjustment among adolescents from authoritative, authoritarian, indulgent, and neglectful homes: A replication in a sample of serious juvenile offenders. *Journal of Research on Adolescence, 16*, 47–58.

Steinberg, L., & Monahan, K. (2007). Age differences in resistance to peer influence. *Developmental Psychology, 43*, 1531–1543.

Steinberg, L., & Silk, J. S. (2002). Parenting adolescents. In M. Bornstein (Ed.), *Handbook of parenting* (2nd ed., Vol. 1). Mahwah, NJ: Erlbaum.

Steiner, J. E. (1979). Human facial expressions in response to taste and smell stimulation. In H. Reese & L. Lipsitt (Eds.), *Advances in child development and behavior* (Vol. 13). New York: Academic Press.

Stephens, J. M. (2008). Cheating. In N. J. Salkind (Ed.), *Encyclopedia of educational psychology*. Thousand Oaks, CA: Sage.

Stern, D. N., Beebe, B., Jaffe, J., & Bennett, S. L. (1977). The infant's stimulus world during social interaction: A study of caregiver behaviors with particular reference to repetition and timing. In H. R. Schaffer (Ed.), *Studies in mother-infant interaction*. London: Academic Press.

Sternberg, R. J. (1986). *Intelligence applied*. Fort Worth, TX: Harcourt Brace.

Sternberg, R. J. (1993). Sternberg Triachic Abilities Test (STAT). Unpublished test, Department of Psychology, Yale University, New Haven, CT.

Sternberg, R. J. (1997). Educating intelligence: Infusing the triarchic theory into instruction. In R. J. Sternberg & E. Grigorenko (Eds.), *Intelligence, heredity, and environment*. New York: Cambridge University press.

Sternberg, R. J. (Ed.). (1998). *Wisdom*. New York: Cambridge University Press.

Sternberg, R. J. (2002). Intelligence: The triarchic theory of intelligence. In J. W. Gutherie (Ed.), *Encyclopedia of education* (2nd ed.). New York: Macmillan.

Sternberg, R. J. (2004). Individual differences in cognitive development. In P. Smith & C. Hart (Eds.), *Blackwell handbook of cognitive development*. Malden, MA: Blackwell.

Sternberg, R. J. (2006). *Cognitive psychology* (4th ed.). Belmont, CA: Wadsworth.

Sternberg, R. J. (2007a). *g. g's*, or jeez: Which is the best model for developing abilities, competencies, and expertise? In P. C. Kyllonen, R. D. Roberts, & L. Stankov (Eds.), *Extending intelligence: Enhancement and new constructs* (pp. 250–265). Mahwah, NJ: Lawrence Erlbaum Associates.

Sternberg, R. J. (2007b). Finding students who are wise, practical, and creative. *The Chronicle of Higher Education, 53* (44), B11.

Sternberg, R. J. (2008a in press). The triarchic theory of successful intelligence. In B. Kerr (Ed.), *Encyclopedia of giftedness, creativity, and talent*. Thousand Oaks, CA: Sage.

Sternberg, R. J. (2009b). The triarchic theory of successful intelligence. In N. Salkind (Ed.), *Encyclopedia of educational psychology*. Thousand Oaks, CA: Sage.

Sternberg, R. J. (2008c). Schools should nurture wisdom. In B. Z. Presseisen (Ed.), *Teaching for intelligence* (2nd ed., pp. 61–88). Thousand Oaks, CA: Corwin.

Sternberg, R. J. (2008d, in press). Successful intelligence as a framework for understanding cultural adaptation. In S. Ang, & L. Van Dyne (Eds.), *Handbook on cultural intelligence*. New York: M. E. Sharpe.

Sternberg, R. J. (2008e, in press). Wisdom, intelligence, creativity, synthesized: A model of giftedness. In T. Balchin, B. Hymer, &

D. Matthews (Eds.), *International companion to gifted education*. London: RoutledgeFalmer.

Sternberg, R. J. (2008f, in press). Teaching for creativity. In R. A. Beghetto & J. C. Kaufman (Eds.), *Nurturing creativity in the classroom*. New York: Cambridge University Press.

Sternberg, R. J. (2009a). *Cognitive psychology* (5th ed.). Belmont, CA: Wadsworth.

Sternberg, R. J. (2009b, in press). Wisdom. In S. J. Lopez (Ed.). *Encyclopedia on positive psychology*. Malden, MA: Blackwell.

Sternberg, R. J. (2009c, in press). The triarchic theory of intelligence. In B. Kerr (Ed.), *Encyclopedia on giftedness, creativity, and talent*. Thousand Oaks, CA: Sage.

Sternberg, R. J. (2009d, in press). Successful intelligence as a framework for understanding cultural adaption. In S. Ang & L. van Dyne (Eds.), *Handbook on cultural intelligence*. New York: M.E. Sharpe.

Sternberg, R. J. (2009e, in press). Wisdom, intelligence, creativity, synthesized: A model of giftedness. In T. Balchin, B. Hymer, & D. Matthews (Eds.), *International companion to gifted education*. London: RoutledgeFalmer.

Sternberg, R. J. (2009f, in press). Teaching for creativity. In R. A. Beghetto & J. C. Kaufman (Eds.), *Nurturing creativity in the classroom*. New York: Cambridge University Press.

Sternberg, R. J., Castejøn, J. L., Prieto, M. D., Hautamämki, J., & Grigorenko, E. L. (2001a). Confirmatory factory analysis of the Sternberg triarchic abilities test in three international samples: An empirical test of the triarchic theory of intelligence. *European Journal of Psychological Assessment, 17* (1), 1–16.

Sternberg, R. J., & Grigorenko, E. L. (2007). *Teaching for successful intelligence* (2nd ed.). Thousand Oaks, CA: Corwin Press.

Sternberg, R. J., & Grigorenko, E. L. (2008a). Ability testing across cultures. In L. A. Suzuki & J. G. Ponterotto (Eds.), *Handbook of multicultural assessment* (3rd ed.). San Francisco: Jossey-Bass.

Sternberg, R. J., & Grigorenko, E. L. (2008b, in press). Ability testing across cultures. In L. Suzuki (ed.), *Handbook of multicultural assessment* (3rd ed.). New York: Jossey-Bass.

Sternberg, R. J., Grigorkenko, E. L., & Singer, J. L. (2004). *Creativity: From potential to realization*. Washington, DC: American Psychological Association.

Sternberg, R. J., Jarvin, L., & Grigorenko, E. L. (in press 2008). *Teaching for intelligence, creativity, and wisdom*. Thousand Oaks, CA: Corwin.

Sternberg, R. J., Jarvin, L., & Reznitskaya, A. (2009). Teaching for wisdom through history: Infusing wise thinking skills in the school

curriculum. In M. Ferrari (Ed.), *Teaching for Wisdom*. Amsterdam: Springer.

Sternberg, R. J., Kaufman, J. C., & Grigorenko, E. L. (2008). *Applied intelligence*. New York: Cambridge University Press.

Sternberg, R. J., Kaufman, J. C., & Pretz, J. E. (2004). A propulsion model of creative leadership. *Creativity and Innovation Management, 13*, 145–153.

Sternberg, R. J., Lipka, J., Newman, T., Wildfeuer, S., & Grigorenko, E. L. (2007). Triarchically-based instruction and assessment of sixth-grade mathematics in a Yup'ik cultural setting in Alaska. *International Journal of Giftedness and Creativity, 21* (2), 6–19.

Sternberg, R. J., Nokes, K., Geissler, P. W., Prince, R., Okatcha, F., Bundy, D. A., & Grigorenko, E. L. (2001b). The relationship between academic and practical intelligence: A case study in Kenya. *Intelligence. 29*, 401–418.

Sternberg, R. J., & O'Hara, L. A. (2000). Intelligence and creativity. In R. J. Sternberg (Ed.), *Handbook of intelligence*. New York: Cambridge University Press.

Sternberg, R. J., & the Rainbow Project Collaborators. (2006). The Rainbow Project: Enhancing the SAT through assessments of analytical, practical, and creative skills. *Intelligence, 34*, 321–350.

Sternberg, R. J., Roediger, H., & Halpern, D. (Eds.). (2007). *Critical thinking in psychology.* New York: Cambridge University Press.

Sternberg, R. J., & Williams, W. M. (1996). *How to develop student creativity*. Alexandria, VA: ASCD.

Sterzer, P., Stadler, C., Krebs, A., Kleinschmidt, A., & Poustka, F. (2005). Abnormal neural responses to emotional visual stimuli in adolescents with conduct disorder. *Biological Psychiatry, 57*, 7–15.

Steur, F. B., Applefield, J. M., & Smith, R. (1971). Televised aggression and the interpersonal aggression of preschool children. *Journal of Experimental Child Psychology, 11*, 442–447.

Stevenson, H. W. (1995). Mathematics achievement of American students: First in the world by the year 2000? In C. A. Nelson (Ed.), *Basic and applied perspectives on learning, cognition, and development*. Minneapolis: University of Minnesota Press.

Stevenson, H. W., Lee, S., Chen, C., Stigler, J. W., Hsu, C., & Kitamura, S. (1990). Contexts of achievement. *Monograph of the Society for Research in Child Development, 55* (Serial No. 221).

Stevenson, H. W., Lee, S., & Stigler, J. W. (1986). Mathematics achievement of Chinese, Japanese, and American children. *Science, 231*, 693–699.

Stevenson, H. W., & Newman, R. S. (1986). Long-term prediction of achievement and atti-

tudes in mathematics and reading. *Child Development, 57*, 646–659.

Stevenson, H. W., & Zusho, A. (2002). Adolescence in China and Japan: Adapting to a changing environment. In B. B. Brown, R. W. Larson, & T. S. Saraswathi (Eds.), *The world's youth*. New York: Cambridge University Press.

Stewart, A., Livingston, M., & Dennison, S. (2008). Transitions and turning points: Examining the links between child maltreatment and juvenile offending. *Child Abuse and Neglect, 32*, 51–66.

Stiggins, R. (2008). *Introduction to student-involved assessment for learning* (5th ed.). Upper Saddle River, NJ: Prentice Hall.

Stipek, D. (2002). *Motivation to learn* (4thed.). Boston: Allyn & Bacon.

Stipek, D. (2004). Head Start: Can't we have our cake and eat it too. *Education Week, 23* (No. 34), 52–53.

Stipek, D. (2005, February 16). Commentary in *USA Today*, p. 1D.

Stoel-Gammon, C. & Sosa, A. V. (2007). Phonological development. In E. Hoff & M. Shatz (Eds.), *Blackwell handbook of language development*. Malden, MA: Blackwell.

Stouthamer-Loeber, M., Loeber, R., Wei, E., Farrington, D. P., & Wikstrom, P. H. (2002). Risk and promotive effects in the explanation of persistent serious delinquency in boys. *Journal of Consulting and Clinical Psychology, 70*, 111–123.

Stoutheimer-Loeber, M., Wei, E., Loeber, R., & Masten, A. (2004). Desistance from serious delinquency in the transition to adulthood. *Development and Psychopathology, 16*, 897–918.

Strasburger, V. C., Wilson, B. J., & Jordan, A. (2008). *Children, adolescents, and the media*. Thousand Oaks, CA: Sage.

Strauss, M. A., Sugarman, D. B., & Giles-Sims, J. (1997). Spanking by parents and subsequent anti-social behavior in children. *Archives of Pediatrics and Adolescent Medicine, 151*, 761–767.

Streib, H. (1999). Off-road religion? A narrative approach to fundamentalist and occult orientations of adolescents. *Journal of Adolescence, 22*, 255–267.

Streissguth, A. P., Martin, D. C., Sandman, B. M., Kirchner, G. L., & Darby, B. L. (1984). Intrauterine alcohol and nicotine exposure: Attention and reaction time in four-year-old children. *Developmental Psychology, 20*, 533–543.

Strenze, T. (2007). Intelligence and socioeconomic success: A meta-analytic review of longitudinal research. *Intelligence, 35*, 401–426.

Streubel, A. H., Donohue, P. K., & Aucott, S. W. (2008). The epidemiology of atypical chronic lung disease in extremely low birth weight infants. *Journal of Perinatology, 28*, 141–148.

Stringer, M., Ratcliffe, S. J., Evans, E. C., & Brown, L. P. (2005). The cost of prenatal care attendance and pregnancy outcomes in low-income working women. *Journal of Obstetrical, Gynecologic, and Neonatal Nursing, 34,* 551–560.

Strong-Wilson, T., & Ellis, J. (2007). Children and place: Reggio Emilia's environment as a third teacher. *Theory Into Practice, 46,* 40–47.

Sturm, R. (2005). Childhood obesity—what we can learn from existing data and social trends. *Prevention of Chronic Diseases, 2,* A12.

Styfco, S. J. (2006). A place for Head Start in a world of universal preschool. In E. Zigler, W. S. Gilliam, & S. M. Jones (Eds.), *A vision for universal preschool education.* New York: Cambridge University Press.

Suarez-Orozco, C. (2007, March). *Immigrant family educational advantages and challenges.* Paper presented at the meeting of the Society for Research in Child Development, Boston.

Suarez-Orozco, C., & Qin, D. B. (2006). Gendered perspectives in psychology: Immigrant origin youth. *International Migration Review, 40,* 165–198.

Subrahmanyam, K., & Greenfield, P. (2008). Online communication and adolescent relationships. *Future of Children, 18* (No. 1), 119–146.

Subrahmanyam, K., Smahel, D., & Greenfield, P. (2006). Connecting developmental constructions on the internet: Identity presentation and sexual exploration in online chat rooms. *Developmental Psychology, 42,* 395–406.

Sue, S. (1990, August). *Ethnicity and culture in psychological research and practice.* Paper presented at the meeting of the American Psychological Association, Boston.

Sue, S., & Morishima, J. K. (1982). *The mental health of Asian Americans: Contemporary issues in identifying and treating mental problems.* San Francisco: Jossey-Bass.

Sugita, Y. (2004). Experience in early infancy is indispensable for color perception. *Current Biology, 14,* 1267–1271.

Sullivan, H. S. (1953). *The interpersonal theory of psychiatry.* New York: W. W. Norton.

Sullivan, K., & Sullivan, A. (1980). Adolescent-parent separation. *Developmental Psychology, 16,* 93–99.

Suman, R. P., Udani, R., & Nanavati, R. (2008). Kangaroo mother care for low birth weight infants: A randomized controlled trial. *Indian Pediatrics, 45,* 17–23.

Sumaroka, M., & Bornstein, M. H. (2008). Play. In M. M. Haith & J. B. Benson (Eds.), *Encyclopedia of infant and early childhood development.* Oxford, UK: Elsevier.

Super, C., & Harkness, S. (1997). The cultural structuring of child development. In J. W. Berry, Y. H. Poortinga, & J. Pandey (Eds.), *Handbook of cross-cultural psychology: Theory and method.* Vol. 2. Boston: Allyn & Bacon.

Suyemoto, K. L. (2009). Multiracial Asian Americans. In N. Tewari & A. Alvarez (Eds.), *Asian American psychology.* Clifton, NJ: Psychology Press.

Sveistrup, H., Schneiberg, S., McKinley, P.A., McGadyen, B. J., & Levin, M. F. (2008, in press). Head, arm, and trunk coordination during reaching in children. *Experimental Brain Research.*

Swaab, D. F., Chung, W. C., Kruijver, F. P., Hofman, M. A., & Ishunina, T. A. (2001). Structural and functional sex differences in the human hypothalamus. *Hormones and Behavior, 40,* 93–98.

Swamy, G. K., Ostbye, T., & Skjaerven, R. (2008). Association of preterm birth with long-term survival, reproduction, and next-generation preterm birth. *Journal of the American Medical Association, 299,* 1429–1436.

Swan, K., Cook, D., Kratcoski, A., Lin, Y., Schenker, J., & van't Hooft, M. (2006). Ubiquitous computing: Rethinking teaching, learning and technology integration. In S. Tettegah & R. Hunter (Eds.), *Educational and technology: Issues and applications, policy, and administration.* New York: Elsevier.

Swanson, B. J., Roman-Shriver, C. R., Shriver, B. J., & Goodell, L. S. (2007). A comparison between improvers and non—improvers among children with anemia enrolled in the WIC program. *Maternal and Child Health Journal, 11,* 447–459.

Sykes, C. J. (1995). *Dumbing down our kids: Why American children feel good about themselves but can't read, write, or add.* New York: St. Martin's Press.

T

Taddio, A. (2008). Circumcision. In M. M. Haith & J. B. Benson (Eds.), *Encyclopedia of infant and early childhood development.* Oxford, UK: Elsevier.

Tager-Flusberg, H. (2005). Putting words together: Morphology and syntax. In J. Berko Gleason (Ed.), *The development of language* (6th ed.). Boston: Allyn & Bacon.

Tager-Flusberg, H., & Zukowski, A. (2009). Putting words together: Morphology and syntax in the preschool years. In J. Berko Gleason & N. Ratner (Eds.), *The development of language* (7th ed.). Boston: Allyn & Bacon.

Takai, Y., Sato, M., Tan, R., & Hirai, T. (2005). Development of stereoscopic acuity: Longitudinal study using a computer-based random-dot stereo test. *Japanese Journal of Ophthalmology, 49,* 1–5.

Talaro, K. P. (2008). *Foundations of microbiology* (6th ed.). New York: McGraw-Hill.

Talge, N. M., Neal, C., Glover, V., and the Early Stress, Translational Research and Prevention Science Network: Fetal and Neonatal Experience on Child and Adolescent Mental Health. (2007). Antenatal maternal stress and long-term effects on neuro-development: How and why? *Journal of Child Psychology and Psychiatry, 48,* 245–261.

Tam, W. H., & Chung, T. (2007). Psychosomatic disorders in pregnancy. *Current Opinion in Obstetrics and Gynecology, 19,* 126–132.

Tamis-LeMonda, C. S., Way, N., Hughes, D., Yoshikawa, H., Kalman, R., & Niwa, E. Y. (2008). Parents' goals for children: The dynamic co-existence of individualism and collectivism in cultures and individuals. *Social Development, 17,* 183–209.

Tannen, D. (1990). *You just don't understand.* New York: Ballantine.

Tantillo, M., Kesick, C. M., Hynd, G. W., & Dishman, R. K. (2006). The effects of exercise on children with attention-deficit hyperactivity disorder. *Medical Science and Sports Exercise, 34,* 203–212.

Tappan, M. B. (1998). Sociocultural psychology and caring psychology: Exploring Vygotsky's "hidden curriculum." *Educational Psychologist, 33,* 23–33.

Tarpley, T. (2001). Children, the Internet, and other new technologies. In D. Singer & J. Singer (Eds.), *Handbook of children and the media.* Thousand Oaks, CA: Sage.

Tasker, F. L., and Golombok, S. (1997). *Growing up in a lesbian family: Effects on child development.* New York: Guilford.

Tauman, R., & Gozal, D. (2006). Obesity and obstructive sleep apnea in children. *Pediatric Respiratory Reviews, 7,* 247–259.

Taveras, E. M., Rifas-Shiman, S. L., Oken, E., Gunderson, E. P., & Gillman, M. W. (2008). Short sleep duration in infancy and risk of childhood overweight. *Archives of Pediatric and Adolescent Medicine, 162,* 305–311.

Taylor, F. M. A., Ko, R., & Pan, M. (1999). Prenatal and reproductive health care. In E. J. Kramer, S. L. Ivey, & Y.-W. Ying (Eds.), *Immigrant women's health.* San Francisco: Jossey-Bass.

Taylor, L. S., & Whittaker, C. R. (2009). *Bridging multiple worlds* (2nd ed.). Boston: Allyn & Bacon.

Taylor, R. D., & Lopez, E. I. (2005). Family management practice, school achievement, and problem behavior in African American adolescents: Mediating processes. *Applied Developmental Psychology, 26,* 39–49.

Taylor, R. L., Smiley, L., & Richards, S. B. (2009). *Exceptional students.* New York: McGraw-Hill.

Taylor, S. E. (2002). *The tending instinct.* New York: Times Books.

te Velde, S. J., De Bourdeaudhuij, I., Throsdottir, I., Rasmussen, M., Hagstromer, M., Klepp, K. I., & Brug, J. (2007). Patterns in sedentary and exercise behaviors and associations with overweight in 9–14-year-old boys and girls-a cross-sectional study. *BMC Public Health, 7,* 16.

Temple, C., Nathan, R., Temple, F., & Burris, N. A. (1993). *The beginnings of writing* (3rd ed.). Boston: Allyn & Bacon.

Templeton, J. L., & Eccles, J. S. (2006). The relation between spiritual development and identity processes. In E. Roehlkepartain, P. E. King, L. Wagener, & P. L. Benson (Eds.), *The handbook of spirituality in childhood and adolescence.* Thousand Oaks, CA: Sage.

Tenenbaum, H. R., Callahan, M., Alba-Speyer, C., & Sandoval, L. (2002). Parent-child science conversations in Mexican descent families: Educational background, activity, and past experience as moderators. *Hispanic Journal of Behavioral Sciences, 24,* 225–248.

Terman, L. (1925). *Genetic studies of genius. Vol. 1: Mental and physical traits of a thousand gifted children.* Stanford, CA: Stanford University Press.

Teti, D. (2001). Retrospect and prospect in the psychological study of sibling relationships. In J. P. McHale & W. S. Grolnick (Eds.), *Retrospect and prospect in the psychological study of families.* Mahwah, NJ: Erlbaum.

Teti, D. M., & Towe-Goodman, N. (2008). Postpartum depression, effects on infant. In M.M. Haith & J. B. Benson (Eds.), *Encyclopedia of infancy and early childhood development.* Oxford, UK: Elsevier.

Tewari, N., & Alvarez, A. (Eds.). (2009). *Asian American psychology.* Clifton, NJ: Psychology Press.

Thapar, A., Fowler, T., Rice, F., Scourfield, J., Van Den Bree, M., Thomas, S., Harold, G., & Hay, D. (2003). Maternal smoking during pregnancy and attention deficit hyperactivity disorder symptoms in offspring. *American Journal of Psychiatry, 160,* 1985–1989.

Tharp, R. G. (1994). Intergroup differences among Native Americans in socialization and child cognition: An erthogenetic analysis. In P. M. Greenfield & R. Cocking (Eds.), *Cross-cultural roots of minority child development.* Mahwah, NJ: Erlbaum.

Tharp, R. G., & Gallimore, R. (1988). *Rousing minds to life: Teaching, learning, and schooling in social context.* New York: Cambridge University Press.

Thelen, E. (1995). Motor development: A new synthesis. *American Psychologist, 50,* 79–95.

Thelen, E. (2000). Perception and motor development. In A. Kazdin (Ed.), *Encyclopedia of psychology.* Washington, DC, & New York: American Psychological Association and Oxford University Press.

Thelen, E. (2001). Dynamic mechanisms of change in early perceptual-motor development.

In J. L. McClelland & R. S. Siegler (Eds.), *Mechanisms of cognitive development.* Mahwah, NJ: Erlbaum.

Thelen, E., Corbetta, D., Kamm, K., Spencer, J. P., Schneider, K., & Zernicke, R. F. (1993). The transition to reaching: Mapping intention and intrinsic dynamics. *Child Development, 64,* 1058–1098.

Thelen, E., & Smith, L. B. (1998). Dynamic systems theory. In W. Damon (Ed.), *Handbook of child psychology* (5th ed., Vol. 1.). New York: Wiley.

Thoma, S. J. (2006). Research on the Defining Issues Test. In M. Killen & J. Smetana (Eds.), *Handbook of moral development.* Mahwah, NJ: Erlbaum.

Thomas, A., & Chess, S. (1991). Temperament in adolescence and its functional significance. In R. M. Lerner, A. C. Petersen, & J. Brooks-Gunn (Eds.), *Encyclopedia of adolescence* (Vol. 2). New York: Garland.

Thomas, M. S. C., & Johnson, M. H. (2008). New advances in understanding sensitive periods in brain development. *Current Directions in Psychological Science, 17,* 1–5.

Thompson, D. R., Obarzanek, E., Franko, D.L., Barton, B. A., Morrison, J., Biro, F.M., Daniels, S. R., & Striegel-Moore, R.H. (2007). Childhood overweight and cardiovascular disease risk factors: The National Heart, Lung, and Blood Institute Growth and Health Study. *Journal of Pediatrics, 150,* 18–25.

Thompson, P. M., Giedd, J. N., Woods, R.P., MacDonald, D., Evans, A. C., & Toga, A. W. (2000). Growth patterns in the developing brain detected by using continuum mechanical tensor maps. *Nature, 404,* 190–193.

Thompson, R. A. (1994). Emotion regulation: A theme in search of a definition. *Monographs of the Society for Research in Child Development, 59* (Serial No. 240), 2–3.

Thompson, R. A. (2006). The development of the person. In W. Damon & R. Lerner (Eds.), *Handbook of child psychology* (6th ed.). New York: Wiley.

Thompson, R. A. (2007). Unpublished review of J. W. Santrock's, *Children,* 10th ed. (New York: McGraw-Hill).

Thompson, R. A. (2008). Unpublished review of J. W. Santrock's *Life-span development,* 12th ed. (New York: McGraw-Hill).

Thompson, R. A. (2009a). Emotional development. In R. A. Schweder (Ed.), *The Chicago companion to the child.* Chicago: University of Chicago Press.

Thompson, R. A. (2009b, in press). Early attachment and later development: Familiar questions, new answers. In J. Cassidy & P. R. Shaver (Eds.), *Handbook of attachment* (2nd Ed.). New York: Guilford.

Thompson, R. A. (2009c). Early foundations: Conscience and the development of moral character. In D. Narvaez & D. Lapsley (Eds.), *Moral personality, identity, and character.* New York: Cambridge University Press.

Thompson, R. A., Easterbrooks, M. A., & Walker, L. (2003). Social and emotional development in infancy. In I. B. Weiner (Ed.), *Handbook of psychology* (Vol. 6). New York: Wiley.

Thompson, R. A., & Goodvin, R. (2005). The individual child: Temperament, emotion, self and personality. In M. J. Bornstein & M. E. Lamb (Eds.) *Developmental psychology* (5th ed.). Mahwah, NJ: Erlbaum.

Thompson, R. A., McGinley, M., & Meyer, S. (2006). Understanding values in relationships. In M. Killen & J. G. Smetana (Eds.), *Handbook of moral development.* Mahwah, NJ: Erlbaum.

Thompson, R. A., & Meyer, S. (2007). Socialization of emotion regulation. In J. J. Gross (Ed.), *Handbook of emotion regulation.* New York: Guilford.

Thompson, R. A., Meyer, S. A., & Jochem, R. (2008). Emotion regulation. In M. M. Haith & J. B. Benson (Eds.), *Encyclopedia of infant and early childhood development.* Oxford, UK: Elsevier.

Thompson, R. A., & Newton, E. (2009, in press). Infant-caregiver communication. In H. T. Reis & S. Sprecher (Eds.), *Encyclopedia of human relationships.* Thousand Oaks, CA: Sage.

Thompson, T., Moore, T., & Symons, F. (2007). Psychotherapeutic medications and positive behavior support. In S. L. Odom, R. H. Horner, M. E. Snell, & J. Blacher (Eds.), *Handbook of developmental disabilities.* New York: Guilford.

Thornton, J. G. (2007). Progesterone and preterm labor—still no definite answers. *New England Journal of Medicine, 357,* 499–501.

Thornton, P. L., Kieffer, E. C., Salbarian-Pena, Y., Odoms-Young, A., Willis, S. K., Kim, H., & Salinas, M. A. (2006). Weight, diet, and physical activity-related health beliefs and practices among pregnant and postpartum Latino women: The role of social support. *Maternal and Child Health Journal, 10,* 95–104.

Timmons, B. W., Naylor, P. J., & Pfeiffer, K. A. (2007). Physical activity for preschool children: How much and how? *Canadian Journal of Public Health, 98* (Suppl. 2), S122–S134.

Tiran, D. (2008). *Bailliere's midwives' dictionary* (11th ed.). Oxford, UK: Elsevier.

Tobin, J. J., Wu, D. Y. H., & Davidson, D. H. (1989). *Preschool in three cultures.* New Haven, CT: Yale University Press.

Toga, A. W., Thompson, P. M., & Sowell, E. R. (2006). Mapping brain Maturation, *Trends in Neuroscience, 29,* 148–159.

Tolani, N., & Brooks-Gunn, J. (2008). Family support, international trends. In M. M. Haith & J. B. Benson (Eds.), *Encyclopedia of infant and early childhood development.* Oxford, UK: Elsevier.

Tomasello, M. (2002). The emergence of grammar in child language. In T. Givon & B. Malle (Eds.), *The evolution of language out of prelanguage.* Amsterdam: John Benjamins.

Tomasello, M. (2003). *Constructing a language: A usage-based theory of language acquisition.* Cambridge, MA: Harvard University Press.

Tomasello, M. (2006). Acquiring linguistic constructions. In W. Damon & R. Lerner (Eds.), *Handbook of child psychology* (6th ed.). New York: Wiley.

Tomasello, M., & Carpenter, M. (2007). Shared intentionality. *Developmental Science, 10,* 121–125.

Tomasello, M., Carpenter, M., & Liszkowski, U. (2007). A new look at infant pointing. *Child Development, 78,* 705–722.

Tong, S., Baghurst, P., Vimpani, G., & McMichael, A. (2007). Socioeconomic position, maternal IQ, home environmental, and cognitive development. *Journal of Pediatrics, 151,* 284–288.

Toth, S. L. (2009, in press). Attachment-based interventions: Comments on Dozier, Egeland, and Benoit. In R. E. Tremblay, R. deV Peters, M. Boivin, & R. G. Barr (Eds.), *Encyclopedia on early childhood development.* Montreal: Centre of Excellence for Early Childhood Development.

Toth, S. L., & Cicchetti, D. (2009, in press). Child maltreatment and its impact on psychosocial development. In R. E. Tremblay, R. deV Peters, M. Boivin, & R. G. Barr (Eds.), *Encyclopedia on early childhood development.* Montreal: Centre of Excellence for Early Childhood Development.

Tough, S. C., Newburn-Cook, C., Johnston, D. W., Svenson, L. W., Rose, S., & Belik, J. (2002). Delayed childbearing and its impact on population rate changes in lower birth weight, multiple birth, and preterm delivery. *Pediatrics, 109,* 399–403.

Trafimow, D., Triandis, H. C., & Goto, S. G. (1991). Some tests of the distinction between the private and collective self. *Journal of Personality and Social Psychology, 60,* 649–655.

Trautner, H. M., Ruble, D. N., Cyphers, L., Kirsten, B., Behrendt, R., & Hartmann, P. (2005). Rigidity and flexibility of gender stereotypes in children: Developmental or differential? *Infant and Child Development, 14,* 365–381.

Treffers, P. E., Eskes, M., Kleiverda, G., & van Alten, D. (1990). Home births and minimal medical interventions. *Journal of the American Medical Association, 246,* 2207–2208.

Trehub, S. E., Schneider, B. A., Thorpe, L. A., & Judge, P. (1991). Observational measures of auditory sensitivity in early infancy. *Developmental Psychology, 27,* 40–49.

Tremblay, R. E. (2009). Development of aggression from early childhood to adulthood. In R. E. Tremblay, R. deV Peters, M. Boivin, & R. G. Barr (Eds.), *Encyclopedia on early childhood development.* Montreal: Center of Excellence for Early Childhood Development.

Triandis, H. C. (1994). *Culture and social behavior.* New York: McGraw-Hill.

Triandis, H. C. (2001). Individualism and collectivism. In D. Matsumoto (Ed.), *Handbook of culture and psychology.* New York: Oxford University Press.

Triandis, H. C. (2007). Culture and psychology: A history of their relationship. In S. Kitayama & D. Cohen (Eds.), *Handbook of cultural psychology.* New York: Guilford.

Trimble, J. E. (1988, August). *The enculturation of contemporary psychology.* Paper presented at the meeting of the American Psychological Association, New Orleans.

Trost, S. G., Fees, B., & Dzewaltowski, D. (2008). Feasibility and efficacy of "move and learn" physical activity curriculum in preschool children. *Journal of Physical Activity and Health, 5,* 88–103.

Trzesniewski, K. H., Donnellan, M. B., Moffitt, T. E., Robins, R. W., Poulton, R., & Caspi, A. (2006). Low self-esteem during adolescence predicts poor health, criminal behavior, and limited economic prospects during adulthood. *Developmental Psychology, 42,* 381–390.

Tseng, V. (2004). Family interdependence and academic adjustment in college: Youth from immigrant and U.S. born families. *Child Development, 75,* 966–983.

Tumeh, P. C., Alavi, A., Houseni, M., Greenfiled, A., Chryssikos, T., Newberg, A., Torigian, D. A., & Moonis, G. (2007). Structural and functional imaging correlates for age-related changes in the brain. *Seminars in Nuclear Medicine, 37,* 69–87.

Turiel, E. (2006). The development of morality. In W. Damon & R. Lerner (Eds.), *Handbook of child psychology* (6th ed.). New York: Wiley.

Turnbull, H. R., Huerta, N., & Stowe, M. (2009). *What every teacher should know about: The Individuals with Disabilities Education Act as amended in 2004* (2nd ed.). Upper Saddle River, NJ: Prentice Hall.

Twenge, J. M., & Campbell, W. K. (2001). Age and birth cohort differences in self-esteem: A cross-temporal meta-analysis. *Personality and Social Psychology Bulletin, 5,* 321–344.

U

U. S. Census Bureau. (2006). *Population Statistics 2006. Washington,* DC: Author.

U.S. Department of Energy. (2001). *The human genome project.* Washington, DC: Author.

U.S. Department of Health and Human Services. (2003). *Child abuse and neglect statistics.* Washington, DC: Author.

U. S. Food and Drug Administration. (2004, March 19). *An important message for pregnant women and women of childbearing age who may become pregnant about the risk of mercury in fish.* Washington, DC: Author.

Uba, L. (1992). Cultural barriers to health care for Southeast Asian refugees. *Public Health Reports, 107,* 544–549.

Udry, J. R., & others. (1985). Serum androgenic hormones motivate sexual behavior in adolescent boys. *Fertility and Sterility, 43,* 90–94.

Uhart, M., Chong, R. Y., Oswald, L., Lin, P. I., & Wand, G. S. (2006). Gender differences in hypothalamic-pituitary-adrenal (HPA) axis reactivity. *Psychoneuroendocrinology, 31,* 642–652.

Ulvund, S. E., & Smith, L. (1996). The predictive validity of nonverbal communicative skills in infants with perinatal hazards. *Infant Behavior and Development, 19,* 441–449.

Umana-Taylor, A. J., Bhanot, R., & Shin, N. (2006). Ethnic identity formation in adolescence: The critical role of families. *Journal of Family Issues, 27,* 390–414.

Umana-Taylor, A. J., Vargas-Changes, D., Garcia, C. D., & Gonzales-Backen, M. (2008). A longitudinal examination of Latino adolescents' ethnic identity, coping with discrimination, and self-esteem. *Journal of Early Adolescence, 28,* 16–50.

Underwood, M. K. (2004). Gender and peer relations: Are the two cultures really all that different? In J. B. Kupersmidt & K. A. Dodge (Eds.), *Children's peer relations: From development to intervention.* Washington, DC: American Psychological Association.

Underwood, M. K. (2007). Introduction to the special issue. Do girls' and boys' friendships constitute different peer cultures, and what are the tradeoffs for development? *Merrill-Palmer Quarterly, 53,* 319–324.

Underwood, M. K., & Hurley, J. C. (1997, April). *Children's responses to angry provocation as a function of peer status and aggression.* Paper presented at the meeting of the Society for Research in Child Development, Washington, DC.

UNICEF. (2003). *State of the world's children: 2003.* Geneva: Author.

UNICEF. (2004). *The state of the world's children 2002.* Geneva: Author.

UNICEF. (2006). *The state of the world's children 2006.* Geneva: Author.

UNICEF. (2007). *The state of the world's children, 2007.* Geneva: Author.

UNICEF. (2008). *The State of the world's children, 2008.* Geneva: Author.

United Nations. (2002). *Improving the quality of life of girls.* Geneva: UNICEF.

Urbano, M. T., & Tait, D. M. (2004). Can the irradiated uterus sustain a pregnancy? *Clinical Oncology, 16,* 24–28.

Urberg, K. (1992). Locus of peer influence: Social crowd and best friend. *Journal of Youth and Adolescence, 21,* 439–450.

USA Today. (2000, October 10). All-USA first teacher team. Retrieved November 15, 2004, from http://www.usatoday.com/life/teacher/teach/htm

V

Vallotton, C. D., & Fischer, K. W. (2008). Cognitive development. In M. M. Haith & J. B. Benson (Eds.), *Encyclopedia of infant and early childhood development.* Oxford, GB: Elsevier.

Valsner, J. (2006). Developmental epistemology and implications for methodology. In W. Damon & R. Lerner (Eds.), *Handbook of child psychology* (6th ed.). New York: Wiley.

Van Beveren, T. T. (2007, January). *Personal conversation.* Richardson, TX: Department of Psychology, University of Texas at Dallas.

Van Buren, E., & Graham, S. (2003). *Redefining ethnic identity: Its relationship to positive and negative school adjustment outcomes for minority youth.* Paper presented at the meeting of the Society for Research in Child Development, Tampa.

van den Boom, D. C. (1989). Neonatal irritability and the development of attachment. In G. A. Kohnstamm, J. E. Bates, & M. K. Rothbart (Eds.), *Temperament in childhood.* New York: Wiley.

van den Heuvel, A., & Marteau, T. M. (2008). Cultural variation in values attached to informed choice in the context of prenatal diagnosis. *Seminars in Fetal and Neonatal Medicine, 13,* 99–102.

van der Schoot, C. E., Hahn, S., & Chitty, L. S. (2008). Non-invasive prenatal diagnosis and determination of fetal Rh status. *Seminars in Fetal and Neonatal Medicine, 13,* 63–68.

van der Sluis, S., & others (2008). Sex differences on the WISC-R in Belgium and the Netherlands. *Intelligence, 36,* 48–67.

Van Dyck, P. C. (2007). Final commentary on the special volume of articles from the National Survey of Children's Health. *Pediatrics, 119,* (Suppl.), S122–S123.

van Hof, P., van der Kamp, J., & Savelsbergh, G. J. (2008). The relation between infants' perception of catchableness and the control of catching. *Developmental Psychology, 44,* 182–194.

van IJzendoorn, M. H., Juffer, F., & Poelhuis, C. W. (2005). Adoption and cognitive development: A meta-analytic comparison of adopted and nonadopted children's IQ and school performance. *Psychological Bulletin, 131,* 301–316.

van IJzendoorn, M. H., & Kroonenberg, P. M. (1988). Cross-cultural patterns of attachment: A meta-analysis of the Strange Situation. *Child Development, 59,* 147–156.

van IJzendoorn, M. H., & Sagi-Schwartz, A. (2009, in press). Cross-cultural patterns of attachment: Universal and contextual dimensions. In J. Cassidy & P. R. Shaver (Eds.), *Handbook of attachment* (2nd Ed.). New York: Guilford.

van Sleuwen, B. E., Engelberts, A. C., Boere-Boonekamp, M. M., Juis, W., Schulpen, T. W., & L'Hoir, M. P. (2007). Swaddling: A systematic review. *Pediatrics, 120,* e1097–e1106.

Vande Vusse, L., Irland, J., Healthcare, W. F., Berner, M. A., Fuller, S., & Adams, D. (2007). Hypnosis for childbirth: A retrospective comparative analysis of outcomes in one obstetrician's practice. *American Journal of Clinical Hypnosis, 50* 109–119.

Vandehey, M., Diekhoff, G., & LaBeff, E. (2007). College cheating: A 20-year follow-up and the addition of an honor code. *Journal of College Development, 48,* 468–480.

Vandell, D. L. (1985, April). *Relationship between infant-peer and infant-mother interactions: What have we learned?* Paper presented at the meeting of the Society for Research in Child Development, Toronto.

Vandell, D. L. (2004). Early child care: The known and unknown. *Merrill-Palmer Quarterly, 50,* 387–414.

Vandell, D. L., & Wilson, K. S. (1988). Infants' interactions with mother, sibling, and peer: Contrasts and relations between interaction systems. *Child Development, 48,* 176–186.

Vasdev, G. (2008). *Obstetric anesthesia.* Oxford, UK: Elsevier.

Vaughan Van Hecke, A., Mundy, P. C., Acra, C. F., Block, J. J., Delgado, E. F., Parlade, M. V., Meyer, J. A., Neal, A. R., & Pomares, Y. B. (2007). Infant joint attention, temperament, and social competence in preschool children. *Child Development, 78,* 53–69.

Vendittelli, F., Riviere, O, Crenn-Herbert, C., Rozan, M. A., Maria, B., Jacquetin, B., & the AUDIPOG Sentinel Network. (2008). Is a breech presentation at term more frequent in woman with a history of cesarean delivery? *American Journal of Obstetrics and Gynecology, 198,* 521e1–521e6.

Venners, S. A., Wang, X., Chen, C., Wang, L., Chen, D., Guang, W., Huang, A., Ryan, L., O'Conner, J., Lasley, B., Overstreet, J., Wilcox, A., & Xu, X. (2004). Paternal smoking and pregnancy loss: A prospective study using a biomarker of pregnancy. *American Journal of Epidemiology, 159,* 993–1001.

Ventura, A. K., Savage, J. S., May, A. L., & Birch, L. L. (2009, in press). Early behavioral, familial, and psychosocial predictors of overweight and obesity. In R. E. Tremblay, R. deV Peters, M. Boivin, & R. G. Barr (Eds.), *Encyclopedia on early childhood development.* Montreal: Centre of Excellence for Early Childhood Development.

Verma, S., & Saraswathi, T. S. (2002). Adolescence in India: Street urchins or Silicon Valley millionaires? In B. B. Brown, R. W. Larson, & T. S. Saraswathi (Eds.), *The world's youth.* New York: Cambridge University Press.

Vermeersch, H., T'Sjoen, G., Kaufman, J. M., & Vincke, J. (2008). The role of testosterone in aggressive and non-aggressive risk-taking in boys. *Hormones and Behavior, 53,* 463–471.

Victor, E., Kellough, R. D., & Tai, R. H. (2008). *Science education* (11th ed.). Upper Saddle River, NJ: Prentice Hall.

Villegas, R., Gao, Y. T., Yang, G., Li, H. L., Elasy, T., Zheng, W., & Shu, X. O. (2008, inpress). Duration of breast-feeding and the incidence of type 2 diabetes mellitus in the Shanghai Women's Health Study. *Diabetologia.*

Visootsak, J., & Sherman, S. (2007). Neuropsychiatric and behavioral aspects of trisomy 21. *Current Psychiatry Reports, 9,* 135–140.

Vitaro, F., Pedersen, S., & Brendgen, M. (2007). Children's disruptiveness, peer rejection, friends' deviancy, and delinquent behaviors: A process-oriented approach. *Development and Psychopathology, 19,* 433–453.

Vogler, G. P. (2006). Behavior genetics and aging. In J. E. Birren & K. W. Schaie (Eds.), *Handbook of the psychology of aging* (6th ed.). San Diego: Academic Press.

Vogler, M. A. (2006). Update: Preventing mother-to-child transmission of HIV. *Current HIV/AIDS Reports, 3,* 59–65.

Vohr, B. R., & Boney, C. M. (2008). Gestational diabetes: The forerunner for the development of maternal and child obesity and metabolic syndrome? *Journal of Maternal-Fetal and Neonatal Medicine, 21,* 149–157.

Volmink, J., Siegfried, N. L., van der Merwe, L., & Brocklkehurst, P. (2007). Antiretrovirals for reducing the risk of mother-to-child transmission of HIV infection. *Cochrane Database of Systematic Reviews, 24,* CD003510.

Von Hofsten, C. (2008). Motor and physical development manual. In M. M. Haith & J. B.

Benson (Eds.), *Encyclopedia of infant and early childhood development*. Oxford, UK: Elsevier.

Votruba-Drzal, E., Coley, R. L., & Chase-Lansdale, P. L. (2004). Child care and low-income children's development: Direct and moderated effects. *Child Development, 75,* 296–312.

Vreeman, R. C., & Carroll, A. E. (2007). A systematic review of school-based interventions to prevent bullying. *Archives of Pediatric and Adolescent Medicine, 161,* 78–88.

Vukelich, C., Christie, J., & Enz, B. J. (2008). *Helping children learn language and literacy.* Boston: Allyn & Bacon.

Vyas, S., Ghani, L., Khazaezadeh, N., & Oteng-Ntim, E. (2008). Pregnancy and obesity. In J. Studd, S. L. Tan, & F. A. Cherenak (Eds.), *Progress in obstetrics and gynecology.* Oxford, UK: Elsevier.

Vygotsky, L. S. (1962). *Thought and language.* Cambridge, MA: MIT Press.

W

Wabitsch, M. (2009, in press). Preventing obesity in young children. In R. E. Tremblay, R. deV Peters, M. Boivin, & R. G. Barr (Eds.), *Encyclopedia on early childhood development.* Montreal: Centre of Excellence for Early Childhood Development. Psychology Press.

Wachs, T. D. (1994). Fit, context and the transition between temperament and personality. In C. Halverson, G. Kohnstamm, & R. Martin (Eds.), *The developing structure of personality from infancy to adulthood.* Hillsdale, NJ: Erlbaum.

Wachs, T. D. (2000). *Necessary but not sufficient.* Washington, DC: American Psychological Association.

Wagner, R. K. (1997). Intelligence, training, and employment. *American Psychologist, 52,* 1059–1069.

Wagner, R. K., & Sternberg, R. J. (1986). Tacit knowledge and intelligent functioning in the everyday world. In R. J. Sternberg & R. K. Wagner (Eds.), *Practical intelligence.* New York: Cambridge University Press.

Wagstaff, A., Bustreo, F., Bryce, J., Claeson, M., and the WHO-World Bank Child Health and Poverty Working Group. (2004). Child health: Reaching the poor. *American Journal of Public Health, 94,* 726–736.

Wainryb, C. (2006). Moral development in culture: Diversity, tolerance, and justice. In M. Killen & J. G. Smetana (Eds.), *Handbook of moral development.* Mahwah, NJ: Erlbaum.

Walden, T. (1991). Infant social referencing. In J. Garber & K. Dogde (Eds.), *The development of emotional regulation and dysregulation.* New York: Cambridge University Press.

Waldrip, A. M., Malcolm, K. T., & Jensen-Campbell, L. A. (2008, in press). With a little help from your friends: The importance of high-quality friendships on adolescent adjustment. *Social Development,*

Walker, L. J. (1982). The sequentiality of Kohlberg's stages of moral development. *Child Development, 53,* 1130–1136.

Walker, L. J. (2002). Moral exemplarity. In W. Damon (Ed.), *Bringing in a new era of character education.* Stanford, CA: Hoover Press.

Walker, L. J. (2004). Progress and prospects in the psychology of moral development. *Merrill-Palmer Quarterly, 50,* 546–557.

Walker, L. J. (2006). Gender and morality. In M. Killen & J. G. Smetana (Eds.), *Handbook of moral development.* Mahwah, NJ: Erlbaum.

Walker, L. J., & Frimer, J. A. (2008a, June). *The diverse personalities of moral heroism.* Paper presented at the meeting of the Canadian Psychological Association, Halifax.

Walker, L. J., & Frimer, J. A. (2008b, in press). Being good for goodness' sake: Transcendence in the lives of moral heroes. In F. K. Oser & W. M. M. H. Veugelers (Eds.), *Getting involved: Global citizenship development and sources of moral values.* Rotterdam, The Netherlands: Sense Publishers.

Walker, L. J., & Hennig, K. H. (2004). Differing conceptions of moral exemplars: Just, brave, and caring. *Journal of Personality and Social Psychology, 86,* 629–647.

Walker, L. J., Henning, K. H., & Krettenauer, T. (2000). Parent and peer contexts for children's moral development. *Child Development, 71,* 1033–1048.

Walker, L. J., & Pitts, R. C. (1998). Naturalistic conceptions of moral maturity. *Developmental Psychology, 34,* 403–419.

Walker, S. (2006). Unpublished review of J. W. Santrock, *Topical life-span development,* 3rd ed. (New York: McGraw-Hill).

Walker, S. P., Wachs, T. D., Gardner, J. M., Lozoff, B., Wasserman, G. A., Pollitt, E., Carter, J. A., & the International Child Development Steering Group. (2007). Child development risk factors for adverse outcomes in developing countries. *Lancet, 369,* 145–157.

Wallerstein, J. S. (2008). Divorce. In M. M. Haith & J. B. Benson (Eds.), *Encyclopedia of infant and early childhood development.* Oxford, UK: Elsevier.

Walper, S., & Beckh, K. (2006). Adolescents' development in high-conflict and separated families: Evidence from a German longitudinal study. In A. Clarke-Stewart & J. Dunn (Eds.), *Families count.* New York: Cambridge University Press.

Walsh, L. A. (2000, Spring). The inside scoop on child development: Interview. *Cutting through the hype.* Minneapolis: College of Education and Human Development, University of Minnesota.

Walsh, L. V. (2006). Beliefs and rituals in traditional birth attendant practice in Guatemala. *Journal of Transcultural Nursing, 17,* 148–154.

Walshaw, C. A., & Owens, J. M. (2006). Low breastfeeding rates and milk insufficiency. *British Journal of General Practice, 56,* 379.

Wang, S. M., DeZinno, P., Fermo, L., William, K., Caldwell-Andrews, A. A., Bravemen, F., & Kain, Z. N. (2005). Complementary and alternative medicine for low-back pain in pregnancy: A cross-sectional survey. *Journal of Alternative and Complementary Medicine, 11,* 459–464.

Ward, L. M. (2004). Wading through stereotypes: Positive and negative associations between media use and black adolescents' conceptions of self. *Developmental Psychology, 40,* 284–294.

Wardlaw, G. M., & Hempl, J. (2007). *Perspectives in nutrition.* (7th ed.). New York: McGraw-Hill.

Wardlaw, G. M., & Smith, A. M. (2009). *Contemporary nutrition* (7th ed.). New York: McGraw-Hill.

Wardle, J., Carnell, S., Haworth, C. M., & Plomin, R. (2008). Evidence for a strong genetic influence on childhood adiposity despite the force of the obesogenic environment. *American Journal of Clinical Nutrition, 87,* 398–404.

Warrington, M., & Younger, M. (2003). "We decided to give it a twirl": Single-sex teaching in English comprehensive schools. *Gender and Education, 15,* 339–350.

Warshak, R. A. (2004, January). Personal communication, Department of Psychology, University of Texas at Dallas, Richardson.

Wartella, E. A. (2007, March). *Children's media research: An overview.* Paper presented at the meeting of the Society for Research in Child Development, Boston.

Wasserman, M., Bender, D., & Lee, S. Y. (2007). Use of preventive maternal and child health services by Latina women: A review of published intervention studies. *Medical Care Research and Review, 64,* 4–45.

Waterman, A. S. (1985). Identity in the context of adolescent psychology. In A. S. Waterman (Ed.), *Identity in adolescence: Processes and contents.* San Francisco: Jossey-Bass.

Waterman, A. S. (1989). Curricula interventions for identity change: Substantive and ethical considerations. *Journal of Adolescence, 12,* 389–400.

Waterman, A. S. (1992). Identity as an aspect of optimal psychological functioning. In G. R. Adams, T. P. Gullotta, & R. Montemayor (Eds.), *Adolescent identity formation.* Newbury Park, CA: Sage.

Waters, E., Kondo-Ikemura, K., Posada, G., & Richters, J. E. (1990). Learning to love: Mechanisms and milestones. In M. Gunnar & L. A. Sroufe (Eds.), *Minnesota symposia on child psychology* (Vol. 23). Mahwah, NJ: Erlbaum.

Watkins, M., Lei, P. W., & Canivez, G. L. (2007). Intelligence and achievement: A cross-lagged panel analysis. *Intelligence, 35,* 59–68.

Watson, D. L. & Tharp, R. G. (2007). *Self-directed behavior* (9th ed.). Belmont, CA: Wadsworth.

Watson, J. B. (1928). *Psychological care of infant and child.* New York: W. W. Norton.

Watson, J. B., & Rayner, R. (1920). Conditioned emotional reactions. *Journal of Experimental Psychology, 3,* 1–14.

Watt, H. M. G. (2008). Gender and occupational outcomes: An introduction. In H. M. G. Watt & J. S. Eccles (Eds.), *Gender and occupational outcomes.* Washington, DC: American Psychological Association.

Watt, H. M. G., & Eccles, J. S. (Eds.). (2008). *Gender and occupational outcomes.* Washington, DC: American Psychological Association.

Waxman, S. (2009). How infants discover distinct word types and map them to distinctive meaning. In J. Colombo, P. McCardle, & L. Freund (Eds.), *Infant pathways to language.* Clifton, NJ: Psychology Press.

Way, N., Santos, C., Niwa, E. Y., & Kim-Gervy, C. (2008). To be or not to be: An exploration of ethnic identity development in context. In M. Asmitia, M. Syed, & K. Radmacher (Eds.), *The intersections of personal and social identities. New Directions for Child and Adolescent Development, 120,* 61–79.

Weaver, R. F. (2008). *Molecular biology* (4th ed.). New York: McGraw-Hill.

Webb, J. T., Gore, J. L., Mend, E. R., & DeVries, A. R. (2007). *A parent's guide to gifted children.* Scottsdale, AZ: Great Potential Press.

Webster, N. S., & Worrell, F. C. (2008). Academically-talented adolescents' attitudes toward service in the community. *Gifted Child Quarterly, 52,* 170–179.

Wegman, M. E. (1987). Annual summary of vital statistics—1986. *Pediatrics, 80,* 817–827.

Wehkalampi, K., Vangonen, K., Laine, T., & Dunkel, L. (2007). Progressive reduction of relative height in childhood predicts adult stature below target heights in boys with constitutional delay of growth and puberty. *Hormone Research, 68,* 99–104.

Weikert, D. P. (1993). [Long-term positive effects in the Perry Preschool Head Start Program.] Unpublished data, High Scope Foundation, Ypsilanti, MI.

Weinstein, R. S. (2004). *Reaching higher: The power of expectations in schooling* (paperback ed.). Cambridge, MA: Harvard University Press.

Weiss, L. A., & others. (2008). Association between microdeletion and microduplication at 16p11.2 and autism. *New England Journal of Medicine, 358,* 667–675.

Wellman, H. M., Cross, D., & Watson, J. (2001). Meta-analysis of theory-of-mind development: The truth about false belief. *Child Development, 72,* 655–684.

Wellman, H. M., Lopez-Duran, S., Labounty, J., & Hamilton, B. (2008). Infant attention to intentional action predicts preschool theory of mind. *Developmental Psychology, 44,* 618–623.

Wellman, H. M., & Woolley, J. D. (1990). From simple desires to ordinary beliefs: The early development of everyday psychology. *Cognition, 35,* 245–275.

Wells, J. C., Hallal, P. C., Reichert, F. F., Menezes, A. M., Araujo, C. L., & Victora, C. G. (2008, in press). Sleep patterns and television viewing in relation to obesity and blood pressure: Evidence from an adolescent Brazilian cohort. *International Journal of Obesity.*

Welti, C. (2002). Adolescents in Latin America: Facing the future with skepticism. In B. B. Brown, R. W. Larson, & T. S. Saraswathi (Eds.), *The world's youth.* New York: Cambridge University Press.

Weng, X., Odouli, R., & Li, D. K. (2008, in press). Maternal caffeine consumption during pregnancy and the risk of miscarriage: A prospective cohort study. *American Journal of Obstetrics and Gynecology.*

Wentzel, K. (1997). Student motivation in middle school: The role of perceived pedagogical caring. *Journal of Educational Psychology, 89,* 411–419.

Wentzel, K. R., & Asher, S. R. (1995). The academic lives of neglected, rejected, popular, and controversial children. *Child Development, 66,* 754–763.

Wentzel, K. R., Barry, C. M., & Caldwell, K. A. (2004). Friendships in middle school: Influences on motivation and school adjustment. *Journal of Educational Psychology, 96,* 195–203.

Werker, J. F., & Tees, R. C. (2005). Speech perception as a window for understanding plasticity and commitment in language systems of the brain. *Developmental Psychobiology, 46,* 233–251.

Wertsch, J. V. (2007). Mediation. In H.Daniels, J. Wertsch, & M. Cole (Eds.), *The Cambridge companion to Vygotsky.* New York: Cambridge University Press.

Westermann, G., Mareschal, D., Johnson, M. H., Sirois, S., Spratling, M. W., & Thomas, M. S. (2007). Neuroconstructivism. *Developmental Science, 10,* 75–83.

Westling, E., Anderes, J. A., Hampson, S.E., & Peterson, M. (2008, in press). Pubertal timing and substance use: The effects of gender, parental monitoring, and deviant peers. *Journal of Adolescent Health.*

Wheeden, A., Scafidi, F. A., Field, T., Ironson, G., Valdeon, C. & Bandstra, E. (1993). Massage effects on cocaine-exposed preterm neonates. *Journal of Developmental and Behavioral Pediatrics, 14,* 318–322.

White, M. (1993). *The material child: Coming of age in Japan and America.* New York: Free Press.

Whitescarver, K. (2006, April). *Montessori rising: Montessori education in the United States, 1955–present.* Paper presented at the meeting of the American Education Research Association, San Francisco.

Whitesell, N. R., & Harter, S. (1989). Children's reports of conflict between simultaneous opposite-valence emotions. *Child Development, 60,* 637–682.

Whiting, J. (1981). Environmental constraint on infant care practices. In R. L. Monroe, R. H. Munroe, & B. Whiting (Eds.), *Handbook of cross-cultural human development.* New York: Garland STPM Press.

Whittle, S., Yap, M. B., Yucel, M., Fornito,A., Simmons, J. G., Sheeber, L., & Allen, N. B. (2008). Prefrontal and amygdala volumes are related to adolescents' affective behaviors during parent-adolescent interactions. *Proceedings of the National Academy of Sciences USA, 105,* 3652–3657.

Wickelgren, I. (1999). Nurture helps to mold able minds. Science, 283, 1832–1834.

Wigfield, A., Eccles, J. S., Schiefele, U., Roeser, R., & Davis-Kean, P. (2006). Development of achievement motivation. In W. Damon & R. Lerner (Eds.), *Handbook of child psychology* (6th ed.). New York: Wiley.

Williams, C. R. (1986). *The impact of television: A natural experiment in three communities.* New York: Academic Press.

Williams, D. D., Yancher, S. C., Jensen, L.C., & Lewis, C. (2003). Character education in a public high school: A multi-year inquiry into unified studies. *Journal of Moral Education, 32,* 3–33.

Williams, J. E., & Best, D. L. (1982). *Measuring sex stereotypes: A thirty-nation study.* Newbury Park, CA: Sage.

Williams, J. E., & Best, D. L. (1989). *Sex and psyche: Self-concept viewed cross-culturally.* Newbury Park, CA: Sage.

Williams, J. H., & Ross, L. (2007). Consequences of prenatal toxin exposure for mental health in children and adolescents: A systematic review. *European Child and Adolescent Psychiatry, 16,* 243–253.

Willoughby, T. (2008). A short-term longitudinal study of internet and computer game use by adolescent boys and girls: Prevalence, frequency of use, and psychosocial predictors. *Developmental Psychology, 44,* 195–204.

Wilson, B. J. (2008). Media and children's aggression, fear, and altruism. *Future of Children, 18* (No. 1), 87–118.

Wilson, M. N. (2007). Poor fathers involvement in the lives of their children. In D. R. Crane & T. B. Heaton (Eds.), *Handbook of families and poverty.* Thousand Oaks, CA: Sage.

Windle, W. F. (1940). *Physiology of the human fetus.* Philadelphia: W. B. Saunders.

Winn, I. J. (2004). The high cost of uncritical teaching. *Phi Delta Kappan, 85,* 496–497.

Winner, E. (1986, August.). Where pelicans kiss seals. *Psychology Today,* pp. 24–35.

Winner, E. (1996). *Gifted children: Myths and realities.* New York: Basic Books.

Winner, E. (2006). Development in the arts: Drawing and music. In W. Damon & R. Lerner (Eds.), *Handbook of child psychology* (6th ed.). New York: Wiley.

Winner, E. (2009). Toward broadening our understanding of giftedness: The spatial domain. In F. D. Horowitz, R. F. Subotnik, & D. J. Matthews (Eds.), *The development of giftedness and talent across the life span.* Washington, DC: American Psychological Association.

Winsler, A., Carlton, M. P., & Barry, M. J. (2000). Age-related changes in preschool children's systematic use of private speech in a natural setting. *Journal of Child Language, 27,* 665–687.

Winsler, A., Diaz, R. M., & Montero, I. (1997). The role of private speech in the transition from collaborative to independent task performance in young children. *Early Childhood Research Quarterly, 12,* 59–79.

Wintre, M. G., & Vallance, D. D. (1994). A developmental sequence in the comprehension of emotions: Intensity, multiple emotions, and valence. *Developmental Psychology, 30,* 509–514.

Witkin, H. A., Mednick, S. A., Schulsinger, R., Bakkestrom, E., Christiansen, K. O., Goodenbough, D. R., Hirchhorn, K., Lunsteen, C., Owen, D. R., Philip, J., Ruben, D. B., & Stocking, M. (1976). Criminality in XYY and XXY men. *Science, 193,* 547–555.

Wittmeier, K. D., Mollar, R. C., & Kriellaars, D. J. (2008). Physical activity intensity and risk of overweight and adiposity in children. *Obesity, 16,* 415–420.

Wolak, J., Mitchell, K., & Finkelhor, D. (2007). Unwanted and wanted exposure to online pornography in a national sample of youth Internet users. *Pediatrics, 119,* 247–257.

Women's Sports Foundation. (2001). *The 10 commandments for parents and coaches in youth sports.* Eisenhower Park, NY: Author.

Wong Briggs, T. (2007, October 18). An early start for learning. *USA Today,* p. 6 D.

Wong, E. C., Kinzie, J. D., & Kinzie, M. (2009). Stress, refugees, and trauma. In N. Tewari & A. Alvarez (Eds.), *Asian American psychology.* Clifton, NJ: Psychology Press.

Wong, Y. J., & Rochlen, A. B. (2008). *The new psychology of men: The emotional side.* Greenwood Publishing Group.

Wood, A. C., Rijsdijk, F., Saudino, K. J., Asherson, P., & Kuntsi, J. (2008, in press). High heritability for a composite index of children's activity level measures. *Behavior Genetics.*

Wood, D., Kaplan, R., & McLoyd, V. C. (2007). Gender differences in educational expectations of urban, low-income African American youth: The role of parents and school. *Journal of Youth and Adolescence, 36,* 417–427.

Woodard, E. (2000). *Media in the Home 2000: The Fifth Annual Survey of Parents and Children.* Philadelphia: The Annenberg Public Policy Center.

Woodhill, B. M., & Samuels, C. A. (2004). Desirable and undesirable androgyny: A prescription for the twenty-first century. *Journal of Gender Studies, 13,* 15–28.

Woodward, A. L., & Markman, E. M. (1998). Early word learning. In D. Kuhn & R. S. Siegler (Eds.), *Handbook of child psychology* (5th ed., Vol. 2). New York: Wiley.

Woodward, A., Markman, E., & Fitzsimmons, C. (1994). Rapid word learning in 13- and 18-month-olds. *Developmental Psychology, 30,* 553–566.

Woolley, J. D., Boerger, E. A., & Markman, A. B. (2004). A visit from the Candy Witch: Factors influencing young children's belief in a novel fantastical being. *Developmental Science, 7,* 456–468.

Worku, B., & Kassir, A. (2005). Kangaroo mother care: A randomized controlled trial on effectiveness of early kangaroo care for low birthweight infants in Addis Ababa, Ethiopia. *Journal of Tropical Pediatrics, 51,* 93–97.

Wu, P., Robinson, C. C., Yang, C., Hart, C. H., Olsen, S. F., & Porter, C. L. (2002). Similarities and differences in mothers' parenting of preschoolers in China and the United States. *International Journal of Behavioural Development, 6,* 481–491.

X

Xu, F., Markowitz, L. E., Gottlieb, S. L., & Berman, S. M. (2007). Seroprevalence of herpes simplex virus types 1 and 2 in pregnant women in the United States. *American Journal of Obstetrics and Gynecology, 196,* e1–e6.

Xue, F., Holzman, C., Rahbar, M. H., Trosko, K., & Fischer, L. (2007). Maternal fish consumption, mercury levels, and risk of preterm delivery. *Environmental Health Perspectives, 115,* 42–47.

Y

Yang, C. K., Kim, J. K., Patel, S. R., & Lee, J. H. (2005). Age-related changes in sleep/wake patterns among Korean teenagers. *Pediatrics, 115* (Suppl, 1), S250–S256.

Yang, Q., Wen, S. W., Leader, A., Chen, X. K., Lipson, J. & Walker, M. (2007). Paternal age and birth defects: How strong is the association? *Human Reproduction, 22,* 696–701.

Yang, S., & Sternberg, R. J. (1997). Taiwanese Chinese people's conceptions of intelligence. *Intelligence, 25,* 21–36.

Yang, S. N., Liu, C. A., Chung, M. Y., Huang, H. C., Yeh, G. C., Wong, C. S., Lin, W. W., Yang, C. H., & Tao, P. L. (2006). Alterations of postsynaptic density proteins in the hippocampus of rat offspring from the morphine-addicted mother: Beneficial effects of dextromethorphan. *Hippocampus, 16,* 521–530.

Yang, Y., May, Y., Ni, L., Zhao, S., Li, L., Zhang, J., Fan, M., Liang, C., Cao, J., & Xu, L. (2003). Lead exposure through gestation-only caused long-term memory deficits in young adult offspring. *Experimental Neurology, 184,* 489–495.

Yell, M. L., & Drasgow, E. (2009). *What every teacher should know about No Child Left Behind* (2nd ed.). Upper Saddle River, NJ: Prentice Hall.

Yin, Y., Buhrmester, D., & Hibbard, D. (1996, March). *Are there developmental changes in the influence of relationships with parents and friends on adjustment during early adolescence?* Paper presented at the meeting of the Society for Research on Adolescence, Boston.

Young, E. L., Boye, A. E., & Nelson, D. A. (2006). Relational aggression: Understanding, identifying, and responding in schools. *Psychology in the Schools, 43,* 297-312.

Young, K. T. (1990). American conceptions of infant development from 1955 to 1984: What the experts are telling parents. *Child. Development, 61,* 17–28.

Youniss, J., & Ruth, A. J. (2002). Approaching policy for adolescent development in the 21st century. In J. T. Mortimer & R. W. Larson (Eds.), *The changing adolescent experience.* New York: Cambridge University Press.

Youniss, J., McLellan, J. A., & Yates, M. (1999). Religion, community service, and identity in American youth. *Journal of Adolescence, 22,* 243–253.

Z

Zagorsky, J. L. (2007). Do you have to be smart to be rich? The impact of IQ on wealth, income, and financial distress. *Intelligence, 35,* 489–501.

Zangl, R., & Mills, D. L. (2007). Increased brain activity to infant-directed speech in 6- and 13-month-old infants. *Infancy, 11,* 31–62.

Zelazo, P. D., & Muller, U. (2004). Executive function in typical and atypical development. In U. Goswami (Ed.), *Blackwell handbook of cognitive development.* Malden, MA: Blackwell.

Zeller, M. H., Reiter-Purtill, J., & Ramey, C. (2008). Negative peer perceptions of obese children in the classroom environment. *Obesity, 16,* 755–762.

Zeskind, P. S. (2009, in press). Impact of the cry of the infant at risk on psychosocial development. In R. E. Tremblay, R. deV Peters,

M. Boivan, & R. G. Barr (Eds.), *Encyclopedia on early childhood development.* Montreal: Center of Excellence for Early Childhood Development.

Zeskind, P. S., Klein, L., & Marshall, T. R. (1992). Adults' perceptions of experimental modifications of durations and expiratory sounds in infant crying. *Developmental Psychology, 28,* 1153–1162.

Zhang, L.-F., & Sternberg, R. J. (2008, in press). Learning in a cross-cultural perspective. In T. Husén & T. N. Postlethwaite (Eds.) *International encyclopedia of education* (3rd ed.), *Learning and cognition).* Oxford: Elsevier.

Zhou, F., Shefer, A., Yuan, K., & Nuorti, J.P. (2008). Trends in acute otitis media—related health care utilization by privately insured young children in the United States, 1997–2004. *Pediatrics, 121,* 253–260.

Zigler, E. F., & Styfco, S. J. (1994). Head Start: Criticisms in a constructive context. *American Psychologist, 49,* 127–132.

Zigler, E. F. (2009, in press). Head Start policy—comments on Currie, and Hustedt and Barnett. In R. E. Tremblay, R. deV Peters, M. Boivin, & R. G. Barr (Eds.), *Encyclopedia on early childhood development.* Montreal: Centre of Excellence for Early Childhood Development.

Zigler, E., Gilliam, W. S., & Jones, S. M. (2006). *A vision for universal preschool education.* New York: Cambridge University Press.

Zimmerman, B. J., Bonner, S., & Kovach, R. (1996). *Developing self-regulated learners.* Washington, DC: American Psychological Association.

Zimmerman, P. (2007, March). *Attachment in adolescence.* Paper presented at the meeting of the Society for Research in Child Development, Boston.

Zimmerman, R. S., Khoury, E., Vega, W. A., Gil, A. G., & Warheit, G. J. (1995). Teacher and student perceptions of behavior problems among a sample of African American, Hispanic and non-Hispanic White students. *American Journal of Community Psychology, 23,* 181–197.

Zinn, M. B., & Wells, B. (2000). Diversity within Latino families: New lessons for family social science. In D. M. Demo, K. R. Allen, & M. A. Fine (Eds.), *Handbook of family diversity.* New York: Oxford University Press.

Zittleman, K. (2006, April). *Being a girl and being a boy: The voice of middle schoolers.* Paper presented at the meeting of the American Educational Research Association, San Francisco.

Zitzer-Comfort, C., Doyle, T. F., Masataka, N., Korenberg, J., & Bellugi, U. (2007). Nature and nurture: Williams syndrome across cultures. *Developmental Science, 10,* 755–762.

Zosuls, K. M., Lurye, L. E., & Ruble, D. N. (2008). Gender: Awareness, identity, and stereotyping. In M. M. Haith & J. B. Benson (Eds.), *Encyclopedia of infant and early childhood development.* Oxford, UK: Elsevier.

CREDITS

Photo Credits

Section Openers

1: © Ariel Skelley/Corbis; 2: © Petit Format/Nestle/ Photo Researchers; 3: © DreamPictures/VStock/Getty RF; 4: © Ariel Skelley/Corbis; 5: © Francisco Cruz/ SuperStock

Chapter 1

Opener: © Francisco Cruz/Superstock; p. 6 (top): © Seana O'Sullivan/Sygma/Corbis; p. 6 (bottom): © AP/Wide World Photos; 1.1: Photo: © Erich Lessing/ Art Resource, NY/Painting by A.I.G. Velasquez, Infanta Margarita Teresa in white garb, Kunsthistorische Museum, Vienna, Austria; p. 7 (bottom): © Wolfgang Flamisch/zefa/Corbis; 1.2: © Archives of the History of American Psychology; p. 10 (top): © Luis Vargas; p. 10 (bottom): National Association for the Education of Young Children, Robert Maust/Photo Agora; p. 11 (top): © Nancy Agostini; p. 11 (left): © Bloomimage/Corbis RF; p. 11 (bottom): © AFP/Getty; p. 14: © Nathan Benn/Corbis; 1.7 Prenatal: Courtesy of Landrum Shettles; Infancy: © John Santrock; Early childhood: © Chromosohn Media, Inc./The Image Works; Middle childhood: © Corbis website; Adolescence: © James L. Shaffer; p. 18: © PhotoDisc/Getty RF; p. 21: © Bettmann/Corbis; p. 22: © Sarah Putnam/Index Stock; p. 23: © Yves deBraine/Black Star/Stock Photo; p. 25 (top): A.R. Lauria/Dr. Michael Cole, Laboratory of Human Cognition, University of California, San Diego; p. 25 (bottom): © Creatas Images/Jupiter Images RF; p. 26: © AP Wide World Photos; p. 27: Courtesy of Albert Bandura; p. 28 (top): Photo by Nina Leen/Timepix/Getty Images; p. 28 (bottom): © Corbis RF; p. 29: Courtesy of Urie Bronfenbrenner; p. 31: © Ray Stott/The Image Works; p. 32: © Bettmann/ Corbis; 1.16: © Sovereign/Phototake; p. 37: © McGraw-Hill Companies, Inc., photographer John Thoeming; p. 39: © Pam Reid; p. 40 (left): © Kevin Fleming/ Corbis; p. 40 (right): © Ed Honowitz/Stone/Getty Images; p. 45: Courtesy of Valerie Pang; p. 48: Courtesy of Katherine Duchen-Smith

Chapter 2

Opener: © Don Hammond/Design Pics/Corbis RF; p. 54: © Enrico Ferorelli; p. 55: © Frans Lemmens/ Corbis; p. 57: © David Wilkie; p. 56: © Alan and Sandy Carey/Getty RF; p. 58: © Rick Rickman; 2.3: © Science Source/Photo Researchers; 2.4a&b: © Custom Medical Stock Photo; p. 61: © Joel Gordon 1989; p. 62: From R. Simensen and R. Curtis Rogers, "Fragile X Syndrome," American Family Physician, 39 (5): 186, May 1989. © American Academy of Family Physicians; p. 63: © Andrew Eccles/JBGPHOTO.COM; p. 64: © Holly Ishmael; p. 65 (top): © J. Pavlovsky/ Sygma/Corbis; 2.7: © Larry Berman; p. 66 (top): © Science Source/Photo Researchers; p. 66 (bottom): © Reuters/Corbis; p. 68: © AP/Wide World Photos; p. 70: © Sonda Dawes/The Image Works; p. 71: © Myrleen Ferguson Cate/Photo Edit; p. 73: © Duomo/Corbis

Chapter 3

Opener: Photo Lennart Nilsson/Albert Bonniers Forlag AB., A Child is Born, Dell Publishing Company; p. 80: © John Santrock; 3.3 (All): Photo Lennart Nilsson/ Albert Bonniers Forlag AB., A Child is Born, Dell Publising Company; 3.4: © Lennart Nilsson/Albert Bonniers

Forlag AB; p. 85 (bottom): © Spina Bifida Association of Greater New Orleans; p. 87: Courtesy of Ann Streissguth from A.P. Streissguth et al., "Teratogenic Effects of Alcohol in Humans and Laboratory Animals" in Science, 209 (18): 353–361, 1980.; p. 88 (top): © Will & Deni McIntyre/Photo Researchers; p. 88 (bottom): © John Chiasson; p. 90: © R.I.A. Novosti/Gamma/H.P.P./ Eyedea; p. 91: © Betty Press/Woodfin Camp; p. 92 (top): © iStock Photos; p. 92 (bottom): © 1990 Alan Reininger/Contact Press Images; p. 94 (top): © David Butow/Corbis; p. 94 (bottom): © Roger Tully/Stone/Getty Images; p. 95: © Sharon Schindler Rising, Centering Pregnancy Program; p. 97: © Viviane Moos/Corbis; p. 98 (top): © SIU/Peter Arnold; p. 98 (bottom): © M. Shostak/Anthro-Photo; p. 99: © Corbis RF; p. 100: © Linda Pugh; p. 101: © Dr. Holly Beckwith; p. 102 (top): © Comstock/Punchstock RF; p. 102 (bottom): © Tom Galliher/Corbis; 3.7: © Stephen Marks, Inc./The Image Bank/Getty Images; p. 104: © Charles Gupton/Stock Boston; p. 106: Courtesy of Dr. Susan Ludington; p. 107: © Dr. Tiffany Field; p. 110: © Ariel Skelley/Corbis; p. 111: © James G. White

Chapter 4

Opener: © Eyewire Vol. EP049/Getty Images RF; p. 119: © Bob Daemmrich/The Image Works; p. 123 (top): © VSS 22/Getty RF; p.123 (bottom): © Jon Feingersh/The Stock Market/Corbis; p. 124: © Corbis RF; 4.5: © A. Glauberman/Photo Researchers; 4.8: © 1999 Kenneth Jarecke/Contact Press Images; 4.9a&b: Courtesy of Dr. Harry T. Chugani, Children's Hospital of Michigan; 4.10a: © David Grubin Productions, Inc. Reprinted by permission; 4.10b: Image courtesy of Dana Boatman, Ph. D., Department of Neurology, John Hopkins University. Reprinted with permission from The Secret Life of the Brain, © 2001 by the National Academy of Sciences. Courtesy of the National Academies Press, Washington, D.C.; 4.11: © Steve Gschmeissner/ Photo Researchers; p. 131: © Davis Turner-Pool/Getty Images; p. 133: © C Squared Studios/Getty RF; p. 134: © Tom Rosenthal/ SuperStock; p. 135: © Jim LoScalzo; p. 138: Courtesy of The Hawaii Family Support Center, Healthy Start Program; p. 139: © AP/Wide World Photos; p. 141: © Vol. DV251 Digital Vision/Getty Images RF; p. 142 (top): © Wendy Stone/Corbis; p. 142 (bottom): © Dave Bartruff/Corbis; p. 143: © Bob Daemmrich/The Image Works; p. 144: © Jules Frazier/Getty RF; p. 145 (top): © L. Perez/zefa/Corbis; p. 145 (bottom): © Corbis RF; p. 146: Courtesy of Barbara Deloin; p. 147: © Dallas Morning News, photographer Vernon Bryant

Chapter 5

Opener: © Philip Kaake/Corbis; p. 154 (top & bottom): © Reuters NewMedia Inc/Corbis; p. 155 (top): Courtesy of Esther Thelen; p. 155 (bottom): © Barbara Peacock/Getty Images; p. 156 (left): © Petit Format/ Photo Researchers; p. 156 (right): © PictureQuest/ Stockbye RF; p. 157: © Fabio Caardosa/zefa/Corbis; 5.2 (top & bottom): © Dr. Karen Adolph, New York University; p. 160: © Michael Greenlar/The Image Works; p. 160 (middle): © Frank Baily Studios; p. 160 (botom): © Joel Gordon 1993; p. 161 (top): © PhotoDisc/Getty RF; p. 161 (middle): © SW Productions/Brand X/Corbis RF; p. 161 (bottom): © Corbis RF; 5.4: Courtesy Amy Needham; p. 163 (top): © Newstockimages/SuperStock RF; p. 163 (bottom): © Digital Vision/Getty RF; p. 165: © Mika/

zefa/Corbis; 5.5: Adapted from "The Origin of Form and Perception" by R.L. Fantz © 1961 by Scientific American. Photo © by David Linton; 5.7 (all): Courtesy of Dr. Charles Nelson; 5.9: © Enrico Ferorelli; p. 170: © Joe McNally; p. 171: © Dr. Bruce Hood, University of Bristol, England; 5.11a: © Michael Siluk; 5.11b: © Dr. Melanie Spence, University of Texas; 5.12: © Jean Guichard/Sygma/Corbis; 5.13 (all): From D. Rosenstein and H. Oster, "Differential Facial Responses to Four Basic Tastes in Newborns" in Child Development, Vol. 59, 1988. Copyright © Society For Research in Child Development, Inc.; p. 175: © Tom Stewart/zefa/Corbis

Chapter 6

Opener: © Gabe Palmer/Corbis; p. 183: © Laura Dwight/Corbis; p. 184: © Elyse Lewin/Brand X/Corbis RF; p. 184: © Archives Jean Piaget, Universite De Geneve, Switzerland; p. 185: © BigStock Photos; p. 186: © PunchStock RF; 6.3a&b: © Doug Goodman/Photo Researchers; p. 189: © Markus Moellenberg/zefa/ Corbis; 6.7: © Paul Fusco/Magnum Photos; p. 195: © David Young-Wolff/Photo Edit; p. 196: © Stewart Cohen/Stone/Getty Images; p. 197: © Gabe Palmer/ Corbis; p. 198: © Archives Jean Piaget, Universite De Geneve, Switzerland; p. 199: © M & E Bernheim/ Woodfin Camp; 6.10: © Elizabeth Crews/The Image Works; p. 201: Courtesy Barbara Rogoff; p. 202 (top): © James Wertsch/Washington University in St. Louis; p. 202 (bottom): © Gabe Palmer/Corbis; 6.11a & b; Images courtesy of E. Bodrova and D.J. Leong, from Tools of the Mind, 2007; 6.12a: A.R. Lauria/Dr. Michael Cole, Laboratory of Human Cognition, University of California, San Diego; 6.12b: © 1999 Yves deBraine/ Black Star/Stock Photo

Chapter 7

Opener: © Ariel Skelley/The Stock Market/Corbis; p. 212: Courtesy of Laura Bickford; p. 214: © LWA-JDC/Corbis; p. 215: © Jose Luis Pelaez/Corbis; pp. 216 & 218: © Tom Stewart/Corbis; 7.2 (left and right): Photos from: Meltzoff, A. N., & Brooks, R. (2007). Intersubjectivity before language: Three windows on preverbal sharing. In S. Bråten (Ed.), On being moved: From mirror neurons to empathy (pp. 149–174). Philadelphia, PA: John Benjamins; p. 219: © John Henley/Corbis; p. 222: © David Butow/SABA/Corbis; p. 223: Courtesy of Dr. Carolyn Rovee-Collier; p. 226: © 2005 James Kamp; 7.11: From Jean Mandler, University of California, San Diego. Reprinted by permission of Oxford University Press; p. 229: © John Santrock; p. 230 (top): © LWA-Sharie Kennedy/Corbis; p. 230 (bottom): Courtesy of Compton-Drew Investigative Learning Center Middle School, St. Louis, MO; p. 231: © Nita Winter Photography; p. 232: © Dale Sparks; p. 234: Courtesy of Judy DeLoache; p. 236: © John Flavell; p. 237: © Joe Baker, Images.com/Corbis; p. 239: © AP/Wide World Photos

Chapter 8

Opener: © Cindy Charles/Photo Edit; p. 247: © The Bettmann Archive/Corbis; p. 250: Courtesy of Robert Sternberg; p. 251: © Jay Gardner, 1998; p. 252: © Joe McNally; p. 255: © Owen Franken/Corbis; p. 257 (left): © David Austin/Stock Boston; p. 257 (right): © Ben Simmons/The Stock Market/Corbis;

Text and Line Art Credits

NAME INDEX

SUBJECT INDEX